Individual Retirement Account Answer Book

Twenty-Eighth Edition

by Bruce J. McNeil and Barry L. Salkin

The continuing popularity and importance of individual retirement accounts as retirement vehicles underscores the necessity for attorneys, accountants, financial planners, and insurance advisors to keep abreast of legislative and regulatory developments in this area. *Individual Retirement Account Answer Book* is the source practitioners rely on for the most comprehensive, authoritative coverage of traditional Individual Retirement Arrangements (IRAs), Roth IRAs, savings incentive match plan for employees (SIMPLE) IRAs, simplified employee pension plan (SEP) IRAs, and Coverdell Education Savings Accounts (ESAs).

Highlights of the Twenty-Eighth Edition

The *Individual Retirement Account Answer Book*, Twenty-Eighth Edition, brings practitioners up to date on important congressional and administrative agency actions and recent judicial decisions that affect all IRAs, and the Coverdell ESA including:

- Numerous changes that affect IRAs made by the Setting Every Community Up for Retirement Enhancement (SECURE) Act, including:
    - The repeal of the maximum age for contributions to a traditional IRA. (Previously, individuals attaining the age of 70½; by the end of the year were unable to make contributions.) This change puts a traditional IRA on the same level playing field as a Roth IRA, which does not have a maximum age for contributions.
    - Increased required beginning date for minimum required distributions from an IRA from age 70½; to age 72. Section 105 of the SECURE Act 2.0 (i.e., HR 2954), which has not yet been enacted, would generally further increase the age for the required beginning date for mandatory distributions to age 75.
    - Parents may now take early withdrawals of up to $5,000 from their retirement accounts without a penalty, an exception to the 10 percent early withdrawal tax, within a year of a child's birth or adoption, referred to as a qualified birth or adoption distribution (QBOAD).

Wolters Kluwer

- — Elimination of the "stretch" IRA, which permitted minimum distributions over the beneficiary's life. Instead, amounts must be distributed by the end of the tenth calendar year following the year of the IRA owner's death, with certain exceptions. (See Chapter 1.)

- The total contributions an individual can make in each year, 2020 and 2021, to all of the individual's traditional IRAs and Roth IRAs. (See Q 1:3.)
- Extended deadlines, due to the COVID-19 pandemic, for making contributions to both traditional and Roth IRAs. [I.R.C. § 219(f)(3)] (See Q 3:2.)
- New information on employer contributions to an employee's SEP IRA, and employee deferrals under a salary reduction simplified employee pension plan (SARSEP), in 2020 and 2021, and a new deferral limit for SIMPLE plans and SIMPLE IRAs. Plus, a new annual compensation limit. [IRS Notice 2020-79, IRS News Rel. IR-2020-244 (Oct. 26, 2020)] (See Q 1:6.)
- Updated IRS guidance on expanded SIMPLE rollover options. (See Chapter 13.)
- New increases for contributions and out-of-pocket limits for HSAs and HDHPs for 2021. [IRS Rev. Proc. 2020-32] (See Q 1:11.)
- Changes that would occur if Section 308 of the SECURE Act 2.0 (H.R. 8696) is enacted, which would permit self-correction of certain inadvertent compliance errors with respect to IRAs at any time before the IRS identified the violations. (See Q 1:65.)
- Expanded definition of compensation under the SECURE Act regarding amounts includible in gross income and paid to an individual to aid in the pursuit of graduate or postdoctoral study; difficulty of care payments; and changes to the treatment of alimony as compensation. (See Q 2:28.)
- For 2021, updated information regarding the income phase-out range for taxpayers making contributions to a Roth IRA, including married couples filing jointly and married individuals filing separately. (See Q 2:30.)
- Updated 2020 and 2021 modified adjusted gross income (MAGI) limits on IRA Owner's Deductions for traditional and Roth IRA contributions (see Qs 3:64, 3:77) and updated Saver's Tax Credit rates for 2021. (See Q 3:143.)
- New life expectancy tables that will apply, effective for required minimum distributions beginning on January 1, 2022, as well as a single life table for eligible designated beneficiaries under the SECURE Act. (See Qs 4:22, 4:25.)
- Modification of the CARES Act by the Consolidated Appropriations Act, 2021, on a retroactive basis, to permit coronavirus-related distributions from a money purchase pension plan without violating Code Section 401(a). (See Q 4:12.)

- Updated 2021 coverage of disaster relief that focuses on the temporary relaxation of tax rules governing retirement plans; includes discussion of the Consolidated Appropriations Act, 2021. (See Chapter 7.)
- Penalties under Code Sections 6721 and 6722 relating to information returns required to be filed in 2022. (See Q 8:25.)
- Discussion of IRS final regulations, issued in November 2020, dealing with determining separate business for purposes of determining the tax on unrelated business taxable income under the Tax Cuts and Jobs Act of 2017. (See Q 8:44.)
- Updated contribution and compensation limits applicable to SEPs (and SARSEPs). (See Chapter 12.)

For the convenience of our readers, IRS Publication 590-A, *Contributions to Individual Retirement Arrangements (IRAs) 2020*, and IRS Publication 590-B, *Distributions from Individual Retirement Arrangements (IRAs) 2020*, which are referenced throughout this work, are reproduced in Appendix A and Appendix B.

11/21

Individual Retirement Account Answer Book

Twenty-Eighth Edition

Bruce J. McNeil
Barry L. Salkin

Wolters Kluwer

Published by Wolters Kluwer in New York.

Wolters Kluwer Legal & Regulatory U.S. serves customers worldwide with CCH and Kluwer Law International products.

Printed in the United States of America

1 2 3 4 5 6 7 8 9 0

ISBN 978-1-5438-3691-2

About Wolters Kluwer Legal & Regulatory U.S.

Wolters Kluwer Legal & Regulatory U.S. delivers expert content and solutions in the areas of law, corporate compliance, health compliance, reimbursement, and legal education. Its practical solutions help customers successfully navigate the demands of a changing environment to drive their daily activities, enhance decision quality and inspire confident outcomes.

Serving customers worldwide, its legal and regulatory portfolio includes products under the CCH Incorporated, Kluwer Law International, ftwilliam.com and MediRegs names. They are regarded as exceptional and trusted resources for general legal and practice-specific knowledge, compliance and risk management, dynamic workflow solutions, and expert commentary.

WOLTERS KLUWER SUPPLEMENT NOTICE

This product is updated on a periodic basis with supplements and/or new editions to reflect important changes in the subject matter.

If you would like information about enrolling this product in the update service, or wish to receive updates billed separately with a 30-day examination review, please contact our Customer Service Department at 1-800-234-1660 or email us at: *customer.service@wolterskluwer.com*. You can also contact us at:

Wolters Kluwer
Distribution Center
7201 McKinney Circle
Frederick, MD 21704

Important Contact Information

- To order any title, go to *www.WoltersKluwerLR.com* or call 1-800-638-8437.
- To reinstate your manual update service, call 1-800-638-8437.
- To contact Customer Service, e-mail *customer.service@wolterskluwer.com*, call 1-800-234-1660, fax 1-800-901-9075, or mail correspondence to: Order Department—Wolters Kluwer, PO Box 990, Frederick, MD 21705.
- To review your account history or pay an invoice online, visit *www.WoltersKluwerLR.com/payinvoices*.

Wolters Kluwer

Preface

Individual Retirement Account Answer Book is designed to provide comprehensive and timely answers to questions pertaining to traditional IRAs that concern accountants, attorneys, financial planners, mutual fund brokers, insurance advisors, and other pension professionals. It also contains discussions of the Roth IRA and Coverdell Education Savings Accounts (ESAs), which continue to be powerful tools for retirement and estate planning and for achieving other long-range financial goals. In addition, a chapter is dedicated to key issues associated with retirement income and state income tax treatment.

To further clarify existing and new legislation, regulations, and rulings that affect traditional Individual Retirement Arrangements (IRAs), Roth IRAs, simplified employee pension plan (SEP) IRAs, savings incentive match plan for employees (SIMPLE) IRAs, and Coverdell ESAs, the book includes practice pointers, worksheets, and numerous examples. Useful addresses and telephone numbers are also provided. Because some federal forms discussed in this volume may have been replaced after preparation of the current edition began, we encourage subscribers to visit the IRS's Web site (*www.irs.gov*) and inquire at local or district IRS offices to obtain the most recent versions of the forms and publications cited in this book.

Format. The question-and-answer format provides specific, concise responses to hundreds of practical questions—a boon for professionals who need clear, concise, and authoritative answers. Citations to authority are provided as research aids for those who wish to pursue particular subjects in greater detail.

Numbering System. Within each chapter, questions are numbered consecutively (e.g., Q 2:1, Q 2:2, Q 2:3).

List of Questions. The list of questions that follow the Contents helps the reader locate areas of immediate interest. A series of subheadings helps to group and organize the questions by topic within each chapter. The list is similar to a detailed table of contents, providing both the question number and the page on which the question appears.

Examples and Practice Pointers. Throughout the book, numerous examples are presented to illustrate important concepts, and useful information for practitioners is presented in the form of practice pointers.

Appendixes. For the convenience of subscribers, IRS Publication 590-A, *Contributions to Individual Retirement Arrangements (IRAs)* and IRS Publication 590-B, *Distributions from Individual Retirement Arrangements (IRAs)* for use in preparing 2020 returns are reproduced in the Appendixes to this edition.

Tables. At the back of the book are tables of statutes and authorities, and a table of cases. References in the tables are to question numbers.

Index. A comprehensive Index is provided as a further aid to locating specific information. References in the Index also are to question numbers.

We hope that the detailed coverage of different types of IRAs provided in this edition proves invaluable for professionals who are advising their clients about the retirement planning opportunities afforded by traditional and Roth IRAs, the Coverdell ESA, and HSAs.

Bruce J. McNeil
Barry L. Salkin

About the Authors

Bruce J. McNeil is a Partner at Leech Tishman Fuscaldo & Lampl and is a member of the firm's Employment & Labor Practice Group. Mr. McNeil focuses his practice on employee benefits, including tax-qualified plans, executive and nonqualified deferred compensation plans, and the tax aspects of equity, phantom equity, and employee benefits litigation. He is a Fellow of the American College of Employee Benefits Counsel and a leading authority on executive and deferred compensation. Mr. McNeil advises his clients on a wide variety of issues with respect to tax-qualified retirement plans, including 401(k), 403(b), and 457 plans, nonqualified deferred compensation arrangements, equity arrangements, split-dollar life insurance arrangements, and COLI and other forms of executive compensation. He counsels clients on all aspects of tax-qualified and executive and nonqualified deferred compensation plans and arrangements for taxable and tax-exempt employers, employee benefit issues in mergers and acquisitions, fiduciary responsibility, and prohibited transaction issues.

Mr. McNeil has practiced before the Internal Revenue Service, the Department of Labor, and the Pension Benefit Guaranty Corporation in examinations, correction programs, and ruling requests. He has served as an expert in federal hearings and investigations and has testified before the U.S. Senate Committee on Finance and the U.S. Department of Labor ERISA Advisory Council. He has also participated in investigations by the U.S. Government Accountability Office regarding nonqualified deferred compensation plans and the impact of mergers and acquisitions on employee benefits.

Mr. McNeil serves on the Board of Directors of the Plan Sponsor Council of America and is Chair of its Nonqualified Deferred Compensation Committee; he is a member of the Board of Directors of the Western Pension & Benefit Council. Mr. McNeil is the Editor-in-Chief of both the *Journal of Pension Planning & Compliance* and the *Journal of Deferred Compensation* (Wolters Kluwer). He is a frequent lecturer on employee benefits matters and the author of more than 40 books, and over 100 articles, on employee benefits matters. Mr. McNeil earned a B.A. from Concordia College, M.A. in English from Georgetown University, J.D. from Drake University Law School, and LL. M. from Georgetown University Law Center.

Barry L. Salkin is Of Counsel at the Wagner Law Group. Mr. Salkin concentrates his practice in ERISA and employee benefits law. He has significant expertise in drafting, amending, and negotiating various ERISA and employee benefit plans, including defined benefit pension plans, profit-sharing plans, 401(k) plans, and qualified and nonqualified deferred compensation programs. Mr. Salkin also has wide-ranging experience in crafting group medical and health plans involving Health Care Reform, HIPAA, and COBRA. In addition, he has represented clients in ERISA litigation and audits.

Mr. Salkin's clients include multinational corporations, closely held companies, high-net-worth individuals, financial institutions, governmental agencies, investment groups, and tax-exempt organizations, such as hospitals and physicians' organizations. Mr. Salkin also advises clients on all aspects of retirement plan tax-qualification requirements and the application of labor and securities laws and regulations to sponsors of employee benefit plans and executive compensation programs. He has extensive experience in establishing, merging, and terminating benefit plans and compensation agreements, and he counsels clients on fiduciary responsibilities and prohibited transactions.

Mr. Salkin is a member of the American College of Employee Benefits Counsel and the New York City Bar Association Employee Benefits Committee, and is an editor of *Benefits Law Journal* and *Journal of Pension Planning and Compliance*. He is a frequent contributor to *Benefits Law Journal, Journal of Pension Plan Compliance*, and *Journal of Deferred Compensation*. He received a B.A. from Rutgers University and an M.A. and Ph.D. in American History from Harvard University. He is also a graduate of Harvard Law School.

Acknowledgments

Individual Retirement Account Answer Book, Twenty-Eighth Edition, is the product of the hard work and dedication of many people.

We are indebted to former authors Jo Ann Lippe, Anthony P. Curatola, Martin Fleisher, Donald R. Levy, Steven G. Lockwood, Gary S. Lesser, and Susan D. Diehl for their major contributions to earlier editions of this work.

Ellen Ros, our Editor at Wolters Kluwer, provided editorial guidance, encouragement, and skills, all of which we gratefully acknowledge.

Contents

TABLES

List of Questions

Chapter 1 Introduction to IRAs

What Is an "IRA"?

Financial Planning

Roth IRA Versus Traditional IRA

Conversions

Attractive Uses for IRAs

Benefit of Establishing an IRA Early

Investment Options

Prohibited Transactions

Listed Transactions

Bankruptcy and Debtor Issues

IRS-Approved Models

Prototype IRAs

IRS Sample Language for Prototypes

Chapter 3 Contributions to Traditional and Roth IRAs

Overview

Contribution Limit

Limit for Spousal IRA Contributions

Compensation Defined

Included Amounts

Recharacterization

Transfer of Allocable Net Income

Election to Recharacterize

Recharacterizing a Pre-2018 Conversion

Excess IRA Contributions

Correcting an Excess Contribution

Saver's Tax Credit for IRA Contributions

Chapter 4 Required Distributions

Distributions in General

Waiver of RMDs for 2020

Mandatory Lifetime Distributions

Lifetime RMDs

Annuity Payments

Qualifying Longevity Annuity Contracts

Distribution for the Year of Death

Distributions After the Year of Death

Step One: Initial Matters

Step Two: Identify Beneficiaries

Beneficiary Categories

The *Designated Beneficiary*

Eligible Designated Beneficiaries

Substantially Equal Periodic Payments

Medical Expenses

Higher Education Expenses

Qualified Reservist Distribution

Qualified First-Time Homebuyer Distribution

Qualified Birth or Adoption Distribution

Disaster and Coronavirus-Related Distributions

Taxation of Roth IRA Distributions

Qualified Roth IRA Distributions

Five-Year Holding Period for Qualified Distribution Purposes

Qualified Reasons

Nonqualified Distributions

Chapter 6 Rollovers and Direct Transfers

Waiver of the 60-Day Limit

Special Considerations

Waiver of RMDs for 2020

Conversions

Transfers After Death

Divorce

Withholding

Transfers from One IRA to Another

Transfers from an Eligible Plan to an IRA

Transfers from a Designated Roth Account to an IRA

Eligible Rollover Distributions

Required Minimum Distributions

Substantially Equal Periodic Payments

Hardship Distributions

After-Tax Assets

Noncash Property

Plan Qualification Issues

Transfers from an IRA to an Eligible Plan

Airline Payments

Chapter 7 Disaster Distributions

Overview of Tax Relief

Qualified Disaster Distributions

Definitions

Dollar Limit on Qualified Disaster Distributions

Tax Relief for Qualified Disaster Distributions

Income Deferral

Exemption from the Early Distribution Penalty

Repayment to an Eligible Retirement Plan

Distributions to Buy or Build a Home

Electronic Filing Requirement

Timely Filing

Predecessor and Successor Reporting

Form 990-T

Form 1040

Form W-2

Form 1098-Q

Form 1099-Q

Form 1099-R

Reporting Distributions on Form 1099-R

Form 5329

Early Distributions

Excess Contributions

Excess Accumulations

Miscellaneous Matters

Form 5330

Form 5498

Filing

Reporting Contributions and the Year-End Value

Death

Closure, Revocation, or Total Loss

Form 5498-ESA

Form 5498-SA

Form 8606

Form 8888

Form 8889

Forms 8915-A Through 8915-E

Chapter 9 Income Tax Planning for IRAs

Planning Goals

Distribution Planning

Income Stability

Minimizing Taxes and Expenses

Maximizing IRA Value

Contribution Planning

Chapter 10 Leaving an IRA to the Spouse

The Spouse as the Favored IRA Beneficiary

Background—IRAs and the Estate Tax

The Marital Deduction

QTIP Exception

Other Exceptions

Effect on Minimum Distributions

Chapter 11 Income in Respect of a Decedent

Income in Respect of a Decedent

Transfer of the IRA by a Trust or the Estate

Retention of the IRA by a Trust or the Estate

Background—Income Taxation of a Trust or Estate

Compensation

Self-employment Compensation

Contributions

Employer Contributions (all SEPs)

Salary Reduction Contributions (SARSEPs only)

Overall Defined Contribution Limit (§ 415)

Elective Deferral Limit (§ 402(g))

Excess Contributions

Distributions

Rollovers, Conversions, and Recharacterizations

Reporting and Disclosure

Debtor Issues

Chapter 13 SIMPLE IRA Arrangements

Overview

Eligible Employers

Establishing a SIMPLE Plan

Contributions and Limits

Salary Reduction Contributions (Elective Deferrals)

Employer Contributions

Matching Employer Contributions

Nonelective Employer Contributions

The Total Contribution

Excess Contributions

Tax Treatment of Contributions

Employer's Deduction

Exclusion from Income

Consequences of an Excess Contribution

Rollovers, Conversions, and Recharacterizations

Distributions

Administrative Matters

Salary Reduction Elections

Notices

Deposit of Contributions

Employer Reports

Trustee Reports

Designated Financial Institutions

Miscellaneous Rules

State Income Tax Issues

Chapter 14 Coverdell Education Savings Account

Comparison with Other Plans

The ESA Beneficiary

Eligibility and Age Limits

Changing the ESA Beneficiary

Death of the ESA Beneficiary

Contributions

Contribution Limits

Donor Income Limit

Excess Contributions

Military Death Payments

Distributions

Qualified Education Expenses

Taxation of Distributions

Additional Tax

Withholding

Rollovers

Estate and Gift Tax Consequences

Contributions

Distributions

New Designated Beneficiary

Death

Establishing an ESA

The Financial Institution

Model ESAs

Prototype ESAs

Disclosure

Revocation

Reporting

Chapter 15 State and Other Jurisdiction Tax Rules Regarding IRAs

Traditional IRA Contributions

Traditional IRA Distributions

Tax on Post-1995 Distributions Received from Traditional IRAs by Former Residents

Tax on Pre-1996 Distributions Received from Traditional IRAs by Former Residents

Roth IRA Distributions

Inherited IRA Distributions

Special Purpose Distributions

Conversion Rollovers to Roth IRAs

SEP IRAs and SIMPLE IRAs

Penalties

Ongoing State Legislation

Ongoing Issues

Chapter 1

Introduction to IRAs

Individual retirement accounts and annuities (IRAs) are tax-favored trust accounts that are generally used for retirement savings. IRAs allow investments to grow tax free, and also provide either an upfront or back-end benefit. With a traditional IRA, contributions are generally deductible but the distributions are taxed. With a Roth IRA, distributions are usually tax free, but there is no deduction for contributions. Some employer plans also use IRAs. A simplified employee pension (SEP) uses SEP IRAs, and a savings incentive match plan for employees (SIMPLE) uses SIMPLE IRAs. Those IRAs operate much like traditional IRAs.

The IRA concept has also been extended to health savings accounts (HSAs) and Coverdell Education Savings Accounts (ESAs). Those trust accounts allow tax-free growth of investments and tax-free distributions for qualified expenses. Contributions to an HSA (but not an ESA) are also deductible. A detailed discussion of HSAs may be found in *Mandated Benefits 2021 Compliance Guide.*

This chapter provides an overview of all those accounts and compares investment in a Roth versus a traditional IRA. Other matters common to IRAs (e.g., prohibited transactions and debtor issues) are also discussed.

What Is an "IRA"?

An IRA (*individual retirement account*) is a tax-exempt trust or custodial account established to benefit one individual, who uses it to save for retirement on a tax-favored basis. Contributions (excluding rollovers) to the account must be made in cash from earned income and may not exceed an annual contribution limit. If they do, the excess amount must be removed, or a 6 percent excise tax applies. The cash restriction and contribution limit do not apply to qualifying rollovers from another IRA or retirement plan.

Q 1:1 Are there different types of IRAs?

There are several kinds of IRAs. They all allow a tax break on either the front end (for contributions) or the back end (for distributions). Earnings grow tax free while they remain in the account. All IRAs are governed by rules in the Internal Revenue Code (Code) which, among other things, proscribe certain investments (e.g., collectibles) and forbid the IRA to engage in prohibited transactions or be pledged as security for a loan. The IRA rules are simpler than the rules for qualified retirement plans.

The term *IRA* is sometimes used to describe financial arrangements that offer similar tax benefits but serve different purposes. One is the education IRA (Coverdell Education Savings Account, or *ESA*), which is used to save for education expenses. The other is the health IRA (Health Savings Account, or *HSA*), used for medical expenses. ESAs and HSAs are also governed by rules found in the Code.

From here on in this book, the term *IRA* refers only to an individual *retirement* account or annuity (IRA annuity). The other savings accounts are called *ESAs* and *HSAs*. (The next series of questions provide summary descriptions only. Details are in subsequent chapters.)

Q 1:2 What is an individual retirement annuity?

An individual retirement annuity (IRA annuity) is an annuity or endowment contract, purchased from an insurance company, that qualifies as either a traditional IRA or a Roth IRA by meeting specific requirements in the Code. The premiums paid to purchase an IRA annuity are considered IRA contributions, and the regular contribution limits apply. Although IRA annuities qualify as standalone IRAs, they can be held as investments within some IRA accounts. A traditional or SEP IRA may hold traditional IRA annuities, and a Roth IRA may hold Roth IRA annuities. [Treas. Reg. § 1.408-3]

Q 1:3 What is a traditional IRA?

A traditional IRA is an IRA that generally receives tax-deductible contributions. The deduction may be limited if an individual or his/her spouse actively participates in an employer's retirement plan. There is no age limit for contributing to a traditional IRA; before 2020, the limit was age 70½.

Minimum distribution requirements apply once an IRA owner reaches age 72 (formerly 70½), and to beneficiaries of the IRA after the owner dies. Distributions are taxed under the annuity rules, which treat basis as investment in the contract and allocate a pro rata amount to every distribution. The rest of a distribution (usually most of it) is taxable income. A 10 percent penalty applies if distributions are made to a traditional IRA owner before age 59½, but there are many exceptions. [I.R.C. §§ 408, 219(b), 72]

For 2021, the contribution limit is $6,000, and an individual who is *catch-up eligible* (age 50 or older) may contribute $1,000 more. The total amount contributed may not exceed earned income, and the contribution limit covers the total amount contributed to both traditional and Roth IRAs. [Notice 2020-79, 2020-46 I.R.B. 1014]

Under Section 107 of the Setting Every Community Up for Retirement Enhancement (SECURE) Act (Pub. L. No. 116-94), which was part of the Further Consolidated Appropriations Act, 2020, and was enacted on December 20, 2019, the maximum age for contributions to a traditional IRA was repealed. (Previously, individuals attaining the age of 70½ by the end of the year were unable to make contributions.) The change under the SECURE Act puts a traditional IRA on the same level playing field as a Roth IRA, which does not have a maximum age for contributions.

Section 114 of the SECURE Act increased the required beginning date for minimum required distributions from an IRA from age 70½ to age 72.

Section 105 of the SECURE Act 2.0 (i.e., HR 2954), which has not yet been enacted, generally further increases the age for the required beginning date for mandatory distributions to age 75.

Also, under the SECURE Act, parents may take early withdrawals of up to $5,000 from their retirement accounts without a penalty, an exception to the 10 percent early withdrawal tax, within a year of a child's birth or adoption, referred to as a qualified birth or adoption distribution (a QBOAD).

Under the prior law, after the death of an IRA owner, a nonspouse beneficiary was permitted to stretch the required minimum distribution date over the beneficiary's life (i.e., a "stretch" IRA). Section 401 of the SECURE Act provides that amounts must be distributed by the end of the 10th calendar year following the year of the IRA owner's death. There are certain exceptions for beneficiaries who are the surviving spouse, disabled or chronically ill, not more than 10 years younger than the IRA owner, or a child under the age of majority.

Q 1:4 What is a Roth IRA?

Contributions to a Roth IRA are not tax deductible, and eligibility to make them is phased out at higher income levels. The contribution limit is shared with traditional IRAs (see Q 1:3). [I.R.C. § 408A]

Qualified distributions are from a Roth IRA always tax free. Nonqualified distributions are taxed according to what they contain, and the components are not prorated (unlike a traditional IRA). Earnings are taxable when distributed, but are not allocated to distributions until every dollar contributed is first removed, so nonqualified distributions are often tax free. A 10 percent penalty applies if a nonqualified distribution includes earnings, but there are exceptions. [I.R.C. § 408A]

Distributions are not required during the Roth IRA owner's lifetime, but the minimum distribution rules apply to the death beneficiaries. [I.R.C. § 408A]

Q 1:5 What is a SEP IRA?

A SEP IRA is a traditional IRA that receives employer contributions made under a Simplified Employer Plan (SEP). The employee (participant) owns the SEP IRA and the employer contributions to it are nonforfeitable. The employer's *contributions* are governed by the SEP rules, but the *SEP IRA* is governed by the traditional IRA rules. [I.R.C. § 408(k)]

A participant can make elective salary deferrals to the SEP IRA if the plan is a *Salary Reduction Simplified Employer Plan* (SARSEP). New SARSEPs have not been allowed since 1997, but old plans were grandfathered and some continue to operate. [I.R.C. § 408(k)(6)]

The employer's contribution is allocated using a written formula that is based on the employee's limited compensation (disregarding amounts over an annual limit) and does not discriminate in favor of highly compensated employees (HCEs). The percentage of compensation an HCE may defer under a SARSEP cannot exceed 125 percent of the average percentage deferred by non-HCEs. [I.R.C. § 408(k)(3), 408(k)(5), 408(k)(6)(A)]

For 2021, an employer may contribute up to $58,000 or 25 percent of a participant's compensation, whichever is less. Salary deferrals under a SARSEP may not exceed $19,500 or, if less, 25 percent of limited compensation. A SARSEP may allow participants age 50 or older to make additional catch-up deferrals, up to $6,500. Compensation over $290,000 is ignored, and an HCE is any person with compensation exceeding $130,000 in 2020. [Notice 2020-79, 2020-46 I.R.B. 1014]

Q 1:6 What is a SIMPLE IRA?

A SIMPLE IRA is an IRA that receives contributions under a Savings Incentive Match Plan for Employees. Only small employers (with fewer than 100 employees) can maintain a SIMPLE. The SIMPLE IRA may receive two kinds of contributions each year: the employer's contribution and the participant's elective salary reduction contributions. Participants may elect to defer a percentage of total compensation to the SIMPLE IRA, subject to an annual limit. The employer decides before each plan year whether to make a matching contribution or a nonelective contribution. The matching contribution matches a participant's deferrals (if any are elected), capped at 3 percent of total compensation (though the cap may be as low as 1 percent for two years out of every five). The nonelective contribution is 2 percent of a participant's limited compensation (disregard ing amounts above an annual limit) and all participants receive it even if they did not elect salary deferrals. For 2021, a participant may defer up to $13,500, and a plan may allow additional catch-up deferrals (for participants age 50 or older) of up to $3,000. If the employer makes the nonelective contribution for 2021, compensation above $290,000 is disregarded. [I.R.C. § 408(p); Notice 2020-79, 2020-46 I.R.B. 1014]

During the first two years of participation, amounts cannot be withdrawn from the SIMPLE IRA or a 25 percent penalty applies. After that, withdrawals are subject to the same rules (including minimum distribution requirements) as a traditional IRA. [I.R.C. §§ 408(p), 72(t)(6), 401(a)(9)]

Contributions an employer can make to an employee's SEP IRA cannot exceed the lesser of: (1) 25 percent of the employee's compensation or (2) $57,000 for 2020 and $58,000 for 2021. An employee may defer under a SARSEP the lesser of: (1) 25 percent of compensation or (2) $19,500 in 2020 and 2021. The annual compensation limit has been increased to $290,000. [IRS Notice 2020-79, IRS News Rel. IR-2020-244 (Oct. 26, 2020)]

Section 114 of the SECURE Act increased the required beginning date for minimum required distributions from an IRA from age 70½ to age 72.

Section 105 of the SECURE Act 2.0 (i.e., HR 2954), which has not yet been enacted, generally further increases the age for the required beginning date for mandatory distributions to age 75.

Q 1:7 Do qualified plan limits apply to a SEP, SARSEP, or SIMPLE?

SEPs, SARSEPs, and SIMPLEs are not qualified plans, but they are defined contribution employer plans. Consequently, they are also subject to the defined contribution limits that apply to qualified plans. The defined contribution limits apply on an aggregate basis to all the plans in which any individual participates.

1. *Exclusion limit for elective deferrals.* An individual's elective deferrals under SARSEPs, SIMPLEs, 401(k) plans, and 403(b) annuities, considered in the aggregate, are excludable from income up to an annual limit. For 2021, the exclusion limit is $19,500 ($26,000 if catch-up eligible), or 100 percent of compensation if less. [I.R.C. § 402(g)]
2. *Limit for an employer's defined contribution plans.* Additions to an individual's accounts in all defined contribution plans of the employer may not exceed an annual limit. *Additions* generally include employer and employee contributions, but *not* elective deferrals and catch-up contributions. For 2021, this limit is $58,000, or 100 percent of compensation if less. [I.R.C. § 415(c)]

[Notice 2020-79, 2020-46 I.R.B. 1014]

The limit for contributions under Section 415(c)(1)(A) was increased from $57,000 to $58,000 for 2021. The annual limit on elective deferrals under Section 402(g)(1) is $19,500 for SARSEPS and, under Section 408(p)(2)(E), $13,500 for SIMPLE plans and SIMPLE IRAs. The annual compensation limit under Sections 401(a)(17) and 408(k) was increased to $290,000. [IRS Notice 2020-79, IRS News Rel. IR-2020-244 (Oct. 26, 2020)]

Q 1:8 What is a deemed IRA?

A qualified employer plan may allow employees to make voluntary contributions to a *deemed IRA*, which is a separate account or annuity in the plan that meets the requirements of a regular IRA (traditional or Roth). If a plan allows deemed IRAs, employees may contribute to them whether or not they are eligible to participate in the plan. Deemed IRAs may not be part of a SEP or SIMPLE plan. [I.R.C. § 408(q); Treas. Reg. § 1.408(q)-1(f)(2)]

A deemed IRA is treated like a regular IRA, and as a separate entity that is not part of the employer plan. An employee's deemed IRA contributions do not reduce his or her compensation income, and are deductible under the normal IRA rules, including the rule that limits traditional IRA deductions based on active participation in a retirement plan, and the income limitation on Roth IRA contributions. Deemed IRA contributions count toward the regular IRA contribution limit, and the regular IRA rules also apply to rollovers and distributions. [I.R.C. § 408(q)]

The limit for contributions under Section 415(c)(1)(A) was increased from $57,000 to $58,000 for 2021. The annual limit on elective deferrals under Section 402(g)(1) is $19,500 for SARSEPS and, under Section 408(p)(2)(E), $13,500 for SIMPLE plans and SIMPLE IRAs. The annual compensation limit under Sections 401(a)(17) and 408(k) was increased to $290,000. [IRS Notice 2020-79, IRS News Rel. IR-2020-244 (Oct. 26, 2020)]

Q 1:9 What is an ESA?

A Coverdell ESA (*ESA*) is a tax-exempt trust established to fund qualified education expenses (kindergarten through college and eligible postsecondary schools) of a particular individual (the trust beneficiary). Contributions are not tax deductible, and no more than $2,000 can be contributed each year to ESAs for a particular individual. Contributions must cease when the beneficiary reaches age 18, unless he/she has special needs. Distributions are not taxed if withdrawn to pay qualified education expenses, but if other distributions are made, the earnings are taxed and subject to a 10 percent penalty. [I.R.C. § 530]

The person in control of the ESA (usually a parent, at least while the beneficiary is a minor) can change the beneficiary without tax consequences if the new and old beneficiaries are members of the same family, and the new one is younger than age 30 or a special needs beneficiary. The ESA must be entirely distributed to the beneficiary at age 30 (unless he or she is a special needs beneficiary) or when the beneficiary dies. [I.R.C. § 530]

Q 1:10 What is an HSA?

A health savings account (*HSA*) is a tax-exempt trust or custodial account established to pay *qualified medical expenses* of the HSA owner (the participant), and his/her spouse and dependents. It is used in conjunction with coverage under a high-deductible health plan.

Contributions are allowed only for periods when the participant is covered by a high-deductible health plan (HDHP), does not have other disqualifying coverage, is not enrolled in Medicare, and cannot be claimed as a dependent on another person's tax return. Eligibility (and the contribution limit) is generally determined on a monthly basis, but an individual who becomes eligible after January can make a full year's contribution based on his/her status in December. In that case, though, eligibility must continue for at least another year, and, if it does not, the extra contributions are recaptured as income and a penalty applies. HSA contributions are tax deductible, or excluded from income if made by the participant's employer. Distributions are tax free if used to pay qualified medical expenses. Other distributions are included in the participant's income and, if made before the participant reaches age 65, becomes disabled, or dies, are subject to a 20 percent penalty. When the participant dies, the account continues as an HSA if the death beneficiary is the decedent's spouse. If there is any other beneficiary, the HSA terminates and the beneficiary is taxed on its fair market value. [I.R.C. § 223]

Table 1-1 shows the HSA limits for 2020 and 2021.

Table 1-1. HSA Limits for 2020 and 2021

	2020		*2021*	
	Single Coverage	*Family Coverage*	*Single Coverage*	*Family Coverage*
Minimum HDHP deductible	$1,400	$2,800	$1,400	$2,800
Maximum HDHP out-of-pocket costs	$6,900	$13,800	$7,000	$14,000
HSA contribution limit if under age 55:				
• Eligible all year	$3,550	$6,900	$3,600	$7,000
• Each eligible month	$295.83	$591.67	$300.00	$600.00
HSA contribution limit if age 55 or older:				
• Eligible all year	$4,550	$7,900	$4,600	$8,000
• Each eligible month	$379.17	$675.00	$383.33	$683.33

[Rev. Proc. 2019-25, 2019-21 I.R.B. 1261; Rev. Proc. 2020-32, 2020-24 I.R.B. 930]

Financial Planning

Roth IRA Versus Traditional IRA

Q 1:11 Which is better to have—a Roth or traditional IRA?

Tax-free Roth IRA distributions are obviously better to receive than distributions from a traditional IRA. But does the upfront cost of a Roth IRA (tax payments on contributed earnings) outweigh that benefit?

Factors to consider when choosing between a Roth or traditional IRA include the following:

1. *Eligibility*. Roth IRA contributions are not an option if an individual's income is too high. A traditional IRA contribution can always be made if there is earned income, but it may not be deductible if there is active participation in an employer retirement plan (see Q 1:3). When other tax-favored retirement plans are fully funded for the year and only a *nondeductible* traditional IRA contribution could still be made, doing so should be weighed against the option of making a taxable investment instead (see Q 1:13).
2. *Future tax bracket (at time of distribution)*. An individual who expects his or her tax bracket to be lower in retirement (frequently the case) may prefer the deductible traditional IRA to the Roth IRA.
3. *Reason for saving*. The Roth IRA allows for easier and earlier access to contribution amounts than does a traditional IRA. A Roth IRA owner may access his or her contribution amounts free of tax and penalty, even if he or she is not making the withdrawal for a qualified reason. Any withdrawal from a traditional IRA is subject to taxes and penalty (unless an exception to the penalty applies). Accordingly, a Roth IRA may be a better vehicle for an individual who wants to save for the long term but also wants an emergency fund. The Roth IRA also provides more estate planning opportunities than a traditional IRA because distributions are not required during the Roth IRA owner's lifetime.
4. *Current financial situation*. The better an individual's current financial position, the more he or she may be willing to forgo a current deduction in exchange for a future tax break. The contrary is also true: if an individual has an immediate, urgent need for the current tax deduction, the attractions of a traditional IRA may outweigh those of a Roth IRA.
5. *Other factors*. Obviously, many other factors—some beyond an individual's control—will help determine which type of IRA should be established. For instance, are taxes expected to go up or down in the next 10, 20, or 30 years? Do state taxes in the taxpayer's state of residence apply to his or her Roth IRA?

Practice Pointer. The "pay taxes now or later" evaluation is an oversimplification of the basic difference between the Roth IRA and the deductible traditional IRA because, as has just been shown, many other factors come into play.

There were some increases for contributions and out-of-pocket limits for HSAs and HDHPs for 2021. The HSA contribution limits for 2021 are $3,600 for self-only and $7,200 for family; the HSA catch-up contribution is (age 55 or older) $1,000; the HDHP minimum deductibles are $1,400 for self-only and $2,800 for family; and the HDHP maximum out-of-pocket amounts for 2021 are $7,000 for self-only and $14,000 for family. [IRS Rev. Proc. 2020-32, 2020-24 I.R.B. 930]

Q 1:12 Whose advice may be helpful when deciding between a Roth or traditional IRA?

Financial planners, accountants, and attorneys are likely to be in the best position to help an individual decide between the Roth IRA and the traditional IRA (and to determine whether to convert a traditional IRA into a Roth IRA). Software is available to aid in the determination, as well. A number of banks, insurance companies, mutual funds, and other financial organizations offer the use of IRA calculators free on their Web pages or make the software available for a nominal charge; many institutions also provide worksheets as tools for completing comparison calculations.

For 2021 and 2020, the total contributions an individual can make each year to all of the individual's traditional IRAs and Roth IRAs remain $6,000 ($7,000 if the individual is age 50 or older) or, if less, the individual's taxable compensation for the year.

Under Section 107 of the Setting Every Community Up for Retirement Enhancement (SECURE) Act (Pub. L. No. 116-94), which was part of the Further Consolidated Appropriations Act, 2020, and was enacted on December 20, 2019, the maximum age for contributions to a traditional IRA was repealed. (Previously, individuals attaining the age of 70½ by the end of the year were unable to make contributions.) The change under the SECURE Act puts a traditional IRA on the same level playing field as a Roth IRA, which does not have a maximum age for contributions.

Section 114 of the SECURE Act increased the required beginning date for minimum required distributions from an IRA from age 70½ to age 72.

Section 105 of the SECURE Act 2.0 (i.e., HR 2954), which has not yet been enacted, generally further increases the age for the required beginning date for mandatory distributions to age 75.

Also, under the SECURE Act, parents may take early withdrawals of up to $5,000 from their retirement accounts without a penalty, an exception to the 10 percent early withdrawal tax, within a year of a child's birth or adoption, referred to as a qualified birth or adoption distribution (a QBOAD).

Under the prior law, after the death of an IRA owner, a nonspouse beneficiary was permitted to stretch the required minimum distribution date over the beneficiary's life (i.e., a "stretch" IRA). Section 401 of the SECURE Act provides that amounts must be distributed by the end of the 10th calendar year following the year of the IRA owner's death. There are certain exceptions for beneficiaries who are the surviving spouse, disabled or chronically ill, not more than 10 years younger than the IRA owner, or a child under the age of majority.

Pursuant to Section 107 of the SECURE Act, age 70½ is no longer a distinguishing factor between a Roth IRA and a traditional IRA.

Q 1:13 Should nondeductible contributions ever be made to a traditional IRA?

Perhaps not, unless the contribution will be converted to a Roth IRA (see Q 1:13) before there is significant appreciation. (See Qs 1:13, 3:105, 3:106.) Contributing to a Roth IRA is always better than making a nondeductible contribution to a traditional IRA. But if a Roth IRA contribution cannot be made (because income is too high; see Qs 1:4, 3:73), and a traditional IRA contribution cannot be deducted (because the individual or spouse actively participates in a retirement plan, and income is too high; see Qs 1:3, 3:49), then making a non-IRA investment may be a better choice.

Without the upfront deduction, the remaining tax benefit of a traditional IRA is tax-free growth during the investment period. But that is enjoyed at the cost of taxation, during the withdrawal period, at ordinary income rates.

By contrast, when a taxable investment is made, income during the investment period (e.g., dividends or interest) is taxed as ordinary income. But when the asset is sold, the gain is taxed at more favorable capital gain rates.

Q 1:14 If tax rates remain constant over a long period of time, does a Roth IRA yield more than a traditional IRA?

No. The assets available for distribution on an after-tax basis will be identical for a Roth IRA and a deductible traditional IRA over any period when the taxpayer's bracket remains *constant*.

> **Example.** Kate will have $6,000 in pre-tax dollars to contribute to an IRA each year. She expects to be in the 24 percent tax bracket for each contribution year, and also when the funds are distributed at retirement. Kate is unsure whether to contribute $6,000 per year to a deductible traditional IRA, or $4,560 (the after-tax amount) per year to a Roth IRA. It turns out that when the tax bracket remains constant over time, either case will yield the same result.

Assumptions

a.	Annual contribution amount:	
	Traditional IRA (deductible)	$6,000
	Roth IRA	$4,560
b.	Number of years until Kate retires	20
c.	Expected annual investment return	5%
d.	Marginal tax rate (contribution phase)	24%
e.	Marginal tax rate (retirement phase)	24%
f.	Full distribution at retirement	

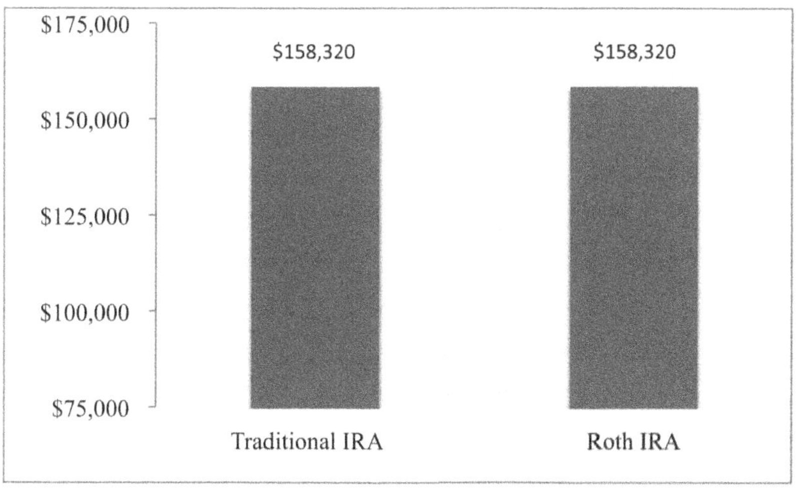

Q 1:15 Which IRA is better if the tax rate will be lower in retirement?

The deductible traditional IRA provides better results than the Roth IRA if the individual's tax rate will be *lower* at the time of distribution than it was during the contribution phase.

> **Example.** The facts are the same as in Q 1:14, except that Kate expects to be in the 32 percent tax bracket for each contribution year (so the after-tax Roth IRA contribution would be $4,560), but in the 24 percent bracket when the funds are distributed. In this case, the deductible traditional IRA is a better choice.

Assumptions

a.	Annual contribution amount:	
	Traditional IRA (deductible)	$6,000
	Roth IRA	$4,080
b.	Number of years until Kate retires	20
c.	Expected annual investment return	5%
d.	Marginal tax rate (contribution phase)	32%
e.	Marginal tax rate (retirement phase)	24%
f.	Full distribution at retirement	

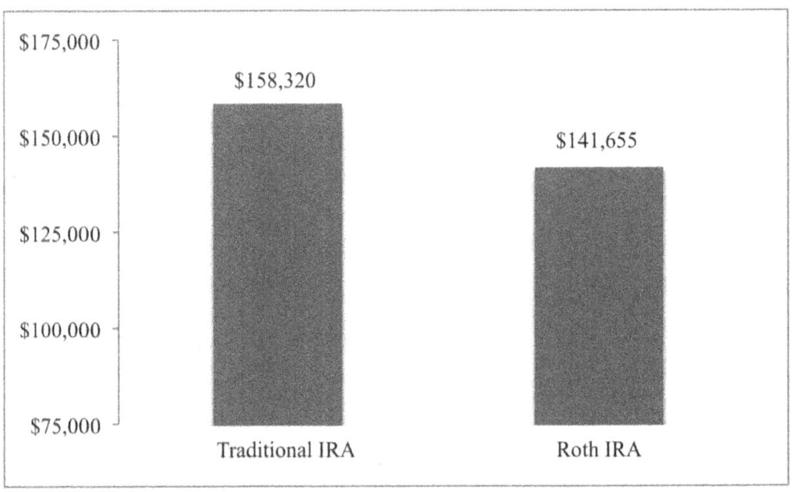

Q 1:16 Which IRA is better if the tax rate in retirement is higher than during the contribution phase?

The Roth IRA provides better results than the deductible traditional IRA if the tax rate in retirement is higher than it was during the contribution phase.

Example. The facts are the same as in Q 1:14, except that Kate expects to be in the 24 percent tax bracket for each contribution year, and the 32 percent bracket at retirement. In this case, the Roth IRA yields more than the traditional IRA.

Assumptions

a.	Annual contribution amount:	
	Traditional IRA (deductible)	$6,000
	Roth IRA	$4,560
b.	Number of years until Kate retires	20
c.	Expected annual investment return	5%
d.	Marginal tax rate (contribution phase)	24%
e.	Marginal tax rate (retirement phase)	32%
f.	Full distribution at retirement	

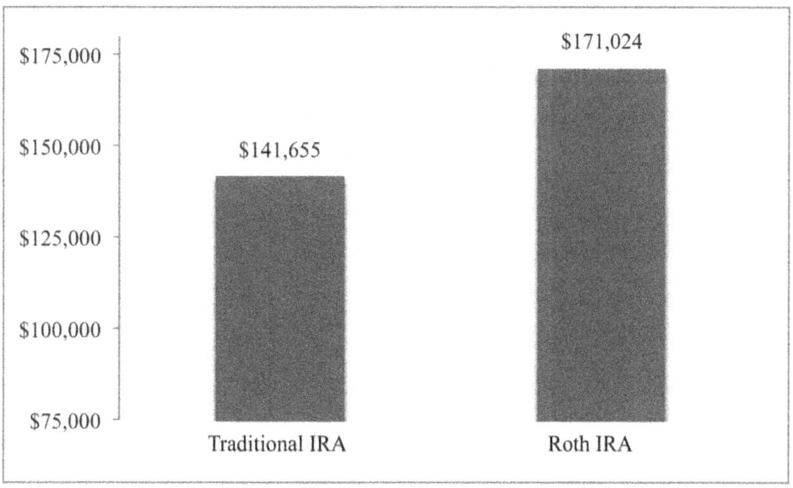

Conversions

Q 1:17 What should be considered when deciding whether to convert a traditional IRA to a Roth IRA?

The decision should take into account a comparison of the current versus expected future tax rate, ability and willingness to pay the conversion tax, whether the assets will be needed in retirement or can be left to accumulate, and how the IRA fits into the estate plan.

Q 1:18 Does conversion to a Roth IRA make IRA assets more accessible?

Yes. One reason an IRA owner may choose to convert a traditional IRA to a Roth IRA is to have easier and earlier access to his or her savings. The assets in a traditional IRA generally are not available without penalty until the owner attains age 59½. The contribution amount (the conversion amount) in a Roth IRA, on the other hand, is available free of tax and penalty after five years (see chapters 2 and 5). Thus, the owner of a traditional IRA who is younger than age 59½ can gain earlier access to the IRA funds by converting them to a Roth IRA.

Q 1:19 Does it make sense to convert a traditional IRA to a Roth IRA and then use IRA assets to pay the taxes on the conversion?

No. It is a bad idea to use IRA assets to pay the conversion tax. An IRA distribution used to cover the tax would reduce the size of the retirement fund, and not only be taxable but also possibly subject to the 10 percent early distribution penalty.

Q 1:20 Over a long savings horizon and with a constant tax rate, does the conversion of a traditional IRA to a Roth IRA result in more dollars available for retirement?

Yes. The conversion of a traditional IRA to a Roth IRA will result in more after-tax assets being available for retirement, when the IRA owner's tax bracket remains constant and he or she has the ability to pay the taxes on the conversion from funds outside the IRA.

> **Example.** Jean converts her $100,000 deductible traditional IRA to a Roth IRA. Jean is in the 24 percent tax bracket and expects to remain in that tax bracket at the time of distribution; she also has $24,000 in other savings earning 7 percent taxable interest. Jean's savings are enough to pay the taxes she owes on the $100,000 conversion. She expects that she will retire in 30 years and will not need to access her Roth IRA before that date. As shown, the Roth IRA will give Jean more assets as a lump-sum distribution after 30 years.

Assumptions

a.	Conversion amount	$100,000
b.	Number of years until Jean retires	30
c.	Expected annual investment return	7%
d.	Marginal tax rate (contribution phase)	24%
e.	Marginal tax rate (retirement phase)	24%
f.	Full distribution at retirement	

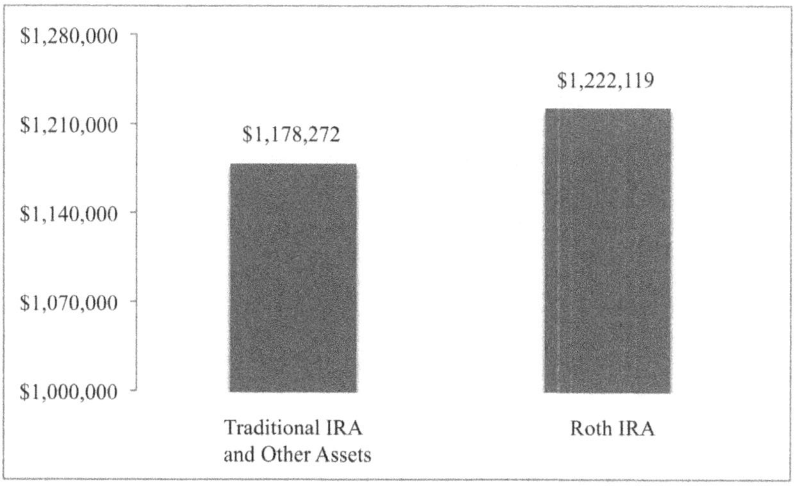

Q 1:21 If an IRA owner's tax bracket will be lower during the distribution phase, does converting from a traditional IRA to a Roth IRA still result in more assets being available at the time of retirement?

Perhaps. If an individual's tax rate is lower during the distribution phase than when contributions were made, the conversion to a Roth IRA may, after the fact, appear to have been the less desirable choice. Given a sufficiently long period of time, however, the conversion probably will result in more after-tax assets being available for retirement as long as sufficient assets exist outside the IRA to pay the conversion tax.

Q 1:22 Why would a traditional IRA owner want to convert to a Roth IRA when doing so creates immediate tax liability?

Converting to a Roth IRA requires the immediate payment of taxes, but avoids tax liability in the future. An individual may want to accelerate taxation—e.g., to avoid taxation of future earnings at ordinary income rates or because the applicable tax rate is expected to rise (see Q 3:111).

Q 1:23 Is conversion to a Roth IRA more desirable when the traditional IRA contains nondeductible contributions?

Yes. The larger the percentage of nondeductible contributions contained in a traditional IRA, the more desirable it is to convert to a Roth IRA because no taxes are owed on the conversion of nondeductible contributions. Only the earnings and the return of deductible contributions will be subject to federal income taxes. Furthermore, the Roth IRA allows for tax-free growth of earnings, whereas the traditional IRA provides for only tax-deferred growth.

> **Note.** An IRA owner is not allowed to convert only the nondeductible contributions. A pro rata share of taxable and nontaxable amounts will be considered converted if an individual does not convert his or her entire traditional IRA balance.

Attractive Uses for IRAs

Q 1:24 Are IRAs useful for general (nonretirement) savings?

IRAs are best suited for retirement savings—the funds can be withdrawn for any purpose, but distributions for nonretirement purposes are often subject to costly penalties. But Roth IRAs also have value as a general savings device because their contributions may always be withdrawn tax free and penalty free. This benefit must be balanced against the loss of tax-free compounding of the amount withdrawn.

Q 1:25 Can savings accumulated under a qualified plan be moved to an IRA?

Yes. Holding rollover assets from a qualified plan is one of the primary uses of a traditional IRA. It is frequently the case that after retirement or termination of employment with a company, an individual will want to move assets from a qualified retirement plan to an IRA to more directly control the investment and distribution of those assets while avoiding the full tax consequences of taking the assets directly. A rollover to a traditional IRA is useful for maintaining a retirement fund that has already been developed under another plan; to avoid 20 percent mandatory withholding on the distribution, a rollover can be made directly from the plan to the IRA (see chapter 6).

Many 401(k) and 403(b) plans now include a qualified Roth IRA contribution program. This feature allows participants to elect the designation of part or all of their elective deferrals to the plan as after-tax Roth contributions. [I.R.C. § 402A; Prop. Treas. Reg. § 1.402A-1] The resulting *designated Roth IRA account* (DRAC) is an account within the qualified plan, not a Roth IRA. DRAC assets may, however, be rolled over to a Roth IRA, where they are exempted from the lifetime minimum distribution requirements and generally less favorable basis recovery rules that apply to qualified plan distributions. The rollover may produce some unfavorable consequences, so caution is warranted (see Q 6:92).

Q 1:26 Can an IRA be used as for emergency funds?

The Code includes special disaster relief provisions that ease access to retirement funds, and allow them to be repaid, by individuals who qualify because of losses due to the coronavirus pandemic, or hurricanes and other national disasters. (See chapter 7.)

Apart from that, a Roth IRA is suitable for holding emergency funds but usually a traditional IRA is not. A Roth IRA owner can always withdraw regular contributions tax free, and distributions of earnings and conversion contributions are often tax free as well. Only nonqualified distributions are subject to tax and penalties. A traditional IRA is unsuitable for emergency savings because distributions are subject to taxes and penalties.

Q 1:27 Are IRA funds easy and cheap to transfer?

Yes. One of the most valuable features of an IRA is the owner's ability to transfer and change investments without tax or penalty. An IRA is a tax-exempt trust, so it may buy and sell assets without generating taxable income. Tax-free transfers to or from an IRA can be done using a trustee-to-trustee transfer, and also (in many cases) using a 60-day rollover. Trustee-to-trustee transfers are unlimited in amount and frequency. Tax-free rollovers from one IRA to another are allowed only once a year. [I.R.C. § 408(d)(4)(B); Treas. Reg. § 1.408-4(b)(4)(ii)]

Benefit of Establishing an IRA Early

Q 1:28 What is the advantage of establishing an IRA as early as possible?

The advantage of beginning IRA savings as early as possible, and thus lengthening the deferral period, is best demonstrated by an example. It should be noted that, although the following example assumes a traditional IRA, the principle of tax deferral on earnings also applies to the Roth IRA and the ESA. Further, the Roth IRA and the ESA have the advantage that qualified distributions will be tax free.

> **Example.** Ed begins to make annual contributions to a traditional IRA when he is age 22. He invests $6,000 each year for nine years until he reaches age 30, and then never adds another penny. The IRA grows at 8 percent each year. At retirement (age 65), as shown in the accompanying table, Ed has $1,196,421 in his account. Lisa, who is the same age as Ed, waits until she is age 35 to begin making annual IRA contributions, and from then on, she contributes $6,000 per year until retirement at age 65. Lisa never catches up with Ed, even though Ed contributes nothing after his nine deposits and even though Lisa contributes $132,000 more than Ed. At age 65, Ed's IRA is 50 percent larger than Lisa's.

Table 1-2. IRA Deposits and Accumulations

Ed			*Lisa*	
Deposit	*Accumulation*	*Age*	*Deposit*	*Accumulation*
$6,000	$ 6,480	22	$ 0	$ 0
$6,000	$ 13,478	23	$ 0	$ 0
$6,000	$ 21,037	24	$ 0	$ 0
$6,000	$ 29,200	25	$ 0	$ 0
$6,000	$ 38,016	26	$ 0	$ 0
$6,000	$ 47,537	27	$ 0	$ 0
$6,000	$ 57,820	28	$ 0	$ 0
$6,000	$ 68,925	29	$ 0	$ 0
$6,000	$ 80,919	30	$ 0	$ 0
$ 0	$ 87,393	31	$ 0	$ 0
$ 0	$ 94,384	32	$ 0	$ 0
$ 0	$101,935	33	$ 0	$ 0
$ 0	$110,090	34	$ 0	$ 0
$ 0	$118,897	35	$6,000	$ 6,480
$ 0	$128,409	36	$6,000	$ 13,478
$ 0	$138,682	37	$6,000	$ 21,037
$ 0	$149,776	38	$6,000	$ 29,200
$ 0	$161,758	39	$6,000	$ 38,016
$ 0	$174,699	40	$6,000	$ 47,537
$ 0	$188,675	41	$6,000	$ 57,820
$ 0	$203,769	42	$6,000	$ 68,925
$ 0	$220,070	43	$6,000	$ 80,919
$ 0	$237,676	44	$6,000	$ 93,873
$ 0	$256,690	45	$6,000	$107,863
$ 0	$277,225	46	$6,000	$122,972
$ 0	$299,403	47	$6,000	$139,290
$ 0	$323,355	48	$6,000	$156,913
$ 0	$349,224	49	$6,000	$175,946
$ 0	$377,162	50	$6,000	$196,501
$ 0	$407,335	51	$6,000	$218,701
$ 0	$439,921	52	$6,000	$242,678
$ 0	$475,115	53	$6,000	$268,572

Table 1-2. IRA Deposits and Accumulations (*cont'd*)

Ed			*Lisa*	
Deposit	*Accumulation*	*Age*	*Deposit*	*Accumulation*
$ 0	$ 513,124	54	$6,000	$296,538
$ 0	$ 554,174	55	$6,000	$326,741
$ 0	$ 598,508	56	$6,000	$359,360
$ 0	$ 646,389	57	$6,000	$394,589
$ 0	$ 698,100	58	$6,000	$432,636
$ 0	$ 753,948	59	$6,000	$473,726
$ 0	$ 814,264	60	$6,000	$518,105
$ 0	$ 879,405	61	$6,000	$566,033
$ 0	$ 949,757	62	$6,000	$617,796
$ 0	$1,025,738	63	$6,000	$673,699
$ 0	$1,107,797	64	$6,000	$734,075
$ 0	$1,196,421	65	$6,000	$799,281

Investment Options

Q 1:29 What are the investment options for an IRA?

Investments that traditional and Roth IRAs may hold include the following:

- Certificates of deposit (CDs);
- Savings accounts;
- Money market mutual funds;
- Mutual funds;
- Stocks (excluding shares of an S corporation), bonds, and annuities;
- A substantial number of other investment vehicles; and
- Certain precious metals which are excluded from the definition of a *collectible*; see Q 1:33.

[I.R.C. §§ 408(m), 1361(c)(2)(A)(vi); Treas. Reg. § 1.1361-1(h)(1)(vii)]

Q 1:30 Must every IRA trustee offer precious metals as an investment option?

No. Most trustees are unlikely to offer them. A simpler alternative is to have the IRA acquire shares of an exchange-traded fund or other security that tracks the price of the precious metals in the physical market. [I.R.C. § 408(m)(3); Priv. Ltr. Rul. 200732026 (Oct. 8, 2007)]

Q 1:31 Are all IRAs subject to the same investment restrictions?

All IRAs are governed by the same *legal* rules determining which assets can or cannot be acquired. But a trustee or custodian might impose *other* asset restrictions in the IRA agreement for its own benefit. For example, to reduce administrative burdens, a trustee could forbid IRAs to acquire real estate. If it did, a purported transfer of prohibited property to the IRA would be invalid. [Dabney v. Commissioner, T.C. Memo. 2014-108 (2014)]

Unconventional assets such as partnerships and real estate are more likely to be allowed for a *self-directed IRA*. The agreement for a self-directed IRA generally assigns all responsibility for investment decisions to the IRA owner, limits the custodian's responsibility to mere administrative and similar matters, and includes an exculpatory clause that expressly relieves the custodian of all fiduciary liability to the owner. The degree of control makes the self-directed IRA owner a fiduciary of the IRA, so care must be taken to avoid prohibited transactions (see Qs 1:37–1:44).

> **Note.** In *Mandelbaum v. FISERV, Inc.* [107 A.F.T.R.2d 2011-1651 (D. Colo. 2011)], self-directed IRA owners unwisely chose to invest in what turned out to be the massive Ponzi scheme orchestrated by Bernard Madoff. They later tried to recoup losses from the IRA custodian based on vague claims of due diligence failures and other fiduciary duty violations. The claims were dismissed, partly because the IRA documents had shifted all fiduciary responsibilities from the custodian to the owners.

As a matter of company policy, a custodian may refuse to *acquire* on behalf of an IRA stock that is not publicly traded—even though it may allow the IRA to *hold* such property. In that case, the owner can still use IRA funds to acquire the stock—either by asking the custodian for a check made payable to the stock issuer (which the custodian or the owner delivers), or by directing the custodian to wire funds to the issuer for the purchase. The stock certificate must be issued in the name of the IRA. [Ancira v. Commissioner, 119 T.C. 135 (2002); McGaugh v. Commissioner, 119 A.F.T.R.2d (RIA) 2017-2359 (7th Cir.), *aff'g* T.C. Memo. 2016-28 (2016)]

Q 1:32 May IRAs be invested in life insurance?

No. Individuals are prohibited from investing in life insurance in their IRAs. [I.R.C. § 408(e)(5)]

Q 1:33 May IRAs acquire collectibles?

No. *Collectibles* include any work of art, rug or antique, metal or gem, stamp or coin, alcoholic beverage, or other tangible property specified by the IRS, and they are strictly off limits for an IRA. If IRA assets are used to purchase a collectible, the amount so used is treated as a distribution. [I.R.C. §§ 408(m), 1361(c)(2)(A)(vi); Treas. Reg. § 1.1361-1(h)(1)(vii)]

Certain precious metals, however, are excluded from the definition of a collectible, and may be acquired by an IRA. The exception covers gold, silver, platinum, and palladium coins and bullion meeting standards of purity described in Code Section 408(m)(3). Bullion, moreover, must be held in the physical possession of a trustee to qualify.

An IRA may invest in an exchange-traded fund that tracks the market price of precious metals. Or, it may acquire shares in a trust that directly invests in such commodities. Ownership of either type of interest is not considered the acquisition of a collectible. But if a redemption of the IRA's shares results in a distribution of the underlying commodity, the IRA will be treated as acquiring a collectible, unless the distributed property is coins covered by the exception. Distributed bullion would always be treated as the acquisition of a collectible, because an IRA may never take physical possession of bullion. [Priv. Ltr. Ruls. 201446030 (Nov. 14, 2014), 200732026 (Oct. 8, 2007)]

Q 1:34 Can IRA assets be pledged as security for a loan?

No. If during any taxable year the owner of an IRA uses the account or any portion thereof as security for a loan, the portion so used is treated as a distribution to that individual. [I.R.C. § 408(e)(4)]

A bankruptcy court most recently held that the anti-assignment provision of an individual retirement annuity contract prevented the annuitant from transferring a valid security interest to his lender. The decision concerned only the lender's claim and did not address potential tax consequences of the failed assignment. [Albracht v. Hamilton State Bank, 505 B.R. 347 (Bankr. N.D. Ga. 2013)]

Q 1:35 Are assets in an IRA forfeitable?

No. The Code requires assets in an IRA to be nonforfeitable. [I.R.C. § 408(a)(4); *see also* IRS Form 5305-R, Article III.]

Q 1:36 Can an IRA owner's personal transactions be matched with transactions inside the IRA under the wash sale rule that governs securities transactions?

They can be. The IRS's position is that Code Section 1091—the wash sale rule—*may* apply to an individual's sale of securities at a loss if his/her IRA (traditional or Roth) acquires substantially identical securities within 30 days before or after the sale. At the very least, the IRS considers the transaction a wash sale if the IRA owner caused the IRA to acquire the replacement securities. [Rev. Rul. 2008-5, 2008-3 I.R.B. 271]

Generally, if a matching pair of transactions is identified under Code Section 1091 (a so-called *wash sale*), the taxpayer cannot deduct the loss, the basis in the sold securities is added to the basis in the replacement securities, and the holding period for the replacement securities includes the holding period for the securities that the taxpayer sold. In effect, there is no recognition of a wash sale loss until the replacement securities are sold. [I.R.C. § 1091(d)]

If a wash sale involves an IRA, however, the loss is never recognizable. Since the IRA owner does not hold the replacement securities, the basis in the original securities is simply lost. It cannot be added to the owner's basis in the IRA. Worse still, a wash sale transaction involving an IRA might be a prohibited transaction; Revenue Ruling 2008-5 expressly warns that conclusions should not be drawn from the IRS's failure to consider that issue in the ruling. [Rev. Rul. 2008-5, 2008-3 I.R.B. 271]

Prohibited Transactions

Q 1:37 Do the prohibited transaction rules apply to IRAs, ESAs, and HSAs?

Yes. IRAs, HSAs, and ESAs are all "plans" subject to the prohibited transaction rules of ERISA and the Code. [I.R.C. § 4975(a), 4975(e)(1); 29 U.S.C. § 1106] Many of the rules are parallel, but the IRS is bound by the Department of Labor's (DOL) regulations and interpretations defining prohibited transactions and their exemptions. The IRS also enforces the tax rules that apply when such transactions occur. [Reorganization Plan No. 4 of 1978, 5 U.S.C. App. 1, 92 Stat. 3790]

Q 1:38 What is a prohibited transaction?

A prohibited transaction occurs generally when a disqualified person (usually the IRA owner) engages in certain transactions (see Q 1:38) involving the plan. [I.R.C. § 4975] If a prohibited transaction occurs, the IRA loses its tax exemption as of the first day of the transaction year, and all the assets in the account on that date are treated as distributed. [I.R.C. § 408(e)] Disqualified persons who participate in the prohibited transaction are required to correct it and must also pay an excise tax. [I.R.C. § 4975(a), 4975(b)]

With some exceptions, a plan and a "disqualified person" may not engage, directly or indirectly, in the following transactions:

- The sale or leasing of property by one to the other;
- The loan of funds or extension of credit by one to the other;
- The furnishing of goods, services, or facilities by one to the other;
- The transfer of plan income or assets to a disqualified person;
- Any dealing with the plan, by a disqualified person who is also a fiduciary, in the fiduciary's own interest (see Q 1:39); and
- Any payment, by a party that transacts with the plan, to a disqualified person who is a fiduciary.

[I.R.C. § 4975(c), 4975(e)(1)]

Q 1:39 Who is a disqualified person?

Disqualified persons include, among others, a plan owner (e.g., owner of a self-directed IRA), who exercises investment discretion over the plan, as well as the spouse, ancestors, and lineal descendants of the owner, and any spouse of a lineal descendant. A corporation is considered a disqualified person if at least 50 percent of either the combined voting power or the value of its stock is owned by disqualified persons. Similarly, a trust or estate is a disqualified person if at least 50 percent of its beneficial ownership is held by a disqualified person. Plan fiduciaries are also disqualified persons. [I.R.C. § 4975(e)(2)]

Q 1:40 Who is a fiduciary?

Generally, a *fiduciary* is a person who exercises discretionary authority or control over the plan's assets or administration, or who renders investment advice to the plan for a fee. [I.R.C. § 4975(e)(3), 4975(e)(2)(A)]

The Department of Labor (DOL) attempted to broaden the scope of fiduciary status in regulations that would have required investment advisors dealing with IRAs to act in their clients' best interests. [29 C.F.R. § 2510.3-21] The rule, issued under the Obama administration, was delayed by the Trump administration and challenged in the courts. In 2018, the Fifth Circuit Court of Appeals struck down the rule. [U.S. Chamber of Commerce v. DOL, 885 F.3d 360 (5th Cir. 2018); Market Synergy Grp. v. DOL, No. 17-3038 (10th Cir. Mar. 13, 2018); DOL Field Assistance Bull. 2018-02 (May 17, 2018)] In February 2021, an updated version of the invalidated DOL fiduciary rule went into effect as a prohibited transaction class exemption.

Q 1:41 What are some examples of disqualified person status that has been attributed under the related party rules?

The Department of Labor (DOL) opined in 2006 that an IRA's investment, at its owner's direction, in notes issued by a corporation would be a prohibited transaction if the majority interest in the corporation is held by the IRA owner's son-in-law and daughter. The arrangement would be both a sale of property (the notes) and an extension of credit, and both transactions are prohibited between an IRA and a disqualified person (the corporation, under the related party rules). [DOL Adv. Op. 2006-09A]

The DOL also concluded that transactions with an entity in which an IRA is invested may be prohibited transactions even if the entity holds no plan assets and the terms are fair. At issue was a limited liability company's (LLC) lease of property to an S corporation on arm's-length terms. The S corporation was majority-owned by a husband and wife, and the husband's IRA owned 49 percent of the LLC. However, the same individual was both comptroller of the S corporation and manager of the LLC, so the DOL did not consider the LLC to be independent of the IRA owner (a disqualified person). Since the IRA owner would have directed his IRA to invest in the LLC with the understanding that the LLC and S corporation would enter into the lease, the DOL found the lease would be a prohibited transaction between the IRA and a party in interest. [DOL Adv. Op. 2006-01A]

Most recent litigation involved an individual who used his retirement savings to start a used car business. He rolled over his 401(k) plan to an IRA, caused the IRA to acquire 98 percent ownership of a new LLC he formed to operate the business, and then became the general manager of the LLC. The Tax Court held that the IRA and the LLC were substantially the same entity, because the IRA only invested in the LLC, and practically all of the LLC's funding came from the IRA. The IRA owner was a disqualified person with respect to the self-directed IRA, and so was the LLC (because a disqualified person—the IRA owner, through the IRA—owned more than 50 percent of the LLC). Thus, by causing the LLC to pay him compensation, the IRA owner transferred plan assets and dealt with the plan for his own benefit—a prohibited transaction. [Ellis v. Commissioner, T.C. Memo. 2013-245 (2013)]

In another case, a self-directed IRA purchased a land tract, transferred half of it to an LLC controlled by the IRA owner and his wife, and provided the funds to develop the tract. Whether the transfer was a loan or capital contribution to the LLC was not clear. Either way, the court held, the transfer was a prohibited transaction. The IRA owner, his wife, and the LLC were all disqualified persons, and IRA assets were used for their benefit. [Kellerman v. Rice, 116 A.F.T.R.2d 2015-6133, 538 B.R. 776 (D. Ark. 2015)]

Q 1:42 What is an *indirect* loan or extension of credit between a disqualified person and the plan?

Code Section 4975(c) defines a prohibited transaction as, among other things, a *direct or indirect* extension of credit between a disqualified person and the IRA. The meaning of *indirect* was explained in a 2013 Tax Court case, *Peek v. Commissioner* [140 T.C. No. 12 (2013)]. The case involved two men who wanted to acquire a business engaged in the sale of fire protection systems. They followed a strategy that was recommended to allow their self-directed traditional IRAs to fund the purchase. In 2001, they organized a corporation (FP) that issued all of its stock to the IRAs in exchange for cash. FP then bought the business assets, paying part of the purchase price in cash and issuing a promissory note for the rest. Unfortunately, the accountant who recommended the strategy and warned the men about prohibited transactions did not know the seller had insisted on securing FP's debt with personal guarantees from the two IRA owners. Then two things occurred. First, the men converted the traditional IRAs to Roth IRAs in 2003 and 2004—and paid income tax on the conversions. Second, in 2006, the Roth IRAs sold the stock of FP and treated the gain as nontaxable. The personal guarantees of the FP debt were still in place at the time of the 2006 sale. The IRS asserted—and the Tax Court agreed—that by securing FP's note with the IRA owners' personal guarantees, each IRA had engaged in a prohibited transaction that caused its termination and a deemed distribution of its assets (the FP stock) in 2001. Thus, in 2006 it was the IRA owners (not the IRAs) who sold FP, and they were personally liable for tax deficiencies because they had not reported the gain. Not only were the individuals stuck with the tax, it was also too late for them to recover their overpayments of tax on the now-fictive conversions of 2003 and 2004. [Peek v. Commissioner, 140 T.C. No. 12 (2013)]

The taxpayers in *Peek* argued that there was no prohibited transaction because the extension of credit was between them and the corporation—not the IRAs. But the Tax Court held that the IRA owners had *indirectly* extended credit to their IRAs, and that the prohibition could be easily avoided if it only targeted a loan or guarantee between a disqualified person and the IRA itself.

In a case with a similar transaction at issue, the IRA owners argued that an exception to the prohibited transaction rules applied, because their personal loan guarantees were given in connection with the acquisition and holding of a security (the stock of the corporation they formed to buy the business). But the Tax Court held that Code Section 4975(d)(3) did not apply, because the purpose of the transaction was to acquire assets, not stock. [Thiessen v. Commissioner, 146 T.C. No. 7 (2016)]

Q 1:43 Can a self-directed IRA be held in a brokerage account?

Yes. But using the account for margin transactions is problematic because certain security arrangements required by the broker are prohibited transactions for the IRA. At present, the DOL is considering whether to issue a new exemption for these transactions.

With a margin account, the investor borrows money from the broker and uses it to make purchases in the account—e.g., securities or futures contracts. The broker demands some form of security for the loan, and indeed may require security as a condition of opening the margin account. The DOL and the IRS have considered some of these arrangements in the context of a self-directed IRA.

In one such case, the DOL opined that an individual whose self-directed IRA is held in a brokerage account cannot pledge his or her personal assets to secure margin debt incurred by the IRA. The pledge would be a prohibited extension of credit between a disqualified person (the self-directed IRA owner) and the IRA. [DOL Op. Ltr. 2009-03A]

In another case, the DOL found that an agreement by the owner of a self-directed IRA to indemnify the broker for investment losses and tax expenses in the IRA's margin account would also be an extension of credit by the disqualified person (the IRA owner) to the IRA, and a prohibited transaction. [DOL Op. Ltr. 2011-09A] The DOL also opined that Prohibited Transaction Exemption (PTE) 80-26 did not cover the indemnification agreement. The DOL issues PTEs that exempt certain transactions from the category of prohibited transactions. PTE 80-26 exempts use of a disqualified person's credit only for ordinary operating expenses of the retirement plan, or for purposes incidental to the plan's ordinary operation. The DOL concluded that investment losses and tax expenses incurred in a margin account are neither ordinary operating expenses nor incidental costs. [DOL Op. Ltr. 2011-09A]

Nonetheless, the DOL is considering whether to issue a new class exemption that would cover pledge and indemnity agreements, as well as cross-collateralization agreements (in which the IRA owner grants a security interest in non-IRA accounts he or she holds with the same broker to cover the IRA's margin debt). Accordingly, the IRS announced in December 2011 that, until further notice, it will evaluate IRAs without regard to any consequences that arise from treating pledges, indemnity agreements, and cross-collateralization agreements like those described in DOL Advisory Opinions 2009-03A and 2011-09A as prohibited transactions—as long as there has not been execution or enforcement of such agreements against the IRA assets. [IRS Ann. 2011-81 (Dec. 12, 2011)]

Pending further action by the DOL and IRS, it seems safe to assume that the mere existence of this kind of cross-collateralization arrangement will not cause an IRA to be treated for tax purposes as having lost its tax-exempt status. However, the assets in the IRA may be vulnerable to creditors.

At least three cases have been decided since IRS Announcement 2011-81. In each, the court held that cross-collateralization language in the IRA agreement does not disqualify an IRA before the event occurs that triggers the collateral. Until then, the lien is only contingent. [*In re* Daley, No. 12-6130, 2013 WL 2922651 (6th Cir. June 17, 2013) (IRA not disqualified, so exempt from bankruptcy estate); *In re* James, 111 A.F.T.R.2d 2013-980 (Bankr. E.D. Tenn. 2013) (same); *Yoshioka v. Charles Schwab Corp.*, No. C-11-1625 EMC, 2012 WL 5932817 (N.D. Cal. July 9, 2012) (claims against broker were premature)]

Q 1:44 Can a self-directed IRA purchase a debt that the IRA owner previously issued to a third party?

No, the debt purchase would be a prohibited transaction. A loan continues to be an extension of credit until it is fully repaid. If a self-directed IRA purchases a note that its owner previously issued to a creditor, the IRA becomes the owner's substitute creditor. The result is the same as if the IRA had been the original lender. In both cases, the acquisition and holding of the owner's note are a prohibited extension of credit between the IRA and a fiduciary. [Employee Benefits Security Administration (EBSA) Adv. Op. 2011-04A]

The transaction would also constitute prohibited self-dealing if the IRA owner, as fiduciary, directs the purchase of the note as part of an arrangement or understanding to use IRA assets for his or her personal benefit. [EBSA Adv. Op. 2011-04A]

Listed Transactions

Q 1:45 What is a listed transaction?

A *listed transaction* is any transaction that is the same as, or substantially similar to, a transaction that the IRS has specifically identified, in published

IRS guidance, as a tax-avoidance transaction. Disclosure requirements apply to listed transactions and there are penalties for noncompliance. [Treas. Reg. §§ 301.6707A-1(a), 1.6011-4(b)(2); T.D. 9492 (July 6, 2010)]

Q 1:46 Has the IRS identified such transactions involving IRAs?

Yes. The IRS has identified as tax abusive certain arrangements that are designed to shift value, or have the effect of doing so, to Roth IRAs in excess of applicable contribution limits. [Notice 2004-8, 2004-4 I.R.B. 333; IRS News Rel. IR-2011-39 (Apr. 7, 2011)] So far, no other type of IRA has been implicated in a listed transaction.

According to Notice 2004-8, abusive Roth IRA transactions generally involve a pre-existing business owned by an individual, a Roth IRA, and a corporation substantially all the shares of which are owned or acquired by the Roth IRA. An arrangement shifting business property to the corporation for less than fair value would be abusive. One example would be a sale of business receivables to the corporation that is not negotiated at arms' length. Another might be a management services agreement that is not fairly negotiated and shifts excessive fees from the business to the corporation. [I.R.S. Chief Counsel Advice 200929005 (July 17, 2009)] (In *United States v. Stover* [108 A.F.T.R.2d 2011-5837 (8th Cir. 2011)], the Eighth Circuit upheld a permanent injunction against a promoter of transactions that were "perfectly" described by Notice 2004-8.)

> **Note.** The IRS Web site provides detailed information about listed transactions. *See http://www.irs.gov/retirement/article/0,,id = 119565,00.html* for listed transactions that involve Roth IRAs, and *http://www.irs.gov/retirement/article/0,,id = 118821,00.html* for those involving other types of retirement plans. Under current tax law, there is less incentive to shift undervalued assets to a traditional, SEP, or SIMPLE IRA because distributions from those IRAs are taxed at ordinary income rates. However, the IRS is studying the potential for tax abuse. [*See* Mark J. Mazur, Assistant Treasury Secretary (Tax Policy), Letter to U.S. Representative George Miller (Sept. 19, 2012), available at *http://online.wsj.com/public/resources/documents/1335_001.pdf*.]

Q 1:47 What requirements apply to a listed transaction?

Various penalties and disclosure requirements apply. Participation in a listed transaction must be disclosed on the IRA owner's (and other participants') income tax returns for the years involved. Any material advisor concerning a listed transaction must maintain a list of all participants and make it available to the IRS. In some cases, material advisors must also register the listed transaction as a tax shelter. [I.R.C. §§ 6664(d)(2)(A), 6011, 6111; Treas. Reg. § 1.6011-4(d)]

If a listed transaction is not properly disclosed, a penalty—equal to 75 percent of the "decrease in tax shown on the return" as a result of the transaction—is payable. [I.R.C. § 6707A(b)] The penalty is determined by looking at the *original* return that should have contained the disclosure, and comparing the tax amount shown there with the amount that would have been shown had the transaction been correctly reported. If the original return included unrelated errors that also affected the tax calculation, those are *not* corrected before calculating the penalty. [*Yari v. Commissioner*, 118 A.F.T.R.2d 2016-6096 (9th Cir. 2016)]

For individuals, the minimum penalty for improperly disclosing a listed transaction is $5,000, and the maximum is $100,000. For entities, the minimum is $10,000 and the maximum is $200,000. [I.R.C. § 6707A(b)]

Listed transactions are also subject to an enhanced understatement penalty (20 percent of the understatement). And if the foregoing disclosure requirements are not met, the understatement penalty is increased to 30 percent (subject to a defense of reasonable cause and good faith).

The excess Roth IRA contribution must be reported annually on Form 5329 until it is removed. If not reported, or if the 6 percent annual excise tax is not paid, penalties are also imposed. [I.R.C. §§ 4973, 6651(a)(1), 6651(a)(2)]

Q 1:48 How does the IRS treat listed transactions involving Roth IRAs?

The IRS generally ignores the form of the listed transaction and recharacterizes it according to the economic substance of what occurred. If the transaction causes a transfer of value to the Roth IRA, the IRS may attempt to recast the steps as an excess contribution or use its authority under Code Section 482 to allocate income, deductions, credits, or allowances among the participants and related parties. In some cases, the IRS may treat the listed transaction as a prohibited transaction that results in termination of IRA status (see Q 1:37). [Notice 2004-8, 2004-4 I.R.B. 333]

In *Paschall v. Commissioner* [137 T.C. No. 2 (2011)], the IRS found that an elaborate series of stock subscriptions and shareholder distributions, which routed traditional IRA funds through shell corporations and into a Roth IRA, was a sham. The Tax Court agreed that the transaction, which had been marketed as a tax-free way to convert traditional IRA funds to a Roth IRA, was in substance an excess Roth IRA contribution. [*See also Polowniak v. Commissioner*, T.C. Memo. 2016-31.] And in *Repetto v. Commissioner* [T.C. Memo. 2012-168], where several Roth IRAs owned a corporation and the corporation received payments—for services never performed—from persons related to the IRA owners, the Tax Court upheld the recasting of the payments as excess Roth IRA contributions. *See also United States v. Stover* [108 A.F.T.R.2d 2011-5837 (8th Cir. 2011)], where the Eighth Circuit upheld a permanent injunction against a promoter of transactions that violated the Roth IRA contribution limits and were "perfectly" described by Notice 2004-8 (see Q 1:46).

However, three Circuit Courts of Appeals, each examining the same transaction (from different parties' perspectives), held that the IRS cannot rely on substance over form to recharacterize a Roth transaction that complies with Code provisions specifically designed to confer tax benefits in the absence of economic substance. [*Benenson, Jr. v. Commissioner*, 122 A.F.T.R.2d 2018-6897

(2d Cir. 2018); Benenson v. Commissioner, 121 A.F.T.R.2d 2018-1350 (1st Cir. 2018); Summa Holdings, Inc. v. Commissioner, 119 A.F.T.R.2d ¶ 2017-447 (6th Cir. 2017); *all rev'g* Summa Holdings, Inc. v. Commissioner, T.C. Memo. 2015-119] The transactions at issue took advantage of the favorable Code rules that govern domestic international sales corporations (DISCs). The DISC rules provide tax subsidies to U.S. exporters by allowing them to route payments through a corporation (the DISC) that essentially conducts only paper activities. The exporter pays commissions to the DISC, which are deductible by the exporter and not taxable to the DISC. Tax is deferred until the DISC pays dividends to its shareholders (who often also own the exporter). In *Summa*, the taxpayers who controlled the exporter inserted Roth IRAs into the ownership chain—the Roth IRAs owned the holding company that owned the DISC—so, when the holding company received dividends from the DISC, it paid the tax on them and distributed the balance to its own shareholders—the Roth IRAs. Claiming a lack of economic substance, the IRS ignored the DISC and recast the entire cash flow—treating the commissions as dividends paid by the exporter to its shareholders, and treating the holding company dividends as excess contributions to the Roth IRAs. The Tax Court held in favor of the IRS but was reversed each time on appeal.

The IRS also used the substance-over-form doctrine to recharacterize a similar transaction that coupled Roth IRAs with a foreign sales corporation (FSC) rather than a DISC. [Mazzei v. Commissioner, 150 T.C. No. 7 (Mar. 5, 2018)] The FSC rules of the Code, now repealed, also subsidized exporters. There, too, the Tax Court upheld the recasting of commission payments as excess Roth contributions. The case is being appealed to the Ninth Circuit. [Mazzei v. Commissioner, No. 0:18-tax-72451 (9th Cir. Sept. 5, 2018)]

Q 1:49 May the IRS respect the form of a transaction for income tax purposes but recharacterize it in order to apply the excise tax?

No. If the IRS respects the form of a transaction for income tax purposes, it may not recharacterize it as a listed Roth IRA transaction for excise tax purposes. Consistent treatment is required. [Repetto v. Commissioner, T.C. Memo. 2012-168; Ohsman v. Commissioner, T.C. Memo. 2011-98; Hellweg v. Commissioner, T.C. Memo. 2011-58; Polowniak v. Commissioner, T.C. Memo. 2016-31]

Bankruptcy and Debtor Issues

Q 1:50 How does federal bankruptcy law apply to IRAs?

Federal law provides substantial protection for IRAs in a bankruptcy proceeding. The Supreme Court held in 2005 that a debtor's retirement savings (including IRAs) must be excluded from the bankruptcy estate to the extent the funds are reasonably needed to support the debtor and any dependents. [Rousey v. Jacoway, 544 U.S. 320 (2005)] The decision placed IRAs on the same footing as other qualified retirement plans—meaning they are equally shielded from creditors—but left bankruptcy courts to make a factual determination in each case as to the amount of funds needed to satisfy the reasonable support standard.

Soon after the *Rousey* decision, the Bankruptcy Abuse Prevention and Consumer Protection Act of 2005 (BAPCPA) was enacted. Among other things, BAPCPA replaced the fact-based reasonable support standard with an objective dollar amount of IRA assets that may be exempted from a debtor's bankruptcy estate regardless of the debtor's need (see Q 1:51).

Q 1:51 Do IRAs enjoy unlimited protection under federal bankruptcy law?

No. Traditional and Roth IRA assets generally may be protected in bankruptcy by exemption from the bankruptcy estate up to a specified dollar amount. There is no limit, however, on the protection of SEP and SIMPLE IRA assets. Qualified rollovers from SEP IRAs, SIMPLE IRAs, and qualified plans also receive unlimited protection—so they should be kept separate from other IRAs. (If rollovers are not commingled with regular contributions, their earnings will qualify for the bankruptcy exemption and be entirely free from the dollar cap. Otherwise, there would have to be some apportionment of earnings between the rollover and regular contributions for purposes of the cap.) [11 U.S.C. § 522(n)]

The dollar limit, originally $1,000,000, is adjusted every three years to reflect changes in the Consumer Price Index. The current dollar limit is $1,362,800 per debtor, and it applies to bankruptcy cases commenced on or after April 1, 2019. The prior limit, $1,283,025, applies to cases begun during the previous three-year period. [11 U.S.C. §§ 104, 522(n); 84 Fed. Reg. 3488–3489 (Feb. 12, 2019); 81 Fed. Reg. 8748–8749 (Feb. 22, 2016)]

It is not clear whether states are preempted from protecting a larger amount of IRA assets. However, given the modest level of contributions permitted annually (currently $6,000, or $7,000 for individuals age 50 or older), only the rare non-rollover IRA will be able to accumulate assets in excess of the exemption amount. For practical purposes, most debtors have an unlimited exemption.

It is also unclear whether the dollar limit applies to deemed IRAs (see Q 1:8). Employers may generally hold deemed IRAs assets and qualified plan assets in the same trust. If deemed IRAs are treated under BAPCPA like employer-related retirement funds, they are protected in bankruptcy without regard to the dollar limit. Otherwise (if they are treated like IRAs that are not employer related), the dollar limit would apply.

Q 1:52 How do state insolvency laws apply to IRAs?

A debtor in bankruptcy is governed by federal bankruptcy law as well as the insolvency laws of his or her state of residence. State insolvency laws also permit exemptions, but sometimes they differ from the federal exemptions (e.g., see Q 1:55).

BAPCPA coordinates the federal and state exemptions by giving states a choice. States may adopt the federal exemptions or enact their own. States that enact separate exemptions may require their exclusive use, or they may allow debtors to choose between federal and state exemptions. A state that requires debtors to use only state law exemptions is said to have "opted out" of the federal exemption scheme. [11 U.S.C. § 522(b)(2), 522(b)(3)]

However, BAPCPA ensures that certain exemptions are available even in opt-out states. One such exemption is for IRAs. Thus, the IRA exemption may be claimed in every state. [11 U.S.C. § 522(b)(3)]

Note. In states that have not opted out of the federal scheme, Section 522(b)(2) authorizes debtors to claim the IRA exemption in Section 522(d)(12). For debtors in opt-out states, the IRA exemption in Section 522(b)(3)(C) is available. Courts have held there is no difference between the two exemptions, which are identically worded. [*In re* Thiem, 443 B.R. 832, 107 A.F.T.R.2d 2011-529 (Bankr. D. Ariz. 2011); *In re* Tabor, 433 B.R. 469, 105 A.F.T.R.2d 2010-2964 (Bankr. M.D. Pa. 2010)]

Q 1:53 Does federal bankruptcy protection extend to inherited IRAs?

No. The Supreme Court held in *Clark v. Rameker* that Section 522 of the Bankruptcy Code does not allow inherited IRAs to be exempted from the bankruptcy estate. The exemption has two requirements—the funds must be in an IRA, and they must be "retirement funds." Inherited IRA funds do not satisfy the second requirement. [Clark v. Rameker, 134 S. Ct. 2242 (2014)]

The Court found that the legal characteristics of an inherited IRA show that its funds are an ordinary pool of money. Unlike an IRA owner, the inherited IRA beneficiary:

1. Cannot add new funds to the account,
2. Must withdraw funds regardless of proximity to retirement, and
3. May withdraw the entire balance without penalty at any time (there is no legal incentive to keep the funds until at least age 59½).

[Clark v. Rameker, 134 S. Ct. at 2247]

Q 1:54 Does the federal bankruptcy exemption cover IRAs acquired in a divorce or marital separation?

The answer depends on whether the IRA funds so acquired have the legal characteristics of retirement funds. [*See* Clark v. Rameker, 134 S. Ct. 2242 (2014)]

The Eighth Circuit Court of Appeals applied the Clark analysis in a case where the debtor acquired an interest in his ex-wife's IRA, but the IRA was not transferred to him. His legal fees owed in the divorce exceeded the value of the IRA, and by the time he filed for bankruptcy a court-ordered lien favoring the lawyer had already been placed on the IRA. The Eight Circuit found that the lien on the account indicated the IRA was a pot of money available to creditors, and not retirement funds, so it held the funds were not exempt under Section 522 of the Bankruptcy Code. [Lerbakken v. Sieloff & Assoc., 949 F.3d 432 (8th Cir. 2020)]

Q 1:55 May a state's bankruptcy or insolvency laws provide a broader exemption that does cover inherited IRAs?

Yes. For example, Idaho exempts a debtor's interest in any employee benefit plan, which is defined to include arrangements that qualify under Code Section 408 or 408A (i.e., IRAs). [Idaho Code § 11-604A] In a most recent case, this exemption was held to apply to inherited IRAs because—unlike the federal exemption—it does not also require the IRA assets to be *retirement funds*. [*In re* Arehart, 66 Bank. Ct. Dec. 185 (Bankr. D. Idaho 2019)]

Q 1:56 If IRA funds are withdrawn during the bankruptcy proceeding, do they lose their exemption?

Under federal bankruptcy law, IRA funds do not cease to qualify for exemption merely because they are eligible for a rollover. (An RMD cannot be rolled over, so a withdrawn RMD is *not* exempt property; see Qs 1:3, 6:59.) [11 U.S.C. § 522(b)(3)(C), 522(b)(4)(D)] IRA funds are thus shielded from creditors during the rollover process (subject to the dollar limit, if it applies; see Q 1:51). Federal bankruptcy law also forbids the use of exempted property to satisfy a debt of the debtor that arose before the case commenced. [11 U.S.C. § 522(c)] This raises the question whether a distribution is still exempt if it is not rolled over within 60 days (the limit for tax-free rollovers) and the bankruptcy case continues past the 60th day.

A debtor in Texas argued that Section 522(c) fixes the status of funds exempted by the debtor—either on the filing date of the bankruptcy petition or when the time for creditors' objections has passed—so that, once fixed, the debtor can liquidate an exempt IRA and freely spend the funds (which he did). But the Fifth Circuit Court of Appeals held Section 522(c) does not prevent exempt property from losing its exempt status. Further, it held, Texas law conditionally exempts a "nontaxable rollover contribution" that is distributed from an exempt IRA—but the exemption expires after 60 days if no rollover occurs. The debtor was ordered to repay the distribution to the bankruptcy estate. [*In re* Hawk, 871 F.3d 287 (5th Cir. 2017)]

Q 1:57 Is bankruptcy protection lost if an IRA is involved in a prohibited transaction, or no longer meets the requirements of the Code?

Yes. An IRA that is involved in a prohibited transaction loses its status as an IRA as of the first day of the year in which the transaction occurs. Consequently, it no longer qualifies for the IRA exemption under the federal bankruptcy laws. [Daniels v. Agin, No. 12-2376, 2013 WL 6153709 (1st Cir. Nov. 25, 2013); *In re* Willis, 104 A.F.T.R.2d 2009-5669 (Bankr. S.D. Fla. 2009)] The same result occurs in states that have opted out (see Q 1:52) of the federal exemption scheme and provide their own exemptions for IRAs. [*E.g.*, Yerian v. Webber, 123 A.F.T.R.2d ¶ 2019-816 (11th Cir.)]

A bankruptcy trustee may challenge a debtor's claim of the IRA exemption on the basis that the asset does not, for some other reason, qualify as an IRA. [*E.g.*, *In re* Joseph Matthias Miller, No. 13-3682, 2015 WL 613833 (8th Cir. Feb. 13, 2015) (upholding the challenged exemption because the annuity purchased using a distribution from the debtor's IRA *did* qualify as an IRA annuity)]

Q 1:58 Are ESAs protected in bankruptcy?

A different protection scheme applies to ESAs. Funds contributed to an ESA more than 720 days before the bankruptcy filing are entirely excluded (with earnings) from the bankruptcy estate. Between 720 days and 365 days before the bankruptcy filing, all amounts contributed for the same designated beneficiary are aggregated and protected only up to $5,850. Amounts contributed less than 365 days before the bankruptcy filing are not protected. [11 U.S.C. § 541(b)(5)]

Q 1:59 Are HSAs protected in bankruptcy?

There is no exemption for HSAs under federal bankruptcy law. [*In re* Lombardy, No. 11-17737, 2012 WL 435816 (Bankr. N.D. Ohio Feb. 9, 2012)] However, some states do treat HSAs as exempt property. Thus, the answer depends on where the petition is filed (i.e., where the debtor resides).

Q 1:60 Are IRAs protected from creditors' claims outside of bankruptcy?

Federal laws (ERISA and BAPCPA) do not shield IRA assets from creditors' claims outside of bankruptcy. For example, a court may order IRA assets to be garnished to satisfy a creditor's lien.

Some states have enacted laws limiting claims against IRA assets outside of bankruptcy. A state may offer such protection for assets in a traditional IRA or Roth IRA. However, it may be beyond the scope of any state law to protect assets in some SEP IRAs and SIMPLE IRAs. This is because ERISA supersedes (preempts) state laws applying to employee benefit plans, and a SEP, SARSEP, or SIMPLE plan that covers at least one employee besides the owner (and spouse) is such a plan. [ERISA §§ 514(a), 3(2)(A); 29 C.F.R. § 2510.3-3(b); DOL Adv. Op. 1999-04A; *In re* Witwer, 148 B.R. 930 (Bankr. C.D. Cal. 1992), *aff'd without opinion*, 163 B.R. 614 (B.A.P. 9th Cir. 1994)]

The ERISA preemption clause guarantees that a state cannot limit ERISA's protection. But are states also precluded from enlarging upon ERISA's protection? The question is still open, but it seems wrong to construe ERISA as preempting a state law that provides more protection for SEP and SIMPLE IRAs outside of bankruptcy.

Q 1:61 Outside of bankruptcy, can the IRS levy on an IRA, ESA, or HSA?

None of these is immune from IRS levy. The agency's official policy is to exercise discretion with respect to the decision to levy on IRAs. [IRS Manual § 5.11.6.2 (Jan. 17, 2017)] But it has no such policy for ESAs and HSAs.

> **Note**. If a law provides a remedy that is enforceable to the same extent as a tax lien, the remedy may be enforced against the obligated individual's IRA. So, since restitution under the Mandatory Victims Restitution Act (MVRA) is enforceable to the same extent as a tax lien, 50 percent of one spouse's IRA (in a state where IRAs are community property) can be garnished to pay restitution the other spouse owes under the MVRA. [United States v. Berry, 951 F.3d 632 (5th Cir. 2020)]

An IRS levy must be on assets that a debtor-taxpayer can withdraw. Only the *beneficiary* can withdraw assets from an HSA or ESA, so the IRS can only levy on those accounts if the beneficiary owes the tax debt. Other individuals (the grantor and other contributors) cannot withdraw contributions, so a levy cannot be used to satisfy their tax liabilities. [I.R.S. Chief Counsel Advice 201017044 (Feb. 24, 2011); I.R.S. Chief Counsel Advice 200927019 (July 2, 2009)]

If an IRA, ESA, or HSA distribution is made pursuant to a levy, the normal taxation rules apply with one exception. The law specifies that the 10 percent penalty on early distributions from an IRA does not apply to an IRS levy. [I.R.C. § 72(t)(2)(A)(vii)] No similar statutory exception exists for the ESA or HSA, so a levy distribution from either of those will incur the 10 percent penalty. [I.R.C. §§ 530(d)(4)(B), 223(f)(4)(A); I.R.S. Chief Counsel Advice 201017044 (Feb. 24, 2011); I.R.S. Chief Counsel Advice CCA 200927019 (July 2, 2009)]

Q 1:62 If an IRA, ESA, or HSA was improperly levied upon, and money or property is later returned, can the payment be restored to the account?

Under a new rule, if the government determines that a levy on an individual's *IRA or eligible retirement plan account* was wrongful, premature, or against administrative procedure, and it returns money (including interest) or property to the individual in accordance with Code Section 6343, the money or property may be timely rolled over to an IRA or an eligible retirement plan that will accept such rollover contributions. This rule is effective for payments in taxable years starting after 2017. [I.R.C. § 6343(f); Bipartisan Budget Act of 2018, Pub. L. No. 115-123, § 41104(b) (Feb. 9, 2018)]

A rollover is not allowed, however, if the levied-upon account was an ESA or HSA. Neither is included in the definition of an *eligible retirement plan*. [I.R.C. §§ 6343(f)(1), 402(c)(8)(B)]

Q 1:63 Do retirement and ESA assets become immune from IRS levy when they are protected in a bankruptcy proceeding?

Not necessarily. Some pre-petition liens are not removed in a bankruptcy proceeding. (In bankruptcy, discharge of a debtor's personal liability, and discharge of liens on his or her property, are separate matters.)

When a federal tax debt is owed, an IRS lien automatically arises on the debtor's property. The IRS may choose to notify other creditors of its lien by publicly filing a notice of federal tax lien (NFTL). A valid NFTL cannot be removed in a bankruptcy proceeding and remains enforceable against the debtor's property even after a discharge. [I.R.C. §§ 6321, 6323(f)]

On the other hand, if the IRS does not file a valid NFTL before the debtor files a bankruptcy petition, the bankruptcy trustee can remove the tax lien—but only if the lien is on property over which the trustee has power. Property must be included in the bankruptcy estate for the trustee to have power over it.

There are two ways to protect retirement and ESA assets in bankruptcy (i.e., allow the debtor to keep them): by excluding or by exempting them from the bankruptcy estate. ERISA qualified plans and ESAs, but not IRAs, are generally *excluded* from the estate, though the debtor may elect instead to *exempt* them. The debtor may also elect to exempt IRAs subject to the limits described above (see Q 1:51). [11 U.S.C. § 541 (exclusion); 11 U.S.C. § 522 (elective exemption)] Excluded assets do not become part of the estate; exempted assets do. Consequently, a bankruptcy trustee only has power over retirement and ESA assets that the debtor elected to exempt. As a result:

- If the IRS filed a valid NFTL before the debtor filed the bankruptcy petition, the tax lien survives discharge. Retirement or ESA assets that the debtor was allowed to keep remaining vulnerable to IRS levy after the bankruptcy.
- If the IRS did not file a valid NFTL, and the debtor elected to *exempt* retirement or ESA assets, the tax lien on those assets is discharged in the bankruptcy. The assets are immune from IRS levy for the prepetition tax debt.
- But if the debtor only *excluded* retirement or ESA assets from the bankruptcy estate (i.e., did not elect exemption), the pre-petition IRS lien survives the bankruptcy even if a valid NFTL was not filed.

[Gross v. Commissioner, 113 A.F.T.R.2d 2014-1017 (9th Cir. 2014); Wadleigh v. Commissioner, 134 T.C. No. 14 (2010); Miles v. Commissioner, 106 A.F.T.R.2d 2010-6563 (9th Cir.), *cert. denied*, 131 S. Ct. 2122 (2011)]

Taxation Under State Law

Q 1:64 Do states treat IRAs the same as federal law?

In general, yes. The majority of states with income tax laws conform to the Internal Revenue Code for IRA contributions and distributions by their residents. Exceptions to the general rule for contributions includes Pennsylvania, New Jersey, and Massachusetts (see Qs 15:1–15:5). In addition, differences occur when a taxpayer changes state residency. The state of residency when a person retires or begins to take withdrawals from a traditional IRA determines the rules that apply for state income tax purposes. (See chapter 16 for further discussion of this issue.)

Corrections of Contribution Errors

Q 1:65 Can inadvertent compliance errors be corrected?

Yes, if Section 308 of the SECURE Act 2.0 (i.e., HR 8696) is enacted. Section 308 would permit self-correction of inadvertent compliance errors at any time before the IRS identified the violations with respect to some IRA errors.

Q 1:66 What would be the process for correcting IRA errors?

Section 308(a) of the SECURE Act 2.0 provides that, except as otherwise provided in the Internal Revenue Code of 1986 (the Code) or regulations issued by the Secretary of the Treasury or the Secretary's delegate, any eligible inadvertent failure to comply with the rules applicable under Section 401(a), 403(a), 403(b), 408(p), or 408(k) of the Code may be self-corrected under the Employee Plans Compliance Resolution System (as described in Revenue Procedure 2019-19 or any successor guidance; the EPCRS), except to the extent that such failure was identified by the Secretary of the Treasury prior to any actions that demonstrate a commitment to implement a self-correction. Revenue Procedure 2019-19 is deemed amended as of the date of the enactment of the SECURE Act 2.0 to provide that the correction period under Section 9.02 of the Revenue Procedure (or any successor guidance) for an eligible inadvertent failure, except as otherwise provided under the Code or in regulations issued by the Secretary of the Treasury, is indefinite and has no last day, other than with respect to failures identified by the Secretary prior to any self-correction as described in the preceding sentence.

Section 308(c) provides that the Secretary of the Treasury will expand the EPCRS to allow custodians of individual retirement plans (as defined in Section 7701(a)(37) of the Code, an individual retirement account described in Section 408(a), and an individual retirement annuity described in Section 408(b)) to address eligible inadvertent failures for which the owner of an individual retirement plan (as so defined) was not at fault, including (but not limited to): (1) waivers of the excise tax that would otherwise apply under

Section 4974 of the Code, (2) under the self-correction component of the EPCRS, waivers of the 60-day deadline for a rollover where the deadline is missed for reasons beyond the reasonable control of the account owner, and (3) rules permitting a nonspouse beneficiary to return distributions to an inherited individual retirement plan described in Section 408(d)(3)(C) of the Code in a case where, due to an inadvertent error by a service provider, the beneficiary had reason to believe that the distribution could be rolled over without inclusion in income of any part of the distributed amount.

Section 308(d) provides that the Secretary of the Treasury will expand the EPCRS to allow plans to which such system applies and custodians and owners of individual retirement plans to self-correct, without an excise tax, any eligible inadvertent failures pursuant to which a distribution is made no more than 180 days after it was required to be made.

Section 308(e) provides that the Secretary of the Treasury will expand the EPCRS to provide additional safe harbor means of correcting eligible inadvertent failures described in subsection (a) of Section 308, including safe harbor means of calculating the earnings that must be restored to a plan in cases where plan assets have been depleted by reason of an eligible inadvertent failure.

Section 308(f) provides that, for purposes of Section 308: (1) in general, except as provided in part, (2) the term "eligible inadvertent failure" means a failure that occurs despite the existence of practices and procedures which (A) satisfy the standards in Section 4.04 of Revenue Procedure 2019-19 (or any successor guidance) or (B) satisfy similar standards in the case of an individual retirement plan; however, (3) the term "eligible inadvertent failure" shall not include any failure that is egregious, relates to the diversion or misuse of plan assets, or is directly or indirectly related to an abusive tax avoidance transaction.

Q 1:67 What are the requirements for correcting IRA errors?

Section 308 will not apply to any failure unless the correction of such failure under Section 308 is made in conformity with the general principles that apply to corrections of such failures under the Code, including regulations or other guidance issued thereunder and including those principles and corrections in Revenue Procedure 2019-19 (or any successor guidance).

Chapter 2

Adopting a Traditional IRA or a Roth IRA

The procedure an individual follows to open (adopt) a new Individual Retirement Arrangement (IRA) is fairly simple. The trustee or custodian, however, must follow comprehensive regulations and use specific forms to properly establish an IRA. This chapter discusses the rules for adopting a traditional IRA and a Roth IRA (in part by answering some common account-opening questions), reviews the duties of the IRA trustee or custodian, and analyzes the IRA documentation requirements.

Common Account-Opening Questions

Q 2:1 What does it mean to adopt (establish) an IRA?

To adopt an IRA is to complete the documentation legally required to make an IRA contribution. The term *establish* is used synonymously with the term *adopt* in this discussion of IRAs.

Q 2:2 When can an IRA be adopted?

An IRA may be adopted at any time. But in order to designate a contribution for a prior calendar year, the IRA must be adopted no later than the contribution deadline, which is the tax filing date (with no extensions) for the contribution year. If an IRA is being established by mail, it may be possible to mail the initial contribution on the due date for filing the return. [*See* Priv. Ltr. Rul. 8551065; I.R.C. § 408(d)(4)(A).]

Example. Larry wants to open an IRA. The latest date he may do so and still make a contribution for 2020 is the tax filing deadline—Thursday, May 17, 2021.

Q 2:3 How is an IRA established?

The individual adopts the IRA by executing an agreement with the trustee or custodian, and receiving from the latter certain disclosure information and a blank copy of the IRA agreement.

1. *IRA Agreement.* The IRA agreement is a contract that sets out the terms and requirements of the IRA (contributions, distributions, etc.). It is executed by both the individual and the trustee or custodian of the IRA and is not filed with the IRS.
2. *The Application.* The trustee or custodian needs certain personal and account-specific information for accurate reporting and administration. This is usually collected on a separate application form (signed by the individual), or it may be included in the IRA agreement itself. Such information includes the individual's name, address, date of birth, Social Security number or appropriate tax identification number, the amount and type of the initial contribution (regular, rollover, or transfer), and the identification of a beneficiary to receive IRA distributions after the individual dies.
3. *The Plain-Language Disclosure.* The financial institution must provide an explanation of the IRA rules and regulations, written in plain and non-technical language (see Q 8:2). It may create its own plain-language disclosure, use one drafted by a document provider, or use IRS Publication 590-A, *Contributions to Individual Retirement Arrangements (IRAs)* 2020 (reproduced in Appendix A).
4. *The Financial Disclosure.* The individual must also be given a financial disclosure statement that projects (to the extent reasonably possible) the future values of an IRA, based on either a fixed annual contribution of $1,000 (for a regular IRA) or a one-time contribution of $1,000 (for a rollover or transfer IRA).

To allow individuals sufficient time to examine the disclosures and blank IRA agreement, these generally must be provided at least seven days before the IRA is established. However, the materials may be provided as late as the IRA establishment date if the financial institution permits the initial contribution to be revoked if the individual decides, upon reconsideration, to cancel the IRA. (Revocation is discussed in Q 2:6.)

An IRA custodian or trustee is assessed a $50 penalty for each failure to provide a copy of an IRA agreement, a plain-language disclosure, or a financial disclosure to persons establishing an IRA, unless the failure is due to reasonable cause. [I.R.C. § 6693(a); Treas. Reg. § 1.408-6(d)(4)(ix)]

Q 2:4 Are all IRA agreements the same?

No. Obviously, traditional IRA agreements have different provisions than Roth IRA agreements. But different forms of agreement also exist for every type of IRA.

Model IRA agreements. The IRS has a series of model IRA agreements that can be used (see Q 2:21).

Prototype IRA agreements. Prototypes are form agreements drafted by IRA sponsors. They may contain provisions not found in the model agreements. Some sponsors obtain IRS approval of their prototypes to ensure the IRA requirements are met. (See Q 2:26.)

Individually designed plans. IRA agreements may also be uniquely drafted to suit individual requirements. (This is not common.) An individually designed IRA is not required to receive an IRA opinion letter in order to receive favorable federal income tax treatment.

Q 2:5 What other disclosures may the document package contain?

The type of investment(s) an IRA owner chooses for the first (or a later) contribution may require additional disclosures or agreements. For example:

- Information about the risks of a particular investment. IRAs may invest in practically any asset except life insurance and collectibles, and special rules apply to the purchase of endowment contracts. Acceptable investments include stocks, bonds, mutual funds, exchange traded funds, annuities, money market accounts, certificates of deposit, common trust funds, common investment funds, and mutual funds. These carry different risks, which may require disclosure.
- Securities laws may require provision of a mutual fund's prospectus or annual report to the fund investors.
- For deposit investments at banks, savings institutions, and credit unions, information about the Truth-in-Savings Act.
- Non-deposit investments may require a disclosure that they are not insured by the Federal Deposit Insurance Corporation (FDIC), and are not deposits or obligations of, and are not guaranteed by, the IRA custodian.

Q 2:6 May an IRA be revoked?

Yes, but only within seven days of receiving the required explanation of basic information from the trustee, custodian, or annuity issuer (see chapter 8). The full amount contributed must be returned if the account is revoked. It is not necessary to provide information about the right to revoke if the trustee, custodian, or annuity issuer supplies a disclosure statement and a copy of the governing instrument to the prospective IRA owner at least seven days before the IRA is established. [Treas. Reg. § 1.408-6(d)(4)(ii)(A)(2)]

> **Note.** If an IRA is timely revoked, the trustee may not deduct any amount for sales commissions, administrative expenses, or fluctuations in market value. [Treas. Reg. § 1.408-6(d)(4)(ii)(A)(2)] While the trustee bears the risk of investment loss during the revocation period, it may keep any gain that is earned unless the IRA document provides otherwise.

> **Practice Pointer.** To avoid investment loss, some IRA trustees require the initial contribution to be invested in a government-guaranteed investment or security until the seven-day revocation period expires.

Q 2:7 Are IRAs covered by federal deposit insurance?

The Federal Deposit Insurance Corporation (FDIC) insures IRAs and certain other retirement accounts if they are held at a bank or savings institution. FDIC insurance does *not* cover IRAs held in mutual funds or brokerage firms (which are not banks).

The maximum coverage is $250,000, which applies in the aggregate to all covered accounts owned by an individual at a single institution. An inherited IRA (which continues in the deceased IRA owner's name) is separately insured from other accounts which the beneficiary holds at the same institution. The $250,000 statutory limit is subject to periodic increase based on inflation. [12 U.S.C. § 1821(a)(1)(F); 12 C.F.R. § 330.14(b)(2); Federal Deposit Insurance Corporation, Deposit Insurance at a Glance, available at *https://www.fdic.gov/deposit/deposits/brochures/deposit-insurance-at-a-glance-english.html* (retrieved Aug. 9, 2020)]

Q 2:8 Can an individual hold several IRAs?

Yes, but holding multiple IRAs of the same type does not allow more to be contributed. Traditional and Roth IRAs are considered together for purposes of the contribution limit. SEP and SIMPLE IRAs, which receive contributions under an employer plan, have separate contribution limits.

> **Example.** Dan understands the benefits of the IRA, but he believes in diversifying institutions as well as investments. He established a traditional IRA at ABC Bank in 2017, another traditional IRA at XYZ Credit Union in 2018, and another at Big Mutual Funds in 2019. Dan opens two new IRAs in 2020, one traditional and one Roth IRA. As long as he contributes no more than his annual maximum ($6,000 or $7,000 if he is age 50 or over by December 31, 2021), Dan has not violated any rule by opening multiple IRAs.

> **Note.** It can be expensive and burdensome to maintain multiple IRAs. Recordkeeping, minimum distribution calculations, cost basis determinations, tracking of rollovers and conversions, and other matters may become significantly complicated. Many trustees and custodians impose minimum

dollar limits or charge a fee for each IRA to discourage individuals from opening multiple IRAs.

Q 2:9 May IRA investments be made jointly with another person?

No. Joint IRA investments are not permitted. For example, a husband and wife may not hold a jointly owned certificate of deposit in a joint IRA account. [I.R.C. § 408(a); Treas. Reg. § 1.408-2(b)]

Q 2:10 Must IRA investments be kept separate from the IRA owner's other investments?

Yes. An IRA is a trust. Assets in an IRA trust may not be combined with the owner's other assets. [I.R.C. § 408(a)(5); Treas. Reg. § 1.408-2(b)(5)]

Q 2:11 How often should IRA documents be reviewed?

Apart from an annual financial review, IRA documents should be reviewed whenever a change is made in the designated beneficiary. A traditional IRA should also be reviewed before the IRA owner reaches age 72 or when a major life event occurs, such as retirement or the incurrence of large expenses. Of course, the documents should be reviewed when the IRA owner dies or when the trustee (or custodian) proposes amendments, as will be required to comply with the SECURE Act.

Q 2:12 Is an IRA a qualified plan?

No. To be a qualified plan, a plan must be sponsored by an employer *and* meet the requirements of Code Section 401(a). An IRA does *not* meet those requirements.

Trustees and Custodians

Q 2:13 Who may serve as the IRA trustee or custodian?

The trustee or custodian of an IRA must be either a bank or a nonbank entity the IRS has approved to serve in that capacity (see Q 2:14). [I.R.C. § 408(a), 408(n); Treas. Reg. § 1.408-2(b), 1.408-2(e)]

The term *bank* is broadly defined as follows:

1. A bank, a trust company, or a domestic savings and loan association [I.R.C. § 408(n)(1)]
2. A corporation that, under the laws of the state of its incorporation or under the laws of the District of Columbia, is subject to both the supervision of, and examination by, the authority in such jurisdiction in charge of the administration of the banking laws [I.R.C. § 408(n)(3)]

3. An insured credit union [I.R.C. § 408(n)(2); Federal Credit Union Act § 101(6), 12 U.S.C. § 1752]

A life insurance company may sponsor IRAs but it must not offer life insurance or endowment contracts as investment options.

Q 2:14 What are the IRS criteria for approving a noninstitutional trustee or custodian?

To gain IRS approval, the nonbank entity must submit a letter ruling request and demonstrate to the satisfaction of the IRS that it will administer IRA trusts in a manner consistent with the requirements of Code Section 408. [Treas. Reg. § 1.408-2(e)] The applicant must provide clear and convincing evidence that the requirements of the regulation are met.

The user fee charged by the IRS to consider such requests is $10,000. [Rev. Proc. 2021-4, 2021-1, I.R.B. 167, § 3.07, Appendix A § .01(4); Treas. Reg. § 1.408-2(e)]

Q 2:15 What is the difference between a trustee and a custodian for purposes of an IRA?

Under the law of trusts, there are distinctions between trustees and custodians. Trustees have greater decision-making authority and wider fiduciary responsibilities than custodians. But for purposes of applying the IRA rules, there is little, if any, meaningful difference between the terms.

The IRS does provide one model agreement for a traditional IRA trust account, and another for a traditional IRA custodial account. Similarly, it provides another pair of model agreements for Roth IRA trust and custodial accounts. However, within each pair, there are no substantive differences between the agreements. Only the use of nomenclature is different (trustees hold assets of grantors, and custodians hold assets of depositors). (See Q 2:21.)

The same institutions may be eligible to serve as trustees or as custodians of IRAs, and the definition of the term *trustee* in Code Section 408(n) includes custodians. [Treas. Reg. § 1.408-2(d)] The IRS also uses the terms interchangeably throughout Publications 590-A, *Contributions to Individual Retirement Arrangements (IRAs)* 2020 (reproduced in Appendix A), and 590-B, *Distributions from Individual Retirement Arrangements (IRAs)* 2020 (reproduced in Appendix B).

Although the IRS model forms make no substantive distinctions between trust and custodial accounts, provisions added to a model agreement (or included in a prototype or individually designed agreement) can determine whether to use a trust or custodial account. For example, a self-directed IRA shifts powers and fiduciary duties from the custodian to the account holder, and should be established as a custodial account. An IRA in which the fiduciary is granted discretion to make investments on the account holder's behalf should be established as a trust account.

Q 2:16 Can the IRA owner serve as its trustee or custodian?

Generally, no. Unlike a qualified plan, an IRA may not have an individual serve as its trustee or custodian unless the IRS approves (see Q 2:13). IRS approval of an individual as an IRA trustee or custodian is extremely unlikely.

Q 2:17 May the trustee or custodian assess fees against the IRA?

Yes, if the IRA agreement specifically allows such fees. In that case, the IRA agreement should also specify the order in which assets will be liquidated for fee payment (e.g., use the most recently purchased asset first).

Q 2:18 After the IRA owner dies, can the death beneficiary move the IRA to a different trustee?

Yes. Any IRA beneficiary (even a nonspouse beneficiary) may change the trustee (or custodian) of an inherited IRA, unless such action was prohibited by the IRA owner.

IRS-Approved Models

Q 2:19 What model forms can be used to establish a traditional or Roth IRA?

The IRS created the 5305 series of model documents, which may be used to establish IRAs. For traditional IRAs there are two models—one for a trust account and another for a custodial account. The same two types are available for Roth IRAs, as well as a third—a model endorsement for a Roth individual retirement annuity. The five models are:

- IRS Form 5305, *Traditional Individual Retirement Trust Account*
- IRS Form 5305-A, *Traditional Individual Retirement Custodial Account*
- IRS Form 5305-R, *Roth Individual Retirement Trust Account*
- IRS Form 5305-RA, *Roth Individual Retirement Custodial Account*
- IRS Form 5305-RB, *Roth Individual Retirement Annuity Endorsement*

The traditional IRA models are identical but for the nomenclature used (*trustee* and *grantor*, versus *custodian* and *depositor*). This is also true of the Roth IRA trust and custodial accounts.

Note. Other model forms are used to establish a SEP or SIMPLE IRA (see chapters 12 and 13). It is not clear why the IRS did not create a model endorsement for a traditional IRA annuity.

An IRA sponsor may reproduce the appropriate model form provisions on its own letterhead or in pamphlets that omit all references to the IRS.

Q 2:20 Does the IRS reissue the model forms whenever the IRA laws are amended?

No. The IRS reissues the model forms periodically, not each time the law is amended. The current model forms were released in April 2017. The prior set was released in 2002, and in the interim the IRA laws were amended numerous times. Nonetheless, every IRA must be operated in a manner consistent with current law.

> **Caution.** The IRS will presumably update the LRMs at some point to reflect important changes made by the Setting Every Community Up for Retirement Enhancement Act (SECURE Act), Div. O of the Further Consolidated Appropriations Act, 2020, Pub. L. No. 116-94 (Dec. 20, 2019):
>
> - The required beginning date for distributions from a traditional IRA is now linked to age 72, not age 70½. (See Q 4:4.)
> - The rules governing distributions to beneficiaries after a traditional or Roth IRA owner dies are significantly changed. (See Qs 4:45, 4:86.)
>
> The SECURE Act also repealed the age limit for contributing to a traditional IRA (formerly age 70½). (See Q 3:46.) The current LRM does not refer to the age limit, however.

Q 2:21 If the IRS amends a model form, must sponsors notify individuals whose IRAs are based on the form?

Yes. If the IRS does reissue a model form, the IRA sponsor must deliver or mail it to each IRA owner within 30 days after either adoption of the required amendments or their effective date, whichever is later. [Treas. Reg. § 1.408-6(d)(4)(ii)(C)]

Q 2:22 Can users modify the model forms?

No. The language in the model IRA forms cannot be changed. However, each model contains a final section that may be used to add other provisions. The added provisions must comply with applicable requirements of state law and the Code.

The blank section is frequently used to insert provisions for payment of the trustee's or custodian's fees. Another common use is to add language providing the right to appoint a successor trustee or custodian in the event one resigns. Financial institutions using a model form often add provisions concerning investments and arbitration of securities law issues.

Q 2:23 If the blank section of a model form is used extensively, should IRS approval be sought?

It is not necessary under normal circumstances. If the drafter follows precedents of law, including letter rulings (which, although not binding, are quite informative), IRS approval should not be needed.

Practice Pointer. It is always possible to seek a letter ruling regarding added language in a special situation or if the IRA is part of a larger program for which approval is desired.

Q 2:24 What does the IRS suggest regarding the blank section?

The instructions for each model form suggest using the blank section to add investment powers, voting rights, exculpatory provisions, amendment and termination provisions, and language pertaining to removal of a trustee, trustees' fees, state-law requirements, acceptance of cash only, treatment of excess contributions, and prohibited transactions with the grantor. Other items, such as detailed reporting requirements, could be provided in supplemental documents that must also comply with the Code (see chapter 8).

Prototype IRAs

Q 2:25 How is IRS approval obtained for a prototype plan?

IRS approval of any prototype IRA agreement is requested using Form 5306, Application for Approval of Prototype or Employer-Sponsored Individual Retirement Account (last revised in August 2013). The IRS user fee for such requests is currently $2,500 per application. For a mass submitter applying on behalf of word-for-word adopters of a particular prototype IRA, only the first 300 of such applications submitted within a 12-month period are subject to the fee. [Rev. Proc. 2021-4, 2021-1 I.R.B. 167, Appendix A § .02]

Q 2:26 What does IRS approval signify?

When the IRS approves a prototype IRA, it issues an opinion letter stating that the *form* of the prototype is acceptable under the Code. [Rev. Proc. 87-50, 1987-2 C.B. 647] The letter is similar to a determination letter issued by the IRS for a qualified retirement plan.

Approval of the form of the prototype IRA means only that it will be acceptable if, in operation, it complies with all of the following rules:

1. The terms of the program are followed.
2. There are no prohibited transactions.
3. The trustee or custodian is a qualified bank or has been approved by the IRS.
4. The required plain-language disclosure statement is provided to each participant.
5. Each adopting individual is provided with annual reports of transactions.
6. The sponsoring institution's telephone number is provided to those adopting the plan.

7. Those adopting the plan are advised to contact the sponsoring institution if there are questions about the plan's operation.
8. A copy of the opinion letter is provided to each affected person.

The IRS provides three caveats to its approval of a prototype IRA. First, that future changes in the Code or regulations may require the prototype to be amended or revised. Second, that the IRS does not evaluate the sponsor's investment program or guarantee the contributions or investments made. Finally, in approving the form of a prototype, the IRS expresses no opinion as to the existence or absence of prohibited transactions.

Q 2:27 Can a single prototype agreement allow either a traditional IRA or a Roth IRA to be established?

Yes. If it is properly drafted, a single prototype document could serve to establish either a Roth IRA or a traditional IRA. The IRS will allow a combined prototype as long as (1) a separate trust, custodial account, or annuity is established for each type of contribution, and (2) the document, as completed by the owner, clearly indicates whether it is to be used as a traditional IRA or as a Roth IRA. [Rev. Proc. 98-59, 1998-2 C.B. 729, *modified by* Rev. Proc. 2010-48, 2010-50 I.R.B. 828; Ann. 97-122, 1997-50 I.R.B. 63]

Practice Pointer. A prototype document could use a check-box system to distinguish traditional IRA contributions from Roth IRA contributions.

IRS Sample Language for Prototypes

Q 2:28 What must a prototype traditional IRA agreement include?

Form 5306 specifies 12 items that must be addressed in a prototype traditional IRA. (For prototype traditional *individual retirement annuity* requirements, see Q 2:29.)

The IRS offers sample language for the 12 items in Part A of the "Traditional Individual Retirement Arrangements (IRA) Listing of Required Modifications (LRM) and Information Package." The LRM was revised in 2010 to incorporate all then-current IRA requirements, and is available on the IRS Web site at *www.irs.gov/pub/irs-tege/tira_lrm.pdf*. The items, shown here with sample language based on the LRM, are:

1. The exclusive benefit provision. [I.R.C. § 408(a)]

> The account is established for the exclusive benefit of the individual or his or her beneficiaries. If this is an inherited IRA within the meaning of Code § 408(d)(3)(C) maintained for the benefit of a designated beneficiary of a deceased individual, references in this document to the "individual" are to the deceased individual.

2. Provision that contributions other than rollovers must be in cash and not exceed the maximum limit. [I.R.C. §§ 72(t)(2)(G), 219(b), 408(a)(1), 408(d)(3)(C), 408(d)(3)(G), 408(p)(1)(B), 408(p)(2)(A)(iv); § 201 of the Gulf Opportunity Zone Act of 2005, Pub. L. No. 109-135; § 15345 of the Food, Conservation, and Energy Act of 2008, Pub. L. No. 110-246; § 702 of Division C of the Emergency Economic Stabilization Act of 2008, Pub. L. No. 110-343]

   (a) Except in the case of a rollover contribution (as permitted by Code Sections 402(c), 402(e)(6), 403(a)(4), 403(b)(8), 403(b)(10), 408(d)(3), and 457(e)(16)) or a contribution made in accordance with the terms of a simplified employee pension (SEP) as described in Code Section 408(k), no contributions will be accepted unless they are in cash, and the total of such contributions shall not exceed $5,000 for any taxable year beginning in 2008 and years thereafter.

   After 2008, the limit will be adjusted by the Secretary of the Treasury for cost-of-living increases under Code Section 219(b)(5)(D). Such adjustments will be in multiples of $500.

   (For 2021, the limit is $6,000.)

   (b) In the case of an individual who is 50 or older, the annual cash contribution limit is increased by $1,000 for any taxable year beginning in 2006 and years thereafter.

   (c) In addition to the amounts described in paragraphs (a) and (b) above, an individual may make additional contributions specifically authorized by statute—such as repayments of qualified reservist distributions, repayments of certain plan distributions made on account of a federally declared disaster, certain amounts received in connection with the *Exxon Valdez* litigation, qualified birth and adoption distributions, and coronavirus-related distributions.

   (d) In addition to the amounts described in paragraphs (a) and (c) above, an individual who was a participant in a § 401(k) plan of a certain employer in bankruptcy described in Code § 219(b)(5)(C) may contribute up to $3,000 for taxable years beginning after 2006 and before 2010 only. An individual who makes contributions under this paragraph (d) may not also make contributions under paragraph (b).

   (This special contribution is not allowed for taxable years 2011 and later; see Q 3:6.)

   (e) No contributions will be accepted under a SIMPLE IRA plan established by any employer pursuant to § 408(p). Also, no transfer or rollover of funds attributable to contributions made by a particular employer under its SIMPLE IRA plan will be accepted from a SIMPLE IRA, that is, an IRA used in conjunction with a SIMPLE IRA plan, prior to the expiration of the 2-year period beginning on the date the individual first participated in that employer's SIMPLE IRA plan.

> (f) If this is an inherited IRA within the meaning of Code Section 408(d)(3)(C), no contributions will be accepted.

3. Provision acknowledging the prohibition of investment by an IRA in collectibles or a statement informing participants in the IRA plan that investment in collectibles will be a taxable distribution. [I.R.C. § 408(m)]

   > If the trust acquires collectibles within the meaning of Code Section 408(m) after December 31, 1981, trust assets will be treated as a distribution in an amount equal to the cost of such collectibles.

   (This provision is *not* required if the IRA precludes any investments that could be construed as collectibles. Note that Code Section 408(m)(3) allows an exception to the rule for certain gold and silver coins.)

4. Prohibition of investment by an individual retirement account in life insurance contracts. [I.R.C. § 408(a)(3)]

   > No part of the trust funds will be invested in life insurance contracts.

5. Statement of required distributions commencing before death. [I.R.C. § 408(a)(6); Treas. Reg. § 1.408-8]

   > (a) Notwithstanding any provision of this IRA to the contrary, the distribution of the individual's interest in the account shall be made in accordance with the requirements of Code § 408(a)(6) and the regulations thereunder, the provisions of which are herein incorporated by reference. If distributions are made from an annuity contract purchased from an insurance company, distributions thereunder must satisfy the requirements of Q&A-4 of § 1.401(a)(9)-6 of the Income Tax Regulations, rather than paragraphs (b), (c) and (d) below and [refer to document provision for distributions at death]. The required minimum distributions calculated for this IRA may be withdrawn from another IRA of the individual in accordance with Q&A-9 of § 1.408-8 of the Income Tax Regulations. If this is an inherited IRA within the meaning of Code § 408(d)(3)(C), the preceding sentence and paragraphs (b), (c) and (d) below do not apply.
   >
   > (b) The entire value of the account of the individual for whose benefit the account is maintained will commence to be distributed no later than the first day of April following the calendar year in which such individual attains age 72 (the "required beginning date") over the life of such individual or the lives of such individual and his or her designated beneficiary.
   >
   > (c) The amount to be distributed each year, beginning with the calendar year in which the individual attains age 72 and continuing through the year of death, shall not be less than the quotient obtained by dividing the value of the IRA, as determined under [refer to IRA provision for distributions at death], as of the end

of the preceding year by the distribution period in the Uniform Lifetime Table in Q&A-2 of § 1.401(a)(9)-9 of the Income Tax Regulations, using the individual's age as of his or her birthday in the year. However, if the individual's sole designated beneficiary is his or her surviving spouse and such spouse is more than 10 years younger than the individual, then the distribution period is determined under the Joint and Last Survivor Table in Q&A-3 of § 1.401(a)(9)-9, using the ages as of the individual's and spouse's birthdays in the year.

(d) The required minimum distribution for the year the individual attains age 72 can be made as late as April 1 of the following year. The required minimum distribution for any other year must be made by the end of such year.

6. Statement of required distributions commencing after death. [I.R.C. § 408(a)(6); Treas. Reg. § 1.408-8; Notice 2007-7, Q&As-17–19, 2007-1 C.B. 395]

(a) Death On or After Required Beginning Date. If the individual dies on or after the required beginning date, the remaining portion of his or her interest will be distributed at least as rapidly as follows:

(1) If the designated beneficiary is someone other than the individual's surviving spouse, the remaining interest will be distributed over the remaining life expectancy of the designated beneficiary, with such life expectancy determined using the beneficiary's age as of his or her birthday in the year following the year of the individual's death, or over the period described in paragraph (a)(3) below if longer.

(2) If the individual's sole designated beneficiary is the individual's surviving spouse, the remaining interest will be distributed over such spouse's life expectancy or over the period described in paragraph (a)(3) below if longer. Any interest remaining after such spouse's death will be distributed over such spouse's remaining life expectancy determined using the spouse's age as of his or her birthday in the year of the spouse's death, or, if the distributions are being made over the period described in paragraph (a)(3) below, over such period.

(3) If there is no designated beneficiary, or if applicable by operation of paragraph (a)(1) or (a)(2) above, the remaining interest will be distributed over the individual's remaining life expectancy determined in the year of the individual's death.

(4) The amount to be distributed each year under paragraph (a)(1), (2) or (3), beginning with the calendar year following the calendar year of the individual's death, is the quotient obtained by dividing the value of the IRA

as of the end of the preceding year by the remaining life expectancy specified in such paragraph. Life expectancy is determined using the Single Life Table in Q&A-1 of § 1.401(a)(9)-9 of the Income Tax Regulations. If distributions are being made to a surviving spouse as the sole designated beneficiary, such spouse's remaining life expectancy for a year is the number in the Single Life Table corresponding to such spouse's age in the year. In all other cases, remaining life expectancy for a year is the number in the Single Life Table corresponding to the beneficiary's or individual's age in the year specified in paragraph (a)(1), (2) or (3) and reduced by 1 for each subsequent year.

(b) Death Before Required Beginning Date. If the individual dies before the required beginning date, his or her entire interest will be distributed at least as rapidly as follows:

(1) If the designated beneficiary is someone other than the individual's surviving spouse, the entire interest will be distributed, starting by the end of the calendar year following the calendar year of the individual's death, over the remaining life expectancy of the designated beneficiary, with such life expectancy determined using the age of the beneficiary as of his or her birthday in the year following the year of the individual's death, or, if elected, in accordance with paragraph (b)(3) below. If this is an inherited IRA within the meaning of Code Section 408(d)(3)(C) established for the benefit of a nonspouse designated beneficiary by a direct trustee-to-trustee transfer from a retirement plan of a deceased individual under Section 402(c)(11), then, notwithstanding any election made by the deceased individual pursuant to the preceding sentence, the nonspouse designated beneficiary may elect to have distributions made under this paragraph (b)(1) if the transfer is made no later than the end of the year following the year of death.

(2) If the individual's sole designated beneficiary is the individual's surviving spouse, the entire interest will be distributed, starting by the end of the calendar year following the calendar year of the individual's death (or by the end of the calendar year in which the individual would have attained age 70½, if later), over such spouse's life expectancy, or, if elected, in accordance with paragraph (b)(3) below. If the surviving spouse dies before distributions are required to begin, the remaining interest will be distributed, starting by the end of the calendar year following the calendar year of the spouse's death, over the spouse's designated beneficiary's remaining life expectancy determined using such beneficiary's age as of his or her birthday in the year

following the death of the spouse, or, if elected, will be distributed in accordance with paragraph (b)(3) below. If the surviving spouse dies after distributions are required to begin, any remaining interest will be distributed over the spouse's remaining life expectancy determined using the spouse's age as of his or her birthday in the year of the spouse's death.

(3) If there is no designated beneficiary, or if applicable by operation of paragraph (b)(1) or (b)(2) above, the entire interest will be distributed by the end of the calendar year containing the fifth anniversary of the individual's death (or of the spouse's death in the case of the surviving spouse's death before distributions are required to begin under paragraph (b)(2) above).

(4) The amount to be distributed each year under paragraph (b)(1) or (2) is the quotient obtained by dividing the value of the IRA as of the end of the preceding year by the remaining life expectancy specified in such paragraph. Life expectancy is determined using the Single Life Table in Q&A-1 of § 1.401(a)(9)-9 of the Income Tax Regulations. If distributions are being made to a surviving spouse as the sole designated beneficiary, such spouse's remaining life expectancy for a year is the number in the Single Life Table corresponding to such spouse's age in the year. In all other cases, remaining life expectancy for a year is the number in the Single Life Table corresponding to the beneficiary's age in the year specified in paragraph (b)(1) or (2) and reduced by 1 for each subsequent year.

(c) The "value" of the IRA includes the amount of any outstanding rollover, transfer and recharacterization under Q&As-7 and -8 of § 1.408-8 of the Income Tax Regulations.

(d) If the sole designated beneficiary is the individual's surviving spouse, the spouse may elect to treat the IRA as his or her own IRA. This election will be deemed to have been made if such surviving spouse makes a contribution to the IRA or fails to take required distributions as a beneficiary.

(e) The required minimum distributions payable to a designated beneficiary from this IRA may be withdrawn from another IRA the beneficiary holds from the same decedent in accordance with Q&A-9 of Section 1.408-8 of the Income Tax Regulations. *Note*: The IRS will likely amend these provisions to comply with the elimination of the stretch IRA provisions under the SECURE Act.

7. Nonforfeitability provision. [I.R.C. § 408(a)(4)]

The interest of an individual in the balance in his or her account is nonforfeitable at all times.

8. Provision acknowledging the prohibition against commingling of assets. [I.R.C. § 408(a)(5)]

   The assets of the trust will not be commingled with other property except in a common trust fund or common investment fund.

9. Requirement for separate accounting for the interest of each individual under an account or annuity established by an employer or employee association. [Treas. Reg. § 1.408-2(c)(3)]

   Separate records will be maintained for the interest of each individual.

   (This provision is required *only* in IRAs that are sponsored by employers or employee associations.)

10. Requirement that trustees or insurers furnish annual calendar-year reports concerning the status of the account or annuity. [Treas. Reg. §§ 1.408-5, 1.408-8]

    The trustee of an individual retirement account shall furnish annual calendar-year reports concerning the status of the account and such information concerning required minimum distributions as is prescribed by the Commissioner of Internal Revenue.

11. Provision that there be substitution for a nonbank trustee or custodian when the Commissioner of Internal Revenue issues a notification. [Treas. Reg. § 1.408-2(e)(6)(v)]

    The nonbank trustee or custodian shall substitute another trustee or custodian if the nonbank trustee or custodian receives notice from the Commissioner of Internal Revenue that such substitution is required because it has failed to comply with the requirements of Treasury Regulations Section 1.408-2(e).

    (This provision is required *only* in IRAs that are sponsored by nonbank trustees or custodians.)

12. Provision describing the type of compensation used for computing deductible limits. [I.R.C. § 219(f)(1); Treas. Reg. § 1.219-1(c)(1)]

    Compensation means wages, salaries, professional fees, or other amounts derived from or received for personal services actually rendered (including, but not limited to, commissions paid to salespersons, compensation for services on the basis of a percentage of profits, commissions on insurance premiums, tips, and bonuses) and includes earned income, as defined in Code Section 401(c)(2) (reduced by the deduction the self-employed individual takes for contributions made to a self-employed retirement plan). For purposes of this definition, Code Section 401(c)(2) shall be applied as if the term *trade or business* for purposes of Code Section 1402 included service described in subsection (c)(6). Compensation does not include amounts derived from or received as earnings or profits from property (including but not limited to interest and dividends) or amounts not

> includable in gross income (determined without regard to Code Section 112). Compensation also does not include any amount received as a pension or annuity or as deferred compensation. The term *compensation* shall include any amount includable in the individual's gross income under Code Section 71 with respect to a divorce or separation instrument described in subparagraph (A) of Code Section 71(b)(2). Such term also includes any differential wage payments as defined in Code Section 3401(h)(2). The SECURE Act expanded this definition in two ways. First, compensation includes amounts included in an individual's gross income and paid to the individual to aid the individual in the pursuit of graduate or postdoctoral study. Second, difficulty of care payments under Code Section 131 are treated as compensation. Additionally, alimony is no longer treated as compensation.
>
> (This provision is optional.)

Caution. The IRS warns that the information and sample provisions included in the LRM may not be appropriate in all cases. Acceptability may depend on the context in which the provisions are used. [Form 5306, Part II; LRM for traditional IRAs, p. 1 (June 2010)]

Q 2:29 What must a prototype individual retirement annuity include?

Ten items must be included. They are listed here, shown with sample language based on that provided in Part B of the revised LRM for traditional IRAs (see Q 2:28).

1. The exclusive benefit provision. [I.R.C. § 408(b)]

   > The contract is established for the exclusive benefit of the individual or his or her beneficiaries. If this is an inherited IRA within the meaning of Code § 408(d)(3)(C) maintained for the benefit of a designated beneficiary of a deceased individual, references in this document to the "individual" are to the deceased individual.

2. Provision that contributions other than rollovers must be in cash and not exceed the maximum limit. [I.R.C. §§ 72(t)(2)(G), 219(b), 408(b)(2), 408(d)(3)(C), 408(d)(3)(G), 408(p)(1)(B), 408(p)(2)(A)(iv); § 201 of the Gulf Opportunity Zone Act of 2005, Pub. L. No. 109-135; § 15345 of the Food, Conservation, and Energy Act of 2008, Pub. L. No. 110-246; § 702 of Division C of the Emergency Economic Stabilization Act of 2008, Pub. L. No. 110-343]

   > (a) Except in the case of a rollover contribution (as permitted by I.R.C. §§ 402(c), 402(e)(6), 403(a)(4), 403(b)(8), 403(b)(10), 408(d)(3) and 457(e)(16)) or a contribution made in accordance with the terms of a Simplified Employee Pension (SEP) as described in § 408(k), no contributions will be accepted unless they are in cash, and the total of such contributions shall not exceed $5,000 for any taxable year beginning in 2008 and years thereafter.

After 2008, the limit will be adjusted by the Secretary of the Treasury for cost-of-living increases under Code § 219(b)(5)(D). Such adjustments will be in multiples of $500.

(For 2021, the limit is $6,000.)

(b) In the case of an individual who is 50 or older, the annual cash contribution limit is increased by $1,000 for any taxable year beginning in 2006 and years thereafter.

(c) In addition to the amounts described in paragraphs (a) and (b) above, an individual may make additional contributions specifically authorized by statute—such as repayments of qualified reservist distributions, repayments of certain plan distributions made on account of a federally declared disaster, certain amounts received in connection with the *Exxon Valdez* litigation, qualified birth and adoption distributions, and coronavirus-related distributions.

(d) In addition to the amounts described in paragraphs (a) and (c) above, an individual who was a participant in a Code § 401(k) plan of a certain employer in bankruptcy described in Code § 219(b)(5)(C) may contribute up to $3,000 for taxable years beginning after 2006 and before 2010 only. An individual who makes contributions under this paragraph (d) may not also make contributions under paragraph (b).

(This special contribution is not allowed for taxable years 2011 and later; see Q 3:6.)

(e) No contributions will be accepted under a SIMPLE IRA plan established by any employer pursuant to § 408(p). Also, no transfer or rollover of funds attributable to contributions made by a particular employer under its SIMPLE IRA plan will be accepted from a SIMPLE IRA, that is, an IRA used in conjunction with a SIMPLE IRA plan, prior to the expiration of the 2-year period beginning on the date the individual first participated in that employer's SIMPLE IRA plan.

(f) If this is an inherited IRA within the meaning of Code § 408(d)(3)(C), no contributions will be accepted.

3. Statement of required distributions commencing before death. [I.R.C. § 408(b)(3); Treas. Reg. § 1.408-8]

(a) Notwithstanding any provision of this IRA to the contrary, the distribution of the individual's interest in the IRA shall be made in accordance with the requirements of Code § 408(b)(3) and the regulations thereunder, the provisions of which are herein incorporated by reference. If distributions are not made in the form of an annuity on an irrevocable basis (except for acceleration), then distribution of the interest in the IRA (as determined under section [refer to document provision that defines "interest" in the IRA]) must satisfy the requirements of Code § 408(a)(6) and the regulations thereunder, rather than paragraphs (b),

(c) and (d) below and section [refer to document provision for distributions at death].

(b) The entire interest of the individual for whose benefit the contract is maintained will commence to be distributed no later than the first day of April following the calendar year in which such individual attains age 72 (the "required beginning date") over (a) the life of such individual or the lives of such individual and his or her designated beneficiary or (b) a period certain not extending beyond the life expectancy of such individual or the joint and last survivor expectancy of such individual and his or her designated beneficiary. Payments must be made in periodic payments at intervals of no longer than 1 year and must be either nonincreasing or they may increase only as provided in Q&As-1 and -4 of § 1.401(a)(9)-6 of the Income Tax Regulations. In addition, any distribution must satisfy the incidental benefit requirements specified in Q&A-2 of § 1.401(a)(9)-6. If this is an inherited IRA within the meaning of Code § 408(d)(3)(C), this paragraph and paragraphs (c) and (d) below do not apply.

(c) The distribution periods described in paragraph (b) above cannot exceed the periods specified in § 1.401(a)(9)-6 of the Income Tax Regulations.

(d) The first required payment can be made as late as April 1 of the year following the year the individual attains age 72 and must be the payment that is required for one payment interval. The second payment need not be made until the end of the next payment interval.

4. Statement of required distributions commencing after death. [I.R.C. § 408(b)(3); Treas. Reg. § 1.408-8; Notice 2007-7, Q&As-17–19, 2007-1 C.B. 395]

(a) Death On or After Required Distributions Commence. If the individual dies on or after required distributions commence, the remaining portion of his or her interest will continue to be distributed under the contract option chosen.

(b) Death Before Required Distributions Commence. If the individual dies before required distributions commence, his or her entire interest will be distributed at least as rapidly as follows:

(1) If the designated beneficiary is someone other than the individual's surviving spouse, the entire interest will be distributed, starting by the end of the calendar year following the calendar year of the individual's death, over the remaining life expectancy of the designated beneficiary, with such life expectancy determined using the age of the beneficiary as of his or her birthday in the year following the year of the individual's death, or, if elected, in accordance with paragraph (b)(3) below. If this is an inherited IRA within the meaning of Code § 408(d)(3)(C) established for the benefit of a nonspouse designated beneficiary by a direct trustee-to-trustee transfer from a retirement plan of a deceased

individual under Code § 402(c)(11), then, notwithstanding any election made by the deceased individual pursuant to the preceding sentence, the nonspouse designated beneficiary may elect to have distributions made under this paragraph (b)(1) if the transfer is made no later than the end of the year following the year of death.

(2) If the individual's sole designated beneficiary is the individual's surviving spouse, the entire interest will be distributed, starting by the end of the calendar year following the calendar year of the individual's death (or by the end of the calendar year in which the individual would have attained age 70½, if later), over such spouse's life expectancy, or, if elected, in accordance with paragraph (b)(3) below. If the surviving spouse dies before required distributions commence to him or her, the remaining interest will be distributed, starting by the end of the calendar year following the calendar year of the spouse's death, over the spouse's designated beneficiary's remaining life expectancy determined using such beneficiary's age as of his or her birthday in the year following the death of the spouse, or, if elected, will be distributed in accordance with paragraph (b)(3) below. If the surviving spouse dies after required distributions commence to him or her, any remaining interest will continue to be distributed under the contract option chosen.

(3) If there is no designated beneficiary, or if applicable by operation of paragraph (b)(1) or (b)(2) above, the entire interest will be distributed by the end of the calendar year containing the fifth anniversary of the individual's death (or of the spouse's death in the case of the surviving spouse's death before distributions are required to begin under paragraph (b)(2) above).

(4) Life expectancy is determined using the Single Life Table in Q&A-1 of § 1.401(a)(9)-9 of the Income Tax Regulations. If distributions are being made to a surviving spouse as the sole designated beneficiary, such spouse's remaining life expectancy for a year is the number in the Single Life Table corresponding to such spouse's age in the year. In all other cases, remaining life expectancy for a year is the number in the Single Life Table corresponding to the beneficiary's age in the year specified in paragraph (b)(1) or (2) and reduced by 1 for each subsequent year.

(c) The "interest" in the IRA includes the amount of any outstanding rollover, transfer and recharacterization under Q&As-7 and -8 of § 1.408-8 of the Income Tax Regulations and the actuarial value of any other benefits provided under the IRA, such as guaranteed death benefits.

(d) For purposes of paragraphs (a) and (b) above, required distributions are considered to commence on the individual's required beginning date or, if applicable, on the date distributions are required to begin to the surviving spouse under paragraph (b)(2) above. However, if distributions start prior to the applicable date in the preceding sentence, on an irrevocable basis (except for acceleration) under an annuity contract meeting the requirements of § 1.401(a)(9)-6 of the Income Tax Regulations, then required distributions are considered to commence on the annuity starting date.

(e) If the sole designated beneficiary is the individual's surviving spouse, the spouse may elect to treat the IRA as his or her own IRA. This election will be deemed to have been made if such surviving spouse makes a contribution to the IRA or fails to take required distributions as a beneficiary.

(f) The required minimum distributions payable to a designated beneficiary from this IRA may be withdrawn from another IRA the beneficiary holds from the same decedent in accordance with Q&A-9 of § 1.408-8 of the Income Tax Regulations. *Note*: This section will need to be amended to reflect the elimination of the stretch IRA under the SECURE Act.

5. Nonforfeitability provision. [I.R.C. § 408(b)(4)]

   The interest of the individual is nonforfeitable.

6. Nontransferability provision. [I.R.C. § 408(b)(1)]

   This contract is nontransferable by the individual.

7. Provision for the application of premium refunds. [I.R.C. § 408(b)(2)]

   Any refund of premiums (other than those attributable to excess contributions) will be applied, before the close of the calendar year following the year of the refund, toward the payment of future premiums or the purchase of additional benefits.

   (This provision is required for annuities that provide for participation in dividends.)

8. Provision for interruption of premium payments. [I.R.C. § 408(b)(2); Prop. Treas. Reg. § 1.408-3(f)]

   If the premium payments are interrupted, the contract will be reinstated at any date prior to maturity upon payment of a premium to the Company, and the minimum premium amount for reinstatement shall be [an amount not to exceed $50], however, the Company may at its option either accept additional future payments or terminate the contract by payment in cash of the then present value of the paid up benefit if no premiums have been received for two full consecutive policy years and the paid up annuity benefit at maturity would be less than $20 per month.

9. Requirement that trustees or issuers furnish annual calendar-year reports. [Treas. Reg. §§ 1.408-5, 1.408-8]

   The issuer of an individual retirement annuity shall furnish annual calendar-year reports concerning the status of the annuity and such information concerning required minimum distributions as is prescribed by the Commissioner of Internal Revenue.

10. Provision describing the type of compensation used for computing deductible limits. [I.R.C. § 219(f)(1), 219(f)(7); Treas. Reg. § 1.219-1(c)(1)]

> Compensation means wages, salaries, professional fees, or other amounts derived from or received for personal services actually rendered (including, but not limited to commissions paid salespersons compensation for services on the basis of a percentage of profits, commissions on insurance premiums, tips, and bonuses) and includes earned income, as defined in Code § 401(c)(2) (reduced by the deduction the self-employed individual takes for contributions made to a self-employed retirement plan). For purposes of this definition, Code § 401(c)(2) shall be applied as if the term trade or business for purposes of Code § 1402 included service described in subsection (c)(6). Compensation does not include amounts derived from or received as earnings or profits from property (including but not limited to interest and dividends) or amounts not includable in gross income (determined without regard to Code § 112). Compensation also does not include any amount received as a pension or annuity or as deferred compensation. The term "compensation" shall include any amount includible in the individual's gross income under Code § 71 with respect to a divorce or separation instrument described in subparagraph (A) of Code § 71(b)(2). The term "compensation" also includes any differential wage payments as defined in Code § 3401(h)(2). The SECURE Act expanded the definition of compensation in two ways. First, compensation includes any amount that is includible in the individual's gross income and paid to the individual to aid the individual in the pursuit of graduate or postdoctoral study. Second, difficulty of care payments, excluded from gross income under Code Section 131, are treated as compensation. Additionally, alimony is no longer treated as compensation.

Caution. The IRS warns that the information and sample provisions included in the LRM may not be appropriate in all cases. Acceptability may depend on the context in which the provisions are used. [Form 5306, Part II; LRM for traditional IRAs, p. 1 (June 2010)]

Q 2:30 What must a prototype Roth IRA agreement include?

Eleven items must be included. They are shown here with sample language based on that provided in a separate LRM for Roth IRAs (also revised in 2010), which is available on the IRS Web site at *http://www.irs.gov/pub/irs-tege/rira_lrm.pdf*.

1. The exclusive benefit provision. [I.R.C. §§ 408A, 408(a), and 408(h)]

> The account is established for the exclusive benefit of the individual or his or her beneficiaries. If this is an inherited IRA within the meaning of Code § 408(d)(3)(C) maintained for the benefit of a designated beneficiary of a deceased individual, references in this document to the "individual" are to the deceased individual.

2. Provision that contributions other than rollovers must be in cash and not exceed the maximum limit. [I.R.C. §§ 72(t)(2)(G), 219(b), 219(f)(1), 219(f)(7), 408(d)(3)(G), 408(p)(1)(B), 408(p)(2)(A)(iv), 408A(c), 408A(d)(6) and 408A(e) and Treas. Reg. §§ 1.219-1(c)(1) and 1.408A-3, -4 and -5; § 201 of the Gulf Opportunity Zone Act of 2005, Pub. L. No. 109-135; § 15345 of the Food, Conservation, and Energy Act of 2008, Pub. L. No. 110-246; § 702 of Division C of the Emergency Economic Stabilization Act of 2008, Pub. L. No. 110-343; § 125 of the Worker, Retiree, and Employer Recovery Act of 2008, Pub. L. No. 110-458]

(a) Maximum Permissible Amount. Except in the case of a qualified rollover contribution (as defined in (g) below) or a recharacterization (as defined in (f) below), no contribution will be accepted unless it is in cash and the total of such contributions to all the individual's Roth IRAs for a taxable year does not exceed the applicable amount (as defined in (b) below), or the individual's compensation (as defined in (h) below), if less, for that taxable year. The contribution described in the previous sentence that may not exceed the lesser of the applicable amount or the individual's compensation is referred to as a "regular contribution." However, notwithstanding the preceding limits on contributions, an individual may make additional contributions specifically authorized by statute—such as repayments of qualified reservist distributions, repayments of certain plan distributions made on account of a federally declared disaster, certain amounts received in connection with the *Exxon Valdez* litigation, qualified birth and adoption distributions, and coronavirus-related distributions. Contributions may be limited under (c) through (e) below.

(b) Applicable Amount. The applicable amount is determined below:

(i) If the individual is under age 50, the applicable amount is $5,000 for any taxable year beginning in 2008 and years thereafter. After 2008, the $5,000 amount will be adjusted by the Secretary of the Treasury for cost-of-living increases under Code § 219(b)(5)(D). Such adjustments will be in multiples of $500.

(The limit for 2021 is $6,000.)

(ii) If the individual is 50 or older, the applicable amount under paragraph (i) above is increased by $1,000 for any taxable year beginning in 2006 and years thereafter.

(iii) If the individual was a participant in a § 401(k) plan of a certain employer in bankruptcy described in Code § 219(b)(5)(C), then the applicable amount under paragraph (i) above is increased by $3,000 for taxable years beginning after 2006 and before 2010 only. An individual who makes contributions under this paragraph (iii) may not also make contributions under paragraph (ii).

(c) Regular Contribution Limit. The maximum regular contribution that can be made to all the individual's Roth IRAs for a taxable year is the smaller amount determined under (i) or (ii) below.

(i) The maximum regular contribution is phased out ratably between certain levels of modified adjusted gross income in accordance with the following table:

Filing Status	*Full Contribution*	*Phase-out Range*	*No Contribution*
		*Modified AGI (for 2006)**	
Single or Head of Household	$95,000 or less	$95,000–$110,000	$110,000 or more
Joint Return or Qualifying Widow(er)	$150,000 or less	$150,000–$160,000	$160,000 or more
Married, Filing Separate Return	$0	$0–$10,000	$10,000 or more

*See Q 3:77 for the MAGI limits effective for 2021.

An individual's modified adjusted gross income ("modified AGI") for a taxable year is defined in Code § 408A(c)(3) and does not include any amount included in adjusted gross income as a result of a qualified rollover contribution. If the individual's modified AGI for a taxable year is in the phase-out range, the maximum regular contribution determined under this table for that taxable year is rounded up to the next multiple of $10 and is not reduced below $200. After 2006, the dollar amounts above will be adjusted by the Secretary of the Treasury for cost-of-living increases under Code § 408A(c)(3). Such adjustments will be in multiples of $1,000. In 2021, the income phase-out range for taxpayers making contributions to a Roth IRA is $125,000 to $140,000. For married couples filing jointly, the income phase-out range is $198,000 to $208,000. The phase-out range for married individuals filing separately who make contributions to a Roth IRA is not subject to an annual cost-of-living adjustment and remains $0 to $10,000.

(ii) If the individual makes regular contributions to both Roth and non-Roth IRAs for a taxable year, the maximum regular contribution that can be made to all the individual's Roth IRAs for that taxable year is reduced by the regular contributions made to the individual's non-Roth IRAs for the taxable year.

(d) SIMPLE IRA Limits. No contributions will be accepted under a SIMPLE IRA plan established by any employer pursuant to Code § 408(p). Also, no transfer or rollover of funds attributable to contributions made by a particular employer under its SIMPLE IRA plan will be accepted from a SIMPLE IRA, that is, an IRA used in conjunction with a SIMPLE IRA plan, prior to the expiration of the 2-year period beginning on the date the individual first participated in that employer's SIMPLE IRA plan.

(e) Inherited IRA. If this is an inherited IRA within the meaning of Code § 408(d)(3)(C), no contributions will be accepted.

(f) Recharacterization. A regular contribution to a non-Roth IRA may be recharacterized pursuant to the rules in § 1.408A-5 of the Income Tax Regulations as a regular contribution to this IRA, subject to the limits in (c) above.

(g) Qualified Rollover Contribution. A "qualified rollover contribution" is a rollover contribution of a distribution from an eligible retirement plan described in Code § 402(c)(8)(B). If the distribution is from an IRA, the rollover must meet the requirements of Code § 408(d)(3), except the one-rollover-per year rule of Code § 408(d)(3)(B) does not apply if the distribution is from a non-Roth IRA. If the distribution is from an eligible retirement plan other than an IRA, the rollover must meet the requirements of Code § 402(c), 402(e)(6), 403(a)(4), 403(b)(8), 403(b)(10), 408(d)(3) or 457(e)(16), as applicable. A qualified rollover contribution also includes (i) and (ii) below.

(i) All or part of a military death gratuity or servicemembers' group life insurance ("SGLI") payment may be contributed if the contribution is made within 1 year of receiving the gratuity or payment. Such contributions are disregarded for purposes of the one-rollover-per-year rule under Code § 408(d)(3)(B).

(ii) All or part of an airline payment (as defined in § 125 of the Worker, Retiree, and Employer Recovery Act of 2008, Pub. L. No. 110-458) received by certain airline employees may be contributed if the contribution is made within 180 days of receiving the payment.

(h) Compensation. For purposes of (a) above, compensation is defined as wages, salaries, professional fees, or other amounts derived from or received for personal services actually rendered (including, but not limited to commissions paid salesmen, compensation for services on the basis of a percentage of profits, commissions on insurance premiums, tips, and bonuses) and includes earned income, as defined in Code § 401(c)(2) (reduced by the deduction the self-employed individual takes for contributions made to a self-employed retirement plan). For purposes of this definition, Code § 401(c)(2) shall be applied as if the term trade or business for purposes of Code § 1402 included service described in subsection (c)(6). Compensation does not include amounts derived from or received as earnings or profits from property (including but not limited to interest and dividends) or amounts not includable in gross income (determined without regard to Code § 112). Compensation also does not include any amount received as a pension or annuity or as deferred compensation. The term "compensation" shall include any amount includible in the individual's gross income under Code § 71 with respect to a divorce or separation instrument described in subparagraph (A) of Code § 71(b)(2). In the case of a married individual filing a joint return, the greater compensation of his or her spouse is treated as his or her own compensation, but only to the extent that such spouse's compensation is not being used for purposes of the spouse making an IRA contribution. The term "compensation" also includes any differential wage payments as defined in Code § 3401(h)(2). The SECURE Act expanded the definition of compensation in two ways. First, compensation includes any amount included in income and paid to the individual to aid the individual in pursuit of graduate or postdoctoral study. Second, compensation now includes difficulty of care payments, which are excluded from gross income under Code Section 131. Additionally, alimony is no longer treated as compensation.

3. Provision acknowledging the prohibition of investment by an IRA in collectibles or a statement informing participants in the IRA plan that investment in collectibles will be a taxable distribution. [I.R.C. § 408(m)]

    If the trust acquires collectibles within the meaning of Code § 408(m) after December 31, 1981, trust assets will be treated as a distribution in an amount equal to the cost of such collectibles.

    (This provision is *not* required if the IRA precludes any investments that could be construed as collectibles. It should be noted that Code Section 408(m)(3) provides an exception to the collectibles prohibition for certain gold and silver coins.)

4. Prohibition of investment by an individual retirement account in life insurance contracts. [I.R.C. § 408(a)(3)]

    No part of the trust funds will be invested in life insurance contracts.

5. Statement of required distributions commencing before death. [I.R.C. § 408A(c)(5)]

    No amount is required to be distributed prior to the death of the individual for whose benefit the account was originally established. If this is an inherited IRA within the meaning of Code § 408(d)(3)(C), this paragraph does not apply.

6. Statement of required distributions commencing after death. [I.R.C. §§ 408(a)(6) and 408A(c)(5) and Treas. Reg. §§ 1.408-8 and 1.408A-6]

(a) Notwithstanding any provision of this IRA to the contrary, the distribution of the individual's interest in the account shall be made in accordance with the requirements of Code § 408(a)(6), as modified by Code § 408A(c)(5), and the regulations thereunder, the provisions of which are herein incorporated by reference. If distributions are made from an annuity contract purchased from an insurance company, distributions thereunder must satisfy the requirements of § 1.401(a)(9)-6 of the Income Tax Regulations (taking into account Code § 408A(c)(5)), rather than the distribution rules in paragraphs (b), (c) and (d) below.

(b) Upon the death of the individual, his or her entire interest will be distributed at least as rapidly as follows:

> (i) If the designated beneficiary is someone other than the individual's surviving spouse, the entire interest will be distributed, starting by the end of the calendar year following the calendar year of the individual's death, over the remaining life expectancy of the designated beneficiary, with such life expectancy determined using the age of the beneficiary as of his or her birthday in the year following the year of the individual's death, or, if elected, in accordance with paragraph (b)(iii) below. If this is an inherited IRA within the meaning of Code § 408(d)(3)(C) established for the benefit of a nonspouse designated beneficiary by a direct trustee-to-trustee transfer from a retirement plan of a deceased individual under Code § 402(c)(11), then, notwithstanding any election made by the deceased individual pursuant to the preceding sentence, the nonspouse designated beneficiary may elect to have distributions made under this paragraph (b)(i) if the transfer is made no later than the end of the year following the year of death.
>
> (ii) If the individual's sole designated beneficiary is the individual's surviving spouse, the entire interest will be distributed, starting by the end of the calendar year following the calendar year of the individual's death (or by the end of the calendar year in which the individual would have attained age 72, if later), over such spouse's life expectancy, or, if elected, in accordance with paragraph (b)(iii) below. If the surviving spouse dies before distributions are required to begin, the remaining interest will be distributed, starting by the end of the calendar year following the calendar year of the spouse's death, over the spouse's designated beneficiary's remaining life expectancy determined using such beneficiary's age as of his or her birthday in the year following the death of the spouse, or, if elected, will be distributed in accordance with paragraph (b)(iii) below. If the surviving spouse dies after distributions are required to begin, any remaining interest will be distributed over the spouse's remaining life expectancy determined using

the spouse's age as of his or her birthday in the year of the spouse's death.

(iii) If there is no designated beneficiary, or if applicable by operation of paragraph (b)(i) or (b)(ii) above, the entire interest will be distributed by the end of the calendar year containing the fifth anniversary of the individual's death (or of the spouse's death in the case of the surviving spouse's death before distributions are required to begin under paragraph (b)(ii) above).

(iv) The amount to be distributed each year under paragraph (b)(i) or (ii) is the quotient obtained by dividing the value of the IRA as of the end of the preceding year by the remaining life expectancy specified in such paragraph. Life expectancy is determined using the Single Life Table in Q&A-1 of § 1.401(a)(9)-9 of the Income Tax Regulations. If distributions are being made to a surviving spouse as the sole designated beneficiary, such spouse's remaining life expectancy for a year is the number in the Single Life Table corresponding to such spouse's age in the year. In all other cases, remaining life expectancy for a year is the number in the Single Life Table corresponding to the beneficiary's age in the year specified in paragraph (b)(i) or (ii) and reduced by 1 for each subsequent year.

(c) The "value" of the IRA includes the amount of any outstanding rollover, transfer and recharacterization under Q&As-7 and -8 of § 1.408-8 of the Income Tax Regulations.

(d) If the sole designated beneficiary is the individual's surviving spouse, the spouse may elect to treat the IRA as his or her own IRA. This election will be deemed to have been made if such surviving spouse makes a contribution to the IRA or fails to take required distributions as a beneficiary.

(e) The required minimum distributions payable to a designated beneficiary from this IRA may be withdrawn from another IRA the beneficiary holds from the same decedent in accordance with Q&A-9 of § 1.408-8 of the Income Tax Regulations. *Note:* This section will need to be modified to reflect the elimination of stretch IRAs under the SECURE Act.

7. Nonforfeitability provision. [I.R.C. § 408(a)(4)]

   The interest of an individual in the balance in his or her account is nonforfeitable at all times.

8. Provision acknowledging the prohibition against commingling of assets. [I.R.C. § 408(a)(5)]

   The assets of the trust will not be commingled with other property except in a common trust fund or common investment fund.

9. Requirement for separate accounting for the interest of each individual under an account or annuity established by an employer or employee association. [Treas. Reg. §§ 1.408-2(c)(3), 1.408A-2]

    Separate records will be maintained for the interest of each individual.

    (This provision is required *only* in Roth IRAs that are sponsored by the employer or employee association.)

10. Requirement that trustees or insurers furnish annual calendar-year reports concerning the status of the account or annuity. [I.R.C. §§ 408(i), 408A(d)(3)(D); Treas. Reg. §§ 1.408-5, 1.408-8]

    The trustee of a Roth individual retirement account shall furnish annual calendar-year reports concerning the status of the account and such information concerning required minimum distributions as is prescribed by the Commissioner of Internal Revenue.

11. Provision that there be substitution for a nonbank trustee or custodian when the Commissioner of Internal Revenue issues a notification. [Treas. Reg. § 1.408-2(e)(6)(v)]

    The nonbank trustee or custodian shall substitute another trustee or custodian if the nonbank trustee or custodian receives notice from the Commissioner of Internal Revenue that such substitution is required because it has failed to comply with the requirements of § 1.408-2(e) of the Income Tax Regulations.

    (This provision is required *only* in IRA accounts that are sponsored by nonbank trustees or custodians.)

Caution. The IRS warns that the information and sample provisions included in the LRM may not be appropriate in all cases. Acceptability may depend on the context in which the provisions are used.

Q 2:31 What must a prototype Roth IRA annuity include?

Nine items are required. They are shown here with sample language based on Part B of the revised LRM for Roth IRAs (available at *http://www.irs.gov/pub/irs-tege/rira_lrm.pdf*).

1. The exclusive benefit provision. [I.R.C. §§ 408A and 408(b)]

    The contract is established for the exclusive benefit of the individual or his or her beneficiaries. If this is an inherited IRA within the meaning of Code § 408(d)(3)(C) maintained for the benefit of a designated beneficiary of a deceased individual, references in this document to the "individual" are to the deceased individual.

2. Provision that contributions other than rollovers must be in cash and not exceed the maximum limit. [I.R.C. §§ 72(t)(2)(G), 219(b), 219(f)(1), 408(d)(3)(G), 408(p)(1)(B), 408(p)(2)(A)(iv), 408A(c), 408A(d)(6) and 408A(e); § 201 of the Gulf Opportunity Zone Act of 2005, Pub. L. No. 109-135; § 15345 of the Food, Conservation, and Energy Act of 2008,

Pub. L. No. 110-246; § 702 of Division C of the Emergency Economic Stabilization Act of 2008, Pub. L. No. 110-343; § 125 of the Worker, Retiree, and Employer Recovery Act of 2008, Pub. L. No. 110-458]

> (a) Maximum Permissible Amount. Except in the case of a qualified rollover contribution (as defined in (g) below) or a recharacterization (as defined in (f) below), no contribution will be accepted unless it is in cash and the total of such contributions to all the individual's Roth IRAs for a taxable year does not exceed the applicable amount (as defined in (b) below), or the individual's compensation (as defined in (h) below), if less, for that taxable year. The contribution described in the previous sentence that may not exceed the lesser of the applicable amount or the individual's compensation is referred to as a "regular contribution." However, notwithstanding the preceding limits on contributions, an individual may make additional contributions specifically authorized by statute—such as repayments of qualified reservist distributions, repayments of certain plan distributions made on account of a federally declared disaster, certain amounts received in connection with the *Exxon Valdez* litigation, qualified birth and adoption distributions, and coronavirus-related distributions. Contributions may be limited under (c) through (e) below.
>
> (b) Applicable Amount. The applicable amount is determined below:
>
> > (i) If the individual is under age 50, the applicable amount is $5,000 for any taxable year beginning in 2008 and years thereafter. After 2008, the $5,000 amount will be adjusted by the Secretary of the Treasury for cost-of-living increases under Code § 219(b)(5)(D). Such adjustments will be in multiples of $500.
> >
> > (The contribution limit for 2021 is $6,000.)
> >
> > (ii) If the individual is 50 or older, the applicable amount under paragraph (i) above is increased by $1,000 for any taxable year beginning in 2006 and years thereafter.
> >
> > (iii) If the individual was a participant in a § 401(k) plan of a certain employer in bankruptcy described in Code § 219(b)(5)(C), then the applicable amount under paragraph (i) above is increased by $3,000 for taxable years beginning after 2006 and before 2010 only. An individual who makes contributions under this paragraph (iii) may not also make contributions under paragraph (ii).
>
> (c) Regular Contribution Limit. The maximum regular contribution that can be made to all the individual's Roth IRAs for a taxable year is the smaller amount determined under (i) or (ii) below.

(i) The maximum regular contribution is phased out ratably between certain levels of modified adjusted gross income in accordance with the following table:

Filing Status	*Full Contribution*	*Phase-out Range*	*No Contribution*
		*Modified AGI (for 2006)**	
Single or Head of Household	$95,000 or less	$95,000–$110,000	$110,000 or more
Joint Return or Qualifying Widow(er)	$150,000 or less	$150,000–$160,000	$160,000 or more
Married, Filing Separate Return	$0	$0–$10,000	$10,000 or more

*See Q 3:77 for the MAGI limits effective for 2020.

An individual's modified adjusted gross income (MAGI) for a taxable year is defined in Code § 408A(c)(3) and does not include any amount included in adjusted gross income as a result of a qualified rollover contribution. If the individual's MAGI for a taxable year is in the phase-out range, the maximum regular contribution determined under this table for that taxable year is rounded up to the next multiple of $10 and is not reduced below $200. After 2006, the dollar amounts above will be adjusted by the Secretary of the Treasury for cost-of-living increases under Code § 408A(c)(3). Such adjustments will be in multiples of $1,000.

(ii) If the individual makes regular contributions to both Roth and non-Roth IRAs for a taxable year, the maximum regular contribution that can be made to all the individual's Roth IRAs for that taxable year is reduced by the regular contributions made to the individual's non-Roth IRAs for the taxable year.

(d) SIMPLE IRA Limits. No contributions will be accepted under a SIMPLE IRA plan established by any employer pursuant to Code § 408(p). Also, no transfer or rollover of funds attributable to contributions made by a particular employer under its SIMPLE IRA plan will be accepted from a SIMPLE IRA, that is, an IRA used in conjunction with a SIMPLE IRA plan, prior to the expiration of the 2-year period beginning on the date the individual first participated in that employer's SIMPLE IRA plan.

(e) Inherited IRA. If this is an inherited IRA within the meaning of Code § 408(d)(3)(C), no contributions will be accepted.

(f) Recharacterization. A regular contribution to a non-Roth IRA may be recharacterized pursuant to the rules in § 1.408A-5 of the Income Tax Regulations as a regular contribution to this IRA, subject to the limits in (c) above.

(g) Qualified Rollover Contribution. A "qualified rollover contribution" is a rollover contribution of a distribution from an eligible retirement plan described in Code § 402(c)(8)(B). If the distribution is from an IRA, the rollover must meet the requirements of Code § 408(d)(3), except the one-rollover-per year rule of Code § 408(d)(3)(B) does not apply if the distribution is from a non-Roth IRA. If the distribution is from an eligible retirement plan other than an IRA, the rollover must meet the requirements of Code § 402(c), 402(e)(6), 403(a)(4), 403(b)(8), 403(b)(10), 408(d)(3), or 457(e)(16), as applicable. A qualified rollover contribution also includes (i) and (ii) below.

(i) All or part of a military death gratuity or servicemembers' group life insurance ("SGLI") payment may be contributed if the contribution is made within 1 year of receiving the gratuity or payment. Such contributions are disregarded for purposes of the one-rollover-per-year rule under Code § 408(d)(3)(B).

(ii) All or part of an airline payment (as defined in § 125 of the Worker, Retiree, and Employer Recovery Act of 2008, Pub. L. No. 110-458) received by certain airline employees may be contributed if the contribution is made within 180 days of receiving the payment.

(h) Compensation. For purposes of (a) above, compensation is defined as wages, salaries, professional fees, or other amounts derived from or received for personal services actually rendered (including, but not limited to commissions paid salesmen, compensation for services on the basis of a percentage of profits, commissions on insurance premiums, tips, and bonuses) and includes earned income, as defined in Code § 401(c)(2) (reduced by the deduction the self-employed individual takes for contributions made to a self-employed retirement plan). For purposes of this definition, Code § 401(c)(2) shall be applied as if the term trade or business for purposes of Code § 1402 included service described in subsection (c)(6). Compensation does not include amounts derived from or received as earnings or profits from property (including but not limited to interest and dividends) or amounts not includable in gross income (determined without regard to Code § 112). Compensation also does not include any amount received as a pension or annuity or as deferred compensation. The term "compensation" shall include any amount includable in the individual's gross income under Code § 71 with respect to a divorce or separation instrument described in subparagraph (A) of Code § 71(b)(2). In the case of a married individual filing a joint return, the greater compensation of his or her spouse is treated as his or her own compensation, but only to the extent that such spouse's compensation is not being used for purposes of the spouse making an IRA contribution. The term "compensation" also includes any differential wage payments as defined in Code § 3401(h)(2). The SECURE Act expanded the definition of compensation in two ways. First, effective for tax years beginning after December 31, 2019, compensation includes any amount included in an individual's gross income and paid to the individual to aid the individual in the pursuit of graduate or postdoctoral study. Second, compensation includes difficulty of care payments that are excludible from gross income under Code Section 131. Additionally, alimony is no longer treated as compensation.

3. Statement of required distributions commencing before death. [I.R.C. § 408A(c)(5)]

   No amount is required to be distributed prior to the death of the individual for whose benefit the contract was originally established. If this is an inherited IRA within the meaning of Code § 408(d)(3)(C), this paragraph does not apply.

4. Statement of required distributions commencing after death. [I.R.C. §§ 408(b)(3), 408A(c)(5); Treas. Reg. §§ 1.408-8 and 1.408A-6]

   (a) Notwithstanding any provision of this IRA to the contrary, the distribution of the individual's interest in the IRA shall be made in accordance with the requirements of Code § 408(b)(3), as modified by Code § 408A(c)(5), and the regulations thereunder, the provisions of which are herein incorporated by reference. If distributions are not made in the form of an annuity on an irrevocable basis (except for acceleration), then distribution of the interest in the IRA (as determined under section [refer to document provision that defines "interest" in the IRA]) must satisfy the requirements of Code § 408(a)(6), as modified by Code § 408A(c)(5), and the regulations thereunder, rather than the distribution rules in paragraphs (b), (c), (d), and (e) below.

   (b) Upon the death of the individual, his or her entire interest will be distributed at least as rapidly as follows:

   (i) If the designated beneficiary is someone other than the individual's surviving spouse, the entire interest will be distributed, starting by the end of the calendar year following the calendar year of the individual's death, over the remaining life expectancy of the designated beneficiary, with such life expectancy determined using the age of the beneficiary as of his or her birthday in the year following the year of the individual's death, or, if elected, in accordance with paragraph (b)(iii) below. If this is an inherited IRA within the meaning of Code § 408(d)(3)(C) established for the benefit of a nonspouse designated beneficiary by a direct trustee-to-trustee transfer from a retirement plan of a deceased individual under Code § 402(c)(11), then, notwithstanding any election made by the deceased individual pursuant to the preceding sentence, the nonspouse designated beneficiary may elect to have distributions made under this paragraph (b)(i) if the transfer is made no later than the end of the year following the year of death.

(ii) If the individual's sole designated beneficiary is the individual's surviving spouse, the entire interest will be distributed, starting by the end of the calendar year following the calendar year of the individual's death (or by the end of the calendar year in which the individual would have attained age 72, if later), over such spouse's life expectancy, or, if elected, in accordance with paragraph (b)(iii) below. If the surviving spouse dies before required distributions commence to him or her, the remaining interest will be distributed, starting by the end of the calendar year following the calendar year of the spouse's death, over the spouse's designated beneficiary's remaining life expectancy determined using such beneficiary's age as of his or her birthday in the year following the death of the spouse, or, if elected, will be distributed in accordance with paragraph (b)(iii) below. If the surviving spouse dies after required distributions commence to him or her, any remaining interest will continue to be distributed under the contract option chosen.

(iii) If there is no designated beneficiary, or if applicable by operation of paragraph (b)(i) or (b)(ii) above, the entire interest will be distributed by the end of the calendar year containing the fifth anniversary of the individual's death (or of the spouse's death in the case of the surviving spouse's death before distributions are required to begin under paragraph (b)(ii) above).

(iv) Life expectancy is determined using the Single Life Table in Q&A-1 of § 1.401(a)(9)-9 of the Income Tax Regulations. If distributions are being made to a surviving spouse as the sole designated beneficiary, such spouse's remaining life expectancy for a year is the number in the Single Life Table corresponding to such spouse's age in the year. In all other cases, remaining life expectancy for a year is the number in the Single Life Table corresponding to the beneficiary's age in the year specified in paragraph (b)(i) or (ii) and reduced by 1 for each subsequent year.

(c) The "interest" in the IRA includes the amount of any outstanding rollover, transfer and recharacterization under Q&As-7 and -8 of § 1.408-8 of the Income Tax Regulations and the actuarial value of any other benefits provided under the IRA, such as guaranteed death benefits.

(d) For purposes of paragraph (b)(ii) above, required distributions are considered to commence on the date distributions are required to begin to the surviving spouse under such paragraph. However, if distributions start prior to the applicable date in the preceding sentence, on an irrevocable basis (except for acceleration) under an annuity contract meeting the requirements of § 1.401(a)(9)-6 of the Income Tax Regulations, then required distributions are considered to commence on the annuity starting date.

(e) If the sole designated beneficiary is the individual's surviving spouse, the spouse may elect to treat the IRA as his or her own IRA. This election will be deemed to have been made if such surviving spouse makes a contribution to the IRA or fails to take required distributions as a beneficiary.

(f) The required minimum distributions payable to a designated beneficiary from this IRA may be withdrawn from another IRA the beneficiary holds from the same decedent in accordance with Q&A-9 of § 1.408-8 of the Income Tax Regulations. *Note*: This section will be updated to reflect the elimination of the stretch IRA by the SECURE Act.

5. Nonforfeitability provision. [I.R.C. § 408(b)(4)]

   The interest of the individual is nonforfeitable.

6. Nontransferability provision. [I.R.C. § 408(b)(1)]

   This contract is nontransferable by the individual.

7. Provision governing the application of premium refunds. [I.R.C. § 408(b)(2)]

   Any refund of premiums (other than those attributable to excess contributions) will be applied, before the close of the calendar year following the year of the refund, toward the payment of future premiums or the purchase of additional benefits.

   (This provision is required for annuities that provide for participation in dividends.)

8. Provision for interruption of premium payments. [I.R.C. § 408(b)(2); Prop. Treas. Reg. § 1.408-3(f)]

   If the premium payments are interrupted, the contract will be reinstated at any date prior to maturity upon payment of a premium to the insurance company, and the minimum premium amount for reinstatement shall be—(not to exceed $50), however, the insurance company may at its option either accept additional future payments or terminate the contract by payment in cash of the then present value of the paid up benefit if no premiums have been received for two full consecutive policy years and the paid up annuity benefit at maturity would be less than $20 per month.

9. Requirement that trustees or issuers furnish annual calendar-year reports. [I.R.C. §§ 408(i), 408A(d)(3)(D); Treas. Reg. §§ 1.408-5, 1.408-8]

> The issuer of a Roth individual retirement annuity shall furnish annual calendar year reports concerning the status of the annuity and such information concerning required minimum distributions as is prescribed by the Commissioner of Internal Revenue.

Caution. The IRS warns that the information and sample provisions included in the LRM may not be appropriate in all cases. Acceptability can depend on context.

Q 2:32 What must a prototype Roth IRA annuity include?

Nine items are required. They are shown here with sample language based on Part B of the revised LRM for Roth IRAs (available at *http://www.irs.gov/pub/irs-tege/rira_lrm.pdf*).

1. The exclusive benefit provision. [I.R.C. §§ 408A and 408(b)]

> The contract is established for the exclusive benefit of the individual or his or her beneficiaries. If this is an inherited IRA within the meaning of Code § 408(d)(3)(C) maintained for the benefit of a designated beneficiary of a deceased individual, references in this document to the "individual" are to the deceased individual.

2. Provision that contributions other than rollovers must be in cash and not exceed the maximum limit. [I.R.C. §§ 72(t)(2)(G), 219(b), 219(f)(1), 408(d)(3)(G), 408(p)(1)(B), 408(p)(2)(A)(iv), 408A(c), 408A(d)(6) and 408A(e); § 201 of the Gulf Opportunity Zone Act of 2005, Pub. L. No. 109-135; § 15345 of the Food, Conservation, and Energy Act of 2008, Pub. L. No. 110-246; § 702 of Division C of the Emergency Economic Stabilization Act of 2008, Pub. L. No. 110-343; § 125 of the Worker, Retiree, and Employer Recovery Act of 2008, Pub. L. No. 110-458]

> (a) Maximum Permissible Amount. Except in the case of a qualified rollover contribution (as defined in (g) below) or a recharacterization (as defined in (f) below), no contribution will be accepted unless it is in cash and the total of such contributions to all the individual's Roth IRAs for a taxable year does not exceed the applicable amount (as defined in (b) below), or the individual's compensation (as defined in (h) below), if less, for that taxable year. The contribution described in the previous sentence that may not exceed the lesser of the applicable amount or the individual's compensation is referred to as a "regular contribution." However, notwithstanding the preceding limits on contributions, an individual may make additional contributions specifically authorized by statute—such as repayments of qualified reservist distributions, repayments of certain plan distributions made on account of a federally declared disaster, certain amounts received in connection with the *Exxon Valdez* litigation, qualified birth and adoption distributions, and coronavirus-related distributions. Contributions may be limited under (c) through (e) below.

(b) Applicable Amount. The applicable amount is determined below:

(i) If the individual is under age 50, the applicable amount is $5,000 for any taxable year beginning in 2008 and years thereafter. After 2008, the $5,000 amount will be adjusted by the Secretary of the Treasury for cost-of-living increases under Code § 219(b)(5)(D). Such adjustments will be in multiples of $500.

(The contribution limit for 2021 is $6,000.)

(ii) If the individual is 50 or older, the applicable amount under paragraph (i) above is increased by $1,000 for any taxable year beginning in 2006 and years thereafter.

(iii) If the individual was a participant in a § 401(k) plan of a certain employer in bankruptcy described in Code § 219(b)(5)(C), then the applicable amount under paragraph (i) above is increased by $3,000 for taxable years beginning after 2006 and before 2010 only. An individual who makes contributions under this paragraph (iii) may not also make contributions under paragraph (ii).

(c) Regular Contribution Limit. The maximum regular contribution that can be made to all the individual's Roth IRAs for a taxable year is the smaller amount determined under (i) or (ii) below.

(i) The maximum regular contribution is phased out ratably between certain levels of modified adjusted gross income in accordance with the following table:

Filing Status	*Full Contribution*	*Phase-out Range*	*No Contribution*
		*Modified AGI (for 2006)**	
Single or Head of Household	$95,000 or less	$95,000–$110,000	$110,000 or more
Joint Return or Qualifying Widow(er)	$150,000 or less	$150,000–$160,000	$160,000 or more
Married, Filing Separate Return	$0	$0–$10,000	$10,000 or more

*See Q 3:77 for the MAGI limits effective for 2021.

An individual's modified adjusted gross income (MAGI) for a taxable year is defined in Code § 408A(c)(3) and does not include any amount included in adjusted gross income as a result of a qualified rollover contribution. If the individual's MAGI for a taxable year is in the phase-out range, the maximum regular contribution determined under this table for that taxable year is rounded up to the next multiple of $10 and is not reduced below $200. After 2006, the dollar amounts above will be adjusted by the Secretary of the Treasury for cost-of-living increases under Code § 408A(c)(3). Such adjustments will be in multiples of $1,000.

(ii) If the individual makes regular contributions to both Roth and non-Roth IRAs for a taxable year, the maximum regular contribution that can be made to all the individual's Roth IRAs for that taxable year is reduced by the regular contributions made to the individual's non-Roth IRAs for the taxable year.

(d) SIMPLE IRA Limits. No contributions will be accepted under a SIMPLE IRA plan established by any employer pursuant to Code § 408(p). Also, no transfer or rollover of funds attributable to contributions made by a particular employer under its SIMPLE IRA plan will be accepted from a SIMPLE IRA, that is, an IRA used in conjunction with a SIMPLE IRA plan, prior to the expiration of the 2-year period beginning on the date the individual first participated in that employer's SIMPLE IRA plan.

(e) Inherited IRA. If this is an inherited IRA within the meaning of Code § 408(d)(3)(C), no contributions will be accepted.

(f) Recharacterization. A regular contribution to a non-Roth IRA may be recharacterized pursuant to the rules in § 1.408A-5 of the Income Tax Regulations as a regular contribution to this IRA, subject to the limits in (c) above.

(g) Qualified Rollover Contribution. A "qualified rollover contribution" is a rollover contribution of a distribution from an eligible retirement plan described in Code § 402(c)(8)(B). If the distribution is from an IRA, the rollover must meet the requirements of Code § 408(d)(3), except the one-rollover-per year rule of Code § 408(d)(3)(B) does not apply if the distribution is from a non-Roth IRA. If the distribution is from an eligible retirement plan other than an IRA, the rollover must meet the requirements of Code § 402(c), 402(e)(6), 403(a)(4), 403(b)(8), 403(b)(10), 408(d)(3) or 457(e)(16), as applicable. A qualified rollover contribution also includes (i) and (ii) below.

(i) All or part of a military death gratuity or servicemembers' group life insurance ("SGLI") payment may be contributed if the contribution is made within 1 year of receiving the gratuity or payment. Such contributions are disregarded for purposes of the one-rollover-per-year rule under Code § 408(d)(3)(B).

(ii) All or part of an airline payment (as defined in § 125 of the Worker, Retiree, and Employer Recovery Act of 2008, Pub. L. No. 110-458) received by certain airline employees may be contributed if the contribution is made within 180 days of receiving the payment.

(h) Compensation. For purposes of (a) above, compensation is defined as wages, salaries, professional fees, or other amounts derived from or received for personal services actually rendered (including, but not limited to commissions paid salesmen, compensation for services on the basis of a percentage of profits, commissions on insurance premiums, tips, and bonuses) and includes earned income, as defined in Code § 401(c)(2) (reduced by the deduction the self-employed individual takes for contributions made to a self-employed retirement plan). For purposes of this definition, Code § 401(c)(2) shall be applied as if the term trade or business for purposes of Code § 1402 included service described in subsection (c)(6). Compensation does not include amounts derived from or received as earnings or profits from property (including but not limited to interest and dividends) or amounts not includable in gross income (determined without regard to Code § 112). Compensation also does not include any amount received as a pension or annuity or as deferred compensation. The term "compensation" shall include any amount includable in the individual's gross income under Code § 71 with respect to a divorce or separation instrument described in subparagraph (A) of Code § 71(b)(2). In the case of a married individual filing a joint return, the greater compensation of his or her spouse is treated as his or her own compensation, but only to the extent that such spouse's compensation is not being used for purposes of the spouse making an IRA contribution. The term "compensation" also includes any differential wage payments as defined in Code § 3401(h)(2). The SECURE Act expanded the definition of compensation in two ways. First, effective for tax years beginning after December 31, 2019, compensation includes amounts included in an individual's gross income and paid to the individual to aid the individual in the pursuit of graduate or postdoctoral study. Second, difficulty of care payments excluded from gross income under Code Section 131(c) are treated as compensation for IRA purposes. Additionally, under the Tax Cuts and Jobs Act of 2017, alimony is no longer treated as compensation.

3. Statement of required distributions commencing before death. [I.R.C. § 408A(c)(5)]

   No amount is required to be distributed prior to the death of the individual for whose benefit the contract was originally established. If this is an inherited IRA within the meaning of Code § 408(d)(3)(C), this paragraph does not apply.

4. Statement of required distributions commencing after death. [I.R.C. §§ 408(b)(3), 408A(c)(5); Treas. Reg. §§ 1.408-8 and 1.408A-6]

   (a) Notwithstanding any provision of this IRA to the contrary, the distribution of the individual's interest in the IRA shall be made in accordance with the requirements of Code § 408(b)(3), as modified by Code § 408A(c)(5), and the regulations thereunder, the provisions of which are herein incorporated by reference. If distributions are not made in the form of an annuity on an irrevocable basis (except for acceleration), then distribution of the interest in the IRA (as determined under section [refer to document provision that defines "interest" in the IRA]) must satisfy the requirements of Code § 408(a)(6), as modified by Code § 408A(c)(5), and the regulations thereunder, rather than the distribution rules in paragraphs (b), (c), (d), and (e) below.

(b) Upon the death of the individual, his or her entire interest will be distributed at least as rapidly as follows:

(i) If the designated beneficiary is someone other than the individual's surviving spouse, the entire interest will be distributed, starting by the end of the calendar year following the calendar year of the individual's death, over the remaining life expectancy of the designated beneficiary, with such life expectancy determined using the age of the beneficiary as of his or her birthday in the year following the year of the individual's death, or, if elected, in accordance with paragraph (b)(iii) below. If this is an inherited IRA within the meaning of Code § 408(d)(3)(C) established for the benefit of a nonspouse designated beneficiary by a direct trustee-to-trustee transfer from a retirement plan of a deceased individual under Code § 402(c)(11), then, notwithstanding any election made by the deceased individual pursuant to the preceding sentence, the nonspouse designated beneficiary may elect to have distributions made under this paragraph (b)(i) if the transfer is made no later than the end of the year following the year of death.

(ii) If the individual's sole designated beneficiary is the individual's surviving spouse, the entire interest will be distributed, starting by the end of the calendar year following the calendar year of the individual's death (or by the end of the calendar year in which the individual would have attained age 72, if later), over such spouse's life expectancy, or, if elected, in accordance with paragraph (b)(iii) below. If the surviving spouse dies before required distributions commence to him or her, the remaining interest will be distributed, starting by the end of the calendar year following the calendar year of the spouse's death, over the spouse's designated beneficiary's remaining life expectancy determined using such beneficiary's age as of his or her birthday in the year following the death of the spouse, or, if elected, will be distributed in accordance with paragraph (b)(iii) below. If the surviving spouse dies after required distributions commence to him or her, any remaining interest will continue to be distributed under the contract option chosen.

(iii) If there is no designated beneficiary, or if applicable by operation of paragraph (b)(i) or (b)(ii) above, the entire interest will be distributed by the end of the calendar year containing the fifth anniversary of the individual's death (or of the spouse's death in the case of the surviving spouse's death before distributions are required to begin under paragraph (b)(ii) above).

(iv) Life expectancy is determined using the Single Life Table in Q&A-1 of § 1.401(a)(9)-9 of the Income Tax Regulations. If distributions are being made to a surviving spouse as the sole designated beneficiary, such spouse's remaining life expectancy for a year is the number in the Single Life Table corresponding to such spouse's age in the year. In all other cases, remaining life expectancy for a year is the number in the Single Life Table corresponding to the beneficiary's age in the year specified in paragraph (b)(i) or (ii) and reduced by 1 for each subsequent year.

(c) The "interest" in the IRA includes the amount of any outstanding rollover, transfer and recharacterization under Q&As-7 and -8 of § 1.408-8 of the Income Tax Regulations and the actuarial value of any other benefits provided under the IRA, such as guaranteed death benefits.

(d) For purposes of paragraph (b)(ii) above, required distributions are considered to commence on the date distributions are required to begin to the surviving spouse under such paragraph. However, if distributions start prior to the applicable date in the preceding sentence, on an irrevocable basis (except for acceleration) under an annuity contract meeting the requirements of § 1.401(a)(9)-6 of the Income Tax Regulations, then required distributions are considered to commence on the annuity starting date.

(e) If the sole designated beneficiary is the individual's surviving spouse, the spouse may elect to treat the IRA as his or her own IRA. This election will be deemed to have been made if such surviving spouse makes a contribution to the IRA or fails to take required distributions as a beneficiary.

(f) The required minimum distributions payable to a designated beneficiary from this IRA may be withdrawn from another IRA the beneficiary holds from the same decedent in accordance with Q&A-9 of § 1.408-8 of the Income Tax Regulations. *Note*: This section will need to be updated to reflect the elimination of the stretch IRA by the SECURE Act.

5. Nonforfeitability provision. [I.R.C. § 408(b)(4)]

   The interest of the individual is nonforfeitable.

6. Nontransferability provision. [I.R.C. § 408(b)(1)]

   This contract is nontransferable by the individual.

7. Provision governing the application of premium refunds. [I.R.C. § 408(b)(2)]

   Any refund of premiums (other than those attributable to excess contributions) will be applied, before the close of the calendar year following the year of the refund, toward the payment of future premiums or the purchase of additional benefits.

   (This provision is required for annuities that provide for participation in dividends.)

8. Provision for interruption of premium payments. [I.R.C. § 408(b)(2); Prop. Treas. Reg. § 1.408-3(f)]

   If the premium payments are interrupted, the contract will be reinstated at any date prior to maturity upon payment of a premium to the insurance company, and the minimum premium amount for reinstatement shall be—(not to exceed $50), however, the insurance company may at its option either accept additional future payments or terminate the contract by payment in cash of the then present value of the paid up benefit if no premiums have been received for two full consecutive policy years and the paid up annuity benefit at maturity would be less than $20 per month.

9. Requirement that trustees or issuers furnish annual calendar-year reports. [I.R.C. §§ 408(i), 408A(d)(3)(D); Treas. Reg. §§ 1.408-5, 1.408-8]

   The issuer of a Roth individual retirement annuity shall furnish annual calendar year reports concerning the status of the annuity and such information concerning required minimum distributions as is prescribed by the Commissioner of Internal Revenue.

Caution. The IRS warns that the information and sample provisions included in the LRM may not be appropriate in all cases. Acceptability can depend on context.

Chapter 3

Contributions to Traditional and Roth IRAs

For 2021, the limit on regular contributions to an IRA is $6,000 or $7,000 for a person who is age 50 or older by the end of the year. Contributions are further limited by the amount of an individual's compensation (generally, wages or self-employment income) for the year. A married couple's contributions may not exceed their combined compensation.

Qualified rollover contributions (see chapter 6) do not count against the IRA contribution limit, nor do contributions made for an individual (including even salary deferrals) under a SEP (chapter 12), SIMPLE (chapter 13), or other employer retirement plan. Separate limits apply to those plans.

An individual may apportion the IRA contribution between traditional and Roth IRAs as long as the total contributions do not exceed the annual limit, and the eligibility requirements are met. Until recently, traditional IRA contributions could only be made by individuals who were younger than age 70½ at the end of the year. The age limit for traditional IRA contributions was repealed, however, by the Setting Every Community Up for Retirement Enhancement Act (SECURE Act), Div. O of the Further Consolidated Appropriations Act, 2020, Pub. L. No. 116-94 (Dec. 20, 2019). There is no age limit for Roth IRA contributions, but at higher income levels, the ability to contribute to a Roth IRA is phased out.

Traditional IRA contributions are generally deductible from gross income. But if an individual (or spouse) actively participates in an employer-sponsored retirement plan, the deduction is phased out as income increases. If a couple is married and only one spouse actively participates, the nonparticipant's deduction is also phased out, but at a higher income level than for the participant.

The owner of a traditional, SEP, or SIMPLE IRA may convert those assets to a Roth IRA. (Special rules apply to conversions from a SIMPLE IRA; see chapter 13.) Conversions do not count against the IRA owner's annual contribution limit, but they are taxable. If the IRA owner is deceased, the only beneficiary who may convert the inherited assets is the surviving spouse.

IRA contributions can be made until the due date of the tax return (without extensions) for the contribution year. Before the contribution deadline for any year, a regular contribution that was designated as one type (e.g., a Roth IRA contribution) may be recharacterized, with earnings, as another type (e.g., a traditional IRA contribution). Recharacterization is essentially a bookkeeping function and does not trigger a tax, although it may affect the deductibility of a contribution. Until recently, timely recharacterization was also available to "undo" a conversion from a non-Roth IRA to a Roth IRA (and negate the conversion tax) or to remedy a failed conversion from an IRA or qualified plan. (It was not clear whether successful conversions from a qualified plan could be recharacterized.) However, successful conversions made after 2017, whether from an IRA or a qualified plan, are permanent—they cannot be recharacterized.

Certain individuals may claim a credit for a percentage of contributions made to a traditional or Roth IRA, as well as for a percentage of salary reduction contributions made to a SEP or SIMPLE IRA. (The tax credit also applies to salary reduction contributions to qualified plans, tax-sheltered annuities, or eligible deferred compensation plans of state and local governments, which are not covered by this book.) Eligibility for the credit is restricted to individuals who are at least age 18 and have adjusted gross income (AGI) below certain limits, excluding students and individuals claimed as an exemption on someone else's return.

Overview

Q 3:1 Do traditional IRAs and Roth IRAs follow the same rules concerning eligibility and contributions?

No. Although many of the contribution rules for the traditional IRA also apply to the Roth IRA, the overall rules are different.

Q 3:2 What contribution rules are the same for traditional IRAs and Roth IRAs?

1. *Contribution amount.* An individual's combined annual contributions to traditional and Roth IRAs are subject to a single contribution limit (see Q 3:4). If both are made for the same year, the traditional IRA contributions count first against the contribution limit (even if they are made later in time). [Treas. Reg. § 1.408A-3, Q&A-3(c)]
2. *Contribution deadline.* Traditional and Roth IRA contributions are both due by the IRA owner's tax filing due date, not including extensions, for the contribution year. However, because of the pandemic, the deadline for 2020 was extended to July 15, 2020, and for 2021, by Notice 2021-21, to May 17, 2021. [I.R.C. § 219(f)(3)]
3. *Spousal IRA rules.* Similar rules regarding the ability to make contributions on behalf of lesser-compensated spouses apply to traditional and Roth IRAs (see Qs 3:12–3:17). [I.R.C. § 219(c)]

4. *No age limit.* Roth IRA contributions were never subject to an age limit, and the age 70½ limit on traditional IRA contributions is repealed for contribution years after 2019. (See Qs 3:45, 3:46.) [I.R.C. §§ 219(d)(1), 408(o)]

Q 3:3 What contribution rules are different?

1. *Tax deductibility.* Roth IRA contributions are never deductible. Traditional IRA contributions are generally deductible, but the deduction is phased out at higher levels of modified adjusted gross income (MAGI) if the individual (or spouse) actively participates in certain retirement plans (see Q 3:47). [I.R.C. § 219]
2. *Income limits.* Eligibility for a Roth IRA contribution is phased out at higher income levels (see Q 3:71). There is no similar restriction for traditional IRAs. [I.R.C. § 408A(c)(3)]
3. *Rollover contributions.* The same rules govern rollovers from one traditional IRA to another and rollovers from one Roth IRA to another. But different rules apply if the source is not the same kind of IRA as the target (e.g., a traditional IRA is rolled over to a Roth IRA) or the source is an employer retirement plan. (See chapter 6.)

Contribution Limit

Q 3:4 How much can be contributed each year to an IRA?

The annual limit for regular contributions to the owner's (*participant's*) traditional and Roth IRAs is the *lesser* of an inflation-adjusted dollar figure ($6,000, for both 2020 and 2021), or 100 percent of the individual's *compensation* (see Q 3:22) includable in gross income. For an individual who will be age 50 or older by the end of the year, the dollar figure is increased by $1,000 (the *catch-up* amount). [I.R.C. §§ 219(b)(1), 219(b)(5), 219(e), 408A(c)(2); Notice 2019-59, 2019-47 I.R.B. 1091; Notice 2020-79, 2020-46 I.R.B. 1014]

Rollovers and trustee-to-trustee transfers into an IRA do not count against the limit. [I.R.C. § 219(f)(6)(B)]

Example. Alan, age 47, is single and lives in a religious community that compensates him $5,000 per year. His contributions to an IRA for any year may not exceed $5,000.

(For rules that allow spouses to share compensation for purposes of the contribution limit, see Qs 3:12–3:17.)

Q 3:5 How does the catch-up contribution work?

To be eligible for the catch-up amount, the IRA owner must be age 50 or older by the end of the calendar year for which the contribution is designated—not the deadline for making the contribution, which is July 15 of the following year (see Q 3:39). The individual must also have enough compensation to cover the catch-up contribution. The $1,000 catch-up amount is never adjusted for inflation. [I.R.C. § 219(b)(1), 219(b)(5)]

Example 1. Mel and his wife, Dorothy, have birthdays several days apart. Mel turns 50 on December 31, 2019, and Dorothy will do so on January 4, 2020. For 2019, Mel may contribute up to $7,000 to his IRA, but Dorothy's IRA contribution is limited to $6,000. She may already be age 50 when she makes the contribution, because the deadline is not until April 15, 2020 (see Q 3:36). Nonetheless, for 2019, Dorothy is not eligible for a catch-up contribution.

Example 2. At age 52, Barbara is eligible for a catch-up contribution for 2020. Her compensation that year is only $6,500, so she cannot use the full catch-up amount. Barbara's IRA contribution for 2020 may not exceed $6,500.

Q 3:6 May an individual contribute to both a traditional IRA and a Roth IRA for the same tax year?

Yes. The combined regular contributions to traditional and Roth IRAs are subject to a single overall limit. (But for the income limits that may limit Roth IRA contributions, see Q 3:71.)

Q 3:7 Do SEP and SIMPLE contributions count against the regular IRA contribution limit?

No. Contributions made on behalf of an individual under an employer's SEP or SIMPLE plan do not reduce the amount he or she may contribute to a traditional or Roth IRA. This is true even if elective salary deferrals are made under the plan, or if the individual is self-employed. [Treas. Reg. § 1.408A-3, Q&A-3(c)(2)]

Participation in a SEP or SIMPLE plan, however, may limit the deductibility of an individual's (and spouse's) traditional IRA contributions. (See Q 3:60.)

Q 3:8 Can an individual contribute less than the full amount one year, and make it up later with a larger contribution?

No. The IRA contribution limit is applied annually and may not be increased even if a contribution was forgone in an earlier year. A contribution in excess of the limit in any year may, however, be *corrected* by contributing less than would otherwise have been permitted in the later year (subject to penalty). Even in that case, no more than the maximum contribution may be claimed for the subsequent year.

Example. For 2018, Andrea could contribute $1,000 (her compensation amount) to her traditional IRA. Instead, she contributed $1,400, causing an excess contribution of $400. Andrea must correct the excess contribution, and since she did not do so by the date her 2018 tax return was due a 6 percent ($24) excise tax is payable for that year (see Q 3:132). The penalty will also be imposed each subsequent year until the excess contribution is corrected.

Andrea's IRA contribution limit for 2019 is $1,500 (that year's compensation). She may correct the outstanding excess contribution of $400 by treating it as a 2019 contribution and depositing only an additional $1,100 to the IRA. In that case, no excise tax will be payable for 2019.

The allowable deductions for these contributions are $1,000 for 2018 (the excess contribution is not deductible), and $1,500 for 2019 (the amount applied to 2019 is deductible then).

Excess contributions and the excise tax are discussed in Qs 3:130–3:137. [*See also* IRS Pub. 590-A, *Contributions to Individual Retirement Arrangements (IRAs)* 2020, in Appendix A.]

Q 3:9 Does the contribution limit apply to rollover contributions and asset transfers between IRAs, or from a qualified plan to an IRA?

The annual contribution limit does not apply to any transfer that is a *qualified rollover* (see chapter 6). If a transfer does not meet that standard, it is treated as a taxable distribution from the source (the IRA or qualified plan) and a regular contribution to the receiving IRA—and in that case the annual limit does apply to the contribution. [I.R.C. § 402(c)]

A qualified rollover is generally made from another IRA or a qualified plan. A rollover made to a Roth IRA is a taxable conversion (see Q 3:83) unless the source is another Roth IRA or a DRAC (designated Roth account within a qualified plan). Qualified rollovers may also come from these other sources (see Qs 6:31, 6:96–6:99):

1. Qualified reservist distributions.
2. Military gratuities and payments received under the Servicemembers Group Life Insurance (SGLI) Program.
3. Repayment of a disaster distribution (see Qs 7:27, 7:39).
4. Payments received in settlement of the *Exxon Valdez* litigation.
5. Settlement payments received by some employees of airlines that filed for bankruptcy after September 11, 2001 and before 2007, or on November 29, 2011. (A 2015 technical amendment extended the rollover period for some of these payments. See Qs 6:121–6:126.)
6. Qualified birth and adoption distributions.
7. Coronavirus-related distributions.

Q 3:10 Can Roth and traditional IRA contributions both be made to the same IRA if there is separate accounting?

No. A Roth IRA cannot be maintained in the same trust, custodial account, or annuity as a traditional IRA. [Ann. 97-122, 1997-50 I.R.B. 63]

Q 3:11 Can property (e.g., stock) be contributed to a traditional or Roth IRA?

No. All regular IRA contributions must be made in cash. However, securities and other property may be transferred to an IRA in a qualified rollover (see chapter 6). [I.R.C. § 219(e)(1)]

> **Example 1.** Corey personally owns 100 shares of appreciated XYZ stock that he wants to transfer directly to an IRA. That is not permitted, but if he sells the stock, he may contribute the cash proceeds to the IRA (subject to the contribution limit).

> **Example 2.** Rita holds appreciated securities in her Roth IRA and wants to transfer them to a new Roth IRA. The securities may be transferred to the new Roth IRA in a qualified rollover.

Limit for Spousal IRA Contributions

Q 3:12 What is a spousal IRA contribution?

A *spousal IRA contribution* is a contribution to a traditional or Roth IRA that one spouse makes on behalf of the other spouse. The rule allows a spouse without sufficient compensation to establish an IRA and receive an IRA contribution. The IRA of the lesser-compensated spouse is called a *Kay Bailey Hutchison spousal IRA* (or a spousal IRA). [I.R.C. § 219(c)(1)]

Q 3:13 What are the rules for spousal contributions to a traditional or Roth IRA?

Couples who take advantage of the spousal IRA rules are subject to the following rules:

1. The spouses must be legally married.
2. They must file a joint federal income tax return.
3. The receiving spouse must have less compensation (or none) than the spouse making the contribution. (See Qs 3:18–3:26 for the definition of compensation.)
4. For contribution years before 2020, one spouse could not contribute to the other's traditional IRA if the receiving spouse was age 70½ or older (see Qs 3:45–3:46). The contributing spouse's age was irrelevant.

5. The contribution limit is separately determined for each spouse. Neither spouse may be credited with a contribution that exceeds his or her limit (taking into account his or her catch-up contribution).

[I.R.C. § 219(c)(2); Treas. Reg. § 1.408A-3, Q&A-4]

Example 1. Jason and Ellen, both age 40, are married and file a joint federal income tax return. Jason works as a swimming coach and earns $30,000 in 2020. Ellen does not work outside the home and has no compensation. Jason may contribute $6,000 to his own Roth IRA and $6,000 to a Roth IRA for Ellen.

Example 2. Felix, age 55, is married to Gloria, age 49. They file a joint federal income tax return for 2020. Felix's compensation is $35,000, and Gloria's is $3,000. Felix may contribute $7,000 to his own IRA. Gloria's IRA (to which Felix may contribute) may not receive more than $6,000.

Example 3. In 2019, Valerie was age 72 and retired, and her wife, Gina, was still working and earned $100,000. Gina could contribute $7,000 to Valerie's Roth IRA ($100,000 is below the applicable MAGI limit; see Qs 3:70, 3:78), but nothing to Valerie's traditional IRA, because the age limit still applied.

Q 3:14 Can a same-sex married couple use the spousal IRA rules?

Yes. The spousal IRA rules apply if the union of two individuals, regardless of gender, is recognized as a *marriage* for federal tax purposes. Same-sex marriage is legal now throughout the United States. [Obergefell v. Hodges, 135 S. Ct. 2584 (2015)] The following should be noted:

- A domestic union of two individuals is recognized as a marriage for federal tax purposes if it is so recognized by the state, possession, or territory of the United States where it was performed (regardless of current domicile).
- The term *marriage* does not include any registered domestic partnership, civil union, or other formal relationship not denominated as marriage under the law of the state where the relationship was entered into.
- A marriage conducted in another country is recognized for federal tax purposes if *at least one* state, possession, or territory of the United States recognizes it (regardless of domicile).

[Treas. Reg. § 301.7701-18]

Q 3:15 Is a spousal IRA different from a regular IRA?

No. The only difference is that one spouse's earned income may be used to fund the other's spousal IRA. The spouse who contributes to the other's IRA does not enjoy special control over it. The trustee or custodian that receives the contribution treats a spousal IRA no differently than any regular contributory IRA.

Q 3:16 Can married spouses establish a joint IRA?

No. Each spouse must establish a separate IRA. Joint accounts are not allowed.

Q 3:17 May a spouse receive a spousal IRA contribution one year and make his or own contribution for the next?

Yes. An individual may have enough compensation to self-fund an IRA one year, but too little the next. The same IRA can receive both an individual's self-funded contributions and contributions made for him or her by the spouse. It is not necessary to establish a separate IRA just for spousal contributions.

Compensation Defined

Included Amounts

Q 3:18 What does compensation include for IRA purposes?

Compensation includes amounts received as wages, salaries, tips, professional fees, commissions, and bonuses, and other amounts received for personal services. In general, compensation refers to monies received in exchange for personal services, as opposed to investment or pension income. The rules that apply to determine compensation are entirely separate from the rules for determining MAGI. [I.R.C. §§ 219, 4408(o), 408A-3; Treas. Reg. § 1.408A-3, Q&A-4; IRS Pub. 590-A, *Contributions to Individual Retirement Arrangements (IRAs)* 2020 (see Appendix A)]

(For amounts excluded from compensation, see Qs 3:27–3:32.)

Q 3:19 Does compensation include self-employment income?

Yes, if a taxpayer's personal services are a material income-producing factor. In that case, whether the business is operated as a sole proprietorship or a partnership, the net earnings from a trade or business are included in compensation for IRA purposes. To determine net earnings, self-employment income is reduced by contributions made on the taxpayer's behalf to any retirement plan other than the IRA, and by the deduction allowed for half of the taxpayer's self-employment taxes. Earnings from self-employment may be included even if no self-employment tax was payable because of religious beliefs. [IRS Pub. 590-A, *Contributions to Individual Retirement Arrangements (IRAs)* 2020 (see Appendix A)]

Q 3:20 May an individual who has a net loss from self-employment contribute to an IRA?

The fact that an individual has a net loss from self-employment does not affect the ability to contribute to an IRA, if the individual has wages reportable on Form W-2, Wage and Tax Statements. [Rev. Rul. 79-286, 1979-2 C.B. 121]

> **Example.** In 2019, John, age 40, was self-employed and had a $10,000 net loss from his plumbing business. He also worked part-time as a clerk in a hardware store and earned W-2 wages of $9,500. John has compensation and is eligible to make a traditional IRA contribution, a Roth IRA contribution, or both.

Q 3:21 If an individual is employed by his/her spouse, do wages received from the spouse count as compensation for IRA purposes?

Yes, if the employment is bona fide.

Q 3:22 Does compensation include combat pay earned by members of the armed forces that is excluded from federal income tax?

Yes. Code Section 219(f)(7) expressly treats tax-free combat pay as compensation for IRA purposes. Thus, members of the U.S. Armed Forces who have no taxable income for a year are allowed to contribute their combat pay to an IRA (most likely a Roth IRA, because the combat pay is tax-free).

Q 3:23 Does compensation include differential wages paid by an employer while the employee is on active military duty?

Yes. *Differential pay* is a supplement some employers pay to an employee during a period of active duty, longer than 30 days, in the U.S. uniformed services. To the extent the payment represents some or all of the wages that would have been paid if the individual were performing services for the employer, it is included in compensation. [I.R.C. § 3401(h)(2)]

> **Note.** Unlike combat pay (see Q 3:30), differential pay is taxable and subject to withholding. [I.R.C. §§ 219(f)(1), 3401(h)]

Q 3:24 Do foster care payments count as compensation for IRA purposes?

Yes, if they are includable in gross income. [I.R.C. § 219(b)(1)] But, not all foster care payments are included in gross income. (For treatment of excluded foster care payments, see Q 3:25.)

Q 3:25 Can foster care payments excluded from income be used for an IRA contribution?

The SECURE Act amended Code Section 408(o) to allow *difficulty of care payments*, which are excludable from gross income, to be used for making *nondeductible* contributions to an IRA. [SECURE Act § 116(a)] The amendment is effective for IRA contributions made after December 20, 2019.

Qualified foster care payments and difficulty of care payments. There are two kinds of qualified foster care payments. The first kind is a payment made to a foster care provider for the general care of a qualified foster individual in the provider's home. [I.R.C. § 131(b)] The second is a difficulty of care payment, which is a separate payment authorized by the state to compensate for additional services the state requires be provided in the home because of a qualified foster individual's physical, mental, or emotional disability. [I.R.C. § 131(c)] A qualified foster individual is any individual living in a foster family home who was placed there by the state (or a political subdivision), or by a licensed or certified foster care placement agency. [I.R.C. § 131(b)(2)]

Difficulty of care payments must be designated as such when paid. [I.R.C. § 131(c)(1)(B)] They are excluded from the recipient's gross income, *except* to the extent they are made, with respect to any time period, for more than 10 qualified foster individuals younger than age 19, or more than five who are age 19 or older. (The second criterion for exclusion also applies to other qualified foster care payments.) [I.R.C. § 131(a), 131(c)(2), 131(b)(4)]

Special rule for IRA contributions. The SECURE Act amends Code Section 408 to add a special rule for individuals who receive difficulty of care payments. If an individual's compensation includible in gross income is less than the IRA contribution limit for the year, and he or she receives a difficulty of care payment that is excluded from gross income, the payment can be used for a *nondeductible* contribution to the IRA, as long as that does not cause the annual contribution limit to be exceeded. [I.R.C. §§ 408(o)(5), 408(o)(2), 408A(c)(2)]

Example. James provides foster care in his home for two children who were placed there under the state's foster care program, and he receives qualified foster care payments for their general care. The state determined that one of the children has mental and emotional disabilities that require extra care in the home. To compensate James for providing it, the state also pays him $1,500 designated as a difficulty of care payment. All of the foster care payments James receives are excluded from gross income. From a separate activity, James earns $2,000 of includible compensation, which he uses to make a deductible traditional IRA contribution. Under the special rule in Code Section 408(o)(5), James may also make a nondeductible contribution of $1,500 to a traditional IRA, or (better yet) a Roth IRA. The other foster care payments he receives cannot be used for an IRA contribution.

Q 3:26 How does the SECURE Act change the treatment of fellowship and stipend payments for purposes of the IRA contribution rules?

Before the SECURE Act, fellowship and stipend payments received by graduate and postdoctoral students were not treated as compensation and could not be used as the basis for an IRA or other retirement plan contribution. The SECURE Act amended Code Section 219(f), which now states that the "term 'compensation' shall include any amount which is included in the individual's gross income and paid to the individual to aid the individual in the pursuit of graduate or postdoctoral study." The provision is effective for taxable years starting after 2019. [SECURE Act § 106]

Excluded Amounts

Q 3:27 What amounts are excluded from compensation for IRA purposes?

Rental, interest, and dividend income, as well as foreign earned income and housing cost amounts that are excluded from U.S. income under Code Section 911, are excluded from compensation for purposes of IRA contributions. Other exclusions include pension or annuity income, deferred compensation, and income from a partnership for which an individual does not provide services that are a material income-producing factor. [I.R.C. § 219(f)(1); IRS Pub. 590-A, *Contributions to Individual Retirement Arrangements (IRAs)* 2020 (see Appendix A)]

Social Security benefits are not compensation. Nor are dividends and interest, unless the taxpayer is a securities dealer. [Kobell v. Commissioner, T.C. Memo. 2011-66 (2011)]

Q 3:28 Do alimony and separate maintenance payments count as compensation for IRA purposes?

Not anymore. The treatment of alimony and separate maintenance payments changed under the Tax Cuts and Jobs Act (TCJA). [Pub. L. No. 115-97, § 11051 (Dec. 22, 2017)]

Before the TCJA, alimony and separate maintenance payments were deductible by the paying spouse (including a former spouse) and were included in the payee spouse's taxable income. As taxable income, the payments were also expressly treated as compensation of the payee for IRA purposes. [I.R.C. §§ 71, 215, and 219(f)(1) (third sentence), all as in effect before amendment by the TCJA] Thus, a payee spouse with no other income could still contribute to an IRA.

The TCJA reversed this tax treatment. Payments covered by the new law are not deductible by the paying spouse and are neither taxable to the payee nor treated as payee compensation for IRA purposes. (TCJA Section 11051 repealed Code Sections 71 and 215, and struck the third sentence of Code section 219(f)(1).)

The effective date provision states that these amendments by the TCJA apply to a divorce or separation agreement (defined in former Code Section 71(b)(2)) executed after December 31, 2018. [TCJA § 11051(c)(1)] The provision also states that the TCJA amendments can be made to apply to an earlier divorce or separation agreement; that would require the parties to execute a modification after 2018. [TCJA § 11051(c)(2)] However, it is not at all clear that a private modification by the parties can change the incidence of taxation and cause payments to be treated as compensation for IRA purposes.

Q 3:29 Are disability payments considered compensation for IRA purposes?

No. Disability payments are considered annuity payments, rather than compensation—even when they are subject to ordinary federal income tax and FICA (Social Security) tax.

Q 3:30 Does compensation for IRA purposes include deferred compensation?

No. In general, payments not made within two and one-half months after the close of a taxable year during which significant services were performed are considered deferred compensation. [*See* I.R.C. § 404(b)(2); Priv. Ltr. Rul. 8519051 (Feb. 13, 1985).]

Code Section 219(f)(1) specifically excludes pension, annuity, and deferred compensation payments from compensation that may be considered when determining an individual's eligibility to make contributions to an IRA.

Q 3:31 Do severance payments count as compensation?

Whether severance payments may support an IRA contribution depends on when the payments are made. Severance payments that are not completed within two and one-half months after the close of the taxable year during which significant services were performed will likely be considered deferred compensation, in which case they could not serve as the basis for IRA contributions.

Q 3:32 What is the safe harbor method of determining compensation for IRA contribution purposes?

As a matter of administrative convenience, the IRS considers an IRA contribution to be supported by sufficient compensation if the contribution does not exceed:

- the amount properly shown in box 1 of an individual's Form W-2 (wages, tips, and other compensation), and
- reduced by the amount (if any) shown in box 11 of that form (nonqualified plan distributions). [Rev. Proc. 91-18, 1991-1 C.B. 522]

Contributions Versus Other Payments

Q 3:33 Do the regular contribution limits apply to payments deposited to an IRA to restore losses?

It depends. Restorative payments, which are made to replace IRA losses resulting from breach of fiduciary duty, fraud, or federal or state securities violations, are not treated as regular contributions and may be deposited into the IRA without regard for the normal contribution limits. By contrast, payments that make up for losses due to market fluctuations or poor investment returns are treated as contributions, not restorative payments, and the usual contribution limits apply. [*See* Priv. Ltr. Rul. 200852034 (Dec. 26, 2008).]

If a payment exceeds the loss due to the breach of fiduciary duty, fraud, or violation of federal or state securities law, the excess is treated as a contribution. Thus, if an IRA owner claims the trustee made unauthorized withdrawals and the claim is settled with an IRA deposit from the trustee, the part of the payment attributable to a reasonable rate of interest on the withdrawals is a contribution. The amount treated as a restorative payment cannot exceed the amount of unauthorized withdrawals. [Priv. Ltr. Rul. 200921039 (May 22, 2009); *see* Rev. Rul. 2002-45, 2002-2 C.B. 116.]

Q 3:34 Is a payment of traditional or Roth IRA account fees using outside funds treated as a contribution?

The answer depends on the type of fee charged and the source of funds used for payment. Annual maintenance fees paid to an IRA trustee or custodian using money outside the IRA are not treated as IRA contributions. But if such fees are paid from funds in the IRA and the participant reimburses the account for the payment, the reimbursement is treated as a regular IRA contribution.

Brokerage commissions charged on a transactional basis (i.e., with respect to purchases or sales of securities held in an IRA) are considered expenses of the account, so if non-IRA funds are used to pay the commissions, the payments are treated as IRA contributions. By contrast, management fees calculated as a percentage of an IRA's total asset value are (like annual maintenance fees) not deemed to be IRA contributions when paid from non-IRA sources. [*See* Rev. Rul. 86-142, 1986-2 C.B. 60; Priv. Ltr. Rul. 200507021 (Feb. 18, 2005).]

Any fee payment deemed to be a contribution counts toward the IRA owner's contribution limit for the year, which the trustee must report on Form 5498 and the IRA owner may be required to report on Form 8606 (see Qs 8:146 (box 1), 8:166). Any deemed contribution that causes the contribution limit to be exceeded for the year is subject to the 6 percent penalty for excess contributions (see Q 3:132). [*E.g.*, Priv. Ltr. Rul. 200507021 (Feb. 18, 2005)]

Q 3:35 How are wrap fees treated?

Some financial institutions offer IRA accounts in which all the services are covered by a single "wrap" fee. The wrap fee may pay for a package of services including investment advice, performance monitoring and review, trade execution, money management, and custodial services.

In two private letter rulings, the IRS concluded that if the wrap fee is calculated as a percentage of the assets under management and bears no relation to the number of transactions executed (and such number is unlimited), then payment of the wrap fee using non-IRA funds is *not* deemed to be a contribution to the IRA. [Priv. Ltr. Ruls. 201104061 (Jan. 28, 2011), 200507021 (Feb. 18, 2005)]

Contribution Deadline

Q 3:36 What is the deadline for making IRA contributions?

Contributions to traditional and Roth IRAs must be made during the tax year to which they relate, or in the following year before the due date for filing the individual's income tax return (not including extensions). For most taxpayers, that deadline is April 15 (or the following Monday, if April 15 falls on a Saturday, Sunday, or holiday) of the year following the tax year of the contribution. However, because of the pandemic, the deadline for making contributions to both traditional and Roth IRA plans for 2019 was extended to July 15, 2020.

An IRA contribution designated for 2020 must be made no later than Thursday, Monday, May 17, 2021.

Q 3:37 When an IRA contribution is made between January 1 and April 15, for which year is it made?

The individual must indicate to the IRA trustee (or custodian) whether a contribution made between January 1 and April 15 applies to the previous year, to the current year, or in stated portions to each. The trustee then reports the contribution accordingly to the IRS. [I.R.C. § 408A(d)(7); Treas. Reg. § 1.408A-3, Q&A-2] If a contribution during this period is not designated as for the prior year, the trustee can assume, and report to the IRS, that it is made for the current year. [IRS Pub. 590-A, *Contributions to Individual Retirement Arrangements (IRAs)* 2020 (see Appendix A)]

Note. The full current and prior year contributions may both be made during this period between January 1 and the filing deadline.

A timely contribution that the taxpayer elects to treat as made for the previous year is deemed to have been made on the last day of the tax year to which it relates. [I.R.C. § 219(c)(1)(F)(3)]

Q 3:38 Is an IRA contribution received or deposited after the tax filing due date timely made?

Yes, if the payment was made in time to satisfy the timely mailing/timely filing rule. If the IRA contribution is sent via U.S. mail, the financial institution is deemed to receive it on the postmark date marked on the envelope (regular mail), or the registration date (registered mail), or the date marked on the sender's receipt (certified mail). The mailing must be correctly addressed with proper postage. [Treas. Reg. § 301.7502-1(c)(1)(iii)(B); Priv. Ltr. Rul. 8536085 (1985)]

Presumably, the IRS's timeliness rules for electronic payments and private delivery services also apply (see Qs 8:35–8:40).

In a private letter ruling request, a financial company serving as an IRA and Coverdell ESA trustee asked the IRS to rule on the timeliness of contributions not processed until after the April 15th deadline. Customers were required to submit a letter of authorization (or its verbal equivalent) indicating the amount of cash contribution, the nonretirement account from which funds were to be transferred, and the tax year of the contribution. The IRS ruled that if a written or verbal authorization is timely made (i.e., the written request is postmarked, or the verbal request transmitted to a company representative, not later than the April 15 contribution deadline), the customer would be deemed to have made a contribution to the IRA (or ESA) on the last day of the preceding taxable year—provided the funds are actually transferred as soon as administratively practicable. [Priv. Ltr. Rul. 201437023 (Sept. 12, 2014)]

Practice Pointer. An individual should follow up with the addressee if the normal confirmation of an IRA contribution is not provided within a reasonable time.

Q 3:39 Is the contribution deadline delayed for individuals serving in (or in support of) the U.S. Armed Forces?

Individuals who serve (or have served) in the U.S. Armed Forces, or in support of such forces, in designated combat or hazardous duty areas have more time to make IRA contributions. The additional time allowed is the period of such service, plus the period of continuous hospitalization (for qualifying injuries), plus 180 days. [I.R.C. § 7508]

(For details about the qualifying geographic areas and reporting instructions for trustees and custodians, *see* IRS Pub. 3, *Armed Forces' Tax Guide* 2020.)

Q 3:40 Can a self-prepared return filed early report an IRA contribution not yet made?

A tax return prepared by the taxpayer and filed early may include a deduction for a traditional IRA contribution not yet made—if the individual expects the contribution will be made before the contribution deadline. [Rev. Rul. 84-18, 1984-1 C.B. 88]

If such a return is filed, but the contribution is made too late, the individual has two choices:

1. File an amended return reversing the deduction (if applicable) and pay the tax; or
2. File an amended return indicating that the contribution is being made in the current year on a return that is expected to be filed in the following year.

Penalties may be imposed, depending on the promptness of the corrective action. [Rev. Rul. 84-18, 1984-1 C.B. 88]

Q 3:41 If someone else prepares the taxpayer's return, can the preparer sign and file the return before the claimed IRA contribution is made?

Possibly. A tax return preparer must exercise due diligence in preparing and filing a client's return and may not take positions that lack a reasonable basis.

Generally, a preparer may rely, in good faith and without verification, on information the client provides—unless the preparer has reason to know the information is incomplete, incorrect, or inconsistent with known or asserted facts. [*See* Treasury Department Circular 230 (June 2014), §§ 10.22, 10.33, 10.34(d).]

This probably means a tax return preparer could sign, and file before the deadline, a return reporting (and deducting) a taxpayer's IRA contribution, if the taxpayer asserts the contribution will be timely made and the preparer has no reason (e.g., based on past experience) to believe the client is unlikely to follow through.

Direct Deposit of Tax Refunds to IRAs

Q 3:42 Can a federal income tax refund be directly deposited into an IRA?

Yes. A taxpayer may direct the deposit of a tax refund into one, two, or three separate accounts at banks or other financial institutions. Traditional, Roth, and SEP IRAs (but not SIMPLE IRAs) and Coverdell ESAs may be designated to receive refunds, along with a broad range of other accounts such as checking and savings accounts, health savings accounts (HSAs), and Archer Medical Savings Accounts (MSAs).

A taxpayer who desires a direct deposit of the tax refund into a single account (IRA or other) would provide the routing and account numbers directly on his or her Form 1040. To direct the deposit into two or three accounts, the taxpayer must file Form 8888, Direct Deposit of Refund to More Than One Account. On lines 1 to 3 of Form 8888, the taxpayer lists the different accounts and indicates how the refund should be allocated among them. A receiving account must be in the taxpayer's name (or the spouse's name, in the case of a joint return). Taxpayers may not request partial payment of a refund by check and the remainder by direct deposit to another account.

Some banks and financial institutions do not permit deposit of joint refunds to individual accounts. If a deposit is rejected for this reason, the IRS will mail the refund check to the taxpayer.

The direct deposit and split-refund options do not change the IRA contribution deadlines or limits in any way. Taxpayers need to verify that the deposit is timely made and instruct the IRA trustee or custodian regarding the year to which it should be assigned. Absent such instruction, the trustee or custodian will apply the contribution to the current year.

Q 3:43 How are contributions affected if the deposited tax refund is adjusted due to math errors on the return?

If a refund is increased or decreased because math errors were made on the return, the contribution of the tax refund is also adjusted. Adjustments are made first to any deposits to the account on line 3, next to any deposits to the account on line 2, and finally to deposits to the account on line 1. If the taxpayer appeals a refund decrease and prevails, the IRS will deposit the resulting refund in the first account listed. [General Instructions for Form 8888, Direct Deposit of Refund to More Than One Account]

Example 1. Annette prepares her 2019 income tax return and determines she is due a refund of $500. She is still eligible to contribute $350 to her Roth IRA account, so she uses Form 8888 to instruct the IRS to deposit $350 of the refund to her Roth IRA (line 1), and the remaining $150 to her checking account (line 2). The IRS corrects a math error on the return and increases the refund to $600. The $100 increase is added to the deposit to the checking account on line 2.

Example 2. Cecil's 2020 return shows he is due a $300 refund. He files Form 8888 requesting the IRS to deposit $100 to his traditional IRA (line 1), $100 to a mutual fund account holding nonretirement assets (line 2), and $100 to his checking account (line 3). The IRS determines there is a math error and reduces the refund to $150. It deposits nothing to the checking account, $50 to the mutual fund account, and $100 to the IRA. If Cecil appeals the adjustment and his calculation is upheld, the resulting refund of $150 will be deposited to his IRA. If the larger deposit causes an excess contribution to be made, Cecil must withdraw the excess or amend his return.

Q 3:44 How are contributions affected if the refund is offset by other obligations of the taxpayer?

It depends on the reason for the offset. A refund that is offset because federal taxes are past due is applied in the same manner as a refund reduction attributable to math errors (see Q 3:43). Refunds are also subject to offset by the Treasury Department's Financial Management Service if certain other amounts are past due (e.g., outstanding state income tax, child support, spousal support, or certain federal nontax debts such as student loans). Those past due amounts are collected from the accounts listed on Form 8888 based on their bank routing numbers, first from the account on line 3, then the account on line 2, and finally the account on line 1. [General Instructions for Form 8888, Direct Deposit of Refund to More Than One Account]

Special Rules for Traditional IRA Contributions

Age Limit Repeal for Traditional IRAs

Q 3:45 What used to be the maximum age for contributing to a traditional IRA?

Previously, an individual who attained age 70½ or more by the end of a calendar could not contribute to a traditional IRA. This age limit did not apply to Roth IRAs, or to contributions made under a SEP or SIMPLE. [I.R.C. § 219(d)(1), as in effect before the Setting Every Community Up for Retirement

Enhancement Act of 2019 (SECURE Act), Div. O of the Further Consolidated Appropriations Act, 2020, Pub. L. No. 116-94 (Dec. 20, 2019)]

Q 3:46 What is the current rule?

The age limit for traditional IRA contributions was repealed by the SECURE Act. The repeal applies to contributions made for taxable years starting after 2019. [SECURE Act § 107, repealing I.R.C. § 219(d)(1)]

(For coordination of the age limit repeal with the exclusion of qualified charitable distributions from gross income, see Q 5:13.)

Deductible Contributions

Q 3:47 Are all traditional IRA contributions deductible?

No. Contributions up to the annual contribution limit (including the earned income restriction) are generally deductible in full. But the deduction may be limited if an individual, or the individual's spouse, *actively participates* (see Qs 3:51, 3:52) in an *employer-sponsored retirement plan* (see Q 3:50).

Q 3:48 If a traditional IRA deduction is limited in one year because of the active participation rule, can the disallowed amount be deducted in the next year?

No. A traditional IRA contribution is deductible only for the year of contribution. If the deduction is denied in whole or part under the active participation rule, it cannot be carried forward. [Dunn v. Commissioner, T.C. Memo. 2015-208 (2015)]

Active Participation Rules

Q 3:49 What individuals do *not* have to be concerned with the active participation rules?

The active participation rules do not apply to:

- Unmarried individuals who do not actively participate (see Qs 3:51, 3:52) in an employer-sponsored retirement plan (see Q 3:50), and
- Married individuals if *neither spouse* (see Q 3:60) actively participates in such a plan.

In all other cases, income limits (see Qs 3:64, 3:65) determine whether, and how much of, a traditional IRA contribution may be deducted. [I.R.C. § 219(g)]

Note. This restriction on the deductibility of traditional IRA contributions does not unconstitutionally discriminate against individuals (and their spouses) who actively participate in a retirement plan. [Shankar v. Commissioner, 143 T.C. No. 5 (2014)]

Q 3:50 What is an *employer-sponsored retirement plan*?

Employer-sponsored retirement plans include:

- Plans qualified under Code Section 401(a)
- SEPs and SARSEPSs (see chapter 12)
- SIMPLEs (see chapter 13)
- Annuity plans qualified under Code Section 403(a)
- Code Section 403(b) tax-sheltered annuity plans
- Plans established for governmental employees (not including Code Section 457 plans)
- Code Section 501(c)(18) plans funded only by employee contributions (this covers certain plans created before June 25, 1959).

[I.R.C. § 219(g)(5)]

Q 3:51 Who *actively participates* in an employer-sponsored retirement plan?

An individual is considered to be an active participant in an employer-sponsored retirement plan (see Q 3:50) if:

- An allocation is made for the individual under a defined contribution plan, or
- The individual is not excluded from participation under the terms of a defined benefit plan.

[Notice 87-16, 1987-1 C.B. 446; *clarified by* Notice 89-25, 1989-1 C.B. 662; *modified by* Notice 98-49, 1998-2 C.B. 365]

The rule is strict and can be unfair. In one case, an individual was held to be an active participant even though he did not know his employer had automatically enrolled him in a plan. It was unclear whether there had been an employer contribution, but if there had been, it would have been forfeited under the vesting rules when the individual was laid off from work. The court applied the active participation rule because the statute does not allow for exceptions, even though in this case the individual did not benefit from the employer plan and denial of the deduction did not advance a congressional purpose. [Corcoran v. Commissioner, T.C. Summary Op. 2012-119 (Dec. 10, 2012)]

Note. An individual who receives an allocation cannot "undo" active plan participation by attempting to include the employer's contribution in gross income. This strategy failed in a case where the employer's $193 contribution caused an individual's $5,000 IRA contribution to be nondeductible. [Gallant v. Commissioner, T.C. Summary Op. 2012-7 (Jan. 10, 2012)]

Example. Jane is self-employed and earns $1 million a year. She established a SEP plan because that allows her to contribute more for retirement than an IRA allows (see chapter 12). For any year that Jane actively participates in the SEP (i.e., receives an allocation under the plan), she may also contribute to a traditional IRA. However, the IRA contribution will not be deductible.

Q 3:52 What does *not* count as active participation in an employer-sponsored retirement plan?

The following situations do not count as active participation in an employer-sponsored retirement plan:

- Coverage under Social Security or a railroad retirement plan;
- Receipt of benefits or payments from an employer retirement plan after the individual is no longer employed [Notice 87-16, 1987-1 C.B. 446];
- Participation in a plan that benefits reservists in U.S. Armed Forces, if service does not exceed 90 days in a year [I.R.C. § 219(g)(6)(A)]; and
- Coverage for volunteer firefighters, if the benefits accrued at the start of the year will not provide more than $1,800 per year at retirement. [I.R.C. § 219(g)(6)(B)]

[IRS Pub. 590-A, *Contributions to Individual Retirement Arrangements (IRAs)* 2020 (see Appendix A)]

Q 3:53 Is active participation in an employer retirement plan indicated on an individual's tax forms?

Yes. Form W-2 provides a box labeled "Retirement Plan" that the employer must mark if the employee actively participates in an employer-sponsored retirement plan.

Q 3:54 If a defined *contribution* plan does not operate on the calendar year, how is the year of active participation determined for IRA purposes?

Defined contribution plans include 401(k) plans, profit-sharing plans, thrift saving plans, stock bonus plans, and money purchase plans. For such plans, active participation begins during the plan year in which a contribution or allocation is made to the employee's account. If the plan *requires* that an allocation be made (i.e., it is nondiscretionary) as of the end of each plan year, the employee is deemed, for purposes of an IRA, to be a participant for the calendar year within which the plan year ends. That is so even if the employment ends before the IRA tax year ends but the plan allocation is not made until the following year. The fact that the employer's contribution is delayed until the next tax year of the employee does not extend participation into that next year. [Notice 87-16, 1987-1 C.B. 446] IRS Pub. 590-A, *Contributions to Individual Retirement Arrangements (IRAs)* 2020, provides an example of a money purchase pension plan (see Appendix A).

A different rule applies if allocations are *discretionary* under a defined contribution plan. In that case, if no amounts have been allocated to the individual's account by the end of the plan year, he or she does not actively participate for IRA purposes in the calendar year within which the plan year ends. If the employer makes a contribution after the plan year ends, the individual is considered an active participant in the plan year when the contribution is made—and, for IRA purposes, in the calendar year within which that plan year ends. [IRS Pub. 590-A, *Contributions to Individual Retirement Arrangements (IRAs)* 2020 (see Appendix A)]

Example 1. On December 30, 2017, Olivia terminates employment with Woolf, Inc., the sponsor of a money purchase plan. The final allocation (nondiscretionary) for the 2017 plan year is made on May 31, 2018. Woolf remits its money purchase plan contribution for the year ending May 31, 2017 on September 17, 2019 (its tax return filing due date). Olivia's participation continues into the 2018 IRA tax year but does not extend into 2018.

Example 2. Meg's employer, Alpha, maintains a 401(k) profit-sharing plan with a plan year that runs from July 1 to June 30. For the plan year ending in 2017, Meg does not meet the length-of-service requirements, so she is not an active participant. She becomes eligible to participate on July 1, 2017 and elects as of that date to defer part of her salary into the plan. Then she terminates her employment on December 31, 2017 to attend graduate school, and she also takes a part-time job with Beta. Meg has enough compensation to contribute to a traditional IRA in both 2017 and 2018.

Because she did not actively participate in the Alpha plan during the *plan year* that ended in 2017, Meg may deduct her traditional IRA contribution for 2017 (even though salary deferrals occurred in the second half of that *calendar year*). But she cannot deduct a traditional IRA contribution for 2018—despite not being employed by Alpha during that calendar year—because she did actively participate in the plan during the plan year that ends in 2018.

Example 3. Emil was covered by a profit-sharing plan when he left his job at the end of 2017. The plan year runs from May 1 through April 30, and employer contributions are discretionary. Contributions that the employer does make are allocated on the last day of the plan year, contributed by the due date for filing the company's tax return, and made for each individual who performed services during the plan year.

As of April 30, 2018, no contributions had been allocated for the plan year just ended, and it was uncertain whether any would be made. However, in December 2018, the company decided it would indeed make contributions for the plan year that ended in April 2018. It made those contributions on February 15, 2019 (during the plan year that ends in 2019), so Emil is treated, for IRA purposes, as an active participant for 2019—but not for 2018.

Q 3:55 How is the year of participation in a defined *benefit* plan determined for IRA purposes?

Defined benefit plans, which include pension plans and annuity plans, work somewhat differently from defined contribution plans because employer contributions are not allocated to individual accounts. An employee who has met the eligibility requirements (usually, one year of service and attainment of age 21) is deemed to have participated for purposes of the IRA contribution deduction rules even though no benefit accruals have begun.

Example. On December 31, 2017, Marcus leaves his job with Sunshine Corp., the sponsor of a defined benefit plan (for which Marcus was eligible). The plan year ends on June 30. Although Marcus was not employed by Sunshine in 2018, for IRA purposes he is considered an active participant in 2018.

A defined benefit plan may condition the accrual of benefits for a particular year on the participant either having worked a minimum number of hours, or having earned a minimum amount of compensation, during the plan year. The two thresholds seem similar, but yield distinctly different results when determining whether a person failing to meet one of them is an active participant. If benefit accrual is conditioned on earning a minimum amount of compensation, an otherwise eligible individual who earns less than that amount in a particular plan year is not considered an active participant for that year. [Treas. Reg. § 1.219-2(b)(1)] On the other hand, if the benefit is conditioned on working a minimum number of hours, an individual who is otherwise eligible is considered to be an active participant even if he or she works too few hours to accrue a benefit. [*See* William Edward Colombell v. Commissioner, T.C. Summary Op. 2006-184 (Nov. 30, 2006).]

Q 3:56 Is an employee who refuses to make plan contributions still subject to the active participation rules?

If the plan is a contributory defined *benefit* plan, the active participation rules still apply. For such a plan, an employee's refusal to contribute does not eliminate active participation for IRA contribution deduction purposes. But for a defined *contribution* plan, benefit entitlement is not established until contributions are made to an individual's defined contribution plan account. [Notice 87-16, 1987-1 C.B. 446]

Thus, if an employee makes no elective deferrals into the employer's 401(k) plan, the employee may not be considered an active participant. The determination is based on whether the employee received any contributions to the plan. If the employer made a profit-sharing contribution on behalf of the employee, the employee is considered an active participant.

Note. Even if an employee shares only in a nominal amount of forfeitures made to a plan for the year, the employee is considered an active participant.

Q 3:57 Does it matter whether the employee is vested in accruals?

No. For IRA purposes, it does not matter whether the employee's benefits in the defined contribution or defined benefit plan are vested. The fact that termination of employment would result in the loss of benefits does not prevent an individual from being considered an active participant for purposes of the IRA contribution deduction rules. The same rule applies to participation in a plan for U.S. government employees. [Priv. Ltr. Rul. 8725094 (Mar. 30, 1987)]

Q 3:58 If an individual's benefits are nonvested and participation terminates before the end of the plan year, is he or she an active participant that year?

Yes. Participation in an eligible retirement plan during any part of the year is sufficient to raise the issue whether traditional IRA contributions may be deducted. In a case on this point, the employee contributions were withdrawn during the year. At the end of the year, there was nothing left to distribute, because employer contributions had been forfeited. The Tax Court held that participation during any part of the year counts for IRA purposes, even it is subsequently and retroactively eliminated. The result would have been the same if the forfeiture has occurred under a regular vesting schedule. [Wartes v. Commissioner, T.C. Memo. 1993-84 (1993)]

Under Code Section 219(g), the income-based restriction of deductions also applies to the spouse of an active participant. In *Wartes*, the spouse argued that, in view of the forfeiture from the qualified plan, there was no possibility of a double tax benefit. But the Tax Court held Code Section 219(g) does not allow such issues to be considered. [*See also* Baumann's v. Commissioner, T.C. Memo. 1995-313 (1995).]

Q 3:59 Do the active participation rules apply to a U.S. military retirement plan?

Yes. In *Morales-Caban v. Commissioner* [T.C. Memo. 1993-466 (1993)], the Tax Court held that a U.S. Air Force retirement plan was to be treated as an employer-sponsored retirement plan. Thus, a husband and wife participating in the plan were subject to IRA contribution deductibility limits. The taxpayers argued that they were not active participants in a retirement plan—the Air Force plan was a "gift" to be awarded after 20 years of service that was unlikely to be attained because of defense force downsizing. The Tax Court rejected this argument.

Q 3:60 How does active participation by one spouse affect the other spouse's ability to deduct traditional IRA contributions?

If only one spouse actively participates in an employer's retirement plan, the *nonparticipating* spouse's ability to deduct a traditional IRA contribution may also be limited. But the income level that triggers that restriction is higher for the nonparticipating spouse. (See Q 3:64.) [I.R.C. § 219(g)(7)]

Q 3:61 How are divorce, remarriage, and death taken into account when determining status under the active participation rule?

To be considered a spouse, a party must be married at the end of the IRA tax year. If there was more than one marriage during that year, the marriage in place at the end of the year is the one taken into account for purposes of the rule. If divorce occurs during the year without remarriage, the individual is deemed to be single for the entire year. If the spouse who is actually covered by the employer plan dies during the IRA tax year and the surviving spouse files a joint return with the deceased spouse (through the executor or administrator), the decedent's coverage before death will affect the survivor's IRA deduction in the same way it would have if the decedent had lived with the marriage intact until the end of the year. [I.R.C. § 6013; IRS Pub. 590-A, *Contributions to Individual Retirement Arrangements (IRAs)* 2020 (see Appendix A)]

Q 3:62 Can the nonparticipating spouse avoid the active participation rules by filing a separate income tax return?

Not usually. But if the spouses live apart from each other throughout the entire tax year, they are treated as single for purposes of the active participation rule. In that case, the nonparticipating spouse's deduction would not be restricted if separate returns are filed. [I.R.C. § 219(g)(4); IRS Pub. 590-A, *Contributions to Individual Retirement Arrangements (IRAs)* 2020 (see Appendix A)]

MAGI Limits on the Traditional IRA Deduction

Q 3:63 How is modified adjusted gross income figured to determine the deductibility of a traditional IRA contribution?

Modified adjusted gross income for this purpose is adjusted gross income (found on line 7 of the new Form 1040), with the following amounts added back:

1. The IRA deduction.
2. Student loan interest deduction (Form 1040, Schedule 1, line 33).
3. Excluded interest from U.S. savings bonds (Series EE and I) issued after 1989 (Form 8815, line 14).
4. Excluded income from employer-paid adoption expenses (Form 8839, line 29).
5. Excluded foreign earned income (Form 2555, line 42).
6. Foreign housing exclusion or deduction (Form 2555, line 36 or line 50).

[I.R.C. §§ 219(g)(3), 211, 135, 139, 911; IRS Pub. 590-A, *Contributions to Individual Retirement Arrangements (IRAs)* 2020 (in Appendix A)]

Q 3:64 What are the MAGI limits on eligibility to deduct a traditional IRA contribution?

Table 3-1 shows the 2020 and 2021 MAGI limits on the deduction for traditional IRA contributions. The limits are adjusted annually for inflation. [I.R.C. § 219(g); Notice 2019-59, 2019-47 I.R.B. 1091; Notice 2020-79, 2020-46 I.R.B. 1014]

The traditional IRA owner determines whether a contribution is deductible by locating his or her status in the first column of Table 3-1 and finding the appropriate MAGI range. If married individuals both contribute to traditional IRAs, the deduction for each must be evaluated separately, first by treating one as the IRA owner and the other as the spouse, and then reversing the process. Whenever a partial deduction is indicated, the reduced limit must be calculated (see Qs 3:65, 3:66).

Table 3-1. 2020 and 2021 MAGI Limits on the IRA Owner's Deduction for Traditional IRA Contributions

Category	*2020*	*2021*
A. *IRA owner IS active participant, and:*		
1. Owner is single or head of household		
• Full deduction	$65,000 or less	$66,000 or less
• Partial deduction	$65,001–$74,999	$66,001–$75,999
• No deduction	$75,000 or more	$76,000 or more
2. Owner is married filing jointly, or qualifying widow(er)		
• Full deduction	$104,000 or less	$105,000 or less
• Partial deduction	$104,001–$123,999	$105,001–$124,999
• No deduction	$124,000 or more	$125,000 or more
3. Owner is married filing separately, and lived with Spouse at any time during the year		
• Partial deduction	$9,999 or less	$9,999 or less
• No deduction	$10,000 or more	$10,000 or more
4. Owner is married filing separately, and lived apart from Spouse the entire year		
• Full deduction • Partial deduction • No deduction	Owner treated as single (category 1)	Owner treated as single (category 1)

Table 3-1. 2020 and 2021 MAGI Limits on the IRA Owner's Deduction for Traditional IRA Contributions (*cont'd*)

Category	*2020*	*2021*
B. *IRA owner is NOT active participant, and:*		
5. Owner is single, head of household, or qualifying widow(er)		
• Full deduction	Any amount	Any amount
6. Owner is married, and Spouse is not active participant (whether they file jointly or separately)		
• Full deduction	Any amount	Any amount
7. Owner is married filing jointly, and Spouse is active participant		
• Full deduction	$196,000 or less	$198,000 or less
• Partial deduction	$196,001–$205,999	$198,001–$207,999
• No deduction	$206,000 or more	$208,000 or more
8. Owner is married filing separately, Spouse is an active participant, and they lived together at any time during the year		
• Partial deduction	$9,999 or less	$9,999 or less
• No deduction	$10,000 or more	$10,000 or more
9. Owner is married filing separately, Spouse is an active participant, and they lived apart the entire year		
• Full deduction • Partial deduction • No deduction	Owner treated as single (category 5)	Owner treated as single (category 5)

[I.R.C. § 219(g)(3)(B)(i), 219(g)(3)(B)(iii), 219(g)(4), 219(g)(3)(B)(ii), 219(g)(7); Notice 2019-59, 2019-47 I.R.B. 1091; Notice 2020-79, 2020-46 I.R.B. 1014]

Q 3:65 What rules govern the phaseout of the traditional IRA deduction?

If MAGI falls *between* the full-deduction and no-deduction levels, the deduction limit (including the catch-up amount) is ratably reduced, then rounded up to the next $10. For example, if the 2020 MAGI of an individual younger than age 50 is 20 percent into the phaseout range, then 20 percent of the normal deduction is disallowed, and the maximum deductible contribution for 2020 is $4,800 (80 percent of $6,000). [I.R.C. § 219(g)(2)(A), 219(g)(2)(C)]

For MAGI at or above the high end of the phaseout range, no deduction is allowed. Otherwise, the minimum deductible amount is $200. For contributions to a spousal IRA (when only one spouse has compensation), the $200 minimum applies to the total deduction on the return. But if both spouses have compensation, the $200 minimum applies separately to each. [I.R.C. § 219(g)(2)(B); IRS Pub. 590-A, *Contributions to Individual Retirement Arrangements (IRAs)* 2020 (see Appendix A)]

If the reduction applies so that one spouse has over-deducted (on an earlier filed return) and the other has contributed less than the maximum deductible, no transfer of the deduction limit is permitted between the spouses. [IRS Pub. 590-A, *Contributions to Individual Retirement Arrangements (IRAs)* 2020 (see Appendix A)] (It would seem that with more careful planning—or replanning, if it is not too late—a different allocation of contributions could produce a higher total deductible amount.)

Q 3:66 How is the partial deduction calculated?

The method for calculating the partial deduction when MAGI is within the phaseout range (see Table 3-1 in Q 3:64) is shown below. The IRS provides a slightly different formula but arrives at the same number. [IRS Pub. 590-A, *Contributions to Individual Retirement Arrangements (IRAs)* 2020 (see Appendix A)] The nondeductible balance may still be contributed to a traditional IRA (if supported by adequate compensation) or a Roth IRA (unless the MAGI limit for a Roth IRA contribution is exceeded; see Qs 3:77–3:79).

1. Start with MAGI.
2. Subtract the amount in line 1 from (using 2021 figures):
   (a) $74,000 if single and an active participant (see Qs 3:51, 3:52);
   (b) $125,000 if the individual is married filing jointly (or a qualifying widower), and an active participant;
   (c) $10,000 if married filing separately and an active participant; or
   (d) $208,000 if the individual is married, filing jointly or living with spouse, and not an active participant but the spouse is.
3. Divide the result in line 2 by $10,000 ($20,000 if filing a joint return and the individual is an active participant).
4. Multiply the maximum contribution limit (before reduction by this adjustment but after reduction for any contributions to Roth IRAs) by the result in line 3.
5. The result, rounded up to the nearest $10, is the reduced contribution limit. If the reduced contribution limit is more than $0 but less than $200, the limit is $200.

Example. Janet and Bernard file a joint return and have combined MAGI of $108,000 for 2019. Each is age 55, earns more than $7,000 compensation, and contributes $7,000 to a traditional IRA. Janet is an active participant in her employer's retirement plan, so her deduction (category 2 in Table 3-1) is calculated as follows:

1. Combined MAGI = $108,000
2. $123,000 – $108,000 = $15,000
3. $15,000 ÷ $20,000 = 0.75
4. $7,000 (contribution limit) × 0.75 = $5,250.

Bernard is not an active participant (category 7 in Table 3-1), so his phase-out range is $193,000–203,000. Since the couple's MAGI is below the bottom of his range, Bernard's $7,000 traditional IRA contribution is fully deductible.

Q 3:67 How are Social Security benefits treated when determining MAGI?

Only 50 percent of an individual's Social Security benefits is included in determining MAGI. The taxability of Social Security benefits is then recalculated, taking into account the portion of the IRA contribution that is determined to be deductible. (The entire process is illustrated in Worksheets 1, 2, and 3 of Appendix B in IRS Pub. 590-A, *Contributions to Individual Retirement Arrangements (IRAs)* 2020 (see Appendix A).)

Q 3:68 How is the deduction claimed?

The deduction for traditional IRA contributions is claimed as an adjustment to income on Form 1040, Schedule 1, line 19. The total adjustments figured on Schedule 1 (line 22) are then taken into account to determine AGI (on Form 1040, line 11).

Q 3:69 May a deductible IRA contribution be designated as nondeductible?

Yes. The election to treat a deductible contribution as nondeductible is made by filing Form 8606, Nondeductible IRAs, and including the designated amount with any other nondeductible contributions made for that year.

Doing so should be considered if the individual is disqualified from making either a Roth IRA contribution or a deductible traditional IRA contribution. One possibility is to make the nondeductible traditional IRA contribution and shortly afterward convert it to a Roth IRA (see Q 3:83). Or, it may be wiser to put the money instead into a taxable investment. (See Q 1:14.)

In almost all instances, an individual will make a Roth IRA contribution instead of a nondeductible traditional IRA contribution if he or she is eligible.

Deductibility Under State Law

Q 3:70 How do states handle the deductible and nondeductible contribution amounts?

Most states follow the Internal Revenue Code rules for determining the deductible and nondeductible contribution amounts. There are some temporary and some permanent differences between the two taxing authorities. For example, some state legislative bodies are not in session when a change at the federal level occurs. As a result, the state generally conforms to the change in the following year and makes the conformity retroactive (see Q 15:2). A permanent difference, on the other hand, affects residents of Pennsylvania, New Jersey, and Massachusetts because these states do not permit residents to deduct IRA contributions for state income tax purposes. In addition, a taxpayer that moves from one state to another may or may not be able to transfer the basis in his or her traditional IRA from the former state of residency to the current state of residency (see Qs 15:11–15:14).

Special Rules for Roth IRA Contributions

Roth IRA Eligibility

Q 3:71 What eligibility rules apply to Roth IRAs?

To establish and make annual contributions to a Roth IRA, an individual must have income (*modified adjusted gross income*, or MAGI) below certain levels and must have compensation. [I.R.C. §§ 219(b), 408A(c)] Failure to meet either requirement could lessen or eliminate an individual's eligibility to make a Roth IRA contribution. Different eligibility rules exist for converting a traditional IRA to a Roth IRA (see Qs 3:83, 3:84).

Q 3:72 Can a married couple establish a joint Roth IRA?

No. The Roth IRA is an individual account. However, special spousal rules are available for married couples, making it easier for both spouses to establish a Roth IRA (see Qs 3:12, 3:13).

Q 3:73 What is MAGI for purposes of determining Roth IRA eligibility?

MAGI determination for Roth IRA purposes is similar to that for traditional IRAs. The difference is that MAGI for Roth purposes requires an additional adjustment to remove conversion income (which is part of AGI). [I.R.C. § 408A(c)(3)(B)(i)]

Starting with AGI (line 11 on the new Form 1040), income from any Roth IRA conversions (see Qs 3:102, 3:103) is subtracted, and the following items are added back:

1. Traditional IRA deduction.
2. Student loan interest deduction (Form 1040, Schedule 1, line 20).
3. Excluded interest from U.S. savings bonds issued after 1989 (Form 8815, line 14).
4. Excluded income from employer-paid adoption expenses (Form 8839, line 29).
5. Excluded foreign earned income (Form 2555, line 42).
6. Foreign housing exclusion or deduction (Form 2555, line 36 or line 50).

[I.R.C. §§ 408A(c)(3), 219(g)(3), 211, 135, 139, 911; Treas. Reg. § 1.408A-3, Q&A-5; IRS Pub. 590-A, *Contributions to Individual Retirement Arrangements (IRAs)* 2020 (see Appendix A)]

Note. Required minimum distributions are included in MAGI for purposes of determining whether a Roth IRA contribution is allowed. [Treas. Reg. § 1.408A-3, Q&A-6]

Q 3:74 Does active participation in another retirement plan affect eligibility to make contributions to a Roth IRA?

No. An individual may actively participate in an employer-sponsored retirement plan without affecting his or her eligibility for a Roth IRA contribution. Anyone with compensation whose MAGI is within the income limits may contribute to a Roth IRA (subject to the annual contribution limit).

Example. Yvonne works for Zane Advertising Company and participates in its 401(k) plan. Whether Yvonne is eligible to make a Roth IRA contribution depends on her MAGI. Her active participation in Zane's 401(k) plan is not relevant.

Q 3:75 Do the MAGI limits prevent high-income individuals from moving assets into Roth IRAs?

No. An individual who cannot make a regular Roth IRA contribution because his or her MAGI is too high may still convert assets into a Roth IRA from a traditional, SEP, or SIMPLE IRA, or from a qualified plan. Large amounts may be transferred this way. [I.R.C. § 408A(c)(3)(B)]

An individual whose MAGI is too high to allow regular Roth IRA contributions may make nondeductible contributions to a traditional IRA and then, in the same or a later year, convert the assets to a Roth IRA. Tax would only be payable on the converted earnings unless the individual had previously made *deductible* contributions to a traditional IRA. (See Qs 3:84, 3:102.)

Roth IRAs may also receive qualified rollovers from DRACs (designated Roth accounts within qualified plans). Rollovers from DRACs are not conversions, nor are they taxable (see chapter 6).

Q 3:76 How does contributing to a traditional IRA affect eligibility to contribute to a Roth IRA?

The annual contribution limit applies to all IRA contributions in the aggregate (see Q 3:4). Since traditional IRA contributions count first against the annual limit, they reduce the amount of any Roth IRA contribution that is allowed for the same year. [IRS Pub. 590-A, *Contributions to Individual Retirement Arrangements (IRAs)* 2020 (see Appendix A)]

MAGI Limits on Roth IRA Contributions

Q 3:77 What are the Roth IRA MAGI limits?

Table 3-2 shows the 2020 and 2021 MAGI limits on eligibility to contribute to a Roth IRA. The limits are adjusted annually for inflation. [I.R.C. § 408A(c)(3); Notice 2019-59, 2019-47 I.R.B. 1091; Notice 2020-79, 2020-46 I.R.B. 1014]

To determine an individual's eligibility to make a Roth IRA contribution, locate his or her status in the first column of Table 3-2 and find the appropriate MAGI range. Whenever a partial deduction is indicated, the reduced limit must be calculated (see Q 3:78).

Table 3-2. 2020 and 2021 MAGI Limits on Roth IRA Contributions

Category	*2020*	*2021*
1. IRA owner is single or head of household		
• Full contribution	$124,000 or less	$125,000 or less
• Partial contribution	$124,001–$138,999	$125,001–$139,999
• No contribution	$139,000 or more	$140,000 or more
2. IRA owner is married filing jointly, or qualifying widow(er)		
• Full contribution	$196,000 or less	$198,000 or less
• Partial contribution	$196,001–$205,999	$198,001–$207,999
• No contribution	$206,000 or more	$208,000 or more
3. IRA owner is married filing separately, and lived with Spouse at any time during the year		
• Full contribution	$0	$0
• Partial contribution	$1–$9,999	$1–$9,999
• No contribution	$10,000 or more	$10,000 or more

Table 3-2. 2020 and 2021 MAGI Limits on Roth IRA Contributions (*cont'd*)

Category	*2020*	*2021*
4. IRA owner is married filing separately, and lived apart from Spouse the entire year		
• Full contribution • Partial contribution • No contribution	Owner treated as single (category 1)	Owner treated as single (category 1)

Example 1. Peter, age 40, is single (category 1 in Table 3-2) and has MAGI of $60,000 for 2020. He earned $50,000 as a professional artist and another $10,000 from investments. Because Peter has at least $6,000 compensation and his MAGI is under $124,000, he may contribute $6,000 to a Roth IRA for 2020 (assuming he does not contribute to a traditional IRA).

Example 2. Quentin is married to Amy, and they file a joint federal income tax return for 2020 (category 2). Quentin's compensation is $80,000, and the couple's MAGI (including Amy's income) is $208,000. Their combined MAGI is too high to allow either Amy or Quentin to contribute to a Roth IRA.

Example 3. Robert earns $100,000 as a pilot and files a joint federal income tax return with his wife, Sarah. She earns $80,000 at her job as a computer programmer. Their combined MAGI for 2020 is $195,000 (including investment income). Robert and Sarah are each eligible for a partial Roth IRA contribution (see Q 3:78 for the calculation procedure).

Example 4. Tim and Ursula are married, but filed separate returns for 2019. They only lived together for two months that year (category 3 in Table 3-2). Tim's MAGI for 2019 was $6,000. He was eligible for a partial Roth IRA contribution for 2019, calculated using the method in Q 3:78. Ursula's 2019 MAGI was $140,000, which was too high to allow any Roth IRA contribution.

Q 3:78 How is the partial contribution limit calculated?

If MAGI is within the range that only allows a partial Roth IRA contribution, the adjusted contribution limit is determined using the following proration procedure:

1. Determine MAGI for Roth IRA purposes (see Q 3:73).
2. Subtract MAGI from the threshold MAGI figure for "no contribution" (from the appropriate category in Table 3-2, Q 3:77).
3. Divide the result by (a) $15,000 for category 1 or (b) $10,000 for categories 2–4.
4. Round the result to three decimal places and multiply by the regular contribution limit for the year (including the catch-up contribution if the individual is age 50 or older at the end of the year).

The resulting figure, rounded up to the nearest $10 (or to at least $200), is the maximum permitted Roth IRA contribution.

> **Example.** In 2020, Jill is single, 45 years of age, and covered by a retirement plan at work. She wants to make the largest possible Roth IRA contribution. Jill's taxable compensation is $118,000, and her MAGI (as computed for both traditional and Roth IRA purposes) is $127,000.
>
> For category 1 in Table 3-2, the Roth IRA contribution is fully phased out when MAGI is $139,000 or more. Jill's largest possible Roth IRA contribution is ($139,000 – $127,000) ÷ $15,000 × $6,000, or $4,800 (after rounding up to the nearest $10). That is the amount she contributes to her Roth IRA for 2020.
>
> Jill could also contribute $1,200 ($6,000 – $4,800) to a traditional IRA, but only as a nondeductible contribution because she actively participates in her employer's retirement plan and her MAGI is too high to allow a deduction (see Table 3-1 in Q 3:64).

Q 3:79 What are the de minimis and rounding rules for determining the reduced Roth IRA contribution limit?

Two rules apply to the calculation procedure in Q 3:78:

1. *$200 threshold.* An individual may contribute $200 to a Roth IRA if the result of the partial contribution calculation is more than $0 but less than $200.
2. *Rounding up to the nearest $10.* The calculation result is rounded up to the next highest $10 increment to determine the allowable contribution.

[I.R.C. §§ 408A(c)(3)(A), 219(g)(2); Treas. Reg. § 1.408A-3, Q&A-3]

Roth IRA Annual Contributions

Q 3:80 Is there a minimum contribution amount for the Roth IRA?

Not under the Code. The law allows an individual to make as small a contribution to a Roth IRA as he or she wishes, but the IRA trustee or custodian may require a minimum contribution to its accounts. That could be significant for a young person who wants to contribute just a small amount to a Roth IRA in order to start the five-year holding period as soon as possible (see chapter 5).

> **Note.** The $200 threshold (see Q 3:79) establishes that *at least* $200 may be contributed if the contribution is not fully phased out. But the individual may contribute less (if allowed by the financial institution). [*See* I.R.C. § 219(g)(2)(B).]

Q 3:81 May a person older than age 70½ contribute to a Roth IRA?

Yes. Roth IRA contributions were never subject to an age limit. [I.R.C. § 408A(c)(4)]

Example. In 2018, Cecilia was 74 years old and earned $4,000 working part-time as a storyteller at the local library. Under the law in effect at the time (see Q 3:45), she could contribute to a Roth IRA, but not a traditional IRA.

Q 3:82 May a Roth IRA contribution be combined with a traditional IRA contribution?

No. The contribution *limit* may be allocated between traditional and Roth IRA contributions, but the contributions must be made to separate IRAs. A Roth IRA may not be maintained in the same trust, custodial account, or annuity, as a traditional IRA. Separate accounting within a single trust, custodial account, or annuity is not permitted. [Ann. 97-122, 1997-50 I.R.B. 63]

Conversions

Q 3:83 What is a Roth IRA conversion?

A *Roth IRA conversion* is a qualifying movement of assets (for methods, see Q 3:96) from a pre-tax IRA (traditional, SEP, or SIMPLE IRA), or from a qualified plan (other than a DRAC), into a Roth IRA. There is a price to be paid: conversions are taxable (see Q 3:102). Roth IRA conversions must satisfy the requirements that apply to rollovers from IRAs and qualified plans (see chapter 6), and the annual IRA contribution limits do not apply to amounts moved in a conversion. [I.R.C. § 408A(c)(6)(B)]

A DRAC (designated Roth account within a qualified plan) is an after-tax account. Consequently, a qualified rollover of assets from a DRAC to a Roth IRA is not a conversion.

Note. Taxable conversions may also occur within qualified plans—e.g., when assets are moved from a pre-tax 401(k) account to a Roth 401(k) account.

A conversion is different from a *recharacterization* (see Qs 3:110, 3:113).

Q 3:84 Who may convert a non-Roth IRA or pre-tax qualified plan interest to a Roth IRA?

These individuals are eligible for a Roth IRA conversion (for details, see chapter 6):

- The owner of a traditional IRA or SEP IRA may convert it to a Roth IRA at any time.
- The owner of a SIMPLE IRA may convert assets from it to a Roth IRA after participating in the SIMPLE plan for at least two years (see Q 3:90).

- The surviving spouse of a deceased traditional, SEP, or SIMPLE IRA owner may convert the assets to a Roth IRA if he or she is the IRA beneficiary. (No other IRA beneficiary may do so; see Q 3:86.) After the conversion, the surviving spouse is treated as owner of the Roth IRA.
- Participants in certain pre-tax qualified plans may convert plan distributions directly to a Roth IRA (see Q 3:94). Eligible plans are qualified employer plans, tax-sheltered annuities (Section 403(b) plans), and deferred compensation plans of a state or local government (Section 457 plans).
- Any beneficiary (not limited to the surviving spouse) of a deceased eligible qualified plan participant may convert plan assets to a Roth IRA. A nonspouse beneficiary may only convert plan assets to an "inherited" Roth IRA.

[I.R.C. §§ 408A(d)(3)(C), 402(c)(11), 402(f)(2)(A); Treas. Reg. § 1.408A-4, Q&A-4; Notice 2009-68, 2009-39 I.R.B. 423; Notice 2008-30, Q&A-7, 2008-12 I.R.B. 638]

Note. Conversions before 2010 were subject to eligibility requirements based on an individual's income and filing status. [I.R.C. § 408A(c)(3)(B)]

Q 3:85 What is the result if any conversion requirement is not satisfied?

There is no Roth IRA conversion unless all the applicable requirements are fulfilled. A failed conversion is just treated as a regular Roth IRA contribution. If that causes the individual's annual contribution limit to be exceeded, an excess contribution results. A failed conversion may be corrected by timely recharacterizing the contribution (see Q 3:111). [Treas. Reg. §§ 1.408A-8, Q&A-1(b)(4); 1.408A-4, Q&A-3; 1.408A-5, Q&A-9(a)(1)]

Note. The prohibition against recharacterizing a *successful* conversion made after 2017 (see Q 3:124) does not prevent the recharacterization of a *failed* conversion.

The conversion methods are described in Q 3:96.

Q 3:86 May a traditional, SEP, or SIMPLE IRA be converted to a Roth IRA after the owner dies if the beneficiary is *not* the surviving spouse?

No. The surviving spouse is the only beneficiary who may convert an IRA after the IRA owner dies. No other IRA beneficiary may convert an IRA to a Roth IRA after the owner dies (see Q 10:10).

Note. The nonspouse beneficiary of an eligible qualified plan interest has a clear advantage in this respect (see Q 3:84).

Q 3:87 May an IRA be converted after required minimum distributions have begun?

Yes. The owner of an IRA may convert it to a Roth IRA even after required minimum distributions (RMDs) have begun. Roth IRA owners are not required to take RMDs, so a conversion would allow all of the IRA funds to accumulate for the owner's beneficiaries. [IRS Pub. 590-A, *Contributions to Individual Retirement Arrangements (IRAs)* 2020 (see Appendix A)]

Practice Pointer. Individuals who wish to use IRAs for estate planning purposes should consider the potential benefits of converting for beneficiaries (since the beneficiaries will be unable to convert). The disadvantage of converting is that a conversion accelerates taxation of the traditional IRA.

Q 3:88 May a required minimum distribution be converted?

No. RMD amounts may not be rolled over into an IRA and therefore cannot be converted to a Roth IRA. [I.R.C. § 408(d)(3)(E); Treas. Reg. § 1.408A-4, Q&A-6]

If a minimum distribution is required, the first dollars distributed during the year are treated as RMD amounts until the full RMD has been distributed. Thus, in a year for which a minimum distribution is required (including the calendar year in which the individual attains age 72), an individual may not convert any amount of an IRA or qualified plan payment until the RMD is distributed. An RMD that is contributed to a Roth IRA is treated as a regular contribution—not a conversion—and the normal contribution rules apply. The same is true for RMDs from qualified plans. [Treas. Reg. § 1.408A-4, Q&A-6; Notice 2009-75, 2009-39 I.R.B. 436]

Example. Lydia, age 75, receives annual RMDs from her traditional IRA. She wants to convert her entire traditional IRA (worth $25,000 at the end of 2019) to a Roth IRA in 2020, but first she must take her 2020 RMD ($1,700). Only then may she convert the balance. *Note*: Under the CARES Act, RMDs for IRAs were waived in 2020.

Q 3:89 May SEP contributions be converted to a Roth IRA?

Employer contributions must be deposited into the participant's SEP IRA, which cannot be a Roth IRA. Once the deposit is made, the participant may convert the assets to a Roth IRA. No waiting period is required, so a conversion may occur immediately after the amount is deposited into the SEP IRA. [Treas. Reg. § 1.408A-4, Q&A-4(a)]

Example 1. HighTech, Inc. provides a SEP retirement plan for its employees. HighTech contributed $35,000 to Sam's SEP (i.e., traditional) IRA over the years, and with earnings the balance has now grown to $50,000. Sam may convert the entire $50,000, or a smaller amount, to a Roth IRA.

Example 2. Sam (from Example 1) converts the entire SEP IRA balance of $50,000. Shortly after the conversion, HighTech announces it will make its annual SEP contributions and Sam's allotment will be $3,000. Sam asks HighTech to contribute the amount directly to his Roth IRA. HighTech must refuse that request, because only traditional IRAs can receive SEP contributions. However, immediately after HighTech deposits the $3,000, Sam may convert it to his Roth IRA.

Q 3:90 May SIMPLE IRA assets be converted to a Roth IRA?

Yes, but only after the individual has completed two years of participation in the employer's SIMPLE plan (for measurement of that period, see Qs 6:64, 13:63). After that, SIMPLE IRA assets may be converted to a Roth IRA. However, new SIMPLE contributions must always be made to a SIMPLE IRA. [Treas. Reg. § 1.408A-4, Q&A-4(b)]

Q 3:91 If nondeductible contributions were made to a SEP or SIMPLE IRA, may they be converted to a Roth IRA?

Yes. Nondeductible contributions in an IRA can be converted to a Roth IRA. A conversion of nondeductible contributions is particularly desirable because contributions that were made on an after-tax basis are converted tax free. Earnings are always taxed on conversion, however. [I.R.C. § 408A(d)(3)(A)(i), 408A(d)(3)(C); Treas. Reg. § 1.408A-4, Q&A-7]

Q 3:92 May an individual selectively convert only the after-tax assets held in a traditional, SEP, or SIMPLE IRA?

Unfortunately, no. Pre-tax assets held in an IRA may not be selectively converted. Distributions from a traditional, SEP, or SIMPLE IRA that contains nondeductible contributions are apportioned by a ratio. Part of each distribution is a return of nondeductible contributions, and the rest is a return of taxable contributions and earnings. (See Q 3:103.) The IRS requires taxpayers to file Form 8606 to determine the taxable portion of a distribution from an IRA that contains nondeductible contributions. [Notice 87-16, Q&As D-2, D-3, D-4, 1987-1 C.B. 446] (Form 8606 is discussed in chapter 8.)

Q 3:93 If all nondeductible contributions are kept in a separate IRA, may just that IRA (along with earnings) be converted?

No. All IRAs are treated as one IRA for the purpose of taxing distributions. An individual who keeps nondeductible contributions in one IRA and deductible contributions in another is no more able to convert just the nondeductible IRA than someone who mixes together deductible and nondeductible contributions in the same IRA. [Treas. Reg. § 1.408A-6, Q&A-9]

Q 3:94 What qualified plan assets may be converted to a Roth IRA?

Any qualified plan assets that are eligible to be transferred in a qualified rollover contribution may be converted to a Roth IRA. The assets must be in an eligible qualified plan; i.e., a qualified employer plan (under Code Section 401(a)), a tax-sheltered annuity (Section 403(b) plan), or a government deferred compensation plan (Section 457 plan). The restrictions that apply to rollover contributions from qualified plans are discussed in detail in chapter 6.

If both pre-tax and after-tax assets are held in a qualified plan account, pro rata amounts of each are included in any eligible rollover distribution. But those distribution components may be isolated, so that (for example) the after-tax part of the distribution is directly transferred to a Roth IRA, and the pre-tax part is moved to a traditional IRA or distributed outright. (See Qs 6:84–6:92.)

> **Note.** DRAC assets may be rolled over to a Roth IRA, but the rollover is not a conversion and no tax applies (see Q 3:83). [I.R.C. § 402A(d)(1)] (DRACs are discussed in chapter 6.)

Q 3:95 May a conversion be "undone" for any reason?

Until 2018, it was possible to use recharacterization (see Qs 3:110, 3:124) to unwind a Roth IRA conversion. But conversions made after 2017 cannot be unwound. [TCJA § 13611]

Conversion Methods

Q 3:96 What is the conversion procedure?

There are three Roth IRA conversion methods, but for some conversions the choice is limited (see Table 3-3). IRA owners, qualified plan participants, and their surviving spouses may use any conversion method. Nonspouse beneficiaries of deceased qualified plan participants must use the direct rollover method (also called a trustee-to-trustee transfer) to convert qualified plan assets, and the receiving account must be denominated as an "inherited" Roth IRA (see Q 3:84). Nonspouse beneficiaries of a deceased IRA owner are not eligible to convert an inherited IRA. [Treas. Reg. § 1.408A-4, Q&A-1; Notice 2008-30, Q&A-7, 2008-12 I.R.B. 638] The conversion methods are:

1. *60-Day rollover.* An amount is distributed from a traditional IRA or qualified plan and contributed (rolled over) to a Roth IRA within 60 days after the distribution. The rollover period may be extended in some cases (see chapter 6).
2. *Direct rollover (trustee-to-trustee transfer).* The trustee of the traditional IRA or qualified plan directly transfers the assets to the trustee of the Roth IRA.
3. *Internal transfer.* An amount in a traditional IRA is transferred to a Roth IRA maintained by the same trustee, or the account is simply redesignated as a Roth IRA.

Table 3-3. Available Conversion Methods

Individual	*60-Day Rollover*	*Direct Rollover*	*Internal Transfer*
IRA owner	Yes	Yes	Yes
Spouse of deceased IRA owner	Yes	Yes	Yes
Nonspouse beneficiary of deceased IRA owner		No conversion	
Qualified plan participant	Yes	Yes	Yes
Spouse of deceased qualified plan participant	Yes	Yes	Yes
Nonspouse beneficiary of deceased qualified plan participant	No	Yes (to inherited Roth IRA)	No

Q 3:97 Must every conversion be completed within 60 days?

Conversions that use the 60-day rollover method obviously must be rolled over to a Roth IRA within 60 days after the distribution from the non-Roth IRA or qualified plan. A Roth IRA contribution that follows the distribution by more than 60 days may qualify for an extension, but the IRS authority to grant extensions is limited (see chapter 6). [I.R.C. § 408A(e)]

If a trustee-to-trustee transfer is used for a conversion, the individual never actually receives a distribution and it is less clear that the 60-day rule applies. An argument can be made that the 60-day rule applies only when the taxpayer actually receives a distribution of the assets.

Practice Pointer. A cautious approach would be to complete all conversions within 60 days, regardless of the form of the transaction.

Q 3:98 Must the entire IRA be converted?

No. An individual may choose to convert only part of a traditional, SEP, or SIMPLE IRA. If an IRA is partly converted, pro rata amounts of the deductible contributions, nondeductible contributions, and earnings in the IRA are included in the conversion (see Q 3:92). [Treas. Reg. § 1.408A-4, Q&A-1]

Q 3:99 May an IRA be converted gradually over a number of years?

Yes. It may be sensible to spread out a conversion for financial planning and tax reasons. Some individuals are certain that conversion will yield long-run benefits, but cannot afford the entire tax at once. Others may conservatively convert just part of an IRA because they are not sure conversion is the right choice. However it is done, each conversion is treated as a separate tax transaction. Through proper financial planning, a comprehensive tax strategy can be devised. [I.R.C. § 408A(d)(3)]

Example. Constance wants to convert her $100,000 traditional IRA to a Roth IRA, but is concerned about the tax impact of such a large conversion. After discussing the situation with her tax advisor, Constance decides to convert $10,000 in 2020 and then convert $10,000 per year for the next 9 years. She must also convert the earnings in the traditional IRA over the same period.

Q 3:100 Is a conversion treated as a rollover or as a transfer?

Regardless of how the transaction is actually completed, a conversion is treated as a rollover of traditional IRA assets into a Roth IRA for reporting and taxation purposes (see Q 3:102). [Treas. Reg. § 1.408A-4, Q&A-1] The transfer is treated as a distribution from the traditional IRA and then a rollover contribution into the Roth IRA—even if there is never an actual distribution because the conversion uses a trustee-to-trustee transfer or internal transfer.

Example. Max receives a brochure from Mutual Funds, Inc., advertising the benefits of converting to a Roth IRA. Max has a traditional IRA with Big Bank. He completes the conversion form included in the marketing material and returns it to Mutual Funds. Mutual Funds forwards the form to Big Bank. The form instructs Big Bank to send Max's IRA assets directly to Mutual Funds. Big Bank forwards the assets and treats the conversion as a taxable distribution. Mutual Funds treats the contribution as a rollover conversion contribution.

Q 3:101 May an individual convert a traditional IRA to a Roth IRA if he or she has already completed a rollover in the last 12 months?

Yes. Conversions are considered rollovers, but the rule that ordinarily limits IRA rollovers to one every 12 months (see chapter 6) does not apply to them. [I.R.C. § 408A(e)]

Example 1. Ken rolls over his traditional IRA from ABC Bank to XYZ Credit Union on March 10, 2019. One month later he decides to convert it to a Roth IRA. The one rollover per 12 months rule does not prevent Ken from converting the IRA.

Example 2. Sally's traditional IRA has $100,000 invested in a mutual fund. She wants to convert it to a Roth IRA and understands that the conversion will be taxable. Since she cannot predict how the market will fluctuate over the next 12 months, she decides to convert one-twelfth of the IRA assets during each month of the year, so the conversion tax will roughly be based on the yearly average of the stock price. She can do that because there is no limit on the number of conversions that can be made in one year.

Taxation of Conversions

Q 3:102 How is a conversion taxed?

As noted above, a Roth IRA conversion is treated as a taxable distribution from the IRA (traditional, SEP, or SIMPLE) or qualified plan, coupled with a qualified rollover of the distribution to a Roth IRA. The converted amount is included in gross income for the distribution year, except to the extent that basis amounts (i.e., non-deducted contributions prorated to the distribution) are included in the distribution. [Treas. Reg. § 1.408A-4, Q&A-7]

Example. In 2019, Frank converts his only IRA, a traditional IRA with a $20,000 balance, to a Roth IRA. Frank had made a total of $8,000 in nondeductible contributions to the traditional IRA, so his taxable amount on conversion is $12,000 ($20,000 less his nondeductible contributions of $8,000).

Q 3:103 How is basis allocated in a conversion?

Basis (i.e., non-deducted contributions) is always prorated to the distribution. However, if the distribution comes from a traditional IRA, all of the individual's traditional IRAs are treated as one IRA and the conversion distribution is treated as coming from that. [I.R.C. § 408(d)(2); Notice 87-16, 1987-1 C.B. 446]

Example 1. Collette has two traditional IRAs. One is worth $20,000 and holds $5,000 of nondeductible contributions. The other is also worth $20,000 but all contributions were deductible. If Collette converts $10,000 from either IRA to a Roth IRA, only $1,250 of the nondeductible contributions will be allocated to the conversion ($5,000 divided by $40,000, multiplied by $10,000). It does not matter which IRA the conversion amount is drawn from; Collette will recognize $8,750 of taxable income.

Example 2. Samuel has a 401(k) account worth $20,000 that holds $5,000 of nondeductible contributions. He also has a traditional IRA worth $20,000 that has only received deductible contributions. Samuel converts half of the 401(k) account to a Roth IRA and rolls over the rest to a new traditional IRA. Half of the nondeductible contributions ($2,500) are allocated to the $10,000 conversion, and Samuel recognizes $7,500 of taxable income. His traditional IRAs are irrelevant to the determination.

Q 3:104 Why would anyone want to convert and accelerate the tax?

An individual may prefer to pay lower taxes now to avoid higher taxes in the future. The Roth IRA and the traditional IRA both allow tax-deferred *accumulation* of earnings, but only the Roth IRA allows the earnings to be *distributed* tax-free (in qualified distributions). Earnings from a traditional IRA are always taxed when distributed—and capital gains rates do not apply to IRA distributions because they are considered compensation. (See chapters 4 and 5.) Conversion may also be favorable if an individual believes his or her tax rate will be higher in the future than now.

Example. Betty has $10,000 in a traditional IRA that she rolled over from a qualified plan from her previous job. If she converts the traditional IRA to a Roth IRA in 2019, she will have to include $10,000 in taxable income that year. She will, however, have $10,000 in her Roth IRA (assuming she uses outside funds to pay the conversion tax). If the return is 8 percent over the next 25 years, Betty will accumulate $77,727. That amount would be completely tax free in the Roth IRA, but only tax deferred in the traditional IRA. Betty may decide it is worth paying some taxes today to avoid taxes in the future.

Q 3:105 What tax rate applies to the conversion amount?

The taxable portion of the conversion is ordinary income and is taxed at the IRA owner's marginal income tax rate. [I.R.C. §§ 408(d)(1), 72; IRS Pub. 590-A, *Contributions to Individual Retirement Arrangements (IRAs)* 2020 (see Appendix A)]

Example. Clark is single and has taxable income of $30,000 for 2019. His income places him in the 12 percent tax bracket. If Clark converts his $65,000 deductible IRA to a Roth IRA in 2019, he will include an additional $65,000 of ordinary income that year. The resulting taxable income of $95,000 will push him into the 24 percent marginal tax bracket. [For 2020 tax brackets, *see* Rev. Proc. 2019-44, 2019-47 I.R.B. 1093. For 2021 tax brackets, *see* Rev. Proc. 2020-45, 2020-46 I.R.B. 1016.]

Q 3:106 How is the tax determined if an annuity contract is converted from a non-Roth IRA to a Roth IRA, or if a non-Roth IRA annuity is converted to a Roth IRA annuity?

Generally, an amount equal to the fair market value of the annuity contract on the date of conversion is deemed to be distributed from the non-Roth IRA and then transferred to the Roth IRA by means of a rollover contribution. If the conversion is accomplished by surrendering the annuity for its cash value and reinvesting the entire cash proceeds in a Roth IRA, and all contractual rights are extinguished in the surrender, then only the cash proceeds are deemed to be distributed. [Temp. Treas. Reg. § 1.408A-4T, Q&A-14]

Guidance for determining the fair market value of an annuity contract on the date of its conversion is provided in Treasury Regulations Section 1.408A-4, Q&A-14(c). Generally:

1. The actual premiums paid for the annuity may be used to establish the contract's fair market value if the conversion occurs soon after the contract is purchased.
2. If the same company that issued the annuity sells a comparable contract, the cost of the latter may be used to measure fair market value.
3. If there are no comparable contracts, fair market value may be established through an approximation based on the interpolated terminal reserve at the date of conversion, plus the proportionate part of the gross

premium last paid before the date of the conversion that covers the period extending beyond that date.

4. For an annuity contract that has not yet been annuitized, a modified version of the accumulation methodology provided in Treasury Regulations Section 1.401(a)(9)-6, Q&A-12 may be used.
5. No valuation method can be used which results, because of the unusual nature of a particular contract, in an approximation that is not reasonably close to the contract's full value.

[Treas. Reg. § 1.408A-4, Q&A-14]

Q 3:107 Are conversions an exception to the 10 percent additional tax on distributions made before age 59½?

Yes. An individual who converts assets to a Roth IRA in a qualified rollover from a traditional, SEP, or SIMPLE IRA, or from a qualified plan, is not subject to the 10 percent additional tax under Code Section 72(t) that is normally associated with distributions before age 59½. [I.R.C. §§ 408A(d)(3), 72(t), 408A(d)(3)(B); Joint Comm. Staff, Technical Explanation of the Pension Protection Act of 2006 (JCX-38-06) (Aug. 3, 2006); Notice 2009-68, 2009-39 I.R.B. 423]

Note. The 10 percent additional tax on early distributions, and the many exceptions that apply to it, are discussed in Qs 5:24–5:66.

Q 3:108 If substantially equal periodic payments are being made, does the 10 percent additional tax exception for such payments continue to apply after a conversion?

Yes. An IRA owner who is taking substantially equal periodic payments from an IRA (an exception to the 10 percent additional tax; see Note below) may convert it to a Roth IRA and then continue the series of payments from the Roth IRA. If the pattern of payments does not change, the payments will remain exempt from the 10 percent additional tax on early distributions because a conversion does not modify the substantially equal periodic payment stream. [Treas. Reg. § 1.408A-4, Q&A-12] The same is true if substantially equal periodic payments are being made from a qualified plan, and the plan interest is converted. [Notice 2009-75, 2009-39 I.R.B. 436]

If the original series of substantially equal periodic payments does not continue to be distributed in the same manner from the Roth IRA after the conversion, the series of payments will have been modified. If that modification occurs within five years of the first series payment or before the individual becomes disabled or attains age 59½, the individual will be subject to the recapture tax of Code Section 72(t)(4)(A) (see Q 5:34). [Treas. Reg. § 1.408A-4, Q&A-12]

Distributions from the Roth IRA that are part of the original series of substantially equal periodic payments will be nonqualified distributions from the Roth IRA (which may be taxable) until they meet the requirements for being a qualified distribution (see Qs 5:68, 5:69). The 10 percent early distribution penalty will not apply to the extent that the nonqualified distributions are part of a series of substantially equal periodic payments.

Note. Individuals under age 59½ may elect to take substantially equal periodic payments from their traditional IRAs as a way to avoid the 10 percent early distribution penalty. This exception requires an individual to continue the periodic payments for five years or until reaching age 59½, whichever period is longer. If the periodic payments are not maintained for the required time period, the individual must retroactively pay the 10 percent early distribution penalty on all previous distributions that were meant to meet the exception.

Q 3:109 Are conversions subject to withholding?

All conversions are treated as distributions and are subject to the withholding rules of Code Section 3405. That means withholding is required from every conversion unless it is waived. It may not be waived for some conversions.

Withholding may be waived for any conversion from a traditional, SEP, or SIMPLE IRA to a Roth IRA. It may also be waived for a conversion from a qualified plan to a Roth IRA if the direct rollover (trustee-to-trustee transfer) method of conversion is used. [I.R.C. § 3405; Treas. Reg. § 1.408A-6, Q&A-13]

Mandatory withholding of 20 percent applies to any conversion from a qualified plan to a Roth IRA that does *not* use the direct rollover method. [I.R.C. § 3405(c)]

Most individuals waive withholding if they are eligible so the entire amount may be converted. The conversion tax is then paid using funds outside the IRA. Any amount that is withheld from the conversion does not enjoy the automatic exception to the 10 percent additional tax (see Q 3:107). If an amount is withheld and the individual is eligible to use the 60-day method of conversion (see Q 3:96), the 10 percent additional tax can still be avoided by depositing outside funds to the Roth IRA to replace the amount withheld from the conversion. A qualified plan beneficiary of a deceased participant, who is limited to the trustee-to-trustee transfer method, cannot avoid paying the 10 percent additional tax on an amount that is withheld unless a Code Section 72(t) exception applies to the plan distribution (see Q 6:48).

Example. Dillon converts his $10,000 traditional IRA to a Roth IRA and elects to have $1,000 withheld as federal tax. He is eligible to use the 60-day rollover method and takes $1,000 from his regular bank account and deposits it to the Roth IRA within 60 days after the conversion. The full $10,000 is now rolled over, and the conversion is completely exempt from the 10 percent additional tax.

Practice Pointer. *Some* method of withholding is probably warranted for most individuals completing conversions, especially in the case of large conversion amounts. Rather than withhold from a conversion, an individual might increase payroll withholding or pay estimated quarterly withholding amounts to cover the tax liability from a conversion.

Recharacterization

Q 3:110 What is recharacterization?

Recharacterization is the process of changing an IRA contribution from one type to another. A regular contribution may be recharacterized at any time before the tax filing deadline (including extensions) for the year for which the contribution was made. Before 2018, recharacterization could also be used to undo some Roth IRA conversions (see Q 3:124). [I.R.C. § 408A(d)(6)]

Recharacterization requires an election (see Q 3:118) and is effected by a trustee-to-trustee transfer of the original contribution (plus allocable earnings; see Q 3:116) from the first IRA to the second IRA. A recharacterized contribution is treated as having been made to the second IRA on the original contribution date, and the actual contribution to the first IRA is ignored. The transfer of the recharacterized contribution and its earnings does not generate taxable income.

The opportunity to recharacterize a contribution is designed to accommodate individuals who make mistakes, change their minds, or find themselves ineligible for one type of contribution and therefore want to switch to the other.

Q 3:111 What IRA contributions may be recharacterized?

The following types of IRA contributions may be recharacterized:

- A traditional IRA contribution may be recharacterized as a Roth IRA contribution if the individual qualifies to make a Roth IRA contribution under the MAGI rules (see Q 3:77). No deduction is allowed for the recharacterized contribution (because Roth IRA contributions are not deductible).
- A Roth IRA contribution may be recharacterized as a traditional IRA contribution. That recharacterized contribution is deductible, subject to the MAGI and active participation rules (see Qs 3:47, 3:64).
- An amount *erroneously* rolled over or transferred from a traditional IRA to a SIMPLE IRA (which is not permitted) may be recharacterized as a contribution back to a traditional IRA. [Treas. Reg. § 1.408A-5, Q&A-4]
- Amounts successfully converted *before 2018* from a traditional, SEP, or SIMPLE IRA to a Roth IRA could generally be recharacterized back to the first type of IRA (see Qs 3:124, 3:126). The effect was to unwind the conversion, and to cancel the income inclusion that otherwise would have resulted. The last date for recharacterizing a 2017 conversion is October 15, 2018.
- A failed conversion to a Roth IRA (see Q 3:85), which is just treated as a regular Roth IRA contribution, may be recharacterized as a traditional IRA contribution (e.g., if the individual's income is too high to allow a Roth IRA contribution). An excess contribution could result, however.

[I.R.C. § 408A(d)(6)]

Q 3:112 What IRA contributions *cannot* be recharacterized?

The following IRA contributions cannot be recharacterized:

- Conversion contributions to a Roth IRA made after 2017 cannot be recharacterized (see Q 3:124). [I.R.C. § 408A(d)(6)(B)(iii)]
- All contributions under a SEP or SIMPLE plan (including elective salary deferrals) are considered to be made by the employer—so they cannot be recharacterized as participant contributions to another type of IRA. [Treas. Reg. § 1.408A-5, Q&A-5]

Q 3:113 If a traditional IRA contribution is recharacterized to a Roth IRA, is that the same as a conversion?

No. There are important differences between a conversion and a recharacterization:

- In a conversion, the transfer of assets from the traditional IRA to the Roth IRA is taxable. The transfer of assets is not taxable in a recharacterization.
- If conversion contributions are distributed from the Roth IRA before being held there for at least five taxable years, a 10 percent additional tax may apply (see Q 5:92). There is no similar rule for recharacterized contributions.

Q 3:114 Is the recharacterization of an IRA contribution treated as a rollover for purposes of the one-rollover-per-year rule?

No. The recharacterization of an IRA contribution is *not* a rollover. It may only be accomplished using a trustee-to-trustee transfer (see Q 3:118), and the one-rollover-per-year limit of Code Section 408(d)(3)(B) (see Q 6:15) does not apply to such transfers. [Treas. Reg. § 1.408A-5, Q&A-8] (For discussion of rollovers, see chapter 6.)

Q 3:115 May a tax-free rollover or a direct transfer be recharacterized?

In general, a tax-free rollover or direct transfer to an IRA cannot be *recharacterized*, because that could allow it to escape taxation. For example, if an amount is rolled over to a traditional IRA, it could only be moved to a Roth IRA in a taxable transaction (i.e., a conversion) (see Q 3:83). [Treas. Reg. § 1.408A-5, Q&A-4, Q&A-10 (Example 4)]

An intervening tax-free transfer may be disregarded, however. Assume a contribution is made to one traditional IRA, and then transferred (with allocable net income) to a second traditional IRA. If the original contribution amount plus all allocable income is then moved to a Roth IRA as a qualified rollover contribution, and both transfers occur within the same year, then the initial contribution may be recharacterized as having been made to the Roth IRA. [Treas. Reg. § 1.408A-5, Q&A-7]

Transfer of Allocable Net Income

Q 3:116 What happens to the earnings on an IRA contribution when the contribution is recharacterized?

The net income attributable to an IRA contribution that is being recharacterized must be transferred along with the contribution. [Treas. Reg. § 1.408A-5, Q&A-2]

Q 3:117 How is allocable net income determined for recharacterization purposes?

If the contribution being recharacterized was made to a separate IRA and no distributions or contributions were subsequently made, then the entire IRA account balance must be transferred in the recharacterization. The net earnings (or loss) attributable to the contribution are simply determined as the difference between the account balance and the original contribution amount.

If the IRA contribution was not kept separate, the net income attributable to it is calculated by allocating a pro rata amount of the earnings accumulated on IRA assets while the contribution was held in the account. This requires an accounting of all amounts that were moved into and out of the account during the relevant period. The following amounts are determined:

1. The fair market value of the account immediately before the contribution being recharacterized is made—Point A (start of the computation period).
2. The fair market value of the account immediately before the recharacterization—Point B (end of the computation period).
3. The total amounts moved *into* the account between Points A and B. That includes the contribution being recharacterized, plus any other amounts that were contributed, transferred, or recharacterized *to* the account during that period.
4. The total amounts moved *out* of the account between Points A and B. They include any distributions, transfers, and recharacterizations *from* the account during that period.

The sum of amounts (1) and (3) is the *adjusted opening balance* (AOB) of the account. The sum of amounts (2) and (4) is the *adjusted closing balance* (ACB) of the account. The net income allocable to the contribution being recharacterized is determined as:

- the contribution being recharacterized, multiplied by
- the fraction [(ACB–AOB)/(AOB)] (rounded to three places).

[Treas. Reg. § 1.408A-5, Q&A-2(c); IRS Pub. 590-A, *Contributions to Individual Retirement Arrangements (IRAs)* 2020 (see Appendix A)]

A special rule is provided for an IRA asset that is not normally valued on a daily basis. In this case, the fair market value of the asset at the beginning of the computation period is deemed to be the most recent, regularly determined, fair market value of the asset, determined as of a date that coincides with or precedes the first day of the computation period. [Treas. Reg. § 1.408A-5, Q&A-2(c)(1)]

> **Example.** On May 1, 2018, Evelyn contributed $5,500 to her traditional IRA, which was valued at $55,000 immediately before the contribution. In January 2019, $100,000 of assets were moved to the IRA by direct (trustee-to-trustee) transfer from Evelyn's 401(k) plan. One month later, Evelyn realized her MAGI for 2018 did not exceed the limit for a Roth IRA contribution, and she asked the IRA trustee to recharacterize the May 1 contribution.
>
> On February 20, 2019, immediately before the recharacterization, the total value of Evelyn's traditional IRA was $170,000. The adjusted opening balance was $160,500 ($55,000 + $5,500 + $100,000). The adjusted closing balance was $170,000 (no distributions were made). The net income allocable to the $5,500 contribution was $324.50 (i.e., $5,500 × ($170,000 – $160,500) ÷ $160,600). The trustee accomplished the recharacterization by directly transferring $5,824.50 (i.e., $5,500 + $324.50) from the traditional IRA to a Roth IRA. Evelyn was treated as having contributed $5,500 to the Roth IRA on May 1, 2018, and her actual contribution to the traditional IRA was disregarded (and could not be deducted). The transfer of earnings was not taxable.

Election to Recharacterize

Q 3:118 How is the election to recharacterize an IRA contribution made?

The election to recharacterize a contribution (e.g., from a traditional IRA to a Roth IRA, or vice versa) is made by sending a notice to both the trustee of the IRA that initially received the contribution, and to the trustee of the IRA to which the contribution will be transferred. The election notice must include the following information:

1. The type and amount of the contribution to the initial IRA that is to be recharacterized;
2. The date on which the contribution was made to the initial IRA and the year for which it was made;
3. A statement of how the individual is electing to treat the contribution for federal income tax purposes;
4. An instruction that the trustee of the initial IRA should transfer, directly to the trustee of the new IRA, the amount of the contribution plus the net income allocable to it;
5. The names of the trustee of the initial IRA and the trustee of the new IRA; and
6. Any additional information needed to make the transfer.

[Treas. Reg. § 1.408A-5, Q&A-6]

Q 3:119 Can the recharacterization deadline be extended?

Yes. Two kinds of extensions are available: automatic and discretionary.

The recharacterization deadline is automatically extended—to the date that is six months after the un-extended due date of the tax return for the year of the contribution—if three requirements are met:

1. The IRA owner timely filed a tax return for the year of the contribution,
2. The owner completes the election procedure (see Q 3:118) during the six-month extension period, and
3. If necessary, the owner files an amended tax return for the contribution year.

[Treas. Reg. § 301.9100-2(b); Ann. 99-57, 1999-1 C.B. 1256]

> **Note.** The automatic extension does not change the deadline in many cases, because an automatic six-month extension of the return filing date is also generally available. However, it may be useful to an individual who files a return by April 15, or who files a return on extension but before October 15, and later decides to recharacterize.

Individuals may apply to the IRS for a discretionary waiver of the recharacterization deadline if they do not meet the automatic waiver requirements. Discretionary waivers are only granted by letter ruling, so the procedures and fees generally attendant to ruling requests must be followed.

Q 3:120 What are the standards for obtaining a discretionary waiver of the recharacterization deadline?

To obtain a discretionary waiver, the individual must show he or she acted reasonably and in good faith, and that the granting of relief will not prejudice any IRS interests. [Treas. Reg. § 301.9100-3] Actions are shown to be reasonable and in good faith if the evidence proves the individual:

- Applied for relief before the IRS discovered the problem,
- Could not timely elect recharacterization because events intervened that were beyond the individual's control,
- Was unaware (despite having exercised reasonable diligence, a subjective standard that depends on the individual's experience and the complexity of the matter) that an election was required,
- Reasonably relied on written advice of the IRS, or
- Reasonably relied on a qualified tax professional who failed to make the election, or never advised that one was needed.

The IRS will *not* grant relief for an individual who was materially informed about recharacterization but chose not to elect it, or who considered recharacterization desirable only in hindsight (because of events that occurred after the deadline—e.g., the converted assets lost value), or wants to extend the deadline because recharacterization would avoid an accuracy-related penalty. [Treas. Reg. § 301.9100-3(b)(3)(iii); *see* Priv. Ltr. Rul. 201024071 (June 18, 2010).]

Prejudice to the government's interests means that granting relief would produce a lower aggregate tax liability (for all the affected years, and taking into account the time value of money) than the taxpayer would have had if the election had been timely made. [Treas. Reg. § 301.9100-3]

Applying these standards, the IRS has granted many favorable recharacterization rulings. [*E.g.*, Priv. Ltr. Ruls. 200331004 (Aug. 1, 2003), 200909073 (Feb. 27, 2009), 201047032 (Nov. 26, 2010), 201024071 (June 18, 2010)]

One example is Private Letter Ruling 201320022 (May 17, 2013), in which the IRA owner's attorney overstated the owner's basis in the IRA when he recommended a conversion. They reviewed the situation before the recharacterization deadline, but the attorney had not yet discovered his error and the IRA owner chose to stay with conversion since only a small amount of gain was expected. The IRS granted relief because the IRA owner's reliance on a qualified tax professional was reasonable, and that professional failed to advise recharacterization. And the government's interests were not prejudiced by the waiver because the tax years affected by the recharacterization were still open.

In 2014, the IRS granted four favorable rulings involving the same scenario. In each, the IRA owner's certified public accountant (CPA) of long standing recommended he convert to a Roth IRA, warning that ability to do so would depend on meeting then-applicable MAGI limits (see Q 3:84, Note). At the time, neither knew the individual's MAGI would be too high. Later, the CPA prepared the individual's income tax return, determined the MAGI figure, and reported the conversion as a taxable distribution—never explaining to the client that the conversion had failed but recharacterization was still possible. Years later, the individual engaged a second CPA to examine the return on an unrelated matter, and the problem finally came to light. The IRS determined that each individual's reliance on the first CPA was reasonable and in good faith, and that the government's interests were not prejudiced because allowing the late recharacterization did not reduce his aggregate tax liability. [Priv. Ltr. Ruls. 201404016 (Jan. 24, 2014), 201404018 (Jan. 24, 2014), 201405033 (Jan. 31, 2014), 201405034 (Jan. 31, 2014)]

The IRS also waived the deadline for a cognitively impaired individual who was unaware that recharacterization was both available and advisable. [Priv. Ltr. Rul. 201423044 (June 6, 2014)]

Q 3:121 May an election be made to recharacterize an IRA contribution on behalf of a deceased IRA owner?

Yes. The election to recharacterize an IRA contribution may be made by the executor, administrator, or other person charged with the duty of filing a deceased IRA owner's final federal income tax return. [Treas. Reg. § 1.408A-5, Q&A-6]

Q 3:122 Is a recharacterization subject to withholding?

No. A recharacterization is not a designated distribution under Code Section 3405 and therefore is not subject to federal income tax withholding. [T.D. 8816, 64 Fed. Reg. 5597, 5599 (Feb. 4, 1999)]

Q 3:123 How are recharacterizations reported for federal income tax purposes?

Any recharacterization of an IRA contribution must be reported on Form 1099-R, Distributions From Pensions, Annuities, Retirement or Profit-Sharing Plans, IRAs, Insurance Contracts, etc., and Form 5498, IRA Contribution Information. (See Qs 8:77, 8:142.)

Recharacterizing a Pre-2018 Conversion

Q 3:124 Can a conversion be recharacterized?

Not anymore. The special rule that allows recharacterizations (Code Section 408A(d)(6)(A)) used to apply not only to regular IRA contributions, but also to conversion contributions from a traditional, SEP, or SIMPLE IRA (and possibly also conversions from a qualified plan; see Q 3:127). It no longer does, because of an amendment of Code Section 408A that was enacted by the TCJA. New Code Section 408A(d)(6)(B)(iii), which is effective for tax years beginning after 2017, prohibits the recharacterization of a conversion contribution to a Roth IRA that is made from an IRA or other eligible retirement plan. [TCJA § 13611; I.R.C. §§ 408A(d)(3), 402(c)(8)(B)]

Since the recharacterization deadline is the due date (including extensions) of the tax return for the conversion year, the last date for recharacterizing a 2017 conversion was October 15, 2018. [I.R.C. § 408A(d)(6); IRS FAQ, *Recharacterization of IRA Contributions* (2018), available at *https://www.irs.gov/retirement-plans/ira-faqs-recharacterization-of-ira-contributions*]

Q 3:125 What was the effect of recharacterizing a pre-2018 conversion?

Recharacterization had the effect of unwinding the conversion. The ability to do so removed some of the tax risk of conversion. If converted assets lost value before the due date of the tax return, the conversion could be undone so that tax would not be paid based on the high conversion-date value of the assets.

Q 3:126 Where were the assets placed when such a conversion was recharacterized?

If assets were converted from a traditional IRA, they were transferred to the same or another traditional IRA in the recharacterization. Assets converted from a SEP IRA (or SIMPLE IRA) to a Roth IRA were recharacterized back to a SEP (or SIMPLE) IRA. [Treas. Reg. § 1.408A-5, Q&A-5]

Q 3:127 Could a pre-2018 conversion of assets from a qualified plan be recharacterized?

It was never clear whether recharacterization could be used to unwind a *successful* pre 2018 conversion from a qualified plan. (Compare the acceptable use of recharacterization to remedy a *failed* qualified plan conversion; see Q 3:111.) [Treas. Reg. § 1.408A-5, Q&A-6, Examples 1 and 2; Treas. Reg. § 1.408A-4, Q&A-3; Notice 2008-30, 2008-12 I.R.B. 638, Q&A-7]

Note. Because of the uncertainty, the prudent course before 2018 was to roll over qualified plan assets first to a traditional IRA, and then convert them to a Roth IRA (although doing so could affect the amount of conversion income; see Q 3:103).

Q 3:128 Could an individual convert, recharacterize, and then reconvert the same contribution to an IRA?

Yes. Before the law was changed, an individual could convert assets (e.g., from a traditional IRA) to a Roth IRA, recharacterize them back to a traditional IRA, and then reconvert them to a Roth IRA. But a waiting period was required before reconverting. The earliest date when a reconversion was allowed was:

- the first day of the year after the taxable year of the (first) conversion, or
- 31 days after the recharacterization, whichever was later.

[Treas. Reg. § 1.408A-5, Q&A-9(a)(1)]

Example 1. John converted his traditional IRA to a Roth IRA in January 2016. He recharacterized the Roth IRA as a traditional IRA one month later. John had to wait until January 1, 2017 to reconvert the traditional IRA.

Example 2. Mindy converted a traditional IRA to a Roth IRA in January 2016. She converted it back to a traditional IRA in a recharacterization on January 18, 2017. The earliest date when Mindy could reconvert the traditional IRA was February 18, 2017 (31 days after the recharacterization date).

Q 3:129 What were the consequences of failing to observe the waiting period before a reconversion?

A premature reconversion (see Q 3:128) was treated as a failed conversion—and considered to be a distribution from the traditional IRA and a regular contribution to the Roth IRA. But for purposes of determining when the individual could make a reconversion, the premature reconversion did count as a conversion. Thus, it could be recharacterized and potentially reconverted at a later date. [Preamble to Treas. Reg. § 1.408A, 64 Fed. Reg. 5597–5611 (1999)]

Excess IRA Contributions

Q 3:130 What is an excess traditional IRA contribution?

For 2020 and 2021, an excess contribution to a traditional IRA is the amount that an individual contributes to his or her traditional IRAs that is more than the smaller of the individual's taxable compensation for the year, or $6,000 ($7,000 if the individual is age 50 or older). This definition applies whether the contributions are deductible or nondeductible. For contribution years before 2020 (see Q 3:45), traditional IRA contributions made by an individual who was age 70½ or older by the end of the year were also considered excess contributions. Other excess contributions may result from a spouse's contribution, an employer's contribution, or an improper rollover contribution. [I.R.C. § 408(a); Treas. Reg. § 1.408-4(c); IRS Pub. 590-A, *Contributions to Individual Retirement Arrangements (IRAs)* 2020 (see Appendix A)]

Q 3:131 What is an excess Roth IRA contribution?

The Code defines an excess Roth IRA contribution as any contribution to a Roth IRA for the taxable year (other than a qualified rollover contribution) in excess of the amount allowable as a contribution to a Roth IRA for that taxable year. [I.R.C. § 4973(f)]

If an excess contribution is caused by an individual's contributing to both a traditional IRA and a Roth IRA, the excess contribution is considered to have occurred in the Roth IRA. That is because an individual's contributions are applied first to the traditional IRA and then to the Roth IRA. [Treas. Reg. § 1.408A-3, Q&A-3; IRS Pub. 590-A, *Contributions to Individual Retirement Arrangements (IRAs)* 2020 (see Appendix A)]

Example 1. Gary, age 42, misunderstands the annual contribution limit and contributes *both* $6,000 to a Roth IRA *and* $6,000 to a traditional IRA for 2019. The traditional IRA contribution counts first against the annual limit, so Gary has made a $6,000 excess contribution to the Roth IRA.

Example 2. Lester contributes $6,000 to his Roth IRA for 2019 though he is only eligible to contribute $5,000 (his MAGI is in the phaseout range; see Q 3:77). Lester has made an excess contribution of $1,000 to the Roth IRA.

Q 3:132 What is the penalty for making an excess IRA contribution?

The penalty is 6 percent of the excess contribution (not to exceed 6 percent of the total IRA value). [I.R.C. § 4973] It can be avoided, however, by making a *corrective distribution* (see Q 3:134).

Correcting an Excess Contribution

Q 3:133 How is an excess contribution corrected?

There are generally three ways to correct an excess contribution—withdraw it in a *corrective distribution* (see Q 3:134), withdraw it but *not* in a corrective distribution, or absorb it as a subsequent-year contribution (see Q 3:136). In some cases, an excess contribution to a Roth IRA can be recharacterized as a traditional IRA contribution (see Q 3:111).

Q 3:134 What is a corrective distribution?

A corrective distribution occurs if three requirements are met:

1. The excess contribution is entirely withdrawn, along with the net income attributable to it. (Net income is calculated using the method described in Q 3:117.) [I.R.C. § 408(d)(4)(C)]
2. The withdrawal occurs by the extended due date of the income tax return for the year the excess contribution was made (year 1). [I.R.C. § 408(d)(4)(A)]
3. No deduction is claimed for the withdrawn contribution. [I.R.C. § 408(d)(4)(B)]

The corrective distribution nullifies the excess contribution. Since it is treated as never having been made, the Code Section 4973 penalty does not apply.

(For reporting of corrective distributions and the calculation of net income, see Qs 8:104–8:112.)

Q 3:135 Must a corrective distribution be taken from the same IRA that received the excess distribution?

The corrective distribution must be taken from the same type of IRA (traditional, Roth, SEP, or SIMPLE) that received the excess contribution. But if there is more than one IRA of the same type, the corrective distribution may be taken from any of them. [IRS Pub. 590-A, *Contributions to Individual Retirement Arrangements (IRAs)* 2020 (see Appendix A)]

Q 3:136 How is a corrective distribution taxed?

The withdrawn contribution is excluded from income because no deduction was claimed. But the net income included with it is taxable:

1. The withdrawn net income is treated as earned in year 1 and is included in that year's taxable income (even if the corrective distribution is made in year 2). [I.R.C. §§ 61, 408(d)(4); Treas. Reg. §§ 1.408A-3, Q&A-7; 1.408A-6, Q&A-1(d)]

2. The withdrawn income is taxable even if the corrective distribution was made from a Roth IRA (because a corrective distribution is not a *qualified distribution*; see Q 5:68). [I.R.C. § 408A(d)(2)(C)]
3. The early distribution penalty of Code Section 72(t) (10 percent of the distributed income) applies to the corrective distribution if the recipient is younger than age 59½, unless an exception to that penalty applies (see Q 5:7). [Notice 87-16, 1987-1 C.B. 446, Q&A-C2; Instructions for Form 5329 (2020), p. 5]

Q 3:137 What happens if a corrective distribution is *not* made?

If a corrective distribution is not made, the excess contribution is added to the IRA owner's basis, and the 6 percent penalty applies for year 1. The penalty also continues to apply each year until the excess contribution is either withdrawn or "absorbed" (as a subsequent-year contribution). [Treas. Reg. § 1.408A-3, Q&A-7]

Withdrawal in year 2. If the excess contribution is distributed in year 2, the penalty does not apply that year. The earnings need not be withdrawn; they may remain in the account. The distribution is taxed according to the regular rules that govern traditional or Roth IRA distributions.

A special rule applies if the excess contribution was made to a traditional IRA, no deduction was claimed for it in year 1, and the contribution was within the annual IRA contribution limit but the individual did not qualify to make it (either because the individual lacked sufficient compensation or was older than age 70½). In that case, the distribution in year 2 is not taxable. [I.R.C. § 408(d)(5); Instructions for Form 8606 (2020)]

Absorption in year 2. Alternatively, the excess contribution from year 1 may be treated as a year 2 contribution, as long as it does not cause that year's limit to be exceeded. The earnings may be left in the IRA, and the penalty is avoided for year 2.

If neither occurs. Failure to withdraw or absorb the excess contribution in year 2 means that the excess contribution penalty must apply for year 2. The same remedial options—withdrawal or absorption—are then available for year 3. But if year 3 passes and the excess contribution is still not removed, the penalty applies for year 3 (and so forth each year). [Treas. Reg. § 1.408A-3, Q&A-7]

The end of the taxable year is the critical date for determining whether the Code Section 4973 penalty applies for any year *after* year 1. If year 2 (or a later year) ends and the excess contribution has not been withdrawn or absorbed, the penalty applies that year. In a most recent case, the taxpayers argued they were not subject to the penalty for year 3 because they removed the excess contribution by the *filing deadline* for the year 3 tax return. They lost. [Wu v. United States, 835 F.3d 711 (7th Cir.), *cert. denied*, 137 S. Ct. 1234 (2017)]

Penalties may not be assessed for any tax year that is closed under the statute of limitations, generally a three-year period. So, if enough years go by without withdrawing or absorbing the excess contribution, the IRS may be foreclosed from assessing the penalty all the way back to year 1. The penalty is still assessable for the open years, however. [Mazzei v. Commissioner, T.C. Memo. 2014-55 (2014)]

Example. Fatima, age 30, exceeded the traditional IRA contribution limit for 2015 by $100. Ignoring the excess, she makes a full contribution for each of 2016 and 2017. Finally, in March 2018, she recognizes the error and withdraws $100 from the traditional IRA. The 6 percent penalty ($6 per year) applies for 2015 through 2017, but not 2018. The same result would occur if Fatima contributes only $5,400 for 2018.

Saver's Tax Credit for IRA Contributions

Q 3:138 What is the saver's tax credit?

An individual who makes eligible contributions (see Qs 3:45, 3:46, 3:4, 3:71) to either a traditional or a Roth IRA (or a combination of both) may be eligible for the saver's tax credit. The credit is determined as a percentage of the eligible contributions, and it can be as much as $1,000 ($2,000 for married couples filing jointly). The lower the individual's income, the higher the percentage (see Q 3:143). [I.R.C. § 25B; IRS Pub. 590-A, *Contributions to Individual Retirement Arrangements (IRAs)* 2020 (see Appendix A)]

The credit is nonrefundable, which means it cannot exceed the tax otherwise payable for the year (disregarding other nonrefundable credits and the adoption credit). [I.R.C. § 25B]

Q 3:139 Who is eligible for the saver's tax credit?

The eligibility requirements for the saver's tax credit are:

1. The taxpayer must be age 18 or older.
2. The taxpayer cannot be a full-time student. A *full-time student* is an individual who at any time during some part of each of five calendar months (not necessarily consecutive) is a full-time student at a school or in an on-farm training course given by a school that has a regular teaching staff, a regular course of study, and a regularly enrolled body of students in attendance. The on-farm training course may also be sponsored by a state, county, or local government.
3. The taxpayer cannot be claimed by another individual as an exemption on his or her individual or joint tax return (e.g., by a parent).
4. The taxpayer's AGI cannot exceed the limit for his or her filing status. (For the 2021 limits, see Q 3:143.) AGI is determined for this purpose by adding back any exclusion or deduction claimed for the year for (1) foreign earned income, (2) foreign housing reimbursement, or (3) excludable income for residents of American Samoa and Puerto Rico.

[I.R.C. § 25B(b); Ann. 2001-106, 2001-2 C.B. 416; Notice 2018-83, 2018-47 I.R.B. 774]

Q 3:140 What contributions are eligible?

Contributions eligible for the saver's tax credit are:

- Traditional and Roth IRA contributions.
- Salary reduction contributions under a SIMPLE plan (see chapter 13) or salary reduction SEP plan (SARSEP; see chapter 12).
- Contributions to an ABLE account by its designated beneficiary (only through December 31, 2025).
- Elective deferrals as defined in Code Section 402(g)(3), or made under an eligible Section 457(b) deferred compensation plan.
- An employee's voluntary contributions to a qualified retirement plan.

[I.R.C. § 25B(d)(1)]

Eligible contributions are reduced by distributions made during the testing period (see below), excluding rollovers and IRA contributions returned (with related income) before the tax return filing due date, including extensions. [I.R.C. § 25B(d)(2); S. Rep. No. 107-30 (Pub. L. No. 107-16) at page 91] For this purpose, distributions include those received by the individual's spouse, if a joint tax return is filed both for the year of distribution and the year for which the credit is claimed. [I.R.C. § 25B(d)(2)(D)]

Q 3:141 What is the testing period?

The *testing period* consists of the year for which the saver's tax credit is claimed (the "credit year"), the period after the end of that year and before the due date (including extensions) for filing the tax return for that year, and the two years before the credit year. [I.R.C. § 25B(d)]

Example. Ruth contributes $2,000 to a Roth IRA in November 2020 and claims the saver's tax credit. The credit year is 2020. The testing period starts on January 1, 2018 and will end on the due date (including extensions) for filing the 2020 tax return. If Ruth takes any distributions during the testing period which she does not roll over, her credit calculation will be affected.

Q 3:142 What is the maximum eligible contribution?

After contributions are reduced (see Q 3:140), the maximum eligible contribution that can be taken into account to determine the credit is $2,000 per person. On a joint return, up to $2,000 per spouse can be considered.

Q 3:143 How is the credit determined?

The saver's credit is determined by multiplying the eligible contribution amount by the applicable credit rate. [I.R.C. § 25B] The income thresholds that determine the applicable credit rate are indexed annually for inflation; the levels effective for 2021 contributions are shown in Table 3-4 below. Since the maximum eligible contribution is $2,000 and the highest credit rate is 50 percent, the saver's tax credit never exceeds $1,000 per person.

Table 3-4. Saver's Tax Credit Rates for 2021

Joint Filers	*Heads of Household*	*All Others*	*Credit Rate*
$0–$39,500	$0–$29,625	$0–$19,750	50%
$39,501–$43,000	$29,626–$32,250	$19,751–$21,500	20%
$43,001–$66,000	$32,251–$49,500	$21,501–$33,000	10%
Over $66,000	Over $49,500	Over $33,000	0%

[Notice 2020-79, 2020-46 I.R.B. 1014]

Chapter 4

Required Distributions

This chapter explains the minimum distribution requirements that apply to IRAs. Most IRAs are subject to the rules that apply to defined contribution plans. Individual retirement annuities, annuitized IRAs, qualifying longevity contracts, and other annuities are governed by the rules applicable to defined benefit plans.

For traditional IRA owners (including owners of SEP and SIMPLE IRAs), the minimum distribution requirements first apply for the year of the individual's 72nd birthday (recently changed from 70½). They continue through the year of death. Required minimum distributions (RMDs) for each year are calculated based on an individual's remaining actuarial life expectancy (or it may be the joint remaining actuarial life expectancy of the individual and spouse who is the sole designated beneficiary and more than 10 years younger). Roth IRA owners are not required to receive lifetime RMDs.

After any IRA owner dies, minimum distribution requirements apply to the beneficiaries. The rules that govern distributions to beneficiaries changed very substantially at the end of 2019. Many who previously could stretch the IRA for a long period of time must now take a full distribution of the interest within 10 years. The changes are effective for distributions with respect to participants who die after 2019. The old distribution rules still apply with respect to beneficiaries of participants who died before 2020.

A large part of chapter 4 is devoted to explaining how these rules apply to benefits left in trust, and what can (and cannot) be done to minimize mandatory distributions to beneficiaries in general. The minimum distribution requirements for annuities are also (more briefly) explained.

The relief measures enacted in response to the coronavirus pandemic include a waiver of the minimum distribution requirements for 2020. Since the waiver was enacted in late March, many individuals had already received distributions that were intended as RMDs. The IRS provided some relief to allow many (not all) of these payments to be returned to a retirement plan. The window for doing so has now closed.

Effective for RMDs beginning on January 1, 2022, new life expectancy tables will apply.

Distributions in General

Q 4:1 What IRAs are subject to mandatory distribution requirements?

Owners of a traditional, SEP, or SIMPLE IRA must make annual withdrawals after reaching a certain age. Roth IRA owners do not have this requirement. After any IRA owner dies, minimum distribution requirements apply to the beneficiaries. [I.R.C. §§ 401(a)(9), 408(a)(6), 408(b)(3), 408A(a), 408A(c)(4)]

Q 4:2 How are minimum distributions determined?

Minimum distributions are required by Code Section 401(a)(9), which contains only a general statement of the requirement. All the details are in the regulations under Section 401(a)(9). They define the minimum requirements that must be satisfied for distributing an *employee's* benefit. But the rules apply to IRAs, too. In applying them to IRAs, the term *employee* means the IRA owner, and *plan administrator* refers to the IRA trustee, custodian, or issuer. [Treas. Reg. § 1.408-8, Q&A-1(b)] (In this book, the term *participant* is often used for the employee or IRA owner.)

One set of minimum distribution rules covers defined contribution plans, and another set of rules covers defined benefit plans and annuities. Most distributions from an IRA resemble those from a defined contribution plan, so the defined contribution rules generally apply to IRAs. But any part of an IRA that has been annuitized (used to purchase an immediate annuity) is governed by the rules for defined benefit plans and annuities. [Treas. Reg. § 1.401(a)(9)-2, Q&A-1(c); Treas. Reg. § 1.401(a)(9)-8, Q&A-2(a)(3); Treas. Reg. § 1.401(a)(9)-6, Q&A-12(a)]

Q 4:3 What IRA distributions count toward satisfying the minimum distribution requirement?

All IRA distributions, whether taxable or not, made during a year for which a minimum distribution is required (a *distribution calendar year*) count toward satisfying that year's requirement, *except* the following:

- IRA contributions returned pursuant to Code Section 408(d)(4) with allocable income by the extended due date of the participant's tax return for the contribution year. [Treas. Reg. § 1.408-8, Q&A-11(b)(1)]
- Excess contributions to any IRA (including employer contributions and salary deferral contributions to a SEP or SIMPLE IRA) that are returned pursuant to Section 408(d)(5) or 408(d)(6) in a corrective distribution. Corrective distributions include the income allocable to the excess contribution and are made by the extended due date of the participant's tax return for the year the excess contribution was made. [Treas. Reg. § 1.408-8, Q&A-11(b)(2) and (3); Treas. Reg. § 1.401(a)(9)-5, Q&A-9(b)(2)]
- Distribution of an annuity contract. [Treas. Reg. § 1.401(a)(9)-8, Q&A-10]

Q 4:4 What is the required beginning date?

The required beginning date (RBD) is the deadline for payment of the first RMD. Other RMDs must be paid by the end of the calendar year for which they are required, but a longer time is allowed to pay the first. The RBD under current law is April 1 of the calendar year after the calendar year that includes the IRA owner's 72nd birthday. For an IRA owner who reached age 70½ before 2020, the RBD is April 1 of the calendar year after the year such age was attained.

[Treas. Reg. § 1.401(a)(9)-5, Q&A-1(c); I.R.C. § 401(a)(9)(C), as amended by the Setting Every Community Up for Retirement Enhancement Act (SECURE Act), § 114(a), Division O of the Further Consolidated Appropriations Act, 2020 (Pub. L. No. 116-94)]

An individual attains age 70½ on the date that is six calendar months after the 70th anniversary of birth. [Treas. Reg. § 1.401(a)(9)-2, Q&A-3] So, anyone born after June 30, 1949 reached age 70½ after 2019 and is subject to the age 72 requirement.

Q 4:5 When is the second RMD due?

The second and each subsequent RMD is due by December 31 of the year for which it is required. So the second RMD is due by December 31 of the calendar year that includes the RBD. [Treas. Reg. § 1.401(a)(9)-5, Q&A-1(c)]

If payment of the first RMD is delayed until the period leading up to the RBD, two RMDs must be paid in the same calendar year.

> **Example**. Effie's 72nd birthday is July 10, 2021. Her first distribution calendar year is 2021, and she waits until March 2022 to take the first RMD. The second distribution calendar year is 2022, so Effie's second RMD is also due in 2022.

Waiver of RMDs for 2020

Q 4:6 Were minimum distributions required in 2020?

No. The minimum distribution requirements for IRAs and most defined contribution plans were suspended for calendar year 2020. [Coronavirus Aid, Relief, and Economic Security (CARES) Act, § 2203, Pub. L. No. 116-136 (Mar. 27, 2020)] The law amends Code Section 401(a)(9), which contains the minimum distribution rules, to include new subparagraph (I) stating the rules for the temporary waiver.

The temporary waiver applies to "individual retirement plans," so inherited IRAs are included. [I.R.C. § 401(a)(9)(I)(i)(III)] That means no RMD is payable for 2020 to any owner or beneficiary of an IRA. A special rule explains how the waiver applies to inherited IRAs being distributed under the 5-year rule (see Q 4:9).

The waiver probably does not apply to annuity payments under an individual retirement annuity contract. Section 401(a)(9) lists the plans covered by the 2020 waiver. They include certain defined contribution plans and "an individual retirement plan." Defined benefit plans are not listed, so the waiver does not apply to them. [I.R.C. § 401(a)(9)(I)(i)] An "individual retirement plan" includes an "individual retirement annuity described in Section 408(b)." [I.R.C. § 7701(a)(37)] If part of an IRA is used to purchase an annuity contract, the annuity contract must satisfy the minimum distribution requirements for defined benefit plans and annuities, and the rest of the IRA must satisfy those for defined contribution plans. [Treas. Reg. § 1.401(a)(9)-8, Q&A-2(a)(3)] So, an individual retirement annuity is an individual retirement plan governed by minimum distribution rules that are not suspended.

Q 4:7 How does the waiver apply to individuals with a required beginning date in 2020?

They are covered by a special rule. If the RBD is April 1, 2020, the first RMD (for 2019) could have been paid either during 2019 or in 2020 on or before the RBD. The CARES Act was enacted on March 27, 2020. Some individuals with a 2020 RBD took the first RMD in 2019, some took it in 2020 before CARES was enacted, and anyone else would have been required to do so within four days.

Under the special rule:

- The first RMD is waived for participants who chose to delay the payment until 2020.
- The first RMD is not waived for participants who took it in 2019.
- For all of them, the second RMD (due by December 31, 2020) is waived.

[I.R.C. § 401(a)(9)(I)(ii); Treas. Reg. § 1.401(a)(9)-5, Q&A-1(b), Q&A-1(c)]

Q 4:8 Does the waiver change anyone's RBD?

No. The suspension does not postpone or otherwise change anyone's RBD. For example, the waiver does not change the determination of whether an individual dies before the RBD (which can affect the payout to beneficiaries). [I.R.C. § 401(a)(9)(I)(iii)(I)]

Q 4:9 How does the waiver apply to an inherited IRA being distributed under the 5-year rule?

If an inherited IRA is being distributed under the 5-year rule, the 5-year period is determined without regard to calendar year 2020. [I.R.C. § 401(a)(9)(I)(iii)(II)]

The 5-year rule applies when a participant dies before the RBD and the IRA has no designated beneficiary. An IRA subject to this rule must be fully distributed by the end of the calendar year that includes the fifth anniversary of the death. No payment is required until the fifth year, and the balance in the fifth year is considered to be the RMD. [I.R.C. § 401(a)(9)(B)(ii); Treas. Reg. § 1.401(a)(9)-3, Q&A-2; Treas. Reg. § 1.401(a)(9)-5, Q&A-5(b); Treas. Reg. § 1.401(a)(9)-2, Q&A-6(a); Treas. Reg. § 54.4974-2, Q&A-3(c); Notice 2007-7, 2007-1 C.B. 395, Q&A-17(b)]

The special waiver rule requires the 5-year period to be determined as if the year 2020 did not exist. This is the result:

If participant died in:	*Inherited IRA must be fully distributed by:*
2015	December 31, 2021 (instead of 2020)
2016	December 31, 2022 (instead of 2021)
2017	December 31, 2023 (instead of 2022)
2018	December 31, 2024 (instead of 2023)
2019	December 31, 2025 (instead of 2024)
2020	December 31, 2025 (no change)

(See Q 4:46 for the meaning of *designated beneficiary* (DB), and Q 4:67 for when trust beneficiaries may be treated as DBs.)

Q 4:10 If an IRA distribution would be the 2020 RMD but for the CARES waiver, can it be returned?

There is no recourse for a person with a 2020 RBD who took the first RMD during 2019, but for anyone else there is relief. For most cases, though, action was required by August 31, 2020. (See Q 4:13 for the methods used to return the payments.)

IRS Notices 2020-51 and 2020-50 offer comprehensive relief that allows most IRA owners, and some of their beneficiaries, to return amounts that would be treated as the 2020 RMD but for the CARES waiver. These are the IRA distributions that can be returned, using one of the methods in Q 4:13:

1. Distributions paid in 2020, to the extent they would be the 2020 RMD but for the CARES waiver.
2. Distributions received in 2020 that would have been treated as the 2019 RMD, if received by an individual whose RBD is April 1, 2020.
3. Distributions, to the extent they include the amount that would be the 2020 RMD but for the CARES Act, and are received in 2020 as part of a series of substantially equal periodic payments (SEPPs) made at least annually over a period expected to last for the life or life expectancy of the participant (or the joint lives or life expectancies of the participant and his or her designated beneficiary), or for at least 10 years.
4. Distributions described in item 3, except they are received in *2021* by an individual whose RBD is April 1, *2021*, to the extent they would be treated as the *2020* RMD but for the CARES Act waiver. The first distributions made in any year are treated as satisfying that year's RMD, even if they are made on or before April 1 to a person whose RBD is in the same year. So, SEPP payments received in 2021 by such a person are first treated as the 2021 RMD, and to the extent those received on or before

April 1 exceed the 2021 RMD, the amount that would be treated as the 2020 RMD but for CARES can be returned. [Treas. Reg. § 1.402(c)-2, Q&A-7; Notice 2020-51, part V, Q&A-5]

5. Any amount distributed in 2020 that qualifies as a coronavirus-related distribution (see Q 4:16).

[Notice 2020-51, 2020-29 I.R.B. (June 23, 2020); Notice 2020-50, 2020-28 I.R.B. 35]

Q 4:11 What are SEPP distributions?

Individuals younger than age 59½ can avoid the 10 percent additional tax on "early" distributions by taking payments from an IRA as a series of substantially equal periodic payments. To qualify for that exception to the tax, the payments must be made at least annually and continue unmodified for at least five years, or (if longer) until age 59½. One method that can be used to calculate SEPPs is based on the RMD rules. [I.R.C. § 72(t)(2)(A)(iv), 72(t)(4); Notice 2002-62, 2002-2 C.B. 710] (For more on this exception to the additional tax, see Qs 5:31–5:41.) In the preamble to the final regulations on November 12, 2020, the IRS indicated that it intended to update Notice 2002-62 to reflect the updated mortality tables.

Q 4:12 What is a coronavirus-related distribution?

Coronavirus-related distributions (CRDs) are distributions totaling $100,000 or less made to a qualified individual from an IRA or other eligible retirement plan on or after January 1, 2020 and before December 31, 2020 (not on December 31). The Consolidated Appropriations Act, 2021, Pub. L. No. 116-260 (Dec. 27, 2020) modified the CARES Act on a retroactive basis to permit coronavirus-related distributions from a money purchase pension plan without violating Code Section 401(a). An individual qualifies for CRDs either because he or she, the spouse, or a dependent is diagnosed with COVID-19, or because the individual experiences adverse financial consequences due to a specified COVID-19-related event. Those events include things like quarantine, job loss, and inability to work due to a lack of childcare that occur because of COVID-19 and that happen to the individual, his or her spouse, or a person who shares the primary residence. (For more details, see Q 7:42.) [CARES Act § 2202; Notice 2020-50, 2020-28 I.R.B. 35]

CRDs get special tax breaks. If the recipient qualifies for a rollover, the CRD can be rolled over within three years from the distribution date. To the extent a CRD is not rolled over, the income is spread evenly over three consecutive years, starting with the distribution year. CRDs are exempt from the additional tax on early distributions. [CARES Act § 2202]

More information about CRDs is in Qs 7:42–7:48.

Q 4:13 What methods can be used to return IRA distributions that would, if not for the waiver, be the 2020 RMD?

Notices 2020-51 and 2020-50 allow three ways to return an IRA distribution that would have been a 2020 RMD but for the CARES waiver:

1. Repay all or part of it to the distributing IRA by August 31, 2020 (see Q 4:14).
2. Roll it over to any IRA, including a Roth IRA as a conversion, by August 31, 2020 (see Q 4:15).
3. Treat the distribution as a coronavirus-related distribution (CRD) and repay it to an IRA within three years (see Q 4:16).

Q 4:14 How does the first method work, and who can use it?

The first method—repayment to the distributing IRA by August 31, 2020—can be used by any IRA owner and by any beneficiary of an inherited IRA, including nonspouse beneficiaries. If the payment that would have been the 2020 RMD was paid to the trustee of a *see-through trust*, the trustee can repay it to the distributing IRA on behalf of the trust beneficiaries (who are treated as the IRA beneficiaries; see Q 4:71).

This is how Notice 2020-51, part III.C, treats the repayment:

- It is treated as a rollover for purposes of Code Section 408(d)(3). That allows the repaid distribution to be excluded from gross income.
- It is not treated as a rollover for purposes of Section 408(d)(3)(B). That is the rule which forbids more than one IRA-to-IRA rollover within a 12-month period. Not treating a repayment as a rollover for purposes of that rule means the repayment is not blocked if the individual did an IRA-to-IRA rollover in the past 12 months, and does not block an IRA-to-IRA rollover in the next 12 months. It also allows a person who receives RMDs in monthly installments to repay all of them to the IRA. Normally, only one installment can be rolled over, because each is treated as a separate distribution for purposes of the 12-month rule.
- The repayment is not treated as a rollover for purposes of Section 408(d)(3)(C), which prohibits 60-day rollovers by a nonspouse beneficiary. (Nonspouse beneficiaries must use a direct or trustee-to-trustee transfer to move amounts from one inherited IRA to another.) Apparently, calling this a *repayment* allows the IRS to avoid the statutory prohibition. [I.R.C. §§ 408(d)(3)(C)(ii), 402(c)(11), 402(f)(2)(A); Notice 2007-7, 2007-5 I.R.B. 395]

Q 4:15 Who can use the conversion method?

Notice 2020-51, Part III.C, extends the 60-day rollover deadline to August 31, 2020, for payments received in 2020 that would have been RMDs but for the CARES waiver. Since this is not a "repayment," the rollover contribution can be made to any IRA. If the payment was from a traditional, SEP, or SIMPLE

IRA, and it is contributed to a Roth IRA, the result is taxable conversion (see Q 3:102). Any IRA owner can use this method. So can a surviving spouse who is a designated beneficiary of the deceased spouse's IRA (the inherited IRA distribution would be converted to a Roth IRA in the surviving spouse's name). But a nonspouse beneficiary *cannot* use this method, because nonspouse beneficiaries of an inherited IRA are ineligible for 60-day rollovers and cannot convert inherited IRA assets. [Notice 2020-51, 2020-29 I.R.B. (June 23, 2020); I.R.C. §§ 408(d)(3)(C), 408A(c)(6)(A), 408A(e)]

The rollover is tax free, unless done as a conversion. [I.R.C. §§ 408(d)(3), 408A(c)(5)(B)]

Q 4:16 Who can use the third method and how does it work?

If the distribution that would be the 2020 RMD, but for the CARES waiver, is paid to a person who is a qualified individual for CRD purposes (see Q 4:12), and who is also eligible to do a rollover, he or she can treat the distribution as a CRD and roll it over within three years. The participant and the surviving spouse of a deceased participant are both eligible for rollovers, but not a nonspouse beneficiary (see Q 4:15).

Notice 2020-50, Part I.C, explicitly allows distributions that would otherwise be the 2020 RMD to be rolled over this way, provided the recipient is a qualified individual for CRD purposes. The notice states:

> . . . periodic payments and distributions that would have been required minimum distributions but for section 2203 of the CARES Act, received by a qualified individual from an eligible retirement plan on or after January 1, 2020, and before December 31, 2020, are permitted to be treated as coronavirus-related distributions and, therefore, permitted to be included in income ratably over 3 years.

[Notice 2020-50, 2020-28 I.R.B. 35]

Example. Dory receives her annual RMDs in monthly installments. She received payments, as usual, in January, February, and March of 2020, which turned out not to be RMDs. Her husband was diagnosed with COVID-19 in 2020 and temporarily quarantined, and he and Dory both lost income as a result. Dory is a qualified individual and can treat the payments as CRDs. That means she has three years to repay them to an IRA and have the repayment be treated as a tax-free rollover. Meanwhile, she includes the distributions ratably in income over three years. (See Qs 7:47, 7:18–7:20.)

Q 4:17 If tax was withheld or property was distributed, what can be returned?

If tax was withheld, the gross distribution that would have been an RMD but for the CARES waiver can be repaid by substituting replacement cash for the withheld tax. If property, rather than cash, was distributed, the same property must be returned to the IRA. [I.R.C. § 408(d)(3)(A)]

Mandatory Lifetime Distributions

Q 4:18 What are the lifetime distribution requirements?

During the life of a traditional, SEP, or SIMPLE IRA owner, distributions must meet two requirements—the minimum distribution requirement of Code Section 401(a)(9)(A) and the incidental benefit requirement of Section 401(a)(9)(G).

To satisfy the first requirement, minimum distributions must begin by the participant's RBD, continue at least annually through the year of death, and be calculated to last over the life expectancy of the participant, or over the joint life expectancies of the participant and a designated beneficiary. To satisfy the incidental benefit requirement, the death benefit and other nonretirement benefits must be *incidental* to the IRA's primary purpose, which is to provide retirement benefits. [Treas. Reg. § 1.401(a)(9)-2, Q&A-1]

There are two ways to meet these requirements. One is to distribute annual RMDs directly from the account. The method for calculating RMDs ensures that both the minimum distribution and incidental benefit requirements are met. [Treas. Reg. § 1.401(a)(9)-5, Q&A-1(a), Q&A-1(d)] The other is to use some or all of the IRA assets to purchase an annuity contract from an insurance company. Payments under the annuity contract must satisfy the minimum distribution requirement, and the death benefit must meet the incidental benefit requirement. [Treas. Reg. § 1.401(a)(9)-5, Q&A-1(e)]

See Qs 4:19–4:26 for how RMDs are calculated, and Qs 4:27–4:36 for the annuity requirements.

Lifetime RMDs

Q 4:19 What is the formula for calculating any lifetime RMD?

The RMD payable for any distribution calendar year during the life of a traditional, SEP, or SIMPLE IRA owner is calculated by dividing the *account value* by the *applicable distribution period*. The amount to be distributed never exceeds the account balance. [Treas. Reg. § 1.401(a)(9)-5, Q&A-1(a)]

Distributions made before a participant's first distribution calendar year (when the minimum distribution requirements first apply) do not count against the first RMD. [Treas. Reg. § 1.401(a)(9)-2, Q&A-6(a)]

Q 4:20 How are RMDs calculated if a participant has more than one IRA?

A separate RMD is calculated for each traditional, SEP, or SIMPLE IRA owned by the participant, and the amounts are combined to determine the total minimum distribution requirement for the year. The total can be withdrawn from any one or more of them. [Treas. Reg. § 1.401(a)(9)-8, Q&A-9, Q&A-2]

Q 4:21 What is the account value?

The account value (the numerator in the RMD calculation) is the account balance on December 31 of the prior calendar year, determined with the following adjustments. If there is more than IRA, the separate account value of each IRA is determined by applying the adjustments to the respective balance in that account. [Treas. Reg. § 1.401(a)(9)-5, Q&A-3]

1. The account balance is increased by the amount of any outstanding rollover contributions. A rollover contribution is outstanding if the distribution is made in one calendar year, but the contribution is not made until the next year. If a rollover of property is outstanding, the fair market value of the property on its actual contribution date (in the next year) is used to adjust the balance of the receiving IRA at the end of the distribution year. [Treas. Reg. § 1.401(a)(9)-5, Q&A-3(e)]

   Example. Mark owns a traditional IRA and a SEP IRA. He withdraws $10,000 from the traditional IRA on December 1, 2019 and rolls it over to the SEP IRA on January 15, 2020. The 2019 RMD for the traditional IRA is computed based on its December 31 account value, which does not include the $10,000 withdrawn earlier that month. To compute the 2019 RMD for the SEP IRA, its account value on December 31 ($500,000) is increased by the $10,000 outstanding rollover contribution, so the numerator used to calculate that RMD is $510,000.

2. To annuitize an IRA means to use some or all of the IRA assets to purchase an immediate individual retirement annuity. If part of an IRA is annuitized, RMDs are determined only for the part that is *not* annuitized. The immediate individual retirement annuity is treated as a separate account for purposes of the minimum distribution requirements, so it is excluded from the account value to calculate RMDs for the rest of the account. [Treas. Reg. § 1.401(a)(9)-8, Q&A-2(a)(3)]
3. If the IRA holds a qualifying longevity annuity contract (QLAC), that contract is also treated as a separate account and its value is excluded in order to determine RMDs for the rest of the account. A QLAC is a deferred annuity under which annuity payments do not commence by the RBD; the terms nonetheless satisfy the minimum distribution and incidental benefit requirements under an exception in the regulations. (See Q 4:33.) [Treas. Reg. § 1.401(a)(9)-5, Q&A-3(d); Treas. Reg. § 1.401(a)(9)-6, Q&A-17]
4. Any other type of annuity held in an IRA account is *not* treated as a separate account. To calculate the RMD payable from the IRA, the value of the annuity as of the end of the calendar year must be determined and included in the year-end account value for the IRA. The resulting RMD can be paid from the other IRA assets (or even from another traditional IRA).
5. There may not be a readily ascertainable fair market value for some assets in an IRA; nonetheless, their value is required to be included in the account value. The regulations provide a method for valuing an

annuity that is not treated as a separate account. Its value is the cash value of the contract, plus the actuarial present value of any additional benefits (with two exceptions) provided under the contract. The first disregarded additional benefit is the right to receive a payment on the annuitant's death that is not more than the aggregate premiums paid minus prior distributions under the contract. The second disregarded benefit is more complicated to describe, but in very general terms it is a benefit valued at not more than 20 percent of the contract's cash value. [Treas. Reg. § 1.401(a)(9)-6, Q&A-12(c)]

Q 4:22 What is the applicable distribution period?

For any distribution calendar year, the applicable distribution period (ADP) used to calculate a participant's lifetime RMD is the number of years of remaining life expectancy (RLE) determined using either the Uniform Lifetime Table or Joint and Last Survivor Table in the regulations. The ADP is redetermined each year. (New life expectancy tables have been issued; see Q 4:25.) In addition to these two tables, there is a single life table for eligible designated beneficiaries under the SECURE Act.

An IRA owner uses the Uniform Lifetime Table if any of the following is true in a distribution calendar year:

- The owner is *not* married,
- The owner is married, and the spouse is *not* the sole DB of the IRA, or
- The spouse is *not* more than 10 years younger than the owner.

But if, throughout the distribution calendar year, the IRA owner is married to a spouse who is more than 10 years younger than the owner, and at all times during the year the spouse is the sole designated beneficiary of the owner's IRA, the ADP for that year is the *longer* of the RLE under the Uniform Lifetime Table, or the RLE under the Joint and Last Survivor Table. [Treas. Reg. § 1.401(a)(9)-5, Q&A-4(b)(1)]

To be the "sole" beneficiary for purposes of computing the participant's lifetime RMDs, the spouse must be the only primary beneficiary of the participant's entire IRA at all times during the year. [Treas. Reg. § 1.401(a)(9)-5, Q&A-4(b)(1)]

Special rules apply if there is a change in the owner's marital status (see Q 4:23).

Q 4:23 How does a mid-year change in the owner's marital status affect the ADP?

If an IRA owner is married on January 1 to a spouse more than 10 years younger who is the sole designated beneficiary (DB) of the owner's IRA, and later that year either spouse dies or they divorce, here is what happens:

- *The IRA owner dies*. The "employee will not fail to have a spouse as the employee's sole beneficiary for that year merely because they are not married throughout that year." [Treas. Reg. § 1.401(a)(9)-5, Q&A-4(a)(2)] So, if the marriage continues until the death and the beneficiary designation does not change, the participant is treated as having been married to a spouse who is the sole DB of the participant's IRA.

Example 1. On January 1, 2020, Meryl and Connie are married, and Connie (who is 10 years younger) is the sole DB of Meryl's IRA. Meryl dies in August 2020. In the interim, they stayed married the entire time, and Meryl did not change the beneficiary designation. For 2020, Meryl is treated as married to a spouse more than 10 years younger who is her sole DB. The ADP for Meryl's last RMD (for 2020) is whichever RLE is longer—that determined under the Uniform Lifetime Table, or the Joint and Last Survivor Table.

- *The spouse dies*. The same rule applies. If the marriage is interrupted by the spouse's death and the spouse remained the sole DB until then, the IRA owner is treated as being married to a spouse who is the sole designated beneficiary of the IRA.

Example 2. The facts are the same, except that Connie is the spouse who dies in August 2020. Meryl's ADP for 2020 is determined the same way as in Example 1 (even if she designates a new DB later in 2020; see Example 4).

- *Either spouse dies or the parties divorce, and the IRA owner designates a new beneficiary later in the year.* "If an employee's spouse predeceases the employee, the spouse will not fail to be the employee's sole beneficiary for the distribution calendar year that includes the date of the spouse's death solely because, for the period remaining in that year after the spouse's death, someone other than the spouse is named as beneficiary." [Treas. Reg. § 1.401(a)(9)-5, Q&A-4(a)(2)] So, the facts after the predeceasing spouse's death do not change the distribution period for the year of death.

Example 3. On January 1, 2020, Anjali and Paul are married, and Paul, who is 11 years younger, is the sole DB of Anjali's IRA. They divorce in April 2020, and Anjali immediately designates her son as the new sole DB. Anjali uses the Uniform Lifetime Table to determine her 2020 ADP.

Example 4. On January 1, 2020, Omar and Eden are married, and Eden, who is 11 years younger, is the sole DB of Omar's IRA. Nothing changes until March 10, 2020, when Eden tragically dies in a car crash. Omar subsequently designates their daughter and son as joint beneficiaries of his IRA. For purposes of determining his 2020 ADP, Omar is treated as married all year to his more than 10-years-younger sole DB.

Example 5. The facts are the same as in Example 3, except that Omar remarries in November and designates his new spouse as sole DB of the IRA. Here, too, Omar is treated as married throughout 2020 to his more-than-10-years-younger sole DB. But not so for 2021. The ADP for 2021 will depend on his marital status, his new wife's age, and whether she remains his sole DB for the whole year.

Q 4:24 How is the RLE determined from the life expectancy tables?

The Uniform Lifetime has one column for the owner's age and another for the corresponding RLE. The ADP for any year is the RLE next to the owner's age to be attained (attained age) on the birthday during that year.

In the Joint and Last Survivor Table, the leftmost column shows the owner's age. The other columns correspond to the spouse's age. The RLE for any year is located where the row showing the owner's attained age intersects with the column showing the spouse's attained age.

Here are two examples. The tables are in Appendix B of IRS Publication 590-B, *Distributions from Individual Retirement Arrangements (IRAs)* 2020. That publication is reproduced as Appendix B to this book. The Uniform Lifetime Table is on page 62, and the Joint and Last Survivor Table begins on page 47, of Publication 590-B's Appendix B. As of March 1, 2021, Publication 590-B has not been revised to reflect the three new life expectancy tables.

> **Example 1**. Melanie's 75th birthday is in June 2020. She is not married. Her ADP for 2020 is 22.9 years, determined from the Uniform Lifetime Table (page 62 of Appendix B to Pub. 590-B). The value of her IRA on December 31, 2020 was $1 million. Melanie's 2020 RMD is $43,668 ($1,000,000 ÷ 22.9).

> **Example 2**. For all of 2020, Horace and Jenny are married, and Jenny is the sole DB of Horace's IRA. Horace will celebrate his 75th birthday, and Jenny her 63rd, during 2020. Horace's ADP for 2020 is the longer of 22.9 years (under the Uniform Lifetime Table) or 24.3 years (under the Joint and Last Survivor Table, at page 55). The value of his IRA on December 31, 2020 was $1 million. His RMD for 2020 is $41,152 ($1,000,000 ÷ 24.3).

Q 4:25 When were the new life expectancy tables released?

They were released on November 12, 2020 for use in calculating 2022 and later RMDs. The life expectancy tables in the current regulations were issued in 2003.

Transition to the new tables will be simple for IRA owners, because their ADPs are redetermined each year. For beneficiaries, the transition will be slightly more complicated, because some use a fixed ADP that is determined at the outset and subsequently adjusted. (For how beneficiaries will transition to the new Single Life Table, see Q 4:84.) [Prop. Treas. Reg. § 1.401(a)(9)(f)]

Q 4:26 What age is used to determine the first RMD?

For a traditional, SEP, or SIMPLE IRA owner who attains age 70½ after 2019, the first distribution calendar year (for which the first RMD is payable) is the calendar year that includes his/her 72nd birthday. [I.R.C. § 401(a)(9)(C), as amended by SECURE Act § 114] Those individuals use age 72 to determine the first ADP.

The rule was different for individuals who attained age 70½ before 2020. Their first distribution calendar year was the calendar year in which age 70½ was attained, and their age on the birthday in that year was used to determine the first ADP. So, that ADP could be based on age 70 or 71, depending on the part of the year in which they were born. [I.R.C. § 401(a)(9)(C), before amendment by SECURE Act § 114(a)]

An individual attains age 70½ on the date six calendar months after the 70th anniversary of his or her birth. [Treas. Reg. § 1.401(a)(9)-2, Q&A-3]

> **Example 1**. Abby was born on January 5, 1940. Her 70th birthday was on January 5, 2010, so she attained age 70½ six months later on June 5, 2010. That makes 2010 her first distribution calendar year. Abby's birthday in 2010 was her 70th, so she used age 70 to determine the first ADP.

> **Example 2**. Liam was born on August 10, 1945. His 70th birthday was on August 10, 2015, and he attained age 70½ on February 10, 2016. Liam's first distribution calendar year was 2016, and his birthday that year was his 71st. Liam used age 71 to determine the first ADP.

Annuity Payments

Q 4:27 What is an annuity?

An annuity is a contract under which the annuitant buys the issuer's promise to make a stream of periodic payments over an agreed term. Boiled down to the most basic terms, the annuitant pays for the contract with a lump sum or periodic payments, and the issuer's payments to the annuitant (annuity payments) can be fixed or variable (dependent on investment performance or an index). Payments under a deferred annuity do not begin until a later *annuity starting date*. A contract under which the annuity payments are not deferred (or were deferred but the annuity starting date has been reached) is an *immediate annuity*. The payment stream can last for a fixed term of years, the annuitant's life, or the joint lives of the annuitant and a beneficiary.

Q 4:28 What is a traditional individual retirement annuity?

An *individual retirement annuity* is an annuity contract issued by an insurance company that meets these requirements in Code Section 408(b):

- It cannot be transferable by the owner.
- Premiums under the contract cannot be fixed and cannot exceed the applicable IRA contribution limit for the year. (The premiums are treated as IRA contributions.) If premiums are refunded for any year, they must be applied, by the end of the succeeding calendar year, toward the payment of future premiums or to purchase additional benefits.

- The terms must include provisions similar to the minimum distribution rules that apply under Section 401(a)(9).
- The contract must satisfy the incidental benefit requirement of Section 401(a)(9)(G).
- The owner's entire interest must be nonforfeitable.

For more details, see the sample provisions in Q 2:29.

A qualifying longevity annuity contract (QLAC) is a type of traditional individual retirement annuity. (See Q 4:33.)

Q 4:29 What are the minimum distribution requirements for a traditional individual retirement annuity?

An individual retirement annuity has the minimum distribution rules built into the contract terms. As a result, every periodic payment under the contract is, in effect, an RMD. The contract must require the following:

1. *Distribution period.* Once they begin, payments must continue for the life of the annuitant (or lives of the annuitant and beneficiary), or for a period certain which is not longer than the annuitant's life expectancy (or the joint life expectancies of the annuitant and beneficiary). Life expectancy is determined for this purpose as of the year when annuity payments begin.
2. *Payment interval.* The annuity must be paid at least annually, and with a uniform interval between payments.
3. *Commencement date.* Annuity payments must begin by the annuitant's required beginning date (determined in the same way as for traditional IRAs).
4. *Payment amount.* Annuity payments must be level (non-increasing) in amount, with some exceptions (e.g., cost-of-living increases).
5. *Incidental benefit rule.* The death and other nonretirement benefits payable under the contract must be incidental to its primary purpose, which is to provide retirement income.

[I.R.C. § 401(a)(9); Treas. Reg. § 1.401(a)(9)-6]

Note. If the entire contract benefit is to be paid as a lump sum, the portion of the payment that is considered to be the RMD is calculated using rules provided in the regulations, and that amount cannot be rolled over to an IRA or other individual retirement annuity. [Treas. Reg. § 1.401(a)(9)-6, Q&A-1(d)]

Q 4:30 What death benefit can an individual retirement annuity provide?

An IRA cannot be invested in life insurance, but it can provide a death benefit subject to the incidental benefit requirement. For an individual retirement annuity to satisfy that requirement, it must be paid over the joint lives of the annuitant and the annuitant's spouse, if the spouse is the sole DB. If any other person is the beneficiary, then the benefits paid after the annuitant's death cannot exceed a particular percentage of the payments made to the annuitant. [I.R.C. §§ 408(a)(3), 401(a)(9)(G); Treas. Reg. § 1.401(a)(9)-6, Q&A-2]

A table in the regulations is used to identify the applicable percentage for death benefits paid to a nonspouse beneficiary. The applicable percentage depends on the "adjusted" age difference between the annuitant and the beneficiary. If the adjusted age difference is 10 years or less, the nonspouse beneficiary may receive 100 percent of the annuitant's payments. As the adjusted age difference increases, the applicable percentage declines. The lowest percentage (52 percent) applies if the adjusted age difference is 44 years or more. [Treas. Reg. § 1.401(a)(9)-6, Q&A-2]

The adjusted age difference is the number of years by which the annuitant is older than the nonspouse beneficiary, reduced by the difference between age 70 and the age the annuitant will attain in the year the annuity payments begin.

> **Example 1.** Rob wants to buy a traditional individual retirement annuity that would pay him $500 a month, starting in the year he attains age 70 and continuing for the rest of his life. After he dies, his daughter Ruth (the DB) would receive $350 per month for the rest of her life. Ruth will be age 40 (she is 30 years younger) when Rob starts receiving the annuity payments. Ruth's monthly payment would be 70 percent of Rob's, but for their adjusted age difference (30 years) the applicable percentage is only 60 percent. The proposed death benefit does not satisfy the incidental benefit rule, so the annuity cannot qualify as an individual retirement annuity.

> **Example 2.** The facts are the same except that the annuity payments will start in the year Rob reaches age 60. Since Rob will be 10 years younger than age 70 in the year the payments begin, the adjusted age difference between Rob and Ruth is 20 years. According to the table in the regulations, for an adjusted age difference of 20 years the applicable percentage is 73 percent. As Ruth's monthly benefit will be only 70 percent of Rob's, the death benefit now satisfies the incidental benefit rule.

Q 4:31 What is a Roth individual retirement annuity?

A Roth individual retirement annuity is similar to a traditional individual retirement annuity, except that the premiums cannot exceed the Roth IRA contribution limits, including the phaseout of contributions at higher income levels (see Q 3:77), and annuity payments are not required during the annuitant's lifetime. But the annuity payments after death must satisfy the minimum distribution and incidental benefit requirements. The annuity contract can incorporate the Roth IRA rules by reference, or include specific provisions that mirror them.

For sample provisions that satisfy the requirements for a Roth individual retirement annuity, see Q 2:31. The IRS also provides a model endorsement that can be used to incorporate Roth IRA provisions into an annuity contract. [IRS Form 5305-RB, *Roth Individual Retirement Annuity Endorsement*]

Qualifying Longevity Annuity Contracts

Q 4:32 What is a longevity contract?

A *longevity contract* is a fixed or variable annuity that does not enter the payout phase until the annuitant reaches a specified, advanced age (e.g., age 80). At that point, a regular stream of payments begins. Depending on the contract, payments may continue for a term of years, the life of the annuitant, or after the annuitant's death to a DB. The contract may also offer options, such as the right to surrender the contract for cash value.

Longevity contracts help mitigate the risk that a person living to very old age will run out of money.

Q 4:33 What is a qualifying longevity annuity contract (QLAC)?

A *qualifying longevity annuity contract* (QLAC) is a longevity annuity that qualifies as a traditional individual retirement annuity despite the fact that payments do not commence by the annuitant's RBD. A special rule in the regulations allows for this exception to the RBD requirement. [Treas. Reg. § 1.401(a)(9)-6, Q&A-17]

A QLAC must require the following:

1. *Annuity commencement by age 85.* Annuity payments must start by the first day of the month following the annuitant's 85th birthday.
2. *Fixed annuity payments.* The periodic payments must be fixed.
3. *Limit on contract premiums.* As of any premium date, the total contract premiums under *all* QLACs purchased by the annuitant cannot exceed the lesser of an inflation-adjusted dollar limit ($135,000 for 2021) or 25 percent of the value, as of the last valuation date in the prior calendar year, of all traditional IRAs that are *owned* by the annuitant. (Inherited IRAs do not count.) [Treas. Reg. § 1.401(a)(9)-6, Q&A-17(b); Notice 2020-79, 2020-46 I.R.B. 1014]
4. *No cash value or commutation option.* The contract cannot offer a commutation benefit, cash surrender value, or similar feature.
5. *Death benefit limitations.* Amounts paid after the annuitant's death must satisfy the incidental benefit requirement (i.e., be incidental to the contract's purpose of providing retirement income (see Q 4:34)).

[Treas. Reg. § 1.401(a)(9)-6, Q&A-17]

Q 4:34 What death benefit can a QLAC provide?

The death benefit and its commencement date depend on the identity of the DB and the contract terms.

If the annuitant's surviving spouse is the sole DB, the life annuity paid to the spouse can be up to 100 percent of the annuity that the annuitant receives.

Payments to the spouse can begin either by the end of the calendar year after the annuitant's death or (if the annuitant dies early) by the annuitant's starting date under the QLAC. Such a death benefit satisfies both the incidental benefit requirement and the post-death minimum distribution rules. [Treas. Reg. § 1.401(a)(9)-6, Q&A-17(c)(1)]

For any other beneficiary (including a surviving spouse who is not the sole DB), annuity payments must start by the end of the calendar year after the annuitant's death. The percentage of the annuitant's periodic payments that can be paid to the death beneficiary is determined using tables in the regulation. The greater the age difference between the annuitant and beneficiary, the lower the percentage that can be paid.

- If the death beneficiary cannot receive benefits under the contract before the annuity starting date, even if the annuitant dies earlier, the applicable table is in Q&A-2 of the regulation. This is the same table that is used for other annuities.
- If the death beneficiary can receive benefits under the contract before the annuity starting date, the applicable table is in Q&A-17(c)(2)(iii)(D).

This second table is more restrictive than the first. For example, if the age difference is 20 years and the beneficiary cannot receive the death benefit before the annuity starting date, even if the annuitant dies earlier, the beneficiary's payments can be up to 73 percent of the annuitant's. But if the contract allows the beneficiary to receive payments before the annuity starting date, only 25 percent of the annuitant's periodic payment can be paid to the beneficiary. [Treas. Reg. § 1.401(a)(9)-6, Q&A-17]

Q 4:35 How are minimum distributions calculated for the rest of the IRA before the QLAC is annuitized?

Until the QLAC becomes an immediate annuity, its value is excluded from the value of the IRA to determine the minimum distributions that must be paid. [Treas. Reg. § 1.401(a)(9)-5, Q&A-3]

Example. Sandra will use her traditional IRA to purchase a QLAC. The contract will provide a lifetime annuity after she reaches age 75, and when she dies it will continue paying benefits to her son, Tim. All contract premiums will be paid from funds within the IRA. When Sarah reaches age 72, she will start taking RMDs from the other assets in the IRA, and they will be calculated without regard to the value of the QLAC.

Q 4:36 Can a QLAC be converted to a Roth IRA?

A QLAC can be rolled over or converted to a Roth IRA, but the periodic annuity payments distributed under the QLAC cannot be converted, because they are minimum distributions. [T.D. 9673, Fed. Reg. Vol. 79, No. 127, p. 37643 (July 2, 2014); Treas. Reg. § 1.408-8, Q&A-12(e); Treas. Reg. § 1.401(a)(9)-6, Q&A-17(d)(3)]

Once a QLAC is converted to a Roth IRA, premiums paid for it are ignored for purposes of determining whether any other QLAC still held satisfies the dollar and percentage limits on premiums. [Treas. Reg. § 1.401(a)(9)-6, Q&A-17(d)(3)(ii)]

If a lump sum is distributed under a QLAC in lieu of periodic annuity payments, only the portion representing the minimum distribution currently payable cannot be converted to a Roth IRA.

Distribution for the Year of Death

Q 4:37 Who gets the participant's RMD for the year of death?

The RMD for the year of death must be paid to the beneficiary of the IRA to the extent it was not paid to the participant before the participant died. [Treas. Reg. § 1.401(a)(9)-5, Q&A-4(a)] It is included in the beneficiary's gross income.

Q 4:38 How is it calculated?

The RMD for the calendar year that includes the participant's death is calculated as if the participant had survived the entire year. So, the prior year-end account balance is divided by the ADP corresponding to the age that was (or would have been) attained on the participant's birthday in the year of death. The rules for deciding whether the Uniform Lifetime Table or the Joint and Last Survivor Table or Single Life Table is used also apply (see Q 4:22). [Treas. Reg. § 1.401(a)(9)-5, Q&A-4(a)]

Distributions After the Year of Death

Q 4:39 What determines how an IRA is distributed after the IRA owner dies?

The beneficiaries selected by the IRA owner determine how the IRA is distributed. A separate minimum distribution rule applies for each type of beneficiary. Some beneficiaries must take minimum distributions at least annually over a period based on life expectancy. Other beneficiaries do not have an annual distribution requirement, but must take a full distribution of the inherited benefit within a 5-year or 10-year period.

Q 4:40 Where are the new post-death distribution rules in amended Code Section 401(a)(9)?

Section 401 of the SECURE Act expanded Code Section 401(a)(9)(E) and added new Section 401(a)(9)(H). The expanded Section 401(a)(9)(E) defines a new category of beneficiaries (eligible designated beneficiaries, or EDBs). The old post-death distribution rules are in Section 401(a)(9)(B). New

Section 401(a)(9)(H) contains rules that modify the old rules in specific cases. Essentially, (H) provides instructions for how to read the rules in (B).

The amendments are effective with respect to participants who die after 2019. The old rules still apply, unmodified, for distributions with respect to participants who died before 2020, except in one case. If the participant died before 2020, and his or her designated beneficiary dies after 2019, the successor to the deceased beneficiary is subject to a special new rule.

Here is how the rest of this chapter is organized:

- First, there is an explanation of the steps to be taken after the IRA owner dies in order to identify beneficiaries, determine how their interest will be distributed, and make adjustments, if possible, to improve the distribution schedule for a beneficiary. How the distribution rules apply to each type of beneficiary is also explained in general terms. (See Qs 4:42–4:82.)
- Second, the specific distribution rule for every case, including the applicable RMD calculation method, is set out with respect to participant deaths after 2019 (Qs 4:83–4:86) and participant deaths before 2020 (Q 4:87).

Q 4:41 What is post-mortem distribution planning?

The minimum distribution requirements apply to beneficiaries starting with the calendar year (Year One) after the calendar year that includes the IRA owner's year of death (YOD). (See Qs 4:37–4:38 for the year-of-death requirements.) During the time between the IRA owner's death and the end of Year One, the regulations allow some actions to be taken that can influence the distribution period and perhaps achieve a better result for the beneficiaries. This process—figuring out whether the result can be improved and taking the actions to achieve it—is post-mortem distribution planning.

Here are the steps to be taken, and the deadlines that must be observed, in post-mortem distribution planning. The details are in the questions that follow.

1. Initial matters (Qs 4:42–4:43):
    a. The IRA should be immediately retitled to indicate its status as an inherited IRA.
    b. Determine whether the IRA owner was required to receive an RMD for the YOD. If yes, then to the extent the RMD was not paid to the owner it must be paid to the IRA beneficiary by December 31 of the YOD.
    c. Consider the special rights of the surviving spouse (SS) if he or she is a beneficiary. These rights do not have to be exercised immediately; the SS can do so at any time. But the SS should know about these rights at the outset.
2. Identify and sort the IRA beneficiaries (Qs 4:44–4:74) to determine whether any:
    a. Is a *designated beneficiary* (DB) or an *eligible designated beneficiary* (EDB);

b. Is not an individual;

c. Has an interest too remote to "count" for purposes of determining the distribution period;

d. Is a trust structured in a way that allows the trust beneficiary to be treated as the plan beneficiary.

3. Consider post-mortem strategies to move or remove a beneficiary (Qs 4:75–4:82). These include:

   a. Timely cashing out a beneficiary (distributing its entire interest) so it does not affect the distribution period for the other beneficiaries (by September 30 of Year One);

   b. Qualified disclaimer of a beneficiary's interest (or part of it) so the interest shifts to another beneficiary (within nine months after the owner's death); and

   c. Dividing the IRA into separate accounts so that (if possible) each is treated as a separate plan with its own distribution period, the surviving spouse of the IRA owner may be the sole beneficiary of his or her separate account, and investments may be optimized to suit each beneficiary's interest (by December 31 of Year One).

4. Apply the distribution rules (Qs 4:83–4:87):

   a. By December 31 of Year One, the minimum distribution method for the IRA or each separate account is set.

   b. If RMDs are payable, determine the applicable distribution period, calculate the first RMD, and pay it by December 31 of Year One.

   c. If the IRA or a separate account will be distributed under the 5-year or 10-year rule, beneficiaries should consider how and when to take their distributions.

Step One: Initial Matters

Q 4:42 How must the IRA be retitled after the owner dies?

When the owner dies, the IRA must be retitled to indicate that the owner is deceased and the IRA is payable to the beneficiary. The owner and beneficiary must be named (e.g., "IRA of Tom Smith, deceased, payable to John Smith as beneficiary").

Q 4:43 What else should be quickly addressed?

If the participant's surviving spouse is a designated beneficiary of the IRA, the spouse should be advised about his or her rights (see Q 4:54). Also, if minimum distribution had commenced to the participant, the YOD RMD must be paid to the beneficiary to the extent it was not already paid. The penalty for failing to withdraw an RMD is steep (50 percent; see Q 4:88). [I.R.C. § 4974(a)]

Step Two: Identify Beneficiaries

Q 4:44 Which beneficiaries must be taken into account for purposes of the minimum distribution rules?

Current and future (contingent) beneficiaries must be taken into account to determine the distribution period, but not beneficiaries whose only interest is as a mere successor. If the only way a contingent beneficiary can receive any of the participant's benefit is for another beneficiary to die, the contingent beneficiary is a *mere successor beneficiary*. The interest is too remote to be taken into account. Mere successors are disregarded for purposes of determining whether there is a DB and which DB has the shortest life expectancy. [Treas. Reg. § 1.401(a)(9)-5, Q&A-7(b), Q&A-7(c)]

Beneficiary Categories

Q 4:45 How are beneficiaries categorized for minimum distribution purposes?

The amended post-death distribution rules create a new category of beneficiary: the eligible designated beneficiary (EDB). [I.R.C. § 401(a)(9)(B)(ii)] Under the new rules, EDBs are the only designated beneficiaries (DBs) who may continue the tax-advantaged status of their inherited benefits for more than 10 years.

The types of beneficiaries that must be identified and sorted are:

- EDBs—a subset of DBs.
- DBs who are not EDBs—here called "simple" DBs, or SDBs.
- Non-DBs—these are beneficiaries who are not DBs, or any beneficiary of an IRA that is treated as not having a DB.
- Beneficiaries of certain trusts—the trust is the IRA beneficiary, but the characteristics of the trust cause the trust beneficiaries (not the trust) to be treated as the plan beneficiaries (for minimum distribution purposes).

Practice Pointer. The meaning of the term *designated beneficiary* does not change under the new rules, so beneficiary designations that were valid before the SECURE Act are still valid. In many cases, however, they will no longer work as intended, so all should be reviewed.

The *Designated Beneficiary*

Q 4:46 Who is a designated beneficiary?

Every individual or entity entitled to receive payments after the IRA owner dies is a beneficiary, but not every beneficiary is a *designated beneficiary* (DB). The post-death minimum distribution requirements greatly depend on whether the IRA has a DB.

A DB is an *individual* who is *designated* as a beneficiary *under the plan*. [I.R.C. § 401(a)(9)(E)] The first part of that definition means that only individuals can be DBs. (For the designation requirements, see Q 4:47.) For example, if an IRA is payable to the participant's estate, it does not have a DB.

In order to count as a DB under the minimum distribution rules, an individual must be a beneficiary on two dates: the decedent's date of death and the beneficiary determination date (which is September 30 of the year after the decedent's year of death). [Treas. Reg. § 1.401(a)(9)-4, Q&A-4(a)]

If any non-individual is an IRA beneficiary on the beneficiary determination date, the IRA is considered to have no DB, even if there are other beneficiaries who are individuals. [Treas. Reg. § 1.401(a)(9)-4, Q&A-3; Treas. Reg. § 1.401(a)(9)-4, Q&A-4] In some cases, it is possible to "remove" non-individual (or other) beneficiaries post-mortem in order to leave the IRA with a DB (see Q 4:75).

An IRA has no DB if it is payable to the participant's estate or charity. The same is generally true if the IRA is payable to a trust, but there are some exceptions. If an IRA is payable to a see-through trust, conduit trust for one DB, or applicable multi-beneficiary trust, the trust beneficiaries, rather than the trust, are treated as the plan beneficiaries, so if they are all individuals the IRA can have a DB. (See Qs 4:67–4:69.)

Q 4:47 What are the designation requirements?

In order to be "designated under the plan," a beneficiary must be identified in writing in the plan documents. The written designation can be in the IRA agreement itself, or in a separate "beneficiary designation" that is filed with the trustee and becomes part of the IRA agreement. The written designation names the individuals and/or entities who will be entitled to receive a portion of the benefit after the IRA owner dies. [Treas. Reg. § 1.401(a)(9)-4, Q&A-1] (In order to be a DB, the beneficiary must be *both* an individual *and* designated under the plan.)

In the beneficiary designation, an IRA owner should name both a *primary beneficiary* and a *contingent beneficiary*. The payments will go to the primary beneficiary after the IRA owner dies. But, if the primary beneficiary dies before the IRA owner and the IRA owner does not name a new primary beneficiary, the contingent beneficiary (if any) succeeds to the primary beneficiary's interest and receives the payments instead. [Treas. Reg. § 1.401(a)(9)-4, Q&A-4(c)]

The IRA owner may also name a *successor beneficiary*, who would receive payments from the IRA if the primary beneficiary survives the IRA owner but dies before the IRA is fully distributed. But, since the primary beneficiary may name his or her own beneficiary to succeed to the interest, the primary beneficiary may override the IRA owner's choice of a successor beneficiary. For true control over the ultimate disposition of an IRA, the owner must either name a trust as the IRA beneficiary, or establish the IRA itself in the form of a trust (a trusteed IRA) instead of as a custodial account.

Some IRA documents provide for a default beneficiary should the owner fail to designate one. But if an IRA owner dies without designating a beneficiary under the plan, the IRA is usually payable to his or her estate, so there is no DB.

Beneficiary designations are not filed with the IRS. A copy should be kept with the IRA owner's files.

Q 4:48 Who can change the designated beneficiary?

Only the participant can change his or her designated beneficiary, and the participant may do so at any time. To be effective, a change must be made in the official beneficiary designation. The most recent beneficiary designation overrides any prior ones.

As noted above, a beneficiary may also designate a beneficiary—but that does not alter the participant's designation.

Q 4:49 If a beneficiary is named in the beneficiary designation, but the decedent's will or a contract names a different beneficiary, which provision controls?

The beneficiary designation in the IRA contract is controlling. The fact that the benefit may pass to a particular individual, under a will or otherwise under state law, does not make that individual a DB. [Treas. Reg. § 1.401(a)(9)-4, Q&A-1]

The U.S. Supreme Court held in *Kennedy v. Plan Administrator for DuPont Savings and Investment Plan* [129 S. Ct. 165 (2009)] that a qualified plan administrator's duty under ERISA is to follow a participant's beneficiary designation, rather than a conflicting common-law contract. Relying on the DuPont decision, the Third Circuit Court of Appeals held that the settlement agreement in a couple's divorce, in which each spouse waived any interest in the other spouse's retirement plan and IRA, did not overcome the beneficiary designation made under the plan documents. The retirement plan benefits had to be paid to the ex-wife, although the decedent's estate could sue her to recover them. [Estate of Kensinger v. URL Pharma, Inc., 674 F.3d 131 (3d Cir. 2012)] An IRA trustee would be similarly required to honor the official beneficiary designation instead of a conflicting agreement.

Although a will does not control the identity of the DB, it can still be very important to the disposition of an IRA. For example, an IRA owner could designate a trust (such as a marital trust) as the beneficiary and establish the terms of the trust in the will.

Q 4:50 Must each beneficiary be specified by name?

No. The IRA owner may name a class of beneficiaries (such as "my children") who are identifiable at the time of his or her death. [Treas. Reg. § 1.401(a)(9)-4, Q&A-1] The members of a class are considered to be identifiable if, at the time the IRA owner dies, it is possible to identify the class member who has the shortest life expectancy. [Treas. Reg. § 1.401(a)(9)-4, Q&A-1]

Q 4:51 Can the DB of an inherited IRA be retroactively changed by agreement or court order?

No. Property transactions are governed by state law, so the beneficiary may assign IRA assets to another party, or a court may order an assignment (for example, to satisfy a community property interest). Such arrangements cannot create a new DB for tax purposes, however. The federal taxation of IRAs is not determined by state law, so if a court orders the assignment of an IRA to someone other than the DB, the assignment is treated for tax purposes as a distribution to the DB. [Priv. Ltr. Ruls. 201628004 (July 8, 2016), 201628005 (July 8, 2016), 201628006 (July 8, 2016), 201623001 (June 3, 2016)]

Since a new DB cannot be retroactively created by court order, it follows that a court order cannot change the payout period for an IRA. A court order may, however, change the identity of the IRA payee, and that can have important federal tax consequences. The IRS ruled privately on such a situation in 2017. [Priv. Ltr. Rul. 201706004 (Feb. 10, 2017)] The decedent named an inter vivos trust as his IRA beneficiary but never created the trust, and his will left the entire estate to his spouse. She asked the IRS to rule on how the IRA would be treated if the probate court reformed the beneficiary designation, substituting herself for the nonexistent trust. The IRS first ruled that the court order would not change the fact that the IRA had no DB. And second, it ruled that if an IRA is paid out under the 5-year rule, only payments made in the fifth year are RMDs (which cannot be rolled over). That meant the SS *could* roll over to her own IRA amounts distributed during the first four years.

Q 4:52 On what date are the DBs finally determined?

The individuals who are the participant's DBs are finally determined on September 30 of the calendar year after the calendar year that includes the participant's date of death (the *beneficiary determination date*). [Treas. Reg. § 1.401(a)(9)-4, Q&A-4(a)]

If an individual is a DB on the participant's date of death, but dies before the beneficiary determination date—and did not disclaim the interest—that person continues to be treated as a beneficiary for purposes of determining the distribution period, and the identity of the successor beneficiary (if any) is irrelevant. [Treas. Reg. § 1.401(a)(9)-4, Q&A-4(c)]

Eligible Designated Beneficiaries

Q 4:53 Who is an eligible designated beneficiary (EDB)?

This is the new category that only exists with respect to participant deaths after 2019. An EDB is a DB who is any of the following on the participant's date of death:

- The participant's surviving spouse,
- A minor child of the participant,
- Disabled (within the meaning of Code Section 72(m)(7)),

- A chronically ill individual (within the meaning of Code Section 7702B(c)(2), subject to an added certification requirement), or
- An individual not more than 10 years younger than the participant.

[I.R.C. § 401(a)(9)(E)(ii)(I) through (V), added by SECURE Act § 401]

Q 4:54 How are benefits distributed to the surviving spouse?

For any SS who is a DB of the participant, the distribution rules are the same no matter the year of the participant's death. The only difference is that, under the new distribution rules, the SS is classified as an EDB. Distributions are made to the SS under the life expectancy rule (that is, annual RMDs are required), and if the participant dies before the RBD, the RMDs do not begin until the year the participant would have attained age 72. [I.R.C. § 401(a)(9)(E)(ii)(I), 401(a)(9)(B)(i), 401(a)(9)(B)(iii), 401(a)(9)(B)(iv)(I)]

But the SS also has extremely valuable special rights. At any time, the SS may roll over his or her share of the inherited benefits to an IRA in the SS's name. Doing so would allow the SS to take RMDs under the lifetime rules (which are more favorable, unless the SS is younger than age 59½), designate his or her own EDB (who would receive benefits under the life expectancy rule after the SS dies), or convert the benefits to a Roth IRA. The SS can also roll them over to his or her own qualified plan account if the plan allows it. [I.R.C. § 408(d)(3)(C); Treas. Reg. § 1.408-8, Q&A-5(a)]

If the SS is the *sole beneficiary* of the decedent's IRA (or of that portion which is payable to the SS's separate account) and has the unlimited right to make withdrawals, the SS may also elect at any time to treat the inherited IRA (or portion) as his or her own. The election causes the SS to be treated as the IRA owner for all purposes. [Treas. Reg. § 1.401(a)(9)-8, Q&A-5]

The advantages and disadvantages of rolling over inherited benefits or treating them as the SS's own, and when it makes sense to do either, are discussed in chapter 10.

Q 4:55 What does it mean for the surviving spouse to be the *sole beneficiary* after the participant's death?

For purposes of determining minimum distributions after the participant's death, the time for determining whether the surviving spouse is the sole beneficiary of the participant's benefit is December 31 of the calendar year after the calendar year that includes the participant's death. The decedent's IRA may be divided into separate accounts on or before that date, and the test is whether the surviving spouse is the sole beneficiary of his or her separate account. [Treas. Reg. § 1.401(a)(9)-8, Q&A-2(a)(2)]

To be considered the sole beneficiary of his or her separate account, the SS must have the unlimited right to withdraw 100 percent of the benefits payable to it. Mere successor beneficiaries, who can only inherit if the spouse dies before withdrawing all the benefits, are ignored (see Qs 4:44, 4:69). [Treas. Reg. § 1.408A-2, Q&A-4]

Q 4:56 How are benefits distributed to other EDBs?

Other EDBs take distributions under the life expectancy rule, except for a minor child of the participant, who does so only until majority is reached. [I.R.C. § 401(a)(9)(H)(ii), 401(a)(9)(E)(iii)]

Q 4:57 Who is a *minor child* of the participant, and how is the child's interest distributed?

Code Section 401(a)(9)(E)(ii)(II) defines this EDB as "a child of the [participant] who has not reached majority (within the meaning of subparagraph (F))." Four points about this:

First, this is a temporary status. The child ceases to be an EDB on the date majority is reached. The year in which that occurs is the last year for which an RMD is paid. After that, annual payments are not required, but the entire interest must be distributed by the end of the calendar year that contains the 10th anniversary of the date when majority is reached (the 10-year rule). [I.R.C. § 401(a)(9)(E)(ii)(II), 401(a)(9)(E)(iii)]

Second, this EDB must be a child *of the participant*, which seems to mean a child by birth or adoption. A grandchild, stepchild (apparently), or other child does not qualify.

Third, this seems to go beyond merely looking at state law where the child resides to find the age of majority. Subparagraph (F) predates the SECURE Act and concerns payments made to the surviving spouse "upon such child reaching majority (or other designated event permitted under regulations)." The only regulation under Section 401(a)(9) that conceivably applies addresses payments under a defined benefit plan or annuity contract that are made to an employee's child until he or she reaches the age of majority. That regulation allows a child to be *treated* as having not reached the age of majority in two cases: (1) until age 26, for a child who has not completed a "specified course of education," or (2) as long as a child who is *disabled* (within the meaning of Code Section 72(m)(7); see Q 4:58) when majority is reached continues to be disabled. [I.R.C. § 401(a)(9)(F); Treas. Reg. § 1.401(a)(9)-6, Q&A-15]

Finally, using retirement funds to benefit young children is now more difficult than ever. A common approach under the old distribution rules was to leave the IRA to a conduit trust for each child and allow the trustee to stretch IRA payments over the child's life expectancy. Now, benefits left to a conduit trust will be withdrawn—and distributed to the child—much sooner, often before it is appropriate to cede control. The result is even worse if retirement benefits are left to a conduit trust for a grandchild (not an EDB), because the 10-year rule will apply immediately when the grandparent dies, not when the grandchild reaches majority. To maintain control over the assets for a longer period of time, it will now be necessary to leave the IRA to an accumulation trust—but that will be expensive, because a trust's income tax brackets are so compressed (for 2021, the highest marginal income tax rate, 37 percent, applies to trust income over $13,050). [Rev. Proc. 2020-45, 2020-46 I.R.B. 1016]

Q 4:58 What does it mean to be *disabled*?

A person is considered to be disabled for EDB purposes if he or she is unable to engage in any substantial gainful activity because of a medically determinable physical or mental impairment that is expected to result in death, or to be of long-continued and indefinite duration. There must exist documentary proof of the condition. (See Qs 5:29–5:30 for more details.) [I.R.C. §§ 401(a)(9)(E)(ii)(III), 72(m)(7)]

Q 4:59 Who is a *chronically ill individual*?

The EDB rule uses a modified version of the definition in Code Section 7702B (regarding long-term care insurance). For Section 401(a)(9) purposes, a *chronically ill individual* is one who has been certified, by a licensed health care practitioner within the previous 12 months, as one of the following:

1. The individual is unable to perform, without substantial assistance from another individual, at least two activities of daily living due to loss of functional capacity, and as of the certification date the period of such inability is indefinite or reasonably expected to be lengthy in nature. The activities of daily living are eating, toileting, transferring, bathing, dressing, and continence.
2. The individual has a level of disability like that described in paragraph 1.
3. The individual requires substantial supervision, due to severe cognitive impairment, for protection from threats to health and safety.

[I.R.C. §§ 401(a)(9)(E)(ii)(IV), 7702B(c)(2)]

Simple DBs

Q 4:60 What is the distribution rule for a Simple DB?

Under the rules that apply with respect to participant deaths after 2019, a DB who is not an EDB (a Simple DB) does not qualify for RMDs. Instead, the interest must be entirely distributed by the end of the calendar year that includes the 10th anniversary of the participant's death (the 10-year rule). [I.R.C. § 401(a)(9)(H)(i), 401(a)(9)(B)(ii)]

The rules for participant deaths before 2020 are more favorable. Any DB qualifies for RMDs, but the manner in which they are calculated depends on whether the participant died before or after the RBD. [I.R.C. § 401(a)(9)(B)(i), 401(a)(9)(B)(iii)]

Q 4:61 Where is the new distribution rule expressed in the amended Code Section 401(a)(9)?

Code Section 401(a)(9)(H)(i) says (emphasis added):

> *Except* in the case of a beneficiary who is *not* a *designated beneficiary*, subparagraph (B)(ii)... shall be applied by substituting "10 years" for "5 years", and... shall apply *whether or not* distributions of the employee's interests have begun in accordance with subparagraph (A).

"Subparagraph (B)(ii)" is the 5-year rule, under which the entire benefit must be distributed by the end of the calendar year including the fifth anniversary of the participant's death. It used to be the general rule for cases where the participant dies before the RBD. Distributions of the employee's interest are considered to "have begun" *on* the RBD. [Treas. Reg. § 1.401(a)(9)-3, Q&A-2; Treas. Reg. § 1.401(a)(9)-2, Q&A-6(a)]

So, when (B)(ii) is read in light of (H)(i), the result is that a Simple DB takes distributions under the 10-year rule, whether the participant dies before or after the RBD. [I.R.C. § 401(a)(9)(H)(i), 401(a)(9)(B)(ii)]

With respect to participants who died before 2020, a Simple DB is just a regular DB. Section 401(a)(9)(B)(iii) provides an exception to the general 5-year rule that allows DBs to take distributions under the life expectancy rule. So, with respect to participant deaths before 2020, a DB gets RMDs whether the participant died before or after the RBD. [I.R.C. § 401(a)(9)(B)(iii)]

Non-DBs

Q 4:62 What is a non-DB?

A non-DB (not a technical term) is a beneficiary that is not a DB. As explained in Q 4:46, there are two ways to be a non-DB:

- Only individuals can be DBs, so a beneficiary that is *not* an individual is a non-DB (e.g., the participant's estate).
- If any beneficiary of an IRA is not an individual, the IRA is determined to have no DB. In that case, distributions to every beneficiary are made under the rules for non-DBs.

Q 4:63 How are benefits distributed to a non-DB?

The distribution rules for non-DBs did not change for participant deaths after 2019. Code Section 401(a)(9)(H)(i), excerpted in Q 4:61, means that the 5-year rule is changed to a 10-year rule *only for beneficiaries who are DBs*. So, there is no change in how Section 401(a)(9)(B) applies to a non-DB. That means, regardless of the year when a participant dies:

- If the participant dies on or after the RBD, distributions are made to the non-DB under the life expectancy rule. [I.R.C. § 401(a)(B)(i)]
- If the participant dies before the RBD, distributions are made to the non-DB under the 5-year rule. [I.R.C. § 401(a)(B)(ii)]

After a Beneficiary Dies

Q 4:64 What happens if an EDB dies before receiving his or her entire interest?

For participant deaths after 2019, if an EDB survives the participant but dies before the interest is fully distributed, and the interest was directly held by the EDB (not through a trust), the remaining benefits are distributed to the successor beneficiary under the 10-year rule, as determined with respect to the EDB's death date. So, the benefits must be distributed to the successor by the end of the calendar year that includes the 10th anniversary of the *EDB's* death. [I.R.C. § 401(a)(9)(H)(iii)] The EDB's last RMD, for the year of death, is paid to the successor beneficiary to the extent it was not paid before the death, but after that there are no more RMDs.

The result is different for a minor-child EDB who reaches majority—at which point the 10-year rule applies—and dies before the end of that 10-year period. In that case, the successor steps into the 10-year period and takes the undistributed benefits by the end of it. A new 10-year period does not start. (See Q 4:57.) [I.R.C. § 401(a)(9)(H)(iii)]

With respect to participant deaths before 2020, an EDB is just a DB. Before the SECURE Act, if a beneficiary was a DB on the participant's date of death, and died before the interest was fully distributed, the distribution method did not change. The successor beneficiary stepped in to take the deceased DB's place. [Treas. Reg. § 1.401(a)(9)-5, Q&A-7(c)(2)]

But now, because of a special provision in the SECURE Act, there is a different result. If the participant died before 2020, then when applying the amendments to a DB of that participant who dies after 2019, the amendments "*shall apply to any beneficiary of such [DB]*" and the DB "*shall be treated as an eligible designated beneficiary*" for purposes of applying new Code Section 401(a)(9)(H)(ii). [SECURE Act § 401(b)(5)(A) (emphasis added)]

Code Section 401(a)(9)(H)(ii) is the rule that says only EDBs qualify to take RMDs. And, under Section 401(a)(9)(H)(iii), if the EDB dies before all benefits are paid, the 10-year rule applies to his or her successor. So, under the special rule, the successor to the participant's DB must take the remaining benefits under the 10-year rule. That means the remaining benefits must be fully distributed by the end of the calendar year that includes the 10th anniversary of the DB's death.

Q 4:65 What happens if the surviving spouse dies before receiving the entire interest?

If the SS dies before receiving the entire interest, the results are exactly the same as in Q 4:64, except in one case. A special rule applies if the participant died before the RBD and the SS is the sole designated beneficiary and dies before RMDs are required to begin (i.e., the SS dies before the year when the participant would have attained age 72). In that case, the SS is treated as the participant for purposes of determining how benefits are distributed to the SS's successor. The status of that successor, with respect to the SS, determines the applicable distribution method. So:

- If the participant died before 2020, and the SS designated his or her own DB, the successor takes the remaining benefits under the life expectancy rule, and a new distribution period is determined based on the DB's life expectancy. If the SS did not designate a DB, distributions to the successor are determined under the applicable non-DB rule.
- If the participant dies after 2019, and the SS names his or her own EDB, distributions to that EDB are made under the life expectancy rule, and a new distribution period is determined using the DB's life expectancy. But if the SS did not designate an EDB, distributions to the successor are made under the 10-year rule.

[I.R.C. § 401(a)(9)(B)(iv)(II), 401(a)(9)(H)(iii); Treas. Reg. § 1.401(a)(9)-3, Q&A-5; Treas. Reg. § 1.401(a)(9)-4, Q&A-4(b)]

Q 4:66 What happens if a Simple DB dies before all the benefits are distributed?

For participant deaths after 2019, the successor beneficiary steps into the Simple DB's 10-year period. The period does not change. For participant deaths *before* 2020, if the DB dies *after* 2019 and before all the benefits are distributed, the successor to the DB takes the remaining benefits under the 10-year rule and they must be fully distributed by the end of the calendar year that includes the 10th anniversary of the DB's death. (See Q 4:64.) [SECURE Act § 401(b)(5)(A); I.R.C. § 401(a)(9)(H)(ii)]

Trusts

Q 4:67 If benefits are payable to a trust, who is the plan beneficiary?

The general rule is that if benefits are payable to a trust, the trust is the plan beneficiary with respect to those benefits and, since only individuals can be DBs, minimum distributions to the trust are determined under the rules for non-DBs. But there are exceptions to this rule. Some trusts can be structured so that the trust beneficiaries (not the trust) are treated as the plan beneficiaries for purposes of the minimum distribution rules.

Of course, the trust beneficiaries do not actually become the plan beneficiaries. They are only treated as such in order to determine the minimum distribution requirements for the trust's share of the IRA. Payments are made from the IRA to the trust, and what happens to the funds after that depends on the terms of the trust and the authority of the trustee.

Q 4:68 If the trust beneficiaries are regarded as the plan beneficiaries, can a separate distribution period be achieved for each of them?

No, there can only be one distribution period for the entire trust. The separate accounts rule does not apply to trusts. [Treas. Reg. § 1.401(a)(9)-8, Q&A-2(a)(2)]

The trust may be divided into subtrusts (for example, to optimize the investment strategy for each trust beneficiary), but doing so does not change the minimum distribution requirements.

Q 4:69 Which trust beneficiaries count, and who must they be to get a life expectancy payout for the IRA?

To get a life expectancy payout for the IRA, two things must be true. First, the IRA owner must have "designated" the trust as a beneficiary under the plan—meaning the IRA owner must have actually named the trust as a beneficiary in the official designation under the plan. Second, the trust beneficiaries must all be EDBs. Otherwise, the IRA will have to be distributed within 10 years.

Current and future (contingent) beneficiaries must be taken into account to determine the distribution period, but not beneficiaries whose only interest is as a mere successor. Thus, if amounts are, or may be, accumulated for the remainder beneficiary's benefit during the life of the trust's income beneficiary, the remainder beneficiary and the income beneficiary must both be taken into account. A person who cannot be a beneficiary unless another beneficiary dies is a mere successor beneficiary, and does not count to determine which beneficiary has the shortest life expectancy. [Treas. Reg. § 1.401(a)(9)-5, Q&A-7(c)]

Example 1. Angel's traditional IRA beneficiary is an irrevocable trust that satisfies the see-through trust requirements. The terms of the trust require all current trust income to be distributed to Angel's surviving wife, Sharon. The trustee is authorized to pay additional amounts to Sharon from the trust corpus for purposes that are defined in the trust document. When Sharon dies, the balance of the trust will be paid to their daughter, Pamela (or to Pamela's children, if any, should Pamela die before Sharon). Sharon and Pamela both count as beneficiaries for RMD purposes. Sharon is the older of the two, so her (shorter) life expectancy is used to measure the distribution period for RMD calculations. The fact that a child of Pamela's may succeed to her interest, or that the benefit may be payable to Pamela's estate if she dies childless, is ignored.

Example 2. The facts are the same except that, when Sharon dies, the remainder of the trust must be distributed to a charitable organization of Sharon's choice. Since amounts are accumulated in the trust for the charity's benefit while Sharon is alive, the charity cannot be ignored. The IRA has no DB and must be distributed under the 5-year rule if Angel dies before his RBD.

Q 4:70 What kind of trust will result in this treatment?

If the participant's benefit is payable to a see-through trust, conduit trust for one beneficiary, or an applicable multi-beneficiary trust, the trust beneficiary (or beneficiaries) who "count" will be treated as the plan beneficiaries, and their identity will determine the minimum distribution requirements.

Q 4:71 What is a see-through trust?

A *see-through trust* (not a term used in the regulations) is a trust that meets four requirements. It must be valid under state law, irrevocable upon the participant's death, have beneficiaries who are all identifiable, and meet certain documentation requirements. [Treas. Reg. § 1.401(a)(9)-4, Q&A-5(b), Q&A-6]

A revocable inter vivos trust that becomes irrevocable, under the trust terms, upon the death of the participant/grantor can qualify as a see-through trust. So can an irrevocable testamentary trust that arises under the participant/grantor's will. [Treas. Reg. § 1.401(a)(9)-4, Q&A-5(b)(2)]

If the IRA is payable to a see-through trust, the trust beneficiaries are treated as the plan beneficiaries for minimum distribution purposes. If the beneficiary of a see-through trust is another see-through trust, the beneficiaries of the second see-through trust are treated as the plan beneficiaries for that purpose. [Treas. Reg. § 1.401(a)(9)-4, Q&A-5(a); Treas. Reg. § 1.401(a)(9)-4, Q&A-5(d)]

> **Note.** If the participant died before 2020 and his or her DB dies after 2019, it is not clear how the special rule in Code Section 401(a)(9)(B)(iv)(II) (see Q 4:65) would apply to a benefit payable to a see-through trust. That special rule applies if the participant dies before the RBD, and the SS who is the sole DB dies before RMDs are required to begin. In that case, the spouse is treated as the participant for purposes of determining distributions to his or her successor—and what is now relevant is whether the successor is an EDB *of the spouse*. For example, if the trust beneficiary who dies after 2019 (the SS) is treated as a DB only because of the see-through trust rules, is the trust beneficiary who succeeds to the deceased SS's interest a "DB of" the SS? Assets that the trust would have distributed to the SS ultimately end up in someone else's hands, but that is determined by the trust instrument and the trustee, and the SS will not have had the opportunity to name a beneficiary. Whether that person is a "beneficiary of" the DB is not clear.

Q 4:72 What is a conduit trust?

Retirement benefits paid to a conduit trust must be passed on to the trust beneficiaries in the same year. The trustee does not have discretion to hold such payments in trust. Since the benefits pass swiftly through, the residuary beneficiary is ignored as a "mere successor," because there is no opportunity to acquire the participant's benefits unless the primary beneficiary dies before emptying them from the plan. The conduit beneficiary is treated as the plan beneficiary in order to determine the distribution period for the benefits. [Treas. Reg. § 1.401(a)(9)-5, Q&A-7(c)(3), Example 2]

The example in the regulations demonstrates a trust with only one conduit beneficiary. The regulations do not address the question of whether a trust for more than one conduit beneficiary would be treated the same way. Given the uncertainty, a trust with two or more conduit beneficiaries should not be named as the IRA beneficiary.

Q 4:73 What is an accumulation trust?

If an IRA is payable to a trust and the receiving trustee is required, or has discretion, to hold any payment from the IRA within the trust for later disposition, the trust is an accumulation trust.

A see-through trust can be structured as an accumulation trust. For example, if the IRA is payable to a trust and the trust instrument directs "all income to my wife, remainder to my children upon her death," the children are not ignored, because principal is reserved for them. If the children are minors when the IRA owner dies, a life expectancy payout will be determined based on the beneficiary with the shortest remaining life expectancy (the surviving spouse). But when the first child reaches majority, the RMDs will cease and whatever remains in the IRA will have to be distributed to the trust within 10 years.

Q 4:74 What is an applicable multi-beneficiary trust?

An *applicable multi-beneficiary trust* is a trust that has more than one beneficiary, all of whom are EDBs and at least one of whom is a disabled or chronically ill EDB. The status of this trust is determined as of date the participant dies. [I.R.C. § 401(a)(9)(H)(v)]

There are two types of applicable multi-beneficiary trusts.

- Type I.
  - First, a Type I trust must, under the trust terms, "be divided immediately upon the death of the employee into *separate trusts for each beneficiary*." [I.R.C. § 401(a)(9)(H)(iv)(I) (emphasis added)]
  - That is clearly a statutory override of the separate accounts rule, which says that dividing a trust into separate accounts does not change the distribution period. There is no reason to expect that the override does away with the separate accounts rule altogether, but at least it does so for a Type I trust.
  - Second, "[section 401(a)(9)(H)(ii), which says that only EDBs can receive RMDs] *shall be applied separately with respect to the portion of the employee's interest that is payable to* any [disabled or chronically ill EDB]." [I.R.C. § 401(a)(9)(H)(iv) (emphasis added)]
  - It is not clear what that means for the Type I trust beneficiaries who are EDBs, but are not disabled or chronically ill. The wording suggests there might be a single distribution period for all the benefits allocated to their separate trusts. If it does mean that, and any of those

beneficiaries is a minor child EDB, then after he/she reaches majority all of their benefits would have to be distributed within the next 10 years.

- Type II.
  - While any disabled or chronically ill beneficiary of a Type II trust is alive, *no* other beneficiary can receive any benefit from the trust. [I.R.C. § 401(a)(9)(H)(iv)(II)]
  - That means only disabled or chronically ill beneficiaries of a Type II trust can be life beneficiaries.
  - Also, Section 401(a)(9)(B)(iii) (which is the *exception* to the *general* 10-year rule that applies when a participant dies before the RBD, and thus allows an EDB to get RMD treatment) "shall apply to the distribution of the employee's interest and any beneficiary who is not [a disabled or chronically ill EDB] shall be treated as a beneficiary of the eligible designated beneficiary upon the death of such eligible designated beneficiary." [I.R.C. § 401(a)(9)(H)(iv)(I)]
  - This is very convoluted. But what it means is that when the last disabled or chronically ill Type II trust beneficiary dies, the rest of the Type II trust beneficiaries cannot qualify for the exception to the 10-year rule. As a result, the IRA must be distributed to the trust within 10 years.
  - It is possible to structure a Type II trust as a conduit trust, so that all payments from the IRA that the trust receives are quickly distributed to the life beneficiaries (the disabled or chronically ill trust beneficiaries). So, in this case at least, a conduit trust *may* have more than one conduit beneficiary and still provide a life expectancy payout.

Step Three: Move or Remove a Beneficiary

Q 4:75 What post-mortem actions can influence the distribution period?

Cashouts, disclaimers, and division of the IRA into separate accounts can accomplish this. Two rules allow these actions to influence the distribution period.

First, the date on which it is finally determined whether there is a designated beneficiary (DB) for the participant's IRA is September 30 of the calendar year (Year One) after the calendar year that includes the participant's date of death (YOD). In order to be a DB, an individual must be designated as a beneficiary under the plan as of when the participant dies *and* must remain a beneficiary on the beneficiary determination date. That means a beneficiary (for example, a charitable entity that is not a DB) who is "removed" before the beneficiary determination date is not taken into account. There are two ways to do that. Either the beneficiary's entire interest can be paid ("cashed out"), or the beneficiary can disclaim the interest. (For a qualified disclaimer also to be effective for gift and estate tax purposes, it must be executed within nine months after the participant's death.) [Treas. Reg. § 1.401(a)(9)-4, Q&A-4(a)]

Second, if an IRA is divided into separate "accounts" by December 31 of Year One (the separate accounts deadline), and the accounts have different beneficiaries, each account is treated as a separate plan for minimum distribution purposes. Consequently, each separate account/plan has its own applicable distribution period (as if each beneficiary were "moved" to his or her own account). For example, if one EDB is much younger than another EDB, and a separate account can be established for each of them, RMDs will be paid to the younger EDB over his or her much longer remaining life expectancy. [Treas. Reg. § 1.401(a)(9)-8, Q&A-2(a)(2)]

Qualified Disclaimer

Q 4:76 What is a qualified disclaimer of a beneficiary's interest in an IRA?

Under the gift and estate tax rules, an individual can refuse a gift by making a qualified disclaimer. If that is done, the disclaimant is treated as having predeceased the person who made the gift, so it passes to someone else. An IRA beneficiary willing to forgo the inheritance can use a qualified disclaimer to refuse the retirement benefits.

To satisfy the requirements of Code Section 2518(a), a qualified disclaimer of retirement benefits must be:

0. in writing,
1. an irrevocable and unqualified refusal to accept the retirement benefits,
2. delivered to the IRA trustee within nine months after the IRA owner dies, and
3. made before the disclaimant has accepted the interest in the IRA or any of its benefits.

A properly disclaimed interest passes without direction either to the decedent's spouse or another individual. If retirement benefits are disclaimed, they pass to the contingent beneficiary.

Q 4:77 When must the qualified disclaimer be made for the disclaimant to be ignored as the DB?

The DBs are not determined until September 30 of the year after the IRA owner's year of death, but the disclaimant will still be a beneficiary on that date unless an effective disclaimer is made. So, a qualified disclaimer must be made within nine months after the IRA dies. [I.R.C. § 2518(a)]

Q 4:78 How will the disclaimer affect the distribution period?

The distribution period will be determined in the usual way, but taking the contingent beneficiary into account.

Example 1. Fern dies in 2018 (so the old distribution rules still apply), having designated her husband, Ralph, age 82, as her primary IRA beneficiary under the plan and her daughter Ellen, age 42, as her contingent IRA beneficiary. In the absence of a qualified disclaimer, Ralph must receive minimum distributions from the IRA beginning in 2019, based on an ADP of 16.3 years, determined under the Uniform Lifetime Table. If Ralph timely disclaims his interest in Fern's IRA, the IRA will pass to Ellen, and she can spread out RMDs over a longer ADP—40.7 years (the life expectancy of a 43-year-old beneficiary).

Example 2. The facts are the same, except that Fern dies in 2020. Ellen does not fit any EDB category, so if Ralph disclaims, the IRA will have to be distributed under the 10-year rule that applies to Simple DBs (see Q 4:60).

Example 3. Phil dies in 2020 at age 50. The primary DB is his wife, Shirley, and Phil's brother Joe (three years younger than Phil) is the contingent DB. Shirley is wealthy and does not need the IRA. She timely disclaims her interest in it, and, since Joe qualifies as an EDB (he is not more than 10 years younger than Phil), Joe not only gets the inherited IRA but also qualifies for a life expectancy payout.

Q 4:79 Can only part of the interest be disclaimed?

Yes. A beneficiary may elect to disclaim a specific pecuniary amount or a percentage of the IRA and claim ownership of the balance. The disclaimed portion will pass to the contingent beneficiary. The amount disclaimed and any income attributable to that amount must be segregated based on the fair market value of the assets on the date of the disclaimer or on a basis that fairly represents the value changes that have occurred between the IRA owner's date of death and the date of disclaimer. [Rev. Rul. 2005-36, 2005-1 C.B. 1368]

Q 4:80 Can the IRA be disclaimed after accepting the IRA owner's previously unpaid year-of-death RMD?

Yes. The RMD and the earnings on it to the date of the disclaimer can be segregated and excluded from the disclaimer. The following examples are based on Revenue Ruling 2005-36. [2005-1 C.B. 1368]

Example 1. Jack owned an IRA at the time of his death in January 2018. The primary beneficiary is his wife, Doris, and the contingent beneficiary is his daughter, Annette. Jack died before receiving his $10,000 RMD for 2018, so in February 2018 the IRA custodian pays the amount to Doris. Shortly afterward, Doris executes a valid disclaimer of the pecuniary amount equal to $60,000 plus whatever income was earned in respect of that amount after the date of Jack's death. The IRA's value was $200,000 at Jack's date of death, and $40,000 income was earned between that date and the date of the disclaimer. The income attributable to the $60,000 portion is $12,000 ($40,000 × ($60,000 ÷ $200,000)). Accordingly, $72,000 ($60,000 + $12,000) passes to Annette.

Example 2. The facts are the same as in Example 1, except that Doris validly disclaims 30 percent of her remaining interest in the principal and income of the IRA after both the $10,000 RMD for 2018 and the income attributable to it since Jack's death have been removed. The income attributable to the RMD is $2,000 ($40,000 × ($10,000 ÷ $200,000)). The disclaimed amount, which passes to Annette, is $68,400 (.30 × ($200,000 + $40,000 − $10,000 − $2,000)).

Example 3. The facts are the same as in Example 1, except that Doris validly disclaims the entire remaining balance in the IRA after a reduction by the income earned since Jack's death in respect of the RMD she received. The IRA custodian segregates $2,000 for Doris' account, and the balance of the IRA passes to Annette.

In a private letter ruling, the IRS allowed a posthumous disclaimer to be made on behalf of a beneficiary who died shortly after the owner. The IRA owner had been receiving RMDs by direct deposit into a joint bank account shared with his wife, the primary IRA beneficiary. The deposits continued after he died. The ruling allowed the executor of the surviving spouse's estate to make a partial disclaimer on her behalf, excluding the RMDs that had been deposited into the account after the husband's death, and their earnings to the date of the wife's death. [Priv. Ltr. Rul. 201125009 (June 24, 2011)]

Separate Accounts

Q 4:81 What goals might be accomplished by dividing an IRA into separate accounts?

If the beneficiaries hold their interests in the IRA outright (not through a trust), separate accounts:

- Can result in a separate distribution period for each IRA share allocated to a separate trust. If there are two beneficiaries, one an EDB and the other a Simple DB, that would allow the EDB to avoid distribution of the interest under the 10-year rule.
- May result in the participant's surviving spouse (SS) being treated as the sole beneficiary of his or her separate account. That would allow the SS to roll over the account to an IRA in his or her own name.

Example. Frank dies in 2018, and his traditional IRA is payable to his wife (40 percent) and son (60 percent). On September 30, 2019, they are determined to be the DBs of Frank's IRA. Frank's wife, Joan, wants to avoid the 10-year rule that would govern if the son (a Simple DB) and she were co-beneficiaries of the same account. The IRA is divided, and the trustee transfers her share into an IRA established in Joan's name.

[Treas. Reg. § 1.401(a)(9)-8, Q&A-2(a)(2)]

Q 4:82 When is it *not* possible to change the distribution period by establishing separate accounts?

The distribution period cannot be changed in the following circumstances:

- Establishing separate accounts cannot change the distribution period of an IRA that is payable to a trust, because the separate accounts rule does not apply to a trust. [Treas. Reg. § 1.401(a)(9)-8, Q&A-2(a)(2)]
- Dividing an IRA does not always achieve a life expectancy payout for all beneficiaries. For example, under the new rules, only an EDB gets to take RMDs.

Step Four: Apply the Distribution Rule

Q 4:83 If the applicable distribution rule requires annual RMDs, how will the distribution period be measured?

In all cases, the Single Life Table is used to determine the RLE of any individual for purposes of calculating RMDs payable to a beneficiary. The ADP is then determined based on the relevant RLE. If the surviving spouse is the sole beneficiary, the ADP is redetermined each year. Otherwise, the ADP is fixed and must be adjusted each year to get the divisor for the RMD calculation. [Treas. Reg. § 1.401(a)(9)-5, Q&A-6, Q&A-5(c)]

Q 4:84 What will be required for a beneficiary to start using the new Single Life Table?

If the SS is the sole DB, the transition will be easy—the RMD for 2022 (i.e., distribution calendar years beginning on or after December 31, 2021) will be calculated using the new Single Life Table (released on November 12, 2020; see Q 4:25). (The proposed regulations would have been effective for the RMD for 2021.) In other cases where RMDs are payable to a beneficiary and there is "fixed" ADP, it will have to be reset. First, a new ADP will be determined by going back in time to the age of the person whose RLE was used to set the ADP—only this time, the *new* Single Life Table will be used to determine a new ADP. Then, moving forward in time, one year will be subtracted from the ADP for each calendar year that has elapsed from that first year to 2022. The result will be the divisor used to calculate the 2022 RMD. [Treas. Reg. § 1.401(a)(9)(f)]

Rules for Participant Deaths After 2019

Q 4:85 How is the ADP measured and adjusted each year to determine RMDs?

This Q 4:85 explains how the ADP is initially measured, and then redetermined or adjusted each distribution calendar year in order to calculate RMDs, once the distribution rule that applies to the beneficiary is known. The applicable distribution rules for each type of beneficiary are in Q 4:86 (participant deaths after 2019) and Q 4:87 (participant deaths before 2020).

- The Single Life Table is always used to determine an individual's remaining life expectancy (RLE).
- With the release of the new Single Life Table on November 12, 2020, beneficiaries for which the ADP is fixed will have to reset it (see Q 4:84).
- If RMDs are payable and the applicable distribution period (ADP) is a *fixed period*, an applicable distribution period (ADP) is first determined. It is based on either the beneficiary's RLE (using the beneficiary's age on the birthday in the calendar year after the participant's death (Year One)), or the participant's RLE (using the age the participant would have attained on the birthday in the year of death (YOD) had death not occurred). The resulting ADP is adjusted to determine the divisor for calculating the RMD for any calendar year:
  - If the ADP is measured by the *beneficiary's* RLE (in Year One), that ADP is the divisor used to calculate the Year One RMD. For any subsequent calendar year, the ADP is reduced by one year for each calendar year that has elapsed since Year One.
  - If the ADP is measured by the *participant's* RLE (in the YOD), the divisor for any calendar year is the ADP reduced by one year for each calendar year that has elapsed since the YOD. (E.g., if the participant's RLE in the YOD is 14.8 years, the divisor for the Year One RMD is 13.8, the divisor for the next year is 12.8, and so on.)
- If the participant's surviving spouse (SS) is the sole DB of the IRA (or a separate account to which a portion of the IRA is payable), the ADP is redetermined for every calendar year. The distribution period is not fixed. (See Q 4:55 for what it means to be the sole DB of the IRA for this purpose.)
- Since there is no RBD for Roth IRAs, the rules that apply to traditional IRAs when the owner dies *before* the RBD also apply to Roth IRAs.

Q 4:86 What are the minimum distribution rules for each type of beneficiary, with respect to participant deaths after 2019?

1. When distributions to a beneficiary commence:
   a. If RMDs are payable to a beneficiary, the first RMD is payable for Year One.
      → Exception: If the SS is an EDB of the IRA (or the portion of it that is payable to the SS's separate account) and the participant died before the RBD, RMDs are not payable to the spouse until the calendar year in which the participant would have attained age 72 (see Q 4:54, first paragraph).

   b. If distributions are under the 5-year or 10-year rule, no distributions are required before the last year of the period. The balance of the account in the last year of the period *is* the RMD (see Q 4:9).
2. Distributions to a nonspouse eligible designated beneficiary, including the SS if *not* the sole beneficiary (EDB):

a. This category includes the SS, if the SS is *not* the sole DB for the IRA, or of a separate account to which a portion of the IRA is payable.

b. Every nonspouse EDB receives annual RMDs.

→ Exception: An EDB who is a minor child of the participant when the participant dies, and only qualifies as an EDB on that basis (for example, is not also disabled), stops being eligible to receive RMDs when majority is reached. The calendar year when that occurs is the last year for which an RMD is paid. After that, the 10-year rule applies. [I.R.C. § 401(a)(9); Treas. Reg. § 1.401(a)(9)-5, Q&A-5]

c. The ADP is a fixed period.

d. If the participant died *on or after* the required beginning date (RBD), the ADP is measured by the RLE of either the EDB or the participant, whichever is *longer*. [I.R.C. § 401(a)(9)(B)(i); Treas. Reg. § 1.401(a)(9)-5, Q&A-5(a), Q&A-5(c)(1), Q&A-5(c)(3), Q&A-6]

e. If the participant died *before* the RBD, or the plan is a Roth IRA, the ADP is measured by the EDB's RLE. [Treas. Reg. § 1.401(a)(9)-5, Q&A-5(b), Q&A-5(c)(1), Q&A-6; Treas. Reg. § 1.408A-6, Q&A-14]

3. Distributions to the SS who is the sole beneficiary of the IRA, or of a separate account to which a portion of the IRA is payable:

a. The ADP is not a fixed period. It is redetermined for each calendar year.

b. For any distribution calendar year, the ADP is measured by the RLE of either the SS or the participant, whichever is *longer*.

c. If the participant died *on or after* the RBD, the first RMD is payable to the SS for Year One. [I.R.C. § 401(a)(9)(H), 401(a)(9)(B)(i); Treas. Reg. § 1.401(a)(9)-5, Q&A-5(a), Q&A-5(c)(2), Q&A-6]

d. If the participant died *before* the RBD or the plan is a Roth IRA, RMDs do not start until the *later of* Year One, or the calendar year when the participant would have attained age 72 had death not occurred. [I.R.C. § 401(a)(9)(H)(ii), 401(a)(9)(B)(iii), 401(a)(9)(B)(iv)(I); Treas. Reg. § 1.401(a)(9)-3, Q&A-3(b); Treas. Reg. § 1.401(a)(9)-5, Q&A-5(b), Q&A-5(c)(2) (first sentence), Q&A-6]

4. Distributions to a "Simple" DB (SDB):

a. Benefits are distributed to an SDB under the 10-year rule. [I.R.C. § 401(a)(9)(H)(i), 401(a)(9)(B)(ii)]

5. Distributions after a beneficiary dies:

a. The beneficiary's last RMD (if any) is for the beneficiary's year of death. There is no change in how it is calculated. To the extent it was not paid before the death, it is paid to the successor beneficiary.

b. If any EDB dies, the successor beneficiary takes the remaining benefits under the 10-year rule—even if the successor is also an EDB. Full distribution is required by the end of the calendar year that includes the 10th anniversary of the beneficiary's death.

→ Exception: If the participant died *before* the RBD, and the SS is the sole DB and also dies before RMDs are required to begin (see paragraph 2.d), the SS is treated as the participant in order to determine distributions to the successor beneficiary. So, if the SS's DB (or other successor beneficiary) is an EDB *with respect to the surviving spouse*, the successor will take distributions under the RMD rules. Otherwise, the 10-year rule will apply to the successor. (This rule cannot apply a second time.) [I.R.C. § 401(a)(9)(B)(iv)(II); Treas. Reg. § 1.401(a)(9)-3, Q&A-5; Treas. Reg. § 1.401(a)(9)-4, Q&A-4(b)]

c. If the beneficiary who dies is an SDB, the successor beneficiary steps into the 10-year distribution period of the deceased SDB. The distribution period does not change.

6. Distributions to a non-DB (including any beneficiary if the IRA is treated as having no DB):
   a. If the participant died *on or after* the RBD, RMDs are payable. The ADP is a fixed period, measured by the participant's RLE. [I.R.C. § 401(a)(B)(ii); Treas. Reg. § 1.401(a)(9)-5, Q&A-5(a), Q&A-5(c)(3)]
   b. If the participant died *before* the RBD, the 5-year rule applies. [I.R.C. § 401(a)(9)(H)(i), 401(a)(9)(B)(iii)]
7. Distributions to a trust:
   a. If the trust is an applicable multi-beneficiary trust, see Q 4:74.
   b. If the trust is a see-through trust, see Qs 4:67–4:71.
   c. If the trust is a trust for one conduit beneficiary, see Qs 4:67–4:70 and Q 4:72.
   d. If the trust is none of those, the trust is a non-DB, and the distribution method is in paragraph 6, above.

Rules for Participant Deaths Before 2020

Q 4:87 What distribution rules apply with respect to participants who died before 2020?

The old post-death distribution rules still apply for distributions with respect to participants who died before 2020. The ADP is initially measured, and redetermined or adjusted each year to calculate RMDs, according to the rules in Q 4:85. Beneficiaries who receive a life expectancy payout must reset the ADP to reflect the new Single Life Table, released on November 12, 2020, effective for the 2022 distribution calendar year (see Q 4:84).

1. Distributions to a DB, including the SS if *not* the sole beneficiary:
   a. If the participant died *on or after* the RBD, RMDs are payable over a fixed period. The ADP is measured by the RLE of either the DB or the participant, whichever is *longer*. [I.R.C. § 401(a)(9)(A) (without regard to § 401(a)(9)(H), which does not apply to deaths before 2020); Treas. Reg. § 1.401(a)(9)-5, Q&A-5(a)(1), Q&A-5(c)(1)]

   b. If the participant died *before* the RBD, or the plan is a Roth IRA, RMDs are payable over a fixed period. The ADP is measured by the DB's RLE. [I.R.C. § 401(a)(9)(B)(iii) (without regard to § 401(a)(9)(H)); Treas. Reg. § 1.401(a)(9)-5, Q&A-5(b), Q&A-5(c)(1)]

2. Distributions to the SS who is the sole beneficiary of the IRA, or of a separate account to which a portion of the IRA is payable:

   a. If the participant died *on or after* the RBD, the ADP is not a fixed period; it is redetermined annually. For each distribution calendar year, the ADP is measured by the RLE of either the SS or the participant, whichever is *longer*. [I.R.C. § 401(a)(9)(A) (without regard to § 401(a)(9)(H)); Treas. Reg. § 1.401(a)(9)-5, Q&A-5(a)(1)]

   b. If the participant died *before* the RBD, or the plan is a Roth IRA, RMDs do not start until the *later of* Year One, or the calendar year when the participant would have attained age 72 had death not occurred. [I.R.C. § 401(a)(9)(B)(iii), 401(a)(9)(B)(iv)(I), both without regard to § 401(a)(9)(H); Treas. Reg. § 1.401(a)(9)-3, Q&A-3(b); Treas. Reg. § 1.401(a)(9)-5, Q&A-5(b), Q&A-5(c)(2), Q&A-6]

3. Distributions to a non-DB (including any beneficiary if the IRA is treated as having no DB):

   a. If the participant died *on or after* the RBD, see Q 4:86, paragraph 6.a.

   b. If the participant died *before* the RBD, see Q 4:86, paragraph 6.b.

4. Distributions after a beneficiary dies:

   a. Regarding the beneficiary's RMD for the year of death, see Q 4:86, paragraph 5.a.

   b. If a beneficiary was a DB when the participant died, and the DB dies *after 2019*, the 10-year rule applies to the DB's successor. (See Q 4:66.)

      → Exception: If the participant's sole DB is the SS, and the SS dies *after* 2019 and before RMDs are required to begin (before the year when the participant would have attained age 72), distributions will depend on *whether the SS designated his or her own EDB*. If the spouse did so, that EDB will take distributions under the life expectancy rule and a new ADP will be determined. Otherwise, the 10-year rule will apply, and the remaining benefit will have to be distributed by the end of the calendar year after the SS's year of death. (See Q 4:65.)

   c. If the beneficiary who dies is an SDB, the successor beneficiary steps into the 10-year distribution period of the deceased SDB. The distribution period does not change.

5. Distributions to a trust:

   a. There is no such thing as an applicable multi-beneficiary trust under the old rules.

   b. The analysis of whether a trust, or the trust beneficiaries, are treated as the plan beneficiaries is the same under old and new rules.

c. If the trust is treated as the plan beneficiary, it is a non-DB; see paragraphs 3.a and 3.b.

d. If the trust beneficiaries are treated as the plan beneficiaries, the applicable distribution rule depends on the identity of the trust beneficiaries. A very important difference between the old and new rules is that it used to be easier to provide a long stretch for children. Now, once a child reaches majority, the 10-year clock begins to tick.

Excess Accumulation Tax

Q 4:88 What penalty applies if a required distribution is not paid?

If the amounts distributed from a qualified retirement plan during a taxable year are "less than the required minimum distribution" for that year, an excise tax applies. The tax is 50 percent of the shortfall, and it is imposed on the payee. IRAs and individual retirement annuities are among the plans subject to the excise tax. [I.R.C. §§ 4974(a), 408(d)(6), 408(b)(3), 401(a)(9)]

The "required minimum distribution" for any year is:

- The RMD required to be paid for the calendar year. [Treas. Reg. § 54.4974-2, Q&A-1]
- Payments that must be distributed for the calendar year under the terms of an individual retirement annuity contract. [Treas. Reg. § 54.4974-2, Q&A-4(a)]
- The fifth-year balance of an IRA being distributed under the 5-year rule. (Payments are not required until the fifth year.) A similar rule will apply to distributions under the 10-year rule. [Treas. Reg. § 54.4974-1, Q&A-3(c), Q&A-5]
- A traditional, SEP, or SIMPLE IRA owner's first RMD, if it is not paid by the RBD. Payment is not required until then, so the penalty applies for the calendar year of the RBD. [Treas. Reg. § 54.4974-2, Q&A-6]

Q 4:89 How is the shortfall reported?

The payee reports the required payment and the actual payment, and calculates the excise tax, on Form 5329, Additional Taxes on Qualified Plans (Including IRAs) and Other Tax Favored Accounts. The result is entered as an additional tax on Schedule 2 to Form 1040. Form 5329 can be attached to the income tax return or filed on its own. [Instructions to Form 5329 (2020), p. 8]

The statute of limitations remains open for any tax year for which a return is not filed. With respect to the excise tax, the relevant "return" that must be filed is Form 5329. The filing of Form 1040 alone does not start the limitations period, because without Form 5329 the IRS cannot determine the excise tax liability. [Paschall v. Commissioner, 137 T.C. 8 (2011)]

Q 4:90 If the shortfall is still not paid in the succeeding year, is it subject to excise tax again?

Not if the succeeding year's minimum distribution is fully paid. The general rule stated in the regulations is that "the required minimum distribution for a calendar year is the required minimum distribution amount required to be distributed during the calendar year." [Treas. Reg. § 54.4974-2, Q&A-1] So, the excise tax is payable if the RMD for a calendar year is not paid, and the amount that should have been withdrawn, which is still in the account, is part of the year-end balance used to calculate the next year's RMD. If that RMD is paid, the excise tax does not apply.

It is not clear whether the excise tax can apply repeatedly with respect to an IRA being distributed under the 5-year rule. Elsewhere the regulation states: "If there is any remaining benefit with respect to an employee (or IRA owner) after the calendar year in which the entire remaining benefit is required to be distributed, *the required minimum distribution for each calendar year subsequent* to such calendar year *is the entire remaining benefit.*" [Treas. Reg. § 54.4974-2, Q&A-5 (emphasis added)] What happens if the IRA is not distributed until eight years after the participant's death? Is 50 percent of the balance payable for each of the fifth, sixth, and seventh years?

> **Note.** If an RMD is missed one year, no distribution in the succeeding year is an eligible rollover distribution until both the second year's RMD and the missed RMD have been paid. [Treas. Reg. 1.402(c), Q&A-7(a)] The excise tax does not seem to be governed by the same principle.

Q 4:91 Can the IRS waive or mitigate the penalty?

The IRS can waive or reduce the penalty on a showing that the shortfall is due to reasonable error and the payee is taking reasonable steps to remedy it. [I.R.C. § 4974(d)]

A taxpayer requests this relief by submitting Form 5329 in this manner:

- Show the required distribution and actual distribution on lines 52 and 53.
- On line 54, enter "RC" (reasonable cause) and the amount of the shortfall for which a waiver is requested, on the dotted line and in parentheses.
- Attach a statement of explanation.

[Instructions for Form 5329 (2020), p. 8]

Q 4:92 Is the penalty ever automatically waived?

The 50 percent penalty is automatically waived in one case: the IRA owner is deceased, the sole beneficiary is an individual who should have received (but did not) a post-death RMD under the life-expectancy rule, and instead the IRA is entirely distributed in accordance with the 5-year rule. [Treas. Reg. § 54.4974-2, Q&A-7(b)]

Chapter 5

Taxation of IRA Distributions

Most traditional IRA distributions are taxed under the annuity rules of the Code, which have two main consequences. First, those rules determine how basis (if any) is allocated, and thus how a distribution is taxed. Second, distributions made to a person younger than age 59½ ("early distributions") are subject to an additional tax unless an exception applies.

Roth IRA distributions are also generally taxed under the annuity rules, but with very different results.

Qualified distributions from a Roth IRA are always tax-free. To be qualified, distributions must satisfy a five-year holding period and be taken for a "qualified reason" (the recipient is age 59½ or older, a death beneficiary or the participant's estate, disabled, or using the distribution to purchase a first home). *Nonqualified* distributions are taxable only if earnings are distributed, and contributions are always distributed first. Nonqualified distributions may also be subject to additional tax.

Traditional IRA Distributions

General Rule

Q 5:1 How are distributions from a traditional IRA or individual retirement annuity taxed?

Distributions from a traditional IRA, and payments under a traditional individual retirement annuity contract, are includible in gross income when received and treated as ordinary income, not capital gains. [I.R.C. § 408(d)(1)] The amount distributed is the amount of cash and the fair market value of any property included in the distribution. [Treas. Reg. § 1.402(a)-1(a)(1)(iii)] Most IRA distributions are taxed according to the annuity rules in Code Section 72, which determine how basis is allocated and whether a 10 percent additional tax on "early" distributions (before age 59½) applies.

The taxable income from a distribution is charged to the person for whom the account is maintained. This is the IRA owner (participant) during his/her lifetime (subject to a state's community property laws) or the beneficiary for whom an inherited IRA is maintained. Distributions paid to a beneficiary are also subject to the rules of Section 691, which governs income in respect of a decedent (see Q 11:4).

Distributions from SEP and SIMPLE IRAs are also governed by the distribution rules in Section 408(d), although some special rules apply. [I.R.C. § 402(h)(3), 402(k)] The term "traditional IRA" also refers to a SEP or SIMPLE IRA, unless otherwise specified.

Q 5:2 What is a participant's basis in the IRA?

A participant acquires basis by making nondeductible contributions to the IRA or by rolling over after-tax amounts to it from another retirement plan. If excess contributions are not returned by the due date of the tax return for the contribution year, they remain in the IRA and add to the participant's basis. When a participant dies, the basis continues in the inherited IRA.

Q 5:3 How is basis allocated to an IRA distribution?

Code Section 72 treats basis amounts as "investment in the contract." The investment in the contract is prorated to each payment from the IRA to determine the taxable amount. In applying Section 72 to an IRA account, these rules apply:

- The account is treated as the contract.
- Nondeductible contributions are treated as the investment in the contract (basis).
- All traditional, SEP, and SIMPLE IRAs are treated as one IRA.
- All distributions from them during any year are treated as one distribution.
- The value of the contract, earnings on the contract, and investment in the contract are all determined as of the end of the calendar year. The value of the contract includes all distributions made during the calendar year.

[I.R.C. §§ 408(d)(1), 72(e)(5)(D)(iii), 72(e)(8)(B)]

Example. June is retired and owns a traditional IRA and a SEP IRA. In February 2020, she takes a $30,000 distribution from the SEP IRA. Before the distribution, the traditional IRA held $10,000 of nondeductible contributions (her only investment in the contract). On December 31, 2020, the value of the traditional IRA is $20,000, and the value of the SEP IRA is $50,000. For purposes of allocating basis to the February distribution, the value of the contract is $100,000 ($20,000 + $50,000 + $30,000). The $30,000 distribution represents 30 percent of the contract value, and takes with it 30 percent of the investment in the contract ($3,000). The rest of the distribution ($27,000) is included in June's gross income. At the start of 2021, her unrecovered basis in the IRAs in $7,000.

Distributions Not Taxed under the Annuity Rules

Q 5:4 What distributions from a traditional IRA are not taxed under the annuity rules of Code Section 72?

These traditional IRA distributions qualify for an exception to the general taxation rule of Code Section 408(d)(1):

- 60-day rollovers (see Q 5:5).
- Contributions returned under Section 408(d)(4) or 408(d)(5) (see Qs 5:7, 5:8).
- Some transfers incident to a divorce or marital separation (see Q 5:10).
- Qualified charitable distributions (see Q 5:12).
- Qualified health savings account funding distributions (see Q 5:17).

Rollover Distributions

Q 5:5 What is a 60-day rollover?

A 60-day rollover occurs when an IRA distribution is contributed to the same or another IRA, or a payment under an individual retirement annuity is contributed to the same or another individual retirement annuity (but not an endowment contract) within 60 days. Many restrictions apply, but if the transfer qualifies, the distribution is not taxable, and the annual contribution limit does not apply to the contribution. [I.R.C. § 408(d)(3)(A)(i), 408(a)(1)]

See chapter 6 for a full discussion of rollovers and the many restrictions that apply to them. Briefly, the principal restrictions on rollovers from one IRA to another are:

- Rollovers from a SIMPLE IRA can only be made to another SIMPLE IRA during the first two years of an individual's participation in an employer's SIMPLE plan. [I.R.C. § 408(d)(3)(G)]
- Only one 60-day rollover from one IRA to another is allowed within any 12-month period. This also applies to rollovers between individual retirement annuities. [I.R.C. § 408(d)(3)(B)]
- Required minimum distributions (RMDs; see chapter 4) cannot be rolled over. [I.R.C. §§ 408(d)(3)(E), 401(a)(9)]
- If property is distributed, only the exact property can be rolled over. The receiving IRA cannot accept cash or other property in substitution for distributed property. [I.R.C. §§ 408A(d)(3)(C), 408(d)(3)(A)]
- Part of a distribution can be rolled over, in which case only the retained amount is taxable subject to the normal basis allocation rules. [I.R.C. § 408(d)(3)(D)]
- After the participant dies, only his or her surviving spouse may use a 60-day rollover for transfers to or from the inherited IRA. Nonspouse beneficiaries are not eligible to do so. [I.R.C. § 408(d)(3)(C)(ii)]

Q 5:6 Can a 60-day rollover be used to convert amounts from a traditional IRA to a Roth IRA?

Yes. In that case, however, the traditional IRA distribution is taxable.

Roth IRAs can only accept *qualified rollover contributions*, and the 60-day rollover of a traditional IRA distribution qualifies as such. But, under the Roth IRA rules, special rules apply to a traditional IRA distribution that is rolled over (converted) to a Roth IRA:

- The traditional IRA distribution is taxed as though it were *not* a qualified rollover contribution. Consequently, the general rule applies, and the distribution is taxed under Code Section 72.
- However, the transfer is not subject to 10 percent additional tax under Section 72(t).
- Section 408(d)(3)(B), which allows only one IRA-to-IRA rollover within a 12-month period, does not apply to the transfer.

[I.R.C. §§ 408A(c)(5)(A), 408A(d)(3)(C), 408A(e)(1)(B), 408(d)(3)(A)]

Returned Contributions

Q 5:7 If contributions are returned before the filing date of the tax return for the contribution year, is the distribution taxable?

If a traditional IRA contribution is returned with its attributable net earnings (see Q 5:9) by the due date (including the automatic 6-month extension) of the tax return for the contribution year, the distribution is not taxed under the general rule, and the distribution is taxed under Code Section 61. For that purpose, the distributed contribution is treated as a deduction, and the earnings are treated as received in the taxable year for which the contribution was made. [I.R.C. § 408(d)(4), 408(d)(7)(B)]

This method can be used to make a *corrective distribution* of a contribution made during the tax year that would otherwise exceed the applicable limit in Code Section 219. If a corrective distribution is made, the original contribution is not deductible, and the 6 percent excess contribution penalty does not apply. [I.R.C. §§ 408(d)(7)(B), 4973] (Corrective distributions are discussed in Qs 3:133–3:136.)

The same method can also be used to withdraw a contribution made during the tax year that the participant wants to "undo." It *cannot* be used, however, to undo any conversion contribution made after 2017. [I.R.C. § 408A(d)(6)(B)]

Q 5:8 If a contribution is returned *after* the filing date of the tax return, how is the distribution taxed?

Under a special rule, a returned contribution is not taxable under the general rule if it is distributed after the extended due date of the tax return for the contribution year, and:

- The contribution did not exceed the "deductible amount" in Code Section 219(b)(1)(A) for the contribution year,
- No deduction was claimed for it, and
- The attributable net earnings are also distributed.

Using the same analysis as in Q 5:7, the distributed earnings are included in gross income, but not the returned contribution. [I.R.C. § 408(d)(5)]

The deductible amount in Section 219(b)(1)(A) is the applicable contribution limit for the year, determined without regard to the earned income requirement. So, this method can be used to return a contribution that was not supported by sufficient earned income but otherwise did not exceed the contribution limit that was in effect for the year. It can also be used to return a traditional IRA contribution made after age 70½ and for a contribution year before 2020. [Instructions for Form 8606, Nondeductible IRAs (2019), p. 5]

Q 5:9 How does one determine the net income attributable to a returned contribution?

The same method is used that applies when a contribution is recharacterized. To compute the attributable net earnings, the returned contribution is multiplied by this fraction: (ACB – AOB) ÷ AOB, where:

- The calculation only takes into account the IRA from which the contribution and earnings are being distributed,
- The computation period opens on the date the excess contribution was made and closes on the date it is distributed with the attributable net earnings,
- ACB is the adjusted closing balance, which is the fair market value of the IRA on the distribution date, plus distributions and transfers made *from* the IRA during the computation period, and
- AOB is the adjusted opening balance, which is the fair market value of the IRA on the date of the contribution, increased by contributions and transfers made *to* the IRA during the computation period.

(See Qs 3:117, 8:111.) [Treas. Reg. § 1.408-11(a)(1); Treas. Reg. § 1.408-11(c)(3); Treas. Reg. § 1.408A-5, Q&A-2(c)(4)]

Marital Transfers

Q 5:10 If all or part of an IRA is transferred to the participant's spouse or former spouse, is the transfer taxable?

The transfer to the spouse or former spouse is not taxable if it is made under a decree of divorce or separate maintenance, or under a written instrument that is incident to such a decree. That is the only way to achieve a tax-free division of an IRA or individual retirement in a divorce. The provisions of the decree or written instrument must be strictly observed. [I.R.C. §§ 408(d)(6), 121(d)(3)(C)(i)]

Q 5:11 What is the result for the receiving spouse?

The transferred interest is treated as belonging to the receiving spouse when the transfer is made. So, the receiving spouse is not taxed on the transfer, and the contributions previously made still count as an investment in the contract. Afterwards, the IRA is considered to be maintained for his or her benefit, so the receiving spouse may contribute to it. [I.R.C. § 408(d)(6)]

Charitable Distributions

Q 5:12 What is a qualified charitable distribution?

A qualified charitable distribution (QCD) is an otherwise taxable distribution from a traditional IRA (but not an ongoing SEP or SIMPLE IRA) that is made directly to a charity by an individual who is age 70½ or older on the distribution date. Distributions up to $100,000 in the aggregate can be donated this way for any taxable year. QCDs are not taxed under the general rule of Code Section 408(d)(1). Instead, they are excluded from gross income subject to an adjustment for contributions made after age 70½ (see Q 5:13). They also count toward satisfying an individual's RMD requirement for the year. [I.R.C. § 408(d)(8)]

The IRA trustee must transfer the QCD directly to the trustee of either a charity qualified under Code Section 170(b)(1)(A) (excluding private foundations) or a donor-advised fund under Code Section 4966(d)(2). The donation must otherwise qualify for a charitable deduction (without regard to the percentage limitations), and the deduction may not also be claimed. [I.R.C. § 408(d)(8)(C), 408(d)(8)(E)]

Q 5:13 How is the excludable amount adjusted for contributions made when an individual is age 70½ or older?

Traditional IRA contributions made for tax years that end on or after the date an individual attains age 70½ are not excluded from income when later distributed in a QCD. [I.R.C. § 408(d)(8)(A)]

The adjustment is in Code Section 408(d)(8)(A), under which the amount that would otherwise (but for the adjustment) be excluded from income is reduced (but not below zero) by the excess of:

- The aggregate deductions *allowed* under Code Section 219 for all taxable years ending on or after the date the IRA owner attains age 70½, over
- The aggregate reductions made under this rule for all prior taxable years. [I.R.C. § 408(d)(8)(A)]

Q 5:14 If an IRA holds nondeductible contributions, are they allocated to a QCD?

No. All of an individual's traditional IRAs are treated as a single IRA, and—under a special allocation rule—amounts that would be taxable when distributed (but for the QCD rule) are allocated first to the distribution. They are the only amounts included in the QCD. [I.R.C. § 408(d)(8)(D)]

> **Example**. At the start of 2019, Toby (age 71) has a traditional IRA worth $100,000 that holds $10,000 of nondeductible contributions. He wants to donate $15,000 (his 2019 RMD plus additional assets) from the IRA to a charitable organization. The IRA custodian follows Toby's instructions and directly transfers $15,000 to the charity's trustee. Toby has satisfied his RMD requirement for 2019, and after the QCD, the traditional IRA still holds $10,000 of nondeductible contributions.

Q 5:15 Can a QCD be made from an inherited IRA?

Yes, if the beneficiary for whom the IRA is maintained is age 70½ or older on the distribution date. [Notice 2007-7, 2007-1 C.B. 395, Q&A-37]

Q 5:16 What is an ongoing SEP IRA or SIMPLE IRA?

A SEP IRA or a SIMPLE IRA is treated as ongoing if it is maintained under a SEP or SIMPLE plan, and the employer makes a contribution to the IRA for the plan year ending with or within the IRA owner's taxable year for the QCD. [Notice 2007-7, 2007-1 C.B. 395, Q&A-36]

Qualified HSA Funding Distribution

Q 5:17 What is a qualified health savings account funding distribution?

A qualified health savings account (HSA) funding distribution is a one-time distribution from a traditional or Roth IRA (including an inherited IRA) that is rolled over to an HSA. The distribution is excluded from the individual's income. Various restrictions apply, including that the distribution cannot exceed the applicable HSA contribution limit for the year, and it must be carried out as a trustee-to-trustee transfer. [I.R.C. § 408(d)(9)]

Deemed Distributions

Investment in Collectibles

Q 5:18 What happens if IRA assets are used to purchase a collectible item?

IRAs may not be invested in "collectibles," so if any such item is purchased by an IRA, the cost of the item is deemed distributed, and the distribution is taxable under the general rule of Code Section 72 [I.R.C. § 408(m)(1), 408(d)(1)]

Q 5:19 What are collectibles?

Collectibles include works of art, rugs, antiques, metals, gems, stamps, coins, alcoholic beverages, and anything else that may be specified in the Treasury regulations. An exception is allowed for certain coins and bullion that meet certain standards of fineness and are held in the physical possession of the IRA trustee. [I.R.C. § 408(m)(2), 408(m)(3)]

Investment in an Endowment Contract

Q 5:20 How does a deemed distribution result from the purchase of an endowment contract using IRA assets?

If IRA assets are used to purchase an endowment contract that benefits the IRA owner:

- The investment is treated as a rollover to the extent the assets are *not* used to purchase life insurance,
- But assets attributable to the purchase of life, health, accident, or other insurance are deemed to be distributed, and the distribution is taxable under Code Section 72.

[I.R.C. § 408(e)(5), 408(d)(1)]

Loan or Pledge

Q 5:21 What deemed distribution occurs if an individual uses an individual retirement annuity contract to obtain a loan?

If an individual borrows under an individual retirement annuity contract or uses the contract to borrow money, the contract ceases to qualify as an individual retirement annuity as of the first day of the calendar year. The fair market value of the contract is deemed distributed on that day, and the distribution is taxable under Code Section 72. [I.R.C. § 408(e)(3), 408(d)(1)]

Q 5:22 What happens if an IRA is pledged as security for a loan?

If all or part of an IRA is pledged as security for a loan, the part that is pledged is deemed to be distributed on the pledge date. The distribution is taxable under Code Section 72. [I.R.C. § 408(e)(4), 408(d)(1)]

Prohibited Transactions

Q 5:23 What deemed distribution results from a prohibited transaction involving an individual's IRA?

If an individual engages in a transaction that is prohibited under Code Section 4975 with respect to his or her IRA, the account ceases to be an IRA as of the first day of the taxable year. A distribution equal to the fair market value of the IRA on such first day is deemed to be distributed, and it is taxable under Code Section 72. [I.R.C. § 408(e)(2), 408(d)(1)]

Additional Tax on Early Distributions

Q 5:24 What is the additional tax on early distributions?

Code Section 72(t) imposes an additional tax on distributions from a "qualified retirement plan," as defined in Section 4974(c), made to a person younger than age 59½. Qualified retirement plans for this purpose include IRAs and individual retirement annuities. The additional tax is 10 percent of the taxable amount distributed, or 25 percent of such amount if the distribution is made from a SIMPLE IRA during the first two years of participation in the employer's SIMPLE plan. [I.R.C. §§ 72(t)(1), 72(t)(6), 4974(c)(4), 4974(c)(5)] Notice 2021-21 automatically postponed to May 17, 2021 the time for reporting and payment of the 10 percent excise tax under Code Section 72(t).

> **Example**. Trevor, age 30, withdraws $2,000 from his traditional IRA. He has made only deductible contributions, so Trevor has no basis, and the entire distribution is taxable. Unless an exception applies, Trevor owes $200 of additional tax.

Q 5:25 Does the additional tax apply to a distribution that is rolled over within 60 days?

No. The additional tax applies to the part of a distribution that is includible in gross income. [I.R.C. § 72(t)] If a distribution is rolled over to the same type of IRA within 60 days, none of it is taxable (see Q 5:6). If a traditional IRA distribution is rolled over (converted) to a Roth IRA, the distribution is taxable, but the penalty does not apply. [I.R.C. § 408A(d)(3)(A)(ii)]

Q 5:26 What are the exceptions to the additional tax?

The following exceptions to the early distribution penalty apply to IRA distributions:

1. *Attainment of age 59½*. The distribution is made on or after the date on which the IRA owner attains age 59½. [I.R.C. § 72(t)(2)(A)(i)] (See Q 5:27.)
2. *Death*. The distribution is made to a beneficiary or to the IRA owner's estate on or after the death of the IRA owner. [I.R.C. § 72(t)(2)(A)(ii)] (See Q 5:28.)
3. *Disability*. The distribution is attributable to the IRA owner's becoming *disabled* (within the meaning of Code Section 72(m)(7)). [I.R.C. § 72(t)(2)(A)(iii)] (See Qs 5:29–5:30.)
4. *Substantially equal periodic payments*. The distribution is part of a series of substantially equal periodic payments made at least annually for the life (or life expectancy) of the IRA owner or the joint lives (or joint life expectancies) of the IRA owner and a designated beneficiary. [I.R.C. § 72(t)(2)(A)(iv)] (See Qs 5:31–5:41.)
5. *Internal Revenue Service (IRS) levy*. The distribution is due to an IRS levy on the IRA. [I.R.C. § 72(t)(2)(A)(vii)]

6. *Medical expenses in excess of the deductible threshold.* The distribution is used to pay the tax-deductible portion of unreimbursed medical expenses, determined without regard to whether an individual itemizes deductions. For 2020 and thereafter, unreimbursed medical expenses are deductible to the extent they exceed 7.5 percent of AGI. [I.R.C. § 72(t)(2)(B); TCJA § 11027(a)] (See Qs 5:42, 5:43.)
7. *Qualified higher education expenses.* The distribution is used for *qualified higher education expenses.* [I.R.C. § 72(t)(2)(E)] (See Qs 5:44–5:48.)
8. *First-time home purchase.* The distribution is a *qualified first-time homebuyer distribution* (also referred to as a qualified special-purpose distribution). [I.R.C. § 72(t)(2)(F)] (See Qs 5:50–5:62.)
9. *Unemployed individual's purchase of health insurance.* The distribution (to the extent of *qualifying health insurance premiums* paid during the year) is made after termination of employment and after the IRA owner has received unemployment compensation for 12 consecutive weeks under any federal or state unemployment compensation law by reason of such termination. [*See* I.R.C. § 72(t)(2)(D) for additional requirements.]
10. *Qualified reservist distribution.* The distribution is to certain military reservists called to active duty. [I.R.C. § 72(t)(2)(G)] (See Q 5:49.)
11. *Qualified health savings account funding distribution.* The distribution is a one-time qualifying withdrawal of IRA funds for rollover to a health savings account. [I.R.C. § 408(d)(9)(E)]
12. *Qualified birth or adoption distribution.* This is a new exception. [I.R.C. § 72(t)(2)(H), added by the SECURE Act § 113] (See Qs 5:63–5:65.)

Age 59½

Q 5:27 Is every IRA distribution to a person older than age 59½ exempt from the additional tax?

Yes. The additional tax does not apply to a distribution made on or after the date the distributee attains age 59½. Although the additional tax is usually referred to as a tax on "early" distributions, attainment of age 59½ is actually the first exception listed. [I.R.C. § 72(t)(2)(A)(i)]

By extrapolation from the minimum distribution rules, age 59½ is attained on the date that is six months after the 59th anniversary of an individual's birth. [Treas. Reg. § 1.401(a)(9)-2, Q&A-3]

Death

Q 5:28 Is every IRA distribution made to a beneficiary or the estate after the IRA owner dies exempt from additional tax?

The exception applies to any distribution made to a *beneficiary* or the participant's estate. But if the participant's surviving spouse is the sole beneficiary of the IRA, he or she has the right to take ownership of the IRA—by either retitling it in the spouse's name or rolling it over to another IRA that the spouse owns. A spouse who does so is then treated as the participant, not a beneficiary, and in that case, the beneficiary exception does not apply. So, if the surviving spouse younger than age 59½ takes ownership of the inherited IRA, the 10 percent additional tax will apply to distributions unless another exception applies. [I.R.C. §§ 72(t)(2), 408(d)(3)(C); Treas. Reg. § 1.408-8, Q&A-5(a); Treas. Reg. § 1.408A-2, Q&A-4; Ozimkoski v. Commissioner, T.C. Memo. 2016-228 (2016)]

Disability

Q 5:29 What is the disability exception to the additional tax on early distributions?

The 10 percent additional tax does not apply to IRA distributions that are "attributable to the employee's being disabled within the meaning of [Code Section 72(m)(7)] . . ." [I.R.C. § 72(t)(2)(A)(iii)] For Code Section 72 purposes, being disabled means having a medically determinable physical or mental impairment that both:

- Leaves one unable to engage in any substantial gainful activity, and
- Is expected to result in death or be of long-continued and indefinite duration.

[I.R.C. § 72(m)(7)]

A *remediable* impairment is not a disability. An impairment is remediable if it can be diminished, safely, and with reasonable effort, enough so that it no longer prevents engagement in the customary (or a comparable) substantial gainful activity. [Treas. Reg. § 1.72-17A(f)(4)] For example, severe compulsive behavior induced as a side effect of prescribed medication, which developed into a serious gambling addiction, took over the patient's life, and nearly destroyed her business, was held to be a remediable impairment because the behavior ceased when she finally stopped the medication with her doctor's help. The early IRA distribution she took during the compulsive phase did not qualify for the disability exception. [Gillette v. Commissioner, T.C. Memo. 2018-185 (2018)]

Documentation must exist to show that the criteria for disability are met (see the first paragraph). The IRS Chief Counsel opined that, for the year the distribution is made, the individual must show that physical or mental impairment left him or her unable to work at any activity comparable to that in which he or she customarily engaged. [Chief Counsel Advice 200922041 (Apr. 16, 2009)]

It is not sufficient to show that an individual qualified for payment under a private contract for disability insurance or was disabled for Social Security or retirement purposes because they are subject to different criteria. [Stipe v. Commissioner, T.C. Memo. 2011-92 (2011); Kowsh v. Commissioner, T.C. Memo. 2008-204 (2008)] There must be proof that the disability preceded the distribution. But, the Tax Court held that disability is proved if the Social Security Administration grants disability benefits after the distribution was made, based on evidence in an application submitted before the distribution date. [Dart v. Commissioner, T.C. Summary Op. 2008-158 (Dec. 16, 2008)]

An example where disability was not proved is *Dollander v. Commissioner* [T.C. Memo. 2009-187 (2009)]. A triage nurse was diagnosed with post-traumatic stress disorder and depression, and a psychiatrist ordered him to be restricted to "light duty." His employer reassigned him to a clerical position, but he continued to work at the same pay grade and salary, was not institutionalized or placed under constant supervision, and managed to carry on separate business activity on the side during the year in which IRA distributions were made. The Tax Court held that the Code Section 72 standard for disability was not met.

Q 5:30 What does it mean for a distribution to be "attributable to being disabled"?

The exception in Code Section 72(t)(2)(A)(iii) applies to distributions that are "attributable to the participant's being disabled." The distributee must be the disabled person; the exception does not apply if his or her spouse is the disabled individual. [Merrell v. Commissioner, T.C. Summary Op. 2020-5 (Jan. 16, 2020)]

The meaning of the phrase "attributable to . . . being disabled" is not clear. The IRS states in Publication 590-B that the distribution must be made "because of your disability." [IRS Pub. 590-B, *Distributions from Individual Retirement Arrangements (IRAs)* 2020, p. 23 (emphasis added; see Appendix B)] But, in a 2001 private letter ruling, it concluded that if an individual was disabled before the distributions commenced, the additional tax would not apply to any of them. [Priv. Ltr. Rul. 200126037 (July 2, 2001)]

Substantially Equal Periodic Payments

Q 5:31 What is a series of substantially equal periodic payments?

A qualifying series of *substantially equal periodic payments* (SEPPs) to an IRA owner is exempt from the 10 percent additional tax. [I.R.C. § 72(t)(2)(A)(iv)] The SEPPs exception allows an IRA owner who is younger than age 59½ to withdraw sums systematically and pay only regular tax on the distributions.

SEPPs are determined based on an IRA owner's life expectancy, using one of the methods set forth in Revenue Ruling 2002-62. [2002-2 C.B. 710] Any series of SEPPs must continue uninterrupted for at least five years or, if later until the individual attains age 59½. If the whole series is not paid or is otherwise interrupted, none of the payments qualifies for the exception (see Q 5:34). [I.R.C. § 72(t)(4)(A); Rev. Rul. 2002-62, 2002-2 C.B. 710]

Q 5:32 How are SEPPs determined?

There are three approved methods for determining a series of SEPPs. They are set forth in Revenue Ruling 2002-62. [2002-2 C.B. 710] If the RMD method is used, the result is a variable series of payments because each year's payment depends on the IRA balance at the end of the prior year. The other methods (fixed amortization and fixed annuitization) generally result in a uniform series of payments.

The method initially chosen must generally be used to calculate all the payments in the series. A one-time change is allowed, however, if either the fixed amortization method or the fixed annuitization method is first used to determine SEPPs, and the individual wants to change to the RMD method. If the one-time change is elected, the RMD method must be used to determine all the remaining payments in the series. [Rev. Rul. 2002-62, § 2.03(b), 2002-2 C.B. 710]

Otherwise, unless the IRA owner dies or becomes disabled, a change in the method of calculating SEPPs during the payment period is an impermissible modification of the series (see Q 5:34). [Rev. Rul. 2002-62, § 1.02(c), 2002-2 C.B. 710]

Q 5:33 How long must the series of SEPPs continue in order to avoid the 10 percent additional tax?

To qualify for the SEPPs exception to the additional tax of Code Section 72(t), the SEPPs must continue without interruption until the *later of* the fifth anniversary of the first SEPP distribution, or the date on which age 59½ is attained. [I.R.C. § 72(t)(4)(A); Arnold v. Commissioner, 111 T.C. 250 (1998)]

> **Example 1.** Arthur begins a series of SEPP distributions on December 15, 2016. The second through fifth SEPPs are paid to him in January of 2017, 2018, 2019, and 2020. In September 2020, he attains age 59½. Believing that the SEPP period has now closed, he takes a sixth distribution in November 2020. The sixth distribution impermissibly modifies the series of SEPPs, because the payment period does not close until December 15, 2020 (the fifth anniversary of the first distribution, which is later than the date Arthur reaches age 59½).

> **Example 2.** Michele turns 54 years old on July 20, 2019, and decides she will take annual SEPP distributions from her IRA. The first distribution is paid to her on October 31, 2019. The fifth anniversary of this distribution is October 31, 2024, but the date when Michele reaches age 59½ is later—July 20, 2025. To qualify for the SEPP exception to the additional tax, Michele must also receive a SEPP in 2025.

Q 5:34 What happens if the series of SEPPs is modified?

There is no penalty if SEPPs are interrupted by the IRA owner's disability or death. [I.R.C. § 72(t)(4)(A)(ii)] Any other deviation from the prescribed series of SEPPs is considered a modification of the series. If there is a modification, no payments in the series qualify for the SEPPs exception, and the additional tax is recaptured on every prior payment in the series—with interest for the period of delay. [I.R.C. § 72(t)(4)(A); Rev. Rul. 2002-62, § 1(c) (2002-2 C.B. 712); Priv. Ltr. Rul. 9821056 (Feb. 24, 1998)]

An incorrect amount being distributed during the required payment period, or an improper switch to a different calculation method for SEPPs, will both trigger a modification. In addition, there is a modification if a SEPP distribution, or any part of the IRA itself, is transferred tax-free to another retirement plan. [Rev. Rul. 2002-62, § 2.02(e); *e.g.*, Priv. Ltr. Rul. 201323045 (June 7, 2013)] There is no modification, however, if there is a trustee-to-trustee transfer of the entire SEPP-paying IRA to another IRA—and no other assets are combined with them. [*See, e.g.*, Priv. Ltr. Rul. 200929021 (July 17, 2009)]

Q 5:35 What changes do *not* cause a modification?

The following changes do not cause a modification:

- Receipt of a coronavirus-related distribution (see Q 7:42). [Notice 2020-50, part 4.H, 2020-28 I.R.B. 35]
- Returning to an IRA the portion of a SEPP that would be the 2020 RMD (but for the waiver under the CARES Act, using one of the approved methods (see Qs 4:10, 4:13)). [Notice 2020-51, 2020-29 I.R.B. (June 23, 2020)]
- Receipt of a qualified disaster distribution (see chapter 7). [Notice 2005-92, 2005-51 I.R.B. 165]
- Interruption of payments after the participant becomes disabled or dies. [I.R.C. § 72(t)(4)(A)(ii)]
- Converting a traditional IRA distribution to a Roth IRA, if the payments continue from the Roth IRA and otherwise as before. [Treas. Reg. § 1.408A-4, Q&A-12]
- Mistakes by the financial institution that result in a different amount or number of payments or a different payment date. (See Q 5:37.)
- Ministerial change by the financial institution (e.g., changing the payment date when switching to a new computer system). [Priv. Ltr. Rul. 9514026 (Jan. 12, 1995)]

Q 5:36 Can an IRA that is paying SEPPs be divided pursuant to a divorce or marital separation agreement without triggering a modification?

An IRA can be divided in a nontaxable transfer incident to a divorce (see Q 5:10), but the transfer can be problematic if SEPPs were being paid from the IRA. Revenue Ruling 2002-62 states: "Under all three methods, substantially equal periodic payments are calculated with respect to an account balance as of the first valuation date.... Thus, a modification to the series of payments will occur if, after such date, there is... (ii) any nontaxable transfer of a portion of the account balance to another retirement plan..."

The IRS does grant favorable rulings if, after the division, subsequent payments in the series are calculated using the same methodology as before, and the calculation takes into account only the account balance that remains after the transfer. [Priv. Ltr. Rul. 201030038 (July 30, 2010)] But, Revenue Ruling 2002-62 seems to indicate it is risky to proceed without first obtaining a private ruling.

Q 5:37 Does a mistake excuse a modification?

It depends. In several private letter rulings, the IRS has drawn the line at whether or not a modification would occur if the IRA owner's instructions were correctly followed. If they were correctly followed, the modification is not excused and cannot be corrected.

Rulings favorable to the IRA owner. The IRS has ruled favorably in several cases where the incorrect amount was paid due solely to errors by the financial institution. [Priv. Ltr. Ruls. 201309020 (Mar. 1, 2013), 201235029 (Aug. 31, 2012), 200929021 (July 17, 2009), 200930053 (July 24, 2009)]

For example, in Private Letter Ruling 201235029 (Aug. 31, 2012), the custodian of an individual retirement annuity erroneously paid a duplicate distribution and failed to offset the error despite several requests by the annuitant. The IRS ruled that there was no modification, and the additional tax did not apply.

Private Letter Ruling 200929021 (July 17, 2009) also concerns an error for which the IRA owner was not responsible. She maintained an IRA from which SEPPs were being paid with one financial institution; the payment period would not end until sometime in the last quarter of 2006. She also participated in three employer retirement plans and consulted with an advisor at another financial institution concerning both her IRA and employer plan accounts. In 2003, she moved assets from two of the employer plan accounts into a tax-sheltered annuity. In 2006, she asked about moving assets out of the third employer plan. The advisor recommended they be moved into the tax-sheltered annuity, not the IRA, to avoid the recapture tax that would result from interrupting the SEPPs. She agreed and directed the transfer, but the advisor's assistant filled out the paperwork incorrectly. So, in August 2006, the assets were moved into the IRA. The IRS concluded that the IRA owner had done everything she could to ensure that the assets would not be transferred to the IRA, and it ruled that no modification occurred. [Priv. Ltr. Rul. 200929021 (July 17, 2009)]

A third example favoring an innocent IRA owner is Private Letter Ruling 200930053 (July 24, 2009). In that case, the custodian of the SEPP-paying IRA regularly paid state taxes from every SEPP installment and distributed the remainder to the IRA owner. One year the custodian forgot to pay the state tax. The IRA owner's distribution was correct (it did not include the tax due), but the tax reserve remained in the IRA, and the full SEPP was not distributed that year. The IRS was asked to rule that the failure to distribute the full amount, along with a makeup distribution of the shortfall plus earnings, would result in no modification for Code Section 72(t) purposes. The IRS complied. [Priv. Ltr. Rul. 200930053 (July 24, 2009)] (For similar rulings, *see* Priv. Ltr. Ruls. 201051025 (Dec. 23, 2010) and 200503036 (Jan. 21, 2005).)

Finally, in Private Letter Ruling 201309020 (Mar. 1, 2013), a SEPP was missed because an employee of the financial custodian retired without leaving proper instructions for carrying on the payments. The IRS allowed a makeup payment and held that there was no modification.

Unfavorable rulings. If the financial institution commits no error, the IRS appears to treat any deviation from the SEPP rules as a modification that cannot be corrected. [Priv. Ltr. Ruls. 201323045 (June 7, 2013), 200925044 (June 19, 2009)]

In Private Letter Ruling 201323045 (June 7, 2013), the IRS ruled that a modification occurred when a portion of the IRA assets were moved to a different IRA before the end of the SEPP period (see Q 5:33). The move occurred because the IRA owner wanted to follow his financial advisor to a different financial institution. He intended to move the entire IRA, but the new financial institution would not accept one of the assets (a share in a real estate investment trust). Unfortunately, the advisor failed to warn the individual that moving only part of the IRA would trigger a modification. The IRS ruled that corrective action was not possible, and the 10 percent tax was payable going back to the *start* of the SEPP stream (years before the move).

Another individual followed bad advice from her financial advisor in Private Letter Ruling 200925044 (June 19, 2009). She consulted with the advisor on a strategy to deal with the market downturn. He recommended she transfer some assets from her IRA (which, he knew, was paying her SEPPs) to certificates of deposit (CDs) she would need to acquire elsewhere because his institution did not offer them. He explicitly advised that she would not sustain a penalty for the transfer. Following his advice, she ordered the transfer. Later, someone more knowledgeable told her that the partial transfer from the IRA interrupted the SEPPs and that she must pay a considerable amount of additional tax. She proposed returning a makeup amount to the IRA (the transferred amount plus earnings) and asked the IRS to rule that there would be no modification. Without explanation, the IRS ruled that there was a modification and corrective action was not possible. [Priv. Ltr. Rul. 200925044 (June 19, 2009)] Thus, reliance on bad professional advice (to the detriment of the IRA owner) is not grounds for a favorable ruling from the IRS—at least with regard to the modification issue.

> **Note.** In the area of rollover deadlines missed because individuals relied on bad professional advice, IRS waiver rulings have been inconsistent. The most recent rulings in that area are sympathetic to the taxpayer. (See Q 6:30.)

Q 5:38 If, in addition to the SEPP, another distribution which qualifies under a different Code Section 72(t) exception is paid during the same year, is there a modification?

No, at least in the case of a distribution used for higher education expenses, which qualifies for the Code Section 72(t)(2)(E) exception to the additional tax (see Q 5:44). In *Benz v. Commissioner* [132 T.C. No. 15 (May 11, 2009)], the Tax Court held that a distribution for higher education expenses that separately qualifies for an exception to the additional tax does not modify a series of substantially equal periodic payments. The opinion suggests that other distributions for which there are statutory exceptions to the additional tax (e.g., qualified medical expense and first-time homebuyer distributions) are also permissible.

Q 5:39 Can the method of calculating SEPPs be changed?

If the RMD method is not initially used, a one-time change to that method is allowed, after which that method must continue to be used until the end of the series. Otherwise, the method cannot be changed. [Rev. Rul. 2002-62, § 2.03(b), 2002-2 C.B. 710]

Q 5:40 Are increases in the cost of living incorporated in SEPP calculations?

No. This has not been allowed since 2002. [Rev. Rul. 2002-62, 2002-2 C.B. 710]

Q 5:41 If an individual has several IRAs, may SEPPs be withdrawn from one IRA but not the others?

An individual may designate which of several IRAs are to be included in the SEPPs calculation, but once the identification is made, the SEPPs must be withdrawn from those and not others. For example, in Private Letter Ruling 9816028 (Jan. 21, 1998), a 49-year-old taxpayer was permitted to annuitize seven of his IRAs without annuitizing the others. Distributions could only be made from the seven accounts; none were permitted from the others. However, the gross annual distribution determined for the seven annuitized IRAs could be drawn from any one or more of the seven specified IRAs in each year.

Medical Expenses

Q 5:42 What is the medical expense exception to the 7.5 percent additional tax?

The additional tax does not apply to IRA distributions to the extent they do not exceed the recipient's deductible amount of medical expenses for the distribution year, determined under Code Section 213, but without regard to whether the recipient itemizes deductions for that taxable year. [I.R.C. § 72(t)(2)(B)]

Medical expenses for this purpose are amounts paid for medical care of the individual, his or her spouse, and any dependents that are not compensated by insurance or otherwise. Only the portion of such payments that exceed 7.5 percent of adjusted gross income is deductible and may be taken into account for purposes of the medical expense deduction. A wide range of costs are qualifying medical expenses—generally, the costs of diagnosing, treating, and preventing disease, transportation for medical care, certain long-term care, and medical insurance. Cosmetic surgery expenses do not qualify unless the surgery is needed to correct a congenital deformity or a disfigurement caused by injury, trauma, or disease. [I.R.C. § 213(d)(1), 213(d)(9)] In a 2011 case, qualifying medical expenses were held to include the cost of sex reassignment surgery, hormonal treatments, and psychological therapy for an individual diagnosed with severe gender identity disorder. [O'Donnabhain v. Commissioner, 134 T.C. No. 4 (2010), *acq.* IRS Action on Decision 2011-03, I.R.B. No. 2011-47]

Q 5:43 When must medical expenses be incurred for a distribution to qualify for the medical expenses exception?

The medical expenses must actually be paid during the distribution year. [I.R.C. §§ 72(t)(2)(B), 213]

Thus, if the medical services are rendered and the IRA distribution is taken in one year, but the expense is not paid until a later year, the medical expense exception to the 10 percent additional tax does not apply. [Kimball v. Commissioner, T.C. Summary Op. 2004-2 (Jan. 8, 2004)]

Nor does the exception apply if an individual takes an IRA distribution in one year to repay a loan of funds used in a prior year to pay medical expenses because the loan repayment (the same-year event) is not the deductible event. [Evers v. Commissioner, T.C. Summary Op. 2008-140 (Nov. 3, 2008)]

Higher Education Expenses

Q 5:44 What are qualified higher education expenses?

For IRA distribution purposes, *qualified higher education expenses* include tuition, fees, books, supplies, and equipment required for the enrollment or attendance of a student at an eligible educational institution (see Q 5:47). For a *special needs beneficiary* (see Q 14:9), the cost of special needs services incurred for enrollment or attendance is also included. Amounts paid for room and board are qualified higher education expenses if the student is enrolled at least half time. The allowed amount is generally the school's posted room and board charge, or, if greater, a fixed annual dollar amount (currently $2,500) for students living off-campus and not at home. [I.R.C. § 529(e)(3); Notice 97-60, 1997-2 C.B. 310]

Particular books, supplies, or equipment (e.g., a laptop computer) may be considered necessary by the IRA owner or student, but an item's cost is not a qualified higher education expense unless the educational institution specifically requires the item. On that basis, the Tax Court recently held that a computer, housewares, appliances, furniture, and bedding purchased for an IRA owner's daughter were not qualified higher education expenses. Nor did book expenses qualify because the purchased books were not shown to be required for courses, and payment for them was not substantiated. [Gorski v. Commissioner, T.C. Summary Op. 2005-112 (Aug. 4, 2005)]

Practice Pointer. An IRA owner should retain documentation (e.g., a course syllabus) to prove that specific items are required by the educational institution, as well as receipts to substantiate their expense.

Q 5:45 When must education expenses be incurred for a distribution to qualify for the exception?

The education expenses must be incurred in the year of the IRA distribution and not in a prior year. [Beckert v. Commissioner, T.C. Memo. 2005-162 (2005)]

Q 5:46 May an IRA owner use the qualified higher education expenses exception for members of his or her family?

Yes. Qualified higher education expenses are qualified expenses of the IRA owner, the owner's spouse, or any child or grandchild of the owner or the owner's spouse. [I.R.C. § 72(t)(7)]

Q 5:47 What is an eligible educational institution for purposes of qualified higher education expenses?

An *eligible educational institution* for purposes of qualified higher education expenses is any college, university, vocational school, or other postsecondary educational institution that is described in Section 481 of the Higher Education Act of 1965 [20 U.S.C. § 1088] and is, therefore, eligible to participate in the student aid programs administered by the Department of Education. The category includes all accredited public, nonprofit, and proprietary postsecondary institutions. [I.R.C. § 529(e)(5); Notice 97-60, 1997-2 C.B. 310]

Q 5:48 Do other tax-favored education programs reduce the amount of education expenses available for penalty-free distributions from an IRA?

Yes. If a student does not need the assets from an IRA for qualified higher education expenses because funds are otherwise available, the exception for such expenses may not apply. Qualified higher education expenses paid with a Pell grant (or other tax-free scholarships), a tax-free distribution from a Coverdell ESA, veteran's educational assistance, or tax-free employer-provided educational assistance are not eligible for a penalty-free distribution from an IRA. [IRS Pub. 970, *Tax Benefits for Education* 2020]

On the other hand, qualified higher education expenses paid with an individual's earnings, a loan, a gift, an inheritance given to the student or the individual claiming the credit, or personal savings (including savings from a qualified state tuition program) are included in determining the amount of the IRA withdrawal that is not subject to the 10 percent early distribution penalty.

Qualified Reservist Distribution

Q 5:49 To what distributions does the qualified reservist exception apply?

This exception applies if (a) the reservist is ordered or called to active duty after September 11, 2001, (b) the order or call is for a period of more than

179 days or an indefinite period because the individual is a member of a *reserve component*, and (c) the reservist receives the distribution on or after the date of the order or call to active duty and by the close of the active-duty period. The term "reserve component" means the Army National Guard of the United States, Army Reserve, Naval Reserve, Marine Corps Reserve, Air National Guard of the United States, Air Force Reserve, Coast Guard Reserve, or Reserve Corps of the Public Health Service. [IRS Pub. 590-B, *Distributions from Individual Retirement Arrangements* (IRAs) 2020 (see Appendix B)]

Code Section 72(t)(2)(G)(i) exempts qualified reservist distributions from the 10 percent additional tax. They are includable in gross income, however, and subject to regular income tax. (See Q 6:119 regarding the special two-year repayment period for qualified reservist distributions.)

Qualified First-Time Homebuyer Distribution

Q 5:50 What is a qualified first-time homebuyer distribution?

The 10 percent additional tax does not apply to a *qualified first-time homebuyer distribution*, which is a distribution used within 120 days to pay for the qualified acquisition costs associated with a first-time homebuyer's principal residence. [I.R.C. § 72(t)(8)]

The term "*first-time homebuyer*" is very broadly defined (see Q 5:52).

Q 5:51 What costs are classified as qualified acquisition costs for purposes of a qualified first-time homebuyer distribution?

For purposes of a qualified first-time homebuyer distribution, qualified acquisition costs include the costs of acquiring, constructing, or reconstructing a residence. They also include any usual or reasonable settlement, financing, or other closing costs. [I.R.C. § 72(t)(8)(C)]

Q 5:52 Who is considered a first-time homebuyer?

The term "*first-time homebuyer*" is generously defined. It covers any individual who did not (and, if married, whose spouse also did not) own a principal residence during the two-year period that ends on the date when the residence at issue is acquired. Thus, ownership of a principal residence that ended more than two years earlier does not disqualify an individual. However, any type of present ownership interest held within the two-year period eliminates use of the exception. [*See* I.R.C. § 72(t)(8)(D).]

For a married couple, the test of first-time home ownership applies separately to each spouse. Consequently, if one newlywed spouse already owned a principal residence during the two-year period, the exception does not apply when the *couple* jointly purchases a principal residence within the same period. [Olup v. Commissioner, T.C. Summary Op. 2005-183 (Dec. 13, 2005)]

Finally, an interest counts as a present ownership interest if it is regarded as such under local law. Thus, individuals who used IRA distributions in 2004 to pay off a mortgage on their residence, contending that the mortgage company owned the property before the payoff, did not qualify for the first-time ownership exception because their joint tenancy interest in the residence (held since 1997) was already a present ownership interest under state law. [Sharma v. Commissioner, T.C. Summary Op. 2008-98 (Aug. 7, 2008)]

Q 5:53 What special rules may apply if a qualified first-time homebuyer distribution is not used for the intended purpose because a natural disaster affected the region?

If a qualified first-time homebuyer distribution was not used for the intended purpose because a natural disaster struck the geographic region where the home was to be bought or built, it may be possible to return the funds tax-free to an IRA or other retirement plan within an extended rollover period. The various disaster relief laws that permit such funds to be returned are discussed in Qs 7:32–7:41. The region must be the subject of a "major disaster area" declaration, and other very specific requirements apply.

An extended rollover period is similarly allowed in some non-disaster cases where the purchase or construction was canceled or delayed (see Q 5:56), but the relief provided is not identical:

- A longer repayment period is allowed under the disaster relief rules (compare Qs 5:56 and 7:37).
- The disaster relief rules allow the qualified first-time homebuyer distribution to be rolled over to an IRA or any other eligible retirement plan (e.g., a 401(k) plan), provided the funds qualify as a tax-free rollover contribution to that plan. Under the non-disaster rule, repayment must be made to an IRA (compare Qs 7:38 and 5:56).

Q 5:54 What is the date of acquisition for purposes of a qualified first-time homebuyer distribution?

For purposes of a qualified first-time homebuyer distribution, the *date of acquisition* is the date on which a binding contract to acquire a principal residence is entered into or the date on which construction or reconstruction of such a principal residence begins. [I.R.C. § 72(t)(8)(D)(iii)]

Q 5:55 Must a qualified first-time homebuyer distribution be used by a certain time?

Yes. A qualified first-time homebuyer distribution must be used before the close of the 120th day after the day on which the distribution is received. [I.R.C. § 72(t)(8)(A)]

Q 5:56 Can the distribution be returned to an IRA if it cannot be used for the intended purpose?

Yes. The qualified first-time homebuyer distribution may be repaid to an IRA within 120 days if the *only* reason for doing so is that the purchase or construction of the residence is either delayed or cancelled. In that case, the repayment is treated as a tax-free rollover contribution and disregarded for purposes of the one-per-year limit on rollovers between IRAs (see Q 6:15). [I.R.C. § 72(t)(8)(E)]

> **Example**. Alex is single and has never before owned a principal residence. He enters into a purchase agreement to buy a home, with the closing scheduled for October. On August 20, Alex takes a $10,000 distribution from his IRA in anticipation of the October closing. Immediately before the closing, his real estate agent tells Alex that the closing will be delayed. In early December, the closing has not yet occurred, and Alex becomes concerned about exceeding the 120-day period for completing the rollover. He may roll over the distribution amount back to the IRA by December 18 (120 days).

Q 5:57 Does the one-rollover-per-year limit apply to the rollover of a qualified first-time homebuyer distribution?

No, the prohibition against more than one rollover within a 12-month period does not apply to rollovers meeting the first-time homebuyer exception.

Q 5:58 What is a principal residence for purposes of a qualified first-time homebuyer distribution?

If an individual uses more than one property as a residence, which property is considered the individual's principal residence depends on the facts and circumstances of the case, including the good faith of the individual. A *principal residence*, for purposes of a qualified first-time homebuyer distribution, may include a houseboat, a house trailer, or stock held by a tenant-stockholder in a cooperative housing corporation. [Treas. Reg. §§ 1.121-3, 1.1034-1(d)(1)]

Q 5:59 For whom may a principal residence be purchased using a qualified first-time homebuyer distribution?

The qualified first-time homebuyer distribution exception is available to pay the qualified acquisition costs of a principal residence for the IRA owner or the owner's spouse, or a child, grandchild, or ancestor of the IRA owner or owner's spouse. It is important to note that the individual who must meet the definition of a first-time homebuyer is the person acquiring the home—not the IRA owner. [I.R.C. § 72(t)(8)(A)]

Q 5:60 Is there a dollar limit on qualified first-time homebuyer distributions?

Yes. There is a lifetime limit of $10,000 on qualified first-time homebuyer distributions. The limit applies to the IRA owner, not necessarily to the individual acquiring the home. [I.R.C. § 72(t)(8)(B)]

Example. Tamara, the daughter of Tom and Wanda, is a qualified first-time homebuyer. Both Tom and Wanda have IRAs. Tom takes a $10,000 distribution from his IRA and gives the money to Tamara to purchase her first home. The next year, Tamara sells the home and moves to a rental apartment in a new city and lives there for three years. Tamara then finds a home she would like to purchase and asks her parents to help out with the down payment. Tom has already exhausted the $10,000 lifetime limit on first-time homebuyer distributions from his IRA. Wanda, however, may take a distribution from her IRA and give the funds to Tamara to acquire her home. Tamara is once again considered to be a qualified first-time homebuyer because she had no present ownership interest in a principal residence during the two-year period ending on the date of acquisition of her new home.

Q 5:61 May an individual take $10,000 from a traditional IRA and $10,000 from a Roth IRA under the first-time homebuyer exception?

Apparently not. The $10,000 lifetime limit on the first-time homebuyer exception appears to apply to an individual's IRAs on a combined basis. [I.R.C. § 72(t)(8)(B)]

Q 5:62 Does a qualified first-time homebuyer distribution count against the $10,000 lifetime limit if the distribution meets another exception to the 10 percent premature distribution penalty?

No. If an IRA owner who takes a qualified first-time homebuyer distribution meets one of the other exceptions to the 10 percent early distribution penalty (see Q 5:26), the first-time homebuyer distribution does not count against the $10,000 lifetime limit on such distributions. [I.R.C. § 72(t)(2)]

Qualified Birth or Adoption Distribution

Q 5:63 What is the exception for a qualified birth or adoption distribution?

Effective for distributions after December 31, 2019, the additional tax under Section 72(t) does not apply to any qualified birth or adoption distribution. [I.R.C. § 72(t)(2)(H), added by the SECURE Act, § 113] A qualified birth or adoption distribution is a distribution made to an individual from an applicable eligible retirement plan during the one-year period starting on the date when a child of the individual is born, or the legal adoption of an eligible adoptee is finalized.

Applicable eligible retirement plans include IRAs, 401(k) and other qualified plans, 403(b) plans, and 457(b) deferred compensation plans, but not defined benefit plans. [I.R.C. §§ 72(t)(2)(H)(vi)(I), 402(c)(8)(B)]

Note. Subject to various restrictions, qualified birth or adoption distributions may be returned (contributed) tax-free to an IRA or other applicable eligible retirement plan. (See Q 6:20.)

Q 5:64 How much can be withdrawn as a qualified birth or adoption distribution?

The largest amount an individual may treat as a qualified birth or adoption distribution is $5,000 for each birth or adoption. But, since this limit applies on an individual basis, both parents (if each participates in an applicable eligible retirement plan) could withdraw up to $5,000 in this way. [I.R.C. § 72(t)(2)(H)(ii)]

Q 5:65 Who is an eligible adoptee?

An eligible adoptee is any individual, other than a child of the taxpayer's spouse, who is younger than age 18 or is physically or mentally incapable of self-support. [I.R.C. § 72(t)(2)(H)(iii)(II)]

Disaster and Coronavirus-Related Distributions

Q 5:66 What distributions authorized under emergency relief measures are exempt from the additional tax?

Qualified disaster distributions and coronavirus-related distributions are both exempt from the additional tax on early distributions. These are distributions that qualify for special tax breaks under laws authorizing emergency relief. The provisions exempting such distributions from the additional tax appear in those laws, rather than in Code Section 72(t). See chapter 7 for an extensive discussion of these distributions. For the specific provision that provides an exemption from the additional tax, see:

- The Disaster Tax Relief and Airport and Airway Extension Act of 2017, Pub. L. No. 115-63 (Sept. 29, 2017), § 502(a)(1).
- The Tax Cuts and Jobs Act, Pub. L. No. 115-97 (Dec. 22, 2017), § 11028(b)(1)(A).
- The Bipartisan Budget Act of 2018, Pub. L. No. 115-123 (Feb. 9, 2018) (2018 Budget Act), § 20102(a)(1).
- Taxpayer Certainty and Disaster Tax Relief Act of 2019, Div. Q of the Further Consolidated Appropriations Act, 2020, Pub. L. No. 116-94 (Dec. 20, 2019), § 202(a)(1).
- The Coronavirus Aid, Relief, and Economic Security Act, Pub. L. No. 116-136 (Mar. 27, 2020), § 2202(a).
- Consolidated Appropriations Act, 2021, Pub. L. No. 116-260 (Dec. 27, 2020).

Taxation of Roth IRA Distributions

Q 5:67 How are Roth IRA distributions taxed?

Different tax rules apply depending on the type of distribution made.

- For qualified distributions, see Q 5:69.

- For nonqualified distributions, see Q 5:85.
- The 60-day rollover of a Roth IRA distribution to the same (or another) Roth IRA is tax-free, provided the requirements in Code Section 408(d)(3) are met (including the 12-month limit on IRA-to-IRA rollovers). Roth IRA distributions cannot be rolled over to any other plan. [I.R.C. § 408A(a), 408A(e); Treas. Reg. § 1.408A-6, Q&A-1(c), Q&A-17; Treas. Reg. § 1.408A-10, Q&A-5] See Qs 6:16 (12-month limit), 6:46 (rollover by the surviving spouse), 6:59 (permitted rollovers), and 6:53 (basis allocation).
- A corrective distribution must be accompanied by allocable net income, and the distributed earnings are includible in gross income (see Q 5:7).

Qualified Roth IRA Distributions

Q 5:68 What is a qualified distribution from a Roth IRA?

A *qualified distribution* from a Roth IRA is any distribution that meets both of these requirements:

1. *Five-year holding period.* The first contribution to a Roth IRA was made at least five taxable years before the distribution (see Q 5:71). [Treas. Reg. § 1.408A-6, Q&A-1], and
2. *Qualified reason.* One of the following is true:
    a. *Attainment of age 59½.* The distribution is made on or after the date when the Roth IRA owner attains age 59½.
    b. *Death.* The distribution is made to a beneficiary, or to the Roth IRA owner's estate, after the owner's death.
    c. *Disability.* The distribution is made because the Roth IRA owner is disabled (within the meaning of Code Section 72(m)(7)). (See Q 5:22.)
    d. *Qualified special purpose distribution.* As defined in the statute, this is a *qualified first-time homebuyer distribution* (see Qs 5:82, 5:50).

[I.R.C. § 408A(d)(1), 408A(d)(2), 408A(d)(5); Treas. Reg. § 1.408A-6, Q&A-1]

Q 5:69 How is a qualified Roth IRA distribution taxed?

Qualified distributions from a Roth IRA are excluded from gross income. They are also exempt from the Code 72(t) additional tax on early distributions because each qualified reason also qualifies for an exemption from the additional tax. [I.R.C. §§ 408A(d)(1), 72(t)(A)(i), 72(t)(A)(ii), 72(t)(A)(iii), 72(t)(2)(F)]

Q 5:70 If a distribution is not qualified, will it be taxed and penalized?

Not necessarily. Contributions may always be withdrawn tax-free, and earnings are not distributed from a Roth IRA until all contributions have been exhausted (see Q 5:88). Also, the penalty applies only to the taxable part of a distribution, so there is no penalty if only contributions are distributed (the rule is slightly different for distributed conversion contributions). In general, the significance of a qualified distribution is that *earnings* may be distributed tax and penalty-free.

Five-Year Holding Period for Qualified Distribution Purposes

Q 5:71 When is the five-year holding period met for qualified distribution purposes?

The five-year holding period requirement is met on the fifth anniversary of the first day of the year for which the first Roth IRA contribution is made. Any properly made contribution (direct, rollover, or conversion) starts the clock. [I.R.C. § 408A(d)(2)(B); Treas. Reg. § 1.408A-6, Q&A-2] Thus, if the initial contribution is made for the 2018 contribution year, the five-year holding period works as follows:

2018	First Year—Initial Contribution (made anytime between January 1, 2018 and April 17, 2019)
2019	Second Year
2020	Third Year
2021	Fourth Year
2022	Fifth Year
2023	Distributions on January 1, 2023 meet the five-year holding period requirement.

Q 5:72 Is the five-year holding period tracked to the day?

No. The five-year holding period is based on the year, not the day. It makes no difference whether the individual made the contribution on the first possible day to make a contribution for a tax year or on the last possible day. The five-year holding period starts on January 1 of the year for which the first contribution is made and ends on December 31 of the fourth consecutive year after that first year. [Treas. Reg. § 1.408A-6, Q&A-2]

Example 1. Louise makes her first Roth IRA contribution on July 1, 2018. Her five-year holding period begins in 2018 and will end on December 31, 2022. Any distribution taken on or after January 1, 2023, will meet the five-year requirement.

Example 2. Lydia makes her first Roth IRA contribution in March 2019 and designates it as made for 2018. Her five-year holding period begins in 2018 and runs through 2022.

Q 5:73 May a qualified distribution include contributions held in the Roth IRA for less than five years?

Yes. The five-year rule does not apply to every contribution—just the first contribution. Once the requirement is met, every distribution with a qualified reason (see Q 5:68) is a qualified distribution. [Treas. Reg. § 1.408A-6, Q&A-2]

> **Example**. On April 13, 2016, Jane opens a Roth IRA and contributes $5,000, which she designates as a 2015 contribution. The five-year period closes at the end of 2019, so starting in 2020, any distribution she takes will have met the first qualified distribution requirement.

Q 5:74 Does the five-year holding period start anew if the individual opens a second Roth IRA?

No. The five-year period begins in the year of an individual's first contribution to *any* Roth IRA. [Treas. Reg. § 1.408A-6, Q&A-2]

> **Example**. Jason opens a Roth IRA at his bank and contributes $5,500 for 2018. For 2021, he contributes to a new Roth IRA opened at his credit union. As of January 1, 2023, a distribution from either Roth IRA will have met the five-year requirement.

Q 5:75 Should a Roth IRA be started as early as possible, even with only a small contribution?

Yes. A young person with any earned income should consider opening a Roth IRA even if only a modest contribution is affordable. No matter how small the contribution, it will start the five-year period.

Q 5:76 If a Roth IRA is liquidated and a new one is opened several years later, does a new five-year period start?

Generally, no. The five-year holding period does not start over after a full distribution of a Roth IRA unless the full distribution was due to a revocation during the seven-day period following establishment of the Roth IRA, a recharacterization (see Q 3:114), or the return of an excess contribution (see chapter 3). [Treas. Reg. § 1.408A-6, Q&A-2]

> **Note**. Roth IRA conversions made after 2017 cannot be recharacterized (see Qs 3:116, 3:128). [Tax Cuts and Jobs Act (TCJA), Pub. L. No. 115-97 (Dec. 22, 2017), § 13611; I.R.C. §§ 408A(d)(3), 402(c)(8)(B)]

> **Example**. Sam establishes a Roth IRA and contributes to it for 2016. He closes the Roth IRA in 2017 because he needs all the funds for a family emergency. (He does not remove the assets as an excess contribution or a recharacterization.) In 2019, Sam opens a new Roth IRA and makes a contribution. The five-year holding period started in 2016, the year of his first Roth IRA contribution.

Q 5:77 Does the five-year requirement also apply to Roth IRA beneficiaries?

Yes. Distributions from an inherited Roth IRA must also satisfy the five-year requirement, or else they are not qualified. The beneficiary's holding period tacks onto that of the deceased owner—that is, the five-year requirement is met on the same date it would have been had the decedent remained alive. [Treas. Reg. § 1.408A-6, Q&A-7]

Beneficiaries must either start taking RMDs one year after the Roth IRA owner dies or take a full distribution under the 5-year or 10-year rule (see Qs 4:86, 4:87). If any RMD is distributed before the five-year holding period is met, it will not be a qualified distribution (even though there would be a qualified reason—payment to a death beneficiary).

Q 5:78 If a Roth IRA owner inherits another person's Roth IRA, are there two different five-year holding periods?

Yes. There is one five-year holding period for the inherited Roth IRA and another for the individual's own Roth IRA. A second inherited Roth IRA acquired from a different decedent would also have its own five-year holding period. The beneficiary must separately keep track of each. [Treas. Reg. § 1.408A-6, Q&A-7]

Example. David establishes a Roth IRA in 2014 and names his daughter Melissa as the beneficiary. Melissa opens her own Roth IRA in 2018. In 2019, David dies, and Melissa inherits his Roth IRA. The five-year period for the inherited IRA has already run, so all distributions from it will be qualified (payment to a beneficiary is a qualified reason). However, the five-year period for Melissa's own Roth IRA will not close until the end of 2022.

Q 5:79 How is the five-year holding period determined if the participant's surviving spouse elects to treat the inherited IRA as the spouse's own?

If the surviving spouse is the sole beneficiary of the decedent spouse's IRA and elects to treat it as the spouse's own, and he or she also owned a Roth IRA at the time of the death, then whichever five-year holding period ends first—the one tracked from the decedent, or the one tracked for the spouse's other Roth IRA—becomes the five-year holding period that applies to all of the surviving spouse's Roth IRAs. [Treas. Reg. § 1.408A-6, Q&A-7] If the spouse continues as a beneficiary of the inherited IRA, the five-year holding periods do not merge. (See Qs 4:54, 4:55, and 10:2 for the surviving spouse's rights as sole beneficiary of the inherited IRA.)

Example 1. Conrad establishes a Roth IRA in 2018 and dies in 2019. He leaves the assets to his wife, Betsy (who previously did not have a Roth IRA). Betsey treats the inherited IRA as her own, and her five-year holding period starts in 2018.

Example 2. Lisa establishes a Roth IRA in 2015. Her husband, John, establishes a Roth IRA in 2017 and names Lisa the beneficiary. In 2020 John dies. Lisa treats John's Roth IRA as her own. She immediately meets the five-year holding period requirement because her own start year (2015) was earlier than her husband's start year (2017).

Example 3. The facts are the same as in Example 2, except that Lisa established her Roth IRA in 2017, and John established his Roth IRA in 2015. When John dies, Lisa treats his Roth IRA as her own. For both of Lisa's Roth IRAs, the five-year holding period begins in 2015 (the earlier start year).

Example 4. Barbara established a Roth IRA in 2014. Her husband, Norman, established his Roth IRA in 2016. In 2017, Norman dies, having named Barbara as beneficiary of his Roth IRA. Barbara elects *not* to treat Norman's Roth IRA as her own. She has two separate five-year holding periods: one for her own Roth IRA, starting in 2014, and one for the Roth IRA she inherits from Norman, with a start year of 2016.

Qualified Reasons

Q 5:80 If the surviving spouse elects to treat the inherited Roth IRA as the spouse's own, can distributions be qualified based on being made to a beneficiary after the participant's death?

No, because treating the decedent's IRA as the spouse's own causes the spouse to be the owner, not a beneficiary, of the IRA for all purposes. [Treas. Reg. § 1.408A-2, Q&A-4; Treas. Reg. § 1.408A-6, Q&A-3]

Q 5:81 For what distributions is *disability* a qualified reason?

These are the same distributions that qualify for the exception to the additional tax on early distributions. So, there is the same lack of clarity as to whether all distributions made to a disabled individual are covered or only distributions that are made "because of" the disability (whatever that means). (See Qs 5:29, 5:30.) [I.R.C. §§ 408A(d)(2)(A)(iii), 72(t)(2)(A)(iii), 72(m)(7)]

Q 5:82 What is a *qualified* special purpose distribution?

Code Section 408A(d)(5) defines this as a distribution to which Section 72(t)(2)(F) applies—that is, a qualified first-time homebuyer distribution. Such distributions cannot exceed $10,000 and must meet other requirements that probably make this a little-used "qualified reason." (See Q 5:50.)

Q 5:83 What is the result if a distribution meets an exception to the additional tax that is not one of the four qualifying reasons?

A distribution without a qualified reason is not a qualified distribution. But the additional tax will not apply if another Code Section 72(t) exception applies.

Nonqualified Distributions

Q 5:84 What is a nonqualified distribution from a Roth IRA?

A *nonqualified distribution* from a Roth IRA is any distribution that is *not*:

- A qualified distribution,
- Contributed to another Roth IRA as a qualified rollover contribution, or
- A corrective distribution.

[Treas. Reg. § 1.408A-6, Q&A-4]

Q 5:85 How is a nonqualified Roth IRA distribution taxed?

A nonqualified Roth IRA distribution is taxed under Code Section 72, subject to ordering and aggregation rules that cause all contributions to be returned before any earnings are distributed. Many nonqualified distributions do not, as a result, include taxable income. If earnings are included in a nonqualified distribution, the additional tax applies to the earnings unless the recipient is age 59½ or older or another Section 72(t) exception applies. The additional tax may also apply to some distributions of conversion contributions (see Q 5:92). [Treas. Reg. § 1.408A-6, Q&A-1(b), Q&A-8]

Q 5:86 What are the aggregation rules?

These aggregation rules apply to determine how a particular nonqualified distribution is taxed.

First, all Roth IRAs are aggregated and treated as one Roth IRA. However, Roth IRAs that an individual holds as the participant are not aggregated with those held as a beneficiary; those held as the beneficiary of one decedent are not aggregated with those held as another decedent's beneficiary; spouses do not aggregate their Roth IRAs, and Roth IRAs are not aggregated with an individual's traditional IRAs. [I.R.C. § 408A(d)(4)(A), 408A(d)(2); Treas. Reg. § 1.408A-6, Q&A-9, Q&A-11]

Second, all Roth IRA distributions (other than disregarded distributions; see last paragraph) made for the same taxable year are aggregated and treated as one distribution. [Treas. Reg. § 1.408A-6, Q&A-9(a)]

Third, all "regular" contributions made for the same taxable year are aggregated and added to the total amount of undistributed regular contributions made in prior taxable years. (See Q 5:87 for the definition of a regular contribution.) [Treas. Reg. § 1.408A 6, Q&A-9(b)]

Fourth, all conversion contributions made during the same taxable year are aggregated, and the portion of each that was includible in gross income at the time of conversion is tracked. With respect to any conversion contribution, the amount converted, reduced by any basis that was included in the conversion, is the amount that was includible in gross income at the time of conversion. [Treas. Reg. § 1.408A-6, Q&A-9(c); Treas. Reg. § 1.408A-4, Q&A-7(a)]

Finally, these are *disregarded*: (1) corrective distributions made from the Roth IRA; (2) Roth IRA contributions that were recharacterized to a traditional IRA (the allocable net income is also ignored); and (3) rollovers from one Roth IRA to another Roth IRA (because all are treated as a single Roth IRA). [Treas. Reg. § 1.408A-6, Q&A-9(e), Q&A-9(g), Q&A-9(d)]

Q 5:87 What are "regular" Roth IRA contributions?

A *regular contribution* is any contribution that is not a qualified rollover contribution. [Treas. Reg. § 1.408A-3, Q&A-1] But since the aggregation rules specifically exclude some contributions and include others that are not "annual" contributions, it is helpful to list the items that count or do not count as regular contributions.

Regular contributions *include*:

- Amounts contributed from compensation subject to the annual contribution limit (including amounts identified as made for a taxable year but timely contributed in the following taxable year). [Treas. Reg. § 1.408A-6, Q&A-9(b)]
- Traditional IRA contributions recharacterized to the Roth IRA (treated as made on the original contribution date and excluding the net earnings transferred in the recharacterization). [Treas. Reg. § 1.408A-6, Q&A-9(f), Q&A-9(h)]
- Qualified distributions rolled over to the Roth IRA from a designated Roth account (DRAC) within a qualified plan. [Treas. Reg. § 1.408A-10, Q&A-3(a)]
- After-tax contributions included in a nonqualified DRAC distribution that is rolled over to the Roth IRA. [Treas. Reg. § 1.408A-10, Q&A-3(a)]
- Excess contributions not removed or recharacterized to a traditional IRA (including "failed" conversion contributions, which result when a conversion is intended, but the transaction does not qualify). [Treas. Reg. §§ 1.408A-4, Q&A-3(b); 1.408A-8, Q&A-1(b)(4)]

Regular contributions *do not* include:

- Qualified rollover contributions (including conversion contributions). [Treas. Reg. § 1.408A-3, Q&A-1]
- Roth IRA contributions recharacterized to a traditional IRA. [Treas. Reg. § 1.408A-6, Q&A-9(g)]
- Net earnings that accompany a traditional IRA contribution when it is recharacterized to the Roth IRA. [Treas. Reg. § 1.408A-6, Q&A-9(h)]
- Contributions removed by a corrective distribution. [Treas. Reg. § 1.408A-6, Q&A-9(e)]

Q 5:88 What are the ordering rules for distributions?

Amounts are distributed from the Roth IRA in the following order:

1. Regular contributions (see Q 5:86, "third" paragraph).
2. Conversion contributions, distributed on a first-in, first-out basis. For those made in any taxable year, the amount that was includible in gross income at the time of the conversion is distributed first.
3. Earnings are distributed last.

[I.R.C. § 408A(d)(4)(B); Treas. Reg. § 1.408A-6, Q&A-8]

Q 5:89 Are the components of a Roth IRA also allocated to qualified distributions in this order?

Yes. Code Section 408A(d)(4)(B) states that these ordering rules apply for purposes of applying "section 72 to *any* distribution from a Roth IRA . . ." (emphasis added). That means contributions returned in a qualified distribution are not available (having been removed) for return in a subsequent nonqualified distribution.

Example. Corey opens his first Roth IRA in March 2016 and immediately contributes $5,500 designated as a 2015 contribution and $5,500 for 2016. He makes no other contributions but withdraws $4,000 in 2019 and $7,000 more in September 2020. The balance in Corey's Roth IRA is $2,500 on December 31, 2020. Both distributions are nonqualified, but neither is taxable. The 2019 distribution returns $4,000 of regular contributions, and the 2020 distribution returns the other $7,000 of regular contributions. Only earnings remain in the Roth IRA.

Q 5:90 How are the components of a Roth IRA allocated to multiple beneficiaries?

Each component of a Roth IRA (regular contributions, conversion contributions, and earnings) is allocated to each beneficiary on a pro-rata basis. [Treas. Reg. § 1.408A-6, Q&A-11] The allocation determines the tax consequences if a nonqualified distribution is received.

Example. When Dean dies, his Roth IRA contains a regular contribution of $4,000, a conversion contribution of $6,000, and earnings of $1,000. Dean had named his four children as equal beneficiaries of the Roth IRA. Dee, Dean's youngest child, takes an immediate distribution of $2,500. It will be deemed to consist of $1,000 of regular contributions (.25 × $4,000) and $1,500 of conversion contributions (.25 × $6,000). Since Dee's share of the contributions has now been entirely distributed to her, all future distributions to Dee will include only earnings.

Additional Tax on Nonqualified Distributions

Q 5:91 How does the additional tax on early distributions apply to a nonqualified Roth IRA distribution?

The additional tax on early distributions applies as follows:

- If a distribution has a qualified reason but is nonqualified because the Roth IRA has been open for less than five years, the additional tax will not apply because each qualified reason is an exception to the additional tax.
- If there is no qualified reason, but another exception under Code Section 72(t) applies, the additional tax does not apply.
- If the nonqualified distribution does not qualify for any exception, there still may not be additional tax because it generally only applies to the taxable part of the nonqualified distribution.
- But additional tax may apply to the nonqualified distribution of a conversion contribution that was held in the Roth IRA for less than five years. (See Q 5:92.)

Q 5:92 What conversion contributions are subject to additional tax when distributed?

If any conversion contribution is distributed within five taxable years of the conversion, the amount of it that was taxed at the time of conversion is subject to the 10 percent additional tax (and all of its exceptions). Normally, the additional tax applies only to the part of a distribution that is includible in gross income, but Code Section 408A(d)(3)(F) overrides that general rule. It applies Section 72(t) to the amount that was includible in gross income at the time of *conversion* as if it were includible in gross income at the time of the *distribution* if the distribution occurs before the end of the five-taxable year period. [I.R.C. §§ 72(t)(1), 408A(d)(3)(F)]

Example. Avi converts his traditional IRA ($20,000, including $2,000 of nondeductible contributions) to a Roth IRA. The amount included in gross income for the year of conversion is $18,000. Under the ordering rules (see Q 5:88), that part of the conversion contribution will be distributed before the $2,000 that was not taxed at the time of conversion.

Q 5:93 What conversion contributions are *not* subject to additional tax when distributed?

The 10 percent additional tax *never* applies to these distributions of conversion contributions from a Roth IRA:

- Any *qualified* distribution of a conversion contribution.
- Any *nonqualified* distribution of a conversion contribution that:

  Was converted more than five taxable years earlier, or

Is paid to either a Roth IRA owner age 59½ or older or a Roth IRA beneficiary, or is covered by another exception to the additional tax, or

Represents the basis amount that was converted.

[I.R.C. § 408A(d)(3)(F); Treas. Reg. § 1.408A-6, Q&A-5, Q&A-8, and Q&A-10, Examples 6 & 9; I.R.C. § 408A(d)(2)(A)(ii)]

Example. Portia has maintained a traditional IRA since 1990 and a Roth IRA since 1999. In 2018, she converts the traditional IRA to a Roth IRA. Portia dies in 2020, and her Roth IRA beneficiary immediately takes a complete distribution. The distribution is qualified (it is made to a beneficiary, and the first contribution was more than five years earlier), so it is irrelevant that Portia's conversion contribution was held for less than five taxable years,

Q 5:94 When does the five-year holding period begin for each conversion contribution?

The five-year holding period for any conversion contribution begins on January 1 of the year when that conversion occurred. [Treas. Reg. § 1.408A-6, Q&A-5(c)] It ends on the last day of the individual's fifth consecutive taxable year in the period beginning with the conversion year. A separate holding period must be tracked for each conversion contribution. Making a conversion contribution does not, however, restart the five-year holding period that applies to determine whether distributions are qualified or nonqualified.

Example 1. Keisha converts $40,000 to a Roth IRA in 2015 and $30,000 more (including $4,000 of nondeductible contributions) in 2016. In 2020, she takes a $60,000 nonqualified distribution from the Roth IRA. The distribution includes $40,000 of sufficiently aged conversion contributions and $20,000 of conversion contributions that were taxed at the time of conversion and have been held less than five taxable years. None of the distribution is includible in gross income, but Keisha must pay $2,000 in additional tax unless an exception applies.

	First date a penalty-free distribution can be made	*Allocation to the 2020 distribution*
2015 conversion:		
$40,000	1/1/2020	$40,000
2016 conversion:		
$26,000 taxed at time of conversion	1/1/2021	$20,000
$4,000 not taxed at conversion	n/a	

Example 2. Max, age 35, establishes a Roth IRA in 2015 at Anchor Bank and immediately makes a $5,000 regular contribution. In 2016, he converts part of his traditional IRA (all pre-tax amounts) to a new Roth IRA at Safeway Credit Union. In 2017, he contributes $5,000 to the Anchor Bank Roth IRA.

And in 2018, he converts the rest of his traditional IRA (all pre-tax amounts) to the Safeway Roth IRA. For qualified distribution purposes, all of Max's Roth IRAs share the same five-year holding period. But if either conversion contribution is returned in a nonqualified distribution before the date shown below (fourth column), it will be treated as an early distribution subject to the 10 percent additional tax (unless an exception applies):

Contribution year	*Type of contribution*	*When qualified distribution can be made (if there is also a qualified reason)*	*When conversion contribution will be held long enough to avoid 10% additional tax if distributed in a nonqualified distribution*
2015	Regular	1/1/2020	n/a
2016	Conversion	1/1/2020	1/1/2021
2017	Regular	1/1/2020	n/a
2018	Conversion	1/1/2020	1/1/2023

Q 5:95 During the five-year holding period, can the 10 percent additional tax be avoided by making a distribution from a different Roth IRA that does not hold the conversion contributions?

No. All Roth IRAs are treated as one IRA under the aggregation rules (see Q 5:86; "first" paragraph), so placing conversion amounts in a separate Roth IRA does not change how a distribution is taxed. [I.R.C. § 408A(d)(4)(A)]

Q 5:96 Should conversion contributions be segregated from regular contributions in separate Roth IRAs for tracking purposes?

There is no reason to do so. A five-year holding period must be separately tracked for each conversion, but the conversion contributions may be commingled with regular contributions. Under the aggregation rules, all Roth IRAs owned by the same individual are treated as one Roth IRA for taxation purposes (see Q 5:46).

Other Issues (Traditional and Roth IRAs)

Withholding

Q 5:97 Are IRA distributions subject to income tax withholding?

Most IRA distributions are subject to withholding requirements, but withholding can usually be waived. (For more information, see Qs 8:23, 8:24.) A payor is not required to withhold tax from any part of an IRA distribution that "it is reasonable to believe" is not includible in the payee's gross income. [Treas. Reg. § 35.3405-1T, Q&A-2]

A payor must withhold tax from an IRA distribution unless:

- The payee provided the payor with a U.S. residential address (including a military or diplomatic post office address) and elected out of withholding (see below);
- The payee is a nonresident alien who certified that status to the payor; or
- The distribution is a qualified disaster distribution or coronavirus-related distribution (see Q 7:4).

If withholding is required, the amount to be withheld is:

- For periodic distributions (i.e., from an annuity), the amount that would be withheld if the distribution were a payment of wages.
- For nonperiodic distributions, 10 percent of the amount distributed from the traditional IRA, or the part of a Roth IRA distribution reasonably believed to be includible in gross income.

[I.R.C. § 3405; Prop. Treas. Reg. § 31.3405(a)-1; Notice of Proposed Rulemaking, 85 Fed. Reg. 31714 (May 27, 2020); Temp. Treas. Reg. § 35.3405-1T; Notice of Proposed Rulemaking, 84 Fed. Reg. 25209 (May 31, 2019); Notice 87-7, 1987-1 C.B. 420; Disaster Tax Relief and Airport and Airway Extension Act of 2017, Pub. L. No. 115-63 (Sept. 29, 2017), § 502(a)(6)(A); Tax Cuts and Jobs Act, Pub. L. No. 115-97 (Dec. 22, 2017), § 11028(b)(1)(F)(i); Bipartisan Budget Act of 2018, Pub. L. No. 115-123 (Feb. 9, 2018), § 20102(a)(6)(A); Consolidated Appropriations Act, 2021, Pub. L. No. 116-260 (Dec. 27, 2000)]

3.8 Percent Tax on Unearned Income

Q 5:98 Does the 3.8 percent tax on unearned income apply to IRA distributions?

Not directly. This tax, imposed by Code Section 1411, is 3.8 percent of the *lesser of* an individual's net investment income, or the amount by which AGI (with some modifications) exceeds a threshold figure. Distributions from IRAs, individual retirement annuities, and qualified plans are excluded from the calculation of net investment income, but included in the modified adjusted gross income calculation. So, the receipt of an IRA distribution may increase an individual's exposure to excise tax on his/her *other* investment income. [I.R.C. § 1411(a), 1411(c)]

Planning aspects of the 3.8 percent tax are discussed in detail in chapter 9.

Loss Recognition

Q 5:99 When can investment losses in an IRA be recognized?

An individual cannot deduct losses recognized inside an IRA. But if an IRA is liquidated and closed, and the final proceeds are less than the remaining investment in the contract (basis), a loss is recognized. If more than one IRA of the same type is held, they must all be liquidated because all IRAs of the same type are treated as a single IRA for purposes of determining the investment in the contract. (See Qs 5:3, 5:86.) [Notice 87-16, 1987-1 C.B. 446, part III.D5; I.R.C. §§ 408(d)(1), 408A(d), 72(e)(5)(D)(iii), 72(e)(8)(B); Treas. Reg. § 1.408A-6, Q&A-9]

Then comes the question of how to deduct the loss. IRS Publication 590-B *used to say* that a loss on liquidation of an IRA is claimed as a miscellaneous itemized deduction. [*See, e.g.*, IRS Pub. 590-B, *Distributions from Individual Retirement Arrangements (IRAs)* 2017] But the miscellaneous itemized deduction is repealed for the years 2018 through 2025. [Tax Cuts and Jobs Act (TCJA), Pub. L. No. 115-97 (Dec. 22, 2017), § 11045] A possible solution is to claim the loss under Code Section 165 as a loss incurred in a transaction entered into for profit, though not connected with a trade or business. [I.R.C. § 165(c)(2)]

Q 5:100 Can a loss be recognized on a conversion?

Yes—provided *all* of an individual's traditional IRAs are converted. Conversions are taxed as if they were not qualified rollover contributions; that is, under Code Section 72. (See Q 5:3.) [I.R.C. § 408A(c)(5)(A), 408A(d)(3)(C), 408A(e)(1)(B), 408(d)(3)(A)]

Q 5:101 Can the "net earnings" transferred with a contribution be negative?

Yes. When a contribution is recharacterized or returned in a corrective or similar distribution, the net earnings allocable to the contribution must also be transferred. But a loss would be allocable to such a contribution if the value of the IRA declines during the "computation period" (see Q 5:9).

Q 5:102 Can transactions occurring inside and outside an IRA be matched to find a "wash sale"?

Yes. If an individual sells stock or securities at a loss and buys substantially identical stock or securities within 30 days before or after the sale date, Code Section 1091 disallows the loss. The transaction is considered a "wash sale." In Revenue Ruling 2008-5, the IRS holds that Section 1091 applies if a purchase (or sale) inside an IRA is matched with a sale (or purchase) outside the IRA. [Rev. Rul. 2008-5, 2008-3 I.R.B. 271]

Normally, a loss disallowed under Code Section 1091 results in a basis adjustment, so it is not gone forever. But the ruling does not allow a basis adjustment if the loss-generating side of the transaction occurs inside the IRA. The loss simply vanishes and cannot be recovered even on liquidation of the IRA. [Rev. Rul. 2008-5, 2008-3 I.R.B. 271]

Chapter 6

Rollovers and Direct Transfers

Rollovers and direct (or trustee-to-trustee) transfers may be used in appropriate cases to transfer retirement benefits from one IRA to another, from an eligible retirement plan to an IRA, or to such a plan from an IRA. Rollovers, which consist of a distribution from the first plan and a contribution to the second, must generally be completed within 60 days, and some types cannot occur more frequently than once in a 12-month period. Direct transfers, which do not allow the assets to come under the participant's control, are not subject to those timing rules. However, both kinds of transfers are subject to requirements that are numerous and specific. When they are met, the assets are moved tax free and the transfer is not subject to regular contribution limits.

Rollovers and direct transfers may also be used to convert pretax retirement assets to a Roth IRA. Those transfers are taxable, but not subject to the regular contribution limits.

Assets may be moved from one Coverdell ESA to another, or from one health savings account to another, using these methods. Special rules also permit limited movements of certain nonretirement assets (e.g., military death gratuities) into an IRA, and (once in a lifetime) some IRA assets into a health savings account.

This chapter explores thoroughly the many complex requirements that must be satisfied to achieve the desired results for these transfers.

Transfer Methods

Q 6:1 How may funds be moved from one IRA to another without incurring tax and penalties?

There are two ways to move funds from one IRA (including individual retirement annuities) to another without incurring tax and penalties—the 60-day rollover and the direct (or trustee-to-trustee) transfer. Most transfers can be accomplished either way, but some—e.g., moving inherited IRA assets for a nonspouse beneficiary—must use a direct transfer.

Q 6:2 Can assets from other retirement plans also be transferred to, or received from, an IRA tax free?

Yes. The other retirement plans that can engage in a tax-free movement of assets with an IRA (including individual retirement annuities) are:

- *Qualified plans* (e.g., 401(k), profit sharing, money-purchase, and 403(a) annuity plans)

- *403(b) annuity plans* (nonqualified plans for employees of a charitable, religious, or educational organization described in Code Section 501(c)(3))
- *Governmental 457(b) plans* (nonqualified deferred compensation plans for employees of a state or local government)

[I.R.C. §§ 402(a), 403(b)(1), 403(b)(8), 457(e)(16), 457(e)(1)(A)]

As with IRA-to-IRA transfers, either a 60-day rollover or a direct transfer is used to move assets between one of these plans (an *Eligible Plan*) and an IRA, and use of the 60-day rollover is restricted in some cases.

Note. The Code uses the term *eligible retirement plan*, which includes IRAs, to describe *all* the retirement plans that are eligible to receive tax-free rollover contributions. [I.R.C. § 402(c)(8)(B)] In this chapter, we use the term *Eligible Plans* to describe only the *non-IRA* defined contribution plans eligible to receive such contributions.

Tax-free asset transfers *between* Eligible Plans (i.e., in which no IRA is involved) are outside the scope of this book and not discussed here.

Q 6:3 What is a rollover?

A *rollover* occurs when an individual takes a distribution from one IRA or Eligible Plan and deposits the assets into another IRA or Eligible Plan within the required time period (usually 60 days). [I.R.C. §§ 408(d)(3), 408A(e)(1), 402(c)(3), 403(a)(4), 403(b)(8), 457(e)(16)] During the interim between the distribution and redeposit, the individual controls the funds and may use them for any purpose. If the trustee makes the distribution by issuing a check, the individual is named as payee.

Certain rollovers cannot occur more frequently than once in any 12-month period (see Qs 6:15–6:19).

Caution. Issuance of a check to make a 60-day rollover distribution is risky. If the beneficiary is inadvertently named as the payee, the rollover will not qualify. That was the unfortunate holding in a Tax Court case that lacks precedential value (only a summary decision was issued) but is nonetheless instructive. [Beech v. Commissioner, T.C. Summary Op. 2012-74 (July 26, 2012)]

Q 6:4 What is a direct or trustee-to-trustee transfer?

Unlike a rollover, a *direct transfer* (also called a *trustee-to-trustee transfer*) does not involve a distribution. Instead, the trustee of one IRA or Eligible Plan directly moves assets to the trustee of another IRA or Eligible Plan on behalf of the individual requesting the transfer. [I.R.C. § 401(a)(31)(A)] If the same trustee serves both plans, the transfer is made internally (within the same financial institution).

The trustee can use any reasonable means of payment that bypasses the individual. For example, a wire transfer may be directed to the trustee of the receiving plan. Or, the transferring plan's trustee may issue a check payable to the receiving plan's trustee on behalf of the named individual. Such a check may be mailed directly to the receiving trustee or provided to the individual (who cannot cash it) for delivery to that trustee. [Treas. Reg. § 1.401(a)(31)-1, Q&A-11, Q&A-12]

Direct transfers are not subject to the timing rules that apply to 60-day rollovers (see Q 6:9).

Note. The terms *trustee-to-trustee transfer* and *direct transfer* are used interchangeably in this book.

Q 6:5 Are the same methods used for conversions?

Yes, but in conversions the transfers are taxable. For example, the direct transfer of a traditional IRA to a Roth IRA is treated as a taxable distribution and recontribution (see Q 6:42).

Q 6:6 When *must* a direct transfer be used?

A direct transfer *must* be used in the following cases:

- when inherited assets are transferred on behalf of a nonspouse beneficiary
- when assets are transferred from a designated Roth account (DRAC; see Q 6:74) to a Roth IRA
- to move assets from an IRA to an HSA (using a *qualified HSA funding distribution*; see Q 6:118)

If a 60-day rollover is attempted in these cases, it will fail to qualify (see Q 6:7).

Q 6:7 What happens if a rollover requirement is not met?

If the 60-day deadline is not met and a waiver is not obtained (see Q 6:25), or if any other rollover requirement is not met, the transfer (or in some cases part of the transfer) is not tax free. Instead, it is treated as a taxable distribution from the first plan and a regular contribution to the second plan. The distribution is taxable in the year it occurs (even if the 60-day period does not end until the succeeding year), and withholding requirements and the 10 percent early distribution penalty may both apply to the taxable part of the distribution. The regular contribution limit applies to the amount deposited into the receiving plan, so an excess contribution can result—possibly triggering the 6 percent excess contribution penalty. Finally, if the failed rollover occurs during payment of a series of substantially equal periodic payments (by either the transferring or the receiving plan), the transaction may be treated as a modification, causing the 10 percent penalty to be payable on every prior payment in the series, with interest for the period of the delay. (See Qs 6:83, 5:34). [I.R.C. §§ 408(d)(3), 72(t)(1), 4973]

Q 6:8 Are there advantages to using a direct transfer rather than a rollover?

Yes. A direct transfer is safer than a rollover because there is no possibility of noncompliance with the timing rules that apply to rollovers (see Q 6:9). Also, withholding is not required when a direct transfer is used. When a rollover is used to transfer assets from an Eligible Plan, the trustee must withhold 20 percent of the taxable part of the distribution (see Q 6:57).

Despite those advantages, an IRA owner or Eligible Plan participant may prefer to use a 60-day rollover so he or she may use the assets during the period between distribution and deposit—in effect, as a short-term loan.

Timing Rules for Rollovers

Q 6:9 What timing rules apply to rollovers?

Every rollover must be completed within 60 days (or the longer period allowed under certain Code exceptions or other laws; see Q 6:20), unless an IRS waiver is obtained (see Q 6:25). Rollovers between certain IRAs are also limited to only one in any one-year period (see Q 6:15).

Note. In lieu of a waiver, some individuals may be able to use a new self-certification procedure to complete the rollover (see Q 6:25).

Q 6:10 Do the timing rules apply to direct transfers?

No. A direct transfer is treated for tax purposes as a distribution and contribution that occur simultaneously, making the 60-day rule irrelevant. Nor is there a limit on the frequency with which direct transfers between IRAs may occur. [Treas. Reg. § 1.402(c)-2, Q&A-1; Rev. Rul. 78-406, 1978-2 C.B. 157]

For example, in Private Letter Ruling 201005057 the IRS ruled that a plan participant could hold a check issued in a direct transfer for more than 60 days before depositing it into the receiving plan. The check was payable to the custodian of the receiving plan for the benefit of the individual, so the individual never had control over the funds. [Priv. Ltr. Rul. 201005057 (Feb. 5, 2010)]

Sixty-Day Deadline

Q 6:11 When does the 60-day rollover period begin?

The 60 day period begins on the date when the individual receives a distribution. In the case of a distribution by check, that means the date the check is received (not when it is deposited or cashed). [I.R.C. §§ 408(d)(3)(A)(ii), 402(c)(8)(B); Treas. Reg. § 1.402(c)-2, Q&A-11]

In one case, an employee was away on vacation, during which time his mail was being held at the post office. Promptly upon returning from vacation, he picked up his mail from the post office, and that date was deemed to be the date he received the distribution. The ruling noted that the mail was not picked up until the day after the employee's return from vacation because the employee had returned too late on his date of return to retrieve his mail. [Priv. Ltr. Rul. 8804014 (Oct. 27, 1987)]

In another case, a distribution check was received 10 months after it was issued because the trustee did not have the employee's correct address from the employer. Because the rollover was made 30 days after the check was finally received, it was timely. [Priv. Ltr. Rul. 8833043 (May 26, 1988)]

Q 6:12 When does it end?

The general rule is that a rollover contribution must be deposited no later than the 60th day after the date on which the distribution is received. [I.R.C. §§ 408(d)(3)(A), 408A(e)(1), 402(c)(3), 403(a)(4), 403(b)(8), 457(e)(16)] This rule is strict and every calendar day is counted—even when the 60th day falls on a weekend or holiday. To be safe, individuals should ensure that any check mailed to the trustee for deposit is *received* by the trustee within the 60-day period.

> **Example.** Victoria plans to withdraw $2,500 from her traditional IRA and then roll it over tax free to another (or the same) IRA. The trustee mails her a distribution check (not an RMD) on November 5, 2019. Victoria receives the check on November 8, 2019. The 60-day period begins on November 8, 2019. It ends on the date that is 60 days later—January 7, 2020. The rollover contribution will be timely if it is made no later than January 7, 2020.

The IRS has issued several private letter rulings in which the 60th day fell on a Sunday or bank holiday, and the rollover contribution was acceptable on the 61st day. But in those rulings, the IRS used its discretionary authority to *waive* the 60-day deadline (see Q 6:27). [Priv. Ltr. Ruls. 200952066 (Dec. 24, 2009), 200930052 (July 24, 2009), 200951044 (Dec. 18, 2009)]

> **Note.** If a rollover is started in one calendar year and completed in the next, the December 31 value of the *receiving* IRA must be adjusted for purposes of calculating the RMD that will be paid from it. For example, assume the *actual* December 31 values in year one are $50,000 for IRA-A and $80,000 for IRA-B, but $5,000 was distributed from A on December 15 and not rolled over to B until January 15 of year two. For purposes of determining the RMD payable from B in year two (which depends on the account balance at the end of year one), the December 31 value of B is $85,000, because it is deemed to include the rollover contribution. [Treas. Reg. § 1.408-8, Q&A-7]

Q 6:13 How does the 60-day rule apply to consecutive distributions?

If two eligible rollover distributions are made on different days, and both of them precede a contribution, each distribution is tested separately to see whether a 60-day rollover has occurred. So, if the contribution is too late to be matched with the first distribution, the analysis does not stop there. It may still qualify as a rollover of the second distribution. [Treas. Reg. § 1.402(c)-2, Q&A-11; Haury v. Commissioner, 113 A.F.T.R.2d 2014-2074 (8th Cir. 2014)]

Example. Rob withdraws $3,000 from his traditional IRA on May 31, and $10,000 more on July 10. On July 31 (61 days after the first distribution, but only 21 days after the second), he returns $3,000 to the IRA. The first distribution is taxable, because it was not returned within 60 days. But the second distribution has been partially rolled over. Rob's combined taxable income from the two distributions is $10,000 ($3,000 plus $7,000).

Q 6:14 Does the IRS grant relief if the 60-day deadline is violated?

Yes, in some circumstances. (See Q 6:25.)

One-Year Limit

Q 6:15 What is the one-year limit for tax-free rollovers?

During any one-year period, an individual may only receive one IRA distribution that is returned to an IRA (the same or another) in a nontaxable 60-day rollover. [I.R.C. § 408(d)(3)(B)]

Q 6:16 To what rollovers does the one-year limit apply?

The one-year limit only applies to tax-free, 60-day, IRA-to-IRA rollovers. It does not apply to rollovers from a traditional IRA to a Roth IRA (which are taxable conversions), rollovers between IRAs and qualified plans, or direct transfers from one IRA to another. [Ann. 2014-32, 2014-48 I.R.B.] Nor does it apply to certain involuntary IRA distributions (see below, after the examples). [IRS Information Letter 2017-0018 (May 31, 2017)]

Example 1. Evelyn owns two traditional IRAs. She received no IRA distributions during 2018. On January 1, 2019, she receives a $5,000 distribution from one IRA which she deposits into the other IRA less than 60 days later. If Evelyn receives another IRA distribution before January 1, 2020, she cannot use a 60-day rollover to return it tax free to an IRA. She could, however, ask the trustee to move the funds using a direct transfer.

Example 2. Harvey takes a distribution from his traditional IRA in January 2020, and two weeks later he rolls it back to the same IRA. In May 2020, he opens a Roth IRA, takes a full distribution of the traditional IRA, and deposits the cash to the Roth IRA less than 60 days later. The second rollover is a taxable conversion, so it is not barred by the one-year limit.

The FDIC, as receiver for a failed financial institution that is also an IRA trustee, may distribute the IRAs if another trustee does not assume them. The one-year rule does not apply to such a distribution, provided neither the failed institution nor the depositor initiated it. [IRS Information Letter 2017-0018 (May 31, 2017)]

Q 6:17 How does the one-year limit apply to an individual who owns more than one IRA?

The one-year limit applies on an aggregate basis to all the IRAs an individual owns. IRAs of all types are considered together—traditional, SEP, SIMPLE, and Roth IRAs. For example, a tax-free 60-day rollover between an individual's traditional IRAs precludes a tax-free 60-day rollover between the individual's Roth IRAs (and vice versa), if both distributions occur within a one-year period. [Ann. 2014-32, 2014-48 I.R.B.]

Example 1. Bob owns a traditional IRA, a SEP IRA, and two Roth IRAs. He wants to consolidate them so he has just one traditional IRA and one Roth IRA. On March 15, 2018, he receives a full distribution of the SEP IRA which he deposits into the traditional IRA within 60 days. If Bob were to receive a Roth IRA distribution before March 15, 2019, he could not roll it over tax free to the other Roth IRA. Instead, Bob should ask the trustee to consolidate the Roth IRAs using a direct transfer, because that is not subject to the one-year limit.

Example 2. Helena, who owns a traditional IRA and a Roth IRA, has a short-term need for cash. She withdraws the needed cash from the traditional IRA on October 1, 2018 and returns it within 60 days to the same IRA. If she takes another distribution from any IRA before October 1, 2019, she will be unable to return it to an IRA as a tax-free 60-day rollover.

Q 6:18 When does the one-year period begin and end?

The one-year period is measured based on the date a distribution is *received.* If the second distribution is received before the same date one year later, it occurs within the period barred by the one-year limit. [I.R.C. § 408(d)(3)(B)]

Example 1. Janis expects to receive a large taxable annuity payment in two weeks, but currently needs cash for bills. She decides to take $10,000 from her traditional IRA and then return that amount from her annuity check when it arrives. The IRA trustee mails the distribution check on March 1, 2019; Janis receives it two days later (March 3) and deposits it into her checking account. The distribution does not violate the one-year limit if *no other distribution* received by Janis on or after March 3, 2018 was rolled over tax free to an IRA. The 2019 rollover will be tax free if Janis restores $10,000 to the IRA within 60 days.

Example 2. Ryan owns two traditional IRAs. He receives a $5,000 distribution from one on June 1, 2019 and deposits it to the other IRA a few days later. This is Ryan's first 60-day rollover, and it qualifies as tax free. No other IRA distribution Ryan receives before June 1, 2020, will be eligible for 60-day rollover to an IRA.

Q 6:19 If a distribution already taken is barred from rollover because of the one-year rule, is relief available?

Tax cannot be avoided if a distribution already taken cannot be rolled over because of the one-year rule. Nor can it be returned to the IRA, except as a regular contribution subject to the annual contribution limit. If the distribution came from a traditional, SEP, or SIMPLE IRA, and the 60-day period has not yet elapsed, it could be rolled over to a Roth IRA as a conversion.

The IRS has no authority to grant relief for violations of the one-year limit, no matter the circumstances. [*See, e.g.*, Priv. Ltr. Rul. 201636050 (Sept. 2, 2016).] (Compare the 60-day deadline, which the IRS has some authority to waive; see Q 6:25.)

Exceptions to the Timing Rules

Q 6:20 What are the exceptions to the timing rules for a 60-day rollover?

The exceptions to the 60-day deadline and the one-year limit are:

1. The 60-day deadline is automatically waived in certain cases involving error by the financial institution (see Q 6:26).
2. The IRS has discretionary authority to waive the 60-day deadline in some hardship cases, upon application by the taxpayer (see Q 6:27).
3. If a qualified first-time homebuyer distribution is made and the funds are not used—only because there is a delay or cancellation of the contract—the deadline for returning the distribution to an IRA is extended to 120 days and the one-year limit does not apply (see Q 6:21).
4. The 60-day rollover period is suspended for *frozen deposits* (distributions temporarily deposited into a taxable account, which then cannot be timely withdrawn for certain reasons related to the bankruptcy or insolvency of a financial institution; see Q 6:22).
5. A *qualified birth or adoption distribution* (see Q 5:63) may be recontributed to an IRA or other Eligible Plan and treated as a tax-free rollover; no time limit applies to the repayment.
6. Within three years after it is made, a *qualified disaster distribution* or coronavirus-related distribution may be repaid to an IRA or Eligible Plan, and treated as a tax-free rollover that is not subject to the one-year limit (see Q 6:23 and chapter 7).
7. The 60-day limit is extended to August 31, 2020 for rollovers of amounts that would be RMDs but for the waiver of RMDs for 2020 by Section 2203 of the Coronavirus Aid, Relief, and Economic Security (CARES) Act, § 2203, Pub. L. No. 116-136 (Mar. 27, 2020). [Notice 2020-51, 2020-29 I.R.B. (June 23, 2020)] (See Q 4:15.)
8. If an amount distributed from an IRA would be an RMD but for the CARES waiver, and it is "repaid" to the distributing IRA by August 31, 2020, the repayment is treated as a rollover for purposes of Code Section 408(d)(3), but *not* for purposes of either Section 408(d)(3)(B)

(the one-year limit) or Section 408(d)(3)(C) (see Q 6:50, re nonspouse beneficiaries). [Notice 2020-51, 2020-29 I.R.B. (June 23, 2020); Notice 2020-50, 2020-28 I.R.B. 35] (See Q 4:14.)

9. During an extended period (with a fixed end date, but not a fixed number of days), some *qualified home acquisition distributions* may be repaid to an IRA or Eligible Plan, and treated as a tax-free rollover to which the one-year limit does not apply (see Q 6:24 and chapter 7).
10. None of the following is subject to the one-year limit—any conversion, recharacterization, or direct (trustee-to-trustee) transfer; any rollover to an IRA from an Eligible Plan; nor any rollover of a qualified reservist distribution, settlement payment received in the *Exxon Valdez* litigation, military death gratuity or SGLI payment (see Qs 6:119–6:121).

Q 6:21 What are the timing rules for recontributing a qualified first-time homebuyer distribution that cannot be used for its intended purpose?

A qualified first-time homebuyer distribution (see Q 5:50) is exempt from the early distribution penalty if it is used within 120 days of receipt to pay certain costs of purchasing a residence (see Qs 5:51, 5:59). If a distribution cannot be used for that purpose *solely* because of a delay or cancellation of the purchase or construction of the residence, the rollover period is automatically extended to 120 days (in lieu of 60 days), and the one-year limit does not apply. [I.R.C. § 72(t)(8)(E); Priv. Ltr. Rul. 200729038 (July 20, 2007)] A private letter ruling may be sought if a longer extension is desired.

Q 6:22 How is the rollover period suspended for frozen deposits?

If an IRA distribution is temporarily deposited in a non-IRA account during the rollover period but cannot be timely withdrawn because it has become a *frozen deposit*, special rules apply. A frozen deposit is an amount that cannot be withdrawn from a financial institution either because the institution is bankrupt or insolvent, or because the state in which it is located has restricted withdrawals on account of the bankruptcy or insolvency (or threat of either) of another financial institution in the state. In the event of a frozen deposit, the period during which the amount is a frozen deposit is not counted in the 60-day period. Also, the 60-day period cannot end earlier than 10 days after the deposit is no longer frozen. [I.R.C. §§ 408A(e), 408(d)(3)(F), 402(c)(7); IRS Pub. 590-A, *Contributions to Individual Retirement Arrangements (IRAs)* 2020 (see Appendix A)]

Q 6:23 What timing rules apply to the repayment of a qualified disaster distribution or coronavirus-related distribution?

To the extent a *qualified disaster distribution* or *coronavirus-related distribution* is eligible for tax-free rollover to an IRA or Eligible Plan (see Qs 6:59, 6:67, 6:101), it may be rolled over to that plan during the three-year period that starts on the day after the distribution. The rollover is disregarded for purposes of the one-year limit. [Disaster Tax Relief and Airport and Airway Extension Act of 2017, Pub. L. No. 115-63 (Sept. 29, 2017) (2017 DTRA), § 502; TCJA § 11028; Bipartisan Budget Act of 2018, Pub. L. No. 115-123 (Feb. 9, 2018) (2018 Budget Act), § 20102; Taxpayer Certainty and Disaster Tax Relief Act of 2019 (2019 DTRA), § 202(a)(3)(A), Div. Q of the Further Consolidated Appropriations Act, 2020, Pub. L. No. 116-94 (Dec. 20, 2019); Consolidated Appropriations Act, 2021, Pub. L. 116-260 (Dec. 27, 2021); CARES Act § 2202; Notice 2020-50, 2020-28 I.R.B. 35]

A qualified disaster distribution is a distribution from an IRA or Eligible Plan that meets certain requirements, including that the recipient sustained economic harm because of a natural disaster that struck in 2016 through 2020. (For the different kinds of qualified disaster distributions, and the periods during which each may be repaid, see Qs 7:3–7:15 and 7:23–7:31. For the ineligibility of a nonspouse beneficiary to repay a qualified disaster distribution, see Q 7:8.)

Q 6:24 What timing rules apply to the repayment of a distribution taken to buy or build a home in an area stricken by a disaster?

Included in the disaster relief is a rule similar to the one described above for unused first-time-homebuyer distributions (see Q 6:21). This rule applies to certain retirement plan distributions that were taken to purchase or construct a principal place of abode, but were not used for that purpose because the area was struck by a natural disaster in 2017, 2018, 2019, or 2020. If various requirements are met, then to the extent such a distribution qualifies for tax-free rollover to an IRA or Eligible Plan, it may be repaid to that plan, and the transfer is treated as a tax-free rollover contribution. [2017 DTRA § 502(b); 2018 Budget Act § 20102(b); 2019 DTRA § 202(b)(2); Consolidated Appropriations Act, 2021]

(For the definition of each disaster area, see Qs 7:11–7:12. For all details concerning these distributions, see Q 7:3 and Qs 7:32–7:42.)

Waiver of the 60-Day Limit

Q 6:25 What are an individual's options if the 60-day rollover deadline is missed?

A taxpayer who misses the 60-day rollover deadline may be able to obtain a hardship waiver. The IRS has statutory authority to extend the rollover period beyond 60 days in cases where the failure to do so would be "against equity or good conscience, including casualty, disaster, or other events beyond the reasonable control of the individual." [I.R.C. §§ 408(d)(3)(I), 402(c)(3)(B); Rev. Proc. 2003-16, 2003-1 C.B. 359] It has used this authority to provide:

- An automatic waiver of the 60-day deadline if certain conditions are met (see Q 6:26).
- A procedure and eligibility requirements for requesting a discretionary waiver, which requires application for a letter ruling (see Qs 6:27, 6:28).

- Waivers granted during examination of the income tax return, if the IRS determines that the taxpayer qualifies for it (see Q 6:29).
- A self-certification procedure, by which an individual claims he or she is eligible for a discretionary waiver, and on which an IRA trustee may generally rely to accept and report the contribution. This is *not* an actual waiver. (See Qs 6:27, 6:28.) [Rev. Proc. 2003-16, 2003-1 C.B. 359; Rev. Proc. 2016-47, 2016-37 I.R.B. 346; Rev. Proc. 2020-46, 2020-45 I.R.B. 945]

Q 6:26 When is the 60-day deadline automatically waived?

The 60-day rule is automatically waived (*without* application to the IRS) when these requirements are met: (1) the taxpayer properly instructed the financial institution concerning the rollover and did everything it required; (2) solely because of financial institution error, the rollover was invalid; and (3) the rollover was completed within one year after the distribution. [Rev. Proc. 2003-16, 2003-1 C.B. 359]

Q 6:27 How is a discretionary waiver of the 60-day rule requested?

If the conditions for an automatic waiver are not met, but the deadline was missed because of hardship (see Q 6:28), an individual may apply to the IRS for a discretionary waiver of the 60-day deadline. A discretionary waiver is requested by applying for a letter ruling.

The submission of a ruling request requires detailed paperwork concerning the retirement account and rollover circumstances, and payment of a user fee ($10,000 for each waiver requested). [Rev. Proc. 2021-4, 2021-1 I.R.B. 157, Appendix A, Category .01(4)]

Q 6:28 What are the grounds for obtaining a discretionary waiver?

To obtain a favorable result, the letter ruling request must convince the IRS that failing to waive the 60-day requirement "would be against equity or good conscience, including casualty, disaster or other events beyond the reasonable control of the taxpayer." The IRS takes into account all relevant facts and circumstances, including:

- Errors committed by a financial institution (if the automatic waiver is unavailable).
- Inability to complete the rollover because of death, disability, hospitalization, incarceration, restrictions imposed by a foreign country, or postal error.
- Whether and how the distributed funds were used.
- The time elapsed since the distribution.

[I.R.C. §§ 408(d)(3)(*l*), 402(c)(3)(B); Rev. Proc. 2003-16, 2003-1 C.B. 359]

Q 6:29 Under what circumstances will the IRS grant a discretionary waiver during examination of the income tax return?

Revenue Procedure 2016-47 [2016-37 I.R.B. 346] states: "In addition to automatic waivers and waivers through application to the IRS under Section 3 of Rev. Proc. 2003-16, the IRS, in the course of examining a taxpayer's individual income tax return, may determine that the taxpayer qualifies for a waiver of the 60-day rollover requirement under § 402(c)(3)(B) or 408(d)(3)(I)."

In a case concerning a late rollover contribution that was made in 2012, the Tax Court held the IRS abused its discretion by failing to grant a waiver during examination. Among other things, the IRS argued it lacked authority to do so because the case predated the 2016 revenue procedure. But the Tax Court held Revenue Procedure 2016-47 was *not* intended to create a *new* authority for the IRS, but rather to make clear that the authority already existed. [Trimmer v. Commissioner, 148 T.C. No. 14 (Apr. 20, 2017)]

Q 6:30 What is the self-certification procedure (in lieu of applying for a discretionary waiver)?

Revenue Procedure 2016-47 [2016-37 I.R.B. 346] also created a new option for taxpayers effective August 24, 2016 (see Q 6:31 for its effect). Instead of going through the letter ruling process to obtain a discretionary waiver, an individual may provide a written self-certification to the IRA trustee (or plan administrator) that the contribution satisfies three conditions. The self-certification procedure was expanded by Revenue Procedure 2020-46, 2020-45 I.R.B. 945, addressing delays that occurred because monies were escheated pursuant to a state's escheatment statute.

First, the IRS must not have previously denied a waiver request with respect to part or all of the distribution to which the contribution relates.

Second, the certification must state that the taxpayer intended to make a timely rollover, but was prevented from doing so because of one or more of 11 acceptable reasons (which must be checked off in the certification):

1. Error committed by the financial institution receiving the contribution or making the related distribution;
2. Distribution was made in the form of a check, which was misplaced and never cashed;
3. The distribution was deposited into, and remained in, an account that the taxpayer erroneously believed was an IRA or Eligible Plan;
4. The taxpayer's principal residence was severely damaged;
5. A member of the taxpayer's family died;
6. The taxpayer or a member of the taxpayer's family was seriously ill;
7. The taxpayer was incarcerated;
8. Restrictions were imposed by a foreign country;

9. A postal error occurred;
10. The distribution was made on account of a levy under Code Section 6331, and the proceeds of the levy have been returned to the taxpayer; or
11. The party making the distribution to which the rollover relates delayed in providing information that the receiving IRA trustee or plan administrator required to accept the contribution, despite the taxpayer's reasonable efforts to obtain it.

Finally, the contribution must be made *as soon as practicable* after the stated reason(s) no longer prevent the taxpayer from making the rollover contribution. A contribution made within 30 days after the obstacle is removed is deemed to have been made as soon as practicable.

The Revenue Procedure includes a model certification form. It may be used word-for-word, or a materially equivalent document may be substituted. [IRS Fact Sheet 2017-1 (Jan. 12, 2017); Rev. Proc. 2016-47, 2016-37 I.R.B. 346]

Q 6:31 What is the effect of the self-certification?

Revenue Procedures 2016-47 and 2020-45 allow the IRA trustee (or plan administrator) to rely on the taxpayer's self-certification when determining whether the contribution meets the statutory standard for a waiver (see Q 6:25 and the factors in Q 6:28), and for purposes of reporting the contribution. However, it may not rely on the self-certification if it has actual knowledge that is contrary to it.

If the trustee accepts the contribution, the taxpayer may report it as a valid rollover. But the certification is *not* a waiver, and upon review the IRS may determine that one or more of the self-certification requirements (see Q 6:30) were not met. If so, there may be added income and penalties (e.g., for failure to pay the correct amount of tax, under Code Section 6651).

A trustee that accepts a late rollover contribution certified by the participant must report it (coded SC) in box 13 of Form 5498, IRA Contribution Information (see Q 8:146). [2020 Instructions for Forms 1099-R and 5498, Distributions from Pensions, Annuities, Retirement or Profit-Sharing Plans, IRAs, Insurance Contracts, etc., and IRA Contribution Information, p. 23]

Q 6:32 How does the IRS rule in situations involving death, disability, or hospitalization?

The IRS is generous in granting discretionary waivers where death, disability, or hospitalization are involved. Evidence that the condition is real (documentation by a physician) must be submitted with the ruling request. The request must also show how the disability or illness prevented timely completion of the rollover.

- Many rulings are granted because the illness, hospitalization, or death of someone close to the taxpayer (spouse, parent, child) caused the taxpayer to be emotionally distraught or preoccupied and unable to cope with financial matters. Other waivers are granted because the taxpayer's own illness or hospitalization prevented completion of the rollover. [*E.g.*, Priv. Ltr. Ruls. 200608025 (Feb. 24, 2006) (care for disabled spouse), 201315036 (Apr. 12, 2013) (prescribed medication impaired the taxpayer's judgment and ability to concentrate)]
- Several waivers were granted based on incapacity caused by Alzheimer's disease. For example, in one case a retiree suffering from Alzheimer's disease, improperly withdrew IRA funds to help pay for a house. The IRS deemed the withdrawal beyond the taxpayer's reasonable control and waived the 60-day deadline to allow redeposit of the amount to an IRA. [Priv. Ltr. Rul. 200401025 (Nov. 5, 2003)]
- A waiver is often granted where an individual took an IRA distribution and died before completing the rollover. The decedent's executor may apply for a waiver if the rollover deadline has passed, in order to deposit the contribution into an IRA in the decedent's name. The ruling request must show the decedent intended to roll over the funds, and they were not used for anything else. [*See, e.g.*, Priv. Ltr. Ruls. 201634026 (Aug. 19, 2016), 200415012 (Jan. 15, 2004).]

Q 6:33 What acts or omissions by a financial institution lead the IRS to grant a discretionary waiver?

Numerous waiver requests concern errors and acts committed by financial institutions, ranging from mistakes, miscommunication, and bad advice, to delay, unavailability, and misappropriation of funds. The taxpayer must show a timely rollover could have been completed but for the financial institution's negligence or erroneous action, and the error or act must be documented. Here are a few examples where waivers were granted because:

- The financial institution made mistakes or did not follow the taxpayer's instructions. [Priv. Ltr. Rul. 200608028 (Feb. 24, 2006)]
- The taxpayer relied on bad advice from the financial institution. [Priv. Ltr. Ruls. 200544026 (Nov. 4, 2005), 200610028 (Mar. 10, 2006)]
- There was miscommunication with the financial institution, or it failed to communicate critical information. [Priv. Ltr. Rul. 200603034 (Jan. 20, 2006) (miscommunication); Priv. Ltr. Rul. 200602049 (Jan. 13, 2006) (the beneficiary/distributee was not told that the distribution came from an individual retirement annuity)]
- The financial institution distributed the wrong amount. [Priv. Ltr. Rul. 200443034 (Oct. 22, 2004) (the trustee miscalculated an RMD and distributed too much); Priv. Ltr. Rul. 201207013 (Feb. 17, 2012) (duplicate RMDs were received because the financial institution asked the IRA owner to submit the withdrawal form twice)]

- The taxpayer's IRA funds were illegally misappropriated by employees of the financial institution. [Priv. Ltr. Ruls. 200531030 (Aug. 5, 2005), 200327064 (July 3, 2003)]
- The financial institution was slow to act, or its personnel were unavailable. [Priv. Ltr. Ruls. 200532061 (Aug. 12, 2005), 200550038 (Dec. 16, 2005)]

Q 6:34 How does the IRS rule in situations where the individual's own advisors gave bad advice?

The IRS will waive the 60-day deadline if the taxpayer relied on bad advice provided by someone other than the financial institution, and that caused the failure to complete a timely rollover. The bad advice must be documented, the reliance must be reasonable, and the taxpayer must show that a rollover was intended. For example:

- The taxpayer kept the traditional IRA distribution because both his tax accountant and a financial advisor advised him (incorrectly) he could use the taxable income to offset other investment losses. [Priv. Ltr. Rul. 201311043 (Mar. 15, 2013)]
- The taxpayer's financial advisor erroneously believed the distribution came from a non-IRA annuity, which would not be taxable because of investment in the contract. [Priv. Ltr. Rul. 201611024 (Mar. 11, 2016)]

Q 6:35 Can a waiver be obtained if the taxpayer's own mistake prevented a timely rollover?

Yes, if a rollover would have occurred but for a *reasonable* mistake of the taxpayer.

An example of a reasonable mistake is Private Letter Ruling 200608026 (Nov. 28, 2005). The taxpayer maintained his IRA with a financial company, and the assets were invested in two company funds—a stock fund and a money market fund. In an Internet transaction, he transferred assets from the stock fund to a *non*-IRA money market fund of the company by mistake, believing it was the money market fund where his IRA was invested. The mistake was discovered two days after the rollover period ended. The IRS viewed the mistake as reasonable and granted a waiver.

The IRS also granted a waiver to a taxpayer who the IRS described as having misunderstood the proper time frame for a rollover. Private Letter Ruling 200606055 (Feb. 10, 2006) is odd because the facts as related seem to show the taxpayer correctly understood the law. According to the ruling, the taxpayer asserted her attempt to deposit rollover funds failed "due to an error on her part in computing the 60-day rollover period . . . she believed that when the 60th day fell on a weekend or holiday, she had until the next business day to accomplish a rollover." The IRS extended the rollover period, because it found the taxpayer had acted in conformance with her belief (she tried to make the contribution the next business day after the 60th day) and had not touched the funds. The ruling briefly mentions serious medical issues the taxpayer faced as additional justification for the waiver.

Q 6:36 In what situations does the IRS refuse to waive the deadline?

The IRS does not waive the 60-day deadline if it is not persuaded that denying the waiver would be "against equity or good conscience, including casualty, disaster, or other events beyond the reasonable control of the individual" (see Q 6:25).

It often reaches this conclusion because the money was used for something else. Even though the rollover rules allow taxpayers to use a distribution for any purpose before returning it to the IRA within 60 days, extreme caution is advised—if the funds are not timely returned, the IRS views their use as evidence that a rollover was never intended. It then rules in conclusory fashion that the money was used as a short-term loan, or to fund a business venture, or for personal expenses, and that the deadline was not missed because of a factor stated in Revenue Procedure 2003-16 (see Q 6:28). Some examples are:

- The taxpayer used retirement distributions to pay bills and personal expenses while waiting for a Social Security determination on his wife's disability and unemployment, which came more than 60 days after the distributions. The IRS concluded the distribution was made as a short-term loan and denied the waiver. [Priv. Ltr. Rul. 200549023 (Sept. 12, 2005)]
- The taxpayer wanted his IRA to purchase a partnership interest, the paperwork prepared by his financial advisor stated that the IRA would hold it, and the custodian issued a check payable to the partnership. But the custodian was unable to hold such property and reported the payment as a distribution. The taxpayer requested a waiver based on reliance upon his financial advisor, who should have chosen a custodian that could hold the partnership interest. The IRS concluded the distribution was used to fund a business venture and denied the waiver. [Priv. Ltr. Rul. 201547010 (Nov. 20, 2015)]
- A husband and wife both took IRA distributions. His was deposited into a checking account and some of the money was used for their living expenses; hers was deposited into another non-IRA account and was left untouched. The IRS granted a waiver for the wife (she claimed reliance on the husband for financial matters) and denied it for the husband. [Priv. Ltr. Rul. 201612017 (Mar. 18, 2016)]

In other cases, the IRS denies the waiver request because (1) evidence to support the claimed factual circumstances was not presented, or it contradicts the taxpayer's assertion; (2) the taxpayer did not exercise reasonable control over the circumstances; (3) a hardship occurred, but it did not *cause* the taxpayer to miss the 60-day deadline; or (4) none of the factors described in Revenue Procedure 2013-16 caused the deadline to be missed. Here is an example of each.

- *Documentation not supportive of claim*: The taxpayer received a distribution of his qualified plan account, and federal tax was withheld from the check. He made a timely contribution of the amount paid by check to a rollover IRA. After the 60-day deadline, he made an online request to transfer funds equal to the withheld tax from his checking account to the IRA (which would have been allowed, if timely; see Q 6:58). He claimed the deadline was missed because of a delayed international mail delivery, but the documentation did not support the claim, and was contradicted by his online transfer request after the deadline had passed. [Priv. Ltr. Rul. 201618014 (Apr. 29, 2016)]
- *Reasonable control not exercised*: The taxpayer believed the rollover period would remain open as long as he did not cash his distribution check, and never bothered to consult a tax professional. [Priv. Ltr. Rul. 200609023 (Mar. 3, 2006)]
- *Financial advisor's error not the cause*: The financial advisor did incorrectly advise that the rollover period was 90 days, but the taxpayer could not have completed the rollover within either 60 or 90 days—the funds were not available. [Priv. Ltr. Rul. 200541050 (July 22, 2005)]
- *Failure to demonstrate a factor enumerated in Revenue Procedure 2013-16*: Fearing his ex-wife was about to attach his IRA, the taxpayer requested an IRA distribution. He set the check aside and forgot about it until after the 60-day period had expired. [Priv. Ltr. Rul. 201548026 (Nov. 27, 2015)]

Q 6:37 Does the IRS have the last word on whether a defective rollover can be cured?

No, the courts do when cases go that far. In a line of decisions, the Tax Court has granted relief for imperfect rollover contributions if the taxpayer acted with full knowledge of the legal requirements, took all steps to comply that were reasonably within his or her control, and achieved substantial compliance with the rules. [*E.g.*, Trimmer v. Commissioner, 148 T.C. No. 14 (Apr. 20, 2017); Wood v. Commissioner, 93 T.C. 114 (1989)]

On the other hand, the Tax Court has denied relief if the defect was not merely *procedural* but concerned a *fundamental element* of the statutory requirements. For example, failing to establish a rollover IRA—that is, depositing the distribution into a regular savings account—is a fundamental defect. So is attempting to use a 60-day rollover for an inherited IRA, because a direct transfer must be used for such a rollover. [Crow v. Commissioner, T.C. Memo. 2002-178; Jankelovits v. Commissioner, T.C. Memo. 2008-285]

Q 6:38 Is a waiver required if a direct transfer is not completed within 60 days?

No, nor will one be granted because the 60-day deadline does not apply to direct transfers. [*E.g.*, Priv. Ltr. Rul. 201035044 (Sept. 3, 2010)]

Special Considerations

Waiver of RMDs for 2020

Q 6:39 Can distributions that would be RMDs but for the CARES waiver be returned to an IRA or other eligible retirement plan?

Relief measures offered in Notices 2020-51 and 2020-50 allow some of these payments (including payments that are part of a series of substantially equal periodic payments) to be returned. (See Qs 4:6–4:17.) [CARES § 2203; Notice 2020-51, 2020-29 I.R.B. (June 23, 2020); Notice 2020-50, 2020-28 I.R.B. 35]

Conversions

Q 6:40 What is a conversion?

A *conversion* occurs when assets are moved to a Roth IRA from a traditional, SEP, or SIMPLE IRA, or from a pre-tax Eligible Plan. A conversion is a taxable transaction; the value transferred is includable in gross income except to the extent basis is allocated to it. (Conversions are discussed in detail in chapters 3 and 10.)

Note. It is not possible anymore to unwind a conversion by recharacterizing it. Conversions made after 2017 cannot be recharacterized (see Q 3:124). [I.R.C. § 408A(d)(6)(B)(iii); TCJA § 13611]

Q 6:41 How is a conversion done?

There are three ways to convert assets to a Roth IRA—by direct transfer, 60-day rollover, or having the trustee redesignate the account as a Roth IRA. These methods are subject to some restrictions (see Table 6-1).

Table 6-1. Conversion Methods

	By		
Convert from:	*Amount Converted:*	*Owner/Participant or Spouse Beneficiary*	*Nonspouse Beneficiary*
Traditional IRA:	Part	• 60-day rollover • Direct transfer	Cannot convert
	All	• 60-day rollover • Direct transfer • Redesignate account as Roth IRA	Cannot convert
SEP IRA:	Part	• 60-day rollover • Direct transfer	Cannot convert

Table 6-1. Conversion Methods (*cont'd*)

	By		
Convert from:	*Amount Converted:*	*Owner/Participant or Spouse Beneficiary*	*Nonspouse Beneficiary*
	All	• 60-day rollover • Direct transfer • Redesignate account as Roth IRA, but then it cannot receive future SEP contributions[1]	Cannot convert
SIMPLE IRA:	Part or all[2]	• 60-day rollover • Direct transfer[3]	Cannot convert
Pre-tax Eligible Plan:	Part	• 60-day rollover or direct transfer to traditional IRA, then redesignate traditional IRA as Roth IRA, *or* • 60-day rollover or direct transfer to Roth IRA	Direct transfer[3] to inherited Roth IRA
	All	• 60-day rollover or direct transfer to traditional IRA, then redesignate traditional IRA as Roth IRA, *or* • 60-day rollover or direct transfer to Roth IRA	Direct transfer[3] to inherited Roth IRA[4]

[1] A SEP IRA cannot receive after-tax contributions.

[2] Conversion is allowed after two years of participation in the SIMPLE (see Q 6:65).

[3] As of 2010, Eligible Plans must also offer a direct transfer on behalf of nonspouse beneficiaries. [Treas. Reg. § 1.401(a)(31)-1, Q&A-1; I.R.C. §§ 408A(c)(3)(B), 408A(d)(3)(B), 402(c)(11), 402(f)(2)(A); Notice 2008-30, 2008-12 C.B. 638, Q&A-4]

[4] A SIMPLE IRA cannot be redesignated as a Roth IRA.

Q 6:42 How is a conversion reported?

No matter how the transaction is completed, a conversion is always treated as a rollover of traditional IRA assets to a Roth IRA for reporting and tax purposes. The IRS has made it clear that a conversion must be reported as a taxable distribution and should not be treated as a trustee-to-trustee transfer from a reporting perspective. [Instructions for Forms 1099-R and 5498 (2020)] The assets are treated as a distribution from the pre-tax IRA or Eligible Plan, and then as a rollover contribution to the Roth IRA. [Treas. Reg. § 1.408A-4, Q&A-1(c)]

Example. Marc receives a brochure from Mutual Funds, Inc., advertising the Roth IRA and in particular the benefits of converting. Marc has a traditional IRA with Big Bank. He completes the conversion form included in the marketing material and returns it to Mutual Funds. Mutual Funds forwards the form to Big Bank. The form asks Big Bank to send Marc's IRA assets directly to Mutual Funds. Big Bank forwards the assets and treats the conversion as a taxable distribution. Mutual Funds treat the contribution as a rollover conversion contribution.

Q 6:43 Does the 60-day deadline apply to assets converted in a rollover?

Yes. In a conversion, assets distributed from a pre-tax IRA or Eligible Plan must be rolled over to the Roth IRA within 60 days of receipt. Of course, there is no 60-day deadline if a direct transfer is used or the account (if a traditional or SEP IRA) is redesignated as a Roth IRA (see Q 6:10). [I.R.C. § 408A(e)]

Q 6:44 Is there a frequency limit on conversions?

No. The one-year limit only applies to certain transfers between IRAs of the *same type* (traditional IRA to traditional IRA, or Roth IRA to Roth IRA). It does not apply to conversions. However, the IRS limits the number of *reconversions* of the same assets to once a year (see chapter 5). [Treas. Reg. § 1.408A-5, Q&A-8]

Example. Sam has $24,000 in a traditional IRA invested in a mutual fund. He would like to convert the traditional IRA to a Roth IRA. Sam understands that the conversion is a taxable distribution and does not want to risk converting the entire amount in the traditional IRA at one time. Like other investors, Sam does not know whether the market will go up or down over the next 12 months. He decides to convert $2,000 per month throughout 2019 in order to obtain a rough yearly average of the stock price. He may do so because there is no limit on the number of conversions an individual may make in a year.

Q 6:45 Are conversions subject to the income limits that apply to regular Roth IRA contributions?

No. The modified adjusted gross income (MAGI) limits on regular Roth IRA contributions do not apply to conversions. So, an individual who cannot contribute directly to a Roth IRA (because his or her income is too high) may still do so through the "back door"—i.e., by making a nondeductible traditional IRA contribution and immediately converting it to a Roth IRA. No waiting period is required. (See Q 3:75.)

Congress, in its Conference Committee Report accompanying the TCJA, acknowledged that this method is used to avoid the income limits on Roth IRA contributions. The statement appears in the discussion of Section 13611 of the TCJA, which repeals the rule that used to allow conversion contributions to be recharacterized (see Q 3:124). [Conference Comm. Rep. on the TCJA, ¶ 5088, n. 269]

Transfers After Death

Q 6:46 Can an inherited IRA be transferred to the beneficiary's own IRA?

Only if the IRA beneficiary is the surviving spouse. For any nonspouse beneficiary, an inherited IRA interest must only be transferred to a properly denominated *inherited IRA* (see Q 6:47). [I.R.C. § 408(d)(3)(C)(ii)] Consequently, if the decedent's IRA is payable to his or her estate and the surviving spouse inherits it through the estate, the IRA may *not* be transferred to the spouse's own IRA. [Priv. Ltr. Rul. 9229022 (Apr. 20, 1992)] But if the surviving spouse is the sole beneficiary of the trust or estate, and as trustee or executor has the unlimited right to compel a distribution of the IRA, then any amounts distributed may be rolled over to the spouse's own IRA. [Treas. Reg. § 1.408-8, Q&A-5; *e.g.*, Priv. Ltr. Ruls. 201612001 (Mar. 18, 2016), 201618011 (Apr. 29, 2016)]

A surviving spouse who is the *contingent* IRA beneficiary may transfer it to his or her own IRA if the primary beneficiary makes a timely qualified disclaimer of the interest (see Qs 4:76–4:80). [Priv. Ltr. Rul. 9247026 (Aug. 24, 1992)]

The distribution rules in Code Section 408 are to be applied without regard to community property laws. [I.R.C. § 408(g)] So if the surviving spouse (SS) holds a community property interest in the decedent's IRA, but the decedent designated someone *else* as the IRA beneficiary, the IRS will treat any transfer of IRA assets to the SS—whether by agreement among the parties or pursuant to a court order—as a taxable distribution to the designated beneficiary, which the SS cannot roll over. [Priv. Ltr. Rul. 201623001 (June 3, 2016)]

Q 6:47 How must an IRA or inherited Eligible Plan interest be transferred for a nonspouse beneficiary?

There are several requirements. First, a direct transfer must be used (and qualified plans are required to offer them), or else the nonspouse beneficiary will be treated as receiving a taxable distribution, and the regular contribution limit will apply to the amount deposited to the IRA. [I.R.C. §§ 408(d)(3)(C)(ii), 402(c)(11), 402(f)(2)(A); Notice 2007-7, 2007-5 I.R.B. 395; WRERA § 108(f)(2)(A), Pub. L. No. 110-458 (2008)] Second, for inherited Eligible Plan Interests, the individual benefited by the transfer must be the *participant's* designated beneficiary (not a beneficiary of that person; see Q 6:69).

Third, the receiving IRA must be titled to identify both the deceased participant and his or her beneficiary (e.g., "Tom Smith as beneficiary of John Smith"), to make clear that it is an inherited IRA (see Q 4:42).

Finally, if the decedent had named a trust as the beneficiary, a direct transfer of the qualified plan benefits to an IRA on behalf of the trust is only tax free to beneficiaries of the trust if the requirements for treating them as designated beneficiaries are satisfied—i.e., the trust is a *see-through trust* (Q 4:71), a *conduit trust* for one beneficiary (Q 4:72), or an *applicable multi-beneficiary trust* (Q 4:74). [Notice 2007-7, Q&A-16, 2007-5 I.R.B. 395]

Q 6:48 If IRA assets are payable to a marital trust, can they be transferred to an IRA in the spouse's name?

No. The spouse of an IRA owner may roll over any distributions from the inherited IRA but may not elect to treat the inherited IRA as his or her own IRA (see Qs 4:54, 10:6). [*E.g.*, Priv. Ltr. Ruls. 201423043 (June 6, 2014), 200807025 (Feb. 15, 2008), 200615032 (Apr. 14, 2006)]

Q 6:49 Can a beneficiary who inherits pre-tax Eligible Plan assets from the participant convert them to a Roth IRA?

Yes. Any beneficiary—spouse or nonspouse—may convert inherited Eligible Plan assets to a Roth IRA. The surviving spouse may use a direct rollover or 60-day rollover. For a nonspouse beneficiary, a direct transfer must be used. [I.R.C. § 408A(e); Notice 2008-30, Q&A-7, 2008-12 I.R.B. 638]

Q 6:50 Can a nonspouse beneficiary of an inherited traditional, SEP, or SIMPLE IRA convert that to a Roth IRA?

No. Nonspouse beneficiaries of *Eligible Plans* have this right, but nonspouse beneficiaries of *IRAs* do not. Under present law, the surviving spouse is the only IRA beneficiary who may convert an inherited IRA to a Roth IRA. [I.R.C. §§ 408A(c)(5)(A), 408A(e), 408(d)(3), 408(d)(3)(C)]

> **Note.** There is no logical reason for treating nonspouse beneficiaries differently if the distribution comes from a qualified plan versus an IRA. Unfortunately, recent legislative proposals have not addressed this inequity.

Q 6:51 Do the disaster relief provisions allow a nonspouse beneficiary to repay a qualified disaster distribution, coronavirus-related distribution, or qualified home acquisition distribution?

No. The rule is the same for all those distributions: Any person who receives the distribution as a *beneficiary*, unless it is the surviving spouse, is not eligible to repay it to an IRA or Eligible Plan. (See Qs 7:8, 7:36.) [IRS Pub. 976, *Disaster Relief* (Feb. 2018)]

Divorce

Q 6:52 Is the transfer of an individual's IRA to a spouse or former spouse tax free?

It is tax free if the transfer to the spouse or former spouse is made under a divorce or separation instrument that meets the requirements in Code Section 408(d)(6). Otherwise, the transfer is treated as a taxable distribution. [I.R.C. §§ 408(d)(6), 408A(a), 121(d)(3)(C); Treas. Reg. § 1.408-4(g)(1); Summers v. Commissioner, T.C. Memo. 2017-125] Divorcing parties should not attempt to divide an IRA on their own, without a court order.

Q 6:53 Is a qualified domestic relations order needed to transfer the IRA?

No. A qualified domestic relations order (QDRO) is used to transfer qualified plan assets tax free in a divorce or marital separation. It has no application to IRAs. [I.R.C. §§ 402(e)(1), 414(p)]

> **Note.** A QDRO is a judgment, decree, or order (including approval of a property settlement agreement) that is issued under the domestic relations law of a state and gives an alternate payee (the spouse, former spouse, child, or other dependent of the participant) the right to receive all or part of the participant's Eligible Plan benefits. A QDRO cannot change the type or form of a benefit. [I.R.C. § 414(p)(1)(B), 414(p)(2), 414(p)(3), 414(p)(8)]

Q 6:54 How should the IRA transfer be carried out?

1. The participant's IRA could be continued and the name of the owner changed to that of the spouse or former spouse. (Both are referred to here as the *Spouse*.) The IRA trustee might require the new owner to sign a new IRA document.
2. A direct transfer could be used to move some or all of the IRA assets to a new or existing IRA of the Spouse.
3. The assets to be retained could be moved by direct transfer to a new or existing IRA in the retaining Spouse's name, and the original IRA could be redesignated in the other Spouse's name.

Q 6:55 Can Eligible Plan benefits be transferred to the Spouse tax free without a QDRO?

No. Transfers of eligible plan benefits without a QDRO would be taxable distributions. Many eligible plans do not allow any transfers to a spouse without a QDRO.

Q 6:56 If the Spouse receives distributions from the participant's Eligible Plan under a QDRO, can they be transferred tax free to an IRA?

Yes, but a tax-free transfer cannot be done for anyone else.

Under a QDRO, an Eligible Plan interest is divided between the participant and one or more *alternate payees* (Spouse, children, and dependents). The QDRO may transfer benefits to an alternate payee either by allocating some or all of the interest to a separate account maintained in the plan, or by directing that part or all of each distribution be paid to the alternate payee.

Either way, a Spouse who receives a distribution as alternate payee under a QDRO is treated like the participant under the rollover rules—so the Spouse may transfer such a payment tax free to an IRA if it is an eligible rollover distribution. [§ 402(e)(1)(B)] Either a 60-day rollover (subject to 20 percent mandatory withholding; see Q 6:57) or a direct transfer may be used.

Withholding

Q 6:57 Must tax be withheld from a rollover distribution?

The general rule is that income tax must be withheld from a *60-day rollover* distribution (though not from a direct transfer). If there is a 60-day rollover from an Eligible Plan, the trustee is required to withhold 20 percent of the distribution. Withholding may be waived, however, when rollover distributions are made from an *IRA*. [I.R.C. §§ 3405, 7701(a)(37)]

To waive withholding from an IRA distribution, the IRA owner or beneficiary must complete Form W-4P, Withholding Certificate for Pension or Annuity Payments, and request zero withholding (see chapter 8). Otherwise, usually 10 percent of the IRA distribution is withheld. If the distribution is made from an individual retirement *annuity* without a withholding waiver, the withheld tax is calculated as though the distribution were a payment of periodic wages. [I.R.C. § 3405(b)]

Q 6:58 Can outside funds be added to a rollover distribution to make up for withheld tax?

Yes—and they should be added. If the full amount of a distribution is not rolled over, the portion that is not is includable in gross income. So if tax is withheld and outside funds are not substituted to make up the difference, tax will be payable on the amount of tax withheld.

If a rollover distribution is received net of withholding tax, outside funds may be added to replace all or part of the withheld tax, but no more. The final amount rolled over cannot exceed the initial gross amount of the distribution eligible for rollover. If withheld tax is replaced, the individual is allowed a credit on the income tax return. [Treas. Reg. § 1.402(c)-2, Q&A-11]

Transfers from One IRA to Another

Q 6:59 What transfers are allowed between IRAs?

Table 6-2 summarizes the *tax-free* transfers that can be made between IRAs subject to satisfaction of applicable requirements. (For taxable conversions, see Table 6-1, Q 6:41.) Except as indicated, either a 60-day rollover or direct transfer can be used to transfer all or part of an account, and to transfer the entire account redesignation by the trustee is also an option.

Both timing rules (the 60-day deadline and the one-year limit) apply to tax-free rollovers (but not direct transfers) from one traditional, SEP, or SIMPLE IRA to another, or from one Roth IRA to another. (See Q 6:16.)

(Qs 6:59 to 6:66 only concern transfers between individual *retirement* accounts. Transfers that involve HSAs or Coverdell ESAs are discussed in Qs 6:113–6:118.)

Table 6-2. Permitted Tax-Free Transfers Between IRAs

	To			
Transfer from:	*Traditional IRA*[1]	*Roth IRA*[1]	*SEP IRA*[1]	*SIMPLE IRA*[1]
Traditional IRA	Yes	No[2]	Yes	Yes[3]
Roth IRA	No	Yes	No	No
SEP IRA	Yes	No[2]	Yes	Yes[3]
SIMPLE IRA	Yes[4]	No[2]	Yes[4]	Yes

[1] A SEP IRA cannot receive after-tax contributions.

[2] Conversion is allowed after two years of participation in the SIMPLE (see Q 6:65).

[3] Eligible Plans must also offer a direct transfer on behalf of nonspouse beneficiaries. [Treas. Reg. § 1.401(a)(31)-1, Q&A-1; I.R.C. §§ 408A(c)(3)(B), 408A(d)(3)(B), 402(c)(11), 402(f)(2)(A); Notice 2008-30, 2008-12 C.B. 638, Q&A-4]

[4] A SIMPLE IRA cannot be redesignated as a Roth IRA.

Q 6:60 What must be excluded from an IRA-to-IRA transfer?

RMDs and excess contributions with earnings must be excluded from a tax-free transfer between IRAs. Also, if noncash property is included in the distribution, the rules described in Qs 6:94 and 6:95 determine what may be rolled over. [I.R.C. §§ 408(d)(3)(A), 408(d)(3)(E), 408(d)(3)(A)(i), 402(c)(6)(A); IRS Pub. 590-A, *Contributions to Individual Retirement Arrangements (IRAs)* 2019 (see Appendix A)]

Transfers from a SIMPLE IRA to any *other* type of IRA are not allowed until the individual has at least two years of participation in the SIMPLE (see Q 6:65). [I.R.C. § 408(d)(3)(G)]

Q 6:61 Who may convert a traditional, SEP, or SIMPLE IRA to a Roth IRA?

The *owner* of a traditional, SEP, or SIMPLE IRA may convert all or part of it to a Roth IRA. After the IRA owner dies, if the surviving spouse is the sole beneficiary, he/she may also convert it. Otherwise, it is *not* possible to convert an inherited IRA. [I.R.C. §§ 408A(c)(5)(A), 408A(e), 408(d)(3)(C)]

Conversions from a SIMPLE IRA cannot occur until two years of participation in the SIMPLE have been completed (see Q 6:65). [I.R.C. §§ 408(d)(3)(G), 72(t), 408A(c)(5)(A)]

Q 6:62 When may IRA conversions occur?

Other than the two-year participation requirement for conversions from a SIMPLE IRA (see Q 6:65), the only restriction is that conversions must occur during the lifetime of the IRA owner (or during the lifetime of the spouse beneficiary who has taken ownership of the IRA). The one-year limitation on tax-free transfers between IRAs does *not* apply to conversions. [I.R.C. § 408A(e)]

Q 6:63 How is basis allocated to a rollover or direct transfer?

If an individual has more than one Roth IRA, they are considered in the aggregate to make any basis determinations. Basis (if any) in traditional, SEP, and SIMPLE IRAs is also determined by considering those on an aggregate basis. (Inherited IRAs are only aggregated with other IRAs that are inherited from the same person.) [I.R.C. §§ 408(d)(2), 72] Consequently, tax-free transfers do not affect basis in an IRA. Conversions are different, however.

Since conversion from a traditional, SEP, or SIMPLE IRA to a Roth IRA is treated as a taxable distribution from the first IRA followed by a contribution to the Roth IRA, basis in the distributing IRA (determined in the aggregate as just described) is allocated pro rata to the distribution to determine the amount of taxable income. (See Qs 5:3, 3:103.)

If an IRA distribution includes both earnings and basis amounts, and only part of the distribution is rolled over, the earnings and basis are each allocated pro rata to the rollover. The basis and earnings cannot be separated and selectively returned to an IRA. [Notice 87-16, 1987-1 C.B. 446, Q&A-D3] (By contrast, pre-tax and after-tax amounts disbursed in a single distribution from an Eligible Plan *can* be separated and selectively transferred to an IRA; see Qs 6:85–6:93.)

Q 6:64 Are transfers between IRAs reversible?

Transfers that are *not* conversions are reversible, subject to the recharacterization rules (see Qs 3:110–3:123). Conversions after 2017 cannot be recharacterized (see Q 3:124).

Q 6:65 What is the two-year participation requirement for transfers to or from a SIMPLE IRA?

Until an employee completes two years of participation in the employer's SIMPLE plan, rollovers and transfers to and from the SIMPLE IRA are restricted, and early distributions suffer a steep penalty. The two-year period begins on the date the first deposit is made into the employee's SIMPLE IRA. [I.R.C. § 72(t)(6); Notice 98-4, 1998-1 C.B. 269]

During that two-year period, rollovers and direct transfers may only occur *between* SIMPLE IRAs. And, for distributions made from the SIMPLE IRA during the first two years, the early distribution penalty for individuals under age 59½ is 25 percent of the taxable amount (instead of the usual 10 percent). [I.R.C. §§ 408(p)(1)(B), 72(t)(6)]

Once the two years of participation are completed, the rules are much freer. SIMPLE IRA assets may then be transferred to a traditional IRA, SEP IRA, or pre-tax Eligible Plan, or converted to a Roth IRA. Also, assets can then be moved *into* the SIMPLE IRA from a traditional or SEP IRA, or from a pre-tax Eligible Plan. [I.R.C. § 408(p)(1)(B); Protecting Americans from Tax Hikes Act of 2015, Pub. L. No. 114-113 (PATH Act), § 306]

Q 6:66 Are transfers from a SIMPLE IRA subject to other special rules?

Yes. Special rules govern the fees and charges that a trustee may impose for SIMPLE IRA transfers. [Notice 98-4, 1998-1 C.B. 269]

Transfers from an Eligible Plan to an IRA

Q 6:67 What transfers are allowed from an Eligible Plan to an IRA?

Eligible rollover distributions (see Q 6:78) may be transferred from an Eligible Plan to an IRA if various requirements are satisfied. Those transfers that are tax free are summarized in Table 6-3; taxable conversions are summarized in Table 6-1 (see Q 6:41). Except as indicated, either a 60-day rollover or direct transfer can be used to transfer all or part of an account, and if the entire account will be transferred another option is redesignation by the trustee. [I.R.C. §§ 402(c)(1), 402(e)(6), 403(b)(8), 457(e)(16)]

The 60-day deadline applies to tax-free rollovers (but not direct transfers) from an Eligible Plan to an IRA (see Q 6:9). These transfers are not subject to a one-year limit.

Table 6-3. Permitted Transfers from an Eligible Plan to an IRA

	To			
Transfer from:	*Traditional IRA*	*Roth IRA*	*SEP IRA*	*SIMPLE IRA*
Pre-tax Eligible Plan[1]	YES	See Table 6-1[2]	YES	YES[3]
Designated Roth Account (DRAC)[4]	NO	YES	NO	NO

[1] A direct transfer is required if the transfer is made on behalf of a nonspouse beneficiary, and the receiving IRA must be properly denominated as an inherited IRA.

[2] This is a taxable conversion; see Table 6-1.

[3] Transfer is allowed after December 18, 2015, and after two years of participation in the employer's SIMPLE. A SIMPLE IRA cannot be redesignated as a traditional, Roth, or SEP IRA, so a 60-day rollover or direct transfer must be used. [I.R.C. §§ 408(p), 72(t)(6); Protecting Americans from Tax Hikes Act of 2015, Pub. L. No. 114-113 (PATH Act), § 306]

[4] Transfer is allowed after two years of participation in the employer's SIMPLE.

Q 6:68 What restrictions apply to the receiving IRA?

There are several restrictions:

- The amount transferred must be an *eligible rollover distribution* (see Q 6:78)
- Eligible rollover distributions from a designated Roth account (*DRAC*; see Q 6:74) may only be transferred to a Roth IRA (including Roth individual retirement annuities)
- For transfers made on behalf of a nonspouse beneficiary, a direct transfer must be used and the receiving IRA must be designated as an inherited IRA (see Q 6:47)
- Eligible Plan assets may only be transferred to a SIMPLE IRA after two years of participation in the SIMPLE plan (see Q 6:65).

[I.R.C. §§ 402(c)(1), 402(c)(8)(B), 402(c)(5), 408(p)(2)(A)(iv), 402(c)(11); Treas. Reg. § 1.402(c)-2; PATH Act of 2015, Pub. L. No. 114-113, § 306]

Q 6:69 For whose benefit can Eligible Plan assets be transferred to an IRA?

An eligible rollover distribution may be transferred to an IRA on behalf of:

- the employee-participant (this includes self-employed individuals)
- the surviving spouse of the employee-participant
- a nonspouse designated beneficiary of the employee-participant (only by direct transfer to an inherited IRA)—but *not* a beneficiary of the participant's designated beneficiary
- the present or former spouse of the employee-participant, pursuant to a qualified domestic relations order.

[I.R.C. §§ 402(i), 402(c)(9), 402(c)(11)(A)(i), 402(e)(1), 403(b)(8), 457(e)(16); IRS Information Letter 2017-0030 (Oct. 11, 2017)]

Q 6:70 What transfer methods may be used?

A direct transfer may be used for permitted transfers from an Eligible Plan to an IRA. A 60-day rollover can also be used (subject to mandatory withholding of 20 percent; see Q 6:57), *unless* the transfer is made:

- on behalf of a nonspouse beneficiary, or
- from a DRAC.

[I.R.C. §§ 402(c)(3), 402(c)(5), 402(e)(6), 403(b)(8), 457(e)(16); Treas. Reg. § 1.401(a)(310-1), Q&A-1(b)]

Q 6:71 Are transfers from an Eligible Plan to an IRA reversible?

No. These transfers are always irrevocable. [Treas. Reg. § 1.402(c)-2, Q&A-13]

Q 6:72 What are the typical circumstances for transfers from an Eligible Plan to an IRA?

Most transfers from an Eligible Plan to an IRA are occasioned by:

1. *Termination of employment.* Although an employer cannot force terminated employees to accept a lump-sum distribution unless an employee's vested account balance is less than $5,000 (or the lesser threshold stated in the Eligible Plan documents), many employees prefer to take their money with them—and employers prefer that they do so for purposes of administration and responsibility. IRAs are generally more flexible and subject to lower administration fees than assets in an Eligible Plan. (The employer may elect whether the $5,000 or lesser mandatory distribution threshold is determined with or without regard to amounts, including earnings, that a participant rolled over to the plan.) [I.R.C. § 411(a)(11)(D)]

2. *Death.* Often when an Eligible Plan participant dies, the surviving spouse will transfer the participant's account to the spouse's own IRA. Other beneficiaries may transfer the account, but only to an inherited IRA (see Qs 6:46, 6:47).
3. *Disability.* Typically, the family of a disabled Eligible Plan participant will need to evaluate resources and medical coverage, as well as proceeds of disability insurance, before deciding how much, if any, of an Eligible Plan distribution should be transferred to an IRA.

Current employees may also want to transfer their plan assets to an IRA as a way to realign investment choices. Eligible Plans are not required to allow in-service withdrawals, however.

Q 6:73 Must an Eligible Plan offer a direct transfer of assets to an IRA, or to multiple IRAs?

An Eligible Plan must offer the plan participant (or the beneficiaries of a deceased participant) a direct transfer of plan assets to *one* traditional, SEP, or Roth IRA. [Treas. Reg. § 1.401(a)(31)-1, Q&A-1; I.R.C. §§ 408A(c)(3)(B), 408A(d)(3)(B), 402(c)(11), 402(f)(2)(A); Notice 2008-30, 2008-12 C.B. 638, Q&A-4]

An Eligible Plan is not required to offer direct transfers to *multiple* IRAs. It may do so, or it may (also not required) offer to make two or more distributions so the participant (or beneficiary) may do 60-day rollovers to multiple IRAs. Nothing in the law requires an Eligible Plan distribution to be transferred to a single traditional IRA. [Rev. Rul. 79-265, 1979-2 C.B. 186]

Transfers from a Designated Roth Account to an IRA

Q 6:74 What is a designated Roth account?

A designated Roth account (DRAC) is a separate account within a 401(k), 403(b), or governmental 457(b) plan that receives only after-tax contributions. Participants may elect to have part or all of their elective deferrals designated in this manner. [I.R.C. § 402A; Prop. Treas. Reg. § 1.402A-1, Q&A-5] DRACs are not subject to the income limitations that apply to Roth IRAs. Distributions from a DRAC may only be rolled over to another DRAC or to a Roth IRA. [I.R.C. §§ 402A, 402(c)(8)(B), 403(b), 457]

Q 6:75 Who can transfer amounts from a DRAC to a Roth IRA?

Any DRAC participant (or the participant's surviving spouse) may transfer an eligible rollover distribution from the DRAC to a Roth IRA—even if he or she is ineligible to make annual contributions to a Roth IRA. [Treas. Reg. § 1.408A-10, Q&A-2] The nonspouse beneficiary of a deceased DRAC participant may transfer amounts from the DRAC to an inherited Roth IRA if a direct transfer is used. [Notice 2009-68, 2009-39 I.R.B. 423; Treas. Reg. § 1.402A-1, Q&A-5(a); Notice 2009-68, 2009-39 I.R.B. 423]

Q 6:76 What are the advantages of making transfers from a DRAC to a Roth IRA?

Roth IRAs are more flexible than DRACs (simpler to manage) and have several tax advantages over a DRAC:

1. *RMD avoidance.* A DRAC participant must take RMDs from the account during his or her lifetime. Roth IRA owners are exempt from the RMD rules. [I.R.C. § 408A(c)(4)]
2. *More favorable taxation of nonqualified distributions.* Roth IRA contributions are distributed first, before earnings, so even nonqualified distributions may be entirely tax free. [I.R.C. § 408A(d)(4)(B); Treas. Reg. § 1.408A-6, Q&A-8] DRAC distributions carry out pro rata amounts of contributions and earnings; thus, if the account has appreciated in value, part of any nonqualified distribution will be taxable. [I.R.C. § 72(e)(8)] (However, see Qs 6:91–6:93 for how a DRAC distribution may be split.)
3. *Credit for lost basis.* A special rule applies if a DRAC that has *depreciated* in value is fully distributed and a portion is then rolled over to a Roth IRA. The "lost" basis (excess of contributions over fair market value) is added to basis in the Roth IRA. [Treas. Reg. § 1.408A-10, Q&A-3(b)]

Example 1. Margaret established a DRAC in 2014, and in 2019 she takes a qualified distribution of $50,000, which she rolls into a new Roth IRA account (her first) that she established for that purpose. The rollover to the new Roth IRA starts the five-year holding period for making qualified distributions from the Roth IRA. Even though no qualified distribution can be made from the Roth IRA until 2024, Margaret can withdraw up to $50,000 tax free at any time, because the ordering rules for Roth IRA distributions treat basis as coming out first.

Example 2. Fran's DRAC account holds $40,000 of contributions, but is worth only $30,000 on the day she takes a full cash distribution. Only contributions are distributed, because there are no earnings. Fran keeps $5,000 of the cash and uses a 60-day rollover to transfer the rest to a Roth IRA. Her basis in the Roth IRA increases by $35,000—$25,000 for the transferred contributions plus $10,000 (the excess of his basis in the DRAC over its fair market value when distributed).

Q 6:77 Is it always beneficial to transfer assets from a DRAC to a Roth IRA?

No. The participant's holding period in the DRAC does *not* carry over to the Roth IRA. Since DRACs and Roth IRAs each have a five-year holding requirement that must be met to have a qualified distribution, this could be problematic if the Roth IRA is new. In that case, it would be necessary to wait until the Roth IRA has been held at least five years before any qualified distributions could be received. (The five-year holding period for a Roth IRA begins on January 1 of the year of the individual's first contribution to any Roth IRA.) [I.R.C. § 408A(d)(2)(B); Treas. Reg. § 1.408A-6, Q&A-2] However, because Roth IRAs distribute contributions before earnings, restarting the five-year clock may have little significance—nonqualified Roth IRA distributions are often tax free anyway.

The rule that does not let the holding period carry over can also be helpful. If an individual who has not fulfilled the five-year requirement for the DRAC transfers assets to a Roth IRA, distributions would then be taxed more favorably—regardless of whether the eligible rollover distribution was qualified or not, or whether the Roth IRA distribution is qualified or not—because contributions could then be distributed before earnings (instead of pro rata, as they would be distributed from the DRAC).

Eligible Rollover Distributions

Q 6:78 What is an eligible rollover distribution?

An *eligible rollover distribution* is a distribution to an employee of all or part of the balance to his or her credit (excluding certain amounts; see Q 6:79) from an Eligible Plan. [I.R.C. § 402(c)(4)]

> **Note.** The term "eligible rollover distribution" (used in the Code) is somewhat misleading because some direct transfers do not involve actual distributions. Also, some transfers fail to qualify as rollovers if a distribution is attempted (e.g., a rollover of inherited qualified plan assets to an inherited IRA).

Q 6:79 What amounts *cannot* be part of an eligible rollover distribution?

The following amounts must be excluded from an eligible rollover distribution that is transferred to an IRA:

- Required minimum distributions (RMDs) (see Q 6:81).
- Substantially equal periodic payments (SEPPs) (see Q 6:83).
- Hardship distributions from a qualified plan (see Q 6:84).
- Corrective distributions of excess contributions, together with allocable income. [Treas. Reg. § 1.402(c)-2, Q&A-4]
- The cost of life insurance paid by a qualified plan. [Notice 2009-68, 2009-39 I.R.B. 423]
- Contributions made under automatic enrollment rules and withdrawn within 90 days of enrollment.
- Deemed distributions (e.g., resulting from an employer loan that was not paid, or from involvement in a prohibited transaction). [Notice 2009-68, 2009-39 I.R.B. 423]
- Inherited retirement assets. Unless the surviving spouse is the decedent's death beneficiary, these cannot be transferred into the beneficiary's own IRA. Eligible Plan assets may be transferred (a direct transfer is required), but only to an "inherited" IRA. (See Qs 6:46–6:47.)
- Property substitutes—if property is distributed, cash or other property may not be substituted (see Qs 6:94–6:96).

[I.R.C. §§ 402(c)(4), 401(a)(31)(C), 403(b)(8), 457(e)(16)]

Required Minimum Distributions

Q 6:80 If an RMD is payable from an Eligible Plan, must it be distributed before assets are rolled over to an IRA?

Yes. Amounts that must be paid to comply with the minimum distribution requirements of Code Section 401(a)(9) are not eligible for transfer to an IRA. The RMD requirements ensure that amounts do not remain indefinitely in tax-favored retirement accounts.

Q 6:81 If a distribution includes an RMD, can the excess amount be transferred to an IRA?

Yes. The RMD itself cannot be rolled over, but the remainder is an eligible rollover distribution unless one of the other exclusions applies. When an RMD is payable from an Eligible Plan, the first distributions are always treated as RMDs until the requirement for the year is fully satisfied. There cannot be an eligible rollover distribution until the current RMD has been distributed. [I.R.C. § 402(c)(4)(B); Treas. Reg. § 1.402(c)-2, Q&A-7; Notice 2007-7, Q&A-17, 2007-5 I.R.B. 395]

Q 6:82 May a participant older than age 70½ roll over an Eligible Plan distribution to a traditional or SEP IRA?

Yes. Even before the SECURE Act repealed the maximum age limit for traditional IRA contributions (see Qs 3:45–3:46), an Eligible Plan distribution could be transferred to a new or existing traditional or SEP IRA after the participant reached that age. [Rev. Rul. 82-153, 1982-2 C.B. 86]

After the transfer, RMDs are calculated for the IRA in the usual way—so if an eligible rollover distribution is transferred to the IRA in one year, a portion of it may be returned as an RMD in the next year (because the RMD calculation depends on the prior year-end balance). (The SECURE Act also delays the start of minimum distributions until age 72; see Q 4:4.)

Substantially Equal Periodic Payments

Q 6:83 What are substantially equal periodic payments?

Substantially equal periodic payments (SEPPs), which must be excluded from an eligible rollover distribution, are Eligible Plan (or IRA) payments that are made at least annually (generally for at least five years) and are computed according to one of three methods—the RMD method, the fixed amortization method, or the fixed annuitization method. An individual younger than age 59½ may initiate a series of SEPP distributions because such payments are not subject to the 10 percent additional tax on early distributions. [I.R.C. §§ 402(c)(4)(A), 72(t)(2)(A)(ii); Rev. Rul. 2002-62, 2002-2 C.B. 710; Treas. Reg. § 1.402(c)-2, Q&A-5] SEPPs are discussed in detail in Qs 5:31–5:41.

Hardship Distributions

Q 6:84 Can hardship distributions from an Eligible Plan be transferred to an IRA?

Generally, hardship distributions from an Eligible Plan *cannot* be transferred to an IRA. [I.R.C. §§ 402(c)(4)(C), 403(b)(8), 457(e)(16)]

However, this transfer restriction is removed once an event occurs that permits without regard to hardship—Eligible Plan distributions to be withdrawn (e.g., separation from service or attainment of age 59½). In that case, the normal rules limiting the transfer of an eligible rollover distribution still apply, but the special restriction on transfers of hardship distributions is lifted. [Notice 99-5, 1999-1 C.B. 319; *modified by* Notice 2000-32, 2000-1 C.B. 1274]

After-Tax Assets

Q 6:85 Does every Eligible Plan account hold both pre-tax and after-tax assets?

No. The *contributions* may be either pre-tax or after-tax assets, depending on the plan. For example, contributions to a DRAC come only from after-tax earnings. And some Eligible Plans that normally take pre-tax contributions (such as a traditional 401(k)) may also accept after-tax contributions. However, the *earnings* within an Eligible Plan account are always pre-tax assets.

Q 6:86 If an Eligible Plan account holds both pre-tax and after-tax assets, how are they allocated to an eligible rollover distribution?

If an Eligible Plan account holds both pre-tax and after-tax assets, a distribution from the account carries out pro rata amounts of each. (This rule does not apply to annuities distributed from Eligible Plan accounts.) [I.R.C. § 72(e)(8)(B), 72(d)]

Example. Diane's account in an Eligible Plan holds $300,000, 20 percent of which ($60,000) is after-tax contributions and 80 percent of which ($240,000) is pre-tax. She requests a direct transfer of $100,000 from the plan to her traditional IRA. The distribution is 20 percent after-tax amounts ($20,000) and 80 percent pre-tax ($80,000). Her plan account is left with $40,000 of after-tax assets, and $160,000 pre-tax assets.

Q 6:87 Can the pre-tax and after-tax amounts in an eligible rollover distribution *both* be transferred to an IRA?

Yes. An eligible rollover distribution that includes both pre-tax and after-tax amounts can be transferred to an IRA, and either a direct transfer or a 60-day rollover may be used. (See Table 6-3, Q 6:67, for which IRAs may accept transfers from Eligible Plans.) [I.R.C. §§ 402(c)(2)(A), 402A]

The rule is different for transfers from one Eligible Plan to another. After-tax amounts included in an eligible rollover distribution may *only* be transferred to another Eligible Plan if a direct transfer is used, and the receiving plan both accepts after-tax amounts and separately accounts for them. [I.R.C. § 402(c)(2)(B)]

Q 6:88 Do pre-tax and after-tax amounts retain the same character after they are transferred to an IRA?

Their treatment depends on whether the eligible rollover distribution comes from a DRAC or a non-DRAC Eligible Plan account.

- If a distribution *not* from a DRAC is transferred to a traditional, SEP, or SIMPLE IRA, the pre-tax and after-tax assets each retain the same character after the transfer.
- Any transfer of a non-DRAC distribution to a Roth IRA is taxed as a conversion. Consequently, those assets are received by the Roth IRA as after-tax assets.
- Eligible rollover distributions from a DRAC may only be transferred to a Roth IRA (or another DRAC). The status of the pre-tax and after-tax components depends on whether the DRAC distribution is qualified or nonqualified. (Determining whether a DRAC distribution is qualified is beyond the scope of this book.)
- If the eligible rollover distribution from the DRAC is qualified, the entire transfer is received by the Roth IRA on an after-tax basis. [Treas. Reg. § 1.408A-10, Q&A-3(a)]
- If the DRAC distribution is nonqualified, however, only the after-tax component is received by the Roth IRA on an after-tax basis. The pre-tax component (representing earnings) of the nonqualified distribution continues to be treated as earnings in the Roth IRA. [§ 402A(d)(1); Treas. Reg. § 1.402A-1, Q&A-2]

In all cases, any earnings that subsequently accumulate on the transferred amounts are pre-tax.

Q 6:89 Can the pre-tax and after-tax parts of the eligible rollover distribution be split, and directed to different "destinations"?

Yes, under current law. According to IRS Notice 2014-54, two or more disbursements from an Eligible Plan may be treated as a single distribution (see Q 6:90), and, if they are, the pre-tax and after-tax components of that single distribution are allocated according to rules that are stated in the same Notice (see Q 6:91). Those rules allocate *pre*-tax amounts first to direct transfers. Taken together, the single distribution and allocation rules of Notice 2014-54 allow the pre-tax and after-tax components of an eligible rollover distribution to be split apart in various ways. [Notice 2014-54, 2014-41 I.R.B. 670]

Q 6:90 What constitutes a single distribution?

The *single distribution rule* of Notice 2014-54 says that:

1. Benefit disbursements that are scheduled to be *made at the same time* are treated as a single distribution—even if the recipient directed they be made to multiple destinations.
2. To determine whether disbursements are scheduled to be made at the same time, reasonable delays to facilitate plan administration are disregarded.

[Notice 2014-54, 2014-50 I.R.B. 937]

Q 6:91 What are the allocation rules for pre-tax and after-tax amounts?

If a single distribution (see Q 6:90) is disbursed to one or more "destinations," the pre-tax and after-tax components are allocated using this hierarchy:

1. Pre-tax amounts are allocated first to any direct transfers.
2. If the pre-tax amount included in the eligible rollover distribution is less than the amount of the direct transfer, it is entirely allocated to the direct transfer. If more than one direct transfer is made (e.g., part to a traditional IRA and part to another Eligible Plan), the recipient can decide how to allocate the pre-tax amount among the direct transfers. The recipient must communicate the desired allocation to the plan administrator *before* the direct rollovers are made.
3. If the pre-tax amount is the same as, or more than the amount of direct transfers, then only pre-tax amounts are allocated to the direct transfers. Any remaining pre-tax amount is next assigned to 60-day rollovers. If there is more than one 60-day rollover, the recipient can decide how to allocate the remaining pre-tax amount among them (and inform the plan administrator).
4. Finally, if any pre-tax amount remains after full allocation to direct transfers and 60-day rollovers, it is included in the recipient's income.

(See the examples in Q 6:92.)

Q 6:92 What distributions are governed by the single distribution and allocation rules of Notice 2014-54?

All Eligible Plan distributions, whether from a DRAC or non-DRAC plan, are now subject to the rules of Notice 2014-54 (which are described in Q 6:91). [Notice 2014-54, 2014-50 I.R.B. 937; T.D. 9769 (May 17, 2016); Treas. Reg. § 1.402A-1, Q&A-5(a)] Those rules became effective at different times:

- For DRAC distributions, on January 1, 2016. (See Example 1.)
- For non-DRAC distributions, on January 1, 2015. (See Examples 2 and 3.)

Example 1. In 2019, when she quits her job, Brianna has $200,000 in a DRAC account within her former employer's qualified plan. That includes after-tax contributions of $160,000 (80 percent) and pre-tax earnings of $40,000 (20 percent). Brianna asks the plan administrator to make two direct transfers—$160,000 to a Roth IRA and $40,000 to a traditional IRA—and allocate all the pre-tax earnings to the traditional IRA. She can do this because both disbursements are treated as a single distribution (see Q 6:90), and she is permitted to allocate all the pre-tax amounts to the traditional IRA (see Q 6:91, rule 2).

Example 2. Maury retires in 2019 with a non-DRAC account balance of $300,000 in his employer's qualified plan. Of that amount, $250,000 is pre-tax and $50,000 is after-tax. He asks the plan administrator to move $250,000 to a traditional IRA and distribute the rest as cash. Both disbursements are treated as a single distribution (see Q 6:90), and all of the pre-tax amounts are allocated to the direct transfer (see Q 6:91). The cash distribution is tax free and withholding is not required.

Example 3. In 2019, when he changes jobs, Dante has an account balance of $300,000 in his old employer's qualified plan. That includes $180,000 of after-tax contributions (60 percent) and $120,000 of pre-tax contributions and earnings (40 percent). Dante wishes to withdraw $20,000 in cash, tax free—which he may accomplish by moving a larger amount of funds and taking advantage of the allocation rules (see Q 6:90). He asks his former employer's plan administrator to remove $100,000 from his account, as a single distribution, and disburse it four ways:

- $20,000 to Dante as a cash distribution,
- $30,000 as a direct transfer to his new employer's qualified plan (which only accepts pre-tax assets from another plan),
- $10,000, including only pre-tax assets, as a direct transfer to a traditional IRA, and
- $40,000, including only after-tax assets, as a direct transfer to a Roth IRA.

Since pre-tax and after-tax assets are removed pro rata from the old plan, 60 percent ($60,000) are after-tax amounts, and 40 percent ($40,000) are pre-tax amounts. The pre-tax amounts are split between the new plan and the traditional IRA. The after-tax assets are split between the Roth IRA and the cash distribution, so Dante is not taxed on receipt of the cash.

Q 6:93 How should plan administrators explain to participants their options for dealing with an eligible rollover distribution?

They are required to provide any recipient of an eligible rollover distribution with a written explanation of all the options. [I.R.C. § 402(f)] Notice 2020-62 includes safe harbor explanations that a plan administrator can provide—one for non-DRAC plans, one for DRACs. [Notice 2020-62, 2020-35 I.R.B. 476]

Noncash Property

Q 6:94 May noncash property be included in an eligible rollover distribution?

Yes, noncash property may be included in an eligible rollover distribution. Or, it may be sold and then the sale proceeds may be rolled over to the IRA. But the distributee may not retain the distributed property and instead transfer cash or property of equivalent value to the IRA—that would not be allowed as a rollover contribution. [I.R.C. § 402(c)(1)(B), 402(c)(1)(C), 402(c)(6); Rev. Rul. 87-77, 1987-2 C.B. 115]

Q 6:95 If the distributed property is sold, must all the proceeds be rolled over to an IRA?

No. But gain or loss will be recognized on the sale of distributed property to the extent any sale proceeds are not rolled over to the IRA. [I.R.C. § 402(c)(6)]

As long as the rollover is completed within 60 days of distribution, the proceeds of sale can be rolled over even if the value of the property changes from the date of distribution to the date of sale. [I.R.C. § 402(c)(6)(A), 402(c)(6)(B)] A property sale will not be taxable, even if there is an increase in value between the date of distribution and the date of rollover, as long as the entire proceeds of the sale are rolled over. [I.R.C. § 402(c)(6)(D)]

If a portion of the distribution is nontaxable (usually a return of after-tax contributions) and the property is sold and only a portion rolled over, the individual may designate which part of the cash or other property is attributable to the nontaxable portion and which part is treated as included in the rollover contribution. The designation, which must be made no later than the due date of the employee's income tax return (including extensions), is irrevocable. If no designation is made, the rollover amount must be allocated pro rata between the cash distribution and the value (determined as of the date of the distribution) of any property received. [I.R.C. § 402(c)(6)(C)]

Q 6:96 Can employer securities distributed from a qualified plan be rolled over to an IRA?

Yes. The main option for a distribution of employer stock (other than rollover) is to pay tax on the cost basis of the stock to the distributing plan. The unrealized appreciation is not taxable until the stock is sold, and then only at capital gains rates. However, it is also possible for the stock (or the proceeds from the sale of the stock) to be rolled over. If the stock is sold and the proceeds are rolled over, there will be no capital gain. [I.R.C. § 402(c)(6)]

Plan Qualification Issues

Q 6:97 Is a rollover to an IRA defective if the distributing trust is no longer a qualified plan?

There are two basic theories regarding the taxing of a distribution from a plan that was originally a qualified plan but becomes disqualified. Three circuit courts, the IRS, and now the Tax Court take the position that once a plan becomes disqualified, no amount is eligible for rollover or income averaging. [*See* Fazi v. Commissioner, 102 T.C. 695 (1994); Priv. Ltr. Rul. 9241008 (July 6, 1992).]

However, under a theory that was previously advanced by the Tax Court, and is still the position of the Second Circuit, it appears that a portion of the distribution is treated as coming from a qualified plan and is eligible for rollover and income-averaging treatment (or capital gains treatment, if applicable), and the remainder of the distribution is currently taxable and is not eligible for rollover or averaging. Of course, one of the difficulties is determining what portion of the distribution can be rolled over or can be eligible for income averaging and what portion cannot. [Greenwald v. Commissioner, 366 F.2d 538, 18 A.F.T.R.2d ¶ 5,645 (2d Cir. 1996)] The Tax Court ruled in favor of the partial disqualification theory in *Baetens v. Commissioner* [777 F.2d 1160 (6th Cir. 1985)], although the Tax Court was later overruled by the Sixth Circuit. In *Fazi v. Commissioner* [102 T.C. 695 (1994)], the Tax Court reconsidered and reversed its original holding in *Baetans* and held that the entire distribution from a disqualified plan was taxable.

Q 6:98 As of when must the distributing plan be qualified for a rollover to be effective?

The distributing plan must be qualified, and its trust must be tax exempt, on the date the distribution is made. A distribution made some time after the plan's termination will probably not be eligible to be rolled over. In one case, a distribution made four years after termination of the plan could not be rolled over. [Priv. Ltr. Rul. 9241008 (July 6, 1992)] In *Boggs v. Commissioner* [83 T.C. 132 (1984)], the Tax Court held that the portion of the distribution consisting of contributions made and trust earnings accrued before the date of a retroactive disqualification remained available for rollover, but subsequent portions were not available for rollover. In *Fazi v. Commissioner* [102 T.C. 695 (1994)], however, the Tax Court found that a distribution from a disqualified plan was taxable, and thus not eligible to be rolled over, even though it included contributions made when the plan was qualified. In *Fazi*, the court found that taxability of the distribution was determined based on the time of the distribution rather than the time the contributions were made. The entire rollover from the plan to Fazi's traditional IRA was disallowed.

Q 6:99 Should a plan participant monitor the rollover process?

A qualified plan participant is well advised to monitor the rollover process. In one case, confusion arose about whether the recipient plan (not a traditional IRA) could or would receive a distribution. The employee relied on a letter from the transferor plan, received before 60 days had elapsed, stating that the application and the employee's check had been forwarded to the plan administrator of the transferee plan at its corporate office. After 60 days had passed without any notification from the transferee plan, the employee contacted a personnel officer at the transferee plan and learned that the check had not been received. Actually, had the check been received, it would not have been accepted because the employee was not eligible to participate in the new plan until the following January 1, the earliest date on which the check could have been accepted. It was then too late to effect a traditional IRA rollover. [Priv. Ltr. Rul. 8819074 (Feb. 17, 1988)]

This case demonstrates that a more efficient approach would have been for the employee to deal directly with the new employer, especially since he was employed within 10 days after terminating employment with his previous employer. If the employee had personally delivered the check to the new employer, he would have immediately learned about the issues involved and would have been able to take the appropriate action to avoid the problem.

Private Letter Ruling 8819074 clearly states that the employee has the burden of verifying that the transferee plan permits the contemplated transfer, and that the employee is eligible for immediate participation in the transferee plan.

Q 6:100 Can qualified plan assets be rolled over to an IRA subject to the participant's pledge to repay the plan if necessary to avoid its termination?

IRA assets may not be pledged to secure a debt, but the IRS has approved a special kind of pledge in one rollover situation. Under a Treasury Department regulation generally referred to as the high-25 rule, certain highly compensated participants in a qualified defined benefit plan are generally restricted from receiving benefits in a lump sum to prevent the premature depletion of the plan's assets should the plan terminate. [Treas. Reg. § 1.401(a)(4)-5(b)(3)] Some highly compensated participants asked the IRS for permission to (1) take lump-sum distributions, (2) roll them over to IRAs, (3) pledge that the money would be repaid if the plan were to terminate without sufficient funds to cover all liabilities, and (4) pledge the rollover IRAs to secure repayment. The IRS agreed that such a pledge would not disqualify the IRAs. [*See* Priv. Ltr. Ruls. 8408063 (Nov. 23, 1983), 9514028 (Jan. 13, 1995); I.R.C. § 408(c)(4).]

Transfers from an IRA to an Eligible Plan

Q 6:101 What transfers may be made from an IRA to an Eligible Plan?

Certain transfers are allowed from an IRA to an Eligible Plan, subject to satisfaction of applicable requirements *and* the Eligible Plan's acceptance of the transfer. Eligible Plans are not required to accept these transfers (see Q 6:104). [I.R.C. § 401(a)(31)(E); Bohner v. Commissioner, 143 T.C. No. 11 (2014)] Table 6-4 summarizes the transfers that the Code allows.

Table 6-4. Transfers from an IRA to an Eligible Plan

	To[1]			
Transfer from:	*Qualified Plan*	*403(b) Plan*	*457(b) Plan*	*DRAC*
Traditional IRA	Yes	Yes	Yes[2]	No
Roth IRA	No	No	No	No[2]
SEP IRA	Yes	Yes	Yes[3]	No
SIMPLE IRA[4]	Yes	Yes	Yes[3]	No

[1] A direct transfer is required if the transfer is made on behalf of a nonspouse beneficiary, and the receiving IRA must be properly denominated as an inherited IRA.

[2] This is a taxable conversion.

[3] *Only* allowed for transfers after two years of participation in the SIMPLE plan (see Q 6:65). [I.R.C. § 408(p); PATH Act of 2015, Pub. L. No. 114-113, § 306]

[4] See Qs 6:74–6:77 for transfers from a DRAC to an IRA.

Q 6:102 May after-tax assets be transferred from an IRA to an Eligible Plan?

After-tax amounts (nondeductible contributions) may only be transferred from an IRA to an Eligible Plan if a direct transfer is used *and* the plan agrees to account separately for the pre-tax and after-tax amounts received. A 60-day rollover cannot be used to transfer the after-tax amounts. The *earnings* on after-tax contributions to a traditional, SEP, or SIMPLE IRA (but *not* a Roth IRA) may be transferred, however—either by direct transfer or 60-day rollover (if the plan allows transfers from a participant's IRA). [I.R.C. § 408(d)(3)(A)(ii); H. Rep. No. 107-51, Part 1 (Pub. L. No. 107-16) June 7, 2001]

If an individual owns more than one traditional IRA, they are all treated as a single IRA for purposes of determining whether a distribution from any of them includes a nondeductible contribution. A special allocation rule applies to transfers from an IRA to an Eligible Plan—such transfers are treated as coming first from the aggregate pre-tax amounts (income and contributions) held in the IRAs. After-tax contributions are not allocated to the IRA transfer until all pre-tax amounts have been removed. [I.R.C. § 408(d)(3)(H)(ii)] The special rule allows more to be transferred from an IRA to an Eligible Plan, because it overrides the general rule that requires basis in traditional IRAs to be prorated to a withdrawal. [I.R.C. §§ 408(d)(2), 72]

Example. Rosalie, age 53, is employed by ABC Company and participates in its 401(k) plan. The plan accepts rollovers from a participant's traditional IRA. Rosalie has two traditional IRAs. The first IRA has a $60,000 balance that is entirely attributable to deductible contributions and earnings. The second IRA holds $125,000—nondeductible contributions ($40,000), pre-tax contributions ($20,000), and earnings on both ($65,000). Considered in the aggregate, the IRAs hold $145,000 of pre-tax assets. That is the maximum amount Rosalie may roll over to a qualified plan, and it does not matter whether she withdraws funds for the rollover from the first or the second IRA.

Q 6:103 If RMDs are payable from the IRA, can they be transferred to an Eligible Plan?

No. The RMD itself may not be rolled over, but other amounts (excluding after-tax amounts) may be transferred from a traditional, SEP, or SIMPLE IRA. (Transfers from a SIMPLE IRA may not occur until the two-year requirement has been satisfied; see Q 6:65.) [I.R.C. §§ 402(c)(4)(B), 408(d)(3)(G), 72(t)(6)]

Q 6:104 What determines whether an Eligible Plan will accept transfers from an IRA?

The transferring IRA owner must participate in the Eligible Plan, and the plan's documents must allow such transfers to be accepted. Acceptance of ineligible transfer contributions could jeopardize an Eligible Plan's tax status. But a plan that inadvertently accepts an ineligible transfer from an IRA trustee will not lose its tax qualification if two requirements are met. First, it must have been reasonable for the Eligible Plan administrator to conclude, based on documentation presented by the IRA owner, that the transfer was proper. And second, within a reasonable time after the plan administrator concludes the contribution was invalid, it is distributed with allocable earnings. [Treas. Reg. § 1.401(a)(31)-1, Q&A-13; Treas. Reg. § 1.401(a)(31)-1, Q&A-14; Rev. Rul. 2014-9, 2014-17 I.R.B. 984]

Example. Emily S. maintains a traditional IRA (not an inherited IRA) that is titled "IRA of Emily S." She asks the IRA trustee to make a direct payment of the entire balance to her employer's qualified plan. The IRA trustee issues a check payable to the qualified plan trustee for the benefit of Emily S., and gives Emily the check. Emily delivers the check to the administrator of the qualified plan, along with a check stub that indicates the funds come from "IRA of Emily S." Emily also certifies to the plan administrator that the funds transferred from the IRA do not include after-tax amounts.

In these circumstances, the administrator for the qualified plan may reasonably conclude that the contribution is valid.

Q 6:105 Must the whole IRA be transferred to the Eligible Plan or can some assets be left behind?

It is possible to transfer just part of an IRA. Code Section 408(d)(3)(A) allows an IRA to distribute "any amount" and transfer it to an Eligible Plan. A direct transfer or a 60-day rollover can be used. [I.R.C. § 408(d)(3)(D); Priv. Ltr. Rul. 9518019 (Feb. 6, 1995)]

Q 6:106 May an Eligible Plan participant transfer to the plan IRA assets that he or she inherited from a deceased spouse?

The participant may do so if the Eligible Plan accepts transfers from a participant's IRA, and the participant inherited the IRA directly (not through a trust) from his or her deceased spouse and was the "sole" beneficiary of that IRA (see Q 4:55). A nonspouse IRA beneficiary does not have this option. [I.R.C. § 408(d)(3)(A), 408(d)(3)(C); IRS Pub. 590-A, *Contributions to Individual Retirement Arrangements (IRAs)* 2020 (see Appendix A)]

Q 6:107 May an independent contractor who does business with an Eligible Plan sponsor transfer IRA assets to the plan?

No. An Eligible Plan may only allow employees to be participants. It cannot accept a rollover from an independent contractor or an individual who does not otherwise have an employment relationship with the employer.

Q 6:108 May an individual older than age 70½ transfer an IRA to an Eligible Plan, and continue to have plan contributions be made on his or her behalf?

Yes. Now that the maximum age limit for contributions to a traditional IRA has been repealed (see Qs 3:45–3:46), there is no age limit on contributions to any Eligible Plan or IRA. Even before the repeal, however, an IRA owner over age 70½ could transfer his or her IRA to an Eligible Plan and still receive contributions under that plan. [I.R.C. § 408(d)(3)(E)]

> **Note.** Minimum distribution requirements now apply once a traditional, SEP, or SIMPLE IRA owner, or a 5 percent owner of the employer maintaining an Eligible Plan, reaches age 72. Other Eligible Plan participants generally are not subject to those rules before retirement. [I.R.C. § 401(a)(9)] Since RMDs are determined based on the prior year-end balance, a portion of any contribution made after age 72 will be returned in an RMD the following year.

Q 6:109 Can an IRA be transferred to an Eligible Plan to delay the start of RMDs?

Yes, unless the individual is a 5 percent owner in the employer that maintains the Eligible Plan (see Note in Q 6:108). Treasury Regulations Section 1.401(a)(9)-7, Q&A-2 provides that if amounts are distributed by one plan and rolled over to a receiving plan, "the benefit of the employee under the receiving plan is increased by the amount rolled over for purposes of determining the required minimum distribution" for the year following the year in which the amount rolled over is distributed.

Based on that regulation, the IRS approved a clever deferral maneuver by an individual who was employed by two companies. He was a 5 percent owner of one company (*Big*), but not the other (*Little*). The IRS allowed him to defer distributions past age 70½ by rolling over his account balance from Big's plan to the plan that Little maintained. As a result, RMDs could be delayed until April 1 of the year after his retirement year. [Priv. Ltr. Rul. 200453015 (Dec. 31, 2005)]

It follows that RMDs would be delayed until after retirement if an employee rolls over a traditional IRA to the employer's Eligible Plan, and the employee is not a 5 percent owner of the company.

Q 6:110 May funds rolled over from an IRA to a qualified plan be used to purchase employer stock?

Yes, and that rollover of IRA funds can be legitimately used to fund a business start-up (a so-called rollover-as-business-start-up, or *ROBS*, transaction). [Powell v. United States, 117 A.F.T.R.2d ¶ 2016-515 (Fed. Cl. 2016)] However, the IRS warns that ROBS transactions have been aggressively promoted and are "questionable because they may solely benefit one individual—the individual who rolls over his or her existing retirement funds to the ROBS plan in a tax-free transaction." [*See* Rollover as Business Start-Ups Compliance Project, available at *https://www.irs.gov/retirement-plans/rollovers-as-business-start-ups-compliance-project* (retrieved May 17, 2019).]

At that webpage, the IRS describes preliminary results from its ROBS Compliance Project, begun in 2009, and warns of several pitfalls:

- Failure to understand that a qualified plan is a separate entity with its own requirements, including the annual filing of plan reports using Form 5500 or Form 5500-EZ.
- Amending the plan, after the ROBS plan sponsor has used rollover funds to purchase the new company's employer stock, to prevent other participants from purchasing stock.
- Amending the plan *after* IRS issuance of a favorable determination letter on it to prevent other employees from participating.
- Fees charged by promoters.
- Asset valuations.
- Failure to issue Form 1099-R, Distributions from Pensions, Annuities, Retirement or Profit-Sharing Plans, IRAs, Insurance Contracts, etc., when the assets are rolled over to the ROBS plan.

[*See also* Memorandum from Michael D. Julianelle (Oct. 1, 2008), available at *http://www.irs.gov/pub/irs-tege/robs_guidelines.pdf* (retrieved May 17, 2019).]

Q 6:111 Once Eligible Plan assets are transferred to an IRA, may they be transferred back to an Eligible Plan?

Yes. All IRA assets (except after-tax contributions) are eligible for transfer to an Eligible Plan without regard to the original source of the funds. [I.R.C. § 408(d)(3)(A)]

If an IRA received transfers from two or more Eligible Plans, assets may be transferred back to one of them (or to another Eligible Plan) from the IRA *if* none of the Eligible Plans transferred after-tax contributions to the IRA, *and* after-tax contributions that were otherwise made to the IRA are excluded. Under the special ordering rule that applies to such transfers from an IRA (see Q 6:102), after-tax amounts would not be allocated to the transfer until all pre-tax amounts held in the individual's IRAs have been exhausted. [I.R.C. § 408(d)(3)(H)(ii)]

Q 6:112 After IRA funds are transferred to an Eligible Plan, can they be used to purchase life insurance?

Yes, if the plan allows it. IRAs cannot purchase life insurance [I.R.C. § 408(a)(3)], but that restriction does not apply after the assets are rolled over to the qualified plan.

Transfers Involving Non-Retirement Assets

Coverdell ESAs

Q 6:113 How are assets moved from one Coverdell ESA to another?

A tax-free direct transfer or 60-day rollover may be used to move assets from one Coverdell ESA (*ESA*) to another. ESAs are generally subject to the same transfer rules as other IRA-to-IRA transfers. [I.R.C. § 530(d)(5)]

Q 6:114 What timing rules apply to a transfer between two ESAs?

The 60-day deadline applies to rollovers (not direct transfers) between ESAs, and only one such rollover is allowed during any one-year period. [I.R.C. § 530(d)(5); IRS Office of Chief Counsel, Program Manager Technical Advice 2016-010 (Dec. 14, 2015)]

Q 6:115 May a transfer be used to change the designated beneficiary of an ESA?

Yes, in some cases. The Code allows the designated beneficiary of an ESA to be changed to another member of the same family without triggering any tax consequences, and either a rollover or direct transfer may be used to accomplish that. [I.R.C. § 530(d)(5)] But the terms of the particular ESA agreement must allow that change (see Qs 14:13, 14:16). [Notice 97-60, 1997-2 C.B. 310] Trustees are not required to include this feature in ESAs that they offer.

Q 6:116 May amounts be moved tax free from an ESA to an IRA?

No. Amounts may not be transferred tax free from an ESA to an IRA. Any transfer of funds from an ESA to an IRA is considered a distribution from the ESA and a regular contribution to the IRA. The distribution is taxable and subject to penalty (because it is not made for qualified education expenses; see

Qs 14:45, 14:41). The regular contribution limit applies to the IRA contribution. [I.R.C. §§ 530(d)(5), 408(a)(1); Treas. Reg. § 1.408A-6, Q&A-18]

Health Savings Accounts

Q 6:117 How are amounts moved tax free from one HSA to another?

Either a direct transfer or a 60-day rollover may be used to move assets from one HSA to another, generally subject to the same transfer rules that apply to IRA-to-IRA transfers. [I.R.C. § 223(f)(5)]

Q 6:118 May assets be rolled over from an IRA to a HSA?

Yes, but only once per lifetime and an election is required. The participant must be an eligible individual, and the withdrawal from the IRA must be a *qualified HSA funding distribution.* If the requirements are satisfied, the transfer is made tax free and without penalty. The rules are extremely complicated, however. [I.R.C. § 408(d)(9); Notice 2008-51, 2008-25 I.R.B. 1163]

Military Payments

Q 6:119 How is a qualified reservist distribution transferred to an IRA?

An individual who receives a qualified reservist distribution (see Q 5:49) has two years, commencing immediately after the end of active duty, to restore the amount to an IRA. No deduction is allowed when a qualified reservist distribution is repaid to an IRA. However, any portion of a qualified reservist distribution that was taxable at receipt constitutes basis when it is repaid to the IRA. [I.R.C. § 72(t)(2)(G)]

> **Note.** A qualified reservist distribution is includable in gross income when received, but exempt from the 10 percent early distribution penalty (see Q 5:49).

Q 6:120 Can military death benefits be rolled over to an IRA?

Yes. Military death gratuities and payments received under the Servicemen's Group Life Insurance Program (SGLI) may be contributed to a Roth IRA or an ESA (see Q 14:35). If they are contributed within one year of receipt, the funds are treated as qualified rollover contributions and are not subject to regular contribution limits. [I.R.C. §§ 408A(e)(2), 530(d)(9)]

Exxon Valdez Settlement Payments

Q 6:121 Can payments received in settlement of the *Exxon Valdez* litigation be transferred to an IRA?

Individuals (or their death beneficiaries) who were plaintiffs in the *Exxon Valdez* litigation (which arose from a 1989 oil spill) may generally transfer to a traditional IRA, Roth IRA, or Eligible Plan up to $100,000 of the settlement payments they receive. [Tax Extenders and Alternative Minimum Tax Relief Act of 2008, § 504(b), Pub. L. No. 110-343, 122 Stat. 3765 (2008); *In re* Exxon Valdez, No. 89-095-CV (HRH) (Consolidated) (D. Alaska)]

The settlement payments may be contributed whether they are received in a lump sum or on a periodic basis, but each must be contributed by the due date (unextended) for filing the return for the taxable year when the payment is made. The payment is treated as a qualified rollover distribution that is deposited into the IRA by a trustee-to-trustee transfer. The one-year limit on rollover contributions (see Q 6:15) does not apply to these contributions.

Exxon Valdez settlement payments that are contributed to a traditional IRA are excluded from gross income and not taxed until they are distributed from the traditional IRA. Payments contributed to a Roth IRA are includable in gross income on receipt, but treated as investment in the contract (i.e., basis) and not taxed when later distributed from the Roth IRA. [Tax Extenders and Alternative Minimum Tax Relief Act of 2008, § 504(b)(3), Pub. L. No. 110-343, 122 Stat. 3765 (2008)]

Airline Payments

Q 6:122 Can settlement proceeds received because of an airline carrier's bankruptcy be transferred to an IRA?

Some airline carriers have been the subject of bankruptcy proceedings filed since September 11, 2001, that adversely affected participants in their defined benefit plans. As a result, court-ordered payments were made to some individuals in order to settle their retirement plan claims. Under laws passed in 2008 and later years, some of those payments could be rolled over to Roth and traditional IRAs.

Q 6:123 What Roth IRA rollovers did the 2008 law allow?

The Worker, Retiree, and Employer Recovery Act of 2008 [Pub. L. No. 110-458 (WRERA)] allowed *qualified airline employees* to transfer *airline payment amounts* to a Roth IRA. To qualify, an individual had to be a current or former employee of a commercial passenger airline carrier that filed for bankruptcy after September 11, 2001, and before January 1, 2007, who participated in a qualified defined benefit plan of the carrier that was terminated or became subject to benefit accrual under the minimum funding rules.

Airline payment amounts (*airline payments*) were money or other property paid to a qualified airline employee by order of a federal bankruptcy court, to settle the individual's bankruptcy claims against the carrier, or against any note or fixed obligation of the carrier to pay a lump-sum amount. WRERA entitled the individual to transfer part or all of the airline payment to a Roth IRA within 180 days of its receipt, or (if later) by June 21, 2009. The transfer was treated as a qualified rollover contribution to a Roth IRA and was not subject to the MAGI requirements that normally (until 2010) restricted such rollovers. But since airline payments were not taxable on receipt, any amount transferred to the Roth IRA was taxed as a conversion. [WRERA § 125(a), 125(b)(2)]

Employment taxes were generally withheld from the airline payment, but the obligation to withhold was ignored when determining the amount eligible for a rollover (i.e., the amount of the withheld tax could also be rolled over). If amounts were paid based on the carrier's future performance, however, those had to be excluded from the rollover. [WRERA § 125(b)(1); Joint Comm. Staff, Tech. Explanation of H.R. 7327, the *Worker, Retiree, and Employer Recovery Act of 2008*, as passed by the House on Dec. 10, 2008]

Q 6:124 How did the 2012 law expand the rollover opportunity to traditional IRAs?

The FAA Air Transportation Modernization and Safety Improvement Act, enacted in 2012, allowed up to 90 percent of the total airline payments received to be transferred to a traditional IRA, treated as a qualified rollover contribution, and retroactively excluded from income. Airline payments that had already been rolled over to a Roth IRA could also be transferred to a traditional IRA (along with allocable income or loss) and recharacterized as though the rollover had originally been made to a traditional IRA. The total amount transferred, whether by rollover, recharacterization, or both (but ignoring any income transferred with a recharacterization), could not exceed 90 percent of the total airline payment received. As under the 2008 law, the total airline payment was determined without regard to employment tax withholding, and amounts based on a carrier's future performance were excluded (see Q 6:123, last paragraph). [FAA Air Transportation Modernization and Safety Improvement Act, § 1106, Pub. L. No. 112-95 (the FAA Act)]

The FAA Act also expanded the term *qualified airline employee* to include the individual's surviving spouse. But it carved out an exception for certain airline carrier executives, so they could not roll over or recharacterize airline payments to a traditional IRA. [FAA Act § 1106(d), 1106(a)(5)]

Any airline payment that was first rolled over to a Roth IRA, and then recharacterized to a traditional IRA, cannot be rolled over again to a Roth IRA for at least five taxable years (see Q 6:126).

To be covered by these rules, an airline payment had to be transferred (by rollover or recharacterization) to a traditional IRA within 180 days of its receipt, or (if later) by August 12, 2012. To claim a refund of tax paid on retroactively excluded income, individuals had to file an amended income tax return. The deadline for doing so was April 15, 2013 (or, if later, the close of the limitations period for credits or refunds under Code Section 6511(a)). [FAA Act § 1106(a)(3)]

Q 6:125 What other rollovers were allowed by the 2014 and 2015 laws?

Section 1106 of the FAA Act was amended in 2014. The effect was to extend the 2012 Act's rollover rules to current and former employees of American

Airlines (excluding some executives), or their surviving spouses. This was accomplished by redefining the term *airline payment amount* to include court-ordered payments under a bankruptcy proceeding filed on November 29, 2011, and the term *qualified airline employee* to include participants in a defined benefit that was frozen as of November 1, 2012. The individuals who became qualified airline employees because of the 2014 Act were given additional time—until April 15, 2015—to amend their tax returns. However, additional time was *not* given for transferring airline payments to an IRA. [FAA Act § 1106, as amended by the Act to Amend Certain Provisions of the FAA Modernization and Reform Act of 2012, Pub. L. No. 113-243, § 1 (the 2014 Act); I.R.S. Ann. 2015-13, 2015-15 I.R.B. 908]

Finally, Section 1106 was amended again in 2015. The 2015 change, which applies only to the individuals swept in by the 2014 Act, allows more time for airline payments to be transferred to an IRA. Those transfers were allowed to occur from December 18, 2014 (when the 2014 Act became effective) through June 15, 2016. [Protecting Americans from Tax Hikes Act of 2015, Pub. L. No. 114-113, Div. Q, § 307 (the PATH Act)]

Q 6:126 Can airline payments that were recharacterized from a Roth to a traditional IRA be converted back to a Roth IRA?

Yes, but only after five taxable years, starting with the taxable year of the recharacterization. [FAA Act § 1106(a)(2), as amended by the 2014 Act § 1 and the PATH Act § 307]

> **Example.** In 2004, Dale, a qualified airline employee, received a $50,000 airline payment, which he rolled over to a Roth IRA. In 2012, after passage of the FAA Act, he timely recharacterized 90 percent of that payment ($45,000), with allocable earnings, as a rollover contribution to a traditional IRA. He also timely filed an amended return for 2004, on which he excluded the recharacterized airline payment ($45,000) from income. Dale may convert the recharacterized payment back to his Roth IRA, although he could not have done so before January 1, 2017.

Q 6:127 Was it possible to recover employment taxes that were withheld from an airline payment rolled over to an IRA?

No. Employment taxes were withheld from airline payments because the payments were treated as wages. Although the withheld employment taxes were ignored to determine the total amount that could be rolled over or recharacterized to an IRA, they could not be recovered. [I.R.C. §§ 3102(a), 3402(a); FAA Act § 1106(c)]

Chapter 7

Disaster Distributions

Congress previously enacted several forms of relief to assist individuals and businesses adversely affected by major disasters that occurred in 2016 and 2017. More recent legislation extended these benefits to cover major disasters in 2018 and 2019, and the coronavirus pandemic and other disasters in 2020. This chapter discusses one form of relief measures—the temporary relaxation of tax rules governing retirement plans, so that qualifying individuals might more easily access, and later restore, their retirement funds.

Tax relief is provided for two groups of retirement plan distributions—qualified disaster distributions and coronavirus-related distributions from an IRA or other eligible retirement plan, and certain other distributions taken to buy or build a principal residence but not used because of a disaster that was declared. For qualified disaster distributions and coronavirus-related distributions, there are three tax breaks: income tax deferral (ratable inclusion of income over three years), exemption from additional tax on early distributions, and the option to roll over the distribution tax free, within three years, to an IRA or other eligible retirement plan.

As to the other group of distributions, qualifying recipients are allowed a shorter period of time to repay the funds to an IRA or other eligible retirement plan. Timely repayments are treated as tax-free rollovers, income inclusions are appropriately reversed, and additional tax paid may be recovered.

Overview of Tax Relief

Q 7:1 What relief does this chapter describe?

Various forms of relief have been enacted to assist individuals and businesses adversely affected by the natural disasters that have occurred since 2016 or the coronavirus pandemic. This chapter describes one type of relief—the temporary relaxation of some federal tax rules governing retirement plans, to ease access by individuals to funds in their retirement accounts and allow them to restore the funds later. The laws authorizing this tax relief are:

- The Disaster Tax Relief and Airport and Airway Extension Act of 2017, Pub. L. No. 115-63 (Sept. 29, 2017) (2017 DTRA), § 502.
- The Tax Cuts and Jobs Act, Pub. L. No. 115-97 (Dec. 22, 2017) (TCJA), § 11028.
- The Bipartisan Budget Act of 2018, Pub. L. No. 115-123 (Feb. 9, 2018) (2018 Budget Act), § 20102.
- Taxpayer Certainty and Disaster Tax Relief Act of 2019 (2019 DTRA), Div. Q of the Further Consolidated Appropriations Act, 2020, Pub. L. No. 116-94 (Dec. 20, 2019).
- The Coronavirus Aid, Relief, and Economic Security Act (CARES Act), Pub. L. No. 116-136 (Mar. 27, 2020).
- Consolidated Appropriations Act, 2021, Pub. L. No. 116-260 (Dec. 27, 2020), Div. EE, Taxpayer Certainty and Disaster Tax Relief Act of 2020, Title III, § 302.

Q 7:2 What is the tax relief offered?

A qualified individual may withdraw up to $100,000 from an IRA or other eligible retirement plan and treat it as a *coronavirus-related distribution* (CRD) or *qualified disaster distribution*. The funds may be used for any purpose. Some distributions can be repaid (rolled over) within three years. To the extent a distribution is not repaid, the income included in the retained portion is spread evenly over three years. The distributions themselves are not subject to withholding or the additional tax on early distributions. (See Qs 7:16, 7:48.)

A three-year rollover period is also allowed for some individuals who withdrew funds from an IRA or eligible retirement plan, which they intended to use to buy or build a principal home in an area where a disaster was declared. Any portion rolled over is exempt from the additional tax. (See Q 7:32.)

Q 7:3 What plans are subject to these rules?

These distributions must be withdrawn from, and can only be repaid to, an eligible retirement plan. *Eligible retirement plan* means any of the following:

- An IRA or IRA annuity (traditional, SEP, SIMPLE, or Roth)
- A qualified pension, profit sharing, or stock bonus plan under Code Section 401(a)
- An annuity contract under Code Section 403(b)
- A qualified annuity plan under Code Section 403(a)
- A deferred compensation plan of a governmental employer under Code section 457(b), or
- A qualified money purchase plan with respect to a coronavirus-related distribution or a qualified disaster distribution under the Consolidated Appropriations Act, 2021, Pub. L. No. 116-260 (Dec. 27, 2020).

IRAs must allow these withdrawals and repayments, but other eligible retirement plans are not required to do so. The terms of a plan may have to be amended to allow them, if that is desired, no later than the last day of the 2022 plan year.

[I.R.C. § 402(c)(8); CARES Act § 2202(a)(4)(C); TCJA § 11028; 2017 DTRA § 502; 2018 Budget Act § 20102; 2019 DTRA § 202(a)(4)(B); Notice 2020-50, 2020-28 I.R.B. 35]

Q 7:4 Can beneficiaries qualify for this relief?

Beneficiaries, which would include alternate payees, who otherwise qualify may withdraw these distributions from an inherited IRA or plan interest. But only the surviving spouse of a deceased participant can repay a distribution. Repayments are treated as rollovers, and nonspouse beneficiaries are not eligible for rollovers. [I.R.C. § 408(d)(3)(C)]

Qualified Disaster Distributions

Definitions

Q 7:5 What is a qualified disaster distribution?

The definition of the term *qualified disaster distribution* recently changed. Under current law, it refers to any of these distributions that an individual withdraws from an IRA or other *eligible retirement plan* (see Q 7:4):

- A qualified 2016 disaster distribution (see Q 7:10),
- A qualified 2017 disaster distribution (see Q 7:11),
- A qualified 2018 or 2019 disaster distribution (see Q 7:12), or
- A qualified 2020 disaster distribution.

Q 7:6 Must a distribution have been made on account of a disaster to qualify?

No. Any distribution meeting the requirements in Qs 7:10–7:12 could be designated as a qualified disaster distribution, even if it would have been made regardless of the disaster. Thus, periodic payments and required minimum distributions (RMDs), which would be paid in any case, may be qualified disaster distributions if they are received by an individual entitled to this relief. [IRS Pub. 590-B, *Distributions from Individual Retirement Arrangements (IRAs)* 2020 (see Appendix B)]

Q 7:7 Who qualifies to receive a qualified disaster distribution?

To be eligible for a qualified disaster distribution, an individual must have:

- Maintained a *principal place of abode* (see Q 7:8) in the major disaster area, on the date or in the time period specified, and
- Sustained an *economic loss* (see Q 7:9) because of that disaster.

Q 7:8 What is a person's principal place of abode?

The principal place of abode is where the person lives most of the time. It does not change merely because of a temporary absence due to special circumstances (e.g., illness, education, business, vacation, or military service).

If a person's principal place of abode was in the disaster area immediately before the disaster struck, and he or she evacuated because of the disaster, that abode is considered still to be there on the date that is required for the qualified disaster distribution. [IRS Pub. 976, *Disaster Relief* (Feb. 2018)]

Q 7:9 What is economic loss?

Economic loss includes, but is not limited to, the following:

- Loss, damage to, or destruction of real or personal property from fire, flooding, looting, vandalism, theft, wind, or other cause;
- Loss related to displacement from one's home; and
- Loss of livelihood due to temporary or permanent layoffs.

[IRS Pub. 976, *Disaster Relief* (Feb. 2018)]

Q 7:10 What is a qualified 2016 disaster distribution?

A qualified 2016 disaster distribution is any distribution from an IRA or other eligible retirement plan:

- made on or after January 1, 2016 and before January 1, 2018,
- to an individual:
  - whose principal place of abode at any time during calendar year 2016 was located in a major disaster area that was declared in 2016 under Section 401 of the Stafford Act, and
  - who sustained an economic loss due to the events that gave rise to that declaration (a *qualified 2016 disaster*).

[TCJA § 11028(b)(1)(D)(i)]

[For a list of the qualified 2016 disasters, *see* IRS Pub. 976, *Disaster Relief* (Feb. 2018).]

Q 7:11 What is a qualified 2017 disaster distribution?

A qualified 2017 disaster distribution is any of the following distributions from an IRA or other eligible retirement plan:

1. For Hurricane Harvey or Tropical Storm Harvey:
   - a distribution made after August 23, 2017 and before January 1, 2019,
   - to an individual whose principal place of abode on August 23, 2017, was located in the Hurricane Harvey and Tropical Storm Harvey disaster area (including Texas and Louisiana), and
   - who sustained an economic loss because of that disaster. [2017 DTRA § 502(a)(4)(A)(i)]
2. For Hurricane Irma:
   - a distribution made after September 4, 2017 and before January 1, 2019,
   - to an individual whose principal place of abode on September 4, 2017, was located in the Hurricane Irma disaster area (including the U.S. Virgin Islands, Puerto Rico, Georgia, Florida, South Carolina, and State of the Seminole Tribe of Florida), and
   - who sustained an economic loss because of that disaster. [2017 DTRA § 502(a)(4)(ii)]
3. For Hurricane Maria:
   - any other distribution made after September 15, 2017 and before January 1, 2019,
   - to an individual whose principal place of abode on September 16, 2017, was located in the Hurricane Maria disaster area (including the U.S. Virgin Islands and Puerto Rico), and

- who sustained an economic loss because of that disaster. [2017 DTRA § 502(a)(4)(iii)]

4. For the California wildfires:
   - a distribution made after October 7, 2017 and before January 1, 2019,
   - to an individual whose principal place of abode was located, at any time during such period, in the California wildfire disaster area (including California), and
   - who sustained an economic loss because of that disaster. [2018 Budget Act § 20102(a)(4)(A)]

Q 7:12 What is a qualified 2018, 2019, or 2020 disaster distribution?

A qualified 2018, 2019, or 2020 disaster distribution is any distribution from an IRA or other eligible retirement plan:

- made on or after the first day of the *incident period* (see below) of a *qualified disaster*, and before June 17, 2020;
- to an individual whose principal place of abode at any time during such incident period was in the respective *qualified disaster area*, and who sustained an economic loss because of that disaster. [2019 DTRA § 202(a)(4)(A)]

The Federal Emergency Management Agency (FEMA) specifies the actual incident period of a disaster (the period when it occurred). But, for purposes of this tax relief, the term *incident period* excludes any part of the actual incident period that is before January 1, 2018 or after January 19, 2020. [2019 DTRA § 201(4)]

The term *qualified disaster* refers to events that gave rise to a Presidential declaration, during the period beginning on January 1, 2018, and ending on January 18, 2020, of a major disaster area under Section 401 of the Stafford Act. For purposes of a qualified 2018 or 2019 disaster distribution, the major disaster area is called the *qualified disaster area*. The California wildfire disaster area is specifically excluded from that term to clarify that double tax benefits are not allowed with respect to the California wildfires (which coincided with part of the same time period; see Q 7:11, paragraph 4). [2019 DTRA § 201(1)(A), 201(3), 201(1)(B)] Under the Consolidated Appropriations Act, Pub. L. No. 116-260 (Dec. 27, 2020), a qualified disaster is a major disaster declared by the President during the period beginning on January 1, 2020 and ending on February 25, 2021, but which must have occurred between December 28, 2019 and on or before December 27, 2020 and during the period specified by FEMA as the period during which the disaster occurred (the Incident Period). However, a major disaster for this purpose does not include any area with respect to which a major disaster was declared only because of a COVID-19 incident. A qualified disaster distribution under the Consolidated Appropriations Act is a distribution made during the Incident Period and after the date on which the area in which the principal place of abode of the individual participant requesting such distribution is declared by FEMA to be a federal disaster area, provided the distribution is made before June 25, 2021.

Dollar Limit on Qualified Disaster Distributions

Q 7:13 What is the dollar limit on qualified disaster distributions?

Generally, there is a $100,000 limit on the total distributions an individual may treat as qualified disaster distributions. This is the aggregate limit for all tax years combined, and from all types of eligible retirement plans. But, for individuals affected by more than one disaster, a separate $100,000 limit applies to each of the following:

- All qualified 2016 disaster distributions;
- All qualified 2017 disaster distributions;
- All qualified 2018 and 2019 disaster distributions made with respect to a particular qualified disaster; and
- All qualified 2020 disaster distributions.

[2017 DTRA § 502(a)(2)(A); TCJA § 11028(b)(1)(B)(i); 2018 Budget Act § 20102(a)(2)(A); 2019 DTRA § 202(a)(2); Consolidated Appropriations Act, 2021, Div. EE, Title III, § 302(a)(2)(A)(i); IRS Pub. 976, *Disaster Relief* (Feb. 2018)]

Q 7:14 May a qualified disaster distribution exceed the individual's actual amount of economic loss?

Yes. A qualified individual must have sustained *some* disaster-related economic loss. But qualified disaster distributions are allowed without regard to need or the actual amount of economic loss. [IRS Pub. 976, *Disaster Relief* (Feb. 2018)]

Q 7:15 If the total distributions exceed $100,000, can the individual choose which to treat as qualified disaster distributions?

Yes. The recipient may designate (see Q 7:17) any distribution that meets the requirements as a qualified disaster distribution, as long as the total amount designated does not exceed $100,000. Thus, if distributions were made from more than one plan, the individual may choose how much of each to designate as a qualified disaster distribution. Similarly, if a qualified disaster distribution is designated for one calendar year and another distribution meeting the requirements is made the following year, the amount designated for the second year cannot cause the total amount of qualified disaster distributions to exceed $100,000.

The excess amount that cannot be designated as a qualified disaster distribution does not qualify for tax relief. The income included in the excess amount is not deferred, and the Code Section 72(t) additional tax also applies if the recipient is younger than age 59½ (unless another exception applies).

Tax Relief for Qualified Disaster Distributions

Q 7:16 What tax relief is provided for qualified disaster distributions?

1. *Income deferral.* They are included in gross income ratably over three years, unless the recipient elects to include all the income in the first year (see Q 7:18). [TCJA § 11028(b)(1)(E)(i); 2017 DTRA § 502(a)(5)(B); 2018 Budget Act § 20102(a)(5)(A); 2019 DTRA § 202(a)(5); Consolidated Appropriations Act 2021, Div. EE, Title III, § 302(a)(6)(A)]
2. *Exemption from the early distribution penalty.* They are exempt from the additional tax under Code Section 72(t) that generally applies to distributions taken before age 59½ (see Qs 7:21–7:22). [TCJA § 11028(b)(1)(A); 2017 DTRA § 502(a)(1); 2018 Budget Act § 20102(a)(1); 2019 DTRA § 202(a)(1); Consolidated Appropriations Act, 2021, Div. EE, Title III, § 302(a)(1)]
3. *Exemption from federal income tax withholding.* [TCJA § 11028(b)(1)(F)(i); 2017 DTRA § 502(a)(6)(A); 2018 Budget Act § 20102(a)(6)(A); 2019 DTRA § 202(a)(6)(A); Consolidated Appropriations Act, 2021, Div. EE, Title III, § 302]
4. *Repayment.* The part of a qualified disaster distribution that is eligible for tax-free rollover to an eligible retirement plan (see Q 7:23) may be repaid to that plan within three years and treated as a tax-free rollover. [TCJA § 11028(b)(1)(C)(i); 2017 DTRA § 502(a)(3)(A); 2018 Budget Act § 20102(a)(3)(A); 2019 DTRA § 202(a)(3); Consolidated Appropriations Act, 2021, Div. EE, Title III, § 302(a)(3)(A)]

Q 7:17 How is the tax relief claimed?

The 8915 series of IRS forms is used to report disaster distributions and repayments.

1. Use the 2019 version of Form 8915-A, Qualified 2016 Disaster Retirement Plan Distributions and Repayments, to report:
   a. *Income*—from a qualified 2016 disaster distribution that was received in 2017, if it is being ratably included in income over a three-year period. Use the 2019 version of the form to report the inclusion for 2019.
   b. *Any repayment*—of a 2016 disaster distribution in 2019.
2. Use the 2019 version of Form 8915-B, Qualified 2017 Disaster Retirement Plan Distributions and Repayments, to report:
   a. *Income*—the income includable for 2019 from a qualified 2017 disaster distribution that was received in either 2017 or 2018, if the income is being ratably included over a three-year period.
   b. *Any repayment*—of a 2017 disaster distribution in 2019.

3. According to IRS Publication 590-B, *Distributions from Individual Retirement Arrangements (IRAs)* 2020, at page 36 (see Appendix B), the IRS will also release:
   a. Form 8915-C, Qualified 2018 Disaster Retirement Plan Distributions and Repayments,
   b. Form 8915-D, Qualified 2019 Disaster Retirement Plan Distributions and Repayments, and
   c. Form 8915-E, Qualified 2020 Disaster Retirement Plan Distributions and Repayments.

Income Deferral

Q 7:18 What are the two ways to include taxable income from a qualified disaster distribution?

The two methods are:

- The default method (ratably include the taxable income over three years), and
- The elective method (include all of it in the distribution year).

An individual who receives more than one qualified disaster distribution in the same year must treat them consistently, using the same method. If the default three-year method is used, the method cannot be changed after the due date (including extensions) for filing the income tax return for the distribution year. [*See* Notice 2005-92, 2005-51 I.R.B. 165.]

Q 7:19 How is the election made to include all the income in the first year?

The election is made on the form used to report the distribution.

Q 7:20 If a person using the three-year inclusion method dies before including the full amount, what happens to the rest of the income?

If a qualified individual using the three-year method dies before all the taxable income is included, the remainder must be included in the decedent's gross income for the year of death. [*See* Notice 2005-92, 2005-51 I.R.B. 165.]

Example. Evan, a qualified individual, received a $30,000 qualified Hurricane Harvey distribution on October 1, 2017. On his 2017 income tax return, he reported $10,000 of taxable income from the distribution. Evan died in November 2018. The rest of the taxable income ($20,000) will be included on the income tax return for his final taxable year.

Exemption from the Early Distribution Penalty

Q 7:21 What is the Code Section 72(t) tax, from which qualified disaster distributions are exempt?

Code Section 72(t) generally imposes an additional tax on IRA and qualified plan distributions taken by a person younger than age 59½. The additional tax is 10 percent of the taxable part of the distribution, or 25 percent of the taxable amount if the distribution is made from a SIMPLE IRA during the first two years of participation in the employer's SIMPLE plan. [I.R.C. § 72(t)(1), 72(t)(6)]

There are many exceptions to the Code Section 72(t) tax (see Q 5:26), but none of them matter when a qualified disaster distribution is taken. All qualified disaster distributions are exempt from the Code Section 72(t) additional tax. [TCJA § 11028(b)(1)(A); 2017 DTRA § 502(a)(1); 2018 Budget Act § 20102(a)(1); 2019 DTRA § 202(a)(1); Consolidated Appropriations Act, 2021, Div. EE, Title III, § 302(a)(1)]

Q 7:22 Can the receipt of a qualified disaster distribution be treated as a change to a series of substantially equal periodic payments?

No. One exception to the Code Section 72(t) additional tax applies to a qualifying series of substantially equal periodic payments. If the whole series is paid without interruption, the series is not subject to additional tax (see Q 5:31). [I.R.C. § 72(t)(2)(A)(iv), 72(t)(4)(A)] Fortunately, if an individual is receiving a series of substantially equal periodic payments from an IRA (or other eligible retirement plan), the IRS does *not* treat the mere receipt of a qualified disaster distribution as a change in the series. Thus, the periodic payments still avoid additional tax unless the series is modified by some other event. [*See* Notice 2005-92, 2005-51 I.R.B. 165.]

> **Note.** Notice 2005-92 concerns similar tax relief that was enacted for Hurricane Katrina victims. The IRS says the principles of Notice 2005-92 also apply to qualified disaster distributions. [IRS Pub. 976, *Disaster Relief* (Feb. 2018), p. 11]

Repayment to an Eligible Retirement Plan

Q 7:23 What is the general rule governing repayment of qualified disaster distributions?

To the extent a qualified disaster distribution is eligible for tax-free rollover to an eligible retirement plan, it may be repaid to that plan within three years, and the repayment is treated as a tax-free rollover. [TCJA § 11028(b)(1)(C); 2017 DTRA § 502(a)(3); 2018 Budget Act § 20102(a)(3); 2019 DTRA § 202(a)(3)(A); Consolidated Appropriations Act, 2021, Div. EE, Title III, § 302(a)(3)]

Whether an amount is eligible for tax-free rollover, and thus repayment, is determined under Code Sections 402(c), 403(a)(4), 403(b)(8), 408(d)(3), and 457(e)(16). (See Q 7:25.)

Q 7:24 Can the repayment be made to any eligible retirement plan?

Repayment can be made to any eligible retirement plan as long as the person making the repayment is a participant in the plan, and the terms of the plan allow it to accept repayments. [TCJA § 11028(b)(1)(C)(i); 2017 DTRA § 502(a)(3)(A); 2018 Budget Act § 20102(a)(3)(A); 2019 DTRA § 202(a)(3)(A); Consolidated Appropriations Act, 2021, Div. EE, Title III, § 302(a)(3)(A); I.R.C. §§ 402(c), 403(a)(4), 403(b)(8), 408(d)(3), 457(e)(16); IRS Pub. 976, *Disaster Relief* (Feb. 2018)]

Q 7:25 What parts of a qualified disaster distribution *cannot* be repaid?

The amounts included in a qualified disaster distribution that are *not* repayable to an eligible retirement plan are shown in Table 7-2.

Table 7-2. Non-Repayable Parts of a Qualified Disaster Distribution

	Repayable to an IRA?	*Repayable to any other eligible retirement plan?*
RMDs	No	No
The whole qualified disaster distribution, if it was received as a beneficiary (unless it is the surviving spouse)	No	No
Periodic payments made for a period of: • at least 10 years, • the life or life expectancy of the participant, or • the lives or joint life expectancies of the participant and his or her designated beneficiary	Yes	No
Hardship distribution from an employer retirement plan[1]	Yes	Yes

[1]A hardship distribution from an employer retirement plan cannot usually be rolled over tax free, but the IRS does not treat qualified disaster distributions as made on account of hardship. [*See* Notice 2005-92, 2005-51 I.R.B. 165; IRS Pub. 976, *Disaster Relief* (Feb. 2018).]

[TCJA § 11028(b)(1)(C)(i); 2017 DTRA § 502(a)(3)(A); 2018 Budget Act § 20102(a)(3)(A); 2019 DTRA § 202(a)(3)(A); Consolidated Appropriations Act, 2021, Div. EE, Title III, § 302; I.R.C. §§ 402(c), 403(a)(4), 403(b)(8), 408(d)(3), 457(e)(16); IRS Pub. 976, *Disaster Relief* (Feb. 2018)]

Q 7:26 How is the three-year period measured?

The three-year repayment period starts on the day after the qualified disaster distribution is made and ends three years later. [TCJA § 11028(b)(1)(C)(i); 2017

DTRA § 502(a)(3)(A); 2018 Budget Act § 20102(a)(3)(A); 2019 DTRA § 202(a)(3)(A); Consolidated Appropriations Act, 2021, Div. EE, Title III, § 302(a)(3)(A)]

> **Example.** Marco, a qualified individual, receives a $40,000 distribution from his 401(k) plan on January 15, 2018 and designates it as a qualified Hurricane Harvey distribution. His repayment period starts on January 16, 2018 and runs through January 15, 2021.

Q 7:27 How is a repayment treated for tax purposes?

To the extent it is timely repaid, a qualified disaster distribution is treated as a trustee-to-trustee transfer to the receiving plan, and not included in income. Specifically:

- The amount repaid is treated as having been received as a *rollover contribution* under Code Section 408(d)(3) if it was distributed from an IRA, or an *eligible rollover distribution* under Code Section 402(c)(4) if it was distributed from any other eligible retirement plan,
- That amount is treated as having been transferred to the receiving plan, within 60 days, in a direct, trustee-to-trustee transfer, and
- Because that transfer qualifies as a tax-free rollover, the part of the qualified disaster distribution so repaid is not includable in income.

[TCJA § 11028(b)(1)(C); 2017 DTRA § 502(a)(3); 2018 Budget Act § 20102(a)(3); 2019 DTRA § 202(a)(3)(B), 202(a)(3)(C); Consolidated Appropriations Act, 2021, Div. EE, Title III, § 302(a)(3)(B), 302(a)(3)(C)]

Q 7:28 Does repayment of a qualified disaster distribution to an IRA count as a rollover for purposes of the one-rollover-per-year rule?

No. A recontributed qualified disaster distribution is not treated as a rollover contribution for purposes of the one-rollover-per-year limitation under Code Section 408(d)(3)(B) (see Q 6:15). [IRS Pub. 976, *Disaster Relief* (Feb. 2018)] So, if the qualified disaster distribution is made from an IRA, it may be repaid to an IRA even if the individual did an IRA-to-IRA rollover in the prior 12 months, and the repayment will not prevent an IRA-to-IRA rollover in the next 12 months.

Q 7:29 How is the repayment treated if the qualified individual elected to use the one-year income inclusion method?

If a qualified individual elects to include all the income from a qualified disaster distribution in the first year, and then timely repays some or all of the distribution to an eligible retirement plan, the repayment reduces the amount to be included in gross income for the distribution year. When the repayment is made after the due date (including extensions) of the tax return for the distribution year, an amended return (including a revised Form 8915; see Q 7:17) must be filed to recover the tax.

Example 1. Yolanda, a qualified individual residing in the Hurricane Irma disaster area, receives a $10,000 distribution from her 401(k) plan on November 1, 2017. In March 2018, she receives a $10,000 payment from her insurance company (reimbursement for her casualty loss from Hurricane Irma) and contributes it to an IRA. On her income tax return for 2017, Yolanda designates the distribution as a qualified Hurricane Irma distribution (using Form 8915-B) and elects to include all the income in the distribution year. None of it is includable in gross income.

Example 2. The facts are the same except Yolanda, after timely requesting a filing extension for the 2017 tax return, waits until July 2018 to make the repayment. She files her 2017 tax return, including Form 8915-B, in August 2018. None of the qualified Hurricane Irma distribution is includable in gross income for 2017, because Yolanda repaid it in 2018 (before timely filing the 2017 tax return).

Example 3. The facts are the same as in Example 1, except that the insurance company does not reimburse Yolanda's loss before the 2017 tax return is due. On Form 8915-B filed with the 2017 return, Yolanda treats the $10,000 distribution as a qualified Hurricane Irma distribution and elects to include the entire amount in gross income for the year. The $10,000 insurance payment arrives in December 2018, and Yolanda contributes it to her IRA. Yolanda must file an amended return for 2017 (including an amended Form 8915-B) to report the repayment and reduce her gross income for 2017 by $10,000.

Q 7:30 How is the repayment treated if the individual uses the default method (three-year ratable inclusion) to report the income?

If income from a qualified disaster distribution is included using the default, three-year method, and part of the distribution is repaid to an eligible retirement plan during the three-year repayment period, then the repayment reduces the ratable portion of income to be included on the return that is next due to be filed. [*See* Notice 2005-92, 2005-51 I.R.B. 165.]

(For treatment of a repayment that *exceeds* the ratable portion of income to be included that year, see Q 7:31.)

Example 1. Terrell, a qualified individual residing in the California wildfire disaster area, withdraws $30,000 from his traditional IRA on December 20, 2017. He treats it as a qualified wildfire distribution and uses the three-year ratable inclusion method to report the income. Terrell makes only one repayment—$10,000, which he contributes to his IRA on April 10, 2019—before filing his tax return for 2018. Terrell should report that repayment on his 2018 tax return (using Form 8915B) and use it to offset the ratable amount of income to be included for 2018. As a result, the portions included in Terrell's income are: $10,000 for 2017, $0 for 2018, and $10,000 for 2019.

Example 2. The facts are the same as in Example 1, except that Terrell makes the $10,000 repayment on July 20, 2019—*after* filing his tax return for 2018 (without an extension). In this case, Terrell should report the repayment on his tax return for 2019, using it to offset the ratable portion of income to be included for 2019. The resulting inclusions of income from the distribution are: $10,000 for 2017, $10,000 for 2018, and $0 for 2019.

Q 7:31 If the three-year method is used and the repayment exceeds the income to be included, can the excess be carried back or forward?

Yes. In that case, the excess amount of the recontribution may either be:

- Carried forward, to reduce the ratable portion of income that will be included on the return for the next year, or
- Carried back to a prior taxable year (or years), to reduce the prior income inclusion; an amended return must be filed to do so.

[*See* Notice 2005-92, 2005-51 I.R.B. 165.]

Example. Lora, a qualified individual residing in the Hurricane Maria disaster area, withdraws $60,000 from her 401(k) plan on February 15, 2018. She treats it as a qualified disaster distribution and, using the default method, reports $20,000 of the income on her 2018 return. On December 20, 2019, she makes her only repayment—$35,000, which she contributes to an IRA. She reports the repayment on her tax return for 2019, and it completely offsets the portion of income ($20,000) to be included for 2019. As to the excess repayment amount ($15,000), Lora has two choices:

1. She could carry the excess repayment forward and use it to reduce the ratable portion of income to be included for 2020. The resulting income inclusions would be: $20,000 for 2018, $0 for 2019, and $5,000 for 2020.
2. She could carry the excess repayment back to 2018. Lora would file an amended return for 2018 and reduce the income included from the distribution that year by $15,000. The resulting income inclusions would be: $5,000 for 2018, $0 for 2019, and $20,000 for 2020.

Distributions to Buy or Build a Home

Q 7:32 What other distributions qualify for disaster-related tax relief?

Tax relief is also available for certain distributions that were intended to be used to buy or build a principal residence, but were not used for that purpose because the area was struck by a major disaster. (See Qs 7:10–7:12 for definitions of the disasters and disaster areas for 2017-19.)

Q 7:33 Who is eligible for this relief?

A person is eligible if he or she meets these requirements:

- The distribution was either a *qualified first-time homebuyer distribution* from an IRA (see Q 5:50) or a *hardship distribution* from a 401(k) plan or tax-sheltered annuity contract.
- The distribution was not received as a beneficiary (other than the surviving spouse).
- The intended use for the funds was to buy or build the principal home in:
  - The Hurricane Harvey (including Tropical Storm Harvey), Hurricane Irma, or Hurricane Maria disaster area, and the distribution was made after February 28, 2017 and before September 21, 2017;
  - The California wildfire disaster area, and the distribution was received after March 31, 2017 and before January 15, 2018; or
  - A *qualified disaster area*, as defined in Q 7:12, and the distribution was received during the period starting 180 days before the first day of the *incident period* (see Q 7:12) of the qualified disaster and ending 30 days after the last day of the incident period.
- And, in all cases, the recipient must have canceled the purchase or construction because of the major disaster in that area.

[2017 DTRA § 502(b); 2018 Budget Act § 20102(b); 2019 DTRA § 202(b)(2); Consolidated Appropriations Act, 2021, Div. EE, Title III, § 302(b)(2)]

Q 7:34 Can a person who lived elsewhere, but planned to move into the area to buy or build the home, qualify for this relief?

Yes. A distribution may qualify for relief if the recipient did not already reside in, but planned to relocate to, the area.

Q 7:35 Is it necessary to sustain economic loss to qualify for tax relief?

No, the distributee need not have sustained economic loss to qualify for this relief.

Q 7:36 What tax relief is available?

The recipient of the distribution may repay it to an IRA or other eligible retirement plan (defined in Q 7:3) within the permitted time period and have the repayment treated as a tax-free rollover. To the extent the repaid amount was already included in gross income, the income inclusion is reversed, and the Code Section 72(t) additional tax (whether the 10 percent or 25 percent additional tax; see Q 7:21) does not apply. [2017 DTRA § 502(b); 2018 Budget Act § 20102(b); 2019 DTRA § 202(b)(1); Consolidated Appropriations Act, Div. EE, Title III, § 302(b)(1)]

Q 7:37 What is the repayment period for such a distribution?

The repayment period is:

- August 23, 2017, through February 28, 2018, if the distribution was taken to buy or construct a home in the Hurricane Harvey, Hurricane Irma, or Hurricane Maria disaster area,
- October 8, 2017, through June 30, 2018, if the distribution was taken to buy or construct a home in the California wildfire disaster area, or
- if the distribution was taken to buy or construct a home in a *qualified disaster area*, the period starting on the first day of that qualified disaster's *incident period* (see Q 7:12 for both definitions), and ending on June 17, 2020.

[2017 DTRA § 502(b)(1)(A); 2018 Budget Act § 20102(b)(1)(A); 2019 DTRA § 202(b)(1)(A), 202(b)(3)]

Note. Ordinarily, a qualified first-time homebuyer distribution must be repaid to an IRA, if at all, within 120 days. [I.R.C. § 72(t)(8)(E)]

Q 7:38 May repayments be made to any eligible retirement plan?

The distribution can be repaid to any eligible retirement plan (including an IRA), but subject to the same restrictions that apply to repayment of a qualified disaster distribution (see Qs 7:23–7:25). That means:

- The individual must be the IRA owner or a participant in the receiving plan;
- Only amounts eligible for tax-free rollover into the receiving plan may be repaid to it; and
- The terms of the receiving plan must allow it to accept the repayment.

[2017 DTRA § 502(b)(1)(A); 2018 Budget Act § 20102(b)(1)(A); 2019 DTRA § 202(a)(3)(A)]

Q 7:39 How is a repayment treated for tax purposes?

Timely repayment of a distribution qualifying for this relief is treated as a rollover (if paid to an IRA) or direct, trustee-to-trustee transfer of the distribution (if paid to another plan). So, that part of the distribution is not includable in income and not subject to additional tax under Code Section 72(t). [2017 DTRA § 502(b)(1)(B); 2018 Budget Act § 20102(b)(1)(B); 2019 DTRA § 202(a)(3)(B); Consolidated Appropriations Act, Div. EE, Title III, § 302(a)(3)(B)]

The 12-month rule (see Q 7:28) does not apply if the repayment is made to an IRA. [IRS Pub. 976, *Disaster Relief* (Feb. 2018)]

Q 7:40 How is the repayment reported?

If the distribution to buy or build a home was not used because of a qualified disaster declared in 2018 or 2019, and it was timely repaid (by June 17, 2020), the repayment is reported on Form 8915-C. The repayment deadline for other distributions to buy or build a home passed before 2020, but those repayments would have been reported on Form 8915-B.

Q 7:41 If a qualifying distribution is not timely repaid, may it still qualify for relief as a qualified disaster distribution?

Yes, if it meets the requirements for a qualified disaster distribution. (See Qs 7:10–7:12.)

Coronavirus-Related Distributions

Q 7:42 What is a coronavirus-related distribution?

A coronavirus-related distribution (CRD) is any distribution from an IRA or other eligible retirement plan made on or after January 1, 2020, and before December 30, 2020 (not on Dec. 31), to an individual (a *qualified individual*) who:

- *Is diagnosed*, or whose spouse or dependent is diagnosed, with the virus SARS-CoV-2 or with coronavirus disease 2019 (together *COVID-19*) by a test approved by the Centers for Disease Control and Prevention (including a test authorized under the Federal Food, Drug, and Cosmetic Act), or
- *Experiences adverse financial consequences* as a result of any of the following, which may occur to the individual, the individual's spouse, or a member of the individual's household (anyone who shares the principal residence):
  - Being quarantined, being furloughed or laid off, or having work hours reduced due to COVID-19;
  - Being unable to work due to lack of childcare due to COVID-19;
  - Closing or reducing hours of a business owned or operated by any such person due to COVID-19;
  - Having a reduction in pay or self-employment income due to COVID-19; or
  - Having a job offer rescinded or start date for a job delayed due to COVID-19.

[CARES Act § 2202(a)(4); Notice 2020-50, 2020-28 I.R.B. 35]

Q 7:43 What financial adversity must be experienced to qualify?

None or very little, depending on the basis for qualifying.

There are two ways to be a qualified individual; only one requires adverse financial consequences. If an individual or an individual's spouse or a dependent is diagnosed with COVID-19 using an authorized test, the diagnosis alone is enough to qualify for a CRD. [CARES Act § 2202(a)(4)(A)]

Other individuals qualify if they "experience adverse financial consequences" as the result of a specified event (see Q 7:42, second main bullet point). Each of the listed events concerns either a business loss or a person's inability to work (at all, or as much or as profitably as before). So, economic loss is built into the events, and if any occurs (to the qualified individual, his or her spouse, or a member of the household), it likely causes enough financial pain to qualify for a CRD. And, as noted in Q 7:45, the amount of a CRD does not have to correlate with actual need. [Notice 2020-50, 2020-28 I.R.B. 35]

Q 7:44 How much can be withdrawn as a CRD?

Up to $100,000 (the total from all plans) may be withdrawn and treated as a CRD. If the total distributions exceed $100,000 in 2020, the individual chooses which to designate as CRDs. [CARES Act § 2202(a)(2)(A)]

Q 7:45 Is the amount limited by actual need?

No. The amount of the CRD does not have to relate to an actual need. Notice 2020-50 says:

> The definition of a coronavirus-related distribution under section 2202(a)(4) of the CARES Act does not limit these distributions to amounts withdrawn solely to meet a need arising from COVID-19. Thus, for example, for an individual who is a qualified individual as a result of experiencing adverse financial consequences as described above, coronavirus-related distributions are permitted without regard to the qualified individual's need for funds, and the amount of the distribution is not required to correspond to the extent of the adverse financial consequences experienced by the qualified individual.

[Notice 2020-50, 2020-28 I.R.B. 35]

Q 7:46 What IRA distributions can be designated as a CRD?

With one exception, any IRA distribution made in 2020 (not on Dec. 31) to a qualified individual (including a nonspouse beneficiary) may be designated as a CRD, no matter how the trustee or plan administrator treats it at the time of the distribution or when reporting it on Form 1099-R. For example, periodic and other distributions that would have been RMDs but for the waiver under CARES Act Section 2203 (see Q 4:6) may be designated as CRDs.

The exception is for amounts described in Treasury Regulations Section 1.402(c)-2, Q&A-4. Any such amount, if distributed, would have to be excluded from the CRD. The only such amounts that could be included in an IRA distribution are:

- Corrective distributions of elective deferrals and employee contributions, with allocable income, that are returned to an employee to comply with Code Section 415 limits, and
- Excess elective deferrals under Section 402(g).

If the distribution is from any other type of eligible retirement plan, other amounts would also have to be excluded. [Notice 2020-50, 2020-29 I.R.B. 35]

Example. Jonas takes RMDs from his IRA on a monthly basis. He received three payments in January, February, and March of 2020 ($10,000 each) that he and the trustee believed were RMDs. (CARES was enacted on Mar. 27). He wants to return $30,000 to the IRA. The rollover deadline for such payments was extended to August 31, 2020 (see Q 4:13), but Jonas misses that deadline because he is busy caring for his wife as she recovers from COVID-19. Since the payments qualify as CRDs, Jonas may return each of them within three years from its distribution date.

Q 7:47 What are the tax breaks for a CRD?

The CRD rules are modeled on the rules for qualified disaster distributions, and the same tax breaks apply. So, a CRD may be repaid (except by a nonspouse beneficiary) to an IRA or other eligible retirement plan within three years from its distribution date, income is included ratably over a three-year period unless the election is made to include it all in the first year, and the distribution itself is subject to neither withholding nor the additional tax on early distributions (see Q 7:16). [CARES Act § 2202(a); Notice 2020-50, 2020-28 I.R.B. 35]

Q 7:48 How are CRDs and their repayments reported?

Recipients of a CRD will use Form 8915-E, *Qualified 2020 Disaster Retirement Plan Distributions and Repayments*, to report the receipt and designation of a CRD, the amount of income included for the current year, the election (if made) to include all the income in the first year, and any repayments. [Notice 2020-50, 2020-28 I.R.B. 35]

Chapter 8

Disclosure, Filings, Penalties, and Withholding

Contributions to and distributions from IRAs, Coverdell ESAs, and HSAs must be reported both to the Internal Revenue Service (IRS) and to the IRA owner. Withholding is required, unless waived. This chapter explains how to comply with the IRS and Department of Labor (DOL) reporting requirements applicable to participants, employers, trustees, and custodians. Substantive issues that may affect reporting are examined, as are rules relating to regular contributions, rollovers, transfers, inherited IRAs, revoked IRAs, and simplified employee pension plan (SEP) and savings incentive match plan for employees (SIMPLE) contributions. Disclosure requirements on the establishment of an IRA are reviewed, as is the seven-day waiting period during which the decision to establish an IRA may be revoked.

This chapter presents the information in two ways. The first part of the chapter is organized as a discussion of topics—opening an IRA (initial disclosure and the right to revoke); annual information reporting of contributions, distributions, and RMDs; payee reporting of distributions; reporting disaster distributions and repayments; withholding requirements; penalties for information reporting violations; and general filing information. The second part of the chapter contains a separate discussion, in numerical order, of each form needed for IRA reporting. These are Forms 990-T, 1040, W-2, 1098-Q, 1099-Q, 1099-R, 1099-SA, 5329, 5330, 5498, 5498-SA, 8606, 8888, 8889, and 8915-A through 8915-E.

Initial Disclosure

Q 8:1 What disclosure must be provided to a prospective IRA owner?

When an IRA is being established, a full disclosure statement must be given to the prospective IRA owner (see Q 8:2) along with a complete set of IRA plan documents. The prospective IRA owner must then be given at least seven days in which to change his or her mind. [Treas. Reg. § 1.408-6(d)(4)(ii)] (During that period, financial and other data regarding the individual establishing the IRA may be completed.)

The foregoing rules also apply to IRAs that are established in connection with a simplified employee pension plan (SEP), a salary reduction simplified employee pension plan (SARSEP), or a savings incentive match plan for employees (SIMPLE). The Roth IRA and the Coverdell education savings account (Coverdell ESA) also require disclosure statements that are slightly different from a traditional IRA disclosure statement.

Q 8:2 What must be included in the disclosure statement?

The disclosure statement for a traditional IRA must include:

1. The requirements for establishing an IRA;
2. Financial projections that indicate whether the return on the IRA is guaranteed;
3. Deductibility rules;
4. Revocation rights, including the name, address, and telephone number of the personal representative of the trustee or custodian (*trustee* refers to either in this chapter) designated to receive revocations;
5. Distribution rules;
6. Prohibited transactions and their consequences;
7. Tax penalties;
8. Estate and gift tax consequences;
9. Whether approval of the IRS has been obtained and, if it has, that the approval does not deal with the financial merits or whether it is advisable for the individual to adopt the plan;
10. Rollover availability;
11. Tax exemption;
12. Nonavailability of forward averaging or capital gains treatment;
13. Advice about commissions payable, expressed as a percentage of an assumed contribution; and
14. Any additional information required by Treasury regulations (that the statement must not be false or misleading).

[Treas. Reg. § 1.408-6(d)(4)(iii)–1.408-6(d)(4)(vii)]

Note. The disclosure statement need not contain specific information pertaining to the benefited individual; however, it must be complete in all other respects. [*See* Treas. Reg. § 1.408-6(d)(4)(ii)(A)(2).]

Q 8:3 What are the rules for mailing an IRA disclosure statement?

Treasury regulations provide that if an IRA disclosure statement, a governing instrument, or an amendment to either is mailed to an individual, it will be deemed to have been received seven days after the date of mailing, unless there is contrary evidence. If the mailing is received in less than seven days before the earlier of the date of the IRA's establishment or the date of investment, the right of revocation must be granted. If an individual's written revocation is required or permitted, the postmark or certification date determines when the revocation was mailed. [Treas. Reg. § 1.408-6(d)(4)]

Generally, a disclosure statement is considered to be mailed on the date of the postmark stamped on the cover in which the document was properly mailed, even if it is received after the date normally required. [Prop. Treas. Reg. §§ 301.7502-1, 301.7502-2] The sender has the burden of proving when the postmark was made. (See Qs 8:35–8:40 for additional mailing rules.)

Right to Revoke

Q 8:4 When may a new IRA be revoked?

A disclosure statement must be provided to anyone who establishes a traditional, SEP, SIMPLE, or Roth IRA, and he or she must have at least seven days to decide whether to proceed with or revoke the IRA. If the disclosure is provided on the same day the IRA is established, the seven-day period commences on that day. If the disclosure is provided at least seven days before the establishment date, no additional revocation period is required.

A timely revocation cancels the IRA agreement. The trustee is obligated to return the entire amount (if any) contributed without any adjustments for sales commissions, administrative fees (including certificate of deposit penalties), or fluctuation in the market value. However, unless the IRA document provides otherwise, investment gains need not be distributed from an IRA that is timely revoked. [Treas. Reg. § 1.408-6(d)(4)]

Note. There is also a seven-day right to revoke when establishing an HSA or Coverdell ESA.

Q 8:5 May a trustee limit investment of IRA contributions until after the revocation period has closed?

Yes. The entire contribution must be returned without adjustment upon a timely revocation, so a trustee may limit its loss exposure by prohibiting investment of contributions during the revocation period in anything that might incur a fee or fluctuate in value. For example, investment of contributions could be limited to an interest-bearing account until the seven-day revocation expires.

Example. The IRA document sponsored by Friendly Mutual Funds provides that contributions during the first seven days after an IRA is established will be invested in the Friendly U.S. Government Cash Fund. After the seven-day period, the IRA assets may be invested in any of the Friendly stock or bond funds. Friendly has avoided its risk of loss if the IRA is revoked.

Q 8:6 What must be reported to the IRS with respect to a revoked IRA?

The revocation of an IRA must be reported because it may have tax consequences. Generally, if contributions were made, the trustee must report them on Form 5498 and report the revocation distribution on Form 1099-R. (See Qs 8:81 (Table 8-2), 8:157.)

Annual Information Reports

Q 8:7 How are IRA contributions, distributions, and year-end values reported to the IRS?

Each year, the IRA trustee must report all contributions and distributions to the IRS. Form 5498 is used to report regular, rollover, conversion, and recharacterized contributions to an IRA. Form 1099-R is used to report distributions from the IRA. For a Coverdell ESA, contributions are reported on Form 5498-ESA and distributions on Form 1099-Q. For an HSA, contributions are reported on Form 5498-SA and distributions on Form 1099-SA.

The year-end value of any IRA, Coverdell ESA, or HSA is reported on the respective version of Form 5498.

Q 8:8 What information must be furnished to the payee?

Besides the initial disclosure statement, the trustee must furnish other information to the payee.

First, the trustee must provide each payee with a statement showing the fair market value of the IRA at the end of each year. The statement must be provided by January 31 of the succeeding year.

Second, by the filing deadline for Form 5498 (May 31), each IRA owner generally must also receive either the official IRS Form 5498 or a qualifying substitute. If reportable contributions were not made during the year, it is not necessary to provide Form 5498, but in that case the fair market value statement must explain what information is being provided to the IRS.

> **Note.** A substitute Form 5498 must satisfy the requirements of IRS Publication 1179, *General Rules and Specifications for Substitute Forms 1096, 1098, 1099, 5498, and Certain Other Information Returns*. Publication 1179 is revised annually and details the required format and content of the substitute form and how it must be furnished to payees.

Finally, an RMD statement must be furnished to any payee subject to the minimum distribution requirements (see Q 8:10). The Setting Every Community Up for Retirement Enhancement Act of 2019, Div. O of the Further Consolidated Appropriations Act, 2020, Pub. L. No. 116-94 (Dec. 20, 2019) (FCAA) (SECURE Act) waived RMDs for 2019 (see Q 4:6).

Q 8:9 What must be reported to the IRS concerning RMDs?

If the owner of a traditional, SEP, or SIMPLE IRA must receive a minimum distribution for any year, that fact (but not the amount) must be indicated by the trustee on the Form 5498 filed for the preceding year. A check box is provided for this purpose. (See discussion of box 11 in Q 8:146.) There is no similar report for a Roth IRA owner because lifetime distributions to the owner are not required.

Nor is an RMD report required with respect to any inherited IRA. None is needed, because all inherited IRAs must distribute RMDs, and the status of an inherited IRA is clear from its title (which names both the decedent and the beneficiary).

Q 8:10 What information must be furnished to the payee concerning the RMD?

An IRA trustee must send to any IRA owner who is alive on December 31 of any year a statement of the IRA's fair market value (FMV) on that day and, if applicable, an RMD statement. Both statements (which may be consolidated into one) must be provided by January 31 of the succeeding year.

The RMD statement is necessary if an RMD distribution will be required in the new year. Two alternatives are available for composing the RMD statement (see Qs 8:11, 8:12), but in either case the statement must inform the IRA owner that the trustee will also notify the IRS (on Form 5498) that an RMD is payable. [Notice 2002-27, § I, 2002-1 C.B. 814, *clarified by* Notice 2003-3, 2003-2 I.R.B. 258, and *modified by* Notice 2009-9, 2009-5 I.R.B. 419]

Q 8:11 What is Alternative One for an RMD Statement?

In Alternative One, the trustee furnishes the IRA owner with a statement of the amount of the RMD for the calendar year and the deadline for distribution. [Notice 2002-27, 2002-1 C.B. 814, *clarified by* Notice 2003-3, 2003-2 I.R.B. 258, and *modified by* Notice 2009-9, 2009-5 I.R.B. 419] The trustee must calculate the RMD amount with respect to each separate IRA maintained by the IRA owner, based on the following criteria for all IRA owners:

1. Use the December 31 account balance without any adjustments for contributions received by that IRA after December 31. This balance will be the same as the amount required to be reported on the year-end FMV statement.
2. Use the Uniform Lifetime Table to determine the IRA owner's life expectancy, based on the IRA owner's attained age during the calendar year for which the RMD is being determined, even though the IRA owner's spouse may be the sole beneficiary and is more than 10 years younger than the IRA owner.

Example. Robert, who attained age 73 in 2019, maintains an IRA with Lone Tree Bank as trustee. Lone Tree Bank has opted for Alternative One in meeting its RMD reporting obligation. On December 31, 2019, the FMV of Robert's IRA is $85,000. Robert's life expectancy factor for 2020 is 24.7 (determined from the Uniform Lifetime Table based on an attained age of 74). (The Uniform Lifetime Table was updated in November 2020, effective for required minimum distributions beginning January 1, 2022.) The December 31, 2019, FMV statement that Lone Tree Bank must furnish to Robert by February 2, 2020, indicates that Robert's RMD for 2020 is $3,441 ($85,000 ÷ 24.7). The statement also indicates that the RMD must be distributed from this IRA or any other traditional IRA for which Robert is the owner no later than December 31, 2020. Finally, the FMV statement informs Robert that Lone Tree Bank is required to report to the IRS (on the 2020 Form 5498 to be filed by May 31, 2020) that an RMD is payable for 2020.

Q 8:12 What is Alternative Two?

In Alternative Two, the trustee provides the IRA owner with a statement that (1) informs the IRA owner that an RMD is required and the deadline for distribution; and (2) includes an offer to calculate the amount of the RMD.

Q 8:13 Can both Alternative One and Alternative Two be used in the same year?

Yes. Notice 2003-3 [2003-1 C.B. 258] clarified that a trustee may simultaneously use Alternative One for some IRA owners and Alternative Two for others.

Q 8:14 May RMD statements be provided electronically?

Yes. Notice 2003-3 [2003-1 C.B. 258] provides that an IRA trustee may transmit the RMD statement electronically if it complies with the procedures described in Treasury Regulations Section 31.6051-1T. These procedures include the consent requirements described in the regulations under Code Section 6051.

For purposes of these procedures, the *furnisher* is the IRA trustee, custodian, or issuer, and the *recipient* is the IRA owner.

1. *Consent*. The recipient must affirmatively consent to receive the RMD statement electronically and must not have withdrawn that consent before the RMD statement is furnished. The consent must be given electronically in a manner that demonstrates the recipient can access the information in the format in which it will be furnished to the recipient. If a change in hardware or software required to access the RMD statement creates a risk that the recipient will not be able to access the information, the furnisher must provide the recipient with a notice prior to changing the hardware or software. That notice must describe the revised hardware or software and inform the recipient that a new consent to the revised electronic format must be provided to the furnisher. After implementing the revised hardware or software, the furnisher must obtain a

new consent from the recipient to receive the RMD statement electronically.

2. *Disclosure.* Prior to, or at the time of, a recipient's consent, the furnisher must provide the recipient with a disclosure statement in which:
   a. The recipient is informed that the RMD statement will be furnished on paper if the recipient does not consent to receiving it electronically.
   b. The recipient is informed of the scope and duration of the consent (e.g., whether the consent applies to the RMD statement every year until consent is withdrawn, or only to the RMD statement required to be furnished by January 31 immediately following the date on which the consent is given).
   c. The recipient is informed of procedures for obtaining a paper copy of the RMD statement after giving consent for an electronic version.
   d. The recipient is informed that he or she may withdraw consent at any time by furnishing the withdrawal in writing, either electronically or on paper, to the person whose name, mailing address, telephone number, and e-mail address is provided in the disclosure statement, and the furnisher must confirm the withdrawal in writing, either electronically or on paper. A withdrawal of consent does not apply to an RMD statement that was furnished electronically before the withdrawal of consent is furnished.
   e. The recipient is informed of the conditions under which a furnisher will cease furnishing statements electronically to the recipient (e.g., termination of the account subject to RMD reporting).
   f. The recipient is informed of the procedures for updating the information needed by the furnisher to contact the recipient.
   g. The recipient is provided with a description of the hardware and software needed to access, print, and retain the RMD statement, and the date when the information will no longer be available on the Web site.
3. *Format.* The electronic version of the RMD statement must contain all required information and comply with applicable revenue procedures relating to substitute statements to recipients.
4. *Posting.* The furnisher must post the RMD statement on a Web site accessible to the recipient on or before the deadline for providing the annual RMD statement (January 31 of the year to which the RMD applies).
5. *Notice Requirements.* The furnisher must notify the recipient that the RMD statement is posted on a Web site no later than the due date for that year's RMD statement. The notice may be delivered by U.S. mail, electronic mail, or in person. The notice must provide instructions on how to access and print the statement, and must include the following legend in capital letters: IMPORTANT TAX RETURN DOCUMENT AVAILABLE. If the notice is provided by electronic mail, the foregoing statement should be on the subject line of the e-mail and the message sent with high importance.

If an electronic notice is returned as undeliverable, and the correct electronic address cannot be obtained from the furnisher's records or from the recipient, the furnisher must then furnish the notice by mail or in person within 30 days after the electronic notice is returned.

The furnisher must also notify a recipient of any corrected RMD statement information posted on its Web site within 30 days of such posting. Such notice must be furnished by mail or in person if (1) an electronic notice of the original posting of the RMD statement was returned as undeliverable, or (2) the recipient did not provide a new e-mail address.

6. *Retention.* The furnisher must provide access to the RMD statements posted on its Web site through October 15 of the year following the calendar year to which the statement relates. The furnisher must also provide access to corrected RMD statements on the Web site for the same time period or, if later than that date, for 90 days after the corrected statements are posted.

Payee Reporting of Distributions

Q 8:15 How does the payee report distributions received from an IRA?

Using the information provided on Form 1099-R, an individual reports IRA distributions received during the year on the income tax return filed for the contribution year. The entire distribution amount is entered on line 4a, and the taxable amount on line 4b, of Form 1040 (2019), U.S. Individual Income Tax Return. (For details, see Q 8:58.)

Q 8:16 How does the payee determine whether any portion of a distribution may be excluded from income because it was rolled over within 60 days to another IRA or to an employer plan?

An IRA-to-IRA rollover should be documented by corresponding copies of Forms 1099-R and 5498. A direct rollover from an employer's plan to an IRA should be represented by a Form 1099-R that is properly coded to show that the distribution is not taxable because it was directly rolled over; Form 5498 will report that the amount was rolled over to an IRA.

If a conduit IRA (an IRA consisting of assets transferred or rolled over from a qualified plan) is rolled over to another employer's plan, the payee does not file Form 5498 to report the amount rolled over. Instead, the payee should attach an explanation to his or her federal income tax return stating that the direct rollover was made to another employer's plan. If a conduit IRA is paid directly to the trustee of the employer's plan, it is reported on Form 1099-R. Code G is placed in box 7 to show that the funds were directly rolled over to an employer's plan.

Rollovers of traditional IRAs (excluding the portion of the IRA consisting of nondeductible IRA contributions) to any employer plan, including a qualified plan, a Section 403(b) plan, and a Section 457(b) plan, are to be reported on Form 1099-R using code G in box 7 (see Q 8:81).

Q 8:17 If any portion of an IRA distribution is not rolled over, is that portion automatically reported as a fully taxable distribution?

Not necessarily. The portion of an IRA distribution that was not rolled over is not automatically reported by the payee as a fully taxable distribution if nondeductible contributions were made to the IRA. In that case, a calculation must be made to determine what portion of the distribution represents a return of after-tax money (i.e., money taxed before being contributed on a nondeductible basis). It should be noted, however, that the IRA trustee will report the amount as taxable; the payee must file Form 8606, Nondeductible IRAs, to prove otherwise.

Q 8:18 Are other IRAs taken into account in the calculation of the portion of a distribution representing a return of after-tax money?

Yes. A payee's entire traditional IRA portfolio (including SEP IRAs, rollovers, and SIMPLE IRAs) must be taken into account when calculating what portion of a distribution represents a return of after-tax contributions. That is so even if none of the other traditional IRAs includes any nondeductible contributions (i.e., those other IRAs were all 100 percent deductible when created). Roth IRAs are treated separately for the purpose of calculating a return of after-tax money.

Reporting Disaster Distributions and Repayments

Q 8:19 What are qualified disaster distributions and repayments?

Federal tax relief has been enacted which allows certain victims of most recent disasters to take special, tax-favored distributions from their IRAs and other eligible retirement plans and, in some cases, repay them tax free. The disasters to which these distributions relate include both the coronavirus pandemic and certain natural disasters declared by the U.S. President under the Stafford Act. (For details, see chapter 7.) For qualifying distributions:

- The early distribution penalty of Code Section 72(t) does not apply;
- Income from the distribution is spread evenly over three years, unless the recipient elects to include all of it in the first year;
- Any part of the distribution that is eligible for tax-free rollover treatment (e.g., not RMDs) may be repaid within three years to the original or another IRA or eligible retirement plan (if the plan allows it); and
- To the extent amounts are timely repaid, the corresponding income inclusion is reversed.

Limited tax relief also exists for some individuals who took a retirement plan distribution to fund the purchase or construction of a main home in a disaster area declared under the Stafford Act, if the disaster prevented them from using the money for that purpose. Distributions qualifying for this relief can be repaid within three years, and the early distribution penalty does not apply to the portion timely repaid. Income from those distributions is not deferred, however (even if repaid).

[Tax Cuts and Jobs Act, Pub. L. No. 115-97 (Dec. 22, 2017) (TCJA), § 11028(b); Disaster Tax Relief and Airport and Airway Extension Act of 2017 (Sept. 29, 2017) (DTRA), § 502; Bipartisan Budget Act of 2018, Pub. L. No. 115-123 (Feb. 9, 2018) (Budget Act), § 20102, 20102(b)(2); Coronavirus Aid, Relief, and Economic Security Act, Pub. L. No. 116-136 (Mar. 27, 2020) (CARES Act), § 2202; Consolidated Appropriations Act, 2021, Pub. L. No. 116-260 (Dec. 27, 2020)]

Q 8:20 How do financial institutions and plan administrators report disaster distributions and repayments?

The financial institution or plan administrator may choose whether to treat a distribution as a qualified disaster distribution, and whether to accept its repayment or rollover. All qualified disaster distributions must be treated consistently under the plan, however. [IRS Pub. 976, *Disaster Relief* (Feb. 2018)]

Payment of a qualified disaster distribution is reported on Form 1099-R—even if the distribution is repaid to the same plan in the same year. If no other code applies, distribution code 2 (early distribution, exception applies) or code 1 (early distribution, no known exception) can be used in box 7 of Form 1099-R. (See Q 8:81, box 7.) [IRS Pub. 976, *Disaster Relief* (Feb. 2018)]

Repayments of qualified disaster distributions are reported on Form 5498, in box 14a. (See Q 8:146.)

Q 8:21 How do individuals report qualified disaster distributions and repayments?

The Form 8915 series is used (see Qs 8:183–8:184).

Withholding

Q 8:22 Is withholding reflected on Form 1099-R?

Yes. Form 1099-R reflects federal income tax withholding. It also provides for state and local tax information (see chapter 16).

Q 8:23 What must be withheld?

Payments from IRAs are subject to different withholding requirements than are payments from qualified plans.

Withholding from IRA distributions. Withholding is generally required with respect to any *designated distribution* from an IRA. That term generally covers all traditional, SEP, and SIMPLE IRA distributions, and Roth IRA distributions only to the extent they are expected to be includible in income. (Qualified 2016 disaster distributions, qualified wildfire distributions, and qualified hurricane distributions are exempt from withholding; see Q 7:4.) [I.R.C. § 3405(e)(1)(B); DTRA § 502(a)(6)(A); TCJA § 11028(b)(1)(F)(i); Budget Act § 20102(a)(6)(A)] But in practical terms, withholding from an IRA distribution is often voluntary, because most payees can waive it (see Q 8:24). If not waived, the amount withheld is usually 10 percent (the rate applicable to a *nonperiodic* distribution), although the recipient can request that a larger percentage be withheld, but if the payment is from an IRA annuity (a *periodic* distribution), withholding is determined as if the distribution were a payment of periodic wages. [I.R.C. § 3405] Withholding is not required from a direct or trustee-to-transfer.

In 2018, the IRS ruled that an *IRA escheatment payment* made by a trustee, from an unclaimed or abandoned traditional IRA to a state unclaimed property fund in accordance with state law, is a nonperiodic, designated distribution from which 10 percent must be withheld—unless a previously made election to waive withholding is on file with the trustee. Further, the ruling states, trustees must report such payments using Form 1099-R. But, under transition relief provided in the 2018 ruling, and extended in 2019, no person was treated as violating these withholding and reporting requirements with respect to any IRA escheatment payment made before the earlier of January 1, 2020, or the date it became "reasonably practicable to comply with" such requirements. [Rev. Rul. 2018-17, 2018-25 I.R.B. 753; Notice 2018-90, 2018-49 I.R.B. 826]

Withholding from qualified plan distributions. Twenty percent withholding is mandatory from a qualified plan distribution. However, if an eligible rollover distribution is directly transferred to an IRA, no withholding is required. [I.R.C. § 3405(c)(2)]

Q 8:24 How is withholding from an IRA distribution waived?

The IRA trustee should provide eligible payees with Form W-4P, Withholding Certificate for Pension or Annuity Payments (or other acceptable form) so that the waiver can be executed before the distribution is made.

The withholding waiver is available only if the IRA distributee:

- Provides the payor with a U.S. residential address (proposed regulations would clarify that a military or diplomatic post office address is treated as a U.S. residential address), or
- Is a nonresident alien and certifies that status to the payor.

[I.R.C. § 3405; Temp. Treas. Reg. § 35.3405-1T; Notice 87-7, 1987-1 C.B. 420; Notice of Proposed Rulemaking, 84 Fed. Reg. 25209 (May 31, 2019)]

Note. Withholding may still be required if a taxpayer identification number (TIN) is missing or incorrect (see Qs 8:84, 8:85).

Information Reporting Penalties

Q 8:25 What penalties apply for failure to file information returns or provide payee statements?

The Code Section 6721 penalty applies to failures to file correct information returns with the IRS. For failures to provide correct statements to payees, the Code Section 6722 penalty applies.

Note. Form 1098-Q is not subject to these penalties (see Q 8:71).

The Code Section 6721 penalty may be imposed for filing information returns:

- After the due date,
- Without all required information,
- With incorrect information,
- With missing, incorrect, or not currently issued TINs or SSNs,
- On paper that is not machine readable, or
- On paper when electronic filing is required.

[I.R.C. § 6721]

The Code Section 6722 penalty may be imposed for:

- Not furnishing a payee statement when it is due,
- Omitting required information, or
- Stating incorrect information.

[I.R.C. § 6722]

The Code Sections 6721 and 6722 penalties are adjusted for inflation. [Rev. Proc. 2019-44, 2019-47 I.R.B. 1093; I.R.C. §§ 6721(f), 6722(f)]

Table 8-1. Penalties Under Code Sections 6721 and 6722 (for Information Returns Required to Be Filed in 2022)

	*Small business**	*Other*
Correct filing not more than 30 days late:		
Each return	$50	$50
Calendar year maximum	$199,500	$571,000
Correct filing more than 30 days late but by August 1:		
Each return	$110	$110
Calendar year maximum	$571,000	$1,713,000
Not correctly filed by August 1:		

Table 8-1. Penalties Under Code Sections 6721 and 6722 (for Information Returns Required to Be Filed in 2022) (*cont'd*)

	*Small business**	*Other*
Each return	$280	$280
Calendar year maximum	$1,142,000	$3,426,000
Intentional disregard of filing requirement:		
Each failure	Greater of $570, or 10% of total items required to be reported correctly	
Calendar year maximum	No limit	

*A filer qualifies as a small business if the average of its annual gross receipts for the three most recent tax years does not exceed $5 million. [I.R.C. §§ 6721(d), 6722(d)]

Q 8:26 Are there exceptions to the Code Section 6721 and 6722 penalties?

Yes. Both penalties are subject to exceptions for reasonable cause, failure that is inconsequential, and de minimis failures. [Internal Revenue Manual § 20.1.7]

Reasonable cause requires a showing that the failure occurred because of events beyond the filer's control or other significant factors. The filer must also show that there was no willful neglect of requirements—that is, actions were taken in a responsible manner to avoid the failure.

An error or omission is inconsequential if it does not hinder the IRS's ability to process the return, correlate its information with the payee's income tax return, or otherwise use the return for its intended purpose. Errors and omissions are *never* inconsequential if they relate to:

1. A TIN, the payee's surname, or any dollar amount (penalty for failure to file a correct information statement)
2. Any dollar amount, a significant part of the payee's address, use of an inadequate substitute form, or furnishing a statement in person that is required to be mailed, or vice versa (penalty for failure to provide a correct payee statement).

The de minimis exception applies if the information or payee statement was timely filed or furnished, but either the correct information was omitted or incorrect information was included, and corrections were made by August 1. Up to 10 such returns (or, if greater, 0.5 percent of the total number of information returns or payee statements required for the calendar year) are exempt from each penalty. [General Instructions for Certain Information Returns (Forms 1096, 1097, 1098, 1099, 3921, 3922, 5498, and W-2G) (2020)]

Q 8:27 What penalties may apply for other IRA reporting violations?

Code Section 6693 imposes the following penalties, each of which is subject to a reasonable cause exception. The penalties are not assessed for inconsequential errors and omissions. [Internal Revenue Manual § 20.1.7]

- Code Section 6693(a)—$50 for each failure by a trustee to report:
  - IRA contributions (Form 5498) and distributions (Form 1099-R)
  - HSA contributions (Form 5498-SA) and distributions (Form 1099-SA)
  - ESA contributions (Form 5498-ESA) and distributions (Form 1099-Q).
- Code Section 6693(b)—an IRA owner is subject to:
  - $50 penalty for each failure to file Form 8606
  - $100 penalty for each overstatement of nondeductible contributions on Form 8606.
- Code Section 6693(c)(1)—$50 for each day that an employer does not provide SIMPLE participants with advance notice about the salary deferral election period.
- Code 6693(c)(2)—$50 for each day that a SIMPLE IRA trustee, or SIMPLE IRA annuity issuer, does not:
  - Report SIMPLE IRA contributions (Form 5498) and distributions (Form 1099-R)
  - Provide the annual summary plan description.

General Filing Information

Q 8:28 How is additional information about IRS reports obtained?

There are several ways to obtain information about IRS reporting.

General Instructions for Certain Information Returns (*Forms 1096, 1097, 1098, 1099, 3921, 3922, 5498*, and *W-2G (2020)*). This contains broad information about the forms listed.

Forms and Publications. IRS forms and publications may be viewed and downloaded online (*www.irs.gov/formspubs*). They may also be ordered by telephone. The number is (800) TAX-FORM, or (800) 829-3676.

Web site. An enormous amount of information is available from the IRS Web site (*www.irs.gov*).

Telephone Queries. The IRS provides assistance for individuals (800-829-1040), businesses (800-829-4933), and retirement plan administrators (877-829-5500).

Information Reporting Program Customer Service Section. There are several numbers for assistance with reporting on Forms 1096, 1097, 1098, 1099, 3921, 5498, W-2, W-2G, W-3: 866-455-7438 (toll free), 304-263-8700 (not toll free), and 304-579-4827 (not toll free; for persons with hearing or speech disability and access to TTY/TDD equipment).

Filing Information Returns Electronically (FIRE). Assistance with electronic filing is provided by telephone at 800-255-0654.

Q 8:29 How is a compliance deadline met if it falls on a weekend or legal holiday?

Generally, if the due date for a specific act of compliance or for filing a return falls on a Saturday, Sunday, or legal holiday, the act or filing is considered timely if it is performed on the earliest succeeding day that is not a Saturday, Sunday, or legal holiday. [I.R.C. § 7503; Treas. Reg. § 301.7503-1(a)]

Q 8:30 What are the legal holidays?

The term *legal holiday* refers to any of the legal holidays in the District of Columbia. For 2021 these are:

- New Year's Day (Friday, January 1)
- Dr. Martin Luther King, Jr.'s Birthday (Monday, January 18)
- Washington's Birthday (Monday, February 15)
- District of Columbia Emancipation Day (Friday, April 16)
- Memorial Day (Monday, May 31)
- Independence Day (Monday, July 5)
- Labor Day (Monday, September 6)
- Columbus Day (Monday, October 11)
- Veterans Day (Thursday, November 11)
- Thanksgiving Day (Thursday, November 25)
- Christmas Day (Friday, December 24)

[I.R.C. § 7503; Treas. Reg. § 301.7503-1(b); D.C. Code Ann. § 28-2701 (1985)]

Q 8:31 What rule applies if the local IRS office is closed on a compliance deadline date?

If a federal compliance or filing deadline occurs on a date when the local IRS office is closed because of a legal state holiday, the act or filing is considered timely if it is performed within that state on the next day that is not a Saturday, Sunday, or federal legal holiday. [Treas. Reg. § 301.7503-1(b)]

Electronic Filing Requirement

Q 8:32 What reports must be filed electronically?

Any payer required to file 250 or more information returns of the same type must file them electronically. The 250-plus requirement applies separately for each type of return, and separately for each type of corrected return. For example, if the payer originally submitted 1,000 returns and will correct 225, the original submission must be electronic, but corrections may be filed on paper.

The electronic filing procedures are detailed in IRS Publication 1220, *Specifications for Filing Forms 1097, 1098, 1099, 3921, 3922, 5498, and W-2G Electronically* (2020). Publication 1220 is updated annually.

Q 8:33 What must first-time electronic filers do?

New electronic filers must file Form 4419, Application for Filing Information Returns Electronically (FIRE), at least 30 days (45 days for some electronic filings) before the due date of the information return. Form 4419 is only filed once, and it covers all types of returns the payer will file electronically. The IRS (Information Returns Branch) processes the form and assigns a transmitter control code for the payer that must be used on all correspondence.

Q 8:34 Can the electronic filing requirement be waived?

A hardship waiver may be requested using Form 8508, Request for Waiver from Filing Information Returns Electronically (Forms W-2, W-2G, 1042-S, 1097-BTC, 1098 Series, 1099 Series, 3921, 3922, 5498 Series, and 8027). The waiver request must be filed at least 45 days before the information return is due.

Timely Filing

Q 8:35 What is the postmark rule?

Generally, if a document or payment subject to a deadline is deposited in the U.S. mail, properly addressed and with the proper postage, the IRS is deemed to have received it on the postmark date that is stamped on the envelope (also called the timely mailing/timely filing rule). Thus, the filing or payment is considered timely even if it is received after the date it is normally required to be received (see Q 8:40). For registered mail, the registration date is considered to be the postmark date; for certified mail, it is the date marked on the sender's receipt. (For electronic filings, see Q 8:37.) [Treas. Reg. § 301.7502-1(a), 301.7502-1(c)(2)]

If a delivery service other than U.S. Postal Service is used the same rule applies, treating the mark on the wrapper (showing the date when the item was given to the service) as the postmark. However, there is an additional requirement—the IRS must receive the document no later than the date when it would ordinarily receive a similar item (same class of mail, sent from the same location, properly addressed) that had been sent through the U.S. mail and postmarked on the filing or payment deadline. [Treas. Reg. § 301.7502-1(c)(1)(iii)(B)]

Q 8:36 What date controls if a document or payment is considered not timely filed or paid?

If a document or payment is considered not timely filed or paid, the date of the postmark stamped on the cover in which it was mailed will *not* be considered the filing or payment date. For purposes of computing any penalties and additions to tax, the date on which the document or payment is received will be taken as the date filed or paid.

Q 8:37 What are the electronic postmark requirements?

The timely mailing/timely filing rule also applies to electronic filings. If an IRS-authorized electronic return transmitter (ERT) is used in a proper and timely manner, the filing is deemed to be made on the date of the electronic postmark.

The electronic postmark is the marker placed by the ERT acknowledging the date, time, and time zone when the ERT received the electronically filed document on its host system. If the filer and the ERT are in different time zones, the filer's time zone determines whether the filing is timely. [Treas. Reg. § 301.7502-1(d)]

Q 8:38 Who bears the risk of an incorrect postmark or delayed delivery?

The sender who relies on the postmark rule bears this risk. If the document arrives late and the postmark is incorrect or illegible, or the postmark is timely, but the item is received later than normal for an item so postmarked, the sender may be required to prove the postmark date. [Treas. Reg. § 301.7502-1(c)(1)(iii)]

A sender may eliminate this risk by using a method of delivery that provides prima facie evidence of a timely postmark. (See Q 8:39.)

Q 8:39 What constitutes prima facie evidence that a postmark is timely?

There are only two ways to obtain prima facie evidence that a postmark is timely. The first way is to use the U.S. Postal Service and send the item by registered or certified mail. For registered mail, a timely registration is prima facie proof of a timely postmark. For certified mail, the prima facie proof is a timely date marked on the sender's receipt. [Treas. Reg. § 301.7502-1(e)(2)(i)]

The other way is to use a delivery method that is substantially equivalent to registered or certified mail but is offered by an IRS-designated private delivery service (PDS). [Treas. Reg. § 301.7502-1(e)(2)(ii)] The IRS has designated certain services, offered by DHL Express, FedEx, and UPS, that may be used to meet the timely mailing/timely filing rule, and users are advised that the PDS providing the service can provide the equivalent of a certified mail sender's receipt. The current IRS-approved PDS list is found at *https://www.irs.gov/filing/private-delivery-services-pds*.

[General Instructions for Certain Information Returns (Forms 1096, 1097, 1098, 1099, 3921, 3922, 5498, and W-2G) (2020)]

Q 8:40 Must a payment actually be received to be considered timely?

Yes. Whether made in the form of currency or other medium, a payment is not treated as paid unless it is actually received and accounted for. If, for example, a check is used as the form of payment, the check does not constitute payment unless it is honored upon presentation.

Predecessor and Successor Reporting

Q 8:41 How is information reporting done when a predecessor entity and a successor entity both have reporting responsibilities?

If a transaction causes both a predecessor entity and a successor entity to have reporting responsibilities for the same reporting period, they can sometimes qualify to use a combined reporting procedure. Otherwise, the predecessor reports all pre-transaction information and the successor reports everything else.

A combined reporting procedure may be used if these requirements are met:

1. The successor business acquires from the predecessor business substantially all the property used in the predecessor's trade or business (or used in a separate unit of the predecessor's trade or business).
2. With respect to some or all of the predecessor's information reporting responsibilities, the predecessor and successor agree that the predecessor must report amounts, including withholding, on information returns for the pre-acquisition portion of the acquisition year, but not for the post-acquisition portion of the acquisition year.
3. The predecessor and the successor agree on the specific forms for which combined reporting will be used. They must also agree that the successor will assume all of the predecessor's information reporting obligations for those forms. Combined reporting may be used for all information forms (5498, 1099, etc.) or just some of them. It may also be used only for specific reporting entities (e.g., a branch within a business entity that files its own separate information returns).

[2020 General Instructions for Forms 1096, 1097, 1098, 1099, 3921, 3922, 5498, and W-2G]

Q 8:42 What is the combined reporting procedure?

If the parties agree to use combined reporting for a particular form (e.g., Form 5498), the successor files one such form for each recipient, combining the predecessor's and successor's reportable amounts (including any withholding). The predecessor does not separately report its share of those amounts for the same period.

The successor must file a statement with the IRS indicating the forms that are being filed on a combined basis under Revenue Procedure 99-50. [1999-2 C.B. 757] The statement must include the predecessor's and successor's names, addresses, telephone numbers, and EINs, as well as the name and telephone number of the person responsible for preparing the statement, and must reflect separately the amount of federal income tax withheld by the predecessor and by the successor for each type of form being filed on a combined basis. The statement must be sent separately (not with the forms), by the forms' due dates, to:

IRS Information Returns Branch
Mail Stop 4360
230 Murall Dr.
Kearneysville, WV 25430

[General Instructions for Forms 1096, 1097, 1098, 1099, 3921, 3922, 5498, and W-2G (2020)]

Form 990-T

Q 8:43 How is Form 990-T used?

Form 990-T, Exempt Organization Business Income Tax Return (and proxy tax under section 6033(e)), is used by tax-exempt organizations and certain IRAs to report their unrelated business taxable income under Code Section 511 and to obtain a refund of income tax held on undistributed long-term capital gains. [I.R.C. §§ 408(e)(1), 852; Treas. Reg. § 1.408-1(b)]

> **Example.** Cathy establishes a large rollover IRA. She purchases shares in an actively managed mutual fund. Gains from trading are reported to her on Form 2439, Notice to Shareholder of Undistributed Long-Term Capital Gains. To obtain a refund of income tax paid on undistributed long-term capital gains, the IRA trustee should make a regulated investment company (RIC) filing on Form 990-T.

Failure to recover undistributed long-term capital gains tax may result in liability to the IRA owner. (For detailed information on Form 990-T and RIC filings, see Qs 8:43–8:57.)

Q 8:44 What is unrelated business taxable income?

Unrelated business taxable income is the taxable income derived from any trade or business that is regularly carried on and not substantially related to an IRA's exempt purpose or function, such as engaging in a business for profit. [I.R.C. §§ 512, 513] It can also arise from debt-financed income under Code Section 514. It may arise when an IRA invests in a limited partnership, a master limited partnership, or an alternative investment. In November 2020, the IRS issued final regulations dealing with determining separate business for purposes of determining the tax on unrelated business taxable income under the Tax Cuts and Jobs Act of 2017.

Example. Myra establishes a large rollover IRA. She purchases an interest in a real estate limited partnership. The partnership invests all its assets in real estate. The partnership borrows $9 out of every $10 it invests in real estate. As a result of the leveraging, the IRA is subject to a tax on its unrelated business taxable income.

Q 8:45 What is the filing threshold for Form 990-T?

The trustee must file Form 990-T for any IRA that has gross income of $1,000 or more from an unrelated trade or business.

Q 8:46 What is the filing deadline and can it be extended?

Form 990-T is due by the 15th day of the fifth month after the end of the tax year (May 17, 2021 for most IRAs). In 2020, the filing date is Wednesday, April 15. An automatic six-month extension of the filing deadline can be obtained by filing Form 8868, Application for Extension of Time to File and Exempt Organization Return.

Q 8:47 When must tax due under Form 990-T be paid?

Any tax due must be paid by the filing deadline (without extension) for Form 990-T (see Q 8:46).

Q 8:48 Is interest charged on an underpayment of taxes due under Form 990-T?

Yes. Interest is charged if the tax due under Form 990-T is not paid by the due date even if an extension of time to file is granted. Interest is also charged on penalties for failure to file, negligence, fraud, gross valuation overstatement, and substantial understatement of tax, from the due date (including extensions) to the date of payment. The interest charge is figured at the underpayment rate determined under Code Section 6621(a)(2).

Q 8:49 What is the penalty for a late filing of Form 990-T?

An IRA trustee that fails to file Form 990-T when due (including extensions of time to file) is subject to a penalty of 5 percent of the unpaid tax for each month or part of a month the return is late, up to a maximum of 25 percent of the unpaid tax, unless it can show reasonable cause for the delay. A trustee filing after the due date (including extensions) must attach an explanation to the return. The minimum penalty for a return that is more than 60 days late is the lesser of the tax due or $135. The penalty will not be imposed if it is shown that the failure to file on time was due to reasonable cause. A statement should be attached to a late return explaining the reasonable cause.

Q 8:50 What is the penalty for late payment of tax due under Form 990-T?

In general, the penalty for late payment of taxes is usually 0.5 percent of the unpaid tax for each month or part of a month the tax is unpaid. The penalty may not exceed 25 percent of the unpaid tax. As described above (see Q 8:49), a penalty will not be imposed if the filer can show that the failure to file on time was due to reasonable cause.

Q 8:51 Which parts of Form 990-T must be completed?

All filers of Form 990-T must complete the applicable items in the heading area at the top of page 1 and the signature area on page 2. Except in the case of an RIC (regulated investment company) filing (see Q 8:52), Part I, Column (A), lines 1 through 13, on page 1 should be completed. If the amount on line 13 of Column (A), is $10,000 or less, only line 13 of Columns (B) and (C), lines 29 through 34 of Part II, and Parts III through V should be completed. Filers who enter $10,000 or less on line 13 of Column (A), do not have to complete Schedules A through K (however, they should refer to applicable schedules when completing Column (A) and in determining the deductible expenses to include on line 13 of Column (B)). If the amount on line 13 of Column (A) is more than $10,000, all lines and schedules that apply should be completed.

Q 8:52 Which parts of Form 990-T should be completed in a regulated investment company filing?

To obtain a refund of income tax paid on undistributed long-term capital gains (only), the IRA trustee should make a regulated investment company (RIC) filing on Form 990-T as follows:

1. Write "Claim for refund shown on Form 2439" at the top of the form;
2. Complete the heading (using the name and employer identification number (EIN) of the exempt trustee);
3. Enter the credit on line 44g;
4. Sign the return; and
5. Attach Copy B of Form 2439, Notice to Shareholder of Undistributed Long-Term Capital Gains.

Q 8:53 May a trustee of multiple IRAs that are invested in regulated investment companies file a composite return?

Yes. Instead of filing a separate Form 990-T for each IRA, an IRA trustee may file a composite return to claim a refund under Code Section 852(b) for IRAs that are invested in RICs that elected to retain a long-term capital gain.

Q 8:54 How is a composite filing accomplished?

A composite filing for multiple IRAs that have invested in RICs is accomplished as follows:

- The trustee must apply to its Internal Revenue Service Center for a special EIN on Form SS-4, Application for Employer Identification Number (EIN). The special EIN will be effective only for making a composite claim for refund of tax under Code Section 852(b) on behalf of the IRAs administered by the trustee. (The trustee should *not* apply for a separate specialized EIN for each year it makes a claim for refund.)
- The trustee must indicate that the application is for a special EIN by writing "Notice 90-18" at the top of the Form SS-4. [Notice 90-18, 1990-1 C.B. 327]
- The trustee must attach a list of the IRAs for which the claim is being made, showing the names and Social Security numbers of the persons who established the IRAs and the allocated shares of tax paid by the RICs.
- The IRAs must be grouped according to the RIC in which each IRA has made an investment.
- Form 2439 must be attached for each RIC according to such grouping.
- The trustee must write at the top of the Form 990-T, "Composite return for each Notice 90-18."
- The trustee must enter the special EIN assigned for the composite return (and only that EIN) in the block provided for EINs.

Q 8:55 Under what circumstances is a composite return not available to an IRA trustee?

A composite return may be filed only by a common trustee of more than one IRA. It may not be filed by a person acting merely as a nominee (owner of record) of RIC shares owned by an IRA.

Furthermore, an IRA that has unrelated business taxable income may not be included in the claim for refund on the composite return. The trustee of such an IRA must file a separate Form 990-T for the IRA reporting the income on that return and claiming a credit for any RIC that elected to retain a long-term capital gain.

Q 8:56 To whom will the refund check awarded under Form 990-T be issued?

The IRS will issue a refund check awarded under Form 990-T to the IRA trustee.

Q 8:57 What is the responsibility of the IRA trustee with respect to the refund issued under Form 990-T?

The trustee must allocate the refund issued under Form 990-T to the IRA trusts in accordance with the amounts due as shown on the composite return. [Notice 90-18, 1990-1 C.B. 327]

Form 1040

Q 8:58 How do individuals report IRA distributions?

If the distributee is an individual, he or she must report the distribution on his or her federal income tax return. On Form 1040, use lines 4a and 4b.

For a distribution that is fully taxable, the entire amount is reported on line 4b. The amount should be the same as that reported in box 1 of Form 1099-R. Line 4a is not used for a fully taxable IRA distribution.

For a distribution that is not fully taxable, the gross amount is entered on line 4a, and the portion that is taxable is entered on line 4b. The gross amount should be the same as the amount reported in box 1 of Form 1099-R, and the taxable amount should be the same as the amount in box 2a of Form 1099-R.

If the payer checked "Tax Amount Not Determined" in box 2b of Form 1099-R, it indicates the payer was unsure of what taxable amount to report in box 2a. That should alert the recipient to check with his or her accountant for assistance in determining the taxable amount.

> **Note.** Qualified health savings account (HSA) funding distributions do not require special reporting on Form 1099-R. [Instructions for Forms 1099-R and 5498 (2020)]

Q 8:59 Is there an exception to using line 4 of Form 1040 to report an IRA distribution?

Yes. There is one exception to using line 4 of Form 1040 to report an IRA distribution. For corrective distributions of excess deferrals, excess contributions, or disallowed deferrals, plus income allocable thereto under a SARSEP, the recipient must report those amounts on the wage line of the tax return for the appropriate year (line 1 of Form 1040). The principal amount is taxable in the year it was deferred; the income allocable thereto is taxable in the year it was distributed.

In most corrective distribution cases, therefore, the payer must issue separate Forms 1099-R because parts of the distribution may be taxed in two or three different years.

Q 8:60 How does an individual request direct deposit of a tax refund into an IRA?

An individual may directly deposit a tax refund into his or her IRA at a bank or other financial institution (such as a mutual fund, brokerage firm, or credit union). The direct deposit is reported on Form 1040. This is accomplished as follows:

If the refund is to be directly deposited into only one individual retirement account, complete lines 20b through 20d on the new Form 1040. Box 20a should not be checked when reporting the deposit of a refund into one IRA.

If the purpose is to split the direct deposit among two or three individual retirement accounts or other accounts, check the box on line 20a, and attach Form 8888, Line 35a-d (see Q 8:177).

Q 8:61 What forms contain the information needed to report a corrective distribution from a SEP IRA?

An individual reports corrective distributions from a SEP IRA (under a SEP or SARSEP plan) on line 7 of Form 1040 or Form 1040A, based on information received from the trustee in one of the following ways:

- Excess salary deferrals (those exceeding the dollar limit on elective contributions (for 2021, $19,500 plus up to $6,500 for catch-up eligible individuals)) are reported as part of the total deferral on Form W-2, Wage and Tax Statement. [Notice 2020-79, 2020-46 I.R.B. 1014]
- Excess contributions (contributions failing the 125 percent actual deferral percentage test) are reported on Form 1099-R.
- Disallowed deferrals (deferrals failing the 50 percent participation rate requirement) are reported on Form 1099-R.
- Deferrals of an ineligible employer (deferrals failing the "fewer than 26 employees in previous year" requirement) are reported on Form 1099-R.
- Nonexcluded contributions (contributions of more than the applicable dollar amount under Code Section 402(h)(2)(B) if the plan is integrated or 25 percent of compensation or earned income) are reported on Form W-2.
- Amounts that exceed the $58,000 (for 2021) or 100 percent of compensation limit under Code Section 415 are reported on Form W-2. [Notice 2020-79, 2020-46 I.R.B. 1014]

Q 8:62 How is a rollover of SEP or SARSEP assets reported on Form 1040?

A SEP or SARSEP IRA participant reports a rollover from one IRA to another IRA on lines 4a and 4b of the new Form 1040. The total distribution from the IRA is entered on line 4a, and the taxable part of such distribution is entered on line 4b. (The taxable amount is figured using Form 8606.)

Q 8:63 How is a rollover from a SEP IRA into an employer plan reported?

Funds in SEP IRAs may be rolled over to an employer plan (including a qualified plan, a Section 403(b) account, or a governmental Section 457(b) account).

The individual should make sure first that the employer's plan has been amended to accept such rollovers. If the plan has been amended, the individual may request a direct rollover from the SEP IRA to the employer's plan, and the SEP IRA plan would report the transaction with the code G in box 7 of Form 1099-R. No reporting of the rollover contribution is required of the employer's plan.

If, however, the individual requests the rollover of the SEP IRA funds, the SEP IRA trustee would report the distribution on Form 1099-R, using code 1 (if the individual is under age 59½) or code 7 (if he or she is age 59½ or older), since the trustee would not know whether the amount will in fact be rolled over within 60 days.

Once the rollover is completed, the SEP IRA assets will take on the characteristics of the plan into which they have been rolled. This means that if the SEP IRA is rolled over into a qualified plan, the assets would become subject to the qualified plan rules (e.g., loans may be taken from the monies; the premature distribution exceptions would be those for qualified plans; and so forth).

Form W-2

Q 8:64 What information concerning a SEP does the employer report on a participant's Form W-2?

Most SEPs only allow employer contributions, which are not reported on Form W-2. However, "retirement plan" must be checked in box 13 to indicate that the individual is an active participant.

Grandfathered SARSEPs do allow employees to make salary deferral contributions. Elective deferrals are excluded from box 1, but included in boxes 3 and 5 because employment taxes apply, the amount of which must be stated in box 12 using code F (elective deferrals under a Section 408(k)(6) salary reduction SEP).

[General Instructions for Forms W-2 and W-3 (Including Forms W-2AS, W-2CM, W-2GU, W-2VI, W-3SS, W-2c, and W-3c) (2020)]

Q 8:65 What does the employer report on a SIMPLE participant's Form W-2?

- The employee's salary reduction contributions are not included in box 1 (wages, tips, or other compensation). But because employment taxes apply to these contributions, they are included in boxes 3 (Social Security wages) and 5 (Medicare wages and tips) (or box 14 if railroad retirement taxes apply). The total amount of the salary reduction contributions is also stated in box 12 with code S (employee salary reduction contributions under a Section 408(p) SIMPLE plan).
- The employer's matching or nonelective contributions to the employee's SIMPLE IRA are not reported on Form W-2.
- "Retirement plan" is checked in box 13 of Form W-2 to identify the individual as an active participant.

[General Instructions for Forms W-2 and W-3 (Including Forms W-2AS, W-2CM, W-2GU, W-2VI, W-3SS, W-2c, and W-3c) (2020)]

Q 8:66 Are employer and employee contributions to an HSA reported on Form W-2?

If HSA contributions are made through the workplace, the employer must report them as follows on the employee's Form W-2:

Boxes 1, 3, and 5.

- *Employer contributions.* Employer contributions to an employee's HSA are excluded from gross income and exempt from employment taxes if the employee is HSA-eligible when the contributions are made, the contribution limits are not exceeded, and other requirements (e.g., comparable treatment of participants) are observed. If it is reasonable for the employer to conclude that these conditions are met, then the employer's contributions are excluded from boxes 1, 3, and 5 of Form W-2. Otherwise, they must be included.
- *Employee contributions made through a cafeteria plan.* An employee's own contributions to an HSA are treated as employer contributions if they are made through a cafeteria plan. Thus, the employer also excludes such contributions from boxes 1, 3, and 5 if it is reasonable to conclude that the conditions described above are met—and also that the elective deferral limits are not exceeded.
- *Employee contributions not made through a cafeteria plan.* Employee HSA contributions that are *not* made under a cafeteria plan are includable as wages and are subject to employment taxes—so they are included in boxes 1, 3, and 5. (In that case, the employee's HSA contributions are deductible on his or her income tax return.)

Box 12.

- *Employer contributions, including employee contributions made through a cafeteria plan.* The total amount of these contributions is stated in box 12 with code W (employer contributions to a health savings account (HSA)).
- *Employee contributions not made through a cafeteria plan.* These are *not* stated in box 12.

[General Instructions for Forms W-2 and W-3 (Including Forms W-2AS, W-2CM, W-2GU, W-2VI, W-3SS, W-2c, and W-3c) (2020)]

Form 1098-Q

Q 8:67 What is Form 1098-Q?

Form 1098-Q, Qualifying Longevity Annuity Contract Information (2021), is a form used to report the status of a contract intended to be a *qualifying longevity annuity contract* (QLAC), that is purchased or held after July 1, 2014, under various retirement plans, including IRAs (but not Roth IRAs). Generally, a QLAC is an annuity contract that satisfies minimum distribution requirements even though payments do not commence until the employee (or traditional IRA owner) reaches an advanced age, as late as age 85. The requirements for a QLAC are in Treasury Regulations Section 1.401(a)(9)-6, Q&A-17. They are also described in the Instructions for Form 1098-Q. (See Qs 4:32–4:36.)

Information to be entered on Form 1098-Q includes the starting date for annuity payments, the periodic annuity that will be payable on the starting date, the individual premiums paid during the calendar year, the cumulative premiums paid to date, and the fair market value of the QLAC at the end of the calendar year.

Q 8:68 Who files Form 1098-Q?

Form 1098-Q is filed, when required, by the issuer of a contract intended to be a QLAC that is purchased or held under a traditional, SEP, or SIMPLE IRA, or under a plan, annuity, or account described in Code Section 401(a), 403(a), 403(b), or 457(b). [Treas. Reg. § 1.6047-2(a)(2)]

Q 8:69 When must it be filed?

The issuer of a QLAC must file Form 1098-Q with the IRS for each calendar year, beginning with the year in which premiums for the contract are first paid, and ending with the year in which the individual in whose name the contract was purchased reaches age 85.

If the individual dies before reaching age 85 and the sole beneficiary under the contract is his or her surviving spouse, the issuer must continue to file Form 1098-Q for each year until the year when payments to the spouse commence or the spouse dies, whichever occurs first.

Form 1098-Q for 2021 is due at the IRS by February 28, 2022, for paper filing, or by March 31, 2022, for electronic filing. [General Instructions for Certain Information Returns (Forms 1096, 1097, 1098, 1099, 3921, 3922, 5498, and W-2G) (2020)]

Q 8:70 Are reports also sent to the individual for whom a contract was purchased?

Yes. If Form 1098-Q must be filed for any year, the issuer must also furnish a copy of it (or a substitute statement) to that individual, or to the beneficiary if the individual has died. Statements for 2021 must be supplied by January 31, 2022. [General Instructions for Certain Information Returns (Forms 1096, 1097, 1098, 1099, 3921, 3922, 5498, and W-2G) (2020)]

Q 8:71 Are QLAC reporting failures subject to penalty?

Unless the failure is due to reasonable cause, a QLAC issuer that does not file Form 1098-Q with the IRS must pay an addition to tax under Code Section 6653(e). The amount is $25 per day that the failure continues, not to exceed $15,000 for one return.

Form 1098-Q is not an *information return* or *payee statement*, so the penalties under Code Sections 6721 and 6722 (see Qs 8:25, 8:26) do not apply. There is no penalty for failing to provide copies of Form 1098-Q to QLAC participants and beneficiaries. [IRS Office of Chief Counsel PMTA 2017-003 (Jan. 4, 2017)]

Form 1099-Q

Q 8:72 What is the purpose of Form 1099-Q?

Form 1099-Q, Payments from Qualified Education Programs (Under Sections 529 and 530), is used to report distributions from a Coverdell ESA to the IRS. To report 2021 distributions, the trustee must file Form 1099-Q by February 28, 2022 (for paper filing) or March 31, 2022 (electronic filing). The trustee must also send a copy of the form to the distributee by January 31, 2022. [General Instructions for Certain Information Returns (Forms 1096, 1097, 1098, 1099, 3921, 3922, 5498, and W-2G) (2020)]

In addition to payments for qualified education expenses, other distributions from a Coverdell ESA also must be reported on Form 1099-Q. These include refunds, payments upon death or disability, and withdrawals of excess contributions plus earnings.

Q 8:73 How are Coverdell ESA distributions reported?

The trustee reports distributions from the Coverdell ESA on Form 1099-Q as follows:

Box 1. The gross distributions from the account during the calendar year are reported in box 1. This amount includes any excess contributions and attributed earnings that are distributed, as well as refunds and payments upon death or disability.

Box 2. The earnings on excess contributions (which are included in box 1) are reported in box 2. The earnings computation uses the same method that is used to calculate net income attributable to a returned IRA contribution (see Q 8:111). If the Coverdell ESA suffers a loss in a year that is not the final year of distributions from the account, or there are no earnings for a year, zero is entered in box 2. A loss is only entered in box 2 if the report is for the final year of distributions from the account.

Box 3. Basis is reported in box 3. It should be the difference between the box 1 and box 2 amounts.

Box 4. This box is checked if a trustee-to-trustee transfer was made from one Coverdell ESA directly to another Coverdell ESA (or to a qualified tuition program). The box may be left blank if the trustee does not know whether the distribution was a trustee-to-trustee transfer. A separate Form 1099-Q must be filed for each trustee-to-trustee transfer.

Box 5. The Coverdell-ESA option is checked in this box 5.

Box 6. This box is checked if the distributee was not the designated beneficiary.

Blank. In the blank space below boxes 5 and 6, the trustee may, but is not required to, include an identifying code for the distribution. (For the list of codes, see Instructions for Form 1099-Q (2019).)

[Instructions for Form 1099-Q, Payments from Qualified Education Programs (Under Sections 529 and 530) (2019); Notice 2003-53, 2003-2 C.B. 362]

Q 8:74 Must the trustee compute the taxable portion of a Coverdell ESA distribution?

No. The trustee of a Coverdell ESA reports the earnings included in a Coverdell ESA distribution, and the basis if that can be determined. [Instructions for Form 1099-Q, Payments from Qualified Education Programs (Under Sections 529 and 530) (2019); *see* IRS Notice 2003-53, 2003-2 C.B. 362.]

Form 1099-R

Reporting Distributions on Form 1099-R

Q 8:75 How does a trustee report an IRA distribution?

A payer's reporting obligations with respect to IRA distributions are twofold: certain information must be reported to the recipient of the distribution and to the IRS. [I.R.C. § 408(i); Treas. Reg. § 1.408-7] Except for certain de minimis distributions, all distributions must be reported, even when the IRA owner exercises his or her right to revoke the initial establishment of the plan.

Q 8:76 When must Form 1099-R be filed with the IRS and furnished to distributees?

Form 1099-R, Distributions from Pensions, Annuities, Retirement or Profit-Sharing Plans, Insurance Contracts, etc., must be filed with the IRS by March 1, 2021 (on paper) or March 31, 2021 (electronic filing) to report distributions made in calendar year 2020. A copy must also be furnished to the distributee by February 1, 2021.

Q 8:77 How is an extension of time to file Forms 1099-R with the IRS obtained?

An automatic 30-day extension of time to file Forms 1099-R with the IRS is granted if the trustee files Form 8809, Application for Extension of Time to File Information Returns, with the IRS by the time Form 1099-R is due (see Q 8:76). This only extends the date for the IRS filing; it does not affect the deadline for providing statements to distributees (see Q 8:78).

Q 8:78 May the deadline for providing Forms 1099-R to distributees be extended?

Yes. An automatic 30-day extension of time to file can be obtained by filing Form 8809, Application for Extension of Time to File Information Returns, on or before the due date of the return. An additional 30-day extension may be requested for certain hardship conditions, but that is discretionary. [General Instructions for Certain Information Returns (Forms 1096, 1097, 1098, 1099, 3921, 3922, 5498, and W-2G) (2020)]

Q 8:79 Does Form 1099-R indicate whether penalties apply to an IRA distribution?

Yes. Distribution codes are entered in box 7 of Form 1099-R that describe the kind of distribution made and the year to which the information relates. The IRS uses these codes to determine the correct tax treatment of the distribution, including whether it may be subject to a penalty. The codes also assist the payee in determining whether Form 5329, Additional Taxes on Qualified Plans (Including IRAs) and Other Tax-Favored Accounts, must be prepared.

Q 8:80 What changes were made to Form 1099-R for 2020 and 2021?

Payers are instructed to use distribution code 1 to report a qualified birth or adoption distribution. Code Section 72(t)(2)(H), added by SECURE Act Section 113, exempts such distributions from the additional tax early distributions. A qualified birth or adoption distribution is a distribution, up to $5,000, made to an individual from an IRA or other eligible retirement plan during the one-year period starting on the date when a child of the individual is born or when his/her legal adoption of an eligible adoptee is finalized. (See Qs 5:63–5:65.) This treatment applies to distributions made after December 31, 2020.

The instructions include information about *qualified birth or adoption distributions*, which may be repaid tax free to an IRA or other eligible retirement plan (if allowed by the plan). (To report repayments, see Q 6:81, box 7, code 1.)

The IRS provides separate guidance to payers of *coronavirus-related distributions* (CRDs; see Q 7:42), which also receive special tax treatment. Such distributions should be reported on Form 1099-R, even if the individual recontributes the CRD to the same plan in the same year. Also, if a payer treats a distribution as a CRD and no other distribution code applies, the payer should use code 2 (early distribution, exception applies) or code 1 (early distribution, no known exception) in box 7. [Notice 2020-50, 2020-28 I.R.B. 35 (June 22, 2020)]

New items in the 2021 instructions for Form 1099-R were the two new model notices for eligible rollover distributions under Code Section 402(f). [*See* Notice 2020-62, 2020-35 I.R.B. 476.]

Q 8:81 How is Form 1099-R completed?

The following are box-by-box instructions for completing Form 1099-R (2021 version) to report distributions made in 2020 from an IRA.

Box 1. Gross Distribution.

Report the total amount of the distribution before any taxes were withheld, but exclude any fees that were charged, such as CD penalties for early withdrawal. For a distribution of property other than cash, report the FMV of the property on the date of distribution. Include rollover distributions in box 1.

Recharacterizations: A Roth IRA *conversion* made on or after January 1, 2018 cannot be recharacterized (see Q 3:124). Recharacterizations of eligible IRA contributions are reportable on Form 1099-R. Enter the amount of the recharacterized IRA contribution, plus earnings, in this box. In the case of a loss on the recharacterized contribution, enter the actual amount recharacterized in this box. Recharacterizations *must* be accomplished via a trustee-to-trustee transfer rather than by a distribution followed by a rollover.

The IRA *from* which the recharacterized amount is being transferred is referred to as the "First IRA"; therefore, the trustee of the First IRA must issue Form 1099-R. (The trustee of the First IRA must also report the original contribution and its character on Form 5498 issued with respect to the First IRA.)

If the First IRA is a traditional IRA, the only type of contribution to it that is eligible to be recharacterized as a Roth IRA contribution is a regular contribution. If the First IRA is a Roth IRA, either a regular contribution, or a conversion contribution to it *made before 2018*, may be recharacterized as a contribution to a traditional IRA.

Earnings (or losses) attributable to the recharacterized contribution must be included in the transfer. Prior-year recharacterizations and same-year recharacterizations must be reported on separate Forms 1099-R because different reporting codes apply for box 7. Code R is used for a prior-year recharacterization; code N is used for a same-year recharacterization.

A *prior-year recharacterization* is a recharacterization of a contribution made *for* 2019 and recharacterized in 2020, even if the 2019 contribution was made in 2020.

A *same-year recharacterization* is a recharacterization of a contribution made *for* 2020 and recharacterized in 2020.

Conversions: The trustee must report an IRA that is converted to a Roth IRA, even if the conversion is accomplished as a trustee-to-trustee transfer or is internally converted with the same trustee.

Revocations and Closures: If a regular or conversion contribution is made to an IRA that is revoked within the plan's first seven days, and the contribution is distributed, the gross amount of the distribution is reported in box 1, the taxable portion (any earnings distributed) in box 2a, and the appropriate code in box 7. This applies to

- A regular contribution made to a traditional or Roth IRA,
- A conversion contribution made to a Roth IRA,
- A rollover or transfer to a traditional IRA or Roth IRA, and
- An employer contribution to a SEP IRA or SIMPLE IRA.

Table 8-2 shows the appropriate code or codes to enter in box 7 when reporting a revoked IRA contribution and the amount to enter in box 2a of Form 1099-R. The gross amount of the revoked contribution is reported in box 1 of the form. The closure of an IRA is reported the same way.

Table 8-2. Revoked Contributions (and IRA Closures)

Source of Contribution	*Box 2a*	*Box 7*
Regular contribution to a traditional IRA without earnings	0	Code 8
Regular contribution to a traditional IRA with earnings	Earnings	Codes 1 and 8 (if applicable)
Regular contribution to a Roth IRA without earnings	0	Code J
Regular contribution to a Roth IRA with earnings	Earnings	Codes J and 8 (if applicable)
Rollover or transfer to a traditional IRA	Same as box 1	Code 1 if under age 59½; code 7 if at least age 59½
Rollover or transfer to a Roth IRA	Same as box 1	Code J
Conversion to a Roth IRA without earnings	0	Code J
Conversion to a Roth IRA with earnings	Earnings	Code J
SEP IRA or SIMPLE IRA	Same as box 1	Code S if SIMPLE IRA established less than 2 years; otherwise, code 1 if under age 59½; code 7 if at least age 59½

Boxes 2a (Taxable Amount) and 2b (Taxable Amount Not Determined).

The payer of distributions from a traditional, SEP, or SIMPLE IRA is not required to compute the taxable amount. Except as noted below, for those distributions the amount in box 1 should also be entered in box 2a and box 2b (taxable amount not determined) should be checked.

Enter 0 (zero) in box 2a for a trustee-to-trustee transfer used to move assets from a traditional, SEP, or SIMPLE IRA to an accepting employer's plan; from a pre-tax employer's plan to a traditional IRA, or from a designated Roth account (DRAC) to a Roth IRA.

Also enter 0 (zero) if a regular traditional IRA contribution is recharacterized as a regular contribution to a Roth IRA.

For a corrective distribution described in Code Section 408(d)(4), enter only the earnings attributable to the returned contribution in this box. However, in accordance with Treasury Regulations Section 1.408-11, the amount of the returned contribution can be reduced by any losses attributable to the contribution. In the case of a loss, enter 0 (zero) in this box. A Section 408(d)(4) distribution is a distribution of an excess (or unwanted) contribution paid to the individual no later than the deadline for filing the federal income tax return (including extensions) for the year *during which* (not *for which*) such contribution was made. Such distribution must include the earnings (or loss) attributable to the returned contribution. Earnings are taxable in the year *during which* the contribution was made rather than in the year they are distributed. The IRS suggests that the trustee advise the participant at the time of the distribution of the year in which the earnings are taxable.

For a corrective distribution described in Code Section 408(d)(5), enter 0 (zero) in this box. A Section 408(d)(5) distribution is a distribution of a "true" excess contribution paid to an individual after the deadline for filing the federal income tax return (including extensions) for the year *during which* such contribution was made. Such corrective distribution of an excess contribution after the tax return filing deadline does *not* include the earnings or loss attributable to it.

For a corrective distribution of certain excess contributions to a SARSEP, parts of the distribution may be taxable in more than one year. Thus, in many cases, two Forms 1099-R are required to show when the different parts are taxable. Note that the correction procedures and reporting requirements for excess SARSEP contributions (excess deferrals, excess contributions, or disallowed deferrals) are different from those for the return of any other excess IRA contributions. The IRS suggests that the trustee advise the participant at the time of the distribution of the year or years in which the distribution is taxable.

If a traditional, SEP, or SIMPLE IRA is converted to a Roth IRA (regardless of the conversion method used), the total amount so treated is reported in boxes 1 and 2a.

If a regular contribution made to a traditional IRA is timely revoked (usually within the first seven days from the date the plan is established) and no earnings are distributed, enter 0 (zero) in this box. If earnings are distributed in the revoked distribution, enter only the earnings. If the trustee knows that the individual deducted the regular contribution, report in this box the same amount as that entered in box 1.

If a rollover, direct rollover, or transfer made to a traditional IRA is timely revoked, report in this box the same amount as that entered in box 1.

If a contribution made to a SEP IRA or SIMPLE IRA is timely revoked, report in this box the same amount as that entered in box 1.

Roth IRAs: Box 2a is generally left blank for all Roth IRA distributions, with a few exceptions. Note that leaving a box blank is different from entering 0 (zero).

If a regular Roth IRA contribution is recharacterized to a traditional IRA, enter 0 (zero) in this box.

If an excess (or unwanted) contribution made to a Roth IRA (including the earnings attributable to the contribution) is distributed by the deadline for filing the individual's federal income tax return (including extensions) for the year *during* which the contribution was made, enter only the earnings in this box. If there are no earnings, enter 0 (zero) in this box. This type of distribution is treated and reported in the same manner as that described under Code Section 408(d)(4).

If a regular contribution made to a Roth IRA is timely revoked (usually within the first seven days from the date the plan is established) and no earnings are distributed, enter 0 (zero) in this box. If earnings in the revoked IRA are distributed, enter only the earnings in this box.

If a rollover or transfer made from one Roth IRA to another Roth IRA is timely revoked, report in this box the same amount as that entered in box 1.

Governmental Section 457(b) Plans and SEP and SIMPLE IRAs: Generally, the taxable amount of the distribution must be entered in this box. But if the payer cannot reasonably obtain the data needed to compute the taxable amount, this box should be left blank. The payer must make every effort to compute the taxable amount.

Second Box 2b. Total Distribution.

Enter an "X" in this box 2b only if the payment shown in box 1 is a total distribution. (A total distribution is one or more distributions within one tax year in which the entire balance of the account is distributed.) If periodic or installment payments are made, mark in this box the year in which the final payment is made.

Box 3. Capital Gain (Included in Box 2a).

Not applicable to traditional, Roth, SEP, SARSEP, or SIMPLE IRAs and should be left blank.

Box 4. Federal Income Tax Withheld.

Enter any federal income tax withheld. This withholding is subject to the deposit rules and to Form 945, Annual Return of Withheld Federal Income Tax. No withholding is required until the annual aggregate distribution exceeds $200.

Traditional IRAs (Including SEP IRAs) and SIMPLE IRAs: All IRA distributions that are "payable upon demand" are generally subject to a flat 10 percent withholding rate, unless the recipient elects to have more than 10 percent withheld. If the recipient is eligible for and elects no withholding, leave this box blank.

For individual retirement *annuities*, the issuer of the annuity contract generally withholds the amount that would be required if the periodic payment were a payment of wages (based on the recipient's Form W-4P).

For withholding purposes, assume that the entire amount of any IRA distribution is taxable, except for the distribution of contributions under Code Section 408(d)(4), in which case only the earnings are taxable, and for Section 408(d)(5) distributions of excess contributions.

A traditional IRA that is converted to a Roth IRA is subject to withholding, unless the recipient is eligible for and elects no withholding. This is true regardless of the method used for the conversion (transfer or rollover) and even if the conversion is accomplished within the same financial institution.

Roth IRAs: Most Roth IRA distributions are exempt from any federal income tax withholding. Therefore, there should be no withholding on Roth IRA distributions, except in the case of a returned contribution plus earnings under Code Section 408(d)(4) or a revoked contribution plus earnings. Such earnings are always treated as taxable distributions—even when they otherwise meet the definition of a qualified distribution. [I.R.C. § 408A(d)(2)(C); Treas. Reg. § 1.408A-6, Q&A-1(d)] Thus, withholding applies only on the earnings being distributed. Of course, the recipient can elect no withholding on the earnings.

Recharacterizations: Do not withhold on any IRA recharacterization. Recharacterizations are not treated as distributions.

Box 5. Employee Contributions/Designated Roth Contributions or Insurance Premiums.

Not applicable to IRAs.

Box 6. Net Unrealized Appreciation in Employer's Securities.

Not applicable to IRAs.

Box 7. Distribution Code.

Enter the code or codes appropriate for the type of distribution made. In certain cases, both a numeric and an alpha code must be entered. For example, for a corrective distribution of an excess contribution plus earnings from a traditional IRA where the earnings are taxable in the prior year and the participant is under age 59½, enter double code 1P in box 7. For a direct rollover from an employer's qualified plan, Section 403(b) plan, or governmental Section 457(b) plan to a traditional IRA for the surviving spouse of a deceased participant, enter double code 4G. For a direct rollover from a designated Roth account to a Roth IRA, use code 4H.

Only three numeric combinations are permitted: codes 8 and 1, 8 and 2, or 8 and 4. If two other numeric codes are applicable, more than one Form 1099-R must be filed. For example, if a participant takes an early distribution during the first part of 2020 and takes another distribution in 2020 upon or after attaining age 59½, two Forms 1099-R must be issued. The early distribution would be coded 1 and the normal distribution would be coded 7.

If a second code is applicable, it is listed under each of the following code descriptions. When an alpha code and a numeric code are used, either code may be placed first (see Table 8-2 above).

Only the distribution codes relevant to IRA distributions are listed below.

Code 1. Early Distribution, No Known Exception. Indicates that the employee or other payee is under age 59½ and none of the exceptions to the 10 percent premature distribution penalty are *known* to apply.

Use code 1 even if the distribution is made for any of the following reasons:

- Medical expenses (applies to IRAs, qualified plans, and Section 403(b) plans)
- Qualified higher education expenses (applies only to IRAs)
- First-time homebuyer expenses (applies only to IRAs)
- Health insurance premiums paid by certain unemployed individuals (applies only to IRAs)
- Qualified reservist distribution
- Qualified birth or adoption distribution

In such cases, the payee may file Form 5329 with his or her federal income tax return to indicate that the 10 percent premature distribution penalty does not apply.

Also use code 1 in these cases:

- If the recipient of the distribution is age 59½ or older and modifies a series of substantially equal periodic payments within five years of the first payment
- For a Section 408(d)(5) distribution if the payee is under age 59½ (see the description of Section 408(d)(5) corrective distributions in the discussion under "Box 2a. Taxable Amounts")

Distributions from a governmental Section 457(b) plan are not subject to the 10 percent premature distribution penalty. Thus, code 1 is not applicable to Section 457(b) plan distributions in most cases. However, if assets from a governmental Section 457(b) plan are rolled over to another plan (e.g., a traditional IRA) that is subject to that penalty, subsequent distributions from the plan that received the governmental Section 457(b) plan's assets will be subject to the 10 percent premature distribution penalty unless the participant satisfies one of the exceptions. Moreover, if a plan distribution subject to the 10 percent premature distribution penalty is rolled over to a Section 457(b) plan, subsequent distributions from that Section 457(b) plan, to the extent they are attributable to the amounts rolled over, will be subject to the 10 percent premature distribution penalty. If the distribution consists solely of assets attributable to the

Section 457(b) plan, use code 2. If the distribution consists solely of assets attributable to a rollover contribution from any plan that is subject to the 10 percent penalty, use code 1. (Use code 7 if the payee is age 59½ or older.) If the distribution comprises amounts from both sources, the plan trustee must file a separate Form 1099-R for each part.

If applicable, use code 1 in conjunction with code 8, B, D, K, L, or P.

Code 2. Early Distribution, Exception Applies. Code 2 is only used for IRA distributions if:

1. A traditional IRA, SEP IRA, or SIMPLE IRA is converted to a Roth IRA, and the participant is under age 59½.
2. A pre-age 59½ distribution is made from the participant's employer's plan or the participant's IRA because of an IRS levy under Code Section 6331.
3. A distribution is one of a series of substantially equal payments (as described in Code Section 72(q), (t), or (v)).

If applicable, use code 8, B, D, K, or P in addition to code 2.

Code 3. Disability. Use code 3 if the employee or other payee is disabled. The instructions for Form 1099-R refer to *disability* as defined under Code Section 72(m)(7). Thus, an individual must be disabled under Code Section 72(m)(7) to avoid the 10 percent early distribution penalty. Because many employer plans use a definition of disability different from the definition under Code Section 72(m)(7), an individual may be subject to the 10 percent early distribution penalty even though he or she meets the plan's definition of disability.

For reporting purposes, code 3 should be used only if the individual is "disabled" as the term is used in Code Section 72(m)(7).

If applicable, use code D in addition to code 3.

Code 4. Death. Use code 4 regardless of the age of the deceased participant or beneficiary to indicate that the distribution was made to the decedent's beneficiary, including an estate or trust. For example, for a trustee-to-trustee transfer of assets on behalf of a nonspouse beneficiary to an inherited IRA, code 4 is used to identify the distribution. If applicable, use one of the following codes in addition to code 4: code 8, G, H, K, or P.

Code 5. Prohibited Transaction. If the trustee knows that the participant or beneficiary of any IRA has engaged in a prohibited transaction (as defined under Code Section 4975(c)), or there has been improper use of the account (as defined under Code Section 408(e)(2)), it is required to report the "deemed" distribution on Form 1099-R. If the prohibited transaction involves a Roth IRA, use code 5 regardless of the payee's age. Code 5 means that the account is no longer an IRA, and no other code should be used with it.

Code 6.* Section 1035 *Exchange. Use code 6 to indicate the tax-free exchange of life insurance, annuity, or endowment contracts under Code Section 1035. For a Section 1035 exchange that is in part taxable, file a separate Form 1099-R to report the taxable amount.

A tax-free Section 1035 exchange is the exchange of

1. A life insurance contract for another life insurance contract, endowment, or annuity contract;
2. An endowment contract for an annuity contract or for another endowment contract that provides for regular payments to begin no later than they would have begun under the old contract; or
3. An annuity contract for another annuity contract.

The distribution of other property at the time of the exchange may be taxable and reportable on a separate Form 1099-R.

All Section 1035 exchanges are reportable on Form 1099-R, except when

1. The exchange occurs within the same insurance company;
2. The exchange is solely a contract-for-contract exchange that does not result in a designated distribution; and
3. The insurance company maintains adequate records of the policyholder's basis in the contracts.

If applicable, use code W in addition to code 6.

Code 7. Normal Distribution. Use code 7 for a normal distribution from an IRA to indicate that the payee is age 59½ or older. Also use code 7 if a traditional IRA (including a SEP IRA) or a SIMPLE IRA is converted to a Roth IRA and the participant is age 59½ or older.

Do not use code 7 for any Roth IRA distribution.

Use code 7 for a Section 408(d)(5) corrective distribution if the payee is age 59½ or older.

Also use code 7 to report a distribution from an annuity contract.

Generally, if no other code applies to the distribution, use code 7.

If applicable, use code K in addition to code 7.

Code 8. Excess Contributions Plus Earnings/Excess Deferrals (and/or Earnings) Taxable in 2020. Use code 8 for a corrective distribution of an excess contribution plus earnings from a traditional IRA, SEP IRA, or Roth IRA when the earnings are taxable in the year of distribution.

Example. An individual contributes $6,000 to a Roth IRA in May 2020. Two months later, he realizes the contribution is improper because his income for the year will exceed the MAGI limit. In December 2020, the IRA trustee makes a corrective distribution of $6,000 plus the earnings on that amount ($100). On the 2020 Form 1099-R, the trustee should enter $6,000 in box 1, $100 in box 2a, and code 8 in box 7 because the earnings included in the distribution are taxable in the year of the distribution (2020).

If the distribution is made from a Roth IRA and the participant is under age 59½, use the double code 8J to indicate that earnings are subject to the 10 percent early distribution penalty. If the participant is age 59½ or older, use code 8 alone.

For a revoked IRA, see Table 8-2 above.

Code 8 also applies to corrective distributions of excess deferrals, excess contributions, and excess aggregate contributions under a SARSEP when the earnings are taxable in the year of distribution. These corrective distributions could be taxable in more than one year; in such a case, separate Forms 1099-R must be issued reporting the year in which each part is taxable and using code 8 (for the portion taxable in the distribution year) or P (for the portion taxable in the prior year).

If applicable, use one of the following codes in addition to code 8: code 1, 2, 4, J, or K.

Codes A, B, C, D, E, and F. These do not apply to IRAs.

Code G. Direct Rollover and Direct Payment. Use code G when a direct rollover is made from an IRA to an employer's qualified plan, 403(b) plan, or governmental 457(b) plan that accepts such rollovers, or from such a plan to an IRA (unless the rollover is from a DRAC to a Roth IRA; see code H). If assets in a traditional IRA or SIMPLE IRA are paid directly to the IRA owner, do not use code G. Instead, use code 1 or code 7, depending on the age of the IRA owner.

If the direct rollover is made for a nonspouse designated beneficiary, code 4 is used in addition to code G.

If the transfer includes assets that do not have a readily available fair market value, code K is used with code G.

If applicable, use code 4 or code K with code G.

Code H. Direct rollover of a designated Roth account distribution to a Roth IRA. Use code H to report a direct rollover from a designated Roth account to a Roth IRA. Use code H with code 4 if the rollover is made for a nonspouse designated beneficiary.

Code J. Early Distribution from a Roth IRA. Use code J generally to report any distribution from a Roth IRA that is made before the participant attains age 59½, dies, or becomes disabled. (For Roth IRA distributions after one of those events, use Code Q or T). In some cases, the payee will need to file Form 5329 to indicate that the 10 percent early distribution penalty does not apply. Use code 5 instead if the Roth IRA engages in a prohibited transaction, or code 2 for an IRS levy.

If applicable, use code 8 or code P (in addition to code J) to indicate a corrective distribution including earnings. For a revoked Roth IRA, see Table 8-2 above.

Code K. Distribution of IRA Assets Not Having a Readily Available FMV. This code is required for assets without a readily available FMV, which may include (but are not limited to):

- interests not readily tradable on an established securities market—e.g., stock, other ownership interest in a corporation, and short or long-term debt obligations,
- ownership interest in a limited liability company (LLC), partnership, trust, or similar entity (unless the interest is traded on an established securities market),
- real estate, and
- option contracts (or similar products) not offered for trade on an established option exchange.

If applicable, code K is used in conjunction with code 1, 2, 4, 7, 8, or G.

Codes L and M. These do not apply to IRAs.

Code N. Recharacterized IRA Contribution Made for 2020. Use code N to indicate a recharacterization of a contribution made for 2020 and recharacterized in 2020 to another type of IRA by a trustee-to-trustee transfer or with the same trustee. (See the discussion under box 1.) Do not use any other code with code N.

Code P. Excess Contributions Plus Earnings/Excess Deferrals Taxable in 2020. Use code P to indicate that the distribution is taxable in the prior year. (See the discussions under box 2a and code 8 above.) For corrective distributions of excess contributions plus earnings for any IRA (including a Roth IRA), the IRS suggests that the trustee advise the payee, at the time of the distribution, that the earnings are taxable in the year *in which* the contributions were made.

> **Example.** Denise (age 54) made a regular contribution of $5,500 to a Roth IRA on November 12, 2020. Because her MAGI exceeded the limit in 2019, the entire amount was an excess Roth IRA contribution. On April 5, 2021, a $5,750 corrective distribution (including earnings of $250) was made to Denise. On the 2021 Form 1099-R, the Roth IRA trustee enters $5,750 in box 1 and $250 in box 2a. Because Denise is younger than age 59½, the double code JP is entered in box 7. Code J identifies the distribution as made before age 59½, and Code P indicates that the earnings distributed are taxable in the prior year (2019).

If applicable, use one of the following codes in addition to code P: code 1, 2, 4, or J.

Code Q. Qualified Distribution from a Roth IRA. This code applies if it is known that the recipient meets the five-year holding period requirement and also has a qualifying reason (attainment of age 59½, death of the owner and distribution to beneficiary, or disability).

Do not use any other code with code Q. If any other code (such as code 8 or P) applies, use code J instead of code Q.

Code R. Recharacterized IRA Contribution Made for 2020. Use code R to indicate a recharacterization of a contribution made for 2020 and recharacterized in 2021 to another type of IRA by a trustee-to-trustee transfer or with the same trustee. (See the discussion of box 1 above.)

Do not use any other code with code R.

Code S. Early Distribution from a SIMPLE IRA in First Two Years, No Known Exception. Use code S to report a distribution from a SIMPLE IRA in the first two years if the participant has not reached age 59½ and none of the exceptions under Code Section 72(t) are known to apply. The two-year period begins on the day contributions are first deposited in the individual's SIMPLE IRA by the employer. Code S indicates that the 25 percent tax under Code Section 72(t)(6) may apply unless the amount is rolled over to another SIMPLE IRA.

Do not use code S if code 3 or 4 applies.

Use code 7 instead of code S if the participant is age 59½ or older. Do not use any other code with code S.

Code T. Roth IRA Distribution, Exception Applies. Use code T for a distribution from a Roth IRA if it is not known whether the five-year holding period requirement has been satisfied but it is known that there is a qualifying reason for the distribution (i.e., the owner is at least age 59½ or is disabled, or the Roth IRA owner died and the distribution is to a beneficiary).

Do not use any other code with code T.

Codes U and W. These do not apply to IRAs.

IRA/SEP/SIMPLE Checkbox. Enter an "X" in the IRA/SEP/SIMPLE checkbox if the distribution is from a traditional IRA, SEP IRA, or SIMPLE IRA, including an IRA that is converted to a Roth IRA. It is not necessary to mark the box for a distribution from a Roth IRA or any recharacterization transfer.

Box 8. Other.

Enter the current actuarial value of an annuity contract that is part of a lump-sum distribution. Do not include such value in box 1 or box 2a. To determine the value of an annuity contract, show the value as an amount equal to the current actuarial value of the annuity contract, reduced by an amount equal to the excess of the employee's contributions over the cash and other property (not including the annuity contract) distributed. If an annuity contract is part of a multiple-recipient lump-sum distribution, enter in box 8, along with the current actuarial value, the percentage of the total annuity contract each Form 1099-R represents.

Box 9a. Percentage of Total Distribution.

Not applicable to IRAs.

Box 9b. Total Employee Contributions.

Not applicable to IRAs.

Box 10. Amount Allocable to IRR (in-plan rollover) within 5 Years.

Not applicable to IRAs.

Box 11. 1st Year of Designated Roth Contribution.

Not applicable to IRAs.

Boxes 12–17. State and Local Information.

These boxes and copies 1 and 2 of Form 1099-R are provided for convenience only and need not be completed for the IRS. The state and local information boxes can be used to report distributions and taxes for two states or localities separated by the dotted line.

Unnumbered Boxes.

The following information is contained in unnumbered boxes:

1. Payer's name, address, and ZIP code.
2. Payer's federal identification number. The same name, address, and EIN used to remit federal income tax withheld and to file Form 945 must be entered here.
3. Recipient's identification number. This box must reflect the taxpayer identification number (TIN) of the person or entity receiving the distribution. In the case of a distribution to an estate or trust, the estate's or trust's TIN is used, not the Social Security number of the decedent. For multiple beneficiary recipients, a separate Form 1099-R is prepared for each beneficiary.
4. Recipient's name, address, and ZIP code. This box reflects the name of the recipient as it is shown on his or her Social Security card. In the case of a distribution made to a beneficiary, the recipient is the beneficiary, not the deceased participant. In some cases, the beneficiary recipient is not an individual (i.e., it may be an estate, a charity, or a university). The appropriate name and TIN of the entity should be provided, not the name and Social Security number of the deceased participant.
5. Account number. The account number box must be completed if the payer has multiple accounts for a recipient for whom it is filing more than one Form 1099-R. Otherwise, designation of an account number is encouraged.

The account number must be unique in order to identify the specific "plan" being reported. The recipient's TIN cannot be used for this purpose. Also, in cases where multiple reportable distributions are made from the same plan for different reasons that require separate Forms 1099-R, the account number must be able to identify the specific Form 1099-R. The purpose of the account number box is to identify the proper form if a correction is filed.

For example, assume that the following distributions were all made during 2020 from the same traditional IRA (Account No. 123456789):

- March distribution was a premature distribution (code 1 applies).

- June distribution was converted to a Roth IRA (code 2 applies).
- IRA owner attains age 59½ on July 14, 2019.
- September distribution was a return of an excess contribution for 2019 (code 8 applies).
- November distribution was a normal distribution (code 7 applies).

Although four distributions were made from the same "plan," separate Forms 1099-R are required because different codes apply. In this example, it would be acceptable to enter "Account No. 123456789" and designate the distributions using numbers (e.g., -1, -2, -3, and -4) or letters (e.g., -G, -J, -N, and -P) or some other sequence.

Q 8:82 Are renewed investments treated as distributions?

No. Whenever existing investments (e.g., certificates of deposit) within an IRA are renewed or reinvested in some other form of investment, no distribution occurs. Therefore, no Form 1099-R is issued in such cases (and they are not reported as contributions on Form 5498).

Filing Corrected Forms 1099-R

Q 8:83 How are corrected Forms 1099-R filed?

If 250 or more Forms 1099-R must be corrected, electronic filing is required. For a lesser number, paper filing is acceptable but electronic filing is encouraged. (See Q 8:32.)

> **Example.** Chuck makes a direct rollover to an eligible recipient plan, and Form 1099-R is filed with the IRS, reporting that none of the direct rollovers is taxable by entering a zero in box 2a. It is later discovered that part of the direct rollover was not eligible to be rolled over; that is, part of the distribution consisted of Chuck's RMD. The original Form 1099-R must be corrected by issuing a new Form 1099-R.

All fields in a corrected Form 1099-R must be completed with the accurate information, not only the data fields needing correction. Completing some types of corrections, such as the correction of an erroneous Social Security number, requires two separate steps. A payer should submit corrections only for the returns filed in error, not all the returns filed. Corrected statements should be furnished to recipients as soon as possible. [IRS Pub. 1220, *Specifications for Electronic Filing of Forms 1097, 1098, 1099, 3921, 3922, 5498, and W-2G* (Oct. 17, 2019)]

If a payer discovers errors that affect a large number of payees, in addition to sending the IRS the corrected forms and notifying the payees, the IRS/IRB underreporter section should be contacted (866-455-7438) for additional requirements. [IRS Pub. 1220]

Q 8:84 What must a payer do if a taxpayer identification number is missing from Form 1099-R?

The payer is required to take these actions if there is no TIN associated with the name on an IRA:

1. When the IRA is opened, the payer must complete an initial solicitation. A solicitation is a request (made by mail, telephone, or approved electronic means) that the payee furnish a correct TIN. If no TIN is received after the initial solicitation, immediately begin backup withholding on reportable payments.
2. Complete a first annual solicitation if a TIN is not provided in response to the initial solicitation. The first annual solicitation must generally be made by December 31 of the year in which the account was opened. However, for accounts opened during December, the first annual solicitation must be made by January 31 of the following year.
3. If the first annual solicitation does not result in the provision of a TIN, a second annual solicitation must be completed by December 31 of the year immediately following the calendar year in which the account was opened.
4. The rate of withholding required when a TIN is missing depends upon the type of payment made from the IRA. If the payment is an eligible rollover distribution that is not directly paid to an eligible retirement plan, 20 percent must be withheld. If the payment is not periodic and it is not an eligible rollover distribution, 10 percent withholding is required. Finally, for a periodic payment that is not an eligible rollover distribution, withholding is required based on the wage withholding tables, using the rate that applies for a single individual who claims zero withholding allowances.

[IRS Pub. 1586, *Reasonable Cause Regulations and Requirements for Missing and Incorrect Name/TINs (including instructions for reading CD/DVDs)* (July 2020)]

Q 8:85 What must a payer do if the taxpayer identification number on a Form 1099-R is incorrect?

The payer must do the following when notified by the IRS that it filed a Form 1099-R providing an incorrect TIN:

1. The payer must complete an initial solicitation when the payee opens the account.
2. Within 30 business days after receiving Notice 972CG, the payer must complete a first annual solicitation.
3. If the payee responds to the first annual solicitation within 45 days, and confirms that the previously provided name/TIN combination is correct, the payer may continue to treat the payee's prior withholding election as valid.

4. If the payee responds to the first annual solicitation within 45 days and furnishes a different name/TIN combination, any existing withholding election based on the prior name/TIN combination must be disregarded. The payee may submit a new withholding election by completing Form W-4P (or a substitute form). The new withholding election will be effective no later than January 1, May 1, July 1, or October 1 after it is received, as long as it is received at least 30 days before that date. [Treas. Reg. § 35.3405-1, Q&A D-21] Until a new withholding election is made, the payer must withhold from distributions based on the wage withholding rate that applies to a married individual claiming three withholding allowances.
5. If the payee does not respond to the first annual solicitation within 45 days, the payer must withhold from any distribution at the appropriate rate.
6. Alternatively, upon receipt of a Notice 972CG in which the IRS notifies the payer of an incorrect name/TIN combination, the payer may choose to disregard any prior withholding elections made by the payees whose name/TIN combinations are identified as incorrect in that notice. In that event, the payer should consider those payees to have no withholding election in effect until new withholding elections are received.
7. The payer must complete a second annual solicitation within the same time frame as required for the first annual solicitation if it is notified of an incorrect name/TIN combination in any calendar year following the first notification (apparently, within 30 business days of receiving the second Notice 972CG).

[IRS Pub. 1586, *Reasonable Cause Regulations and Requirements for Missing and Incorrect Name/TINs (including instructions for reading CD/DVDs)* (July 2020)]

Q 8:86 How does the IRS detect a missing or incorrect taxpayer identification number on Form 1099-R?

Form 1099-R is included in the Information Returns Name/TIN Matching Program. The IRS performs a verification check when Form 1099-R is filed to determine whether the name/TIN combination reported on the form matches information in the Social Security Administration's files. If the information does not match, the IRS sends Notice 972CG, *Notice of Proposed Civil Penalty*, to the filer of the information statement.

Notice 972CG lists each submission in which a name/TIN combination is missing or incorrect, states the proposed penalty, and explains how the filer should respond. Details concerning this procedure are explained in IRS Publication 1586, *Reasonable Cause Regulations and Requirements for Missing and Incorrect Name/TINs (including instructions for reading CD/DVDs)* (July 2020).

Revoked IRAs

Q 8:87 Is Form 1099-R issued when an IRA is revoked?

Yes, if any distribution is made. If nothing was contributed before the revocation, nothing is distributed and Form 1099-R is not used.

Q 8:88 Do distribution reporting requirements vary according to the type of IRA contribution being revoked?

Yes. Proper distribution reporting depends on the type of IRA contribution being revoked. For details, see the discussion of box 1 (on Form 1099-R) in Q 8:81.

Fees Deducted from IRAs

Q 8:89 Is the deduction of fees from an IRA treated as a distribution?

No. When fees such as annual maintenance fees or transaction fees are deducted from an IRA, they are not treated as distributions and are not reportable on Form 1099-R. In addition, once fees are deducted from the plan, a participant may not reimburse those amounts back to the plan. That is, if fees are reimbursed to the plan, they are treated as regular IRA contributions, and they must be reported in box 1 of Form 5498. Such amounts would thus count toward the IRA owner's contribution limit for the year. (For discussion of outside funds used to pay account fees, including wrap fees, see Qs 3:37, 3:38.)

Q 8:90 If a financial penalty is assessed on an IRA investment, is the amount reported as a distribution?

No. A financial penalty assessed by contract with respect to an IRA investment (e.g., an early withdrawal fee on a certificate of deposit, or CD), is not included in the distribution amount. The distribution amount reported on line 1 is *net* of any such fee.

> **Example 1.** Beth requests a distribution from her IRA in the amount of $1,000. This is *not* a withdrawal of an unwanted contribution with earnings. The trustee institution imposes an early withdrawal CD penalty of $50. The trustee gives Beth a check for $1,000 and takes the $50 CD penalty from the remaining IRA balance. The reportable distribution is $1,000, even though $1,050 came out of Beth's IRA. Any withholding is assessed on the reportable distribution amount of $1,000.

> **Example 2.** The facts are the same as in Example 1, except the trustee reduces the $1,000 by the $50 CD penalty, resulting in a check to Beth of $950 net. The reportable distribution is $950, even though $1,000 came out of Beth's IRA. Withholding is assessed on the reportable distribution amount of $950.

Miscellaneous Matters

Q 8:91 If an IRA is directly transferred from one trustee to another, is that reported to the IRS?

The receiving trustee generally does not file either Form 1099-R or Form 5498 to report a trustee-to-trustee transfer from one IRA to another, because there is no payment or distribution to the IRA owner.

There are exceptions. If a SIMPLE IRA is transferred to a non-SIMPLE IRA before the employee has participated in the SIMPLE for a two-year period measured from the date the first SIMPLE contribution was deposited into the SIMPLE IRA, reporting is required on both Form 1099-R (as a taxable distribution) and Form 5498 (as a regular contribution). Reporting is also required for recharacterizations made using to a trustee-to-trustee transfer. (See Qs 8:81, 8:146.) Also, a direct transfer which is a conversion is taxable, and treated as a distribution, so Forms 1099-R and 5498 must both be filed.

Reporting on these forms is also required for any trustee-to-trustee transfer from an IRA to a qualified plan, or from a qualified plan to an IRA.

[Instructions for Forms 1099-R and 5498 (2021), Direct Rollovers, p. 4; Transfers p. 6]

Q 8:92 How long should copies of Form 1099-R be kept?

Copies of information returns filed with the IRS (including Form 1099-R) should be kept for at least three years from the due date of the return.

Q 8:93 May Form 1099-R be enclosed in the same envelope with other forms?

Yes, but not with other material. If a trustee combines Forms 1099-R with returns for interest, dividend, and royalty payments, strict mailing requirements must be followed. For example, no enclosures are permitted for promotional material or a quarterly or annual report. Even a sentence on the year-end statement describing new services being offered is not permitted. Logos are permitted on the envelope and on any nontax enclosures. If, however, Form 1099-R is being mailed without such forms, a combined mailing may be allowed. Payee statements that are related may be included in the same envelope; related forms include Form 1099, Form 1098, and Form 5498 (or the account balance on a Form 5498). In addition, Form W-2 may also be included in the single mailing because it is related to the payee statements. [Notice 87-17, 1987-1 C.B. 454]

Q 8:94 Must the account number box on Form 1099-R be completed?

Yes. The account number is a unique identifier; it must not appear anywhere else on the form, and it must not be a Social Security number. In the event that multiple reportable distributions are made from the same plan for different reasons that require separate Forms 1099-R, and the payer files a corrected form, the account number will allow the IRS to identify the specific Form 1099-R that is being corrected.

Q 8:95 Are there other requirements that trustees or other payers of distributions should be aware of?

Yes. The instructions for Form 1099-R contain the following important reminders:

Trustee-to-Trustee Transfers. Form 1099-R is not to be used to report direct transfers between trustees for the same type of plan (i.e., traditional IRA to traditional IRA (including SEP IRA to SEP IRA), SIMPLE IRA to SIMPLE IRA, Roth IRA to Roth IRA, qualified plan to qualified plan, 403(b) plan to 403(b) plan, and 457 plan to 457 plan). However, recharacterization transfers must be reported on Form 1099-R.

The trustee must report as a taxable distribution on Form 1099-R any trustee-to-trustee transfer from a SIMPLE IRA to any IRA (other than another SIMPLE IRA) during the two-year period beginning on the day employer contributions are first deposited in the participant's SIMPLE IRA. The IRS needs this information because tax-free transfers (and rollovers) are not permitted from a SIMPLE IRA to an IRA other than another SIMPLE IRA during the first two years regardless of the participant's age. Since the original SIMPLE IRA trustee will know that assets are transferring to a non-SIMPLE IRA before the two-year period has expired, it can prepare and file Form 1099-R.

Roth Conversions. If a traditional IRA (including a SEP IRA) or SIMPLE IRA is converted to a Roth IRA, it must be reported even if the assets are transferred in a trustee-to-trustee transfer or the assets are transferred within the same financial institution. A SIMPLE IRA is not eligible to convert to a Roth IRA until the participant has satisfied the two-year holding period applicable to SIMPLE IRAs.

Divorce and Marital Separation. IRA transfers pursuant to a Code-compliant divorce or separation instrument are tax free, and not reported on Form 1099-R. This may include the transfer of an interest from one spouse's IRA to an IRA in the other spouse's name, or simply the redesignation of an IRA in the name of the other spouse.

Nonresident Aliens. If income tax is withheld under Code Section 3405 (the normal retirement plan withholding section), the distribution and withholding must be reported on Form 1099-R and the annual withholding return must be filed with Form 945. If income tax is withheld under Code Section 1441 (the nonresident alien section), the distribution and withholding must be reported on Forms 1042-S and 1042.

Attaching Form 1099-R to Tax Return. Recipients of distributions from an IRA are required to attach Form 1099-R to their federal income tax returns *only if* federal income tax withholding is shown in box 4.

How to Treat an IRA Plan for Reporting Distributions. An IRA includes all investments under one IRA plan or account. Thus, only one Form 1099-R is filed for all distributions from all investments that are paid in one year to one recipient under one plan, unless different codes must be entered in box 7. The trustee, custodian, or other payer need not file a separate Form 1099-R for each distribution under the same plan using the same code. If multiple distributions from an IRA are made during a year one recipient and all the distributions use the same code in box 7, only one Form 1099-R should be filed.

When Form 1099-R Is Not Required. Form 1099-R is not required when aggregate distributions to an individual during the year are less than $10. Negative amounts also need not be entered in any box on the form (e.g., Form 1099-R is not required for a distribution of worthless property). However, the recipient of a negative amount may enter 0 (zero) in boxes 1 and 2a, and, in the case of an employer's plan, enter any after-tax employee contributions in box 5.

Form 1099-SA

Q 8:96 What is the purpose of Form 1099-SA?

HSA trustees report distributions to the IRS on Form 1099-SA, Distributions from an HSA, Archer MSA, or Medicare Advantage MSA. The filing deadline to report 2020 HSA distributions is March 1, 2021 (for paper filing) or March 31, 2021 (electronic filing). The trustee must also furnish a copy to the distributee by January 31, 2021. [Instructions for Forms 1098-SA and 5498-SA (2020)]

Trustee-to-trustee transfers are not reported on Form 1099-SA.

Q 8:97 How are HSA distributions reported?

Box 1. The gross amount of the distribution, including earnings, is reported in box 1. The trustee is not required to determine the taxable part of the distribution.

If the account owner received a corrective distribution of excess HSA contributions (which must include allocable earnings), the gross amount is reported in box 1. (Withdrawals of excess employer contributions, with earnings, that are returned to the employer are not reported on Form 1099-SA.)

Box 2. This box is used only if a corrective distribution was reported in box 1. In that case, the earnings portion of the corrective distribution is separately stated in box 2.

Box 3. The distribution code is placed in box 3. Use:

- Normal distribution—code 1.
- Corrective distribution—code 2.
- Distribution on account of disability—code 3.
- Distribution to the deceased HSA owner's estate, whether during or after the year of death—code 4.
- Deemed distribution because of a prohibited transaction—code 5.

- Distribution to a deceased HSA owner's *nonspouse* beneficiary, if made after the year of death and not paid to the estate—code 6.

Box 4. If applicable, report in this box the fair market value of the HSA on the account owner's date of death.

Form 5329

Q 8:98 Who must file Form 5329?

An *IRA owner* generally must file Form 5329, Additional Taxes on Qualified Retirement Plans (Including IRAs) and Other Tax-Favored Accounts, if any of the following applies (for exceptions, see Q 8:99):

1. An early distribution was made from a Roth IRA, the amount on Form 8606, line 30, is more than zero, and the owner is required to enter an amount that is more than zero on line 1 (of Form 5329).
2. An early distribution was made from an IRA (excluding a Roth IRA) and no exception to the additional tax on such distributions is applicable. However, Form 5329 need not be filed if distribution code 1 is correctly shown on all Forms 1099-R for the same year and additional tax is owed with respect to each of those forms (in that case the additional tax is reported on Form 1040).
3. An exception to the tax on early IRA distributions applies, and distribution code 1 is shown in box 7 of Form 1099-R.
4. An excess contribution was made to a traditional IRA (Part III must be completed), Roth IRA (Part IV must be completed), Coverdell ESA (Part V must be completed), MSA (Part VI must be completed), HSA (Part VII must be completed), or qualified retirement plan (Part VII must be completed), or there is a tax due from an excess contribution on line 17, 25, 33, 41, 49, or 53 of the prior year's Form 5329.
5. A distribution from a Coverdell ESA was made in excess of amounts spent for qualified higher education expenses.
6. An RMD was required from an IRA but not distributed. (Part VIII must be completed.)

Q 8:99 Are there exceptions to the filing requirement?

Yes. Form 5329 need not be filed if any of the following applies:

1. Only the 10 percent tax is owed on early distributions (distribution code 1 must be shown in box 7 of Form 1099-R). (If Form 1040 is filed, 10 percent of the taxable part of the distribution should be entered on line 60 and "no" written under the heading "Other Taxes" to the left of line 60 to indicate that Form 5329 does not have to be filed.)

2. An early distribution was received from an IRA, but the distributee meets an exception to the tax (distribution code 2, 3, or 4 must be correctly shown on Form 1099-R).
3. The taxable part of all qualifying distributions was rolled over.

Q 8:100 How is Form 5329 filed?

Form 5329 is ordinarily filed as an attachment to Form 1040. However, an individual must file Form 5329 on its own if he or she is not required to file Form 1040. In that case, Form 5329 is due at the time and place that would be applicable for Form 1040.

Q 8:101 What is reported on Form 5329?

An individual uses Form 5329 to report distributions and accumulations that are subject to additional tax (see Qs 8:102–8:126). There are eight parts to Form 5329, each for a different kind of distribution. The distributions are reported and any additional tax due on them is also figured. The distributions reportable on Form 5329 are:

- Distributions to a payee younger than age 59½ (part I)
- Coverdell ESAs distributions not used for qualified educational expenses (part II)
- Excess contributions to a traditional IRA (part III)
- Excess contributions to a Roth IRA (part IV)
- Excess contributions to a Coverdell ESA (part V)
- Excess contributions to an Archer MSA (part VI)
- Excess contributions to an HSA (part VII)
- Excess amounts accumulated in an IRA because RMDs were not taken (part VIII).

Early Distributions

Q 8:102 How are early IRA distributions reported on Form 5329?

Taxable IRA distributions that are made before the payee has reached age 59½ are reported in Part I of Form 5329. Only the taxable portion of the distribution is included, so basis allocated to the distribution and excess contributions withdrawn are excluded. The additional tax on the early distributions is also figured in Part I.

Deemed distributions that are subject to the additional tax are also to be reported in Part I. For example, if an IRA invests in a collectible, the collectible is deemed distributed on the day of the investment. A deemed distribution also results if an IRA engages in a prohibited transaction. In that case, the IRA is disqualified and its entire value is deemed distributed as of the first day of the year.

If the "payee" is younger than age 59½, the early distribution penalty may apply.

Note. A prohibited transaction must be reported on Form 5330, Return of Excise Taxes Related to Employee Benefit Plans (see Q 8:125).

Q 8:103 If an exception applies to the additional tax on early distributions, how is that reported?

If an early distribution is covered by an exception to the additional tax, the amount is entered on line 2, and the applicable exception is identified by the number assigned to it in the instructions.

Q 8:104 What is reported on Form 5329 if a distribution was incorrectly designated on Form 1099-R as made to a payee younger than age 59½?

The distribution should be included on both line 1 (early distributions included in income) and line 2 (early distributions not subject to additional tax). The instructions include a special "exception" to the additional tax for this purpose, and its number is also entered on line 2.

Excess Contributions

Q 8:105 What excess contributions are reported on Form 5329?

Two kinds of excess contributions are reported on Form 5329—those made during the current year, and those made in a prior year that were not previously recovered. Excess contributions not corrected by the end of the year are subject to the 6 percent additional tax.

Q 8:106 How are excess contributions corrected?

There are generally three methods for correcting excess contributions to an IRA (see Q 3:137):

1. Withdraw an excess contribution made for the current year before the tax return is due (as a corrective distribution).
2. Withdraw an excess contribution after the tax return for the contribution year is due.
3. Treat a prior-year excess contribution as made for the current year.

Note. If the excess contribution is withdrawn, it may be necessary to report the distribution elsewhere on Form 5329 (e.g., as an early distribution) and additional tax may apply.

Q 8:107 How is an excess contribution corrected before the tax return is due for the contribution year?

Both the excess contribution and any earnings attributable to it must be distributed by the due date (including extensions) for the IRA owner's tax return for the contribution year. (For the method of calculating the earnings that must be distributed, see Q 8:111.)

Note. The IRA owner may not deduct the excess contribution.

If this method is used, the distribution of the excess contribution is not taxable, but the earnings distribution is includable in income (and may be subject to additional tax).

Example 1. Harriet makes an IRA contribution for 2020 on January 10, 2021. She has until the deadline for filing her 2020 federal income tax return, including extensions, to remove the excess or unwanted contribution (whether or not deductible) because the contribution was made for 2020.

Example 2. On January 1, 2020, Arnold (age 49) contributes $7,000 to his traditional IRA. On April 3, 2020, when the account value is $7,920, Arnold realizes he was entitled to contribute only $6,000 for 2020, and he asks the trustee to return the $1,000 excess contribution. The earnings attributable to the excess contribution must also be returned. Using the formula in Q 8:111, the trustee determines that $70 of earnings must be distributed. The total corrective distribution will be $1,070, and on his 2020 return Arnold will deduct $6,000 for his IRA contribution (if he qualifies for the deduction) and include earnings of $70 in gross income. Arnold will also pay an early distribution penalty of $7 for 2020.

Q 8:108 How is an excess contribution corrected by withdrawing it after the tax return is due for the contribution year?

If the time to file the IRA owner's tax return for the contribution year has expired, the excess contribution may be corrected by withdrawal. [Treas. Reg. § 1.408-11]

1. Because the tax return due date has passed, the owner is immediately subject to the 6 percent excise tax. The excise tax applies first to the year in which the excess contribution was made and then to each subsequent year until the excess is corrected.
2. This method does not require any earnings on the excess contribution to be withdrawn. Only the excess amount is distributed.
3. No deduction is allowed for the excess contribution.

The withdrawal of an excess IRA contribution in this manner may be a taxable distribution (unlike the method in Q 8:107). It is not a taxable distribution if the individual's aggregate contributions for the year in which the excess contribution was made did not exceed $5,000 (the $5,000 rule). Otherwise, the distribution is taxable and additional tax may also apply if the individual is younger than age 59½. [I.R.C. § 408(d)(5)]

There are two exceptions to the $5,000 rule.

1. If an employer makes an excess contribution to an employee's IRA under a SEP or SARSEP arrangement, the $5,000 amount is increased by the excess SEP contribution.
2. If an individual makes an excess rollover contribution based on erroneous information received from his or her employer with respect to the amount eligible to be rolled over, the $5,000 amount is increased by the portion of the rollover contribution attributable to the erroneous information.

Example. Lewis, age 43, inadvertently contributes $6,500 to his traditional IRA for 2020. His contribution limit for the year is $6,000, so Lewis has made a $500 excess contribution. If he does not correct the excess by using the method in Q 8:107, Lewis is immediately subject to the 6 percent excess contribution penalty on the $500 excess.

If Lewis withdraws the $500 on October 31, 2021, the $500 distribution is includable in income for the year in which the distribution occurs, and it also may be subject to the 10 percent early distribution penalty because Lewis is not yet age 59½. Since the contribution amount exceeds $5,000 and Lewis cannot deduct the excess contribution, he is paying taxes twice on the same money. If eligible, Lewis may be better off using the method in Q 8:109 (even though 6 percent additional tax would then be payable on the $500 excess contribution).

Assuming, however, that Lewis does use this method, it would be reported as follows:

1. Lewis would report the distribution on his Form 1040 for 2020 (the year when the excess contribution was made) as follows—
   a. $6,000 as a regular contribution and
   b. $30 ($500 × 6%) as the excess contribution penalty.
2. Lewis would complete Form 5329 and attach it to Form 1040. He would complete Part III and report the 6 percent excess contribution penalty of $30.
3. The trustee would
   a. Report the full amount contributed ($6,000) on Form 5498 for 2020 (the year in which the excess contribution was made) and
   b. Report the gross distribution as $500 and the taxable distribution as zero on Form 1099-R (2020 version).

Although no earnings are distributed with respect to the excess contribution, the trustee would enter the gross amount in box 1 on Form 1099-R, and zero in box 2a. Codes P and 8 do not apply to the distribution of an excess contribution after the tax return filing deadline, because no earnings are distributed. Instead, the trustee would enter the early distribution code (code 1) because of Lewis's age.

Q 8:109 How is an excess contribution corrected by treating it as a contribution made for a subsequent year?

This method does not involve a distribution from the IRA. The IRA owner merely undercontributes in the subsequent year and applies so much of the excess contribution as does not cause the contribution limit for that year to be exceeded. This is repeated each year until the excess contribution is exhausted.

The 6 percent additional tax applies for the year the excess contribution is made, and continues to apply in each subsequent year to the uncorrected portion of the excess contribution. [I.R.C. § 219(f)(6)]

Practice Pointer. The 6 percent penalty may be less costly here than if the method in Q 8:108 is used. That method requires a distribution of earnings that is taxable and may also be subject to the 10 percent additional tax on early distributions.

Example. Lucy, age 23, made a $5,500 contribution to her IRA for 2018. Since Lucy's compensation for the year was only $4,700, she made a 2018 excess IRA contribution of $800.

If Lucy decides not to withdraw the $800 excess under Method 1, she is immediately subject to the 6 percent excess contribution penalty for the year in which the excess contribution was made. Lucy's compensation for 2019 is $9,500, making her eligible to contribute the maximum of $6,000. Lucy makes a new contribution of $5,200 for 2019, and notifies the trustee that the prior-year excess amount of $800 should be applied toward her overall limit of $6,000 for 2019. Because she uses up her entire prior-year excess in the following year, the 6 percent penalty is not reapplied.

The following would occur:

1. Lucy would report the contribution on her Form 1040 for 2018 (the year in which the excess contribution was made) as follows—
    a. $4,700 as a regular contribution and
    b. $48 ($800 × 6%) as the excess contribution penalty.
2. She would complete Form 5329, and attach it to the 2018 Form 1040. The excess contribution penalty ($48) would be figured in part III.
3. The trustee would report the full amount contributed ($5,500) on Form 5498 for 2018 (when the excess contribution was made). No further reporting would be required because no corrective distribution would be made.
4. Lucy would report $6,000 ($5,200 + $800) as a regular contribution on her Form 1040 for 2019.

Q 8:110 What guidance has the IRS offered on this topic?

Notice 2000-39 [2000-2 C.B. 132] and the regulations provided the following relevant information concerning distributions from an IRA:

1. "Net income" may include a negative number; therefore, investment losses may be allocated to an excess or recharacterized contribution.
2. Earnings are determined based on an IRA's entire balance, not on an investment account balance within the IRA.
3. Recharacterized contributions are taken into account for the period they are actually held in a traditional IRA or Roth IRA for purposes of calculating earnings.
4. If an IRA owner has made regular contributions to an IRA, the last contribution made is deemed to be the contribution being distributed (i.e., the last-in, first-out method).
5. If an individual maintains multiple IRAs, the earnings calculation is made with respect to the IRA designated by the individual and the corrective distribution must be made from that IRA.
6. An individual who has an IRA must recharacterize the dollar amount of his or her account balance. Property (e.g., a specific number of shares of stock) may not be recharacterized.

Q 8:111 How is net income calculated and who is required to determine it?

The IRA trustee is responsible for calculating the net income to distribute with the IRA owner's excess contribution. [Treas. Reg. § 1.408-11(d)]

The formula for calculating the net income on a returned contribution or a recharacterized contribution is:

$$\text{Net income}^{1} = \text{Contribution}^{2} \times \frac{(\text{Adjusted closing balance}^{3} - \text{Adjusted opening balance}^{4})}{\text{Adjusted opening balance}}$$

[1] Net income can be positive or negative.

[2] The amount of the contribution that is being returned or recharacterized.

[3] Adjusted closing balance (ACB) is the fair market value (FMV) of the IRA at the end of the computation period plus the amount of any distributions or transfers (including recharacterizations) made *from* the IRA during the computation period.

[4] Adjusted opening balance (AOB) is the FMV of the IRA at the beginning of the computation period, plus the amount of any contributions (including the contribution that is being returned) or transfers (including recharacterizations) made *to* the IRA during the computation period.

The computation period is the period beginning immediately before the time when the contribution being returned or recharacterized was made to the IRA and ending immediately prior to the removal of the contribution (or transfer in the case of a recharacterization). If a series of regular contributions was made, and consecutive contributions in the series are being recharacterized, then the computation period begins immediately before the first contribution being recharacterized was made. [Treas. Reg. § 1.408A-5, Q&A-2(c)(2)(iii)]

The preamble to the regulations implies that if an IRA is valued on a daily basis, for purposes of determining the AOB the computation period begins the exact day before the contribution was made that is being returned or recharacterized. If the IRA is not valued on a daily basis, for purposes of determining the AOB the FMV at the beginning of the computation period is deemed to be the most recent, regularly determined, FMV of the asset as of a date that coincides with or precedes the first day of the computation period (i.e., the most recent statement value). The IRS believes that if an IRA asset is normally valued on a daily basis, these values must be used so that the calculation of the amount of net income is based on the actual earnings and losses during the time the IRA actually held the contribution. The IRS also believes that using the most recent statement value would produce anomalous results.

Two regulations control the calculation of net income associated with returned contributions:

1. Regulations Section 1.408-11 governs the net income calculation for returned contributions under Code Section 408(d)(4). Returned contributions can be either excess contributions or "unwanted" contributions made to a traditional IRA or to a Roth IRA.
2. Regulations Section 1.408A-5, Q&A-2(c) governs the net income calculation for recharacterized contributions. Recharacterized contributions include regular contributions made to either a traditional IRA or a Roth IRA.

In general, both regulations are identical except in the following areas:

1. For returned contributions under Code Section 408(d)(4), where a series of regular contributions were made, the contribution being returned is deemed to be the last contribution made, up to the amount of the contribution identified as the amount to be distributed.
2. For recharacterized contributions under Code Section 408A(d)(6), where a series of contributions were made that are eligible for recharacterization, the IRA owner can choose by date and by dollar amount which contribution, or portion thereof, is to be recharacterized. (However, the IRA owner may not identify by a specific asset acquired with those dollars.)

The regulations clarify that the net income calculation is performed only on "the IRA" containing the particular contribution being returned or recharacterized, and that IRA is the IRA from which the distribution or recharacterizing transfer must be made. Although the regulations do not specifically define the term "the IRA," it is the author's interpretation that this means all assets associated with the particular IRA agreement and for which a separate Form 5498 is issued.

The regulations also clarify that if regular and conversion contributions are commingled in a single Roth IRA, the calculation of net income must be performed on the entire IRA, and any net income, including losses, must be prorated.

Example 1. Shannon contributes $1,600 to her traditional IRA on May 1, 2019; immediately before the contribution, the FMV of the IRA was $4,000. On February 1, 2020, Shannon requests a distribution under Code Section 408(d)(4) to return $400 of that contribution. The FMV of her IRA on February 1, 2020, is $7,600. During the computation period (May 1, 2019, through February 1, 2020), no other contributions are made and no distributions are taken.

The AOB is $6,400 ($4,800 + $1,600) and the ACB is $7,600. The earnings attributable to the excess are determined as follows:

$$\text{Net income} = \$400 \times \frac{(\$7{,}600 - \$6{,}400)}{\$6{,}400} = \$75$$

Therefore, the distribution must be $475, of which $75 is taxable to Shannon on her 2019 tax return.

Example 2. Beginning in 2013, Jackie contributed $500 to a Roth IRA on the 15th of each month through payroll deduction. As a result, she made an excess contribution of $1,000 for 2013. The last two contributions made for 2013 are the excess contributions. The balance in Jackie's IRA immediately before the first excess contribution (on November 15) was $11,000. On March 1, 2014, Jackie requested a distribution of the $1,000 excess contribution with attributable earnings. The balance of the IRA immediately before the corrective distribution on March 1, 2014, was $16,000. No distributions were taken during the computation period November 15, 2013, through March 1, 2014. The only other contributions made during the computation period consisted of $1,000 ($500 × 2), contributed on January 15, 2014, and February 15, 2014.

Since the excess contribution resulted from two monthly payments that were part of a series of regular payments, the total excess contribution is considered made during a single computation period, which began immediately before the first excess payment (November 15).

The AOB for this computation period is $13,000 ($11,000 + (4 × $500)), and the ACB is $16,000.

$$\text{Net income} = \$1{,}000 \times \frac{(\$16{,}000 - \$13{,}000)}{\$13{,}000} = \$231$$

Therefore, the total to be distributed on March 1, 2014, is $1,231 ($500 + $500 + $231). Of this amount $231 is taxable to Jackie on her 2013 tax return.

Q 8:112 How are excess contributions to a Roth IRA or a Coverdell ESA reported on Form 5329?

Part IV of Form 5329 is used to report the tax on excess contributions to a Roth IRA, and Part V of Form 5329 is used to report the tax on excess contributions to a Coverdell ESA. (For a Coverdell ESA, it is the *beneficiary* (not the donor) who files Form 5329.) If the excess contribution is withdrawn, no penalty will apply provided (1) the withdrawal is made by the tax return filing due date (including extensions) and (2) the withdrawal includes any income earned on the withdrawn contributions.

Q 8:113 How is the 6 percent penalty tax on excess contributions computed?

The penalty tax is computed as 6 percent of the total excess contribution remaining at the end of the year. However, it may not exceed 6 percent of the IRA or Coverdell ESA value as determined at the end of the year. [I.R.C. § 4973(a)] The penalty is figured on Form 5329.

Excess Accumulations

Q 8:114 Is the excess accumulations tax ever waived?

Yes. There is a reasonable cause exception to the excess accumulations tax, so in appropriate circumstances the IRS may waive it. The individual must demonstrate that the failure to take the full RMD (this is what causes an excess accumulation) was due to reasonable error, and that responsible steps were or are being taken to remedy the shortfall. [I.R.C. § 4974(d)]

Q 8:115 How is a waiver requested?

A reasonable cause waiver of the excess accumulations tax is requested by filing Form 5329, attaching a letter of explanation, and paying the excise tax that is due. If the IRS grants the waiver it will refund the tax.

Q 8:116 If the RMD could not be withdrawn for reasons relating to an insurer's delinquency, does the excess accumulation tax apply?

The tax may not apply if the RMD could not be withdrawn because the IRA is invested in a contract issued by an insurance company that is involved in state insurer delinquency proceedings. To qualify for the exemption, it must be shown that the assets in the IRA include an "affected investment" and other IRA assets were not available to be used for the RMD. [I.R.C. § 4974(d); Rev. Proc. 92-10, 1992-1 C.B. 661, *clarified by* Rev. Proc. 92-16, 1992-1 C.B. 673 and Rev. Proc. 95-52, 1995-2 C.B. 439]

Q 8:117 What is an affected investment?

An *affected investment* is an annuity contract or a guaranteed investment contract (GIC) (with an insurance company) for which payments under the terms of the contract have been reduced or suspended because of state insurer delinquency proceedings against the contracting insurance company. [Rev. Proc. 92-10, 1992-1 C.B. 661, *clarified by* Rev. Proc. 92-16, 1992-1 C.B. 673 and Rev. Proc. 95-52, 1995-2 C.B. 439]

Q 8:118 Must the RMD have been paid to the extent possible?

Yes. If the IRA includes other assets in addition to the affected investment, all of them must have been used to satisfy as much as possible of the minimum distribution requirement. In addition, if the affected investment included an "available portion" (see Q 8:119), that too must have been used to fulfill the RMD requirement.

An individual with several traditional IRAs would be required to use all of his or her assets to the extent possible to make up the RMD.

Q 8:119 What is the available portion of an affected investment?

The *available portion* of an affected investment is the amount of payment remaining after they have been reduced or suspended because of state insurer delinquency proceedings.

Q 8:120 What action must be taken if the reduction or suspension of payments under the annuity contract or GIC is canceled?

If the reduction or suspension of payments is canceled, the increased payments under the annuity contract or GIC must be used to make up the prior RMD shortfall. Increased payments received during one year must be applied to the shortfall by December 31 of the next year. The process must continue until the shortfall is eliminated.

Miscellaneous Matters

Q 8:121 Does the filing of Form 5329 affect reporting on Form 1040?

Yes. With respect to Part I of Form 5329, because a distribution may be fully taxable even if it is not subject to the 10 percent premature distribution penalty, the distribution (but not the penalty) should be reported in full on lines 4a and 4b of Form 1040. The penalty tax, if applicable, is reported on Form 1040, Schedule 4, line 59.

Parts III–V of Form 5329 reflect the fact that any excess contribution may be left in an IRA as long as the 6 percent penalty is regularly (annually) paid. Nonetheless, a taxable distribution reported on line 4b of Form 1040 should reflect the elimination of an excess contribution.

Q 8:122 Which version of Form 5329 is used to pay a tax for a previous year?

To pay a tax for a previous year, that year's version of Form 5329 must be used. For example, to pay tax for 2020, the 2020 version of the form must be used.

Q 8:123 How is additional tax owed for a previous year reported?

If tax is owed for a previous year because of an early distribution, Part I of Form 5329 for that year should be completed and attached to Form 1040X, Amended U.S. Income Tax Return. The individual should include the distribution as additional income on Form 1040X if it has not previously been reported. If a tax other than the tax on early distributions for a previous year is owed, Form 5329 should be filed by itself for that year. The other tax (e.g., excess contribution penalty tax) would be paid on Form 5329 for the current year.

Q 8:124 How is Form 5329 prepared if both spouses owe penalty taxes and file a joint return?

Each spouse must complete a separate Form 5329 for taxes attributable to his or her own IRA or SEP IRA. If both spouses owe penalty taxes and are filing a joint return, they should enter the combined total tax from Forms 5329 on Form 1040, Schedule 4, line 59.

Q 8:125 How is a prohibited transaction reported on Form 5329?

If a prohibited transaction took place—for example, borrowing from an IRA or pledging an individual retirement annuity as security for a loan—the IRA is no longer qualified as an IRA on the first day of the tax year the borrowing or pledging occurred. The IRA owner is considered to have received a distribution of the entire value of his or her IRA at that time. If the prohibited transaction occurs in the year in which the IRA is established, presumably the amount treated as a distribution is the amount initially contributed to the IRA. In that case, the full amount must be reported on line 1 of Form 5329.

Q 8:126 Must Form 5329 be filed if an IRA invests in collectibles?

Yes. If an IRA trustee invested IRA funds in collectibles, the IRA owner is considered to have received a distribution equal to the cost of those collectibles. If the owner was under age 59½ when the funds were invested, the cost of the collectibles is included on line 1 of Form 5329. Collectibles generally include works of art, rugs, antiques, metals, gems, stamps, coins, alcoholic beverages, and certain other tangible personal property purchased after 1981.

Nevertheless, an IRA trustee may invest IRA funds in U.S. one-ounce, one-half-ounce, one-quarter-ounce, and one-tenth-ounce gold coins; one-ounce silver coins; and certain platinum coins minted after September 30, 1986. Certain state-issued coins are also permissible IRA investments. [I.R.C. § 408(m)(3)]

Furthermore, a registered security such as a mutual fund share is not treated as a collectible, even if the fund holds coins or precious metals. Nonetheless, if the issuer distributes coins or metals to the IRA in a redemption of shares or otherwise, it will cause the IRA to acquire a prohibited collectible unless the foregoing exception applies. [Priv. Ltr. Rul. 200732026 (Oct. 8, 2007)]

Note. The IRA owner must include the total cost of the collectibles in income on line 4b of his or her Form 1040. [I.R.C. § 408(m)]

Form 5330

Q 8:127 What is the purpose of Form 5330?

With regard to IRAs, Form 5330, Return of Excise Taxes Related to Employee Benefit Plans, is used to report the excise tax on the following:

- Nondeductible employer contributions to SEP, SARSEP, and SIMPLE IRAs [I.R.C. § 4972(d)(1)(A)(ii)].
- Prohibited transactions—15 percent first tier excise tax [I.R.C. § 4975(a), 4975(e)(1)].
- Excess contributions under plans with a cash or deferred arrangement (CODA) [I.R.C. § 4979(a), 4979(e)(4)].

The nondeductible contributions are computed as of the end of the employer's tax year. The current-year nondeductible contributions are equal to the amount contributed during the employer's tax year in excess of the amount of contributions allowable as a deduction under Code Section 404. In addition, prior-year nondeductible SEP contributions continue to be subject to the 10 percent excise tax annually until eliminated by a carryforward deduction in years after the nondeductible contributions are made.

Q 8:128 May more than one type of excise tax be reported on the same Form 5330?

Yes. Generally, a single return may be filed for different excise taxes with the same due date. Thus, an employer may use one Form 5330 to report the prohibited transaction tax and the tax on nondeductible employer contributions. It should be noted, however, that more than one "person" may be required to file Form 5330 in the event of a prohibited transaction.

Note. The due date for the payment of tax on excess contributions to plans with CODAs falls after the due date for the payment of taxes on prohibited transactions and nondeductible employer contributions. Furthermore, the IRS requires a separate filing for reporting the tax on excess contributions to plans with CODAs.

Q 8:129 Who must file Form 5330?

Form 5330 must be filed by the following:

1. Any employer that is liable for the tax under Code Section 4972 for non-deductible contributions made under SEP, SARSEP, and SIMPLE plans;
2. Any disqualified person (see Q 8:131) who is liable for the tax under Code Section 4975 for participating in a prohibited transaction (other than a fiduciary acting only as such or an individual (or his or her beneficiary) who engages in a prohibited transaction with respect to his or her IRA); and
3. Any employer that is liable for the tax under Code Section 4979 on excess contributions to plans with a CODA.

Q 8:130 Why is an individual (or his or her beneficiary) who engages in a prohibited transaction with respect to his or her IRA not required to file Form 5330?

Form 5330 need not be filed by an individual (or his or her beneficiary) who engages in a prohibited transaction with respect to his or her IRA because by that action the IRA is disqualified. As a result, the IRA itself becomes taxable (see Q 8:102).

Q 8:131 Who is a disqualified person?

A *disqualified person* is any one of the following:

1. A fiduciary;
2. A person providing services to the plan;
3. An employer, any of whose employees are covered by the plan;
4. An employee organization, any of whose members are covered by the plan;
5. Any direct or indirect owner of 50 percent or more of
   a. The combined voting power of all classes of stock entitled to vote,
   b. The total value of shares of all classes of stock of a corporation,
   c. The capital interest or the profits interest of a partnership,
   d. The beneficial interest of a trust or unincorporated enterprise that is an employer or an employee organization described in item 3 or 4, respectively, or
   e. Any direct or indirect owner of 50 percent or more of (i) the combined voting power of all classes of stock entitled to vote or the total value of shares of all classes of stock of a corporation, (ii) the capital interest or the profits interest of a partnership, or (iii) the beneficial interest of a trust or unincorporated enterprise that is an employer or an employee organization described in item 3 or 4, respectively;

6. A family member of any individual described in item 1, 2, 3, or 5 (a family member is a spouse, an ancestor, a lineal descendant, or a spouse of a lineal descendant);
7. A corporation, partnership, or trust or estate of which (or in which) any direct or indirect owner holds 50 percent or more of the interest described in item 5e(i), (ii), or (iii) (for purposes of (iii), the beneficial interest of the trust or estate is owned directly or indirectly or held by persons described in items 1 through 5);
8. An officer or director (or an individual having powers or responsibilities similar to those of an officer or director), 10 percent or more shareholder, or highly compensated employee (earning 10 percent or more of the yearly wages of an employer) of a person described in item 3, 4, 5, or 7; or
9. A 10 percent or more (in capital or profits) partner or joint venturer in a person described in item 3, 4, 5, or 7.

[Instructions to Form 5330, p. 7 (rev. Dec. 2020)]

Q 8:132 When must Form 5330 be filed?

For the tax on nondeductible contributions under SEP and SARSEP plans, and for the tax on engaging in a prohibited transaction, Form 5330 must be filed by the last day of the seventh month after the end of the tax year of the employer or other person that must file the return. [Instructions to Form 5330, p. 2 (rev. Dec. 2020)]

Q 8:133 How may an extension to file Form 5330 be requested?

Form 5558, Application for Extension of Time to File Certain Employee Plan Returns, can be filed to request an extension of time to file Form 5330. If the request is approved, an extension of up to six months may be granted.

Q 8:134 What is the penalty for not filing Form 5330 by the due date?

If Form 5330 is not filed by the due date, including extensions, there may be a penalty of 5 percent of the unpaid tax for each month or part of a month the return is late, up to a maximum of 25 percent of the unpaid tax. The minimum penalty for a return that is more than 60 days late is the lesser of the tax due or $100.

The penalty for late filing will not be imposed if failure to file on time can be shown to have a reasonable cause. A request for abatement of any late filing penalties requires a statement explaining the reasonable cause to be attached to Form 5330. [Instructions to Form 5330, p. 3 (rev. Dec. 2020)]

Q 8:135 What is the penalty for late payment of tax due on Form 5330?

If the tax due on Form 5330 is not paid when due, there may be a penalty of 0.5 percent of the unpaid tax for each month or part of a month the tax is not paid, up to a maximum of 25 percent of the unpaid tax. This penalty may also apply to any additional tax not paid within 10 days of the date of the notice and demand for payment. The penalty will not be imposed if it can be shown that the failure to pay on time was for reasonable cause. [Instructions to Form 5330, p. 3 (rev. Dec. 2020)]

Q 8:136 May interest and other penalties be charged if the tax due under Form 5330 is not paid by the due date?

Yes. Even if an extension of time to file is granted (see Q 8:133), interest (determined under Code Section 6621) is charged on taxes not paid by the due date. Interest is also charged on penalties imposed for failure to file, negligence, fraud, gross valuation overstatements, and substantial understatements of tax from the due date (including extensions) to the date of payment. Interest and penalties will be billed separately after the return is filed.

Form 5498

Q 8:137 What is reported on Form 5498?

Each calendar year, IRA trustees and custodians must report to the IRS any contributions made to an IRA, and its value at the end of the year. Form 5498 is used for that purpose. [I.R.C. § 408(i); Prop. Treas. Reg. § 1.408-5] (For contributions to a Coverdell ESA, see Qs 8:159–8:162; or to an HSA, see Qs 8:163, 8:164.)

Filing

Q 8:138 When must Form 5498 be filed?

To report 2020 contributions and year-end value, Form 5498 must be filed with the IRS by June 30, 2021, to reflect IRS Notice 2020-21. Generally, a copy or qualifying substitute Form 5498 must also be provided to the individual by the same date. But the copy of Form 5498 need not be provided to the participant if zero reportable (including rollover) contributions were made during 2020, and the statement described in Q 8:10 (of the account value on December 31, 2020, and any RMD payable in 2021) was furnished to the participant by January 31, 2021. [General Instructions for Certain Information Returns (Forms 1096, 1097, 1098, 1099, 3921, 3922, 5498, and W-2G) (2020)]

Q 8:139 Can the filing deadline for Form 5498 be extended?

An automatic 30-day extension of time to file Form 5498 can be obtained by filing Form 8809, Request for Extension of Time to File Information Returns, with the IRS. The IRS suggests filing Form 8809 as soon as the need is apparent, but in any case it must be filed by the date Form 5498 is due (June 30, 2021).

For certain hardship conditions, an additional 30 days may be requested by submitting another Form 8809 before the end of the initial extension period.

Note. The approved extension request will apply only to the due date for filing the returns with the IRS. Such approval will not extend the due date for providing statements to IRA owners.

Q 8:140 Can more time be requested to deliver the payee copies of Form 5498?

An extension of time to provide copies of Forms 5498 to payees can be requested by submitting a letter to:

IRS, Attn: Extension of Time Coordinator, 240 Murall Drive, Mail Stop 4360, Kearneysville, WV 25430.

The letter should state:

- Payer's name, TIN, and address
- Type of return
- A statement that the request is for an extension for providing statements to recipients
- Reason for the delay
- Payer's signature

The request must be postmarked by the due date of the return (June 1, 2021). If the request for extension is approved, an additional 30 days to furnish the statements to IRA owners will be granted.

Q 8:141 How are corrected Forms 5498 submitted?

Sometimes it is necessary to correct a Form 5498 after the original has been submitted to the IRS. All corrections for a year should be submitted to the IRS in accordance with the rules that apply to corrected Forms 1099-R (see Q 8:83).

Q 8:142 May Form 5498 be enclosed in the same envelope with other forms?

It may be enclosed with other IRS forms, but no extraneous material. If a trustee combines Form 5498 with returns for interest, dividend, and royalty payments, strict mailing requirements must be followed. For example, no enclosures are permitted for promotional material or a quarterly or annual report. Even a sentence on the year-end statement describing new services being offered is not permitted. Logos are permitted on the envelope and on any nontax enclosures. If, however, Form 5498 is being mailed without any related forms, a combined mailing may be allowed. Payee statements that are related may be included in a single mailing; related forms include Form 1099 and Form 1098.

In addition, Forms W-2 and W-2P may be included in the single mailing because they are related to the payee statements. [Notice 87-17, 1987-1 C.B. 454]

Q 8:143 How long should copies of Form 5498 be kept?

Copies of information returns filed with the IRS (including Form 5498) should be kept for at least three years from the due date of the return.

Reporting Contributions and the Year-End Value

Q 8:144 What changes were made to Form 5498 for 2019?

There are two changes:

1. New code "BA" has been added to report a repayment of a qualified birth or adoption distribution (in box 14b).
2. The SECURE Act increased the age for starting minimum distributions from age 70½ to 72. This is effective for individuals who attain age 70½ after December 31, 2019. (See Q 8:146, box 11.)

Q 8:145 What "Account Number" is used to identify the IRA on Form 5498?

If an individual holds several accounts with the same institution, the trustee must assign a unique number to each one. It is not necessary to assign an account number if the individual holds only one account with the trustee. However, the IRS encourages the assignment of account numbers in all cases. The individual's Social Security number may *not* be used as an account number.

Q 8:146 How is the 2020 Form 5498 completed?

The following are box-by-box instructions for correctly completing the 2020 Form 5498.

Box 1: IRA Contributions (Other Than Amounts in Boxes 2–4, 8–10, 13a, and 14a).

Enter all contributions to a traditional IRA made in 2020 and from January 1 through April 15, 2021, that are designated for 2020. Regular contributions include catch-up contributions made by eligible individuals who are age 50 or older by December 31, 2020. Report catch-up contributions made to a traditional IRA in this box.

Report gross contributions, including excess contributions, even if the excess contributions are subsequently withdrawn. Also include in box 1 a regular traditional IRA contribution even if the regular contribution (plus earnings) has been recharacterized as a regular Roth IRA contribution.

For excess contributions that are being treated by the IRA owner as a regular contribution made in a subsequent year, do *not* report the contribution on Form

5498 for the subsequent year. It will have been reported on the Form 5498 for the year the contribution was originally made to the IRA.

Report in this box any regular traditional IRA contributions (referred to as *employee contributions*) made to a SEP IRA. Such contributions are treated as the employee's regular traditional IRA contributions for the year and not as employer contributions to the SEP.

These contributions are *not* reported in box 1: contributions to a SIMPLE IRA (box 9), contributions to a Roth IRA (box 10), rollover contributions (box 2), conversion contributions (box 3), and recharacterized contributions (box 4).

Box 2: Rollover Contributions.

Box 2 is for entry of rollover contributions, and contributions treated as rollover contributions, to any IRA (traditional, Roth, SEP, or SIMPLE) during 2020. This includes 60-day rollover contributions made from one IRA to another, direct or indirect rollovers from a qualified plan (including a governmental Section 457(b) plan) or Section 403(b) plan to an IRA, and contributions of military death gratuities, SGLI payments, qualified settlement income received in connection with the Exxon Valdez litigation, and airline payment amounts. If the rollover consists of property other than cash, its value as of the day the trustee receives it is entered (this may differ from the value on the day it was distributed from the original plan).

Late rollover contributions are reported in box 13, not box 2.

Box 3: Roth IRA Conversion Amount.

Enter the amount converted from a traditional IRA, SEP IRA, or SIMPLE IRA (that has met the two-year period requirement) to a Roth IRA during 2019, regardless of how the conversion was accomplished. (Rollovers from one Roth IRA to another, and qualified rollover contributions from a qualified plan, are *not* entered in this box.)

Box 4: Recharacterized Contributions.

Report in this box a recharacterization transfer from a traditional IRA to a Roth IRA or from a Roth IRA to a traditional IRA, plus earnings. All recharacterization transfers received by the same IRA during the same year are aggregated and reported on a single Form 5498. Mark the appropriate checkbox in box 7 to indicate the type of IRA that received the recharacterization transfer.

Box 5: Fair Market Value of Account.

Enter in this box the fair market value (FMV) of a traditional, Roth, SEP, or SIMPLE IRA as of December 31, 2020 (but for inherited IRAs, see Qs 8:152–8:154). The December 31, 2020, FMV does not include regular contributions made in 2021 for 2020.

Box 6: Life Insurance Cost Included in Box 1.

This box is used for endowment contracts only. Enter the amount included in box 1 allocable to the cost of life insurance.

Box 7: Checkboxes.

This series of checkboxes is used to identify the type of IRA for which contributions are being reported—traditional IRA (the *IRA* box; also for conduit IRAs), SEP IRA, SIMPLE IRA, or Roth IRA.

Box 8: SEP Contributions.

In box 8, report any amount that the employer contributed to a SEP IRA *during* 2020; amounts contributed by a self-employed individual to his or her own account, and salary deferral contributions made under a SARSEP, are treated as employer contributions for this purpose. Contributions made in 2020 for 2019 are included, but not contributions made in 2021 for 2020. (The trustee does *not* report the year for which contributions have been made.) Report the dollar amount of employer SEP contributions paid to the IRA during the year.

Employee contributions to a SEP IRA are not reported in box 8. Since those contributions are treated as regular IRA contributions, and are subject (or deemed subject) to the 100 percent of compensation or $6,500 limit (for 2021) of Code Section 219, they are reported in box 1. (Note that salary deferrals under a SARSEP are treated as *employer*, not *employee*, contributions.)

Box 9: SIMPLE Contributions.

Enter any amount that the employer contributed to a SIMPLE IRA (including salary deferrals and employer matching or nonelective contributions) *during* 2020. (The trustee does *not* report based on the employer's tax year for which these contributions are being made.) Report the dollar amount of employer SIMPLE contributions paid to the SIMPLE IRA during the year.

Box 10: Roth IRA Contributions.

Enter any regular contributions made to a Roth IRA in 2020 and from January 1 through May 17, 2021, that are designated for 2020.

Box 11: Check if RMD for 2021.

Check this box on the *2020* Form 5498 if a traditional, SEP, or SIMPLE IRA owner must take an RMD in 2021. This box must be checked if the individual attained age 70½ on or before December 31, 2019.

The SECURE Act changed the reference age for starting RMDs from age 70½ to age 72. The change is effective for distributions required after December 31, 2019, with respect to individuals who attain age 70½ after such date. Consequently, no individual subject to the new rule will have an RMD for 2021. (See Q 4:4.) [I.R.C. § 401(a)(9)(C), as amended by SECURE Act § 114]

Boxes 12a and 12b: RMD Date and Amount.

The IRA trustee must give advance notice to participants of the dates and amounts of RMDs to be paid in 2021. Boxes 12a and 12b may be used for this purpose, but alternative means of notice are also available. Instead of using boxes 12a and 12b in this way, the trustee may provide the information in a separate Form 5498, or in a separate RMD statement delivered to the participant before January 31, 2021, in accordance with Alternative One or Alternative Two (see Qs 8:11–8:12).

Boxes 13a, 13b, and 13c: Postponed Contribution.

If the trustee accepted a late rollover contribution that was certified by the participant (see Qs 6:30, 6:31), the contribution is reported here. Late rollover contributions and postponed contributions cannot be reported on the same Form 5498. If the participant contributed both types, a separate form is required for each.

Postponed contributions. Enter in box 13a the amount of any postponed contribution made in 2020 for a prior year. If contributions are made for more than one prior year, each prior year's postponed contribution must be reported on a separate form. The year for which the postponed contribution was made is entered in box 13b. Finally, in box 13c, enter the code for the reason for the participant's postponed contribution:

- For participants' service in the combat zone or hazardous duty area, report as described in Q 8:148.
- For participants who are "affected taxpayers," as described in an IRS News Release relating to a federally designated disaster area, enter FD.

Late rollover contributions. Enter in box 13a the amount of the late rollover contribution certified by the participant and accepted by the trustee during 2020. No entry is made in box 13b. Code SC (for "self-certified") is entered in box 13c. (For information about certifying a late rollover, see Qs 6:30, 6:31.) [Rev. Proc. 2016-47, 2016-37 I.R.B. 346] Revenue Procedure 2020-46, 2020-45 I.R.B. 945 extended the self-certifying relief under Revenue Procedure 2016-47 due to delays caused by escheats pursuant to state escheat law.

Boxes 14a and 14b: Repayments.

These boxes are used to report any repayment of a qualified reservist distribution, a qualified disaster distribution (e.g., a qualified 2019 disaster distribution; see Qs 8:19–8:21), or a qualified birth or adoption distribution. The amount repaid is reported in box 14a, and the code for the type of payment is entered in box 14b—code QR for a qualified reservist distribution, code DD for a qualified disaster distribution (see chapter 7), or code BA for a qualified birth or adoption distribution.

Boxes 15a and 15b: FMV of Specified Assets.

The trustee is responsible for ensuring that *all* IRA assets are valued annually. This includes assets without a readily available FMV, which now must be valued as a group in box 15a, and coded to identify them in box 15b. The new codes are:

Code A. Stock or other ownership interest in a corporation that is not readily tradable on an established securities market.

Code B. Short or long-term debt obligation that is not traded on an established securities market.

Code C. Ownership interest in a limited liability company or similar entity (unless the interest is traded on an established securities market).

Code D. Real estate.

Code E. Ownership interest in a partnership, trust, or similar entity (unless the interest is traded on an established securities market).

Code F. Option contract or similar product that is not offered for trade on an established option exchange.

Code G. Other asset that does not have a readily available FMV.

Code H. More than two types of assets (listed in A through G) are held in the IRA.

Q 8:147 What special reporting requirements does a trustee have if the owner of a traditional, SEP, or SIMPLE IRA will receive an RMD in 2021?

Notice 2002-27, § 1, 2002-1 C.B. 814, *clarified by* Notice 2003-3, 2003-2 I.R.B. 258, and *modified by* Notice 2009-9, 2009-5 I.R.B. 419, requires trustees, custodians, and issuers to send a notice annually to each participant who must receive an RMD that either states the amount of the RMD, or offers to calculate it for the participant. Participants must receive the statement by January 31 of the year for which the RMD is due. This reporting applies to traditional IRAs (regular and rollover), SEP IRAs, and SIMPLE IRAs. (See Q 8:8.)

Q 8:148 What is the reporting procedure for contributions made during the extended time periods allowed for military personnel in certain combat zones?

Individuals who serve in or support the Armed Forces in a designated combat zone or qualified hazardous duty area may make IRA contributions for a prior year after the normal contribution due date (May 17, 2021 for 2020 contributions). "IRA contributions" for this purpose encompass contributions to a traditional IRA, Roth IRA, SEP IRA, or SIMPLE IRA. The additional time allowed includes the time that the individual was in the designated zone or area plus at least 180 days. The individual must designate the contribution for a prior year. If a qualifying individual makes an IRA contribution after May 17 and designates the contribution for a prior year, the trustee must report the contribution either on Form 5498 for the year for which the contribution was made or on Form 5498 for a subsequent year.

If the trustee reports the contribution for the year in which it is made, no special reporting is required. The contribution is included in the appropriate box on the original Form 5498 or, if an original form had been filed for that individual, on a corrected Form 5498.

If the contribution is reported on Form 5498 for a prior year, the trustee must include the year for which the contribution was made, the amount of the contribution, and one of the following indicators:

- *EO13239* for Afghanistan and those countries in direct support.
- *EO12744* for the Arabian Peninsula, including air space, adjacent waters, and Jordan that are in direct support.
- *EO13119* or *PL106-21* (reference to Pub. L. No. 106-21) for the Federal Republic of Yugoslavia (Serbia and Montenegro), Albania, Kosovo, the Adriatic Sea, and the Ionian Sea north of the 39th parallel.
- *PL115-97* for the Sinai Peninsula of Egypt.

The information is entered on Form 5498 in boxes 13a, 13b, and 13c (see Q 8:146). For a detailed statement of the specific geographic areas included in each of the above regions, see Instructions for Forms 1099-R and 5498 (2020), p. 21.

Q 8:149 Does Form 5498 indicate which contributions, if any, are deductible?

No. Form 5498 does not address the issue of whether a contribution is deductible or nondeductible or whether the amount is excludable from income under Code Section 402(h).

Q 8:150 Must an IRA owner inform the trustee, the issuer, or his or her employer whether an IRA contribution is deductible?

No. An IRA owner must determine whether a contribution is deductible or nondeductible in order to complete his or her Form 1040, but is not required to inform the IRA trustee, the issuer, or his or her employer whether a contribution is deductible or nondeductible.

Q 8:151 Are separate Forms 5498 required for each investment under a single IRA plan?

No, a separate Form 5498 need not be filed for each investment under one IRA plan. For example, if a participant has three CDs under one IRA plan, only one Form 5498 is required for all contributions and the fair market values of the CDs under the plan. In contrast, if an individual has established more than one IRA plan with the same financial organization, a separate Form 5498 must be filed for each plan.

Because the definition of an individual retirement account includes all assets within the same trust or custodial agreement, a trustee should reflect all information that is associated with that same agreement on one Form 5498. On the other hand, in an individual retirement annuity, each contract is a separate plan.

Death

Q 8:152 What is reported when the IRA owner dies?

For the year of death, the trustee must issue Form 5498 and an annual statement for the decedent and also for each beneficiary. The versions are not identical.

Reports as to the decedent. Generally, the date-of-death fair market value of the IRA is reported in box 5 of Form 5498 and on the annual statement prepared with respect to the decedent. However, the trustee may choose instead to report the IRA's fair market value as of the end of the death year. If this alternate method is used, the value shown on the report for the decedent is usually zero (because the year-end value will be shown on the beneficiary's report and should not also be shown on the decedent's report). A trustee that uses the alternate method must also inform the decedent's executor or administrator that it will provide, upon request, a date-of-death valuation.

If the trustee only learns of the death after the filing deadline for Form 5498 (June 1, 2021) has passed, it is not necessary to issue corrected versions of Form 5498 or the annual statement, but the date-of-death valuation must be timely provided if the executor or administrator requests it.

Reports for the beneficiary (with respect to the inherited IRA). On the beneficiary's Form 5498 and annual statement prepared for the year of death, the "participant's name" must name both the decedent and the beneficiary. This indicates that the IRA is an inherited IRA. However, if the surviving spouse is the sole designated beneficiary and elects to treat the IRA as his or her own, the spouse is identified as the participant (because the IRA is not an inherited IRA and the spouse is not considered a beneficiary). The naming procedure for an inherited IRA must also be used for an IRA established to receive a rollover for a nonspouse beneficiary (or spouse beneficiary who does not elect to be treated as owner).

The trustee must prepare Form 5498 and an annual statement for the beneficiary for every year that the inherited IRA exists—except the year when the beneficiary's share is fully distributed. If the beneficiary's share is fully distributed by the end of the decedent's death year, these reports are never issued for the beneficiary. [Instructions for Forms 1099-R and 5498 (2020)]

Example 1. Albert Ames maintains an IRA and his designated beneficiary is Barbara Baxter. Albert dies in 2021, and on all reports for the inherited IRA the trustee uses "Barbara Baxter as beneficiary of Albert Ames" as the participant's name.

Example 2. Diane Smith established a new IRA with Big Bank to receive a direct rollover of $70,000 from her 401(k) plan, which was accomplished in June 2020. She named her two nephews (Ian and Kevin O'Brien) as the designated beneficiaries, with each to receive a one-half share. Diane dies in September 2020. In November 2020, Joe withdraws his full share from the IRA. Ian withdraws nothing in 2020.

Two Forms 5498 will be issued for 2020. One will be issued in Diane Smith's name, and her Social Security number will identify her as the participant. The entry in box 2 will be $70,000 (for the rollover from the 401(k) plan), and zero will be entered in box 5 because this trustee uses the alternative method to report fair market value.

The second Form 5498 will be issued for Ian's share of the inherited IRA. The participant's name on the form is "Ian O'Brien as beneficiary of Diane Smith," but Ian's Social Security number is also entered. In box 5, the year-end 2019 fair market value of the inherited IRA (all Ian's share) will be entered.

No Form 5498 will be issued for Kevin's share, because it was fully distributed during the year and there were no contributions to report (the rollover contribution was reported on Diane's Form 5498).

Form 1099-R will be filed with respect to Kevin's share. The participant's name will be "Kevin O'Brien as beneficiary of Diane Smith," and Kevin's Social Security number will be entered. The total distribution of Kevin's share will be reported on this form.

Q 8:153 What is the procedure for reporting the direct rollover of inherited qualified plan assets into an IRA that was established to receive them?

No reporting is required if the direct rollover is made to a traditional IRA, because no distribution is made (see Q 8:91). However, the beneficiary could choose instead to have the qualified plan assets directly transferred to a new Roth IRA. In that case, the transfer would be treated as a conversion and the qualified distribution from the qualified plan would be taxable (and reported by the plan's trustee). The IRA trustee would report the transfer as a conversion contribution to the inherited Roth IRA.

Note. A trustee-to-trustee transfer must be used for any rollover on behalf of a nonspouse beneficiary. Also, the conversion would not be allowed if the assets of the deceased were in a traditional IRA (rather than a qualified plan).

Q 8:154 What must be reported if the designated beneficiary dies before his or her inherited share is fully distributed?

The reporting requirements are described in Q 8:152, except for this purpose the deceased beneficiary is the decedent, and the successor beneficiary is the beneficiary. [Instructions for Forms 1099-R and 5498 (2020)]

Example. The facts are the same as in Q 8:152 (Example 1), except Barbara Baxter named Carol Curtin as her successor beneficiary for the inherited IRA. The primary beneficiary (Barbara Baxter) dies in 2022. For 2022, the trustee issues Form 5498 and an annual statement with respect to Barbara, designating the inherited IRA participant as "Barbara Baxter as beneficiary of Albert Ames." On all reports issued for Carol, the trustee names the inherited IRA participant "Carol Curtin as beneficiary of Barbara Baxter."

Closure, Revocation, or Total Loss

Q 8:155 Must Form 5498 be filed if an IRA is closed before the end of the year?

Form 5498 must be filed if contributions of any kind (regular, rollover, conversion, or recharacterized) were made during the year of closure, and a year-end value of zero would be shown. If no contributions were made during the final year, Form 5498 is not filed, and there is also no need to issue an annual payee statement with respect to that year.

In rare cases, a trustee may be legally required to force the closure of an IRA. For example, this may occur pursuant to the USA PATRIOT Act because the individual fails to satisfy the Customer Identification Program requirements. [USA PATRIOT Act of 2001, § 326, Pub. L. No. 107-56] If an IRA is closed for any reason, Form 1099-R and Form 5498 must be filed to report contributions and distributions for the final year.

Q 8:156 If the IRA has no value on December 31 because of investment loss, must Form 5498 be filed?

Yes, if contributions were made during the year. The rules described in Q 8:155 apply here as well.

Q 8:157 Must Form 5498 be filed if an IRA is revoked during the year?

Again, the same rules apply. Form 5498 must be filed if contributions were made before the revocation (their distribution would also be reported on Form 1099-R). If the IRA was revoked before any contributions were made, Form 5498 is not filed.

Q 8:158 How is a revocation reported if it straddles two years?

If the seven-day revocation period starts in one year and ends in the next, Form 5498 must be filed for the first year if a contribution was made during the first year. The year-end value of the IRA would be reported on Form 5498, and the revocation distribution would be reported on Form 1099-R for the second year.

Neither report would be necessary if no contribution was made.

Form 5498-ESA

Q 8:159 What is reported on Form 5498-ESA?

Form 5498-ESA is used to report regular contributions, rollovers, and trustee-to-trustee transfers to a Coverdell ESA.

Q 8:160 How are Coverdell ESA contributions reported?

The trustee enters the Coverdell ESA contribution amount in box 1 of the form, and the rollover contribution or trustee-to-trustee transfer in box 2.

Q 8:161 When is Form 5498-ESA due?

Form 5498-ESA is a three-part form. Copy A is filed with the IRS by June 1, 2021 (for 2020 contributions). Copy B is furnished to the beneficiary by April 30, 2021. Copy C is retained by the trustee of the Coverdell ESA. [General Instructions for Forms 1096, 1097, 1098, 1099, 3921, 3922, 5498, and W-2G (2020)]

Q 8:162 How are contributions and earnings tracked in a Coverdell ESA?

The responsible individual should save the Forms 5498-ESA to keep track of contributions. A distribution may not be taxable if it was used to pay for qualified educational expenses (see Qs 14:45–14:53). [*See* IRS Pub. 970, *Tax Benefits for Education* 2020.]

Form 5498-SA

Q 8:163 What is the purpose of Form 5498-SA?

An HSA trustee uses Form 5498-SA to report contributions to, and the fair market value of, the HSA. Reportable amounts include regular and rollover contributions, and trustee-to-trustee transfers of *qualified HSA funding distributions* from an IRA to the HSA. However, trustee-to-trustee transfers from one HSA to another are *not* reported on Form 5498-SA.

To report 2020 contributions, the IRS filing deadline is June 1, 2021. That is also the deadline for furnishing a copy to the owner of the HSA account. But if there are no reportable contributions for 2020, the trustee may instead provide a statement of the account's year-end 2020 fair market value, provided the participant receives it by January 1, 2021. [Instructions for Forms 1099-SA and 5498-SA (2020)]

(Form 5498-SA is also used to report on Archer MSAs and Medicare Advantage MSAs.)

Q 8:164 How are HSA contributions reported?

HSA contributions are reported as follows:

Box 1. Not used for HSAs.

Box 2. Include in this box the total regular contributions and trustee-to-trustee transfers from an IRA (see Q 8:163) that the HSA trustee received *during 2020*. This includes amounts contributed by May 17, 2021 and designated for 2020.

Exclude rollover contributions from box 2 (they are reported in box 4). Also omit excess *employer* contributions made in 2020 if they were withdrawn (with earnings) and returned to the employer. Any other excess contributions should be included in box 2.

Box 3. Report in this box contributions received during *2021* (by May 17) and designated for 2020.

Box 4. Rollover contributions are reported in this box.

Box 5. Enter the fair market value of the account on December 31, 2020.

Form 8606

Q 8:165 Which form is used to determine the portion of an IRA distribution that is a tax-free return of nondeductible contributions?

Form 8606, Nondeductible IRAs, is used to determine the portion of an IRA distribution that is a tax-free return of nondeductible contributions. It must be filed with an IRA owner's federal tax return (Form 1040) unless there have been no nondeductible contributions to the owner's traditional IRA or IRAs and the owner has no Roth IRAs. If a portion of a current contribution is nondeductible, Form 8606 starts or continues the data history that will be needed to determine the nontaxable portion of a distribution when it occurs.

> **Practice Pointer.** It is likely that Form 8606 will be needed long after the individual tax return is discarded. Therefore, Form 8606 or the information it contains should be kept as part of a permanent tax record (see Q 8:168).

Q 8:166 Is Form 8606 also used for reporting nondeductible contributions to the Roth IRA?

Yes. Parts II and III of Form 8606 are used to report nondeductible contributions to the Roth IRA and the Coverdell ESA:

1. *Conversion section.* Part II is used for figuring the taxable amount of conversions from a traditional IRA or a SIMPLE IRA to a Roth IRA. Part II is also used to show a recharacterization of amounts that were converted before 2018 to a Roth IRA.
2. *Roth IRA distribution section.* Part III is used for reporting distributions from a Roth IRA and to report a recharacterization involving a Roth IRA contribution.

Q 8:167 Must an IRA owner file Form 8606 if neither a nondeductible traditional IRA contribution nor a traditional IRA distribution occurs in a particular year?

If an IRA owner has never made a nondeductible contribution to a traditional IRA, there is no need to file Form 8606. If, however, there is a history of nondeductible contributions to preserve, there seems to be no harm in filing Form 8606 to keep the file current, even if the owner did not make a nondeductible contribution or take a distribution in a particular year. Whether to file Form 8606 under such circumstances is a matter for the owner's tax preparer to determine.

If an IRA owner is not filing a Form 1040 for the year, but nondeductible contributions or distributions (or both) have occurred, Form 8606 must still be filed—at the time and place the Form 1040 would have been filed.

Q 8:168 What recordkeeping is suggested for Form 8606 filers?

In the instructions for Form 8606, the IRS provides a list of records that are to be kept:

1. Page 1 of each year's Form 1040 for years in which nondeductible contributions were made to a traditional IRA;
2. Confirmation of the contributions made each year (Forms 5498 or other contribution records);
3. Forms 5498 or similar statements to confirm year-end values for each year in which a distribution occurred;
4. Forms 1099-R and W-2P for each year in which a distribution was received. (Form W-2P, formerly used for partial distributions from IRAs, was discontinued and has been replaced by Form 1099-R.); and
5. Forms 8606 and any supporting statements, attachments, and worksheets for all applicable years.

Practice Pointer. It is advisable to maintain a separate IRA file that contains photocopies of the items needed for filing Form 8606, rather than removing the items from the IRA owner's general tax return files.

Q 8:169 Should information similar to that needed to file Form 8606 be kept for all IRAs, even those for which Form 8606 never needs to be filed?

Information like that needed to complete Form 8606 should also be maintained for Roth IRAs, because the rules for determining the taxation of *nonqualified* distributions are quite complex (see Q 5:85). Basis, taxable amounts, and conversion contributions must all be allocated to a nonqualified Roth IRA distribution, and records will be needed to perform and substantiate the allocation.

Q 8:170 Does the IRA owner report after-tax monies that were rolled over from an employer plan into a traditional IRA?

Yes, also on Form 8606. The instructions to Form 8606 provide for amounts rolled over from any nontaxable portion of a qualified employer plan to a traditional or SEP IRA to be entered on line 2. The legend on line 2 of the form merely reads, "Enter your total basis in traditional IRAs."

> **Example.** Before 2020, Sam had made nondeductible contributions of $10,000 to a traditional IRA. During 2020, Sam made a $6,000 current-year IRA contribution that is all nondeductible, and he rolled over to the IRA $5,000 of the after-tax employee contributions that he had made to his employer's qualified plan. On Sam's 2020 Form 8606, lines 1, 2, and 3 would be completed as follows:
>
> Line 1: $6,000 (2020 regular contribution)
>
> Line 2: $15,000 ($10,000 basis for prior years + $5,000 after-tax rolled over amount)
>
> Line 3: $21,000

Q 8:171 Why may it become crucial to maintain separate Form 8606 records for each IRA owned when IRAs have separate beneficiaries?

If an IRA owner dies owning more than one traditional IRA, the beneficiary of one of the IRAs might wish to continue that IRA and not accelerate its distribution. If the decedent had made nondeductible contributions, the basis would not have been fully recovered, and at least some of it would remain because the IRA itself remains. In that event, Form 8606 must continue to be filed for distributions from the inherited IRA, which is effectively owned by the beneficiary.

If, for example, there were two traditional IRAs and separate beneficiaries, the beneficiary of each IRA would file a separate Form 8606. The decedent's basis would therefore need to be split between the two traditional IRAs; separately maintained Form 8606 records would facilitate that process. If either beneficiary also maintained one or more IRAs that were not inherited, distributions from such IRAs would be combined under the IRA owner's Form 8606, but not with the Form 8606 of the inherited traditional IRA, which would continue to have its own separate basis.

Q 8:172 What penalties may arise from a failure to follow the requirements of Form 8606?

Unless reasonable cause can be established, a $50 fine results from failing to file Form 8606 in a year when nondeductible contributions are made. Further, unless reasonable cause is shown, there is a $100 fine for each overstatement of nondeductible contributions on Form 8606.

Q 8:173 In addition to the penalties for failing to file Form 8606 correctly, what other consequences may result from the failure to follow the requirements of Form 8606?

An IRA owner who fails to file Form 8606 correctly may lose out on recovery of basis. In the absence of evidence to the contrary, the IRS will assume that all distributions are of amounts previously deducted and that the entire distribution is fully taxable.

Q 8:174 When is basis fully recovered?

Because basis and income are prorated to each traditional IRA distribution (and an individual's traditional IRAs are considered in the aggregate for this purpose), basis is not fully recovered until the last traditional IRA has been fully distributed. That may happen many years hence. In any event, it would seem reasonable to correct any mathematical errors in the final distribution by applying the basis recovery formula so that 100 percent of the unapplied nondeductible contributions is used as a setoff at that time. Before 2018, if there had been a loss, the unamortized basis might become a deductible loss, subject to the limitation on miscellaneous itemized deductions. However, the TCJA repealed the miscellaneous itemized deduction for the years 2018 through 2025. Possibly, the loss could be claimed under Code Section 165(c)(2), as a loss incurred in a transaction entered into for profit, though not connected with a trade or business. [IRS Pub. 590-B, *Distributions from Individual Retirement Arrangements (IRAs)* 2020 (see Appendix B); TCJA § 11045, repealing I.R.C. § 67]

Q 8:175 What is the procedure to follow when redesignating a nondeductible contribution as a deductible contribution?

To change a nondeductible contribution to a deductible contribution, the IRA owner must file a new Form 8606 along with Form 1040X, Amended U.S. Individual Income Tax Return.

Q 8:176 How are distributions from IRAs reflected on Form 1040 (Form 1040A)?

Total taxable distributions from IRAs are entered on line 4b of Form 1040. If the distribution has been rolled over, line 4a of Form 1040 will show the total distributed, and line 4b will show only the portion not rolled over reduced by the basis recovery amount calculated on Form 8606 (which will in effect be used to subtract the nondeductible contributions from the amount shown on line 4b).

Form 8888

Q 8:177 What is the purpose of Form 8888?

An individual who is due a refund of income tax may instruct the IRS to deposit the refund directly into one, two, or three IRAs, mutual funds, or other financial accounts. The instruction is given on Form 1040 if the entire refund is to be deposited in a single account (see Q 8:60). Form 8888 is required if the individual wants the direct deposit to be split among two or three accounts. The IRS will not deposit a tax refund into more than three accounts, and individuals may not request partial payment of a refund by check. [Form 8888, Allocation of Refund (Including Savings Bond Purchases) (2019)]

The financial accounts designated on Form 8888 must be in the individual's own name (or the spouse's name if a joint return is filed). Direct deposit is allowed into a traditional IRA, Roth IRA, or SEP IRA, but not a SIMPLE IRA. The year for which the IRA contribution is to be made should be indicated on the form. It will not be valid for such year, however, unless it is actually deposited to the account by the due date of the return (without regard to extensions).

Example. Irene completes her income tax return for 2020 and determines that a $6,000 tax refund is due. She attaches Form 8888, instructing the IRS to deposit $4,000 to her Roth IRA at Bank X and $2,000 to her Roth IRA at Bank Y, and designating the amounts as 2020 IRA contributions. Irene files the return on March 1, 2021, allowing ample time for the IRS to make the direct deposits before the May 17, 2021 deadline for 2020 IRA contributions. She also confirms with the financial institutions that the deposits were actually made in time.

If a requested deposit is not actually made by the contribution deadline for the designated year, it will not qualify as a contribution for that year and the individual must file an amended return.

Some banks and financial institutions do not permit deposit of joint refunds to individual accounts. If a deposit is rejected for this reason, the IRS will mail a check to the individual.

If an income tax refund that was directly deposited to an IRA is later adjusted due to math errors on the return or offset by other obligations of the individual, the IRA contribution must also be adjusted. (For detailed discussion of these matters, see Qs 3:45–3:47.)

Form 8889

Q 8:178 Who files Form 8889?

The owner of a health savings account (HSA), and after the owner's death the person who acquires an interest in the HSA, may be required to file Form 8889. [Instructions for Form 8889, Health Savings Account (HSAs) (2020)]

Q 8:179 What is the purpose of Form 8889?

Form 8889, Health Savings Accounts (HSAs), is used to report contributions and distributions from an HSA, determine the deduction for contributions, determine income and additional tax that may be due, and figure income that may be due if ownership is transferred upon the HSA owner's death.

The HSA owner. The HSA owner files Form 8889 if there was HSA activity for the return year:

- Contributions—by the owner, or by another person (e.g., the employer) on the owner's behalf for the return year. The owner reports these even if all the contributions were made by others. Contributions may be made for the return year until the filing date (without extensions) of the return. Form 8889 is also used to calculate the owner's contribution limit for the year and determine whether excess contributions were made.
- Distributions—distributions used for qualified medical expenses, and any other distributions. Income that may be attributable to the distributions is also determined.
- The owner failed to remain an "eligible individual" throughout the testing period of Code Section 223(b)(8)—This may be an issue if contributions were made for the prior year based on the owner's deemed eligibility (see Q 8:17, regarding Part III of Form 8889). The income and additional tax due because of the failure are calculated.

If married spouses file jointly and each has an HSA, a separate Form 8889 is completed for each and both forms are attached to the joint return.

Death of an HSA owner. The designated beneficiary of the HSA (if there is one) completes Form 8889 and attaches it to his or her income tax return for the year of death. If there is no designated beneficiary, or if the estate is the named beneficiary, all the HSA activity for the year of death is reported on Form 8889, and the form is included as part of the decedent's final income tax return.

Q 8:180 How does an HSA owner report activity on Form 8889?

The information needed to fill out Form 8889 should all be shown on the individual's copy of Form 1099-SA, HSA, Archer MSA, or Medicare Advantage MSA Information. That is the form the HSA trustee uses to report HSA activity to the IRS.

Part I of Form 8889 is where HSA contributions are reported and the deduction is calculated.

- The type of HDHP coverage (self-only or family) that the individual had, or was treated as having, for the year is checked on line 1. If the coverage changed during the year, the box for the coverage held longer is checked.
- Contributions are grouped by source and reported.
- The contribution limit (including the catch-up amount, if any) is figured, taking into account any Archer MSA contributions that were made for the same year (they apply first against the contribution limit).
- The allowable deduction is determined.

Part II is for distributions reporting.

- The total distributions received during the year are reported. The taxable portion of the distributions is determined by excluding rollovers to another HSA and returns of excess contributions and their earnings and reducing distributions by unreimbursed qualified medical expenses.
- The 20 percent additional tax applicable to distributions not made for qualified medical expenses is computed.

Part III is used to determine income and additional tax due because of a failure with respect to any HSA testing period. The failure triggers an income inclusion, and a 10 percent additional tax may be payable. The income and additional tax are determined and reported on Form 8889.

- Testing period for a qualified HSA distribution—After a rollover from a health flexible spending arrangement (FSA) or health reimbursement arrangement (HRA) to an HSA, the HSA owner must continuously satisfy HSA eligibility requirements throughout a testing period. The testing period begins with the month of the rollover and ends on the last day of the 12th month after that. If the requirement is not met, the rollover amount is included in income and a 10 percent additional tax applies (unless the failure was because of death or disability).
- Testing period for the last month rule—An individual who meets the HSA eligibility requirements on the first day of the last month of the year is treated as having been eligible all year, and for some individuals the result is a higher contribution limit for the year. However, the individual must remain HSA-eligible continuously during the testing period, which runs from such first day through the last day of the subsequent year. If the requirement is not met, any contributions made that would not have been allowed but for the last month rule are included in income and a 10 percent additional tax applies (unless the failure was because of death or disability).
- Testing period for a qualified HSA funding distribution—A rollover from a traditional or Roth IRA to an HSA is tax free but subject to the HSA contribution limit. The HSA owner must remain HSA-eligible throughout a testing period that begins with the month of the rollover and ends on the last day of the 12th month following it. If the individual fails to remain HSA-eligible throughout the testing period, the rollover amount is included in gross income and a 10 percent additional tax applies (unless the failure was because of death or disability).

Q 8:181 When an HSA owner dies, how is Form 8889 completed if the spouse is the designated beneficiary?

If the designated beneficiary of an HSA is the owner's surviving spouse, the spouse acquires ownership of the HSA immediately upon the owner's death. Thus, the spouse completes Form 8889 in the same manner as any owner does.

Q 8:182 How is Form 8889 completed if the surviving spouse is not the designated beneficiary?

If the surviving spouse is not the designated beneficiary, the account ceases to be an HSA upon the owner's death and its fair market value on that date is treated as a taxable distribution. This is reported on Form 8889.

The instructions to Form 8889 require the following if there is a designated beneficiary (who must be an individual) for the HSA:

1. "Death of HSA account beneficiary" is written across the top of the form.
2. The designated beneficiary's name and Social Security number are entered in the top spaces on the form.
3. The fair market value of the HSA on the owner's date of death is entered (as a distribution) on line 14a.
4. Any qualified medical expenses that the decedent incurred and the designated beneficiary paid within one year after the date of death are entered on line 15.
5. The taxable distribution is determined by reducing the amount on line 14a (but not below zero) by the line 15 amount. The result is entered on line 16 and also included on the Form 1040 as an item of gross income.
6. The box on line 17a is checked because the death exception to the 10 percent additional tax applies to this distribution.

Alternatively, if the death beneficiary is the decedent's estate, the taxable distribution attributable to the loss of HSA status is reported on Form 8889 and attached to the decedent's final income tax return. Accordingly:

1. Entries are made as indicated in steps 1 through 6 above, except that (a) the decedent's name and Social Security number are entered (step 2); the entry for line 14a also includes distributions that were made before the owner died (step 3); and there is no entry for line 15 because qualified medical expenses paid after the date of death are deductible by the estate and cannot be reported on the decedent's final income tax return (step 4).
2. Part 1 is completed if there were contributions made for the year of death.

Forms 8915-A Through 8915-E

Q 8:183 How is the Form 8915 series used?

Special tax treatment applies to *qualified disaster distributions* and *coronavirus-related distributions*, and a recipient of either uses the Form 8915 series to report various events. (See chapter 7 for details concerning these distributions.)

Recipients use these forms to report the receipt and designation of a QDD from an eligible retirement plan; the taxable amount to be included in income for the current year, and any repayments. (See Qs 8:15–8:18 and chapter 7 regarding taxation and repayment of QDDs, and repayment of qualified distributions used to buy or build a principal residence in a disaster area.) There is a separate form for each type of distribution, and in each case events that occur during any year are reported on that year's version of the form. For example, the 2019 series is used as follows to report events that occurred in 2019.

If the distribution is received from an IRA, reporting is coordinated with Form 8606.

Use *Form 8915-A, Qualified 2016 Disaster Retirement Plan Distributions and Repayments* (2019) if you:

- received a qualified 2016 disaster distribution (2016 QDD) in 2017, are using the ratable inclusion method, and need to report the inclusion for year three, and/or
- repaid all or part of a 2016 QDD during 2019.

Use *Form 8915-B, Qualified 2017 Disaster Retirement Plan Distributions and Repayments* (2019) if you:

- received a qualified 2017 disaster distribution (2017 QDD) in 2017, are using the ratable inclusion method, and need to report the inclusion for year three,
- received a 2017 QDD in 2018, are using the ratable inclusion method, and need to report the year two inclusion, or
- repaid all or part of a 2017 QDD during 2019.

Use *Form 8915-C, Qualified 2018 Disaster Retirement Plan Distributions and Repayments* (2019) if you:

- received a qualified 2018 disaster distribution (2018 QDD) in 2019, and need to designate the amount, determine the taxable part of the distribution, and either report the income inclusion for year one or elect to include all the income in 2019,
- received a 2018 QDD in 2018, are using the ratable inclusion method, and need to report the year two inclusion,
- repaid all or part of a 2018 QDD during 2019, or
- received a qualified distribution (see Qs 8:19–8:21, and chapter 7) in 2019 to buy or build your main home in a 2018 disaster area, and repaid any part of it during 2019.

At the end of 2020, IRS released new *Form 8915-E, Qualified 2020 Disaster Retirement Plan Distributions and Repayments* (2020). This will be used to report events like those above for a coronavirus-related distribution received during 2020. [Notice 2020-50, 2020-28 I.R.B. (June 22, 2020)] The IRS provides a form in the 8915 series addressing the qualified disaster relief provisions under the Consolidated Appropriations Act, 2021.

Q 8:184 What is reported if an individual using the three-year inclusion method dies before the end of that period?

If the three-year inclusion method is used and the individual dies before all the taxable income is included, further deferral is not allowed. Form 8915 would show that the remaining taxable income is included in the decedent's gross income for the year of death. (See Q 7:20.)

Chapter 9

Income Tax Planning for IRAs

IRAs are tax-sheltered investments. To obtain the most value from them, the consequences of holding, contributing to, and taking distributions from an IRA should be fully considered. These include not only direct consequences (tax and otherwise), but also indirect effects that may occur beyond the IRA itself.

This chapter focuses on issues affecting IRAs that can be managed or at least mitigated by understanding the governing income tax rules and taking appropriate actions. Other issues explored are the ideal order of asset withdrawal from an individual's various accounts, the best assets to place in retirement accounts, the interaction between IRA distributions and the Medicare surtaxes on net investment income, compensation, and self-employment income, and how IRAs bear on both Medicaid eligibility and Medicare Part B insurance premiums. The impact of the temporary tax reforms enacted in 2017 is also considered.

The chapter is a kind of checklist of planning tips.

Planning Goals

Q 9:1 What kind of planning does this chapter cover?

This chapter examines aspects of retirement planning that specifically relate to IRAs. A balanced, diversified financial portfolio should have a mix of assets (cash, growth and income equities, and fixed-income assets), allocated among:

- Taxable accounts (e.g., brokerage)
- Tax-deferred accounts (traditional, SEP, and SIMPLE IRAs, and pre-tax plans such as a 401(k)), and
- Tax-exempt accounts (Roth IRAs and other after-tax plans, such as a Roth 401(k)).

Retirement planning involves many considerations, not all of them financial. Assets must be carefully evaluated in light of the individual's personal needs and goals. That kind of planning is beyond the scope of this book. Readers should always consult their personal tax and financial advisors.

Q 9:2 How is IRA planning affected by the temporary federal tax reforms enacted in 2017?

The rules governing IRAs and other tax-favored retirement plan were largely left intact. But the Tax Cuts and Jobs Act changed some other things that bear on IRA planning. [Tax Cuts and Jobs Act (TCJA), Pub. L. No. 115-97 (Dec. 22, 2017)] Most of the non-business changes made by the TCJA are only effective for the years 2018 through 2025 (unless Congress acts to extend them). The 2026 sunset adds considerable uncertainty to the planning process.

Table 9-1 shows items that bear on IRA planning in three groups—temporary changes made by the TCJA (which sunset in 2026), permanent changes made by the TCJA, and items that are not changed by tax reform.

Table 9-1. Selected Effects of 2017 Federal Income Tax Reform

Changes that expire after 2025:	
• Personal income tax rates are lower; some changes are made to the bracket thresholds.	I.R.C. § 1; TCJA § 11001
• Standard deduction is roughly doubled.	I.R.C. § 63; TCJA § 11021(a)
• Personal exemption is eliminated.	I.R.C. § 151(d); TCJA § 11041(a)(2)
• Miscellaneous itemized deduction is eliminated (e.g., cannot deduct investment expenses).	I.R.C. § 67(g); TCJA § 11045(a)

Table 9-1. Selected Effects of 2017 Federal Income Tax Reform (*cont'd*)

• Inflation adjustment method is changed to "chained CPI-U"—which will result in slower increases than before (e.g., the income limit for making Roth IRA contributions will increase less frequently).	TCJA § 11002
• The estate tax exemption amount is doubled (making estate planning largely unnecessary for all but the wealthiest individuals). (See chapter 11.)	I.R.C. § 2010; TCJA § 11061(a)
• There is now a 20 percent deduction for *qualified business income* of certain passthrough entities, which (in the case of personal service businesses) is not available at higher income levels. (See Q 9:19.)	I.R.C. § 199A; TCJA § 11011(e)
Permanent changes (no sunset):	
• IRA conversions made after 2017 cannot be unwound by recharacterization.	I.R.C. § 408A(d)(6); TCJA § 13611
Unchanged items:	
• The rules governing tax-favored retirement plans are the same as before.	
• Capital gains are subject to the same favorable tax rates as before. (But the income bracket for each rate is now tied to an inflation-adjusted dollar amount of taxable income, rather than the marginal income tax rate.)	I.R.C. § 1(j); TCJA § 11001(a)
• Social security benefits are still taxable on a sliding scale, based on taxable income. (See Q 9:9.)	
• The 3.8 percent Medicare surtax on net investment income is unchanged. (See Q 9:7.)	

Distribution Planning

Income Stability

Q 9:3 Can lifetime RMDs be delayed beyond age 72?

Other than by converting to a Roth IRA, the only way to delay RMDs past age 72 is to invest part of the traditional IRA in a qualifying longevity annuity contract (QLAC). Payments under a QLAC do not begin until age 85 or later. RMDs are not entirely avoided; no more than $125,000, as indexed (or 25 percent of the IRA, whichever is less), can be used to purchase a QLAC. The limit for 2021 is $135,000. [Notice 2020-79, 2020-46 I.R.B. 1014] Assets invested in the QLAC are not taken into account to determine the RMDs payable from the rest of the IRA. (See Qs 4:33–4:36.)

Minimizing Taxes and Expenses

Q 9:4 What consequences may result from receiving an IRA distribution?

Receiving a *taxable* IRA distribution (or otherwise increasing taxable income) can have any of the effects listed below:

- Push taxable income into a higher tax bracket.
- Cause capital gains to be taxed at the 20 percent rate.
- Increase the Medicare surtax on net investment income.
- Cause Medicare premiums to increase.
- Cause Social Security benefits to be taxable.
- Affect eligibility for Medicaid.
- Affect eligibility for college tuition assistance programs (this could also result from a nontaxable Roth IRA distribution).

Q 9:5 When should IRA assets be withdrawn?

As a basic guideline, assets should generally be used in this order:

1. Required minimum distributions (RMDs), which must be paid in any case.
2. Taxable assets that generate the least tax (loss assets, and long-term capital gain assets (held more than one year)).
3. Tax-deferred assets (pre-tax IRAs—traditional, SEP, or SIMPLE; and other pre-tax retirement plans).
4. Tax-exempt assets (Roth IRAs, Roth 401(k) plans).

This is just a guideline, however. Drawing on a mix of assets may be optimal in individual circumstances (e.g., those described in Qs 9:5–9:11).

Q 9:6 Why might it be useful to withdraw some IRA assets earlier?

At times, an individual may expect to be taxed at a higher rate in the future than at present. At those times, to minimize tax and preserve assets, it can be helpful to take distributions from a traditional IRA or other tax-deferred account. (A Roth IRA conversion might also be considered; see chapter 10.)

A higher future tax rate can result because more income is generated in the future, the tax rates are raised, or both. For example:

- A person may believe a future Congress will raise the tax rates on ordinary income or capital gains. Or, that Congress will not act to extend the current ordinary income rates, which otherwise will automatically increase in 2026 (see Q 9:2). (Such predictions are inherently uncertain.)
- Temporary circumstances such as a business loss or market downturn may cause taxable income to be unusually low in the current year.
- Large RMDs may be expected in the future by a person not yet required to receive them (because he or she is younger than age 72). For example, a very large balance may be held in a SEP IRA or 401(k) account. In that case, drawing now from the tax-deferred account offers two advantages: distributions are taxed at the relatively low current rate; and the account balance is diminished, leading to smaller RMDs in the future.

Q 9:7 Can it be helpful to spend both pre-tax and after-tax IRA assets in the same year?

Yes. Distributions from a tax-deferred account such as a traditional IRA that are not rolled over will increase the recipient's taxable income, and thus increase the tax that is due. [Lashua, 2020 TCM 152] But as long as the distribution does not push taxable income into the next tax bracket, it will not increase the applicable tax rate. If a larger distribution is needed, it may be helpful to supplement the draw with a nontaxable Roth IRA distribution.

Roth IRA distributions are not taxable if they are qualified distributions (see Q 5:69), or do not include earnings or conversion contributions (see Q 5:70).

> **Example 1.** Margo and Bill are married and filed a joint federal income tax return for 2018. They expected to have $65,000 of income that year, all taxable. Taking into account the 2018 standard deduction ($24,000) and federal income tax brackets, they anticipated taxable income of $41,000, which would have been taxed at the marginal rate of 12 percent. The resulting federal income tax would have been $6,825. But Margo and Bill had living expenses (excluding federal tax) of $85,000 in 2018. Without supplementary income, they would have had a cash shortfall of $26,825 ($65,000 – $6,825 – $85,000).
>
> Margo and Bill decided to cover the shortfall by taking a distribution from Bill's traditional IRA. The distribution was taxable, so it had to be large enough to cover the additional tax due. Accordingly, Bill withdrew a $31,000 distribution from his traditional IRA. Now their taxable income for

2018 was $72,000 ($65,000 + $31,000 – $24,000). The upper limit for the 12 percent marginal rate was $77,400, so the distribution did not push them into the next tax bracket. The resulting federal tax was $10,545. With cash totaling $96,000 ($65,000 + $31,000), and expenditures of $95,545 ($85,000 + $10,545), Margo and Bill were able to cover their expenses and have some cash left over ($455).

Example 2. The facts are the same as in Example 1, except that Margo and Bill had living expenses of $95,000 (i.e., $10,000 higher) for 2018. Now, without an IRA distribution, the cash shortfall would have been $36,825 ($10,000 higher than before). They decided to take a larger distribution from Bill's traditional IRA, but not large enough to push them into the next tax bracket, which is subject to a much higher marginal tax rate (22 percent). Bill took a $34,000 traditional IRA distribution (instead of $31,000, in Example 1). Their resulting taxable income was $75,000 (instead of $72,000), which was still within the 12 percent tax bracket. The federal tax on that amount was $10,905, so there was still a cash shortfall of $6,905 ($65,000 + $34,000 – $10,905). To cover it, Margo withdrew that amount tax free from her Roth IRA.

Q 9:8 Can IRA distributions be managed to minimize the 3.8 percent surtax on net investment income?

Yes. As explained below, taxable IRA distributions may increase the 3.8 percent surtax on net investment income, but Roth IRA distributions are neutral in this regard. There is no way to avoid taking taxable RMDs from a traditional IRA, but if larger amounts will be withdrawn, the effect on the surtax should be considered.

For individuals, the 3.8 percent surtax applies to net investment income only to the extent that modified adjusted gross income (MAGI) exceeds a base amount (see Table 9-2). (Regarding trusts and estates, see the footnote to Table 9-2.) IRA distributions are not considered investment income, so they are never directly subject to the surtax. But since taxable IRA distributions are included in MAGI, they can subject more of an individual's net investment income to the surtax. [I.R.C. § 1411]

Note. The 3.8 percent surtax on *net investment income* is distinct from the Medicare surtax on *compensation and self-employment income* (see Q 9:21). An individual can be subject to both. [I.R.C. § 1411(a)(1) ("imposed in addition to any other tax imposed by this subtitle")]

For surtax purposes, a good year for taking a large traditional IRA distribution (above the RMD) would be one in which either net investment income or MAGI is lower than usual. Otherwise, if the funds are needed immediately and a Roth IRA is also maintained, it may be preferable to use that as the source. It may be useful to consult a financial expert if a large amount of surtax is at stake.

Table 9-2. 3.8 Percent Surtax on Net Investment Income

Filing Status	*Surtax Is 3.8% of Net Investment Income, Capped at the Excess of MAGI over:*
Married filing jointly or surviving spouse	$250,000
Single or head of household	$200,000
Married filing separately	$125,000
Estate or trust	(See determination procedure.[1])

[1] The surtax cap is calculated differently for an estate or trust. It is determined by subtracting, from the entity's undistributed net investment income, the dollar amount of taxable income at which the highest income tax rate (37 percent) begins to apply. For 2021, the 37 percent rate applies to all taxable income of a trust or estate over $13,050. [I.R.C. § 1411(a)(2), 1(e); Rev. Proc. 2020-45, 2020-46 I.R.B. 1016]

Q 9:9 Do IRA distributions affect the cost of Medicare Part B insurance?

They can affect the cost. The receipt of *taxable* IRA distributions may result in higher Medicare Part B insurance premiums, but there is usually a two-year delay between cause and effect. (The premiums depend on an individual's MAGI reported on the most recently filed tax return—so 2021 premiums are typically based on the return filed in 2020 reporting 2019 income.) Nontaxable Roth IRA distributions do not have this effect.

MAGI is the sum of adjusted gross income plus tax-exempt interest income, if any. The lowest Medicare Part B premium is set at $148.50 per month for 2021. An IRA distribution would only cause a jump in premiums if the taxable amount pushes MAGI into the next level. (See Table 9-3.)

Table 9-3. Medicare Part B Premiums (2021)

2019 MAGI (If Filed Individual Return and Was Not Married)	*2019 MAGI (If Filed Joint Return)*	*2019 MAGI (If Was Married and Filed Separate Return)*	*Monthly Premium in 2021*
Up to $88,000	Up to $176,000	$88,000 or less	$148.50
$88,001–$111,000	$176,001–$222,000	n/a	$207.90
$111,001–$138,000	$222,001–$276,000	n/a	$297.00
$138,001–$165,000	$276,001–$330,000	n/a	$386.10
$165,001–$499,999	$333,001–$749,999	$88,001–$411,999	$475.20
$500,000 or over	$750,000 or over	$412,000 or over	$504.90

[Social Security Administration, *Medicare Premiums: Rules for Higher Income Beneficiaries* (2021), available at *https://www.ssa.gov/benefits/medicare/medicare-premiums.html*]

Q 9:10 Do IRA distributions affect the taxation of Social Security benefits?

Social Security benefits may be taxable, depending on income. Taxable IRA and qualified plan distributions count as income for this purpose. Nontaxable Roth IRA and Roth 401(k) distributions do not cause Social Security income (SSI) to be taxed.

If modified AGI (adjusted to include tax-exempt interest, half the SSI, and certain other amounts) exceeds a base amount, then a portion of the SSI payment is taxable income that must be reported on the Form 1040 (see Table 9-4). [IRS Pub. 915, *Social Security and Equivalent Railroad Retirement Benefits* (2020)]

Table 9-4. Taxable Portion of the Social Security Benefit

Filing Status	*Up to 50 Percent Is Taxable If Modified AGI Is:*	*Up to 85 Percent Is Taxable If Modified AGI Is:*
Married filing jointly	$32,000 to $44,000	Above $44,000
Single, head of household, or qualifying widow(er)	$25,000 to $34,000	Above $34,000
Married filing separately and lived apart from spouse for entire year	$25,000 to $34,000	Above $34,000
Married filing separately and lived with spouse at all during year	n/a	Above $0

Consequently, a taxable IRA or qualified plan distribution that is large enough to push the recipient's modified AGI over the 50 or 85 percent limit will increase the tax on SSI. This is an additional cost to be considered if a large taxable IRA distribution or Roth IRA conversion is planned.

Q 9:11 When should the first RMD be taken?

All of the issues discussed above are exacerbated if the first RMD is taken from a traditional IRA during the grace period (January 1 through April 1 of the year that includes the required beginning date, or RBD). That is because the second RMD must be paid by the end of the same year. [Treas. Reg. § 1.401(a)(9)-5, Q&A-1(c)]

If bunching two RMDs into the same year would increase taxable income enough to produce adverse consequences, it is better not to wait until the grace period to take the first RMD. However, if taxable income is expected to be lower in the year of the grace period (e.g., because the individual is retiring in the prior year), it makes sense to delay the first RMD until then.

The RMD waiver for calendar year 2020 included a special rule for individuals with an RBD in 2020. Unfortunately, it treated some of them unfairly. The first RMD is waived only if the payment was delayed until 2020. Those who did not delay, and took the first RMD in 2019, were stuck with it. (See Qs 4:7, 4:10.) [I.R.C. § 401(a)(9)(I)(i), added by § 2203 of the Coronavirus Aid, Relief, and Economic Security Act (CARES Act), Pub. L. No. 116-136 (Mar. 27, 2020)]

Note.

No IRA owner not already receiving RMDs will have a 2021 RBD. Going forward, the new RBD is April 1 of the calendar year following the year in which age 72 is attained. It applies to traditional, SEP, and SIMPLE IRA owners born after June 30, 1949 (see Q 4:4). The first of them will reach age 72 in 2021 and have an RBD in 2022. [I.R.C. § 401(a)(9)(C), as amended by § 114 of the Setting Every Community Up for Retirement Enhancement Act of 2019 (SECURE Act), Div. O of the Further Consolidated Appropriations Act, 2020, Pub. L. No. 116-94 (Dec. 20, 2019)]

Q 9:12 What can be done with an IRA if it will be necessary to apply for Medicaid assistance?

A detailed answer to the question is beyond the scope of this book because Medicaid rules vary from state to state. In general, however, the following is true.

Medicaid provides health coverage for low-income individuals. A person covered by a long-term care policy or other health insurance is usually required to pay some part of the cost (a co-payment). However, some needs are so catastrophic that that they may drain a relatively wealthy person's financial resources. Such individuals would then apply for Medicaid assistance.

Income, assets, and expenses are all taken into account to determine eligibility for Medicaid. An IRA that is not yet required to pay RMDs (i.e., it is not in *payout status*) is valued as an asset, with no discount for taxes that will be payable. Once the IRA is in payout status, however, it is viewed as a payment stream and only the RMDs are taken into account (as income).

This is straightforward in the case of a traditional IRA, but a Roth IRA is never in payout status during its owner's lifetime. For that reason, the Roth IRA is probably always considered an asset for Medicaid purposes.

People often "spend down" their assets on items other than medical care before applying for Medicaid. Generally, there is a five-year lookback period for such spending. So one way to deal with a large IRA is to withdraw and spend the funds early enough to avoid the lookback. This presents an obvious drawback: catastrophic expenses are unpredictable.

An alternative to spending down is to place assets in a trust that is structured to exclude the assets from Medicaid consideration.

The issue is complicated and an attorney specializing in elder law should be consulted.

Q 9:13 Should a qualified charitable distribution be considered if an RMD is not needed for expenses?

Yes. The amount distributed as a qualified charitable contribution (QCD) is generally not taxed and counts toward satisfying the RMD, so this is an excellent way to use an RMD. (RMDs are waived for calendar year 2020; see Q 4:6.)

A QCD is an otherwise taxable distribution from an IRA—including an inherited IRA, but not an ongoing SEP or SIMPLE IRA—that the IRA trustee transfers directly to a qualified charity. An IRA owner or inherited IRA beneficiary who is age 72 or older may donate up to $100,000 per year this way. Since the first dollars distributed during any year count toward satisfying that year's RMD, a QCD must precede other distributions to count for that purpose. [I.R.C. § 408(d)(8); Treas. Reg. § 1.402(c)-2, Q&A-7]

QCDs are excluded from income and cannot also be deducted as a charitable contribution—with one exception. Deductible traditional IRA contributions that are made after age 70½ are not excluded from income when subsequently distributed as a QCD. [I.R.C. § 408(d)(8)(A)]

Maximizing IRA Value

Q 9:14 What is essential to preserving the value of an IRA?

The answer is simple—avoid penalties and unwanted distributions. The penalty for failing to take RMDs is costly—50 percent of the shortfall (see Q 4:88). Other penalties to avoid include the 6 percent excise tax on excess contributions, the 10 percent additional tax on early distributions, the 10 percent additional tax on early distribution of conversion contributions, and the most disastrous penalty of all—loss of IRA status for participating in a prohibited transaction.

The penalty for underpayment of estimated tax can be avoided by ensuring that adequate amounts are withheld from taxable IRA distributions.

Finally, failing to carefully observe the 60-day rollover rules is another costly mistake. Amounts can be withdrawn from an IRA as (in effect) a short-term loan, but only if they are returned within 60 days. Also, no more than one nontaxable 60-day rollover between IRAs can occur within any 12-month period (see Qs 6:15–6:19 for details concerning this rule).

Q 9:15 To minimize penalties, when should a surviving spouse roll over the decedent spouse's traditional IRA?

A young surviving spouse who inherits the decedent spouse's traditional IRA should generally wait until age 59½ to roll it over. The 10 percent early distribution penalty does not apply to distributions received by a beneficiary. If an early distribution is taken after the IRA is rolled over, the penalty will apply to the taxable part of the distribution (unless another exception applies) because the surviving spouse is then regarded as the owner, not the beneficiary. (For a more detailed review of the surviving spouse's options, see Qs 5:134–5:145.)

Q 9:16 Should an IRA owner take a discretionary distribution from a traditional IRA or a Roth IRA if both are maintained?

The question assumes that a distribution will be made *after* payment of any RMDs due for the year from the traditional IRA. Consider taking a taxable distribution from the traditional IRA if the tax rates are lower (or expected to be lower) in retirement than they were when contributions were made, the early distribution penalty will not apply, and the resulting increase in taxable income does not cause any of the adverse consequences described in Q 9:4.

Otherwise, consider taking only RMDs from the traditional IRA and other distributions from the Roth IRA.

Q 9:17 Should a person younger than age 59½ take discretionary distributions from an inherited IRA, or from his or her own traditional or Roth IRA?

A person younger than age 59½ who inherited an IRA and also maintains his or her own traditional and/or Roth IRA should take discretionary distributions (above the RMD) from the inherited IRA in most cases. An inherited IRA must be paid out faster than one's own IRA, so if any IRA is to be drained it should be the inherited IRA.

As compared with a distribution from one's own traditional IRA, the tax cost of a distribution from the inherited IRA (traditional or Roth) may also be lower because the early distribution penalty does not apply to beneficiaries. And if the comparison is between an inherited traditional IRA and one's own Roth IRA, the distribution should probably be taken from the inherited IRA even though the short-term tax cost will be greater. Funds can remain longer in the Roth IRA and will compound and be distributed tax free.

Contribution Planning

Q 9:18 What assets should be placed in IRAs?

Generally, to optimize the tax advantages of an IRA (tax-free compounding of earnings, and tax-free distributions in the case of a Roth IRA):

- Dividend-paying equities, higher-yielding fixed income assets, and assets that will be frequently bought and sold are best placed in an IRA, because the income and gains will not be taxed within the account.

- Assets that produce little taxable income—growth equities held for the long term, lower-yielding fixed income assets, and municipal bonds—can be held in taxable accounts, provided low turnover is expected.

Q 9:19 How may IRA contributions indirectly affect taxes and expenses incurred for other items?

Some of the consequences considered above are triggered by taxable income; they may be mitigated by deductible IRA contributions. An example is the Medicare surtax on net investment income, which is tied to MAGI. The deduction for a traditional IRA contribution would likely have only a trivial effect, but deferral contributions to SEP and SIMPLE IRAs (which have higher limits) may be significant.

Q 9:20 How can SEP contributions help some individuals qualify for the new deduction for qualified business income from a pass-through entity?

The TCJA introduced a new deduction that provides an incentive, in some cases, to establish or increase contributions to a SEP or other pre-tax retirement plan. Under Code Section 199A, an individual's taxable income may be offset by 20 percent of his or her qualified business income from a partnership, S corporation, or sole proprietorship (pass-through entity). If the entity engages in a personal service business, the individual's deduction is phased out generally at higher income levels. For 2021, those levels (adjusted for inflation) are $164,900 for single and head of household filers; $329,800 for married individuals filing a joint return with the spouse; and $164,925 for married individuals filing separate from the spouse. [I.R.C. § 199A; TCJA § 11011; Rev. Proc. 2020-45, 2020-46 I.R.B. 1016]

Some individuals engaged in a service business through a pass-through entity will need to reduce taxable income in order to qualify for the 20 percent deduction. If the business maintains a SEP or 401(k) plan, contributions under the plan may accomplish that goal.

Q 9:21 What are the options if a deductible IRA contribution cannot be made?

If an individual cannot make a deductible contribution to a traditional IRA (because income exceeds the MAGI limit for a deduction, or there is active participation in a retirement plan), there are three options:

1. Contribute to a Roth IRA;
2. If income is above the MAGI limits for a Roth IRA contribution, make a nondeductible contribution to a traditional IRA and consider immediately converting it to a Roth IRA; or
3. Invest instead in a taxable account.

(For the advantages and disadvantages of these options, see Q 1:13.)

Q 9:22 Does the Medicare surtax on compensation and self-employment income affect deferrals to a SEP or SIMPLE IRA?

No. Payroll and self-employment taxes (including the surtax in question), which are payable on an individual's total compensation and net earnings from self-employment (NESE), have no effect on the amounts deferred to a SEP or SIMPLE IRA. The surtax on NESE may cause the income tax on self-employment income to increase, however.

The basic Medicare component of the payroll tax is 2.9 percent of total compensation. But for compensation that exceeds a threshold amount (see Table 9-5), an additional tax of 0.9 percent applies. The employer pays half of the basic tax (1.45 percent). The employee is responsible for the rest of the basic tax (1.45 percent), and all of the surtax payable. The employee's share is collected through withholding, which reduces the compensation paid as cash. Any elective deferral amounts are transferred in full to the SEP or SIMPLE IRA. [I.R.C. §§ 3111(b), 3101(b)]

The Medicare component of the self-employment tax is similar, except that the self-employed individual pays all of it. The amount payable is 2.9 percent of NESE, with an additional tax of 0.9 percent payable on the amount of NESE over the threshold. [I.R.C. § 1401(b)(1)]

For income tax purposes, half of the basic (2.9 percent) self-employment tax paid is deductible. However, *none* of the additional tax is deductible. [I.R.C. § 1401(b)(2)] The effect is to somewhat increase the amount of income tax payable on self-employment income.

Table 9-5. Medicare Surtax on Compensation and Self-Employment Income

Filing Status	*Surtax Applies to Compensation or NESE over:*
Married filing jointly or surviving spouse	$250,000
Single or head of household	$200,000
Married filing separately	$125,000

Q 9:23 If savings will be needed before age 59½, should they be invested in a Roth or traditional IRA?

In general, several factors bear on the decision whether to contribute to a Roth or traditional IRA—whether tax rates will be higher or lower when funds are withdrawn versus contributed (see chapter 1), and the utility of deductible contributions (see Q 9:18)—but there is one case in which the Roth IRA is the clear winner. A person likely to need withdrawals from the IRA before age

59½ should contribute to a Roth IRA, if possible, because those contributions may always be withdrawn without tax or penalty.

Of course, early withdrawals work against the important goal of saving for retirement.

Q 9:24 May a person still working after age 70½ continue to make annual contributions?

Yes. The age limit for contributions to a traditional IRA (formerly 70½) has been repealed, effective for contribution years after 2019. So as long as there is sufficient earned income, those contributions may continue. Roth IRA contributions and elective salary deferrals under a SARSEP or SIMPLE plan have always been allowed to continue past age 70½.

Traditional, SEP, and SIMPLE IRA owners must start taking minimum distributions when they reach age 72 (age 70½, for individuals who attained age 70½ before 2020). Once minimum distributions begin, continued contributions (including salary deferrals) to those IRAs are somewhat inefficient because a portion of each contribution made in one year is returned in the next year as part of the RMD. Even so, they may be worthwhile. Salary deferrals under a SARSEP or SIMPLE reduce AGI and may mitigate some of the negative consequences considered above. Moreover, a regular IRA contribution (traditional or Roth) can also be made for the same year, because the limits are separate.

Q 9:25 Should a parent consider a cash gift to fund the child's IRA?

Absolutely. Young people with earned income should start contributing early to an IRA, because the value of tax-free compounding is enormous. But they often cannot afford to do so. A parent (or anyone) with sufficient means could make a gift of cash to fund the contribution amount. The annual gift tax exclusion ($15,000 for 2021) would be available. [I.R.C. § 2503; Rev. Proc. 2020-45, 2020-46 I.R.B. 1016]

Q 9:26 Can payments from an individual retirement annuity be rolled over to an IRA?

No. To qualify as an individual retirement annuity, the stream of payments must satisfy the minimum distribution rules. As a result, the entire payment received from the annuity each year *is* the RMD. None of it can be rolled over, and if a rollover is attempted (and not caught by the IRA trustee) the excess contribution penalty will apply.

Chapter 10

Leaving an IRA to the Spouse

Retirement benefits are often a significant part of an individual's estate, and a participant who is married usually wants to leave all or part of them to the surviving spouse. A surviving spouse who is a designated beneficiary of the participant's IRA has rights that other beneficiaries do not have, and as a result can obtain more value from them. The most powerful tool of the surviving spouse is the ability to roll over benefits from the inherited IRA to an IRA in the spouse's name—which allows the benefits to remain in the IRA for a longer period of years and continue to grow tax deferred (or tax exempt, if it is a Roth IRA).

This chapter considers the different ways that an IRA can be left to benefit the surviving spouse, whether outright or through a trust, and the impact of each transfer method on the estate tax incurred at the participant's death.

The Setting Every Community Up for Retirement Enhancement Act of 2019, Div. O of the Further Consolidated Appropriations Act, 2020, Pub. L. No. 116-94 (Dec. 20, 2019) (FCAA) (SECURE) completely changed the minimum distribution rules that apply after the death of an IRA or other defined contribution plan participant. The SECURE amendments require most IRAs to be distributed to beneficiaries within 10 years after the participant dies. Only eligible designated beneficiaries (EDBs), which include the surviving spouse and a few other individuals, are entitled to stretch payments from the IRA over their life expectancy. IRAs payable to a trust (for example, a QTIP trust) are now subject to post-death minimum distribution rules that can be extremely unfavorable. So, the final section of this chapter explains which methods of transferring an IRA to the surviving spouse produce suitable income tax results, and which should be avoided.

The Spouse as the Favored IRA Beneficiary

Q 10:1 How do the tax laws favor designating the spouse as the IRA beneficiary?

A surviving spouse (SS) who is the designated beneficiary of the deceased spouse's IRA has rights that other beneficiaries do not. The most important of these is the right to roll over the decedent's IRA to an IRA in the SS's name. [I.R.C. § 408(d)(3)(C); Treas. Reg. § 1.408-8, Q&A-5(a)] A rollover can be done at any time.

A SS who rolls over the deceased spouse's IRA is then treated as the participant for all purposes. [Treas. Reg. § 1.408-8, Q&A-5(b) and (c)] That allows the SS to:

- Take smaller RMDs, calculated using the Uniform Lifetime Table, rather than the less favorable Single Life Table. Longer life expectancies under the Uniform Lifetime Table translate to a larger divisor for each year's RMD calculation, and more opportunity to defer income tax. (See Q 4:22.) [Treas. Reg. § 1.401(a)(9)-5, Q&A-4(a)]
- Designate a new eligible designated beneficiary (EDB), who will be able to take RMDs when the spouse dies based on the EDB's own life expectancy. Otherwise, when the SS dies, the IRA would have to be distributed to the successor beneficiary under the 10-year rule (by December 31 of the calendar year containing the 10th anniversary of the SS's death). [I.R.C. § 401(a)(9)(H)(ii), 401(a)(9)(H)(iii)]
- Postpone the start of RMDs if the deceased spouse dies before RMDs have begun, the SS is younger than the deceased spouse, and the SS is also the *sole* beneficiary of the inherited IRA. A rollover by the SS would postpone the start of RMDs until the year of the SS's 72nd birthday. As a beneficiary of the inherited IRA, the SS would have to commence RMDs when the deceased spouse would have reached age 72, which will occur earlier. [Treas. Reg. § 1.401(a)(9)-3, Q&A-3(b)] For purposes of determining minimum distributions, a participant is considered to die before distributions are "required to begin" if he or she dies before the required beginning date for RMDs, which is April 1 of the calendar year following the calendar year in which age 72 is attained. [Treas. Reg. § 1.401(a)(9)-2, Q&A-6(a)]

- If the first spouse's IRA is a Roth IRA, a rollover allows the SS to avoid lifetime RMDs altogether. [I.R.C. § 408A(c)(4)] If the spouse does not yet meet the five-year holding period requirement for qualified distributions from a Roth IRA, the decedent's holding period (if longer than the SS's) will carry over with the rollover (see Q 5:79). [Treas. Reg. § 1.408A-6, Q&A-7(b)]
- The SS may convert the decedent's IRA to a Roth IRA. [I.R.C. §§ 408A(c)(5)(A), 408A(e), 408(d)(3), 408(d)(3)(C)]

Q 10:2 If the surviving spouse is the *sole* designated beneficiary, what are his or her other rights?

A SS who is the sole DB can elect to treat the deceased spouse's IRA as the SS's own. A SS is the *sole beneficiary* if no other person (disregarding mere successor beneficiaries; see Q 4:44) is also a beneficiary and the SS has the unlimited right to withdraw all amounts from the IRA. If there is more than one beneficiary but the IRA is divided into separate accounts by December 31 of the calendar year after the deceased spouse's year of death (the *separate accounts deadline*), the determination of whether the SS is the sole beneficiary is made with respect to the SS's separate account. [Treas. Reg. § 1.401(a)(9)-8, Q&A-2]

Q 10:3 How does the surviving spouse make the election to treat the decedent's IRA as his or her own?

There are three ways to make this election. [Treas. Reg. § 1.408-8, Q&A-5(a), Q&A-5(b); Treas. Reg. § 1.408A-2, Q&A-4]

1. Retitle the decedent's IRA in the spouse's own name as the account owner.
2. Make a contribution to the inherited IRA. A beneficiary cannot make contributions to an inherited IRA, so this is deemed to be an election to treat the IRA as the SS's own.
3. Fail to withdraw an RMD that would be payable to the spouse as a beneficiary of the IRA. (This is the only completely passive way for the spouse to take ownership of the decedent's IRA.)

Q 10:4 When can the surviving spouse roll over the decedent's IRA or elect to treat it as the spouse's own?

The SS may roll over the decedent's IRA or elect to treat it as his or her own (if eligible), at any time. However, if the participant's year-of-death RMD (if any) was not paid before death, it must first be paid to the SS. The SS cannot roll over that or any other RMD he or she receives. [Treas. Reg. § 1.408-8, Q&A-5(a); T.D. 8987, 2002-1 C.B. 852]

Q 10:5 If the surviving spouse dies before rolling over the IRA, can the executor of his/her estate do so on her behalf?

If the SS received a distribution before his or her death, the executor for the SS's estate may complete the rollover. If more than 60 days have elapsed since the distribution, the executor may even be able to obtain a discretionary waiver of the rollover deadline if circumstances show that hardship (including death) prevented timely completion of the rollover. [Rev. Proc. 2003-16, 2003-1 C.B. 359] Unfortunately, however, the executor *cannot* designate a beneficiary for the rollover IRA. Only a living participant may do that. [*See, e.g.*, Priv. Ltr. Rul. 201334036 (Aug. 23, 2013).]

The executor of the SS's estate cannot initiate a rollover, however, nor may it elect to treat the IRA inherited from the first spouse as the (deceased) SS's own. [Treas. Reg. § 1.408-8, Q&A-5; Priv. Ltr. Rul. 200126036 (July 2, 2001)]

Q 10:6 If the spouse is not the sole beneficiary, or holds the interest through a trust, is a rollover possible?

The SS *cannot* roll over the decedent's IRA or elect to treat it as the SS's own if the IRA is payable to a trust or the decedent's estate. However, if a trust is the IRA beneficiary and the SS is the sole beneficiary of that trust with an unlimited right to compel distribution of the IRA to the trust and distributions from the trust to the SS, and no other person has the power to appoint the IRA payments to anyone besides the SS, then the SS may roll over to his or her own IRA any payments from the decedent's IRA to the trust that are actually distributed to the SS. [T.D. 8987, 2002-1 C.B. 852; *e.g.*, Priv. Ltr. Rul. 200242044 (Oct. 18, 2002)]

The same is true if the IRA is payable to the decedent's estate, the SS is the sole estate beneficiary, and no person has the power to appoint the IRA to anyone besides the SS. The SS can compel the estate to take a full distribution of the IRA, and then roll over the payment to the SS's own IRA. [*See, e.g.*, Priv. Ltr. Rul. 200406048 (Feb. 6, 2004).]

Q 10:7 Is it always advisable for the surviving spouse to roll over the deceased spouse's IRA?

No. If the SS is younger than age 59½, rolling over the IRA will expose the SS to the 10 percent additional tax on early distributions. [I.R.C. § 72(t)(2)(A)(i)] There are several ways to deal with this:

- The SS can remain as a beneficiary until he or she reaches age 59½ and roll it over after that. The RMDs (and other distributions) paid from an inherited IRA are not subject to additional tax. [I.R.C. § 72(t)(2)(A)(ii)]
- The SS can roll over the IRA and take RMDs as part of a series of substantially equal periodic payments (SEPPs). SEPPs qualify as an exception to the additional tax. The series of payments must continue, without modifi-

cation, for at least five years or, if later, until age 59½ is reached (see Q 5:31). [I.R.C. § 72(t)(4)(A); Rev. Rul. 2002-62, 2002-2 C.B. 710]

- The SS can roll over the entire IRA but segregate a portion of it (the funds he or she expects to need until age 59½) in a separate IRA and elect to withdraw a series of SEPPs from that IRA only. (See Q 5:41.) [*See, e.g.*, Priv. Ltr. Rul. 200943044 (Oct. 23, 2009).]
- The SS can leave some funds in the inherited IRA (if he/she does not expect to require more than the beneficiary RMDs before age 59½) and roll over the rest to the SS's own IRA.

Q 10:8 How does the presence of after-tax money in the IRA factor into the decision?

If the deceased spouse's IRA has after-tax money and the SS's own (pre-existing) IRA does not, the SS may want to convert the inherited IRA directly to a Roth IRA to take advantage of the basis. If the SS were to roll it over and then convert, the after-tax money would be "diluted" (since all traditional IRAs owned by a participant are treated as one IRA for purposes of allocating basis) and the conversion tax would be higher. [I.R.C. §§ 408(d)(1), 72(e)(5)(D)(iii), 72(e)(8)(B)]

For the same reason, if the reverse is true, the SS should consider converting his or her own traditional IRA to a Roth IRA before doing a rollover.

Q 10:9 Might creditor issues affect the choice of whether to roll over the IRA?

Absolutely. If the SS were to declare bankruptcy, the SS's interest in an inherited IRA would *not* be protected from the reach of creditors. The bankruptcy exemption is allowed only for IRAs held as the owner (see Q 1:53). [Clark v. Rameker, 134 S. Ct. 2242 (2014)]

Q 10:10 Should the surviving spouse convert the decedent's traditional IRA to a Roth IRA?

A Roth IRA is a great thing to have, but conversion is an expensive way to obtain it. Still, it may be worthwhile.

If the SS is wealthy, does not need the decedent's IRA, and wants to leave tax-free assets to beneficiaries, conversion can be useful. The conversion removes assets from the SS's own estate and can lead to a lower estate tax bill when the SS dies. Conversion also allows the SS's death beneficiaries to take distributions free of income tax.

The Setting Every Community Up for Retirement Enhancement Act of 2019, Div. O of the Further Consolidated Appropriations Act, 2020, Pub. L. No. 116-94 (Dec. 20, 2019) (FCAA) (SECURE), also tilts the balance somewhat in favor of conversion. Most beneficiaries must now take distribution of an inherited IRA within 10 years, which both accelerates the income tax on a traditional IRA and likely increases it, due to the bunching of income into a higher tax bracket. Beneficiaries are relieved of this burden if a Roth IRA is inherited.

A SS should consider converting the IRA if his or her IRA beneficiary will be taxed at a higher rate than the SS currently faces. That is likely to be the case if the IRA will be left to an accumulation trust. (See Q 4:57, last sentence.)

One disadvantage of converting to a Roth IRA is that the tax deduction for income received in respect of a decedent (IRD) may be lost. Payments from an IRA are considered to be IRD, and a recipient of IRD is allowed to claim, as an income tax deduction, the amount of estate tax that was paid with respect to including that item of IRD in the decedent's estate. Also, if the traditional IRA passing to the SS qualifies for the marital deduction (see Q 10:16), none of the estate tax paid by the decedent's estate will be attributable to the IRA, so none will be deductible by the SS as an offset to the conversion income. [I.R.C. § 691]

Background—IRAs and the Estate Tax

Q 10:11 Is the decedent's IRA included in the gross estate?

Yes. Federal estate tax is imposed on the transfer at death of all of a decedent's property, real or personal, tangible or intangible. [I.R.C. § 2031] Property generally includes the value of an annuity or other payment receivable by a beneficiary by reason of surviving the decedent, if the decedent possessed the right to receive the payment for a period that does not end before his or her death. [I.R.C. § 2039] That includes IRAs, which are included in the gross estate at their value on the date of death. The value is not adjusted for future tax liability that will be payable by the beneficiary. [Estate of Doris F. Kahn v. Commissioner, 125 T.C. 227; Instructions to IRS Form 706, United States Estate (and Generation-Skipping Transfer) Tax Return (rev. Sept. 2020), p. 30]

Q 10:12 What tax breaks can apply to the IRA in calculating the estate tax?

Retirement benefits (including an IRA) transferred to the surviving spouse may be deductible from the gross estate under Code Section 2056. Transfers that do not qualify for the deduction may still be shielded from estate tax by the unified credit, which is allowed under Code Section 2010.

Q 10:13 How does the unified credit work?

The unified credit (also called the applicable credit amount) is an offset to both the gift taxes imposed on lifetime transfers and the estate tax incurred on transfers at death. [I.R.C. §§ 2001, 2010, 2505] The credit is the sum of two amounts: the *basic exclusion amount* (BEA), which every individual gets, and the *deceased spousal unused exemption amount* (DSUE). Since 2011, a married couple have been able to share their unified credits by means of the DSUE. If the BEA is not fully used on the first-to-die spouse's estate tax return, his or her executor may elect on that return to transfer the unused amount (the DSUE) to the surviving spouse. This is called "portability." [I.R.C. § 2010(c)]

The Tax Cuts and Jobs Act (TCJA) temporarily doubled the BEA from $5 million to $10 million, before adjustment for inflation, for the years 2018 through 2025. [TCJA, Pub. L. No. 115-97 (Dec. 22, 2017), § 11061] Unless Congress acts, the BEA will revert in 2026 to $5 million plus the inflation adjustment. For deaths (and taxable gift transfers) in 2021, the inflation-adjusted BEA is $11,700,000. [I.R.C. §§ 2010, 2505; Rev. Proc. 2020-45, 2020-46 I.R.B. 1016] Consequently, if both spouses die in 2020, up to $23,400,000 of taxable property transfers can be shielded from their estates.

Note. The generation-skipping transfer (GST) tax also has an exemption amount equal to the BEA, but that tax is not unified with the estate and gift taxes. The GST exemption is not portable, and taxable transfers are taxed only at the highest rate that applies to the taxable estate and gift transfers (40 percent). The GST tax exemption will also revert in 2026 to $5 million (before the inflation adjustment). [I.R.C. §§ 2631, 2010(c)]

Q 10:14 What will happen to the unified credit when the temporary increase sunsets in 2026?

The BEA increase is temporary, but portability is permanent. Final Treasury regulations issued in late 2019 clarify how the BEA and DSUE will work when the temporary increase sunsets at the end of 2025:

- A special rule ensures that the estate of a decedent who dies after 2025 will not be inappropriately taxed with respect to gifts that were sheltered from gift tax by the increased BEA when made. [T.D. 9884, 84 Fed. Reg. 64995 (Nov. 26, 2019)]
- The BEA increase is a "use it or lose it" benefit, and the applicable exemption amount is consumed in the following order: first the DSUE, then the permanent part of one's own exemption, and finally the temporary BEA increase. If taxable gifts do not absorb the entire BEA credit before 2025, the unused temporary increase is lost. For example, suppose the first spouse's estate transfers a DSUE of $3 million to the surviving spouse, and the surviving spouse makes a $12 million taxable gift in 2020. That gift uses the $3 million DSUE, the surviving spouse's entire "permanent" BEA (half of the inflation-adjusted 2020 exclusion, or $5,850,000), and $3,150,100 of the "temporary" BEA. If no more taxable gifts are made before the spouse dies in 2026, the unused temporary BEA ($2,580,000) is lost. [Treas. Reg. § 20.2010-1(c)(2)(i)]
- A DSUE election made during the period of the BEA increase (2018 through 2025) will not be reduced when the temporary increase sunsets at the end of 2025. So, if the first spouse dies during this period and the executor makes the portability election, the transferred DSUE may exceed

the second spouse's own BEA if he or she dies after 2025. [Treas. Reg. § 20.2010-1(c)(2)(iii) and (iv)]

Q 10:15 If retirement benefits are a large part of the estate, should an exemption trust be part of the estate plan?

An exemption trust (also known as a credit shelter or bypass trust) used to be a common feature of spousal estate planning, but is much less likely to be used now. Its purpose was to ensure use of both spouses' estate tax exemptions, but the cost was often high. When the first spouse died, property with a value equal to the estate tax exemption would be transferred to the exemption trust. The SS would receive income from the trust for life, and upon his or her later death the trust would not be part of the SS's estate. The SS's estate tax exemption could be used to shield other assets from estate tax.

But where retirement benefits were a large part of a spouse's wealth and were used to fund the exemption trust, there were three bad income tax results. First, IRA and other retirement benefits are most valuable when left outright to the SS, because then the SS can roll them over (see Q 10:1). The SS cannot roll over an IRA left to an exemption trust. Second, payments received by an exemption trust are taxed at a much higher rate than when received by an individual. For 2021, the highest marginal rate of income tax (37 percent) applies to trust income above $13,050; for a single individual, that rate applies only to income above $523,600. [Rev. Proc. 2020-45, 2020-46 I.R.B. 1016] Finally, the income taxes paid by the trust reduce the assets left for the trust remaindermen without lowering estate tax when the SS dies. Highly taxed assets (like an IRA) are more efficiently shielded with the marital deduction, because those tax payments remove assets from the SS's estate and reduce the exposure to estate tax when the SS dies.

Fortunately, the federal tax impetus for the exemption trust is now gone:

- Due to serial increases in the estate tax exemption, few estates now have estate tax liability. For example, in 2000 the estate tax exemption was $675,000. In 2017, before the exemption was temporarily doubled, it was $5,490,000. [Rev. Proc. 2016-55, 2016-45 I.R.B. 707]
- The portable exemption simplifies planning. Trusts are no longer needed to preserve both spouses' exemptions.
- Before same-sex marriage was legalized in the U.S., exemption trusts were used to reduce estate tax because the marital deduction was unavailable. [United States v. Windsor, 570 U.S. 744 (2013)]

Exemption trusts may still be useful in estate planning to lower state inheritance taxes (which typically apply at a lower threshold and do not allow for portability) or for nontax reasons. Fortunately, the federal tax incentive for them is gone.

The Marital Deduction

Q 10:16 What is required for an IRA to qualify for the marital deduction?

Property qualifies for the marital deduction if it is included in the decedent's gross estate, passes to the surviving spouse who is a U.S. citizen, and is not a terminable interest (see Q 10:17). [I.R.C. § 2056(a), 2056(b)]

Q 10:17 What is a terminable interest?

A terminable interest is an interest in property that will terminate or fail on lapse of time or on the occurrence or failure to occur of some contingency. For example, a life estate is a terminable interest. [I.R.C. § 2056(b)(1)]

The marital deduction defers estate tax on property transfers within the marital unit. Deferral ends when the second spouse dies, and the property (to the extent not consumed) is included in his or her estate. But if the interest transferred to the SS will terminate and pass to someone other than the SS (or the SS's estate), estate tax would be entirely avoided were it not for the terminable interest rule.

But, as with many rules, there are exceptions.

Q 10:18 What are the exceptions to the terminable interest rule?

Some property is treated as transferred to the SS, and not to any other person, under exceptions to the terminable interest rule. Thus, they are eligible for the marital deduction. The exceptions relevant to IRAs are for:

- Qualified terminable interest property (QTIP; see Q 10:19). [I.R.C. § 2056(b)(7)(B)]
- Survivor annuity (this is the exception that applies to an IRA passed outright to the SS; see Q 10:23). [I.R.C. § 2056(b)(7)(C)]
- Life estate with general power of appointment (see Q 10:25). [I.R.C. § 2056(b)(5)]
- Charitable remainder trust (see Q 10:26). [I.R.C. § 2056(b)(8)]

QTIP Exception

Q 10:19 What is qualified terminable interest property?

QTIP is property passing from the decedent in which the SS has a qualifying income interest for life, payable at least annually, and for which a QTIP election is made on the decedent's estate tax return. [I.R.C. § 2056(b)(7)(B)(i)]

The SS has a qualifying interest for life if the SS is entitled to all the income from the property, payable at least annually, and no person has the power to appoint any part of the property to someone other than the SS (ignoring an appointment power that is only exercisable at or after the death of the SS).

When the SS dies, whatever is left of the QTIP (or other property in which the SS had a qualifying income interest for life) is included in the gross estate. [I.R.C. § 2044]

Q 10:20 What is a QTIP trust?

A trust named as the IRA beneficiary is a QTIP trust if:

- The SS has a qualifying income interest for life, payable at least annually, in all the income from *both* the IRA and the trust,
- No person can appoint the property to any person other than the SS, and
- A QTIP election is made for *both* the IRA and the trust.

[I.R.C. § 2056(b)(7)(B)(ii)]

The IRA and the trust are regarded as separate items of QTIP, so the requirements must be separately met. [Rev. Rul. 2006-26, 2006-1 C.B. 939]

A basic QTIP trust would require all the income to be paid annually to the SS, and the remainder would pass to the donor's issue when the SS dies. This kind of trust is often used after a second marriage, so the SS is benefited during his or her life, and children from the participant's first marriage receive the trust assets when the SS dies. A QTIP trust named as the IRA beneficiary may be structured as either a conduit trust or an accumulation trust (see Qs 10:30–10:33).

Q 10:21 How is "income" determined?

The "income" to which the SS must be entitled for life is both the income internal to the IRA and the income of the trust. In both cases, "income" means accounting income—which differs from both taxable income and the RMD. For example, an IRA distribution to the trust is income for tax purposes, but may be allocated to the trust principal for accounting purposes. The trust is always required to withdraw the RMD, and that amount is not likely to be the same as the internal income (profitability) of the IRA for the same period. So, to meet the standard, the trust may be required to withdraw either the IRA income or the RMD, whichever is greater (but see Q 10:22, regarding the SS's right to compel the withdrawal). [Rev. Rul. 2006-26, 2006-1 C.B. 939; Treas. Reg. § 20.2056(b)-7(d)]

A properly drafted trust instrument includes a definition of trust income. If it does not, state law controls. Most states have adopted a version of the Uniform Fiduciary Income and Principal Act (UFIPA). The UFIPA provides a rule that specifically applies to a marital deduction trust named as beneficiary of an IRA or other retirement plan. It was drafted in response to Revenue Ruling 2006-26, which held that the prior rule did not meet the proper QTIP standard. [UFIPA, Comment of the National Conference of Commissioners on Uniform State Laws to Section 409, p. 69 (2018)] UFIPA Section 409(d) treats the IRA as a separate fund within the trust and requires accounting income to be separately determined for that fund, and for the rest of the trust.

Q 10:22 What does it mean to be "entitled to" all the income for life?

There are two ways to meet this requirement. The first is for all the income to be distributed to the SS at least annually. The second is for the SS to have the right, exercisable at least annually, to compel such distribution, and to the extent the right is not exercised the trust income must be accumulated and added to principal. [Rev. Rul. 2006-26, 2006-1 C.B. 939; Treas. Reg. §§ 20.2056(b)-7(d)(2), 20.2056(b)-5(f)(1), 20.2056(b)-5(f)(8)]

This second method allows the trustee to leave the internal IRA income (see Q 10:21) in the plan to the extent it exceeds the RMD, unless the SS asks for it to be withdrawn and distributed.

Other Exceptions

Q 10:23 What is the exception to the terminable interest rule for a survivor annuity?

The QTIP rules include a separate exception to the terminable interest rule for a "survivor annuity." A survivor annuity is defined as an annuity included in the decedent's gross estate under Section 2039, where only the SS can receive payments during his/her life. The interest of the SS is treated as a qualifying income interest for life, *and* the executor is treated as having made a QTIP election for it (unless the executor otherwise elects) on the decedent's estate tax return. The election, or the election to opt out, is irrevocable. [I.R.C. § 2056(b)(7)(C)]

Q 10:24 Is an IRA transferred outright to the surviving spouse a survivor annuity?

Yes. IRAs are treated as annuities under the estate tax rules, so if the SS is the sole DB of an IRA, it should qualify as a survivor annuity, and the executor will be deemed to have made the QTIP election. [I.R.C. § 2039; Instructions to IRS Form 706, United States Estate (and Generation-Skipping Transfer) Tax Return (rev. Sept. 2020), p. 30]

Q 10:25 How is a general power of appointment used to qualify an IRA transfer for the marital deduction?

The participant can designate a trust as beneficiary that gives the SS a qualifying income interest for life payable at least annually, but also gives the SS a general power to appoint the trust principal to the SS or his or her estate. The power must be exercisable by the SS alone, and no person can have the power to appoint any of the property to someone other than the SS. So, a general power trust is similar to a QTIP trust, but gives the SS more power. The general power trust qualifies for the marital deduction, but is rarely used because it offers no advantage over an outright transfer to the SS, at a greater cost. [I.R.C. § 2056(b)(5)]

Q 10:26 What is a charitable remainder trust?

A charitable remainder trust is a type of split-interest trust. If the SS is the only non-charitable beneficiary of a charitable remainder trust, and the other beneficiary is a qualified charity, the interest passing to the SS is not treated as a terminable interest and can qualify for the marital deduction. The value of the charitable interest qualifies for a charitable deduction from the gross estate. [I.R.C. § 2056(b)(8)]

There are two kinds of charitable remainder trusts: *charitable remainder annuity trusts* (CRATs) and *charitable remainder unitrusts* (CRUTs). If the IRA is transferred to a CRAT, the SS receives a fixed sum paid at least annually from the trust, over the life of the SS or a term not more than 20 years. The payment is fixed at the outset as a percentage (at least 5 percent, not more than 50 percent) of the IRA's initial fair market value when it is transferred to the trust. A CRUT is similar, except that payments to the SS are a fixed percentage (at least 5 percent, not more than 50 percent) of the net fair market value of the IRA, valued annually. [I.R.C. § 664(d)] When the SS dies (or the term ends), the trust assets pass to the charitable beneficiary.

The charitable remainder trust is a tax-exempt entity. That means no income tax is paid on IRA distributions to the trust, and the assets are fully available to be invested by the trust—and produce higher unitrust payments for the SS (in the case of a CRUT). The SS is taxed on the fixed or unitrust payments, which are received as IRD and can be offset by a deduction for the share of the estate tax (if any) that was attributable to inclusion of the SS's split interest in the first spouse's estate. [I.R.C. §§ 664(b), 664(c), 691]

Effect on Minimum Distributions

Q 10:27 How is estate planning for retirement benefits affected by SECURE?

SECURE completely changed the minimum distribution rules that apply to IRAs and most defined contribution plans after the participant dies. The new rules apply with respect to deaths after 2019, but also reach back to some deaths before 2020 (see Q 4:87, paragraph 4.b). The old system, under which designated beneficiaries (DBs) were entitled to life expectancy payouts, is gone. Only a small group of beneficiaries (*eligible designated beneficiaries*, or EDBs) now qualifies for payouts based on life expectancy, and when an EDB dies, the remaining benefits must be distributed to the successor within 10 years. EDBs include the participant's SS, a minor child of the participant (only until majority; then the 10-year rule applies), an individual who is disabled or chronically ill, and a person not more than 10 years younger than the participant. Nearly everyone else is required to take a full distribution of the benefits within 10 years after the participant dies. [SECURE § 401(b)(5)(A); I.R.C. § 401(a)(9)(H)(i), 401(a)(9)(B)(ii)] For details, see chapter 4.

As a result, many beneficiary designations, and most trusts for retirement benefits, will not work as was intended when they were drafted.

This section of the chapter 10 reviews the impact of the new minimum distribution rules on the different methods used to transfer retirement benefits to the SS. The discussion only addresses IRA benefits left to the SS, but other defined contribution plan benefits left to the SS can generally be rolled over to an IRA, subject to rules explained in chapter 6.

Q 10:28 What aspects of estate planning for retirement benefits are *not* affected by SECURE?

The SS who is designated as an IRA beneficiary continues to have all the same options as before (see Qs 10:1, 10:2) and remains subject to the same minimum distribution rules. The rules that govern beneficiary designations and see-through trusts are not changed, though of course the results of both are now quite different.

Q 10:29 What minimum distribution rule applies if the surviving spouse is designated as the beneficiary of an IRA?

This is an outright transfer of the IRA to the SS, so:

- The SS receives RMDs based on his/her life expectancy, which is recalculated each year. RMDS start in the calendar year when the participant would have reached age 72. [I.R.C. § 401(a)(9)(E)(ii)(I), 401(a)(9)(B)(i), 401(a)(9)(B)(iii), 401(a)(9)(B)(iv)(I)]
- After the SS dies, the balance of the IRA must be distributed to the successor beneficiary under the ten-year rule, even if the successor is an EDB. (For the special rule that applies if both the participant and the surviving spouse each die before the respective RBD, and the SS is the sole beneficiary, see Q 4:65.) [I.R.C. § 401(a)(9)(H)(iii)]
- The IRA also qualifies for the marital deduction as a survivor annuity (and the QTIP election is deemed to be made for it). (See Q 10:24.)

Q 10:30 How is the IRA distributed if it is payable to a conduit trust for the surviving spouse?

If the participant designates a conduit trust as the IRA beneficiary, and the SS is the conduit beneficiary, the result is the same as if the SS were designated as the IRA beneficiary:

- The SS is treated as the sole trust beneficiary and the sole plan beneficiary. The remainder beneficiaries are disregarded for purposes of the minimum distribution rules and may even include a charity or the SS's estate. [Treas. Reg. § 1.401(a)(9)-5, Q&A-7(c)(3), Example 2]
- The distribution rules are the same as in Q 10:29.

- The trust also qualifies for the marital deduction, on the same basis as an IRA transferred outright to the SS. But the QTIP election must be affirmatively made for both the IRA and the trust.

Q 10:31 How is the IRA distributed if is payable to a see-through accumulation trust?

An accumulation trust is a see-through trust if all the countable beneficiaries are individuals who are identifiable. Mere successor beneficiaries are ignored. (See Q 4:69.) [Treas. Reg. § 1.401(a)(9)-5, Q&A-7(c)(1)] If an IRA is payable to such a trust, it appears the IRA would have to be distributed under the 10-year rule—that is, within 10 years after the *participant* dies.

The result is uncertain because the SECURE amendments do not fit seamlessly with the rest of Code Section 401(a)(9) and the regulations.

- Section 401(a)(9)(H)(ii) provides that "subparagraph (B)(iii)" (which is now the 10-year rule) "shall apply only in the case of *an* [EDB]" (emphasis added).
- Section 401(a)(9)(H)(iii) states: "If *an* [EDB] dies before the... employee's interest... is entirely distributed, the exception under [Section 401(a)(9)(B)(ii)] shall not apply to *any beneficiary of such* [EDB] and the remainder... shall be distributed within 10 years after the death of *such* [EDB]." (emphasis added).

These provisions raise two issues. First, if the life beneficiary (perhaps the SS) is one EDB, and the remainder beneficiary is another EDB, is the life beneficiary subject to the life expectancy rule or the 10-year rule? That is, does (H)(ii) apply only if there is *one* EDB?

And, Second: if the life beneficiary does qualify for the life expectancy rule, does the remainder beneficiary also qualify for it? Or is the remainder beneficiary (who is an EDB) a "beneficiary" *of the life beneficiary* (which would require the 10-year rule to apply), even though he/she was chosen by the settlor, not the life beneficiary?

Without IRS guidance, new regulations, or a statutory amendment, it should be expected that such a trust would be required to take full distribution of the IRA within 10 years, so the tax on the IRA would be accelerated (unless it is a Roth IRA). The trust fiduciary could invest the assets, but the growth would no longer be tax free, and a high rate of income tax would apply with respect to assets accumulated in the trust.

Q 10:32 What distribution rule applies if the IRA is payable to an accumulation trust that is *not* a see-through trust?

The result in this case is the same as it was before the SECURE amendments. The IRA would have no designated beneficiary, so:

- If the participant dies on or after the RBD and the IRA is a traditional, SEP, or SIMPLE IRA, minimum distributions would be payable over the participant's remaining life expectancy (determined as if he/she had survived).

- If the participant dies before the RBD or the IRA is a Roth IRA, the IRA would have to be distributed to the trust within five years after the participant dies.

[I.R.C. § 401(a)(9)(B)(i), 401(a)(9)(B)(ii)]

Q 10:33 How will IRA benefits be distributed if they are paid to a QTIP trust?

A QTIP trust named as the IRA beneficiary may be structured as either a conduit or an accumulation trust. Only the conduit structure will guarantee a life expectancy payout for the IRA.

To qualify the QTIP trust as a conduit, the trustee must be required—by the trust terms—to distribute *currently* (in the taxable year of receipt) to the SS *all* payments it receives from the IRA. That means, with respect to the IRA, giving the SS a qualifying income interest for life is not enough. The SS must also (1) actually *receive* all the income each year (conduit status will fail if the second method described in Q 10:22, the "right to compel," is allowed), and (2) if any IRA payments to the trust exceed income they must also be distributed annually to the SS. [Treas. Reg. § 1.401(a)(9)-5, Q&A-7(c)(3), Example 2]

After SECURE, a QTIP trust should *not* be named as the IRA beneficiary if the trustee may keep any payment received from the IRA in the trust. If the QTIP accumulation trust qualifies as a see-through trust, the results in Q 10:31 apply. If it is not a see-through trust, the results in Q 10:32 apply. Either way, naming an "accumulation" type QTIP trust as the IRA beneficiary is an income tax disaster. The trust may qualify for the marital deduction, but this is a Pyrrhic victory.

Q 10:34 If the surviving spouse is disabled or chronically ill, what distribution rule applies if the IRA is payable to an applicable multi-beneficiary trust?

The applicable multi-beneficiary trust is a new kind of trust that qualifies for a life expectancy payout under the SECURE amendments. All trust beneficiaries must be EDBs, and at least one (the SS, in this case) must be chronically ill or disabled. The IRA will be paid to the trust over the life expectancy of the SS. (See Q 4:74 for details.)

Q 10:35 What distribution rule applies to an individual retirement trust?

An individual retirement trust (also called a trusteed IRA) will have to be fully distributed within 10 years after the participant dies. The beneficiary who succeeds to the interest after the SS dies cannot be disregarded, so the trust has no DB. [I.R.C. § 401(a)(9)(B)(i), 401(a)(9)(B)(ii)]

Chapter 11

Income in Respect of a Decedent

Jo Ann Lippe, Esq.

The value of an IRA on the date of the IRA owner's death represents gross income that he/she was entitled to collect, but did not collect while alive. The right to collect that income passes to the beneficiary of the inherited IRA. As the beneficiary receives distributions from the IRA, the amounts are received as "income in respect of a decedent" (IRD). The beneficiary includes them in gross income just as the decedent would have done.

The right to collect IRD is a property right, so its value as of the date of death is included in the decedent's gross estate. If estate tax is paid as a result of including that right in the estate, the beneficiary who collects and pays income tax on the IRD is allowed to deduct the amount of estate tax that was attributable to it.

This chapter explains how IRD is taken into account for income tax purposes when distributions are made from an inherited IRA to an individual beneficiary, a trust, or the decedent's estate. Since the situation is more complex in the case of a trust or estate, a general description of how a trust or estate is taxed is also included.

Income in Respect of a Decedent

Q 11:1 What is income in respect of a decedent?

Income in respect of a decedent (IRD) is an amount the decedent was entitled to receive as gross income, that was not properly includible in income for his/her last, or any prior, taxable year. [I.R.C. § 691(a); Treas. Reg. § 1.691(a)-1(b)] The right to receive income is a property right. So, the value of the right on the date of death is included in the decedent's gross estate. [I.R.C. § 2033]

Q 11:2 How is IRD taxable when other inheritances are not?

Except as otherwise provided (for example, in Code Section 102, which says that inheritances are not taxed), gross income means all income from whatever source derived, including (but not limited to) income in respect of a decedent, and income from an interest in an estate or trust. [I.R.C. § 61(a)(13), 61(a)(14)]

Q 11:3 What part of an inherited IRA is IRD?

The balance of the IRA on the date of death, less the decedent's basis in the IRA (generally, nondeductible contributions), is IRD. Post-death appreciation is not IRD. [Treas. Reg. § 1.691(a)-1(b); Rev. Rul. 92-47, 1992-1 C.B. 198; Treas. Reg. § 1.663(c)-5, Example 9]

Q 11:4 When is IRD included in income, and by whom?

IRD is included in income when received by:

- The estate of the decedent, if the estate acquired the right to receive it from the decedent. An example would be an IRA that is payable to the decedent's estate.
- Or, if the estate did not acquire the right from the decedent, then the person who acquired the right by reason of the decedent's death. This would apply, for example, if the decedent designated his/her surviving spouse as the IRA beneficiary.
- Or, the person who acquires the right from the decedent by bequest, devise, or inheritance, if the amount is received after a distribution by the decedent's estate of such right. This would apply, for example, if the decedent failed to designate a beneficiary for the IRA, the will requires the estate residue to go to the surviving spouse, and the estate transfers the IRA to the surviving spouse.

[I.R.C. § 691(a)]

Q 11:5 What deduction is allowed with respect to IRD?

The person who includes IRD in gross income is entitled to deduct, for income tax purposes, the share of the estate tax that was paid with respect to that IRD. The deduction is allowed in the same year that the IRD is collected and included in gross income. [I.R.C. § 691(c)]

Since the IRD is both subject to estate tax and includible in gross income when collected, there is the potential for double taxation. The deduction is allowed to mitigate the burden. But the deduction is inefficient. It limits, but does not eliminate, the double taxation. Also, the estate tax on the IRD may have been paid from non-IRD assets (and thus paid by another person).

Q 11:6 How is the deduction computed?

This is best explained with an example. Assume that Alice dies in 2020, leaving a $5 million taxable estate, and the only IRD asset in the estate is her $1,000,000 traditional IRA (with zero basis). Her husband, Rex, is the only designated beneficiary of the IRA.

1. The estate tax attributable to the inclusion of all IRD items in the estate is determined. Start with the estate tax actually paid by the estate. Then refigure the tax that would result if the IRD items were not part of the estate. The difference is the IRD attributable to all items of IRD. (This is a favorable method because it assigns the highest marginal estate tax rate to the IRD items.)
   - Alice's IRA is the only IRD item in her estate. Its value on the date of her death is all IRD (because only deductible contributions were made). The difference between the actual estate tax paid and the tax refigured without including the IRA in the estate is $400,000. This is the total 691(c) deduction that Rex is allowed.
2. If there is more than one IRD item in the estate, the total estate tax attributable to all IRD items is allocated among them in proportion to their relative values in the estate. The result for each IRD asset is the total 691(c) deduction allowed for that asset.
   - This does not apply to Alice's estate.
3. Divide the total 691(c) deduction by the estate value of the IRD item. The result is the fraction of each IRD payment that can be claimed as a 691(c) deduction:
   - The date-of-death value of Alice's IRA is $1,000,000. The total 691(c) deduction will be $400,000. Consequently, for each payment of IRD that Rex receives, he will claim (and reduce his total 691(c) deduction by) an amount equal to 40 percent of such IRD payment.
4. Determine the amount of each payment that is IRD. Surprisingly, there is no official guidance for how to do this. (There is a rule for allocating IRD to payments received under a joint survivor annuity contract,

but an IRA is not such a contract.) In the absence of guidance, the common approach taken is to treat IRD as being distributed first from the IRA.

- Assume that the IRA value has grown to $1,100,000 on December 31, 2020, and that the distribution period used to calculate Rex's first RMD (at age 72) will be 25.6 years. Rex's first RMD, paid in 2021, will be $42,969. He will include that amount in gross income as IRD. He will also claim a 691(c) deduction of $17,187 (40 percent of the IRD inclusion).
- Rex will continue to do that each year until the entire 691(c) deduction is consumed.

Q 11:7 What happens to the deduction if the IRA depreciates after the date of death?

This can cause some of the deduction to be lost. Suppose the value of Alice's IRA (in Q 11:6) fell to $900,000 on December 31, 2020. If Rex were to cash it out on that date, only $900,000 of IRD would be recognized. Rex's 691(c) deduction would be limited to $360,000 (40 percent of $900,000). The other $40,000 of estate tax paid with respect to the IRA could not be recouped.

Q 11:8 How is the deduction claimed?

The Code Section 691(c) deduction is claimed as an itemized deduction. [I.R.C. § 67(g)] An individual must have deductions in excess of the standard deduction to gain any benefit from it. The standard deduction is temporarily doubled (through 2025) doubled and will return to the prior level (with inflation adjustments) in 2026. [I.R.C. § 63] Also in 2026, the 691(c) deduction will again be subject to the income-based limitation of Code Section 68 (which is temporarily repealed through 2025).

The Section 691(c) deduction is allowed in computing the alternative minimum tax.

Transfer of the IRA by a Trust or the Estate

Q 11:9 Is the transfer of an IRA taxable if made to fulfill a specific or residuary bequest?

No, because such a transfer is not a "sale." [I.R.C. § 691(b)(2)]

The transfer of the decedent's IRA is the transfer of a right to receive income in respect of the decedent. If the right to receive IRD is transferred by the estate of the decedent, or a person who received the right by reason of the decedent's death, or by bequest, devise, or inheritance from the decedent, then the transferor must include the fair market value of the right (at the time of transfer) in gross income. [I.R.C. § 691(a)(2), first sentence]

Example 1. The executor of Rhea's estate sells her uncollected accounts receivable for cash. The estate includes the sale price in gross income as IRD.

But the second sentence of Section 691(a)(2) says: "the term "transfer" . . . does not include transmission at death to the estate of the decedent or a transfer to a person pursuant to the right of such person to receive such amount by reason of the death of the decedent or by bequest, devise, or inheritance from the decedent." The regulations under Section 691 also say: "If a trust to which is bequeathed a right of a decedent to certain payments of income terminates and transfers the right to a beneficiary, only the beneficiary must include such income in gross income when received." [Treas. Reg. § 1.691(a)-4(b)(3)]

Example 2. Maury's IRA is payable to a trust established under his will. His sister and brother each have a 50% share of the IRA, which is a trust asset. Instead of cashing out the IRA, the trustee asks the IRA administrator to divide it into two equal shares and transfer each share to a separate inherited IRA. One inherited IRA will be titled with Maury's sister as beneficiary, and the other with his brother as beneficiary. The trust transfers each inherited IRA to the respective beneficiary. The transfer is not taxable to the trust. Each beneficiary will include the IRD in gross income as distributions are taken.

Q 11:10 Is the transfer of the IRA taxable if it is made pursuant to a pecuniary bequest?

This depends on whether the bequest is determined by a formula or is a specific dollar amount that does not depend on the value of the decedent's property.

If the bequest is a specific dollar amount, the transfer of the right to receive IRD is treated as a sale. But if it is determined by a formula, it is not a sale, and not taxable. An example of a formula bequest is a will that directs the executor to fund a trust with the maximum amount of property that can be transferred without being subject to estate tax (i.e., the decedent's exemption amount). The executor cannot determine how much of the exemption will be used until expenses of the estate and other items are taken into account, so this is not treated as a sale.

Retention of the IRA by a Trust or the Estate

Background—Income Taxation of a Trust or Estate

Q 11:11 How are amounts received by a trust or the decedent's estate taxed?

In general, a trust is taxed on income that it retains. Beneficiaries are taxed on income that the trust receives and passes through currently (in the same taxable year) to the beneficiaries entitled to receive it. Distributions that exceed the trust's income are not taxed to the beneficiaries. [I.R.C. §§ 651, 652, 661, 662]

Q 11:12 What determines whether an amount set aside for or distributed to a beneficiary is taxable to the beneficiary?

This is determined by the fiduciary and tax accounting that are conducted by the trustee.

- The allocation of amounts to fiduciary accounting income (FAI) determines the total amount of trust income that is available for distribution to the beneficiaries who are entitled to receive income currently (in the taxable year the trust receives it).
- The allocation of the trust's distributable net income (DNI) determines who bears the tax burden. An amount properly paid or credited to a beneficiary, or a distribution required to be made (whether or not it is made) is only taxed to the extent it carries out DNI. (See Qs 11:16, 11:17.)

Q 11:13 What is fiduciary accounting income?

FAI is an accounting concept. Amounts received by a trust are allocated between the income and corpus ("principal" in accounting language) portions of a trust according to the fiduciary accounting rules. FAI is not the same as taxable income.

A well-drafted trust instrument defines "income." If no definition is included, then the allocation of amounts to income is determined under applicable state law. Most states have adopted a version of the Uniform Fiduciary Income and Principal Act (UFIPA). Section 409 of the UFIPA prescribes rules for allocating retirement distributions between FAI and corpus, in cases where the trust is the IRA beneficiary.

The UFIPA treats the IRA as a separate trust within the trust that actually receives the IRA distributions. If more than one retirement plan is payable to the trust, each is treated as a separate trust within the trust. [UFIPA § 409(a)(4)]

For each accounting period, the trustee:

1. Determines the "internal income" of the IRA as if it were a separate trust subject to the UFIPA rules. If the trustee is unable to do so, such income is presumed to be a set percentage (not less than 3 percent, nor more than 5 percent, and defined in the trust instrument) of the IRA's fair market value at the end of the prior accounting period. If the trustee cannot determine the fair market value, the internal income is presumed to be the present value of the expected future payments from the IRA, as determined under Code Section 7520. [UFIPA § 409(b)]
2. Allocates distributions received by the trust between FAI and corpus. An IRA distribution is allocated to FAI to the extent of the IRA's internal income for that accounting period. If the distribution exceeds the IRA's internal income for the period, the balance is allocated to corpus. For example, if the trust collects a required minimum distribution (RMD) that exceeds the IRA's internal income for the period, the amount that is equal to the internal income is allocated to FAI, and the rest is allocated to corpus. [UFIPA § 409(c)]

3. What happens next depends on whether or not the trust is a marital deduction trust (Qs 10:16–10:22), UFIPA Section 409(d) was specifically amended in 2018 to assure compliance with the IRS's interpretation of the marital deduction requirements. [UFIPA, Final Act with Comments by the National Conference of Commissioners on Uniform State Laws, Comment on Section 409, p. 69 (2018), available at *https://www.uniformlaws.org/viewdocument/final-act-with-comments-41?CommunityKey = 1105f9bb-eb93-4d4d-a1ab-a535ef73de0c&tab = librarydocuments* (retrieved Oct. 25, 2020)]
   a. For a trust that is *not* a marital deduction trust, if the IRA distribution is less than the IRA's internal income for the period, and more than one trust beneficiary is entitled to a distribution of *all* the current FAI from the IRA, then the trustee transfers the shortfall amount from corpus to income. [UFIPA § 409(e)]
   b. But if the IRA is payable to a marital deduction trust, the trustee must allocate the withdrawn RMD to FAI, and distribute that amount to the SS. [Code § 401(a)(9); UFIPA § 409(d)] If the RMD is less than the IRA's internal income for the same period, the surviving spouse (SS) can compel the trustee (under the trust terms) to make up the difference by withdrawing more from the IRA. [UFIPA § 409(d)(1); Rev. Rul. 2006-26, 2006-1 C.B. 939]
      i. If the SS exercises that right and asks the trustee to withdraw the shortfall (or at least part of it), the trustee must withdraw the amount requested from the IRA, allocate it to FAI, and distribute it to the SS. [UFIPA § 409(d)(2)]
      ii. If the SS does not exercise that right, or asks for less than the full shortfall, and the trustee withdraws more from the IRA, then the trustee can allocate its additional withdrawal to FAI, and distribute that to the SS, too. But, the sum of (1) the amount requested by the SS, plus (2) the additional withdrawal by the trustee, cannot exceed the shortfall of the RMD from the IRA's internal income for the accounting period. [UFIPA § 409(d)(2) and (3)]

Q 11:14 What is distributable net income?

DNI is a tax concept. DNI is the taxable income of a trust, determined without regard to the deduction allowed for certain distributions to trust beneficiaries, tax-exempt interest, and the trust's personal exemption. Capital gains and losses are also usually excluded from the computation. [I.R.C. § 643(a)]

Q 11:15 What is the separate share rule?

If a trust has more than one beneficiary, then "substantially separate and independent shares" of different beneficiaries in the trust are treated as if they were separate trusts. [I.R.C. § 663(c)]

Example. The beneficiary of Pete's IRA is a trust established under his will. The trust also holds various securities that Pete owned at the time he died. The trust has two beneficiaries. Until the respective 30th birthday of each, Caroline is entitled to current payment of all dividend and interest income from the securities, and Mina is entitled to current payment of all RMDs distributed from the IRA. As soon as practicable after each reaches age 30, the trustee will distribute the securities to Caroline, and the IRA to Mina. Caroline and Mina have separate and independent shares of the trust. Dividends and interest received by the trust can only be distributed to Caroline, so all DNI attributable to such income passes through to her. All DNI attributable to RMDs passes through to Mina.

Q 11:16 How is DNI allocated to distributions from a simple trust?

The terms of a simple trust require the trustee to distribute all FAI currently to the beneficiaries. A simple trust cannot reserve any income, and cannot pay or reserve any amounts for charitable purposes. In computing its taxable income, such a trust is allowed to deduct the amount of FAI for the taxable year which is required to be distributed currently or, if less, the trust's DNI for the taxable year. [I.R.C. § 651]

The trust's FAI required to be distributed currently is included in the gross income of the beneficiaries who are required to receive it. If that amount exceeds DNI, then DNI is prorated among the beneficiaries entitled to receive FAI, in proportion to the amount each is entitled to receive. [I.R.C. § 652]

Q 11:17 How is DNI allocated to distributions from a complex trust, or the decedent's estate?

A complex trust is not required to distribute all of its FAI currently. FAI may be distributed, accumulated, or used for charitable purposes, in accordance with the particular terms of the trust and applicable state law. The trust instrument determines the amounts that must be or are permitted to be distributed. Estates are taxed according to the same rules as complex trusts. [I.R.C. § 651]

In computing its taxable income, a complex trust is allowed a deduction for the sum of "Tier 1" and "Tier 2" amounts or, if less, the trust's DNI for the taxable year:

- Tier 1 is the FAI for the taxable year (current FAI) that is required to be distributed currently. If any amount that must be distributed can be paid from either FAI or corpus, it is included in Tier 1 to the extent it is paid from current FAI.
- Tier 2 is "other amounts properly paid or credited or required to be distributed for such taxable year." [I.R.C. § 661(a)]

(Charitable distributions are also taken into account but are ignored here for simplicity.)

A trust beneficiary includes in gross income his/her share of the trust's Tier 1 and Tier 2 amounts. If the sum of the trust's Tier 1 and Tier 2 amounts allocable to *all* trust beneficiaries for the taxable year exceeds DNI, then DNI is allocated as follows:

- DNI is allocated first to Tier 1 amounts. If more than one beneficiary is entitled to Tier 1 amounts and the total amount in Tier 1 for all beneficiaries exceeds the trust's DNI, then DNI is allocated in proportion to the share of Tier 1 amounts that the beneficiary is entitled to receive—taking into account the separate share rule if it applies.
- Any DNI that is left after the allocation to Tier 1 is allocated to Tier 2 in the same manner. That is, if DNI exceeds the combined Tier 2 amounts, then DNI is allocated to Tier 2 beneficiaries in proportion to the Tier 2 amounts they receive. [I.R.C. § 662; Treas. Reg. § 1.662(a)-3(c)]

Since DNI determines allocation of the tax burden, a beneficiary is taxed on allocations of DNI. Amounts properly set aside, credited, or distributed that do *not* carry DNI are not taxed; they are considered to come from the trust corpus.

The exclusion of capital gains from DNI (with some exceptions) means that the tax burden with respect to capital gains is not shifted from the trust to the beneficiaries.

Passthrough of IRD

Q 11:18 How is IRD allocated to distributions from a trust or the decedent's estate?

Four factors determine how IRD is allocated to distributions from a trust or the decedent's estate.

1. If there is more than one beneficiary, do they have separate and independent shares? Are there separate shares (under the 663(c) rule)?
2. Is the amount FAI or corpus?
3. Does the governing document provide for the allocation of the item among beneficiaries?
4. If not, does applicable state law?

Q 11:19 How is the IRD taxed if an IRA distribution to the trust is allocated to fiduciary accounting income?

The part of the IRA payment to the trust that is IRD is included in the trust's gross income, and (since it is ordinary income) is also included in DNI. Like any other amount that the trust receives, it is allocated to either FAI or corpus. If the IRD amount is FAI, then the IRD (and the 691(c) deduction) pass to the beneficiary to whom the amount is required to be distributed (or paid or credited) in the same taxable year. [Treas. Reg. § 1.691(c)-2(a)(1)]

Q 11:20 How is the IRD taxed if the IRA distribution is allocated to corpus?

If the amount that is IRD is allocated to corpus in the taxable year when it is received, and there are separate shares, there are four possible scenarios (see Qs 11:21–11:24). This can arise, for example, if the IRA is cashed out. The proceeds would be allocated to corpus.

Corpus and the Separate Share Rule

Q 11:21 How is the IRD taxed if the separate share rule applies and the trust instrument allocates the IRA to only one share?

If the trust instrument allocates the IRA proceeds to a particular share, and they are distributed (from corpus) to the beneficiary of that share in the same year, the distribution carries out all of the IRD. The beneficiary includes the IRD in gross income and is entitled to the 691(c) deduction. [I.R.C. § 663(c); Treas. Reg. § 1.663(c)-5, Example 9]

Example 1. Paula's will establishes a testamentary trust that is funded with her IRA (with a zero basis) and real estate. The trust provides for the real property to be distributed to Esme, and the IRA to be distributed to Frank, when each reaches age 35. Until then, all rents are paid currently to Esme, and RMDs are all paid currently to Frank. When Paula dies, Esme is age 32, and Frank is 35. The trustee cashes out the IRA (it is allocated to corpus) and distributes the proceeds ($1 million) in the same year to Frank. All the IRD is allocated to Frank, who includes it in income and is entitled to the 691(c) deduction.

Example 2. Krishna dies in 2021 and his will directs the executor to divide the estate residue into two equal shares, one for each of his children. The date-of-death value of the residue (allocated to corpus) is $15 million. The will requires the executor to fund the older child's share first with Krishna's IRA. The executor takes a full distribution of the IRA in 2021 and allocates the proceeds ($2 million) to corpus. If any distribution is made to *either* child during 2021, *all* the IRD must be allocated to the older child's share.

Instead of cashing out the IRA, the executor could distribute the IRA intact to the older child. The transfer would not be a taxable event (see Q 11:9), and the child would recognize the IRD as distributions are taken.

Q 11:22 What is the result if the trust instrument specifies the percentage of the IRA that is allocated to each share?

If the trust instrument allocates a percentage of the IRA to each share, and the trustee cashes it out (the proceeds are allocated to corpus) and distributes the entire proceeds to one of the beneficiaries in the same year, then the distribution only carries out that share's percentage of the IRA as IRD. The trust must include the rest of the IRD in its gross income. The 691(c) deduction follows with the IRD. [I.R.C. § 663(c)]

Example 3. The facts are the same as Q 11:21, Example 1, except the trust instrument entitles Frank and Esme to half of each asset (the real estate and the IRA). The trust still cashes out the IRA and distributes all the proceeds ($1 million) to Frank. In this case, the distribution to Frank only carries out half of the IRD. The rest of the IRD stays with the trust. The trust and Frank each have $500,000 of gross income from IRD, and each can claim half of the 691(c) deduction.

Q 11:23 What is the result if state law requires shares to be funded from assets on a pro rata basis?

If the trust document is silent as to which assets will be used to fund the shares, but applicable state law requires shares to be funded from trust assets on a pro rata basis, the result is the same as in Q 11:22.

Q 11:24 If the trust instrument gives the trustee discretion to choose the assets that will fund each share, how is the IRD taxed?

If the trust document gives the trustee discretion to choose the assets to fund each share, then when the IRA is cashed out, the trustee must use a reasonable and equitable method to allocate the IRD among the separate shares *that could potentially be funded with such amount* (whether or not the share is entitled to FAI) using a "reasonable and equitable method." [Treas. Reg. §§ 1.663(c)-2(b)(3), 1.663(c)-5, Example 6]

Example 4. Ken's estate has two beneficiaries—his surviving spouse, and an exemption trust for his child. The will includes a formula bequest for the trust. It is to be funded with the largest amount of assets that can pass to the trust without estate tax (i.e., the estate tax exemption amount). Ken's surviving spouse gets the residue of the estate, and all the income from it. The IRA is distributed to the estate. The estate receives an IRA distribution of $900,000 (all IRD). Local law requires allocation of the $900,000 to corpus.

Since either share may potentially be funded with the IRA, the trustee must allocate the IRD to the two shares of the estate based upon the relative values of the two separate shares, using a reasonable and equitable method. The trust includes in gross income the IRD allocated to its share. The estate includes the rest of the IRD in gross income. The 691(c) deduction follows the IRD.

Chapter 12

Simplified Employee Pension Plans

The simplified employee pension (SEP) plan was created so that small employers could use IRAs to provide retirement benefits for their employees without being subject to the complex disclosure, funding, and approval requirements of a qualified ERISA plan. A SEP may be adopted by any employer, whether a corporation, a limited liability company, a general partnership, a limited liability partnership, or a sole proprietorship. Once a SEP is in place, all eligible employees of the employer must be covered by the SEP, even seasonal and part-time workers.

Some employers may permit eligible employees to make elective contributions under its SEP; this type of SEP is commonly called a salary reduction SEP (SARSEP). Although SARSEPs were repealed by the Small Business Job Protection Act of 1996 (SBJPA), a SARSEP established before January 1, 1997, may continue to receive contributions.

The Setting Every Community Up for Retirement Enhancement Act (SECURE Act), Div. O of the Further Consolidated Appropriations Act, 2020, Pub. L. No. 116-94 (Dec. 20, 2019) made many changes that affect IRA distributions, particularly those made to beneficiaries after the participant's death.

Overview

Q 12:1 What is a simplified employee pension plan?

A *simplified employee pension plan* (SEP) is a written arrangement under which an IRA (*SEP IRA*) is established for each participant and the employer makes contributions to it based on the participant's compensation. The employer is not required to make contributions every year. A SEP IRA may be established as a traditional IRA (or traditional individual retirement annuity), but not as a Roth IRA. The contributions are deductible by the employer and excluded from the participant's income until they are distributed. [I.R.C. § 408(k)(1); Prop. Treas. Reg. § 1.408-7(a)]

Internal Revenue Code (Code) Section 408(a), (b), and (c) set forth the requirements for a valid IRA that is part of a SEP arrangement. Code Section 408(k)(2) through 408(k)(5) and Code Section 416(c)(2) (if the plan is top heavy) are specific to SEPs.

Typically, an employee selects, establishes, and maintains the IRA into which employer SEP contributions are made. Group IRAs, which may be established by an employer or by an employee association under Section 408(c) of the Code, may qualify as SEPs if additional requirements are met.

Q 12:2 What is a salary reduction SEP, or SARSEP?

A *salary reduction SEP* (also called a SARSEP) is a SEP plan that includes an elective salary deferral feature. It is no longer possible to establish a new

SARSEP, but SARSEPs that were established and effective before January 1, 1997, are grandfathered and may continue to operate if they meet all requirements (see Q 12:52). [I.R.C. § 408(k)(6)(H)]

The 1997 cutoff date does not apply to determine participant eligibility. Recently hired individuals may participate in a grandfathered SARSEP.

Example 1. Sound Company has had a SEP since 1991. It established a SARSEP effective January 1, 1996, and all employees elected to participate. Sound can continue to maintain its SARSEP after December 31, 1996, because it has been grandfathered.

Example 2. Light Company has never maintained a retirement program. As of December 31, 1996, it established a SARSEP using Form 5305A-SEP but none of the employees established an IRA. Because Light did not completely establish a SARSEP by December 31, 1996, the grandfather rules do not apply to it (or to any successor company).

Q 12:3 How are SEP contributions taxed?

For federal income tax purposes, SEP contributions (including elective salary deferrals under a SARSEP) that do not exceed applicable limits are excluded from a participant's income, and deductible by the employer. [I.R.C. §§ 408(k), 402(g), 402(h), 404(h)(1)(C)] (For the treatment of excess contributions, see Qs 12:80–12:85.)

Q 12:4 Are SEP contributions subject to Social Security and Medicare?

Employer contributions are *not* subject to Social Security and Medicare taxes. However, salary reduction contributions (including catch-up contributions) made by a SARSEP participant are subject to those taxes. [I.R.C. §§ 3121(a)(5)(C), 3306(b)(5)(C)]

Establishing a SEP

Q 12:5 What employers may have a SEP plan?

Any employer, whether a corporation, a limited liability company, a general partnership, a limited liability partnership, or a sole proprietorship, may establish and maintain a SEP plan. Self-employed individuals may have a SEP even if they also participate in another employer's retirement plan.

Q 12:6 How is a SEP established?

To establish a new SEP, an employer must adopt a written plan agreement, provide written information about the plan to all employees (see Q 12:93), and ensure that each eligible employee has a SEP IRA. A tax credit is available to offset the employer's costs of establishing a new SEP plan (see Q 12:20).

Q 12:7 What is the deadline for establishing a SEP?

A new SEP can be established until the due date (including extensions) of the employer's income tax return for the first year.

Q 12:8 What is a SEP's plan year?

Most SEPs are maintained on the basis of the calendar year. For some SEPs, the employer may use its own tax year as the plan year. [I.R.C. § 408(k)(7)(C)]

Plan Agreement

Q 12:9 Does the IRS have a model SEP agreement?

Yes. The model agreement is Form 5305-SEP, Simplified Employee Pension-Individual Retirement Accounts Contribution Agreement. A SEP established using Form 5305-SEP has automatic IRS approval as to its form (but not its operation).

An employer may *not* use Form 5305-SEP to establish a SEP plan if any of the following is true:

1. The employer currently maintains a qualified plan. [IRS Form 5305-SEP, instructions]
2. The employer is not willing to pay the cost of the SEP contribution.
3. Any eligible employee does not have an IRA. [IRS Form 5305-SEP, instructions]
4. The employer uses the services of any leased employees. [I.R.C. § 414(n)]
5. The employer is not willing to include all eligible employees, including employees of related, controlled, and affiliated employers (see Qs 12:30, 12:31). [IRS Form 5305-SEP, instructions]

Q 12:10 Does the IRS have a model SARSEP agreement?

Yes, but it cannot be used to establish a new SARSEP. The model form can only be used to *update* a grandfathered SARSEP plan. [Form 5305A-SEP, Salary Reduction and Other Elective Simplified Employee Pension-Individual Retirement Accounts Contribution Agreement.]

The current version of the model agreement (rev. June 2006) must be used to update a SARSEP. [SARSEP Fix-It Guide, available at *https://www.irs.gov/Retirement-Plans/SARSEP-Plan-Fix-It-Guide*] But an employer may *not* use Form 5305A-SEP if any of the following is true:

1. The employer has leased employees as defined in Code Section 414(n)(2). [IRS Form 5305A-SEP, instructions]
2. The employer currently maintains a qualified plan. [IRS Form 5305A-SEP, instructions]

3. The employer had more than 25 employees eligible to participate in the SEP at any time during the prior calendar year. For affiliated employers that are treated as a single employer (see Qs 12:30, 12:31), all their employees eligible to participate in the prior year are aggregated. [IRS Form 5305A-SEP, instructions]
4. The employer has an eligible employee who does not have an IRA.
5. The employer is a state or local government or a tax-exempt organization. [IRS Form 5305A-SEP, instructions]

Q 12:11 What may be included in a prototype or individually designed SEP plan?

Some features not allowed in a model plan may be included in a prototype or individually designed plan. Prototype SEPs are generally offered to employers by financial institutions, which may also provide administrative and technical services to employers.

Qualifying organizations may file Form 5306-A, Application for Approval of Prototype Simplified Employee Pension (SEP), with the IRS for approval of a prototype SEP. The IRS will not issue opinion letters on prototype SEPs that consolidate a SEP plan and an IRA into one document.

A prototype SEP may also be drafted and submitted by a mass submitter to the IRS National Office for approval. Once approved, the prototype plan may be sponsored by banks or other financial institutions for their customers.

The IRS provides sample language that may be used to draft a prototype SEP plan or amend an existing SARSEP plan. There is a separate document, called a *Listing of Required Modifications and Information Package* (LRM), for each. [LRM for prototype SEPs (rev. Mar. 2002), available at *http://www.irs.gov/pub/irs-tege/sep_lrm.pdf*; LRM for prototype SARSEPs (rev. Mar. 2002), available at *http://www.irs.gov/pub/irs-tege/sarsep_lrm.pdf*]

Practice Pointer. A copy of the IRS opinion letter approving the prototype SEP must be furnished to employers that use that agreement.

Q 12:12 What organizations qualify to sponsor a prototype SEP?

An organization seeking to qualify as a sponsor of a prototype SEP must be one of the following:

- A trade or professional organization (other than an employee association) having characteristics similar to those described in Treasury Regulations Section 1.501(c)(6)-1;
- A bank (as defined in Code Section 581);
- An insured credit union (within the meaning of Section 101(6) of the Federal Credit Union Act);
- A regulated investment company (as defined in Code Section 851);

- An investment advisor under a contract with one or more regulated investment companies;
- A principal underwriter that has a principal underwriting contract with one or more regulated investment companies; or
- A person that, under the Treasury regulations, may act as a trustee or custodian of an IRA (nonbank trustee or custodian).

When the sponsoring organization is an insurance company, the IRS will issue an opinion letter, if requested to do so, as to whether a specific prototype individual annuity contract, within the meaning of the regulations, meets the requirements of Code Section 408(b).

Q 12:13 May an employer adopting a prototype SEP rely on the IRS opinion letter that was issued to the prototype sponsor?

Yes. If a particular employer adopts a prototype SEP arrangement in accordance with the form approved by the IRS and observes its provisions, that employer may rely on the opinion letter as long as:

1. SEP contributions are made to a model IRA or an IRS-approved master or prototype IRA, and
2. Contributions under the SEP arrangement do not (in combination with another SEP arrangement or any terminated qualified defined benefit plan of the employer) fail to satisfy the requirements of Code Section 415 (see Q 12:70).

Q 12:14 May a prototype SEP be used by an employer that currently maintains a master or prototype defined contribution plan?

Yes. If an employer maintains a master or prototype defined contribution plan, the plan document most likely contains language that will coordinate contributions under that plan with any other master or prototype defined contribution plan or SEP maintained by the same employer. [*See, e.g.*, Defined Contribution LRM, item 31 (8-2005), available at *http://www.irs.gov/pub/irs-tege/dc_lrm.pdf*.] If a qualified plan does not contain language that coordinates contributions made under it with a SEP and is maintained with a SEP, it may not satisfy Code Section 415.

Q 12:15 How may a sponsor of a prototype SEP ensure relief from ERISA's reporting requirements?

Under Title I of ERISA, relief from the annual reporting requirements is *not* available to an employer that selects, recommends, or in any other way influences employees to choose a particular IRA or type of IRA to which contributions under the SEP will be made if those IRAs are subject to restrictions that prohibit the withdrawal of funds for any period (other than restrictions imposed by the Code that apply to all IRAs). If, however, an employer that sponsors a nonmodel (i.e., prototype) SEP selects the IRAs to which contributions will be made and such IRAs make available to participants an option that imposes a restriction on withdrawals, the plan administrator for that SEP (generally the employer) is not precluded from using the alternative method of compliance under Department of Labor (DOL) Regulations Section 2520.104-49, provided:

1. Other meaningful investment options that do not restrict withdrawals are available to participants;
2. The employer does not select, recommend, or otherwise influence any participant's choice of an available investment option under the IRAs; and
3. All other conditions of the regulation are satisfied.

[DOL Reg. §§ 2520.104-48(c), 2520.104-49(a)(1)(iv); IRS Forms 5305-SEP, 5305A-SEP]

Example. The Five Cents Savings Bank (Bank) establishes a nonmodel SEP for its employees. The terms of the SEP require all eligible employees to establish their IRAs with the Bank. In most other respects, the terms of the IRA and SEP follow Form 5305 and Form 5305-SEP, which contain no restrictions on withdrawals, and the Bank has not added withdrawal restrictions. Investments under the plan are at the direction of the participant and are not under the control of any other person.

Through its IRAs, the Bank offers various investment options to participants, including regular savings, term certificates, and "special notice accounts." Neither the regular savings nor the term certificates impose any restrictions on withdrawals by the participant; however, the special notice accounts do not allow withdrawal of funds held on deposit for less than 90 days.

The Bank is not precluded from using the alternative method of compliance for its SEP, because meaningful investment options that do not restrict withdrawals are available to participants. The Bank does not select, recommend, or otherwise influence any participant's choice of an investment option available under the IRAs, and all other conditions of the applicable regulation are satisfied.

Q 12:16 How may IRS approval be requested for an individually designed SEP?

An employer may submit a request for a letter ruling to the National Office of the IRS regarding the acceptability of an individually designed SEP or SARSEP arrangement. The IRS imposes a one-time user fee of $2,500 per application. If a mass submitter applies on behalf of word-for-word adopters of a particular prototype SEP IRA, only the first 300 of such applications submitted within a 12-month period ending January 31 are subject to the fee. [Rev. Proc. 2021-4, 2021-1 I.R.B. 157, Appendix A § .02]

SEP IRAs

Q 12:17 What is a SEP IRA?

The SEP IRA is the traditional IRA established with a bank, insurance company, or other financial institution that receives SEP contributions made by the employer on the participant's behalf. If the plan is a SARSEP, the SEP IRA also receives the participant's elective salary reduction contributions. Every SEP participant must have a SEP IRA. The employer may help with setting it up, but each participant owns and controls his/her SEP IRA.

A Roth IRA cannot be used as a SEP IRA. [I.R.C. § 408A(f)(1)]

Q 12:18 Does the IRS have model SEP IRA forms?

The employer may use one of the IRS model forms for a traditional IRA. [Form 5305, Individual Retirement Trust Account; Form 5305-A, Individual Retirement Custodial Account]

Q 12:19 May a participant's *regular* traditional IRA contributions be deposited into the SEP IRA?

Yes, subject to the annual contribution limit for traditional IRA contributions. Such contributions are not subject to SEP contribution limits.

Incentive Tax Credits

Q 12:20 What tax credit is an employer allowed for establishing a new SEP?

A small business that adopts a new retirement plan (SEP, SIMPLE, defined contribution plan, or defined benefit plan) can generally claim the *small employer pension plan startup cost credit* against income tax. Until recently, the credit was 50 percent of the first $1,000 in administrative and retirement-education expenses incurred for each of the first three years of the plan. Now, for tax years beginning after 2019, the credit is increased for each such year to the *greater* of:

- $500, or
- The lesser of $250 for each employee who is not a highly compensated employee (HCE; see Q 12:46), or $5,000.

[I.R.C. § 45E, as amended by the Setting Every Community Up for Retirement Enhancement Act of 2019 (SECURE Act), Div. O of the Further Consolidated Appropriations Act, 2020, Pub. L. No. 116-94 (Dec. 20, 2019)]

To be eligible for the credit, an employer must have had 100 or fewer employees with compensation in excess of $5,000 during the previous tax year. The employer must also have had at least one non-highly compensated employee (NHCE). For these determinations, employers that are members of a controlled group are treated as a single employer (see the aggregation rules in Qs 12:31, 12:32). [I.R.C. §§ 45E(e)(1), 408(p)(2)(C)(i)]

The credit is not allowed, however, if the new plan covers substantially the same employees as were covered by another plan of the employer (or a member of the same controlled group) during the three-taxable-year period immediately preceding the first year for which the credit would otherwise be allowed. [I.R.C. § 45E(c)(2)]

The small employer pension plan startup cost credit is taken as a general business credit on the employer's tax return. To claim it, the employer uses Form 8881, Credit for Small Employer Plan Startup Costs. Expenses for which the credit is claimed are not tax deductible. However, the non-credited portion of those expenses may be taken as a business deduction. [I.R.C. §§ 45E, 38(b)(14)]

The Section 45E credit may be claimed in addition to the credit described in Q 12:21 if the new plan includes an auto-enrollment feature.

Q 12:21 What tax credit is allowed for including an automatic enrollment feature in the plan?

For tax years starting after 2019, eligible small business employers are allowed a $500 income tax credit for each of the first three taxable years in which an eligible automatic contribution arrangement is included in a SEP, SIMPLE, defined contribution plan, or defined benefit plan. [I.R.C. §§ 38(b)(33), 45T (as added by SECURE Act § 105)] This retirement automatic enrollment credit is allowed in addition to the credit for plan start-up expenses under Code Section 45E.

Generally, a plan has an eligible automatic contribution arrangement if the employer can unilaterally enroll participants and contribute on their behalf a specified percentage of compensation each year and participants may elect either to receive cash in lieu of deferral or to defer at a different percentage. Notice requirements also apply. [I.R.C. §§ 45T(b)(1), 414(w)(3)]

The eligibility requirements for employers are the same as for the Section 45E credit (see Q 12:20)—that is, 100 or fewer employees with compensation greater than $5,000 during the prior tax year, and at least one NCHE (taking into account the controlled group aggregation rules). [I.R.C. §§ 45T(c), 408(p)(2)(C)(i)]

Practice Pointer. Code Section 45T appears to allow an employer to claim the credit for 2020 if the automatic enrollment feature was first established in the tax year that started in 2018. Or, it would allow the credit for 2020 and 2021 if the feature was first included in the 2019 tax year.

Participation

Eligible Employees

Q 12:22 Who must be allowed to participate in an employer's SEP?

Employees who are age 21 or older, have worked for the employer during at least three of the previous five years, and earn compensation of at least $600 *must* be allowed to participate in the employer's SEP plan. A plan's eligibility requirements may be less restrictive, but not more so. For example, a plan could reduce the service requirement to one year, but could not raise it to four years. [I.R.C. § 408(k)(2); Notice 2020-79, 2020-46 I.R.B. 1014] The age and service requirements are satisfied if they are met at any time during the plan year. [Prop. Treas. Reg. § 1.408-7(d)(1)]

(For how to determine *compensation* for SEP purposes, see Qs 12:34–12:44.)

Note. Eligible employees who die or terminate employment before the employer contribution is made for the year in which death or termination occurred must be included in the allocation of that contribution based on compensation received in that year.

Leased employees who are otherwise eligible must be included in a SEP if they are treated as regular employees under Code Section 414(n). Other leased employees could be included in a prototype SEP.

Example 1. Gladiator Corporation maintains a SEP for its employees. The plan year is the calendar year, and the SEP requires that participants be at least age 21 and have performed services for at least three of the immediately preceding five calendar years.

Jane worked for Gladiator in 2015, 2016, and 2017, while attending college. She never worked more than 25 days in any one year. In October 2018, Jane begins to work for Gladiator on a full-time basis; she earns $25,000 from Gladiator in 2018. Jane turns 21 on December 31, 2018. She is entitled to share in any SEP contributions made by Gladiator with respect to 2018. As of December 31, 2018, Jane meets the minimum age and service requirements because she worked for Gladiator in three of the five years preceding 2018. [Prop. Treas. Reg. § 1.408-7(d)(5)] Had Jane started working for Gladiator in 2017, she would not have satisfied the plan's three-year eligibility requirement, because she would have completed only two years of prior service as of December 31, 2018.

Example 2. Wizard Software, Inc. adopted a SEP that required an employee to have performed services for at least three of the immediately preceding five calendar years. Tommy had been continuously employed by Wizard since 1993 and shared in Wizard's SEP contribution for each year through 2014. Tommy performed no service during 2015, 2016, and 2017, but returned to work in 2018. He is not entitled to share in Wizard's contributions for 2018 because he worked during only two of the immediately preceding five years—2013 and 2014.

Example 3. Timely Tours adopted a SEP that requires at least two prior calendar years of service, and compensation of at least $500 in the plan year. Sandra, the owner's spouse, has performed services for Timely Tours every year since 2000, when the business started, but without compensation until 2018. In December 2018, she received $1,000 compensation. Sandra will receive a SEP contribution for 2018.

Example 4. Great Falls, Inc. maintains a grandfathered SARSEP that required an employee to be age 21 to qualify for participation. The plan is maintained on a calendar-year basis. Joy will attain age 21 on December 31, 2018. Her participation commences on January 1, 2018, the first day of the plan year that contains her first date of eligibility.

Q 12:23 May a person who is employed on the effective date of the plan be treated as satisfying the age and/or service requirements specified in the SEP?

Yes. The IRS has allowed a prototype plan sponsor to include a provision that allows an employer to waive the age and/or service requirement for an individual employed on the effective date of the plan.

Q 12:24 Must all eligible employees participate in the SEP?

Yes. Employees who meet the eligibility requirements *must* receive the employer contribution. They cannot refuse to participate (see Q 12:25). Consequently, every eligible employee must have a valid SEP IRA, and the employer should set one up for any employee who has not done so. Otherwise, the SEP may be disqualified, the employer's tax deduction for contributions may be lost, and the employees may no longer be able to exclude from income the contributions that were deposited to their SEP IRAs. Employees might also be subject to a 6 percent penalty for the excess contributions to their SEP IRAs. [Prop. Treas. Reg. § 1.408-7(d); Notice 81-1, 1981-1 C.B. 610; IRS Pub. 560, *Retirement Plans for Small Businesses (SEP, SIMPLE, and Qualified Plans)* 2020]

Example. Mort, an employee of Aardvarks, Inc., becomes eligible to receive a SEP contribution for 2019 but dies before establishing an IRA. Aardvarks should establish an IRA in Mort's name. Mort's estate should be designated as the IRA beneficiary, or the default option under the IRA, if any, should be selected. (An interest-bearing investment is generally chosen for an IRA established in such a manner.)

Q 12:25 Why might an individual not want to participate in a SEP?

Participation in a SEP counts as *active participation in a retirement plan* for traditional IRA purposes. As a result, the deductibility of any traditional IRA contributions that a SEP participant (and his or her spouse) makes would be phased out at higher income levels (see Q 3:64). [I.R.C. § 219(g)]

SEP participation does not affect the ability to *make* traditional IRA contributions. It only affects the deduction amount.

Q 12:26 Can an employee older than age 70½ participate?

Yes, and the employer *must* make SEP contributions for them. Code Section 219(d)(1), which used to prohibit annual traditional IRA contributions beyond age 70½, did not apply to SEP or SARSEP contributions. [I.R.C. § 219(b)(2), 219(b)(4)] (Code Section 219(d)(1) is repealed by Section 107 of the SECURE Act, effective for tax years starting after 2019.)

If participation continues after the age when required distributions begin, the employer would continue to make SEP contributions even while the employee receives RMDs. Since RMDs are calculated based on the prior year-end balance in the SEP IRA, each such contribution winds up being partly distributed in the succeeding year's RMD.

For the commencement of RMDs at age 72, rather than age 70½ (see Q 4:4).

Q 12:27 May a U.S. citizen employed by a foreign government establish and contribute to a SEP?

No. U.S. citizens employed by a foreign government do pay U.S. self-employment tax, but that does not mean they are self-employed. Only an employer may establish a SEP, and to be an employer, one must have an ownership interest in the enterprise. [Rosenfeld v. Commissioner, 112 A.F.T.R.2d 2013-5638 (9th Cir. 2013)]

> **Note.** Code Section 3121(b)(11) and Treasury Regulations Section 1.402(c)-3(d) require U.S. citizens employed by foreign governments to pay self-employment tax on those earnings. Otherwise, the "employer" share of the tax would not be paid. (The United States cannot ask a foreign government to withhold and remit U.S. employment tax.)

Q 12:28 May an individual simultaneously participate in one employer's SEP and another employer's SIMPLE, and also make regular IRA contributions?

Yes. Participation in a SEP does not preclude participation in a SIMPLE, and participants may also contribute to their traditional or Roth IRAs without the contribution limits being affected (see Q 12:61). Contributions under the SIMPLE are not limited by the contributions made under the SEP (and vice versa) if the plans are maintained by different employers. [IRS *Employee Plans News*, Issue 2011-7 (Oct. 12, 2011)]

> **Example.** Adam, who is employed by a bakery, operates a catering business on the side. He participates in the bakery's SIMPLE plan and maintains his own SEP through the catering business. The contribution limits for the two plans are completely independent. Adam may make a full SEP contribution,

even though a full contribution is also made to his SIMPLE IRA. He may also contribute to his Roth IRA if he has sufficient compensation.

Excludable Employees

Q 12:29 May otherwise eligible employees be excluded from a SEP?

A SEP plan may exclude otherwise eligible employees if:

1. The retirement benefits of those employees were collectively bargained for in good faith and the employees are under a union agreement with the employer; or
2. The employees are nonresident aliens with no U.S. source income from the employer.

[I.R.C. § 408(k)(2)]

A prototype SEP or SARSEP may also include plan provisions regarding the exclusion of "acquired" employees (during the transition period after a business acquisition; see Q 12:33).

Q 12:30 If two businesses are related, can one offer a SEP that excludes the other's employees?

It depends on the relationship. Code Section 414 contains a rule that treats certain affiliated employers as a single employer for SEP, SIMPLE, and qualified plan purposes. If the rule applies, a SEP or SIMPLE that one employer maintains must also be offered to the other's employees subject to the same eligibility and participation requirements.

Q 12:31 What relationships cause the single employer rule to apply?

The single employer rule applies to corporations that are members of a controlled group, businesses (incorporated or not) that are under common control, and organizations that belong to an affiliated service group. [I.R.C. §§ 414(b), 414(c), 414(m), 1563(a)] For purposes of applying the 415 limit to SEPs (and SIMPLEs), corporations are generally members of a controlled group if they are linked by stock ownership of at least 50 percent (voting power or value), either through a common parent corporation or by the same five or fewer individuals, trusts, and estates. [I.R.C. §§ 414(b), 415(h)] Similarly, business organizations are under common control if there is linked ownership, through a common parent organization or the same five or fewer persons, of 50 percent or more (of the vote or value of a corporation's stock, the profit or capital interest in a partnership, or the actuarial interest of a trust or estate). For linkage without a common parent, the five or fewer owners (individuals, trusts, and estates) must also effectively control each organization, meaning that their aggregate ownership of each entity, taking into account only their identical interests, must be at least 50 percent. [I.R.C. §§ 414(c), 415(h)] Finally, two service organizations form an affiliated group if one is a shareholder or partner in the other and regularly performs services for it (or for other persons). An affiliated service group also exists if highly compensated employees of a service organization own at least 10 percent of another entity, and that entity regularly provides the kind of services to the first organization that employees would typically perform. [I.R.C. § 414(m)]

> **Example.** Nate, age 35, is the sole proprietor of a printing shop with five employees; it does not maintain a SEP. Last month, Nate began selling life insurance through a new, solely owned corporation. He wants to establish a corporate SEP with no service requirements (so he may immediately participate). But since Nate controls both businesses, the corporation may only have a SEP if the printing shop employees (at least those age 21 or older) are also immediately eligible to participate.

Q 12:32 Is service with related employers aggregated to determine eligibility?

Yes. For purposes of a SEP, *service* includes service with any related entity; that is, service with an entity under common control or with a member of a controlled group must be aggregated. Service with a member of an affiliated service group must also be counted. [I.R.C. § 414(b), 414(c), 414(m)(4)(B); Prop. Treas. Reg. § 1.414(m)-3(a)(5); Priv. Ltr. Ruls. 9033061 (May 24, 1990), 9026056 (Apr. 3, 1990), 8945070 (Aug. 17, 1989), 8928008 (Nov. 12, 1989)]

> **Example 1.** The 100 percent owner of Rusty Sleigh Company (which has a SEP) plans to acquire 80 percent of the common stock of Slick Sleds, Inc. If the transaction closes in December 2019, employees of Slick Sleds who satisfy the plan's age, service, and compensation requirements become eligible to participate in the SEP for 2019.
>
> **Example 2.** Kitty Corporation has 20 employees and sponsors a calendar year SARSEP. Only Kitty's employees are eligible to participate. On November 3, 2017, Cat Company (Catco) acquired all of Kitty Corporation's stock, and the two companies became a controlled group. Catco has 100 employees who satisfy the plan's eligibility rules.
>
> The transaction causes the controlled group to have more than 25 employees in 2017 who meet the plan's eligibility requirements. This invalidates the SARSEP's grandfathered status as of January 1, 2017. The only alternative is to discontinue contributions under the plan as soon as possible. There are no transition or grace period rules for SEP plans.

Prototype and model SEP documents may be used in related employer situations. Individually designed SEPs that provide for coverage of a related employer's employees have also been accepted by the IRS. [*See, e.g.*, Priv. Ltr. Rul. 200003059 (Jan. 24, 2000)]

Q 12:33 May an employee "acquired" by business acquisition or other similar transaction be excluded from participation in a SEP or SARSEP?

Yes. The IRS allows the sponsor of a prototype SEP or SARSEP to include a provision that excludes acquired employees from participation during a transition period. An *acquired employee* is an employee (of the employer that maintains the SEP; i.e., the *first employer*) who would be employed by another employer that was involved in a business acquisition or other similar transaction with the first employer, had the transaction not occurred. The plan may provide that an acquired employee would not be eligible to become a participant in the SEP during a transition period beginning on the date of the transaction and ending on the last day of the first plan year beginning after the transaction. For the exclusion to apply, the minimum coverage requirements (see Q 12:22) must have been met before the acquisition, and coverage under the plan must not significantly change during the transition period other than by reason of the change in members of the group. [I.R.C. § 410(b)(6)(C)(i); Treas. Reg. § 1.410(b)-2(a), 1.410(b)-2(b)]

Compensation

Q 12:34 What does compensation include for SEP purposes?

The compensation of any nonowner employee of a business that maintains a SEP generally consists of the wages, tips, and other amounts received from the employer as payment for services performed, to the extent these amounts are includable in gross income.

Compensation for SEP purposes excludes items that receive special tax benefits, such as nontaxable premiums for group term life insurance. It also generally excludes items not includable in gross income. But income that native American Indians derive from the exercise of tribal fishing rights is treated as compensation for SEP purposes, even though it is exempt from federal income and employment taxes. [§§ 408(k)(7)(B), 414(s), 415(c)(3), 7873; Treas. Reg. § 1.415(c)-2(c); Prop. Treas. Reg. § 1.415(c)-2(g)]

(For self-employment compensation, see Qs 12:41–12:44.)

Q 12:35 Are elective deferrals under a SARSEP included in compensation?

Compensation determined for SARSEP purposes generally includes the salary a participant elects to defer to the SEP IRA. However, the employer may elect to exclude elective deferrals from compensation. [I.R.C. § 414(s)(2)]

Q 12:36 For what period is compensation taken into account?

Contributions are based on compensation of a participant for the plan year. For a SEP established using the model forms, the plan year is the calendar year. An employer that uses a prototype SEP may elect to use its own tax year as the plan year. [I.R.C. § 408(k)(7)(C); Form 5305-SEP, Simplified Employee Pension—Individual Retirement Accounts Contribution Agreement under Code Section 408(k)]

Compensation is taken into account for a particular year if it is actually paid or made available to the employee (or, if earlier, is includible in the employee's gross income) within the year. Compensation under certain cash or deferred arrangements (e.g., cafeteria plans) is taken into account as of the date when the employee would have received it as a cash payment, but for the election to defer. [Treas. Reg. § 1.415(c)-2(e)]

Q 12:37 Can compensation include amounts paid after the end of the year?

Compensation paid after the end of the year may be taken into account if all of the following circumstances are met:

1. The plan provides that compensation for a year includes amounts earned during the year but paid afterward solely because of the timing of pay periods and pay dates.
2. The compensation at issue was earned during the year but is paid in the first few weeks of the succeeding year.
3. All such amounts are included on a uniform and consistent basis with respect to all similarly situated employees.
4. The same amount is not included for more than one year.

[Treas. Reg. § 1.415(c)-2(e)(2)]

Example. Jean defers part of her salary into her employer's SARSEP during 2020. The plan allows compensation paid after the limitation year to be taken into account when the four circumstances described above are met. On January 15, 2021, Jean receives a check for the pay period that ended on December 31, 2020. Jean may defer compensation from that check, and the deferral will be treated as a contribution for the 2020 plan year. (See Qs 12:51–12:57 for an explanation of elective deferrals under a SARSEP.)

Q 12:38 Does compensation include severance payments?

Severance payments are generally not considered compensation for SEP purposes. But a plan can allow certain payments after termination from employment to be treated as compensation. The plan document's definition of *compensation* is determinative. [*See* Treas. Reg. § 1.415(c)-2(e)(3).]

Q 12:39 Does compensation include differential wage payments made for employees on active military duty?

Yes. *Differential wage payments* are considered compensation for SEP purposes. Differential wages are amounts that some employers pay an employee during a period of active duty service with the military that lasts more than 30 days, representing at least some of the wages that would have been earned if the individual continued to provide services for the employer. [Notice 2010-15, 2010-6 I.R.B. 390; I.R.C. §§ 408(k)(7)(B), 414(s), 415(c)(3), 3401(h); Treas. Reg. § 1.415(c)-2(d)(3)]

> **Example.** Ben, an employee of The Bender Company, is a member of the National Guard and called to active military service for the period July 2018 through December 2019. Bender's corporate policy is to supplement the military pay of its employees who are deployed in the military. The pay supplements Ben receives in 2018 and 2019 are taken into account when Bender allocates its SEP contributions for those years.

Q 12:40 Are salary continuation payments made after a disability treated as compensation?

Yes. A rule almost identical to the one for differential wage payments (see Q 12:39) applies with respect to contributions on behalf of disabled employees. The employee must be disabled within the meaning of Code Section 22(e)(3), which requires total and permanent *inability* to engage in any substantial gainful activity by reason of any medically determinable physical or mental impairment which can be expected to result in death or which has lasted or can be expected to last for a continuous period of not less than 12 months. In that case the employer is permitted to base a SEP contribution on the amount of compensation the participant would have received if he or she were paid at the rate of compensation received immediately before becoming permanently and totally disabled. [Treas. Reg. § 1.415(c)-2(e)(4)] Also, the participant must not be an HCE (see Q 12:46) or the plan sponsor must make contributions for all disabled participants. [I.R.C. § 415(c)(3)(C)]

Self-employment Compensation

Q 12:41 How is compensation determined for a sole proprietor?

For SEP purposes, a sole proprietor's compensation is his or her earned income—i.e., the net earnings from self-employment from an unincorporated business in which his or her personal services are a material income-producing factor. If an individual has more than one business, only earned income from the business with the SEP plan is taken into account. [I.R.C. §§ 408(k)(7)(B), 1402(a), 401(c)(2), 401(a)(17), 404(*l*)]

An individual's net earnings from self-employment is determined as the gross income from the business, less allowable business deductions. These include the deductible part (one-half) of the self-employment tax allowed by Code Section 164(f), the deduction for SEP contributions made by the plan on the self-employed individual's behalf, and the owner's share of the business' allowable expense for SEP contributions made on behalf of nonowner participants.

The calculation of net earnings from self-employment is circular, because the SEP contribution is allocated based on the self-employed individual's earned income, but that cannot be determined without knowing the amount of the SEP contribution. Fortunately, the problem is solved with algebra. The SEP contribution (C) is calculated with this formula:

$$C = (\text{Unadjusted Compensation} - \S\,164(\text{f})\ \text{Deduction} - \text{Share of Nonowner Contribution Expense}) \times \frac{\text{Plan Contribution \%}}{(100\% + \text{Plan Contribution \%})}$$

Example: Stan owns a graphic design business and has one nonowner employee (Sarah). Both Stan and Sarah participate in the company's SEP plan. For 2019, the plan will contribute 10 percent of plan compensation. Sarah's salary is $40,000, and Stan has earnings (before adjustment) of $80,000.

The plan will contribute $4,000 (.10 × $40,000) for Sarah. Stan's earnings for self-employment tax purposes are $76,000 ($80,000 – $4,000), so his self-employment tax liability is $11,628 ($76,000 × .153). Applying the formula above, the SEP contribution for Stan will be $6,381 [($80,000 – $5,814 – $4,000) × (.10 ÷ 1.10)].

Practice Pointer. Calculating earned income for both plan and self-employment tax purposes can be extremely complicated because the owner's compensation fluctuates as the plan is being designed. Even practitioners with a thorough understanding of how plan limits are applied and how earned income is calculated will find the process of designing plans, calculating contributions, and applying limits a complex, if not impossible, task. Until there is a legislative change, the practitioner must use caution. Custom illustrations and spreadsheet software are available to practitioners who need to design plans for unincorporated business owners with common-law employees.

Q 12:42 If an S corporation has a SEP plan, can the shareholders share in contributions?

For SEP purposes, compensation does *not* include income passed through to shareholders of an S corporation. Personal services are required for plan participation. So, if an S corporation shareholder is also an employee of the business, his or her employee compensation (salary) is the basis for receiving a SEP contribution.

Q 12:43 How is a partner's net earnings from self-employment determined for SEP purposes?

To determine the net earnings from self-employment from a partnership where the individual's personal services are a material income-producing factor, earned income includes:

- A partner's distributive share of partnership income or loss (other than separately stated items, such as capital gains and losses) (e.g., see Joe, Lou, Tom, and Jan in the Example in Q 12:44), and
- Guaranteed payments to a partner for his or her personal services (e.g., see Roz in the Example in Q 12:44).

However, distributions of other income or loss to a limited partner are *not* included.

[IRS Pub. 560, *Retirement Plans for Small Businesses (SEP, SIMPLE, and Qualified Plans)* 2020]

Q 12:44 If a self-employed individual has unrelated earned income, what adjustment is needed to determine compensation for SEP purposes?

If an individual is self-employed in a business that maintains a SEP, and also has unrelated *income earned as an employee* (i.e., W-2 wages), then the Social Security contributions deducted from those wages are allowed as a credit when self-employment tax is determined. Since the credit reduces the self-employment tax, and thus also the Code Section 164(f) deduction (see Q 12:41), a somewhat larger compensation amount results for SEP purposes. That may cause the individual's allocable share of the employer's SEP contribution to be larger (e.g., compare Lou with Joe in the Example below).

On the other hand, if an individual is self-employed in more than one business, one of which maintains a SEP, the total self-employment tax liability must be apportioned between the businesses. Only the self-employment tax attributed to the business with the SEP may be taken into account under Code Section 164(f) to determine the net earnings from self-employment for SEP purposes. (See, e.g., the effect of Tom's unrelated self-employment loss, and of Jan's unrelated self-employment income, in the Example below.)

Example. Unusual Facts, a partnership, maintains a SEP plan for its employees. The partnership makes a contribution for 2020 equal to 25 percent of the participants' compensation. There are three nonowner-employees who have combined wages of $40,000. The following chart shows the determination of each partner's compensation for SEP purposes, and the resulting allocation of the plan contribution.

Table 12-1. Partnership's SEP Calculations

	A	B	C	D	E
Employee Name/ Status	*Pre-Plan Compensation*	*Share of $10,000 Nonowner Contribution Expense*	*Self-Employment Income for SE Tax*	*Deduction for Self-Employment Tax Attributed to Partnership*	*25% Contribution*
Owners					
Joe Normal	$140,000	$2,000	$138,000	$10,385	$25,523
Lou—has $20,000 of W-2 income from an unrelated entity	$140,000	$2,000	$138,000	$6,665*	$26,267
Tom—has a $10,000 loss from self-employment from an unrelated entity	$140,000	$2,000	$128,000	$10,251**	$25,550
Jan—has a $10,000 gain from self-employment from an unrelated entity	$140,000	$2,000	$148,000	$10,519***	$25,636
Abe—is ineligible to participate	$140,000	$2,000	n/a	n/a	Ineligible
Roz—is a guaranteed payment partner with a $90,000 of guaranteed payment	$90,000	none allocated	$90,000	$6,358	$16,728
Nonowners					
Employees (combined)	$40,000	n/a	n/a	n/a	$10,000

Table 12-1. Partnership's SEP Calculations (*cont'd*)

* In computing his self-employment tax, Lou is allowed a $2,480 credit for the amount of Social Security tax paid on his wages ($20,000 × 12.4% = $2,480).

** Tom's 2020 net earnings from self-employment are $128,000 ($140,000 – $10,000 – $2,000). The self-employment tax payable is $20,503, and Tom is allowed to deduct half of that amount ($10,251). Since Tom's outside activity generated a loss, the deduction is entirely attributable to Tom's partnership earnings. Tom's adjusted partnership compensation (on which the SEP contribution is based) is $127,749 ($140,000 – $2,000 – $10,251). Tom's SEP contribution is one-fifth of that amount ($25,550).

*** Jan's 2020 net earnings from self-employment are $148,000 ($140,000 + $10,000 – $2,000), resulting in self-employment tax liability of $21,038. She may deduct half of that amount ($10,519). To determine the part of the deduction that is attributable to Jan's partnership earnings, the total deduction is multiplied by.9333 (her pre-plan earned income of $140,000, divided by $150,000 (the sum of the pre-plan earned income and outside earned income)). The result, $9,818, is the deduction taken into account to determine Jan's SEP contribution. Jan's adjusted partnership compensation is $128,182 ($140,000 – $2,000 – $9,818), and her SEP contribution from the partnership is one-fifth of that amount ($25,636).

Practice Pointer. Frequently, partners have different tax preparers. Information from the uncompleted federal income tax returns of some partners may be needed to compute the contributions to be made under the plan and to complete the federal income tax returns of the partnership, which, in turn, are needed for the completion of the federal income tax returns of the individual partners. When all the partners and the partnership use the same tax preparer, return preparation is facilitated and confidentiality issues are minimized.

Contributions

Employer Contributions (all SEPs)

Q 12:45 What are the general rules for making employer contributions?

SEP contributions are discretionary, in that an employer is not required to make them every year. But when they are made, contributions must be made for all participants according to a written allocation formula that does not discriminate in favor of highly compensated employees (HCEs). The formula must specify the requirements participants must meet to share in the allocation, and how allocations will be calculated. Allocations must bear a uniform relationship to *compensation*, ignoring amounts above $290,000 (the limit for 2021). [I.R.C. § 408(k)(3), 408(k)(5); Notice 2019-59, 2019-47 I.R.B. 1091] (For how *compensation* is determined, see Qs 12:34–12:44. The corresponding compensation limit for 2020 was $285,000.) [Notice 2019-59, 2019-47 I.R.B. 774]

Salary reduction contributions are only allowed under a grandfathered SARSEP plan (see Q 12:51). [I.R.C. § 408(k)(4), 408(k)(6)]

(For SEP and SARSEP contribution limits, see Q 12:60.)

Q 12:46 What is a highly compensated employee (HCE)?

For 2021, an HCE is an individual who:

1. Was a 5 percent owner (determined using the ownership attribution rules of Code Section 318) at any time during the current year or preceding ("look back") year, *or*
2. Received from the employer during the preceding year (2020) compensation exceeding $130,000 and in the preceding year, if the employer so elected, was in the top 20 percent of employees ranked by compensation.

[I.R.C. §§ 408(k)(6)(G), 414(q); Notice 2020-79, 2020-46 I.R.B. 1014]

The dollar threshold for HCE status is adjusted annually for inflation. For HCE status in 2020, the 2019 compensation must also have exceeded $130,000. [I.R.C. § 414(q)(1); Notice 2019-59, 2019-46 I.R.B. 1014]

Q 12:47 Must the same percentage of compensation be contributed for every participant?

Not necessarily. The SEP contributions must bear a *uniform relationship* to compensation. Generally, this requirement is met by contributing the same percentage of the compensation taken into account for each participant (see Q 12:62), but it is also acceptable to use a *permitted disparity formula* for a plan that is integrated with Social Security (see Q 12:48). [I.R.C. §§ 408(k)(3)(D), 401(*l*)(2)]

Q 12:48 What disparity is permitted for contributions under a plan integrated with Social Security?

For a SEP plan that is integrated with Social Security, the disparity between employer contributions for HCEs versus those for other employees can be as much as 5.7 percent. [I.R.C. §§ 408(k)(3)(D), 401(*l*)(2)]

In theory, the integration rules avoid the duplication of benefits by not requiring that contributions be made twice on the same compensation. Social Security integration (sometimes called *permitted disparity*) is allowed under the same rules that apply to defined contribution plans. That is, the contribution based on compensation above the taxable wage base (TWB) for the current year may not be more than twice the rate that is applied to the portion of compensation subject to the base. For example, instead of providing a flat 8 percent of pay for each participant, a SEP could provide 5 percent on the portion of pay covered by Social Security (the TWB for 2021 is $142,800), and 10 percent on the portion in excess of such pay. [Social Security Press Rel., *Social Security Administration Announces 1.3 Percent Benefit Increase for 2021* (Oct. 13, 2020)]

Generally, only one plan of an employer may be integrated with Social Security. Model Form 5305A-SEP does not allow for integration.

The spread or disparity rate depends on the integration level selected for the plan year. The maximum percentage rate of 5.7 percent may be used when the plan is integrated at the TWB or when the integration amount is set at 20 percent or less of the TWB. If the integration level is set above $10,000 (or 20 percent of the TWB if that amount is greater) and below the TWB, the maximum spread factor of 5.7 percent must be reduced. [I.R.C. § 408(k)(3)(D); Treas. Reg. § 1.401(l)-2(d)] Table 12-2 summarizes these rules.

Table 12-2. Adjusting the Maximum Disparity Rate

If the Integration Level Is More Than	*But Not More Than*	*The 5.7% Maximum Disparity Rate Is Reduced To*
20% of the TWB	80% of the TWB	4.3%
80% of the TWB	An amount less than 100% of the TWB	5.4%

Calculated from the 2021 TWB of $142,800, the maximum 5.7 percent spread would be as shown in Table 12-3.

Table 12-3. Adjustments Based on 2021TWB of $142,800

If the Integration Level Is More Than	*But Not More Than*	*The 5.7% Maximum Disparity Rate*
$ 0	$ 28,560	Remains at 5.7%
$ 28,560	$114,240	Is reduced to 4.3%
$114,240	$142,800	Is reduced to 5.4%

Caution. Code Section 402(h)(2)(B), regarding the exclusion of an employer's SEP contribution, provides for a reduction of the dollar limit ($58,000 for 2021; see Q 12:63) if the plan is integrated with Social Security. The amount by which the $58,000 limit is reduced in an integrated SEP is equal to the plan's spread (disparity) percentage multiplied by the amount of the HCE's compensation not in excess of the plan's integration level or the TWB, whichever is less. Compensation in excess of $290,000 (the 2021 limit) is not considered. In the case of an NHCE, the $58,000 limit is not reduced.

For 2021, the maximum offset applicable to an HCE results in a contribution limit, under an integrated plan, of $49,886 ($58,000 − (the maximum integration level of $142,800 × .057)). This compares to a contribution limit of $58,000 under a nonintegrated plan.

Practice Pointer. An employer with few employees (or employees who do not earn significant amounts) should consider the additional nonowner cost to provide an owner with a $58,000 contribution rather than the reduced limit. The additional cost of the nonowner contributions may be insignificant, especially if there is more than one owner.

Example 1. The Darn Knit Store established a prototype SEP for its employees, who are Donna (the owner) and Mona. Under the plan, SEP contributions are integrated with Social Security. The plan's integration level is set at $10,000, and it uses the maximum permitted spread of 5.7 percent. For 2021, Donna has W-2 compensation of $290,000, and Mona's is $10,000. Darn Knit contributes to the plan the smallest amount that will result in the maximum allocation to Donna ($49,886; i.e., $58,000 – (.057 × $142,800)). Expressed as a formula, the SEP contribution for each employee is approximately 11.70 percent of total compensation, plus 5.70 percent of compensation over $10,000 (the integration level).

Under the integration formula, Donna receives a contribution of $49,886 ($290,000 × .1170) + (($280,000 – $10,000) × .0570). Mona receives $1,170 ($10,000 × .1170).

If the plan were *not* integrated, Donna's contribution would be $58,000 ($290,000 × .20), and Mona's would be $2,000 ($10,000 × .20).

Analysis. As shown in the table, the total SEP contributions would be higher (more costly for the business) with a nonintegrated plan, but 90 percent of the cost difference would redound to Donna, the owner. From her point of view, a nonintegrated plan would be more cost-effective.

	Donna (owner)	*Mona*	*Total Plan Cost*
Integrated plan contribution	$48,425	$1,180	$49,605
Nonintegrated plan contribution	$56,000	$2,000	$58,000
Additional benefit paid under nonintegrated plan	$7,575	$820	$8,395
Allocation of additional benefit	90%	10%	100%

Example 2. Beaver Hat Shop maintains a SEP for its employees, who are Clarence (the owner) and five other individuals. In 2019, Clarence earns a salary of $280,000, and each other employee earns $80,000. Contributions under the SEP plan are integrated with Social Security. The integration level is set at the TWB ($132,900 for 2019), and the maximum permitted spread of 5.7 percent is used. Beaver Hat's contribution for 2019 is the smallest amount that results in the maximum allocation to Clarence ($48,425; i.e., $56,000 – (.057 × $132,900)). Expressed as a formula, each employee's contribution is 14.3 percent of total compensation, plus 5.7 percent of any compensation over $132,900 (the integration level).

Clarence receives a contribution of $48,425 (($280,000 × .143) + ($280,000 – $132,900) × .057). Each other employee receives a contribution of $11,440 ($80,000 × .143).

If the plan were *not* integrated, Clarence would receive a $56,000 contribution, and each other employee would receive $16,000 ($80,000 × .2).

Analysis. As seen below, the total cost would be $30,119 higher under a nonintegrated plan, and only 25 percent of the additional cost would benefit Clarence personally. From a purely economic perspective, Clarence may consider employer contributions to be more efficiently allocated with an integrated plan.

	Clarence (Owner)	*Each Other Employee*	*Total Plan Cost*
Integrated plan contribution	$48,425	$11,440	$105,625
Nonintegrated plan contribution	$56,000	$16,000	$136,000
Additional benefit paid under nonintegrated plan	$7,575	$4,560	$30,119
Allocation of additional benefit	25%	15%	100%

Q 12:49 Can the employer make conditional or restricted contributions?

No. An employer may *not*:

- Restrict in any way an employee's right to a contribution made by the employer,
- Require employees to make their own contributions (for a SARSEP) in order to receive an employer contribution,
- Require employees to maintain any balance in the SEP-IRA as a condition of receiving employer contributions, or
- Prohibit withdrawals.

Q 12:50 Can SEP contributions be made in an unprofitable year?

Yes. Contributions to a SEP may exceed profits for the year and can even be made when there are no profits. A contribution on behalf of a *self-employed* individual (including a partner in a partnership) may not, however, create a net operating loss; that is, the contribution may not exceed the individual's earned income (determined without regard to the deduction for the contribution). Contributions made to *nonowner*-employees may, however, exceed the owner's earned income and create a net loss from self-employment. [I.R.C. § 404(a)(8)(C), 404(h)(2); Temp. Treas. Reg. § 1.404(a)(8)-1T]

Salary Reduction Contributions (SARSEPs only)

Q 12:51 What contributions are made under a grandfathered SARSEP?

Two kinds of contributions are allowed under a SARSEP:

1. Employer contributions, which are made on behalf of participants according to the SEP rules explained above, and
2. Elective salary reduction contributions (deferrals).

Q 12:52 What conditions must a SARSEP meet to be grandfathered?

There are four requirements:

1. The SARSEP must have existed before January 1, 1997.
2. At any time in the preceding year, no more than 25 employees can have been eligible to participate in the SARSEP.
3. The elective deferrals of all HCEs (see Q 12:46) must meet the *actual deferral percentage test* (see Q 12:54).
4. The other SEP qualification requirements must also be met.

Q 12:53 Can an employer require participants to elect salary deferrals?

No. An employer cannot require or pressure an employee to make elective SARSEP contributions.

Q 12:54 What is the actual deferral percentage (ADP) test?

The actual deferral percentage (ADP) test is a nondiscrimination rule that applies to SARSEPs. It limits the percentage of total compensation that a highly compensated employee (HCE) may elect to defer for the current year. According to the rule, the maximum deferral an eligible HCE may elect for the current year is the average of the individual percentages, computed separately, for all eligible employees who are not HCEs (the NHCEs) multiplied by 1.25. [I.R.C. § 408(k)(6)(A)(iii)] (See Q 12:78 for the treatment of catch-up contributions for purposes of the ADP test.)

Example 1. Nutmeg Corporation's employees earn the following amounts and elect to defer the following percentages of compensation for 2020:

NHCE 1	$10,000/8%
NHCE 2	$10,000/4%
NHCE 3	$10,000/4%
NHCE 4	$10,000/0%

Nutmeg Corporation maintains a prototype SARSEP that defines compensation for ADP testing purposes as gross compensation (before reduction for elective deferrals). The average of the NHCEs' deferral percentages is computed as follows:

$$(8\% + 4\% + 4\% + 0\%) \div 4 = 4\%$$

The amount that may be deferred by each eligible HCE is computed as follows: 4% × 1.25 = 5%, up to $19,500 for 2021 (see Q 12:75), plus catch-up contribution if eligible.

Note. The percentage that an eligible HCE may defer is not dependent (as is generally the case in a 401(k) plan) on the percentages or dollar amounts that other HCEs elect to defer.

Example 2. Sunfish Corporation maintains a grandfathered SARSEP for its employees. Sunfish has three non-highly compensated employees (NHCEs) who elect to defer 2 percent, 3 percent, and 4 percent, respectively. The only other eligible employee is the company's owner, Marsha, and she contributes her allowed maximum of 3.75 percent (the average of the ADPs of each eligible NHCE, determined separately for each employee, multiplied by 1.25). Because Marsha, a key employee, is a plan participant, the SARSEP is deemed to be top heavy, and Sunfish must contribute 3 percent (i.e., the lesser of 3 percent or 3.75 percent) for each non-key employee who has made an excess SEP contribution. Elective contributions must be reduced if the 25-percent-of-includable-compensation limit is exceeded (see Q 12:84).

Example 3. Bonefish Corporation maintains a grandfathered model SARSEP for its employees. All the employees are under age 50. Each of the company's three NHCEs elects to defer 1 percent. The only other eligible employee is the company's owner, Arthur, and he contributes his allowed maximum of 1.25 percent (the average of the ADPs of each eligible NHCE, determined separately for each employee, multiplied by 1.25). Because Arthur, a key employee, is a plan participant, the SARSEP is deemed top heavy, and Bonefish must contribute 1.25 percent (i.e., the lesser of 3 percent or 1.25 percent) to each non-key employee. Normal elective contributions (but not catch-up contributions) must be reduced if the 25-percent-of-includable-compensation limit is exceeded (see Q 12:84).

Caution. In a model SARSEP (that uses Form 5305A-SEP), the term *compensation* generally excludes elective contributions that are made by the participant to the plan. Under the model document, the ADP percentage for an employee who deferred $400 from gross wages of $10,000 would be 4.1766667 percent ($400 ÷ $9,600) rather than 4 percent ($400 ÷ $10,000) as used in this example. The 25 percent participant exclusion limit is always based on reduced compensation.

Q 12:55 Do elective deferrals continue after an employee reaches age 70½?

The employer *must* allow elective deferrals to continue after an individual reaches age 70½, *unless* the particular SARSEP prohibits it. [IRS *Employee Plans News*, Issue 2011-7 (Oct. 12, 2011)] (See Q 12:26.)

Q 12:56 May a SARSEP plan include an automatic contribution arrangement?

Yes. If the written plan includes an automatic contribution arrangement, a default percentage of salary will be deferred to a participant's SARSEP IRA unless he or she affirmatively elects to make either no contribution or a different contribution. Participants must be given notice and the opportunity to withdraw the default contribution. A default contribution that is withdrawn is included in the participant's gross income, but the 10 percent additional tax does not apply. [I.R.C. § 414(w)]

Q 12:57 Is the saver's tax credit available for salary reduction contributions under a SARSEP?

Yes. A qualifying SARSEP participant may claim the saver's tax credit for salary reduction contributions made under the plan. (For qualification and other details about the saver's tax credit, see Qs 3:138–3:143.) [I.R.C. § 25B]

Deposit of Contributions

Q 12:58 When must a participant's allocable share of the employer's SEP contribution for the year be deposited into the SEP IRA?

Allocable shares of the employer's nonelective SEP contributions must be deposited to a participant's SEP IRAs by the due date, including extensions, of the employer's federal income tax return for the year (see the timing rules in Q 12:67).

Q 12:59 For a SARSEP, when must a participant's salary reduction contributions be deposited into the SEP IRA?

A SARSEP participant's elective deferrals (salary reduction contributions) must be remitted to the trustee as soon as possible, but not later than 15 days after the month in which the participant would otherwise have received the payment.

> **Note.** All contributions to a SEP are plan assets. [DOL Reg. § 2510.3-102(a)] ERISA regulations generally require employee contributions to a SARSEP to be deposited as soon as they can reasonably be segregated from the employer's general assets, but in any event within 15 business days after the end of the month in which the payroll deduction is made. [DOL Reg. § 2510.3-102] Thus, the 15-day period (30 days in the case of a SIMPLE) is not a safe

harbor. Under some circumstances, one day may be sufficient time to segregate and deposit contributions.

Contribution Limits

Q 12:60 What are the numerical limits on SEP and SARSEP contributions?

Other than the eligibility requirements described elsewhere (participation requirements in Q 12:22, and the SARSEP ADP test in Q 12:54), SEPs and SARSEPs are subject to the following numerical limits:

- The maximum compensation of any participant that can be taken into account for a year [I.R.C. § 408(k)(6)] (see Q 12:62);
- The largest contribution to a SEP IRA that may be excluded from a participant's income [I.R.C. § 402(h)] (see Q 12:63);
- The maximum deduction an employer may claim annually for SEP contributions [I.R.C. § 404(h)] (see Q 12:66);
- The overall exclusion limit for annual additions to a participant's accounts in defined contribution plans of the employer [I.R.C. § 415] (see Q 12:70); and
- The annual exclusion limit for an individual's combined elective deferrals under plans that allow them [I.R.C. § 402(g)] (see Q 12:75).

Q 12:61 May a SEP participant also make regular contributions to a traditional or Roth IRA?

Yes. Regular IRA contributions can also be made. The regular traditional IRA (but not Roth IRA) contribution may even be deposited into the SEP IRA, subject to the regular IRA limits. Contributions to a traditional IRA may not be deductible, however (whether contributed to a traditional IRA of the participant or his or her spouse), because of the active participation rule (see Q 3:49).

Compensation Limit (§ 408(k)(6))

Q 12:62 How much compensation can be taken into account for SEP purposes?

An annual inflation-adjusted limit applies to the amount of compensation that may be taken into account for SEP (and SARSEP) purposes. For 2021, compensation over $290,000 is disregarded for any employee. (The corresponding limit for 2020 was $285,000.) [I.R.C. § 408(k)(3)(C); Notice 2020-79, 2020-46 I.R.B. 1014; Notice 2019-59, 2019-47 I.R.B. 1091]

Maximum Contribution to a SEP IRA (§ 402(h))

Q 12:63 How much can an employer contribute to the SEP IRA of any nonowner employee participant?

The most an employer can contribute for a plan year on behalf of any *nonowner employee* is the lesser of two amounts—an inflation-adjusted dollar figure ($58,000 for 2021, increased from $57,000 for 2020), or *25* percent of the participant's limited compensation (i.e., only considering compensation up to $290,000 for 2021, or $285,000 for 2020). Compensation for this purpose does *not* include the employer's SEP contribution. [I.R.C. §§ 402(h)(2), 408(k)(7)(B), 414(s); Notice 2020-79, 2020-46 I.R.B. 1014; Notice 2019-59, 2019-47 I.R.B. 1091]

(But for how *elective deferrals* under a SARSEP are taken into account in determining compensation, see Q 12:35.)

Q 12:64 Does the same limit apply to contributions for a self-employed person?

Yes, but a special computation is required to determine the maximum contribution for a self-employed individual. The limit works out to the lesser of $58,000 (for 2021) or *20* percent of the net earnings from self-employment. The corresponding dollar figure for 2020 was $57,000. (See Q 12:41.)

Q 12:65 Are elective deferrals under a SARSEP also subject to the Section 402(h) limit?

Yes. The 402(h) limit covers not only the employer's contribution to the SEP IRA, but also any salary reduction contributions elected by a SARSEP participant. Thus, for a SARSEP, the employer contribution made on the participant's behalf, plus the participant's own salary reduction contributions, may not exceed $58,000 (for 2021) or 25 percent of compensation (ignoring compensation over $290,000). (See Q 12:63.)

As noted in Q 12:35, for purposes of the 25 percent limit, compensation is *not* reduced by the SARSEP participant's salary reduction contributions (elective deferrals)—*unless* the employer has elected to exclude them from compensation. [I.R.C. § 414(s)(2)]

Employer's Deduction Limit (§ 404(h))

Q 12:66 What is the employer's deduction limit?

An employer's SEP contributions are generally deductible to the extent they do not exceed 25 percent of the total limited compensation (see Q 12:63) of all participants. [I.R.C. § 404(h)(1)(C)]

Self-employed individuals can make deductible SEP contributions on their own behalf, but the calculation is more complicated. The deductible limit for those contributions is generally 20 percent of the business owner's net income from self-employment (see Q 12:41). [I.R.C. §§ 404(h)(1)(C), 408(k)(3)(C)]

Elective deferrals and catch-up contributions made under a SARSEP are treated as elective *employer* contributions, so they are also deductible. [I.R.C. § 408(k)(6)(A)(i)]

> **Note.** Contributions made for certain domestic employees are not deductible because they are not trade or business expenses. (See Note in Q 13:57.)

Q 12:67 What are the timing rules for the employer's deduction?

The timing rules for the employer's deduction are as follows:

- If the SEP is maintained on a calendar-year basis, and the calendar year is also the employer's tax year, then contributions are deductible for the calendar year (Example 1).
- If the SEP is maintained on a calendar-year basis, but the employer uses a different tax year, then contributions are deductible for the employer's tax year *with or within which* the plan year ends (Example 2).
- If the SEP is maintained on the basis of the employer's tax year (see Q 12:8), then contributions are deductible for that tax year (Example 3).

To be deductible, however, contributions must be deposited with the plan by the due date (including extensions) of the employer's federal income tax return for that year. (For carryover of nondeductible amounts, see Q 12:68.) [I.R.C. §§ 402(h), 404(h)(1)(B)]

> **Example 1.** Clarity Corporation is a calendar-year corporation that maintains a calendar-year SEP. Contributions made for the 2020 SEP plan year are deductible on Clarity's 2020 federal income tax return, provided they are actually deposited with the plan by the filing deadline (as extended) for that return.

> **Example 2.** Westside Corporation's tax year ends on May 31. Its SEP is maintained according to the calendar year. The 2020 plan year ends within Westside's tax year that ends May 31, 2021. Westside pays its employer contribution for the 2020 plan year on August 31, 2021. The contribution is deductible on Westside's federal tax return for the tax year that ends on May 31, 2021.

> **Example 3.** The tax year of the Timely Reporting Corporation runs from April 1 through March 31. The plan year of its SEP is the same. Timely's contributions for the plan year ending on March 31, 2020 are deductible on Timely's federal income tax return for the same period, assuming the contributions are actually paid to the plan no later than the due date (including extensions) for that return.

Q 12:68 Can a SEP contribution that is not deductible in one tax year be carried forward and deducted in the next year?

Yes. Nondeductible contributions are carried forward to the next year and are deductible then to the extent the current contributions for the later year do not "use up" that year's deduction limit. Any amount still not deductible carries forward again to the next year. [I.R.C. § 404(h)(1)(C)]

> **Example.** The Crane Corporation is a calendar-year business with a SEP plan for its two employees, each of whom earns $60,000 in 2019. Crane makes a 10 percent SEP contribution current with each salary payment (so $6,000 is contributed for each employee during 2019). In January 2020, Crane makes an additional contribution, intending to bring the total contribution for each employee up to the 25-percent-of-compensation limit. To reach that limit, Crane should contribute another $9,000 (15 percent of salary) for each employee. However, too much is accidentally contributed—$12,000 (20 percent of salary) for each employee.
>
> Crane can rectify the situation by contributing less for the 2020 plan year. The nondeductible amount of 2019 contributions ($6,000) carries forward to 2020. If the contributions for 2020 are at least $6,000 below the deductible limit for that year, the carryover will be used and the 2020 contributions will also be fully deductible.

Q 12:69 Is the employer penalized for making nondeductible contributions?

Yes. Unless a nondeductible contribution is timely removed, the employer is subject to a 10 percent excise tax on the excess contribution. [I.R.C. § 4972(a), 4972(d)(1)(A)(iii)] (See Q 12:80 regarding excess contributions.)

Overall Defined Contribution Limit (§ 415)

Q 12:70 What is the overall limit that applies to defined contribution plans?

The total amount of benefits and contributions an individual may receive in any year, taking into account all of an employer's defined contribution plans, is subject to an overall limit. This is the *415 limit*—so-called because it appears in Section 415 of the Code. Qualified plans and certain other plans, including SEPs, must comply with the 415 limit or risk disqualification. [I.R.C. § 415(c), 415(a)(1)(B), 415(a)(2)(C)]

The rule specifically imposes a ceiling on *annual additions* made for a *limitation year* to a participant's accounts in *defined contribution plans* of the employer (or related employers; see Qs 12:30, 12:31). The 415 limit for 2021 is $58,000 (up from $57,000 for 2020), or (if less) 100 percent of the participant's compensation. [I.R.C. § 415(c)(1), 415(c)(10); Notice 2020-79, 2020-46 I.R.B. 1014; Notice 2019-59, 2019-47 I.R.B. 1091] (For definitions, see Q 12:72 (annual additions), Q 12:73 (limitation year), Q 12:71 (defined contribution plan), and Qs 12:34–12:44 (compensation).)

The 415 limit only matters to a SEP participant if he or she *also* participates in another defined contribution plan of the employer. The dollar limit is the same as for the maximum SEP contribution (see Q 12:63). Only the percentage limit differs. Under a SEP plan, the employer may not contribute more than 25 percent of an individual's compensation. But if the employer has two or more plans in which the individual participates, up to 100 percent of compensation may be contributed on a combined basis.

Q 12:71 What defined contribution plans are covered by the 415 limit?

The plans treated as defined contribution plans for purposes of the 415 limit are SEPs, SIMPLEs, qualified plans (i.e., plans qualified under Code Section 401(a) with an exempt trust under Code Section 501(a)), and annuity plans described in Code Section 403(a). Certain other amounts are also treated as additions made under a defined contribution plan:

- Mandatory employee contributions made under a defined benefit plan (unless they are picked up by the employer),
- Contributions allocated to an individual medical benefits account, if the account is part of a pension or annuity plan established under Code Section 401(h),
- Amounts allocated to a key employee's account for postretirement medical benefits, and
- Annual additions under an annuity plan described in Code Section 403(b).

[Treas. Reg. § 1.415(c)-1(a)]

Q 12:72 What are annual additions?

The total *annual addition* to a participant's account is the sum of employer contributions (even excess contributions, whether or not a corrective distribution is made), some employee contributions, and forfeitures credited to a participant's account for the *limitation year* (see Q 12:73). Annual additions do *not* include:

- Investment earnings in the account,
- Salary deferrals elected under a SARSEP (see Q 12:51),
- Catch-up contributions,
- Benefits and employee contributions directly transferred to an account from a qualified plan,
- Rollovers of employee contributions,
- Dividends on employer securities reinvested under an employee stock ownership plan,
- Excess deferrals (if distributed),
- Certain repayments,
- Employee contributions under a qualified cost of living arrangement, and
- Restorative payments made to cover losses resulting from a fiduciary breach.

[Treas. Reg. § 1.415(c)-1(b)]

Q 12:73 What is a limitation year?

A *limitation year* is the annual period to which the 415 limit applies. It is the calendar year, unless the plan provides otherwise. It need not be the same as the employer's tax year, *nor* the year on which the plan is maintained.

If a plan's limitation year is not the calendar year, the applicable inflation-adjusted 415 limit is the one announced for the calendar year in which the limitation year *ends*. [Treas. Reg. § 1.415(d)-1(b)(2)(iii)]

> **Example.** The Calendar Company's SEP plan has a limitation year that runs from February 1 through January 31. For the limitation year that ends on January 31, 2021, the dollar-adjusted 415 limit that is announced for calendar year 2021 will apply. (The IRS generally announces the limit for a year in late October of the prior year.)

Q 12:74 What are the timing rules for annual additions?

Generally, an annual addition is taken into account for a particular limitation year if it is allocated to the participant's account, under the plan's terms, as of any date within that limitation year. [Treas. Reg. §§ 1.415(c)-1(b), 1.415(c)-1(b)(6)(i)(A)]

However, if the allocation depends on any condition being satisfied (e.g., continued employment) and the condition is not yet satisfied on the allocation date under the plan, then the annual addition is considered allocated for this purpose only when the condition is satisfied. [Treas. Reg. § 1.415(c)-1(b)(6)(i)(A)]

Employer contributions are not treated as credited to a participant's account for a particular limitation year unless they are timely made. That means they must be actually paid to the plan not more than 30 days after the due date of the employer's tax return (including extensions) for the limitation year with or within which the limitation year ends. [I.R.C. § 404(h)(1)(B), 404(a)(6); Treas. Reg. § 1.415(c)-1(b)(6)(i)(B)]

> **Example 1.** The Green Company's tax year runs from June 1 through May 31. It maintains a SEP that uses the calendar year as both its plan year and limitation year. The plan requires Green's annual contribution to be made to the plan two months after Green's tax year ends. It also requires the plan to allocate the contribution to participants' accounts as of the last day of the plan year ending within that tax year. The allocation does not depend on any condition being satisfied.
>
> The 2019 plan year ends within Green's tax year that ends on May 31, 2020. Green makes its contribution on July 31, 2020, and plan allocations are made as of the end of the 2019 plan year (December 31, 2019). The employer contribution is actually made within the time required by statute (not more than 30 days after the due date, including extensions, for Green's tax return for the period that ends in July 2020). Consequently, the plan

allocations made as of December 31, 2019, are treated as annual additions for the SEP's *2019* limitation year.

Example 2. The facts are the same as Example 1, except that Green's SEP has a plan year that runs from February 1 through January 31. The limitation year is still the calendar year. The employer contribution that Green makes on July 31, 2020 is allocated by the SEP as of January 31, 2020 (the end of the plan year that ends within Green's tax year for which the contribution is made). Since January 31, 2020, falls within the SEP's 2020 limitation year, the allocations are annual additions for the plan's *2020* limitation year.

Elective Deferral Limit (§ 402(g))

Q 12:75 How much compensation may a participant defer under the SARSEP rules?

For 2021, a SARSEP participant may defer up to $19,500, or (if less) *25* percent of compensation earned from the employer that maintains the SARSEP. As explained in Q 12:62, compensation over $290,000 (the 2021 limit) is ignored. [Notice 2020-79, 2020-46 I.R.B. 114; Notice 2018-83, 2018-47 I.R.B. 774; I.R.C. § 402(g)] A SARSEP plan may also allow catch-up contributions (see Q 12:76).

(For the employer's election to exclude elective deferrals from compensation, see Q 12:35.)

Q 12:76 What catch-up deferrals do the SARSEP rules allow?

SARSEP plans are not required to allow catch-up deferrals, but they can allow them for participants who will be age 50 or older by the end of the year. For 2021, an eligible participant may defer up to $6,500 (the figure for 2020 was $6,500), or the lesser amount allowed by the plan, as a catch-up contribution. Catch-ups are not subject to the 25-percent-of-compensation limit (see Q 12:75), but the total amount deferred, including the catch-up amount, may not exceed 100 percent of compensation. [Notice 2020-79, 2020-46 I.R.B. 1014; Notice 2019-59, 2019-47 I.R.B. 1091; I.R.C. §§ 402(h)(2), 414(v)(3)(A); Treas. Reg. §§ 1.414(v)-1(c)(2)(i), 414(v)(2), 414(v)(5); Treas. Reg. § 1.414(v)-1(g)(3)]

Q 12:77 Are catch-up deferrals subject to the SEP and SARSEP nondiscrimination rules?

No. An elective deferral that is a catch-up contribution is not subject to the nondiscrimination rules and will not cause the plan to be treated as failing those rules. Catch-up contributions are disregarded in applying the limits of certain Code Sections, including Code Sections 401(a)(30), 402(h), 403(b), 404(h), 408, 415, and 457(b)(2) (determined without regard to Section 457(b)(3)), to other contributions or benefits under the plan offering catch-up contributions or to any other plan of the employer. [I.R.C. § 414(v)(3); Treas. Reg. § 1.414(v)-1(d)(1)]

Q 12:78 How are catch-up contributions treated for purposes of ADP testing?

Any elective deferral for the plan year that is treated as a catch-up contribution because it exceeds a statutory or employer-provided limit is disregarded in calculating a participant's actual deferral percentage (ADP) under a SARSEP. [Treas. Reg. § 1.414(v)-1(d)(2)(i)]

> **Caution.** Because an amount treated as a catch-up contribution is not taken into account in calculating the ADP, the ADP may have to be recalculated if unanticipated catch-up amounts are determined to exist for any participating non-highly compensated employee (NHCE).

Q 12:79 Do elective deferrals made under a SARSEP plan count as *annual additions* for purposes of the Code Section 415 limit?

No. The employer's nonelective contributions under the SARSEP are subject to the Code Section 415 limit, but the participant's salary reduction contributions are not. [I.R.C. § 415(c)(2)]

Excess Contributions

Q 12:80 What is an excess SEP contribution?

An *excess contribution* is made if the total amounts contributed for the year by or for the participant to eligible retirement plans of the employer exceed the annual limit.

A SEP plan may restrict total contributions to an amount less than what the Code allows, in which case amounts in excess of the plan's limit are excess contributions. Amounts paid to HCEs that fail the ADP test (see Q 12:54) are also excess contributions. [I.R.C. § 402(h); IRS Pub. 560, *Retirement Plans for Small Businesses (SEP, SIMPLE, and Qualified Plans)* 2020]

Q 12:81 What happens if an excess contribution is made?

If not corrected (see Q 12:82), excess contributions have consequences for both the employer and the employee.

For the employer, the excess contribution is nondeductible and subject to a 10 percent excise tax. [I.R.C. §§ 404(h), 4972(d)(1)(A)(iii)]

For the employee, any excess contribution that the employer did not correct is included in gross income and treated as a contribution that the employee has made. Unless the employee withdraws it, with earnings, by the due date of the employee's federal income tax return, a 6 percent excise tax is payable yearly until the amount is removed. [I.R.C. §§ 402(h)(1), 4973; I.R.S. Ann. 97-41, 1997-16 I.R.B. 28]

Example 1. Theo's sole proprietorship has no employees and makes a 26 percent SEP contribution for 2020. There is no carryforward. The excess employer SEP contribution is not deductible for 2020 under the SEP rules. Theo should include the excess amount on line 7 of his Form 1040 for 2020

Example 2. Max, a sole proprietor, makes a 25 percent SEP contribution for himself and all eligible employees. Max overestimated his earned income; in fact, he had no earned income for the year. The contributions made on behalf of only the nonowner-employees create a net operating loss that Max may use to offset personal income. Any balance attributable to the nonowner-employees may be carried forward.

Q 12:82 How is an excess SEP contribution corrected?

There are two correction methods. The first is to distribute the excess SEP contribution back to the employer, along with all earnings calculated to the date of the distribution. The distributed amount is not taxed to the participant, but should be reported on Form 1099-R with a taxable amount of zero. If it is not feasible to determine the earnings, a reasonable rate of interest should be used. [IRS SEP Plan Fix-It Guide, available at *https://www.irs.gov/Retirement-Plans/SEP-Fix-It-Guide-Common-Problems-Real-Solutions*]

The other method is for employers that use the IRS Voluntary Correction Program (VCP). Generally, the VCP allows a plan sponsor, at any time before audit, to pay a fee and receive IRS approval for correction of plan failures. A VCP user may leave the excess amount in the SEP-IRA if an additional compliance fee is paid (10 percent of the excess amount, excluding earnings; but no fee is charged if the excess amount is less than $100). [IRS SEP Plan Fix-It Guide]

(For correction of excess elective deferrals under a SARSEP, see Q 12:84.)

Q 12:83 What is an excess elective deferral under a SARSEP?

Excess elective deferrals are elective deferrals that exceed the Section 402(g) limit (see Q 12:75). For example, elective SARSEP deferrals exceeding $19,500 (for 2021), for a participant who is not catch-up eligible, would be excess elective deferrals. If an individual participates in more than one SARSEP (whether with the same or another employer), or also makes deferrals under a SIMPLE or other salary reduction arrangement, the combined elective deferrals may not exceed the Section 402(g) limit. [Notice 2020-79, 2020-46 I.R.B. 1014]

Excess elective deferrals may also result from failure to satisfy the ADP test for HCE contributions.

Q 12:84 How is an excess elective deferral corrected?

An individual who made an excess elective deferral under a SARSEP may correct it by timely withdrawal. The excess deferral amount, adjusted to include all earnings for the deferral year, must be withdrawn by April 15 of the year following the year of the excess deferral. The excess deferral is included in income for the year of the deferral, but the earnings (for the deferral year only) are included in income for the year they are distributed. The earnings are not subject to employment taxes. [Instructions for Forms 1099-R and 5498 (2020), p. 7 (Excess Deferrals)]

However, if the participant does not withdraw the excess amount by the April 15 deadline, the excess deferral is considered a regular IRA contribution and is subject to the contribution limit for traditional IRAs. If an excess IRA contribution results, a 6 percent excise tax applies until the excess contribution (with attributable earnings) is withdrawn. [I.R.C. § 4973] Further, if the excess is not timely corrected, a participant who is younger than age 59½ when the amount is finally distributed will be subject to the 10 percent early distribution penalty. [I.R.C. § 72(t); Instructions for Forms 1099-R and 5498 (2020), p. 7 (Excess Deferrals); IRS SARSEP Plan Fix-It Guide, available at *http://www.irs.gov/Retirement-Plans/SARSEP-Plan-Fix-It-Guide*]

(For correction of excess contributions that are *not* elective deferrals, see Q 12:82.)

Q 12:85 What notice must the employer provide concerning excess contributions?

The employer must provide a clear written notice to the affected employees which states:

1. The amount of the excess contributions attributable to the employee's elective deferrals;
2. The calendar year for which the excess contributions were made;
3. That the excess contributions are includable in the affected employee's gross income for the specified calendar year; and
4. That failure to withdraw the excess SEP contributions and income attributable to it by April 15 of the tax year following the year of notification may result in significant penalties.

The employer's notice must be given within two and one-half months after the end of the plan year. An employer's failure to notify affected employees of excess SEP contributions or disallowed deferrals in no way alters the fact that the amounts are includable in the employees' gross income and may also be subject to the IRA contribution limits (and thus may be considered excess IRA contributions). Although, in a sense, the employer has 12 months to act, failure to make a proper and timely notification within two and one-half months will cost the employer a 10 percent penalty under Code Section 4979. [I.R.C. § 4979(f); Treas. Reg. § 54.4979-1(a)(4)(i), 54.4979-1(a)(4)(ii)]

Distributions

Q 12:86 When must distributions from the SEP IRA begin?

The minimum distribution rules that apply to traditional IRAs (see chapter 4) also apply to SEP IRAs, so minimum distributions must begin by the employee's required beginning date (RBD). If distributions do not commence by the RBD, the 50 percent excess accumulation penalty applies. [I.R.C. § 4974(a)]

Note. The minimum distribution requirements are suspended for 2020. (See Qs 4:6–4:17.) [I.R.C. § 401(a)(9)(I)(i), added by Coronavirus Aid, Relief, and Economic Security Act (CARES Act), Pub. L. No. 116-136 (Mar. 27, 2020), § 2203]

The SECURE Act changed the definition of the RBD. For anyone who attains age *70½* after 2019 (everyone born *after* June 30, 1949), the RBD is April 1 of the calendar year following the year when age *72* is attained. For anyone who attained age 70½ before 2020 (everyone born *on or before* June 30, 1949), the old RBD definition still applies, and the RBD is April 1 of the calendar year after age 70½ was attained. [I.R.C. § 401(a)(9)(C)(i)(I), as amended by SECURE Act § 114]

After the participant dies, the SEP IRA is subject to the same minimum distribution requirements that apply to beneficiaries of traditional IRAs (see chapter 4). [Treas. Reg. § 1.408-8, Q&A-2] The SECURE Act changed these rules significantly. (See Qs 4:40, 4:53, 4:86.)

Q 12:87 When may an employee withdraw the employer's contributions?

Employees who are not HCEs may always withdraw employer contributions (and salary deferral contributions under a SARSEP). An HCE may not withdraw or transfer elective deferrals under a SARSEP until March 15 of the year after the limitation year (or an earlier determination by the employer that the ADP test (see Q 12:54) is satisfied). The trustee or custodian of the IRA may enforce the restriction; failure to do so could result in penalties to the employee and possible loss of SEP status for the arrangement.

Until the employer determines that the ADP test has been met, any transfer or distribution from a SARSEP of restricted funds (salary reduction contributions and income attributable to such contributions) by an HCE is taxable and may be subject to the 10 percent early distribution penalty, regardless of whether an exception to the penalty would otherwise apply. [I.R.C. § 408(k)(6)(F)] Indeed, any distribution, transfer, or rollover of the restricted funds before the earlier of employer certification or March 15 following the end of the plan year will not be treated as an excess contribution permitted to be withdrawn without penalty. [*See* IRS Form 5305A-SEP (rev. June 2006), Instructions for the Employer—Restrictions on Withdrawals, at 4, and Instructions for the Employee—Excess SEP Contributions (containing references to HCEs), at 6]

Practice Pointer. The tax, if any, is reported in Part I of Form 5329, Additional Taxes on Qualified Plans (Including IRAs) and Other Tax-Favored Accounts.

Rollovers, Conversions, and Recharacterizations

Q 12:88 What tax-free rollovers to or from a SEP IRA are permitted?

Tax-free rollovers are generally permitted *to* a SEP IRA from another SEP IRA, or from a traditional IRA, SIMPLE IRA (after participating at least two years in the employer's SIMPLE plan; see Q 13:68), governmental 457(b) plan, pre-tax qualified plan, or 403(b) plan. SEP IRAs may not receive transfers from a Roth IRA or a designated Roth account (DRAC) within a qualified plan. (See chapter 6.)

Tax-free rollovers *from* a SEP IRA can generally be made to another SEP IRA, or to a traditional IRA, governmental 457(b) plan (provided the accepting plan agrees to account separately for the rollover), pre-tax qualified plan, or 403(b) plan. Rollovers may also occur from a SEP IRA to a SIMPLE IRA after participating in the employer's SIMPLE for at least two years—but only for transfers after December 18, 2015. (See chapter 6.)

IRA-to-IRA transfers are subject to the one-rollover-per-year requirement. (See Qs 6:15–6:19.)

Q 12:89 May a SEP IRA be converted to a Roth IRA?

Yes. The SEP participant (or the participant's surviving spouse who is the designated beneficiary) may convert the SEP IRA to a Roth IRA. [Treas. Reg. § 1.408A-4] No other beneficiary is eligible to convert an inherited IRA under current law. (See Q 3:84.)

Note. By contrast, qualified plan beneficiaries are allowed to convert qualified plan assets to a Roth IRA. [Notice 2008-30, Q&A-7, 2008-12 I.R.B. 638]

Q 12:90 May SEP IRA contributions be made to a SEP IRA that has been converted to a Roth IRA?

If the entire SEP IRA is redesignated as a Roth IRA, it is no longer a SEP IRA and cannot receive new SEP contributions. But if assets are withdrawn from the SEP IRA and converted to a Roth IRA, the SEP IRA may continue to receive SEP contributions. [Treas. Reg. § 1.408A-4, Q&A-1(b)]

Q 12:91 If SEP assets are converted to a Roth IRA, can the conversion be reversed by recharacterizing the assets back to the SEP IRA?

It was previously possible to unwind a conversion of SEP assets by timely recharacterizing the converted assets back to the SEP IRA. However, no conversion made after 2017 can be recharacterized. [Tax Cuts and Jobs Act, Pub. L. No. 115-97, § 13611 (Dec. 22, 2017); I.R.C. § 408A(d)(3), 408A(d)(6)(B); Treas. Reg. § 1.408A-5, Q&A-5]

The deadline for recharacterizing a conversion made in 2017 was October 15, 2018. [I.R.C. § 408A(d)(6); IRS FAQ, *Recharacterization of IRA Contributions (2018)*, available at *https://www.irs.gov/retirement-plans/ira-faqs-recharacterization-of-ira-contributions*]

Q 12:92 May SEP contributions be recharacterized to a different type of IRA?

No. All contributions under a SEP are considered to be made by the employer. They cannot be recharacterized as contributions that the participant makes to another IRA. [Treas. Reg. § 1.408A-5]

Reporting and Disclosure

Q 12:93 What are the employer's reporting and disclosure responsibilities?

The employer must provide employees with information about the plan when it is first established, and after that on an annual basis.

Initially, all employees must receive a notice stating that the plan has been adopted, the requirements an employee must meet to receive a contribution, and how the employer's contribution will be allocated among employees. A copy of the plan agreement must also be provided. If the IRS model agreement (Form 5305-SEP) was used to establish the plan, a copy of the form's instructions should also be provided. [Treas. Reg. § 1.408-9(a); Instructions to Form 5305-SEP (rev. 2004)]

The same information must be given to each new employee who becomes eligible to participate in the plan.

Subsequently, on an annual basis, the employer must also provide an annual written statement about the plan to all employees. This must include a description of the plan's terms, how they can be changed, and when participants will be informed about contributions made to their SEP IRAs (see Q 12:94). [Prop. Treas. Reg. § 1.408-9(b)]

Annual reports to the IRS about the *plan* are generally not required. On each participant's Form W-2, however, the employer must check "retirement plan" in box 13. Also, if the plan is a SARSEP, the employer excludes the participant's elective salary reduction contributions from box 1 (wages, etc., subject to income tax), but includes them in boxes 3, 5, and 7 (Social Security and Medicare wages and tips). SEP contributions are never included in box 1. [General Instructions for Forms W-2 and W-3 (2020)]

Q 12:94 What annual notice must the employer give to participants about its SEP contribution?

The employer must provide each employee with a written statement indicating the amount of the employer's contribution for the year, and it must be furnished within 30 days of the contribution or by January 31 of the year following the calendar year for which the contribution is made. [Prop. Treas. Reg. § 1.408-9(b)]

Note. SEP contributions are not coded by year when they are reported by the trustee to the IRS.

Example. Maxgate maintains a calendar year SEP. Its federal income tax return for the 2020 tax year is due on March 15, 2021. On February 1, 2021, Maxgate makes its 2020 contribution and notifies the trustee that the contribution is being made for the prior year. On April 5, 2021, Maxgate's bookkeeper discovers that the company had already made its 2020 contribution on January 25, 2021 and that the SEP is now overfunded by $10,000. Although the SEP trustee will report both contributions as made in 2021, there is no requirement that the report indicate for which year the contributions are made. Arguably, a SEP contribution made between January 1 and April 15, 2021 could be for either 2020 or 2021. Maxgate might not have a problem at all, unless participant compensation for 2020 cannot support the additional $10,000 contribution.

Although it was issued a few years before the existence of SEPs, Revenue Ruling 76-28 [1976-1 C.B. 106, *modified slightly by* Rev. Rul. 76-77, 1976-1 C.B. 107] would appear to support the reasoning in the preceding example, because the language of Code Section 404(h) is similar to the "special rules for SEPs" under Code Section 404 regarding the time contributions are deemed made. [I.R.C. § 404(h), 404(a)(6)] On the other hand, the IRS might consider whether employees were notified that the contribution was made for the current year or prior taxable year. In the example, Maxgate's contribution notice to its employees would be required by January 31, 2020, or within 30 days after the contribution is made.

Q 12:95 What are the reporting and disclosure responsibilities of the plan trustee?

The financial institution serving as trustee for the plan must report annually to the IRS with respect to each SEP IRA. On Form 5498, the trustee reports contributions made to, and the year-end fair market value of, the SEP IRA. A box on the form is also checked if an RMD will be required for the next year. On Form 1099-R, the trustee reports any distributions made from the SEP IRA. Copies of Forms 5498 and 1099-R must also be provided to the participants. Under IRS Notice 2021-21, the reporting deadline for 2020 was extended until June 30, 2021.

Debtor Issues

Q 12:96 Are SEP IRAs protected in bankruptcy?

Yes. If a SEP or SARSEP participant is the debtor in bankruptcy, the IRA enjoys full exemption from the bankruptcy estate under the federal Bankruptcy Code (see Q 1:52). (Regarding protection for inherited IRAs, see Q 1:54.)

Q 12:97 In a nonbankruptcy situation, may the IRS or another creditor assert claims against a SEP IRA?

Outside of bankruptcy, federal laws do not protect IRA assets from creditors' claims. Some state laws do so, but whether such laws extend to every SEP IRA is not clear.

The federal laws that may protect retirement assets from creditors' claims are the Bankruptcy Abuse Prevention and Consumer Protection Act of 2005 (BAPCPA) and ERISA. BAPCPA does not apply outside of bankruptcy. ERISA contains an anti-alienation provision that provides such protection, but it does not apply to IRAs. [29 U.S.C. §§ 1003(b), 1051; 29 C.F.R. § 2510.3-2(d)]

Another ERISA provision preempts state laws relating to *employee benefit plans*. [ERISA § 514(a)] A SEP plan is an employee benefit plan for this purpose if it covers at least one employee, not counting the business owner and his or her spouse. [ERISA § 3(2)(A); 29 C.F.R. § 2510.3-3(b); DOL Adv. Op. 1999-04A; *In re* Witwer, 148 B.R. 930 (Bankr. C.D. Cal. 1992), *aff'd without opinion*, 163 B.R. 614 (B.A.P. 9th Cir. 1994)]

Clearly, the preemption clause guarantees that a state cannot diminish ERISA's protection. But it seems wrong to conclude that a state is also precluded from enlarging upon ERISA's protection. In the author's view, ERISA should be construed as allowing all SEP IRAs to be covered under a state law that protects IRAs outside of bankruptcy.

Chapter 13

SIMPLE IRA Arrangements

The savings incentive match plan for employees (SIMPLE) is a simplified tax-favored retirement plan for small employers that is available under Section 408(p) of the Internal Revenue Code (Code). Employees may choose to make salary reduction contributions to a SIMPLE individual retirement account or annuity (IRA) rather than receive those amounts as part of their regular compensation. The employer makes either a matching contribution or a nonelective contribution on behalf of eligible employees.

Plan contributions are deposited with a financial institution authorized to accept IRA deposits. The employer may stipulate the financial institution that employees must use to establish their SIMPLE IRAs.

This chapter examines the rules for setting up a SIMPLE plan, employer and employee eligibility, employee notifications, salary reduction arrangements, summary descriptions, the time and manner of making contributions and elections, and the administrative requirements and deposit rules for financial institutions and employers.

A SIMPLE IRA can accept rollovers from another SIMPLE IRA at any time. Once the participant has completed at least two years of participation in the employer's SIMPLE, rollovers from a traditional IRA, SEP IRA, or pre-tax qualified plan are also allowed.

The Setting Every Community Up for Retirement Enhancement Act (SECURE Act), Div. O of the Further Consolidated Appropriations Act, 2020, Pub. L. No. 116-94 (Dec. 20, 2019) made many changes that affect IRA distributions, particularly those made to beneficiaries after the participant's death.

Overview

Q 13:1 What is a SIMPLE plan?

A Savings Incentive Match Plan for Employees of Small Employers (SIMPLE) is a retirement plan specifically for businesses with 100 or fewer employees. It is generally less expensive and easier to administer than other employer-sponsored plans. The employer establishes a SIMPLE IRA for each eligible employee and makes mandatory annual contributions. The employee may also defer a portion of salary to the SIMPLE IRA. SIMPLE plans are governed by Section 408(p) of the Internal Revenue Code (Code or I.R.C.).

Q 13:2 How does a SIMPLE plan work?

The employer chooses before each plan year whether to make a matching contribution or a nonelective contribution for every participant. A matching contribution is generally the lesser of 3 percent of a participant's compensation (for some years the percentage may be lower) or the amount of the participant's salary deferral. A nonelective contribution is 2 percent of the participant's compensation, although compensation taken into account for this purpose (but not the matching contribution) may not exceed an annual limit.

SIMPLE plans are subject to various requirements concerning establishment, vesting rights, participation, notice, administration, distributions, and taxation. For a general overview of SIMPLE IRAs, *see* SIMPLE IRA Plans (IRS, July 6, 2021); SIMPLE IRA Checklist and Plan Fix-It Guide (IRS, June 6, 2021); and SIMPLE IRA Plan FAQs (IRS, July 8, 2021).

Eligible Employers

Q 13:3 What employers can have a SIMPLE plan?

An employer must meet two requirements to be eligible in any year for a SIMPLE plan. One, it must not have had more than 100 employees in the *preceding* year who earned more than $5,000 in compensation. And two, the employer cannot also have a qualified plan that covers service for the same year as the SIMPLE, unless the qualified plan is only for collective bargaining employees. [I.R.C. § 408(p)(2)(C)(i)(I), 408(p)(2)(D)]

(For the grace periods that apply for failures to meet the 100-employee test, see Qs 13:6, 13:7.)

Q 13:4 Is every employee counted?

Yes. Every person employed at any time during the prior calendar year must be counted, regardless of whether they are eligible to participate in the SIMPLE. Self-employed individuals who received earned income from the employer during the year must also be counted. Even employees whom the employer excludes from participation in the SIMPLE (see Q 13:32) must be counted for purposes of the 100-employee limit. [I.R.C. §§ 401(c)(1), 408(p)(2)(C)(i)(I), 408(p)(4)(A)]

Leased employees must also be counted under the SIMPLE rules if they are treated, under Code Section 414(n), as employees of the employer. [I.R.C. § 414(b), 414(c), 414(m), 414(n), 414(o)]

Q 13:5 If two employers are related, must all their employees be counted to determine whether one or both may have a SIMPLE plan?

Code Section 414 contains a rule that treats certain affiliated employers as a single employer for SIMPLE, SEP, and qualified plan purposes. Consequently, all individuals who work for that single employer are counted to determine whether the 100-employee limit (and all other SIMPLE requirements) are met. (See Qs 12:30–12:32.)

Related employers include the following:

- A controlled group of corporations under Code Section 414(b)
- Any business (whether or not incorporated) under common control under Code Section 414(c)
- An affiliated service group under Code Section 414(m)

Example. Pam owns Peach, a computer rental agency with 80 employees who each received more than $5,000 in compensation in 2020. Pam also owns Pear, a company that repairs computers and has 60 employees who each received more than $5,000 in compensation in 2020. Pam is the sole proprietor of both businesses. Code Section 414(c) provides that the employees of partnerships and sole proprietorships under common control are treated as employees of the same employer. Thus, for purposes of the SIMPLE rules, all 140 employees are treated as employed by the same employer, and neither Peach nor Pear may establish a SIMPLE for 2020 (see Q 13:3).

Q 13:6 What grace period applies to the 100-employee limit?

Once an employer has maintained a SIMPLE for at least one year, it is treated as automatically satisfying the 100-employee limit for the next two calendar years after each calendar year in which that requirement is met. This grace period gives the employer time to correct overages. [I.R.C. § 408(p)(2)(C)(i)(II)] A special transition rule applies if the failure to satisfy the 100-employee limit results from an acquisition, disposition, or similar transaction involving the employer (see Q 13:7).

Example. Since 2013, Train Associates has maintained a steady work force of 70 employees with very little turnover. Its SIMPLE plan (for employees who earned at least $5,000 in any prior year) has been operational since 2014. In 2020, however, Train hired 40 new employees, bringing the total who earned at least $5,000 that year to more than 100. Were it not for the grace period, Train would be disqualified from maintaining a SIMPLE for 2021. However, because of the grace period, Train is treated as satisfying the 100-employee limit for both 2020 and 2021 (since it met the requirement in 2019).

Q 13:7 What grace period applies after a merger, acquisition, or disposition by the employer?

If an acquisition, disposition, or similar transaction causes an employer to exceed the 100-employee limit, the employer is still treated as meeting the requirement, for the year of the transaction and the next two years, if two requirements are met:

- Coverage under the plan does not change significantly during the grace period, and

- The plan would have continued to qualify if the employer had remained as a separate employer.

[I.R.C. §§ 408(p)(10), 410(b)(6)(C)]

Q 13:8 Can an employer maintain both a qualified plan and a SIMPLE?

They cannot be concurrently maintained. A SIMPLE must be the employer's only plan. If the employer (or a predecessor employer) does maintain a defined contribution or defined benefit plan (see Q 13:9), under which *any* employee receives an allocation of contributions, or an increase in accrued benefits, for a particular plan year, then for the calendar year in which that plan year begins and ends SIMPLE contributions cannot also be made. If they are made, the SIMPLE contributions made are considered excess contributions, which the employer must report as wages on Form W-2, Wage and Tax Statement.

There is one exception. An employer may maintain a qualified plan that covers only collectively bargained employees, if those employees are excluded from participating in the SIMPLE (see Q 13:9). [I.R.C. § 408(p)(2)(D)]

(For contributions that are disregarded to determine whether a qualified plan is concurrently maintained, see Q 13:10.)

Q 13:9 What types of employer-sponsored plans disqualify an employer from making contributions under a SIMPLE plan?

An employer may not make SIMPLE contributions if it concurrently (see Q 13:8) maintains any of the plans described in Code Section 219(g)(5). These are:

1. A qualified pension, profit sharing, or stock bonus plan under Code Section 401(a) that includes a tax-exempt trust under Code Section 501(a);
2. An annuity plan under Code Section 403(a);
3. A tax-sheltered annuity contract described in Code Section 403(b);
4. A governmental plan (i.e., a plan established by the United States, a state, an agency of a state, or a political subdivision of a state) other than an eligible deferred compensation plan under Code Section 457(b);
5. Certain trusts funded solely with employee contributions under Code Section 501(c)(18);
6. A SEP or SARSEP; and
7. A SIMPLE within the meaning of Code Section 408(p)—i.e., the employer may maintain only one SIMPLE.

[I.R.C. §§ 219(g)(5)(A), 408(p)(2)(D)]

Q 13:10 What amounts are disregarded to determine whether a qualified plan contribution was made?

Forfeitures (except to the extent they replace otherwise-required contributions), transfers, and rollovers are disregarded to determine whether a contribution has been made to a qualified plan. [Notice 98-4, Q&A B-3, 1998-1 C.B. 269]

Q 13:11 May a tax-exempt organization or governmental entity establish a SIMPLE?

Yes. Tax-exempt organizations and governmental entities may establish SIMPLEs. They may even do so while offering 457(b) plans to their employees. (A 457(b) plan is similar to a 401(k) plan, but it is not a qualified plan.) [I.R.C. §§ 408(k)(6)(E), 408(p)(2)(D)(ii), 219(g)(5)(A), 219(g)(5)(B); Notice 98-4, Q&A B-4, 1998-1 C.B. 269]

Note. Employer contributions and salary deferrals made under a SIMPLE plan are not counted for purposes of the contribution limits that apply to 457(b) plans. [I.R.C. § 457(c)]

Establishing a SIMPLE Plan

Q 13:12 How is a SIMPLE plan established?

An employer establishes a SIMPLE plan by adopting a written plan agreement, opening SIMPLE IRAs for eligible employees, and giving information (see Q 13:82) about the plan to all employees. [IRS Pub. 560, *Retirement Plans for Small Business (SEP, SIMPLE, and Qualified Plans)* 2020]

Q 13:13 Must a SIMPLE plan be maintained on a calendar-year basis?

Yes. Contributions under a SIMPLE plan are determined on a calendar-year basis. So is the determination of whether an employer has met the eligibility requirements for a SIMPLE (see Q 13:3). [I.R.C. § 408(p)(6)(C)] A SIMPLE can be started during the year, however (see Q 13:15).

Q 13:14 What is the deadline for setting up a SIMPLE plan?

A new SIMPLE plan must become effective on or before October 1 if contributions are to be made for the same year. Otherwise, the next calendar year must be the first plan year. [IRS Pub. 560, *Retirement Plans for Small Business (SEP, SIMPLE, and Qualified Plans)* 2020]

There is one exception to this rule. If a *new* employer comes into existence after October 1 and establishes the SIMPLE as soon as administratively feasible, contributions can be made for that first year.

Note. The IRS model forms do not allow for an adoption date later than October 1 of the applicable year.

Q 13:15 Must the first plan year begin on January 1?

Not necessarily. An existing employer may establish a SIMPLE effective on any date from January 1 through October 1 if it (or any predecessor employer; see Q 13:17) did not previously maintain a SIMPLE. But if the employer or a predecessor employer previously maintained a SIMPLE, a new SIMPLE may only be established with an effective date of January 1. [Notice 98-4, Q&A K-1, 1998-1 C.B. 269]

Q 13:16 Can an employer terminate one SIMPLE plan and start another in the same year?

No. An employer (or predecessor employer; see Q 13:17) that terminates a SIMPLE cannot establish a new SIMPLE and have it become effective during the same calendar year. The new SIMPLE may not become effective until at least January 1 of the next year. [Notice 98-4, Q&A K-1, 1998-1 C.B. 269]

Q 13:17 What is a predecessor employer?

The term *predecessor employer* has not been defined for SIMPLE purposes. However, a regulation under Code Section 415 (not applicable to SIMPLE IRAs) generally would find the existence of a predecessor employer if:

1. A plan maintained by the current employer continues a benefit that a participant accrued while performing services for a former employer, or
2. The current employer constitutes (taking facts and circumstances into account) a continuation of all or a portion of the trade or business of a former entity that predated the current employer.

[Treas. Reg. § 1.415(f)-1(c); *see* Treasury Decision 9319 (Apr. 5, 2007)]

Plan Agreement

Q 13:18 What written agreement is needed for a SIMPLE plan?

Every SIMPLE plan must have a written agreement that states the governing rules of the plan. The employer may use an IRS model form, or adopt a prototype or individually designed SIMPLE plan. [I.R.C. § 408(a)–408(c), 408(p)(1), 408(p)(2)(A)] (For a general discussion of the differences between model forms and prototypes, and the procedure for obtaining IRS approval of a prototype, see Qs 2:25–2:26.)

Q 13:19 What model forms does the IRS provide?

There are two IRS model forms. An employer that will select the custodian of the SIMPLE IRAs uses Form 5305-SIMPLE, Savings Incentive Match Plan for Employees of Small Employers (SIMPLE)—for Use With a Designated Financial Institution. If the plan will allow participants to choose any financial institution for their SIMPLE IRAs, the employer uses Form 5304-SIMPLE, Savings Incentive

Match Plan for Employees of Small Employers (SIMPLE)—Not for Use With a Designated Financial Institution. (DFIs are discussed in Qs 13:99–13:106.)

The basic language of the model forms cannot be amended. However, some provisions include options for the employer to select:

- Whether to make all employees eligible to participate, or set a minimum compensation threshold (not to exceed $5,000)
- Whether to exclude employees who are covered by a collective bargaining agreement for which retirement benefits were fairly negotiated
- The timing of employee salary deferral elections
- For years when the employer chooses to make the nonelective contribution (2 percent of compensation), whether all participants will receive an allocation or only those with a specified minimum compensation (not to exceed $5,000)
- The details of the withdrawal procedure

The model forms also include a model for the annual notice that must be given to employees. The annual notice tells the employees what contribution the employer will make for the next year under the plan. It also includes a blank salary deferral agreement that employees can use to update their elections.

Q 13:20 Do the model forms include an automatic enrollment option?

No. The IRS stated in 2009 that it would probably add an automatic enrollment option to the model forms, but the latest forms (revised March 2012) do not include that. [Notice 2009-67, 2009-39 I.R.B. 420] If an automatic enrollment option is desired, the employer must adopt a prototype or individually designed plan agreement. Such agreements must contain, at minimum, all the provisions needed to satisfy Code requirements for a SIMPLE plan. Drafters may use their own language, or use the IRS-provided sample language found in the IRS Listing of Required Modifications (LRM) for SIMPLEs. [Savings Incentive Match Plan for Employees of Small Employers (SIMPLE IRA Plan) under Section 408(p) of the Internal Revenue Code (Apr. 2005), found at *http://www.irs.gov/pub/irs-tege/simpleplan_lrm.pdf*]

A new tax credit available to employers for the first three taxable years in which the plan includes automatic enrollment (see Q 13:27). [I.R.C. § 45T, added by the Setting Every Community Up for Retirement Enhancement Act of 2019 (SECURE Act), Div. O of the Further Consolidated Appropriations Act, 2020, Pub. L. No. 116-94 (Dec. 20, 2019)]

Q 13:21 How is the agreement adopted?

If a model form (Form 5305-SIMPLE or Form 5304-SIMPLE) is used to establish a SIMPLE (see Q 13:9), the plan is adopted when the form is completed and executed by the employer (and also by the DFI, if one is used). For prototype and individually designed SIMPLEs, the SIMPLE is adopted when all instructions for adopting it have been followed.

Q 13:22 Is IRS approval needed for a SIMPLE plan?

No. The model forms are pre-approved by the IRS—i.e., the form (but not the operation) of a model SIMPLE plan meets all the legal requirements. IRS approval is not required for prototype and individually designed SIMPLE plans, but it may be sought using the letter ruling process. If an employer adopts a prototype that has received a favorable IRS opinion letter, the employer may rely on the opinion letter as approval of identical versions of the prototype.

If IRS approval is not obtained for a prototype or individually designed plan or agreement, there is no assurance that the form of the document establishing the SIMPLE or SIMPLE IRA will result in deferral of income taxes and the deductibility of employer contributions.

SIMPLE IRAs

Q 13:23 What is a SIMPLE IRA?

Every employee eligible to participate in a SIMPLE plan must have a SIMPLE IRA, which is the IRA (or IRA annuity) that receives employer contributions made on the participant's behalf, as well as salary reduction contributions the participant elects.

A SIMPLE IRA is similar to, but not the same as, a traditional IRA. The only amounts that can be deposited into a SIMPLE IRA are contributions made under the plan and certain rollover contributions (see Q 13:67). Distributions from a SIMPLE IRA are also restricted during the first two years of participation (see Q 13:74). A SIMPLE IRA cannot be a Roth IRA. [I.R.C. § 408(p); Notice 98-4, 1998-1 C.B. 269]

> **Note.** Like any IRA, a SIMPLE IRA can be taxed on unrelated business taxable income. And if a SIMPLE IRA were to become involved in a prohibited transaction (e.g., a pledge of the account as security for a loan), it would cease to be treated as an IRA and the assets would be deemed distributed in a taxable transaction. The 15 percent prohibited transaction tax would not apply, however. [I.R.C. §§ 408(e), 511, 4975(c)(3)]

Q 13:24 Does the IRS have model forms for SIMPLE IRAs?

Yes. The IRS has two model forms that can be used to set up a participant's SIMPLE IRA. They are Form 5305-S, SIMPLE Individual Retirement Trust Account, and Form 5305-SA, SIMPLE Individual Retirement Custodial Account. Both forms were revised in April 2017. The model SIMPLE IRA forms are similar to the models for traditional IRAs (Forms 5305 and 5305-A).

An employer that prefers different terms than are included in the model forms may adopt a prototype or individually designed SIMPLE IRA agreement. The IRS provides suggested language for such agreements in its Listing of Required Modifications and Information Package (LRM) for SIMPLE Individual Retirement Arrangements (rev. June 2010), available at *http://www.irs.gov/pub/irs-tege/sira_lrm.pdf*.

Q 13:25 When must a participant's SIMPLE IRA be opened?

A participant's SIMPLE IRA must be opened by the first date on which a contribution must be deposited. [Notice 98-4, Q&A K-2, 1998-1 C.B. 269]

Q 13:26 What if an eligible employee is unwilling or unable to establish a SIMPLE IRA?

If an eligible employee is unwilling or unable to establish a SIMPLE IRA with any financial institution before the date on which the SIMPLE contribution must be made, the employer may execute the necessary documents to establish a SIMPLE IRA on the employee's behalf, with a financial institution selected by the employer. [Notice 98-4, Q&A G-4, 1998-1 C.B. 269] Under such circumstances, the employee's estate should be named beneficiary of the SIMPLE IRA (unless the plan provides for a default beneficiary).

Incentive Tax Credits

Q 13:27 What tax credits are available to employers who establish a new SIMPLE plan or include a new automatic enrollment feature?

There are two such credits:

- The small employer pension plan startup cost credit (under Code Section 45E)
- The retirement automatic enrollment credit (under Code Section 45T, added by SECURE Act § 105).

These are discussed in detail in Qs 12:20 and 12:21.

Participation

Eligible Employees

Q 13:28 Who may be covered under a SIMPLE plan?

Only *employees* of the employer that maintains a SIMPLE may participate in it. The common-law definition of an employee applies for this purpose, and it includes self-employed individuals and leased employees described in Code Section 414(n). [I.R.C. § 408(p)(6)(B)] An independent contractor is not considered an employee. A household employee may be covered under a SIMPLE (see Q 13:57). [I.R.C. § 4972(c)(6)]

Q 13:29 What are the participation requirements?

Generally, all *employees* (including anyone treated as an employee under the tax laws) who received at least $5,000 in compensation from the employer during any two preceding calendar years (whether or not consecutive), and who are reasonably expected to receive at least $5,000 in compensation during the current calendar year, must be allowed to participate in the employer's SIMPLE plan during the current calendar year. The plan may have eligibility requirements that are less restrictive, but not more so. Restrictions based on age are not permitted. [I.R.C. § 408(p)(4)(A), 408(p)(6)(B)]

However, certain employees may be excluded from participation (see Q 13:32).

Note. The law does not define what it means to *reasonably expect* that an employee will receive the minimum compensation necessary for participation.

Example 1. Plane Company, an eligible employer, establishes a SIMPLE plan effective for 2019. A plan provision defines a *participant* as any current employee who received $500 or more in compensation from Plane in any prior year. Joe earned $1,000 working for Plane in 2017 and then took the next year off. If he returns to work in 2019, he will be eligible to participate in Plane's SIMPLE plan.

Example 2. Harry's long-time employer maintains a SIMPLE plan in 2020. The plan uses the most restrictive eligibility requirement (at least $5,000 compensation in any two prior years) allowed by law. Harry earned $10,000 in 2016 and 2017, but only $4,000 for each of 2018 and 2019. For 2020, he is reasonably expected to earn $7,000. He is eligible to participate in 2020.

Example 3. Donna has been a full-time employee of Giant Motor Company for 18 years. Her current salary (for 2020) is $36,000. Giant's SIMPLE requires at least $5,000 of current year compensation in order to participate. Before the plan's annual election period (November 2 to December 31), Donna requests and is granted an 11-month personal leave of absence starting January 1, 2021. Since Donna is reasonably expected to earn only $3,000 in 2021, she may not participate in the SIMPLE that year.

Example 4. The facts are the same as in Example 3, except that on January 2, 2021, Donna decides not to take the leave of absence. She is still unable to participate in the plan for 2021 because, during the election period for that year (the 60-day period before January 1, 2021), it was not reasonably expected that she would earn $5,000 in 2021.

Q 13:30 Can SIMPLE IRA contributions be made for an individual still employed after age 70½?

Yes. Contributions to a SIMPLE IRA are not subject to a maximum age requirement. Code Section 219(d)(1), which used to prohibit traditional IRA contributions beyond age 70½, did not apply to SIMPLE IRAs. [I.R.C. § 219(b)(4)] (Code Section 219(d)(1) is repealed by SECURE Act Section 107, effective for tax years starting after 2019.)

Q 13:31 Can a person with two jobs participate in a retirement plan with each employer, if one of them is a SIMPLE plan?

Yes. For example, an individual might work for a company and participate in its retirement plan, while operating a business on the side that maintains its own SIMPLE plan. However, the combined elective deferrals under all plans (across employers) may not exceed the limit under Code Section 402(g) (see Q 13:62). The Code Section 402(g) limit for 2021 is $19,500.

Excludable Employees

Q 13:32 What employees can be excluded from participation?

A SIMPLE plan may exclude certain employees from participation. [I.R.C. § 408(p)(4)(B)] The plan document must affirmatively exclude them by classification. Employees who may be excluded are:

1. An employee who is included in a unit of employees covered by a collective bargaining agreement between employee representatives and one or more employers, if there is evidence that retirement benefits were the subject of good-faith bargaining between such employee representatives and such employer or employers;
2. In the case of a trust established or maintained pursuant to a collective bargaining agreement between air pilots represented in accordance with Title II of the Railway Labor Act and one or more employers, all employees *not* covered by that agreement; and
3. An employee who is a nonresident alien and who received no earned income from the employer that constitutes income from U.S. sources.

The related employer rules (see Q 13:5) and leased employee rules (see Q 13:4) apply for purposes of Code Section 408(p). Thus, for example, if two related employers must be aggregated under the rules of Code Section 414(b), all employees of either employer who satisfy the eligibility criteria must be allowed to participate in the SIMPLE.

The IRS model forms (see Q 13:19) automatically exclude from participation nonresident alien employees who do not receive earnings that constitute income from sources within the United States, but allow an employer to choose whether to exclude employees covered under a collective bargaining agreement in which retirement benefits were the subject of good-faith bargaining.

Q 13:33 May an employer use a rolling eligibility period to exclude employees who become eligible?

It is unclear whether a SIMPLE may be amended each year to increase the number of years of service needed to participate.

Example. Marvin, the owner and only employee of a newly established small business, creates a SIMPLE in 2018 using an IRS model SIMPLE form. The plan does not have a service requirement. A new employee, Carl, is hired in June, and Marvin amends the plan to require one year of service so that Carl will not be eligible to participate until the following year. In 2019, Marvin amends the plan again, this time effective January 1, 2020. The amendment is timely and conforms to the summary plan description (see Q 13:83) previously provided to eligible employees (i.e., himself only). The new amendment provides for a two-year service requirement. Again, Carl is ineligible. Such serial amendments would be prohibited in a qualified plan, and it seems unlikely they would pass muster under a SIMPLE.

Compensation

Q 13:34 What is compensation for SIMPLE purposes?

For SIMPLE purposes, an employee's compensation includes:

- Wages, tips, and other amounts received from the employer that are subject to income tax withholding under Code Section 3401(a)
- Deferred compensation (elective deferrals made under a SIMPLE and compensation deferred under an eligible 457(b) plan)
- Differential pay (after 2008)—this is the supplement some employers pay an employee for his or her period (lasting at least 30 days) of active duty in the U.S. uniformed services (to make up for wages that would have been earned working for the employer during that period).
- For tax years starting after 2019, compensation also includes taxable nontuition fellowship and stipend payments, and difficulty-of-care payments that are excluded from income. (See Qs 3:24–3:26.)

[I.R.C. §§ 408(p)(6)(A)(i), 3401(a), 6051(a)(3), 6051(a)(8), 219(f)(1), 408(o)(5), 415(c)(8)]

To apply the 100-employee limit, and to determine an employee's eligibility to participate based on past compensation, compensation also includes elective deferrals under a 401(k) plan, a SARSEP, or a Section 403(b) annuity contract. [I.R.C. §§ 408(p)(6)(A), 6051(a)(3), 6051(a)(8)]

Example. Ian, an eligible employee of Nuts and Bolts, Inc., earned $10,000 and elected to defer 5 percent of compensation ($500) under the company's SIMPLE. Only $9,500 is reported on his Form W-2, but Ian's compensation for plan purposes is $10,000 (the $500 elective deferral is included). If Nuts and Bolts makes a 2 percent nonelective contribution for the year (see Q 13:49), Ian's allocation will be $200.

Q 13:35 How does a self-employed individual determine compensation?

Compensation for a self-employed individual means the net earnings from self-employment (determined under Code Section 1402(a) without regard to Code Section 1402(c)(6)). It *includes* the contributions made on his or her behalf. [I.R.C. § 408(p)(6)(A)]

SIMPLE contributions that a self-employed individual makes on behalf of *nonowner* employees are deductible, however, as an expense of the business, to determine his or her net earnings from self-employment. [I.R.C. §§ 404(a), 404(m), 1402(a)]

> **Example 1.** Gina is a sole proprietor and maintains a SIMPLE in which she is the only participant. In 2019, she has $10,000 of personal service income from self-employment. After deducting half of the self-employment taxes payable ($10,000 ×.153 ÷ 2 = $765), Gina's net earnings from self-employment—and compensation for SIMPLE purposes—are $9,235.

> **Example 2.** Willie owns an unincorporated print shop that maintains a SIMPLE plan. He and one other employee (Andy) perform all the services. Willie's compensation for SIMPLE purposes is his net earnings from self-employment, determined *without* deducting contributions he makes on his own behalf. But contributions that Willie makes for Andy *are* deducted (along with other business expenses of the shop).

Contributions and Limits

Q 13:36 What contributions are made under a SIMPLE plan?

The employer pays two amounts into each participant's SIMPLE IRA:

- The salary reduction contributions the participant elected to defer (or which were elected for the employee by default; see Qs 13:39, 13:43), and
- The employer's contribution—either a matching contribution (see Q 13:46) or a nonelective contribution (see Q 13:49).

Q 13:37 What numerical limits govern SIMPLE contributions?

- The maximum compensation a participant can elect to defer under a qualified salary reduction agreement. [I.R.C. §§ 408(p)(2)(A)(ii), 402(g)(1)(C)] (See Q 13:39.)
- The maximum catch-up deferral a plan may allow annually for participants age 50 or older. [I.R.C. § 402(g)(1)(C)] (See Q 13:39.)
- The percentage of participant deferrals an employer will match, if a matching contribution is made. [I.R.C. § 408(p)(2)(C)] (See Qs 13:46–13:48.)
- The percentage of compensation an employer will contribute if it makes a nonelective contribution. [I.R.C. § 408(p)(2)(B)(i)] (See Q 13:49.)
- The maximum compensation taken into account, if the employer makes a nonelective contribution. [I.R.C. § 408(p)(2)(B)(ii)] (See Q 13:49.)
- The annual exclusion limit for an individuals' combined elective deferrals under plans that allow them. [I.R.C. § 402(g)] (See Q 13:62.)

Salary Reduction Contributions (Elective Deferrals)

Q 13:38 How do participants elect salary deferrals?

Each participant makes a written election (see Q 13:81) that tells the employer how much salary to defer. The amount is expressed as either a percentage or a dollar amount of compensation, and the total deferral for the year may not exceed the applicable limit (see Q 13:39).

Q 13:39 How much salary can be deferred?

Any participant may elect to defer compensation up to the *applicable dollar limit* ($10,000 plus an inflation adjustment). A plan may also allow participants who will be age 50 or older by the end of the year to defer more compensation as a *catch-up deferral*. A plan is not required to allow catch-up deferrals, and if it does it may restrict them to an amount that is below the statutory limit (which is $2,500 plus an inflation adjustment). [I.R.C. §§ 408(p)(2)(A)(ii), 408(p)(2)(E), 402(g)(1)(C), 414(v)(2)(B)(i)]

For 2021, the applicable dollar limit is $13,500 (no change from 2020), and the largest catch-up deferral a plan may allow is $3,000 (no change from 2020). [Notice 2020-79, 2020-46 I.R.B. 1014]

Example 1. Alice, age 25, works for Round Corp. and participates in its SIMPLE plan. For 2021, she elected to defer 10 percent of her $36,000 compensation to the SIMPLE IRA. Each pay period, Round will contribute 10 percent of Alice's gross salary to the SIMPLE IRA. The total salary reduction contribution for 2021 will be $3,600.

Example 2. Kirk, age 60, participates in a SIMPLE plan that allows the maximum catch-up deferrals. Kirk elects to defer $16,500 of his $120,000 salary for 2021 (13.75 percent).

Q 13:40 Can compensation earned before the election is made be contributed as a salary deferral?

No. A salary reduction election may not apply to compensation that an employee received, or had a right to immediately receive, before entering into the qualified salary reduction arrangement.

Q 13:41 Can the employer restrict a participant's salary reduction contribution?

No, except as necessary to comply with the statutory limits (see Q 13:39). [Notice 98-4, Q&A D-2, 1998-1 C.B. 269]

Example. Edward, age 45, has compensation of $162,000 ($13,500 per month) in 2020. He wants to frontload his elective contributions for the year, so he chooses a deferral percentage of 20 percent under his employer's SIMPLE. The employer defers $2,700 per month to Edward's SIMPLE IRA for January through May, but nothing for the rest of the year because Edward's deferral limit for 2020 has then been reached ($13,500).

Q 13:42 Are elective deferrals limited to what an employee could receive in cash after FICA and FUTA taxes are subtracted?

No. The participant's elective contribution is subject to FICA and FUTA taxes, but the taxes are withheld from the paycheck. They do not reduce the contribution. The employer's contribution is not subject to FICA and FUTA taxes. [Notice 98-4, 1998-1 C.B. 269]

Q 13:43 May a SIMPLE include an automatic salary contribution arrangement?

Yes. Under an *automatic contribution arrangement*, a default salary reduction contribution is made for the participant unless he or she affirmatively elects to make either no contribution or a different contribution. If a SIMPLE plan includes an automatic contribution arrangement, the default elective contribution is made to the SIMPLE IRA instead of being paid to the participant in cash. SIMPLE plans are not required to include an automatic contribution arrangement. [I.R.C. § 414(w); Notice 2009-66, Q&A-1, 2009-39 I.R.B. 418]

The arrangement may provide for a default contribution that increases depending on the participant's years of participation in the plan. [Notice 2009-66, Q&A-3, 2009-39 I.R.B. 418]

If the SIMPLE includes an automatic contribution arrangement, the employer must provide notice of the default contribution and must allow participants to elect not to have it be made. [Notice 2009-66, Q&A-4, 2009-39 I.R.B. 418]

Employer Contributions

Q 13:44 Must the employer make a SIMPLE contribution each year?

Yes. For every plan year, the employer must make either:

- A matching contribution (capped generally at 3 percent of a participant's *total* compensation; see Q 13:46), or
- A nonelective contribution (always 2 percent of a participant's *covered* compensation; see Q 13:49).

The employer must choose one or the other for each plan year, and apply it to all participants. Participants must receive advance notice of the employer's decision before the annual election period, so they may take that information into account when making their salary deferral elections. (See Qs 13:78, 13:83.) [I.R.C. § 408(p)(2), 408(p)(5)(C)]

Q 13:45 May an employee elect *not* to receive matching or nonelective contributions?

No. Eligible employees cannot opt out of participation in a SIMPLE. They may choose not to elect salary deferral, but cannot refuse the employer's matching contribution or nonelective contribution. [I.R.C. § 408(p)(4)(A)]

Note. The potential downside of participating in a SIMPLE or SEP is that it may limit the tax deduction for any traditional IRA contributions made by the employee (and spouse). (See Q 3:70.)

Matching Employer Contributions

Q 13:46 What is a matching contribution?

The employer's matching contribution is a dollar-for-dollar match, subject to a cap, of the compensation that each participant elected to defer for the plan year. The cap is usually 3 percent of compensation, but the employer may choose a lower percentage (not less than 1 percent) for two years out of every five (see Q 13:48). [I.R.C. § 408(p)(2)(A), 408(p)(2)(C)]

A participant must elect to defer salary in order to receive a matching contribution from the employer.

Example. Astro Enterprises maintains a SIMPLE plan and has chosen to make a 3 percent matching contribution for 2020. The plan allows participants age 50 or older to make the maximum catch-up deferrals allowed by law. All five of its employees participate. Their ages, compensation, and salary deferral elections for 2020 are shown below. The contributions to be made for 2020 (taking into account the applicable deferral limits; see Q 13:39) are shown in the last three rows.

Employee	*Amber*	*Kyle*	*Anthony*	*Emily*	*Eric*
Age	45	35	20	60	25
Compensation	$140,000	$60,000	$15,000	$80,000	$50,000
Deferral election	10%	5%	0%	25%	2%
Salary deferral	$13,500	$3,000	$ 0	$16,500	$1,000
Employer contribution	$4,200	$1,800	$ 0	$2,400	$1,000
Total contributed	$17,700	$4,800	$ 0	$18,900	$2,000

Q 13:47 How often can the employer make less than a 3 percent match?

The employer may elect to make a reduced matching contribution (less than 3 percent, but not less than 1 percent) for no more than two years out of any five consecutive plan years. The testing period is always the five-year period that *ends with and includes* the year for which the election will be effective. [I.R.C. § 408(p)(2)(C)(ii)]

Q 13:48 How does the two-years-out-of-five test work if no salary reduction arrangement was in effect for one or more of those years?

If no salary reduction arrangement was in effect for any year within the five-year period, the employer is treated as having made a 3 percent contribution for that year. This arises if the SIMPLE plan is first established within that period. [I.R.C. § 408(p)(2)(C)(ii)(III), 408(p)(2)(B)(i)]

Example 1. Alex formed the Alpha Company in 2008, but did not establish a SIMPLE until 2018. For the years before 2018, Alpha is treated as having made a 3 percent matching contribution. Consequently, Alpha can elect a reduced matching contribution (less than 3 percent, but not less than 1 percent) for 2018.

Example 2. Alpha elects the following matching contributions for 2018 through 2021:

2018—1 percent (testing period 2014 through 2018)

2019—3 percent (testing period 2015 through 2019)

2020—2 percent (testing period 2016 through 2020)

2021—3 percent (testing period 2017 through 2021)

Alpha also elects to make a matching contribution for 2022. Since it already made reduced matching contributions for two of the five years in that testing period (2018 through 2022), its matching contribution for 2022 must be 3 percent.

Example 3. For 2023, the relevant testing period is 2019 through 2023, so the first reduced-contribution year (2018) is no longer taken into account. Alpha may elect a reduced matching contribution (less than 3 percent, but not less than 1 percent) for 2023.

Nonelective Employer Contributions

Q 13:49 How is an employer's nonelective contribution determined?

The employer's nonelective contribution is always 2 percent of a participant's compensation (*limited compensation*) for the year, taking into account only compensation up to the limit in Code Section 401(a)(17) (which is $200,000 with an inflation adjustment). For 2021, that limit is $290,000 (up from $285,000 for 2020). [I.R.C. § 408(p)(2)(B); Notice 2020-79, 2020-46 I.R.B. 1014] This means the largest nonelective contribution a participant could receive for 2021 is $5,800 (2 percent of $290,000).

(By contrast, compensation is *not* limited for purposes of determining the amount of an employer's *matching contribution* (see Q 13:46).)

If the employer chooses to make a nonelective contribution for a plan year (see Q 13:83 regarding notice), all participants receive it whether or not they elect to defer salary.

Q 13:50 May the employer make nonelective contributions every year?

Yes, as long as participants receive proper notice that the employer will make the 2 percent nonelective contribution instead of a matching contribution. Written notice must be provided within a reasonable period of time before the period when employees make their salary deferral elections. (See Q 13:78.)

The Total Contribution

Q 13:51 What is the largest possible combined contribution for 2021 if the employer makes a nonelective contribution?

If the employer makes the nonelective contribution for 2021, the plan allows catch-up deferrals up to the statutory limit, and the participant defers as much salary as possible:

- The largest possible salary reduction contribution is $13,500 for a participant younger than age 50, or $16,500 for a participant age 50 or older. (See Q 13:39.)
- A participant with compensation of $290,000 or more would be able to obtain the maximum employer contribution of $5,800 (which is 2 percent of $290,000). (See Q 13:49.)
- So, for a participant with sufficient compensation the largest combined contribution is either $19,300 (if younger than age 50) or $22,300 (if age 50 or older).

Q 13:52 What is the largest possible combined contribution for 2021 if the employer makes a matching contribution?

If the employer makes the largest possible matching contribution (3 percent), the plan allows catch-up deferrals up to the statutory limit, and the participant defers as much salary as possible:

- The largest possible salary reduction contribution is the amount in Q 13:51 (first bullet).
- If that amount is at least 3 percent of the participant's total compensation, it will be matched dollar-for-dollar. (See Q 13:46.)
- So, a participant younger than age 50 would need compensation of at least $450,000 to obtain a $13,500 matching contribution ($13,500 is 3 percent of $450,000), and in that case would obtain the largest possible combined contribution: $27,000.

- And, a participant age 50 or older would need compensation of at least $550,000 to obtain a $16,500 matching contribution, and in that case would obtain the largest combined contribution: $33,000.

Q 13:53 Can SIMPLE contributions be forfeited?

No. All contributions under a SIMPLE are fully vested and nonforfeitable when made. [I.R.C. § 408(a)(4), 408(b)(4), 408(p)(3)]

Q 13:54 Can someone who participates in an employer's SIMPLE plan also make regular contributions to an IRA?

Yes. Completely separate limits apply, so the SIMPLE contributions made for an individual do not reduce the amount he or she may contribute annually to a traditional or Roth IRA. Regular IRA contributions cannot be placed in the SIMPLE IRA, however. [I.R.C. §§ 219(g)(5), 408(p)(1)(B)]

Active participation in a SIMPLE does affect the *deductibility* of traditional IRA contributions (see Qs 3:48, 3:53). To determine the year of an individual's active participation, nonelective contributions made by the employer after the end of the year are treated as though they were made on the last day of the previous year. [Notice 87-16, 1987-1 C.B. 446, *clarified by* Notice 89-25, 1989-1 C.B. 662, and *modified by* Notice 98-49, 1998-2 C.B. 365; I.R.C. § 219(g)(5)(A)(vi)]

Example 1. Reliance Corporation established a SIMPLE IRA plan and elected to make a 2 percent nonelective contribution (instead of a matching contribution) for 2018. Though the contribution is made in January 2019, it is nonelective—so employees are treated as active participants in the SIMPLE for 2018.

Example 2. Beehive Corporation establishes a cash-bonus SIMPLE. Under the SIMPLE, employees may elect in writing to have all or a portion of their annual bonuses treated as elective contributions under the SIMPLE or to receive their bonuses in cash on December 31. The employees who make elective contributions based on their 2018 bonuses are treated as active participants for 2018, even though the amounts may be deposited into their SIMPLE IRAs after the end of the year.

Excess Contributions

Q 13:55 What is an excess contribution to a SIMPLE IRA?

An excess SIMPLE IRA contribution is an employer contribution or salary deferral contribution that exceeds the permitted amounts. (All contributions are excess contributions if the employer does not qualify to establish or maintain a SIMPLE; see Qs 13:3, 13:6, 13:7.)

Q 13:56 What action is required if an excess contribution is made?

The excess contribution must be corrected. An excess matching or nonelective contribution is not deductible by the employer. It is corrected by returning the excess amount (adjusted for income or loss) to the employer and reporting the distribution as nontaxable on Form 1099-R. An excess salary reduction contribution is corrected by distributing the amount (adjusted for income or loss) to the participant, filing Form 1099-R to report the distribution as includable in the participant's gross income for the year of the distribution, and notifying the participant that no part of the corrective distribution is eligible for a rollover. [IRS, *SIMPLE IRA Plan Fix-it Guide*, Mistake 6, available at *http://www.irs.gov/Retirement-Plans/SIMPLE-IRA-Plan-Fix-It-Guide*]

(For the tax consequences of making an excess contribution, see Q 13:66.)

Note. Sponsors may generally correct plan deficiencies using the IRS' Employee Plans Compliance Resolution System (EPCRS). For details of the EPCRS, *see* Rev. Proc. 2021-30, §§ 4.01(1)(c), 4.03(2), 5.07, 6.02, 6.11, 7.01; 2021-31 I.R.B. 172; *see also* EPCRS Overview, available at *https://www.irs.gov/Retirement-Plans/EPCRS-Overview*.

Tax Treatment of Contributions

Employer's Deduction

Q 13:57 Are SIMPLE contributions deductible by the employer?

Yes. The employer deducts SIMPLE contributions as a trade or business expense. This applies not only to the employer's matching or nonelective contribution, but also the salary deferral contributions deposited for participants. Excess contributions are not deductible, however; nor are SIMPLE contributions for certain domestic workers (see Note). The deduction is claimed on the business's income tax return (Form 1120 for a corporation, Form 1065 for a partnership, or Form 1040 Schedule C for a sole proprietorship).

For a sole proprietor or business partner, both the salary deferral contribution and the nonelective or matching contribution made on his or her behalf are deductible. The deduction is claimed on Form 1040, Schedule 1, line 28.

Participants who are not self-employed do not claim any deduction; the contributions are simply excluded from their income.

[IRS, *SIMPLE IRA Plan FAQs—Contributions*, available at *https://www.irs.gov/retirement-plans/retirement-plans-faqs-regarding-simple-ira-plans*]

Note. A SIMPLE plan may cover domestic workers who are not family members, but those contributions are not deductible, because they are not connected with a trade or business. The 10 percent excise tax that normally applies when an employer makes a nondeductible contribution to a SIMPLE IRA does not apply in this case. [I.R.C. § 4972(c)(6)] (These rules do not apply to an employer whose business (such as a cleaning service) is to provide domestic services to *clients*. Such an employer may make deductible SIMPLE contributions for its employees.)

Q 13:58 When are contributions deductible?

For deduction purposes, matching or nonelective contributions must be made to the financial institution maintaining the SIMPLE IRA no later than the due date for filing the employer's income tax return, including extensions, for the taxable year that includes the last day of the calendar year for which the contributions are made. [I.R.C. § 408(p)(5)(A)(ii)]

Example 1. Webster Corporation's taxable year ends on November 30. Webster adopts a SIMPLE for 2017. On March 15, 2018 (just before its tax return due date), Webster makes a nonelective contribution for all employees for the 2017 plan year. Webster may deduct these contributions on its federal income tax return for the taxable year ending on November 30, 2017.

Example 2. Complex Corporation, whose taxable year ends on November 30, adopts a SIMPLE for 2017. On August 30, 2017, Complex files Form 7004 and receives an automatic six-month extension to file its federal income tax return. Thus, its 2017 federal income tax return, normally due on March 15, 2018, is due on September 15, 2018. On September 10, 2018, Complex makes a matching contribution for all employees for the 2017 plan year. For its contribution made on September 10, 2018, Complex may claim a deduction on its federal income tax return for the taxable year ending on November 30, 2017.

Q 13:59 Can SIMPLE contributions that a self-employed individual makes for nonowner employees create a deductible loss?

Yes. [I.R.C. § 1402(a)] Contributions made on behalf of nonowner-employees in an unincorporated business reduce the owner's income. A loss could result.

Q 13:60 Can SIMPLE contributions made on the self-employed individual's behalf create a deductible loss or an excess contribution?

The IRS has not issued guidance on this matter, so it is unclear whether a self-employed individual may claim a loss for a SIMPLE contribution made on his or her behalf.

Example. Jane is self-employed and does not have other employees. Her compensation for 2019 is $4,000. Her SIMPLE provides a matching contribution of up to 3 percent of compensation. Jane contributes $4,000 and also receives a $120 matching contribution. The combined contributions exceed her compensation by $120. It is not clear (1) whether Jane can deduct the $120 matching contribution and (2) whether the 10 percent excise tax applies to it.

Note. Under a qualified defined contribution plan, contributions that exceed a self-employed individual's earned income are not deductible because of Code Section 404(a)(8)(C)—but that provision does not apply to a SIMPLE.

Exclusion from Income

Q 13:61 How is a SIMPLE participant taxed on contributions?

Contributions to a SIMPLE IRA are excluded from the participant's gross income to the extent of the respective contribution limits. That is, the employer's matching or nonelective contribution is excluded up to the applicable limit described in Q 13:46 or Q 13:49; and salary deferrals are excluded to the extent of the applicable limit (Q 13:39). (The annual exclusion limit for elective deferrals may apply to some participants; see Q 13:62.) Tax withholding is not required for contributions properly made under a SIMPLE plan. [I.R.C. §§ 402(g), 402(k), 3401(12)(D)]

Excess contributions are taxable and may be subject to an excise tax. The specific consequences depend on whether and when they are corrected. (See Qs 13:55, 13:56.)

Q 13:62 Are a SIMPLE participant's salary deferrals subject to the Code Section 402(g) exclusion limit?

Yes, but the Code Section 402(g) limit is irrelevant for most participants. Section 402(g) provides that if the aggregate amount of an individual's elective deferrals under all plans (excluding catch-up deferrals) exceeds an inflation-adjusted applicable dollar amount ($15,000 before adjustment), the excess is includable in gross income. For 2021, this exclusion limit is $19,500 (the same amount for 2019). [Notice 2020-79, 2020-46 I.R.B. 1014]

Since the Section 402(g) exclusion limit is higher than the elective deferrals allowed under a SIMPLE (ignoring catch-up deferrals), it does not affect most SIMPLE participants. But if any SIMPLE participant *also* makes elective deferrals under another employer's plan, the exclusion limit could be significant.

> **Example.** Laurie, age 45, works for the Cable Company, and also runs her own, unrelated business. Each has a SIMPLE plan in which Laurie participates. If she makes elective deferrals under both plans for 2021, no more than $19,500 could be excluded from gross income.

Q 13:63 Are salary reduction contributions under a SIMPLE subject to payroll and self-employment taxes?

Yes. Salary reduction contributions to a SIMPLE IRA are subject to FICA and FUTA taxes as well as the tax imposed under the Railroad Retirement Tax Act [Pub. L. No. 89-97, 79 Stat. 335] (RRTA). However, the full contribution (unreduced by tax) is made to the SIMPLE IRA (see Q 13:42). [I.R.C. §§ 3121(a)(5)(H), 3306(b)(5)(H); Notice 98-4, Q&A I-1, 1998-1 C.B. 269]

Q 13:64 Do those taxes apply to the employer's matching or nonelective contribution?

No. Matching and nonelective contributions to a SIMPLE IRA are not subject to FICA, FUTA, or RRTA taxes. [I.R.C. §§ 3121(a)(5)(H), 3121(v)(2)(C), 3231(e)(8)(B), 3306(b)(5)(H); Notice 98-4, Q&A I-1, 1998-1 C.B. 269]

Q 13:65 Can participants claim the saver's credit for salary deferrals made under a SIMPLE plan?

They can if they meet the income limits for that credit. The credit ranges from 10 percent to 50 percent, depending on adjusted gross income. [I.R.C. § 25B; IRS Pub. 590-A, *Contributions to Individual Retirement Arrangements (IRAs)* 2020 (see Appendix A)] (For further discussion of the saver's tax credit, see Qs 3:142–3:147.)

Consequences of an Excess Contribution

Q 13:66 What are the tax consequences of an excess contribution?

Both the employer and the participant may realize tax consequences if an excess contribution is made to a SIMPLE IRA.

If there is an excess *employer* contribution, the employer cannot deduct it. The excess contribution is not taxed on its return to the employer, but the earnings included in the corrective distribution are included in the employer's gross income. [I.R.C. § 408(d)(4), (5)]

When an excess *salary reduction* contribution is corrected, the distribution (including the excess contribution and its earnings) is generally taxable to the participant for the year of the distribution. It is taxable for the year of the contribution, however, if the distribution is made by the participant's deadline (including extensions) for filing his or her tax return for the year for which the contribution was made. The Code Section 72(t) additional tax on early distributions is also generally levied on the distribution if the participant is younger than age 59½. In that case, the additional tax is computed as a percentage of the entire distribution (not just the earnings). The rate is 25 percent if the distribution occurs before the participant has completed two years of participation in the SIMPLE. If it occurs later, the rate is 10 percent (see Q 13:74). [I.R.C. §§ 408(d), 72(t)]

Also, for either type of excess contribution the participant must pay a 6 percent excise tax for each year in which an excess contribution remains in the SIMPLE IRA. There is one exception—the excise tax is avoided with respect to an excess contribution that is returned, with earnings, by the participant's filing deadline (including extensions) for the tax return for the year for which the excess contribution was made. [I.R.C. § 4973(a)]

Rollovers, Conversions, and Recharacterizations

Q 13:67 What rollovers can be made *to* a SIMPLE IRA?

Until recently, rollover contributions to a SIMPLE IRA were only acceptable if they came from another SIMPLE IRA owned by the same individual. Section 306 of the Protecting Americans from Tax Hikes Act, enacted on December 8, 2015, expanded the types of plans from which SIMPLE IRAs can accept rollovers.

The new law distinguishes between rollovers that occur before versus after an individual has completed two years of participation in the employer's SIMPLE plan. For rollovers during the first two years, the rule remains as it was before—i.e., only rollovers from another SIMPLE IRA that the individual owns are permitted. But after the two-year period, assets can be moved into the SIMPLE IRA from a traditional or SEP IRA, or from a pre-tax qualified plan (see Q 6:65). [I.R.C. § 408(p); Protecting Americans from Tax Hikes Act of 2015, Pub. L. No. 114-113 (PATH Act), § 306] *See also* Issue Snapshot—Expansion of Rollover Options Includes Savings Incentive Match Plan for Employees (SIMPLE) IRA Plans (IRS, Aug. 13, 2021).

The two-year participation period starts when contributions are first deposited into the participant's SIMPLE IRA. [I.R.C. §§ 408(p)(1)(B), 72(t)(6)]

Q 13:68 What plans may receive rollovers *from* a SIMPLE IRA?

Amounts may be rolled over from one SIMPLE IRA to another SIMPLE IRA at any time (both must be owned by the same individual). After completion of the two-year participation period (see Q 13:67), distributions may also be rolled over to another IRA or to a qualified plan, Section 403(b) annuity or custodial account plan, or governmental Section 457(b) plan in which the SIMPLE IRA owner participates. [I.R.C. § 408(d)(3)(A)(ii), 408(d)(3)(G)] *See also* Issue Snapshot—Expansion of Rollover Options Includes Savings Incentive Match Plan for Employees (SIMPLE) IRA Plans (IRS, Aug. 13, 2021).

If the participant is deceased and the two-year period has closed, the beneficiary may transfer the inherited interest to a traditional IRA according to the rollover rules that generally apply to beneficiaries. In short, a surviving spouse who is the sole beneficiary may roll over the SIMPLE IRA to a traditional IRA in the beneficiary's name or may convert it to a Roth IRA in the beneficiary's name. Any other beneficiary may transfer the SIMPLE IRA to an "inherited" traditional IRA but must use a trustee-to-trustee transfer to do so. (See chapter 6.)

Q 13:69 What happens if an improper transfer occurs during the first two years of participation?

If, during the two-year period, an amount is paid from a SIMPLE IRA directly to the trustee or custodian of an IRA or other plan that is not a SIMPLE IRA (i.e., a qualified plan, a governmental Section 403(b) plan, a traditional IRA, or a Roth IRA), the payment is neither a tax-free trustee-to-trustee transfer nor a rollover contribution. It is treated as a distribution from the SIMPLE IRA and a contribution to the other IRA or other plan. Since the contribution does not qualify as a rollover, it is a subject to the annual contribution limit that applies to the receiving plan or IRA.

Q 13:70 Can a SIMPLE IRA be converted to a Roth IRA?

During the participant's lifetime, amounts held in a SIMPLE IRA may be converted to a Roth IRA. A conversion is not permitted during the initial two-year period, however (see Q 13:67). [Treas. Reg. § 1.408A-4, Q&A-4(b); Notice 98-4, 1998-1 C.B. 269]

After the participant dies, only the surviving spouse may convert the SIMPLE IRA to a Roth IRA. Other beneficiaries may not do so. [I.R.C. §§ 408A(c)(5)(A), 408A(e), 408(d)(3)(C)]

Q 13:71 Can a conversion of SIMPLE IRA assets be undone by recharacterizing the assets back to a SIMPLE IRA?

Not anymore. Until recently, a conversion of SIMPLE IRA assets to a Roth IRA could be unwound by timely recharacterizing the converted assets back to a SIMPLEIRA. However, no conversion made after 2017 can be recharacterized. [Tax Cuts and Jobs Act, Pub. L. No. 115-97, § 13611 (Dec. 22, 2017); I.R.C. § 408A(d)(3), 408A(d)(6)(B); Treas. Reg. § 1.408A-5, Q&A-5]

The deadline for recharacterizing a 2017 conversion was October 15, 2018. [I.R.C. § 408A(d)(6); IRS FAQ, *Recharacterization of IRA Contributions* (2018), available at *https://www.irs.gov/retirement-plans/retirement-plans-faqs-regarding-iras*]

Q 13:72 May new SIMPLE contributions be deposited after a SIMPLE IRA is converted to a Roth IRA?

It depends on how the conversion is accomplished. If the conversion is done by redesignating the SIMPLE IRA as a Roth IRA, then the SIMPLE IRA becomes a Roth IRA and ceases to be part of the SIMPLE plan, and additional SIMPLE contributions cannot be made to it. [Treas. Reg. § 1.408A-4] However, if the conversion is accomplished by transferring the assets from the SIMPLE IRA to a separate Roth IRA, then the SIMPLE IRA may still receive employer contributions. [Treas. Reg. § 1.408A-4, Q&A-4(b) and Q&A-4(c)]

Q 13:73 May any contributions made to a SIMPLE IRA be recharacterized?

No. All contributions under a SIMPLE plan, including salary deferral contributions, are considered to be made by the employer. They cannot be recharacterized as contributions that are made by the participant to another type of IRA. [Treas. Reg. § 1.408A-5, Q&A-5]

Distributions

Q 13:74 How are distributions from a SIMPLE IRA taxed?

SIMPLE IRA distributions are generally taxed like traditional IRA distributions—they are taxable except to the extent of pro rata basis recovery, the 50 percent excess accumulation penalty applies to missed RMDs, and early distributions that are not protected by a Code Section 72(t) exception are subject to additional tax. (See chapters 4 and 5.) However, the additional tax applies at a special rate—25 percent rather than 10 percent—if the distribution is made during the first two years of an individual's participation in the employer's SIMPLE. [I.R.C. §§ 408(d), 4974(a), 72(t)(6)] This two-year period starts on the day the employer makes the first contribution to the individual's SIMPLE IRA, and ends exactly two years later. [Notice 98-4, Q&A I-2, 1998-1 C.B. 269] IRS Notice 2021-21 automatically postponed until May 17, 2021 the time for reporting and payment of the 10 percent excise tax under Code Section 72(t).

(For the tax consequences of a corrective distribution from the SIMPLE IRA, see Q 13:66.)

Q 13:75 Do the minimum distribution requirements apply to a SIMPLE IRA?

Yes. All the rules that govern minimum distributions from a traditional IRA (see chapter 4) apply to SIMPLE IRAs. Consequently, minimum distributions must begin by the employee's required beginning date (RBD). If distributions do not commence by the RBD, the 50 percent excess accumulation penalty applies. [Treas. Reg. § 408-(8), Q&A-2; I.R.C. §§ 408(a)(6), 408(b)(4), 408(p)(1), 4974(a)]

Note. The minimum distribution rules were suspended for 2020. (See Qs 4:6–4:17.) [I.R.C. § 401(a)(9)(I)(i), added by Coronavirus Aid, Relief, and Economic Security Act (CARES Act), Pub. L. No. 116-136 (Mar. 27, 2020), § 2203]

The SECURE Act changed the definition of the RBD. (For details, see Q 4:4.) As a result, distributions must commence by April 1 of the calendar year after the year the employee attains:

- Age 70½, for anyone born *on or before* June 30, 1949.
- Age 72, for anyone born *after* June 30, 1949.

[I.R.C. § 401(a)(9)(C)(i)(I), as amended by SECURE Act § 114]

A participant who is still employed after minimum distributions begin may continue to defer salary, and the employer must continue to make the matching or nonelective contribution. Since RMDs are calculated based on the prior year end balance in the SIMPLE IRA, a portion of the contributions deposited during the prior year would then be distributed as part of the current year's RMD. [I.R.C. § 72]

The delayed payout rules that apply to qualified plans do not apply to IRAs, so RMDs from a SIMPLE IRA may not be delayed until after retirement. [I.R.C. § 401(a)(9)(C); Notice 96-67, 1996-2 C.B. 235]

Q 13:76 How are minimum distributions determined for beneficiaries after the SIMPLE IRA owner dies?

They are subject to the same minimum distribution requirements that apply to beneficiaries of traditional IRAs (see chapter 4). [Treas. Reg. § 1.408-8, Q&A-2]

The SECURE Act changed these rules significantly (see Qs 4:40, 4:53, 4:86).

Q 13:77 Can the employer restrict or impose penalties on an employee's withdrawals from a SIMPLE IRA?

No. An employer may not require an employee to retain any portion of the contributions in his or her SIMPLE IRA or otherwise impose any withdrawal restrictions. [I.R.C. § 408(p)(3); Treas. Reg. § 1.408-6(d)(4)(ii)]

Administrative Matters

Salary Reduction Elections

Q 13:78 When are salary reduction elections made?

Salary reduction elections must be made during an official election period, though a participant must be able to *discontinue* salary deferrals at any time (see Q 13:80). The minimum requirements are:

- All participants must have an annual opportunity to make or change salary reduction elections. There must be an official election period for this purpose that includes the last 60 days of each plan year (November 2 through December 31). (An employer may allow longer or more frequent election periods.)
- The 60-day period preceding an employee's first date of eligibility must always be allowed as the initial election period.
- If new or rehired employees are immediately eligible to participate in the plan, their initial election period must run at least 60 days, starting from the date when official notice of the plan is received, and including the first day of eligibility (or the day before).

[I.R.C. § 408(p)(5)(C); Notice 98-4, Q&As E-1, E-2, 1998-1 C.B. 269]

Example 1. On November 1, 2017, Precision Company decides to establish its first retirement plan. It adopts a SIMPLE with no service or compensation requirements, and all 40 of its employees are eligible. The plan is duly adopted and becomes effective on January 1, 2018. The employees are given a summary description, a model notice, and a model salary reduction agreement on November 1, 2017. The election period starts on that date and extends to December 31, 2017. After that, an election may not be made or modified until the next notice period, which begins on November 1, 2018. However, a participant may stop the deferrals at any time.

Example 2. Crawdad Company establishes a SIMPLE effective July 1, 2018. The first election period must begin by July 1 and may not end before August 30, 2018.

Example 3. Stacy, an architect, accepts a job with Better Design, Inc. Better Design maintains a SIMPLE that covers all its employees, and participation starts on the first day of employment. Stacy's first day at Better Design is May 1, 2019. On that day, she is given a copy of the plan's annual notice and salary reduction election form. The normal election period for employees of Better Design begins in November, but Stacy's first election period runs from May 1 through June 29, and her election will be effective for 2019.

Q 13:79 Can the new election be modified within the 60-day period?

Yes. An election made during the 60-day election period may be modified, without restriction, before the period ends.

Any such modification of an election is prospective and should be implemented by the employer as soon as administratively feasible, or in accordance with the documentation submitted to the employer.

Q 13:80 If an employee terminates salary reduction contributions, can they be restarted before the next year begins?

The plan document determines when a terminated election may resume. It could provide that an employee may not elect to resume a terminated election until the beginning of the next year. [I.R.C. § 408(p)(5)(B)] Or it could allow salary reductions to resume on an earlier date (e.g., the start of the next calendar quarter).

Example 1. Lunar Company's SIMPLE permits participants to elect to make or modify a salary reduction election on the first day of any month. Cecil terminates his deferrals on August 1. On September 1, he may elect to resume them.

Example 2. Solar Inc.'s SIMPLE allows participants to elect to make or modify a salary reduction election during the first week of any month. However, the plan provides that a participant who terminates deferrals outside of the normal cycle may not resume them until the following year. Larry terminates his deferral contributions in the third week of August 2018. He may not restart salary deferrals until 2019.

Q 13:81 What is the form of the election?

The employee enters into a *qualified salary reduction arrangement* with the employer. This is a written agreement in which:

- The employee may elect whether to have the employer defer compensation to the employee's SIMPLE IRA or pay it directly to the employee in cash.
- The amount to be deferred (if any) is stated as either a percentage of the employee's compensation or a dollar amount, which in either case cannot exceed the applicable limit for the year (see Q 13:39).
- The employee's election is made subject to requirements of the plan—among which is the employer's obligation to make the matching or nonelective contribution specified in the notice (see Q 13:83).

[I.R.C. § 408(p)(2)(A)]

Practice Pointer. The IRS model forms for establishing a SIMPLE plan (Forms 5304-SIMPLE and 5305-SIMPLE) include both a model salary reduction arrangement and a model notice to eligible employees.

Q 13:82 How long does a qualified salary reduction arrangement remain in effect?

A new qualified salary reduction arrangement replaces any earlier arrangements and remains in effect as long as the employee is eligible to participate, or until:

- The employee asks to terminate all salary reduction contributions,
- The employee submits a new salary reduction arrangement (during an election period; see Q 13:78), or
- The plan is terminated.

An eligible employee can request termination of a salary reduction arrangement at any time. The termination request must be in writing, and it must become effective as soon as practicable after its receipt by the employer or, if later, the date specified in the termination request. [I.R.C. § 408(p)(5)(B)]

Notices

Q 13:83 What notice must the employer provide before the election period starts?

Within a reasonable time before the election period begins, the employee must receive written notice stating:

- That the employee can make or modify a salary reduction election during the election period.
- Whether the employer has decided to (1) match the employee's contribution, up to 3 percent of his/her compensation (or up to a lesser stated percentage, not below 1 percent), or (2) contribute 2 percent of the employee's compensation (ignoring compensation above the applicable limit under Code Section 401(a)(17)). (See Qs 13:46–13:49.)
- Whether the employee can select a financial institution to serve as trustee of his/her SIMPLE IRA, or the employer has designated a financial institution to serve as trustee for all the SIMPLE IRAs. If the employer uses a designated financial institution (DFI), the notice must also state that the employee may request a balance transfer to another financial institution at no cost or penalty (subject to reasonably restrictions). (See Qs 13:99–13:106.)
- If the plan includes an automatic contribution arrangement (see Q 13:43), the notice must explain (1) that a default salary reduction contribution will be made if the employee does not affirmatively elect a contribution percentage or amount; (2) that the employee can terminate a default contribution; (3) how default contributions will be invested; and (4) the specific period during which an employee may withdraw or transfer a default contribution (adjusted for income or loss) without cost.

- A summary description of the plan (often provided by the financial institution serving as trustee). For plans established using an IRS model form, this requirement can be met giving each employee a copy of the completed form (Form 5305-SIMPLE or 5304-SIMPLE, whichever was used), with a copy of the procedures for withdrawing or transferring amounts from the SIMPLE IRA.

[I.R.C. §§ 408(*l*)(2)(C), 6693(c); ERISA § 101(g); Notice 2009-67, 2009-39 I.R.B. 420]

Q 13:84 What is a reasonable period of notice that the employer will not make a 3 percent matching contribution?

An employer is deemed to have provided reasonable notice that a different contribution will be made (either a reduced matching contribution or the 2 percent nonelective contribution) if the notice is included with the notice that informs employees they may enter into or modify their salary reduction arrangement. [I.R.C. § 408(p)(2)(C)(ii)(II)] Thus, a reasonable period can be as short as one day. [Notice 98-4, Q&A G-2, 1998-1 C.B. 269]

Q 13:85 May an employer alter the matching percentage or change to a nonelective contribution after the 60-day election period begins?

No. Once the election period starts, the employer may not change the matching percentage or the type of contribution. Employees must have all the correct information in time to properly evaluate the election.

Example. Ezra adopts a SIMPLE for his business. It provides a dollar-for-dollar matching contribution (not to exceed 1 percent of compensation), but none of his employees participate. Realizing he can take advantage of the situation, Ezra increases the matching contribution to 3 percent, effective for the current year. The portion attributable to the 2 percent increase is an excess contribution.

Q 13:86 What penalties apply if an employer does not provide a required notice?

An employer that fails to provide a required notice is liable for a penalty of $50 per day until the notice is provided. The IRS will not impose the penalty if the employer can show that the failure was attributable to reasonable cause.

For example, a failure to provide the summary description when required is attributable to reasonable cause if the employee may select his or her own SIMPLE IRA trustee and is notified of that right, but the trustee's name and address and its withdrawal procedures are not available to the employer when the summary description must be provided. [I.R.C. §§ 408(*l*)(2)(C), 6693(c)(1)]

Q 13:87 What happens if the employer does not make the matching or nonelective contributions that were promised in the notice?

An employer that fails to make the SIMPLE IRA contributions promised in the plan notice must take corrective action. For example, if the contributions were too small, the shortfall must be adjusted for earnings from the date of the mistake to the correction date, and the adjusted amounts must be deposited to the participants' SIMPLE IRAs. [IRS, *SIMPLE IRA Plan Fix-It Guide*, available at *http://www.irs.gov/Retirement-Plans/SIMPLE-IRA-Plan-Fix-It-Guide*]

> **Note.** An employer may use the EPCRS (see Note in Q 13:56) to remedy a whole range of possible mistakes and avoid the consequences of disqualifying its plan. [*See* Rev. Proc. 2021-30, §§ 4.01(1)(c), 4.03(2), 5.07, 6.02, 6.11, 7.01; 2021-31 I.R.B. 172.] See Q 13:107 for illustrative corrections.

Deposit of Contributions

Q 13:88 When must the employer's matching or nonelective contribution be deposited into the SIMPLE IRAs?

The employer's matching or nonelective contribution for any plan year must be deposited with the plan trustee by the due date for filing the income tax return (including extensions) for the employer's taxable year including the last day of the calendar year for which the contributions are made. [I.R.C. § 408(p)(5)(A)(ii)]

> **Example.** Bizco, whose taxable year runs from April through March, maintains a SIMPLE plan for its employees. Capital Bank is the plan trustee. For the plan year that ends on December 31, 2018, Bizco must deposit its matching or nonelective contribution with Capital Bank by the due date (as extended) for filing Bizco's income tax return for the taxable year that ends on March 31, 2019. Consequently, the deposit is required by July 15, 2020 (or by January 15, 2021, if Bizco requests a filing extension).

Q 13:89 When must salary reduction contributions be deposited?

Participants' salary reduction contributions must be deposited with the financial institution more frequently—as soon as the amounts can "reasonably be segregated" from the employer's general assets, and in no event later than 30 days after the date when the amounts would have been paid to employees in cash. [I.R.C. § 408(p)(5)(A)(i); DOL Reg. § 2510.3-102(b)(2)] Under a safe harbor, deposits made within seven business days after the date amounts would have been paid to employees in cash are deemed to satisfy the "reasonably be segregated" standard. [DOL Reg. § 2510.3-102(a)(2)(i)]

> **Example.** Bizco (from Q 13:88) pays its employees on the last day of each month. After each payday, Bizco must deposit the plan participants' salary reduction contributions with Capital Bank as soon as the amounts can reasonably be segregated from Bizco's general assets. To be sure it meets this

requirement, Bizco makes the deposit each month within seven business days after the respective payday. For example, salary deferrals from paychecks issued on April 30, 2019, will be deposited within the next seven business days.

Employer Reports

Q 13:90 Must an employer file a Form 5500 annual return/report for a SIMPLE?

No. An employer is not required to file any annual information returns, such as Form 5500 or Form 5500-EZ, for a SIMPLE. [I.R.C. § 408(i), 408(*l*)(2)(A); ERISA § 101(g)]

Q 13:91 Does the employer report SIMPLE IRA contributions to the IRS?

The employer's matching and nonelective contribution amounts are not reported to the IRS. But since salary deferrals are subject to employment taxes, the employer must include them in the appropriate box on the employee's Form W-2 (see Qs 8:65, 13:56).

Trustee Reports

Q 13:92 What information must a SIMPLE IRA trustee provide to an employer?

Each year, a SIMPLE IRA trustee must provide the employer sponsoring the SIMPLE with a summary description containing the following information:

1. Name and address of the employer and of the trustee;
2. Requirements for eligibility for participation;
3. Benefits provided with respect to the SIMPLE;
4. Time and method of making elections with respect to the SIMPLE; and
5. Procedures for, and effects of, withdrawals (including rollovers) from the SIMPLE IRA.

The trustee must provide the summary description to the employer early enough to allow the employer to meet its notification obligation to its employees (see Q 13:83). A trustee is not, however, required to provide the summary description for the SIMPLE before agreeing to be the trustee of a SIMPLE IRA. [Notice 98-4, Q&A H-1(2), 1998-1 C.B. 269]

A trustee may satisfy its obligation for a SIMPLE established using Form 5305-SIMPLE or Form 5304-SIMPLE by providing an employer with a current copy of the model form, with instructions; the information required for completion of Article VI of the model form (regarding the procedure for withdrawal); and the name and address of the financial institution. The trustee should provide guidance to the employer concerning the need to complete the first two pages of the model form in accordance with its plan's terms and to distribute completed copies to eligible employees. A procedure similar to that used for the model forms applies to prototype SIMPLEs. [Notice 98-4, Q&A G-1(4), 1998-1 C.B. 269]

An employer is relieved from providing the procedures for withdrawal if the information is provided directly to the employee by the financial institution.

Q 13:93 What is the penalty if a SIMPLE IRA trustee does not timely provide the summary description?

Under the Code, a SIMPLE IRA trustee that fails to provide an employer with a summary description of the plan incurs a $50 penalty for each day the failure continues, unless the trustee shows that the failure is a result of reasonable cause. [I.R.C. § 6693(c); Notice 98-4, Q&A H-1(3), 1998-1 C.B. 269]

To the extent that the employer or trustee provides the information contained in a summary description by the deadline prescribed by law (see Q 13:83) to the employee for whom the SIMPLE IRA is established, the trustee of that SIMPLE IRA is deemed to have shown reasonable cause for failure to provide that information to the employer. Thus, for example, if an employer provides its name and address and other necessary information and the effects of withdrawal to all eligible employees in a SIMPLE, and the trustee provides its name and address and its procedures for withdrawal to each eligible employee for whom a SIMPLE IRA is established with the trustee, the trustee will be deemed to have shown reasonable cause for failing to provide the employer with that information. [Notice 98-4, Q&As G-1, H-1, 1998-1 C.B. 269]

Q 13:94 Is the trustee required to report to the employer concerning a *transfer SIMPLE IRA*?

No. A *transfer SIMPLE IRA* is a SIMPLE IRA established by an employee to hold assets from another employer's SIMPLE IRA. The current employer is not involved with it. [Notice 98-4, Q&A H-1, 1998-1 C.B. 269]

Q 13:95 What information must the trustee provide to the plan participants?

Within 31 days after the close of each calendar year, the trustee must provide to each individual on whose behalf an account is maintained, a statement of the account balance as of the close of that calendar year and the account activity during that calendar year. For each failure to provide such a statement, the trustee incurs a $50 penalty under Code Section 6693 for each day the failure continues, unless reasonable cause for the failure is shown.

The trustee must also provide the other information that IRA holders are required to receive, such as the disclosure statements referred to in Treasury Regulations Section 1.408-6 (see Q 2:3). [I.R.C. § 408(i)]

Q 13:96 Does the trustee report SIMPLE IRA contributions to the IRS?

Yes. Code Section 408(i) requires the trustee of a SIMPLE IRA to file Form 5498, IRA Contribution Information, with the IRS to report the amount of contributions and rollovers (including a direct rollover) to a SIMPLE IRA. The fair market value of the account or annuity is also indicated on Form 5498. [Ann. 97-10, 1997-10 I.R.B. 64] A trustee or custodian that fails to file the reports incurs a $50 penalty under the Code for each failure, unless it is shown that the failure is attributable to reasonable cause. [I.R.C. § 6693(c); Notice 98-4, Q&A H-1(3), 1998-1 C.B. 269] A copy of Form 5498 must be furnished to the participant and the information provided to the IRS by June 1, 2021 to report 2020 contributions, or by June 1, 2022 to report 2021 contributions. (See chapter 8 for details concerning Form 1099-R.)

Q 13:97 Are SIMPLE IRA distributions reported on Form 1099-R?

Yes. Pursuant to Code Section 6047 and Treasury Regulations Section 35.3405-1, the payer of any designated distribution from an IRA (including SIMPLE IRAs) must report the distribution on Form 1099-R, Distributions From Pensions, Annuities, Retirement or Profit-Sharing Plans, IRAs, Insurance Contracts, etc.

The penalty under the Code for failure to report a designated distribution from an IRA (including a SIMPLE IRA) is $50 for each failure (but not more than $50,000) unless the failure is attributable to reasonable cause (rather than willful neglect). [I.R.C. §§ 6047(f), 6704]

(See chapter 8 for a discussion of distribution codes for Form 1099-R.)

Q 13:98 Is special coding required to report a SIMPLE IRA distribution made during the initial two-year period of an individual's participation?

Yes. If a distribution is made to a participant during the first two years of participation in the SIMPLE, the trustee must mark code S in box 7 of Form 1099-R (see chapter 8).

The trustee generally prepares that report based on its own records of the SIMPLE IRA. However, if other adequately substantiated information is provided to the trustee regarding the individual's first date of participation in any SIMPLE plan maintained by the same employer, the trustee may (but is not required to) also take that into account. [Notice 98-4, Q&A H-5, 1998-1 C.B. 269]

Designated Financial Institutions

Q 13:99 Must an employee be allowed to choose the trustee for his or her SIMPLE IRA?

Generally, yes. Under Code Section 408(p), an employer must allow every participant to designate the financial institution to receive contributions for the participant's SIMPLE IRA. There is one exception, however. The plan may specify that all the SIMPLE IRAs will be maintained by a single financial institution of the employer's choosing—a *designated financial institution* (DFI). If a plan does not include that specification, every participant must be allowed to choose the financial institution to which the employer must direct his or her SIMPLE IRA contributions.

Only certain financial institutions (banks, savings and loan associations, insured credit unions), insurance companies that issue insurance contracts, and IRS-approved nonbank trustees may serve as DFIs under a SIMPLE. [I.R.C. § 408(n)]

Q 13:100 What circumstances allow an employer to use a DFI?

The employer may select a DFI to serve as the trustee for all SIMPLE IRAs under the plan if the following requirements are met:

1. The SIMPLE plan agreement must state that the employer will use a DFI.
2. The employer and the financial institution must agree that the financial institution will be the DFI for the plan (as defined in Code Section 408(p)(7)).
3. The financial institution must agree that if a participant so requests, the SIMPLE IRA balance will be transferred without cost or penalty to another SIMPLE IRA or, after the initial two-year participation period, to any IRA, at a financial institution selected by the participant.
4. Each participant must be given written notice that describes the procedure for requesting such a transfer.

[I.R.C. § 408(p)(7)]

Example 1. A representative of Lucky Investment Financial Institution approaches Top Brass Manufacturing Company about establishing a SIMPLE. Top Brass agrees to establish a SIMPLE for its employees. Top Brass prefers to avoid writing checks to more than one financial institution, so it wants to choose a single financial institution to maintain all the SIMPLE IRAs. Top Brass and Lucky agree that Lucky will be the DFI, and Lucky agrees to transfer any participant's balance, upon request and without cost or penalty, to another SIMPLE IRA, or after the two-year period to any IRA, at a financial institution selected by the participant.

Top Brass executes a SIMPLE agreement that requires all SIMPLE IRAs under the plan to be maintained with the DFI it chooses. A SIMPLE IRA is then established at Lucky for each eligible employee of Top Brass. All participants receive a written description of how and when they may direct a transfer of the SIMPLE IRA balance without cost or penalty. Lucky is the DFI for the plan, and the participants must abide by the arrangement.

Example 2. A representative of Metro Financial Institution approaches Mirror Company to discuss establishing a SIMPLE. Mirror invites Metro to give a presentation to the Mirror employees describing the investment options that will be available for the SIMPLE IRAs it maintains. Each eligible employee receives a notice that states that he or she must select the financial institution that will serve as the trustee of his or her SIMPLE IRA. The plan does not require Mirror to select a single DFI, but all the employees who are eligible to participate voluntarily select Metro to serve as their trustee. Nonetheless, Metro is not a DFI. It is *not* required to offer cost-free balance transfers to the participants.

Example 3. The facts are the same as in Example 2, except that two Mirror employees, Lance and Gwen, elected to make salary reduction contributions but failed to open SIMPLE IRAs in time to receive Mirror's first contribution. Mirror establishes SIMPLE IRAs for them at Metro and contributes the appropriate amounts. If Lance and Gwen want to transfer their balances to another financial institution, Metro may charge them a fee or penalty for doing so, because Metro is not a DFI.

Q 13:101 May the DFI limit the period for accommodating balance transfer requests at no cost or penalty to the participant?

Yes. The DFI is not required to accommodate cost-free transfers at all times of the year. It may limit them to a reasonable period of time each year. [I.R.C. § 408(p)(7)]

Example 1. Orange Computer first establishes a SIMPLE plan effective January 1, 2018. It intends to make all contributions to Starship Financial Institution, which has agreed to serve as the DFI. The first election period for participants runs from November 2 through December 31, 2017. Each participant receives notice of his or her right to request a balance transfer to another financial institution, but the notice states that transfers will only be without cost and penalty if they are requested during the 60-day period before January 1 of each year (or during a participant's first election period if it occurs at a different time of year). The restriction is reasonable.

Example 2. The facts are the same as in Example 1. Linda, a participant, does not request a balance transfer until July 1, 2018. Starship is not required to transfer her balance without cost or penalty, because the request was not timely. However, if Linda withdraws her request and resubmits it during the 60-day period before January 1, 2019, Starship will accommodate the new request at no cost to Linda.

Example 3. The facts are the same as in Example 1. Eli is hired on June 1, 2018, and on that date he becomes eligible to participate in the SIMPLE. His first election period runs from June 1 through July 30, 2018. If he asks Starship during that period to transfer his SIMPLE IRA balance to another financial institution, Starship must do so at no cost or penalty to Eli.

Q 13:102 May the DFI limit the frequency of such transfers?

Yes. If the participant acts within the reasonable time limits set by the DFI, he or she may request *reasonably frequent* transfers, which the DFI must accommodate without charge or penalty. A participant's request to transfer the balance on a monthly basis is considered reasonable. [I.R.C. § 408(p)(7); Notice 98-4, Q&A J-3, 1998-1 C.B. 269]

Q 13:103 How must the DFI's restrictions be disclosed?

The DFI's limitation of cost-free and penalty-free balance transfer requests to a reasonable period of time each year must be disclosed in the section of the annual written notice to participants that describes a participant's rights with respect to the DFI (see Q 13:83).

A SIMPLE that uses a DFI may have been established using Form 5305-SIMPLE, Savings Incentive Match Plan for Employees of Small Employers (SIMPLE)—for Use With a Designated Financial Institution. In that case, the employer may satisfy its annual notice requirements by providing a copy of the completed form. Article VI of the form (Procedures for Withdrawal) must contain a clear explanation of the DFI's restrictions on cost and penalty free balance transfers.

Q 13:104 When is a balance transfer considered to be made without cost or penalty?

A transfer of a SIMPLE IRA balance is deemed to be made without cost or penalty if none of the following (or similar amounts) is charged based with respect to the balance transferred:

- Liquidation, transaction, redemption, or termination fees;
- Commissions;
- Loads (front-end or back-end); or
- Surrender charges.

The DFI may require that contributions the participant wants transferred must be placed in a specific investment until the transfer is made.

> **Example 1.** Sound Financial Institution serves as the DFI for Cement Company's SIMPLE plan. It offers several investment options for SIMPLE IRAs, some of which carry a sales charge. The plan's notice to eligible employees explains that if a balance transfer is requested during the 60-day election period that begins each year on November 2, Sound will transfer balances accordingly on a monthly basis with no cost or penalty to the employee. However, from the time Sound receives a contribution until the date of its transfer to another financial institution, it must be placed in an investment for which there is no sales charge. Any other amounts in the SIMPLE IRA that the employee does not require to be transferred may be invested without this restriction. All of this is stated in the written plan notice. Sound's restriction is appropriate, because otherwise it would have to absorb the sales charge. The restriction may cause the employee to forgo some income, but that does not violate the requirement that balance transfers be made without cost to the employee.

Example 2. The facts are the same as in Example 1. Sound Financial Institution generally charges its IRAs a reasonable annual administration fee. Sound also charges that fee with respect to SIMPLE IRAs, including SIMPLE IRAs from which balances must be transferred in accordance with participants' transfer elections. The requirement that participants' balances be transferred without cost or penalty is not violated merely because a reasonable *annual* administration fee is charged to SIMPLE IRAs from which balances must be transferred in accordance with participants' transfer elections.

[Notice 98-4, Q&A J-4, 1998-1 C.B. 269]

Q 13:105 Is the without-cost-or-penalty requirement violated if a DFI charges the employer for the transfer of a participant's SIMPLE IRA balance?

No. The DFI may charge the *employer* a reasonable amount for the transfer without violating the requirement that a transfer be made without cost to the *employee.* [Notice 98-4, Q&A J-5, 1998-1 C.B. 269]

Q 13:106 May the employer pass the charge on to its employees?

No. If the DFI charges the employer for a balance transfer and the employer passes it through to plan participants, the without-cost-or-penalty requirement is violated. In that case the employer may not require the use of a DFI for the SIMPLE IRAs. It would have to allow employees to choose their own financial institution.

Miscellaneous Rules

Q 13:107 How are defects in a SIMPLE IRA plan corrected under any of the IRS compliance programs?

Employers may use the IRS Voluntary Correction Program to correct many qualification failures, e.g., problems with the plan document, plan operation, or employee eligibility. [Rev. Proc. 2021-30, 2021-31 I.R.B. 172] See also the following IRS documents: (1) SIMPLE IRA Plan Fix-It Guide—You used the wrong compensation definition to calculate deferrals and contributions to SIMPLE IRAs (Aug. 4, 2021); (2) Fixing Common Plan Mistakes—SIMPLE IRA Sponsor with a Related Business (Aug. 9, 2021); (3) SIMPLE IRA Plan Fix-It Guide—You have more than 100 employees who earned $5,000 or more in compensation for the prior year (July 27, 2021); and (4) SIMPLE IRA Plan Fix-It Guide—You made incorrect employer contributions for eligible employees (Aug. 4, 2021).

Q 13:108 Are SIMPLE IRA plans subject to ERISA bonding requirements?

Possibly. In most cases, an employer that handles funds or other property that belongs to an ERISA plan is required to be bonded. The basic standard is determined by the possibility of risk of loss in each situation; thus, it is based on the facts and circumstances of each situation. The amount of a bond is determined at the beginning of each year. The bond amount may not be less than 10 percent of the amount of funds handled. The minimum bond amount is $1,000. Contributions made by withholding from an employee's salary are not considered funds or other property of a SIMPLE IRA plan for purposes of the bonding provisions as long as they are retained in, and not segregated in any way from, the general assets of the withholding employer. Because employer contributions are made into SIMPLE IRAs established by each employee (and are outside of the control of an employer, once made), bonding would not generally apply. [ERISA §§ 404(c), 412; DOL Reg. §§ 2510.3-3, 2550.412-5]

Q 13:109 Is a SIMPLE subject to minimum funding standards?

No. The minimum funding standards under ERISA and Code Section 412 do not apply to a SIMPLE. Under ERISA, employee deferrals must be deposited in a timely manner (see Q 13:89).

State Income Tax Issues

Q 13:110 How are SIMPLE IRA contributions made by a self-employed individual treated for state income tax purposes?

In most states, contributions made by self-employed individuals on behalf of themselves and their employees are deductible for state income tax purposes. Exceptions to this general rule exist for Pennsylvania, New Jersey, and Massachusetts, where contributions on behalf of the self-employed taxpayer are not deductible on the personal tax return but contributions on behalf of their employees are deductible (see Qs 15:65–15:69).

Chapter 14

Coverdell Education Savings Account

The Coverdell education savings account (ESA) was originally created to encourage saving for higher education expenses through the granting of federal tax benefits. It was subsequently expanded to cover expenses for secondary and elementary school education.

An ESA may accept contributions on behalf of a child younger than 18, or a beneficiary of any age with special needs. Undistributed earnings accumulate tax free, and there is no tax on distributions that are used to pay qualified education expenses. Other distributions are taxable and subject to a 10 percent additional tax on the distributed earnings.

The contribution limit for an ESA is severely limited by comparison to a Code Section 529 savings plan. For any year, no more than $2,000 may be contributed to the ESAs of any beneficiary, taking into account contributions from all sources. ESA assets must also be managed for the interest of the beneficiary, unlike a 529 savings account, which can be revoked by the owner (and the assets recovered) at any point. But ESAs have some advantages over 529 plans. ESAs cover more of the expenses of kindergarten through high school (still true, even after the recent expansion of 529 account benefits), and they offer superior investment options.

Contributions to an ESA are not tax deductible, and individuals must have income below a specified limit to qualify as donors. Contributors need not be related to the beneficiary.

Unless the beneficiary has special needs, assets in an ESA that are not used or needed for educational purposes must be distributed by the time the child reaches age 30, or else rolled over tax free to another family member's ESA.

Comparison with Other Plans

Q 14:1 What is a Coverdell education savings account?

The *Coverdell education savings account* (ESA) is a tax-advantaged trust or custodial account established to fund the qualified education expenses of a beneficiary (the ESA beneficiary) at an eligible institution. Such expenses include tuition and many other costs of education from kindergarten through secondary school, college, and postgraduate education. Earnings grow tax free inside the ESA, and distributions are free of federal income tax unless they exceed the beneficiary's qualified education expenses (see Q 14:45). Other withdrawals are taxed, and a 10 percent penalty may apply (see Qs 14:51, 14:54). Anyone may contribute to the account, but the total amount is limited annually. Contributions to the ESA are not tax deductible.

Q 14:2 How is an ESA different from a 529 plan?

Both are tax-favored education savings plans, but there are important differences. Among them: A *529 plan* (so-called because it is established under Code Section 529) can receive much larger contributions than an ESA, and its benefits were just expanded by Congress under the Tax Cuts and Jobs Act (TCJA) (see Q 14:3). But an ESA still offers some advantages over a 529 plan (see Q 14:4), so for many families it is useful to maintain both.

Note. There are two kinds of 529 plans—savings plans, and prepaid tuition plans. Only 529 savings plans are considered here.

Their features are compared in Table 14-1.

Table 14-1. Comparison Between a 529 Savings Plan and a Coverdell ESA

	529 savings plan	*Coverdell ESA*
Type of plan	State-sponsored investment account	Trust account established through brokerage or financial institution Similar to an IRA
Account ownership and control	Owner is person who establishes the account (usually a parent) Owner may always revoke account and take back the assets (though tax and penalty would be owed)	Same (usually), but account must be managed for benefit of the designated beneficiary
Contributions	Not deductible	*Same*
Contribution limits	Each plan sets a lifetime limit; typically, $400,000–$500,000 Some also have an annual contribution limit (typically set at annual gift tax exclusion amount, which is $15,000 for 2021)	$2,000 per year total, from all donors Donor limit is $2,000 (or less based on adjusted gross income) per beneficiary
Age limits	None	No contributions after beneficiary is age 18 Must distribute account to beneficiary at age 30 (or change beneficiary before then) Age limits do not apply for a special needs beneficiary

Table 14-1. Comparison Between a 529 Savings Plan and a Coverdell ESA (*cont'd*)

	529 savings plan	*Coverdell ESA*
Earnings	Grow tax free inside account	*Same*
Qualified education expenses: *Kindergarten through high school*	*Tuition—* • $10,000 annual limit • For public, private, or religious school (not homeschool)	*Incurred for enrollment or attendance—* • Tuition (actual cost) and fees, for public, private, or religious school—may include homeschool under state law • Books, supplies, equipment • Academic tutoring *For special needs beneficiary—* • Special needs services incurred for enrollment or attendance *Required or provided by school—* • Room and board • Uniforms • Transportation • Extended day programs • Supplementary items, services *Computer-related—* • Cost of computer or peripheral equipment, computer software, or Internet access and related services, *if* for use by beneficiary and family during any year beneficiary is at the school • Generally excludes sports, gaming, and hobby software

Table 14-1. Comparison Between a 529 Savings Plan and a Coverdell ESA (*cont'd*)

	529 savings plan	*Coverdell ESA*
Qualified education expenses: *College and other post-secondary school*	*Expenses required for enrollment and attendance—* • Tuition and fees • Books, supplies, equipment *For special needs beneficiary—* • Special needs services incurred for enrollment or attendance *Room and board—* • For student enrolled at least half-time • The greater of the (i) actual cost, if student lives in campus housing, or (ii) amount stated by school for federal financial aid purposes *Computer-related—* • Cost of computer or peripheral equipment, computer software, or Internet access and related services, *if* for primary use by beneficiary during any year at school • Generally excludes sports, gaming, and hobby software *New for distributions after 2018—* • Fees, books, supplies, and equipment required for participation in registered apprenticeship program • Repayment of qualified education loan (of beneficiary or sibling, up to	*Same, excluding items marked new for distributions after 2018*

Table 14-1. Comparison Between a 529 Savings Plan and a Coverdell ESA (*cont'd*)

	529 savings plan	*Coverdell ESA*
	$10,000 over lifetime of that individual)	
Distributions for qualified education expenses	No federal income tax	*Same*
Nonqualified distributions	Distributed earnings taxed as ordinary income Penalty also applies (10 percent of distributed earnings) Penalty exceptions (but earnings are still taxed): • Distribution after beneficiary's death or disability • Amount equal to scholarship award can be withdrawn without penalty • Military school attendance	*Same*
Investment choices	Pre-defined, managed asset allocation portfolios, often age-based Fees tend to be higher than for ESAs Only two investment changes per year	Parent chooses and manages investments Same broad investment options as for IRAs No limit on investment changes
Beneficiary	Can be changed at any time Change is tax free, if new beneficiary is member of beneficiary's family	Same, except new beneficiary must be younger than age 30 or have special needs
Beneficiary's death	Options: • Owner withdraws assets (nonqualified distribution, so taxable, but no penalty), or • Transfer account tax free to new beneficiary (must be family member of decedent)	Options: • Transfer account tax free to new beneficiary (must be family member of decedent, and be younger than age 30 or have special needs), or • Distribute assets to beneficiary's estate

Table 14-1. Comparison Between a 529 Savings Plan and a Coverdell ESA (*cont'd*)

	529 savings plan	*Coverdell ESA*
Gift tax	Contributions qualify for annual gift tax exclusion ($15,000 for 2021) If combined 529 and ESA gifts exceed exclusion amount, donor may elect to spread gift ratably over 5 years	*Same*
Estate tax	Account excluded from account owner's estate (unless owner revokes account and takes assets back)	*Same*
State tax	Some states offer tax benefits for their own plans	*Not applicable*
Financial aid impact	Treated as assets of the owner (usually the parent)	*Same*

[I.R.C. §§ 529, 530]

Q 14:3 How has recent legislation expanded 529 plans?

529 plans have been expanded twice in the last few years.

First, before 2018, tax-free 529 plan distributions could only be used for qualified *higher* education expenses. No elementary or high school expenses were covered. Now, because of the TCJA, up to $10,000 per year may be withdrawn tax free to pay a 529 account beneficiary's *tuition* for kindergarten through high school education at a public, private, or religious school. The $10,000 limit applies on a per-student basis across all 529 accounts and is effective for distributions after December 31, 2017. [Tax Cuts and Jobs Act (TCJA), Pub. L. No. 115-97 (Dec. 22, 2017), § 11032(a); I.R.C. § 529(c)(7), 529(e)(3)(A)] (ESAs already had such coverage, and more.)

Second, for 529 plan distributions (*but not ESA distributions*) after 2018, the following are now qualified higher education expenses:

- Fees, books, supplies, and equipment required for the beneficiary's participation in an apprenticeship program registered and certified with the Secretary of Labor, and
- Repayments of principal and interest on qualified education loans of the beneficiary, or a sibling of the beneficiary, with a lifetime limit of $10,000 per individual.

[Setting Every Community Up for Retirement Enhancement Act of 2019 (SECURE Act), Div. O of the Further Consolidated Appropriations Act, 2020, Pub. L. No. 116-94 (Dec. 20, 2019), § 302 (adding I.R.C. § 529(c)(8), 529(c)(9))]

Q 14:4 So after these expansions, what are the reasons to continue using an ESA?

The ESA still retains two advantages over the 529 account:

1. *Kindergarten through high school.* Tax-free ESA distributions can be used to pay tuition plus a broad range of other expenses. Since 2018, tax-free 529 account distributions may be used to pay only tuition, and that is limited to $10,000 per year.
2. *Investment choices.* The parent (or other responsible individual) makes the investment decisions for the ESA and can choose from the same wide array of investment that are available to IRA owners. The 529 account owner is limited to choosing among pre-set asset allocation portfolios (which tend to be conservative) and can change investments only twice a year.

Q 14:5 Can a child have both plans?

Yes. ESAs and 529 plans are not mutually exclusive. A child can have both an ESA and a 529 account, and contributions can be made to both accounts in the same year. [I.R.C. § 530(d)(2)(C)(ii)] Many families find it optimal to contribute the first $2,000 for the year to the ESA, and the rest to a 529 plan.

Q 14:6 How do ESAs compare to Roth IRAs for education savings?

Using a Roth IRA to save for education expenses could actually be better than using an ESA or 529 plan. Roth IRA distributions are tax free—no reason required—once the owner reaches age 59½ and the Roth IRA has been held at least five years (see Qs 5:67, 5:68). And even before age 59½, contributions to the Roth IRA may be withdrawn tax free. Also, a Roth IRA can grow to be much richer than an ESA, not only because larger annual contributions are permitted, but also because the Roth IRA can accept sizeable rollovers from other retirement plans. Even larger amounts may accumulate in a 529 plan, but those are subject to many restrictions that do not apply to IRAs.

Getting sizeable funds into a Roth IRA from a *pre*-tax qualified plan may be expensive, however, because conversions are taxable. Special rules also apply if conversion contributions are distributed within five years. (See Qs 5:92–5:96.) The other downside of using a Roth IRA for education expenses is that it diminishes the amount of tax-favored savings available at retirement.

The ESA Beneficiary

Eligibility and Age Limits

Q 14:7 How many beneficiaries can be named for an ESA?

There are two kinds of ESA beneficiaries. Each ESA must have one—and only one—*ESA beneficiary* for whom the account is maintained. One or more *death beneficiaries* should also be named (see Q 14:18).

Q 14:8 Who can be an ESA beneficiary?

Anyone younger than age 18, or with qualifying special needs (see Q 14:9), may be designated as the ESA beneficiary. The designation is made by the person who opens the ESA.

Q 14:9 What is a special needs beneficiary?

Treasury regulations are expected to be issued that will define a *special needs beneficiary* as an individual who requires additional time to complete his or her education because of a physical, mental, or emotional condition (including a learning disability). [H.R. Conf. Rep. No. 107-84 § IV.A (2001)] However, as of this writing, in May 2021, those regulations have not been issued, and it is not clear that those provisions can be used until the IRS adopts regulations. When the IRS issues regulations, the following rules will apply: (1) contributions will be permitted even after the individual turns 18; (2) the Coverdell account can continue in existence (without transfer to another beneficiary) after the beneficiary turns 30; and (3) the account established for a different beneficiary can be transferred to a special needs beneficiary who is over age 30.

Q 14:10 When the ESA beneficiary reaches age 18, can new contributions still be made?

No, unless the ESA beneficiary has special needs. Rollovers are allowed, however (see Q 14:57).

Q 14:11 What happens when the beneficiary reaches age 30?

The ESA must terminate unless it has a special needs beneficiary. All unused ESA funds must be distributed to the ESA beneficiary within 30 days after his or her 30th birthday. [I.R.C. § 530(b)(1)]

(For how to avoid a mandatory distribution by changing the beneficiary, see Qs 14:13, 14:39.)

Q 14:12 Can an unborn child be designated as the ESA beneficiary?

No. A child must already be born to be designated as an ESA beneficiary. (Code Section 530(b)(1) uses the word *individual* to clarify the issue.)

Changing the ESA Beneficiary

Q 14:13 What are the requirements for changing the ESA beneficiary?

Four requirements must be met to change the ESA beneficiary:

1. *Terms of the ESA.* The ESA trust or custodial agreement must allow the beneficiary to be changed (this is not always allowed). (See Q 14:15.)
2. *Timing.* The change must generally occur *before* the current ESA beneficiary's 30th birthday (not applicable to a special needs beneficiary). [I.R.C. § 530(b)(1)]
3. *Eligibility.* The new ESA beneficiary must be younger than age 30 or have special needs, and must also be a member of the current ESA beneficiary's family (see Q 14:14). [I.R.C. § 530(b)(1)]
4. *Procedure.* The correct procedure must be followed (see Q 14:16).

Q 14:14 Who are the members of an ESA beneficiary's family?

The ESA beneficiary's family includes these relatives:

- Spouse;
- Son, daughter, stepchild, foster child, adopted child, or a descendant of any of them;
- Brother, sister, stepbrother, or stepsister;
- Father or mother or ancestor of either;
- Stepfather or stepmother;
- Son or daughter of a brother or sister;
- Brother or sister of father or mother;
- Son-in-law, daughter-in-law, father-in-law, mother-in-law, brother-in-law, or sister-in-law;
- The spouse of any individual listed above; and
- First cousin.

[I.R.C. §§ 152(a), 529(e)(2), 530(d)(6); IRS Pub. 970, *Tax Benefits for Education* 2020]

Q 14:15 Who has authority to make the change?

This is determined by the ESA agreement. In the model IRS agreements, the *responsible individual* is the only person who *may* have authority to change the ESA beneficiary. The person who opens the account (the grantor) chooses whether to grant or withhold such authority. [IRS Form 5305-E, Coverdell Education Trust Savings Account]

Note. Under the model IRS agreements, the responsible individual has sole authority to manage and control the account after it is opened and must be *one* parent or legal guardian of the ESA beneficiary, at least until the latter reaches the age of majority. [*See* IRS Form 5305-E, Coverdell Education Trust Savings Account.]

Q 14:16 What is the procedure for changing the ESA beneficiary?

If the change is allowed, there are two ways to designate a new ESA beneficiary—appoint a different beneficiary for the existing account, or roll over the funds to another ESA maintained for the new beneficiary (see Qs 14:57–14:60). In either case, the responsible individual must follow the custodian's procedures for making the change.

Q 14:17 Are there tax consequences if the ESA beneficiary is changed?

Changing the ESA beneficiary has no federal income tax consequences if the requirements stated in Q 14:13 are met. [I.R.C. § 530(d)(6); Notice 97-60, 1997-2 C.B. 310] (For gift and estate tax consequences, see Q 14:67.)

> **Example.** Erica has $7,000 left in her ESA when she graduates from college. Her mother (the responsible individual named in the ESA agreement) may transfer the full $7,000 balance to an ESA for Erica's younger sister, Stacey, who is still in high school, and no taxes will be owed on the transfer. [IRS Pub. 970, *Tax Benefits for Education* 2020]

Death of the ESA Beneficiary

Q 14:18 What happens if the ESA beneficiary dies before the funds are exhausted?

In most cases, if the beneficiary dies before the ESA assets are exhausted, the account must be closed, and its assets distributed to the decedent's estate, within 30 days after the death. The distributed earnings would be taxable as ordinary income, but the 10 percent additional tax would not apply. [I.R.C. § 530(d)(4)]

But if the ESA has a *death beneficiary* who is the decedent's surviving spouse or family member (see Q 14:14), and that person is younger than age 30 or has special needs when the death occurs, then the account continues as an ESA, and the death beneficiary is substituted as the current beneficiary. The transfer of the ESA to the new beneficiary is tax free. [I.R.C. § 530(b)(1)(E), 530(d)(7)]

(For what the model ESA agreements require when an ESA beneficiary dies, see Q 14:83.)

Contributions

Q 14:19 What is the deadline for making ESA contributions?

ESA contributions (other than rollovers) can be made until the deadline (without extensions) for filing the income tax return for the contribution year—generally, April 15 of the year after the contribution year. The deadline is the following Monday if April 15 falls on a Saturday, Sunday, or holiday. The last day for making an ESA contribution for 2020 is April 15, 2021. [I.R.C. § 530(b)(4)] However, IRS Notice 2021-21 extended the deadline for 2020 contributions to May 17, 2021.

One way to contribute to an ESA is to deliver cash or a check to the trustee. Another is to authorize the trustee to withdraw funds from a taxable account of the donor and contribute them to the ESA. If the donor's authorizing instructions are timely submitted to the trustee, but due to processing time the contribution is not deposited until after April 15, is the contribution timely? The IRS ruled privately (meaning it cannot be relied upon as precedent) that if a written authorization is postmarked, or a verbal request is transmitted to a company representative, on or before the April 15 contribution deadline, and the trustee transfers the funds to the ESA (or IRA) as soon as administratively practicable, the contribution will be deemed to be timely made. [Priv. Ltr. Rul. 201437023 (Sept. 12, 2014)]

Q 14:20 Can securities or other property be contributed to an ESA?

No. Property may be rolled over from one ESA to another, but otherwise all ESA contributions must be made in cash. [I.R.C. § 530(b)(1)(A)(i)]

> **Example.** Steve and Linda are short of cash but own stock that is worth $2,000. They want to transfer the stock directly to their daughter's ESA, but that is not allowed. Steve and Linda must first sell the stock or liquidate other assets to raise cash for the ESA contribution.

Q 14:21 Can a federal income tax refund be directly deposited into an ESA?

Yes. A taxpayer may instruct the IRS to deposit a tax refund directly into an ESA. However, the annual contribution limit still applies.

Contribution Limits

Q 14:22 What are the ESA contribution limits?

There are two contribution limits.

- *Beneficiary limit.* Contributions for an ESA beneficiary may not exceed $2,000 per year from all donors combined. If a beneficiary has more than one ESA, the aggregate contributions are limited to $2,000. [I.R.C. § 530(b)(1)(A)(iii)]
- *Donor limit.* A donor may not contribute more than $2,000 per year to any beneficiary's ESA, but may contribute that much to ESAs for any number of beneficiaries. The contribution limit is lower for donors with higher income (see Qs 14:22, 14:23).

The $2,000 limit does not apply to rollovers from another ESA (see Q 14:57). Military gratuities and life insurance proceeds paid under the Servicemembers'

Group Life Insurance (SGLI) program may also be deposited without regard to the $2,000 limit (see Q 14:35). [I.R.C. § 530(b)(1)(A), 530(c)(1)]

Q 14.23 Who can be a donor?

Any individual, including the ESA beneficiary, who satisfies the donor income limit can make contributions (see Qs 14:25–14:27). Corporations and other entities may also contribute, and they are not subject to income limits. [I.R.C. § 530(b)(1), 530(c)(1); Notice 97-60, 1997-2 C.B. 310]

Note. The IRS has not issued guidance on contributions by nonindividuals.

Q 14:24 Is there a minimum contribution threshold for an ESA?

The law does not impose a minimum threshold for contributions. The trustee or custodian may place a minimum contribution requirement on its accounts.

Donor Income Limit

Q 14:25 What income counts for purposes of the donor limit?

Donors cannot make ESA contributions if their *modified adjusted gross income* (MAGI) is too high. MAGI is adjusted gross income (AGI) determined with some modifications. For most individuals, MAGI is the same as AGI. (Note that MAGI is determined differently for IRA purposes.) MAGI for ESA purposes is AGI *increased* by:

1. Foreign earned income of U.S. citizens or residents living abroad;
2. Housing costs of U.S. citizens or residents living abroad; and
3. Income from sources in Puerto Rico, Guam, American Samoa, the Virgin Islands, or the Northern Mariana Islands.

[I.R.C. § 530(c)(2)]

Q 14:26 What are the MAGI limits?

The MAGI limits are shown in Table 14-2. If MAGI is within the phaseout range, a donor's contribution limit is ratably reduced (see Q 14:27). Unlike many retirement plan limits, these are *not* adjusted for inflation. [I.R.C. § 530(c)]

Table 14-2. MAGI Limits for ESA Donors

Filing Status	*Full Contribution*	*Phaseout Range*	*No Contribution*
Single, or married filing separately	$0 to $94,999	$95,000 to $109,999	$110,000 or more
Married filing jointly	$0 to $189,999	$190,000 to 219,999	$220,000 or more

Example 1. Alice is single, her MAGI for 2020 is $60,000, and she wants to make ESA contributions for her nieces. She may contribute up to $2,000 to each girl's ESA (subject to the $2,000 limit on contributions from all donors that applies to each niece).

Example 2. Bruce and Jenny are married and file a joint federal income tax return. Their MAGI for 2020 is $350,000. Neither spouse can make a 2020 ESA contribution. (They can make gifts, however, to enable contributions by other donors; see Q 14:28.)

Q 14:27 How is the contribution limit reduced if MAGI is within the phaseout range?

The donor's contribution limit is ratably reduced when MAGI is within the phaseout range. [I.R.C. § 530(c)] The IRS instructs that the nominal contribution limit ($2,000) should be multiplied by the fraction whose numerator equals MAGI minus $95,000 ($190,000 if the donor files a joint return), and whose denominator is $15,000 ($30,000 for a joint return). After rounding to three decimal places, the result is subtracted from $2,000. The calculation yields the reduced contribution limit for an individual with MAGI in the phaseout range.

Another way to think about it is to figure how far into the phaseout range a donor's MAGI lies. The contribution limit is phased out to the same extent. (For single filers and married individuals filing separately, the phaseout range is $15,000. It is $30,000 for married couples filing jointly.)

Example 1. Mark wants to contribute as much as he can to his nephew's ESA. He is single, and his MAGI for 2019 is $98,250. His maximum contribution to an ESA for any one child is $1,567, determined as follows.

1. $98,250 – $95,000 = $3,250
2. $3,250 ÷ $15,000 = 0.217
3. 0.217 × $2,000 = $433
4. $2,000 – $433 = $1,567

Example 2. Ken, a single filer, has MAGI of $100,000 for 2020. That exceeds the MAGI limit for a full contribution by $5,000. Since $5,000 is one-third of the way into the phaseout range, his contribution limit is reduced by one-third. For 2020, Ken may contribute $1,334 to his daughter's ESA.

Q 14:28 Can a person with high MAGI make a cash gift to fund another person's ESA contribution?

Yes. For example, parents with high MAGI may give $2,000 to their child to fund the child's own ESA contribution. (Earned income is not required for an ESA contribution.)

Excess Contributions

Q 14:29 What is an excess contribution?

An *excess contribution* is generally any contribution, excluding rollovers, that exceeds the prescribed contribution limits. Thus, if aggregate contributions on behalf of an ESA beneficiary exceed $2,000 per year or, if less, the combined maximum contributions that the donors were eligible to make that year, the surplus amount is an excess contribution. Undistributed excess contributions may be "absorbed" by unused contribution capacity in a later year. They are not absorbed, though, by unused contribution capacity from a former year. [I.R.C. § 4973(e)(1)]

For any year, the excess contributions (which are subject to a 6 percent excise tax; see Q 14:30) are determined as the sum of two amounts:

1. The current year's excess contribution, which is the amount by which the aggregate current year contributions of all donors to ESAs having the same ESA beneficiary exceeds the lesser of $2,000 or the combined maximum contributions that donors were eligible to make.
2. The preceding year's unmitigated excess contribution, which is the amount of excess contributions that were subject to excise tax in the preceding year, reduced (but not below zero) by (a) distributions (not including rollovers) during the current year from the beneficiary's ESAs, and (b) the amount, if any, by which the current year's contributions are less than the maximum amount that the donors could have contributed.

[I.R.C. § 4973(e)(1)]

Q 14:30 How is an excess contribution taxed and corrected?

A 6 percent excise tax is charged against any excess contribution that remains in an ESA at the end of the year. The *beneficiary* (not the donor) must pay it.

The excise tax does not apply if the excess contribution is withdrawn, with earnings, within five months after the end of the contribution year (by May 31, 2021, for an excess contribution in 2020). The withdrawn earnings must be included in the beneficiary's gross income for the year of the contribution. [I.R.C. §§ 4973(a), 530(d)(4)(C)] If an excess contribution is not withdrawn within five months after the contribution year ends, the excise tax applies for the contribution year and continues to apply each year until it is removed. [I.R.C. § 4973(e)]

In lieu of withdrawing an excess contribution and its earnings, the total may be redesignated as a contribution for the succeeding year (subject to normal contribution limits). The income and excise tax consequences are the same unless the full amount is redesignated within five months after the contribution year ends.

Example. In 2019, Ray's mother, Elena, and grandfather, Thomas, respectively contribute $500 and $2,000 to ESAs on Ray's behalf. Neither contribution is restricted by the MAGI limits, but in combination they result in a $500 excess contribution for 2019. There is no distribution before June 1, 2020, so Ray has to pay a $30 excise tax when he files his 2019 tax return. For 2020, Elena contributes nothing, and Thomas contributes $1,500, which is $500 less than his individual contribution limit based on MAGI. The excess contribution from 2019 is now absorbed and exempt from further excise tax.

The ESA beneficiary reports an excess contribution, and figures the excise tax payable, using IRS Form 5329, Additional Taxes on Qualified Retirement Plans (Including IRAs) and Other Tax-Favored Accounts (see Qs 8:98–8:101).

Q 14:31 Does the excise tax apply if an ESA contribution is made after the beneficiary reaches age 18?

An ESA contribution made for a beneficiary older than age 18 who is not a special needs beneficiary (see Q 14:9) must be removed from the account (with earnings), but it appears the excise tax would not apply. Code Section 4973(e), which defines excess contributions for purposes of the excise tax, does not describe this kind of improper contribution.

Q 14:32 Are excess contributions likely in an ESA?

Excess contributions can easily be made to an ESA because anyone may contribute without knowing what other donors are doing. The responsible individual of an ESA is notified when it is established, but a child could have several ESAs with responsible individuals who are not communicating with one another.

Example. Marge and her former husband, Rick, have joint custody over their son, Jim. Marge opens an ESA for Jim and contributes $2,000. In the same year, Rick's parents open another ESA for Jim and contribute $2,000. If there is no communication between Marge and Rick's parents, the excess may go unnoticed. The IRS may catch the error and send out penalty letters.

Q 14:33 How is an excess contribution discovered?

An excess contribution may be discovered from the contribution information reported on Form 5498-ESA. That is the form each ESA trustee must prepare and send to the beneficiary, the responsible individual, and the IRS. (See Qs 14:97, 14:98.)

Q 14:34 Who receives the money when an excess contribution is distributed from an ESA?

The withdrawn contribution and earnings are paid by default to the beneficiary, who also pays any excise tax due, but the IRS model ESA forms specifically allow language to be added concerning treatment of excess contributions.

Military Death Payments

Q 14:35 Can survivor benefits paid because of the death of a member of the armed forces be deposited into an ESA?

Yes. The recipient of a military death payment may contribute some or all of it to one or more ESAs, Roth IRAs, or both. The payments are the *military death gratuity* (MDG) and life insurance proceeds paid under the Servicemembers Group Life Insurance (SGLI) program of the U.S. Veterans Administration. (Regarding transfers of such payments to a Roth IRA, see Q 6:120.)

Any transfer of such a payment to an ESA must occur within one year after the date it is received, and the ESA beneficiary must be a family member (see Q 14:14) of the person who received the payment. The transfer is treated as a tax-free rollover, not a new contribution—so the limit on annual contributions for the beneficiary does not apply (see Q 14:22). [I.R.C. § 530(d)(9)]

The 12-month rule that normally limits the frequency of rollovers (see Q 14:60) does not apply to these contributions. An MDG or SGLI payment rolled over to an ESA is included in basis, so it will not be taxed when later distributed. [I.R.C. § 530(d)(9); IRS Office of Chief Counsel PMTA 2016-010 (Dec. 14, 2015)]

> **Note.** The MDG is a $100,000 payment that the U.S. Department of Defense provides to eligible survivors of a servicemember who dies during active duty or in other specified circumstances. SGLI is a life insurance program offered by the U.S. Veterans Administration that provides coverage of up to $400,000 for certain members of the uniformed services. [*See* U.S. Dept. of Defense websites: Death Gratuity at *https://militarypay.defense.gov/Benefits/Death-Gratuity/* (retrieved Aug. 12, 2020); and Servicemembers Group Life Insurance (SGLI) at *https://militarypay.defense.gov/Benefits/Servicemembers-Group-Life-Insurance/* (retrieved Aug. 12, 2020).]

Distributions

Q 14:36 When may distributions be taken from an ESA?

The beneficiary (or the responsible person, if the beneficiary is a minor) may take distributions at any time and for any purpose that is in the beneficiary's interest, even if there are no education expenses. For some investments, the financial institution may impose restrictions and fees for early withdrawal. (For mandatory distributions from the ESA, see Q 14:38.)

Q 14:37 Who decides when distributions will be taken?

The ESA agreement determines who controls the ESA and may take distributions. For a minor beneficiary, this is usually the parent.

Q 14:38 When *must* the ESA be distributed?

Normally, the ESA must be fully distributed within 30 days after the beneficiary reaches age 30. This requirement does not apply for special needs beneficiaries. (See Q 14:9.) A full distribution is also required within 30 days after the beneficiary dies, unless the ESA has a death beneficiary meeting the requirements described in Q 14:18. [I.R.C. § 530(b)(1)(E), 530(d)(7)]

Q 14:39 Can ESA funds be withdrawn to avoid their mandatory distribution to the beneficiary at age 30?

No. The ESA is a trust established for the benefit of the designated beneficiary and his or her education needs. Unlike a 529 account, it cannot be revoked by the account owner (except within seven days after opening the ESA; see Q 14:96) or responsible individual, and the assets may not be withdrawn to benefit any person who is not the beneficiary.

However, before the beneficiary reaches age 30, it is perfectly acceptable for the responsible individual to roll over the ESA to another beneficiary who is a member of the current beneficiary's family, and who is younger than age 30 or has special needs (see Q 14:13). That would not be a violation of the trust.

> **Note.** In many cases, the beneficiary will have become the account owner by the time of his or her 30th birthday. The terms of the ESA may cause ownership to transfer to the beneficiary upon reaching the age of majority (18 years). A beneficiary who is the owner may, of course, take the assets at any time for personal benefit, but if they are not used for qualified education expenses the distribution will be taxable and subject to penalty.

Qualified Education Expenses

Q 14:40 What expenses are taken into account for ESA purposes?

Only *qualified education expenses* (QEEs) are taken into account for ESA purposes. Some expenses that qualify under the ESA rules do not qualify under the rules for 529 plans (see Table 14-1 in Q 14:2).

Q 14:41 What are qualified education expenses for ESA purposes?

Expenses that qualify for tax-free ESA distributions include the following:

For elementary, secondary, and higher education:

- Tuition, fees, academic tutoring, special needs services in the case of a special needs beneficiary, books, supplies, and other equipment required for the enrollment or attendance of the ESA beneficiary at a public, private, or religious school. [I.R.C. §§ 529(e)(3)(A)(i), 530(b)(4)(A)(i)]
- Room and board. [I.R.C. §§ 529(e)(3)(B), 530(b)(4)(A)(ii)]
- The purchase of computer technology or equipment or Internet access or any related service, if it is used by the beneficiary and his or her family

during any year when the beneficiary is in school (excluding computer software designed for sports, games, or hobbies unless the software is educational in nature). [I.R.C. § 530(b)(4)(A)(iii)]

- Amounts contributed to a qualified state tuition program (529 account; see Q 14:2). [I.R.C. § 529(e)(3)(B)(i)]

For higher education only:

- Expenses for room and board at an *eligible educational institution* where the student is enrolled at least half time (see Qs 14:42, 14:43). The qualified expenses may not exceed the school's posted room and board charge (for students residing on campus), or $2,500 per year (for students living off campus and not at home). [I.R.C. § 529(e)(3)(B)]
- Expenses for uniforms, transportation, and supplementary items or services (including extended day programs) that are required by an elementary or secondary school in connection with enrollment or attendance. [I.R.C. § 530(b)(4)(A)(ii)]

[*See* IRS Pub. 970, *Tax Benefits for Education* 2020.]

Q 14:42 What is half-time enrollment?

Half-time enrollment means enrollment for at least half of the full-time academic workload, based on the institution's standards for the particular course of study. The institution's standard for a full-time workload must be at least as stringent as those established by the Department of Education under the Higher Education Act. [Notice 97-60, 1997-2 C.B. 310; 34 C.F.R. § 674.2(b)]

Q 14:43 What is an eligible educational institution?

Virtually all accredited public, nonprofit, and proprietary schools—from kindergarten on through postsecondary institutions—are *eligible educational institutions*. If the school is eligible to participate in student aid programs administered by the Department of Education, it is an eligible institution. [Notice 97-60, 1997-2 C.B. 310; 20 U.S.C. § 1088] A school's status as an eligible educational institution may be verified online at *https://ope.ed.gov/dapip/#/home*.

Q 14:44 What happens if there are no qualified education expenses?

If the ESA beneficiary will not incur further (or any) qualified education expenses, the responsible individual (who may be the ESA beneficiary) has two options. The assets in the ESA could be paid to the ESA beneficiary or used for his or her other expenses—but they will be subject to taxes and the 10 percent penalty (see Q 14:45). Or, it may be possible to change the ESA beneficiary (see Q 14:13). [Notice 97-60, 1997-2 C.B. 310]

Taxation of Distributions

Q 14:45 What ESA distributions are tax free?

ESA distributions are completely tax free if the total amount distributed during the year is not more than the beneficiary's *adjusted qualified education expenses* (AQEE) (see Q 14:47). If the distributions exceed AQEE, then any earnings from the ESA that are included in the excess distribution are taxable. A 10 percent additional tax may also apply (see Q 14:54). [I.R.C. § 530(d)(2)]

Q 14:46 Where is the necessary information found?

All of the figures needed to determine the taxation of an ESA distribution are found in information reports filed with the IRS, copies of which are provided to the beneficiary or the responsible person.

1. *ESA distributions:*
   - *Gross amount distributed.* Each ESA trustee prepares Form 1099-Q, Payments from Qualified Education Programs (Under Sections 529 and 530), box 1.
   - *Earnings in the ESA.* Form 1099-Q, box 2.
   - *Basis in the ESA.* Form 1099-Q, box 3.
   - *Fair market value (FMV) at the end of the previous year.* Form 1099-Q, blank box below box 5.
   - *Regular contributions made during the distribution year.* The ESA trustee also prepares Form 5498-ESA, Coverdell ESA Contribution Information. Regular contributions for the year are reported in box 1.
   - *529 account distributions.* The plan trustee similarly prepares Form 1099-liQ.
2. *Qualified education expenses (QEE).* The educational institution reports these expenses on Form 1098-T, Tuition Payments. There are two possible reporting methods, and the form indicates which is used:
   - *Payments received.* If the preparer uses this method, box 1 shows the total payments received from all sources, less reimbursements and refunds, for QEE in the calendar year. Scholarships and grants are included in box 1.
   - *Amounts billed.* If this method is used, box 2 shows the total amounts billed for QEE, less any reductions in those charges, during the calendar year. The figure in box 2 is not reduced by scholarships and grants.
3. *Scholarships and grants.* These are reported in box 5 of Form 1098-T. The preparer generally includes all amounts received from third parties, that is, governmental entities and private civic, religious, and nonprofit entities. (The figure in box 5 excludes, however, (1) payments from family members, (2) loan proceeds, and (3) payments for a student whose QEEs are fully waived, fully paid by scholarships, or completely covered under a formal billing agreement between the school and an employer or governmental entity.)

4. *Insurance refunds and reimbursements.* If payment of a student's QEEs is insured under a contract, the insurer prepares Form 1098-T to report, in box 10, any reimbursements or refunds made under the contract during the calendar year.
5. *Expenses taken into account for credit purposes.* If eligible, the parent or student who pays the QEE can claim either the American Opportunity Credit (AOC) or the Lifetime Learning Credit (LLC). Both credits are figured on Form 8863, Education Credits (American Opportunity and Lifetime Learning Credits), which the claimant attaches to his or her income tax return.
    - The AOC is for college and post-graduate education expenses. The credit is 100 percent of the first $2,000 of QEE, plus 25 percent of the next $2,000. The maximum credit is $2,500.
    - The LLC is for expenses of all post-secondary education, and education to acquire or improve job skills. The credit is 100 percent of the first $2,000 of QEE, plus 25 percent of the next $10,000 of QEE. The maximum credit is $2,000.

Q 14:47 How is AQEE determined?

To determine AQEE, adjustments are made to the beneficiary's total qualified education expenses (QEE). These adjustments are needed to avoid double counting any expense that is already taken into account for other benefits. Two amounts are subtracted from QEE to determine AQEE:

- The tax-free part of any educational assistance payments, and
- Any QEE taken into account to claim the AOC or the LLC (see Q 14:46, item 5). [I.R.C. § 530(d)(2)(A)]

(For allocating AQEE when both ESA and 529 account distributions are received in the same calendar year, see Q 14:52.)

Q 14:48 What are educational assistance payments?

Educational assistance payments include:

- Scholarships and fellowship grants (tax-free portion only)
- Veterans' educational assistance
- Pell grants
- Employer-provided educational assistance
- Other nontaxable educational assistance payments—*excluding* gifts and inheritances

(Gifts and inheritances, though tax free, are *not* taken into account to determine AQEE; *see* I.R.C. § 530(d)(2).)

Q 14:49 What part of a grant or scholarship is tax free?

The tax-free part of a grant or scholarship is the entire amount reduced by:

- The amount (if any) of the payment that is more than the student's total QEE,
- Any part of the payment that is designated for another purpose (cannot be used to cover QEEs), and
- Any part of the payment that is for teaching, research, or other services, if the payment is conditioned on any of those services.

[IRS Pub. 970, *Tax Benefits for Education* 2020]

Q 14:50 How are QEEs adjusted when an education tax credit is claimed?

If either the AOC or the LLC is claimed (both cannot be claimed), the expenses taken into account to determine the credit must be subtracted as an adjustment to QEE. [I.R.C. § 530(d)(2)(C); IRS Pub. 970, *Tax Benefits for Education* 2019]

Q 14:51 How is the taxable part of an ESA distribution determined?

If the total ESA distributions for the year exceed AQEE, the earnings included in the excess distribution are taxable, and the 10 percent additional tax may also apply (see Q 14:54). [I.R.C. §§ 530(d), 72] There are several steps for calculating the taxable part of an ESA distribution:

1. Determine whether the total ESA distributions exceed AQEE. If not, stop—the distributions are tax free. If there is an excess distribution, it is necessary to continue.
2. Figure the amount of basis in the ESA, without regard to current year distributions. (This is the total amount of ESA contributions made in the current and prior years, less basis previously distributed.)
3. Determine the amount of basis distributed from the ESA. (This is the current year distributions, multiplied by a fraction. The numerator is the amount determined in step 2 (total basis at year-end). The denominator is the FMV of the ESA at the end of the prior year, increased by distributions made in the current year.)
4. Determine the amount of earnings included in the current year distributions. (This is the total distribution amount less the amount from step 3 (distributed basis).)
5. Figure the tax-free part of the distributed earnings. (Multiply the total distributed earnings by a fraction. The numerator is AQEE. The denominator is the total amount distributed.)
6. Subtract the tax-free distributed earnings from the total earnings distributed. The result is the amount included in income.

Example 1. Tammy, an ESA beneficiary, incurs AQEE of $1,000 for 2019. The total amount contributed to her ESA in prior years is $5,000, and no contributions were made in 2019. The value of the ESA at the end of 2018 was $7,200. During 2019, $1,100 was withdrawn from Tammy's ESA.

There is an excess distribution of $100 from the ESA ($1,100 − $1,000). Tammy's basis in the ESA at the end of 2019—before the distribution is taken into account—is $5,000 (the total contributions made for all years). The basis allocated to the 2019 distribution is $663 ($1,100 × $5,000 ÷ ($7,200 + $1,100)). The rest of the distribution ($437; i.e., $1,100 − $663) is earnings. The tax-free portion of the earnings is $398 ($437 × ($1,000 ÷ $1,100)). That leaves $39 ($437 − $398) of taxable earnings for Tammy to include in income.

Example 2. In 2018, Sam attended college on scholarship and paid his own way for the rest. He incurred $8,500 of QEE. The tax-free scholarship covered $3,500 of the QEE, and Sam paid the rest using $3,900 saved from previous job earnings, and $1,100 withdrawn from his ESA. On his 2018 tax return, he will claim a full AOC for $4,000 of the QEE. At the end of 2017, the value of his ESA was $6,200, including $5,500 of contributions. No contributions were made in 2018.

Sam's AQEE is $1,000 ($8,500 − $3,500 − $4,000). There is an excess distribution of $100 ($1,100 − $1,000) from the ESA. Before the distribution, his basis in the ESA was $5,500. The 2018 distribution removes $829 of that basis ($1,100 × $5,500 ÷ ($6,200 + $1,100)). The rest of the distribution ($271) comes from earnings. The tax-free part of the distributed earnings is $247 ($271 × $1,000 ÷ $1,100). The rest of the distributed earnings ($25) are taxable.

Q 14:52 If both ESA and 529 account distributions are made, how is AQEE allocated?

The total AQEE is compared with the combined amount of ESA and 529 account distributions. Generally, if the total distributions exceed AQEE, then AQEE is apportioned between the two to determine the taxable amounts distributed from the ESA and the 529 account. [I.R.C. § 530(d)(2)(C)(ii)]

However, education expenses for lower and secondary school are qualified for ESA purposes (see Q 14:41) but *not* for 529 plan purposes (other than tuition expense, up to $10,000 of which is now allowed each year for 529 plan purposes; see Q 14:3). Those can be allocated only to ESA distributions. If some expenses are incurred that qualify only under the ESA rules, and others are incurred that qualify for ESA and 529 account purposes, a special allocation is necessary:

- The portion of AQEE that is *only* qualified for ESA purposes is entirely allocated to the ESA distributions.
- The rest of the AQEE is apportioned between distributions from the ESA (excluding the amount already matched with AQEE) and the 529 plan.

Example 1. In 2019, Marie attended college full time. She incurred $9,500 of AQEE and $500 of nonqualifying expenses. To pay these expenses, she used a $4,000 distribution from her ESA and a $6,000 distribution from her 529 account. The $9,500 of AQEE is allocated in proportion to the distributions—40 percent to the ESA distribution ($3,800), and 60 percent ($5,700) to the 529 distribution. The result is an excess distribution of $200 ($4,000 - $3,800) from the ESA, the taxable part of which is determined according to the procedure in Q 14:51. (Taxation of the 529 distribution is beyond the scope of this book.)

Example 2. Sydney graduated from high school (a private academy) in May 2019 and started his freshman year at college three months later. He incurred AQEE of $1,500 for high school room and board (which is not a qualified expense for 529 plan purposes), and $6,000 for college, and paid for these with distributions of $1,200 from his ESA and $6,200 from his 529 account. To figure the taxable part of each distribution, AQEE is first allocated between the two distributions. However, the high school AQEE can only be allocated to the ESA distribution, and it is less than the total amount distributed from the ESA—so the ESA distribution is tax free. All the college AQEE is allocated to the 529 distribution.

Example 3. The facts are the same as in Example 2, except that Sydney took $2,800 from the ESA and $5,000 from the 529 account. Since the ESA distribution was more than the high school AQEE, some of the college AQEE must be allocated between the 529 distribution and the "unused" part of the ESA distribution. As shown below, allocation of the AQEE results in an excess distribution of $62 from the ESA, which is taxed in accordance with the procedure in Q 14:51.

High school AQEE	$1,500
College AQEE	$6,000
ESA distribution	$2,800
529 distribution	$5,000
High school AQEE allocated to ESA distribution	$1,500
"Unused" ESA distribution	$1,300
Total distributions to which college AQEE is allocated:	
Unused ESA distribution	$1,300
529 distribution	$5,000
Proportional allocation of college AQEE:	
To unused ESA distribution	$1,238
To 529 distribution	$4,762
Taxation of ESA distribution:	
Total distribution	$2,800
Total allocated AQEE (high school and college)	$2,738
Excess distribution	$ 62

Q 14:53 If an ESA distribution exceeds basis, is the loss deductible?

Losses within an ESA are not deductible until all amounts have been finally distributed. (If a beneficiary has more than one ESA, they are all treated as one ESA for taxation purposes, so a loss cannot be recognized until they have all been fully distributed.) At that point, the beneficiary may be allowed an income tax deduction for the amount of any contributions that were not returned.

Until 2018, that loss would be claimed as a miscellaneous itemized deduction, subject to the 2-percent-of-adjusted-gross-income limit. [IRS Pub. 970, *Tax Benefits for Education* 2020; I.R.C. § 67] However, the Tax Cuts and Jobs Act (TCJA) eliminated the miscellaneous itemized deduction for the years 2018 through 2025. It may be possible to claim the loss under Code Section 165(c)(2), as a loss incurred in a transaction entered into for profit, though not connected with a trade or business. [TCJA § 11045]

Additional Tax

Q 14:54 What ESA distributions are subject to additional tax?

Additional tax generally applies if an excess distribution is made from an ESA. The additional tax is 10 percent of the amount included in income. However, the excise tax is not payable if an exception applies (see Q 14:55). [I.R.C. § 530(d)(4)] Under IRS Notice 2021-21, the 10 percent additional tax is not required to be reported and paid until May 17, 2021.

Example. Donna, age 19, serves as the responsible individual for her own ESA. She has $2,200 in her account, which represents a $2,000 contribution (basis) plus $200 in earnings. She takes a distribution of the entire $2,200 to take a vacation unrelated to education. Donna will owe taxes and penalties on the distributed earnings ($200), plus additional tax ($20).

Q 14:55 What are the exceptions to the 10 percent additional tax?

A distribution from an ESA is not subject to the 10 percent penalty, even if it is otherwise subject to federal income tax, if it meets one of these exceptions:

1. *Death.* The distribution is made to the estate of the deceased ESA beneficiary. [I.R.C. § 530(d)(4)(B)(i)]
2. *Disability.* The distribution is attributable to the ESA beneficiary's being disabled (within the meaning of Code Section 72(m)(7)). To be disabled means the individual cannot perform substantial gainful activity as a result of a mental or physical condition that is expected to last for an indefinite duration or result in death. [I.R.C. § 530(d)(4)(B)(ii)]
3. *Nontaxable Scholarship, Allowance, or Payment.* The distribution does not exceed the amount of an otherwise nontaxable scholarship, allowance, or payment covering eligible education expenses, that is received in the same year (see Q 14:49). [I.R.C. § 530(d)(4)(B)(iii)]
4. *Waiver.* The tax-free nature of the distribution is waived so that the individual or his or her parents can claim the AOC or LLC (see Q 14:47, item

5). [I.R.C. § 530(d)(4)(B)(iv); IRS Pub. 970, *Tax Benefits for Education* 2020]

5. *Attendance at a U.S. Military Academy.* The distribution is made because the ESA beneficiary attends a U.S. military academy (e.g., West Point). The exception applies only to the extent a distribution does not exceed the costs of advanced education at the academy. [IRS Pub. 970, *Tax Benefits for Education* 2020]
6. *Excess Contribution.* The last exception applies to the corrective distribution, before June 1, 2020, of an excess 2019 contribution and its associated earnings. (If the June 1 deadline falls on a Sunday or a holiday in any year, it is extended to the next day.) The distributed earnings are included in gross income for the year when the excess contribution was made. [I.R.C. § 530(d)(4)(C); IRS Pub. 970, *Tax Benefits for Education* 2020]

Withholding

Q 14:56 Is federal income tax withheld from an ESA distribution?

No, there is no requirement to withhold federal income tax from ESA distributions.

Rollovers

Q 14:57 How are assets moved tax free from one ESA to another?

If a direct (trustee-to-trustee) transfer or a 60-day rollover is used, cash and other property in an ESA may be transferred tax free to another ESA on behalf of:

- The same beneficiary, or
- Another beneficiary who is a member of the same family as the first beneficiary (see Q 14:14), if the new beneficiary is younger than age 30 or has special needs.

[I.R.C. § 530(d)(5)]

Q 14:58 How is a direct transfer accomplished?

Generally, to accomplish a direct transfer, the responsible individual (see Q 14:74) selects a new trustee for the ESA, signs a new ESA agreement, and authorizes the transfer in writing. The new trustee sends the authorization to the current trustee with instructions for sending the ESA assets directly to the new trustee.

Or, the first trustee might issue a check payable to the new trustee which is delivered by the responsible individual. The key feature of a trustee-to-trustee transfer is that the responsible individual and the ESA beneficiary never have direct access to the funds as they are moved. As a result, there is no distribution.

Q 14:59 What are the requirements for a 60-day rollover?

A 60-day rollover of ESA assets is done the same way as for an IRA (see Q 6:3). The ESA assets are paid directly to the responsible individual (who controls the ESA), who then deposits them into a new ESA (which may or may not be maintained by the same trustee or custodian). The deposit must occur no later than 60 days after the distribution. [I.R.C. § 530(d)(5)]

The IRS waives the 60-day limit in some cases (e.g., after a casualty, a disaster, or other event beyond the reasonable control of the individual). [I.R.C. § 530(d)(5)] (See chapter 6 for a complete discussion of the 60-day rule and IRS waivers.)

Q 14:60 How frequently can rollovers occur?

Sixty-day rollovers between ESAs are limited to one every 12 months, but there is no limit on the number of trustee-to-trustee transfers that may occur between ESAs. The 12-month limit on 60-day rollovers applies *on an aggregate basis* to all ESAs held for the same beneficiary. [I.R.C. § 530(d)(5); IRS Office of Chief Counsel PMTA 2016-010 (Dec. 14, 2015); *see* Bobrow v. Commissioner, T.C. Memo. 2014-21 (Jan. 28, 2014).]

The 12-month limit does not apply, however, to rollovers of either military death or SGLI payments to an ESA (see Q 14:35). [I.R.C. § 530(d)(9)]

Estate and Gift Tax Consequences

Contributions

Q 14:61 Are contributions to an ESA subject to gift tax?

An ESA contribution made for another person is a completed gift, but in most cases not a taxable gift because of the annual gift tax exclusion—which is $15,000 for 2018 through 2021. That means, for example, there is only a taxable gift to the extent the 2021 ESA contribution amount, combined with other completed gifts by the donor to the same ESA beneficiary for 2021, exceeds $15,000. The annual exclusion amount is adjusted annually for inflation. [I.R.C. §§ 530(d)(3), 529(c)(2)(A)(i), 2503(b), 2503(e); Rev. Proc. 2019-44, 2019-47 I.R.B. 1093; Rev. Proc. 2020-45, 2020-46 I.R.B. 1016; Rev. Proc. 2018-57, 2018-49 I.R.B. 827; Rev. Proc. 2017-58, 2017-45 I.R.B. 489]

If a taxable gift is made, the donor must file a gift tax return but usually there is no immediate tax (because of the unified credit against the gift and estate taxes). [I.R.C. §§ 2505, 2010(c)]

Q 14:62 Do contributions made to a 529 plan in the same year also count against the annual exclusion limit?

Yes. Since 529 plan contributions are also treated as completed gifts when made, they are also subject to the annual gift tax exclusion. If a donor contributes to an ESA plan and a 529 plan in the same year, and both plans are held for the same ESA beneficiary, the combined contributions must be taken into account (together with other gifts from the donor to that donee) for purposes of the annual gift tax exclusion. [I.R.C. §§ 530(d)(3), 529(c)(2)(A)]

However, if a donor's contributions to an individual's 529 plans and ESAs exceed the annual gift tax exclusion limit (see Q 14:61), the donor may elect to treat all or part of the gift as spread evenly over five years. If the election is made, one-fifth of the gift is shielded by each year's annual exclusion limit. Without taking into account future adjustments of the exclusion limit for inflation, a gift in 2021 of $75,000 (five times the $15,000 annual exclusion limit) may be entirely shielded this way. (If a donor who makes this election dies before the end of the five-year period, the contribution amounts allocable to periods after death are included in his or her gross estate.) [I.R.C. §§ 530(d)(3), 529(c)(5)(B), 529(c)(2)(B), 529(c)(4)(C)]

The donor makes the five-year averaging election on a gift tax return filed for the actual contribution year. [2019 Instructions for Form 709, p. 7]

> **Example.** Horace contributes $2,000 to his daughter's ESA and $43,000 to her 529 plan in 2020. He also gives her some shares of stock worth $4,000. His total completed gifts to her ($49,000) exceed the exclusion amount ($15,000) by $34,000. Instead of reporting $34,000 of taxable gifts, Horace elects to treat the ESA and 529 plan gifts ($45,000) as made evenly over five years. Because of the election (which he makes on a gift tax return filed for 2020), Horace is deemed to make $9,000 of ESA and 529 plan gifts for each year from 2020 through 2024. Thus, for 2020, the total amount of Horace's completed gifts to his daughter is only $13,000 ($9,000 plus $4,000 of stock), which is less than the $15,000 exclusion amount. There is no taxable gift for 2020.

Q 14:63 Are contributions subject to generation skipping transfer tax?

The generation skipping transfer (GST) tax may only apply if the gift is taxable, and most ESA contributions are not taxable because of the annual gift tax exclusion limit (see Q 14:61). If the contribution is over the exclusion limit and the ESA beneficiary is a generation or more below the donor, the transfer is a direct skip subject to GST tax. [I.R.C. §§ 530(d)(3), 529(c)(2), 2642(c)(1)]

Q 14:64 Is an excess contribution treated the same way?

Yes. An excess contribution that is not removed is treated as a completed gift, and the same rules apply. The election described in Q 14:62 is also available to a donor whose excess contributions to a 529 plan, ESA, or both, on behalf of the same individual cause the gift to exceed the annual gift tax exclusion limit. [I.R.C. § 529(c)(2), 529(c)(4)(C)]

Distributions

Q 14:65 During the ESA beneficiary's lifetime, do distributions from the ESA have gift tax consequences?

No. ESA *contributions* are completed gifts (see Q 14:61). A *distribution* from the ESA is not treated as a gift. [I.R.C. §§ 530(d)(3), 529(c)(5)(A)]

(For the consequences of a deemed distribution when the ESA beneficiary dies, see Q 14:69.)

Q 14:66 Are the ESA assets deemed distributed when the beneficiary dies?

There is a deemed distribution of assets only if the beneficiary's death causes the ESA to terminate. (For whether the ESA may continue, see Qs 14:68, 14:69.)

New Designated Beneficiary

Q 14:67 Is there a taxable gift if the ESA beneficiary is changed from one person to another?

There may be. It depends on the generational assignments of the two beneficiaries under the transfer tax laws.

There is no taxable gift if the new beneficiary is a member of the old beneficiary's family, and is assigned to the same generation as (or a generation higher than) the old beneficiary. It does not matter whether the change is made by redesignating the beneficiary on the same account, or by rolling the account over to an ESA for the new beneficiary. [I.R.C. §§ 530(d)(6), 529(c)(5)(B)]

But if the new beneficiary is assigned to a generation below (younger than) the old beneficiary, the old beneficiary is treated as making a completed gift (the value of the account) to the new one. Even so, there would not be a taxable gift or direct skip for GST purposes if the amount is covered by the annual gift tax exclusion.

Finally, if the gift does exceed the annual exclusion limit, a taxable gift (and direct skip) may still be avoidable. The old beneficiary could make a five-year averaging election for the gift (see Q 14:62). [I.R.C. §§ 530(d)(6), 529(c)(5)(B), 529(c)(2)(B)]

Death

Q 14:68 If the ESA beneficiary dies and the ESA terminates, are there estate tax consequences?

Yes. An ESA generally terminates and is deemed distributed when the ESA beneficiary dies. In that case, the value of the ESA is included in the deceased beneficiary's gross estate for estate tax purposes. [I.R.C. §§ 530(d)(3), 529(c)(4)(B)]

Q 14:69 Is the ESA included in the deceased ESA beneficiary's gross estate if the account does not terminate?

No. If there is an ESA death beneficiary who is a member of the decedent's family, and who either is younger than age 30 or has special needs, then the account survives and the death beneficiary is substituted as the new ESA beneficiary. The value of the account would *not* be included in the decedent's gross estate. [I.R.C. §§ 530(d)(3), 529(c)(4)(A)]

Establishing an ESA

Q 14:70 How is an ESA established?

An ESA is established as a trust or custodial account for the benefit of a particular eligible individual (the ESA beneficiary). The grantor (who establishes the account) chooses a financial institution to serve as the account trustee or custodian, receives a plain-language disclosure statement, enters into a governing agreement that sets out the important terms and conditions of the account, and makes the first contribution.

Q 14:71 Must a child have a Social Security number or a taxpayer identification number to establish an ESA?

Yes. The trustee or custodian of an ESA is required to report certain information to the government using the child's Social Security number (SSN) or taxpayer identification number (TIN). Most trustees and custodians will require the child's SSN or TIN at the time the ESA is established; others will require it to be provided within a certain number of days after establishment.

Q 14:72 Whose Social Security numbers must be provided to the financial institution?

The Social Security numbers (SSNs) of the contributor (grantor or depositor) and the ESA beneficiary are required. If the contributor is a nonresident alien without an SSN, "Foreign" should be entered in the block where the number is requested. [IRS Form 5305-E, Coverdell Education Savings Account, *General Instructions* (Oct. 2016)]

The ESA beneficiary's SSN also serves as the identification number of the ESA. However, if the ESA will have unrelated business taxable income to report, it must acquire its own employer identification number (EIN). An EIN is also needed if a common fund is created for ESAs. [IRS Form 5305-E, *General Instructions* (Oct. 2016)]

Q 14:73 Is Form W-9 TIN certification required for an ESA?

No. The ESA trustee or custodian must collect the ESA beneficiary's SSN, but need not use Form W-9, Request for Taxpayer Identification Number and Certification, to do so.

Q 14:74 Who controls the ESA once it is opened?

The person who controls the account after it is opened is the *responsible individual*. The grantor names the responsible individual, usually a parent or the legal guardian of the ESA beneficiary, in the ESA agreement. [IRS Pub. 970, *Tax Benefits for Education* 2020]

Unless the ESA agreement provides otherwise, a grantor who is not also the responsible individual only controls the opening of the account and its initial contribution.

Q 14:75 How many ESAs may one individual establish?

There is no limit on the number of ESAs an individual may establish, but the total annual contribution to all ESAs for a particular ESA beneficiary is limited to $2,000. [IRS Pub. 970, *Tax Benefits for Education* 2020]

The Financial Institution

Q 14:76 What institutions may serve as an ESA trustee or custodian?

Any financial organization authorized to accept traditional IRA contributions is automatically approved to accept ESA contributions and act as a trustee or custodian. Thus, banks, credit unions, savings associations, insurance companies, mutual funds, brokerages, and other financial institutions already approved by the IRS to offer IRAs are automatically approved by the IRS to offer ESAs. Any other organization must submit an application to the IRS for approval to serve as a trustee or custodian of an ESA in accordance with the procedures set forth in Treasury Regulations Section 1.408-2(e) and Section 3.07 of Revenue Procedure 2021-4. [2021-1 I.R.B. 167]

Note. Individuals may not serve as ESA trustees or custodians.

Q 14:77 May a federal credit union offer the ESA?

Yes. ESAs offered by federal credit unions are insured under the banking regulations. [12 C.F.R. § 745.9-1]

Model ESAs

Q 14:78 What model agreements does the IRS supply?

Yes. The IRS provides two model agreements—Form 5305-E, Coverdell Education Savings Trust Account, and Form 5305-EA, Coverdell Education Savings

Custodial Account. As with the IRA models, the ESA models are identical but for the nomenclature used (see Q 2:21). Trust departments and trust companies generally use the trust agreement (Form 5305-E), and other financial institutions generally use the custodial agreement (Form 5305-EA).

Q 14:79 Who signs the model agreement?

The model agreements have signature lines for the contributor (grantor or depositor), the financial institution (trustee or custodian), and a witness. There is no signature line for the responsible individual, but to ensure that he or she is also bound by the agreement some financial institutions require the responsible person to sign and return a copy of the agreement or other acknowledgment form. Nor is the ESA beneficiary required to sign, as usually he or she is a minor.

Q 14:80 What do the IRS model agreements contain?

The IRS model ESA forms—Form 5305-E and Form 5305-EA—have the same look and organization as the IRS model IRA agreements. They contain the following:

1. Contributor information: the name and the Social Security number (SSN) or individual taxpayer identification number (TIN) of the person establishing the ESA.
2. Designated beneficiary information: the name, SSN or TIN, date of birth, and address of the ESA beneficiary.
3. Responsible individual information: the name and address of the responsible individual.
4. Trustee or custodian information: the name and address of the trustee or custodian.
5. Contribution information: the amount of the initial contribution.
6. Legal document: the required IRS provisions that must be adopted word for word in Articles I through X of the form.
7. Instructions: a description of how to use the form.
8. Signature lines: signature lines for the contributor (grantor or depositor), the trustee or custodian, and a witness.

Neither of the IRS model ESA forms contains a disclosure statement, but each indicates that one is required.

Q 14:81 Who are the parties involved in a model ESA?

The model ESA agreements refer to these individuals and entities:

1. *Designated beneficiary.* The person on whose behalf an ESA is established. [I.R.C. § 530(b)(1)]

2. *Trustee or custodian.* The financial institution accepting an ESA contribution. [I.R.C. § 530(b)(1)(B) (trustee); Notice 97-60, 1997-2 C.B. 310 (custodian)]
3. *Grantor or depositor.* The person who establishes the ESA on behalf of the ESA beneficiary and makes the first contribution. Individuals, corporations, and other entities may all do so.
4. *Responsible individual.* The individual named by the grantor to control the ESA. This must be a parent or legal guardian of the ESA beneficiary, at least until he or she reaches the age of majority. Only one person at a time may be the responsible individual.
5. *Successor responsible individual.* The individual who takes over as the responsible individual when the current one becomes incapacitated or dies, or when the ESA beneficiary reaches majority or dies.
6. *Contributor.* Anyone who contributes to the ESA. Contributors may be individuals, corporations, or other entities.
7. *Designated death beneficiary.* The person, if any, named to receive the ESA assets upon the ESA beneficiary's death.

Q 14:82 What powers does the responsible individual hold?

Under the model forms, the responsible individual can redirect investment of the ESA assets and direct investment of all new contributions and their earnings. He or she may direct the trustee or custodian concerning the administration, management, and distribution of the account. Finally, the responsible individual may transfer the assets of the ESA to a different trustee or custodian in order to change the investment selections or the terms of the trust or custodial agreement. [IRS Forms 5305-E, 5305-EA]

Example. Grandfather establishes an ESA on behalf of Grandson at Bank XYZ, contributes $2,000, and selects investment in a five-year CD earning 3 percent annually. Grandfather names Grandson's Mother as the responsible individual. Shortly after Mother receives notification of her role as responsible individual, she transfers the assets in the ESA to ABC Mutual Fund and invests in an international index fund. Bank XYZ imposes a loss-of-earnings penalty on the ESA CD because Mother withdrew the assets before maturity. Grandfather becomes angry at Mother's actions and demands that the assets be transferred back to Bank XYZ and placed back into the CD. Neither ABC Mutual Fund nor Bank XYZ may honor Grandfather's request. Grandfather has no authority over the ESA. Mother, as the responsible individual, may complete the transfer of the ESA assets.

Under a model ESA, the responsible individual also has the power (unless denied under the terms established by the grantor) to change the beneficiary designation at any time. The new beneficiary must be a qualifying member of the former ESA beneficiary's family who is younger than age 30 (or older if a special needs beneficiary). [IRS Forms 5305-E and 5305-EA] (See Q 14:14.)

Q 14:83 What do the model agreements require in the event of the ESA beneficiary's death?

If the designated ESA beneficiary (DB) dies, and there is a designated ESA death beneficiary (DDB) younger than age 30 who is a member of the deceased DB's family (see Q 14:14), the DDB automatically becomes the DB on the date of death.

If the DDB is age 30 or older or not a member of family, or there is no DDB, the account must be distributed within 30 days of death. (This will be a taxable distribution; see Q 14:18.)

Q 14:84 Who is authorized to change the ESA beneficiary of a model ESA?

The grantor decides at the outset whether to allow any *voluntary* change of the DB during the DB's lifetime. The model agreements contain the following provision, and the grantor must check one of the options:

> The responsible individual ___ may or ___ may not change the beneficiary designated under this agreement to another member of the ESA beneficiary's family described in Section 529(e)(2) in accordance with the trustee's procedures.

Example. Grandfather establishes an ESA on behalf of his grandson, Jimmy. Grandfather names Jimmy's dad as the responsible individual. Jimmy has always been Grandfather's favorite grandson, and Grandfather does not want the ESA assets transferred to one of his other grandchildren. Grandfather could check the box stipulating that the responsible individual may not change the ESA beneficiary.

Q 14:85 How do the model agreements provide for a successor to the responsible individual?

Both model agreements start with the requirement that there must be only one responsible individual (RI) at a time, and the person originally named as the RI must be a parent or legal guardian of the DB. After that:

If the RI dies or becomes incapacitated while the DB is still a minor, the successor RI (who must have been named in a witnessed writing) takes over as RI. If none was named, the DB's other parent or legal guardian takes over.

If the DB dies and another member of his or her family (see Q 14:14) younger than age 30 was properly named as the designated ESA death beneficiary (DDB), the DDB automatically becomes the new DB as of the date of death—and a parent or legal guardian of the DDB takes over as the RI.

A default rule in the model agreements provides that the DB automatically becomes the RI upon reaching the age of majority under state law. There is an exception—if the DB has special needs, none of the age limits apply. (The Code requires this exception, and it is reiterated in the instructions for the model agreements.)

The grantor may change the default "age of majority" rule by checking a box. If the box is checked, the RI continues to serve until there are no more assets and the account is terminated. But if the RI dies or is incapacitated before that endpoint, the default rule comes back—i.e., the DB automatically becomes the RI. (Again, an exception would apply if the DB has special needs, in which case a successor RI would take over.)

Q 14:86 Can provisions be added to the IRS model agreements?

Yes. The language of the model agreement may not be changed, but a blank article is included where provisions may be added. For example, it may be used to add definitions, investment powers, voting rights, exculpatory provisions, amendment and termination procedures, processes for removal of the trustee or custodian, fee clauses, state law requirements, procedures for excess contributions, and cautionary language about prohibited transactions. [Forms 5305-E and 5305-EA, *General Instructions* (Oct. 2016)]

Q 14:87 May the trustee or custodian preselect options in the IRS model agreements?

Yes. An ESA trustee or custodian may preselect the model agreement options instead of leaving the choice to the contributor. For example, a trustee may want to simplify administration by requiring uniform terms for all its ESAs.

Prototype ESAs

Q 14:88 May a financial institution create a prototype ESA agreement?

Presumably. However, the IRS has not yet established an approval process for prototype ESA agreements.

Q 14:89 What must be stated in the ESA agreement?

The ESA agreement must be in writing, and state the following:

- The trust must be created and organized in the United States.
- The trustee must be a bank or an entity approved by the IRS.
- The trustee may accept only a contribution that:
  - Is in cash;
  - Is made before the beneficiary reaches age 18; and
  - Would not result in total contributions for the tax year (not including rollover contributions) of more than the legal maximum (currently $2,000).

- The account funds cannot be invested in life insurance contracts or collectibles.
- Money in the account cannot be combined with other property except in a common trust fund or common investment fund.

[I.R.C. § 530; *see also* IRS Pub. 970, *Tax Benefits for Education* 2019]

Q 14:90 May prototype documents alter the roles of the parties to an ESA?

To a limited extent, drafters of prototype ESA documents may change the terminology and roles for the various parties to the ESA. The roles of the trustee or custodian and of the ESA beneficiary are well established in the law and not subject to much change by a prototype drafter. The provisions designating the responsible individual and the responsible individual's role and responsibilities are more apt to be changed in a prototype document. In all events, the agreements must be consistent with the requirements of the Code.

Q 14:91 Must a prototype ESA follow the model agreement's notion of the responsible individual?

Probably not. Trustees and custodians who draft their own prototype documents should be able to draft their own rules to govern the individual controlling an ESA. It is conceivable that the rules for the responsible individual only apply to users of the model ESA agreements. The IRS has not yet issued a listing of required modifications (LRM) or a process for submitting prototype ESA documents.

Disclosure

Q 14:92 What must be disclosed about the ESA before it is established?

The model agreements require a written disclosure statement that uses plain language to describe the ESA [Forms 5305-E, 5305-EA (Oct. 2016)] There are no regulations concerning disclosure for an ESA, but the IRS model agreements indicate that providing a copy of IRS Notice 97-60 [1997-2 C.B. 310] satisfies the disclosure requirement.

Q 14:93 To whom is the disclosure provided?

The disclosure is provided to the contributor (grantor or depositor) when the ESA is established. The trustee or custodian must also provide it to the responsible individual if that is a different individual. [IRS Forms 5305-E and 5305-EA (Oct. 2016)]

Q 14:94 Is financial disclosure also required?

Not at this time. The rules for financial disclosure when IRAs are established do not apply to ESAs.

Q 14:95 Who receives a copy of the ESA agreement?

The person who establishes the ESA agreement should keep a copy of it. The financial institution also sends a copy to the responsible individual (if that is a different person).

Revocation

Q 14:96 May an ESA be revoked?

Yes. Like any IRA, an ESA may be revoked within seven days after the disclosure information (see Q 14:92) is received from the trustee. The full amount contributed must be returned.

Reporting

Q 14:97 What reports must the trustee or custodian file with the IRS?

For each calendar year, the trustee or custodian is required to report to the IRS concerning distributions from, contributions to, and the earnings of every ESA. The distribution report is made using Form 1099-Q, Payments From Qualified Education Programs (Under Sections 529 and 530), which breaks out the earnings and basis amounts distributed. The report is not required if distributions were not made. Contributions (regular, rollover, and trustee-to-trustee transfers) and earnings in the account are reported using Form 5498-ESA, Coverdell ESA Contribution Information. The IRS has authority to require additional reporting in the future. [I.R.C. § 530(h)] (See Qs 8:72–8:74, 8:159–8:162.)

Q 14:98 Who else must receive information reports?

Each year, the beneficiary and the responsible individual must each receive a statement from the trustee or custodian that includes the information reported to the IRS in Forms 1099-Q and 5498-ESA. The statement for the first year of the ESA must also be provided to the person who established the account. Other contributors are not entitled to receive reports.

Q 14:99 What other tax filings are required?

The ESA *beneficiary* must complete Form 5329, Additional Taxes on Qualified Plans (Including IRAs) and Other Tax-Favored Accounts, to figure any additional tax payable with respect to the ESA. The form is filed as an attachment to the beneficiary's income tax return for the same year.

For excess contributions to the ESA, a 6 percent excise tax is payable (see Q 14:30). For an ESA distribution *not* used for qualified education expenses, an additional tax equal to 10 percent of the taxable portion of the distribution is payable, unless an exception applies. (See Qs 14:45, 14:54.)

Chapter 15

State and Other Jurisdiction Tax Rules Regarding IRAs

Individual taxpayers in 43 states, the District of Columbia, and the five U.S. Possessions (American Samoa, Guam, the Commonwealth of Puerto Rico, the Commonwealth of the Northern Mariana Islands, and the U.S. Virgin Islands) pay some form of income tax to these jurisdictions. The states and other jurisdictions differ in how they tax retirement income—whether before or after retirement; whether from qualified retirement plans, traditional IRAs, Roth IRAs, or nonqualified retirement plans; and whether retirement income is received as a lump sum or as an annuity. The purpose of this chapter, therefore, is to provide insight into the income tax treatment of retirement income by the states, the District of Columbia, and the five U.S. possessions.

At the federal level, a great deal of guidance is provided by the Internal Revenue Code, Treasury Regulations, Revenue Rulings, Revenue Procedures, cases, and plenty of other government and commercial resources to assist in the understanding and implementation of the tax rules on retirement income. At the state level, the District of Columbia, and the U.S. Possessions, there is far less guidance than what the federal government provides, not only on retirement income, but also on most income tax topics, and these jurisdictions may even be silent on many other topics. This is not because these jurisdictions are not concerned to produce better guidance, but the resources available to them to promulgate their rules are limited. Consequently, the best picture of retirement income rules below the federal level must be pieced together by drawing on each jurisdiction's Web site, published tax guides, recent tax booklets, tax laws, tax regulations, and case law. It is very possible that a given jurisdiction may not even offer any guidance on an issue that is not considered significant enough to that jurisdiction's revenue department.

To make matters even more difficult to research is the fact that income tax laws at every level—state and federal—are ever-changing. For a historical perspective at the federal level, the Economic Growth and Tax Relief Reconciliation Act of 2001 (EGTRRA) changed the federal law on contribution limits to, distributions from, and even transfers between qualified retirement plans (including IRAs) beginning in 2002. The Job Creation and Worker Assistance Act of 2002 (JCWAA) made several technical corrections to several tax provisions in EGTRRA. The Katrina Emergency Tax Relief Act of 2005 (KETRA) and Gulf Opportunity Zone Act of 2005 (GOZA) provided special relief for those affected by hurricanes. In addition, the Tax Increase Protection and Reconciliation Act of 2005 (TIPRA) repealed the adjusted gross income (AGI) limit for Roth conversions after 2009 and provided an optional two-year recognition rule for the converted interest. The Tax Relief, Unemployment Insurance Reauthorization, and Job Creation Act of 2010 (Tax Relief Act of 2010) extended the exclusion from gross income for qualified charitable distributions of up to $100,000 received from traditional and Roth IRAs in 2010 and 2011. Then in January 2013, the American Taxpayer Relief Act of 2012 (ATRA) extended the qualified charitable distribution (QCD) provisions for 2012 and 2013. In December 2014, the Tax Increase Prevention Act of 2014 (TIPA) extended many of the tax benefits that would have expired in 2013, and the Achieving a Better Life Experience (ABLE) Act of 2014 created a new savings account for persons with disabilities that is generally exempt from income tax. Significant in 2015, the Surface Transportation and Veterans Health Care Choice Improvement Act of 2015 modified the due date of business returns, and the Protecting Americans from Tax Hikes Act (PATH Act) of 2015 again extended most of the tax benefits of individuals and made many of them permanent. In 2016, the Trade Facilitation and Trade Enforcement Act of 2015 increased the penalty for failure to timely file a return, effective for returns required to be filed in calendar years after 2015. The Setting Every Community up for Retirement Enhancement Act (SECURE Act) extended the required commencement date until age 72, allowed contributions to a traditional IRA after a participant attained age 72, and eliminated the "stretch IRA" for most beneficiaries.

The IRS issued Revenue Procedure 2016-47, which revised guidance for requesting waiver of the 60-day rollover rule by issuing a self-certification to the IRA trustee.

These federal changes are not only significant at the national level, they affect individual taxpayers at other governmental levels. Some states and jurisdictions adopt federal income tax provisions in the year of enactment; others adopt them in later years; and still others allow early adoption pending their legislative sessions.

Traditional IRA Contributions

Q 15:1 Do all states permit a deduction for traditional IRA contributions?

No. Three states do not permit a deduction for traditional IRA contributions: Massachusetts, New Jersey, and Pennsylvania. Seven states (Alaska, Florida, Nevada, South Dakota, Texas, Washington, and Wyoming) do not have a state personal income tax, and two states (New Hampshire and Tennessee) impose a personal income tax on interest and dividends only. The remaining 38 states and the District of Columbia permit a deduction for contributions made to a traditional IRA on a taxpayer's state income tax form.

Q 15:2 Do states that permit a deduction for traditional IRA contributions follow the federal tax law?

In general, yes. The majority of those states use the federal income tax return information as a starting point, then apply their own rates and some state adjustments. When changes in federal tax law occur, however, the states do not always respond immediately or in the same manner. For example, although contributions to a traditional IRA have been deductible on the federal tax return since 1975, they have been deductible in Alabama and the District of Columbia only since 1982, and in Minnesota only since 1985 (see Qs 15:9, 15:10).

EGTRRA increased the contribution limit for traditional IRAs and Roth IRAs to $3,000 beginning in 2002, $4,000 in 2005, $5,000 in 2008, $5,500 in 2013, and $6,000 in 2019, where it remains as of May 1, 2021, as a result of the cost of living adjustment (see Q 3:4). EGTRRA allowed an even higher contribution limit (additional $1,000) for taxpayers who are age 50 or over by December 31 of the current year (see Qs 3:4, 3:5).

Q 15:3 Do states that permit a deduction for traditional IRA contributions generally follow the federal tax law on nondeductible contributions?

Yes. States that permit a deduction for contributions to traditional IRAs generally follow the federal tax law on nondeductible contributions.

Q 15:4 Do states that permit a deduction for traditional IRA contributions generally follow the federal tax law on catch-up contributions?

Yes. States that permit an income tax deduction for traditional IRA contributions generally follow the federal tax law on catch-up contributions that apply to individuals who are age 50 or older by December 31 of the current year.

Q 15:5 Do states tax earnings on traditional IRA contributions in the year of accrual?

No. States follow the federal rules; that is, earnings on traditional IRA contributions are taxed only in the year of distribution.

Traditional IRA Distributions

Q 15:6 How are traditional IRA distributions taxed by states?

In most states, distributions from a traditional IRA that are included on the recipient's federal income tax return are also included on his or her state income tax return. The exceptions include states that do not permit a deduction for a contribution to a traditional IRA (e.g., Massachusetts and New Jersey) or permit, in some years, a lesser or greater deduction for a traditional IRA contribution (e.g., Arkansas, California, District of Columbia, Georgia, and Minnesota). Although Pennsylvania does not permit a deduction for contributions to a traditional IRA, that state also does not tax any form of retirement income received by a retiree who is age 59½ or older (see Q 15:9).

Illinois (as of 1989), and Mississippi (as of 1994) exclude retirement benefits from gross income, including traditional IRA distributions received by a retiree, spouse, or other beneficiary at the death of the primary retiree. [35 Ill. Comp. Stat. Ann. 5/203(a)(2)(F); Miss. Code Ann. § 27-7-15(4)(*l*)] Other states provide an exclusion amount for retirement income, including IRA distributions (see Q 15:8).

Q 15:7 Does state taxation of distributions apply to traditional IRAs in the same way that it does to other types of retirement benefits?

Most states tax distributions from a traditional IRA and a qualified plan in the same manner. Of course, there are some exceptions whereby qualified retirement benefits receive preferential treatment.

Three states (Louisiana, Michigan, and Ohio) do not tax lump-sum distributions from qualified plans if the taxpayer elects 10-year forward averaging for federal income tax calculations.

Note. Only taxpayers born before 1936 are eligible for 10-year averaging.

States that have their own version of the federal 10-year averaging rules are Arkansas (Form AR1000TD), California (Form 540 Schedule G-1), Delaware (Form 329), Kentucky (Form 4972-K), Minnesota (Schedule M1LS), New York (Form IT-230), and South Carolina (Form SC4972). North Dakota was included in this group of states in prior years.

Lump-sum distributions from traditional IRAs have never been eligible for forward averaging for federal income tax calculations.

Q 15:8 Do states tax a lump-sum distribution from a traditional IRA differently than they tax an annuity distribution from a traditional IRA?

Generally, no. New York, however, allows taxpayers who are age 59½ or older a $20,000 annual exclusion for annuity distributions, including annuity distributions from traditional IRAs. Lump-sum distributions from IRAs qualify for the annual exclusion, but payments derived from contributions made after retirement do not. [*See* NY State Dep't of Taxation and Finance Publication 36, *General Information for Senior Citizens and Retired Persons* (Mar. 2015); some of the information therein is out of date, but not the rule applicable to lump-sum distributions from IRAs, pp. 13–16.] If the taxpayer attains age 59½ during the tax year, the exclusion is allowed only for the amount of pension or annuity income received on or after the taxpayer attains age 59½. Note that lump-sum payments from an HR 10 (Keogh) plan qualify for the exclusion, but only if the taxpayer does not use federal Form 4972, Tax on Lump-Sum Distributions (from qualified plans of participants born before January 2, 1936).

Q 15:9 What is the state income tax effect on a distribution from a traditional IRA if a state does not permit a deduction for a traditional IRA contribution?

Currently, there are only three states with a personal income tax that do not permit a deduction for a traditional IRA contribution (Massachusetts, New Jersey, and Pennsylvania).

For a Pennsylvania resident, a retirement distribution is not taxable if it is made on or after the person's retirement and the attainment of age 59½. Otherwise, the distribution, less previously taxed contributions, is totally taxable.

A Massachusetts or New Jersey resident must maintain records of all contributions to his or her traditional IRA. Because a traditional IRA owned by a resident of those states may have two bases, separate records are needed to determine which portion of the traditional IRA distribution is subject to federal tax and which portion is subject to state tax. In the case of a New Jersey resident, New Jersey Income Tax Publication Bulletin GIT-2, *IRA Withdrawals* (rev. Dec. 2018), provides that the taxpayer must calculate the New Jersey taxable portion of a periodic distribution annually. The calculation specifics, however, are given in New Jersey Income Tax Publication Bulletin GIT-1, *Pension and Annuity* (rev. Dec. 2018), and provide that a taxpayer must use the Three-Year Rule Method, if qualified, or the General Rule Method. The Three-Year Method allows a person to recover previously taxed contributions before including any distribution amount in New Jersey gross income if it can be totally recovered within three years. Otherwise, the General Rule applies, which prorates the previously taxed contribution over the taxpayer's expected return on the contract. These methods are discussed in detail in Publication Bulletin GIT-1 available at *www.state.nj.us/treasury/taxation/pdf/pubs/tgi-ee/git1.pdf*. A Massachusetts resident, on the other hand, may recover previously taxed contributions before including any distribution amounts in Massachusetts gross income. [Instructions for Form 1, Schedule X, p. 18]

Q 15:10 What is the state income tax effect on a distribution from a traditional IRA if a state permitted a greater or lesser deduction than the federal deduction for a traditional IRA contribution?

A few states have permitted a deduction that, in some years, was different from the federal deduction. As a result, an IRA owned by a taxpayer in those states has two bases: one for federal purposes and one for state purposes. Therefore, taxpayers in those states need to keep separate records to determine which portion of the distribution is subject to federal tax and which portion is subject to state tax (see Qs 15:6, 15:9).

Q 15:11 Does a taxpayer's state basis in a traditional IRA transfer to another state when the taxpayer takes a distribution from the traditional IRA as a resident of that other state?

Generally, no. South Carolina, for example, issued Private Letter Ruling 89-4 (Apr. 7, 1989) holding that a "taxpayer's withdrawals from an IRA are fully taxable even though amounts contributed while a nonresident were not deductible due to another State's laws." The taxpayer had made the contributions while residing in Pennsylvania.

However, Oregon and Virginia permit a resident taxpayer a subtraction for distributions from a traditional IRA, Keogh, or simplified employee pension (SEP) plan for the contributions to the plan that have already been taxed by another state. Oregon allows the subtraction only if several conditions are satisfied. [Or. Rev. Stat. § 316.159(1); Or. Admin. R. 150-316-0230] The conditions are:

- The distributions consist of contributions made during a period in which the taxpayer was a nonresident of Oregon;

- The distributions consist of contributions made during a period in which the taxpayer was a resident of a state that imposes an income tax;
- The distributions consist of contributions for which no deduction, exclusion, or exemption for the contributions was allowed or allowable in the state in which the taxpayer was a resident prior to becoming an Oregon resident; and
- No deduction, exclusion, subtraction, or other tax benefit has been allowed for the distributions by another state before the taxpayer becomes a resident of Oregon.

Example 1. In 1997, Sam was a resident of a state that imposes no income tax. He made a deductible IRA contribution in 1997. In 1998, Sam converted his regular IRA of $2,000 to a Roth IRA. The distribution will be reported over a four-year period. Sam became a permanent Oregon resident on April 1, 1998. Sam is not entitled to a subtraction, because the contributions were not previously taxed. Sam will be taxed on $375 (¾ of $500 for the period April through December 1998) on his 1998-part year Oregon return. If Sam remains an Oregon resident, he will be taxed on $500 in 1999, 2000, and 2001.

California provides a partial step-up in basis to a taxpayer's IRA assets upon establishing residency in the state. Beginning in 2002, the IRA basis for California purposes is the taxpayer's IRA contributions in excess of $1,500 that were made in years 1982 through 1986. This rule applies to taxpayers regardless of when they established residency in the state. [*See* State of California Franchise Tax Board Publication 1100 (Rev. 05-2020).]

Example 2. An individual became a California resident on January 1, 2001. The fair market value of the individual's IRA on January 1, 2001 was $9,000. The individual's contributions in excess of California deduction limits during 1982–1986 were $2,500. If the individual received IRA distributions of $1,500 in 2001 and $3,000 in 2002, then the individual's taxation is determined as follow:

Taxable year 2001 (prior law):			
CA IRA basis, January 1, 2001	$9,000 (FMV on 1/1/01)		
Less: IRA distribution	1,500		
CA IRA basis, December 31, 2001	$7,500		
Taxable year 2002 (new law):			
IRA distribution, 2002			$3,000
Less: CA IRA basis			
Contributions more than CA deduction limits		$2,500	
Less: CA IRA basis recovered in 2001		1,500	
CA IRA basis available in 2002			1,000
Taxable year 2002 (new law):			$2,000

Note. More information regarding IRAs can be found in FTB Publication 1005.

Q 15:12 If a state denies a deduction for a traditional IRA contribution, will the IRA owner (when retired) be able to claim that state's state tax basis after he or she has moved to a state that allows a deduction for a traditional IRA contribution?

The answer varies from state to state. Three states (Massachusetts, New Jersey, and Pennsylvania) do not permit a deduction for a contribution to an IRA. Depending on the state of relocation, the retired IRA owner may or may not be permitted an adjustment for the state tax basis in the IRA that he or she would have had if he or she had not moved (see Q 15:11). If such an adjustment is granted, only the accumulated earnings on the IRA will be taxed by the state to which the IRA owner has moved.

Q 15:13 Is double taxation of a traditional IRA distribution possible at the state level?

Yes. Double taxation is possible on part but not all of a distribution from a traditional IRA. This is true even after the enactment of the ban on source taxes (see Q 15:25). In certain situations, the amount of a traditional IRA contribution can be taxed twice. For example, if the owner of a traditional IRA residing in a state that does not permit a deduction for a traditional IRA contribution moves to another state upon retirement, and the new state of residence does not recognize the prior state's state basis in the IRA, the contribution portion of any distribution from the IRA will be taxed by the new state of residence. Since the contribution has already been taxed by the former state of residence, it will have been taxed twice. [*See, e.g.*, South Carolina Priv. Ltr. Rul. 89-4 (Apr. 7, 1989).]

Q 15:14 Is negative taxation of a traditional IRA distribution possible at the state level?

Yes. Negative taxation is possible on part but not all of a distribution from a traditional IRA. Negative taxation can occur with respect to the IRA contribution amount. For example, if the owner of a traditional IRA residing in a state that permits a deduction for a traditional IRA contribution moves at retirement to a state that does not have a state income tax, the contribution portion of any distribution from the owner's traditional IRA will not be taxed by the new state of residence. The contribution will have been awarded a tax subsidy in the former state of residence and no tax cost in the current state of residence.

Similarly, if the owner moves to a state with a lower state income tax rate, the owner pays less in state taxes on the distribution of the contribution amount than the tax benefits received on the contribution amount from the higher tax rate state. For example, if a taxpayer contributed $5,000 to his or her IRA in a state with a 6 percent tax rate and moved to a state with a 4 percent tax rate, the taxpayer would enjoy a tax benefit of $100 (($5,000 × 6%) – ($5,000 × 4%)).

Q 15:15 Do traditional IRA distributions qualify for a state's pension exclusion?

It depends. The taxable portion of a traditional IRA distribution is generally eligible for the pension exclusion in states that have a pension exclusion provision; however, not all states have a pension exclusion provision, and the amount and eligibility requirements in the states that have one generally vary. For example, South Carolina provides a $3,000 annual deduction per spouse for retirement income received before age 65 and a $10,000 annual deduction per spouse at age 65 or over. [S.C. Code Ann. § 12-6-1170] Wisconsin provides an exemption for up to $5,000 of certain retirement income if the taxpayer is age 65 or older on December 31st and the taxpayer's federal AGI is less than $15,000 (or $30,000, if married filing jointly). The Wisconsin exemption applies to each spouse; thus, if both spouses qualify and have taxable income from a qualified retirement plan or an IRA, then up to $10,000 may be excluded on a joint return. [Wis. Stat. § 71.05(1)(ae)] Delaware provides a pension exclusion of up to $12,500 per person for taxpayers who are age 60 or older and up to $2,000 per person for taxpayers who are under age 60. [Del. Code Ann. tit. 30, § 1106(b)(3)] (See Q 15:43.) Maryland provides a pension exclusion for taxpayers who are 65 or over or totally disabled, or in instances where the taxpayer's spouse is totally disabled on the last day of the tax year and the taxable income from the retirement plan is included on the taxpayer's federal income tax return. The pension exclusion, however, does not apply to a traditional IRA, a Roth IRA, a SEP, or a Keogh plan. [Md. Code Ann. § 10-209]

Q 15:16 Where can a state's retirement exclusion amount be found?

A state's retirement exclusion amount and the criteria for exclusion are posted on the state's Web site. See a list of state Web sites in Q 15:87.

For a broad-based appreciation of the treatment of IRA distributions by state, readers should consult Appendix C, State by State Comparison of IRA Tax Rules 2020. Because state tax laws change frequently, state Web sites should be consulted for the most up-to-date provisions.

Q 15:17 Is an individual's age for qualifying under a state's pension exclusion provision determined on December 31 of the taxable year or January 1 of the following year?

It depends on the state. Colorado residents qualify if they are over age 55 as of December 31 of the taxable year. Delaware residents qualify for an exclusion of $2,000 on pension income if they were under 60 on December 31, and up to $12,500 if they were 60 or over on December 31 of the taxable year. South Carolina, on the other hand, does not stipulate the date but it states that beginning in the year in which the taxpayer reaches age 65, the taxpayer may make a deduction. (see Q 15:43).

Q 15:18 Do states treat traditional IRA rollovers or direct transfers to another IRA as taxable distributions?

No. All states treat rollovers, direct transfers, and trustee-to-trustee transfers as nontaxable transactions. It should be noted, however, that some states give favorable tax treatment to distributions from qualified retirement plans. Thus, a rollover to a traditional IRA from a qualified retirement plan may defer taxation but result in taxation at a less favorable state income tax rate when distributions are taken from the IRA.

For example, a taxpayer in Louisiana (or Michigan or Ohio) who takes a lump-sum distribution from a qualified plan and elects 10-year forward averaging for federal income tax calculations would pay no state income tax on the distribution. If the same taxpayer rolls over the distribution from the qualified plan to a traditional IRA, the withdrawal from the traditional IRA in a later year will be treated as ordinary income on both the federal and state tax returns. (For other situations with similar state laws, see Q 15:7.)

In *Bobrow v. Commissioner* [No. 7022-11, T.C. Memo. 2014-21 (Jan. 28, 2014)], the Tax Court held that a successful 60-day rollover means one rollover per year per person from the date the rollover is completed, not one rollover per IRA. Many tax advisors and even the IRS as initially seen in former IRS Publication 590 assumed that the "once per year" rule applied to each IRA independently. As a result of the decision, failing to complete a rollover in a timely manner carries income tax consequences at both the federal and state income tax levels. (IRS Publication 590, which is now published in two volumes, Publication 590-A, *Contributions to Individual Retirement Arrangements (IRAs)* 2020 and Publication 590-B, *Distributions from Individual Retirement Arrangements (IRAs)* 2020, are reproduced in this edition as Appendix A and Appendix B.)

A failed rollover is treated as an IRA distribution, which triggers state income tax in the year of distribution (see Qs 15:7–15:14) with the exception of those taxpayers residing in states without an income tax. In addition, some states assess penalties for an early withdrawal from an IRA (see Qs 15:71–15:75). However, taxpayers might enjoy some relief if their state excludes or provides an exclusion amount for IRA distributions received after a certain age, such as 55, 59½, or 65 depending on the state (see Qs 15:15–15:17).

Q 15:19 Do states conform to the federal tax laws concerning traditional IRA rollovers or direct transfers to a qualified plan?

For the most part state laws conform to the federal law. Massachusetts, for example, follows federal law for workplace retirement plans, effective January 1, 2002, including the provisions of Internal Revenue Code (Code; I.R.C.) Sections 72 and 401 through 420 (but excluding Code Sections 402A (elective deferral of Roth IRA contributions) and 408(q) (deemed IRAs)) and Sections 457, 3401, and 3405. [Mass. Dep't of Rev., Technical Information Release (TIR)

02-18, I.D. (Nov. 6, 2002)] Some states are unable to conform to federal tax law until their next legislative session. In these situations, the state legislature must decide to conform to the tax law either prospectively or retroactively. Moreover, the state's department of revenue must decide whether or not to issue a position statement on how taxpayers should handle such a situation on the current-year tax return (see Q 15:51).

Q 15:20 Is a distribution from a traditional IRA taxable by the IRA owner's former state of residence when the individual moves out of the state and claims residency in another state?

The answer depends on the former state of residence and on the year in which the distribution was made (i.e., after 1995 or before 1996). Another important factor is the relationship that the taxpayer has or has not maintained with the former state of residency. These issues are discussed in the following sections.

Q 15:21 Is there a waiver available of the 60-day rollover requirement for transferring amounts from one retirement plan to another in order to avoid inclusion in gross income?

Yes, EGTRRA authorized the IRS to waive the 60-day rollover requirement where the failure to waive would be against equity or good conscience (e.g., a casualty, disaster, or other event beyond the reasonable control of the individual subject to the rollover requirement). This is important at the federal level and below it, since many states and other jurisdictions have adopted the federal rules. If a taxpayer does not comply with the 60-day rollover requirement, he or she may incur not only a large federal tax liability, but also a large tax liability at the state or other jurisdiction level.

The IRS issued Revenue Procedure 2020-46 in October 2020, which revised guidance for requesting waiver of the 60-day rollover rule. If the taxpayer satisfies the conditions set forth in the procedure, the taxpayer can issue a self-certification to the IRA trustee instead of needing to request a private letter ruling (see Qs 6:30 and 6:31). The IRS expanded the self-certification relief in 2020 to address the situation in which IRA assets were transferred to a state's unclaimed property fund.

Under the federal rules, a person can make a late rollover contribution if the person is entitled to an automatic waiver of the 60-day rollover requirement, request and receive a private letter ruling waiver of the 60-day requirement, or qualify for and use a self-certification procedure for a waiver of the 60-day requirement. As previously noted, Revenue Procedure 2016-47 provides for a self-certification procedure (subject to verification upon audit) that may be used by a taxpayer claiming eligibility for a waiver under Code Section 402(c)(3)(B) or 408(d)(3)(1) with respect to a rollover into a plan or IRA.

Q 15:22 Do state revenue departments waive the 60-day rollover requirement for transferring amounts from one retirement plan to another in order to avoid inclusion in gross income?

Indirectly yes. Although no state has issued a ruling concerning a waiver of the 60-day rollover requirement, states have adopted the federal rules. Thus, one would assume that if the rollover is a qualified rollover at the federal level, it is likewise a qualified rollover at the state level. Conversely, if the rollover is not a qualified rollover at the federal income tax level, it similarly is not a qualified rollover at the state income tax level.

Q 15:23 How does an individual apply for the waiver of the 60-day rollover requirement?

If an individual does not qualify for an automatic waiver (see Q 15:24), he or she can apply to the IRS for a waiver of the 60-day rollover requirement. This is done by submitting a request for a private letter ruling under the appropriate IRS revenue procedure outlined in Revenue Procedure 2016-47 and Revenue Procedure 2021-4. This revenue procedure is generally published in the first Internal Revenue Bulletin of the year. A user fee accompanies this application. In determining whether or not to grant a waiver, the IRS will consider all relevant facts and circumstances.

Q 15:24 How is the 60-day rollover requirement waived automatically?

On the IRS Web site "Retirement Plans FAQs relating to Waivers of the 60-Day Rollover Requirement" (*www.irs.gov/Retirement-Plans/Retirement-Plans-FAQs-relating-to-Waivers-of-the-60-Day-Rollover-Requirement*), question #3 lists the criteria that apply to all who receive the automatic waiver. The IRS states that these FAQs provide general information and should not be cited as any type of legal authority. In essence, the list of criteria points to bank error as the reason why a rollover is not completed in the 60-day period and it is not the individual taxpayer's fault. Thus, without further guidance from the IRS, it appears that the bank or financial institution must justify to the taxpayer if the institution is not at fault for the error. If the bank or financial institution is at fault, the taxpayer should document the transaction by asking the bank or financial institution for a letter admitting the error and a detailed record of the entire transaction to be kept in the taxpayer's records (see Qs 6:25, 6:26).

Tax on Post-1995 Distributions Received from Traditional IRAs by Former Residents

Q 15:25 If an individual moves out of a state permanently, does that end the possibility that the former state of residence will tax a traditional IRA distribution made to that individual in the new domicile?

Yes, if the taxpayer has truly left the former state of domicile, then, for traditional IRA distributions, Public Law No. 104-95, which is known as the ban on source taxes, prevents states, the District of Columbia, and U.S. Possessions from taxing former residents on retirement income from qualified retirement plans, traditional IRAs, and, in some cases, nonqualified retirement plans. [*See also* Title 4 U.S.C. § 114.] However, if the distribution from the traditional IRA occurs during the year that the taxpayer moves out of the state, the right to tax may depend on the timing of the distribution and move (see Q 15:29).

Q 15:26 What is a domicile?

A *domicile* is a residence intended as an individual's permanent and primary home. Whether a residence qualifies as a domicile may be verified in a number of ways, including the following:

- The amount of time the individual is physically present in the residence
- The home address listed on the individual's
  - — Car registration,
  - — Driver's license,
  - — Voter registration, and
  - — State and federal tax returns (as well as where the returns are filed)
- The location of the individual's
  - — Real estate holdings,
  - — Club memberships,
  - — Business connections, and
  - — Polling place

All facts and circumstances are considered. Unless care is exercised, a dispute over the location of the domicile may lead to expensive litigation. [*See, e.g.*, Reichstetter, New York Div. of Tax Appeals, DTA No. 818356 (Oct. 31, 2002).]

Other factors that may be relevant in determining an individual's state of domicile are the location of the individual's checking account, savings account, stockbroker, and cemetery plot.

The Idaho State Tax Commission has prepared a nine-page brochure, *Idaho Residency Status* (Apr. 19, 2018), and a second nine-page brochure, *Idaho Source Income* (Jan. 29, 2018), which provide lengthy discussions of these topics, with illustrations. The brochures are available on the Web sites at *https://tax.idaho.gov/i-2015.cfm* and *https://tax.idaho.gov/aguideidsourceincome.pdf*, respectively.

Minnesota has prepared Income Tax Fact Sheet 1, Residency (rev. Jan. 2020). This fact sheet provides the criteria for individuals, military personnel, students, and non-U.S. citizens as well as several examples to illustrate some of the more complex issues. The fact sheet can be found on the state's Web site at *https://www.revenue.state.mn.us/sites/default/files/2020-01/fact_sheets_fs1.pdf*.

Q 15:27 What is a "source state"?

The term *source state* refers to the state in which an individual's traditional IRA was initially established, or in which the individual's pension was earned or funded. A source state seeks to tax the income that was deferred and, in most cases, to tax the tax benefit that was given while the individual was working or living in the source state.

Q 15:28 May an individual continue to have a residence in a state in which he or she formerly had a domicile?

Yes. Maintaining such a residence, however, may demonstrate that the individual continues to be domiciled in that state and, therefore, may still be considered a resident of that state. A possible outcome is that the individual's traditional IRA distributions may be taxable by the former state of domicile (the source state) because the individual is not deemed to be a "former resident," as required for relief under federal law. From a tax standpoint, therefore, it is even more desirable now than it was previously to cleanly sever ties with the source state (to establish "former residency" status) and keep contacts with the source state to a minimum.

A person can have more than one residence but can have only one domicile. The difficulty is that a person must prove that he or she has taken up a new domicile and, in so doing, has abandoned the former domicile.

Minnesota, for example, provides income tax fact sheets explaining residency and non-residency. As defined in fact sheet 1, "domicile" is the place a taxpayer intends to make his or her home permanently or for an indefinite period. Once a person establishes domicile in Minnesota, it continues until the person takes action to change it. If a person moves out of Minnesota, but does not intend to permanently remain in another state or country, the person continues to be a Minnesota resident. Several factors (no single factor determines domicile) used to determine domicile include physical presence, family and community connections, professional and business, housing, statements and declarations of legal residence.

Q 15:29 Does it matter whether a traditional IRA distribution is taken out of the state in the year of the move rather than in subsequent years?

Yes. Most states include a distribution from a traditional IRA in a taxpayer's gross income if the taxpayer takes the distribution while he or she is still a resident of the state. In addition, if a taxpayer maintains residency (e.g., by voting or keeping a residence) in a state, the distribution could be taxed by that state even if the distribution was taken after the taxpayer moved out of the state. For example, New York law leans toward the automatic taxation of distributions that are received before the end of the year of relocation. To ensure that a distribution is not taxable by the former state of residence, a taxpayer would be wise to delay the distribution until the year after the relocation (see Q 15:28).

Q 15:30 Are all forms of nonqualified retirement income protected by the ban on source taxes?

No. The ban on source taxes shelters nonqualified retirement income from any plan, program, or arrangement described in Code Section 3121(v)(2)(C), as noted in Title 4 U.S.C. § 114, only if such income is part of a series of substantially equal periodic payments made not less frequently than annually for:

- The life or life expectancy of the recipient (or joint lives or joint life expectancies of the recipient and his or her designated beneficiary), or
- A period of not less than 10 years.

In addition, income from a nonqualified plan is protected by the ban on source taxes if the plan was established solely to provide benefits in excess of the qualified plan limits and the benefits are paid after the employee terminates.

The effect of a nonqualified plan on the ban on sources taxes raises some questions. For example, does the term *terminate* have the same meaning as *separate from service*, which is found in Code Section 402? Does a nonqualified plan that provides a participant with the option to take a lump-sum payment or an annuity payment satisfy the ban on source taxes if the employer's qualified plan provides only an annuity option? These and other questions are still to be resolved.

Wisconsin highlights this issue in Publication 106, *Wisconsin Tax Information for Retirees* (Jan. 2020):

> If you worked in Wisconsin but are now a resident of another state, payments you received from a *nonqualified* pension or annuity or a *nonqualified* deferred compensation plan are taxable by Wisconsin unless (1) the distribution is paid out in annuity form over your life expectancy or for a period of not less than 10 years or (2) the distribution is paid in either an annuity form or lump-sum from arrangements known commonly as "mirror plans."

[*See https://www.revenue.wi.gov/DOR%20Publications/pb106.pdf.*]

Tax on Pre-1996 Distributions Received from Traditional IRAs by Former Residents

Q 15:31 If an individual leaves a state entirely, does that end the possibility that the individual will be taxed by the former state of residence on a distribution made to that individual in the new state of residence?

Not necessarily. Public Law No. 104-95 (Jan. 10, 1996), the ban on source taxes (see Q 15:25), is effective for IRA distributions taken *after* 1995. Thus, complete relocation does not necessarily end the possibility that an individual will be taxed by his or her former state of residence on IRA distributions taken before January 1, 1996.

It is true that the state from which the individual departed may no longer be able to claim him or her as a resident, and, as a nonresident, the individual may leave behind no assets on which taxes can be levied. The former resident may not even be physically present to be served with process. Nevertheless, there have been cases where state tax authorities successfully moved against former residents in their new domiciles.

Q 15:32 If an individual maintains a residence in his or her former state of residence, will that individual cease to be taxed by the former state on IRA distributions made in the new state of residence?

It depends. Maintaining a residence may demonstrate that the individual continues to be domiciled in the former state. As such, the individual may be deemed to be a current resident, not a former resident (see Q 15:28). For example, New York State Tax Bulletin, Personal Income Tax, TB-IT-690 (Dec. 15, 2011), discusses this issue in depth and states that:

> Whether you are considered a New York State resident or nonresident for personal income tax purposes depends, in some instances, on whether you maintain a permanent place of abode inside or outside the state. For example, if you are domiciled outside New York State, but you maintain a permanent place of abode in New York State, you are a resident for income tax purposes if you spend 184 or more days in New York State.

Q 15:33 May a taxpayer's former state of residence attach assets in the taxpayer's new state of residence?

Yes. Nevertheless, a number of states—including Arizona, Colorado, Illinois, Louisiana, New Mexico, New York, Oregon (to a limited extent), and Virginia—have adopted legislation or regulations that specifically preclude judgments against retirement income and bar the state from such action against former residents, particularly involving retirement income.

Q 15:34 On what theory may a state tax an individual after his or her change of domicile from that state to another state?

The theory is quite clear. The individual, having been allowed by the state in which he or she was domiciled to deduct contributions and to defer tax on earnings accruing on the contributions (which are otherwise taxable income), should not be allowed to avoid that state's tax permanently by moving to another state.

Q 15:35 What is the claim of the state to which the taxpayer moves?

Domicile or residency in a state is a valid basis for a state to impose an income tax. By claiming domicile or residency, a taxpayer enjoys various services and privileges provided by the new state—roads, police, firefighting, social services, welfare, and the protection of its laws. Because most of a retiree's income may come from Social Security benefits, IRA distributions, or pension payments, there might be little other income for the new state of domicile to tax to support its efforts on behalf of the new resident.

Q 15:36 Which states have sought to tax former residents and in what ways?

Various states have sought to tax different types of retirement income of former residents. California and Oregon have attempted to tax traditional IRA and pension distributions. New York has attempted to tax distributions from non-annuity IRAs. [*See, e.g.*, Wolf, New York Div. of Tax Appeals, Tax Appeals Tribunal, DTA No. 812738 (Mar. 7, 1996).] Minnesota, New York, and Vermont have claimed authority to tax non-IRA distributions.

Q 15:37 How long is the statute of limitations for seeking tax on a traditional IRA distribution received by a former state resident?

The answer is unclear. The general rule is three years; however, the three-year statute of limitations applies only to timely filed tax returns. An individual who has not filed a state tax return for pre-1996 retirement income should not rely on the three-year statute of limitations. The reason is that if a state tax return has not been filed for a prior year, the clock has not begun to run. Thus, a state may be within its rights to seek tax on those prior distributions.

Q 15:38 How is tax apportioned when more than one state makes a claim on an individual's distributions based on being the source state?

In Iowa, it had been proposed that the allocation for a state be based on the number of years the taxpayer worked in that state. This would have been calculated using a fraction whose denominator was the number of years lived in all states. Iowa rescinded those proposed rules, which would have become effective in 1993. Furthermore, in 1994 Iowa acted to end its taxation of pensions received by former residents.

Q 15:39 Must states follow the federal law requiring nonresident aliens to report only U.S. source income?

No. States are not required to follow the same rules as the federal government for nonresident aliens. California law, for example, requires nonresident aliens to report their adjusted income from all sources even though the federal law requires nonresident aliens to report only their U.S. source income. Therefore, it is important to understand the state rules for domicile and residency (see Qs 15:25–15:38).

Roth IRA Distributions

Q 15:40 How are Roth IRA distributions taxed by states?

In most states, Roth IRA distribution amounts that are included on, or excluded from, the federal income tax return are likewise included on, or excluded from, the state income tax return. Pennsylvania holds that "distributions are includable in income to the extent that contributions were not previously included if made before the individual for whom the account is maintained obtains age 59½ and retires from service or if the plan makes no provision for payments at regularly recurring intervals continuing at least until the participant's death." [Pa. Ltr. Rul. PIT-98-048, Pennsylvania Department of Revenue (Aug. 27, 1999)] Similarly, Massachusetts excludes from gross income distributions from a Roth IRA so long as the taxpayer is at least age 59½ but adds the provisions "(or disabled or a 'first-time homebuyer') and the account [must be] at least 5 years old." [TIR 98-8, Massachusetts 1998 Reducing Income Taxes Act, Dep't of Revenue (Oct. 6, 1998)]

Q 15:41 Do states treat Roth IRA rollovers or direct transfers to another Roth IRA as taxable distributions?

No. All states treat rollovers, direct transfers, and trustee-to-trustee transfers as nontaxable transfers. Rollovers between Roth IRAs may be made only once every 365 days, whereas direct rollovers (i.e., trustee-to-trustee transfers) may be made as often as trustees will permit. (See Q 15:18.)

Q 15:42 Is a taxable Roth IRA distribution taxable by a former state of residence if an individual moves out of the state and claims residency in another state?

The answer is no if the taxable distribution occurs in a year other than the year in which the taxpayer relocates. The answer also depends on the state and the timing of the distribution if the distribution occurs in the year in which the taxpayer is a part-year resident of the source state. In New York, for example, if a taxable distribution from a Roth IRA is received during the change-of-residence year, the income portion of the distribution is included in the recipient's New York AGI for the change-of-residence year. If the individual receives the taxable distribution when he or she is a resident of New York, the income portion of the distribution is included in New York source income. If the taxable distribution is received when the individual is not a resident of New York, the income portion of the distribution is not included in New York source income. [N.Y. TSB-M-98(7)I (Dec. 24, 1998)]

Q 15:43 Do Roth IRA distributions qualify for a state's pension exclusion?

The portion of a Roth IRA distribution that is taxable is generally eligible for a state's pension exclusion; the portion of a Roth IRA distribution that is not taxable is generally not eligible for a state's pension exclusion (see Qs 15:15–15:17). Not all states have a pension exclusion provision.

Inherited IRA Distributions

Q 15:44 Is a distribution from an inherited traditional IRA excludable from state income taxes?

In general, no. Distributions from a traditional IRA that are included on the recipient's federal income tax return are also included on his or her state income tax return. This would be equally true for distributions made from an inherited IRA whereby the distribution amount is included in the beneficiary's federal gross income.

Maryland, for example, includes in income the total amounts received from pensions, IRAs, and annuities that are reported on lines 15b and 16b of the taxpayer's federal income tax return. Moreover, Maryland provides a pension exclusion amount for those taxpayers who are 65 or older or totally disabled, or whose spouse was totally disabled, on the last day of the tax year *and* the taxpayer included on his or her federal return taxable income received as a pension, annuity, or endowment from an "employee retirement system" qualified under Section 401(a), 403, or 457(b) of the Internal Revenue Code. However, a traditional IRA, a Roth IRA, a simplified employee plan (SEP), a Keogh plan, an ineligible deferred compensation plan, or foreign retirement income does not qualify for the pension exclusion. Hence, distributions from an IRA or inherited IRA are totally includable in Maryland's gross income.

Pennsylvania, on the other hand, provides an exception to the general rule. Specifically, a retirement distribution received by a Pennsylvania resident is not taxable if it is made on or after the person's retirement and the attainment of age 59½ (see Q 15:9). However, Section 10 of the Pennsylvania Department of Revenue Personal Income Tax Bulletin 2008-1 (Jan. 16, 2008) states that distributions from an IRA are not taxable if the payments are paid to the estate, or designated beneficiary, of the participant by reason of the participant's death. Thus, the age of the beneficiary, unlike that of the owner, is not a relevant factor. This includes amounts attributable to income on plan assets that accrues after the death of the plan participant. But this exclusion is not available for a surviving spouse who elects to apply his or her distributions from an inherited IRA to his or her own individual retirement plan or for any amount rolled over into the surviving spouse's own individual retirement plan on a tax-free basis. As noted in Section 2 of this bulletin, the current regulations [61 Pa. Code § 101.6(c)(8)] do not address all of the issues that are unique to these accounts or annuities. The Department proposes to address them by regulation. This bulletin is being published to provide guidance pending the adoption of the regulations. Because those regulations have not been adopted yet, the tax bulletin is the current authority.

In the case of a New York resident, taxpayers who are age 59½ or older are allowed a $20,000 annual exclusion for annuity distributions, including annuity distributions from traditional IRAs (see Q 15:8). New York allows this subtraction for a taxpayer who receives the pension or annuity income of a deceased individual regardless of the taxpayer's age, if the deceased would have been entitled to it had the deceased individual continued to live. Thus, the deceased owner's age is relevant in the case of distributions to the beneficiary. If the deceased individual has more than one beneficiary, the $20,000 maximum amount of the pension and annuity exclusion must be allocated among the beneficiaries. Each beneficiary's share of the $20,000 exclusion is determined by multiplying the $20,000 by a fraction whose numerator is the value of the pensions and annuities inherited by the beneficiary, and whose denominator is the total value inherited by all beneficiaries of the deceased individual's pensions and annuities. More details and examples are provided in the NY State Dep't of Taxation and Finance Publication 36, *General Information for Senior Citizens and Retired Persons* (Mar. 2015), pp. 14–16.

As already noted for Illinois, retirement benefits are excluded from gross income, including traditional IRA distributions received by a retiree, spouse, or other beneficiary at the death of the primary retiree (see Q 15:6). The Illinois Department of Revenue has reinforced that this exclusion is available for a dependent taxpayer who inherits an IRA where income tax is paid at the federal level by the dependent taxpayer in the Department's General Information Letter IT 00-0052-GIL. This letter held that, to the extent that payments from an IRA to a dependent beneficiary are included in the beneficiary's federal AGI, the same amount may be subtracted in the computation of the Illinois base income as provided in 35 Ill. Comp. Stat. Ann. 5/203(a)(2)(F).

Colorado allows a pension subtraction for IRA income that is included in federal taxable income if the taxpayer is age 55 or older as of December 31 of that year per "FYI—Income 25: Pension/Annuity Subtraction (updated Feb. 2020)" (see Qs 15:60 and 15:64 for Colorado rollover discussion). That pension subtraction includes taxpayers who are under 55 years old if the IRA income was received as a beneficiary because of the death of the person who earned the IRA and those distributions were not subject to the IRS premature distribution penalty.

In December 2019, Congress enacted the SECURE Act, which affects inherited IRAs. Under the SECURE Act, a nonspouse beneficiary of an IRA, with some exceptions, is required to directly roll over the assets of an inherited IRA and will be required to withdraw all of the assets from the IRA by the end of the 10th year after the date of death. An individual who inherits an IRA may still stretch out the required distribution over the individual's lifetime if the individual is the participant's spouse or is less than 10 years younger than the participant. If the nonspouse beneficiary is a minor child, distributions can continue until the individual reaches the age of majority (to be determined by the IRS). If the beneficiary is disabled or chronically ill, the distribution can continue for so long as those conditions remain in effect.

Q 15:45 Is a distribution from an inherited Roth IRA excludable from state income taxes?

In general, yes. Qualified distributions from a Roth IRA are not included on the owner's federal income tax return and likewise are not included on the owner's state income tax return. This also would be true for qualified distributions made from an inherited Roth IRA.

In the rare situation whereby the distribution to the owner is not a qualified distribution (see Q 5:51) at the time of death (i.e., fails to satisfy the five-year holding period requirement), the beneficiary owner may need to include some of the distribution amount into both the federal and state gross incomes. Of course, the ordering rules for Roth IRAs (see Q 5:88) apply. Although a beneficiary may need to include the unqualified portion of a Roth distribution, not all states will require this amount to be added into the state's gross income of the beneficiary. Section 10 of the Pennsylvania Department of Revenue Personal Income Tax Bulletin 2008-1 (Jan. 16, 2008) states that distributions from an IRA are not taxable if the payments are paid to the estate, or designated beneficiary, of the participant by reason of the participant's death.

Q 15:46 Does a taxpayer's state basis in a traditional IRA transfer to a beneficiary residing in another state?

Generally, no. The California Board of Equalization noted in an appeal case that a beneficiary will inherit any California basis associated with an inherited IRA but will not inherit any non-California basis associated with an inherited IRA. In the appeal case of Dennis and Martha Maddix [Case No. 552996 (May 25, 2011)], the Board held that the beneficiary, a California resident, does not inherit any California basis from her uncle's IRA, a resident of Texas, since it is doubtful the uncle had any California basis in his IRA.

As noted in Q 15:11, South Carolina issued Private Letter Ruling 89-4 (Apr. 7, 1989), holding that a "taxpayer's withdrawals from an IRA are fully taxable even though amounts contributed while a nonresident were not deductible due to another State's laws." The taxpayer had made the contributions while residing in Pennsylvania. Presumably, South Carolina would hold the same position if the beneficiary is a South Carolina resident and the deceased owner was a resident of Pennsylvania or any other state.

Oregon and Virginia, on the other hand, permit a resident taxpayer a subtraction for distributions from a traditional IRA, Keogh, or simplified employee pension (SEP) plan for the contributions to the plan that have already been taxed by another state. Oregon allows the subtraction only if several conditions are satisfied. [Or. Rev. Stat. § 316.159(1); Or. Admin. R. 150-316.159]

Special Purpose Distributions

Q 15:47 Are distributions from a traditional IRA for a first-time home purchase taxable at the state level?

Generally, yes. In most states, traditional IRA distribution amounts that are included in the gross income of an individual's federal income tax return are likewise included in the gross income reported on the individual's state income tax return (see Q 15:6). Many states have specifically adopted the provisions of the IRA regulations of 1997 and 1998. Although other states have not specifically adopted those regulations, they base their state taxable income on the taxpayer's federal return, giving the taxpayer the same result.

Federal law includes in gross income any taxable distribution amounts from traditional IRAs used for first-time home purchases but, under Code Section 72(t)(2)(F), exempts up to $10,000 of that taxable amount from the 10 percent premature distribution penalty. [*See* Exceptions for First Home in IRS Publication 590-B, *Distributions from Individual Retirement Arrangements (IRAs)* 2020 (reproduced as Appendix A of this volume).]

Q 15:48 Are distributions from a Roth IRA for a first-time home purchase taxable at the state level?

Generally, no. Most states exclude from taxation Roth IRA distributions that are excluded from federal income taxation (see Q 15:40). Contributions returned from a Roth IRA are never taxable. Beginning in 2003, earnings distributed from a Roth IRA are exempted for "qualified" first-time home purchases.

Of the states that do not follow the federal treatment of IRAs, Massachusetts and New Jersey have adopted the federal treatment of Roth IRA qualified distributions. Massachusetts, for example, issued TIR 98-8, Massachusetts 1998 Reducing Income Taxes Act, Department of Revenue, October 6, 1998, which states that distributions [from Roth IRAs] are tax free so long as the taxpayer is at least age 59½ (or disabled, or a "first-time homebuyer") and the account satisfies the Internal Revenue Service's "five year rule." New Jersey provides conformity in its statute for qualified first-time homebuyers. [NJ § 54A:6-28.b.(4); *see also* NJ TB-44R (Feb. 9, 2010).] At present, Pennsylvania taxes all distributions from any type of IRA after the recovery of contributions unless the distribution is received on or after the participant retires and attains age 59½.

Q 15:49 Are distributions from a traditional IRA or Roth IRA for education expenses taxable at the state level?

Generally, yes. The distributed amount is included in state gross income. Federal income tax law, however, exempts from the 10 percent premature distribution penalty taxable IRA distribution amounts that are used to pay "qualified higher education expenses" of the taxpayer or the taxpayer's spouse, children, or grandchildren. [I.R.C. § 72(t)(7)]

Michigan, for example, had provided that for tax years beginning after December 31, 1999, a taxpayer may deduct, to the extent included in AGI, the amount of a distribution from an IRA that qualifies under Code Section 408 as long as that distribution is used to pay "qualified higher education expenses" as that term is defined in the Michigan Education Savings Program Act (MESP) per MCL §§ 390.1471 to 390.1486 per § 206.30(1)(t) and 206.30(1)(u). However, this deduction is not available after January 1, 2012.

Under federal law, a withdrawal from an IRA may be made if it is for higher education expenses without having to pay the 10 percent early withdrawal penalty under Code Section 72(t)(2)(e).

Q 15:50 Are distributions from a traditional IRA for medical expenses taxable at the state level?

Yes. Many states, however, allow deductions for contributions to medical savings accounts (MSAs) and tax-free withdrawals from such accounts. In addition, under federal law, a withdrawal from an IRA may be made if it is for medical expenses without having to pay the 10 percent early withdrawal penalty under Code Section 72(t)(2)(B).

Q 15:51 Do states conform to special short-term provisions of the federal income tax law for distributions from traditional or Roth IRAs?

In general, yes. But because of their respective legislative schedules, not all states adopt federal income tax provisions immediately. For example, North Carolina's Department of Revenue (DOR) announced that it would follow the changes made by the Deficit Reduction Act of 2005 [Pub. L. No. 109-171 (Feb. 9, 2006)], Heroes Earned Retirement Opportunities Act [Pub. L. No. 109-227 (May 18, 2006)], Pension Protection Act of 2006 [Pub. L. No. 109-280 (Aug. 19, 2006)], and Tax Relief and Health Care Act of 2006 [Pub. L. No. 109-432 (Dec. 20, 2006)] for 2006 filers. The North Carolina DOR also stated that if the state's General Assembly elected not to adopt some or all of the provisions during its 2007 legislative session, the DOR would assess any income tax plus applicable interest due as a result of a taxpayer using provisions not adopted by the General Assembly in determining the taxpayer's income tax liability. [North Carolina Important Notice About 2006 Federal Tax Legislation (Jan. 4, 2007)]

Minnesota, on the other hand, provides a tab on its Web site for individuals called "What's New," which has a list of items, including information on federal adjustments, to update taxpayers on how a tax provision is currently treated on the state's income tax return. (*See http://www.revenue.state.mn.us/federal-adjustments.*)

South Carolina amended S.C. Code Ann. § 12-6-40(A)(1)(a) to conform with the Internal Revenue Code as amended through December 31, 2016, including the effective dates, except where otherwise provided. In addition, South

Carolina provided an extension for expiring federal provision. That is, Code Section 12-6-40(A)(1)(c) provides that if during 2017 the federal government extends, without otherwise amending, Internal Revenue Code provisions that expired on December 31, 2016, then these sections or portions of sections which have been adopted by South Carolina will be extended in the same manner that they are for federal income tax purposes. (Senate Bill 250 (Act No. 4).) [*See https://dor.sc.gov/resources-site/lawandpolicy/Advisory%20Opinions/IL17-15.pdf#search=conformity.*]

Q 15:52 Do states provide a tax credit comparable to the saver's credit under Code Section 25B?

In general, no.

Q 15:53 Do all states permit taxpayers age 70½ or older to make up to $100,000 tax-free qualified charitable gifts from their IRA?

No. Many states have conformed to the provisions provided under the Pension Protection Act of 2006 [Pub. L. No. 109-280, 120 Stat. 780], known as the PPA. In those states, taxpayers who are age 70½ or older could exclude from income up to $100,000 of distributions from their traditional and Roth IRAs for qualified charitable gifts in tax years 2006 and 2007. This provision was extended first by the Tax Relief Act of 2010 through 2011, then by the American Taxpayer Relief Act of 2012 (ATRA) through 2012 and 2013, then by the Tax Increase Prevention Act of 2014 (TIPA) through 2014, and subsequently this exclusion was made permanent by the Protecting Americans from Tax Hikes Act (PATH Act) of 2015. California, for example, did not adopt all of the provisions under the PPA, but it did adopt the tax-free distribution provision for IRA distributions for charitable gifts. [*See* the California Conformity Archive under Additional Information at *https://www.ftb.ca.gov/tax-pros/law/conformity.html.*] New Jersey, on the other hand, announced that it would not adopt this provision.

The SECURE Act increased the required beginning date for minimum required distributions from age 70½ to age 72. Section 105 of the SECURE Act 2.0 (i.e., HR 2954), which had not been enacted as of May 1, 2021, generally further increases the age for the required beginning date for mandatory distributions to age 75.

Q 15:54 Do all states conform to the disaster relief provisions for taxpayers taking early distributions from an IRA?

No. In general, those states specifically addressed by disaster relief provisions adopted the provisions. Alabama, Florida, Louisiana, and Mississippi, for example, are identified in GOZA and KETRA, and, as such, they did adopt the provisions. Florida is not germane to this discussion, because the state does not have an individual income tax. Mississippi provides that early distributions from retirement accounts withdrawn as a result of Hurricane Katrina are excluded from Mississippi gross income. [*See http://www.dor.ms.gov/Pages/Provisions-of-KATRINA.aspx*.] Louisiana adopted the federal treatment since it begins its calculation with the taxpayer's federal adjusted gross income.

Q 15:55 Have all states conformed to the Pension Protection Act provision relating to reservists called to active duty who elect to take an early distribution?

Yes, with some limitations. Wisconsin adopted this provision (PPA § 827) retroactively in 2007. Minnesota adopted on March 7, 2008, the federal tax provisions enacted after May 18, 2006, retroactive to the federal effective date, with a few exceptions (see Q 15:51). This was posted on Minnesota's Web site for tax law changes and updated on April 11, 2008. California adopted the provision beginning on January 1, 2005 (but not retroactive to January 11, 2001, as provided for by the PPA).

Q 15:56 Did states permit taxpayers who participated in an employer's 401(k) plan that went bankrupt to make additional contributions to their IRAs?

It depends on the state and its conformity date. For example, California has a conformity date of January 1, 2005, and it has not incorporated amendments made to Code Section 219(b)(5) by the Pension Protection Act of 2006 (PPA) that allow qualifying individuals who participated in a bankrupt employer's 401(k) plan to make additional IRA contributions of up to $3,000 for each year from 2007 through 2009.

Conversion Rollovers to Roth IRAs

Q 15:57 Do states follow the federal income tax rules for conversion rollovers to Roth IRAs?

In general, yes. There are, however, some notable exceptions. Massachusetts [M.G.L. chapter 62, § 2(a)(3)(C)] and New Jersey include in state gross income only the state taxable portion of the conversion distribution, which in general differs from the federal taxable portion (see Qs 15:1, 15:6). Illinois and Pennsylvania do not include the taxable portion of a qualified conversion in state gross income. The position of both states is consistent with the fact that both exclude from state gross income distributions from qualified traditional IRAs. [Illinois Department of Revenue, Informational Bulletin FY 99-5 (Nov. 1, 1998); Pa. Ltr. Rul. PIT-98-048, Pennsylvania Department of Revenue (Aug. 27, 1999)]

Q 15:58 Did states follow the four-year averaging rule for 1998 conversion rollovers?

In general, yes.

An Illinois resident, however, could exclude from state gross income any amount included in AGI for federal income tax purposes due to a conversion rollover. [Illinois Department of Revenue, Informational Bulletin FY 99-5 (Nov. 1, 1998)]

Q 15:59 Did states follow the two-year averaging rule for 2010 conversion rollovers?

Yes, with exceptions. Hawaii law does not conform with Code Section 408A(d)(3)(A)(iii). It is inoperative for income tax purposes per Hawaii Revised Statutes, Section 235-2.4(m). Beginning after 2009, taxpayers in Hawaii have been able to convert eligible non-Roth IRAs to Roth IRAs regardless of income, but the income resulting from such conversions counts as income in the taxable year of conversion rather than over a two-year period.

New Jersey taxpayers who converted a traditional IRA to a Roth IRA during 2010 and elected to report the income resulting from the conversion in equal amounts in 2011 and 2012 on their federal income tax returns were required to report the amount that was taxable for New Jersey in equal installments in 2011 and 2012. If a taxpayer elected to include the entire amount of income from the conversion on the 2010 federal return, then the same was done on the 2010 New Jersey tax return. [*See http://www.state.nj.us/treasury/taxation/new2010.shtml.*] The taxable amounts for the federal and New Jersey tax returns may or may not have been the same.

Q 15:60 Do states permit taxpayers to apply exclusion amounts for retirement income to the taxable portion of a conversion rollover?

It depends on the state. Iowa and Kentucky, for example, permit taxpayers who are eligible to elect retirement exclusion to apply the exclusion to all or part of the taxable portion of a conversion rollover. Illinois and Pennsylvania (see Q 15:57) exclude the entire taxable portion of a conversion rollover. As of tax year 2014, North Carolina has repealed the $2,000 private retirement deduction as part of its Tax Simplification and Reduction Act.

Colorado, for example, provides in "FYI—Income 25: Pension/Annuity Subtraction (updated December 2016)" that the rollover amount included in federal adjusted gross income as an IRA distribution qualifies for the pension subtraction in the year the amount is received in gross income if the taxpayer is age 55 or older as of December 31 of that year. More importantly, this provision applies whether the rollover is reported in full in the year of the conversion or reported over a four-year period. Considering this provision, one can only conclude that the two-year carryover provision for conversions will receive similar treatment. (See Q 15:58.)

Q 15:61 If an individual moves to another state and during that year converts a traditional IRA to a Roth IRA, is that individual required to include the taxable portion of the conversion in his or her state gross income?

It depends on the state and the timing of the conversion. Oregon, for example, requires the entire taxable amount of a conversion to a Roth IRA to be included in state gross income if the taxpayer is a resident of Oregon at the time of the conversion. [*See* Pub. 17, Individual Income Tax Guide, No. 150-101-431 (Rev. 12-17).] Kentucky requires that the entire taxable amount be included in state gross income in the case of an "inbound" taxpayer who has already moved into the state, or an "outbound" taxpayer who has not yet left the state, at the time of the conversion. [Ky. Tax Alert, Vol. 18, No. 1 (Jan. 1, 1999)]

Iowa requires a taxpayer who resides in the state for part of the year to include only the portion of the taxable amount of the conversion attributable to the months of residence. For this purpose, a month is a period longer than half a month spent in Iowa. Thus, a taxpayer who spends 16 or more days of the month (15 days for February) in Iowa is credited with being a resident of Iowa for that month. [Iowa Reg. Rule 701-40.54(2)]

California was like Iowa where it taxed the portion of the current year's taxable income based on the taxpayer's residency in the state and California based its allocation on residency days, not residency months. However currently, the taxable amount of a distribution for a part-year resident from a traditional IRA that is being converted to a Roth IRA is included in the California source income only if the taxpayer was a resident of California on the date of the distribution. [California Franchise Tax Board (FTB) Publication 1005, Pension and Annuity Guidelines (Rev. 2019)]

Q 15:62 Do states provide an adjustment for previously taxed IRA conversion amounts?

In general, an IRA conversion is taxable in the year of conversion (see Q 15:57), and the state's exclusion amount for retirement income may or may not apply to the taxable portion of the conversion (see Q 15:60).

Q 15:63 Does the two-year averaging rule provide tax planning opportunities for some taxpayers?

In general, yes. A taxpayer residing in a state with an exclusion amount (Q 15:60) may want to spread the taxable conversion amount over two years and thereby reduce the total state income tax on the conversion. For example, a taxpayer living in a state with a 5 percent income tax rate that also provides a $30,000 annual exclusion could save up to $1,500 ($30,000 in year 2 × 5%) by electing the two-year averaging rule.

In addition, a taxpayer moving from a state with a low state income tax rate or no state income tax to a state with a higher state income tax rate may opt out of the two-year averaging rule and thereby reduce his or her overall state income taxes as a result of the move. Conversely, a taxpayer moving from a state with a high state income tax rate to one with a low state income tax rate or no state income tax, may want to elect the two-year averaging rule and reduce his or her overall state income taxes as a result of the move.

Example 1. Alex converts his traditional IRA to a Roth IRA in 2010; the taxable portion of the conversion is $100,000. If Alex moves from State A, which does not tax IRA conversions to State B, which has a 6 percent state income tax rate, he avoids paying $6,000 ($100,000 × 6%) on the conversion to State B by electing to include the entire $100,000 in his 2010 federal income tax return.

Example 2. Betty makes an IRA conversion in 2010; the taxable portion of the conversion is $100,000. If Betty moves from State C, which has an 8 percent state income tax rate, to State D, which has a 3 percent state income tax rate, she reduces her overall state income taxes by $5,000 ($50,000 (8% – 3%) × 2 years) on the conversion by electing that two-year averaging rule on her 2010 federal income tax return.

Q 15:64 If an individual moved out of a state during the four-year averaging period for a 1998 conversion rollover and took up residency in another state, could the former state of residence tax the conversion rollover?

It depended on the state. New York, for example, required the inclusion of any remaining deferred taxable portion from the conversion on the individual's part-year state tax return. Thus, the tax was collected before the individual left the state.

Iowa's allocation was based on residency months, and California's allocation used to be based on residency days (see Q 15:61).

Wisconsin, on the other hand, did not require the inclusion of any remaining deferred taxable portion from a 1998 conversion upon a person's moving out of the state. Rather, the state required the former resident to continue filing state income tax returns in the proper year. For taxpayers who moved into the state during the four-year averaging period, none of the deferred conversion amount was subject to Wisconsin income tax. [*See* Wis. Tax Bull. No. 112 (Jan. 1999).]

Colorado provides in "FYI—Income 25: Pension/Annuity Subtraction (updated December 2016)" that the rollover amount included in federal adjusted gross income as an IRA distribution qualifies for the pension subtraction in the year the amount is received in gross income if the taxpayer is age 55 or older as of December 31 of that year. This provision applies whether the rollover is reported in full in the year of the conversion or reported over a four-year period. In light of this provision, it would appear that a taxpayer would report income over 2011 and 2012 for a 2010 conversion but claim the deduction on the entire conversion amount in 2011. If the taxpayer relocates in 2012, however, the question will be whether any part of the pension subtraction taken in 2011 must be added back to income as a result of the income being partly reported in 2011 and 2012.

SEP IRAs and SIMPLE IRAs

Q 15:65 Do all states permit a deduction for employer contributions to SEP IRA and SIMPLE IRA plans?

Yes, with a few notable exceptions. Contributions made by self-employed individuals to SEP IRA and SIMPLE IRA plans on behalf of themselves are not deductible for personal income tax purposes in Pennsylvania [Reg. 101.6], New Jersey [Reg. 18:35-2.5], and Massachusetts. [Dep't of Revenue, Dir. 99-7 (May 28, 1999)] However, contributions made by employers on behalf of their employees are deductible.

Q 15:66 Do all states permit a deduction for employee contributions to SEP IRA and SIMPLE IRA plans?

No. Self-employed taxpayers and employees in some states are not eligible to deduct from their state gross income the amounts employers contributed to SEP IRA and SIMPLE IRA plans on their behalf (see Q 15:65).

In the case of Massachusetts, the deductibility rules were more complicated for tax years prior to 2002.

For tax years beginning on or after January 1, 2002, all amounts of retirement plan contributions and distributions that are excluded from gross income under the sections of the current Code enumerated are excluded from Massachusetts gross income. In the case of contributions to and distributions from qualified plans, 401(k) plans, 403(b) plans, 457 plans, SEPs, and SIMPLE IRAs, the amount excluded from Massachusetts gross income is the amount excluded from federal gross income by the current Code. Thus, for those plans, Massachusetts conforms to federal law in the treatment of elective deferrals, catch-up contributions, and qualified rollovers of plan proceeds. [TIR 02-18 (Nov. 6, 2002)]

Q 15:67 Do all states permit a deduction for contributions to a SIMPLE IRA plan on behalf of a domestic employee?

No. The majority of states conform to the federal income tax rules; thus, they would not permit a deduction for such contributions. New Jersey and Pennsylvania do not permit a deduction in any case (see Q 15:65).

Q 15:68 Do all states permit a deduction for catch-up contributions to SEP IRA and SIMPLE IRA plans by individuals age 50 or older?

No. Catch-up contribution amounts are not deductible from gross income for New Jersey, Pennsylvania, and Massachusetts. (See Q 15:65.)

Q 15:69 Do states tax earnings on contributions to SEP IRA and SIMPLE IRA plans in the year of accrual?

No. Earnings on contributions to SEP IRA and SIMPLE IRA plans are taxed only in the year of distribution. (See Q 15:5.)

Penalties

Q 15:70 Do some states concentrate on penalizing wealthy, self-employed individuals more than retired employees?

State laws do not make any discernible distinction. Regulators and enforcers, however, seem to be more vocal when the recipient of a distribution has control over the timing of personal transactions and defers the realization and receipt of an asset due for distribution so that it can be "earned" in the lower-tax or no-tax state to which he or she has moved. Transactions that occur shortly before a move, and even in the same tax year, are highly suspect.

Q 15:71 Do states tax and impose penalties on distributions that are taken before the IRA owner attains age 59½?

Yes. Treatment varies from state to state. Some states provide different exclusion amounts for retirement benefits, including IRA distributions that are received before a stated age. The stated age may be 55, 59½, or 65, depending on the state.

Moreover, some states determine the attainment of age as of December 31 of the taxable year; others determine it as of January 1 of the following year.

Some states do not impose a penalty for early distributions. Kentucky, for example, does not assess a similar penalty for Kentucky individual income tax purposes. Instead, the state requires these taxpayers to include the amount of the early IRA withdrawal in their gross income. This amount is then subject to tax at the regular Kentucky income tax rates. [Kentucky Revenue Cabinet Tax Policy No. 42P280 (June 1, 1983)]

Q 15:72 Why should the age of a recipient at the time of distribution be a factor?

Congress provided tax incentives to encourage individuals to participate in qualified retirement plans and IRAs and thereby have resources available at retirement. To discourage people from withdrawing funds from a retirement plan for nonretirement purposes, Congress placed an additional 10 percent penalty on certain early (pre-age-59½) distributions.

Q 15:73 Do states have their own version of the federal early distribution penalty tax found in Code Section 72(t)?

Some states penalize monies withdrawn "early" from qualified plans and IRAs. (The definition of *early* varies among the states.) For example, Alabama, Colorado, Hawaii, Illinois, Indiana, Michigan, Minnesota, Mississippi, Montana, New Jersey, New York, Pennsylvania, and South Carolina require the taxpayer to include the distribution amount in gross income.

Other states impose an additional state tax that is calculated as a percentage of the federal early distribution tax found in Code Section 72(t) (e.g., 10 percent in Arkansas, 29.6 percent in Nebraska, 24 percent in Vermont, and 33 percent in Wisconsin). California does not tax a portion of the federal early distribution tax, but simply levies a 2.5 percent tax on the taxable distribution amount. Maine had a 15 percent early distribution tax calculated as a percentage of the federal early distribution tax that was lowered to 7.5 percent for 2012, and then finally repealed for tax years beginning after 2012.

Some states do not impose any penalties for early distributions. Kentucky, for example, does not assess a similar penalty for Kentucky individual income tax purposes. Instead, the state requires these taxpayers to include the amount of the early IRA withdrawal in their gross income. This amount is then subject to tax at the regular Kentucky income tax rates. [Kentucky Revenue Cabinet Tax Policy No. 42P280 (June 1, 1983)]

Q 15:74 Can an IRA owner deduct from federal income tax penalties imposed by a state on distributions that are taken before he or she attains age 59½?

Yes. The Office of Chief Counsel issued IRS Memorandum 20072201F on June 1, 2007, which ruled in the case of California's penalty. The Office of Chief Counsel held, in part, that "since it is apparent that the 2½ percent additional amount is properly considered a tax, it is deductible under IRC § 164."

Therefore, one must assume that if the California penalty is deductible, then the Arkansas, Nebraska, Vermont, and Wisconsin penalties also must be deductible. However, the Tax Cuts and Jobs Act of 2017 limits the deductibility of taxes to $10,000 as an itemized deduction. As a result, the state penalty may be deductible, but the taxpayer may not be able to deduct the amount because of the itemized deduction limitation.

Q 15:75 Are there any exceptions to the state penalties on distributions before age 59½?

Yes, but the exceptions vary among the states. Pennsylvania, for example, does not penalize a retirement distribution that is made on or after the recipient has retired and reached the age of 59½. Other states follow the federal tax provisions, which contain several exceptions to the 10 percent premature distribution penalty (e.g., a distribution made to an employee who is disabled or as part of a series of substantially equal periodic payments).

Kentucky does not assess a penalty for individual income tax purposes. However, the state does require these taxpayers to include the amount of the early IRA withdrawal in their gross income. This amount is then subject to tax at the regular Kentucky income tax rates. [Kentucky Revenue Cabinet Tax Policy No. 42P280 (June 1, 1983)]

Health Savings Accounts

Q 15:76 Do all states permit a deduction for contributions to a health savings account?

No. Two states do not recognize health savings accounts (HSAs): California and New Jersey. Seven states (Alaska, Florida, Nevada, South Dakota, Texas, Washington, and Wyoming) do not have a state personal income tax, and two states (New Hampshire and Tennessee) have a state personal income tax on interest and dividends only. The remaining 38 states and the District of Columbia permit a deduction for contributions made to an HSA.

Q 15:77 Do states that permit a deduction for contributions to a health savings account follow the federal tax law?

Yes. Those states generally use the federal adjusted gross income (AGI) as a starting point for calculating state income.

Q 15:78 What is the state income tax effect on a rollover from a medical savings account to a health savings account?

Generally, a rollover from a medical savings account (MSA) to an HSA is tax free. If the state follows the federal regulation, the rollover will be tax free. There are three states that do not apply this rule; Alabama, California, and New Jersey (see Q 15:76).

In California, the rollover from an MSA to an HSA is treated as a nonqualified MSA distribution and is subjected to income tax plus a 10 percent penalty. Even though New Jersey does not recognize HSAs, the state allows an exclusion for amounts distributed from an MSA.

Q 15:79 Are distributions from health savings accounts taxed by the states?

In general, HSA distributions are not taxable. Amounts distributed from an HSA that are used to pay the qualified medical expenses of the account beneficiary are not subject to tax. The two states that do not recognize HSA accounts are the exceptions: California and New Jersey (see Q 15:76).

Q 15:80 Do states tax earnings on health savings accounts?

No. Earnings from HSAs are excluded from a state's gross income, except for those two states that do not permit a deduction for HSA contributions: California and New Jersey (see Q 15:76).

Withholding and Estimated Taxes

Q 15:81 Do states practice mandatory withholding?

Not all states practice mandatory withholding, which was introduced in federal tax law in 1992 for certain distributions from qualified retirement plans but not from IRAs.

Q 15:82 Do states have mandatory withholding on distributions from IRAs?

Generally, no. Most states follow the federal rule that allows a taxpayer to waive withholding on a distribution from an IRA. A few states, however, have mandatory withholding: Georgia (if the payments are periodic, unless the payee elects to not have withholding, which and that will remain in effect until it is revoked by the payee) [Ga. Code § 48-7-101(h)], Iowa (if federal income tax is withheld) [Iowa Reg. Rule 701-46.1(422)], and Oregon (unless the taxpayer opts out of withholding) [Or. Admin. R. 150-316.189].

Q 15:83 Does the IRA trustee withhold state income tax on IRA distributions?

The IRA trustee usually follows the directions of the IRA owner. The IRA owner may elect either to pay estimated tax on the distribution or to have the trustee withhold tax on the distribution. Of course, any underpayment penalty incurred is the responsibility of the IRA owner.

Q 15:84 Is the IRA owner responsible for making estimated tax payments on IRA distributions?

Yes, unless the IRA owner directs the IRA trustee to withhold taxes on the distributions (see Q 15:83). If the withholding amounts are adequate, there should be no need to make estimated tax payments. Any underpayment penalty incurred is the responsibility of the IRA owner.

Q 15:85 How are IRA trustees reacting to the myriad withholding rules that have evolved?

In light of the ban on source taxes (see Q 15:25), IRA trustees should be less frequently caught between the IRA owner's source state and his or her current state of residence. Withholding has not been a major issue for post-1995 distributions from IRAs, simplified employee pension plans, or savings incentive match plans for employees.

Choosing a State for Retirement

Q 15:86 Do individuals choose a state for retirement on the basis of whether their retirement income from IRAs and other sources will be taxed more favorably, or possibly not at all?

State income taxation of retirement income is surely a factor in the choice of a state in which to retire, but should not be the only factor considered. Property tax rates, sales tax levels, and old-age exemptions are also important. Some people would argue that taxation of any kind should be one of the last things to consider in selecting a retirement community. Location of one's family, health facilities, and recreational areas are sometimes regarded as more important considerations than taxes.

Q 15:87 Where can one obtain income tax information about a state?

One quick way of obtaining information about state income taxes and current or previous tax forms is to check the Web site of the state's revenue department or the revenue department of the District of Columbia:

State	*Web site*
Alabama	revenue.alabama.gov
Alaska	tax.alaska.gov
Arizona	azdor.gov
Arkansas	dfa.arkansas.gov
California	ftb.ca.gov
Colorado	colorado.gov/revenue
Connecticut	ct.gov/drs/
Delaware	revenue.delaware.gov/
District of Columbia	otr.cfo.dc.gov/
Florida	Floridarevenue.com
Georgia	dor.ga.gov
Hawaii	tax.hawaii.gov
Idaho	tax.idaho.gov/
Illinois	revenue.state.il.us
Indiana	in.gov/dor
Iowa	iowa.gov/tax/
Kansas	ksrevenue.org

State	*Web site*
Kentucky	revenue.ky.gov/
Louisiana	rev.state.la.us/
Maine	maine.gov/revenue/
Maryland	marylandtaxes.com
Massachusetts	mass.gov/dor/
Michigan	michigan.gov/taxes
Minnesota	revenue.state.mn.us
Mississippi	dor.ms.gov/
Missouri	dor.mo.gov/
Montana	revenue.mt.gov/
Nebraska	revenue.ne.gov/
Nevada	tax.nv.gov
New Hampshire	revenue.nh.gov/
New Jersey	state.nj.us/treasury/taxation/
New Mexico	tax.newmexico.gov/
New York	tax.ny.gov/
North Carolina	dornc.com/
North Dakota	nd.gov/tax/
Ohio	tax.ohio.gov/
Oklahoma	oktax.state.ok.us/
Oregon	oregon.gov/dor
Pennsylvania	revenue.state.pa.us/
Rhode Island	tax.ri.gov/
South Carolina	dor.sc.gov
South Dakota	dor.sd.gov
Tennessee	tn.gov/revenue/
Texas	comptroller.texas.gov/taxes
Utah	tax.utah.gov/
Vermont	tax.vermont.gov
Virginia	tax.virginia.gov/
Washington	dor.wa.gov/
West Virginia	tax.wv.gov
Wisconsin	revenue.wi.gov/
Wyoming	revenue.wyo.gov

Certain U.S. Possessions

Q 15:88 If individuals choose to retire in any of the U.S. Possessions, could there be issues regarding IRAs?

Yes. Each of the five U.S. Possessions (American Samoa, Guam, the Commonwealth of Puerto Rico, the Commonwealth of the Northern Mariana Islands (CNMI), and the U.S. Virgin Islands (USVI)) has its own independent tax department. Taxpayers who receive income from one of these possessions must file either the U.S. tax return only, or a possession tax return only, or both returns—depending on whether the taxpayer is considered a resident of one of the possessions. In some cases, a taxpayer may have to file a U.S. tax return, but is able to exclude the income earned in the U.S. possession. [*See* IRS Pub. 570, *Tax Guide for Individuals with Income from U.S. Possessions* 2020.]

Q 15:89 Can taxpayers in the U.S. Possessions obtain a deduction for traditional IRA contributions?

Yes, if a taxpayer is able to exclude U.S. Possession income from the U.S. tax return, the excluded income is not taken into account when calculating deductible IRA contributions. [*See* IRS Pub. 570, *Tax Guide for Individuals with Income from U.S. Possessions* 2020.]

Q 15:90 Are adjustments to add back U.S. Possessions income excluded income necessary for taxpayers who receive Social Security benefits and contribute to a traditional IRA?

Yes, taxpayers who receive U.S. Possessions income that is excluded from their federal AGI, receive Social Security benefits, and contribute to a traditional IRA must complete a separate worksheet to compute their modified adjusted gross income (MAGI). [*See* Appendix B in IRS Pub. 590-A, *Contributions to Individual Retirement Arrangements* (IRAs) 2020 (reproduced as Appendix A of this volume).]

Q 15:91 Can taxpayers obtain assistance to resolve issues due to inconsistent tax treatment between the IRS and the tax agencies in the U.S. Possessions?

Procedures are available to taxpayers needing assistance from the U.S. competent authority under the provisions of tax authority agreements entered into between the IRS and each of the tax agencies of the U.S. Possessions: American Samoa, Guam, the Commonwealth of the Northern Mariana Islands, the United States Virgin Islands, and Puerto Rico. Each tax coordination agreement contains provisions allowing the competent authorities of the United States and the possession to resolve, by mutual agreement, inconsistent tax treatment by the two jurisdictions. [*See* IRS Rev. Proc. 2006-23, 2006-20 I.R.B. 900 (May 1, 2006).]

Q 15:92 Where can one obtain income tax information about a U.S. Possession?

Information about income taxes in the U.S. Possessions is available on the following Web sites:

U.S. Possession	*Web site*
American Samoa	https://www.americansamoa.gov/tax-office-page
Guam	https://www.guamtax.com/
Northern Mariana Islands	https://www.finance.gov.mp/revenue-taxation.php
Puerto Rico (in local language)	https://www.hacienda.gobierno.pr/
U.S. Virgin Islands	https://bir.vi.gov/

Ongoing State Legislation

Q 15:93 Is further taxation of retirement benefits by states possible?

Additional income taxes are always possible. Studies on the tax dollars lost by federal and state governments through employee benefits programs are published continually. IRAs continue to be popular among wage earners. For tax years 2008 through 2020, the limit for spousal IRA contributions increased from $8,000 to $12,000 (total for both spouses, if younger than 50) and $10,000 to $14,000 (total for both spouses, if age 50 or older). [*See* Notice 2020-79 for I.R.C. § 219(b)(5)(A) and How Much Can Be Contributed? IRS Pub. 590-A, *Contributions to Individual Retirement Arrangements (IRAs)* 2020 (reproduced as Appendix A in this volume).]

On the other hand, state treasuries may experience a revenue increase because of the tax law changes passed by Congress. The Roth IRA has been available to wage earners since 1998. Contributions to a Roth IRA are nondeductible, but withdrawals and distributions are nontaxable. If taxpayers divert to Roth IRAs part of their contributions to qualified plans (e.g., 401(k) plans), federal AGI and state gross income will increase. Hence, state income tax revenue will increase. Further, many taxpayers converted their traditional IRAs to Roth IRAs in 1998. The taxable portion of the conversion was included in federal AGI and in state gross income over four years. State income tax revenues were expected to increase and did increase during the period 1995 through 2001. In fact, individual income tax revenues increased at an average of 9 percent per year, peaking at 12.3 percent in FY 2000. This trend, however, reversed itself in 2002 (decrease of 11.4 percent) and 2003 (decrease of 2.4 percent). State tax revenues from individuals increased in fiscal years 2004 (9.5 percent), 2005 (12.4 percent), 2006 (11.8 percent), 2007 (7.2 percent), and 2008 (5.5 percent). This trend, not surprisingly, reversed itself in 2002 (decrease of 11.4 percent) and 2003 (decrease of 2.4 percent).

Prior to 2018, a taxpayer was able to undo a traditional IRA to a Roth IRA conversion by recharacterizing it (see Qs 3:124–3:129). This action allowed individuals to undo a conversion and then reconvert after satisfying the appropriate waiting period when the market value of the IRA assets is lower, which also allowed individuals to pay lower income taxes to both the United States Treasury and their respective state revenue department. The Tax Cuts and Jobs Act repealed the recharacterization provision for conversions made after December 31, 2017. As a result, the fluctuation of state tax revenues resulting from taxpayers converting, then recharacterizing, and then reconverting is eliminated.

For the most recent state collections data, *see* U.S. Census Bureau, Quarterly Summary of State and Local Government Tax Revenue, available at *https://www.census.gov/programs-surveys/qtax4.html*.

Ongoing Issues

Q 15:94 What are the state tax implications regarding IRAs in same-sex marriages?

It may depend on the state, but at the federal level there appears to be uniformity. The IRS released guidance on the application of the U.S. Supreme Court decision which made it unconstitutional that same-sex marriages were not recognized under the Internal Revenue Code, in respect to qualified retirement plans in *United States v. Windsor* [570 U.S. 12 (2013)]. Specifically, IRS guidance includes: Revenue Ruling 2013-17, 2013-38 I.R.B. 201 (Sept. 16, 2013), *amplified by* Notice 2014-19, 2014-17 I.R.B. 979 (Apr. 21, 2014); Notice 2014-37, 2014-24 I.R.B. 1100 (June 9, 2014); and Notice 2015-86, 2015-52 I.R.B. 887 (Dec. 28, 2015) in light of the U.S. Supreme Court ruling in *Obergefell v. Hodges* [135 S. Ct. 2584 (2015)] that requires a state to license a marriage between two people of the same sex and to recognize a marriage between two people of the same sex when their marriage was lawfully licensed and performed out-of-state. The IRS has provided guidance since 2013 for the federal rules of recognition to assist employers and plan administrators that operate in more than one state to reduce potential and substantial financial and administrative burdens. This action was necessary because several Internal Revenue Code sections provide special rules with respect to married participants in qualified retirement plans, such as the need for and validity of spousal elections, consents, and notices that could change every time an employee, former employee, participant, or spouse moved to a state with different marriage recognition rules.

According to the IRS, the guidance listed above for retirement plans requires that a qualified retirement plan treat a same-sex spouse as a spouse for purposes of satisfying the federal tax laws relating to qualified retirement plans; that a qualified retirement plan recognize a same-sex marriage that was validly entered into in a jurisdiction whose laws authorize the marriage, even if the married couple lives in a domestic or foreign jurisdiction that does not recognize the validity of same-sex marriages; and that a person who is in a registered domestic partnership or civil union is not considered to be a spouse for purposes of applying the federal tax law requirements relating to qualified retirement plans, regardless of whether that person's partner is of the opposite sex or same sex.

At the state level in view of the federal guidance as described above, the only significant issue appeared to be whether a same-sex couple will be allowed to file a joint return in those states that did not recognize same-sex couples and the subsequent effect on such calculations as the modified adjusted gross income (MAGI) for deductible IRA contributions. Moreover, in those states that had recognized same-sex couples before, a same-sex couple may have been required to file a joint return. As a result of the *Obergefell v. Hodges* [135 S. Ct. 2584 (2015)] decision, states must now recognize same-sex marriages.

For example, Michigan was a state that did not recognize same-sex couples. On July 1, 2015, the Michigan Department of Treasury issued a Notice to Taxpayers that the U.S. Supreme Court in *Obergefell v. Hodges* invalidated the Michigan Constitution's definition of marriage as the union of one man and one woman. As a result, Michigan, and all states, now recognize the marriages of same-sex spouses, and same-sex marriages may no longer be an issue.

[*https://www.michigan.gov/documents/taxes/Notice_US_Supreme_Court_Obergefell_493269_7.pdf*]

Q 15:95 What are the state tax implications regarding qualified longevity annuity contract issues within an IRA?

There do not appear to be any state tax implications with the final regulations issued on July 1, 2014 (TD 9673) with Correcting Amendment 2014 ARD 151-1 on August 6, 2014 or any previous guidance regarding the use of the qualified longevity annuity contract (QLAC) within a tax-qualified defined contribution plan, a Section 403(b) plan, or an IRA. Although some states impose the early withdrawal penalty on monies withdrawn from qualified plans and IRAs like the federal rules (see Q 15:73), there are no required minimum distribution (RMD) rules for older taxpayers at the state level comparable to the federal rules. The QLAC provides a guaranteed life annuity to a retiree while providing some protection for the premium paid and reduces the RMDs that a plan participant needs to withdraw annually.

Q 15:96 What are the state tax implications of the ABLE Act's creation of a new savings account for persons with disabilities that is generally exempt from income tax?

The ABLE Act created Internal Revenue Code Section 529A, which permits a state to establish and maintain a new type of tax-advantaged savings program, a qualified ABLE program, under which contributions may be made to an account (an ABLE account) that is established for the purpose of meeting the qualified disability expenses of the designated beneficiary of the account who is a resident of that state and who is disabled. Moreover, these accounts also receive favorable treatment for purposes of certain means-tested federal programs. If a state does not establish and maintain its own qualified ABLE program, it may enter into a contract with another state to provide its residents with access to a qualified ABLE program.

The Section 529A proposed regulations note that the ABLE Act was "loosely modeled" to the Section 529 plan. The Section 529 plan, otherwise known as a Qualified Tuition Program (QTP), is an existing program established and maintained by a state that allows a contributor either to prepay a beneficiary's qualified higher education expenses at an eligible educational institution or to contribute to an account for paying those expenses (see chapter 14).

The Tax Cuts and Jobs Act of 2017 (TCJA) [Pub. L. No. 115-97 (Dec. 22, 2017)] makes two changes to the ABLE account, beginning on December 22, 2017 and continuing through December 31, 2025. The first change allows the beneficiary of the ABLE account to add to his or her account, after the maximum contribution limit ($15,000 in 2018) is reached, the lesser of (1) the federal poverty line for a one-person household, or (2) the individual's compensation for the taxable year. In addition, the designated beneficiary of the ABLE account is allowed to claim the saver's credit for the contributions made to the ABLE account. The second change permits amounts from a 529 plan to be rolled over to an ABLE account without penalty if the ABLE account is owned by the designated beneficiary of the 529 plan, or a member of such designated beneficiary's family.

Contributions made to the ABLE account are not deductible for federal income tax purposes. All states with personal income tax laws follow the federal rules pertaining to the non-deductibility of contributions made to an ABLE account, with Ohio being the exception. Effective January 1, 2017, a deduction from federal AGI is allowed for amounts contributed during the taxable year to an ABLE savings account opened pursuant to Ohio Rev. Code Ann. §§ 113.50 to 113.56 to the extent that the amounts contributed have not been deducted in computing the contributor's federal AGI for the taxable year. [Ohio Rev. Code Ann. § 5747.78; Ohio Rev. Code Ann. § 5747.01(A)(32)] The total amount of contributions deducted for any taxable year by a taxpayer or the taxpayer and the taxpayer's spouse cannot exceed the annual contribution limit for each beneficiary for whom contributions are made. If the total annual contributions for a beneficiary exceed the annual contribution limit, the excess may be carried forward and deducted in future taxable years until the contributions have been fully deducted. [Ohio Rev. Code Ann. § 5747.78] *Annual contribution limit* means the limit set forth in Ohio Rev. Code Ann. § 5747.70 on the dollar amount of contributions and purchases that a taxpayer, or a taxpayer and the taxpayer's spouse, may deduct during a taxable year for each beneficiary, or $2,000 (beginning January 1, 2018, $4,000). [Ohio Rev. Code Ann. § 5747.78]

At the time of publishing, not all states have enacted legislation to conform to the changes resulting from the TCJA. Some states have adopted many of the changes affecting individual taxpayers, including the increased contributions to ABLE accounts and the rollover to ABLE programs from 529 plans. Wisconsin, for example, specifically acknowledged the adoption of these changes and put out a table indicating which provisions are adopted. [*See https://www.revenue.wi.gov/DORFAQ/IRCProvisions2017.pdf.*]

Appendix A

IRS Publication 590-A—Contributions To Individual Retirement Arrangements (IRAs) (2020)

Department of the Treasury
Internal Revenue Service

Publication 590-A
Cat. No. 66302J

Contributions to Individual Retirement Arrangements (IRAs)

For use in preparing

2020 Returns

Feb 26, 2021

Contents

What's New for 2020

Coronavirus-related tax relief. Recent legislation provides for tax-favored withdrawals from IRAs for certain individuals who were impacted by the coronavirus in 2020. See Coronavirus Relief in Publication 590-B, Distributions from Individual Retirement Accounts (IRAs), for more information.

Contribution deadline extension. The 2019 traditional and Roth IRA contribution deadline was extended to July 15, 2020.

Modified AGI limit for traditional IRA contributions. For 2020, if you are covered by a retirement plan at work, your deduction for contributions to a traditional IRA is reduced (phased out) if your modified AGI is:

- More than $104,000 but less than $124,000 for a married couple filing a joint return or a qualifying widow(er),
- More than $65,000 but less than $75,000 for a single individual or head of household, or
- Less than $10,000 for a married individual filing a separate return.

Modified AGI limit for certain married individuals. If you are married and your spouse is covered by a retirement plan at work and you aren't, and you live with your spouse or file a joint return, your deduction is phased out if your modified AGI is more than $196,000 (up from $193,000 for 2019) but less than $206,000 (up from $203,000 for 2019). If your modified AGI is $206,000 or more, you can't take a deduction for contributions to a traditional IRA.

Modified AGI limit for Roth IRA contributions. For 2020, your Roth IRA contribution limit is reduced (phased out) in the following situations.

- Your filing status is married filing jointly or qualifying widow(er) and your modified AGI is at least $196,000. You can't make a Roth IRA contribution if your modified AGI is $206,000 or more.
- Your filing status is single, head of household, or married filing separately and you didn't live with your spouse at any time in 2020 and your modified AGI is at least $124,000. You can't make a Roth IRA contribution if your modified AGI is $139,000 or more.
- Your filing status is married filing separately, you lived with your spouse at any time during the year, and your modified AGI is more than zero. You can't make a Roth IRA contribution if your modified AGI is $10,000 or more.

Difficulty of care payments. You may be able to make additional nondeductible IRA contributions after December 20, 2019, if you received difficulty of care payments, which are a type of qualified foster care payment. For more information, see *Difficulty of care payments*, later.

Maximum age for making traditional IRA contributions repealed. For tax years beginning after 2019, the rule that you are not able to make contributions to your traditional IRA for the year in which you reach age 70½ and all later years has been repealed.

Required minimum distributions (RMDs). For distributions required to be made after 2019, the age for the required beginning date for mandatory distributions is changed to age 72 for taxpayers reaching age 70½ after December 31, 2019.

Certain taxable non-tuition fellowship and stipend payments. For tax years beginning after 2019, certain taxable non-tuition fellowship and stipend payments are treated as compensation for the purpose of IRA contributions. Compensation will include any amount included in your gross income and paid to aid in your pursuit of graduate or postdoctoral study.

What's New for 2021

Modified AGI limit for traditional IRA contributions increased. For 2021, if you are covered by a retirement plan at work, your deduction for contributions to a traditional IRA is reduced (phased out) if your modified AGI is:

- More than $105,000 but less than $125,000 for a married couple filing a joint return or a qualifying widow(er),
- More than $66,000 but less than $76,000 for a single individual or head of household, or
- Less than $10,000 for a married individual filing a separate return.

Modified AGI limit for certain married individuals increased. If you are married and your spouse is covered by a retirement plan at work and you aren't, and you live with your spouse or file a joint return, your deduction is phased out if your modified AGI is more than $198,000 (up from $196,000 for 2020) but less than $208,000 (up from $206,000 for 2020). If your modified AGI is $208,000 or more, you can't take a deduction for contributions to a traditional IRA.

Modified AGI limit for Roth IRA contributions increased. For 2021, your Roth IRA contribution limit is reduced (phased out) in the following situations.

- Your filing status is married filing jointly or qualifying widow(er) and your modified AGI is at least $198,000. You can't make a Roth IRA contribution if your modified AGI is $208,000 or more.
- Your filing status is single, head of household, or married filing separately and you didn't live with your spouse at any time in 2021 and your modified AGI is at least $125,000. You can't make a Roth IRA contribution if your modified AGI is $140,000 or more.
- Your filing status is married filing separately, you lived with your spouse at any time during the year, and your modified AGI is more than zero. You can't make a Roth IRA contribution if your modified AGI is $10,000 or more.

Reminders

Future developments. For the latest information about developments related to Pub. 590-A, such as legislation enacted after it was published, go to *IRS.gov/Pub590A*.

Divorce or separation instruments after 2018. Amounts paid as alimony or separate maintenance payments under a divorce or separation instrument executed after 2018 won't be deductible by the payer. Such amounts also won't be includible in the income of the recipient. The same is true of alimony paid under a divorce or separation instrument executed before 2019 and modified after 2018, if the modification expressly states that the alimony isn't deductible to the payer or includible in the income of the recipient. For more information, see Pub. 504.

Qualified disaster tax relief. Special rules provide for tax-favored withdrawals and repayments from certain retirement plans for taxpayers who suffered economic losses as a result of Hurricane Harvey, Tropical Storm Harvey, Hurricane Irma, Hurricane Maria, or the 2017 California wildfires and certain major disasters that occurred in 2018, 2019, and early 2020. For more information, see Form 8915-B (for qualified 2017 disasters), Form 8915-C (for qualified 2018 disasters), Form 8915-D (for qualified 2019 disasters), and Form 8915-E (Use for Coronavirus-Related and Other Qualified 2020 Disaster Distributions).

Disaster tax relief is also available for taxpayers who suffered economic losses as a result of disasters declared by the President under section 401 of the Robert T. Stafford Disaster Relief and Emergency Assistance Act during calendar year 2016. See the Instructions for Form 8915-A, Qualified 2016 Disaster Retirement Plan Distributions and Repayments, for more information on these provisions.

IRAs and unrelated business income. An IRA is subject to tax on unrelated business income if it carries on an unrelated trade or business. An unrelated trade or business means any trade or business regularly carried on by the IRA or by a partnership of which it is a member. For more information, see *Unrelated business income* under *What Acts Result in Penalties or Additional Taxes*, later.

IRA interest. Although interest earned from your IRA is generally not taxed in the year earned, it isn't tax-exempt interest. Tax on your traditional IRA is generally deferred until you take a distribution. Don't report this interest on your return as tax-exempt interest. For more information on tax-exempt interest, see the instructions for your tax return.

Extended rollover period for qualified plan loan offsets in 2018 or later. For distributions made in tax years beginning after December 31, 2017, you have until the due date (including extensions) for your tax return for the tax year in which the offset occurs to roll over a qualified plan loan offset amount. For more information, see *Time Limit for Making a Rollover Contribution* in chapter 1.

No recharacterizations of conversions made in 2018 or later. A conversion of a traditional IRA to a Roth IRA, and a rollover from any other eligible retirement plan to a Roth IRA, made after December 31, 2017, cannot be recharacterized as having been made to a traditional IRA. For more information, see *Recharacterizations* in chapter 1.

Photographs of missing children. The IRS is a proud partner with the *National Center for Missing & Exploited Children® (NCMEC)*. Photographs of missing children selected by the Center may appear in this publication on pages that would otherwise be blank. You can help bring these children home by looking at the photographs and calling 1-800-THE-LOST (1-800-843-5678) if you recognize a child.

Introduction

This publication discusses contributions to individual retirement arrangements (IRAs). An IRA is a personal savings plan that gives you tax advantages for setting aside money for retirement. For information about distributions (including rollovers) from an IRA, see Pub. 590-B.

What are some tax advantages of an IRA? Two tax advantages of an IRA are that:

- Contributions you make to an IRA may be fully or partially deductible, depending on which type of IRA you have and on your circumstances; and
- Generally, amounts in your IRA (including earnings and gains) aren't taxed until distributed. In some cases, amounts aren't taxed at all if distributed according to the rules.

What's in this publication? This publication discusses contributions to traditional and Roth IRAs. It explains the rules for:

- Setting up an IRA,
- Contributing to an IRA,
- Transferring money or property to and from an IRA, and
- Taking a credit for contributions to an IRA.

It also explains the penalties and additional taxes that apply when the rules aren't followed. To assist you in complying with the tax rules for IRAs, this publication contains worksheets and sample forms which can be found throughout the publication and in the appendices at the back of the publication.

How to use this publication. The rules that you must follow depend on which type of IRA you have. Use *Table I-1* to help you determine which parts of this publication to read. Also use Table I-1 if you were referred to this publication from instructions to a form.

Comments and suggestions. We welcome your comments about this publication and suggestions for future editions.

You can send us comments through *IRS.gov/FormComments*. Or, you can write to the Internal Revenue Service, Tax Forms and Publications, 1111 Constitution Ave. NW, IR-6526, Washington, DC 20224.

Although we can't respond individually to each comment received, we do appreciate your feedback and will consider your comments and suggestions as we revise our tax forms, instructions, and publications. Do **not** send tax questions, tax returns, or payments to the above address.

Getting answers to your tax questions. If you have a tax question not answered by this publication or the *How To Get Tax Help* section at the end of this publication, go to the IRS Interactive Tax Assistant page at *IRS.gov/Help/ITA* where you can find topics by using the search feature or viewing the categories listed.

Getting tax forms, instructions, and publications. Visit *IRS.gov/Forms* to download current and prior-year forms, instructions, and publications.

Ordering tax forms, instructions, and publications. Go to *IRS.gov/OrderForms* to order current forms, instructions, and publications; call 800-829-3676 to order prior-year forms and instructions. The IRS will process your order for forms and publications as soon as possible. Do not resubmit requests you've already sent us. You can get forms and publications faster online.

Useful Items

You may want to see:

Publications

- ❑ **590-B** Distributions from Individual Retirement Arrangements (IRAs)
- ❑ **560** Retirement Plans for Small Business (SEP, SIMPLE, and Qualified Plans)
- ❑ **571** Tax-Sheltered Annuity Plans (403(b) Plans)
- ❑ **575** Pension and Annuity Income
- ❑ **939** General Rule for Pensions and Annuities

Forms (and Instructions)

- ❑ **W-4P** Withholding Certificate for Pension or Annuity Payments
- ❑ **1099-R** Distributions From Pensions, Annuities, Retirement or Profit-Sharing Plans, IRAs, Insurance Contracts, etc.
- ❑ **5304-SIMPLE** Savings Incentive Match Plan for Employees of Small Employers (SIMPLE)—Not for Use With a Designated Financial Institution
- ❑ **5305-S** SIMPLE Individual Retirement Trust Account
- ❑ **5305-SA** SIMPLE Individual Retirement Custodial Account
- ❑ **5305-SIMPLE** Savings Incentive Match Plan for Employees of Small Employers (SIMPLE)—for Use With a Designated Financial Institution
- ❑ **5329** Additional Taxes on Qualified Plans (Including IRAs) and Other Tax-Favored Accounts
- ❑ **5498** IRA Contribution Information
- ❑ **8606** Nondeductible IRAs
- ❑ **8815** Exclusion of Interest From Series EE and I U.S. Savings Bonds Issued After 1989
- ❑ **8839** Qualified Adoption Expenses
- ❑ **8880** Credit for Qualified Retirement Savings Contributions
- ❑ **8915-A** Qualified 2016 Disaster Retirement Plan Distributions and Repayments
- ❑ **8915-B** Qualified 2017 Disaster Retirement Plan Distributions and Repayments
- ❑ **8915-C** Qualified 2018 Disaster Retirement Plan Distributions and Repayments
- ❑ **8915-D** Qualified 2019 Disaster Retirement Plan Distributions and Repayments
- ❑ **8915-E** Qualified 2020 Disaster Retirement Plan Distributions and Repayments (Use for Coronavirus-Related and Other Qualified 2020 Disaster Distributions)

See *How To Get Tax Help* for information about getting these publications and forms.

Table I-1. **Using This Publication**

IF you need information on...	**THEN see...**
traditional IRAs	chapter 1.
Roth IRAs	chapter 2, and parts of chapter 1.
the credit for qualified retirement savings contributions (the saver's credit)	chapter 3.
how to keep a record of your contributions to, and distributions from, your traditional IRA(s)	Appendix A.
SEP IRAs, SIMPLE IRAs, and 401(k) plans	Pub. 560.
Coverdell education savings accounts (ESAs) (formerly called education IRAs)	Pub. 970.

IF for 2020, you: • received ***social security*** benefits, • had taxable compensation, • contributed to a traditional IRA, and • you or your spouse was covered by an employer retirement plan, and you want to...	**THEN see...**
first figure your modified adjusted gross income (AGI)	Appendix B, Worksheet 1.
then figure how much of your traditional IRA contribution you can deduct	Appendix B, Worksheet 2.
and finally figure how much of your social security is taxable	Appendix B, Worksheet 3.

Table I-2. **How Are a Traditional IRA and a Roth IRA Different?**

This table shows the differences between traditional and Roth IRAs. Answers in the middle column apply to traditional IRAs. Answers in the right column apply to Roth IRAs.

Question	Answer	
	Traditional IRA?	**Roth IRA?**
Is there an age limit on when I can open and contribute to a	No. For tax years after 2019, you are able to contribute to your IRA even if you have reached age 70½ or older. See *Who Can Open a Traditional IRA?* in chapter 1.	No. You can be any age. See *Can You Contribute to a Roth IRA?* in chapter 2.
If I earned more than $6,000 in 2020 ($7,000 if I was 50 or older by the end of 2020), is there a limit on how much I can contribute to a	Yes. For 2020, you can contribute to a traditional IRA up to: • $6,000, or • $7,000 if you were age 50 or older by the end of 2020. There is no upper limit on how much you can earn and still contribute. See *How Much Can Be Contributed?* in chapter 1.	Yes. For 2020, you may be able to contribute to a Roth IRA up to: • $6,000, or • $7,000 if you were age 50 or older by the end of 2020, but the amount you can contribute may be less than that depending on your income, filing status, and if you contribute to another IRA. See *How Much Can Be Contributed?* and *Table 2-1* in chapter 2.
Can I deduct contributions to a	Yes. You may be able to deduct your contributions to a traditional IRA depending on your income, filing status, whether you are covered by a retirement plan at work, and whether you receive social security benefits. See *How Much Can You Deduct?* in chapter 1.	No. You can never deduct contributions to a Roth IRA. See *What Is a Roth IRA?* in chapter 2.
Do I have to file a form just because I contribute to a	Not unless you make nondeductible contributions to your traditional IRA. In that case, you must file Form 8606. See *Nondeductible Contributions* in chapter 1.	No. You don't have to file a form if you contribute to a Roth IRA. See *Contributions not reported* in chapter 2.

1.

Traditional IRAs

Introduction

This chapter discusses the original IRA. In this publication, the original IRA (sometimes called an ordinary or regular IRA) is referred to as a "traditional IRA." A traditional IRA is any IRA that isn't a Roth IRA or a SIMPLE IRA. The following are two advantages of a traditional IRA.

- You may be able to deduct some or all of your contributions to it, depending on your circumstances.
- Generally, amounts in your IRA, including earnings and gains, aren't taxed until they are distributed.

Who Can Open a Traditional IRA?

You can open and make contributions to a traditional IRA if you (or, if you file a joint return, your spouse) received taxable compensation during the year.

You can have a traditional IRA whether or not you are covered by any other retirement plan. However, you may not be able to deduct all of your contributions if you or your spouse is covered by an employer retirement plan. See *How Much Can You Deduct*, later.

TIP *For tax years beginning after December 31, 2019, the rule that you are not able to make contributions to your traditional IRA for the year in which you reach age 70½ and all later years has been repealed.*

Both spouses have compensation. If both you and your spouse have compensation, each of you can open an IRA. You can't both participate in the same IRA. If you file a joint return, only one of you needs to have compensation.

What Is Compensation?

Generally, compensation is what you earn from working. For a summary of what compensation does and doesn't include, see Table 1-1. Compensation includes all of the items discussed next (even if you have more than one type).

Wages, salaries, etc. Wages, salaries, tips, professional fees, bonuses, and other amounts you receive for providing personal services are compensation. The IRS treats as compensation any amount properly shown in box 1 (Wages, tips, other compensation) of Form W-2, Wage and Tax Statement, provided that amount is reduced by any amount properly shown in box 11 (Nonqualified plans). Scholarship and fellowship payments are compensation for IRA purposes only if shown in box 1 of Form W-2.

Commissions. An amount you receive that is a percentage of profits or sales price is compensation.

Self-employment income. If you are self-employed (a sole proprietor or a partner), compensation is the net earnings from your trade or business (provided your personal services are a material income-producing factor) reduced by the total of:

- The deduction for contributions made on your behalf to retirement plans, and
- The deduction allowed for the deductible part of your self-employment taxes.

Compensation includes earnings from self-employment even if they aren't subject to self-employment tax because of your religious beliefs.

Self-employment loss. If you have a net loss from self-employment, don't subtract the loss from your salaries or wages when figuring your total compensation.

Alimony and separate maintenance. For IRA purposes, compensation includes any taxable alimony and separate maintenance payments you receive under a decree of divorce or separate maintenance but only with respect to divorce or separation instruments executed on or before December 31, 2018, that have not been modified to exclude such amounts.

Nontaxable combat pay. If you were a member of the U.S. Armed Forces, compensation includes any nontaxable combat pay you received. This amount should be reported in box 12 of your 2020 Form W-2 with code Q.

Graduate or postdoctoral study. Compensation includes any income paid to you to aid you in the pursuit of graduate or postdoctoral study.

Table 1-1. **Compensation for Purposes of an IRA**

Includes...	Doesn't include...
wages, salaries, etc.	earnings and profits from property.
commissions.	interest and dividend income.
self-employment income.	pension or annuity income.
taxable alimony and separate maintenance.	deferred compensation.
nontaxable combat pay.	income from certain partnerships.
taxable non-tuition fellowship and stipend payments	any amounts you exclude from income.

What Isn't Compensation?

Compensation doesn't include any of the following items.

- Earnings and profits from property, such as rental income, interest income, and dividend income.
- Pension or annuity income.
- Deferred compensation received (compensation payments postponed from a past year).
- Income from a partnership for which you don't provide services that are a material income-producing factor.
- Conservation Reserve Program (CRP) payments reported on Schedule SE (Form 1040), line 1b.
- Any amounts (other than combat pay) you exclude from income, such as foreign earned income and housing costs.

When Can a Traditional IRA Be Opened?

You can open a traditional IRA at any time. However, the time for making contributions for any year is limited. See *When Can Contributions Be Made*, later.

How Can a Traditional IRA Be Opened?

You can open different kinds of IRAs with a variety of organizations. You can open an IRA at a bank or other financial institution or with a mutual fund or life insurance company. You can also open an IRA through your stockbroker. Any IRA must meet Internal Revenue Code requirements. The requirements for the various arrangements are discussed below.

Kinds of traditional IRAs. Your traditional IRA can be an individual retirement account or annuity. It can be part of either a SEP or an employer or employee association trust account.

Individual Retirement Account

An individual retirement account is a trust or custodial account set up in the United States for the exclusive benefit of you or your beneficiaries. The account is created by a written document. The document must show that the account meets all of the following requirements.

- The trustee or custodian must be a bank, a federally insured credit union, a savings and loan association, or an entity approved by the IRS to act as trustee or custodian.
- The trustee or custodian generally can't accept contributions of more than the deductible amount for the year. However, rollover contributions and employer contributions to a SEP can be more than this amount.
- Contributions, except for rollover contributions, must be in cash. See *Rollovers*, later.
- You must have a nonforfeitable right to the amount at all times.
- Money in your account can't be used to buy a life insurance policy.
- Assets in your account can't be combined with other property, except in a common trust fund or common investment fund.
- You must start receiving distributions by April 1 of the year following the year in which you reach age 72. See Pub. 590-B for more information about required minimum distributions (RMDs) and other distribution rules.

Individual Retirement Annuity

You can open an individual retirement annuity by purchasing an annuity contract or an endowment contract from a life insurance company.

An individual retirement annuity must be issued in your name as the owner, and either you or your beneficiaries who survive you are the only ones who can receive the benefits or payments.

An individual retirement annuity must meet all the following requirements.

- Your entire interest in the contract must be nonforfeitable.
- The contract must provide that you can't transfer any portion of it to any person other than the issuer.
- There must be flexible premiums so that if your compensation changes, your payment can also change. This provision applies to contracts issued after November 6, 1978.
- The contract must provide that contributions can't be more than the deductible amount for an IRA for the year, and that you must use any refunded premiums to pay for future premiums or to buy more benefits before the end of the calendar year after the year in which you receive the refund.
- Distributions must begin by April 1 of the year following the year in which you reach age 72. See Pub. 590-B for more information about required minimum distributions (RMDs) and other distribution rules.

Individual Retirement Bonds

The sale of individual retirement bonds issued by the federal government was suspended after April 30, 1982. The bonds have the following features.

- They stop earning interest when you reach age 70½. If you die, interest will stop 5 years after your death, or on the date you would have reached age 70½, whichever is earlier.
- You can't transfer the bonds.

If you cash (redeem) the bonds before the year in which you reach age 59½, you may be subject to a 10% additional tax. See Pub. 590-B for more information about the age 59½ rule for early distributions and other distribution rules. You can roll over redemption proceeds into IRAs.

SIMPLE IRAs

A SIMPLE IRA plan is a tax-favored retirement plan that certain small employers (including self-employed employees) can set up for the benefit of their employees. Your participation in your employer's SIMPLE IRA plan doesn't prevent you from making contributions to a traditional or Roth IRA. See Pub. 560 for more information about SIMPLE IRAs.

Simplified Employee Pension (SEP)

A SEP is a written arrangement that allows your employer to make deductible contributions to a traditional IRA (a SEP IRA) set up for you to receive such contributions. Generally, distributions from SEP IRAs are subject to the withdrawal and tax rules that apply to traditional IRAs. See Pub. 560 for more information about SEPs.

Employer and Employee Association Trust Accounts

Your employer or your labor union or other employee association can set up a trust to provide individual retirement accounts for employees or members. The requirements for individual retirement accounts apply to these traditional IRAs.

Required Disclosures

The trustee or issuer (sometimes called the sponsor) of your traditional IRA must generally give you a disclosure statement at least 7 days before you open your IRA. However, the sponsor doesn't have to give you the statement until the date you open (or purchase, if earlier) your IRA, provided you are given at least 7 days from that date to revoke the IRA.

The disclosure statement must explain certain items in plain language. For example, the statement should explain when and how you can revoke the IRA, and include the name, address, and telephone number of the person to receive the notice of cancellation. This explanation must appear at the beginning of the disclosure statement.

If you revoke your IRA within the revocation period, the sponsor must return to you the entire amount you paid. The sponsor must report on the appropriate IRS forms both your contribution to the IRA (unless it was made by a trustee-to-trustee transfer) and the amount returned to you. These requirements apply to all sponsors.

How Much Can Be Contributed?

There are limits and other rules that affect the amount that can be contributed to a traditional IRA. These limits and rules are explained below.

Community property laws. Except as discussed later under Kay Bailey Hutchison Spousal IRA Limit, each spouse figures his or her limit separately, using his or her own compensation. This is the rule even in states with community property laws.

Brokers' commissions. Brokers' commissions paid in connection with your traditional IRA are subject to the contribution limit. For information about whether you can deduct brokers' commissions, see Brokers' commissions, later, under *How Much Can You Deduct.*

Trustees' fees. Trustees' administrative fees aren't subject to the contribution limit. For information about whether you can deduct trustees' fees, see Trustees' fees, later, under *How Much Can You Deduct.*

Qualified reservist repayments. If you were a member of a reserve component and you were ordered or called to active duty after September 11, 2001, you may be able to contribute (repay) to an IRA amounts equal to any qualified reservist distributions (defined under *Early Distributions* in Pub. 590-B) you received. You can make these repayment contributions even if they would cause your total contributions to the IRA to be more than the general limit on contributions. To be eligible to make these repayment contributions, you must have received a qualified reservist distribution from an IRA or from a section 401(k) or 403(b) plan or a similar arrangement. See Pub. 590-B under *Early Distributions* for more information on qualified reservist distributions.

Limit. Your qualified reservist repayments can't be more than your qualified reservist distributions.

When repayment contributions can be made. You can't make these repayment contributions later than the date that is 2 years after your active duty period ends.

No deduction. You can't deduct qualified reservist repayments.

Reserve component. The term "reserve component" means the:

- Army National Guard of the United States,
- Army Reserve,
- Naval Reserve,
- Marine Corps Reserve,
- Air National Guard of the United States,
- Air Force Reserve,
- Coast Guard Reserve, or
- Reserve Corps of the Public Health Service.

Figuring your IRA deduction. The repayment of qualified reservist distributions doesn't affect the amount you can deduct as an IRA contribution.

Reporting the repayment. If you repay a qualified reservist distribution, include the amount of the repayment with nondeductible contributions on line 1 of Form 8606.

Example. In 2020, your IRA contribution limit is $6,000. However, because of your filing status and AGI, the limit on the amount you can deduct is $3,500. You can make a nondeductible contribution of $2,500 ($6,000 − $3,500). In an earlier year, you received a $3,000 qualified reservist distribution, which you would like to repay this year.

For 2020, you can contribute a total of $9,000 to your IRA. This is made up of the maximum deductible contribution of $3,500; a nondeductible contribution of $2,500; and a $3,000 qualified reservist repayment. You contribute the maximum allowable for the year. Since you are making a nondeductible contribution ($2,500) and a qualified reservist repayment ($3,000), you must file Form 8606 with your return and include $5,500 ($2,500 + $3,000) on line 1 of Form 8606. The qualified reservist repayment isn't deductible.

CAUTION *Contributions on your behalf to a traditional IRA reduce your limit for contributions to a Roth IRA. See chapter 2 for information about Roth IRAs.*

General Limit

For 2020, the most that can be contributed to your traditional IRA is generally the smaller of the following amounts.

- $6,000 ($7,000 if you are age 50 or older).
- Your taxable compensation (defined earlier) for the year.

Note. This limit is reduced by any contributions to a section 501(c)(18) plan (generally, a pension plan created before June 25, 1959, that is funded entirely by employee contributions).

This is the most that can be contributed regardless of whether the contributions are to one or more traditional IRAs or whether all or part of the contributions are nondeductible. (See *Nondeductible Contributions*, later.) Qualified reservist repayments don't affect this limit.

Examples. George, who is 34 years old and single, earns $24,000 in 2020. His IRA contributions for 2020 are limited to $6,000.

Danny, an unmarried college student working part time, earns $3,500 in 2020. His IRA contributions for 2020 are limited to $3,500, the amount of his compensation.

More than one IRA. If you have more than one IRA, the limit applies to the total contributions made on your behalf to all your traditional IRAs for the year.

Annuity or endowment contracts. If you invest in an annuity or endowment contract under an individual retirement annuity, no more than $6,000 ($7,000 if you are age 50 or older) can be contributed toward its cost for the tax year, including the cost of life insurance coverage. If more than this amount is contributed, the annuity or endowment contract is disqualified.

Kay Bailey Hutchison Spousal IRA Limit

For 2020, if you file a joint return and your taxable compensation is less than that of your spouse, the most that can be contributed for the year to your IRA is the smaller of the following two amounts.

1. $6,000 ($7,000 if you are age 50 or older).
2. The total compensation includible in the gross income of both you and your spouse for the year, reduced by the following two amounts.
   a. Your spouse's IRA contribution for the year to a traditional IRA.
   b. Any contributions for the year to a Roth IRA on behalf of your spouse.

This means that the total combined contributions that can be made for the year to your IRA and your spouse's IRA can be as much as $12,000 ($13,000 if only one of you is age 50 or older, or $14,000 if both of you are age 50 or older).

Note. This traditional IRA limit is reduced by any contributions to a section 501(c)(18) plan (generally, a pension plan created before June 25, 1959, that is funded entirely by employee contributions).

Example. Kristin, a full-time student with no taxable compensation, marries Carl during the year. Neither of them was age 50 by the end of 2020. For the year, Carl has taxable compensation of $30,000. He plans to contribute (and deduct) $6,000 to a traditional IRA. If he and Kristin file a joint return, each can contribute $6,000 to a traditional IRA. This is because Kristin, who has no compensation, can add Carl's compensation, reduced by the amount of his IRA contribution ($30,000 − $6,000 = $24,000), to her own compensation (-0-) to figure her maximum contribution to a traditional IRA. In her case, $6,000 is her contribution limit, because $6,000 is less than $24,000 (her compensation for purposes of figuring her contribution limit).

Filing Status

Generally, except as discussed earlier under *Kay Bailey Hutchison Spousal IRA Limit*, your filing status has no effect on the amount of allowable contributions to your traditional IRA. However, if during the year either you or your spouse was covered by a retirement plan at work, your deduction may be reduced or eliminated, depending on your filing status and income. See *How Much Can You Deduct*, later.

Example. Tom and Darcy are married and both are 53. They both work and each has a traditional IRA. Tom earned $3,800 and Darcy earned $48,000 in 2020. Because of the Kay Bailey Hutchison Spousal IRA limit rule, even though Tom earned less than $7,000, they can contribute up to $7,000 to his IRA for 2020 if they file a joint return. They can contribute up to $7,000 to Darcy's IRA. If they file separate returns, the amount that can be contributed to Tom's IRA is limited by his earned income, $3,800.

Less Than Maximum Contributions

If contributions to your traditional IRA for a year were less than the limit, you can't contribute more after the due date of your return for that year to make up the difference.

Example. Rafael, who is 40, earns $30,000 in 2020. Although he can contribute up to $6,000 for 2020, he contributes only $3,000. After April 15, 2021, Rafael can't make up the difference between his actual contributions for 2020 ($3,000) and his 2020 limit ($6,000). He can't contribute $3,000 more than the limit for any later year.

More Than Maximum Contributions

If contributions to your IRA for a year were more than the limit, you can apply the excess contribution in one year to a later year if the contributions for that later year are less than the maximum allowed for that year. However, a penalty or additional tax may apply. See Excess Contributions, later, under *What Acts Result in Penalties or Additional Taxes*.

When Can Contributions Be Made?

As soon as you open your traditional IRA, contributions can be made to it through your chosen sponsor (trustee or other administrator). Contributions must be in the form of money (cash, check, or money order). Property can't be contributed.

Although property can't be contributed, your IRA may invest in certain property. For example, your IRA may purchase shares of stock. For other restrictions on the use of funds in your IRA, see Prohibited Transactions, later in this chapter. You may be able to transfer or roll over certain property from one retirement plan to another. See the discussion of rollovers and other transfers later in this chapter under Can You Move Retirement Plan Assets.

TIP *You can make a contribution to your IRA by having your income tax refund (or a portion of your refund), if any, paid directly to your traditional IRA, Roth IRA, or SEP IRA. For details, see the instructions for your income tax return or Form 8888, Allocation of Refund (Including Savings Bond Purchases).*

Contributions can be made to your traditional IRA for each year that you receive compensation. For any year in which you don't work, contributions can't be made to your IRA unless you receive taxable alimony, nontaxable combat pay, military differential pay, or file a joint return with a spouse who has compensation. See Who Can Open a Traditional IRA, earlier. Even if contributions can't be made for the current year, the amounts contributed for years in which you did qualify can remain in your IRA. Contributions can resume for any years that you qualify.

Contributions must be made by due date. Contributions can be made to your traditional IRA for a year at any time during the year or by the due date for filing your return for that year, not including extensions. For most people, this means that contributions for 2020 must be made by April 15, 2021.

TIP *For tax years beginning after 2019, the rule that you are not able to make contributions to your traditional IRA for the year in which you reach age 70½ and all later years has been repealed.*

Designating year for which contribution is made. If an amount is contributed to your traditional IRA between January 1 and April 15, you should tell the sponsor which year (the current year or the previous year) the contribution is for. If you don't tell the sponsor which year it is for, the sponsor can assume, and report to the IRS, that the contribution is for the current year (the year the sponsor received it).

Filing before a contribution is made. You can file your return claiming a traditional IRA contribution before the contribution is actually made. Generally, the contribution must be made by the due date of your return, not including extensions.

Contributions not required. You don't have to contribute to your traditional IRA for every tax year, even if you can.

How Much Can You Deduct?

Generally, you can deduct the lesser of:

- The contributions to your traditional IRA for the year, or
- The general limit (or the Kay Bailey Hutchison Spousal IRA limit, if applicable) explained earlier under How Much Can Be Contributed.

However, if you or your spouse was covered by an employer retirement plan, you may not be able to deduct this amount. See Limit if Covered by Employer Plan, later.

TIP *You may be able to claim a credit for contributions to your traditional IRA. For more information, see chapter 3.*

Trustees' fees. Trustees' administrative fees that are billed separately and paid in connection with your traditional IRA aren't deductible as IRA contributions. You are also not able to deduct these fees as an itemized deduction.

Brokers' commissions. These commissions are part of your IRA contribution and, as such, are deductible subject to the limits.

Full deduction. If neither you nor your spouse was covered for any part of the year by an employer retirement plan, you can take a deduction for total contributions to one or more of your traditional IRAs of up to the lesser of:

- $6,000 ($7,000 if you are age 50 or older), or
- 100% of your compensation.

This limit is reduced by any contributions made to a 501(c)(18) plan on your behalf.

Kay Bailey Hutchison Spousal IRA. In the case of a married couple with unequal compensation who file a joint return, the deduction for contributions to the traditional IRA of the spouse with less compensation is limited to the lesser of:

1. $6,000 ($7,000 if the spouse with the lower compensation is age 50 or older), or
2. The total compensation includible in the gross income of both spouses for the year reduced by the following three amounts.

a. The IRA deduction for the year of the spouse with the greater compensation.

b. Any designated nondeductible contribution for the year made on behalf of the spouse with the greater compensation.

c. Any contributions for the year to a Roth IRA on behalf of the spouse with the greater compensation.

This limit is reduced by any contributions to a section 501(c)(18) plan on behalf of the spouse with the lesser compensation.

Note. If you were divorced or legally separated (and didn't remarry) before the end of the year, you can't deduct any contributions to your spouse's IRA. After a divorce or legal separation, you can deduct only the contributions to your own IRA. Your deductions are subject to the rules for single individuals.

Covered by an employer retirement plan. If you or your spouse was covered by an employer retirement plan at any time during the year for which contributions were made, your deduction may be further limited. This is discussed later under Limit if Covered by Employer Plan. Limits on the amount you can deduct don't affect the amount that can be contributed.

Are You Covered by an Employer Plan?

The Form W-2 you receive from your employer has a box used to indicate whether you were covered for the year. The "Retirement plan" box should be checked if you were covered.

Reservists and volunteer firefighters should also see Situations in Which You Aren't Covered, later.

If you aren't certain whether you were covered by your employer's retirement plan, you should ask your employer.

Federal judges. For purposes of the IRA deduction, federal judges are covered by an employer plan.

For Which Year(s) Are You Covered?

Special rules apply to determine the tax years for which you are covered by an employer plan. These rules differ depending on whether the plan is a defined contribution plan or a defined benefit plan.

Tax year. Your tax year is the annual accounting period you use to keep records and report income and expenses on your income tax return. For almost all people, the tax year is the calendar year.

Defined contribution plan. Generally, you are covered by a defined contribution plan for a tax year if amounts are contributed or allocated to your account for the plan year that ends with or within that tax year. However, also see Situations in Which You Aren't Covered, later.

A defined contribution plan is a plan that provides for a separate account for each person covered by the plan. In a defined contribution plan, the amount to be contributed to each participant's account is spelled out in the plan. The level of benefits actually provided to a participant depends on the total amount contributed to that participant's account and any earnings and losses on those contributions. Types of defined contribution plans include profit-sharing plans, stock bonus plans, and money purchase pension plans.

Example. Company A has a money purchase pension plan. Its plan year is from July 1 to June 30. The plan provides that contributions must be allocated as of June 30. Bob, an employee, leaves Company A on December 31, 2019. The contribution for the plan year ending on June 30, 2020, is made February 15, 2021. Because an amount is contributed to Bob's account for the plan year, Bob is covered by the plan for his 2020 tax year.

A special rule applies to certain plans in which it isn't possible to determine if an amount will be contributed to your account for a given plan year. If, for a plan year, no amounts have been allocated to your account that are attributable to employer contributions, employee contributions, or forfeitures, by the last day of the plan year, and contributions are discretionary for the plan year, you aren't covered for the tax year in which the plan year ends. If, after the plan year ends, the employer makes a contribution for that plan year, you are covered for the tax year in which the contribution is made.

Example. Mickey was covered by a profit-sharing plan and left the company on December 31, 2019. The plan year runs from July 1 to June 30. Under the terms of the plan, employer contributions don't have to be made, but if they are made, they are contributed to the plan before the due date for filing the company's tax return. Such contributions are allocated as of the last day of the plan year, and allocations are made to the accounts of individuals who have any service during the plan year. As of June 30, 2020, no contributions were made that were allocated to the June 30, 2020, plan year, and no forfeitures had been allocated within the plan year. In addition, as of that date, the company wasn't obligated to make a contribution for such plan year and it was impossible to determine whether or not a contribution would be made for the plan year. On December 31, 2020, the company decided to contribute to the plan for the plan year ending June 30, 2020. That contribution was made on February 15, 2021. Mickey is an active participant in the plan for his 2021 tax year but not for his 2020 tax year.

No vested interest. If an amount is allocated to your account for a plan year, you are covered by that plan even if you have no vested interest in (legal right to) the account.

Defined benefit plan. If you are eligible to participate in your employer's defined benefit plan for the plan year that ends within your tax year, you are covered by the plan. This rule applies even if you:

- Declined to participate in the plan,
- Didn't make a required contribution, or
- Didn't perform the minimum service required to accrue a benefit for the year.

A defined benefit plan is any plan that isn't a defined contribution plan. In a defined benefit plan, the level of benefits to be provided to each participant is spelled out in the plan. The plan administrator figures the amount needed to provide those benefits and those amounts are contributed to the plan. Defined benefit plans include pension plans and annuity plans.

Example. Nick, an employee of Company B, is eligible to participate in Company B's defined benefit plan, which has a July 1 to June 30 plan year. Nick leaves Company B on December 31, 2019. Because Nick is eligible to participate in the plan for its year ending June 30, 2020, he is covered by the plan for his 2020 tax year.

No vested interest. If you accrue a benefit for a plan year, you are covered by that plan even if you have no vested interest in (legal right to) the accrual.

Situations in Which You Aren't Covered

Unless you are covered by another employer plan, you aren't covered by an employer plan if you are in one of the situations described below.

Social security or railroad retirement. Coverage under social security or railroad retirement isn't coverage under an employer retirement plan.

Benefits from previous employer's plan. If you receive retirement benefits from a previous employer's plan, you aren't covered by that plan.

Reservists. If the only reason you participate in a plan is because you are a member of a reserve unit of the Armed Forces, you may not be covered by the plan. You aren't covered by the plan if both of the following conditions are met.

1. The plan you participate in is established for its employees by:
   a. The United States,
   b. A state or political subdivision of a state, or
   c. An instrumentality of either (a) or (b) above.
2. You didn't serve more than 90 days on active duty during the year (not counting duty for training).

Volunteer firefighters. If the only reason you participate in a plan is because you are a volunteer firefighter, you may not be covered by the plan. You aren't covered by the plan if both of the following conditions are met.

1. The plan you participate in is established for its employees by:
   a. The United States,
   b. A state or political subdivision of a state, or
   c. An instrumentality of either (a) or (b) above.
2. Your accrued retirement benefits at the beginning of the year won't provide more than $1,800 per year at retirement.

Limit if Covered by Employer Plan

As discussed earlier, the deduction you can take for contributions made to your traditional IRA depends on whether you or your spouse was covered for any part of the year by an employer retirement plan. Your deduction is also affected by how much income you had and by your filing status. Your deduction may also be affected by social security benefits you received.

Reduced or no deduction. If either you or your spouse was covered by an employer retirement plan, you may be entitled to only a partial (reduced) deduction or no deduction at all, depending on your income and your filing status.

Your deduction begins to decrease (phase out) when your income rises above a certain amount and is eliminated altogether when it reaches a higher amount. These amounts vary depending on your filing status.

To determine if your deduction is subject to the phaseout, you must determine your modified AGI and your filing status, as explained later under *Deduction Phaseout*. Once you have determined your modified AGI and your filing status, you can use Table 1-2 or Table 1-3 to determine if the phaseout applies.

Social Security Recipients

Instead of using Table 1-2 or Table 1-3 and Worksheet 1-2, complete the worksheets in Appendix B of this publication if, for the year, all of the following apply.

- You received social security benefits.
- You received taxable compensation.
- Contributions were made to your traditional IRA.
- You or your spouse were covered by an employer retirement plan.

Use the worksheets in Appendix B to figure your IRA deduction, your nondeductible contribution, and the taxable portion, if any, of your social security benefits. Appendix B includes an example with filled-in worksheets to assist you.

Deduction Phaseout

The amount of any reduction in the limit on your IRA deduction (phaseout) depends on whether you or your spouse was covered by an employer retirement plan.

Covered by a retirement plan. If you are covered by an employer retirement plan and you didn't receive any social security retirement benefits, your IRA deduction may be reduced or eliminated depending on your filing status and modified AGI, as shown in Table 1-2.

If your spouse is covered. If you aren't covered by an employer retirement plan, but your spouse is, and you didn't receive any social security benefits, your IRA deduction may be reduced or eliminated entirely depending on your filing status and modified AGI as shown in Table 1-3.

Filing status. Your filing status depends primarily on your marital status. For this purpose, you need to know if

Table 1-2. **Effect of Modified AGI[1] on Deduction if You Are Covered by a Retirement Plan at Work**

If you are covered by a retirement plan at work, use this table to determine if your modified AGI affects the amount of your deduction.

IF your filing status is...	AND your modified AGI is...	THEN you can take...
single or **head of household**	$65,000 or less	a full deduction.
	more than $65,000 but less than $75,000	a partial deduction.
	$75,000 or more	no deduction.
married filing jointly or **qualifying widow(er)**	$104,000 or less	a full deduction.
	more than $104,000 but less than $124,000	a partial deduction.
	$124,000 or more	no deduction.
married filing separately[2]	less than $10,000	a partial deduction.
	$10,000 or more	no deduction.

[1] Modified AGI (adjusted gross income). See *Modified adjusted gross income (AGI)*, later.
[2] If you didn't live with your spouse at any time during the year, your filing status is considered Single for this purpose (therefore, your IRA deduction is determined under the "Single" filing status).

Table 1-3. **Effect of Modified AGI[1] on Deduction if You Aren't Covered by a Retirement Plan at Work**

If you aren't covered by a retirement plan at work, use this table to determine if your modified AGI affects the amount of your deduction.

IF your filing status is...	AND your modified AGI is...	THEN you can take...
single, **head of household,** or **qualifying widow(er)**	any amount	a full deduction.
married filing jointly or **separately** with a spouse who ***isn't*** covered by a plan at work	any amount	a full deduction.
married filing jointly with a spouse who ***is*** covered by a plan at work	$196,000 or less	a full deduction.
	more than $196,000 but less than $206,000	a partial deduction.
	$206,000 or more	no deduction.
married filing separately with a spouse who ***is*** covered by a plan at work[2]	less than $10,000	a partial deduction.
	$10,000 or more	no deduction.

[1] Modified AGI (adjusted gross income). See *Modified adjusted gross income (AGI)*, later.
[2] You are entitled to the full deduction if you didn't live with your spouse at any time during the year.

your filing status is single or head of household, married filing jointly or qualifying widow(er), or married filing separately. If you need more information on filing status, see Pub. 501, Exemptions, Standard Deduction, and Filing Information.

Lived apart from spouse. If you didn't live with your spouse at any time during the year and you file a separate return, your filing status, for this purpose, is single.

Modified adjusted gross income (AGI). You can use Worksheet 1-1 to figure your modified AGI. If you made contributions to your IRA for 2020 and received a distribution from your IRA in 2020, see *Both contributions for 2020 and distributions in 2020*, later.

CAUTION *Don't assume that your modified AGI is the same as your compensation. Your modified AGI may include income in addition to your compensation (discussed earlier) such as interest, dividends, and income from IRA distributions.*

Form 1040 or 1040-SR. If you file Form 1040 or 1040-SR, refigure the amount on line 11, the "adjusted gross income" line, without taking into account any of the following amounts.

- IRA deduction.
- Student loan interest deduction.
- Tuition and fees deduction.
- Foreign earned income exclusion.
- Foreign housing exclusion or deduction.
- Exclusion of qualified savings bond interest shown on Form 8815.
- Exclusion of employer-provided adoption benefits shown on Form 8839.

This is your modified AGI.

Form 1040-NR. If you file Form 1040-NR, refigure the amount on line 11, the "adjusted gross income" line, without taking into account any of the following amounts.

- IRA deduction.
- Student loan interest deduction.
- Exclusion of qualified savings bond interest shown on Form 8815.
- Exclusion of employer-provided adoption benefits shown on Form 8839.

This is your modified AGI.

Income from IRA distributions. If you received distributions in 2020 from one or more traditional IRAs and your traditional IRAs include only deductible contributions, your distributions are fully taxable and are included in your modified AGI. See Pub. 590-B for more information on distributions.

Both contributions for 2020 and distributions in 2020. If all three of the following apply, any IRA distributions you received in 2020 may be partly tax free and partly taxable.

- You received distributions in 2020 from one or more traditional IRAs.
- You made contributions to a traditional IRA for 2020.
- Some of those contributions may be nondeductible contributions. (See *Nondeductible Contributions* and Worksheet 1-2, later.)

If this is your situation, you must figure the taxable part of the traditional IRA distribution before you can figure your modified AGI. To do this, you can use Worksheet 1-1 in Pub. 590-B.

If at least one of the above doesn't apply, figure your modified AGI using Worksheet 1-1.

How To Figure Your Reduced IRA Deduction

If you or your spouse is covered by an employer retirement plan and you didn't receive any social security benefits, you can figure your reduced IRA deduction by using Worksheet 1-2. The Instructions for Forms 1040 and 1040-SR include a similar worksheet that you can use instead of the worksheet in this publication.

If you or your spouse is covered by an employer retirement plan, and you received any social security benefits, see *Social Security Recipients*, earlier.

Note. If you were married and both you and your spouse contributed to IRAs, figure your deduction and your spouse's deduction separately.

Reporting Deductible Contributions

If you file Schedule 1 (Form 1040), enter your IRA deduction on line 19 of that form.

Self-employed. If you are self-employed (a sole proprietor or partner) and have a SIMPLE IRA, enter your deduction for allowable plan contributions on Schedule 1 (Form 1040), line 15.

Nondeductible Contributions

Although your deduction for IRA contributions may be reduced or eliminated, contributions can be made to your IRA of up to the general limit or, if it applies, the Kay Bailey Hutchison Spousal IRA limit. The difference between your total permitted contributions and your IRA deduction, if any, is your nondeductible contribution.

Example. Tony is 29 years old and single. In 2020, he was covered by a retirement plan at work. His salary is $72,000. His modified AGI is $90,000. Tony makes a $6,000 IRA contribution for 2020. Because he was covered by a retirement plan and his modified AGI is above $75,000, he can't deduct his $6,000 IRA contribution. He must designate this contribution as a nondeductible contribution by reporting it on Form 8606.

Repayment of reservist distributions. Nondeductible contributions may include repayments of qualified reservist distributions. For more information, see *Qualified reservist repayments* under *How Much Can Be Contributed*, earlier.

Difficulty of care payments. For contributions after December 20, 2019, you are able to elect to increase the nondeductible IRA contribution limit by some or all of the amount of difficulty of care payments, which are a type of qualified foster care payment, received. If you receive difficulty of care payments, then those amounts may increase the amount of nondeductible IRA contributions you can make but not above the $6,000 IRA deductible amount ($7,000 if you are age 50 or older). The increase to the nondeductible IRA contribution limit equals the lesser of (i) the amount of difficulty of care payments excluded from gross income, or (ii) the amount by which the deductible limit for IRA contributions exceeds the amount of the taxpayer's compensation included in gross income for the tax year.

Form 8606. To designate contributions as nondeductible, you must file Form 8606.

You don't have to designate a contribution as nondeductible until you file your tax return. When you file, you can even designate otherwise deductible contributions as nondeductible contributions.

You must file Form 8606 to report nondeductible contributions even if you don't have to file a tax return for the year.

CAUTION *A Form 8606 isn't used for the year that you make a rollover from a qualified retirement plan to a traditional IRA and the rollover includes nontaxable amounts. In those situations, a Form 8606 is completed for the year you take a distribution from that IRA. See* Form 8606 *under* Distributions Fully or Partly Taxable *in Pub. 590-B.*

Failure to report nondeductible contributions. If you don't report nondeductible contributions, all of the contributions to your traditional IRA will be treated like deductible contributions when withdrawn. All distributions from

Worksheet 1-1.**Figuring Your Modified AGI** *Keep for Your Records*

Use this worksheet to figure your modified AGI for traditional IRA purposes.

1.	Enter your adjusted gross income (AGI) from Form 1040, 1040-SR, or Form 1040-NR, line 11, figured without taking into account the amount from Schedule 1 (Form 1040), line 19	1.	
2.	Enter any student loan interest deduction from Schedule 1 (Form 1040), line 20	2.	
3.	Enter any tuition and fees deduction from Schedule 1 (Form 1040), line 21	3.	
4.	Enter any foreign earned income exclusion and/or housing exclusion from Form 2555, line 45	4.	
5.	Enter any foreign housing deduction from Form 2555, line 50	5.	
6.	Enter any excludable savings bond interest from Form 8815, line 14	6.	
7.	Enter any excluded employer-provided adoption benefits from Form 8839, line 28	7.	
8.	Add lines 1 through 7. This is your **Modified AGI** for traditional IRA purposes	8.	

your IRA will be taxed unless you can show, with satisfactory evidence, that nondeductible contributions were made.

Penalty for overstatement. If you overstate the amount of nondeductible contributions on your Form 8606 for any tax year, you must pay a penalty of $100 for each overstatement, unless it was due to reasonable cause.

Penalty for failure to file Form 8606. You will have to pay a $50 penalty if you don't file a required Form 8606, unless you can prove that the failure was due to reasonable cause.

Tax on earnings on nondeductible contributions. As long as contributions are within the contribution limits, none of the earnings or gains on contributions (deductible or nondeductible) will be taxed until they are distributed.

Cost basis. You will have a cost basis in your traditional IRA if you made any nondeductible contributions. Your cost basis is the sum of the nondeductible contributions to your IRA minus any withdrawals or distributions of nondeductible contributions.

CAUTION *Commonly, distributions from your traditional IRAs will include both taxable and nontaxable (cost basis) amounts. See Pub. 590-B for more information on distributions.*

RECORDS **Recordkeeping.** There is a recordkeeping worksheet, Appendix A. Summary Record of Traditional IRA(s) for 2020, that you can use to keep a record of deductible and nondeductible IRA contributions.

Examples—Worksheet for Reduced IRA Deduction for 2020

The following examples illustrate the use of Worksheet 1-2.

Example 1. For 2020, Tom and Betty file a joint return on Form 1040. They are both 39 years old. They are both employed. Tom is covered by his employer's retirement plan. However, Betty isn't covered by her employer's retirement plan. Tom's salary is $62,000, and Betty's is $34,500. They each have a traditional IRA and their combined modified AGI, which includes $9,000 interest and dividend income, is $105,500. Because their modified AGI is between $104,000 and $124,000 and Tom is covered by an employer plan, Tom is subject to the deduction phaseout discussed earlier under *Limit if Covered by Employer Plan*.

For 2020, Tom contributed $6,000 to his IRA, and Betty contributed $6,000 to hers. Even though they file a joint return, they must figure their IRA deduction separately.

Tom can take a deduction of only $5,550. Using Worksheet 1-2, Figuring Your Reduced IRA Deduction for 2020, Tom figures his deductible and nondeductible amounts as shown on Worksheet 1-2. Figuring Your Reduced IRA Deduction for 2020—Example 1 Illustrated.

He can choose to treat the $5,550 as either deductible or nondeductible contributions. He can either leave the $450 ($6,000 − $5,550) of nondeductible contributions in his IRA or withdraw them by April 15, 2021. He decides to treat the $5,550 as deductible contributions and leave the $450 of nondeductible contributions in his IRA.

Betty figures her IRA deduction as follows. Betty can treat all or part of her $6,000 contribution as either deductible or nondeductible. This is because she isn't covered by her employer's retirement plan, and their combined modified AGI isn't between $196,000 and $206,000. Therefore, she isn't subject to the deduction phaseout discussed earlier under *Limit if Covered by Employer Plan*, and she doesn't need to use Worksheet 1-2. Betty decides to treat her $6,000 IRA contributions as deductible.

The IRA deductions of $5,550 and $6,000 on the joint return for Tom and Betty total $11,550.

Example 2. For 2020, Ed and Sue file a joint return on Form 1040. They are both 39 years old. Ed is covered by his employer's retirement plan. Ed's salary is $45,000. Sue had no compensation for the year and didn't contribute to an IRA. Sue isn't covered by an employer plan. Ed contributed $6,000 to his traditional IRA and $6,000 to a traditional IRA for Sue (a Kay Bailey Hutchison Spousal IRA). Their combined modified AGI, which includes $2,000 interest and dividend income and a large capital gain from the sale of stock, is $198,555.

Because the combined modified AGI is $124,000 or more and Ed is covered by his employer's plan, he can't deduct any of the contribution to his traditional IRA. He can either leave the $6,000 of nondeductible contributions in his IRA or withdraw them by April 15, 2021.

Sue figures her IRA deduction as shown on Worksheet 1-2. Figuring Your Reduced IRA Deduction for 2020—Example 2 Illustrated.

Worksheet 1-2. **Figuring Your Reduced IRA Deduction for 2020**

Keep for Your Records

(Use only if you or your spouse is covered by an employer plan and your modified AGI falls between the two amounts shown below for your coverage situation and filing status.)

Note. If you were married and both you and your spouse contributed to IRAs, figure your deduction and your spouse's deduction separately.

IF you...	AND your filing status is...	AND your modified AGI is over...	THEN enter on line 1 below...
are **covered** by an employer plan	single or head of household	$65,000	$75,000
	married filing jointly or qualifying widow(er)	$104,000	$124,000
	married filing separately	$0	$10,000
aren't covered by an employer plan, but your spouse is **covered**	married filing jointly	$196,000	$206,000
	married filing separately	$0	$10,000

1. Enter applicable amount from table above . . . . . 1. ________
2. Enter your ***modified AGI*** (that of both spouses, if married filing jointly) . . . . . 2. ________

   Note. If line 2 is equal to or more than the amount on line 1, **stop here.** Your IRA contributions aren't deductible. See *Nondeductible Contributions*, earlier.
3. Subtract line 2 from line 1. **If line 3 is $10,000 or more ($20,000 or more if married filing jointly or qualifying widow(er) and you are covered by an employer plan), stop here.** You can take a full IRA deduction for contributions of up to $6,000 ($7,000 if you are age 50 or older) or 100% of your (and if married filing jointly, your spouse's) compensation, whichever is less . . . . . 3. ________
4. Multiply line 3 by the percentage below that applies to you. If the result isn't a multiple of $10, round it to the next highest multiple of $10. (For example, $611.40 is rounded to $620.) However, if the result is less than $200, enter $200.
   - Married filing jointly or qualifying widow(er) **and** you are covered by an employer plan, multiply line 3 by 30% (0.30) (by 35% (0.35) if you are age 50 or older).
   - All others, multiply line 3 by 60% (0.60) (by 70% (0.70) if you are age 50 or older). . . . . . 4. ________
5. Enter your compensation minus any deductions on Schedule 1 (Form 1040), line 14 (deductible part of self-employment tax), and Schedule 1 (Form 1040), line 15 (self-employed SEP, SIMPLE, and qualified plans). If you are filing a joint return and your compensation is less than your spouse's, include your spouse's compensation reduced by his or her traditional IRA and Roth IRA contributions for this year. If you file Form 1040, 1040-SR, or 1040-NR, don't reduce your compensation by any losses from self-employment . . . . . 5. ________
6. Enter contributions made, or to be made, to your IRA for 2020, but **don't** enter more than $6,000 ($7,000 if you are age 50 or older). If contributions are more than $6,000 ($7,000 if you are age 50 or older), see *Excess Contributions*, later . . . . . 6. ________
7. **IRA deduction.** Compare lines 4, 5, and 6. Enter the smallest amount (or a smaller amount if you choose) here and on your Schedule 1 (Form 1040), line 19. If line 6 is more than line 7 and you want to make a nondeductible contribution, go to line 8 . . . . . 7. ________
8. **Nondeductible contribution.** Subtract line 7 from line 5 or 6, whichever is smaller. Enter the result here and on line 1 of your Form 8606 . . . . . 8. ________

Worksheet 1-2. **Figuring Your Reduced IRA Deduction for 2020—Example 1 Illustrated**

(Use only if you or your spouse is covered by an employer plan and your modified AGI falls between the two amounts shown below for your coverage situation and filing status.)

Note. If you were married and both you and your spouse contributed to IRAs, figure your deduction and your spouse's deduction separately.

IF you...	**AND your filing status is...**	**AND your modified AGI is over...**	**THEN enter on line 1 below...**
are **covered** by an employer plan	single or head of household	$65,000	$75,000
	married filing jointly or qualifying widow(er)	$104,000	$124,000
	married filing separately	$0	$10,000
aren't covered by an employer plan, but your spouse is **covered**	married filing jointly	$196,000	$206,000
	married filing separately	$0	$10,000

1. Enter applicable amount from table above **1.** 124,000

2. Enter your ***modified AGI*** (that of both spouses, if married filing jointly) **2.** 105,500

   Note. If line 2 is equal to or more than the amount on line 1, **stop here.** Your IRA contributions are not deductible. See *Nondeductible Contributions*, earlier.

3. Subtract line 2 from line 1. **If line 3 is $10,000 or more ($20,000 or more if married filing jointly or qualifying widow(er) and you are covered by an employer plan), stop here.** You can take a full IRA deduction for contributions of up to $6,000 ($7,000 if you are age 50 or older) or 100% of your (and if married filing jointly, your spouse's) compensation, whichever is less **3.** 18,500

4. Multiply line 3 by the percentage below that applies to you. If the result isn't a multiple of $10, round it to the next highest multiple of $10. (For example, $611.40 is rounded to $620.) However, if the result is less than $200, enter $200.
   - Married filing jointly or qualifying widow(er) **and** you are covered by an employer plan, multiply line 3 by 30% (0.30) (by 35% (0.35) if you are age 50 or older). **4.** 5,550
   - All others, multiply line 3 by 60% (0.60) (by 70% (0.70) if you are age 50 or older).

5. Enter your compensation minus any deductions on Schedule 1 (Form 1040), line 14 (deductible part of self-employment tax) and Schedule 1 (Form 1040), line 15 (self-employed SEP, SIMPLE, and qualified plans). If you are filing a joint return and your compensation is less than your spouse's, include your spouse's compensation reduced by his or her traditional IRA and Roth IRA contributions for this year. If you file Form 1040, 1040-SR, or 1040-NR, don't reduce your compensation by any losses from self-employment **5.** 62,000

6. Enter contributions made, or to be made, to your IRA for 2020, but **don't** enter more than $6,000 ($7,000 if you are age 50 or older). If contributions are more than $6,000 ($7,000 if you are age 50 or older), see *Excess Contributions*, later **6.** 6,000

7. **IRA deduction.** Compare lines 4, 5, and 6. Enter the smallest amount (or a smaller amount if you choose) here and on your Schedule 1 (Form 1040), line 19. If line 6 is more than line 7 and you want to make a nondeductible contribution, go to line 8 . . . . . **7.** 5,550

8. **Nondeductible contribution.** Subtract line 7 from line 5 or 6, whichever is smaller. Enter the result here and on line 1 of your Form 8606 . . . . . **8.** 450

Page 18 Chapter 1 **Traditional IRAs**

Worksheet 1-2. **Figuring Your Reduced IRA Deduction for 2020—Example 2 Illustrated**

(Use only if you or your spouse is covered by an employer plan and your modified AGI falls between the two amounts shown below for your coverage situation and filing status.)

Note. If you were married and both you and your spouse contributed to IRAs, figure your deduction and your spouse's deduction separately.

IF you...	**AND your filing status is...**	**AND your modified AGI is over...**	**THEN enter on line 1 below...**
are **covered** by an employer plan	single or head of household	$65,000	$75,000
	married filing jointly or qualifying widow(er)	$104,000	$124,000
	married filing separately	$0	$10,000
aren't covered by an employer plan, but your spouse is **covered**	married filing jointly	$196,000	$206,000
	married filing separately	$0	$10,000

1. Enter applicable amount from table above **1.** 206,000

2. Enter your ***modified AGI*** (that of both spouses, if married filing jointly) **2.** 198,555

   Note. If line 2 is equal to or more than the amount on line 1, **stop here.** Your IRA contributions aren't deductible. See *Nondeductible Contributions*, earlier.

3. Subtract line 2 from line 1. **If line 3 is $10,000 or more ($20,000 or more if married filing jointly or qualifying widow(er) and you are covered by an employer plan), stop here.** You can take a full IRA deduction for contributions of up to $6,000 ($7,000 if you are age 50 or older) or 100% of your (and if married filing jointly, your spouse's) compensation, whichever is less **3.** 7,445

4. Multiply line 3 by the percentage below that applies to you. If the result isn't a multiple of $10, round it to the next highest multiple of $10. (For example, $611.40 is rounded to $620.) However, if the result is less than $200, enter $200.
   - Married filing jointly or qualifying widow(er) **and** you are covered by an employer plan, multiply line 3 by 30% (0.30) (by 35% (0.35) if you are age 50 or older).
   - All others, multiply line 3 by 60% (0.60) (by 70% (0.70) if you are age 50 or older). **4.** 4,470

5. Enter your compensation minus any deductions on Schedule 1 (Form 1040), line 14 (deductible part of self-employment tax) and Schedule 1 (Form 1040), line 15 (self-employed SEP, SIMPLE, and qualified plans). If you are filing a joint return and your compensation is less than your spouse's, include your spouse's compensation reduced by his or her traditional IRA and Roth IRA contributions for this year. If you file Form 1040, 1040-SR, or 1040-NR, don't reduce your compensation by any losses from self-employment **5.** 39,000

6. Enter contributions made, or to be made, to your IRA for 2020, but **don't** enter more than $6,000 ($7,000 if you are age 50 or older). If contributions are more than $6,000 ($7,000 if you are age 50 or older), see *Excess Contributions*, later **6.** 6,000

7. **IRA deduction.** Compare lines 4, 5, and 6. Enter the smallest amount (or a smaller amount if you choose) here and on your Schedule 1 (Form 1040), line 19, whichever applies. If line 6 is more than line 7 and you want to make a nondeductible contribution, go to line 8 . . . . . **7.** 4,470

8. **Nondeductible contribution.** Subtract line 7 from line 5 or 6, whichever is smaller. Enter the result here and on line 1 of your Form 8606 . . . . . **8.** 1,530

What if You Inherit an IRA?

If you inherit a traditional IRA, you are called a beneficiary. A beneficiary can be any person or entity the owner chooses to receive the benefits of the IRA after he or she dies. Beneficiaries of a traditional IRA must include in their gross income any taxable distributions they receive.

Inherited From Spouse

If you inherit a traditional IRA from your spouse, you generally have the following three choices. You can do one of the following.

1. Treat it as your own IRA by designating yourself as the account owner.
2. Treat it as your own by rolling it over into your IRA, or to the extent it is taxable, into a:
   a. Qualified employer plan,
   b. Qualified employee annuity plan (section 403(a) plan),
   c. Tax-sheltered annuity plan (section 403(b) plan), or
   d. Deferred compensation plan of a state or local government (section 457 plan).
3. Treat yourself as the beneficiary rather than treating the IRA as your own.

Treating it as your own. You will be considered to have chosen to treat the IRA as your own if:

- Contributions (including rollover contributions) are made to the inherited IRA, or
- You don't take the required minimum distribution for a year as a beneficiary of the IRA.

You will only be considered to have chosen to treat the IRA as your own if:

- You are the sole beneficiary of the IRA, and
- You have an unlimited right to withdraw amounts from it.

However, if you receive a distribution from your deceased spouse's IRA, you can roll that distribution over into your own IRA within the 60-day time limit, as long as the distribution isn't a required distribution, even if you aren't the sole beneficiary of your deceased spouse's IRA. For more information, see *When Must You Withdraw Assets? (Required Minimum Distributions)* in Pub. 590-B for more information on required minimum distributions.

Inherited From Someone Other Than Spouse

If you inherit a traditional IRA from anyone other than your deceased spouse, you can't treat the inherited IRA as your own. This means that you can't make any contributions to the IRA. It also means you can't roll over any amounts into or out of the inherited IRA. However, you can make a trustee-to-trustee transfer as long as the IRA into which amounts are being moved is set up and maintained in the name of the deceased IRA owner for the benefit of you as beneficiary. See Pub. 590-B for more information.

Like the original owner, you generally won't owe tax on the assets in the IRA until you receive distributions from it. You must begin receiving distributions from the IRA under the rules for distributions that apply to beneficiaries.

More information. For more information about rollovers, required distributions, and inherited IRAs, see:

- Rollovers, later, under *Can You Move Retirement Plan Assets;*
- *When Must You Withdraw Assets? (Required Minimum Distributions)* in Pub. 590-B; and
- The discussion of IRA Beneficiaries under *When Must You Withdraw Assets? (Required Minimum Distributions)* in Pub. 590-B.

Can You Move Retirement Plan Assets?

You can transfer, tax free, assets (money or property) from other retirement programs (including traditional IRAs) to a traditional IRA. You can make the following kinds of transfers.

- Transfers from one trustee to another.
- Rollovers.
- Transfers incident to a divorce.

This chapter discusses all three kinds of transfers.

Transfers to Roth IRAs. Under certain conditions, you can move assets from a traditional IRA or from a designated Roth account to a Roth IRA. For more information about these transfers, see Converting From Any Traditional IRA Into a Roth IRA, later in this chapter, and Can You Move Amounts Into a Roth IRA? in chapter 2.

Transfers to Roth IRAs from other retirement plans. Under certain conditions, you can move assets from a qualified retirement plan to a Roth IRA. For more information, see Can You Move Amounts Into a Roth IRA? in chapter 2.

Trustee-to-Trustee Transfer

A transfer of funds in your traditional IRA from one trustee directly to another, either at your request or at the trustee's request, isn't a rollover. This includes the situation where the current trustee issues a check to the new trustee but gives it to you to deposit. Because there is no distribution to you, the transfer is tax free. Because it isn't a rollover, it isn't affected by the 1-year waiting period required between rollovers. This waiting period is discussed later under Rollover From One IRA Into Another.

For information about direct transfers from retirement programs other than traditional IRAs, see Direct rollover option, later.

Rollovers

Generally, a rollover is a tax-free distribution to you of cash or other assets from one retirement plan that you contribute to another retirement plan within 60 days you received the payment or distribution. The contribution to the second retirement plan is called a "rollover contribution."

Note. An amount rolled over tax free from one retirement plan to another is generally includible in income when it is distributed from the second plan.

Kinds of rollovers to a traditional IRA. You can roll over amounts from the following plans into a traditional IRA.

- A traditional IRA.
- An employer's qualified retirement plan for its employees.
- A deferred compensation plan of a state or local government (section 457 plan).
- A tax-sheltered annuity plan (section 403 plan).

Also, see Table 1-4.

Treatment of rollovers. You can't deduct a rollover contribution, but you must report the rollover distribution on your tax return as discussed later under Reporting rollovers from IRAs and Reporting rollovers from employer plans.

Rollover notice. A written explanation of rollover treatment must be given to you by the plan (other than an IRA) making the distribution. See Written explanation to recipients, later, for more details.

Kinds of rollovers from a traditional IRA. You may be able to roll over, tax free, a distribution from your traditional IRA into a qualified plan. These plans include the Federal Thrift Savings Plan (for federal employees), deferred compensation plans of state or local governments (section 457 plans), and tax-sheltered annuity plans (section 403(b) plans). The part of the distribution that you can roll over is the part that would otherwise be taxable (includible in your income). Qualified plans may, but aren't required to, accept such rollovers.

Tax treatment of a rollover from a traditional IRA to an eligible retirement plan other than an IRA. Ordinarily, when you have basis in your IRAs, any distribution is considered to include both nontaxable and taxable amounts. Without a special rule, the nontaxable portion of such a distribution couldn't be rolled over. However, a special rule treats a distribution you roll over into an eligible retirement plan as including only otherwise taxable amounts if the amount you either leave in your IRAs or don't roll over is at least equal to your basis. The effect of this special rule is to make the amount in your traditional IRAs that you can roll over to an eligible retirement plan as large as possible.

Eligible retirement plans. The following are considered eligible retirement plans.

- IRAs.
- Qualified trusts.
- Qualified employee annuity plans under section 403(a).
- Deferred compensation plans of state and local governments (section 457 plans).
- Tax-sheltered annuities (section 403(b) annuities).

Time Limit for Making a Rollover Contribution

You must generally make the rollover contribution by the 60th day after the day you receive the distribution from your traditional IRA or your employer's plan.

Example. You received an eligible rollover distribution from your traditional IRA on June 30, 2020, that you intend to roll over to your 403(b) plan. To postpone including the distribution in your income, you must complete the rollover by August 29, 2020, the 60th day following June 30.

The IRS may waive the 60-day requirement where the failure to do so would be against equity or good conscience, such as in the event of a casualty, disaster, or other event beyond your reasonable control. For exceptions to the 60-day period, see Ways to get a waiver of the 60-day rollover requirement, later.

Plan loan offset. A plan loan offset is the amount your employer plan account balance is reduced, or offset, to repay a loan from the plan. How long you have to complete the rollover of a plan loan offset depends on what kind of plan loan offset you have. For tax years beginning after December 31, 2017, if you have a qualified plan loan offset, you will have until the due date (including extensions) for your tax return for the tax year in which the offset occurs to complete your rollover. A qualified plan loan offset occurs when a plan loan in good standing is offset because your employer plan terminates, or because you sever from employment. If your plan loan offset occurs for any other reason, then you have 60 days from the date the offset occurs to complete your rollover.

Rollovers completed after the 60-day period. In the absence of a waiver, amounts not rolled over within the 60-day period don't qualify for tax-free rollover treatment. You must treat them as a taxable distribution from either your IRA or your employer's plan. These amounts are taxable in the year distributed, even if the 60-day period

Table 1-4. **Rollover Chart**

The following chart indicates the rollovers that are permitted between various types of plans.

		Roll To							
		Roth IRA	**Traditional IRA**	**SIMPLE IRA**	**SEP IRA**	**Govern-mental 457(b) Plan**	**Qualified Plan[1] (pre-tax)**	**403(b) Plan (pre-tax)**	**Designated Roth Account (401(k), 403(b), or 457(b))**
Roll From	**Roth IRA**	Yes[2]	No	No	No	No	No	No	No
	Traditional IRA	Yes[3]	Yes[2]	Yes[2, 7], after 2 years	Yes[2]	Yes[4]	Yes	Yes	No
	SIMPLE IRA	Yes[3], after 2 years	Yes[2], after 2 years	Yes[2]	Yes[2], after 2 years	Yes[4], after 2 years	Yes, after 2 years	Yes, after 2 years	No
	SEP IRA	Yes[3]	Yes[2]	Yes[2, 7], after 2 years	Yes[2]	Yes[4]	Yes	Yes	No
	Govern-mental 457(b) Plan	Yes[3]	Yes	Yes[7], after 2 years	Yes	Yes	Yes	Yes	Yes,[3, 5]
	Qualified Plan[1] (pre-tax)	Yes[3]	Yes	Yes[7], after 2 years	Yes	Yes[4]	Yes	Yes	Yes,[3, 5]
	403(b) Plan (pre-tax)	Yes[3]	Yes	Yes[7], after 2 years	Yes	Yes[4]	Yes	Yes	Yes,[3, 5]
	Designated Roth Account (401(k), 403(b), or 457(b))	Yes	No	No	No	No	No	No	Yes[6]

[1] Qualified plans include, for example, profit-sharing, 401(k), money purchase, and defined benefit plans.
[2] Only one rollover in any 12-month period.
[3] Must include in income.
[4] Must have separate accounts.
[5] Must be an in-plan rollover.
[6] Any nontaxable amounts distributed must be rolled over by direct trustee-to-trustee transfer.
[7] Applies to rollover contributions after December 18, 2015. For more information regarding retirement plans and rollovers, go to *Tax Information for Retirement Plans*.

expires in the next year. You may also have to pay a 10% additional tax on early distributions as discussed under *Early Distributions* in Pub. 590-B.

Unless there is a waiver or an extension of the 60-day rollover period, any contribution you make to your IRA more than 60 days after the distribution is a regular contribution, not a rollover contribution.

Example. You received a distribution in late December 2020 from a traditional IRA that you don't roll over into another traditional IRA within the 60-day limit. You don't qualify for a waiver. This distribution is taxable in 2020 even though the 60-day limit wasn't up until 2021.

Ways to get a waiver of the 60-day rollover requirement. There are three ways to obtain a waiver of the 60-day rollover requirement.

- You qualify for an automatic waiver.
- You self-certify that you met the requirements of a waiver.
- You request and receive a private letter ruling granting a waiver.

How do you qualify for an automatic waiver? You qualify for an automatic waiver if all of the following apply.

- The financial institution receives the funds on your behalf before the end of the 60-day rollover period.
- You followed all of the procedures set by the financial institution for depositing the funds into an IRA or other eligible retirement plan within the 60-day rollover period (including giving instructions to deposit the funds into a plan or IRA).
- The funds aren't deposited into a plan or IRA within the 60-day rollover period solely because of an error on the part of the financial institution.

- The funds are deposited into a plan or IRA within 1 year from the beginning of the 60-day rollover period.
- It would have been a valid rollover if the financial institution had deposited the funds as instructed.

If you don't qualify for an automatic waiver, you can use the self-certification procedure to make a late rollover contribution or you can apply to the IRS for a waiver of the 60-day rollover requirement.

How do you self-certify that you qualify for a waiver? Pursuant to Revenue Procedure 2016-47 in Internal Revenue Bulletin 2016-37, available at *IRB 2016-37*, you may make a written certification to a plan administrator or an IRA trustee that you missed the 60-day rollover contribution deadline because of one or more of the 11 reasons listed in Revenue Procedure 2016-47. A plan administrator or an IRA trustee may rely on the certification in accepting and reporting receipt of the rollover contribution. You may make the certification by using the model letter in the appendix to the revenue procedure or by using a letter that is substantially similar. There is no IRS fee for self-certification. A copy of the certification should be kept in your files and be available if requested on audit.

Note. A self-certification is not a waiver by the IRS of the 60-day rollover requirement. If the IRS subsequently audits your income tax return, it may determine that you do not qualify for a waiver, in which case you may owe additional taxes and penalties.

How do you apply for a waiver and what is the fee? You can request a ruling according to the procedures outlined in Revenue Procedure 2003-16 and Revenue Procedure 2021-4. The appropriate user fee of $10,000 must accompany every request for a waiver of the 60-day rollover requirement (see the user fee chart in Appendix A of Revenue Procedure 2021-4).

How does the IRS determine whether to grant a waiver in a private letter ruling? In determining whether to issue a favorable letter ruling granting a waiver, the IRS will consider all of the relevant facts and circumstances, including:

- Whether errors were made by the financial institution, that is, the plan administrator, or IRA trustee, issuer or custodian;
- Whether you were unable to complete the rollover within the 60-day period due to death, disability, hospitalization, incarceration, serious illness, restrictions imposed by a foreign country, or postal error;
- Whether you used the amount distributed; and
- How much time has passed since the date of the distribution.

Note. The IRS can waive only the 60-day rollover requirement and not the other requirements for a valid rollover contribution. For example, the IRS can't waive the IRA one-rollover-per-year rule.

For more information on waivers of the 60-day rollover requirement, go to *RetirementPlans-FAQs*.

Amount. The rules regarding the amount that can be rolled over within the 60-day time period also apply to the amount that can be deposited due to a waiver. For example, if you received $6,000 from your IRA, the most that you can deposit into an eligible retirement plan due to a waiver is $6,000.

Extension of rollover period. If an amount distributed to you from a traditional IRA or a qualified employer retirement plan is a frozen deposit at any time during the 60-day period allowed for a rollover, two special rules extend the rollover period.

- The period during which the amount is a frozen deposit isn't counted in the 60-day period.
- The 60-day period can't end earlier than 10 days after the deposit is no longer frozen.

Frozen deposit. This is any deposit that can't be withdrawn from a financial institution because of either of the following reasons.

- The financial institution is bankrupt or insolvent.
- The state where the institution is located restricts withdrawals because one or more financial institutions in the state are (or are about to be) bankrupt or insolvent.

Rollover From One IRA Into Another

You can withdraw, tax free, all or part of the assets from one traditional IRA if you reinvest them within 60 days in the same or another traditional IRA. Because this is a rollover, you can't deduct the amount that you reinvest in an IRA.

TIP *You may be able to treat a contribution made to one type of IRA as having been made to a different type of IRA. This is called recharacterizing the contribution. See* Recharacterizations *in this chapter for more information.*

Waiting period between rollovers. Generally, if you make a tax-free rollover of any part of a distribution from a traditional IRA, you can't, within a 1-year period, make a tax-free rollover of any later distribution from that same IRA. You also can't make a tax-free rollover of any amount distributed, within the same 1-year period, from the IRA into which you made the tax-free rollover.

The 1-year period begins on the date you receive the IRA distribution, not on the date you roll it over into an IRA. Rules apply to the number of rollovers you can have with your traditional IRAs. See *Application of one-rollover-per-year limitation*, later.

Example. You have two traditional IRAs, IRA-1 and IRA-2. In 2020, you made a tax-free rollover of a distribution from IRA-1 into a new traditional IRA (IRA-3). You can't, within 1 year of the distribution from IRA-1, make a tax-free rollover of any distribution from either IRA-1 or IRA-3 into another traditional IRA.

For 2020, the rollover from IRA-1 into IRA-3 prevents you from making a tax-free rollover from IRA-2 into any other traditional IRA. This is because in 2020 you are only allowed to make one rollover within a 1-year period. So when you make a rollover from IRA-1 to IRA-3, you can't make a rollover from IRA-2 to any other traditional IRA.

Exception. An IRA distribution made from a failed financial institution by the Federal Deposit Insurance Corporation as receiver is not treated as a rollover for purposes of the one-rollover-per-year limitation, provided:

1. Neither the failed financial institution nor the depositor initiated the distribution, and
2. No financial institution has assumed the IRAs of the failed financial institution.

Application of one-rollover-per-year limitation. You can make only one rollover from an IRA to another (or the same) IRA in any 1-year period regardless of the number of IRAs you own. The limit will apply by aggregating all of an individual's IRAs, including SEP and SIMPLE IRAs as well as traditional and Roth IRAs, effectively treating them as one IRA for purposes of the limit. However, trustee-to-trustee transfers between IRAs aren't limited and rollovers from traditional IRAs to Roth IRAs (conversions) aren't limited.

Example. John has three traditional IRAs: IRA-1, IRA-2, and IRA-3. John didn't take any distributions from his IRAs in 2020. On January 1, 2021, John took a distribution from IRA-1 and rolled it over into IRA-2 on the same day. For 2021, John can't roll over any other 2021 IRA distribution, including a rollover distribution involving IRA-3. This wouldn't apply to a conversion.

The same property must be rolled over. If property is distributed to you from an IRA and you complete the rollover by contributing property to an IRA, your rollover is tax free only if the property you contribute is the same property that was distributed to you.

Partial rollovers. If you withdraw assets from a traditional IRA, you can roll over part of the withdrawal tax free and keep the rest of it. The amount you keep will generally be taxable (except for the part that is a return of nondeductible contributions). The amount you keep may be subject to the 10% additional tax on early distributions discussed later under *What Acts Result in Penalties or Additional Taxes*.

Required distributions. Amounts that must be distributed during a particular year under the required distribution rules (discussed in Pub. 590-B) aren't eligible for rollover treatment.

Inherited IRAs. If you inherit a traditional IRA from your spouse, you can generally roll it over, or you can choose to make the inherited IRA your own as discussed earlier under *What if You Inherit an IRA*.

Reporting rollovers from IRAs. Report any rollover from one traditional IRA to the same or another traditional IRA on Form 1040, 1040-SR, or 1040-NR, lines 4a and 4b.

Enter the total amount of the distribution on Form 1040, 1040-SR, or 1040-NR, line 4a. If the total amount on Form 1040, 1040-SR or 1040-NR, line 4a, was rolled over, enter zero on Form 1040, 1040-SR, or 1040-NR, line 4b. If the total distribution wasn't rolled over, enter the taxable portion of the part that wasn't rolled over on Form 1040, 1040-SR, or 1040-NR, line 4b. Enter "Rollover" next to line 4b. See your tax return instructions.

If you rolled over the distribution into a qualified plan (other than an IRA) or you make the rollover in 2021, attach a statement explaining what you did.

For information on how to figure the taxable portion, see *Are Distributions Taxable?* in Pub. 590-B.

Rollover From Employer's Plan Into an IRA

You can roll over into a traditional IRA all or part of an eligible rollover distribution you receive from your (or your deceased spouse's):

- Employer's qualified pension, profit-sharing, or stock bonus plan;
- Annuity plan;
- Tax-sheltered annuity plan (section 403(b) plan); or
- Governmental deferred compensation plan (section 457 plan).

A qualified plan is one that meets the requirements of the Internal Revenue Code.

Eligible rollover distribution. Generally, an eligible rollover distribution is any distribution of all or part of the balance to your credit in a qualified retirement plan except the following.

1. A required minimum distribution (explained under *When Must You Withdraw Assets? (Required Minimum Distributions)* in Pub. 590-B).
2. A hardship distribution.
3. Any of a series of substantially equal periodic distributions paid at least once a year over:
   a. Your lifetime or life expectancy,
   b. The lifetimes or life expectancies of you and your beneficiary, or
   c. A period of 10 years or more.
4. Corrective distributions of excess contributions or excess deferrals, and any income allocable to the excess, or of excess annual additions and any allocable gains.
5. A loan treated as a distribution because it doesn't satisfy certain requirements either when made or later (such as upon default), unless the participant's accrued benefits are reduced (offset) to repay the loan. See the discussion earlier of plan loan offsets (including qualified plan loan offsets) under *Time Limit for Making a Rollover Contribution*.
6. Dividends on employer securities.
7. The cost of life insurance coverage.

Your rollover into a traditional IRA may include both amounts that would be taxable and amounts that wouldn't be taxable if they were distributed to you, but not rolled over. To the extent the distribution is rolled over into a traditional IRA, it isn't includible in your income.

TIP *Any nontaxable amounts that you roll over into your traditional IRA become part of your basis (cost) in your IRAs. To recover your basis when you take distributions from your IRA, you must complete Form 8606 for the year of the distribution. See* Form 8606 *under* Distributions Fully or Partly Taxable *in Pub. 590-B.*

Rollover by nonspouse beneficiary. If you are a designated beneficiary (other than a surviving spouse) of a deceased employee, you can roll over all or part of an eligible rollover distribution from one of the types of plans listed above into a traditional IRA. You must make the rollover by a direct trustee-to-trustee transfer into an inherited IRA.

You will determine your required minimum distributions in years after you make the rollover based on whether the employee died before his or her required beginning date for taking distributions from the plan. For more information, see *Distributions after the employee's death* under *Tax on Excess Accumulation* in Pub. 575.

Written explanation to recipients. Before making an eligible rollover distribution, the administrator of a qualified retirement plan must provide you with a written explanation. It must tell you about all of the following.

- Your right to have the distribution paid tax free directly to a traditional IRA or another eligible retirement plan.
- The requirement to withhold tax from the distribution if it isn't paid directly to a traditional IRA or another eligible retirement plan.
- The tax treatment of any part of the distribution that you roll over to a traditional IRA or another eligible retirement plan within 60 days after you receive the distribution.
- Other qualified retirement plan rules, if they apply, including those for lump-sum distributions, alternate payees, and cash or deferred arrangements.
- How the plan receiving the distribution differs from the plan making the distribution in its restrictions and tax consequences.

The plan administrator must provide you with this written explanation no earlier than 90 days and no later than 30 days before the distribution is made.

However, you can choose to have a distribution made less than 30 days after the explanation is provided as long as both of the following requirements are met.

- You are given at least 30 days after the notice is provided to consider whether you want to elect a direct rollover.
- You are given information that clearly states that you have this 30-day period to make the decision.

Contact the plan administrator if you have any questions regarding this information.

Withholding requirement. Generally, if an eligible rollover distribution is paid directly to you, the payer must withhold 20% of it. This applies even if you plan to roll over the distribution to a traditional IRA. You can avoid withholding by choosing the direct rollover option, discussed later.

Exceptions. The payer doesn't have to withhold from an eligible rollover distribution paid to you if either of the following conditions applies.

- The distribution and all previous eligible rollover distributions you received during your tax year from the same plan (or, at the payer's option, from all your employer's plans) total less than $200.
- The distribution consists solely of employer securities, plus cash of $200 or less in lieu of fractional shares.

CAUTION *The amount withheld is part of the distribution. If you roll over less than the full amount of the distribution, you may have to include in your income the amount you don't roll over. However, you can make up the amount withheld with funds from other sources.*

Other withholding rules. The 20% withholding requirement doesn't apply to distributions that aren't eligible rollover distributions. However, other withholding rules apply to these distributions. The rules that apply depend on whether the distribution is a periodic distribution or a nonperiodic distribution. For either of these types of distributions, you can still choose not to have tax withheld. For more information, see Pub. 575.

Direct rollover option. Your employer's qualified plan must give you the option to have any part of an eligible rollover distribution paid directly to a traditional IRA. The plan isn't required to give you this option if your eligible rollover distributions are expected to total less than $200 for the year.

Withholding. If you choose the direct rollover option, no tax is withheld from any part of the designated distribution that is directly paid to the trustee of the traditional IRA.

If any part is paid to you, the payer must withhold 20% of that part's taxable amount.

Choosing an option. Table 1-5 may help you decide which distribution option to choose. Carefully compare the effects of each option.

Table 1-5. **Comparison of Payment to You Versus Direct Rollover**

Affected item	Result of a payment to you	Result of a direct rollover
Withholding	The payer must withhold 20% of the taxable part.	There is no withholding.
Additional tax	If you are under age 59½, a 10% additional tax may apply to the taxable part (including an amount equal to the tax withheld) that isn't rolled over.	There is no 10% additional tax. See *Early Distributions* in Pub. 590-B.
When to report as income	Any taxable part (including the taxable part of any amount withheld) not rolled over is income to you in the year paid.	Any taxable part isn't income to you until later distributed to you from the IRA.

TIP *If you decide to roll over any part of a distribution, the direct rollover option will generally be to your advantage. This is because you won't have 20%*

withholding or be subject to the 10% additional tax under that option.

If you have a lump-sum distribution and don't plan to roll over any part of it, the distribution may be eligible for special tax treatment that could lower your tax for the distribution year. In that case, you may want to see Pub. 575 and Form 4972, Tax on Lump-Sum Distributions, and its instructions to determine whether your distribution qualifies for special tax treatment and, if so, to figure your tax under the special methods.

You can then compare any advantages from using Form 4972 to figure your tax on the lump-sum distribution with any advantages from rolling over all or part of the distribution. However, if you roll over any part of the lump-sum distribution, you can't use the Form 4972 special tax treatment for any part of the distribution.

Contributions you made to your employer's plan. You can roll over a distribution of voluntary deductible employee contributions (DECs) you made to your employer's plan. Prior to January 1, 1987, employees could make and deduct these contributions to certain qualified employers' plans and government plans. These aren't the same as an employee's elective contributions to a 401(k) plan, which aren't deductible by the employee.

If you receive a distribution from your employer's qualified plan of any part of the balance of your DECs and the earnings from them, you can roll over any part of the distribution.

No waiting period between rollovers. The once-a-year limit on IRA-to-IRA rollovers doesn't apply to eligible rollover distributions from an employer plan. You can roll over more than one distribution from the same employer plan within a year.

IRA as a holding account (conduit IRA) for rollovers to other eligible plans. If you receive an eligible rollover distribution from your employer's plan, you can roll over part or all of it into one or more conduit IRAs. You can later roll over those assets into a new employer's plan. You can use a traditional IRA as a conduit IRA. You can roll over part or all of the conduit IRA to a qualified plan, even if you make regular contributions to it or add funds from sources other than your employer's plan. However, if you make regular contributions to the conduit IRA or add funds from other sources, the qualified plan into which you move funds won't be eligible for any optional tax treatment for which it might have otherwise qualified.

Property and cash received in a distribution. If you receive both property and cash in an eligible rollover distribution, you can roll over part or all of the property, part or all of the cash, or any combination of the two that you choose.

The same property (or sales proceeds) must be rolled over. If you receive property in an eligible rollover distribution from a qualified retirement plan, you can't keep the property and contribute cash to a traditional IRA in place of the property. You must either roll over the property or sell it and roll over the proceeds, as explained next.

Sale of property received in a distribution from a qualified plan. Instead of rolling over a distribution of property other than cash, you can sell all or part of the property and roll over the amount you receive from the sale (the proceeds) into a traditional IRA. You can't keep the property and substitute your own funds for property you received.

Example. You receive a total distribution from your employer's plan consisting of $10,000 cash and $15,000 worth of property. You decide to keep the property. You can roll over to a traditional IRA the $10,000 cash received, but you can't roll over an additional $15,000 representing the value of the property you choose not to sell.

Treatment of gain or loss. If you sell the distributed property and roll over all the proceeds into a traditional IRA, no gain or loss is recognized. The sale proceeds (including any increase in value) are treated as part of the distribution and aren't included in your gross income.

Example. On September 6, Mike received a lump-sum distribution from his employer's retirement plan of $50,000 in cash and $50,000 in stock. The stock wasn't stock of his employer. On September 24, he sold the stock for $60,000. On October 6, he rolled over $110,000 in cash ($50,000 from the original distribution and $60,000 from the sale of stock). Mike doesn't include the $10,000 gain from the sale of stock as part of his income because he rolled over the entire amount into a traditional IRA.

Note. Special rules may apply to distributions of employer securities. For more information, see *Figuring the Taxable Amount* under *Taxation of Nonperiodic Payments* in Pub. 575.

Partial rollover. If you received both cash and property, or just property, but didn't roll over the entire distribution, see *Rollovers* in Pub. 575.

Life insurance contract. You can't roll over a life insurance contract from a qualified plan into a traditional IRA.

Distributions received by a surviving spouse. If you receive an eligible rollover distribution (defined earlier) from your deceased spouse's eligible retirement plan (defined earlier), you can roll over part or all of it into a traditional IRA. You can also roll over all or any part of a distribution of DECs.

Distributions under divorce or similar proceedings (alternate payees). If you are the spouse or former spouse of an employee and you receive a distribution from a qualified retirement plan as a result of divorce or similar proceedings, you may be able to roll over all or part of it into a traditional IRA. To qualify, the distribution must be:

- One that would have been an eligible rollover distribution (defined earlier) if it had been made to the employee, and
- Made under a qualified domestic relations order.

Qualified domestic relations order. A domestic relations order is a judgment, decree, or order (including approval of a property settlement agreement) that is issued under the domestic relations law of a state. A "qualified domestic relations order" gives to an alternate payee (a spouse, former spouse, child, or dependent of a participant in a retirement plan) the right to receive all or part of the benefits that would be payable to a participant under the plan. The order requires certain specific information, and it can't alter the amount or form of the benefits of the plan.

Tax treatment if all of an eligible distribution isn't rolled over. Any part of an eligible rollover distribution that you keep is taxable in the year you receive it. If you don't roll over any of it, special rules for lump-sum distributions may apply. See *Lump-Sum Distributions* under *Taxation of Nonperiodic Payments* in Pub. 575. The 10% additional tax on early distributions, discussed later under *What Acts Result in Penalties or Additional Taxes*, doesn't apply.

Keogh plans and rollovers. If you are self-employed, you are generally treated as an employee for rollover purposes. Consequently, if you receive an eligible rollover distribution from a Keogh plan (a qualified plan with at least one self-employed participant), you can roll over all or part of the distribution (including a lump-sum distribution) into a traditional IRA. For information on lump-sum distributions, see *Lump-Sum Distributions* under *Taxation of Nonperiodic Payments* in Pub. 575.

More information. For more information about Keogh plans, see chapter 4 of Pub. 560.

Distribution from a tax-sheltered annuity. If you receive an eligible rollover distribution from a tax-sheltered annuity plan (section 403(b) plan), you can roll it over into a traditional IRA.

Receipt of property other than money. If you receive property other than money, you can sell the property and roll over the proceeds as discussed earlier.

Rollover from bond purchase plan. If you redeem retirement bonds that were distributed to you under a qualified bond purchase plan, you can roll over tax free into a traditional IRA the part of the amount you receive that is more than your basis in the retirement bonds.

Reporting rollovers from employer plans. Enter the total distribution (before income tax or other deductions were withheld) on Form 1040, 1040-SR, or 1040-NR, line 5a. This amount should be shown in box 1 of Form 1099-R. From this amount, subtract any contributions (usually shown in box 5 of Form 1099-R) that were taxable to you when made. From that result, subtract the amount that was rolled over either directly or within 60 days of receiving the distribution. Enter the remaining amount, even if zero, on Form 1040, 1040-SR, or 1040-NR, line 5b. Also, enter "Rollover" next to line 5b of Form 1040, 1040-SR, or 1040-NR.

Transfers Incident to Divorce

If an interest in a traditional IRA is transferred from your spouse or former spouse to you by a divorce or separate maintenance decree or a written document related to such a decree, the interest in the IRA, starting from the date of the transfer, is treated as your IRA. The transfer is tax free. For information about transfers of interests in employer plans, see *Distributions under divorce or similar proceedings (alternate payees)* under *Rollover From Employer's Plan Into an IRA*, earlier.

Transfer methods. There are two commonly used methods of transferring IRA assets to a spouse or former spouse. The methods are:

- Changing the name on the IRA, and
- Making a direct transfer of IRA assets.

Changing the name on the IRA. If all the assets are to be transferred, you can make the transfer by changing the name on the IRA from your name to the name of your spouse or former spouse.

Direct transfer. Under this method, you direct the trustee of the traditional IRA to transfer the affected assets directly to the trustee of a new or existing traditional IRA set up in the name of your spouse or former spouse.

If your spouse or former spouse is allowed to keep his or her portion of the IRA assets in your existing IRA, you can direct the trustee to transfer the assets you are permitted to keep directly to a new or existing traditional IRA set up in your name. The name on the IRA containing your spouse's or former spouse's portion of the assets would then be changed to show his or her ownership.

CAUTION *If the transfer results in a change in the basis of the traditional IRA of either spouse, both spouses must file Form 8606 and follow the directions in the instructions for that form.*

Converting From Any Traditional IRA Into a Roth IRA

Allowable conversions. You can withdraw all or part of the assets from a traditional IRA and reinvest them (within 60 days) in a Roth IRA. The amount that you withdraw and timely contribute (convert) to the Roth IRA is called a conversion contribution. If properly (and timely) rolled over, the 10% additional tax on early distributions won't apply. However, a part or all of the distribution from your traditional IRA may be included in gross income and subjected to ordinary income tax.

You must roll over into the Roth IRA the same property you received from the traditional IRA. You can roll over part of the withdrawal into a Roth IRA and keep the rest of it. The amount you keep will generally be taxable (except for the part that is a return of nondeductible contributions) and may be subject to the 10% additional tax on early distributions. See *When Can You Withdraw or Use Assets*, later, for more information on distributions from traditional IRAs and *Early Distributions* in Pub. 590-B for more information on the tax on early distributions.

Periodic distributions. If you started taking substantially equal periodic payments from a traditional IRA, you can convert the amounts in the traditional IRA to a Roth IRA and then continue the periodic payments. The 10% additional tax on early distributions won't apply even if the distributions aren't qualified distributions (as long as they are part of a series of substantially equal periodic payments).

Required distributions. You can't convert amounts that must be distributed from your traditional IRA for a particular year (including the calendar year in which you reach age 72) under the required distribution rules (discussed in Pub. 590-B).

Income. You must include in your gross income distributions from a traditional IRA that you would have had to include in income if you hadn't converted them into a Roth IRA. These amounts are normally included in income on your return for the year that you converted them from a traditional IRA to a Roth IRA.

You don't include in gross income any part of a distribution from a traditional IRA that is a return of your basis, as discussed under *Are Distributions Taxable* in Pub. 590-B.

CAUTION *If you must include any amount in your gross income, you may have to increase your withholding or make estimated tax payments. See Pub. 505, Tax Withholding and Estimated Tax.*

Recharacterizations

You may be able to treat a contribution made to one type of IRA as having been made to a different type of IRA. This is called recharacterizing the contribution.

To recharacterize a contribution, you must generally have the contribution transferred from the first IRA (the one to which it was made) to the second IRA in a trustee-to-trustee transfer. If the transfer is made by the due date (including extensions) for your tax return for the tax year for which the contribution was made, you can elect to treat the contribution as having been originally made to the second IRA instead of to the first IRA. If you recharacterize your contribution, you must do all three of the following.

- Include in the transfer any net income allocable to the contribution. If there was a loss, the net income you must transfer may be a negative amount.
- Report the recharacterization on your tax return for the year during which the contribution was made.
- Treat the contribution as having been made to the second IRA on the date that it was actually made to the first IRA.

No recharacterizations of conversions made in 2018 or later. A conversion of a traditional IRA to a Roth IRA, and a rollover from any other eligible retirement plan to a Roth IRA, made in tax years beginning after December 31, 2017, cannot be recharacterized as having been made to a traditional IRA. If you made a conversion in the 2017 tax year, you had until the due date (with extensions) for filing the return for that tax year to recharacterize it.

No deduction allowed. You can't deduct the contribution to the first IRA. Any net income you transfer with the recharacterized contribution is treated as earned in the second IRA. The contribution won't be treated as having been made to the second IRA to the extent any deduction was allowed for the contribution to the first IRA.

Conversion by rollover from traditional to Roth IRA. You receive a distribution from a traditional IRA in 1 tax year. You then roll it over into a Roth IRA within 60 days of the distribution from the traditional IRA but in the next year. For recharacterization purposes, you would treat this transaction as a contribution to the Roth IRA in the year of the distribution from the traditional IRA.

Effect of previous tax-free transfers. If an amount has been moved from one IRA to another in a tax-free transfer, such as a rollover, you generally can't recharacterize the amount that was transferred. However, see *Traditional IRA mistakenly moved to SIMPLE IRA*, next.

Traditional IRA mistakenly moved to SIMPLE IRA. If you mistakenly roll over or transfer an amount from a traditional IRA to a SIMPLE IRA, you can later recharacterize the amount as a contribution to another traditional IRA.

Recharacterizing excess contributions. You can recharacterize only actual contributions. If you are applying excess contributions for prior years as current contributions, you can recharacterize them only if the recharacterization would still be timely with respect to the tax year for which the applied contributions were actually made.

Example. You contributed more than you were entitled to in 2020. You can't recharacterize the excess contributions you made in 2020 after April 15, 2021, because contributions after that date are no longer timely for 2020.

Recharacterizing employer contributions. You can't recharacterize employer contributions (including elective deferrals) under a SEP or SIMPLE plan as contributions to another IRA. SEPs are discussed in chapter 2 of Pub. 560. SIMPLE plans are discussed in chapter 3 of Pub. 560.

Recharacterization not counted as rollover. The recharacterization of a contribution is not treated as a rollover for purposes of the 1-year waiting period described earlier in this chapter under *Rollover From One IRA Into Another*. This is true even if the contribution would have been treated as a rollover contribution by the second IRA if it had been made directly to the second IRA rather than as a result of a recharacterization of a contribution to the first IRA.

How Do You Recharacterize a Contribution?

To recharacterize a contribution, you must notify both the trustee of the first IRA (the one to which the contribution was actually made) and the trustee of the second IRA (the one to which the contribution is being moved) that you have elected to treat the contribution as having been made to the second IRA rather than the first. You must make the notifications by the date of the transfer. Only one notification is required if both IRAs are maintained by the same trustee. The notification(s) must include all of the following information.

- The type and amount of the contribution to the first IRA that is to be recharacterized.
- The date on which the contribution was made to the first IRA and the year for which it was made.
- A direction to the trustee of the first IRA to transfer in a trustee-to-trustee transfer the amount of the contribution and any net income (or loss) allocable to the contribution to the trustee of the second IRA.

Worksheet 1-3. **Determining the Amount of Net Income Due to an IRA Contribution and Total Amount To Be Recharacterized**

Keep for Your Records

1.	Enter the amount of your IRA contribution for 2021 to be recharacterized	1.	
2.	Enter the fair market value of the IRA immediately prior to the recharacterization (include any distributions, transfers, or recharacterizations made while the contribution was in the account)	2.	
3.	Enter the fair market value of the IRA immediately prior to the time the contribution being recharacterized was made, including the amount of such contribution and any other contributions, transfers, or recharacterizations made while the contribution was in the account	3.	
4.	Subtract line 3 from line 2	4.	
5.	Divide line 4 by line 3. Enter the result as a decimal (rounded to at least three places)	5.	
6.	Multiply line 1 by line 5. This is the net income attributable to the contribution to be recharacterized	6.	
7.	Add lines 1 and 6. This is the amount of the IRA contribution plus the net income attributable to it to be recharacterized	7.	

- The name of the trustee of the first IRA and the name of the trustee of the second IRA.
- Any additional information needed to make the transfer.

In most cases, the net income you must transfer is determined by your IRA trustee or custodian. If you need to determine the applicable net income on IRA contributions made after 2020 that are recharacterized, use Worksheet 1-3. See Regulations section 1.408A-5 for more information.

Timing. The election to recharacterize and the transfer must both take place on or before the due date (including extensions) for filing your tax return for the tax year for which the contribution was made to the first IRA.

Extension. Ordinarily, you must choose to recharacterize a contribution by the due date of the return or the due date plus extensions. However, if you miss this deadline, you can still recharacterize a contribution if:

- Your return was timely filed for the year the choice should have been made, and
- You take appropriate corrective action within 6 months from the due date of your return, excluding extensions. For returns due April 15, 2021, this period ends on October 15, 2021. When the date for doing any act for tax purposes falls on a Saturday, Sunday, or legal holiday, the due date is delayed until the next business day.

Appropriate corrective action consists of:

- Notifying the trustee(s) of your intent to recharacterize,
- Providing the trustee with all necessary information, and
- Having the trustee transfer the contribution.

Once this is done, you must amend your return to show the recharacterization. You have until the regular due date for amending a return to do this. Report the recharacterization on the amended return and write "Filed pursuant to section 301.9100-2" on the return. File the amended return at the same address you filed the original return.

Decedent. The election to recharacterize can be made on behalf of a deceased IRA owner by the executor, administrator, or other person responsible for filing the decedent's final income tax return.

Election can't be changed. After the transfer has taken place, you can't change your election to recharacterize.

Same trustee. Recharacterizations made with the same trustee can be made by redesignating the first IRA as the second IRA, rather than transferring the account balance.

Reporting a Recharacterization

If you elect to recharacterize a contribution to one IRA as a contribution to another IRA, you must report the recharacterization on your tax return as directed by Form 8606 and its instructions. You must treat the contribution as having been made to the second IRA.

More than one IRA. If you have more than one IRA, figure the amount to be recharacterized only on the account from which you withdraw the contribution.

When Can You Withdraw or Use Assets?

You can withdraw or use your traditional IRA assets at any time. However, a 10% additional tax generally applies if you withdraw or use IRA assets before you are age $59^1/_2$. This is explained under *Age $59^1/_2$ Rule* under *Early Distributions* in Pub. 590-B.

You can generally make a tax-free withdrawal of contributions if you do it before the due date for filing your tax return for the year in which you made them. This means that, even if you are under age $59^1/_2$, the 10% additional tax may not apply. These withdrawals are explained later.

Contributions Returned Before Due Date of Return

If you made IRA contributions in 2020, you can withdraw them tax free by the due date of your return. If you have an extension of time to file your return, you can withdraw them tax free by the extended due date. You can do this if, for each contribution you withdraw, both of the following conditions apply.

- You didn't take a deduction for the contribution.
- You withdraw any interest or other income earned on the contribution. You can take into account any loss on the contribution while it was in the IRA when calculating the amount that must be withdrawn. If there was a loss, the net income earned on the contribution may be a negative amount.

Note. If you timely filed your 2020 tax return without withdrawing a contribution that you made in 2020, you can still have the contribution returned to you within 6 months of the due date of your 2020 tax return, excluding extensions. If you do, file an amended return with "Filed pursuant to section 301.9100-2" written at the top. Report any related earnings on the amended return and include an explanation of the withdrawal. Make any other necessary changes on the amended return (for example, if you reported the contributions as excess contributions on your original return, include an amended Form 5329 reflecting that the withdrawn contributions are no longer treated as having been contributed).

In most cases, the net income you must withdraw is determined by the IRA trustee or custodian. If you need to determine the applicable net income on IRA contributions made after 2020 that are returned to you, use Worksheet 1-4. See Regulations section 1.408-11 for more information.

Example. On May 2, 2021, when her IRA is worth $4,800, Cathy makes a $1,600 regular contribution to her IRA. Cathy requests that $400 of the May 2, 2021, contribution be returned to her. On February 2, 2022, when the IRA is worth $7,600, the IRA trustee distributes to Cathy the $400 plus net income attributable to the contribution. No other contributions have been made to the IRA for 2021 and no distributions have been made.

The adjusted opening balance is $6,400 ($4,800 + $1,600) and the adjusted closing balance is $7,600. The net income due to the May 2, 2021, contribution is $75 ($400 x ($7,600 − $6,400) ÷ $6,400). Therefore, the total to be distributed on February 2, 2022, is $475. This is shown on Worksheet 1-4. Example—Illustrated.

Worksheet 1-4. **Determining the Amount of Net Income Due to an IRA Contribution and Total Amount To Be Withdrawn From the IRA** *Keep for Your Records*

1.	Enter the amount of your IRA contribution for 2021 to be returned to you	1.	
2.	Enter the fair market value of the IRA immediately prior to the removal of the contribution, plus the amount of any distributions, transfers, and recharacterizations made while the contribution was in the IRA	2.	
3.	Enter the fair market value of the IRA immediately before the contribution was made, plus the amount of such contribution and any other contributions, transfers, and recharacterizations made while the contribution was in the IRA	3.	
4.	Subtract line 3 from line 2	4.	
5.	Divide line 4 by line 3. Enter the result as a decimal (rounded to at least three places)	5.	
6.	Multiply line 1 by line 5. This is the net income attributable to the contribution to be returned	6.	
7.	Add lines 1 and 6. This is the amount of the IRA contribution plus the net income attributable to it to be returned to you	7.	

Worksheet 1-4. **Example—Illustrated** *Keep for Your Records*

1.	Enter the amount of your IRA contribution for 2021 to be returned to you	1.	400
2.	Enter the fair market value of the IRA immediately prior to the removal of the contribution, plus the amount of any distributions, transfers, and recharacterizations made while the contribution was in the IRA	2.	7,600
3.	Enter the fair market value of the IRA immediately before the contribution was made, plus the amount of such contribution and any other contributions, transfers, and recharacterizations made while the contribution was in the IRA	3.	6,400
4.	Subtract line 3 from line 2	4.	1,200
5.	Divide line 4 by line 3. Enter the result as a decimal (rounded to at least three places)	5.	0.1875
6.	Multiply line 1 by line 5. This is the net income attributable to the contribution to be returned	6.	75
7.	Add lines 1 and 6. This is the amount of the IRA contribution plus the net income attributable to it to be returned to you	7.	475

Last-in first-out rule. If you made more than one regular contribution for the year, your last contribution is considered to be the one that is returned to you first.

Earnings Includible in Income

You must include in income any earnings on the contributions you withdraw. Include the earnings in income for the year in which you made the contributions, not the year in which you withdraw them.

CAUTION *Generally, except for any part of a withdrawal that is a return of nondeductible contributions (basis), any withdrawal of your contributions after the due date (or extended due date) of your return will be treated as a taxable distribution. Excess contributions can also be recovered tax free as discussed under What Acts Result in Penalties or Additional Taxes, later.*

Early Distributions Tax

The 10% additional tax on distributions made before you reach age 59½ doesn't apply to these tax-free withdrawals of your contributions. However, the distribution of interest or other income must be reported on Form 5329 and, unless the distribution qualifies as an exception to the age 59½ rule, it will be subject to this tax. See *Early Distributions* under *What Acts Result in Penalties or Additional Taxes?* in Pub. 590-B.

Excess Contributions Tax

If any part of these contributions is an excess contribution for 2019, it is subject to a 6% excise tax. You won't have to pay the 6% tax if any 2019 excess contribution was withdrawn by April 17, 2020 (plus extensions), and if any 2020 excess contribution is withdrawn by April 15, 2021 (plus extensions). See *Excess Contributions* under *What Acts Result in Penalties or Additional Taxes*, later.

TIP *You may be able to treat a contribution made to one type of IRA as having been made to a different type of IRA. This is called recharacterizing the contribution. See Recharacterizations, earlier, for more information.*

What Acts Result in Penalties or Additional Taxes?

The tax advantages of using traditional IRAs for retirement savings can be offset by additional taxes and penalties if you don't follow the rules. There are additions to the regular tax for using your IRA funds in prohibited transactions. There are also additional taxes for the following activities.

- Investing in collectibles.
- Making excess contributions.
- Taking early distributions. See Pub. 590-B.
- Allowing excess amounts to accumulate (failing to take required distributions). See Pub. 590-B.
- Having unrelated business income.

There are penalties for overstating the amount of nondeductible contributions and for failure to file Form 8606, if required.

This chapter discusses those acts that you should avoid and the additional taxes and other costs, including loss of IRA status, that apply if you don't avoid those acts.

Prohibited Transactions

Generally, a prohibited transaction is any improper use of your traditional IRA account or annuity by you, your beneficiary, or any disqualified person.

Disqualified persons include your fiduciary and members of your family (spouse, ancestor, lineal descendant, and any spouse of a lineal descendant).

The following are some examples of prohibited transactions with a traditional IRA.

- Borrowing money from it.
- Selling property to it.
- Using it as security for a loan.
- Buying property for personal use (present or future) with IRA funds.

CAUTION *If your IRA is invested in nonpublicly traded assets or assets that you directly control, the risk of engaging in a prohibited transaction in connection with your account may be increased.*

Fiduciary. For these purposes, a fiduciary includes anyone who does any of the following.

- Exercises any discretionary authority or discretionary control in managing your IRA or exercises any authority or control in managing or disposing of its assets.
- Provides investment advice to your IRA for a fee, or has any authority or responsibility to do so.
- Has any discretionary authority or discretionary responsibility in administering your IRA.

Effect on an IRA account. Generally, if you or your beneficiary engages in a prohibited transaction in connection with your traditional IRA account at any time during the year, the account stops being an IRA as of the first day of that year.

Effect on you or your beneficiary. If your account stops being an IRA because you or your beneficiary engaged in a prohibited transaction, the account is treated as distributing all its assets to you at their fair market values on the first day of the year. If the total of those values is more than your basis in the IRA, you will have a taxable gain that is includible in your income. For information on figuring your gain and reporting it in income, see *Are Distributions Taxable* in Pub. 590-B. The distribution may be subject to additional taxes or penalties.

Borrowing on an annuity contract. If you borrow money against your traditional IRA annuity contract, you must include in your gross income the fair market value of the annuity contract as of the first day of your tax year. You may have to pay the 10% additional tax on early distributions discussed in Pub. 590-B.

Pledging an account as security. If you use a part of your traditional IRA account as security for a loan, that part is treated as a distribution and is included in your gross income. You may have to pay the 10% additional tax on early distributions discussed in Pub. 590-B.

Trust account set up by an employer or an employee association. Your account or annuity doesn't lose its IRA treatment if your employer or the employee association with whom you have your traditional IRA engages in a prohibited transaction.

Owner participation. If you participate in the prohibited transaction with your employer or the association, your account is no longer treated as an IRA.

Taxes on prohibited transactions. If someone other than the owner or beneficiary of a traditional IRA engages in a prohibited transaction, that person may be liable for certain taxes. In general, there is a 15% tax on the amount of the prohibited transaction and a 100% additional tax if the transaction isn't corrected.

Loss of IRA status. If the traditional IRA ceases to be an IRA because of a prohibited transaction by you or your beneficiary, you or your beneficiary aren't liable for these excise taxes. However, you or your beneficiary may have to pay other taxes as discussed under *Effect on you or your beneficiary*, earlier.

Exempt Transactions

The Department of Labor has authority to grant administrative exemptions from the prohibited transaction provisions of ERISA and the Code for a class of transactions or for individual transactions. In order to grant an administrative exemption, the Department must make the following three determinations.

1. The exemption must be administratively feasible;
2. In the interest of the plan and its participants; and,
3. Protective of the rights of plan participants and beneficiaries.

For additional information on prohibited transaction exemptions, see the Department of Labor publication, *Exemption Procedures under Federal Pension Law*.

The following two types of transactions aren't prohibited transactions if they meet the requirements that follow.

- Payments of cash, property, or other consideration by the sponsor of your traditional IRA to you (or members of your family).
- Your receipt of services at reduced or no cost from the bank where your traditional IRA is established or maintained.

Payments of cash, property, or other consideration. Even if a sponsor makes payments to you or your family, there is no prohibited transaction if all three of the following requirements are met.

1. The payments are for establishing a traditional IRA or for making additional contributions to it.
2. The IRA is established solely to benefit you, your spouse, and your or your spouse's beneficiaries.
3. During the year, the total fair market value of the payments you receive isn't more than:
   a. $10 for IRA deposits of less than $5,000, or
   b. $20 for IRA deposits of $5,000 or more.

If the consideration is group term life insurance, requirements (1) and (3) don't apply if no more than $5,000 of the face value of the insurance is based on a dollar-for-dollar basis on the assets in your IRA.

Services received at reduced or no cost. Even if a sponsor provides services at reduced or no cost, there is no prohibited transaction if all of the following requirements are met.

- The traditional IRA qualifying you to receive the services is established and maintained for the benefit of you, your spouse, and your or your spouse's beneficiaries.
- The bank itself can legally offer the services.
- The services are provided in the ordinary course of business by the bank (or a bank affiliate) to customers who qualify but don't maintain an IRA (or a Keogh plan).
- The determination, for a traditional IRA, of who qualifies for these services is based on an IRA (or a Keogh plan) deposit balance equal to the lowest qualifying balance for any other type of account.
- The rate of return on a traditional IRA investment that qualifies isn't less than the return on an identical investment that could have been made at the same time at the same branch of the bank by a customer who isn't eligible for (or doesn't receive) these services.

Investment in Collectibles

If your traditional IRA invests in collectibles, the amount invested is considered distributed to you in the year invested. You may have to pay the 10% additional tax on early distributions discussed in Pub. 590-B.

Any amounts that were considered to be distributed when the investment in the collectible was made, and which were included in your income at that time, aren't included in your income when the collectible is actually distributed from your IRA.

Collectibles. These include:

- Artworks,
- Rugs,
- Antiques,
- Metals,
- Gems,
- Stamps,
- Coins,
- Alcoholic beverages, and

- Certain other tangible personal property.

Exception. Your IRA can invest in one, one-half, one-quarter, or one-tenth ounce U.S. gold coins, or one-ounce silver coins minted by the Treasury Department. It can also invest in certain platinum coins and certain gold, silver, palladium, and platinum bullion.

Unrelated Business Income

An IRA is subject to tax on unrelated business income if it carries on an unrelated trade or business. An unrelated trade or business means any trade or business regularly carried on by the IRA or by a partnership of which it is a member. If the IRA has $1,000 or more of unrelated trade or business gross income, the IRA trustee is required to file a Form 990-T, Exempt Organization Business Income Tax Return. The Form 990-T must be filed by the 15th day of the 4th month after the end of the IRA's tax year. See Pub. 598, Tax on Unrelated Business Income of Exempt Organizations, for more information.

Excess Contributions

Generally, an excess contribution is the amount contributed to your traditional IRAs for the year that is more than the smaller of:

- $6,000 ($7,000 if you are age 50 or older), or
- Your taxable compensation for the year.

The taxable compensation limit applies whether your contributions are deductible or nondeductible.

An excess contribution could be the result of your contribution, your spouse's contribution, your employer's contribution, or an improper rollover contribution. If your employer makes contributions on your behalf to a SEP IRA, see chapter 2 of Pub. 560.

Tax on Excess Contributions

In general, if the excess contributions for a year aren't withdrawn by the date your return for the year is due (including extensions), you are subject to a 6% tax. You must pay the 6% tax each year on excess amounts that remain in your traditional IRA at the end of your tax year. The tax can't be more than 6% of the combined value of all your IRAs as of the end of your tax year.

The additional tax is figured on Form 5329. For information on filing Form 5329, see *Reporting Additional Taxes*, later.

Example. For 2020, Paul Jones is 45 years old and single, his compensation is $31,000, and he contributed $6,500 to his traditional IRA. Paul has made an excess contribution to his IRA of $500 ($6,500 minus the $6,000 limit). The contribution earned $5 interest in 2020 and $6 interest in 2021 before the due date of the return, including extensions. He doesn't withdraw the $500 or the interest it earned by the due date of his return, including extensions.

Paul figures his additional tax for 2020 by multiplying the excess contribution ($500) shown on Form 5329, line 16, by 0.06, giving him an additional tax liability of $30. He enters the tax on Form 5329, line 17, and on Schedule 2 (Form 1040), line 6. See Paul's filled-in Form 5329, later.

Excess Contributions Withdrawn by Due Date of Return

You won't have to pay the 6% tax if you withdraw an excess contribution made during a tax year and you also withdraw any interest or other income earned on the excess contribution. You must complete your withdrawal by the date your tax return for that year is due, including extensions.

How to treat withdrawn contributions. Don't include in your gross income an excess contribution that you withdraw from your traditional IRA before your tax return is due if both of the following conditions are met.

- No deduction was allowed for the excess contribution.
- You withdraw the interest or other income earned on the excess contribution.

You can take into account any loss on the contribution while it was in the IRA when calculating the amount that must be withdrawn. If there was a loss, the net income you must withdraw may be a negative amount.

In most cases, the net income you must transfer will be determined by your IRA trustee or custodian. If you need to determine the applicable net income you need to withdraw, you can use the same method that was used in Worksheet 1-3.

If you timely filed your 2020 tax return without withdrawing a contribution that you made in 2020, you can still have the contribution returned to you within 6 months of the due date of your 2020 tax return, excluding extensions. If you do, file an amended return with "Filed pursuant to section 301.9100-2" written at the top. Report any related earnings on the amended return and include an explanation of the withdrawal. Make any other necessary changes on the amended return (for example, if you reported the contributions as excess contributions on your original return, include an amended Form 5329 reflecting that the withdrawn contributions are no longer treated as having been contributed).

How to treat withdrawn interest or other income. You must include in your gross income the interest or other income that was earned on the excess contribution. Report it on your return for the year in which the excess contribution was made. Your withdrawal of interest or other income may be subject to an additional 10% tax on early distributions discussed in Pub. 590-B.

Form 1099-R. You will receive Form 1099-R indicating the amount of the withdrawal. If the excess contribution was made in a previous tax year, the form will indicate the year in which the earnings are taxable.

Example. Maria, age 35, made an excess contribution in 2020 of $1,000, which she withdrew by April 15, 2021, the due date of her return. At the same time, she also withdrew the $50 income that was earned on the $1,000. She must include the $50 in her gross income for 2020 (the year in which the excess contribution was made). She must also pay an additional tax of $5 (the 10% additional tax on early distributions because she isn't yet 59½ years old), but she doesn't have to report the excess contribution as income or pay the 6% excise tax. Maria receives a Form 1099-R showing that the earnings are taxable for 2020.

Excess Contributions Withdrawn After Due Date of Return

In general, you must include all distributions (withdrawals) from your traditional IRA in your gross income. However, if the following conditions are met, you can withdraw excess contributions from your IRA and not include the amount withdrawn in your gross income.

- Total contributions (other than rollover contributions) for 2020 to your IRA weren't more than $6,000 ($7,000 if you are age 50 or older).
- You didn't take a deduction for the excess contribution being withdrawn.

The withdrawal can take place at any time, even after the due date, including extensions, for filing your tax return for the year.

Excess contribution deducted in an earlier year. If you deducted an excess contribution in an earlier year for which the total contributions weren't more than the maximum deductible amount for that year (see the following table), you can still remove the excess from your traditional IRA and not include it in your gross income. To do this, file Form 1040-X for that year and don't deduct the excess contribution on the amended return. Generally, you can file an amended return within 3 years after you filed your return, or 2 years from the time the tax was paid, whichever is later.

Year(s)	Contribution limit	Contribution limit if age 50 or older at the end of the year
2019	$6,000	$7,000
2013 through 2018	$5,500	$6,500
2008 through 2012	$5,000	$6,000
2006 or 2007	$4,000	$5,000
2005	$4,000	$4,500
2002 through 2004	$3,000	$3,500
1997 through 2001	$2,000	—
before 1997	$2,250	—

Excess due to incorrect rollover information. If an excess contribution in your traditional IRA is the result of a rollover and the excess occurred because the information the plan was required to give you was incorrect, you can withdraw the excess contribution. The limits mentioned above are increased by the amount of the excess that is due to the incorrect information. You will have to amend your return for the year in which the excess occurred to correct the reporting of the rollover amounts in that year. Don't include in your gross income the part of the excess contribution caused by the incorrect information.

Deducting an Excess Contribution in a Later Year

You can't apply an excess contribution to an earlier year even if you contributed less than the maximum amount allowable for the earlier year. However, you may be able to apply it to a later year if the contributions for that later year are less than the maximum allowed for that year.

You can deduct excess contributions for previous years that are still in your traditional IRA. The amount you can deduct this year is the lesser of the following two amounts.

- Your maximum IRA deduction for this year minus any amounts contributed to your traditional IRAs for this year.
- The total excess contributions in your IRAs at the beginning of this year.

This method lets you avoid making a withdrawal. It doesn't, however, let you avoid the 6% tax on any excess contributions remaining at the end of a tax year.

To figure the amount of excess contributions for previous years that you can deduct this year, see Worksheet 1-5.

Worksheet 1-5. **Excess Contributions Deductible This Year**

Use this worksheet to figure the amount of excess contributions from prior years you can deduct this year.

1.	Maximum IRA deduction for the current year	1. _______
2.	IRA contributions for the current year	2. _______
3.	Subtract line 2 from line 1. If zero or less, enter -0-	3. _______
4.	Excess contributions in IRA at beginning of year	4. _______
5.	Enter the lesser of line 3 or line 4. This is the amount of excess contributions for previous years that you can deduct this year	5. _______

Example. Teri was entitled to contribute to her traditional IRA and deduct $1,000 in 2019 and $1,500 in 2020 (the amounts of her taxable compensation for these years). For 2019, she actually contributed $1,400 but could deduct only $1,000. In 2019, $400 is an excess contribution subject to the 6% tax. However, she wouldn't have to pay the 6% tax if she withdrew the excess (including any earnings) before the due date of her 2019 return. Because Teri didn't withdraw the excess, she owes excise tax of $24 for 2019. To avoid the excise tax for 2020, she can correct the $400 excess amount from 2019 in 2020 if her actual contributions are only $1,100 for 2020 (the allowable deductible contribution of $1,500 minus the $400 excess from 2019 she wants to treat as a deductible contribution in 2020). Teri can deduct $1,500 in 2020 (the $1,100 actually contributed plus the $400 excess contribution from 2019). This is shown on Worksheet 1-5. Example—Illustrated.

Worksheet 1-5. **Example—Illustrated**

Use this worksheet to figure the amount of excess contributions from prior years you can deduct this year.

1.	Maximum IRA deduction for the current year	**1.**	1,500
2.	IRA contributions for the current year	**2.**	1,100
3.	Subtract line 2 from line 1. If zero or less, enter -0-	**3.**	400
4.	Excess contributions in IRA at beginning of year	**4.**	400
5.	Enter the lesser of line 3 or line 4. This is the amount of excess contributions for previous years that you can deduct this year	**5.**	400

Form **5329** (Rev. February 2021) Department of the Treasury Internal Revenue Service

Additional Taxes on Qualified Plans (Including IRAs) and Other Tax-Favored Accounts

▶ Attach to Form 1040, 1040-SR, or 1040-NR.

▶ Go to *www.irs.gov/Form5329* for instructions and the latest information.

OMB No. 1545-0074 | 2020 | Attachment Sequence No. **29**

Name of individual subject to additional tax. If married filing jointly, see instructions.		Your social security number
Paul Jones		003-00-0000
Fill in Your Address Only if You Are Filing This Form by Itself and Not With Your Tax Return	Home address (number and street), or P.O. box if mail is not delivered to your home	Apt. no.
	City, town or post office, state, and ZIP code. If you have a foreign address, also complete the spaces below. See instructions.	If this is an amended return, check here ▶ ☐
	Foreign country name / Foreign province/state/county	Foreign postal code

If you **only** owe the additional 10% tax on the full amount of the early distributions, you may be able to report this tax directly on Schedule 2 (Form 1040), line 6, without filing Form 5329. See instructions.

Part I **Additional Tax on Early Distributions.** Complete this part if you took a taxable distribution before you reached age 59½ from a qualified retirement plan (including an IRA) or modified endowment contract (unless you are reporting this tax directly on Schedule 2 (Form 1040)—see above). You may also have to complete this part to indicate that you qualify for an exception to the additional tax on early distributions or for certain Roth IRA distributions. See instructions.

1	Early distributions includible in income (see instructions). For Roth IRA distributions, see instructions	1	
2	Early distributions included on line 1 that are not subject to the additional tax (see instructions). Enter the appropriate exception number from the instructions: ______	2	
3	Amount subject to additional tax. Subtract line 2 from line 1	3	
4	**Additional tax.** Enter 10% (0.10) of line 3. Include this amount on Schedule 2 (Form 1040), line 6	4	
	Caution: If any part of the amount on line 3 was a distribution from a SIMPLE IRA, you may have to include 25% of that amount on line 4 instead of 10%. See instructions.		

Part II **Additional Tax on Certain Distributions From Education Accounts and ABLE Accounts.** Complete this part if you included an amount in income, on Schedule 1 (Form 1040), line 8, from a Coverdell education savings account (ESA), a qualified tuition program (QTP), or an ABLE account.

5	Distributions included in income from a Coverdell ESA, a QTP, or an ABLE account	5	
6	Distributions included on line 5 that are not subject to the additional tax (see instructions)	6	
7	Amount subject to additional tax. Subtract line 6 from line 5	7	
8	**Additional tax.** Enter 10% (0.10) of line 7. Include this amount on Schedule 2 (Form 1040), line 6	8	

Part III **Additional Tax on Excess Contributions to Traditional IRAs.** Complete this part if you contributed more to your traditional IRAs for 2020 than is allowable or you had an amount on line 17 of your 2019 Form 5329.

9	Enter your excess contributions from line 16 of your 2019 Form 5329. See instructions. If zero, go to line 15			9	
10	If your traditional IRA contributions for 2020 are less than your maximum allowable contribution, see instructions. Otherwise, enter -0-	10			
11	2020 traditional IRA distributions included in income (see instructions)	11			
12	2020 distributions of prior year excess contributions (see instructions)	12			
13	Add lines 10, 11, and 12			13	
14	Prior year excess contributions. Subtract line 13 from line 9. If zero or less, enter -0-			14	
15	Excess contributions for 2020 (see instructions)			15	500
16	Total excess contributions. Add lines 14 and 15			16	500
17	**Additional tax.** Enter 6% (0.06) of the **smaller** of line 16 **or** the value of your traditional IRAs on December 31, 2020 (including 2020 contributions made in 2021). Include this amount on Schedule 2 (Form 1040), line 6			17	30

Part IV **Additional Tax on Excess Contributions to Roth IRAs.** Complete this part if you contributed more to your Roth IRAs for 2020 than is allowable or you had an amount on line 25 of your 2019 Form 5329.

18	Enter your excess contributions from line 24 of your 2019 Form 5329. See instructions. If zero, go to line 23			18	
19	If your Roth IRA contributions for 2020 are less than your maximum allowable contribution, see instructions. Otherwise, enter -0-	19			
20	2020 distributions from your Roth IRAs (see instructions)	20			
21	Add lines 19 and 20			21	
22	Prior year excess contributions. Subtract line 21 from line 18. If zero or less, enter -0-			22	
23	Excess contributions for 2020 (see instructions)			23	
24	Total excess contributions. Add lines 22 and 23			24	
25	**Additional tax.** Enter 6% (0.06) of the **smaller** of line 24 **or** the value of your Roth IRAs on December 31, 2020 (including 2020 contributions made in 2021). Include this amount on Schedule 2 (Form 1040), line 6			25	

For Privacy Act and Paperwork Reduction Act Notice, see your tax return instructions. Cat. No. 13329Q Form **5329** (2020)

Page 36 Chapter 1 **Traditional IRAs**

Closed tax year. A special rule applies if you incorrectly deducted part of the excess contribution in a closed tax year (one for which the period to assess a tax deficiency has expired). The amount allowable as a traditional IRA deduction for a later correction year (the year you contribute less than the allowable amount) must be reduced by the amount of the excess contribution deducted in the closed year.

To figure the amount of excess contributions for previous years that you can deduct this year if you incorrectly deducted part of the excess contribution in a closed tax year, see Worksheet 1-6.

Worksheet 1-6. **Excess Contributions Deductible This Year if Any Were Deducted in a Closed Tax Year**

Use this worksheet to figure the amount of excess contributions for prior years that you can deduct this year if you incorrectly deducted excess contributions in a closed tax year.

1.	Maximum IRA deduction for the current year	1. ____
2.	IRA contributions for the current year	2. ____
3.	If line 2 is less than line 1, enter any excess contributions that were deducted in a closed tax year. Otherwise, enter -0-	3. ____
4.	Subtract line 3 from line 1	4. ____
5.	Subtract line 2 from line 4. If zero or less, enter -0-	5. ____
6.	Excess contributions in IRA at beginning of year	6. ____
7.	Enter the lesser of line 5 or line 6. This is the amount of excess contributions for previous years that you can deduct this year	7. ____

Reporting Additional Taxes

Generally, you must use Form 5329 to report the tax on excess contributions, early distributions, and excess accumulations.

Filing a tax return. If you must file an individual income tax return, complete Form 5329 and attach it to your Form 1040, 1040-SR, or 1040-NR. Enter the total additional taxes due on Schedule 2 (Form 1040), line 6.

Not filing a tax return. If you don't have to file a return, but do have to pay one of the additional taxes mentioned earlier, file the completed Form 5329 with the IRS at the time and place you would have filed Form 1040, 1040-SR, or 1040-NR. Be sure to include your address on page 1 and your signature and date on page 2. Enclose, but don't attach, a check or money order payable to "United States Treasury" for the tax you owe, as shown on Form 5329. Write your social security number and "2020 Form 5329" on your check or money order.

Form 5329 not required. You don't have to use Form 5329 if either of the following situations exists.

- Distribution code 1 (early distribution) is correctly shown in box 7 of Form 1099-R. If you don't owe any other additional tax on a distribution, multiply the taxable part of the early distribution by 10% and enter the result on Schedule 2 (Form 1040), line 6. Enter "No" to the left of the line to indicate that you don't have to file Form 5329. You must file Form 5329 to report your additional taxes.
- If you rolled over part or all of a distribution from a qualified retirement plan, the part rolled over isn't subject to the tax on early distributions.

2.

Roth IRAs

Reminders

Deemed IRAs. For plan years beginning after 2002, a qualified employer plan (retirement plan) can maintain a separate account or annuity under the plan (a deemed IRA) to receive voluntary employee contributions. If the separate account or annuity otherwise meets the requirements of an IRA, it will be subject only to IRA rules. An employee's account can be treated as a traditional IRA or a Roth IRA.

For this purpose, a "qualified employer plan" includes:

- A qualified pension, profit-sharing, or stock bonus plan (section 401(a) plan);
- A qualified employee annuity plan (section 403(a) plan);
- A tax-sheltered annuity plan (section 403(b) plan); and
- A deferred compensation plan (section 457 plan) maintained by a state, a political subdivision of a state, or an agency or instrumentality of a state or political subdivision of a state.

Designated Roth accounts. Designated Roth accounts are separate accounts under 401(k), 403(b), or 457(b) plans that accept elective deferrals that are referred to as Roth contributions. These elective deferrals are included in your income, but qualified distributions from these accounts aren't included in your income. Designated Roth accounts aren't IRAs and shouldn't be confused with Roth IRAs. Contributions, up to their respective limits, can be made to Roth IRAs and designated Roth accounts according to your eligibility to participate. A contribution to one doesn't impact your eligibility to contribute to the other. See Pub. 575 for more information on designated Roth accounts.

Introduction

Regardless of your age, you may be able to establish and make nondeductible contributions to an individual retirement plan called a Roth IRA.

Contributions not reported. You don't report Roth IRA contributions on your return.

What Is a Roth IRA?

A Roth IRA is an individual retirement plan that, except as explained in this chapter, is subject to the rules that apply to a traditional IRA (defined next). It can be either an account or an annuity. Individual retirement accounts and annuities are described in chapter 1 under *How Can a Traditional IRA Be Opened*.

To be a Roth IRA, the account or annuity must be designated as a Roth IRA when it is opened. A deemed IRA can be a Roth IRA, but neither a SEP IRA nor a SIMPLE IRA can be designated as a Roth IRA.

Unlike a traditional IRA, you can't deduct contributions to a Roth IRA. But, if you satisfy the requirements, qualified distributions (discussed in chapter 2 of Pub. 590-B) are tax free, and if you choose, you can leave amounts in your Roth IRA as long as you live.

Traditional IRA. A traditional IRA is any IRA that isn't a Roth IRA or SIMPLE IRA. Traditional IRAs are discussed in chapter 1.

When Can a Roth IRA Be Opened?

You can open a Roth IRA at any time. However, the time for making contributions for any year is limited. See *When Can You Make Contributions*, later, under *Can You Contribute to a Roth IRA*.

Can You Contribute to a Roth IRA?

Generally, you can contribute to a Roth IRA if you have taxable compensation (defined later) and your modified AGI (defined later) is less than:

- $206,000 for married filing jointly or qualifying widow(er);
- $139,000 for single, head of household, or married filing separately and you didn't live with your spouse at any time during the year; and
- $10,000 for married filing separately and you lived with your spouse at any time during the year.

TIP *You may be able to claim a credit for contributions to your Roth IRA. For more information, see chapter 3.*

Is there an age limit for contributions? Contributions can be made to your Roth IRA regardless of your age.

Can you contribute to a Roth IRA for your spouse? You can contribute to a Roth IRA for your spouse provided the contributions satisfy the Kay Bailey Hutchison Spousal IRA limit discussed in chapter 1 under *How Much Can Be Contributed*, you file jointly, and your modified AGI is less than $206,000.

Compensation. Compensation includes wages, salaries, tips, professional fees, bonuses, and other amounts received for providing personal services. It also includes commissions, self-employment income, nontaxable combat pay, military differential pay, and taxable alimony and separate maintenance payments. For more information, see *What Is Compensation* under *Who Can Open a Traditional IRA?* in chapter 1.

Modified AGI. Your modified AGI for Roth IRA purposes is your adjusted gross income (AGI) as shown on your return with some adjustments. Use Worksheet 2-1 to determine your modified AGI.

CAUTION *Don't subtract conversion income when figuring your other AGI-based phaseouts and taxable income, such as your deduction for medical and dental expenses. Subtract them from AGI only for the purpose of figuring your modified AGI for Roth IRA purposes.*

How Much Can Be Contributed?

The contribution limit for Roth IRAs generally depends on whether contributions are made only to Roth IRAs or to both traditional IRAs and Roth IRAs.

Roth IRAs only. If contributions are made only to Roth IRAs, your contribution limit is generally the lesser of:

- $6,000 ($7,000 if you are age 50 or older), or
- Your taxable compensation.

However, if your modified AGI is above a certain amount, your contribution limit may be reduced, as explained later under *Contribution limit reduced*.

Roth IRAs and traditional IRAs. If contributions are made to both Roth IRAs and traditional IRAs established for your benefit, your contribution limit for Roth IRAs is generally the same as your limit would be if contributions were made only to Roth IRAs, but then reduced by all contributions for the year to all IRAs other than Roth IRAs. Employer contributions under a SEP or SIMPLE IRA plan don't affect this limit.

This means that your contribution limit is the lesser of:

- $6,000 ($7,000 if you are age 50 or older) minus all contributions (other than employer contributions under a SEP or SIMPLE IRA plan) for the year to all IRAs other than Roth IRAs, or
- Your taxable compensation minus all contributions (other than employer contributions under a SEP or

Worksheet 2-1. **Modified Adjusted Gross Income for Roth IRA Purposes**

Use this worksheet to figure your modified adjusted gross income for Roth IRA purposes.

1.	Enter your adjusted gross income from Form 1040, 1040-SR, or 1040-NR, line 11	**1.**	
2.	Enter any income resulting from the conversion of an IRA (other than a Roth IRA) to a Roth IRA (included on Form 1040, 1040-SR, or 1040-NR, line 4b) and a rollover from a qualified retirement plan to a Roth IRA (included on Form 1040, 1040-SR, or 1040-NR, line 5b)	**2.**	
3.	Subtract line 2 from line 1	**3.**	
4.	Enter any traditional IRA deduction from Schedule 1 (Form 1040), line 19	**4.**	
5.	Enter any student loan interest deduction from Schedule 1 (Form 1040), line 20	**5.**	
6.	Enter any tuition and fees deduction from Schedule 1 (Form 1040), line 21	**6.**	
7.	Enter any foreign earned income exclusion and/or housing exclusion from Form 2555, line 45	**7.**	
8.	Enter any foreign housing deduction from Form 2555, line 50	**8.**	
9.	Enter any excludable qualified savings bond interest from Form 8815, line 14	**9.**	
10.	Enter any excluded employer-provided adoption benefits from Form 8839, line 28	**10.**	
11.	Add the amounts on lines 3 through 10	**11.**	
12.	Enter: • $206,000 if married filing jointly or qualifying widow(er), • $10,000 if married filing separately and you lived with your spouse at any time during the year, or • $139,000 for all others	**12.**	

Is the amount on line 11 more than the amount on line 12?
If "Yes", see the *Note* below.
If "No", the amount on line 11 is your ***modified adjusted gross income*** for Roth IRA purposes.

Note. If the amount on line 11 is more than the amount on line 12 and you have other income or loss items, such as social security income or passive activity losses, that are subject to AGI-based phaseouts, you can refigure your AGI solely for the purpose of figuring your modified AGI for Roth IRA purposes. (If you receive social security benefits, use Worksheet 1 in Appendix B to refigure your AGI.) Then go to line 3 above in this Worksheet 2-1 to refigure your modified AGI. If you don't have other income or loss items subject to AGI-based phaseouts, your modified adjusted gross income for Roth IRA purposes is the amount on line 11 above.

SIMPLE IRA plan) for the year to all IRAs other than Roth IRAs.

However, if your modified AGI is above a certain amount, your contribution limit may be reduced, as explained later under *Contribution limit reduced*.

Simplified employee pensions (SEPs) and savings incentive match plans for employees (SIMPLE plans) are discussed in Pub. 560.

Repayment of reservist distributions. You can repay qualified reservist distributions even if the repayments would cause your total contributions to the Roth IRA to be more than the general limit on contributions. However, the total repayments can't be more than the amount of your distribution.

Note. If you make repayments of qualified reservist distributions to a Roth IRA, increase your basis in the Roth IRA by the amount of the repayment. For more information, see *Qualified reservist repayments* under *How Much Can Be Contributed?* in chapter 1.

Contribution limit reduced. If your modified AGI is above a certain amount, your contribution limit is gradually reduced. Use Table 2-1 to determine if this reduction applies to you.

Figuring the reduction. If the amount you can contribute must be reduced, use Worksheet 2-2 to figure your reduced contribution limit.

TIP *Round your reduced contribution limit up to the nearest $10. If your reduced contribution limit is more than $0, but less than $200, increase the limit to $200.*

Example. You are a 45-year-old, single individual with taxable compensation of $125,000. You want to make the maximum allowable contribution to your Roth IRA for 2020. Your modified AGI for 2020 is $125,000. You haven't contributed to any traditional IRA, so the maximum contribution limit before the modified AGI reduction is $6,000. You figure your reduced Roth IRA contribution of $5,600 as shown on Worksheet 2-2. Example—Illustrated.

Table 2-1. **Effect of Modified AGI on Roth IRA Contribution**

This table shows whether your contribution to a Roth IRA is affected by the amount of your modified adjusted gross income (modified AGI).

IF you have taxable compensation and your filing status is...	**AND your modified AGI is...**	**THEN...**
married filing jointly or **qualifying widow(er)**	less than $196,000	you can contribute up to $6,000 ($7,000 if you are age 50 or older) as explained under *How Much Can Be Contributed*, earlier.
	at least $196,000 but less than $206,000	the amount you can contribute is reduced as explained under *Contribution limit reduced*, earlier.
	$206,000 or more	you can't contribute to a Roth IRA.
married filing separately (and you lived with your spouse at anytime during the year)	zero (-0-)	you can contribute up to $6,000 ($7,000 if you are age 50 or older) as explained under *How Much Can Be Contributed*, earlier.
	more than zero (-0-) but less than $10,000	the amount you can contribute is reduced as explained under *Contribution limit reduced*, earlier.
	$10,000 or more	you can't contribute to a Roth IRA.
single, head of household, or **married filing separately** (and you didn't live with your spouse at any time during the year)	less than $124,000	you can contribute up to $6,000 ($7,000 if you are age 50 or older) as explained under *How Much Can Be Contributed*, earlier.
	at least $124,000 but less than $139,000	the amount you can contribute is reduced as explained under *Contribution limit reduced*, earlier.
	$139,000 or more	you can't contribute to a Roth IRA.

Worksheet 2-2. **Determining Your Reduced Roth IRA Contribution Limit**

Before using this worksheet, check Table 2-1 to determine whether or not your Roth IRA contribution limit is reduced. If it is, use this worksheet to determine how much it is reduced.

1. Enter your modified AGI for Roth IRA purposes (Worksheet 2-1, line 11)	**1.**	______
2. Enter: • $196,000 if filing a joint return or qualifying widow(er), • $-0- if married filing a separate return and you lived with your spouse at any time in 2020, or • $124,000 for all others	**2.**	______
3. Subtract line 2 from line 1	**3.**	______
4. Enter: • $10,000 if filing a joint return or qualifying widow(er) or married filing a separate return and you lived with your spouse at any time during the year, or • $15,000 for all others	**4.**	______
5. Divide line 3 by line 4 and enter the result as a decimal (rounded to at least three places). If the result is 1.000 or more, enter 1.000	**5.**	______
6. Enter the lesser of: • $6,000 ($7,000 if you are age 50 or older), or • Your taxable compensation	**6.**	______
7. Multiply line 5 by line 6	**7.**	______
8. Subtract line 7 from line 6. Round the result up to the nearest $10. If the result is less than $200, enter $200	**8.**	______
9. Enter contributions for the year to other IRAs	**9.**	______
10. Subtract line 9 from line 6	**10.**	______
11. Enter the lesser of line 8 or line 10. This is your **reduced Roth IRA contribution limit**	**11.**	______

When Can You Make Contributions?

You can make contributions to a Roth IRA for a year at any time during the year or by the due date of your return for that year (not including extensions).

TIP *You can make contributions for 2020 by the due date (not including extensions) for filing your 2020 tax return. This means that most people can make contributions for 2020 by April 15, 2021.*

What if You Contribute Too Much?

A 6% excise tax applies to any excess contribution to a Roth IRA.

Excess contributions. These are the contributions to your Roth IRAs for a year that equal the total of:

1. Amounts contributed for the tax year to your Roth IRAs (other than amounts properly and timely rolled over from a Roth IRA or properly converted from a traditional IRA or rolled over from a qualified retirement plan, as described later) that are more than your contribution limit for the year (explained earlier under How Much Can Be Contributed); plus
2. Any excess contributions for the preceding year, reduced by the total of:
   a. Any distributions out of your Roth IRAs for the year, plus
   b. Your contribution limit for the year minus your contributions to all your IRAs for the year.

Withdrawal of excess contributions. For purposes of determining excess contributions, any contribution that is withdrawn on or before the due date (including extensions) for filing your tax return for the year is treated as an amount not contributed. This treatment only applies if any earnings on the contributions are also withdrawn. The earnings are considered earned and received in the year the excess contribution was made.

If you timely filed your 2020 tax return without withdrawing a contribution that you made in 2020, you can still

Worksheet 2-2. **Example—Illustrated**

Before using this worksheet, check Table 2-1 to determine whether or not your Roth IRA contribution limit is reduced. If it is, use this worksheet to determine how much it is reduced.

1. Enter your modified AGI for Roth IRA purposes (Worksheet 2-1, line 11)	**1.**	125,000
2. Enter: • $196,000 if filing a joint return or qualifying widow(er), • $-0- if married filing a separate return and you lived with your spouse at any time in 2020, or • $124,000 for all others	**2.**	124,000
3. Subtract line 2 from line 1	**3.**	1,000
4. Enter: • $10,000 if filing a joint return or qualifying widow(er) or married filing a separate return and you lived with your spouse at any time during the year, or • $15,000 for all others	**4.**	15,000
5. Divide line 3 by line 4 and enter the result as a decimal (rounded to at least three places). If the result is 1.000 or more, enter 1.000	**5.**	0.067
6. Enter the lesser of: • $6,000 ($7,000 if you are age 50 or older), or • Your taxable compensation	**6.**	6,000
7. Multiply line 5 by line 6	**7.**	402
8. Subtract line 7 from line 6. Round the result up to the nearest $10. If the result is less than $200, enter $200	**8.**	5,600
9. Enter contributions for the year to other IRAs	**9.**	0
10. Subtract line 9 from line 6	**10.**	6,000
11. Enter the lesser of line 8 or line 10. This is your **reduced Roth IRA contribution limit**	**11.**	5,600

have the contribution returned to you within 6 months of the due date of your 2020 tax return, excluding extensions. If you do, file an amended return with "Filed pursuant to section 301.9100-2" written at the top. Report any related earnings on the amended return and include an explanation of the withdrawal. Make any other necessary changes on the amended return.

Applying excess contributions. If contributions to your Roth IRA for a year were more than the limit, you can apply the excess contribution in 1 year to a later year if the contributions for that later year are less than the maximum allowed for that year.

Can You Move Amounts Into a Roth IRA?

You may be able to convert amounts from either a traditional, SEP, or SIMPLE IRA into a Roth IRA. You may be able to roll over amounts from a qualified retirement plan to a Roth IRA. You may be able to recharacterize contributions made to one IRA as having been made directly to a different IRA. You can roll amounts over from a designated Roth account or from one Roth IRA to another Roth IRA.

Conversions

You can convert a traditional IRA to a Roth IRA. The conversion is treated as a rollover, regardless of the conversion method used. Most of the rules for rollovers, described in chapter 1 under Rollover From One IRA Into Another, apply to these rollovers. However, the 1-year waiting period doesn't apply.

Conversion methods. You can convert amounts from a traditional IRA to a Roth IRA in any of the following three ways.

- ***Rollover.*** You can receive a distribution from a traditional IRA and roll it over (contribute it) to a Roth IRA within 60 days after the distribution.
- ***Trustee-to-trustee transfer.*** You can direct the trustee of the traditional IRA to transfer an amount from the traditional IRA to the trustee of the Roth IRA.
- ***Same trustee transfer.*** If the trustee of the traditional IRA also maintains the Roth IRA, you can direct the trustee to transfer an amount from the traditional IRA to the Roth IRA.

Same trustee. Conversions made with the same trustee can be made by redesignating the traditional IRA as a Roth IRA, rather than opening a new account or issuing a new contract.

Income. You must include in your gross income distributions from a traditional IRA that you would have had to include in income if you hadn't converted them into a Roth IRA. These amounts are normally included in income on your return for the year that you converted them from a traditional IRA to a Roth IRA.

CAUTION *If you must include any amount in your gross income, you may have to increase your withholding or make estimated tax payments. See Pub. 505, Tax Withholding and Estimated Tax.*

More information. For more information on conversions, see Converting From Any Traditional IRA Into a Roth IRA in chapter 1.

Rollover From Employer's Plan Into a Roth IRA

You can roll over into a Roth IRA all or part of an eligible rollover distribution you receive from your (or your deceased spouse's):

- Employer's qualified pension, profit-sharing, or stock bonus plan (including a 401(k) plan);
- Annuity plan;
- Tax-sheltered annuity plan (section 403(b) plan); or
- Governmental deferred compensation plan (section 457 plan).

Any amount rolled over is subject to the same rules for converting a traditional IRA into a Roth IRA. See Converting From Any Traditional IRA Into a Roth IRA in chapter 1. Also, the rollover contribution must meet the rollover requirements that apply to the specific type of retirement plan.

Rollover methods. You can roll over amounts from a qualified retirement plan to a Roth IRA in one of the following ways.

- ***Rollover.*** You can receive a distribution from a qualified retirement plan and roll it over (contribute) to a Roth IRA within 60 days after the distribution. Because the distribution is paid directly to you, the payer must generally withhold 20% of it. For rules about making a rollover of a plan loan offset, including a qualified plan loan offset, see Time Limit for Making a Rollover Contribution in chapter 1.
- ***Direct rollover option.*** Your employer's qualified plan must give you the option to have any part of an eligible rollover distribution paid directly to a Roth IRA. Generally, no tax is withheld from any part of the designated distribution that is directly paid to the trustee of the Roth IRA.

Rollover by nonspouse beneficiary. If you are a designated beneficiary (other than a surviving spouse) of a deceased employee, you can roll over all or part of an eligible rollover distribution from one of the types of plans listed above into a Roth IRA. You must make the rollover by a direct trustee-to-trustee transfer into an inherited Roth IRA.

You will determine your required minimum distributions in years after you make the rollover based on whether the employee died before his or her required beginning date for taking distributions from the plan. For more information, see *Distributions after the employee's death* under *Tax on Excess Accumulation* in Pub. 575.

Income. You must include in your gross income distributions from a qualified retirement plan that you would have had to include in income if you hadn't rolled them over into a Roth IRA. You don't include in gross income any part of a distribution from a qualified retirement plan that is a return of basis (after-tax contributions) to the plan that were taxable to you when paid. These amounts are normally included in income on your return for the year of the rollover from the qualified employer plan to a Roth IRA.

CAUTION *If you must include any amount in your gross income, you may have to increase your withholding or make estimated tax payments. See Pub. 505, Tax Withholding and Estimated Tax.*

For more information on eligible rollover distributions from qualified retirement plans and withholding, see Rollover From Employer's Plan Into an IRA in chapter 1.

Military Death Gratuities and Servicemembers' Group Life Insurance (SGLI) Payments

If you received a military death gratuity or SGLI payment with respect to a death from injury that occurred after October 6, 2001, you can contribute (roll over) all or part of the amount received to your Roth IRA. The contribution is treated as a qualified rollover contribution.

The amount you can roll over to your Roth IRA can't exceed the total amount that you received reduced by any part of that amount that was contributed to a Coverdell ESA or another Roth IRA. Any military death gratuity or SGLI payment contributed to a Roth IRA is disregarded for purposes of the 1-year waiting period between rollovers.

The rollover must be completed before the end of the 1-year period beginning on the date you received the payment.

The amount contributed to your Roth IRA is treated as part of your cost basis (investment in the contract) in the Roth IRA that isn't taxable when distributed.

Rollover From a Roth IRA

You can withdraw, tax free, all or part of the assets from one Roth IRA if you contribute them within 60 days to another Roth IRA. Most of the rules for rollovers, described in chapter 1 under Rollover From One IRA Into Another, apply to these rollovers. However, rollovers from retirement plans other than Roth IRAs are disregarded for purposes of the 1-year waiting period between rollovers.

A rollover from a Roth IRA to an employer retirement plan isn't allowed.

A rollover from a designated Roth account can only be made to another designated Roth account or to a Roth IRA.

If you roll over an amount from one Roth IRA to another Roth IRA, the 5-year period used to determine qualified distributions doesn't change. The 5-year period begins with the first tax year for which the contribution was made to the initial Roth IRA. See *What Are Qualified Distributions?* in chapter 2 of Pub. 590-B.

3.

Retirement Savings Contributions Credit (Saver's Credit)

What's New

Modified AGI limit for retirement savings contributions credit increased. For 2020, you may be able to claim the retirement savings contributions credit if your modified AGI isn't more than:

- $65,000 if your filing status is married filing jointly;
- $48,750 if your filing status is head of household; or
- $32,500 if your filing status is single, married filing separately, or qualifying widow(er).

Introduction

You may be able to take a tax credit if you make eligible contributions (defined later) to a qualified retirement plan, an eligible deferred compensation plan, or an IRA. You may be able to take a credit of up to $1,000 (up to $2,000 if filing jointly). This credit could reduce the federal income tax you pay dollar for dollar.

Can you claim the credit? If you make eligible contributions to a qualified retirement plan, an eligible deferred compensation plan, or an IRA, you can claim the credit if all of the following apply.

1. You were born before January 2, 2003.
2. You aren't a full-time student (explained later).
3. No one else, such as your parent(s), claims an exemption for you on their tax return.
4. Your adjusted gross income (defined later) isn't more than:
   a. $65,000 if your filing status is married filing jointly;
   b. $48,750 if your filing status is head of household; or
   c. $32,500 if your filing status is single, married filing separately, or qualifying widow(er).

Full-time student. You are a full-time student if, during some part of each of 5 calendar months (not necessarily consecutive) during the calendar year, you are either:

- A full-time student at a school that has a regular teaching staff, course of study, and regularly enrolled body of students in attendance, or
- A student taking a full-time, on-farm training course given by either a school that has a regular teaching staff, course of study, and regularly enrolled body of students in attendance, or a state, county, or local government.

You are a full-time student if you are enrolled for the number of hours or courses the school considers to be full time.

Adjusted gross income. This is generally the amount on line 11 of your 2020 Form 1040, 1040-SR, or 1040-NR. However, you must add to that amount any exclusion or deduction claimed for the year for:

- Foreign earned income,
- Foreign housing costs,
- Income for bona fide residents of American Samoa, and
- Income from Puerto Rico.

Eligible contributions. These include:

1. Contributions to a traditional or Roth IRA;
2. Salary reduction contributions (elective deferrals, including amounts designated as after-tax Roth contributions) to:
   a. A 401(k) plan (including a SIMPLE 401(k)),
   b. A section 403(b) annuity,
   c. An eligible deferred compensation plan of a state or local government (a governmental 457 plan),
   d. A SIMPLE IRA plan, or
   e. A salary reduction SEP; and
3. Contributions to a section 501(c)(18) plan.

They also include voluntary after-tax employee contributions to a tax-qualified retirement plan or section 403(b) annuity. For purposes of the credit, an employee contribution will be voluntary as long as it isn't required as a condition of employment.

Reducing eligible contributions. Reduce your eligible contributions (but not below zero) by the total distributions you received during the testing period (defined later) from any IRA, plan, or annuity included above under *Eligible contributions.* Also reduce your eligible contributions by any distribution from a Roth IRA that isn't rolled over, even if the distribution isn't taxable.

Don't reduce your eligible contributions by any of the following.

1. The portion of any distribution which isn't includible in income because it is a trustee-to-trustee transfer or a rollover distribution.
2. Distributions that are taxable as the result of an in-plan rollover to your designated Roth account.

3. Any distribution that is a return of a contribution to an IRA (including a Roth IRA) made during the year for which you claim the credit if:
   a. The distribution is made before the due date (including extensions) of your tax return for that year,
   b. You don't take a deduction for the contribution, and
   c. The distribution includes any income attributable to the contribution.
4. Loans from a qualified employer plan treated as a distribution.
5. Distributions of excess contributions or deferrals (and income attributable to excess contributions and deferrals).
6. Distributions of dividends paid on stock held by an employee stock ownership plan under section 404(k).
7. Distributions from an eligible retirement plan that are converted or rolled over to a Roth IRA.
8. Distributions from a military retirement plan.
9. Distributions from an inherited IRA by a nonspousal beneficiary.

Distributions received by spouse. Any distributions your spouse receives are treated as received by you if you file a joint return with your spouse both for the year of the distribution and for the year for which you claim the credit.

Testing period. The testing period consists of the year for which you claim the credit, the period after the end of that year and before the due date (including extensions) for filing your return for that year, and the 2 tax years before that year.

Example. You and your spouse filed joint returns in 2018 and 2019, and plan to do so in 2020 and 2021. You received a taxable distribution from a qualified plan in 2018 and a taxable distribution from an eligible deferred compensation plan in 2019. Your spouse received taxable distributions from a Roth IRA in 2020 and tax-free distributions from a Roth IRA in 2021 before April 15. You made eligible contributions to an IRA in 2020 and you otherwise qualify for this credit. You must reduce the amount of your qualifying contributions in 2020 by the total of the distributions you received in 2018, 2019, 2020, and 2021.

Maximum eligible contributions. After your contributions are reduced, the maximum annual contribution on which you can base the credit is $2,000 per person.

Effect on other credits. The amount of this credit won't change the amount of your refundable tax credits. A refundable tax credit, such as the earned income credit or the refundable amount of your child tax credit, is an amount that you would receive as a refund even if you didn't otherwise owe any taxes.

Maximum credit. This is a nonrefundable credit. The amount of the credit in any year can't be more than the amount of tax that you would otherwise pay (not counting any refundable credits) in any year. If your tax liability is reduced to zero because of other nonrefundable credits, such as the credit for child and dependent care expenses, then you won't be entitled to this credit.

How to figure and report the credit. The amount of the credit you can get is based on the contributions you make and your credit rate. Your credit rate can be as low as 10% or as high as 50%. Your credit rate depends on your income and your filing status. See Form 8880 to determine your credit rate.

The maximum contribution taken into account is $2,000 per person. On a joint return, up to $2,000 is taken into account for each spouse.

Figure the credit on Form 8880. Report the credit on Schedule 3 (Form 1040), line 4, and attach Form 8880 to your return.

How To Get Tax Help

If you have questions about a tax issue, need help preparing your tax return, or want to download free publications, forms, or instructions, go to *IRS.gov* and find resources that can help you right away.

Preparing and filing your tax return. After receiving all your wage and earnings statements (Form W-2, W-2G, 1099-R, 1099-MISC, 1099-NEC, etc.); unemployment compensation statements (by mail or in a digital format) or other government payment statements (Form 1099-G); and interest, dividend, and retirement statements from banks and investment firms (Forms 1099), you have several options to choose from to prepare and file your tax return. You can prepare the tax return yourself, see if you qualify for free tax preparation, or hire a tax professional to prepare your return.

Free options for tax preparation. Go to *IRS.gov* to see your options for preparing and filing your return online or in your local community, if you qualify, which include the following.

- **Free File.** This program lets you prepare and file your federal individual income tax return for free using brand-name tax-preparation-and-filing software or Free File fillable forms. However, state tax preparation may not be available through Free File. Go to *IRS.gov/FreeFile* to see if you qualify for free online federal tax preparation, e-filing, and direct deposit or payment options.
- **VITA.** The Volunteer Income Tax Assistance (VITA) program offers free tax help to people with low-to-moderate incomes, persons with disabilities, and limited-English-speaking taxpayers who need help preparing their own tax returns. Go to *IRS.gov/VITA*, download the free IRS2Go app, or call 800-906-9887 for information on free tax return preparation.
- **TCE.** The Tax Counseling for the Elderly (TCE) program offers free tax help for all taxpayers, particularly those who are 60 years of age and older. TCE volunteers specialize in answering questions about pensions and retirement-related issues unique to seniors. Go to *IRS.gov/TCE*, download the free IRS2Go app,

or call 888-227-7669 for information on free tax return preparation.

- **MilTax.** Members of the U.S. Armed Forces and qualified veterans may use MilTax, a free tax service offered by the Department of Defense through Military OneSource.

  Also, the IRS offers Free Fillable Forms, which can be completed online and then filed electronically regardless of income.

Using online tools to help prepare your return. Go to *IRS.gov/Tools* for the following.

- The *Earned Income Tax Credit Assistant* (*IRS.gov/EITCAssistant*) determines if you're eligible for the earned income credit (EIC).
- The *Online EIN Application* (*IRS.gov/EIN*) helps you get an employer identification number (EIN).
- The *Tax Withholding Estimator* (*IRS.gov/W4app*) makes it easier for everyone to pay the correct amount of tax during the year. The tool is a convenient, online way to check and tailor your withholding. It's more user-friendly for taxpayers, including retirees and self-employed individuals. The features include the following.
  - Easy to understand language.
  - The ability to switch between screens, correct previous entries, and skip screens that don't apply.
  - Tips and links to help you determine if you qualify for tax credits and deductions.
  - A progress tracker.
  - A self-employment tax feature.
  - Automatic calculation of taxable social security benefits.
- The *First Time Homebuyer Credit Account Look-up* (*IRS.gov/HomeBuyer*) tool provides information on your repayments and account balance.
- The *Sales Tax Deduction Calculator* (*IRS.gov/SalesTax*) figures the amount you can claim if you itemize deductions on Schedule A (Form 1040).

Getting answers to your tax questions. On IRS.gov, you can get up-to-date information on current events and changes in tax law.

- *IRS.gov/Help*: A variety of tools to help you get answers to some of the most common tax questions.
- *IRS.gov/ITA*: The Interactive Tax Assistant, a tool that will ask you questions on a number of tax law topics and provide answers.
- *IRS.gov/Forms*: Find forms, instructions, and publications. You will find details on 2020 tax changes and hundreds of interactive links to help you find answers to your questions.
- You may also be able to access tax law information in your electronic filing software.

Need someone to prepare your tax return? There are various types of tax return preparers, including tax preparers, enrolled agents, certified public accountants (CPAs), attorneys, and many others who don't have professional credentials. If you choose to have someone prepare your tax return, choose that preparer wisely. A paid tax preparer is:

- Primarily responsible for the overall substantive accuracy of your return,
- Required to sign the return, and
- Required to include their preparer tax identification number (PTIN).

Although the tax preparer always signs the return, you're ultimately responsible for providing all the information required for the preparer to accurately prepare your return. Anyone paid to prepare tax returns for others should have a thorough understanding of tax matters. For more information on how to choose a tax preparer, go to *Tips for Choosing a Tax Preparer* on IRS.gov.

Coronavirus. Go to *IRS.gov/Coronavirus* for links to information on the impact of the coronavirus, as well as tax relief available for individuals and families, small and large businesses, and tax-exempt organizations.

Tax reform. Tax reform legislation affects individuals, businesses, and tax-exempt and government entities. Go to *IRS.gov/TaxReform* for information and updates on how this legislation affects your taxes.

Employers can register to use Business Services Online. The Social Security Administration (SSA) offers online service at *SSA.gov/employer* for fast, free, and secure online W-2 filing options to CPAs, accountants, enrolled agents, and individuals who process Form W-2, Wage and Tax Statement, and Form W-2c, Corrected Wage and Tax Statement.

IRS social media. Go to *IRS.gov/SocialMedia* to see the various social media tools the IRS uses to share the latest information on tax changes, scam alerts, initiatives, products, and services. At the IRS, privacy and security are paramount. We use these tools to share public information with you. **Don't** post your SSN or other confidential information on social media sites. Always protect your identity when using any social networking site.

The following IRS YouTube channels provide short, informative videos on various tax-related topics in English, Spanish, and ASL.

- *Youtube.com/irsvideos*.
- *Youtube.com/irsvideosmultilingua*.
- *Youtube.com/irsvideosASL*.

Watching IRS videos. The IRS Video portal (*IRSVideos.gov*) contains video and audio presentations for individuals, small businesses, and tax professionals.

Online tax information in other languages. You can find information on *IRS.gov/MyLanguage* if English isn't your native language.

Free interpreter service. Multilingual assistance, provided by the IRS, is available at Taxpayer Assistance Centers (TACs) and other IRS offices. Over-the-phone interpreter service is accessible in more than 350 languages.

Getting tax forms and publications. Go to *IRS.gov/Forms* to view, download, or print all of the forms, instructions, and publications you may need. You can also download and view popular tax publications and instructions (including the Instructions for Forms 1040 and 1040-SR) on mobile devices as an eBook at *IRS.gov/eBooks*. Or you can go to *IRS.gov/OrderForms* to place an order.

Access your online account (individual taxpayers only). Go to *IRS.gov/Account* to securely access information about your federal tax account.

- View the amount you owe, pay online, or set up an online payment agreement.
- Access your tax records online.
- Review your payment history.
- Go to *IRS.gov/SecureAccess* to review the required identity authentication process.

Using direct deposit. The fastest way to receive a tax refund is to file electronically and choose direct deposit, which securely and electronically transfers your refund directly into your financial account. Direct deposit also avoids the possibility that your check could be lost, stolen, or returned undeliverable to the IRS. Eight in 10 taxpayers use direct deposit to receive their refunds. The IRS issues more than 90% of refunds in less than 21 days.

Getting a transcript of your return. The quickest way to get a copy of your tax transcript is to go to *IRS.gov/Transcripts*. Click on either "Get Transcript Online" or "Get Transcript by Mail" to order a free copy of your transcript. If you prefer, you can order your transcript by calling 800-908-9946.

Reporting and resolving your tax-related identity theft issues.

- Tax-related identity theft happens when someone steals your personal information to commit tax fraud. Your taxes can be affected if your SSN is used to file a fraudulent return or to claim a refund or credit.
- The IRS doesn't initiate contact with taxpayers by email, text messages, telephone calls, or social media channels to request personal or financial information. This includes requests for personal identification numbers (PINs), passwords, or similar information for credit cards, banks, or other financial accounts.
- Go to *IRS.gov/IdentityTheft*, the IRS Identity Theft Central webpage, for information on identity theft and data security protection for taxpayers, tax professionals, and businesses. If your SSN has been lost or stolen or you suspect you're a victim of tax-related identity theft, you can learn what steps you should take.
- Get an Identity Protection PIN (IP PIN). IP PINs are six-digit numbers assigned to eligible taxpayers to help prevent the misuse of their SSNs on fraudulent federal income tax returns. When you have an IP PIN, it prevents someone else from filing a tax return with your SSN. To learn more, go to *IRS.gov/IPPIN*.

Checking on the status of your refund.

- Go to *IRS.gov/Refunds*.
- The IRS can't issue refunds before mid-February 2021 for returns that claimed the EIC or the additional child tax credit (ACTC). This applies to the entire refund, not just the portion associated with these credits.
- Download the official IRS2Go app to your mobile device to check your refund status.
- Call the automated refund hotline at 800-829-1954.

Making a tax payment. The IRS uses the latest encryption technology to ensure your electronic payments are safe and secure. You can make electronic payments online, by phone, and from a mobile device using the IRS2Go app. Paying electronically is quick, easy, and faster than mailing in a check or money order. Go to *IRS.gov/Payments* for information on how to make a payment using any of the following options.

- *IRS Direct Pay*: Pay your individual tax bill or estimated tax payment directly from your checking or savings account at no cost to you.
- *Debit or Credit Card*: Choose an approved payment processor to pay online, by phone, or by mobile device.
- *Electronic Funds Withdrawal*: Offered only when filing your federal taxes using tax return preparation software or through a tax professional.
- *Electronic Federal Tax Payment System*: Best option for businesses. Enrollment is required.
- *Check or Money Order*: Mail your payment to the address listed on the notice or instructions.
- *Cash*: You may be able to pay your taxes with cash at a participating retail store.
- *Same-Day Wire*: You may be able to do same-day wire from your financial institution. Contact your financial institution for availability, cost, and cut-off times.

What if I can't pay now? Go to *IRS.gov/Payments* for more information about your options.

- Apply for an *online payment agreement* (*IRS.gov/OPA*) to meet your tax obligation in monthly installments if you can't pay your taxes in full today. Once you complete the online process, you will receive immediate notification of whether your agreement has been approved.
- Use the *Offer in Compromise Pre-Qualifier* to see if you can settle your tax debt for less than the full amount you owe. For more information on the Offer in Compromise program, go to *IRS.gov/OIC*.

Filing an amended return. You can now file Form 1040-X electronically with tax filing software to amend 2019 Forms 1040 and 1040-SR. To do so, you must have e-filed your original 2019 return. Amended returns for all prior years must be mailed. See *Tips for taxpayers who need to file an amended tax return* and go to *IRS.gov/Form1040X* for information and updates.

Checking the status of your amended return. Go to *IRS.gov/WMAR* to track the status of Form 1040-X amended returns. Please note that it can take up to 3 weeks from the date you filed your amended return for it to show up in our system, and processing it can take up to 16 weeks.

Understanding an IRS notice or letter you've received. Go to *IRS.gov/Notices* to find additional information about responding to an IRS notice or letter.

Contacting your local IRS office. Keep in mind, many questions can be answered on IRS.gov without visiting an IRS Taxpayer Assistance Center (TAC). Go to *IRS.gov/LetUsHelp* for the topics people ask about most. If you still need help, IRS TACs provide tax help when a tax issue can't be handled online or by phone. All TACs now provide service by appointment, so you'll know in advance that you can get the service you need without long wait times. Before you visit, go to *IRS.gov/TACLocator* to find the nearest TAC and to check hours, available services, and appointment options. Or, on the IRS2Go app, under the Stay Connected tab, choose the Contact Us option and click on "Local Offices."

The Taxpayer Advocate Service (TAS) Is Here To Help You

What Is TAS?

TAS is an ***independent*** organization within the IRS that helps taxpayers and protects taxpayer rights. Their job is to ensure that every taxpayer is treated fairly and that you know and understand your rights under the *Taxpayer Bill of Rights*.

How Can You Learn About Your Taxpayer Rights?

The Taxpayer Bill of Rights describes 10 basic rights that all taxpayers have when dealing with the IRS. Go to *TaxpayerAdvocate.IRS.gov* to help you understand what these rights mean to you and how they apply. These are ***your*** rights. Know them. Use them.

What Can TAS Do For You?

TAS can help you resolve problems that you can't resolve with the IRS. And their service is free. If you qualify for their assistance, you will be assigned to one advocate who will work with you throughout the process and will do everything possible to resolve your issue. TAS can help you if:

- Your problem is causing financial difficulty for you, your family, or your business;
- You face (or your business is facing) an immediate threat of adverse action; or
- You've tried repeatedly to contact the IRS but no one has responded, or the IRS hasn't responded by the date promised.

How Can You Reach TAS?

TAS has offices *in every state, the District of Columbia, and Puerto Rico*. Your local advocate's number is in your local directory and at *TaxpayerAdvocate.IRS.gov/Contact-Us*. You can also call them at 877-777-4778.

How Else Does TAS Help Taxpayers?

TAS works to resolve large-scale problems that affect many taxpayers. If you know of one of these broad issues, please report it to them at *IRS.gov/SAMS*.

TAS for Tax Professionals

TAS can provide a variety of information for tax professionals, including tax law updates and guidance, TAS programs, and ways to let TAS know about systemic problems you've seen in your practice.

Low Income Taxpayer Clinics (LITCs)

LITCs are independent from the IRS. LITCs represent individuals whose income is below a certain level and need to resolve tax problems with the IRS, such as audits, appeals, and tax collection disputes. In addition, clinics can provide information about taxpayer rights and responsibilities in different languages for individuals who speak English as a second language. Services are offered for free or a small fee for eligible taxpayers. To find a clinic near you, visit *www.TaxpayerAdvocate.IRS.gov/about-us/Low-Income-Taxpayer-Clinics-LITC/* or see IRS Pub. 4134, *Low Income Taxpayer Clinic List*.

Appendices

To help you complete your tax return, use the following appendices that include worksheets and tables.

1. **Appendix A**—Summary Record of Traditional IRA(s) for 2020.
2. **Appendix B**—Worksheets you use if you receive social security benefits and are subject to the IRA deduction phaseout rules. A filled-in example is included.
   a. Worksheet 1, Computation of Modified AGI.
   b. Worksheet 2, Computation of Traditional IRA Deduction for 2020.
   c. Worksheet 3, Computation of Taxable Social Security Benefits.
   d. Comprehensive Example and completed worksheets.

Appendix A. Summary Record of Traditional IRA(s) for 2020

Keep for Your Records

Name ______________________________

I was ☐ covered ☐ not covered by my employer's retirement plan during the year.

I became 59½ on ______________________________ (month) (day) (year)

Contributions

Name of traditional IRA	Date	Amount contributed for 2020	Check if rollover contribution	Fair market value of IRA as of December 31, 2020, from Form 5498
1.				
2.				
3.				
4.				
5.				
6.				
7.				
8.				
Total				

Total contributions deducted on tax return . . . . $ ________

Total contributions treated as nondeductible on Form 8606 . . . . $ ________

Distributions

Name of traditional IRA	Date	Amount of distribution	Reason (for example, retirement, rollover, conversion, withdrawal of excess contributions)	Income earned on IRA	Taxable amount reported on income tax return	Nontaxable amount from Form 8606, line 13
1.						
2.						
3.						
4.						
5.						
6.						
7.						
8.						
Total						

Basis of all traditional IRAs for 2020 and earlier years (from Form 8606, line 14) . . . . $ ________

Note. You should keep copies of your income tax return, and Forms W-2, 8606, and 5498.

Appendix B. Worksheets for Social Security Recipients Who Contribute to a Traditional IRA

Keep for Your Records

If you receive social security benefits, have taxable compensation, contribute to your traditional IRA, and you or your spouse is covered by an employer retirement plan, complete the following worksheets. (See *Are You Covered by an Employer Plan?* in chapter 1.)

Use Worksheet 1 to figure your modified adjusted gross income. This amount is needed in the computation of your IRA deduction, if any, which is figured using Worksheet 2.

The IRA deduction figured using Worksheet 2 is entered on your tax return.

Worksheet 1
Computation of Modified AGI
(For use only by taxpayers who receive social security benefits)

Filing Status—Check only one box:
☐ **A.** Married filing jointly
☐ **B.** Single, Head of Household, Qualifying Widow(er), or Married filing separately and ***lived apart*** from your spouse during the ***entire year***
☐ **C.** Married filing separately and ***lived with*** your spouse at ***any time*** during the year

1. Adjusted gross income (AGI) from Form 1040 or 1040-SR
(For purposes of this worksheet, figure your AGI without taking into account any social security benefits from Form SSA-1099 or RRB-1099, any deduction for contributions to a traditional IRA, any student loan interest deduction, any tuition and fees deduction, or any exclusion of interest from savings bonds to be reported on Form 8815.) . . . . . **1.** ________

2. Enter the amount in box 5 of all Forms SSA-1099 and Forms RRB-1099 . . . . . **2.** ________

3. Enter one-half of line 2 . . . . . **3.** ________

4. Enter the amount of any foreign earned income exclusion, foreign housing exclusion, U.S. possessions income exclusion, exclusion of income from Puerto Rico you claimed as a bona fide resident of Puerto Rico, or exclusion of employer-provided adoption benefits . . . . . **4.** ________

5. Enter the amount of any tax-exempt interest reported on Form 1040 or 1040-SR, line 2a . . . . **5.** ________

6. Add lines 1, 3, 4, and 5 . . . . . **6.** ________

7. Enter the amount listed below for your filing status.
- **$32,000** if you checked box **A** above.
- **$25,000** if you checked box **B** above.
- **$0** if you checked box **C** above . . . . . **7.** ________

8. Subtract line 7 from line 6. If zero or less, enter -0- on this line . . . . . **8.** ________

9. If line 8 is zero, skip to line 17, enter -0-, and continue with line 18.
If line 8 is more than zero, enter the amount listed below for your filing status.
- **$12,000** if you checked box **A** above.
- **$9,000** if you checked box **B** above.
- **$0** if you checked box **C** above . . . . . **9.** ________

10. Subtract line 9 from line 8. If zero or less, enter -0- . . . . . **10.** ________

11. Enter the smaller of line 8 or line 9 . . . . . **11.** ________

12. Enter one-half of line 11 . . . . . **12.** ________

13. Enter the smaller of line 3 or line 12 . . . . . **13.** ________

14. Multiply line 10 by 0.85. If line 10 is zero, enter -0- . . . . . **14.** ________

15. Add lines 13 and 14 . . . . . **15.** ________

16. Multiply line 2 by 0.85 . . . . . **16.** ________

17. **Taxable benefits** to be included in modified AGI for traditional IRA deduction purposes. Enter the smaller of line 15 or line 16 . . . . . **17.** ________

18. Enter the amount of any employer-provided adoption benefits exclusion and any foreign earned income exclusion and foreign housing exclusion or deduction that you claimed . . . . . **18.** ________

19. **Modified AGI** for determining your reduced traditional IRA deduction—add lines 1, 17, and 18. Enter here and on line 2 of Worksheet 2 next . . . . . **19.** ________

Appendix B. (Continued)

Keep for Your Records

Worksheet 2
Computation of Traditional IRA Deduction for 2020
(For use only by taxpayers who receive social security benefits)

IF your filing status is...	AND your modified AGI is over...	THEN enter on line 1 below...
married filing jointly or qualifying widow(er)	$104,000*	$124,000
married filing jointly (you are not covered by an employer plan but your spouse is)	$196,000*	$206,000
single, or head of household	$65,000*	$75,000
married filing separately**	$0*	$10,000

*If your modified AGI **isn't** over this amount, you can take an IRA deduction for your contributions of up to the lesser of $6,000 ($7,000 if you are age 50 or older) or your taxable compensation. Skip this worksheet, proceed to Worksheet 3, and enter your IRA deduction on line 2 of Worksheet 3.
If you **didn't live with your spouse **at any time** during the year, consider your filing status as single.
Note. If you were married and you or your spouse worked and you both contributed to IRAs, figure the deduction for each of you separately.

1.	Enter the applicable amount from above	**1.** ________
2.	Enter your **modified AGI** from Worksheet 1, line 19	**2.** ________
	Note. If line 2 is equal to or more than the amount on line 1, **stop here;** your traditional IRA contributions aren't deductible. Proceed to Worksheet 3.	
3.	Subtract line 2 from line 1	**3.** ________
4.	Multiply line 3 by the percentage below that applies to you. If the result isn't a multiple of $10, round it to the next highest multiple of $10. (For example, $611.40 is rounded to $620.) However, if the result is less than $200, enter $200. • Married filing jointly or qualifying widow(er) **and** you are covered by an employer plan, multiply line 3 by 30% (0.30) (by 35% (0.35) if you are age 50 or older). • All others, multiply line 3 by 60% (0.60) (by 70% (0.70) if you are age 50 or older).	**4.** ________
5.	Enter your compensation minus any deductions on Schedule 1 (Form 1040), line 14 (deductible part of self-employment tax) and Schedule 1 (Form 1040), line 15 (self-employed SEP, SIMPLE, and qualified plans). If you are the lower-income spouse, include your spouse's compensation reduced by his or her traditional IRA and Roth IRA contributions for this year	**5.** ________
6.	Enter contributions you made, or plan to make, to your traditional IRA for 2020, but don't enter more than $6,000 ($7,000 if you are age 50 or older)	**6.** ________
7.	**Deduction.** Compare lines 4, 5, and 6. Enter the smallest amount here (or a smaller amount if you choose). Enter this amount on your Schedule 1 (Form 1040), line 19. (If the amount on line 6 is more than the amount on line 7, complete line 8.)	**7.** ________
8.	**Nondeductible contributions.** Subtract line 7 from line 5 or 6, whichever is smaller. Enter the result here and on line 1 of your Form 8606, Nondeductible IRAs	**8.** ________

Appendix B. (Continued)

Keep for Your Records

Worksheet 3
Computation of Taxable Social Security Benefits
(For use by taxpayers who receive social security benefits and take a traditional IRA deduction)

Filing Status—Check only one box:

☐ **A.** Married filing jointly

☐ **B.** Single, Head of Household, Qualifying Widow(er), or Married filing separately and ***lived apart*** from your spouse during the ***entire year***

☐ **C.** Married filing separately and ***lived with*** your spouse at ***any time*** during the year

1. Adjusted gross income (AGI) from Form 1040 or 1040-SR (For purposes of this worksheet, figure your AGI without taking into account any IRA deduction, any student loan interest deduction, any tuition and fees deduction, or any social security benefits from Form SSA-1099 or RRB-1099, or any exclusion of interest from savings bonds to be reported on Form 8815.) **1.** ______

2. Deduction(s) from line 7 of Worksheet(s) 2 **2.** ______

3. Subtract line 2 from line 1 **3.** ______

4. Enter amount in box 5 of all Forms SSA-1099 and Forms RRB-1099 **4.** ______

5. Enter one-half of line 4 **5.** ______

6. Enter the amount of any foreign earned income exclusion, foreign housing exclusion, exclusion of income from U.S. possessions, exclusion of income from Puerto Rico you claimed as a bona fide resident of Puerto Rico, or exclusion of employer-provided adoption benefits **6.** ______

7. Enter the amount of any tax-exempt interest reported on line 2a of Form 1040 or 1040-SR **7.** ______

8. Add lines 3, 5, 6, and 7 **8.** ______

9. Enter the amount listed below for your filing status.
- **$32,000** if you checked box **A** above.
- **$25,000** if you checked box **B** above.
- **$0** if you checked box **C** above **9.** ______

10. Subtract line 9 from line 8. If zero or less, enter -0- on this line **10.** ______

11. If line 10 is zero, **stop here.** None of your social security benefits are taxable. If line 10 is more than zero, enter the amount listed below for your filing status.
- **$12,000** if you checked box **A** above.
- **$9,000** if you checked box **B** above.
- **$0** if you checked box **C** above **11.** ______

12. Subtract line 11 from line 10. If zero or less, enter -0- **12.** ______

13. Enter the smaller of line 10 or line 11 **13.** ______

14. Enter one-half of line 13 **14.** ______

15. Enter the smaller of line 5 or line 14 **15.** ______

16. Multiply line 12 by 0.85. If line 12 is zero, enter -0- **16.** ______

17. Add lines 15 and 16 **17.** ______

18. Multiply line 4 by 0.85 **18.** ______

19. **Taxable social security benefits.** Enter the smaller of line 17 or line 18 **19.** ______

Appendix B. (Continued)

Keep for Your Records

Comprehensive Example
Determining Your Traditional IRA Deduction and the Taxable Portion of Your Social Security Benefits

John Black is married and files a joint return. He is 65 years old and had 2020 wages of $98,700. His wife didn't work in 2020. He also received social security benefits of $12,000 and made a $7,000 contribution to his traditional IRA for the year. He had no foreign income, no tax-exempt interest, and no adjustments to income on lines 10 through 22 on his Schedule 1 (Form 1040). He participated in a section 401(k) retirement plan at work.

John completes Worksheets 1 and 2. Worksheet 2 shows that his 2020 IRA deduction is $5,290. He must either withdraw the contributions that are more than the deduction (the $1,710 shown on line 8 of Worksheet 2), or treat the excess amounts as nondeductible contributions (in which case he must complete Form 8606 and attach it to his Form 1040-SR).

The completed worksheets that follow show how John figured his modified AGI to determine the IRA deduction and the taxable social security benefits to report on his Form 1040-SR.

Worksheet 1
Computation of Modified AGI
(For use only by taxpayers who receive social security benefits)

Filing Status—Check only one box:

☑ **A.** Married filing jointly
☐ **B.** Single, Head of Household, Qualifying Widow(er), or Married filing separately and ***lived apart*** from your spouse during the ***entire year***
☐ **C.** Married filing separately and ***lived with*** your spouse at ***any time*** during the year

1. Adjusted gross income (AGI) from Form 1040 or 1040-SR (For purposes of this worksheet, figure your AGI without taking into account any social security benefits from Form SSA-1099 or RRB-1099, any deduction for contributions to a traditional IRA, any student loan interest deduction, any tuition and fees deduction, or any exclusion of interest from savings bonds to be reported on Form 8815.)	1.	98,700
2. Enter the amount in box 5 of all Forms SSA-1099 and Forms RRB-1099	2.	12,000
3. Enter one-half of line 2	3.	6,000
4. Enter the amount of any foreign earned income exclusion, foreign housing exclusion, U.S. possessions income exclusion, exclusion of income from Puerto Rico you claimed as a bona fide resident of Puerto Rico, or exclusion of employer-provided adoption benefits	4.	0
5. Enter the amount of any tax-exempt interest reported on Form 1040 or 1040-SR, line 2a	5.	0
6. Add lines 1, 3, 4, and 5	6.	104,700
7. Enter the amount listed below for your filing status. • **$32,000** if you checked box **A** above. • **$25,000** if you checked box **B** above. • **$0** if you checked box **C** above	7.	32,000
8. Subtract line 7 from line 6. If zero or less, enter -0- on this line	8.	72,700
9. If line 8 is zero, skip to line 17, enter -0-, and continue with line 18. If line 8 is more than zero, enter the amount listed below for your filing status. • **$12,000** if you checked box **A** above. • **$9,000** if you checked box **B** above. • **$0** if you checked box **C** above	9.	12,000
10. Subtract line 9 from line 8. If zero or less, enter -0-	10.	60,700
11. Enter the smaller of line 8 or line 9	11.	12,000
12. Enter one-half of line 11	12.	6,000
13. Enter the smaller of line 3 or line 12	13.	6,000
14. Multiply line 10 by 0.85. If line 10 is zero, enter -0-	14.	51,595
15. Add lines 13 and 14	15.	57,595
16. Multiply line 2 by 0.85	16.	10,200
17. **Taxable benefits** to be included in modified AGI for traditional IRA deduction purposes. Enter the smaller of line 15 or line 16	17.	10,200
18. Enter the amount of any employer-provided adoption benefits exclusion and any foreign earned income exclusion and foreign housing exclusion or deduction that you claimed	18.	0
19. **Modified AGI** for determining your reduced traditional IRA deduction—add lines 1, 17, and 18. Enter here and on line 2 of Worksheet 2 next	19.	108,900

Appendix B. (Continued)

Keep for Your Records

Worksheet 2
Computation of Traditional IRA Deduction for 2020
(For use only by taxpayers who receive social security benefits)

IF your filing status is...	AND your modified AGI is over...	THEN enter on line 1 below...
married filing jointly or qualifying widow(er)	$104,000*	$124,000
married filing jointly (you aren't covered by an employer plan but your spouse is)	$196,000*	$206,000
single, or head of household	$65,000*	$75,000
married filing separately**	$0*	$10,000

*If your modified AGI **isn't** over this amount, you can take an IRA deduction for your contributions of up to the lesser of $6,000 ($7,000 if you are age 50 or older) or your taxable compensation. Skip this worksheet, proceed to Worksheet 3, and enter your IRA deduction on line 2 of Worksheet 3.
If you **didn't live with your spouse **at any time** during the year, consider your filing status as single.
Note. If you were married and you or your spouse worked and you both contributed to IRAs, figure the deduction for each of you separately.

1.	Enter the applicable amount from above	1.	124,000
2.	Enter your **modified AGI** from Worksheet 1, line 19	2.	108,900
	Note. If line 2 is equal to or more than the amount on line 1, **stop here;** your traditional IRA contributions aren't deductible. Proceed to Worksheet 3.		
3.	Subtract line 2 from line 1	3.	15,100
4.	Multiply line 3 by the percentage below that applies to you. If the result isn't a multiple of $10, round it to the next highest multiple of $10. (For example, $611.40 is rounded to $620.) However, if the result is less than $200, enter $200. • Married filing jointly or qualifying widow(er) **and** you are covered by an employer plan, multiply line 3 by 30% (0.30) (by 35% (0.35) if you are age 50 or older). • All others, multiply line 3 by 60% (0.60) (by 70% (0.70) if you are age 50 or older).	4.	5,290
5.	Enter your compensation minus any deductions on Schedule 1 (Form 1040), line 14 (deductible part of self-employment tax) and Schedule 1 (Form 1040), line 15 (self-employed SEP, SIMPLE, and qualified plans). If you are the lower-income spouse, include your spouse's compensation reduced by his or her traditional IRA and Roth IRA contributions for this year	5.	98,700
6.	Enter contributions you made, or plan to make, to your traditional IRA for 2020, but don't enter more than $6,000 ($7,000 if you are age 50 or older)	6.	7,000
7.	**Deduction.** Compare lines 4, 5, and 6. Enter the smallest amount here (or a smaller amount if you choose). Enter this amount on your Schedule 1 (Form 1040), line 19. (If the amount on line 6 is more than the amount on line 7, complete line 8)	7.	5,290
8.	**Nondeductible contributions.** Subtract line 7 from line 5 or 6, whichever is smaller. Enter the result here and on line 1 of your Form 8606, Nondeductible IRAs	8.	1,710

Appendix B. (Continued)

Keep for Your Records

Worksheet 3
Computation of Taxable Social Security Benefits
(For use by taxpayers who receive social security benefits and take a traditional IRA deduction)

Filing Status—Check only one box:

☑ **A.** Married filing jointly

☐ **B.** Single, Head of Household, Qualifying Widow(er), or Married filing separately and ***lived apart*** from your spouse during the ***entire year***

☐ **C.** Married filing separately and ***lived with*** your spouse at ***any time*** during the year

1. Adjusted gross income (AGI) from Form 1040 or 1040-SR (For purposes of this worksheet, figure your AGI without taking into account any IRA deduction, any student loan interest deduction, any tuition and fees deduction, any social security benefits from Form SSA-1099 or RRB-1099, or any exclusion of interest from savings bonds to be reported on Form 8815.)	1.	98,700
2. Deduction(s) from line 7 of Worksheet(s) 2	2.	5,290
3. Subtract line 2 from line 1	3.	93,410
4. Enter the amount in box 5 of all Forms SSA-1099 and Forms RRB-1099	4.	12,000
5. Enter one-half of line 4	5.	6,000
6. Enter the amount of any foreign earned income exclusion, foreign housing exclusion, exclusion of income from U.S. possessions, exclusion of income from Puerto Rico you claimed as a bona fide resident of Puerto Rico, or exclusion of employer-provided adoption benefits	6.	0
7. Enter the amount of any tax-exempt interest reported on Form 1040 or 1040-SR, line 2a	7.	0
8. Add lines 3, 5, 6, and 7	8.	99,410
9. Enter the amount listed below for your filing status. • **$32,000** if you checked box **A** above. • **$25,000** if you checked box **B** above. • **$0** if you checked box **C** above	9.	32,000
10. Subtract line 9 from line 8. If zero or less, enter -0- on this line	10.	67,410
11. If line 10 is zero, **stop here.** None of your social security benefits are taxable. If line 10 is more than zero, enter the amount listed below for your filing status. • **$12,000** if you checked box **A** above. • **$9,000** if you checked box **B** above. • **$0** if you checked box **C** above	11.	12,000
12. Subtract line 11 from line 10. If zero or less, enter -0-	12.	55,410
13. Enter the smaller of line 10 or line 11	13.	12,000
14. Enter one-half of line 13	14.	6,000
15. Enter the smaller of line 5 or line 14	15.	6,000
16. Multiply line 12 by 0.85. If line 12 is zero, enter -0-	16.	47,099
17. Add lines 15 and 16	17.	53,099
18. Multiply line 4 by 0.85	18.	10,200
19. **Taxable social security benefits.** Enter the smaller of line 17 or line 18	19.	10,200

Index

To help us develop a more useful index, please let us know if you have ideas for index entries. See "Comments and Suggestions" in the "Introduction" for the ways you can reach us.

Appendix B

IRS Publication 590-B—Distributions From Individual Retirement Arrangements (IRAs) (2020)

Department of the Treasury
Internal Revenue Service

Publication 590-B
Cat. No. 66303U

Distributions from Individual Retirement Arrangements (IRAs)

For use in preparing
2020 Returns

Get forms and other information faster and easier at:
- *IRS.gov* (English)
- *IRS.gov/Spanish* (Español)
- *IRS.gov/Chinese* (中文)
- *IRS.gov/Korean* (한국어)
- *IRS.gov/Russian* (Русский)
- *IRS.gov/Vietnamese* (Tiếng Việt)

Mar 25, 2021

Contents

What's New

Coronavirus-related distributions. Recent legislation contains special rules that provide for tax-favored withdrawals, income inclusion, and repayments for certain individuals who were impacted by the coronavirus in 2020. See *Coronavirus Relief*, later.

Special rules for qualified disaster distributions and repayments expanded. The special rules for qualified disaster distributions and repayments are expanded to apply to those disasters described in the Taxpayer Certainty and Disaster Tax Relief Act of 2020. A qualified disaster is now expanded to include a major disaster that was declared before February 26, 2021, by the President under section 401 of the Stafford Act and that occurred on or after December 28, 2019, and on or before December 27, 2020, and continued no later than January 26, 2021.

However, this change does not include a major disaster that has been declared only by reason of COVID-19.

See *Disaster-Related Relief*, later, for more information.

RMDs not required in 2020. New legislation temporarily waives the requirement to make required minimum distributions (RMDs) in 2020 in response to the coronavirus pandemic. Whether that distribution is one in a series of RMDs or the initial RMD that would be required by April 1 for a taxpayer reaching age 70½ in tax year 2019, no RMD is required. See *When Must You Withdraw Assets? (Required Minimum Distributions)*, later, for more information.

Qualified birth or adoption distribution. Beginning in tax years after December 31, 2019, you can take a distribution from your IRA without it being subject to the 10% additional tax for early distributions if that distribution is for a qualified birth or adoption. For more information, see *Qualified birth or adoption distribution* under *Exceptions*, later.

Qualified plan loan offsets. A qualified plan loan offset is a type of plan loan offset that meets certain requirements. In order to be a qualified plan loan offset, the loan, at the time of the offset, must be a loan in good standing and the offset must be solely by reason of (1) the termination of the qualified employer plan, or (2) the failure to meet the repayment terms is because the employee has a severance from employment. If you meet the requirements of a qualified plan loan offset, you have until the due date, including extensions, to file your tax return for the tax year in which the offset occurs to roll over the qualified plan loan offset amount.

This revision is effective for tax years beginning January 1, 2018.

Modification of required distribution rules for designated beneficiaries. There are new required minimum distribution rules for certain beneficiaries who are designated beneficiaries when the IRA owner dies in a tax year beginning after December 31, 2019. All distributions must be made by the end of the 10th year after death, except for distributions made to certain eligible designated beneficiaries. See *10-year rule*, later, for more information.

Required minimum distributions (RMDs). For distributions required to be made after December 31, 2019, the age for beginning mandatory distributions is changed to age 72 for IRA owners reaching age 70½ after December 31, 2019. The required beginning date for IRA owners who haven't reached age 70½ by the end of 2019 is April 1 of the year following the year of the owner's 72nd birthday. See *When Must You Withdraw Assets? (Required Minimum Distributions)*, later, for more information.

Future Developments

For the latest information about developments related to Pub. 590-B, such as legislation enacted after it was published, go to *IRS.gov/Pub590B*.

Reminders

Tax relief for qualified disaster distributions and repayments. Special rules provide for tax-favored withdrawals and repayments to certain retirement plans (including IRAs) for taxpayers who suffered economic losses as a result of certain major disasters that occurred in 2018 and 2019.

Special rules also provide for tax-favored withdrawals and repayments from certain retirement plans (including IRAs) for taxpayers who suffered economic losses as a result of Hurricane Harvey or Tropical Storm Harvey, Hurricane Irma, Hurricane Maria, or the 2017 California wildfires.

Disaster tax relief is also available for taxpayers who suffered economic losses as a result of disasters declared by the President under section 401 of the Robert T. Stafford Disaster Relief and Emergency Assistance Act during calendar year 2016.

See *Disaster-Related Relief*, later, for information on these special rules.

Simplified employee pension (SEP). SEP IRAs aren't covered in this publication. They are covered in Pub. 560, Retirement Plans for Small Business.

Deemed IRAs. A qualified employer plan (retirement plan) can maintain a separate account or annuity under the plan (a deemed IRA) to receive voluntary employee contributions. If the separate account or annuity otherwise meets the requirements of an IRA, it will be subject only to IRA rules. An employee's account can be treated as a traditional IRA or a Roth IRA.

For this purpose, a "qualified employer plan" includes:

- A qualified pension, profit-sharing, or stock bonus plan (section 401(a) plan);
- A qualified employee annuity plan (section 403(a) plan);
- A tax-sheltered annuity plan (section 403(b) plan); and
- A deferred compensation plan (section 457 plan) maintained by a state, a political subdivision of a state, or an agency or instrumentality of a state or political subdivision of a state.

Statement of required minimum distribution (RMD). If an RMD is required from your IRA, the trustee, custodian, or issuer that held the IRA at the end of the preceding year must either report the amount of the RMD to you, or offer to calculate it for you. The report or offer must include the date by which the amount must be distributed. The report is due January 31 of the year in which the minimum distribution is required. It can be provided with the year-end fair market value statement that you normally get each year. No report is required for section 403(b) contracts (generally tax-sheltered annuities) or for IRAs of owners who have died.

IRA interest. Although interest earned from your IRA is generally not taxed in the year earned, it isn't tax-exempt interest. Tax on your traditional IRA is generally deferred until you take a distribution. Don't report this interest on your return as tax-exempt interest. For more information on tax-exempt interest, see the instructions for your tax return.

Net Investment Income Tax (NIIT). For purposes of the NIIT, net investment income doesn't include distributions from a qualified retirement plan (for example, 401(a), 403(a), 403(b), or 457(b) plans, and IRAs). However, these distributions are taken into account when determining the modified adjusted gross income threshold. Distributions from a nonqualified retirement plan are included in net investment income. See Form 8960, Net Investment Income Tax—Individuals, Estates, and Trusts, and its instructions for more information.

Photographs of missing children. The IRS is a proud partner with the *National Center for Missing & Exploited Children® (NCMEC)*. Photographs of missing children selected by the Center may appear in this publication on pages that would otherwise be blank. You can help bring these children home by looking at the photographs and calling 1-800-THE-LOST (1-800-843-5678) if you recognize a child.

Introduction

This publication discusses distributions from individual retirement arrangements (IRAs). An IRA is a personal savings plan that gives you tax advantages for setting aside money for retirement. For information about contributions to an IRA, see Pub. 590-A.

What are some tax advantages of an IRA? Two tax advantages of an IRA are that:

- Contributions you make to an IRA may be fully or partially deductible, depending on which type of IRA you have and on your circumstances; and
- Generally, amounts in your IRA (including earnings and gains) aren't taxed until distributed. In some cases, amounts aren't taxed at all if distributed according to the rules.

What's in this publication? This publication discusses traditional and Roth IRAs. It explains the rules for:

- Handling an inherited IRA, and
- Receiving distributions (making withdrawals) from an IRA.

It also explains the penalties and additional taxes that apply when the rules aren't followed. To assist you in complying with the tax rules for IRAs, this publication contains worksheets, sample forms, and tables, which can be found throughout the publication and in the appendices at the back of the publication.

How to use this publication. The rules that you must follow depend on which type of IRA you have. Use Table I-1 to help you determine which parts of this publication to read. Also use Table I-1 if you were referred to this publication from instructions to a form.

Comments and suggestions. We welcome your comments about this publication and suggestions for future editions.

You can send us comments through *IRS.gov/FormComments*. Or, you can write to the Internal Revenue Service, Tax Forms and Publications, 1111 Constitution Ave. NW, IR-6526, Washington, DC 20224.

Although we can't respond individually to each comment received, we do appreciate your feedback and will consider your comments and suggestions as we revise our tax forms, instructions, and publications. Do **not** send tax questions, tax returns, or payments to the above address.

Getting answers to your tax questions. If you have a tax question not answered by this publication or the *How To Get Tax Help* section at the end of this publication, go to the IRS Interactive Tax Assistant page at *IRS.gov/Help/ITA* where you can find topics by using the search feature or viewing the categories listed.

Getting tax forms, instructions, and publications. Visit *IRS.gov/Forms* to download current and prior-year forms, instructions, and publications.

Ordering tax forms, instructions, and publications. Go to *IRS.gov/OrderForms* to order current forms, instructions, and publications; call 800-829-3676 to order prior-year forms and instructions. The IRS will process your order for forms and publications as soon as possible. Do not resubmit requests you've already sent us. You can get forms and publications faster online.

Useful Items

You may want to see:

Publications

- ❑ **590-A** Contributions to Individual Retirement Accounts (IRAs)
- ❑ **560** Retirement Plans for Small Business (SEP, SIMPLE, and Qualified Plans)
- ❑ **571** Tax-Sheltered Annuity Plans (403(b) Plans)
- ❑ **575** Pension and Annuity Income
- ❑ **939** General Rule for Pensions and Annuities
- ❑ **976** Disaster Relief

Forms (and Instructions)

- ❑ **W-4P** Withholding Certificate for Pension or Annuity Payments
- ❑ **1099-R** Distributions From Pensions, Annuities, Retirement or Profit-Sharing Plans, IRAs, Insurance Contracts, etc.
- ❑ **5304-SIMPLE** Savings Incentive Match Plan for Employees of Small Employers (SIMPLE)—Not for Use With a Designated Financial Institution
- ❑ **5305-S** SIMPLE Individual Retirement Trust Account
- ❑ **5305-SA** SIMPLE Individual Retirement Custodial Account

- ❑ **5305-SIMPLE** Savings Incentive Match Plan for Employees of Small Employers (SIMPLE)—for Use With a Designated Financial Institution
- ❑ **5329** Additional Taxes on Qualified Plans (Including IRAs) and Other Tax-Favored Accounts
- ❑ **5498** IRA Contribution Information
- ❑ **8606** Nondeductible IRAs
- ❑ **8815** Exclusion of Interest From Series EE and I U.S. Savings Bonds Issued After 1989
- ❑ **8839** Qualified Adoption Expenses
- ❑ **8880** Credit for Qualified Retirement Savings Contributions
- ❑ **8915-A** Qualified 2016 Disaster Retirement Plan Distributions and Repayments
- ❑ **8915-B** Qualified 2017 Disaster Retirement Plan Distributions and Repayments
- ❑ **8915-C** Qualified 2018 Disaster Retirement Plan Distributions and Repayments
- ❑ **8915-D** Qualified 2019 Disaster Retirement Plan Distributions and Repayments
- ❑ **8915-E** Qualified 2020 Disaster Retirement Plan Distributions and Repayments (Use for Coronavirus-Related and Other Qualified 2020 Disaster Distributions)

See *How To Get Tax Help*, later, for information about getting these publications and forms.

Table I-1. **Using This Publication**

IF you need information on...	**THEN** see...
Traditional IRAs	chapter 1.
Roth IRAs	chapter 2, and parts of chapter 1.
Coronavirus Relief	chapter 3.
Disaster-Related Relief	chapter 4.
SEP IRAs, SIMPLE IRAs, and 401(k) plans	Pub. 560.
Coverdell education savings accounts (formerly called education IRAs)	Pub. 970.

Table I-2. **How Are a Traditional IRA and a Roth IRA Different?**

This table shows the differences between traditional and Roth IRAs. Answers in the middle column apply to traditional IRAs. Answers in the right column apply to Roth IRAs.

Question	**Answer**	
	Traditional IRA?	**Roth IRA?**
Do I have to start taking distributions when I reach a certain age from a	Yes. You must begin receiving required minimum distributions by April 1 of the year following the year you reach age 72. See *When Must You Withdraw Assets? (Required Minimum Distributions)* in chapter 1.	No. If you are the original owner of a Roth IRA, you don't have to take distributions regardless of your age. See *Are Distributions Taxable?* in chapter 2. However, if you are the beneficiary of a Roth IRA, you may have to take distributions. See *Distributions After Owner's Death* in chapter 2.
How are distributions taxed from a	Distributions from a traditional IRA are taxed as ordinary income, but if you made nondeductible contributions, not all of the distribution is taxable. See *Are Distributions Taxable?* in chapter 1.	Distributions from a Roth IRA aren't taxed as long as you meet certain criteria. See *Are Distributions Taxable?* in chapter 2.
Do I have to file a form just because I receive distributions from a	Not unless you have ever made a nondeductible contribution to a traditional IRA. If you have, file Form 8606. See *Nondeductible Contributions* in Pub. 590-A.	Yes. File Form 8606 if you received distributions from a Roth IRA (other than a rollover, qualified charitable distribution, one-time distribution to fund an HSA, recharacterization, certain qualified distributions, or a return of certain contributions).

1.

Traditional IRAs

Introduction

This chapter discusses distributions from an IRA. In this publication, the original IRA (sometimes called an ordinary or regular IRA) is referred to as a "traditional IRA." A traditional IRA is any IRA that isn't a Roth IRA or a SIMPLE IRA.

What if You Inherit an IRA?

If you inherit a traditional IRA, you are called a beneficiary. A beneficiary can be any person or entity the owner chooses to receive the benefits of the IRA after he or she dies. Beneficiaries of a traditional IRA must include in their gross income any taxable distributions they receive.

Inherited from spouse. If you inherit a traditional IRA from your spouse, you generally have the following three choices. You can:

1. Treat it as your own IRA by designating yourself as the account owner;
2. Treat it as your own by rolling it over into your IRA, or to the extent it is taxable, into a:
   a. Qualified employer plan,
   b. Qualified employee annuity plan (section 403(a) plan),
   c. Tax-sheltered annuity plan (section 403(b) plan),
   d. Deferred compensation plan of a state or local government (section 457 plan); or
3. Treat yourself as the beneficiary rather than treating the IRA as your own.

Treating it as your own. You will be considered to have chosen to treat the IRA as your own if:

- Contributions (including rollover contributions) are made to the inherited IRA, or
- You don't take the required minimum distribution for a year as a beneficiary of the IRA.

You will only be considered to have chosen to treat the IRA as your own if:

- You are the sole beneficiary of the IRA, and
- You have an unlimited right to withdraw amounts from it.

However, if you receive a distribution from your deceased spouse's IRA, you can roll that distribution over into your own IRA within the 60-day time limit, as long as the distribution isn't a required distribution, even if you aren't the sole beneficiary of your deceased spouse's IRA. For more information, see *When Must You Withdraw Assets? (Required Minimum Distributions)*, later.

Inherited from someone other than spouse. If you inherit a traditional IRA from anyone other than your deceased spouse, you can't treat the inherited IRA as your own. This means that you can't make any contributions to the IRA. It also means you can't roll over any amounts into or out of the inherited IRA. However, you can make a trustee-to-trustee transfer as long as the IRA into which amounts are being moved is set up and maintained in the name of the deceased IRA owner for the benefit of you as beneficiary.

Like the original owner, you generally won't owe tax on the assets in the IRA until you receive distributions from it. You must begin receiving distributions from the IRA under the rules for distributions that apply to beneficiaries.

IRA with basis. If you inherit a traditional IRA from a person who had a basis in the IRA because of nondeductible contributions, that basis remains with the IRA. Unless you are the decedent's spouse and choose to treat the IRA as your own, you can't combine this basis with any basis you have in your own traditional IRA(s) or any basis in traditional IRA(s) you inherited from other decedents. If you take distributions from both an inherited IRA and your IRA, and each has basis, you must complete separate Forms 8606 to determine the taxable and nontaxable portions of those distributions.

Federal estate tax deduction. A beneficiary may be able to claim a deduction for estate tax resulting from certain distributions from a traditional IRA. The beneficiary can deduct the estate tax paid on any part of a distribution that is income in respect of a decedent. He or she can take the deduction for the tax year the income is reported. For information on claiming this deduction, see *Estate Tax Deduction* under *Other Tax Information* in Pub. 559.

Any taxable part of a distribution that isn't income in respect of a decedent is a payment the beneficiary must include in income. However, the beneficiary can't take any estate tax deduction for this part.

A surviving spouse can roll over the distribution to another traditional IRA and avoid including it in income for the year received.

More information. For more information about rollovers, required distributions, and inherited IRAs, see:

- *Rollovers* under *Can You Move Retirement Plan Assets?* in chapter 1 of Pub. 590-A;
- *When Must You Withdraw Assets? (Required Minimum Distributions)*, later; and
- The discussion of *IRA Beneficiaries*, later, under *When Must You Withdraw Assets? (Required Minimum Distributions).*

When Can You Withdraw or Use Assets?

You can withdraw or use your traditional IRA assets at any time. However, a 10% additional tax generally applies if you withdraw or use IRA assets before you reach age 59½. This is explained under *Age 59½ Rule* under *Early Distributions*, later.

If you were affected by a qualified disaster, see chapter 4.

You can generally make a tax-free withdrawal of contributions if you do it before the due date for filing your tax return for the year in which you made them. This means that even if you are under age 59½, the 10% additional tax may not apply. These distributions are explained in Pub. 590-A.

When Must You Withdraw Assets? (Required Minimum Distributions)

You can't keep funds in a traditional IRA (including SEP and SIMPLE IRAs) indefinitely. Eventually, they must be distributed. If there are no distributions, or if the distributions aren't large enough, you may have to pay a 50% excise tax on the amount not distributed as required. See *Excess Accumulations (Insufficient Distributions)*, later, under *What Acts Result in Penalties or Additional Taxes*. The requirements for distributing IRA funds differ, depending on whether you are the IRA owner or the beneficiary of a decedent's IRA.

Required minimum distribution (RMD). The amount that must be distributed each year is referred to as the required minimum distribution.

Note. A qualified charitable distribution will count towards your required minimum distribution. See *Qualified charitable distributions* under *Are Distributions Taxable*, later.

Distributions not eligible for rollover. Amounts that must be distributed (required minimum distributions) during a particular year aren't normally eligible for rollover treatment. But see *Special rule for RMDs and rollovers in 2020*, later.

IRA Owners

If you are the owner of a traditional IRA, you must generally start receiving distributions from your IRA by April 1 of the year following the year in which you reach age 72. April 1 of the year following the year in which you reach age 72 is referred to as the "required beginning date."

Distributions by the required beginning date. You must receive at least a minimum amount for each year starting with the year you reach age 72. If you don't receive that minimum distribution amount in the year you become age 72, you must receive that distribution by April 1 of the year following the year you become age 72.

If an IRA owner dies after reaching age 72, but before April 1 of the next year, no minimum distribution is required for that year because death occurred before the required beginning date.

RMDs not required in 2020. You are not required to make RMDs in tax year 2020, whether that distribution is one required after the initial RMD in a series of required distributions or the distribution that would be required by April 1 for a taxpayer reaching age 70½ in tax year 2019.

TIP *For tax years 2019 and earlier, you were required to begin receiving distributions by April 1 of the year following the year in which you reached age 70½. If you reach age 70½ in tax year 2020 or later, you must generally begin receiving distributions from your IRA by April 1 of the year following the year in which you reach age 72.*

TIP *If you have a RMD for 2020 due by April 1, 2021, you are not required to take that distribution in 2021. You are only required to take the distribution due by December 31, 2021.*

Special rule for RMDs and rollovers in 2020. If you receive a distribution in 2020, whether an RMD for the initial required distribution or a distribution in a series of RMDs, you can roll that distribution over and the 60-day rollover period is extended in that the end of that 60-day period cannot occur before August 31, 2020.

Permitted repayments of RMDs previously distributed from an IRA in 2020. If you received a distribution from your IRA that would have normally counted as an RMD in 2020, and that cannot be rolled over without violating the one-rollover-per-year rule, you can repay the amount back to that IRA as long as the repayment is made no later than August 31, 2020.

CAUTION *Even if you begin receiving distributions before you reach age 72, you must begin calculating and receiving RMDs by your required beginning date.*

More than minimum received. If, in any year, you receive more than the required minimum distribution for that year, you won't receive credit for the additional amount when determining the required minimum distributions for future years. This doesn't mean that you don't reduce your IRA account balance. It means that if you receive more than your required minimum distribution in one year, you can't treat the excess (the amount that is more than the required minimum distribution) as part of your required minimum distribution for any later year. However, any amount distributed in the year you become age 72 will be credited toward the amount that must be distributed by April 1 of the following year.

Distributions after the required beginning date. The required minimum distribution for any year after the year you reach age 72 must be made by December 31 of that later year.

Distributions from individual retirement accounts. If you are the owner of a traditional IRA that is an individual retirement account, you or your trustee must figure the required minimum distribution for each year. See *Figuring the Owner's Required Minimum Distribution* below.

Distributions from individual retirement annuities. If your traditional IRA is an individual retirement annuity, special rules apply to figuring the required minimum distribution. For more information on rules for annuities, see Regulations section 1.401(a)(9)-6. These regulations can be read in many libraries, and IRS offices, and online at the *IRS.gov*.

Change in marital status. For purposes of figuring your required minimum distribution, your marital status is determined as of January 1 of each year. If your spouse is a beneficiary of your IRA on January 1, he or she remains a beneficiary for the entire year even if you get divorced or your spouse dies during the year. For purposes of determining your distribution period, a change in beneficiary is effective in the year following the year of death or divorce.

Change of beneficiary. If your spouse is the sole beneficiary of your IRA, and he or she dies before you, your spouse won't fail to be your sole beneficiary for the year that he or she died solely because someone other than your spouse is named a beneficiary for the rest of that year. However, if you get divorced during the year and change the beneficiary designation on the IRA during that same year, your former spouse won't be treated as the sole beneficiary for that year.

Figuring the Owner's Required Minimum Distribution

Figure your required minimum distribution for each year by dividing the IRA account balance (defined next) as of the close of business on December 31 of the preceding year by the applicable distribution period or life expectancy. Tables showing distribution periods and life expectancies are found in Appendix B and are discussed later.

IRA account balance. The IRA account balance is the amount in the IRA at the end of the year preceding the year for which the required minimum distribution is being figured.

Contributions. Contributions increase the account balance in the year they are made. If a contribution for last year isn't made until after December 31 of last year, it increases the account balance for this year, but not for last year. Disregard contributions made after December 31 of last year in determining your required minimum distribution for this year.

Outstanding rollovers. The IRA account balance is adjusted by outstanding rollovers that aren't in any account at the end of the preceding year.

For a rollover from a qualified plan or another IRA that wasn't in any account at the end of the preceding year, increase the account balance of the receiving IRA by the rollover amount valued as of the date of receipt.

No recharacterizations of conversions made in 2018 or later. A conversion of a traditional IRA to a Roth IRA, and a rollover from any other eligible retirement plan to a Roth IRA, made in tax years beginning after December 31, 2017, cannot be recharacterized as having been made to a traditional IRA.

Distributions. Distributions reduce the account balance in the year they are made. A distribution for last year made after December 31 of last year reduces the account balance for this year, but not for last year. Disregard distributions made after December 31 of last year in determining your required minimum distribution for this year.

Distribution period. This is the maximum number of years over which you are allowed to take distributions from the IRA. The period to use for 2021 is listed next to your age as of your birthday in 2021 in Table III in Appendix B.

Life expectancy. If you must use Table I, your life expectancy for 2021 is listed in the table next to your age as of your birthday in 2021. If you use Table II, your life expectancy is listed where the row or column containing your age as of your birthday in 2021 intersects with the row or column containing your spouse's age as of his or her birthday in 2021. Both Table I and Table II are in Appendix B.

Distributions during your lifetime. Required minimum distributions during your lifetime are based on a distribution period that is generally determined using Table III (Uniform Lifetime) in Appendix B. However, if the sole beneficiary of your IRA is your spouse who is more than 10 years younger than you, see *Sole beneficiary spouse who is more than 10 years younger* below.

To figure the required minimum distribution for 2021, divide your account balance at the end of 2020 by the distribution period from the table. This is the distribution period listed next to your age (as of your birthday in 2021) in Table III in Appendix B, unless the sole beneficiary of your IRA is your spouse who is more than 10 years younger than you.

Example. You own a traditional IRA. Your account balance at the end of 2020 was $100,000. You are married and your spouse, who is the sole beneficiary of your IRA, is 6 years younger than you. You turn 75 years old in 2021. You use Table III. Your distribution period is 22.9. Your required minimum distribution for 2021 would be $4,367 ($100,000 ÷ 22.9).

Sole beneficiary spouse who is more than 10 years younger. If the sole beneficiary of your IRA is your spouse and your spouse is more than 10 years younger than you, use the life expectancy from Table II (Joint Life and Last Survivor Expectancy) in Appendix B.

The life expectancy to use is the joint life and last survivor expectancy listed where the row or column containing your age as of your birthday in 2021 intersects with the row or column containing your spouse's age as of his or her birthday in 2021.

You figure your required minimum distribution for 2021 by dividing your account balance at the end of 2020 by the life expectancy from Table II (Joint Life and Last Survivor Expectancy) in Appendix B.

Example. You own a traditional IRA. Your account balance at the end of 2020 was $100,000. You are married and your spouse, who is the sole beneficiary of your IRA, is 11 years younger than you. You turn 75 in 2021 and your spouse turns 64. You use Table II. Your joint life and last survivor expectancy is 23.6. Your required minimum distribution for 2021 would be $4,237 ($100,000 ÷ 23.6).

Distributions in the year of the owner's death. The required minimum distribution for the year of the owner's death depends on whether the owner died before the required beginning date, defined earlier.

If the owner died before the required beginning date, there is no required minimum distribution in the year of the owner's death. For years after the year of the owner's death, see *Owner Died Before Required Beginning Date*, later, under *IRA Beneficiaries.*

If the owner died on or after the required beginning date, the IRA beneficiaries are responsible for figuring and distributing the owner's required minimum distribution in the year of death. The owner's required minimum distribution for the year of death is generally based on Table III (Uniform Lifetime) in Appendix B. However, if the sole beneficiary of the IRA is the owner's spouse who is more than 10 years younger than the owner, use the life expectancy from Table II (Joint Life and Last Survivor Expectancy).

Note. You figure the required minimum distribution for the year in which an IRA owner dies as if the owner lived for the entire year.

IRA Beneficiaries

The rules for determining required minimum distributions for beneficiaries depend on the following.

- The beneficiary is the surviving spouse.
- The beneficiary is an individual (other than the surviving spouse).
- The beneficiary isn't an individual (for example, the beneficiary is the owner's estate). (But see *Trust as beneficiary*, later, for a discussion about treating trust beneficiaries as designated beneficiaries.)
- The IRA owner died before the required beginning date, or died on or after the required beginning date.

The following paragraphs explain the rules for required minimum distributions and beneficiaries.

CAUTION *If distributions to the beneficiary from an inherited traditional IRA are less than the required minimum distribution for the year, discussed in this chapter under* When Must You Withdraw Assets? (Required Minimum Distributions)*, you may have to pay a 50% excise tax for that year on the amount not distributed as required. For details, see* Excess Accumulations (Insufficient Distributions) *under* What Acts Result in Penalties or Additional Taxes*, later in this chapter.*

Surviving spouse. If you are the surviving spouse who is the sole beneficiary of your deceased spouse's IRA, you may elect to be treated as the owner and not as the beneficiary. If you elect to be treated as the owner, you determine the required minimum distribution (if any) as if you were the owner beginning with the year you elect or are deemed to be the owner. For details, see *Inherited from spouse* under *What if You Inherit an IRA*, earlier in this chapter.

Note. If you become the owner in the year your deceased spouse died, don't determine the required minimum distribution for that year using your life; rather, you must take the deceased owner's required minimum distribution for that year (to the extent it wasn't already distributed to the owner before his or her death).

CAUTION *You can never make a rollover contribution of an RMD; however, RMDs are waived for 2020 and you can roll over an RMD for 2020. The rollover must be completed within 60 days after the distribution, except that for distributions made before July 2, 2020, the 60-day rollover period was extended to August 31, 2020. Normally, any rollover contribution of an RMD is subject to the 6% tax on excess contributions. See chapter 1 of Pub. 590-A for more information on the tax on excess contributions.*

TIP *For any year after the owner's death, where a surviving spouse is the sole designated beneficiary of the account and he or she fails to take a required minimum distribution (if one is required) by December 31 under the rules discussed below for beneficiaries, he or she will be deemed the owner of the IRA. For details, see* Inherited from spouse *under* What if You Inherit an IRA*, earlier in this chapter.*

Date the designated beneficiary is determined. Generally, the designated beneficiary is determined on September 30 of the calendar year following the calendar year of the IRA owner's death. In order to be a designated beneficiary, an individual must be a beneficiary as of the date of death. Any person who was a beneficiary on the date of the owner's death, but isn't a beneficiary on September 30 of the calendar year following the calendar year of the owner's death (because, for example, he or she disclaimed entitlement or received his or her entire benefit), won't be taken into account in determining the designated beneficiary. An individual may be designated as a beneficiary either by the terms of the plan or, if the plan permits, by affirmative election by the employee specifying the beneficiary.

Note. If a person who is a beneficiary as of the owner's date of death dies before September 30 of the year following the year of the owner's death without disclaiming entitlement to benefits, that individual, rather than his or her successor beneficiary, continues to be treated as a beneficiary for determining the distribution period.

For the exception to this rule, see *Death of surviving spouse prior to date distributions begin*, later.

Death of a beneficiary. In general, the beneficiaries of a deceased beneficiary must continue to take the required minimum distributions after the deceased beneficiary's death. However, the beneficiaries of a deceased beneficiary don't calculate required minimum distributions using their own life expectancies. Instead, the deceased beneficiary's remaining interest must be distributed within 10 years after the beneficiary's death, or in some cases within 10 years after the owner's death. See *10-year rule*, later.

More than one beneficiary. If an IRA has more than one beneficiary or a trust is named as beneficiary, see *Miscellaneous Rules for Required Minimum Distributions*, later.

Eligible designated beneficiaries. An IRA beneficiary is an eligible designated beneficiary if the beneficiary is the owner's surviving spouse, the owner's minor child, a disabled individual, a chronically ill individual, or any other individual who is not more than 10 years younger than the IRA owner.

Owner Died On or After Required Beginning Date

If the owner died on or after his or her required beginning date (defined earlier), and you are an eligible designated beneficiary, you must base required minimum distributions for years after the year of the owner's death on the longer of:

- Your single life expectancy shown in Table I in Appendix B, as determined under *Beneficiary an individual* later; or
- The owner's life expectancy as determined under *Death on or after required beginning date* under *Beneficiary not an individual* later.

Surviving spouse is sole designated beneficiary. If the owner died on or after his or her required beginning date and his or her spouse is the sole designated beneficiary, the life expectancy the spouse must use to figure his or her required minimum distribution may change in a future distribution year. This change will apply where the spouse is older than the deceased owner or the spouse treats the IRA as his or her own.

Designated beneficiary who is not an eligible designated beneficiary. Distributions to a designated beneficiary who is not an eligible designated beneficiary must be completed within 10 years of the death of the owner. See *10-year rule*, later.

Owner Died Before Required Beginning Date

If the owner died before his or her required beginning date (defined earlier), and you are an eligible designated beneficiary, you must generally base required minimum distributions for years after the year of the owner's death using your single life expectancy shown in Table I in Appendix B, as determined under *Beneficiary an individual*, later.

However, there are situations where an individual designated beneficiary may be required to take the entire account by the end of the 10th year following the year of the owner's death. See *10-year rule*, later.

If the owner's beneficiary isn't an individual (for example, if the beneficiary is the owner's estate), the *5-year rule*, discussed later, applies.

Special rules for surviving spouse. If the owner died before his or her required beginning date and the surviving spouse is the sole designated beneficiary, the following rules apply.

Year of first required distribution. If the owner died before the year in which he or she reached age 72 (age 70½ if the owner died in tax year 2019 or an earlier year), distributions to the spouse don't need to begin until the year in which the owner would have reached age 72 (or age 70½, if applicable).

Death of surviving spouse prior to date distributions begin. If the surviving spouse dies before December 31 of the year he or she must begin receiving required minimum distributions, the surviving spouse will be treated as if he or she were the owner of the IRA.

This rule doesn't apply to the surviving spouse of a surviving spouse.

Example 1. Your spouse died in 2017, at age 65. You are the sole designated beneficiary of your spouse's traditional IRA. You don't need to take any required minimum distribution until December 31 of 2024, the year your spouse would have reached age 72. If you die prior to that date, you will be treated as the owner of the IRA for purposes of determining the required distributions to your beneficiaries. For example, if you die in 2020, your beneficiaries won't have any required minimum distribution for 2020 (because you, treated as the owner, died prior to your required beginning date). They must start taking distributions under the general rules for an owner who died prior to the required beginning date.

Example 2. Same as *Example 1*, except your sole beneficiary upon your death in 2020 is your surviving spouse. Your surviving spouse can't wait until the year you would have turned 72 to take distributions using his or her life expectancy. Also, if your surviving spouse dies prior to the date he or she is required to take a distribution, he or she isn't treated as the owner of the account. Just like any other individual beneficiary of an owner who dies before the required beginning date, your surviving spouse must start taking distributions in 2021 based on his or her life expectancy (or elect to fully distribute the account under the 10-year rule by the end of 2030).

TIP *The second surviving spouse from* Example 2 *above can still elect to treat the IRA as his or her own IRA or roll over any distributions that aren't required minimum distributions into his or her own IRA. See* Inherited from spouse *under* What if You Inherit an IRA, *earlier in this chapter.*

5-year rule. The 5-year rule requires the IRA beneficiaries who are not taking life expectancy payments to withdraw 100% of the IRA by December 31 of the year containing the fifth anniversary of the owner's death. For example, if the owner died in 2019, the beneficiary would have to fully distribute the plan by December 31, 2024. The beneficiary is allowed, but not required, to take distributions prior to that date. The 5-year rule never applies if the owner died on or after his or her required beginning date.

The 5-year rule generally applies to all beneficiaries if the owner died in a year ending before 2020, and to beneficiaries who are not individuals if the owner died in a year ending after 2019. For beneficiaries who are individuals, see *10-year rule*, next.

CAUTION *The 5-year rule generally applies to all beneficiaries if the owner died in a year ending before 2020. It also applies to beneficiaries who are not individuals (such as a trust) if the owner died in a year ending after 2019. If the owner died in a year ending after 2019 and the beneficiary is an individual, see* 10-year rule *next.*

10-year rule. The 10-year rule applies if the beneficiary is an eligible designated beneficiary who elects the 10-year rule, if the owner died before reaching his or her required beginning date.

In all other cases, the 10-year rule applies if the beneficiary is a designated beneficiary who is not an eligible designated beneficiary, regardless of whether the owner died before reaching his or her required beginning date.

The 10-year rule also applies upon the death of an eligible designated beneficiary or upon a minor child beneficiary reaching the age of majority except that the 10-year period ends on the 10th anniversary of the beneficiary's death or the child's attainment of majority.

Individual designated beneficiaries. The terms of most IRA plans require individual designated beneficiaries, who are eligible designated beneficiaries, to take required minimum distributions using the life expectancy rules (explained later) unless such beneficiaries elect to take distributions using the 5-year rule or the 10-year rule, whichever rule applies. The deadline for making this election is December 31 of the year the beneficiary must take the first required distribution using his or her life expectancy (or December 31 of the year containing the 5th anniversary (or 10th anniversary for the 10-year rule) of the owner's death, if earlier).

If the individual designated beneficiary is not an eligible designated beneficiary, the beneficiary is required to fully distribute the IRA by the 10th anniversary of the owner's death under the 10-year rule.

Beneficiary not an individual. The 5-year rule applies in all cases where there is no individual designated beneficiary by September 30 of the year following the year of the owner's death or where any beneficiary isn't an individual (for example, the owner named his or her estate as the beneficiary).

TIP *Review the IRA plan documents or consult with the IRA custodian or trustee for specifics on the 5- or 10-year rule provisions, where applicable, of any particular plan.*

CAUTION *If the 5-year rule applies, the amount remaining in the IRA, if any, after December 31 of the year containing the 5th anniversary of the owner's death is subject to the 50% excise tax detailed in* Excess Accumulations (Insufficient Distributions), *later.*

CAUTION *If the 10-year rule applies, the amount remaining in the IRA, if any, after December 31 of the year containing the 10th anniversary of the owner's death is subject to the 50% excise tax detailed in* Excess Accumulations (Insufficient Distributions), *later.*

Figuring the Beneficiary's Required Minimum Distribution

How you figure the required minimum distribution depends on whether the beneficiary is an individual or some other entity, such as a trust or estate.

Beneficiary an individual. If the beneficiary is an individual, to figure the required minimum distribution for 2021, divide the account balance at the end of 2020 by the appropriate life expectancy from Table I (Single Life Expectancy) in Appendix B. Determine the appropriate life expectancy as follows.

Spouse as sole designated beneficiary. Use the life expectancy listed in the table next to the spouse's age (as of the spouse's birthday in 2021). Use this life expectancy even if the spouse died in 2021.

If the spouse died in 2020 or a prior year, use the life expectancy listed in the table next to the spouse's age as of his or her birthday in the year he or she died. Reduce the life expectancy by 1 for each year since the year following the spouse's death.

CAUTION *You can't make a rollover contribution of your required minimum distributions in years after the owner's death. Such contribution is subject to the 6% tax on excess contributions. See chapter 1 of Pub. 590-A for more information on the tax on excess contributions.*

Other designated beneficiary. Use the life expectancy listed in the table next to the beneficiary's age as of his or her birthday in the year following the year of the owner's death. Reduce the life expectancy by 1 for each year since the year following the owner's death. However, if you are a designated beneficiary who is not an eligible designated beneficiary, the entire account balance must be fully distributed within 10 years after the owner's death.

As discussed in *Death of a beneficiary*, earlier, if the designated beneficiary dies before his or her portion of the account is fully distributed, continue to use the designated beneficiary's remaining life expectancy to determine the amount of distributions. However, if the deceased beneficiary was an eligible designated beneficiary, any remaining balance in the account must be distributed within 10 years of the beneficiary's death.

Example. Your father died in 2020. You are the designated beneficiary of your father's traditional IRA. You are 53 years old in 2021, which is the year following your father's death. You use Table I and see that your life expectancy in 2021 is 31.4. If the IRA was worth $100,000 at the end of 2020, your required minimum distribution for 2021 would be $3,185 ($100,000 ÷ 31.4).

Beneficiary not an individual. If the beneficiary isn't an individual, determine the required minimum distribution for 2021 as follows.

Death on or after required beginning date. Divide the account balance at the end of 2020 by the appropriate life expectancy from Table I (Single Life Expectancy) in Appendix B. Use the life expectancy listed next to the owner's age as of his or her birthday in the year of death. Reduce the life expectancy by 1 for each year after the year of death.

Death before required beginning date. If the IRA owner dies before the required beginning date and the beneficiary isn't an individual (for example, the owner named his or her estate as the beneficiary), the 5-year rule applies. No distribution is required for any year before the fifth year. See *5-year rule*, earlier.

Note. The required beginning date was defined earlier under *Distributions by the required beginning date*.

Example. The owner died in 2020 at the age of 80. The owner's traditional IRA went to his estate. The account balance at the end of 2020 was $100,000. In 2021, the required minimum distribution would be $10,870 ($100,000 ÷ 9.2). (The owner's life expectancy in the year of death, 10.2, reduced by 1.)

If the owner had died in 2020 at the age of 70 (before their required beginning date), the entire account would have to be distributed by the end of 2025. See *Death on or after required beginning date* and *Death before required beginning date* for more information.

Which Table Do You Use To Determine Your Required Minimum Distribution?

There are three different life expectancy tables. The tables are found in Appendix B of this publication. You use only one of them to determine your required minimum distribution for each traditional IRA. Determine which one to use as follows.

Reminder. In using the tables for lifetime distributions, marital status is determined as of January 1 each year. Divorce or death after January 1 is generally disregarded until the next year. However, if you divorce and change the beneficiary designation in the same year, your former spouse can't be considered your sole beneficiary for that year.

Table I (Single Life Expectancy). Use Table I for years after the year of the owner's death if either of the following applies.

- You are an individual and a designated beneficiary, but not the owner's surviving spouse and sole designated beneficiary.
- The beneficiary isn't an individual and the owner died on or after the required beginning date, defined earlier.

Surviving spouse. If you are the owner's surviving spouse and sole designated beneficiary, you will also use Table I for your required minimum distributions. However, if the owner hadn't reached age 72 when he or she died, and you don't elect to be treated as the owner of the IRA, you don't have to take distributions until the year in which the owner would have reached age 72.

Table II (Joint Life and Last Survivor Expectancy). Use Table II if you are the IRA owner and your spouse is both your sole designated beneficiary and more than 10 years younger than you.

Note. Use this table in the year of the owner's death if the owner died after the required beginning date and this is the table that would have been used had he or she not died.

Table III (Uniform Lifetime). Use Table III if you are the IRA owner and your spouse isn't both the sole designated beneficiary of your IRA and more than 10 years younger than you.

Note. Use this table in the year of the owner's death if the owner died after the required beginning date and this is the table that would have been used had he or she not died.

No table. Don't use any of the tables if either the 5-year rule or the 10-year rule (discussed earlier) applies.

What Age(s) Do You Use With the Table(s)?

The age or ages to use with each table are explained below.

Table I (Single Life Expectancy). If you are a designated beneficiary figuring your first distribution, use your age as of your birthday in the year distributions must begin.

This is usually the calendar year immediately following the calendar year of the owner's death. After the first distribution year, reduce your life expectancy by 1 for each subsequent year. If you are the owner's surviving spouse and the sole designated beneficiary, this is generally the year in which the owner would have reached age 72. After the first distribution year, use your age as of your birthday in each subsequent year.

Example 1. You are an eligible designated beneficiary figuring your first required minimum distribution. Distributions must begin in 2021. You become age 57 years old in 2021. You use Table I.

Example 2. You are the owner's surviving spouse and the sole designated beneficiary. The owner would have turned age 72 in 2021. Distributions begin in 2021. You become 69 years old in 2021. You use Table I. Your distribution period for 2021 is 17.8.

Owner's life expectancy. You use the owner's life expectancy to calculate required minimum distributions when the owner dies on or after the required beginning date and there is no designated beneficiary as of September 30 of the year following the year of the owner's death. In this case, use the owner's life expectancy for his or her age as of the owner's birthday in the year of death and reduce it by 1 for each subsequent year.

Or use the owner's life expectancy in the year of death (reduced by 1 for each subsequent year) if the owner is younger than you.

Table II (Joint Life and Last Survivor Expectancy). For your first distribution by the required beginning date, use your age and the age of your designated beneficiary as of your birthdays in the year you become age 72. Your combined life expectancy is at the intersection of your ages.

If you are figuring your required minimum distribution for 2021, use your ages as of your birthdays in 2021. For each subsequent year, use your and your spouse's ages as of your birthdays in the subsequent year.

Table III (Uniform Lifetime). For your first distribution by your required beginning date, use your age as of your birthday in the year you become age 72.

If you are figuring your required minimum distribution for 2021, use your age as of your birthday in 2021. For each subsequent year, use your age as of your birthday in the subsequent year.

Miscellaneous Rules for Required Minimum Distributions

The following rules may apply to you.

Installments allowed. The yearly required minimum distribution can be taken in a series of installments (monthly, quarterly, etc.) as long as the total distributions for the year are at least as much as the minimum required amount.

More than one IRA. If you have more than one traditional IRA, you must determine a separate required minimum distribution for each IRA. However, you can total these minimum amounts and take the total from any one or more of the IRAs.

More than minimum received. If, in any year, you receive more than the required minimum amount for that year, you won't receive credit for the additional amount when determining the minimum required amounts for future years. This doesn't mean that you don't reduce your IRA account balance. It means that if you receive more than your required minimum distribution in one year, you can't treat the excess (the amount that is more than the required minimum distribution) as part of your required minimum distribution for any later year. However, any amount distributed in your age 72 year will be credited toward the amount that must be distributed by April 1 of the following year.

Multiple individual beneficiaries. If, as of September 30 of the year following the year in which the owner dies, there is more than one beneficiary, the beneficiary with the shortest life expectancy will be the designated beneficiary if both of the following apply.

- All of the beneficiaries are individuals.
- The account or benefit hasn't been divided into separate accounts or shares for each beneficiary.

Separate accounts. A single IRA can be split into separate accounts or shares for each beneficiary. These separate accounts or shares can be established at any time, either before or after the owner's required beginning date. Generally, these separate accounts or shares are combined for purposes of determining the minimum required distribution. However, these separate accounts or shares won't be combined for required minimum distribution purposes after the death of the IRA owner if the separate accounts or shares are established by the end of the year following the year of the IRA owner's death.

The separate account rules can't be used by beneficiaries of a trust.

Trust as beneficiary. A trust can't be a designated beneficiary even if it is a named beneficiary. However, the beneficiaries of a trust will be treated as having been designated beneficiaries for purposes of determining required minimum distributions after the owner's death (or after the death of the owner's surviving spouse described in *Death of surviving spouse prior to date distributions begin*, earlier) if all of the following are true.

1. The trust is a valid trust under state law, or would be but for the fact that there is no corpus.
2. The trust is irrevocable or became, by its terms, irrevocable upon the owner's death.
3. The beneficiaries of the trust who are beneficiaries with respect to the trust's interest in the owner's benefit are identifiable from the trust instrument.

4. The trustee of the trust provides the IRA custodian or trustee with the documentation required by that custodian or trustee. The trustee of the trust should contact the IRA custodian or trustee for details on the documentation required for a specific plan.

The deadline for the trustee to provide the beneficiary documentation to the IRA custodian or trustee is October 31 of the year following the year of the owner's death.

Trust beneficiary is another trust. If the beneficiary of the trust (which is the beneficiary of the IRA) is another trust and both trusts meet the above requirements, the beneficiaries of the other trust will be treated as having been designated as beneficiaries for purposes of determining the distribution period.

Note. The separate account rules, discussed earlier, can't be used by beneficiaries of a trust.

TIP *You may want to contact a tax advisor to comply with this complicated area of the tax law.*

Annuity distributions from an insurance company. Special rules apply if you receive distributions from your traditional IRA as an annuity purchased from an insurance company. See Regulations sections 1.401(a)(9)-6 and 54.4974-2. These regulations can be found in many libraries, and IRS offices, and online at *IRS.gov*.

Are Distributions Taxable?

In general, distributions from a traditional IRA are taxable in the year you receive them.

Failed financial institutions. Distributions from a traditional IRA are taxable in the year you receive them even if they are made without your consent by a state agency as receiver of an insolvent savings institution. This means you must include such distributions in your gross income unless you roll them over.

Exceptions. Exceptions to distributions from traditional IRAs being taxable in the year you receive them are:

- Rollovers (see chapter 1 of Pub. 590-A);
- Qualified charitable distributions, discussed later;
- Tax-free withdrawals of contributions (see chapter 1 of Pub. 590-A); and
- The return of nondeductible contributions, discussed later under *Distributions Fully or Partly Taxable*.

CAUTION *Although a conversion of a traditional IRA is considered a rollover for Roth IRA purposes, it isn't an exception to the rule that distributions from a traditional IRA are taxable in the year you receive them. Conversion distributions are includible in your gross income subject to this rule and the special rules for conversions explained in chapter 1 of Pub. 590-A.*

Qualified charitable distributions. A qualified charitable distribution (QCD) is generally a nontaxable distribution made directly by the trustee of your IRA (other than a SEP or SIMPLE IRA) to an organization eligible to receive tax-deductible contributions. You must be at least age 70½ when the distribution was made. Also, you must have the same type of acknowledgment of your contribution that you would need to claim a deduction for a charitable contribution. See *Substantiation Requirements* in Pub. 526.

The maximum annual exclusion for QCDs is $100,000. Any QCD in excess of the $100,000 exclusion limit is included in income as any other distribution. If you file a joint return, your spouse can also have a QCD and exclude up to $100,000. The amount of the QCD is limited to the amount of the distribution that would otherwise be included in income. If your IRA includes nondeductible contributions, the distribution is first considered to be paid out of otherwise taxable income.

TIP *A QCD will count towards your required minimum distribution, discussed earlier.*

CAUTION *You can't claim a charitable contribution deduction for any QCD not included in your income.*

Example. On December 23, 2020, Jeff, age 75, directed the trustee of his IRA to make a distribution of $25,000 directly to a qualified 501(c)(3) organization (a charitable organization eligible to receive tax-deductible contributions). The total value of Jeff's IRA is $30,000 and consists of $20,000 of deductible contributions and earnings and $10,000 of nondeductible contributions (basis). Since Jeff is at least age 70½ and the distribution is made directly by the trustee to a qualified organization, the part of the distribution that would otherwise be includible in Jeff's income ($20,000) is a QCD.

In this case, Jeff has made a QCD of $20,000 (his deductible contributions and earnings). Because Jeff made a distribution of nondeductible contributions from his IRA, he must file Form 8606 with his return. Jeff includes the total distribution ($25,000) on line 4a of Form 1040-SR. He completes Form 8606 to determine the amount to enter on line 4b of Form 1040-SR and the remaining basis in his IRA. Jeff enters -0- on line 4b. This is Jeff's only IRA and he took no other distributions in 2020. He also enters "QCD" next to line 4b to indicate a qualified charitable distribution.

After the distribution, his basis in his IRA is $5,000. If Jeff itemizes deductions and files Schedule A (Form 1040) with Form 1040-SR, the $5,000 portion of the distribution attributable to the nondeductible contributions can be deducted as a charitable contribution, subject to AGI limits. He can't take the charitable contribution deduction for the $20,000 portion of the distribution that wasn't included in his income.

One-time qualified Health Savings Account (HSA) funding distribution. You may be able to make a qualified HSA funding distribution from your traditional IRA or Roth IRA to your HSA. You can't make this distribution from an ongoing SEP IRA or SIMPLE IRA. For this purpose, a SEP IRA or SIMPLE IRA is ongoing if an employer contribution is made for the plan year ending with or within your tax year in which the distribution would be made. The distribution must be less than or equal to your maximum annual HSA contribution.

This distribution must be made directly by the trustee of the IRA to the trustee of the HSA. The distribution isn't included in your income, isn't deductible, and reduces the amount that can be contributed to your HSA. You must make the distribution by the end of the year; the special rule allowing contributions to your HSA for the previous year if made by your tax return filing deadline doesn't apply. The qualified HSA funding distribution is reported on Form 8889 for the year in which the distribution is made.

One-time transfer. Generally, only one qualified HSA funding distribution is allowed during your lifetime. If you own two or more IRAs, and want to use amounts in multiple IRAs to make a qualified HSA funding distribution, you must first make an IRA-to-IRA transfer of the amounts to be distributed into a single IRA, and then make the one-time qualified HSA funding distribution from that IRA.

Testing period rules apply. If at any time during the testing period you cease to meet all requirements to be an eligible individual, the amount of the qualified HSA funding distribution is included in your gross income. The qualified HSA funding distribution is included in gross income in the tax year you first fail to be an eligible individual. This amount is subject to the 10% additional tax (unless the failure is due to disability or death).

More information. See Pub. 969 for additional information about this distribution.

Ordinary income. Distributions from traditional IRAs that you include in income are taxed as ordinary income.

No special treatment. In figuring your tax, you can't use the 10-year tax option or capital gain treatment that applies to lump-sum distributions from qualified retirement plans.

TIP *If you were affected by a qualified disaster, see chapter 4.*

Distributions Fully or Partly Taxable

Distributions from your traditional IRA may be fully or partly taxable, depending on whether your IRA includes any nondeductible contributions.

Fully taxable. If only deductible contributions were made to your traditional IRA (or IRAs, if you have more than one), you have no basis in your IRA. Because you have no basis in your IRA, any distributions are fully taxable when received. See *Reporting and Withholding Requirements for Taxable Amounts*, later.

Partly taxable. If you made nondeductible contributions or rolled over any after-tax amounts to any of your traditional IRAs, you have a cost basis (investment in the contract) equal to the amount of those contributions. These nondeductible contributions aren't taxed when they are distributed to you. They are a return of your investment in your IRA.

Only the part of the distribution that represents nondeductible contributions and rolled over after-tax amounts (your cost basis) is tax free. If nondeductible contributions have been made or after-tax amounts have been rolled over to your IRA, distributions consist partly of nondeductible contributions (basis) and partly of deductible contributions, earnings, and gains (if there are any). Until all of your basis has been distributed, each distribution is partly nontaxable and partly taxable.

Form 8606. You must complete Form 8606, and attach it to your return, if you receive a distribution from a traditional IRA and have ever made nondeductible contributions or rolled over after-tax amounts to any of your traditional IRAs. Using the form, you will figure the nontaxable distributions for 2020, and your total IRA basis for 2020 and earlier years. See the illustrated Forms 8606 in this chapter.

Note. If you are required to file Form 8606, but you aren't required to file an income tax return, you must still file Form 8606. Complete Form 8606, sign it, and send it to the IRS at the time and place you would otherwise file an income tax return.

Figuring the Nontaxable and Taxable Amounts

If your traditional IRA includes nondeductible contributions and you received a distribution from it in 2020, you must use Form 8606 to figure how much of your 2020 IRA distribution is tax free.

Note. When figuring the nontaxable and taxable amounts of distributions made prior to death in the year the IRA account owner dies, the value of all traditional (including SEP) and SIMPLE IRAs should be figured as of the date of death instead of December 31.

Contribution and distribution in the same year. If you received a distribution in 2020 from a traditional IRA and you also made contributions to a traditional IRA for 2020 that may not be fully deductible because of the income limits, you can use Worksheet 1-1 to figure how much of your 2020 IRA distribution is tax free and how much is taxable. Then you can figure the amount of nondeductible contributions to report on Form 8606. Follow the instructions under *Reporting your nontaxable distribution on Form 8606* next to figure your remaining basis after the distribution.

Reporting your nontaxable distribution on Form 8606. To report your nontaxable distribution and to figure the remaining basis in your traditional IRA after distributions, you must complete Worksheet 1-1 before completing Form 8606. Then follow these steps to complete Form 8606.

Worksheet 1-1. **Figuring the Taxable Part of Your IRA Distribution**

Keep for Your Records

Use only if you made contributions to a traditional IRA for 2020 that may not be fully deductible and have to figure the taxable part of your 2020 distributions to determine your modified AGI. See *Limit if Covered by Employer Plan* in chapter 1 of Pub. 590-A.

Form 8606 and the related instructions will be needed when using this worksheet.

Note. When used in this worksheet, the term "**outstanding rollover**" refers to an amount distributed from a traditional IRA as part of a rollover that, as of December 31, 2020, hadn't yet been reinvested in another traditional IRA, but was still eligible to be rolled over tax free.

1.	Enter the basis in your traditional IRAs as of December 31, 2019	**1.** ______
2.	Enter the total of all contributions made to your traditional IRAs during 2020 and all contributions made during 2021 that were for 2020, ***whether or not deductible***. Don't include rollover contributions properly rolled over into IRAs. Also, don't include certain returned contributions described in the instructions for line 7 of Form 8606	**2.** ______
3.	Add lines 1 and 2	**3.** ______
4.	Enter the value of all your traditional IRAs as of December 31, 2020 (include any outstanding rollovers from traditional IRAs to other traditional IRAs). Subtract any repayments of qualified disaster distributions	**4.** ______
5.	Enter the total distributions from traditional IRAs (including amounts converted to Roth IRAs that will be shown on line 16 of Form 8606) received in 2020. (Don't include outstanding rollovers included on line 4 or any rollovers between traditional IRAs completed by December 31, 2020. Also, don't include certain returned contributions described in the instructions for line 7 of Form 8606.) Do include repayments of qualified disaster distributions	**5.** ______
6.	Add lines 4 and 5	**6.** ______
7.	Divide line 3 by line 6. Enter the result as a decimal (rounded to at least three places). If the result is 1.000 or more, enter 1.000	**7.** ______
8.	**Nontaxable portion of the distribution.** Multiply line 5 by line 7. Enter the result here and on lines 13 and 17 of Form 8606	**8.** ______
9.	**Taxable portion of the distribution (before adjustment for conversions).** Subtract line 8 from line 5. Enter the result here, and if there are no amounts converted to Roth IRAs, **stop here** and enter the result on line 15a of Form 8606	**9.** ______
10.	Enter the amount included on line 9 that is allocable to amounts converted to Roth IRAs by December 31, 2020. (See ***Note*** at the end of this worksheet.) Enter here and on line 18 of Form 8606	**10.** ______
11.	**Taxable portion of the distribution (after adjustments for conversions).** Subtract line 10 from line 9. Enter the result here and on line 15a of Form 8606	**11.** ______

Note. If the amount on line 5 of this worksheet includes an amount converted to a Roth IRA by December 31, 2020, you must determine the percentage of the distribution allocable to the conversion. To figure the percentage, divide the amount converted (from line 16 of Form 8606) by the total distributions shown on line 5. To figure the amounts to include on line 10 of this worksheet and on line 18 of Form 8606, multiply line 9 of the worksheet by the percentage you figured.

1. Use Worksheet 1-2 in chapter 1 of Pub. 590-A, or the IRA Deduction Worksheet in the Form 1040 or 1040-SR, or 1040-NR instructions to figure your deductible contributions to traditional IRAs to report on Schedule 1 (Form 1040), line 19.
2. After you complete Worksheet 1-2 in chapter 1 of Pub. 590-A or the IRA Deduction Worksheet in the form instructions, enter your nondeductible contributions to traditional IRAs on line 1 of Form 8606.
3. Complete lines 2 through 5 of Form 8606.
4. If line 5 of Form 8606 is less than line 8 of Worksheet 1-1, complete lines 6 through 15c of Form 8606 and stop here.
5. If line 5 of Form 8606 is equal to or greater than line 8 of Worksheet 1-1, follow instructions 6 and 7 next. Don't complete lines 6 through 12 of Form 8606.
6. Enter the amount from line 8 of Worksheet 1-1 on lines 13 and 17 of Form 8606.
7. Complete line 14 of Form 8606.
8. Enter the amount from line 9 of Worksheet 1-1 (or, if you entered an amount on line 11, the amount from that line) on line 15a of Form 8606.

Worksheet 1-1. **Figuring the Taxable Part of Your IRA Distribution—Illustrated**

Use only if you made contributions to a traditional IRA for 2020 that may not be fully deductible and have to figure the taxable part of your 2020 distributions to determine your modified AGI. See *Limit if Covered by Employer Plan* in chapter 1 of Pub. 590-A.

Form 8606 and the related instructions will be needed when using this worksheet

Note. When used in this worksheet, the term "**outstanding rollover** " refers to an amount distributed from a traditional IRA as part of a rollover that, as of December 31, 2020, hadn't yet been reinvested in another traditional IRA, but was still eligible to be rolled over tax free.

1. Enter the basis in your traditional IRAs as of December 31, 2019	1.	300
2. Enter the total of all contributions made to your traditional IRAs during 2020 and all contributions made during 2021 that were for 2020, ***whether or not deductible***. Don't include rollover contributions properly rolled over into IRAs. Also, don't include certain returned contributions described in the instructions for line 7 of Form 8606	**2.**	2,000
3. Add lines 1 and 2	**3.**	2,300
4. Enter the value of all your traditional IRAs as of December 31, 2020 (include any outstanding rollovers from traditional IRAs to other traditional IRAs). Subtract any repayments of qualified disaster distributions	**4.**	20,000
5. Enter the total distributions from traditional IRAs (including amounts converted to Roth IRAs that will be shown on line 16 of Form 8606) received in 2020. (Don't include outstanding rollovers included on line 4 or any rollovers between traditional IRAs completed by December 31, 2020. Also, don't include certain returned contributions described in the instructions for line 7 of Form 8606.) Do include repayments of qualified disaster distributions	**5.**	5,000
6. Add lines 4 and 5	**6.**	25,000
7. Divide line 3 by line 6. Enter the result as a decimal (rounded to at least three places). If the result is 1.000 or more, enter 1.000	**7.**	0.092
8. Nontaxable portion of the distribution. Multiply line 5 by line 7. Enter the result here and on lines 13 and 17 of Form 8606	**8.**	460
9. Taxable portion of the distribution (before adjustment for conversions). Subtract line 8 from line 5. Enter the result here, and if there are no amounts converted to Roth IRAs, **stop here** and enter the result on line 15a of Form 8606	**9.**	4,540
10. Enter the amount included on line 9 that is allocable to amounts converted to Roth IRAs by December 31, 2020. (See ***Note*** at the end of this worksheet.) Enter here and on line 18 of Form 8606	**10.**	4,540
11. Taxable portion of the distribution (after adjustments for conversions). Subtract line 10 from line 9. Enter the result here and on line 15a of Form 8606	**11.**	-0-

Note. If the amount on line 5 of this worksheet includes an amount converted to a Roth IRA by December 31, 2020, you must determine the percentage of the distribution allocable to the conversion. To figure the percentage, divide the amount converted (from line 16 of Form 8606) by the total distributions shown on line 5. To figure the amounts to include on line 10 of this worksheet and on line 18 of Form 8606, multiply line 9 of the worksheet by the percentage you figured.

Example. Rose Green has made the following contributions to her traditional IRAs.

Year	Deductible	Nondeductible
2013	2,000	-0-
2014	2,000	-0-
2015	2,000	-0-
2016	1,000	-0-
2017	1,000	-0-
2018	1,000	-0-
2019	700	300
Totals	**$9,700**	**$300**

Rose needs to complete Worksheet 1-1 to determine if her IRA deduction for 2020 will be reduced or eliminated. In 2020, she makes a $2,000 contribution that may be partly nondeductible. She also receives a distribution of $5,000 for conversion to a Roth IRA. She completed the conversion before December 31, 2020, and didn't recharacterize any contributions. At the end of 2020, the fair market values of her accounts, including earnings, total $20,000. She didn't receive any tax-free distributions in earlier years. The amount she includes in income for 2020 is figured on Worksheet 1-1.

The illustrated Form 8606 for Rose shows the information required when you need to use Worksheet 1-1 to figure your nontaxable distribution. Assume that the $500 entered on Form 8606, line 1, is the amount Rose figured using instructions 1 and 2 given earlier under *Reporting your nontaxable distribution on Form 8606*.

Form **8606**

Department of the Treasury
Internal Revenue Service (99)

Nondeductible IRAs

▶ Go to *www.irs.gov/Form8606* for instructions and the latest information.
▶ For coronavirus-related distributions, see the instructions.
▶ Attach to 2020 Form 1040, 1040-SR, or 1040-NR.

OMB No. 1545-0074
2020
Attachment Sequence No. **48**

Name. If married, file a separate form for each spouse required to file 2020 Form 8606. See instructions.	Your social security number
Rose Green	001-00-0000

Fill in Your Address Only if You Are Filing This Form by Itself and Not With Your Tax Return

Home address (number and street, or P.O. box if mail is not delivered to your home)		Apt. no.
City, town or post office, state, and ZIP code. If you have a foreign address, also complete the spaces below (see instructions).		
Foreign country name	Foreign province/state/county	Foreign postal code

Part I **Nondeductible Contributions to Traditional IRAs and Distributions From Traditional, SEP, and SIMPLE IRAs**
Complete this part only if one or more of the following apply.

- You made nondeductible contributions to a traditional IRA for 2020.
- You took distributions from a traditional, SEP, or SIMPLE IRA in 2020 **and** you made nondeductible contributions to a traditional IRA in 2020 or an earlier year. For this purpose, a distribution does not include a rollover (other than a repayment of a qualified disaster distribution (see 2020 Forms 8915-C, 8915-D, and 8915-E)), qualified charitable distribution, one-time distribution to fund an HSA, conversion, recharacterization, or return of certain contributions.
- You converted part, but not all, of your traditional, SEP, and SIMPLE IRAs to Roth IRAs in 2020 **and** you made nondeductible contributions to a traditional IRA in 2020 or an earlier year.

1	Enter your nondeductible contributions to traditional IRAs for 2020, including those made for 2020 from January 1, 2021, through April 15, 2021. See instructions			1	500
2	Enter your total basis in traditional IRAs. See instructions			2	300
3	Add lines 1 and 2			3	800
	In 2020, did you take a distribution from traditional, SEP, or SIMPLE IRAs, or make a Roth IRA conversion? — **No** ▶ Enter the amount from line 3 on line 14. Do not complete the rest of Part I. — **Yes** ▶ Go to line 4.				
4	Enter those contributions included on line 1 that were made from January 1, 2021, through April 15, 2021			4	0
5	Subtract line 4 from line 3			5	800
6	Enter the value of **all** your traditional, SEP, and SIMPLE IRAs as of December 31, 2020, plus any outstanding rollovers. Subtract any repayments of qualified disaster distributions (see 2020 Forms 8915-C, 8915-D, and 8915-E)	6			
7	Enter your distributions from traditional, SEP, and SIMPLE IRAs in 2020. **Do not** include rollovers (other than repayments of qualified disaster distributions (see 2020 Forms 8915-C, 8915-D, and 8915-E)), qualified charitable distributions, a one-time distribution to fund an HSA, conversions to a Roth IRA, certain returned contributions, or recharacterizations of traditional IRA contributions (see instructions)	7			
8	Enter the net amount you converted from traditional, SEP, and SIMPLE IRAs to Roth IRAs in 2020. Also enter this amount on line 16	8			
9	Add lines 6, 7, and 8 — 9				
10	Divide line 5 by line 9. Enter the result as a decimal rounded to at least 3 places. If the result is 1.000 or more, enter "1.000"	10	× .		
11	Multiply line 8 by line 10. This is the nontaxable portion of the amount you converted to Roth IRAs. Also enter this amount on line 17	11			
12	Multiply line 7 by line 10. This is the nontaxable portion of your distributions that you did not convert to a Roth IRA	12			
13	Add lines 11 and 12. This is the nontaxable portion of all your distributions			13	460*
14	Subtract line 13 from line 3. This is **your total basis in traditional IRAs for 2020 and earlier years**			14	340
15a	Subtract line 12 from line 7			15a	
b	Enter the amount on line 15a attributable to qualified disaster distributions from 2020 Forms 8915-C, 8915-D, and 8915-E (see instructions). Also, enter this amount on 2020 Form 8915-C, line 23; 2020 Form 8915-D, line 22; **or** 2020 Form 8915-E, line 13, as applicable			15b	
c	**Taxable amount.** Subtract line 15b from line 15a. If more than zero, also include this amount on 2020 Form 1040, 1040-SR, **or** 1040-NR, line 4b			15c	0
	Note: You may be subject to an additional 10% tax on the amount on line 15c if you were under age 59½ at the time of the distribution. See instructions.				

For Privacy Act and Paperwork Reduction Act Notice, see separate instructions. Cat. No. 63966F Form **8606** (2020)

* From Worksheet 1 - 1 in Publication 590-B

Form 8606 (2020) Page **2**

Part II **2020 Conversions From Traditional, SEP, or SIMPLE IRAs to Roth IRAs**

Complete this part if you converted part or all of your traditional, SEP, and SIMPLE IRAs to a Roth IRA in 2020.

16	If you completed Part I, enter the amount from line 8. Otherwise, enter the net amount you converted from traditional, SEP, and SIMPLE IRAs to Roth IRAs in 2020	16	5,000
17	If you completed Part I, enter the amount from line 11. Otherwise, enter your basis in the amount on line 16 (see instructions)	17	460
18	**Taxable amount.** Subtract line 17 from line 16. If more than zero, also include this amount on 2020 Form 1040, 1040-SR, or 1040-NR, line 4b	18	4,540*

Part III **Distributions From Roth IRAs**

Complete this part only if you took a distribution from a Roth IRA in 2020. For this purpose, a distribution does not include a rollover (other than a repayment of a qualified disaster distribution (see 2020 Forms 8915-C, 8915-D, and 8915-E)), qualified charitable distribution, one-time distribution to fund an HSA, recharacterization, or return of certain contributions (see instructions).

19	Enter your total nonqualified distributions from Roth IRAs in 2020, including any qualified first-time homebuyer distributions, and any qualified disaster distributions (see instructions). Also see 2020 Forms 8915-C, 8915-D, and 8915-E	19	
20	Qualified first-time homebuyer expenses (see instructions). **Do not** enter more than $10,000 reduced by the total of all your prior qualified first-time homebuyer distributions	20	
21	Subtract line 20 from line 19. If zero or less, enter -0-	21	
22	Enter your basis in Roth IRA contributions (see instructions). If line 21 is zero, **stop here**	22	
23	Subtract line 22 from line 21. If zero or less, enter -0- and skip lines 24 and 25. If more than zero, you may be subject to an additional tax (see instructions)	23	
24	Enter your basis in conversions from traditional, SEP, and SIMPLE IRAs and rollovers from qualified retirement plans to a Roth IRA. See instructions	24	
25a	Subtract line 24 from line 23. If zero or less, enter -0- and skip lines 25b and 25c	25a	
b	Enter the amount on line 25a attributable to qualified disaster distributions from 2020 Forms 8915-C, 8915-D, and 8915-E (see instructions). Also, enter this amount on 2020 Form 8915-C, line 24; 2020 Form 8915-D, line 23; **or** 2020 Form 8915-E, line 14, as applicable	25b	
c	**Taxable amount.** Subtract line 25b from line 25a. If more than zero, also include this amount on 2020 Form 1040, 1040-SR, **or** 1040-NR, line 4b	25c	

Sign Here Only if You Are Filing This Form by Itself and Not With Your Tax Return

Under penalties of perjury, I declare that I have examined this form, including accompanying attachments, and to the best of my knowledge and belief, it is true, correct, and complete. Declaration of preparer (other than taxpayer) is based on all information of which preparer has any knowledge.

▶ Your signature ▶ Date

Paid Preparer Use Only	Print/Type preparer's name	Preparer's signature	Date	Check ☐ if self-employed	PTIN
	Firm's name ▶			Firm's EIN ▶	
	Firm's address ▶			Phone no.	

*From Worksheet 1 - 1 in Publication 590-B

Form **8606** (2020)

Other Special IRA Distribution Situations

Two other special IRA distribution situations are discussed next.

Distribution of an annuity contract from your IRA account. You can tell the trustee or custodian of your traditional IRA account to use the amount in the account to buy an annuity contract for you. You aren't taxed when you receive the annuity contract (unless the annuity contract is being converted to an annuity held by a Roth IRA). You are taxed when you start receiving payments under that annuity contract.

Tax treatment. If only deductible contributions were made to your traditional IRA since it was opened (this includes all your traditional IRAs, if you have more than one), the annuity payments are fully taxable.

If any of your traditional IRAs include both deductible and nondeductible contributions, the annuity payments are taxed as explained earlier under *Distributions Fully or Partly Taxable*.

Cashing in retirement bonds. When you cash in retirement bonds, you are taxed on the entire amount you receive. Unless you have already cashed them in, you will be taxed on the entire value of your bonds in the year in which you reach age 70½. The value of the bonds is the amount you would have received if you had cashed them in at the end of that year. When you later cash in the bonds, you won't be taxed again.

Reporting and Withholding Requirements for Taxable Amounts

If you receive a distribution from your traditional IRA, you will receive Form 1099-R, or a similar statement. IRA distributions are shown in boxes 1 and 2a of Form 1099-R. A number or letter code in box 7 tells you what type of distribution you received from your IRA.

Number codes. Some of the number codes are explained below. All of the codes are explained in the instructions for recipients on Form 1099-R.

1—Early distribution, no known exception (in most cases, under age 59½).

2—Early distribution, exception applies (under age 59½).

3—Disability.

4—Death.

5—Prohibited transaction.

7—Normal distribution.

8—Excess contributions plus earnings/ excess deferrals (and/or earnings) taxable in 2020.

CAUTION *If code 1, 5, or 8 appears on your Form 1099-R, you are probably subject to a penalty or additional tax. If code 1 appears, see* Early Distributions, *later. If code 5 appears, see* Prohibited Transactions, *later. If code 8 appears, see* Excess Contributions *in chapter 1 of Pub. 590-A.*

Letter codes. Some of the letter codes are explained below. All of the codes are explained in the instructions for recipients on Form 1099-R.

B—Designated Roth account distribution.

G—Direct rollover of a distribution to a qualified plan, a section 403(b) plan, a governmental section 457(b) plan, or an IRA.

H—Direct rollover of a designated Roth account distribution to a Roth IRA.

J—Early distribution from a Roth IRA, no known exception (in most cases, under age 59½).

N—Recharacterized IRA contribution made for 2020 and recharacterized in 2020.

P—Excess contributions plus earnings/ excess deferrals (and/or earnings) taxable in 2019.

Q—Qualified distribution from a Roth IRA.

R—Recharacterized IRA contribution made for 2019 and recharacterized in 2020.

S—Early distribution from a SIMPLE IRA in the first 2 years, no known exception (under age 59½).

T—Roth IRA distribution, exception applies.

If the distribution shown on Form 1099-R is from your IRA, SEP IRA, or SIMPLE IRA, the small box in box 7 (labeled *IRA/SEP/SIMPLE*) should be marked with an "X."

CAUTION *If code J, P, or S appears on your Form 1099-R, you are probably subject to a penalty or additional tax. If code J appears, see* Early Distributions, *later. If code P appears, see* Excess Contributions *in chapter 1 of Pub. 590-A. If code S appears, see* Distributions (Withdrawals) *in chapter 3 of Pub. 560.*

Withholding. Federal income tax is withheld from distributions from traditional IRAs unless you choose not to have tax withheld.

The amount of tax withheld from an annuity or a similar periodic payment is based on your marital status and the number of withholding allowances you claim on your withholding certificate (Form W-4P). If you haven't filed a certificate, tax will be withheld as if you are a married individual claiming three withholding allowances.

Generally, tax will be withheld at a 10% rate on nonperiodic distributions.

IRA distributions delivered outside the United States. In general, if you are a U.S. citizen or resident alien and your home address is outside the United States or its possessions, you can't choose exemption from withholding on distributions from your traditional IRA.

To choose exemption from withholding, you must certify to the payer under penalties of perjury that you aren't a

U.S. citizen, a resident alien of the United States, or a tax-avoidance expatriate.

Even if this election is made, the payer must withhold tax at the rates prescribed for nonresident aliens.

More information. For more information on withholding on pensions and annuities, see *Pensions and Annuities* in chapter 1 of Pub. 505. For more information on withholding on nonresident aliens and foreign entities, see *Pensions, Annuities, and Alimony* under *Withholding on Specific Income* in Pub. 515.

Reporting taxable distributions on your return. Report fully taxable distributions, including early distributions, on Form 1040, 1040-SR, or 1040-NR, line 4b (no entry is required on line 4a). If only part of the distribution is taxable, enter the total amount on Form 1040, 1040-SR, or 1040-NR, line 4a, and enter the taxable part on Form 1040, 1040-SR, or 1040-NR, line 4b.

Estate tax. Generally, the value of an annuity or other payment receivable by any beneficiary of a decedent's traditional IRA that represents the part of the purchase price contributed by the decedent (or by his or her former employer(s)) must be included in the decedent's gross estate. For more information, see the instructions for Form 706, Schedule I.

What Acts Result in Penalties or Additional Taxes?

The tax advantages of using traditional IRAs for retirement savings can be offset by additional taxes and penalties if you don't follow the rules. There are additions to the regular tax for using your IRA funds in prohibited transactions. There are also additional taxes for the following activities.

- Investing in collectibles.
- Having unrelated business income.
- Taking early distributions.
- Allowing excess amounts to accumulate (failing to take required distributions).
- Making excess contributions.

There are penalties for overstating the amount of nondeductible contributions and for failure to file Form 8606, if required.

This chapter discusses those acts (relating to distributions) that you should avoid and the additional taxes and other costs, including loss of IRA status, that apply if you don't avoid those acts.

Prohibited Transactions

Generally, a prohibited transaction is any improper use of your traditional IRA account or annuity by you, your beneficiary, or any disqualified person.

Disqualified persons include your fiduciary and members of your family (spouse, ancestor, lineal descendant, and any spouse of a lineal descendant).

The following are some examples of prohibited transactions with a traditional IRA.

- Borrowing money from it.
- Selling property to it.
- Using it as security for a loan.
- Buying property for personal use (present or future) with IRA funds.

CAUTION *If your IRA invested in nonpublicly traded assets or assets that you directly control, the risk of engaging in a prohibited transaction in connection with your IRA may be increased.*

Fiduciary. For these purposes, a fiduciary includes anyone who does any of the following.

- Exercises any discretionary authority or discretionary control in managing your IRA or exercises any authority or control in managing or disposing of its assets.
- Provides investment advice to your IRA for a fee, or has any authority or responsibility to do so.
- Has any discretionary authority or discretionary responsibility in administering your IRA.

Effect on an IRA account. Generally, if you or your beneficiary engages in a prohibited transaction in connection with your traditional IRA account at any time during the year, the account stops being an IRA as of the first day of that year.

Effect on you or your beneficiary. If your account stops being an IRA because you or your beneficiary engaged in a prohibited transaction, the account is treated as distributing all its assets to you at their fair market values on the first day of the year. If the total of those values is more than your basis in the IRA, you will have a taxable gain that is includible in your income. For information on figuring your gain and reporting it in income, see *Are Distributions Taxable*, earlier. The distribution may be subject to additional taxes or penalties.

Borrowing on an annuity contract. If you borrow money against your traditional IRA annuity contract, you must include in your gross income the fair market value of the annuity contract as of the first day of your tax year. You may have to pay the 10% additional tax on early distributions, discussed later.

Pledging an account as security. If you use a part of your traditional IRA account as security for a loan, that part is treated as a distribution and is included in your gross income. You may have to pay the 10% additional tax on early distributions, discussed later.

Trust account set up by an employer or an employee association. Your account or annuity doesn't lose its IRA treatment if your employer or the employee association with whom you have your traditional IRA engages in a prohibited transaction.

Owner participation. If you participate in the prohibited transaction with your employer or the association, your account is no longer treated as an IRA.

Taxes on prohibited transactions. If someone other than the owner or beneficiary of a traditional IRA engages in a prohibited transaction, that person may be liable for certain taxes. In general, there is a 15% tax on the amount of the prohibited transaction and a 100% additional tax if the transaction isn't corrected.

Loss of IRA status. If the traditional IRA ceases to be an IRA because of a prohibited transaction by you or your beneficiary, you or your beneficiary isn't liable for these excise taxes. However, you or your beneficiary may have to pay other taxes as discussed under Effect on you or your beneficiary, earlier.

Exempt Transactions

The Department of Labor has authority to grant administrative exemptions from the prohibited transaction provisions of ERISA and the Code for a class of transactions or for individual transactions. In order to grant an administrative exemption, the Department must make the following three determinations.

1. The exemption must be administratively feasible.
2. In the interest of the plan and its participants and beneficiaries.
3. Protective of the rights of plan participants and beneficiaries.

For additional information on prohibited transaction exemptions, see the Department of Labor publication, Exemption Procedures under Federal Pension Law.

Transactions Not Prohibited

The following two types of transactions aren't prohibited transactions if they meet the requirements that follow.

- Payments of cash, property, or other consideration by the sponsor of your traditional IRA to you (or members of your family).
- Your receipt of services at reduced or no cost from the bank where your traditional IRA is established or maintained.

Payments of cash, property, or other consideration. Even if a sponsor makes payments to you or your family, there is no prohibited transaction if all three of the following requirements are met.

1. The payments are for establishing a traditional IRA or for making additional contributions to it.
2. The IRA is established solely to benefit you, your spouse, and your or your spouse's beneficiaries.
3. During the year, the total fair market value of the payments you receive isn't more than:
   a. $10 for IRA deposits of less than $5,000, or
   b. $20 for IRA deposits of $5,000 or more.

If the consideration is group-term life insurance, requirements (1) and (3) don't apply if no more than $5,000 of the face value of the insurance is based on a dollar-for-dollar basis on the assets in your IRA.

Services received at reduced or no cost. Even if a sponsor provides services at reduced or no cost, there is no prohibited transaction if all of the following requirements are met.

- The traditional IRA qualifying you to receive the services is established and maintained for the benefit of you, your spouse, and your or your spouse's beneficiaries.
- The bank itself can legally offer the services.
- The services are provided in the ordinary course of business by the bank (or a bank affiliate) to customers who qualify but don't maintain an IRA (or a Keogh plan).
- The determination, for a traditional IRA, of who qualifies for these services is based on an IRA (or a Keogh plan) deposit balance equal to the lowest qualifying balance for any other type of account.
- The rate of return on a traditional IRA investment that qualifies isn't less than the return on an identical investment that could have been made at the same time at the same branch of the bank by a customer who isn't eligible for (or doesn't receive) these services.

Investment in Collectibles

If your traditional IRA invests in collectibles, the amount invested is considered distributed to you in the year invested. You may have to pay the 10% additional tax on early distributions, discussed later.

Any amounts that were considered to be distributed when the investment in the collectible was made, and which were included in your income at that time, aren't included in your income when the collectible is actually distributed from your IRA.

Collectibles. These include:

- Artworks,
- Rugs,
- Antiques,
- Metals,
- Gems,
- Stamps,
- Coins,
- Alcoholic beverages, and

- Certain other tangible personal property.

Exception. Your IRA can invest in one, one-half, one-quarter, or one-tenth ounce U.S. gold coins, or one-ounce silver coins minted by the Treasury Department. It can also invest in certain platinum coins and certain gold, silver, palladium, and platinum bullion.

Unrelated Business Income

An IRA is subject to tax on unrelated business income if it carries on an unrelated trade or business. An unrelated trade or business means any trade or business regularly carried on by the IRA or by a partnership of which it is a member, and not substantially related to the IRA's exempt purpose or function. If the IRA has $1,000 or more of unrelated trade or business gross income, the IRA must file a Form 990-T, Exempt Organization Business Income Tax Return. An IRA trustee is permitted to file Form 990-T on behalf of the IRA. In the case of an IRA that operates on a calendar year, the Form 990-T must be filed by the 15th day of April following the close of the calendar year. In the case of an IRA that operates on a fiscal year, the Form 990-T must be filed by the 15th day of the 4th month following the close of the fiscal year. See Pub. 598 for more information.

Early Distributions

You must include early distributions of taxable amounts from your traditional IRA in your gross income. Early distributions are also subject to an additional 10% tax, as discussed later.

Early distributions defined. Early distributions are generally amounts distributed from your traditional IRA account or annuity before you are age 59$^1/_2$, or amounts you receive when you cash in retirement bonds before you are age 59$^1/_2$.

TIP *If you were affected by a qualified disaster, see chapter 4.*

Age 59$^1/_2$ Rule

Generally, if you are under age 59$^1/_2$, you must pay a 10% additional tax on the distribution of any assets (money or other property) from your traditional IRA. Distributions before you are age 59$^1/_2$ are called early distributions.

The 10% additional tax applies to the part of the distribution that you have to include in gross income. It is in addition to any regular income tax on that amount.

A number of exceptions to this rule are discussed later under Exceptions. Also see *Contributions Returned Before Due Date of Return* in chapter 1 of Pub. 590-A.

After age 59$^1/_2$ and before age 72. After you reach age 59$^1/_2$, you can receive distributions without having to pay the 10% additional tax. Even though you can receive distributions after you reach age 59$^1/_2$, distributions aren't required until you reach age 72. See *When Must You Withdraw Assets? (Required Minimum Distributions)*, earlier.

Exceptions

There are several exceptions to the age 59$^1/_2$ rule. Even if you receive a distribution before you are age 59$^1/_2$, you may not have to pay the 10% additional tax if you are in one of the following situations.

- You have unreimbursed medical expenses that are more than 7.5% of your adjusted gross income.
- The distributions aren't more than the cost of your medical insurance due to a period of unemployment.
- You are totally and permanently disabled.
- You are the beneficiary of a deceased IRA owner.
- You are receiving distributions in the form of an annuity.
- The distributions aren't more than your qualified higher education expenses.
- You use the distributions to buy, build, or rebuild a first home.
- The distribution is due to an IRS levy of the qualified plan.
- The distribution is a qualified reservist distribution.
- The distribution is a qualified birth or adoption distribution.

Most of these exceptions are explained below.

Note. Distributions that are timely and properly rolled over, as discussed in chapter 1 of Pub. 590-A, aren't subject to either regular income tax or the 10% additional tax. Certain withdrawals of excess contributions after the due date of your return are also tax free and therefore not subject to the 10% additional tax. (See *Excess Contributions Withdrawn After Due Date of Return* in chapter 1 of Pub. 590-A.) This also applies to transfers incident to divorce, as discussed under *Can You Move Retirement Plan Assets?* in chapter 1 of Pub. 590-A.

Receivership distributions. Early distributions (with or without your consent) from savings institutions placed in receivership are subject to this tax unless one of the above exceptions applies. This is true even if the distribution is from a receiver that is a state agency.

Unreimbursed medical expenses. Even if you are under age 59$^1/_2$, you don't have to pay the 10% additional tax on distributions that aren't more than:

- The amount you paid for unreimbursed medical expenses during the year of the distribution, minus
- 7.5% of your adjusted gross income (defined next) for the year of the distribution.

You can only take into account unreimbursed medical expenses that you would be able to include in figuring a deduction for medical expenses on Schedule A (Form 1040). You don't have to itemize your deductions to take advantage of this exception to the 10% additional tax.

Adjusted gross income. This is the amount on Form 1040, 1040-SR, or 1040-NR, line 11.

Medical insurance. Even if you are under age 59½, you may not have to pay the 10% additional tax on distributions during the year that aren't more than the amount you paid during the year for medical insurance for yourself, your spouse, and your dependents. You won't have to pay the tax on these amounts if all of the following conditions apply.

- You lost your job.
- You received unemployment compensation paid under any federal or state law for 12 consecutive weeks because you lost your job.
- You receive the distributions during either the year you received the unemployment compensation or the following year.
- You receive the distributions no later than 60 days after you have been reemployed.

Disabled. If you become disabled before you reach age 59½, any distributions from your traditional IRA because of your disability aren't subject to the 10% additional tax.

You are considered disabled if you can furnish proof that you can't do any substantial gainful activity because of your physical or mental condition. A physician must determine that your condition can be expected to result in death or to be of long, continued, and indefinite duration.

Beneficiary. If you die before reaching age 59½, the assets in your traditional IRA can be distributed to your beneficiary or to your estate without either having to pay the 10% additional tax.

However, if you inherit a traditional IRA from your deceased spouse and elect to treat it as your own (as discussed under *What if You Inherit an IRA*, earlier), any distribution you later receive before you reach age 59½ may be subject to the 10% additional tax.

Annuity. You can receive distributions from your traditional IRA that are part of a series of substantially equal payments over your life (or your life expectancy), or over the lives (or the joint life expectancies) of you and your beneficiary, without having to pay the 10% additional tax, even if you receive such distributions before you are age 59½. You must use an IRS-approved distribution method and you must take at least one distribution annually for this exception to apply. The "required minimum distribution method," when used for this purpose, results in the exact amount required to be distributed, not the minimum amount.

There are two other IRS-approved distribution methods that you can use. They are generally referred to as the "fixed amortization method" and the "fixed annuitization method." These two methods aren't discussed in this publication because they are more complex and generally require professional assistance. For information on these methods, see Revenue Ruling 2002-62, which is on page 710 of Internal Revenue Bulletin 2002-42 at *IRS.gov/pub/irs-irbs/irb02-42.pdf*.

Recapture tax for changes in distribution method under equal payment exception. You may have to pay an early distribution recapture tax if, before you reach age 59½, the distribution method under the equal periodic payment exception changes (for reasons other than your death or disability). The tax applies if the method changes from the method requiring equal payments to a method that wouldn't have qualified for the exception to the tax. The recapture tax applies to the first tax year to which the change applies. The amount of tax is the amount that would have been imposed had the exception not applied, plus interest for the deferral period.

You may have to pay the recapture tax if you don't receive the payments for at least 5 years under a method that qualifies for the exception. You may have to pay it even if you modify your method of distribution after you reach age 59½. In that case, the tax applies only to payments distributed before you reach age 59½.

Report the recapture tax and interest on line 4 of Form 5329. Attach an explanation to the form. Don't write the explanation next to the line or enter any amount for the recapture on line 1 or 3 of the form.

One-time switch. If you are receiving a series of substantially equal periodic payments, you can make a one-time switch to the required minimum distribution method at any time without incurring the additional tax. Once a change is made, you must follow the required minimum distribution method in all subsequent years.

Higher education expenses. Even if you are under age 59½, if you paid expenses for higher education during the year, part (or all) of any distribution may not be subject to the 10% additional tax. The part not subject to the tax is generally the amount that isn't more than the qualified higher education expenses (defined next) for the year for education furnished at an eligible educational institution (defined below). The education must be for you, your spouse, or the children or grandchildren of you or your spouse.

When determining the amount of the distribution that isn't subject to the 10% additional tax, include qualified higher education expenses paid with any of the following funds.

- Payment for services, such as wages.
- A loan.
- A gift.
- An inheritance given to either the student or the individual making the withdrawal.
- A withdrawal from personal savings (including savings from a qualified tuition program).

Don't include expenses paid with any of the following funds.

- Tax-free distributions from a Coverdell education savings account.
- Tax-free part of scholarships and fellowships.
- Pell grants.
- Employer-provided educational assistance.

- Veterans' educational assistance.
- Any other tax-free payment (other than a gift or inheritance) received as educational assistance.

Qualified higher education expenses. Qualified higher education expenses are tuition, fees, books, supplies, and equipment required for the enrollment or attendance of a student at an eligible educational institution. They also include expenses for special needs services incurred by or for special needs students in connection with their enrollment or attendance. In addition, if the individual is at least a half-time student, room and board are qualified higher education expenses.

Eligible educational institution. This is any college, university, vocational school, or other postsecondary educational institution eligible to participate in the student aid programs administered by the U.S. Department of Education. It includes virtually all accredited, public, nonprofit, and proprietary (privately owned profit-making) postsecondary institutions. The educational institution should be able to tell you if it is an eligible educational institution.

For more information, see chapter 9 of Pub. 970.

First home. Even if you are under age 59½, you don't have to pay the 10% additional tax on up to $10,000 of distributions you receive to buy, build, or rebuild a first home. To qualify for treatment as a first-time homebuyer distribution, the distribution must meet all the following requirements.

1. It must be used to pay qualified acquisition costs (defined next) before the close of the 120th day after the day you received it.
2. It must be used to pay qualified acquisition costs for the main home of a first-time homebuyer (defined below) who is any of the following.
   a. Yourself.
   b. Your spouse.
   c. Your or your spouse's child.
   d. Your or your spouse's grandchild.
   e. Your or your spouse's parent or other ancestor.
3. When added to all your prior qualified first-time homebuyer distributions, if any, total qualifying distributions can't be more than $10,000.

TIP *If both you and your spouse are first-time homebuyers (defined later), each of you can receive distributions up to $10,000 for a first home without having to pay the 10% additional tax.*

Qualified acquisition costs. Qualified acquisition costs include the following items.

- Costs of buying, building, or rebuilding a home.
- Any usual or reasonable settlement, financing, or other closing costs.

First-time homebuyer. Generally, you are a first-time homebuyer if you had no present interest in a main home during the 2-year period ending on the date of acquisition of the home which the distribution is being used to buy, build, or rebuild. If you are married, your spouse must also meet this no-ownership requirement.

Date of acquisition. The date of acquisition is the date that:

- You enter into a binding contract to buy the main home for which the distribution is being used, or
- The building or rebuilding of the main home for which the distribution is being used begins.

TIP *If you received a distribution to buy, build, or rebuild a first home and the purchase or construction was canceled or delayed, you could generally contribute the amount of the distribution to an IRA within 120 days of the distribution and not pay income tax or the 10% additional tax on early distributions. This contribution is treated as a rollover contribution to the IRA.*

Qualified reservist distributions. A qualified reservist distribution isn't subject to the additional tax on early distributions.

Definition. A distribution you receive is a qualified reservist distribution if the following requirements are met.

- You were ordered or called to active duty after September 11, 2001.
- You were ordered or called to active duty for a period of more than 179 days or for an indefinite period because you are a member of a reserve component.
- The distribution is from an IRA or from amounts attributable to elective deferrals under a section 401(k) or 403(b) plan or a similar arrangement.
- The distribution was made no earlier than the date of the order or call to active duty and no later than the close of the active duty period.

Reserve component. The term "reserve component" means the:

- Army National Guard of the United States,
- Army Reserve,
- Naval Reserve,
- Marine Corps Reserve,
- Air National Guard of the United States,
- Air Force Reserve,
- Coast Guard Reserve, or
- Reserve Corps of the Public Health Service.

Qualified birth or adoption distribution. A qualified birth or adoption distribution is any distribution from an applicable eligible retirement plan if made during the 1-year period beginning on the date on which your child was born or the date on which the legal adoption of your child was finalized.

A qualified birth or adoption distribution must not exceed $5,000 per adoption or birth. In addition, an eligible adoptee is any individual (other than the child of the taxpayer's spouse) who has not reached age 18 or is physically or mentally incapable of self-support.

Amount may be repaid. If you receive a qualified birth or adoption distribution, you can make one or more contributions to an eligible retirement plan if you are a beneficiary of that plan, the plan accepts rollover contributions, and the total of those contributions does not exceed the amount of the qualified birth or adoption distribution.

Additional 10% Tax

The additional tax on early distributions is 10% of the amount of the early distribution that you must include in your gross income. This tax is in addition to any regular income tax resulting from including the distribution in income.

Use Form 5329 to figure the tax. See the discussion of Form 5329, later, under *Reporting Additional Taxes* for information on filing the form.

Example. Tom Jones, who is 35 years old, receives a $3,000 distribution from his traditional IRA account. Tom doesn't meet any of the exceptions to the 10% additional tax, so the $3,000 is an early distribution. Tom never made any nondeductible contributions to his IRA. He must include the $3,000 in his gross income for the year of the distribution and pay income tax on it. Tom must also pay an additional tax of $300 (10% (0.10) × $3,000). He files Form 5329. See the filled-in Form 5329, later.

CAUTION *Early distributions of funds from a SIMPLE retirement account made within 2 years of beginning participation in the SIMPLE are subject to a 25%, rather than a 10%, early distributions tax.*

Nondeductible contributions. The tax on early distributions doesn't apply to the part of a distribution that represents a return of your nondeductible contributions (basis).

Excess Accumulations (Insufficient Distributions)

You can't keep amounts in your traditional IRA (including SEP and SIMPLE IRAs) indefinitely. Generally, you must begin receiving distributions by April 1 of the year following the year in which you reach age 72. The required minimum distribution for any year after the year in which you reach age 72 must be made by December 31 of that later year.

Tax on excess. If distributions are less than the required minimum distribution for the year, discussed earlier under *When Must You Withdraw Assets? (Required Minimum Distributions)*, you may have to pay a 50% excise tax for that year on the amount not distributed as required.

Reporting the tax. Use Form 5329 to report the tax on excess accumulations. See the discussion of Form 5329, later, under *Reporting Additional Taxes* for more information on filing the form.

Request to waive the tax. If the excess accumulation is due to reasonable error, and you have taken, or are taking, steps to remedy the insufficient distribution, you can request that the tax be waived. If you believe you qualify for this relief, attach a statement of explanation and complete Form 5329 as instructed under *Waiver of tax for reasonable cause* in the Instructions for Form 5329.

Exemption from tax. If you are unable to take required distributions because you have a traditional IRA invested in a contract issued by an insurance company that is in state insurer delinquency proceedings, the 50% excise tax doesn't apply if the conditions and requirements of Revenue Procedure 92-10 are satisfied. Those conditions and requirements are summarized below. Revenue Procedure 92-10 is in Cumulative Bulletin 1992-1. You can read the revenue procedure at most IRS offices, at many public libraries, and online at *IRS.gov*.

Conditions. To qualify for exemption from the tax, the assets in your traditional IRA must include an affected investment. Also, the amount of your required distribution must be determined as discussed earlier under *When Must You Withdraw Assets? (Required Minimum Distributions)*.

Affected investment defined. Affected investment means an annuity contract or a guaranteed investment contract (with an insurance company) for which payments under the terms of the contract have been reduced or suspended because of state insurer delinquency proceedings against the contracting insurance company.

Requirements. If your traditional IRA (or IRAs) includes assets other than your affected investment, all traditional IRA assets, including the available portion of your affected investment, must be used to satisfy as much as possible of your IRA distribution requirement. If the affected investment is the only asset in your IRA, as much of the required distribution as possible must come from the available portion, if any, of your affected investment.

Form **5329** (Rev. February 2021) Department of the Treasury Internal Revenue Service

Additional Taxes on Qualified Plans (Including IRAs) and Other Tax-Favored Accounts

▶ Attach to Form 1040, 1040-SR, or 1040-NR.
▶ Go to *www.irs.gov/Form5329* for instructions and the latest information.

OMB No. 1545-0074 — **2020** — Attachment Sequence No. **29**

Name of individual subject to additional tax. If married filing jointly, see instructions.	Your social security number
Tom Jones	001 00 0000

Fill in Your Address Only if You Are Filing This Form by Itself and Not With Your Tax Return ▶

Home address (number and street), or P.O. box if mail is not delivered to your home		Apt. no.
City, town or post office, state, and ZIP code. If you have a foreign address, also complete the spaces below. See instructions.		If this is an amended return, check here ▶ ☐
Foreign country name	Foreign province/state/county	Foreign postal code

If you **only** owe the additional 10% tax on the full amount of the early distributions, you may be able to report this tax directly on Schedule 2 (Form 1040), line 6, without filing Form 5329. See instructions.

Part I Additional Tax on Early Distributions. Complete this part if you took a taxable distribution before you reached age 59½ from a qualified retirement plan (including an IRA) or modified endowment contract (unless you are reporting this tax directly on Schedule 2 (Form 1040)—see above). You may also have to complete this part to indicate that you qualify for an exception to the additional tax on early distributions or for certain Roth IRA distributions. See instructions.

1	Early distributions includible in income (see instructions). For Roth IRA distributions, see instructions	1	3000
2	Early distributions included on line 1 that are not subject to the additional tax (see instructions). Enter the appropriate exception number from the instructions: _______	2	-0-
3	Amount subject to additional tax. Subtract line 2 from line 1	3	3000
4	**Additional tax.** Enter 10% (0.10) of line 3. Include this amount on Schedule 2 (Form 1040), line 6	4	300
	Caution: If any part of the amount on line 3 was a distribution from a SIMPLE IRA, you may have to include 25% of that amount on line 4 instead of 10%. See instructions.		

Part II Additional Tax on Certain Distributions From Education Accounts and ABLE Accounts. Complete this part if you included an amount in income, on Schedule 1 (Form 1040), line 8, from a Coverdell education savings account (ESA), a qualified tuition program (QTP), or an ABLE account.

5	Distributions included in income from a Coverdell ESA, a QTP, or an ABLE account	5	
6	Distributions included on line 5 that are not subject to the additional tax (see instructions)	6	
7	Amount subject to additional tax. Subtract line 6 from line 5	7	
8	**Additional tax.** Enter 10% (0.10) of line 7. Include this amount on Schedule 2 (Form 1040), line 6	8	

Part III Additional Tax on Excess Contributions to Traditional IRAs. Complete this part if you contributed more to your traditional IRAs for 2020 than is allowable or you had an amount on line 17 of your 2019 Form 5329.

9	Enter your excess contributions from line 16 of your 2019 Form 5329. See instructions. If zero, go to line 15			9	
10	If your traditional IRA contributions for 2020 are less than your maximum allowable contribution, see instructions. Otherwise, enter -0-	10			
11	2020 traditional IRA distributions included in income (see instructions)	11			
12	2020 distributions of prior year excess contributions (see instructions)	12			
13	Add lines 10, 11, and 12			13	
14	Prior year excess contributions. Subtract line 13 from line 9. If zero or less, enter -0-			14	
15	Excess contributions for 2020 (see instructions)			15	
16	Total excess contributions. Add lines 14 and 15			16	
17	**Additional tax.** Enter 6% (0.06) of the **smaller** of line 16 **or** the value of your traditional IRAs on December 31, 2020 (including 2020 contributions made in 2021). Include this amount on Schedule 2 (Form 1040), line 6			17	

Part IV Additional Tax on Excess Contributions to Roth IRAs. Complete this part if you contributed more to your Roth IRAs for 2020 than is allowable or you had an amount on line 25 of your 2019 Form 5329.

18	Enter your excess contributions from line 24 of your 2019 Form 5329. See instructions. If zero, go to line 23			18	
19	If your Roth IRA contributions for 2020 are less than your maximum allowable contribution, see instructions. Otherwise, enter -0-	19			
20	2020 distributions from your Roth IRAs (see instructions)	20			
21	Add lines 19 and 20			21	
22	Prior year excess contributions. Subtract line 21 from line 18. If zero or less, enter -0-			22	
23	Excess contributions for 2020 (see instructions)			23	
24	Total excess contributions. Add lines 22 and 23			24	
25	**Additional tax.** Enter 6% (0.06) of the **smaller** of line 24 **or** the value of your Roth IRAs on December 31, 2020 (including 2020 contributions made in 2021). Include this amount on Schedule 2 (Form 1040), line 6			25	

For Privacy Act and Paperwork Reduction Act Notice, see your tax return instructions. Cat. No. 13329Q Form **5329** (2020)

Available portion. The available portion of your affected investment is the amount of payments remaining after they have been reduced or suspended because of state insurer delinquency proceedings.

Make up of shortfall in distribution. If the payments to you under the contract increase because all or part of the reduction or suspension is canceled, you must make up the amount of any shortfall in a prior distribution because of the proceedings. You make up (reduce or eliminate) the shortfall with the increased payments you receive.

You must make up the shortfall by December 31 of the calendar year following the year that you receive increased payments.

Reporting Additional Taxes

Generally, you must use Form 5329 to report the tax on excess contributions, early distributions, and excess accumulations.

Filing a tax return. If you must file an individual income tax return, complete Form 5329 and attach it to your Form 1040, 1040-SR, or 1040-NR. Enter the total additional taxes due on Schedule 2 (Form 1040), line 6.

Not filing a tax return. If you don't have to file a return, but do have to pay one of the additional taxes mentioned earlier, file the completed Form 5329 with the IRS at the time and place you would have filed Form 1040, 1040-SR, or 1040-NR. Be sure to include your address on page 1 and your signature and date on page 2. Enclose, but don't attach, a check or money order payable to "United States Treasury" for the tax you owe, as shown on Form 5329. Write your social security number and "2020 Form 5329" on your check or money order.

Form 5329 not required. You don't have to use Form 5329 if any of the following situations exists.

- Distribution code 1 (early distribution) is correctly shown in box 7 of Form 1099-R. If you don't owe any other additional tax on a distribution, multiply the taxable part of the early distribution by 10% and enter the result on Schedule 2 (Form 1040), line 6. Enter "No" to the left of the line to indicate that you don't have to file Form 5329. However, if you owe this tax and also owe any other additional tax on a distribution, don't enter this 10% additional tax directly on your Form 1040, 1040-SR, or 1040-NR. You must file Form 5329 to report your additional taxes.
- If you rolled over part or all of a distribution from a qualified retirement plan, the part rolled over isn't subject to the tax on early distributions.
- You have a qualified disaster distribution.

2.

Roth IRAs

Reminders

Disaster relief. If you were affected by a qualified disaster, see chapter 4.

Deemed IRAs. For plan years beginning after 2002, a qualified employer plan (retirement plan) can maintain a separate account or annuity under the plan (a deemed IRA) to receive voluntary employee contributions. If the separate account or annuity otherwise meets the requirements of an IRA, it will be subject only to IRA rules. An employee's account can be treated as a traditional IRA or a Roth IRA.

For this purpose, a "qualified employer plan" includes:

- A qualified pension, profit-sharing, or stock bonus plan (section 401(a) plan);
- A qualified employee annuity plan (section 403(a) plan);
- A tax-sheltered annuity plan (section 403(b) plan); and
- A deferred compensation plan (section 457 plan) maintained by a state, a political subdivision of a state, or an agency or instrumentality of a state or political subdivision of a state.

Designated Roth accounts. Designated Roth accounts are separate accounts under 401(k), 403(b), or 457(b) plans that accept elective deferrals that are referred to as Roth contributions. These elective deferrals are included in your income, but qualified distributions from these accounts aren't included in your income. Designated Roth accounts aren't IRAs and shouldn't be confused with Roth IRAs. Contributions, up to their respective limits, can be made to Roth IRAs and designated Roth accounts according to your eligibility to participate. A contribution to one doesn't impact your eligibility to contribute to the other. See Pub. 575 for more information on designated Roth accounts.

Introduction

Regardless of your age, you may be able to establish and make nondeductible contributions to an individual retirement plan called a Roth IRA.

Contributions not reported. You don't report Roth IRA contributions on your return.

What Is a Roth IRA?

A Roth IRA is an individual retirement plan that, except as explained in this chapter, is subject to the rules that apply to a traditional IRA (defined next). It can be either an account or an annuity. Individual retirement accounts and annuities are described in *How Can a Traditional IRA Be Opened?* in chapter 1 of Pub. 590-A.

To be a Roth IRA, the account or annuity must be designated as a Roth IRA when it is opened. A deemed IRA can be a Roth IRA, but neither a SEP IRA nor a SIMPLE IRA can be designated as a Roth IRA.

Unlike a traditional IRA, you can't deduct contributions to a Roth IRA. But, if you satisfy the requirements, qualified distributions (discussed later) are tax free and you can leave amounts in your Roth IRA as long as you live.

Traditional IRA. A traditional IRA is any IRA that isn't a Roth IRA or SIMPLE IRA. Traditional IRAs are discussed in chapter 1.

Are Distributions Taxable?

You don't include in your gross income qualified distributions or distributions that are a return of your regular contributions from your Roth IRA(s). You also don't include distributions from your Roth IRA that you roll over tax free into another Roth IRA. You may have to include part of other distributions in your income. See *Ordering Rules for Distributions*, later.

Basis of distributed property. The basis of property distributed from a Roth IRA is its fair market value (FMV) on the date of distribution, whether or not the distribution is a qualified distribution.

Withdrawals of contributions by due date. If you withdraw contributions (including any net earnings on the contributions) by the due date of your return for the year in which you made the contribution, the contributions are treated as if you never made them. If you have an extension of time to file your return, you can withdraw the contributions and earnings by the extended due date. The withdrawal of contributions is tax free, but you must include the earnings on the contributions in income for the year in which you made the contributions.

What Are Qualified Distributions?

A qualified distribution is any payment or distribution from your Roth IRA that meets the following requirements.

1. It is made after the 5-year period beginning with the first tax year for which a contribution was made to a Roth IRA set up for your benefit.
2. The payment or distribution is:
   a. Made on or after the date you reach age 59½,
   b. Made because you are disabled (defined earlier),
   c. Made to a beneficiary or to your estate after your death, or
   d. One that meets the requirements listed under *First home* under *Exceptions* in chapter 1 (up to a $10,000 lifetime limit).

TIP *If you were affected by a qualified disaster, see chapter 4.*

Additional Tax on Early Distributions

If you receive a distribution that isn't a qualified distribution, you may have to pay the 10% additional tax on early distributions as explained in the following paragraphs.

Distributions of conversion and certain rollover contributions within 5-year period. If, within the 5-year period starting with the first day of your tax year in which you convert an amount from a traditional IRA or roll over an amount from a qualified retirement plan to a Roth IRA, you take a distribution from a Roth IRA, you may have to pay the 10% additional tax on early distributions. You must generally pay the 10% additional tax on any amount attributable to the part of the amount converted or rolled over (the conversion or rollover contribution) that you had to include in income (recapture amount). A separate 5-year period applies to each conversion and rollover. See *Ordering Rules for Distributions*, later, to determine the recapture amount, if any.

The 5-year period used for determining whether the 10% early distribution tax applies to a distribution from a conversion or rollover contribution is separately determined for each conversion and rollover, and isn't necessarily the same as the 5-year period used for determining whether a distribution is a qualified distribution. See *What Are Qualified Distributions*, earlier.

For example, if a calendar-year taxpayer makes a conversion contribution on February 25, 2020, and makes a regular contribution for 2019 on the same date, the 5-year period for the conversion begins January 1, 2020, while the 5-year period for the regular contribution begins on January 1, 2019.

Unless one of the exceptions listed later applies, you must pay the additional tax on the portion of the distribution attributable to the part of the conversion or rollover contribution that you had to include in income because of the conversion or rollover.

You must pay the 10% additional tax in the year of the distribution, even if you had included the conversion or rollover contribution in an earlier year. You must also pay the additional tax on any portion of the distribution attributable to earnings on contributions.

Other early distributions. Unless one of the exceptions listed below applies, you must pay the 10% additional tax on the taxable part of any distributions that aren't qualified distributions.

Exceptions. You may not have to pay the 10% additional tax in the following situations.

- You have reached age 59½.
- You are totally and permanently disabled.
- You are the beneficiary of a deceased IRA owner.
- You use the distribution to buy, build, or rebuild a first home.
- The distributions are part of a series of substantially equal payments.
- You have unreimbursed medical expenses that are more than 7.5% of your adjusted gross income (defined earlier) for the year.
- You are paying medical insurance premiums during a period of unemployment.
- The distributions aren't more than your qualified higher education expenses.
- The distribution is due to an IRS levy of the qualified plan.
- The distribution is a qualified reservist distribution.

Most of these exceptions are discussed earlier in chapter 1 under Early Distributions.

TIP *If you were affected by a qualified disaster, see chapter 4.*

Ordering Rules for Distributions

If you receive a distribution from your Roth IRA that isn't a qualified distribution, part of it may be taxable. There is a set order in which contributions (including conversion contributions and rollover contributions from qualified retirement plans) and earnings are considered to be distributed from your Roth IRA. For these purposes, disregard the withdrawal of excess contributions and the earnings on them (discussed under *What if You Contribute Too Much?* in chapter 2 of Pub. 590-A). Order the distributions as follows.

1. Regular contributions.
2. Conversion and rollover contributions, on a first-in, first-out basis (generally, total conversions and rollovers from the earliest year first). See *Aggregation (grouping and adding) rules*, later. Take these conversion and rollover contributions into account as follows.
   a. Taxable portion (the amount required to be included in gross income because of the conversion or rollover) first.
   b. Nontaxable portion.
3. Earnings on contributions.

Disregard rollover contributions from other Roth IRAs for this purpose.

Aggregation (grouping and adding) rules. Determine the taxable amounts distributed (withdrawn), distributions, and contributions by grouping and adding them together as follows.

- Add all distributions from all your Roth IRAs during the year together.
- Add all regular contributions made for the year (including contributions made after the close of the year, but before the due date of your return) together. Add this total to the total undistributed regular contributions made in prior years.
- Add all conversion and rollover contributions made during the year together. For purposes of the ordering rules, in the case of any conversion or rollover in which the conversion or rollover distribution is made in 2020 and the conversion or rollover contribution is made in 2021, treat the conversion or rollover contribution as contributed before any other conversion or rollover contributions made in 2021.

Add any recharacterized contributions that end up in a Roth IRA to the appropriate contribution group for the year that the original contribution would have been taken into account if it had been made directly to the Roth IRA.

Disregard any recharacterized contribution that ends up in an IRA other than a Roth IRA for the purpose of grouping (aggregating) both contributions and distributions. Also, disregard any amount withdrawn to correct an excess contribution (including the earnings withdrawn) for this purpose.

Example. On October 15, 2016, Justin converted all $80,000 in his traditional IRA to his Roth IRA. His Forms 8606 from prior years show that $20,000 of the amount converted is his basis.

Justin included $60,000 ($80,000 − $20,000) in his gross income.

On February 23, 2020, Justin made a regular contribution of $5,000 to a Roth IRA. On November 8, 2020, at age 60, Justin took a $7,000 distribution from his Roth IRA.

The first $5,000 of the distribution is a return of Justin's regular contribution and isn't includible in his income.

The next $2,000 of the distribution isn't includible in income because it was included previously.

Figuring your recapture amount. If you had an early distribution from your Roth IRAs in 2020, you must allocate the early distribution by using the Recapture Amount—Allocation Chart located in Appendix C.

Figure 2-1. **Is the Distribution From Your Roth IRA a Qualified Distribution?**

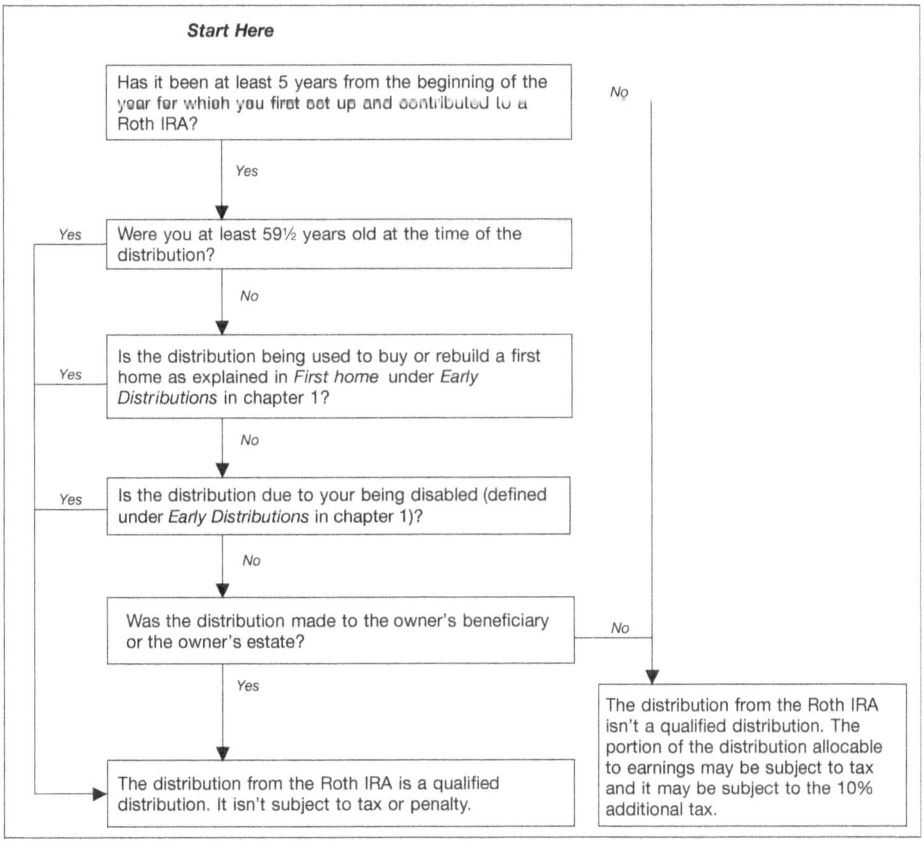

Illustrated Recapture Amount—Allocation Chart

Enter the amount from your 2020 Form 8606, line 19 . . . . **$85,500**

Before you begin: You will need your prior year Form(s) 8606 and income tax return(s) if you entered an amount on any line(s) as indicated below.

You will now allocate the amount you entered above (2020 Form 8606, line 19) in the order shown, to the amounts on the lines listed below (to the extent a prior year distribution wasn't allocable to the amount). The maximum amount you can enter on each line below is the amount entered on the referenced lines of the form for that year. **Note.** Once you have allocated the full amount from your 2020 Form 8606, line 19, **STOP**. See the *Example* below.

Tax Year	Your Form			
2020	Form 8606, line 20	**$10,000**	Form 8606, line 22	**$55,500**
2005	Form 8606, line 18	**$10,000**	Form 8606, line 17	**$-0-**
2016	Form 8606, line 18; and Form 1040, line 16b; Form 1040A, line 12b; or Form 1040NR, line 17b*	**$20,000**	Form 8606, line 17; and Form 1040, line 16a; Form 1040A, line 12a; or Form 1040NR, line 17a**	**$20,000**
2020	Form 8606, line 25c			

* Only include those amounts rolled over to a Roth IRA.

** Only include any contributions (usually box 5 of Form 1099-R) that were taxable to you when made and rolled over to a Roth IRA.

Amount to include on Form 5329, line 1. Include on line 1 of your 2020 Form 5329 the following four amounts from the Recapture Amount—Allocation Chart that you filled out.

- The amount you allocated to line 20 of your 2020 Form 8606.
- The amount(s) allocated to your 2015 through 2020 Forms 8606, line 18.
- The amount(s) allocated to your 2020 Form 1040, 1040-SR or 1040-NR, line 5b; 2019 Form 1040 or 1040-SR, line 4d; your 2018 Form 1040, line 4b; your 2016 and 2017 Forms 1040, line 16b; Forms 1040A, line 12b; or 2015 through 2019 Form 1040-NR, line 17b.
- The amount from your 2020 Form 8606, line 25c.

Also, include any amount you allocated to line 20 of your 2020 Form 8606 on your 2020 Form 5329, line 2, and enter exception number 09.

Example. Ishmael, age 32, opened a Roth IRA in 2000. He made the following transactions into his Roth IRA.

- In 2005, he converted $10,000 from his traditional IRA into his Roth IRA. He filled out a 2005 Form 8606 and attached it with his 2005 Form 1040. He entered $0 on line 17 of Form 8606 because he took a deduction for all the contributions to the traditional IRA; therefore, he has no basis. He entered $10,000 on line 18 of Form 8606. He also entered zero on Form 1040, line 15a, and $10,000 on line 15b.
- In 2016, he rolled over the balance of his qualified retirement plan, $20,000, into a Roth IRA when he changed jobs. He used a 2016 Form 1040 to file his taxes. He entered $20,000 on line 16a of Form 1040 because that was the amount reported in box 1 of his 2016 Form 1099-R. Box 5 of his 2016 Form 1099-R reported $0 since he didn't make any after-tax contributions to the qualified retirement plan. He entered $20,000 on line 16b of Form 1040 since that is the taxable amount that was rolled over in 2016.

The total balance in his Roth IRA as of January 1, 2020, was $105,000 ($50,000 in contributions from 2000 through 2019 + $10,000 from the 2005 conversion + $20,000 from the 2016 rollover + $25,000 from earnings). He hasn't taken any early distribution from his Roth IRA before 2020. In 2020, he made a contribution of $5,500 to his Roth IRA.

In August of 2020, he took a $85,500 early distribution from his Roth IRA to use as a down payment on the purchase of his first home. See his filled out *Illustrated Recapture Amount—Allocation Chart* to see how he allocated the amounts from the above transactions. Based on his allocation, he would enter $20,000 on his 2020 Form 5329, line 1 (see *Amount to include on Form 5329, line 1*, earlier). He should also report $10,000 on his 2020 Form 5329, line 2, and enter exception 09 because that amount isn't subject to the 10% additional tax on early distributions.

How Do You Figure the Taxable Part?

To figure the taxable part of a distribution that isn't a qualified distribution, complete Form 8606, Part III.

Must You Withdraw or Use Assets?

You aren't required to take distributions from your Roth IRA at any age. The minimum distribution rules that apply to traditional IRAs don't apply to Roth IRAs while the owner is alive. However, after the death of a Roth IRA owner, certain of the minimum distribution rules that apply to traditional IRAs also apply to Roth IRAs as explained later under *Distributions After Owner's Death*.

Minimum distributions. You can't use your Roth IRA to satisfy minimum distribution requirements for your traditional IRA. Nor can you use distributions from traditional IRAs for required distributions from Roth IRAs. See *Distributions to beneficiaries*, later.

Distributions After Owner's Death

If a Roth IRA owner dies, the minimum distribution rules that apply to traditional IRAs apply to Roth IRAs as though the Roth IRA owner died before his or her required beginning date. See *When Can You Withdraw or Use Assets?* in chapter 1.

Distributions to beneficiaries. Generally, the entire interest in the Roth IRA must be distributed by the end of the 5th or 10th calendar year, as applicable, after the year of the owner's death unless the interest is payable to an eligible designated beneficiary over the life or life expectancy of the eligible designated beneficiary. See *When Must You Withdraw Assets? (Required Minimum Distributions)* in chapter 1.

If paid as an annuity, the entire interest must be payable over a period not greater than the designated beneficiary's life expectancy and distributions must begin before the end of the calendar year following the year of death. Distributions from another Roth IRA can't be substituted for these distributions unless the other Roth IRA was inherited from the same decedent.

If the sole beneficiary is the spouse, he or she can either delay distributions until the decedent would have reached age 72 or treat the Roth IRA as his or her own.

Combining with other Roth IRAs. A beneficiary can combine an inherited Roth IRA with another Roth IRA maintained by the beneficiary only if the beneficiary either:

- Inherited the other Roth IRA from the same decedent, or
- Was the spouse of the decedent and the sole beneficiary of the Roth IRA and elects to treat it as his or her own IRA.

Distributions that aren't qualified distributions. If a distribution to a beneficiary isn't a qualified distribution, it is generally includible in the beneficiary's gross income in the same manner as it would have been included in the owner's income had it been distributed to the IRA owner when he or she was alive.

If the owner of a Roth IRA dies before the end of:

- The 5-year period beginning with the first tax year for which a contribution was made to a Roth IRA set up for the owner's benefit, or
- The 5-year period starting with the year of a conversion contribution from a traditional IRA or a rollover from a qualified retirement plan to a Roth IRA,

each type of contribution is divided among multiple beneficiaries according to the pro-rata share of each. See *Ordering Rules for Distributions*, earlier in this chapter under *Are Distributions Taxable*.

Example. When Ms. Hibbard died in 2020, her Roth IRA contained regular contributions of $4,000, a conversion contribution of $10,000 that was made in 2016, and earnings of $2,000. No distributions had been made from her IRA. She had no basis in the conversion contribution in 2016.

When she established this Roth IRA (her first) in 2016, she named each of her four children as equal beneficiaries. Each child will receive one-fourth of each type of contribution and one-fourth of the earnings. An immediate distribution of $4,000 to each child will be treated as $1,000 from regular contributions, $2,500 from conversion contributions, and $500 from earnings.

In this case, because the distributions are made before the end of the applicable 5-year period for a qualified distribution, each beneficiary includes $500 in income for 2020. The 10% additional tax on early distributions doesn't apply because the distribution was made to the beneficiaries as a result of the death of the IRA owner.

CAUTION *If distributions from an inherited Roth IRA are less than the required minimum distribution for the year, discussed in chapter 1 under* When Must You Withdraw Assets? (Required Minimum Distributions), *you may have to pay a 50% excise tax for that year on the amount not distributed as required. For the tax on excess accumulations (insufficient distributions), see* Excess Accumulations (Insufficient Distributions) *under* What Acts Result in Penalties or Additional Taxes? *in chapter 1. If this applies to you, substitute "Roth IRA" for "traditional IRA" in that discussion.*

3.

Coronavirus Relief

Introduction

New rules provide for special distributions, during tax year 2020, from IRAs and other retirement plans. These rules provide tax-favored withdrawals, income inclusion, and repayments for certain individuals who are impacted by the coronavirus. See *Qualified Coronavirus-Related Distributions* next.

Qualified Coronavirus-Related Distributions

Coronavirus-related distributions. A coronavirus-related distribution is a retirement plan distribution that was made:

1. In 2020 before December 31, 2020; and
2. To a qualified individual. See *Qualified individuals* next for details.

If (1) and (2) apply, you can generally designate any distribution (including periodic payments and required minimum distributions) from an eligible retirement plan as a coronavirus-related distribution, regardless of why the distribution was made. Coronavirus-related distributions are permitted without regard to your need. See *Eligible retirement plan*, later, for the list of plans from which coronavirus-related distributions can be made.

A reduction or offset of your account balance in an eligible retirement plan (other than an IRA) in order to repay a loan can also be designated as a qualified 2020 disaster distribution. For more information, see *Distribution of plan loan offsets* under *Types of Qualified 2020 Disaster Distributions* in the Instructions for Form 8915-E.

Qualified individuals. You are a qualified individual if you are an individual meeting any of the following criteria.

1. You were diagnosed with the virus SARS-CoV-2 or with coronavirus disease 2019 (referred to collectively in these instructions as coronavirus) by a test approved by the Centers for Disease Control and Prevention (including a test authorized under the Federal Food, Drug, and Cosmetic Act).
2. Your spouse or dependent (as defined in section 152) was diagnosed with coronavirus by a test approved by the Centers for Disease Control and Prevention (including a test authorized under the Federal Food, Drug, and Cosmetic Act).
3. You experienced adverse financial consequences as a result of you, your spouse, or a *Member of your household* (as defined later):
   - Being quarantined, being furloughed or laid off, or having work hours reduced due to coronavirus;
   - Being unable to work due to lack of childcare due to coronavirus;
   - Having to close or reduce the hours of a business you, your spouse, or a member of your household owned or operated due to coronavirus; or
   - Having a reduction in pay (or self-employment income) due to coronavirus or having a job offer rescinded or start date for a job delayed due to coronavirus.

Member of your household. For purposes of determining whether you are a qualified individual, anyone who shares your principal residence is a member of your household.

Eligible retirement plan. An eligible retirement plan can be any of the following.

- A qualified pension, profit-sharing, or stock bonus plan (including a 401(k) plan).
- The federal Thrift Savings Plan.
- A qualified annuity plan.
- A tax-sheltered annuity contract.
- A governmental section 457 deferred compensation plan.
- A traditional, SEP, SIMPLE, or Roth IRA.

Taxation of Qualified Coronavirus-Related Distributions

Qualified coronavirus-related distributions are included in income in equal amounts over 3 years. However, if you elect, you can include the entire distribution in your income in the year it was received.

Qualified coronavirus-related distributions aren't subject to the 10% additional tax (or the additional 25% tax for certain distributions from SIMPLE IRAs) on early distributions from qualified retirement plans (including IRAs). Also, if you are receiving substantially equal periodic payments from a qualified retirement plan, the receipt of a qualified coronavirus-related distribution from that plan won't be treated as a change in those substantially equal payments merely because of the qualified coronavirus-related distribution. However, any distributions you received in excess of the $100,000 qualified coronavirus-related distribution limit may be subject to the additional tax on early distributions.

Note. If a qualified taxpayer dies before the full taxable amount of the coronavirus-related distribution has been included in gross income (or repaid), the remainder must be included in income for the tax year of the taxpayer's death.

Repayment and Inclusion in Income of Qualified Coronavirus-Related Distributions

If you choose, you can generally repay any portion of a qualified coronavirus-related distribution that is eligible for tax-free rollover treatment to an eligible retirement plan. Also, you can repay a qualified coronavirus-related distribution made on account of a hardship from a retirement plan.

You have 3 years from the day after the date you received the qualified coronavirus-related distribution to make a repayment. The amount of your repayment can't be more than the amount of the original distribution. Amounts that are repaid are treated as trustee-to-trustee transfers and are not included in income. Also, for purposes of the one-rollover-per-year limitation for IRAs, a repayment to an IRA is not considered a rollover.

For more information on how to report distributions and repayments, see the Instructions for Form 8915-E.

Repayment of qualified coronavirus-related distributions if reporting in income under the 1-year election. If you elect to include all of your qualified coronavirus-related distributions received in a year in income for that year and then repay any portion of the distribution during the allowable 3-year period, the amount repaid will reduce the amount included in income for the year of distribution.

If the repayment is made after the due date (including extensions) for your return for the year of distribution, you will need to file, with an amended return, a revised Form 8915-E. See *Amending Your Return*, later.

Example. Maria received a $45,000 qualified coronavirus-related distribution on November 1, 2020. Maria repays $45,000 of the qualified distribution on March 31, 2021. She reports the distribution and the repayment on Form 8915-E, which she files with her timely filed 2020 tax return. As a result, no portion of the distribution is included in income on her return.

Repayment of qualified coronavirus-related distributions if reporting in income under the 3-year method. If you are reporting the qualified coronavirus-related distribution in income over a 3-year period and you repay any portion of the qualified coronavirus-related distribution to an eligible retirement plan before filing your 2020 tax return, the repayment will reduce the portion of the distribution that is included in income in 2020.

If you repay a portion after the due date (including extensions) for filing your 2020 return, the repayment will reduce the portion of the distribution that is included in income on your 2020 return. If, during a year in the 3-year period, you repay more than is otherwise includible in income for that year, the excess may be carried forward or back to reduce the amount included in income for the year.

If the repayment is made after the due date (including extensions) for your return for the year of distribution, you will need to file, with an amended return, a revised Form 8915-E. See *Amending Your Return*, later.

Example. John received a $90,000 qualified coronavirus-related distribution from his IRA on March 15, 2020. He doesn't elect to include the entire distribution in his 2020 income but elects to include $30,000 in each of his 2020, 2021, and 2022 returns. John decides to repay $45,000 on November 10, 2020. He makes no other repayments during the allowable 3-year period. John reports $0 in income on his 2020 return and carries the $15,000 excess repayment ($45,000 – $30,000) forward to 2021 and reduces the amount reported in that year to $15,000. John will report $30,000 on his 2022 tax return.

4. Disaster-Related Relief

Introduction

Recent legislation contains new rules that provide for tax-favored withdrawals, income inclusion, and repayments for individuals who suffered economic losses as a result of certain major disasters that occurred in 2018, 2019, and 2020. See *Qualified 2018, 2019, and 2020 disaster distributions*, later, for more information.

Previously enacted legislation contains rules that provide for tax-favored withdrawals, income inclusion, and repayments for individuals who suffered economic losses as a result of disasters in 2016 and certain disasters in 2017.

The principles set forth in Notice 2005-92, 2005-51 I.R.B. 1165, available at *IRS.gov/IRB/2005-51_IRB* (which provides guidance on the tax-favored treatment of distributions for victims of Hurricane Katrina), and Notice 2020-50, 2020-28 I.R.B. 35, available at *IRS.gov/IRB/2020-28_IRB*, generally also apply to these rules.

If you received a qualified disaster distribution (defined later), it is taxable, but isn't subject to the 10% additional tax on early distributions. The taxable amount is figured in the same manner as other IRA distributions. However, the distribution is included in income ratably over 3 years unless you elect to report the entire amount in the year of distribution. For example, if you received a $60,000 qualified disaster distribution in 2018, you can include $20,000 in your income in 2018, 2019, and 2020. However, you can elect to include the entire distribution in your income in the year it was received. Also, you can repay the distribution and not be taxed on the distribution. See *Qualified Disaster Distributions*, later.

If you received a distribution from an eligible retirement plan to purchase or construct a main home but didn't purchase or construct a main home because of certain major disasters in 2018, 2019, or 2020, you may be able to repay the distribution and not pay income tax or the 10% additional tax on early distributions. See *Repayment of Qualified 2018, 2019, and 2020 Distributions for the Purchase or Construction of a Main Home*, later.

Form 8915-C, Qualified 2018 Disaster Retirement Plan Distributions and Repayments, and Form 8915-D, Qualified 2019 Disaster Retirement Plan Distributions and Repayments, and Form 8915-E, Qualified 2020 Disaster Retirement Plan Distributions and Repayments, are used to report qualified disaster distributions and repayments. Also report repayments of qualified distributions for home purchases and construction that were canceled because of qualified 2018, 2019, or 2020 disasters on Form 8915-C, Form 8915-D, or Form 8915-E, as applicable.

Qualified Disaster Distributions

Qualified 2016 disaster distribution. A qualified 2016 disaster distribution is any distribution you received from an eligible retirement plan made on or after January 1, 2016, and before January 1, 2018, if at any time during the calendar year 2016 your main home was located in a major disaster area declared in 2016 by the President under section 401 of the Robert T. Stafford Disaster Relief and Emergency Assistance Act and you sustained an economic loss by reason of the events giving rise to such Presidential declaration. If the previous sentence applied to you, you could generally designate any distribution (including a periodic payment or a required minimum distribution) from an eligible retirement plan as a qualified 2016 disaster distribution, regardless of whether the distribution was made on account of a federally declared disaster in calendar year 2016. Qualified 2016 disaster distributions were permitted without regard to your need or the actual amount of your economic loss, described later.

See *Qualified 2016 Disasters* in Pub. 976 for a list of disasters declared by the President in 2016. Also, see Form 8915-A, Qualified 2016 Disaster Retirement Plan Distributions and Repayments, for more information on reporting qualified 2016 disaster distributions.

Qualified 2017 disaster distribution. A qualified 2017 disaster distribution is any distribution you received from an eligible retirement plan if all of the following conditions apply.

1. The distribution was made:
   a. After August 22, 2017, and before January 1, 2019, for Hurricane Harvey or Tropical Storm Harvey;
   b. After September 3, 2017, and before January 1, 2019, for Hurricane Irma;
   c. After September 15, 2017, and before January 1, 2019, for Hurricane Maria; or
   d. After October 7, 2017, and before January 1, 2019, for the California wildfires.
2. Your main home was located in a qualified disaster area listed below on the date or any date in the period shown for that area.
   a. August 23, 2017, for the Hurricane Harvey and Tropical Storm Harvey disaster area. For this purpose, that area includes the states of Texas and Louisiana.
   b. September 4, 2017, for the Hurricane Irma disaster area. For this purpose, that area includes the U.S. Virgin Islands and Puerto Rico; the states of Georgia, Florida, and South Carolina; and the Seminole Tribe of Florida and associated lands.
   c. September 16, 2017, for the Hurricane Maria disaster area. For this purpose, that area includes the U.S. Virgin Islands and Puerto Rico.
   d. October 8, 2017, to December 31, 2017, for the California wildfire disaster area. For this purpose, that area includes the state of California.
3. You sustained an economic loss because of the disaster(s) in (2) above.

If (1) through (3) above apply, you could generally designate any distribution (including a periodic payment or a required minimum distribution) from an eligible retirement plan (including IRAs) as a qualified 2017 disaster distribution, regardless of whether the distribution was made on account of Hurricane Harvey, Tropical Storm Harvey, Hurricane Irma, Hurricane Maria, or the California wildfires. Qualified 2017 disaster distributions were permitted without regard to your need or the actual amount of your economic loss.

Qualified 2018, 2019, and 2020 disaster distributions. The definition of a qualified disaster distribution has been expanded to include distributions made from an eligible retirement plan to an individual whose main home was in a qualified disaster area (described next) at any time during that disaster's incident period and who sustained an economic loss because of the disaster.

Qualified disaster area. Any area with respect to which a major disaster was declared after 2017 and before February 19, 2020, by the President under section 401 of the Robert T. Stafford Disaster Relief and Emergency Assistance Act, except the California wildfire disaster area defined in the Bipartisan Budget Act of 2018, and any area with respect to which a major disaster has been declared solely due to COVID-19.

Incident period. The incident period for any qualified disaster is the period specified by the Federal Emergency Management Agency (FEMA) as the period during which the disaster occurred, but not including any dates before 2018.

Qualified disaster distribution. Qualified disaster distributions for 2018, 2019, and 2020 disasters are those distributions from an eligible retirement plan:

1. Made on or after the first day of the incident period of a qualified disaster and before June 17, 2020 (before June 25, 2021, for a qualified 2020 disaster);

2. Made to an individual whose main home at any time during the incident period of such qualified disaster was in the qualified disaster area; and
3. That individual sustained an economic loss because of the disaster.

Economic loss. Qualified disaster distributions are permitted without regard to your need or the actual amount of your economic loss. Examples of an economic loss include, but aren't limited to:

1. Loss, damage to, or destruction of real or personal property from fire, flooding, looting, vandalism, theft, wind, or other cause;
2. Loss related to displacement from your home; or
3. Loss of livelihood due to temporary or permanent layoffs.

Distribution limit for 2018, 2019, and 2020 disaster distributions. The total of your qualified disaster distributions from all plans is limited to $100,000 per disaster for certain major disasters that occurred in 2018, 2019, and 2020. If you take distributions from more than one type of plan, such as a 401(k) plan and an IRA, and the total amount of your distributions exceeds $100,000 for a single disaster, you may allocate the $100,000 limit among the plans by any reasonable method you choose.

Example. In 2019, you received a distribution of $50,000. In 2020, you receive a distribution of $125,000 for the same disaster. Separately, each distribution meets the requirements for a qualified disaster distribution. If you decide to treat the entire $50,000 received in 2019 as a qualified disaster distribution, only $50,000 of the 2020 distribution can be treated as a qualified disaster distribution for the same disaster.

Eligible retirement plan. An eligible retirement plan can be any of the following.

- A qualified pension, profit-sharing, or stock bonus plan (including a 401(k) plan).
- The federal Thrift Savings Plan.
- A qualified annuity plan.
- A tax-sheltered annuity contract.
- A governmental section 457 deferred compensation plan.
- A traditional, SEP, SIMPLE, or Roth IRA.

Main home. Generally, your main home is the home where you live most of the time. A temporary absence due to special circumstances, such as illness, education, business, military service, evacuation, or vacation, won't change your main home.

Taxation of Qualified Disaster Distributions

Qualified disaster distributions are included in income in equal amounts over 3 years. However, if you elect, you can include the entire distribution in your income in the year it was received.

Qualified disaster distributions aren't subject to the 10% additional tax (or the additional 25% tax for certain distributions from SIMPLE IRAs) on early distributions from qualified retirement plans (including IRAs). Also, if you are receiving substantially equal periodic payments from a qualified retirement plan, the receipt of a qualified disaster distribution from that plan won't be treated as a change in those substantially equal payments merely because of the qualified disaster distribution. However, any distributions you received in excess of the $100,000 qualified disaster distribution limit may be subject to the additional tax on early distributions.

Repayment of Qualified Disaster Distributions

If you choose, you can generally repay any portion of a qualified disaster distribution that is eligible for tax-free rollover treatment to an eligible retirement plan. Also, you can repay a qualified disaster distribution made on account of a hardship from a retirement plan. However, see Exceptions, later, for qualified disaster distributions you cannot repay.

You have 3 years from the day after the date you received the qualified disaster distribution to make a repayment. The amount of your repayment can't be more than the amount of the original distribution. Amounts that are repaid are treated as trustee-to-trustee transfers and are not included in income. Also, for purposes of the one-rollover-per-year limitation for IRAs, a repayment to an IRA is not considered a rollover.

For more information on how to report distributions and repayments, see the Instructions for Form 8915-A (in the case of qualified 2016 disasters), the Instructions for Form 8915-B (in the case of qualified 2017 disasters), the Instructions for Form 8915-C (in the case of qualified 2018 disasters), the Instructions for Form 8915-D (in the case of qualified 2019 disasters), or the Instructions for Form 8915-E (in the case of qualified 2020 disasters).

Exceptions. You cannot repay the following types of distributions.

1. Qualified disaster distributions received as a beneficiary (other than as a surviving spouse).
2. Required minimum distributions.
3. Periodic payments (other than from an IRA) that are for:
    a. A period of 10 years or more,
    b. Your life or life expectancy, or

c. The joint lives or joint life expectancies of you and your beneficiary.

Repayment of distributions if reporting under the 1-year election. If you elect to include all of your qualified disaster distributions received in a year in income for that year and then repay any portion of the distribution during the allowable 3-year period, the amount repaid will reduce the amount included in income for the year of distribution. If the repayment is made after the due date (including extensions) for your return for the year of distribution, you will need to file, with an amended return, a revised Form 8915-A (if the repayment is for a qualified 2016 disaster distribution), a revised Form 8915-B (if the repayment is for a qualified 2017 disaster distribution), a revised Form 8915-C (if the repayment is for a qualified 2018 disaster distribution), a revised Form 8915-D (if the repayment is for a qualified 2019 disaster distribution), or a revised Form 8915-E (in the case of a qualified 2020 disaster distribution). See *Amending Your Return*, later.

Example. Maria received a $45,000 qualified disaster distribution on November 1, 2020. After receiving reimbursement from her insurance company for a casualty loss, Maria repays $45,000 of the qualified distribution on March 31, 2021. She reports the distribution and the repayment on Form 8915-E, which she files with her timely filed 2020 tax return. As a result, no portion of the distribution is included in income on her return.

Repayment of qualified disaster distributions if reporting under the 3-year method. If you are reporting the qualified disaster distribution in income over a 3-year period and you repay any portion of the qualified disaster distribution to an eligible retirement plan before filing your 2020 tax return, the repayment will reduce the portion of the distribution that is included in income in 2020. If you repay a portion after the due date (including extensions) for filing your 2020 return, the repayment will reduce the portion of the distribution that is included in income on your 2021 return, unless you are eligible to amend your 2018, 2019, or 2020 return, as applicable. If, during a year in the 3-year period, you repay more than is otherwise includible in income for that year, the excess may be carried forward or back to reduce the amount included in income for the year.

Example. John received a $90,000 qualified disaster distribution from his pension plan on November 15, 2019. He doesn't elect to include the entire distribution in his 2019 income, but elects to include $30,000 in each of his 2019, 2020, and 2021 returns. On November 10, 2020, John repays $45,000. He makes no other repayments during the allowable 3-year period. John may report the distribution and repayment in either of the following ways.

- Report $0 in income on his 2020 return, and carry the $15,000 excess repayment ($45,000 – $30,000) forward to 2021 and reduce the amount reported in that year to $15,000.
- Report $0 in income on his 2020 return, report $30,000 on his 2021 return, and file an amended return for 2019 to reduce the amount previously included in income to $15,000 ($30,000 – $15,000).

Repayment of Qualified 2018, 2019, and 2020 Distributions for the Purchase or Construction of a Main Home

If you received a qualified distribution to purchase or construct a main home in certain major disaster areas, you can repay all or any part of that distribution to an eligible retirement plan during the period beginning on the first day of the incident period of a qualified disaster and ending on June 17, 2020 (June 25, 2021, for qualified 2020 distributions).

To be a qualified distribution, the distribution must meet all of the following requirements.

1. The distribution is a hardship distribution from a 401(k) plan, a hardship distribution from a tax-sheltered annuity plan (403(b) plan), or a qualified first-time homebuyer distribution from an IRA.
2. The distribution was received during the period beginning on the date which is 180 days before the first day of the incident period of the qualified disaster and ending on the date which is 30 days after the last day of such incident period.
3. The distribution was to be used to purchase or construct a main home in the disaster area and was not purchased or constructed because of the disaster.

Any amount that is repaid during the period beginning on the first day of the incident period of such qualified disaster and ending on June 17, 2020 (June 25, 2021, for qualified 2020 distributions), is treated as a trustee-to-trustee transfer and is not included in income. Also, for purposes of the one-rollover-per-year limitation for IRAs, a repayment to an IRA is not considered a rollover.

A qualified distribution not repaid before June 18, 2020 (June 25, 2021, for qualified 2020 distributions), may be taxable for 2020 (the year distributed) and subject to the additional 10% tax (or the additional 25% tax for certain SIMPLE IRAs) on early distributions.

See Form 8915-C (for qualified 2018 disaster distributions), Form 8915-D (for qualified 2019 disaster distributions), or Form 8915-E (for qualified 2020 disaster distributions) if you received a qualified distribution that you repaid, in whole or in part, before June 18, 2020 (June 25, 2021, for qualified 2020 distributions).

Amending Your Return

If, after filing your original return, you make a repayment, the repayment may reduce the amount of your qualified disaster distributions that were previously included in income. Depending on when a repayment is made, you may need to file an amended tax return to refigure your taxable income.

If you make a repayment by the due date of your original return (including extensions), include the repayment on your amended return.

If you make a repayment after the due date of your original return (including extensions), include it on your amended return only if either of the following applies.

- You elected to include all of your qualified disaster distributions in income in the year of the distribution (not over 3 years) on your original return.
- The amount of the repayment exceeds the portion of the qualified disaster distributions that are includible in income for 2021 and you choose to carry the excess back to your 2019 or 2020 tax return.

Example. You received a qualified disaster distribution in the amount of $90,000 on October 16, 2019. You choose to spread the $90,000 over 3 years ($30,000 in income for 2019, 2020, and 2021). On November 19, 2021, you make a repayment of $45,000. For 2021, none of the qualified disaster distribution is includible in income. The excess repayment of $15,000 can be carried back to 2020 or 2019, as applicable.

File Form 1040-X to amend a return you have already filed. Generally, Form 1040-X must be filed within 3 years after the date the original return was filed, or within 2 years after the date the tax was paid, whichever is later.

How To Get Tax Help

If you have questions about a tax issue, need help preparing your tax return, or want to download free publications, forms, or instructions, go to *IRS.gov* and find resources that can help you right away.

Preparing and filing your tax return. After receiving all your wage and earnings statements (Form W-2, W-2G, 1099-R, 1099-MISC, 1099-NEC, etc.); unemployment compensation statements (by mail or in a digital format) or other government payment statements (Form 1099-G); and interest, dividend, and retirement statements from banks and investment firms (Forms 1099), you have several options to choose from to prepare and file your tax return. You can prepare the tax return yourself, see if you qualify for free tax preparation, or hire a tax professional to prepare your return.

Free options for tax preparation. Go to *IRS.gov* to see your options for preparing and filing your return online or in your local community, if you qualify, which include the following.

- **Free File.** This program lets you prepare and file your federal individual income tax return for free using brand-name tax-preparation-and-filing software or Free File fillable forms. However, state tax preparation may not be available through Free File. Go to *IRS.gov/FreeFile* to see if you qualify for free online federal tax preparation, e-filing, and direct deposit or payment options.
- **VITA.** The Volunteer Income Tax Assistance (VITA) program offers free tax help to people with low-to-moderate incomes, persons with disabilities, and limited-English-speaking taxpayers who need help preparing their own tax returns. Go to *IRS.gov/VITA*, download the free IRS2Go app, or call [illegible] for information on free tax return preparation.
- **TCE.** The Tax Counseling for the Elderly (TCE) program offers free tax help for all taxpayers, particularly those who are 60 years of age and older. TCE volunteers specialize in answering questions about pensions and retirement-related issues unique to seniors. Go to *IRS.gov/TCE*, download the free IRS2Go app, or call 888-227-7669 for information on free tax return preparation.
- **MilTax.** Members of the U.S. Armed Forces and qualified veterans may use MilTax, a free tax service offered by the Department of Defense through Military OneSource.

  Also, the IRS offers Free Fillable Forms, which can be completed online and then filed electronically regardless of income.

Using online tools to help prepare your return. Go to *IRS.gov/Tools* for the following.

- The *Earned Income Tax Credit Assistant* (*IRS.gov/EITCAssistant*) determines if you're eligible for the earned income credit (EIC).
- The *Online EIN Application* (*IRS.gov/EIN*) helps you get an employer identification number (EIN).
- The *Tax Withholding Estimator* (*IRS.gov/W4app*) makes it easier for everyone to pay the correct amount of tax during the year. The tool is a convenient, online way to check and tailor your withholding. It's more user-friendly for taxpayers, including retirees and self-employed individuals. The features include the following.
  - Easy to understand language.
  - The ability to switch between screens, correct previous entries, and skip screens that don't apply.
  - Tips and links to help you determine if you qualify for tax credits and deductions.
  - A progress tracker.
  - A self-employment tax feature.
  - Automatic calculation of taxable social security benefits.
- The *First Time Homebuyer Credit Account Look-up* (*IRS.gov/HomeBuyer*) tool provides information on your repayments and account balance.
- The *Sales Tax Deduction Calculator* (*IRS.gov/SalesTax*) figures the amount you can claim if you itemize deductions on Schedule A (Form 1040).

Getting answers to your tax questions. On IRS.gov, you can get up-to-date information on current events and changes in tax law.

- *IRS.gov/Help*: A variety of tools to help you get answers to some of the most common tax questions.
- *IRS.gov/ITA*: The Interactive Tax Assistant, a tool that will ask you questions on a number of tax law topics and provide answers.
- *IRS.gov/Forms*: Find forms, instructions, and publications. You will find details on 2020 tax changes and hundreds of interactive links to help you find answers to your questions.
- You may also be able to access tax law information in your electronic filing software.

Need someone to prepare your tax return? There are various types of tax return preparers, including tax preparers, enrolled agents, certified public accountants (CPAs), attorneys, and many others who don't have professional credentials. If you choose to have someone prepare your tax return, choose that preparer wisely. A paid tax preparer is:

- Primarily responsible for the overall substantive accuracy of your return,
- Required to sign the return, and
- Required to include their preparer tax identification number (PTIN).

Although the tax preparer always signs the return, you're ultimately responsible for providing all the information required for the preparer to accurately prepare your return. Anyone paid to prepare tax returns for others should have a thorough understanding of tax matters. For more information on how to choose a tax preparer, go to *Tips for Choosing a Tax Preparer* on IRS.gov.

Coronavirus. Go to *IRS.gov/Coronavirus* for links to information on the impact of the coronavirus, as well as tax relief available for individuals and families, small and large businesses, and tax-exempt organizations.

Tax reform. Tax reform legislation affects individuals, businesses, and tax-exempt and government entities. Go to *IRS.gov/TaxReform* for information and updates on how this legislation affects your taxes.

Employers can register to use Business Services Online. The Social Security Administration (SSA) offers online service at *SSA.gov/employer* for fast, free, and secure online W-2 filing options to CPAs, accountants, enrolled agents, and individuals who process Form W-2, Wage and Tax Statement, and Form W-2c, Corrected Wage and Tax Statement.

IRS social media. Go to *IRS.gov/SocialMedia* to see the various social media tools the IRS uses to share the latest information on tax changes, scam alerts, initiatives, products, and services. At the IRS, privacy and security are paramount. We use these tools to share public information with you. **Don't** post your SSN or other confidential information on social media sites. Always protect your identity when using any social networking site.

The following IRS YouTube channels provide short, informative videos on various tax-related topics in English, Spanish, and ASL.

- *Youtube.com/irsvideos*.
- *Youtube.com/irsvideosmultilingua*.
- *Youtube.com/irsvideosASL*.

Watching IRS videos. The IRS Video portal (*IRSVideos.gov*) contains video and audio presentations for individuals, small businesses, and tax professionals.

Online tax information in other languages. You can find information on *IRS.gov/MyLanguage* if English isn't your native language.

Free interpreter service. Multilingual assistance, provided by the IRS, is available at Taxpayer Assistance Centers (TACs) and other IRS offices. Over-the-phone interpreter service is accessible in more than 350 languages.

Getting tax forms and publications. Go to *IRS.gov/Forms* to view, download, or print all of the forms, instructions, and publications you may need. You can also download and view popular tax publications and instructions (including the Instructions for Forms 1040 and 1040-SR) on mobile devices as an eBook at *IRS.gov/eBooks*. Or you can go to *IRS.gov/OrderForms* to place an order.

Access your online account (individual taxpayers only). Go to *IRS.gov/Account* to securely access information about your federal tax account.

- View the amount you owe, pay online, or set up an online payment agreement.
- Access your tax records online.
- Review your payment history.
- Go to *IRS.gov/SecureAccess* to review the required identity authentication process.

Using direct deposit. The fastest way to receive a tax refund is to file electronically and choose direct deposit, which securely and electronically transfers your refund directly into your financial account. Direct deposit also avoids the possibility that your check could be lost, stolen, or returned undeliverable to the IRS. Eight in 10 taxpayers use direct deposit to receive their refunds. The IRS issues more than 90% of refunds in less than 21 days.

Getting a transcript of your return. The quickest way to get a copy of your tax transcript is to go to *IRS.gov/Transcripts*. Click on either "Get Transcript Online" or "Get Transcript by Mail" to order a free copy of your transcript. If you prefer, you can order your transcript by calling 800-908-9946.

Reporting and resolving your tax-related identity theft issues.

- Tax-related identity theft happens when someone steals your personal information to commit tax fraud. Your taxes can be affected if your SSN is used to file a fraudulent return or to claim a refund or credit.
- The IRS doesn't initiate contact with taxpayers by email, text messages, telephone calls, or social media channels to request personal or financial information. This includes requests for personal identification numbers (PINs), passwords, or similar information for credit cards, banks, or other financial accounts.
- Go to *IRS.gov/IdentityTheft*, the IRS Identity Theft Central webpage, for information on identity theft and data security protection for taxpayers, tax professionals, and businesses. If your SSN has been lost or stolen or you suspect you're a victim of tax-related identity theft, you can learn what steps you should take.
- Get an Identity Protection PIN (IP PIN). IP PINs are six-digit numbers assigned to eligible taxpayers to help prevent the misuse of their SSNs on fraudulent federal income tax returns. When you have an IP PIN, it prevents someone else from filing a tax return with your SSN. To learn more, go to *IRS.gov/IPPIN*.

Checking on the status of your refund.

- Go to *IRS.gov/Refunds*.
- The IRS can't issue refunds before mid-February 2021 for returns that claimed the EIC or the additional child tax credit (ACTC). This applies to the entire refund, not just the portion associated with these credits.
- Download the official IRS2Go app to your mobile device to check your refund status.
- Call the automated refund hotline at 800-829-1954.

Making a tax payment. The IRS uses the latest encryption technology to ensure your electronic payments are safe and secure. You can make electronic payments online, by phone, and from a mobile device using the IRS2Go app. Paying electronically is quick, easy, and faster than mailing in a check or money order. Go to *IRS.gov/Payments* for information on how to make a payment using any of the following options.

- *IRS Direct Pay*: Pay your individual tax bill or estimated tax payment directly from your checking or savings account at no cost to you.
- *Debit or Credit Card*: Choose an approved payment processor to pay online, by phone, or by mobile device.
- *Electronic Funds Withdrawal*: Offered only when filing your federal taxes using tax return preparation software or through a tax professional.
- *Electronic Federal Tax Payment System*: Best option for businesses. Enrollment is required.
- *Check or Money Order*: Mail your payment to the address listed on the notice or instructions.
- *Cash*: You may be able to pay your taxes with cash at a participating retail store.
- *Same-Day Wire*: You may be able to do same-day wire from your financial institution. Contact your financial institution for availability, cost, and cut-off times.

What if I can't pay now? Go to *IRS.gov/Payments* for more information about your options.

- Apply for an *online payment agreement* (*IRS.gov/OPA*) to meet your tax obligation in monthly installments if you can't pay your taxes in full today. Once you complete the online process, you will receive immediate notification of whether your agreement has been approved.
- Use the *Offer in Compromise Pre-Qualifier* to see if you can settle your tax debt for less than the full amount you owe. For more information on the Offer in Compromise program, go to *IRS.gov/OIC*.

Filing an amended return. You can now file Form 1040-X electronically with tax filing software to amend 2019 Forms 1040 and 1040-SR. To do so, you must have e-filed your original 2019 return. Amended returns for all prior years must be mailed. See *Tips for taxpayers who need to file an amended tax return* and go to *IRS.gov/Form1040X* for information and updates.

Checking the status of your amended return. Go to *IRS.gov/WMAR* to track the status of Form 1040-X amended returns. Please note that it can take up to 3 weeks from the date you filed your amended return for it to show up in our system, and processing it can take up to 16 weeks.

Understanding an IRS notice or letter you've received. Go to *IRS.gov/Notices* to find additional information about responding to an IRS notice or letter.

Contacting your local IRS office. Keep in mind, many questions can be answered on IRS.gov without visiting an IRS Taxpayer Assistance Center (TAC). Go to *IRS.gov/LetUsHelp* for the topics people ask about most. If you still need help, IRS TACs provide tax help when a tax issue can't be handled online or by phone. All TACs now provide service by appointment, so you'll know in advance that you can get the service you need without long wait times. Before you visit, go to *IRS.gov/TACLocator* to find the nearest TAC and to check hours, available services, and appointment options. Or, on the IRS2Go app, under the Stay Connected tab, choose the Contact Us option and click on "Local Offices."

The Taxpayer Advocate Service (TAS) Is Here To Help You

What Is TAS?

TAS is an ***independent*** organization within the IRS that helps taxpayers and protects taxpayer rights. Their job is to ensure that every taxpayer is treated fairly and that you know and understand your rights under the *Taxpayer Bill of Rights*.

How Can You Learn About Your Taxpayer Rights?

The Taxpayer Bill of Rights describes 10 basic rights that all taxpayers have when dealing with the IRS. Go to *TaxpayerAdvocate.IRS.gov* to help you understand what these rights mean to you and how they apply. These are ***your*** rights. Know them. Use them.

What Can TAS Do For You?

TAS can help you resolve problems that you can't resolve with the IRS. And their service is free. If you qualify for their assistance, you will be assigned to one advocate who will work with you throughout the process and will do everything possible to resolve your issue. TAS can help you if:

- Your problem is causing financial difficulty for you, your family, or your business;
- You face (or your business is facing) an immediate threat of adverse action; or
- You've tried repeatedly to contact the IRS but no one has responded, or the IRS hasn't responded by the date promised.

How Can You Reach TAS?

TAS has offices *in every state, the District of Columbia, and Puerto Rico*. Your local advocate's number is in your local directory and at *TaxpayerAdvocate.IRS.gov/Contact-Us*. You can also call them at 877-777-4778.

How Else Does TAS Help Taxpayers?

TAS works to resolve large-scale problems that affect many taxpayers. If you know of one of these broad issues, please report it to them at *IRS.gov/SAMS*.

TAS for Tax Professionals

TAS can provide a variety of information for tax professionals, including tax law updates and guidance, TAS programs, and ways to let TAS know about systemic problems you've seen in your practice.

Low Income Taxpayer Clinics (LITCs)

LITCs are independent from the IRS. LITCs represent individuals whose income is below a certain level and need to resolve tax problems with the IRS, such as audits, appeals, and tax collection disputes. In addition, clinics can provide information about taxpayer rights and responsibilities in different languages for individuals who speak English as a second language. Services are offered for free or a small fee for eligible taxpayers. To find a clinic near you, visit *www.TaxpayerAdvocate.IRS.gov/about-us/Low-Income-Taxpayer-Clinics-LITC/* or see IRS Pub. 4134, *Low Income Taxpayer Clinic List*.

Appendices

To help you complete your tax return, use the following appendices that include worksheets and tables.

1. **Appendix A**—Worksheet for Determining Required Minimum Distributions.
2. **Appendix B**—Life Expectancy Tables. These tables are included to assist you in computing your required minimum distribution amount if you haven't taken all your assets from all your traditional IRAs before age 70½ or age 72, whichever applies.
   a. Table I (Single Life Expectancy).
   b. Table II (Joint Life and Last Survivor Expectancy).
   c. Table III (Uniform Lifetime)
3. **Appendix C**—Recapture Amount—Allocation Chart. This chart allocates amounts that comprise an early distribution.

Appendix A. Worksheet for Determining Required Minimum Distributions

Keep for Your Records

1. Age	70½	71½	72½	73½	74½
2. Year age was reached					
3. Value of IRA at the close of business on December 31 of the year immediately prior to the year on line 2[1]					
4. Distribution period from Table III or life expectancy from Life Expectancy Table I or Table II[2]					
5. Required distribution (divide line 3 by line 4)[3]					

1. Age	75½	76½	77½	78½	79½
2. Year age was reached					
3. Value of IRA at the close of business on December 31 of the year immediately prior to the year on line 2[1]					
4. Distribution period from Table III or life expectancy from Life Expectancy Table I or Table II[2]					
5. Required distribution (divide line 3 by line 4)[3]					

1. Age	80½	81½	82½	83½	84½
2. Year age was reached					
3. Value of IRA at the close of business on December 31 of the year immediately prior to the year on line 2[1]					
4. Distribution period from Table III or life expectancy from Life Expectancy Table I or Table II[2]					
5. Required distribution (divide line 3 by line 4)[3]					

1. Age	85½	86½	87½	88½	89½
2. Year age was reached					
3. Value of IRA at the close of business on December 31 of the year immediately prior to the year on line 2[1]					
4. Distribution period from Table III or life expectancy from Life Expectancy Table I or Table II[2]					
5. Required distribution (divide line 3 by line 4)[3]					

[1] If you have more than one IRA, you must figure the required distribution separately for each IRA.

[2] Use the appropriate life expectancy or distribution period for each year and for each IRA.

[3] If you have more than one IRA, you must withdraw an amount equal to the total of the required distributions figured for each IRA. You can, however, withdraw the total from one IRA or from more than one IRA.

Appendix B. Life Expectancy Tables

Table I
(Single Life Expectancy)
(For Use by Beneficiaries)

Age	Life Expectancy	Age	Life Expectancy
0	82.4	28	55.3
1	81.6	29	54.3
2	80.6	30	53.3
3	79.7	31	52.4
4	78.7	32	51.4
5	77.7	33	50.4
6	76.7	34	49.4
7	75.8	35	48.5
8	74.8	36	47.5
9	73.8	37	46.5
10	72.8	38	45.6
11	71.8	39	44.6
12	70.8	40	43.6
13	69.9	41	42.7
14	68.9	42	41.7
15	67.9	43	40.7
16	66.9	44	39.8
17	66.0	45	38.8
18	65.0	46	37.9
19	64.0	47	37.0
20	63.0	48	36.0
21	62.1	49	35.1
22	61.1	50	34.2
23	60.1	51	33.3
24	59.1	52	32.3
25	58.2	53	31.4
26	57.2	54	30.5
27	56.2	55	29.6

Appendix B. (Continued)

Table I
(Single Life Expectancy)
(For Use by Beneficiaries)

Age	Life Expectancy	Age	Life Expectancy
56	28.7	84	8.1
57	27.9	85	7.6
58	27.0	86	7.1
59	26.1	87	6.7
60	25.2	88	6.3
61	24.4	89	5.9
62	23.5	90	5.5
63	22.7	91	5.2
64	21.8	92	4.9
65	21.0	93	4.6
66	20.2	94	4.3
67	19.4	95	4.1
68	18.6	96	3.8
69	17.8	97	3.6
70	17.0	98	3.4
71	16.3	99	3.1
72	15.5	100	2.9
73	14.8	101	2.7
74	14.1	102	2.5
75	13.4	103	2.3
76	12.7	104	2.1
77	12.1	105	1.9
78	11.4	106	1.7
79	10.8	107	1.5
80	10.2	108	1.4
81	9.7	109	1.2
82	9.1	110	1.1
83	8.6	111 and over	1.0

Appendix B. Life Expectancy Tables (Continued)

Table II
(Joint Life and Last Survivor Expectancy)
(For Use by Owners Whose Spouses Are More Than 10 Years Younger and Are the Sole Beneficiaries of Their IRAs)

Ages	20	21	22	23	24	25	26	27	28	29
20	70.1	69.6	69.1	68.7	68.3	67.9	67.5	67.2	66.9	66.6
21	69.6	69.1	68.6	68.2	67.7	67.3	66.9	66.6	66.2	65.9
22	69.1	68.6	68.1	67.6	67.2	66.7	66.3	65.9	65.6	65.2
23	68.7	68.2	67.6	67.1	66.6	66.2	65.7	65.3	64.9	64.6
24	68.3	67.7	67.2	66.6	66.1	65.6	65.2	64.7	64.3	63.9
25	67.9	67.3	66.7	66.2	65.6	65.1	64.6	64.2	63.7	63.3
26	67.5	66.9	66.3	65.7	65.2	64.6	64.1	63.6	63.2	62.8
27	67.2	66.6	65.9	65.3	64.7	64.2	63.6	63.1	62.7	62.2
28	66.9	66.2	65.6	64.9	64.3	63.7	63.2	62.7	62.1	61.7
29	66.6	65.9	65.2	64.6	63.9	63.3	62.8	62.2	61.7	61.2
30	66.3	65.6	64.9	64.2	63.6	62.9	62.3	61.8	61.2	60.7
31	66.1	65.3	64.6	63.9	63.2	62.6	62.0	61.4	60.8	60.2
32	65.8	65.1	64.3	63.6	62.9	62.2	61.6	61.0	60.4	59.8
33	65.6	64.8	64.1	63.3	62.6	61.9	61.3	60.6	60.0	59.4
34	65.4	64.6	63.8	63.1	62.3	61.6	60.9	60.3	59.6	59.0
35	65.2	64.4	63.6	62.8	62.1	61.4	60.6	59.9	59.3	58.6
36	65.0	64.2	63.4	62.6	61.9	61.1	60.4	59.6	59.0	58.3
37	64.9	64.0	63.2	62.4	61.6	60.9	60.1	59.4	58.7	58.0
38	64.7	63.9	63.0	62.2	61.4	60.6	59.9	59.1	58.4	57.7
39	64.6	63.7	62.9	62.1	61.2	60.4	59.6	58.9	58.1	57.4
40	64.4	63.6	62.7	61.9	61.1	60.2	59.4	58.7	57.9	57.1
41	64.3	63.5	62.6	61.7	60.9	60.1	59.3	58.5	57.7	56.9
42	64.2	63.3	62.5	61.6	60.8	59.9	59.1	58.3	57.5	56.7
43	64.1	63.2	62.4	61.5	60.6	59.8	58.9	58.1	57.3	56.5
44	64.0	63.1	62.2	61.4	60.5	59.6	58.8	57.9	57.1	56.3
45	64.0	63.0	62.2	61.3	60.4	59.5	58.6	57.8	56.9	56.1
46	63.9	63.0	62.1	61.2	60.3	59.4	58.5	57.7	56.8	56.0
47	63.8	62.9	62.0	61.1	60.2	59.3	58.4	57.5	56.7	55.8
48	63.7	62.8	61.9	61.0	60.1	59.2	58.3	57.4	56.5	55.7
49	63.7	62.8	61.8	60.9	60.0	59.1	58.2	57.3	56.4	55.6
50	63.6	62.7	61.8	60.8	59.9	59.0	58.1	57.2	56.3	55.4
51	63.6	62.6	61.7	60.8	59.9	58.9	58.0	57.1	56.2	55.3
52	63.5	62.6	61.7	60.7	59.8	58.9	58.0	57.1	56.1	55.2
53	63.5	62.5	61.6	60.7	59.7	58.8	57.9	57.0	56.1	55.2
54	63.5	62.5	61.6	60.6	59.7	58.8	57.8	56.9	56.0	55.1
55	63.4	62.5	61.5	60.6	59.6	58.7	57.8	56.8	55.9	55.0
56	63.4	62.4	61.5	60.5	59.6	58.7	57.7	56.8	55.9	54.9
57	63.4	62.4	61.5	60.5	59.6	58.6	57.7	56.7	55.8	54.9
58	63.3	62.4	61.4	60.5	59.5	58.6	57.6	56.7	55.8	54.8
59	63.3	62.3	61.4	60.4	59.5	58.5	57.6	56.7	55.7	54.8

Appendix B. (Continued)

Table II (continued)
(Joint Life and Last Survivor Expectancy)
(For Use by Owners Whose Spouses Are More Than 10 Years Younger and Are the Sole Beneficiaries of Their IRAs)

Ages	20	21	22	23	24	25	26	27	28	29
60	63.3	62.3	61.4	60.4	59.5	58.5	57.6	56.6	55.7	54.7
61	63.3	62.3	61.3	60.4	59.4	58.5	57.5	56.6	55.6	54.7
62	63.2	62.3	61.3	60.4	59.4	58.4	57.5	56.5	55.6	54.7
63	63.2	62.3	61.3	60.3	59.4	58.4	57.5	56.5	55.6	54.6
64	63.2	62.2	61.3	60.3	59.4	58.4	57.4	56.5	55.5	54.6
65	63.2	62.2	61.3	60.3	59.3	58.4	57.4	56.5	55.5	54.6
66	63.2	62.2	61.2	60.3	59.3	58.4	57.4	56.4	55.5	54.5
67	63.2	62.2	61.2	60.3	59.3	58.3	57.4	56.4	55.5	54.5
68	63.1	62.2	61.2	60.2	59.3	58.3	57.4	56.4	55.4	54.5
69	63.1	62.2	61.2	60.2	59.3	58.3	57.3	56.4	55.4	54.5
70	63.1	62.2	61.2	60.2	59.3	58.3	57.3	56.4	55.4	54.4
71	63.1	62.1	61.2	60.2	59.2	58.3	57.3	56.4	55.4	54.4
72	63.1	62.1	61.2	60.2	59.2	58.3	57.3	56.3	55.4	54.4
73	63.1	62.1	61.2	60.2	59.2	58.3	57.3	56.3	55.4	54.4
74	63.1	62.1	61.2	60.2	59.2	58.2	57.3	56.3	55.4	54.4
75	63.1	62.1	61.1	60.2	59.2	58.2	57.3	56.3	55.3	54.4
76	63.1	62.1	61.1	60.2	59.2	58.2	57.3	56.3	55.3	54.4
77	63.1	62.1	61.1	60.2	59.2	58.2	57.3	56.3	55.3	54.4
78	63.1	62.1	61.1	60.2	59.2	58.2	57.3	56.3	55.3	54.4
79	63.1	62.1	61.1	60.2	59.2	58.2	57.2	56.3	55.3	54.3
80	63.1	62.1	61.1	60.1	59.2	58.2	57.2	56.3	55.3	54.3
81	63.1	62.1	61.1	60.1	59.2	58.2	57.2	56.3	55.3	54.3
82	63.1	62.1	61.1	60.1	59.2	58.2	57.2	56.3	55.3	54.3
83	63.1	62.1	61.1	60.1	59.2	58.2	57.2	56.3	55.3	54.3
84	63.0	62.1	61.1	60.1	59.2	58.2	57.2	56.3	55.3	54.3
85	63.0	62.1	61.1	60.1	59.2	58.2	57.2	56.3	55.3	54.3
86	63.0	62.1	61.1	60.1	59.2	58.2	57.2	56.2	55.3	54.3
87	63.0	62.1	61.1	60.1	59.2	58.2	57.2	56.2	55.3	54.3
88	63.0	62.1	61.1	60.1	59.2	58.2	57.2	56.2	55.3	54.3
89	63.0	62.1	61.1	60.1	59.1	58.2	57.2	56.2	55.3	54.3
90	63.0	62.1	61.1	60.1	59.1	58.2	57.2	56.2	55.3	54.3
91	63.0	62.1	61.1	60.1	59.1	58.2	57.2	56.2	55.3	54.3
92	63.0	62.1	61.1	60.1	59.1	58.2	57.2	56.2	55.3	54.3
93	63.0	62.1	61.1	60.1	59.1	58.2	57.2	56.2	55.3	54.3
94	63.0	62.1	61.1	60.1	59.1	58.2	57.2	56.2	55.3	54.3
95	63.0	62.1	61.1	60.1	59.1	58.2	57.2	56.2	55.3	54.3
96	63.0	62.1	61.1	60.1	59.1	58.2	57.2	56.2	55.3	54.3
97	63.0	62.1	61.1	60.1	59.1	58.2	57.2	56.2	55.3	54.3
98	63.0	62.1	61.1	60.1	59.1	58.2	57.2	56.2	55.3	54.3
99	63.0	62.1	61.1	60.1	59.1	58.2	57.2	56.2	55.3	54.3

Page 48 **Publication 590-B (2020)**

Appendix B. (Continued)

Table II (continued)
(Joint Life and Last Survivor Expectancy)
(For Use by Owners Whose Spouses Are More Than 10 Years Younger and Are the Sole Beneficiaries of Their IRAs)

Ages	20	21	22	23	24	25	26	27	28	29
100	63.0	62.1	61.1	60.1	59.1	58.2	57.2	56.2	55.3	54.3
101	63.0	62.1	61.1	60.1	59.1	58.2	57.2	56.2	55.3	54.3
102	63.0	62.1	61.1	60.1	59.1	58.2	57.2	56.2	55.3	54.3
103	63.0	62.1	61.1	60.1	59.1	58.2	57.2	56.2	55.3	54.3
104	63.0	62.1	61.1	60.1	59.1	58.2	57.2	56.2	55.3	54.3
105	63.0	62.1	61.1	60.1	59.1	58.2	57.2	56.2	55.3	54.3
106	63.0	62.1	61.1	60.1	59.1	58.2	57.2	56.2	55.3	54.3
107	63.0	62.1	61.1	60.1	59.1	58.2	57.2	56.2	55.3	54.3
108	63.0	62.1	61.1	60.1	59.1	58.2	57.2	56.2	55.3	54.3
109	63.0	62.1	61.1	60.1	59.1	58.2	57.2	56.2	55.3	54.3
110	63.0	62.1	61.1	60.1	59.1	58.2	57.2	56.2	55.3	54.3
111	63.0	62.1	61.1	60.1	59.1	58.2	57.2	56.2	55.3	54.3
112	63.0	62.1	61.1	60.1	59.1	58.2	57.2	56.2	55.3	54.3
113	63.0	62.1	61.1	60.1	59.1	58.2	57.2	56.2	55.3	54.3
114	63.0	62.1	61.1	60.1	59.1	58.2	57.2	56.2	55.3	54.3
115+	63.0	62.1	61.1	60.1	59.1	58.2	57.2	56.2	55.3	54.3

Appendix B. (Continued)

Table II (continued)
(Joint Life and Last Survivor Expectancy)
(For Use by Owners Whose Spouses Are More Than 10 Years Younger and Are the Sole Beneficiaries of Their IRAs)

Ages	30	31	32	33	34	35	36	37	38	39
30	60.2	59.7	59.2	58.8	58.4	58.0	57.6	57.3	57.0	56.7
31	59.7	59.2	58.7	58.2	57.8	57.4	57.0	56.6	56.3	56.0
32	59.2	58.7	58.2	57.7	57.2	56.8	56.4	56.0	55.6	55.3
33	58.8	58.2	57.7	57.2	56.7	56.2	55.8	55.4	55.0	54.7
34	58.4	57.8	57.2	56.7	56.2	55.7	55.3	54.8	54.4	54.0
35	58.0	57.4	56.8	56.2	55.7	55.2	54.7	54.3	53.8	53.4
36	57.6	57.0	56.4	55.8	55.3	54.7	54.2	53.7	53.3	52.8
37	57.3	56.6	56.0	55.4	54.8	54.3	53.7	53.2	52.7	52.3
38	57.0	56.3	55.6	55.0	54.4	53.8	53.3	52.7	52.2	51.7
39	56.7	56.0	55.3	54.7	54.0	53.4	52.8	52.3	51.7	51.2
40	56.4	55.7	55.0	54.3	53.7	53.0	52.4	51.8	51.3	50.8
41	56.1	55.4	54.7	54.0	53.3	52.7	52.0	51.4	50.9	50.3
42	55.9	55.2	54.4	53.7	53.0	52.3	51.7	51.1	50.4	49.9
43	55.7	54.9	54.2	53.4	52.7	52.0	51.3	50.7	50.1	49.5
44	55.5	54.7	53.9	53.2	52.4	51.7	51.0	50.4	49.7	49.1
45	55.3	54.5	53.7	52.9	52.2	51.5	50.7	50.0	49.4	48.7
46	55.1	54.3	53.5	52.7	52.0	51.2	50.5	49.8	49.1	48.4
47	55.0	54.1	53.3	52.5	51.7	51.0	50.2	49.5	48.8	48.1
48	54.8	54.0	53.2	52.3	51.5	50.8	50.0	49.2	48.5	47.8

Appendix B. (Continued)

Table II (continued)
(Joint Life and Last Survivor Expectancy)
(For Use by Owners Whose Spouses Are More Than 10 Years Younger and Are the Sole Beneficiaries of Their IRAs)

Ages	30	31	32	33	34	35	36	37	38	39
49	54.7	53.8	53.0	52.2	51.4	50.6	49.8	49.0	48.2	47.5
50	54.6	53.7	52.9	52.0	51.2	50.4	49.6	48.8	48.0	47.3
51	54.5	53.6	52.7	51.9	51.0	50.2	49.4	48.6	47.8	47.0
52	54.4	53.5	52.6	51.7	50.9	50.0	49.2	48.4	47.6	46.8
53	54.3	53.4	52.5	51.6	50.8	49.9	49.1	48.2	47.4	46.6
54	54.2	53.3	52.4	51.5	50.6	49.8	48.9	48.1	47.2	46.4
55	54.1	53.2	52.3	51.4	50.5	49.7	48.8	47.9	47.1	46.3
56	54.0	53.1	52.2	51.3	50.4	49.5	48.7	47.8	47.0	46.1
57	54.0	53.0	52.1	51.2	50.3	49.4	48.6	47.7	46.8	46.0
58	53.9	53.0	52.1	51.2	50.3	49.4	48.5	47.6	46.7	45.8
59	53.8	52.9	52.0	51.1	50.2	49.3	48.4	47.5	46.6	45.7
60	53.8	52.9	51.9	51.0	50.1	49.2	48.3	47.4	46.5	45.6
61	53.8	52.8	51.9	51.0	50.0	49.1	48.2	47.3	46.4	45.5
62	53.7	52.8	51.8	50.9	50.0	49.1	48.1	47.2	46.3	45.4
63	53.7	52.7	51.8	50.9	49.9	49.0	48.1	47.2	46.3	45.3
64	53.6	52.7	51.8	50.8	49.9	48.9	48.0	47.1	46.2	45.3
65	53.6	52.7	51.7	50.8	49.8	48.9	48.0	47.0	46.1	45.2
66	53.6	52.6	51.7	50.7	49.8	48.9	47.9	47.0	46.1	45.1
67	53.6	52.6	51.7	50.7	49.8	48.8	47.9	46.9	46.0	45.1
68	53.5	52.6	51.6	50.7	49.7	48.8	47.8	46.9	46.0	45.0
69	53.5	52.6	51.6	50.6	49.7	48.7	47.8	46.9	45.9	45.0
70	53.5	52.5	51.6	50.6	49.7	48.7	47.8	46.8	45.9	44.9
71	53.5	52.5	51.6	50.6	49.6	48.7	47.7	46.8	45.9	44.9
72	53.5	52.5	51.5	50.6	49.6	48.7	47.7	46.8	45.8	44.9
73	53.4	52.5	51.5	50.6	49.6	48.6	47.7	46.7	45.8	44.8
74	53.4	52.5	51.5	50.5	49.6	48.6	47.7	46.7	45.8	44.8
75	53.4	52.5	51.5	50.5	49.6	48.6	47.7	46.7	45.7	44.8
76	53.4	52.4	51.5	50.5	49.6	48.6	47.6	46.7	45.7	44.8
77	53.4	52.4	51.5	50.5	49.5	48.6	47.6	46.7	45.7	44.8
78	53.4	52.4	51.5	50.5	49.5	48.6	47.6	46.6	45.7	44.7
79	53.4	52.4	51.5	50.5	49.5	48.6	47.6	46.6	45.7	44.7
80	53.4	52.4	51.4	50.5	49.5	48.5	47.6	46.6	45.7	44.7
81	53.4	52.4	51.4	50.5	49.5	48.5	47.6	46.6	45.7	44.7
82	53.4	52.4	51.4	50.5	49.5	48.5	47.6	46.6	45.6	44.7
83	53.4	52.4	51.4	50.5	49.5	48.5	47.6	46.6	45.6	44.7
84	53.4	52.4	51.4	50.5	49.5	48.5	47.6	46.6	45.6	44.7
85	53.3	52.4	51.4	50.4	49.5	48.5	47.5	46.6	45.6	44.7
86	53.3	52.4	51.4	50.4	49.5	48.5	47.5	46.6	45.6	44.6
87	53.3	52.4	51.4	50.4	49.5	48.5	47.5	46.6	45.6	44.6
88	53.3	52.4	51.4	50.4	49.5	48.5	47.5	46.6	45.6	44.6

Appendix B. (Continued)

Table II (continued)
(Joint Life and Last Survivor Expectancy)
(For Use by Owners Whose Spouses Are More Than 10 Years Younger and Are the Sole Beneficiaries of Their IRAs)

Ages	30	31	32	33	34	35	36	37	38	39
89	53.3	52.4	51.4	50.4	49.5	48.5	47.5	46.6	45.6	44.6
90	53.3	52.4	51.4	50.4	49.5	48.5	47.5	46.6	45.6	44.6
91	53.3	52.4	51.4	50.4	49.5	48.5	47.5	46.6	45.6	44.6
92	53.3	52.4	51.4	50.4	49.5	48.5	47.5	46.6	45.6	44.6
93	53.3	52.4	51.4	50.4	49.5	48.5	47.5	46.6	45.6	44.6
94	53.3	52.4	51.4	50.4	49.5	48.5	47.5	46.6	45.6	44.6
95	53.3	52.4	51.4	50.4	49.5	48.5	47.5	46.5	45.6	44.6
96	53.3	52.4	51.4	50.4	49.5	48.5	47.5	46.5	45.6	44.6
97	53.3	52.4	51.4	50.4	49.5	48.5	47.5	46.5	45.6	44.6
98	53.3	52.4	51.4	50.4	49.5	48.5	47.5	46.5	45.6	44.6
99	53.3	52.4	51.4	50.4	49.5	48.5	47.5	46.5	45.6	44.6
100	53.3	52.4	51.4	50.4	49.5	48.5	47.5	46.5	45.6	44.6
101	53.3	52.4	51.4	50.4	49.5	48.5	47.5	46.5	45.6	44.6
102	53.3	52.4	51.4	50.4	49.5	48.5	47.5	46.5	45.6	44.6
103	53.3	52.4	51.4	50.4	49.5	48.5	47.5	46.5	45.6	44.6
104	53.3	52.4	51.4	50.4	49.5	48.5	47.5	46.5	45.6	44.6
105	53.3	52.4	51.4	50.4	49.4	48.5	47.5	46.5	45.6	44.6
106	53.3	52.4	51.4	50.4	49.4	48.5	47.5	46.5	45.6	44.6
107	53.3	52.4	51.4	50.4	49.4	48.5	47.5	46.5	45.6	44.6
108	53.3	52.4	51.4	50.4	49.4	48.5	47.5	46.5	45.6	44.6
109	53.3	52.4	51.4	50.4	49.4	48.5	47.5	46.5	45.6	44.6
110	53.3	52.4	51.4	50.4	49.4	48.5	47.5	46.5	45.6	44.6
111	53.3	52.4	51.4	50.4	49.4	48.5	47.5	46.5	45.6	44.6
112	53.3	52.4	51.4	50.4	49.4	48.5	47.5	46.5	45.6	44.6
113	53.3	52.4	51.4	50.4	49.4	48.5	47.5	46.5	45.6	44.6
114	53.3	52.4	51.4	50.4	49.4	48.5	47.5	46.5	45.6	44.6
115+	53.3	52.4	51.4	50.4	49.4	48.5	47.5	46.5	45.6	44.6

Appendix B. (Continued)

Table II (continued)
(Joint Life and Last Survivor Expectancy)
(For Use by Owners Whose Spouses Are More Than 10 Years Younger and Are the Sole Beneficiaries of Their IRAs)

Ages	40	41	42	43	44	45	46	47	48	49
40	50.2	49.8	49.3	48.9	48.5	48.1	47.7	47.4	47.1	46.8
41	49.8	49.3	48.8	48.3	47.9	47.5	47.1	46.7	46.4	46.1
42	49.3	48.8	48.3	47.8	47.3	46.9	46.5	46.1	45.8	45.4
43	48.9	48.3	47.8	47.3	46.8	46.3	45.9	45.5	45.1	44.8
44	48.5	47.9	47.3	46.8	46.3	45.8	45.4	44.9	44.5	44.2
45	48.1	47.5	46.9	46.3	45.8	45.3	44.8	44.4	44.0	43.6
46	47.7	47.1	46.5	45.9	45.4	44.8	44.3	43.9	43.4	43.0
47	47.4	46.7	46.1	45.5	44.9	44.4	43.9	43.4	42.9	42.4

Appendix B. (Continued)

Table II (continued) (Joint Life and Last Survivor Expectancy) (For Use by Owners Whose Spouses Are More Than 10 Years Younger and Are the Sole Beneficiaries of Their IRAs)										
Ages	**40**	**41**	**42**	**43**	**44**	**45**	**46**	**47**	**48**	**49**
48	47.1	46.4	45.8	45.1	44.5	44.0	43.4	42.9	42.4	41.9
49	46.8	46.1	45.4	44.8	44.2	43.6	43.0	42.4	41.9	41.4
50	46.5	45.8	45.1	44.4	43.8	43.2	42.6	42.0	41.5	40.9
51	46.3	45.5	44.8	44.1	43.5	42.8	42.2	41.6	41.0	40.5
52	46.0	45.3	44.6	43.8	43.2	42.5	41.8	41.2	40.6	40.1
53	45.8	45.1	44.3	43.6	42.9	42.2	41.5	40.9	40.3	39.7
54	45.6	44.8	44.1	43.3	42.6	41.9	41.2	40.5	39.9	39.3
55	45.5	44.7	43.9	43.1	42.4	41.6	40.9	40.2	39.6	38.9
56	45.3	44.5	43.7	42.9	42.1	41.4	40.7	40.0	39.3	38.6
57	45.1	44.3	43.5	42.7	41.9	41.2	40.4	39.7	39.0	38.3
58	45.0	44.2	43.3	42.5	41.7	40.9	40.2	39.4	38.7	38.0
59	44.9	44.0	43.2	42.4	41.5	40.7	40.0	39.2	38.5	37.8
60	44.7	43.9	43.0	42.2	41.4	40.6	39.8	39.0	38.2	37.5
61	44.6	43.8	42.9	42.1	41.2	40.4	39.6	38.8	38.0	37.3
62	44.5	43.7	42.8	41.9	41.1	40.3	39.4	38.6	37.8	37.1
63	44.5	43.6	42.7	41.8	41.0	40.1	39.3	38.5	37.7	36.9
64	44.4	43.5	42.6	41.7	40.8	40.0	39.2	38.3	37.5	36.7
65	44.3	43.4	42.5	41.6	40.7	39.9	39.0	38.2	37.4	36.6
66	44.2	43.3	42.4	41.5	40.6	39.8	38.9	38.1	37.2	36.4
67	44.2	43.3	42.3	41.4	40.6	39.7	38.8	38.0	37.1	36.3
68	44.1	43.2	42.3	41.4	40.5	39.6	38.7	37.9	37.0	36.2
69	44.1	43.1	42.2	41.3	40.4	39.5	38.6	37.8	36.9	36.0
70	44.0	43.1	42.2	41.3	40.3	39.4	38.6	37.7	36.8	35.9
71	44.0	43.1	42.2	41.3	40.3	39.4	38.6	37.7	36.8	35.9
72	43.9	43.0	42.0	41.1	40.2	39.3	38.4	37.5	36.6	35.7
73	43.9	43.0	42.0	41.1	40.1	39.2	38.3	37.4	36.5	35.6
74	43.9	42.9	42.0	41.1	40.1	39.2	38.3	37.4	36.5	35.6
75	43.8	42.9	42.0	41.0	40.1	39.2	38.3	37.4	36.5	35.6
76	43.8	42.9	42.0	41.0	40.1	39.2	38.3	37.3	36.5	35.6
77	43.8	42.9	41.9	41.0	40.1	39.1	38.2	37.3	36.4	35.5
78	43.8	42.8	41.9	40.9	40.0	39.1	38.2	37.2	36.3	35.4
79	43.8	42.8	41.9	40.9	40.0	39.1	38.1	37.2	36.3	35.4
80	43.7	42.8	41.8	40.9	40.0	39.0	38.1	37.2	36.3	35.4
81	43.7	42.8	41.8	40.9	40.0	39.0	38.1	37.2	36.3	34.3
82	43.7	42.8	41.8	40.9	39.9	39.0	38.0	37.1	36.2	36.2
83	43.7	42.7	41.8	40.9	39.9	39.10	38.0	37.0	36.2	35.3
84	43.7	42.7	41.8	40.8	39.9	38.9	38.0	37.1	36.2	35.2
85	43.7	42.7	41.8	40.8	39.9	38.9	38.0	37.1	36.2	35.2
86	43.7	42.7	41.8	340.8	39.9	38.9	38.0	37.0	36.1	35.2
87	43.7	42.7	41.8	40.8	39.9	38.9	38.0	37.0	36.1	35.2

Appendix B. (Continued)

Table II (continued)
(Joint Life and Last Survivor Expectancy)
(For Use by Owners Whose Spouses Are More Than 10 Years Younger and Are the Sole Beneficiaries of Their IRAs)

Ages	40	41	42	43	44	45	46	47	48	49
88	43.7	42.7	41.8	40.8	39.9	38.9	38.0	37.0	36.1	35.2
89	43.7	42.7	41.7	40.8	39.8	38.9	38.0	37.0	36.1	35.2
90	43.7	42.7	41.7	40.8	39.8	38.9	38.0	37.0	36.1	35.2
91	43.7	42.7	41.7	40.8	39.8	38.9	37.9	37.0	36.1	35.2
92	43.7	42.7	41.7	40.8	39.8	38.9	37.9	37.0	36.1	35.1
93	43.7	42.7	41.7	40.8	39.8	38.9	37.9	37.0	36.1	35.1
94	43.7	42.7	41.7	40.8	39.8	38.9	37.9	37.0	36.1	35.1
95	43.6	42.7	41.7	40.8	39.8	38.9	37.9	37.0	36.1	35.1
96	43.6	42.7	41.7	40.8	39.8	38.9	37.9	37.0	36.1	35.1
97	43.6	42.7	41.7	40.8	39.8	38.9	37.9	37.0	36.1	35.1
98	43.6	42.7	41.7	40.8	39.8	38.9	37.9	37.0	36.0	35.1
99	43.6	42.7	41.7	40.8	39.8	38.9	37.9	37.0	36.0	35.1
100	43.6	42.7	41.7	40.8	39.8	38.9	37.9	37.0	36.0	35.1
101	43.6	42.7	41.7	40.8	39.8	38.9	37.9	37.0	36.0	35.1
102	43.6	42.7	41.7	40.8	39.8	38.9	37.9	37.0	36.0	35.1
103	43.6	42.7	41.7	40.8	39.8	38.9	37.9	37.0	36.0	35.1
104	43.6	42.7	41.7	40.8	39.8	38.8	37.9	37.0	36.0	35.1
105	43.6	42.7	41.7	40.8	39.8	38.8	37.9	37.0	36.0	35.1
106	43.6	42.7	41.7	40.8	39.8	38.8	37.9	37.0	36.0	35.1
107	43.6	42.7	41.7	40.8	39.8	38.8	37.9	37.0	36.0	35.1
108	43.6	42.7	41.7	40.8	39.8	38.8	37.9	37.0	36.0	35.1
109	43.6	42.7	41.7	40.7	39.8	38.8	37.9	37.0	36.0	35.1
110	43.6	42.7	41.7	40.7	39.8	38.8	37.9	37.0	36.0	35.1
111	43.6	42.7	41.7	40.7	39.8	38.8	37.9	37.0	36.0	35.1
112	43.6	42.7	41.7	40.7	39.8	38.8	37.9	37.0	36.0	35.1
113	43.6	42.7	41.7	40.7	39.8	38.8	37.9	37.0	36.0	35.1
114	43.6	42.7	41.7	40.7	39.8	38.8	37.9	37.0	36.0	35.1
115+	43.6	42.7	41.7	40.7	39.8	38.8	37.9	37.0	36.0	35.1

Appendix B. (Continued)

Table II (continued)
(Joint Life and Last Survivor Expectancy)
(For Use by Owners Whose Spouses Are More Than 10 Years Younger and Are the Sole Beneficiaries of Their IRAs)

Ages	50	51	52	53	54	55	56	57	58	59
50	40.4	40.0	39.5	39.1	38.7	38.3	38.0	37.6	37.3	37.1
51	40.0	39.5	39.0	38.5	38.1	37.7	37.4	37.0	36.7	36.4
52	39.5	39.0	38.5	38.0	37.6	37.2	36.8	36.4	36.0	35.7
53	39.1	38.5	38.0	37.5	37.1	36.6	36.2	35.8	35.4	35.1
54	38.7	38.1	37.6	37.1	36.6	36.1	35.7	35.2	34.8	34.5
55	38.3	37.7	37.2	36.6	36.1	35.6	35.1	34.7	34.3	33.9
56	38.0	37.4	36.8	36.2	35.7	35.1	34.7	34.2	33.7	33.3

Appendix B. (Continued)

Table II (continued)
(Joint Life and Last Survivor Expectancy)
(For Use by Owners Whose Spouses Are More Than 10 Years Younger and Are the Sole Beneficiaries of Their IRAs)

Ages	50	51	52	53	54	55	56	57	58	59
57	37.6	37.0	36.4	35.8	35.2	34.7	34.2	33.7	33.2	32.8
58	37.3	36.7	36.0	35.4	34.8	34.3	33.7	33.2	32.8	32.3
59	37.1	36.4	35.7	35.1	34.5	33.9	33.3	32.8	32.3	31.8
60	36.8	36.1	35.4	34.8	34.1	33.5	32.9	32.4	31.9	31.3
61	36.6	35.8	35.1	34.5	33.8	33.2	32.6	32.0	31.4	30.9
62	36.3	35.6	34.9	34.2	33.5	32.9	32.2	31.6	31.1	30.5
63	36.1	35.4	34.6	33.9	33.2	32.6	31.9	31.3	30.7	30.1
64	35.9	35.2	34.4	33.7	33.0	32.3	31.6	31.0	30.4	29.8
65	35.8	35.0	34.2	33.5	32.7	32.0	31.4	30.7	30.0	29.4
66	35.6	34.8	34.0	33.3	32.5	31.8	31.1	30.4	29.8	29.1
67	35.5	34.7	33.9	33.1	32.3	31.6	30.9	30.2	29.5	28.8
68	35.3	34.5	33.7	32.9	32.1	31.4	30.7	29.9	29.2	28.6
69	35.2	34.4	33.6	32.8	32.0	31.2	30.5	29.7	29.0	28.3
70	35.1	34.3	33.4	32.6	31.8	31.1	30.3	29.5	28.8	28.1
71	35.0	34.2	33.3	32.5	31.7	30.9	30.1	29.4	28.6	27.9
72	34.9	34.1	33.2	32.4	31.6	30.8	30.0	29.2	28.4	27.7
73	34.8	34.0	33.1	32.3	31.5	30.6	29.8	29.1	28.3	27.5
74	34.8	33.9	33.0	32.2	31.4	30.5	29.7	28.9	28.1	27.4
75	34.7	33.8	33.0	32.1	31.3	30.4	29.6	28.8	28.0	27.2
76	34.6	33.8	32.9	32.0	31.2	30.3	29.5	28.7	27.9	27.1
77	34.6	33.7	32.8	32.0	31.1	30.3	29.4	28.6	27.8	27.0
78	34.5	33.6	32.8	31.9	31.0	30.2	29.3	28.5	27.7	26.9
79	34.5	33.6	32.7	31.8	31.0	30.1	29.3	28.4	27.6	26.8
80	34.5	33.6	32.7	31.8	30.9	30.1	29.2	28.4	27.5	26.7
81	34.4	33.5	32.6	31.8	30.9	30.0	29.2	28.3	27.5	26.6
82	34.4	33.5	32.6	31.7	30.8	30.0	29.1	28.3	27.4	26.6
83	34.4	33.5	32.6	31.7	30.8	29.9	29.1	28.2	27.4	26.5
84	34.3	33.4	32.5	31.7	30.8	29.9	29.0	28.2	27.3	26.5
85	34.3	33.4	32.5	31.6	30.7	29.9	29.0	28.1	27.3	26.4
86	34.3	33.4	32.5	31.6	30.7	29.8	29.0	28.1	27.2	26.4
87	34.3	33.4	32.5	31.6	30.7	29.8	28.9	28.1	27.2	26.4
88	34.3	33.4	32.5	31.6	30.7	29.8	28.9	28.0	27.2	26.3
89	34.3	33.3	32.4	31.5	30.7	29.8	28.9	28.0	27.2	26.3
90	34.2	33.3	32.4	31.5	30.6	29.8	28.9	28.0	27.1	26.3
91	34.2	33.3	32.4	31.5	30.6	29.7	28.9	28.0	27.1	26.3
92	34.2	33.3	32.4	31.5	30.6	29.7	28.8	28.0	27.1	26.2
93	34.2	33.3	32.4	31.5	30.6	29.7	28.8	28.0	27.1	26.2
94	34.2	33.3	32.4	31.5	30.6	29.7	28.8	27.9	27.1	26.2
95	34.2	33.3	32.4	31.5	30.6	29.7	28.8	27.9	27.1	26.2
96	34.2	33.3	32.4	31.5	30.6	29.7	28.8	27.9	27.0	26.2

Appendix B. (Continued)

Table II (continued) (Joint Life and Last Survivor Expectancy) (For Use by Owners Whose Spouses Are More Than 10 Years Younger and Are the Sole Beneficiaries of Their IRAs)										
Ages	50	51	52	53	54	55	56	57	58	59
97	34.2	33.3	32.4	31.5	30.6	29.7	28.8	27.9	27.0	26.2
98	34.2	33.3	32.4	31.5	30.6	29.7	28.8	27.9	27.0	26.2
99	34.2	33.3	32.4	31.5	30.6	29.7	28.8	27.9	27.0	26.2
100	34.2	33.3	32.4	31.5	30.6	29.7	28.8	27.9	27.0	26.1
101	34.2	33.3	32.4	31.5	30.6	29.7	28.8	27.9	27.0	26.1
102	34.2	33.3	32.4	31.4	30.5	29.7	28.8	27.9	27.0	26.1
103	34.2	33.3	32.4	31.4	30.5	29.7	28.8	27.9	27.0	26.1
104	34.2	33.3	32.4	31.4	30.5	29.6	28.8	27.9	27.0	26.1
105	34.2	33.3	32.3	31.4	30.5	29.6	28.8	27.9	27.0	26.1
106	34.2	33.3	32.3	31.4	30.5	29.6	28.8	27.9	27.0	26.1
107	34.2	33.3	32.3	31.4	30.5	29.6	28.8	27.9	27.0	26.1
108	34.2	33.3	32.3	31.4	30.5	29.6	28.8	27.9	27.0	26.1
109	34.2	33.3	32.3	31.4	30.5	29.6	28.7	27.9	27.0	26.1
110	34.2	33.3	32.3	31.4	30.5	29.6	28.7	27.9	27.0	26.1
111	34.2	33.3	32.3	31.4	30.5	29.6	28.7	27.9	27.0	26.1
112	34.2	33.3	32.3	31.4	30.5	29.6	28.7	27.9	27.0	26.1
113	34.2	33.3	32.3	31.4	30.5	29.6	28.7	27.9	27.0	26.1
114	34.2	33.3	32.3	31.4	30.5	29.6	28.7	27.9	27.0	26.1
115+	34.2	33.3	32.3	31.4	30.5	29.6	28.7	27.9	27.0	26.1

Appendix B. (Continued)

Table II (continued) (Joint Life and Last Survivor Expectancy) (For Use by Owners Whose Spouses Are More Than 10 Years Younger and Are the Sole Beneficiaries of Their IRAs)										
Ages	60	61	62	63	64	65	66	67	68	69
60	30.9	30.4	30.0	29.6	29.2	28.8	28.5	28.2	27.9	27.6
61	30.4	29.9	29.5	29.0	28.6	28.3	27.9	27.6	27.3	27.0
62	30.0	29.5	29.0	28.5	28.1	27.7	27.3	27.0	26.7	26.4
63	29.6	29.0	28.5	28.1	27.6	27.2	26.8	26.4	26.1	25.7
64	29.2	28.6	28.1	27.6	27.1	26.7	26.3	25.9	25.5	25.2
65	28.8	28.3	27.7	27.2	26.7	26.2	25.8	25.4	25.0	24.6
66	28.5	27.9	27.3	26.8	26.3	25.8	25.3	24.9	24.5	24.1
67	28.2	27.6	27.0	26.4	25.9	25.4	24.9	24.4	24.0	23.6
68	27.9	27.3	26.7	26.1	25.5	25.0	24.5	24.0	23.5	23.1
69	27.6	27.0	26.4	25.7	25.2	24.6	24.1	23.6	23.1	22.6
70	27.4	26.7	26.1	25.4	24.8	24.3	23.7	23.2	22.7	22.2
71	27.2	26.5	25.8	25.2	24.5	23.9	23.4	22.8	22.3	21.8
72	27.0	26.3	25.6	24.9	24.3	23.7	23.1	22.5	22.0	21.4
73	26.8	26.1	25.4	24.7	24.0	23.4	22.8	22.2	21.6	21.1
74	26.6	25.9	25.2	24.5	23.8	23.1	22.5	21.9	21.3	20.8
75	26.5	25.7	25.0	24.3	23.6	22.9	22.3	21.6	21.0	20.5

Appendix B. (Continued)

Table II (continued)
(Joint Life and Last Survivor Expectancy)
(For Use by Owners Whose Spouses Are More Than 10 Years Younger and Are the Sole Beneficiaries of Their IRAs)

Ages	60	61	62	63	64	65	66	67	68	69
76	26.3	25.6	24.8	24.1	23.4	22.7	22.0	21.4	20.8	20.2
77	26.2	25.4	24.7	23.9	23.2	22.5	21.8	21.2	20.6	19.9
78	26.1	25.3	24.6	23.8	23.1	22.4	21.7	21.0	20.3	19.7
79	26.0	25.2	24.4	23.7	22.9	22.2	21.5	20.8	20.1	19.5
80	25.9	25.1	24.3	23.6	22.8	22.1	21.3	20.6	20.0	19.3
81	25.8	25.0	24.2	23.4	22.7	21.9	21.2	20.5	19.8	19.1
82	25.8	24.9	24.1	23.4	22.6	21.8	21.1	20.4	19.7	19.0
83	25.7	24.9	24.1	23.3	22.5	21.7	21.0	20.2	19.5	18.8
84	25.6	24.8	24.0	23.2	22.4	21.6	20.9	20.1	19.4	18.7
85	25.6	24.8	23.9	23.1	22.3	21.6	20.8	20.1	19.3	18.6
86	25.5	24.7	23.9	23.1	22.3	21.5	20.7	20.0	19.2	18.5
87	25.5	24.7	23.8	23.0	22.2	21.4	20.7	19.9	19.2	18.4
88	25.5	24.6	23.8	23.0	22.2	21.4	20.6	19.8	19.1	18.3
89	25.4	24.6	23.8	22.9	22.1	21.3	20.5	19.8	19.0	18.3
90	25.4	24.6	23.7	22.9	22.1	21.3	20.5	19.7	19.0	18.2
91	25.4	24.5	23.7	22.9	22.1	21.3	20.5	19.7	18.9	18.2
92	25.4	24.5	23.7	22.9	22.0	21.2	20.4	19.6	18.9	18.1
93	25.4	24.5	23.7	22.8	22.0	21.2	20.4	19.6	18.8	18.1
94	25.3	24.5	23.6	22.8	22.0	21.2	20.4	19.6	18.8	18.0
95	25.3	24.5	23.6	22.8	22.0	21.1	20.3	19.6	18.8	18.0
96	25.3	24.5	23.6	22.8	21.9	21.1	20.3	19.5	18.8	18.0
97	25.3	24.5	23.6	22.8	21.9	21.1	20.3	19.5	18.7	18.0
98	25.3	24.4	23.6	22.8	21.9	21.1	20.3	19.5	18.7	17.9
99	25.3	24.4	23.6	22.7	21.9	21.1	20.3	19.5	18.7	17.9
100	25.3	24.4	23.6	22.7	21.9	21.1	20.3	19.5	18.7	17.9
101	25.3	24.4	23.6	22.7	21.9	21.1	20.2	19.4	18.7	17.9
102	25.3	24.4	23.6	22.7	21.9	21.1	20.2	19.4	18.6	17.9
103	25.3	24.4	23.6	22.7	21.9	21.0	20.2	19.4	18.6	17.9
104	25.3	24.4	23.5	22.7	21.9	21.0	20.2	19.4	18.6	17.8
105	25.3	24.4	23.5	22.7	21.9	21.0	20.2	19.4	18.6	17.8
106	25.3	24.4	23.5	22.7	21.9	21.0	20.2	19.4	18.6	17.8
107	25.2	24.4	23.5	22.7	21.8	21.0	20.2	19.4	18.6	17.8
108	25.2	24.4	23.5	22.7	21.8	21.0	20.2	19.4	18.6	17.8
109	25.2	24.4	23.5	22.7	21.8	21.0	20.2	19.4	18.6	17.8
110	25.2	24.4	23.5	22.7	21.8	21.0	20.2	19.4	18.6	17.8
111	25.2	24.4	23.5	22.7	21.8	21.0	20.2	19.4	18.6	17.8
112	25.2	24.4	23.5	22.7	21.8	21.0	20.2	19.4	18.6	17.8
113	25.2	24.4	23.5	22.7	21.8	21.0	20.2	19.4	18.6	17.8
114	25.2	24.4	23.5	22.7	21.8	21.0	20.2	19.4	18.6	17.8
115+	25.2	24.4	23.5	22.7	21.8	21.0	20.2	19.4	18.6	17.8

Page 56 Publication 590-B (2020)

Appendix B. (Continued)

Table II (continued)
(Joint Life and Last Survivor Expectancy)
(For Use by Owners Whose Spouses Are More Than 10 Years Younger and Are the Sole Beneficiaries of Their IRAs)

Ages	70	71	72	73	74	75	76	77	78	79
70	21.8	21.3	20.9	20.6	20.2	19.9	19.6	19.4	19.1	18.9
71	21.3	20.9	20.5	20.1	19.7	19.4	19.1	18.8	18.5	18.3
72	20.9	20.5	20.0	19.6	19.3	18.9	18.6	18.3	18.0	17.7
73	20.6	20.1	19.6	19.2	18.8	18.4	18.1	17.8	17.5	17.2
74	20.2	19.7	19.3	18.8	18.4	18.0	17.6	17.3	17.0	16.7
75	19.9	19.4	18.9	18.4	18.0	17.6	17.2	16.8	16.5	16.2
76	19.6	19.1	18.6	18.1	17.6	17.2	16.8	16.4	16.0	15.7
77	19.4	18.8	18.3	17.8	17.3	16.8	16.4	16.0	15.6	15.3
78	19.1	18.5	18.0	17.5	17.0	16.5	16.0	15.6	15.2	14.9
79	18.9	18.3	17.7	17.2	16.7	16.2	15.7	15.3	14.9	14.5
80	18.7	18.1	17.5	16.9	16.4	15.9	15.4	15.0	14.5	14.1
81	18.5	17.9	17.3	16.7	16.2	15.6	15.1	14.7	14.2	13.8
82	18.3	17.7	17.1	16.5	15.9	15.4	14.9	14.4	13.9	13.5
83	18.2	17.5	16.9	16.3	15.7	15.2	14.7	14.2	13.7	13.2
84	18.0	17.4	16.7	16.1	15.5	15.0	14.4	13.9	13.4	13.0
85	17.9	17.3	16.6	16.0	15.4	14.8	14.3	13.7	13.2	12.8
86	17.8	17.1	16.5	15.8	15.2	14.6	14.1	13.5	13.0	12.5
87	17.7	17.0	16.4	15.7	15.1	14.5	13.9	13.4	12.9	12.4
88	17.6	16.9	16.3	15.6	15.0	14.4	13.8	13.2	12.7	12.2
89	17.6	16.9	16.2	15.5	14.9	14.3	13.7	13.1	12.6	12.0
90	17.5	16.8	16.1	15.4	14.8	14.2	13.6	13.0	12.4	11.9
91	17.4	16.7	16.0	15.4	14.7	14.1	13.5	12.9	12.3	11.8
92	17.4	16.7	16.0	15.3	14.6	14.0	13.4	12.8	12.2	11.7
93	17.3	16.6	15.9	15.2	14.6	13.9	13.3	12.7	12.1	11.6
94	17.3	16.6	15.9	15.2	14.5	13.9	13.2	12.6	12.0	11.5
95	17.3	16.5	15.8	15.1	14.5	13.8	13.2	12.6	12.0	11.4
96	17.2	16.5	15.8	15.1	14.4	13.8	13.1	12.5	11.9	11.3
97	17.2	16.5	15.8	15.1	14.4	13.7	13.1	12.5	11.9	11.3
98	17.2	16.4	15.7	15.0	14.3	13.7	13.0	12.4	11.8	11.2
99	17.2	16.4	15.7	15.0	14.3	13.6	13.0	12.4	11.8	11.2
100	17.1	16.4	15.7	15.0	14.3	13.6	12.9	12.3	11.7	11.1
101	17.1	16.4	15.6	14.9	14.2	13.6	12.9	12.3	11.7	11.1
102	17.1	16.4	15.6	14.9	14.2	13.5	12.9	12.2	11.6	11.0
103	17.1	16.3	15.6	14.9	14.2	13.5	12.9	12.2	11.6	11.0
104	17.1	16.3	15.6	14.9	14.2	13.5	12.8	12.2	11.6	11.0
105	17.1	16.3	15.6	14.9	14.2	13.5	12.8	12.2	11.5	10.9
106	17.1	16.3	15.6	14.8	14.1	13.5	12.8	12.2	11.5	10.9
107	17.0	16.3	15.6	14.8	14.1	13.4	12.8	12.1	11.5	10.9
108	17.0	16.3	15.5	14.8	14.1	13.4	12.8	12.1	11.5	10.9
109	17.0	16.3	15.5	14.8	14.1	13.4	12.8	12.1	11.5	10.9

Appendix B. (Continued)

Table II (continued)
(Joint Life and Last Survivor Expectancy)
(For Use by Owners Whose Spouses Are More Than 10 Years Younger and Are the Sole Beneficiaries of Their IRAs)

Ages	70	71	72	73	74	75	76	77	78	79
110	17.0	16.3	15.5	14.8	14.1	13.4	12.7	12.1	11.5	10.9
111	17.0	16.3	15.5	14.8	14.1	13.4	12.7	12.1	11.5	10.8
112	17.0	16.3	15.5	14.8	14.1	13.4	12.7	12.1	11.5	10.8
113	17.0	16.3	15.5	14.8	14.1	13.4	12.7	12.1	11.4	10.8
114	17.0	16.3	15.5	14.8	14.1	13.4	12.7	12.1	11.4	10.8
115+	17.0	16.3	15.5	14.8	14.1	13.4	12.7	12.1	11.4	10.8

Page 58 Publication 590-B (2020)

Appendix B. (Continued)

Table II (continued)
(Joint Life and Last Survivor Expectancy)
(For Use by Owners Whose Spouses Are More Than 10 Years Younger and Are the Sole Beneficiaries of Their IRAs)

Ages	80	81	82	83	84	85	86	87	88	89
80	13.8	13.4	13.1	12.8	12.6	12.3	12.1	11.9	11.7	11.5
81	13.4	13.1	12.7	12.4	12.2	11.9	11.7	11.4	11.3	11.1
82	13.1	12.7	12.4	12.1	11.8	11.5	11.3	11.0	10.8	10.6
83	12.8	12.4	12.1	11.7	11.4	11.1	10.9	10.6	10.4	10.2
84	12.6	12.2	11.8	11.4	11.1	10.8	10.5	10.3	10.1	9.9
85	12.3	11.9	11.5	11.1	10.8	10.5	10.2	9.9	9.7	9.5
86	12.1	11.7	11.3	10.9	10.5	10.2	9.9	9.6	9.4	9.2
87	11.9	11.4	11.0	10.6	10.3	9.9	9.6	9.4	9.1	8.9
88	11.7	11.3	10.8	10.4	10.1	9.7	9.4	9.1	8.8	8.6
89	11.5	11.1	10.6	10.2	9.9	9.5	9.2	8.9	8.6	8.3
90	11.4	10.9	10.5	10.1	9.7	9.3	9.0	8.6	8.3	8.1
91	11.3	10.8	10.3	9.9	9.5	9.1	8.8	8.4	8.1	7.9
92	11.2	10.7	10.2	9.8	9.3	9.0	8.6	8.3	8.0	7.7
93	11.1	10.6	10.1	9.6	9.2	8.8	8.5	8.1	7.8	7.5
94	11.0	10.5	10.0	9.5	9.1	8.7	8.3	8.0	7.6	7.3
95	10.9	10.4	9.9	9.4	9.0	8.6	8.2	7.8	7.5	7.2
96	10.8	10.3	9.8	9.3	8.9	8.5	8.1	7.7	7.4	7.1
97	10.7	10.2	9.7	9.2	8.8	8.4	8.0	7.6	7.3	6.9
98	10.7	10.1	9.6	9.2	8.7	8.3	7.9	7.5	7.1	6.8
99	10.6	10.1	9.6	9.1	8.6	8.2	7.8	7.4	7.0	6.7
100	10.6	10.0	9.5	9.0	8.5	8.1	7.7	7.3	6.9	6.6
101	10.5	10.0	9.4	9.0	8.5	8.0	7.6	7.2	6.9	6.5
102	10.5	9.9	9.4	8.9	8.4	8.0	7.5	7.1	6.8	6.4
103	10.4	9.9	9.4	8.8	8.4	7.9	7.5	7.1	6.7	6.3
104	10.4	9.8	9.3	8.8	8.3	7.9	7.4	7.0	6.6	6.3
105	10.4	9.8	9.3	8.8	8.3	7.8	7.4	7.0	6.6	6.2
106	10.3	9.8	9.2	8.7	8.2	7.8	7.3	6.9	6.5	6.2
107	10.3	9.8	9.2	8.7	8.2	7.7	7.3	6.9	6.5	6.1
108	10.3	9.7	9.2	8.7	8.2	7.7	7.3	6.8	6.4	6.1
109	10.3	9.7	9.2	8.7	8.2	7.7	7.2	6.8	6.4	6.0
110	10.3	9.7	9.2	8.6	8.1	7.7	7.2	6.8	6.4	6.0
111	10.3	9.7	9.1	8.6	8.1	7.6	7.2	6.8	6.3	6.0
112	10.2	9.7	9.1	8.6	8.1	7.6	7.2	6.7	6.3	5.9
113	10.2	9.7	9.1	8.6	8.1	7.6	7.2	6.7	6.3	5.9
114	10.2	9.7	9.1	8.6	8.1	7.6	7.1	6.7	6.3	5.9
115+	10.2	9.7	9.1	8.6	8.1	7.6	7.1	6.7	6.3	5.9

Appendix B. (Continued)

Table II (continued)
(Joint Life and Last Survivor Expectancy)
(For Use by Owners Whose Spouses Are More Than 10 Years Younger and Are the Sole Beneficiaries of Their IRAs)

Ages	90	91	92	93	94	95	96	97	98	99
90	7.8	7.6	7.4	7.2	7.1	6.9	6.8	6.6	6.5	6.4
91	7.6	7.4	7.2	7.0	6.8	6.7	6.5	6.4	6.3	6.1
92	7.4	7.2	7.0	6.8	6.6	6.4	6.3	6.1	6.0	5.9
93	7.2	7.0	6.8	6.6	6.4	6.2	6.1	5.9	5.8	5.6
94	7.1	6.8	6.6	6.4	6.2	6.0	5.9	5.7	5.6	5.4
95	6.9	6.7	6.4	6.2	6.0	5.8	5.7	5.5	5.4	5.2
96	6.8	6.5	6.3	6.1	5.9	5.7	5.5	5.3	5.2	5.0
97	6.6	6.4	6.1	5.9	5.7	5.5	5.3	5.2	5.0	4.9
98	6.5	6.3	6.0	5.8	5.6	5.4	5.2	5.0	4.8	4.7
99	6.4	6.1	5.9	5.6	5.4	5.2	5.0	4.9	4.7	4.5
100	6.3	6.0	5.8	5.5	5.3	5.1	4.9	4.7	4.5	4.4
101	6.2	5.9	5.6	5.4	5.2	5.0	4.8	4.6	4.4	4.2
102	6.1	5.8	5.5	5.3	5.1	4.8	4.6	4.4	4.3	4.1
103	6.0	5.7	5.4	5.2	5.0	4.7	4.5	4.3	4.1	4.0
104	5.9	5.6	5.4	5.1	4.9	4.6	4.4	4.2	4.0	3.8
105	5.9	5.6	5.3	5.0	4.8	4.5	4.3	4.1	3.9	3.7
106	5.8	5.5	5.2	4.9	4.7	4.5	4.2	4.0	3.8	3.6
107	5.8	5.4	5.1	4.9	4.6	4.4	4.2	3.9	3.7	3.5
108	5.7	5.4	5.1	4.8	4.6	4.3	4.1	3.9	3.7	3.5
109	5.7	5.3	5.0	4.8	4.5	4.3	4.0	3.8	3.6	3.4
110	5.6	5.3	5.0	4.7	4.5	4.2	4.0	3.8	3.5	3.3
111	5.6	5.3	5.0	4.7	4.4	4.2	3.9	3.7	3.5	3.3
112	5.6	5.3	4.9	4.7	4.4	4.1	3.9	3.7	3.5	3.2
113	5.6	5.2	4.9	4.6	4.4	4.1	3.9	3.6	3.4	3.2
114	5.6	5.2	4.9	4.6	4.3	4.1	3.9	3.6	3.4	3.2
115+	5.5	5.2	4.9	4.6	4.3	4.1	3.8	3.6	3.4	3.1

Page 60 Publication 590-B (2020)

Appendix B. (Continued)

Table II (continued)
(Joint Life and Last Survivor Expectancy)
(For Use by Owners Whose Spouses Are More Than 10 Years Younger and Are the Sole Beneficiaries of Their IRAs)

Ages	100	101	102	103	104	105	106	107	108	109
100	4.2	4.1	3.9	3.8	3.7	3.5	3.4	3.3	3.3	3.2
101	4.1	3.9	3.7	3.6	3.5	3.4	3.2	3.1	3.1	3.0
102	3.9	3.7	3.6	3.4	3.3	3.2	3.1	3.0	2.9	2.8
103	3.8	3.6	3.4	3.3	3.2	3.0	2.9	2.8	2.7	2.6
104	3.7	3.5	3.3	3.2	3.0	2.9	2.7	2.6	2.5	2.4
105	3.5	3.4	3.2	3.0	2.9	2.7	2.6	2.5	2.4	2.3
106	3.4	3.2	3.1	2.9	2.7	2.6	2.4	2.3	2.2	2.1
107	3.3	3.1	3.0	2.8	2.6	2.5	2.3	2.2	2.1	2.0
108	3.3	3.1	2.9	2.7	2.5	2.4	2.2	2.1	1.9	1.8
109	3.2	3.0	2.8	2.6	2.4	2.3	2.1	2.0	1.8	1.7
110	3.1	2.9	2.7	2.5	2.3	2.2	2.0	1.9	1.7	1.6
111	3.1	2.9	2.7	2.5	2.3	2.1	1.9	1.8	1.6	1.5
112	3.0	2.8	2.6	2.4	2.2	2.0	1.9	1.7	1.5	1.4
113	3.0	2.8	2.6	2.4	2.2	2.0	1.8	1.6	1.5	1.3
114	3.0	2.7	2.5	2.3	2.1	1.9	1.8	1.6	1.4	1.3
115+	2.9	2.7	2.5	2.3	2.1	1.9	1.7	1.5	1.4	1.2

Appendix B. (Continued)

Table II (continued)
(Joint Life and Last Survivor Expectancy)
(For Use by Owners Whose Spouses Are More Than 10 Years Younger and Are the Sole Beneficiaries of Their IRAs)

Ages	110	111	112	113	114	115+
110	1.5	1.4	1.3	1.2	1.1	1.1
111	1.4	1.2	1.1	1.1	1.0	1.0
112	1.3	1.1	1.0	1.0	1.0	1.0
113	1.2	1.1	1.0	1.0	1.0	1.0
114	1.1	1.0	1.0	1.0	1.0	1.0
115+	1.1	1.0	1.0	1.0	1.0	1.0

Appendix B. Uniform Lifetime Table

Table III
(Uniform Lifetime)

(For Use by:
- **Unmarried Owners,**
- **Married Owners Whose Spouses aren't More Than 10 Years Younger, and**
- **Married Owners Whose Spouses aren't the Sole Beneficiaries of Their IRAs)**

Age	Distribution Period	Age	Distribution Period
70	27.4	93	9.6
71	26.5	94	9.1
72	25.6	95	8.6
73	24.7	96	8.1
74	23.8	97	7.6
75	22.9	98	7.1
76	22.0	99	6.7
77	21.2	100	6.3
78	20.3	101	5.9
79	19.5	102	5.5
80	18.7	103	5.2
81	17.9	104	4.9
82	17.1	105	4.5
83	16.3	106	4.2
84	15.5	107	3.9
85	14.8	108	3.7
86	14.1	109	3.4
87	13.4	110	3.1
88	12.7	111	2.9
89	12.0	112	2.6
90	11.4	113	2.4
91	10.8	114	2.1
92	10.2	115 and over	1.9

Appendix C. Recapture Amount—Allocation Chart

Enter the amount from your 2020 Form 8606, line 19 . . . . ____________

Before you begin: You will need your prior year Form(s) 8606 and income tax return(s) if you entered an amount on any line(s) as indicated below. You will now allocate the amount you entered above (2020 Form 8606, line 19) in the order shown, to the amounts on the lines listed below (to the extent a prior year distribution wasn't allocable to the amount). The maximum amount you can enter on each line below is the amount entered on the referenced lines of the form for that year. **Note.** Once you have allocated the full amount from your 2020 Form 8606, line 19, **STOP**.

Tax Year	Your Form			
2020	Form 8606, line 20	____________	Form 8606, line 22	____________
1998	Form 8606, line 16	____________	Form 8606, line 15	____________
1999	Form 8606, line 16	____________	Form 8606, line 15	____________
2000	Form 8606, line 16	____________	Form 8606, line 15	____________
2001	Form 8606, line 18	____________	Form 8606, line 17	____________
2002	Form 8606, line 18	____________	Form 8606, line 17	____________
2003	Form 8606, line 18	____________	Form 8606, line 17	____________
2004	Form 8606, line 18	____________	Form 8606, line 17	____________
2005	Form 8606, line 18	____________	Form 8606, line 17	____________
2006	Form 8606, line 18	____________	Form 8606, line 17	____________
2007	Form 8606, line 18	____________	Form 8606, line 17	____________
2008	Form 8606, line 18; and Form 1040, line 16b; Form 1040A, line 12b; or Form 1040NR, line 17b*	____________	Form 8606, line 17; and Form 1040, line 16a; Form 1040A, line 12a; or Form 1040NR, line 17a**	____________
2009	Form 8606, line 18; and Form 1040, line 16b; Form 1040A, line 12b; or Form 1040NR, line 17b*	____________	Form 8606, line 17; and Form 1040, line 16a; Form 1040A, line 12a; or Form 1040NR, line 17a**	____________
2010	Form 8606, lines 18 and 23*	____________	Form 8606, lines 17 and 22**	____________
2011	Form 8606, line 18; and Form 1040, line 16b; Form 1040A, line 12b; or Form 1040NR, line 17b*	____________	Form 8606, line 17; and Form 1040, line 16a; Form 1040A, line 12a; or Form 1040NR, line 17a**	____________
2012	Form 8606, line 18; and Form 1040, line 16b; Form 1040A, line 12b; or Form 1040NR, line 17b*	____________	Form 8606, line 17; and Form 1040, line 16a; Form 1040A, line 12a; or Form 1040NR, line 17a**	____________
2013	Form 8606, line 18; and Form 1040, line 16b; Form 1040A, line 12b; or Form 1040NR, line 17b*	____________	Form 8606, line 17; and Form 1040, line 16a; Form 1040A, line 12a; or Form 1040NR, line 17a**	____________
2014	Form 8606, line 18; and Form 1040, line 16b; Form 1040A, line 12b; or Form 1040NR, line 17b*	____________	Form 8606, line 17; and Form 1040, line 16a; Form 1040A, line 12a; or Form 1040NR, line 17a**	____________
2015	Form 8606, line 18; and Form 1040, line 16b; Form 1040A, line 12b; or Form 1040NR, line 17b*	____________	Form 8606, line 17; and Form 1040, line 16a; Form 1040A, line 12a; or Form 1040NR, line 17a**	____________
2016	Form 8606, line 18; and Form 1040, line 16b; Form 1040A, line 12b; or Form 1040NR, line 17b*	____________	Form 8606, line 17; and Form 1040, line 16a; Form 1040A, line 12a; or Form 1040NR, line 17a**	____________
2017	Form 8606, line 18; and Form 1040, line 16b; Form 1040A, line 12b; or Form 1040NR, line 17b*	____________	Form 8606, line 17; and Form 1040, line 16a; Form 1040A, line 12a; or Form 1040NR, line 17a**	____________
2018	Form 8606, line 18; and Form 1040, line 4b or Form 1040NR, line 17b*	____________	Form 8606, line 17; and Form 1040, line 4a or Form 1040NR, line 17a**	____________
2019	Form 8606, line 18; and Form 1040 or 1040-SR, line 4d or Form 1040-NR, line 17b*	____________	Form 8606, line 17; and Form 1040 or 1040-SR, line 4c or Form 1040-NR, line 17a**	____________
2020	Form 8606, line 18; and and Form 1040, 1040-SR, or 1040-NR, line 5b	____________	Form 8606, line 17; and Form 1040, 1040-SR, or 1040-NR, line 5a	____________
2020	Form 8606, line 25c	____________		

* Only include those amounts rolled over to a Roth IRA.

** Only include any contributions (usually box 5 of Form 1099-R) that were taxable to you when made and rolled over to a Roth IRA.

Index

To help us develop a more useful index, please let us know if you have ideas for index entries. See "Comments and Suggestions" in the "Introduction" for the ways you can reach us.

Appendix C

State by State Comparison of IRA Tax Rules—2021

State by State Comparison of IRA Tax Rules—2021

State	Contribution by Taxpayer to IRA	IRA Distribution by Owner	State Exclusion Amounts for IRA Distribution by Owner
Alabama	Deductible (3)	Incl deductible state part (5)	No exclusion for retirement income
Alaska	(1)	(1)	Not applicable
Arizona	Deductible	Amt incl'd in Fed AGI	No exclusion for retirement income
Arkansas	Deductible	Amt incl'd in Fed AGI	$6,000 after 59½
California	Deductible (6)	Amt incl'd in Fed AGI (6)	No exclusion for retirement income
Colorado	Deductible	Amt incl'd in Fed Taxable Income	Up to $24,000 per spouse if 65 or $20,000 if 55–64
Connecticut	Deductible (4)	Amt incl'd in Fed AGI	No exclusion for retirement income
Delaware	Deductible	Amt incl'd in Fed AGI	Up to $12,500 per spouse if 60 or $2,000 if under 60
District of Columbia	Deductible (3)	Incl deductible state part (5)	No exclusion for retirement income
Florida	(1)	(1)	Not applicable
Georgia	Deductible	Amt incl'd in Fed AGI	Up to $35,000 if 62–64 or $65,000 per spouse if 65 or older
Hawaii	Deductible	Amt incl'd in Fed AGI	No exclusion for IRA distributions

State by State Comparison of IRA Tax Rules—2021 (*cont'd*)

State	Contribution by Taxpayer to IRA	IRA Distribution by Owner	State Exclusion Amounts for IRA Distribution by Owner
Idaho	Deductible	Amt incl'd in Fed AGI	No exclusion for retirement income
Illinois	Deductible	Amt incl'd in Fed AGI	Not taxed
Indiana	Deductible	Amt incl'd in Fed AGI	No exclusion for retirement income unless disabled
Iowa	Deductible	Amt incl'd in Fed AGI	Up to $12k (married) & up to $6k (other) if 55 or older
Kansas	Deductible	Amt incl'd in Fed AGI	No exclusion for retirement income
Kentucky	Deductible	Amt incl'd in Fed AGI per spouse	Beg in 2018, $31,110 and prior to 2018 the amount was indexed for inflation
Louisiana	Deductible	Amt incl'd in Fed AGI	Up to $6k if age 65 or older per spouse
Maine	Deductible	Amt incl'd in Fed AGI	Beg in 2016, ($10k - SSBs - RRBs) per spouse
Maryland	Deductible	Amt incl'd in Fed AGI	No exclusion for IRAs
Massachusetts	Not Deductible	Incl deductible state part (5)	No exclusion for IRA distributions
Michigan	Deductible	All: Ord. Inc.	All or some is excludible depending age

State by State Comparison of IRA Tax Rules—2021 (*cont'd*)

State	Contribution by Taxpayer to IRA	IRA Distribution by Owner	State Exclusion Amounts for IRA Distribution by Owner
Minnesota	Deductible (7)	Incl deductible state part (5)	No exclusion for retirement income
Mississippi	Deductible	Amt incl'd in Fed AGI	Not taxed
Missouri	Deductible	Amt incl'd in Fed AGI	Up to $6k of retirement income (excl SSB) per spouse below MO income thresholds of $32k (MJ), $16k (MS); $25k (Others)
Montana	Deductible	Amt incl'd in Fed AGI	Up to $4,370 if over age 59½ and below threshold amount
Nebraska	Deductible	Amt incl'd in Fed AGI	No exclusion for retirement income
Nevada	(1)	(1)	Not applicable
New Hampshire	(2)	(2)	Not applicable
New Jersey	Not Deductible	Incl deductible state part (5)	Various exclusion amounts, depending on income
New Mexico	Deductible	Amt incl'd in Fed AGI	No exclusion for retirement income
New York	Deductible	Amt incl'd in Fed AGI	Up to $20k per spouse if age 59½ or older
North Carolina	Deductible	Amt incl'd in Fed AGI	No exclusion after 2013

State by State Comparison of IRA Tax Rules—2021 (*cont'd*)

State	Contribution by Taxpayer to IRA	IRA Distribution by Owner	State Exclusion Amounts for IRA Distribution by Owner
North Dakota	Deductible	Amt incl'd in Fed AGI	No exclusion for retirement income
Ohio	Deductible	Amt incl'd in Fed AGI	Various tax credits for retirees, depending on qualifying income
Oklahoma	Deductible	Amt incl'd in Fed AGI	Up to $10k of retirement income
Oregon	Deductible	Amt incl'd in Fed AGI	No exclusion for IRA distributions unless another state has already taxed certain contributions
Pennsylvania	Not Deductible	All if prior to age 59½; None after age 59½ (8);	Not applicable
Rhode Island	Deductible	Amt incl'd in Fed AGI	No exclusion for IRA distributions
South Carolina	Deductible	Amt incl'd in Fed Taxable Income	Up to $10k per spouse if 65 or older or $3k if under 65
South Dakota	(1)	(1)	Not applicable
Tennessee	(2)	(2)	Not taxable
Texas	(1)	(1)	Not applicable
Utah	Deductible	Amt incl'd in Fed AGI	A credit of up to $450 if age 65 or older and below threshold amount per filing status

State by State Comparison of IRA Tax Rules—2021 (*cont'd*)

State	Contribution by Taxpayer to IRA	IRA Distribution by Owner	State Exclusion Amounts for IRA Distribution by Owner
Vermont	Deductible	VT % of adjusted Fed AGI amt	No exclusion for retirement income
Virginia	Deductible	Amt incl'd in Fed AGI	Up to $12k if age 65 or older per spouse and below threshold amount
Washington	(1)	(1)	Not applicable
West Virginia	Deductible	Amt incl'd in Fed AGI	Up to $8k if age 65 or older per spouse
Wisconsin	Deductible	Amt incl'd in Fed AGI	Up to $5k if 65 or older and Fed AGI is less than $15k or $30K if MJ or MS
Wyoming	(1)	(1)	Not applicable

(1) These states do not have a state income tax.
(2) These states do not have a state income tax, however, do have a tax on dividends and income from investments.
(3) Deductible since 1982.
(4) Deductible since 1991 when state income tax was enacted.
(5) Amount included in ordinary income is the distributed amount less nondeducted state contributions.
(6) Deduction differed from federal IRA rules for pre-1975; hence the amount included in the federal AGI may need adjusting for CA
(7) Deductible since 1985.
(8) Title 61 Pa. Code Sec. 101.6(c)(iii) provides special tax forgiveness provisions for distributions received under certain circumstances.

Internal Revenue Code Sections

[*References are to question numbers.*]

I.R.C. §

I.R.C. §

I.R.C. §

I.R.C. §

I.R.C. §

I.R.C. §

I.R.C. §

I.R.C. §

I.R.C. §

I.R.C. §

Treasury Regulations Sections

[References are to question numbers.]

Treasury Regulations

Treas. Reg. §

Treas. Reg. §

Treas. Reg. §

Treas. Reg. §

Treas. Reg. §

Treas. Reg. §

Temporary Treasury Regulations

Temp. Treas. Reg. §

Proposed Treasury Regulations

Prop. Treas. Reg. §

Prop. Treas. Reg. §

Prop. Treas. Reg. §

Revenue Procedures and Rulings

[*References are to question numbers.*]

Revenue Procedures

Rev. Proc.

Rev. Proc.

Revenue Rulings

Rev. Rul.

Rev. Rul.

Rev. Rul.

IRS Announcements, Notices, General Counsel Memoranda, and News Releases

[*References are to question numbers.*]

Announcements

Ann.

Notices

Notice

Notice

Notice

General Counsel Memoranda

G.C.M.

News Releases

Private Letter Rulings

[References are to question numbers.]

Priv. Ltr. Rul.

Priv. Ltr. Rul.

Priv. Ltr. Rul.

Internal Revenue Service Forms and Publications

[References are to question numbers.]

IRS Forms

Form No.

Form No.

Form No.

Form No.

IRS Publications

Pub. No.

ERISA Sections

[References are to question numbers.]

Department of Labor Regulations, Advisory Opinions, and Technical Releases

[*References are to question numbers.*]

DOL Regulations

Proposed DOL Regulations

Department of Labor (DOL) Advisory Opinions

Employee Benefits Security Administration (EBSA) Information Letters

Employee Benefits Security Administration (EBSA) Technical Release

Cases

[References are to question numbers.]

A

B

C

D

E

P

R

S

T

U

W

Y

Index

References are to question numbers.

A

C

D

E

F

I

J

K

L

M

N

O

P

Q

R

S

T

U